Thomas CONSTABLE'S NOTES

on the Bible

Volume VI Matthew – Mark

Thomas L. Constable

Thomas Constable's Notes on the Bible
Volume VI: Matthew - Mark
(print edition)
©2016 Tyndale Seminary Press
Fort Worth, TX

ISBN-10: 1-938484-16-9
ISBN-13: 978-1-938484-16-2

For electronic access to notes from Dr. Thomas L. Constable, visit **www.soniclight.com**

This volume is dedicated to serious students of the Bible around the world, for whom I have written these notes, especially my students at Dallas Theological Seminary. Many of them have taught me much - as they have asked questions about various passages of Scripture - that have led me to try to help them.

Contents

Thomas Constable's Notes on the Bible
Volume VI: Matthew - Mark

Constable's Notes
on Matthew

Introduction

THE SYNOPTIC PROBLEM

The synoptic problem is intrinsic to all study of the Gospels, especially the first three. ("Gospel" capitalized in these notes refers to a book of the Bible, whereas "gospel" lowercased refers to the good news, the gospel message.) The word "synoptic" comes from two Greek words, *syn* and *opsesthai*, meaning, "to see together." Essentially the synoptic problem involves all the difficulties that arise because of the similarities and differences between the Gospel accounts. Matthew, Mark, and Luke have received the title "Synoptic Gospels" because they present the life and ministry of Jesus Christ similarly. The content and purpose of John's Gospel are sufficiently distinct to put it in a class by itself. It is not one of the so-called Synoptic Gospels.

Part of the synoptic problem is determining the sources the Holy Spirit led the evangelists to use in producing their Gospels. There is internal evidence (within the individual Gospels themselves) that the writers used source materials as they wrote. The most obvious example of this is the Old Testament passages to which each one referred directly or indirectly. Since Matthew and John were disciples of Jesus Christ, many of their statements represent eyewitness accounts of what happened. Likewise, Mark had close connections with Peter, and Luke was an intimate associate of Paul as well as a careful historian (Luke 1:1-4). Information that the writers obtained verbally (oral tradition) and in writing (documents) undoubtedly played a part in what they wrote. Perhaps the evangelists also received special revelations from the Lord before and or when they wrote their Gospels.

Some scholars have devoted much time and attention to the study of the other sources the evangelists may have used. They are the "source critics" and their work constitutes "source criticism." Because source criticism and its development are so crucial to Gospel studies, a brief introduction to this subject follows.[1]

In 1776 and 1779, two posthumously published essays by A. E. Lessing became known, in which he argued for a single written source for the Synoptic Gospels. He called this source the *Gospel of the Nazarenes*, and he believed its writer had composed it in the Aramaic language. To him, one original source best explained the parallels and differences between the Synoptics. This idea of an original source or primal Gospel caught the interest of many other scholars. Some of them believed there was a written source, but others held it was an oral source.

As one might expect, the idea of two or more sources occurred to some scholars as the best solution to the synoptic problem (e.g., H. J. Holtzmann and B. H. Streeter). Some favored the view that Mark was one of the primal sources, because over 90 percent of the material in Mark also appears in Matthew and or Luke. Some posited another primary source, "Q," an abbreviation of the German word for source, *quelle*. It supposedly contained the material in Matthew and Luke that does not appear in Mark.

Gradually, source criticism gave way to "form criticism." The "form critics" concentrated on the process involved in transmitting what Jesus said and did to the primary sources. They assumed that the process of transmitting this information followed patterns of oral communication that are typical in primitive societies. Prominent New Testament form critics include K. L. Schmidt, Martin Dibelius, and Rudoph Bultmann. Typically, oral communication has certain characteristic effects on stories. It tends to shorten narratives, to retain names, to balance teaching, and to elaborate on stories about miracles, to name a few results. The critics also adopted other criteria from secular philology to assess the accuracy of statements in the Gospels. For example, they viewed as distinctive to Jesus only what was dissimilar to what Palestinian Jews or early Christians might have said. Given the critics' view of inspiration it is easy to see how most of them concluded that the Gospels in their present form do not accurately represent what Jesus said and did. However, some conservative scholars used the same literary method but held a much higher view of the Gospel: for example, Vincent Taylor, who wrote *The Gospel According to St. Mark*.

The next wave of critical opinion, "redaction criticism," began to influence the Christian world shortly after World War II. A redactor is an editor. The German scholar Gunther Bornkamm began this "school" with an essay in 1948, which appeared in English in 1963.[2] Redaction critics generally accept the tenets of source and form criticism. However, they also believe that the Gospel evangelists altered the traditions they received in order to make their own theological emphases. They viewed the writers not simply as compilers of the church's oral traditions, but as theologians who adapted the material for their own purposes. They viewed the present Gospels as containing both traditional material and edited material. There is a good aspect and a bad aspect to this view. Positively, it recognizes the individual evangelist's distinctive purpose for writing. Negatively, it permits an interpretation of the Gospel that allows for historical error, and even deliberate distortion. Redaction scholars have been more or less liberal, depending on their view of Scripture generally. Redaction critics also characteristically show more interest in the early Christian community, out of which the Gospels came, and the beliefs of that community, than they do in Jesus' historical context. Their interpretations of the early Christian community vary greatly, as one would expect. In recent years the trend in critical scholarship has been conservative, to recognize more rather than less Gospel material as having a historical basis.

---

[1] For a longer discussion, see Donald A. Carson and Douglas J. Moo, *An Introduction to the New Testament*, pp. 54-73, 79-112.

[2] Gunther Bornkamm, "The Stilling of the Storm in Matthew," In *Tradition and Interpretation in Matthew*, pp. 52-57.

Some knowledge of the history of Gospel criticism is helpful to the serious student who wants to understand the text. Questions of the historical background out of which the evangelists wrote, their individual purposes, and what they simply recorded or what they commented on—all affect interpretation. Consequently, the conservative expositor can profit somewhat from the studies of scholars who concern themselves with these questions primarily.[3]

Most critics have concluded that one source the writers used was one or more of the other Gospels. Currently most source critics believe that Matthew and Luke drew information from Mark's Gospel. Mark's accounts are generally longer than those of Matthew and Luke, suggesting that Matthew and Luke condensed Mark. To them, it seems more probable that they condensed him, than that he elaborated on them. There is no direct evidence, however, that one evangelist used another as a source. Since they were either personally disciples of Christ, in close contact with eyewitnesses of His activities, they may not have needed to consult an earlier Gospel.

Most source critics also believe that the unique material in each Gospel goes back to Q. This may initially appear to be a document constructed out of thin air. However, the early church father Papias (A.D. 80-155) may have referred to the existence of such a source. Eusebius, the fourth-century church historian, wrote that Papias had written, "Matthew composed the *logia* [sayings? Gospel?] in the *hebraidi* [Hebrew? Aramaic?] *dialekto* [dialect? language? style?]."[4] This is an important statement for several reasons, but here note that Papias referred to Matthew's *logia*. This may be a reference to Matthew's Gospel, but many source critics believe it refers to a primal document that became a source for one or more of our Gospels. Most of them do not believe Matthew wrote Q. They see in Papias' statement support for the idea that primal documents such as Matthew's *logia* were available as sources, and they conclude that Q was the most important one.

Another major aspect of the synoptic problem is the order in which the Gospels appeared as finished products. This issue has obvious connections with the question of the sources the Gospel writers may have used.

Until after the Reformation, almost all Christians believed that Matthew wrote his Gospel before Mark and Luke wrote theirs; they held Matthean priority. From studying the similarities and differences between the Synoptics, some source critics also concluded that Matthew and Luke came into existence before Mark. They viewed Mark as a condensation of the other two. Some of the leaders in this movement were J. A. Eichorn, J. G. Herder, and J. J. Griesbach. The Tübingen school in Germany was also influential. However, the majority of source critics today, as well as many evangelical scholars, believe that Mark was the first Gospel and that Matthew and Luke wrote later. As explained above, they hold this view because they believe it is more probable that Matthew and Luke drew from and condensed Mark, than that Mark expanded on Matthew and Luke. However, the number of scholars who hold Matthean priority is increasing.[5]

Since source criticism is highly speculative, many conservative expositors today continue to lean toward Matthean priority. We do so because there is no solid evidence to contradict this traditional view—that Christians held almost consistently for the church's first 17 centuries.

While the game of deducing which Gospel came first, and who drew from whom, appeals to many students, these issues are essentially academic ones. They have little to do with the meaning of the text. Consequently I do not plan to discuss them further, but will refer interested students to the vast body of literature that is available. I will, however, deal with problems involving the harmonization of the Gospel accounts at the appropriate places in the exposition that follows. The Bible expositor's basic concern is not the nature and history of the stories in the text, but their primary significance in their contexts. One conservative scholar spoke for many others when he wrote the following.

> ". . . it is this writer's opinion that there is no evidence to postulate a tradition of literary dependence among the Gospels. The dependence is rather a parallel dependence on the actual events which occurred."[6]

A much more helpful critical approach to the study of the Bible is "literary criticism," the current wave of interest. This approach analyzes the text in terms of its literary structure, emphases, and unique features. It seeks to understand the canonical text as a piece of literature by examining how the writer wrote it. Related to this approach is "rhetorical criticism," which analyzes the text as a piece of rhetoric. This approach is helpful because there are so many speeches in the Gospels.

GENRE

Genre refers to the type of literature that a particular document fits within. Certain types of literature have features that affect their interpretation. For example, we interpret letters differently than poems. So it is important to identify the genre or genres of a book of the Bible.

The Gospels are probably more like ancient Greco-Roman biographies than any other type of literature.[7] This category is quite broad and encompasses works of considerable diversity, including the Gospels. Even Luke, with its characteristic historiographic connections to Acts,

---

[3]For a conservative evaluation of the usefulness of redaction criticism, see D. A. Carson, "Redaction Criticism: On the Legitimacy and Illegitimacy of a Literary Tool," in *Scripture and Truth*, pp. 119-42.

[4]*The Ecclesiastical History of Eusebius Pamphilus*, 3:39:16.

[5]E.g., William R. Farmer, *The Synoptic Problem*.

[6]Charles H. Dyer, "Do the Synoptics Depend on Each Other?" *Bibliotheca Sacra* 138:551 (July-September 1981):244.

qualifies as ancient biography. Unlike this genre, however, the Gospels "combine teaching and action in a preaching-oriented work that stands apart from anything else in the ancient world."[8] They also are anonymous, in the sense that the writers did not identify themselves as the writers, as Paul did in his epistles, for example, and they are not as pretentious as most ancient biographies.

WRITER

External evidence strongly supports the Matthean authorship of the first Gospel. The earliest copies of the Gospel we have begin "*KATA MATTHAION*" ("according to Matthew"). Several early church fathers referred to Matthew (lit. "gift of God" or "faithful") as the writer, including: Clement of Rome, Polycarp, Justin Martyr, Clement of Alexandria, Tertullian, and Origen.[9] Papias' use of the term *logia* to describe Matthew's work, cited above, is not a clear attestation to Matthean authorship of the first Gospel. Since Matthew was a disciple of Jesus and one of the 12 Apostles, his work carried great influence and enjoyed much prestige from its first appearance. We might expect a more prominent disciple such as Peter or James to have written it. The fact that the early church accepted it as from Matthew further strengthens the likelihood that he indeed wrote it.

Internal evidence of Matthean authorship is also strong. As a tax collector for Rome, Matthew would have had to be able to write capably. His profession forced him to keep accurate and detailed records, which skill he put to good use in composing his Gospel. There are more references to money—and to more different kinds of money—in this Gospel, than in any of the others.[10] Matthew humbly referred to himself as a tax collector, a profession with objectionable connotations in his culture, whereas the other Gospel writers simply called him Matthew (or Levi). Matthew called his feast for Jesus "a dinner" (Matt. 9:9-10), but Luke referred to it as "a great banquet" (Luke 5:29). All these details confirm the testimony of the early church fathers.

According to tradition, Matthew ministered in Palestine for several years after Jesus' ascension to heaven. He also made missionary journeys to the Jews who lived among the Gentiles outside Palestine, Diaspora Jews. There is evidence that he visited Persia, Ethiopia, Syria, and Greece.[11]

LANGUAGE

Papias' statement, cited above, refers to a composition by Matthew in the *hebraidi dialekto* (the Hebrew or possibly Aramaic language or dialect, the same Greek word referring to both cognate languages). This may not be a reference to Matthew's Gospel. Four other church fathers mentioned that Matthew wrote in Aramaic and that translations followed in Greek: Irenaeus (A.D. 130-202), Origen (A.D. 185-254), Eusebius (4th century), and Jerome (6th century).[12] However, they may have been referring to something other than our first Gospel. These references have led many scholars to conclude that Matthew composed his Gospel in Aramaic, and that someone else, or he himself, later translated it into Greek. This is the normal meaning of the fathers' statements. If Matthew originally wrote his Gospel in Aramaic, it is difficult to explain why he sometimes, but not always, quoted from a Greek translation of the Old Testament, the Septuagint. The Hebrew Old Testament would have been the normal text for a Hebrew or Aramaic author to use. A Greek translator might have used the Septuagint (abbreviated LXX) to save himself some work, but if he did so—why did he not use it consistently? Matthew's Greek Gospel contains many Aramaic words. This solution also raises some questions concerning the reliability and inerrancy of the Greek Gospel that has come down to us.

There are several possible solutions to the problem of the language of Matthew's Gospel.[13] The best seems to be that Matthew wrote a Hebrew document—that God did not inspire—that is no longer extant. He also composed an inspired Greek Gospel that has come down to us in the New Testament. Many competent scholars believe that Matthew originally wrote his Gospel in Greek. They do so mainly because of his Greek.[14]

DATE AND PLACE OF COMPOSITION

Dating Matthew's Gospel is difficult for many reasons, even if one believes in Matthean priority. The first extra-biblical reference to it occurs in the writings of Ignatius (ca. A.D. 110-115).[15] However, Matthew's references to Jerusalem and the Sadducees point to dates of composition (for both the Hebrew and Greek Gospels) before A.D. 70, when the Romans destroyed Jerusalem. His references to Jerusalem assume its existence

---

[7]Carson and Moo, pp. 112-15.

[8]Ibid., p. 115.

[9]For further attestation, see Norman L. Geisler and William E. Nix, *A General Introduction to the Bible*, p. 193.

[10]See Werner G. Marx, "Money Matters in Matthew," *Bibliotheca Sacra* 136:542 (April-June 1979):148-57.

[11]Warren W. Wiersbe, *The Bible Exposition Commentary*, 1:13.

[12]Louis A. Barbieri Jr., "Matthew," in *The Bible Knowledge Commentary: New Testament*, p. 15.

[13]See Stanley D. Toussaint, *Behold the King: A Study of Matthew*, pp. 329-33, for five views.

[14]See, for example, D. A. Carson, "Matthew," in *Matthew-Luke*, vol. 8 of *The Expositor's Bible Commentary*, p. 13.

[15]*To the Smyrneans* 1:1.

(e.g., 4:5; 27:53). Matthew recorded more warnings about the Sadducees than all the other New Testament writers combined, but after A.D. 70 they no longer existed as a significant authority in Israel.[16] Consequently, Matthew probably wrote before A.D. 70.[17]

References in the text to the customs of the Jews continuing "to this day" (27:8; 28:15) imply that some time had elapsed between the crucifixion of Jesus Christ and the composition of the Gospel. Since Jesus probably died in A.D. 33, Matthew may have composed his Gospel perhaps a decade or more later. A date between A.D. 40 and 70 is very probable. Some other dates proposed by reliable scholars include between A.D. 50 and 60,[18] or in the 60s,[19] though most scholars favor a date after A.D. 70.[20]

Matthew appears first among the four Gospels in our canon, because when the church established the canon, Matthew was believed to have been the first one written, and the one with the most developed connection to the Old Testament.[21]

Since Matthew lived and worked in Palestine, we would assume that he wrote while living there. There is no evidence that excludes this possibility. Nevertheless, scholars love to speculate. Other sites they have suggested include Antioch of Syria (Ignatius was bishop of Antioch), Alexandria, Edessa, Syria, Tyre, and Caesarea Maratima. These are all guesses.

DISTINCTIVE FEATURES

"If a Bible reader were to jump from Malachi into Mark, or Acts, or Romans, he would be bewildered. Matthew's Gospel is the bridge that leads us out of the Old Testament and into the New Testament."[22]

Compared with the other Gospels, Matthew's is distinctively Jewish. He used parallelisms, as did many of the Old Testament writers, and his thought patterns and general style are typically Hebrew.[23] Matthew's vocabulary (e.g., kingdom of heaven, holy city, righteousness, etc.) and subject matter (e.g., the Law, defilement, the Sabbath, Messiah, etc.) are also distinctively Jewish. Matthew referred to the Old Testament more than any other evangelist.[24] The United Bible Society's *Greek New Testament* lists 54 direct citations of the Old Testament in Matthew, plus 262 widely recognized allusions and verbal parallels. Usually Matthew referred to the Old Testament, or quoted someone doing so, to prove a point to his readers. The genealogy in chapter 1 traces Jesus' ancestry back to Abraham, the father of the Jewish race. Matthew gave prominent attention to Peter, the apostle to the Jews.[25] The writer also referred to many Jewish customs without explaining them, evidently because he believed most of his original readers would not need an explanation.

Another distinctive emphasis in Matthew is Jesus' teaching ministry. No other Gospel contains as many of Jesus' discourses and instructions. These include the Sermon on the Mount (chs. 5—7), the charge to the apostles (ch. 10), the parables of the kingdom (ch. 13), the lesson on forgiveness (ch. 18), the denunciation of Israel's leaders (ch. 23), and the Olivet Discourse (chs. 24—25).[26] About 60 percent of the book focuses on Jesus' teachings. However, Matthew presented Jesus as a doer as well as a teacher. He referred to more than 20 miracles that Jesus performed.[27] Ryrie counted 35 separate miracles of Christ recorded in the Gospels: 20 related in Matthew, 18 in Mark, 20 in Luke, and seven in John.[28] I have listed 39 references to His miracles in Appendix 6, at the end of these notes.

The transitional nature of this Gospel is also evident in that Matthew alone, among the Gospel writers, referred to the church (16:18; 18:17). He recorded Jesus' prediction of the church, as well as instruction about how His disciples should conduct themselves in the church. The Lord created the church in view of Israel's rejection of her Messiah (cf. 16:13-18; Rom. 11), though it was always in the eternal plan of God.

---

[16]Carson, "Matthew," pp. 20-21.

[17]See also Carson and Moo, pp. 152-56.

[18]Mark L. Bailey, in *The New Testament Explorer*, p. 2.

[19]R. T. France, *The Gospel of Matthew*, p. 19.

[20]Ibid.

[21]Darrell L. Bock, *Jesus according to Scripture*, p. 31. For a brief discussion of the New Testament canon, see Carson and Moo, pp. 726-43.

[22]Wiersbe, 1:10.

[23]A. T. Robertson, *A Grammar of the Greek New Testament in the Light of Historical Research*, p. 119.

[24]W. Graham Scroggie, *A Guide to the Gospels*, p. 270.

[25]Willoughby C. Allen, *A Critical and Exegetical Commentary on the Gospel According to S. Matthew*, p. lxxxi.

[26]Robert H. Gundry, *Matthew: A Commentary on His Literary and Theological Art*, is an evangelical who believed in inerrancy, but he argued that parts of Matthew's Gospel present events that did not really happen in Jesus' life. This is a position that many liberal scholars have taken who refer to these non-historical stories as myth, legend, or heroic biography. Gundry called them midrash, a Jewish embellishment that was common in non-biblical writings of Matthew's time. See Scott Cunningham and Darrell L. Bock, "Is Matthew Midrash?" *Bibliotheca Sacra* 144:574 (April-June 1987):157-80, for a refutation of Gundry's position.

[27]See Mark J. Larson, "Three Centuries of Objections to Biblical Miracles," *Bibliotheca Sacra* 160:637 (January-March 2003):77-100.

[28]Charles C. Ryrie, *The Miracles of our Lord*, p. 11.

AUDIENCE AND PURPOSES

Several church fathers (i.e., Irenaeus, Origen, and Eusebius) stated what we might suppose from the distinctively Jewish emphases of this book, namely: that Matthew wrote his Gospel primarily for his fellow Jews.[29]

He wrote, under the inspiration of the Holy Spirit, for a specific purpose or, more accurately, specific purposes. He did not state these purposes concisely, as John did in his Gospel (John 20:30-31). Nevertheless they are clear from his content and his emphases.

> "Matthew has a twofold purpose in writing his Gospel. Primarily he penned this Gospel to prove Jesus is the Messiah, but he also wrote it to explain God's kingdom program to his readers. One goal directly involves the other. Nevertheless, they are distinct."[30]

> "Matthew's purpose obviously was to demonstrate that Jesus Christ was the promised Messiah of the Old Testament, that He fulfilled the requirements of being the promised King who would be a descendant of David, and that His life and ministry fully support the conclusion that He is the prophesied Messiah of Israel. . . .

> "As a whole, the gospel is not properly designated as only an apologetic for the Christian faith. Rather, it was designed to explain to the Jews, who had expected the Messiah when He came to be a conquering king, why instead Christ suffered and died, and why there was the resulting postponement of His triumph to His second coming."[31]

Matthew presented three aspects to God's kingdom program. First, Jesus presented Himself to the Jews as the king that God had promised in the Old Testament. Second, Israel's leaders rejected Jesus as their king. This resulted in the postponement, not the cancellation, of the messianic kingdom that God had promised Israel. Third, because of Israel's rejection, Jesus is now building His church in anticipation of His return to establish the promised messianic kingdom on the earth.

There are at least three wider purposes that Matthew undoubtedly hoped to fulfill with his Gospel. First, he wanted to instruct Christians and non-Christians concerning the person and work of Jesus.[32] Second, he wanted to provide an apologetic to aid his Jewish brethren in witnessing to other Jews about Christ. Third, he wanted to encourage all Christians to witness for Christ boldly and faithfully. It is interesting that Matthew is the only Gospel writer to use the Greek verb *matheteuo*, "to disciple" (13:52; 27:57; 28:19; cf. Acts 14:21 for its only other occurrence in the New Testament). This fact shows his concern for making disciples of Christ.[33]

Carson identified nine major themes in Matthew. They are: Christology, prophecy and fulfillment, law, church, eschatology, Jewish leaders, mission, miracles, and the disciples' understanding and faith.[34]

PLAN AND STRUCTURE

Matthew often grouped his material into sections: so that three, five, six, or seven events, miracles, sayings, or parables appear together.[35] Jewish writers typically did this to help their readers remember what they had written. The presence of this technique reveals Matthew's *didactic* (instructional) intent. Furthermore, it indicates that his arrangement of material was somewhat topical, rather than strictly chronological. Generally, chapters 1—4 are in chronological order, chapters 5—13 are topical, and chapters 14—28 are again chronological.[36] Matthew is the least chronological of the Gospels.

Not only Matthew, but the other Gospel writers as well, present the life of Jesus Christ in three major stages. These stages are: His presentation to the people, their consideration of His claims, and their rejection and its consequences.

---

[29]Scroggie, p. 248.

[30]Toussaint, p. 18. See also Bailey, pp. 2-3.

[31]John F. Walvoord, *Matthew: Thy Kingdom Come*, pp. 12, 13. On the kind of Messiah that the Jews expected, see Alfred Edersheim, *The Life and Times of Jesus the Messiah*, 1:160-79.

[32]See David K. Lowery, "A Theology of Matthew," in *A Biblical Theology of the New Testament*, p. 25.

[33]See Martin L. Franzmann, *Follow Me: Discipleship According to Saint Matthew*.

[34]Carson, "Matthew," pp. 26-38.

[35]See Allen, p. lxv; and Alfred Plummer, *An Exegetical Commentary on the Gospel According to S. Matthew*, pp. xix-xxiii.

[36]Henry C. Thiessen, *Introduction to the New Testament*, p. 139.

A key phrase in Matthew's Gospel enables us to note the major movements in the writer's thought. It is the phrase "and it came about that when Jesus had finished" (7:28; 11:1; 13:53; 19:1; 26:1). This phrase always occurs at the end of one of Jesus' major addresses. A different address, therefore, concludes each major section of the Gospel, and they are climactic. Matthew evidently used the narrative sections to introduce Jesus' discourses, which he regarded as especially important in his book. Mark, on the other hand, gave more detailed information concerning the narrative material in his Gospel. In addition to each major section, there is a prologue and an epilogue to the Gospel according to Matthew.

Narrative	Teaching	Transition
1—4	5:1—7:27	7:28-29
8:1—9:34	9:35—10:42	11:1a
11:1b—12:50	13:1-52	13:53a
13:53b—17:27	18	19:1a
19:1b—23:39	24—25	26:1a
26:1b—28:20		

One writer believed Matthew constructed his Gospel as an eleven-part chiasm, with the center panel occurring in chapter 13. He argued that this structure highlights the postponement of the kingdom.

"A. Demonstration of Jesus' Qualifications as King (chaps. 1—4)
    B. Sermon on the Mount: Who Can Enter His Kingdom (chaps. 5—7)
        C. Miracles and Instruction (chaps 8—9)
            D. Instruction to the Twelve: Authority and Message for Israel (chap. 10)
                E. Opposition: The Nation's Rejection of the King (chaps. 11—12)
                    F. Parables of the Kingdom: The Kingdom Postponed (chap. 13)
                E.' Opposition: The Nation's Rejection of the King (chaps. 14—17)
            D.' Instruction to the Twelve: Authority and Message for the Church (chap. 18)
        C.' Miracles and Instruction (chaps. 19—23)
    B.' Olivet Discourse: When the Kingdom Will Come (chaps. 24—25)
A.' Demonstration of Jesus' Qualifications as King (chaps. 26—28)"[37]

OUTLINE

I.   The introduction of the King 1:1—4:11

      A.   The King's genealogy 1:1-17
      B.   The King's birth 1:18-25
      C.   The King's childhood ch 2

            1.   The prophecy about Bethlehem 2:1-12
            2.   The prophecies about Egypt 2:13-18
            3.   The prophecies about Nazareth 2:19-23

      D.   The King's preparation 3:1—4:11

            1.   Jesus' forerunner 3:1-12
            2.   Jesus' baptism 3:13-17
            3.   Jesus' temptation 4:1-11

II.   The authority of the King 4:12—7:29

      A.   The beginning of Jesus' ministry 4:12-25

            1.   The setting of Jesus' ministry 4:12-16
            2.   Jesus' essential message 4:17
            3.   The call of four disciples 4:18-22
             4.   A summary of Jesus' ministry 4:23-25

---

[37] Gary W. Derickson, "Matthew's Chiastic Structure and Its Dispensational Implications," *Bibliotheca Sacra* 163:652 (October-December 2006):426.

B.   Jesus' revelations concerning participation in His kingdom chs. 5—7

1.   The setting of the Sermon on the Mount 5:1-2
2.   The subjects of Jesus' kingdom 5:3-16
3.   The importance of true righteousness 5:17—7:12
4.   The false alternatives 7:13-27
5.   The response of the audience 7:28-29

III.   The manifestation of the King 8:1—11:1

A.   Demonstrations of the King's power 8:1—9:34

1.   Jesus' ability to heal 8:1-17
2.   Jesus' authority over His disciples 8:18-22
3.   Jesus' supernatural power 8:23—9:8
4.   Jesus' authority over His critics 9:9-17
5.   Jesus' ability to restore 9:18-34

B.   Declarations of the King's presence 9:35—11:1

1.   Jesus' compassion 9:35-38
2.   Jesus' commissioning of 12 disciples 10:1-4
3.   Jesus' charge concerning His apostles' mission 10:5-42
4.   Jesus' continuation of His work 11:1

IV.   The opposition to the King 11:2—13:53

A.   Evidences of Israel's opposition to Jesus 11:2-30

1.   Questions from the King's forerunner 11:2-19
2.   Indifference to the King's message 11:20-24
3.   The King's invitation to the repentant 11:25-30

B.   Specific instances of Israel's rejection of Jesus ch. 12

1.   Conflict over Sabbath observance 12:1-21
2.   Conflict over Jesus' power 12:22-37
3.   Conflict over Jesus' sign 12:38-45
4.   Conflict over Jesus' kin 12:46-50

C.   Adaptations because of Israel's rejection of Jesus 13:1-53

1.   The setting 13:1-3a
2.   Parables addressed to the multitudes 13:3b-33
3.   The function of these parables 13:34-43
4.   Parables addressed to the disciples 13:44-52
5.   The departure 13:53

V.   The reactions of the King 13:54—19:2

A.   Opposition, instruction, and healing 13:54—16:12

1.   The opposition of the Nazarenes and Romans 13:54—14:12
2.   The withdrawal to Bethsaida 14:13-33
3.   The public ministry at Gennesaret 14:34-36
4.   The opposition of the Pharisees and scribes 15:1-20
5.   The withdrawal to Tyre and Sidon 15:21-28
6.   The public ministry to Gentiles 15:29-39
7.   The opposition of the Pharisees and Sadducees 16:1-12

B.   Jesus' instruction of His disciples around Galilee 16:13—19:2

        1.   Instruction about the King's person 16:13-17
        2.   Instruction about the King's program 16:18—17:13
        3.   Instruction about the King's principles 17:14-27
        4.   Instruction about the King's personal representatives ch. 18
        5.   The transition from Galilee to Judea 19:1-2

VI.   The official presentation and rejection of the King 19:3—25:46

A.   Jesus' instruction of His disciples around Judea 19:3—20:34

        1.   Instruction about marriage 19:3-12
        2.   Instruction about childlikeness 19:13-15
        3.   Instruction about wealth 19:16—20:16
        4.   Instruction about Jesus' passion 20:17-19
        5.   Instruction about serving 20:20-28
        6.   An illustration of illumination 20:29-34

B.   Jesus' presentation of Himself to Israel as her King 21:1-17

        1.   Jesus' preparation for the presentation 21:1-7
        2.   Jesus' entrance into Jerusalem 21:8-11
        3.   Jesus' entrance into the temple 21:12-17

C.   Israel's rejection of her King 21:18—22:46

        1.   The sign of Jesus' rejection of Israel 21:18-22
        2.   Rejection by the chief priests and the elders 21:23—22:14
        3.   Rejection by the Pharisees and the Herodians 22:15-22
        4.   Rejection by the Sadducees 22:23-33
        5.   Rejection by the Pharisees 22:34-46

D.   The King's rejection of Israel ch. 23

        1.   Jesus' admonition of the multitudes and His disciples 23:1-12
        2.   Jesus' indictment of the scribes and the Pharisees 23:13-36
        3.   Jesus' lamentation over Jerusalem 23:37-39

E.   The King's revelations concerning the future chs. 24—25

        1.   The setting of the Olivet Discourse 24:1-3
        2.   Jesus' warning about deception 24:4-6
        3.   Jesus' general description of the future 24:7-14
        4.   The abomination of desolation 24:15-22
        5.   The second coming of the King 24:23-31
        6.   The responsibilities of disciples 24:32—25:30
        7.   The King's judgment of the nations 25:31-46

VII.   The crucifixion and resurrection of the King chs. 26—28

A.   The King's crucifixion chs. 26—27

        1.   Preparations for Jesus' crucifixion 26:1-46
        2.   The arrest of Jesus 26:47-56
        3.   The trials of Jesus 26:57—27:26
        4.   The crucifixion of Jesus 27:27-56
        5.   The burial of Jesus 27:57-66

  B.   The King's resurrection ch. 28

    1.   The empty tomb 28:1-7
    2.   Jesus' appearance to the women 28:8-10
    3.   The attempted cover-up 28:11-15
    4.   The King's final instructions to His disciples 28:16-20

MESSAGE

The four Gospels are foundational to Christianity because they record the life of Jesus Christ and His teachings. Each of the four Gospels fulfills a unique purpose. They are not simply four versions of the life of Jesus. If one wants to study the life of Jesus Christ, the best way to do that is with a "Harmony of the Gospels" that correlates all the data chronologically.[38] However, if one wants to study only one of the Gospel accounts, then one needs to pay attention to the uniqueness of that Gospel. The unique material, what the writer included and excluded, reveals the purpose for which he wrote and the points he wanted to stress. It also reveals the writer's distinctive message: what he wanted to say.

By the way, when referring to the four Gospels, or one or more of them, it is customary to capitalize the word "Gospel." When one refers to the gospel message, the good news, or the whole New Testament as the Christian gospel, most writers do not capitalize it.

What is the unique message of Matthew's Gospel? How does it differ from the other three Gospels? What specific emphasis did Matthew want his readers to gain as they read his record of Jesus' life and ministry?

Matthew wanted his readers to do what John the Baptist and Jesus called the people of their day to do, namely: "Repent, for the kingdom of heaven is at hand." This was the message of the King to His people, and the message of the King's herald, John the Baptist, as John called the King's people to prepare for the King's coming.

This is not the final message of Christianity, but it is the message that Matthew wanted his readers to understand. When John the Baptist and Jesus originally issued this call, they faced a situation that was different from the situation we face today. They called the people of their day to trust in and follow Jesus because the messianic kingdom was immediately at hand, coming soon. If the Jews had responded positively to Jesus, He would have established His kingdom immediately. He would have died on the cross, risen from the dead, ascended into heaven, ushered in the Tribulation, returned to the earth, and established His kingdom. All these things are the subjects of Old Testament messianic prophecy that had to be fulfilled.

The messianic kingdom is at hand for us today in a different sense. Jesus Christ has died, risen from the dead, and ascended into heaven. The Tribulation is still future, but following those seven years Jesus will return and establish His messianic kingdom on earth.

The commission that Jesus has given us as His disciples is essentially to prepare people for the King's return. To do this we must go into all the world and herald the gospel to everyone. We must call them to trust in and follow the King as His disciples.

Essentially the message of Matthew is: "The kingdom of heaven is at hand." The proper response to this message is: "Repent." We will consider first the message, and then the proper response. Note three things about the message.

First, "the kingdom of heaven is at hand" is the statement of a fact. "At hand" means that it is coming soon. The subject of this statement is the kingdom. The kingdom is the theme of Matthew's Gospel. The word "kingdom" occurs about 50 times in Matthew. Since "kingdom" is such a prominent theme, it is not surprising to discover that this Gospel presents Jesus as the great King.

Matthew presents the kingship of Jesus. Kingship involves the fact that Jesus is the great King that the Old Testament prophets predicted would come and rule over all the earth in Israel's golden age. It points to the universal sovereignty of God's Son, who would rule over all people on earth. He was to be a "Son of David" who would also rule over Israel.

The word "kingdom" refers to the realm over which the King reigns. This is usually what we think of when we think of Jesus' messianic kingdom: the sphere over which He will rule. However, it is important that we not stress the sphere to the detriment of the sovereignty with which He will rule. Both ideas are essential to the concept of the kingdom that Matthew presents: sphere and sovereignty.

The little-used phrase in Matthew's Gospel "kingdom of God" stresses the fact that it is God who rules. The King is God, and He will reign over all of His creation eventually. The kingdom belongs to God, and it will extend over all that God sovereignly controls.

Matthew, of all the Gospel evangelists, was the only one to use the phrase "kingdom of heaven." John the Baptist and Jesus never explained this phrase, but their audiences knew what they meant by it. Ever since God gave His great promises to Abraham, the Jews knew what the kingdom of heaven meant. It meant God's rule over His people who lived on the earth. As time passed, God gave the Israelites more information about His

---

[38]See Appendix 1 "A Harmony of the Gospels," at the end of these notes, or A. T. Robertson, *A Harmony of the Gospels for Students of the Life of Christ*, or Ernest Burton and Edgar Goodspeed, *A Harmony of the Synoptic Gospels in Greek*.

rule over them. He told them that He would provide a descendant of David who would be their King. This king would rule over the Israelites, who would live in the Promised Land. His rule would include the whole earth, however, and the Gentiles, too, would live under His authority. The kingdom of heaven that the Old Testament predicted was an *earthly* kingdom over which God would rule through His Son. It would not just be God's rule over His people from heaven. When the Jews in Jesus' day heard John the Baptist and Jesus calling them to "Repent, for the kingdom of heaven is at hand," what did they think? They understood that the earthly messianic kingdom predicted in the Old Testament was very near. They needed to get ready for it by making some changes.

The simple meaning of "kingdom of heaven," then, is God's establishment of heaven's order over all the earth. Every created being and every human authority would be in subjection to God. God would overturn everyone and everything that did not recognize His authority. It is the establishment of divine order on earth administered by a Davidic King. It is the supremacy of God's will over human affairs. The establishment of the kingdom of heaven on earth, then, is the hope of humanity. It is impossible for people to bring in this kingdom. Only God can bring it in. People just need to get ready, because it is coming.

Second, Matthew's Gospel interprets the kingdom. It does not just affirm the coming of the kingdom, but it also explains the order of the kingdom. Specifically, it reveals the principle of the kingdom, the practice of the kingdom, and the purpose of the kingdom.

The principle of the kingdom is *righteousness*. Righteousness is one of the major themes in Matthew. Righteousness in Matthew refers to righteous conduct, righteousness in practice—rather than positional righteousness, about which the Apostle Paul wrote much. Righteousness is necessary to enter the kingdom, and to serve in the kingdom, under the King. The words of the King in Matthew constitute the law of the kingdom. They proclaim the principle of righteousness (cf. 5:20).

The practice of the kingdom is peace. Peace is another major theme in Matthew. When we think of the Sermon on the Mount, we should think of these two major themes: righteousness and peace. The kingdom would come, not by going to war with Rome and defeating it. It would come by peaceful submission to the King: Jesus. These two approaches to inaugurating the kingdom contrast starkly, as we think of Jesus hanging on the cross between two insurrectionists. They tried to establish the kingdom the way most people in Israel thought it would come: by violence. Jesus, on the other hand, submitted to His Father's will, and even though He died, He rose again and will inaugurate the kingdom one day. He secured the future establishment of the kingdom. Jesus' example of peaceful submission to God's will is to be the model for His disciples. Greatness in the kingdom does not come by self-assertion, but by self-sacrifice. The greatest in the kingdom will be the servant of all. The works of the King, in Matthew, demonstrate the powers of the kingdom moving toward peace (cf. 26:52).

The purpose of the kingdom is joy. God will establish His kingdom on earth to bring great joy to humankind. His kingdom rule will be the time of greatest fruitfulness and abundance in earth's history. God's will has always been to bless people. It is by rebelling against God that people lose their joy. The essence of joy is intimate fellowship with God. This intimate fellowship will be a reality during the kingdom to a greater extent than ever before in history. The will of the King in Matthew is to bless humankind.

Third, Matthew's Gospel stresses the method by which the King will administer the kingdom. It is a threefold method.

In the first five books of the Old Testament, the Law or Torah, God revealed the need for a high priest to offer a final sacrifice for humankind to God. The last part of Matthew's Gospel, the passion narrative, presents Jesus as the Great High Priest who offered that perfect sacrifice.

In the second part of the Old Testament, the Historical Books, the great need and expectation is a king who will rule over Israel and the nations in righteousness. The first part of Matthew's Gospel presents Jesus as that long expected King, Messiah, God's anointed ruler.

In the last part of the Old Testament, the Prophets, we see the great need for a prophet who could bring God's complete revelation to mankind. The middle part of Matthew's Gospel presents Jesus as the Prophet who would surpass Moses and bring God's final revelation to mankind (cf. Heb. 1:1).

God will administer His kingdom on earth through this Person who, as King, has all authority; as Prophet, reveals God's final word of truth; and as Priest, has dealt with sin finally. God's administration of His kingdom is in the hands of a King who is both the great High Priest and the completely faithful Prophet.

The central teaching of Matthew's Gospel then concerns the kingdom of heaven. The needed response to this Gospel is: "Repent."

In our day Christians differ in their understanding of the meaning of repentance. This difference arises because there are two Greek verbs, each of which means "to repent." One of these verbs is *metamelomai*. When it occurs, it usually describes an active change. The other word is *metanoeo*. When it occurs, it usually describes a contemplative change. Consequently, when we read "repent" or "repentance" in our English Bibles, we have to ask ourselves whether a change of behavior is in view primarily or a change of mind. Historically the Roman Catholic Church has favored an active interpretation of the nature of repentance, whereas Protestants have favored a contemplative interpretation. Catholics emphasize that repentance involves a change of behavior, while Protestants emphasize that it involves a change of thinking essentially. One interpretation stresses the need for a sense of sorrow, and the other stresses the need for a sense of awareness. This confusion also surfaces in the "Lordship

Salvation" controversy within evangelical Protestantism. That is why some critics of Lordship Salvation say advocates of Lordship Salvation are leading Protestants back to Rome.

According to Matthew, the word that John the Baptist and Jesus used, when they called their hearers to repentance, was *metanoeo*. We could translate it, "Think again." They were calling their hearers to consider the implications of the imminent messianic kingdom.

Consideration that the kingdom of heaven was at hand would result in a conviction of sin and a sense of sorrow. These are the inevitable consequences of considering these things. Conviction of a need to change is the consequence of genuine repentance. John the Baptist called for the fruits of repentance, a change of behavior that arose from a change of mind. But note that the fruits of repentance, a change of behavior, are not the same as repentance, a change of mind.

Consideration leads to conviction, and conviction leads to conversion. "Conversion" describes turning from rebellion to submission, from self to the Savior. In relation to the coming kingdom, it involves becoming humble and childlike, rather than proud and independent. It involves placing confidence in Jesus rather than in self for salvation.

To summarize, we can think of the kind of repenting that John the Baptist, Jesus, and later Jesus' disciples, were calling on their hearers to demonstrate as involving consideration, conviction, and conversion. Repentance begins with consideration of the facts. Awareness of these facts brings conviction of personal need. Feeling these personal needs leads to conversion, or a turning from what is bad to what is good (cf. Peter's sermon in Acts).

Now let us combine "repent" with "the kingdom of heaven is at hand." Matthew's Gospel calls the reader to consider the King and the kingdom. This should produce the conviction that one is not ready for such a kingdom, nor is one ready to face such a King, because our righteousness is inadequate. Then we should submit our lives to the rule of the King and the standards of the kingdom.

Matthew's Gospel proclaims the kingdom. It interprets the kingdom as righteousness, peace, and joy. It reveals that a perfect King who is a perfect Prophet and a perfect Priest will administer the kingdom. It finally appeals to people to repent in view of these realities: to consider, to feel conviction, and to turn in conversion. As readers of this Gospel, we need to get ready, to think again, because the kingdom of heaven is coming.

The Christian church now has the task of calling the world to "Repent, for the kingdom of heaven is at hand." The church, as I am using the term here, consists of Jesus' disciples collectively. The King is coming back to rule and to reign. People need to prepare for that event. The church's job is to spread the good news of the King and the kingdom to those who have very different ideas about the ultimate ruler and the real utopia. We face the same problem that Jesus did in His day. Therefore, Matthew's Gospel is a great resource for us as we seek to carry out the commission that the King has given us. Matthew 1:23 ("Immanuel, God with us") and 28:19-20 ("Lo, I am with you always") enclose the book like bookends. In the person of Jesus Christ, God has drawn near to abide forever with His people.

Individually, we have a responsibility to consider the King and the kingdom, to gain conviction by what we consider, and to change our behavior. Our repentance should involve submission to the King's authority, and preparation for kingdom service. We submit to the King's authority as we observe all that He has commanded us. We prepare for kingdom service as we faithfully persevere in the work that He has given us to do, rather than pursuing our own personal agendas. We can do God's will joyfully because we have the promise of the King's presence with us, and the enablement of His authority behind us (28:18, 20).[39]

---

[39]Adapted from G. Campbell Morgan, *Living Messages of the Books of the Bible*, 2:1:9-22.

Exposition

I. THE INTRODUCTION OF THE KING 1:1—4:11

"Fundamentally, the purpose of this first part is to introduce the reader to Jesus on the one hand and to the religious leaders on the other."[40]

The first two chapters of this section prepare the reader for Jesus' ministry. Consequently they serve as a prologue to the Gospel.

A. THE KING'S GENEALOGY 1:1-17 (CF. LUKE 3:23-38)

Matthew began his Gospel with a record of Jesus' genealogy because the Christians claimed that Jesus was the Messiah promised in the Old Testament. To qualify as such He had to be a Jew from the royal line of David (Isa. 9:6-7). Matthew's genealogy proves that Jesus descended not only from Abraham, the father of the Israelite nation, but also from David, the founder of Israel's royal dynasty.

1:1   This verse is obviously a title, but is it a title of the whole Gospel, a title for the prologue (chs. 1—2), or a title for the genealogy that follows (1:1-17)? Probably it refers to the genealogy. There is no other ancient Near Eastern book-length document extant that uses the expression *biblos geneseos* (book or record of the generation) as its title.[41] While the noun *genesis* (birth) occurs again in verse 18, there it introduces the birth narrative of Jesus. In the Septuagint, the same phrase—*biblos geneseos*—occurs in Genesis 2:4 and 5:1, where in each case a narrative follows it, as here. Genealogies are quite common in the Old Testament, of course, and the presence of one here introduces a Jewish flavor to Matthew's Gospel immediately.

"Each use of the formula [in the Bible] introduces a new stage in the development of God's purpose in the propagation of the Seed through which He planned to effect redemption."[42]

The last Old Testament messianic use of this phrase is in Ruth 4:18, where the genealogy ends with David. Matthew reviewed David's genealogy and extended it to Jesus.

"The plan which God inaugurated in the creation of *man* is to be completed by *the Man*, Christ Jesus."[43]

This is "the genealogy of Jesus" Christ. The name "Jesus" is the Greek form of the Hebrew name "Joshua," and it means "Yahweh is salvation" (*yehoshua*, the long form) or "Yahweh saves" (*Yeshua*, the short form). The two major Joshuas in the Old Testament both anticipated Jesus Christ by providing salvation (cf. Heb. 3—4; Zech. 6:11-13).

"Jesus" occurs no fewer than 150 times in Matthew, but human characters never use it when addressing Jesus Himself in this book. Matthew evidently reserved the use of this name for himself, in order to establish the closest possible association between himself as the narrator, and Jesus, so that his point of view might coincide with that of Jesus.[44]

The name "Christ" is the rough equivalent of the Hebrew "Messiah," or "Anointed One." In the Old Testament, it refers generally to people anointed for a special purpose, including: priests, kings, the patriarchs (metaphorically), and even the pagan king Cyrus. It came to have particular reference to the King whom God would provide from David's line who would rule over Israel and the nations eventually (cf. 2 Sam. 7:12-16; Ps. 2:2: 105:15; et al.). The early Christians believed that Jesus of Nazareth was the Christ of the Old Testament. Because they used both names together, "Christ" became a virtual name for Jesus, a titulary (title turned name). Paul, for example, used it this way frequently in his writings.

Matthew introduced Jesus Christ as the descendant of "David" and "Abraham." Why did he select these two ancestors for special mention, and why did he name David before Abraham?

Abraham and David are important because God gave each of them a covenant. God vowed that He would unconditionally provide seed, land, and blessing to Abraham and his descendants (Gen. 12:1-3, 7; 15; et al.). Abraham would not only receive blessing from God, but he would also be a source of blessing to the whole world. God's covenant with David guaranteed that his descendants would rule over the kingdom of Israel forever. The house or dynasty of David would always have the right to

[40]Jack Dean Kingsbury, *Matthew as Story*, p. 5. He believed the first major section of the book ends with 4:16.
[41]Carson, "Matthew," p. 61.
[42]Merrill C. Tenney, *The Genius of the Gospels*, p. 52.
[43]Toussaint, p. 36.
[44]Kingsbury, pp. 45-46.

rule, symbolized by the throne (2 Sam. 7:12-16). Thus Matthew's reference to these two men should remind the reader of God's promises regarding a King who would rule over Israel and the universal blessing that He would bring (cf. Isa. 11:1).[45]

"What is emphasized is the fact that the Messiah has His historical roots in Abraham and that He has come as a Davidic king in response to the promises to the patriarchs."[46]

"He is the Son of Abraham both because it is in him that the entire history of Israel, which had its beginning in Abraham, attains its goal (1:17) and because he is the one through whom God will extend to the nations his blessing of salvation (8:11; 28:18-20). . . .

"Just as the title 'Son of Abraham' characterizes Jesus as the one in whom the Gentiles will find blessing, so the title 'Son of David' characterizes Jesus as the One in whom Israel will find blessing."[47]

The non-chronological order of David first, and then Abraham, indicates that Matthew had more in mind than a simple chronological list of Jesus' ancestors. As the Gospel unfolds, it becomes clear that the Jews needed to accept Jesus as the promised Son of David before He would bring the blessings promised to Abraham (cf. 9:27; 12:23; 15:22; 20:30-31; 21:9, 15; 22:42, 45). Jesus presented Himself to the Jews first. When they rejected Him, He turned to the Gentiles. Yet He explained that their rejection was only temporary. When He returns, the Jews will acknowledge Him as their Messiah, and then He will rule on the earth and bless all humankind (cf. Zech. 12:10-14; 14:4, 9-11; Rom. 11:26).

"Christ came with all the reality of the kingdom promised to David's Son. But if He were refused as the Son of David, still, as the Son of Abraham, there was blessing not merely for the Jew, but for the Gentile. He is indeed the Messiah; but if Israel will not have Him, God will during their unbelief bring the nations to taste of His mercy."[48]

"By this brief superscription Matthew discloses the theme of his book. Jesus is the One who shall consummate God's program."[49]

"First He is Sovereign, then Savior [in Matthew]."[50]

"This introduction clearly demonstrates that Matthew's purpose in writing the gospel is to provide adequate proof for the investigator that the claims of Christ to be King and Saviour are justified. For this reason, the gospel of Matthew was considered by the early church one of the most important books of the New Testament and was given more prominence than the other three gospels."[51]

The Old Testament prophets predicted that the Messiah would be born of a woman (Gen. 3:15), of the seed of Abraham (Gen. 22:18), through the tribe of Judah (Gen. 49:10), and of the family of David (2 Sam. 7:12-13). Jesus qualified in every respect.

1:2-6a   In tracing Jesus' genealogy, why did Matthew begin with Abraham rather than with Adam, as Luke did? Matthew wanted to show Jesus' Jewish heritage, and to do this he only needed to go back as far as Abraham, the father of the Jewish race. Significantly, Matthew called him "Abraham" rather than "Abram." The longer name connotes the covenant privileges that God made to Abraham when He changed his name.

The writer separated "Judah and his brothers" (v. 2), because the messianic promise of rulership went to Judah alone (Gen. 49:10). This allusion to the 12 tribes of Israel provides another clue that Matthew's interests were strongly royal (cf. 8:11; 19:28).

Matthew also mentioned Perez's brother ("Zerah," v. 3), perhaps because he was his twin. But he probably did so because "Perez" was a key figure in both the Old Testament genealogies (Ruth 4; 1 Chron. 4) and in Jewish tradition.[52]

---

[45]See J. Dwight Pentecost, "The Biblical Covenants and the Birth Narratives," in *Walvoord: A Tribute*, p. 262.

[46]Eugene H. Merrill, "The Book of Ruth: Narration and Shared Themes," *Bibliotheca Sacra* 142:566 (April-June 1985):137.

[47]Kingsbury, pp. 47-48.

[48]William Kelly, *Lectures on the Gospel of Matthew*, p. 14.

[49]Toussaint, p. 37.

[50]S. Lewis Johnson Jr., "The Argument of Matthew," *Bibliotheca Sacra* 112:446 (April-June 1955):143.

[51]Walvoord, p. 17.

[52]For discussion of these traditions, see Alfred Edersheim, *Sketches of Jewish Social Life in the Days of Christ*, ch. xviii: "Ancient Jewish Theological Literature."

"Jewish tradition traced the royal line to Perez (Ruth iv. 12, 18ff.), and 'son of Perez' is a Rabb[inic]. expression for the Messiah."[53]

The inclusion of Tamar (v. 3), Rahab (v.5), and Ruth (v. 5) as well as Bathsheba (v. 6b)—is unusual—because the Jews traced their heritage through their male ancestors (until the Middle Ages). Matthew's mention of each of these women reveals his emphases.

"Of the four mentioned two—Rahab and Ruth—are foreigners, and three—Tamar, Rahab and Bathsheba—were stained with sin."[54]

"Of these four, two (Tamar and Rahab) were Canaanites, one (Ruth) a Moabite, and one (Bathsheba) presumably a Hittite. Surely they exemplify the principle of the sovereign grace of God, who not only is able to use the foreign (and perhaps even the disreputable) to accomplish his eternal purposes, but even seems to delight in doing so."[55]

The writer had several purposes for including these women. First, he showed that Jesus came to include sinners in the family of God by seeking and saving the lost (cf. v. 21).[56] Second, their inclusion shows the universal character of Jesus' ministry and kingdom.[57] After the Jews rejected Jesus as their Messiah, God opened the doors of the church to Gentiles equally with Jews. Matthew's Gospel records the beginning of this change. Third, reference to these women prepares the reader for the significant role Mary will play in the messianic line though, of course, she was neither a great sinner nor a foreigner.[58] All five women became partakers in the messianic line through strange and unexpected divine providence. Matthew may have mentioned these women to disarm criticism by showing that God countenanced irregular marital unions in Messiah's legal ancestry.[59]

"The word 'King' with 'David' [v. 6a] would evoke profound nostalgia and arouse eschatological hope in first-century Jews. Matthew thus makes the royal theme explicit: King Messiah has appeared. David's royal authority, lost at the Exile, has now been regained and surpassed by 'great David's greater son' . . ."[60]

"The addition of the title, *the king*, marks the end of this period of waiting, and points forward to Jesus, *the Son of David, the Christ, the King of the Jews*."[61]

A fourth reason was apparently to highlight four Old Testament stories that illustrate a common point. That point is that, in each case, a Gentile showed extraordinary faith in contrast to Jews, who were greatly lacking in their faith.[62]

"The allusions to these stories accomplish four theological purposes.

"First, they demonstrate God's providential hand in preserving Messiah's line, even in apostate times. This naturally led to Matthew's account of the virgin conception, through which God brought the Messiah into the world.

"Second, they demonstrate God's heart for godly Gentiles and the significant role of their faith at crucial times in Israel's history.

"Third, they demonstrate the importance of the Abrahamic and Davidic covenants in understanding Messiah's mission, with a focus on faith and obedience, not a racial line.

---

[53]A. H. M'Neile, *The Gospel According to St. Matthew*, p. 1.

[54]A. Carr, *The Gospel According To St. Matthew*, p. 81.

[55]Eugene H. Merrill, *Kingdom of Priests: A History of Old Testament Israel*, p. 188. See also idem, "The Book . . .," p. 138.

[56]*A Dictionary of Christ and the Gospels*, s.v. "Genealogies of Jesus Christ," by P. M. Barnard, 1:638.

[57]Edwin D. Freed, "The Women in Matthew's Genealogy," *Journal for the Study of the New Testament* 29 (1987):3-19.

[58]Raymond Brown, *The Birth of the Messiah*, pp. 64-74.

[59]M'Neile, p. 5; M. D. Johnson, *The Purpose of Biblical Genealogies*, pp. 176-79.

[60]Carson, "Matthew," p. 66.

[61]J. C. Fenton, *Saint Matthew*, p. 38.

[62]John C. Hutchison, "Women, Gentiles, and the Messianic Mission in Matthew's Genealogy," *Bibliotheca Sacra* 158:630 (April-June 2001):152-64.

"Fourth, they call Matthew's readers to repentance and humility, and to accepting Gentiles into the body of Christ, thereby affirming an important theme of Matthew's Gospel."[63]

1:6b-11   Matthew did not refer to Solomon or the other kings of Israel as kings. Probably he wanted to focus attention on David and on Jesus as the fulfillment of the promises God gave to David. Solomon did not fulfill these promises.

The writer's reference to "Bathsheba" is unusual (v. 6b). It draws attention to the heinousness of David's sin. Perhaps he wanted to stress that "Uriah" was not an Israelite but a "Hittite" (2 Sam. 11:3; 23:39). Evidently Bathsheba was the daughter of an Israelite (cf. 1 Chron. 3:5), but the Jews would have regarded her as a Hittite since she married Uriah.

Five kings do not appear where we would expect to find them. Three are absent between Joram and Uzziah: Ahaziah, Joash, and Amaziah (v. 8), and two are lacking between Josiah and Jehoiachin, namely, Jehoahaz and Jehoiakim. As we shall note below (v. 17), Matthew deliberately constructed his genealogy in three groups of 14 names. Why did he omit reference to these five kings? The first three were especially wicked. They all had connections with Ahab, Jezebel, and Athaliah. Moreover, all of them experienced violent deaths. The second two were also evil, and Jehoiakim's reign was very short—only three months. Matthew did not sanitize his genealogy completely, however, as his references to Tamar, Rahab, and David's sin indicate.

"This man [Jehoiachin] is called Coniah in Jer. 22:24-30, where a curse is pronounced upon him. There it is predicted that none of his seed should prosper sitting upon David's throne. Had our Lord been the natural son of Joseph, who was descended from Jeconiah, He could never reign in power and righteousness because of the curse. But Christ came through Mary's line, not Joseph's. As the adopted son of Joseph, the curse upon Coniah's seed did not affect Him."[64]

Jehoiachin's brothers (v. 11), Jehoiakim and Zedekiah, also ruled over Judah. Zedekiah's reign lasted 11 years, but he was a puppet of the Babylonians. The royal line passed through Jehoiachin.

"There is pathos in this second allusion to brotherhood [cf. v. 2]. 'Judah and his brethren,' partakers in the promise (also in the sojourn in Egypt); 'Jeconiah and his brethren,' the generation of the promise eclipsed."[65]

1:12-16   Most of the names in this section occur nowhere else in the Bible. Matthew probably knew them from oral tradition and or written sources.

"While no twentieth-century Jew could prove he was from the tribe of Judah, let alone from the house of David, that does not appear to have been a problem in the first century, when lineage was important in gaining access to temple worship."[66]

Verse 16 contains careful and unusual wording. Matthew was preparing for what he later explained, the virgin birth of Jesus (v. 23). The phrase "who is called" (*ho legomenos*) does not imply doubt about Jesus' messiahship. It just identifies the Jesus whose genealogy preceded. This is one of Matthew's favorite expressions in this Gospel. It announces the names of persons or places 12 times (cf. 1:16; 2:23; 4:18; 10:2; 13:55; 26:3, 14, 36; 27:16, 17, 22, 33). As this verse shows, Jesus was *legally* Joseph's son, even though He was *virgin-born* by Mary.

1:17   Clearly, the three groups of 14 generations Matthew recorded do not represent a complete genealogy from Abraham to Jesus (cf. v. 8). Luke recorded several names from the exile to Jesus' birth that Matthew omitted (Luke 3:23-27). "All the generations" (NASB) then must mean all the generations that Matthew listed. The Greek text literally says "all the generations from Abraham to David . . . to Christ." Matthew's summary statement does not constitute an error in the Bible. Jewish writers frequently arranged genealogies so their readers could remember them easily. Perhaps Matthew chose his arrangement because the numerical equivalent of the Hebrew consonants in David's name total 14. In Hebrew the letter equivalent to "d" also stands for the number "4," and "v" represents "6." Matthew did not need to present an unbroken genealogy to establish Jesus' right to the Davidic throne.

Before leaving this genealogy, note that each of the three sections ends with a significant person or event connected with the Davidic dynasty.

---

[63]Ibid., p. 164.

[64]*The New Scofield Reference Bible*, pp. 991-92.

[65]A. B. Bruce, "The Synoptic Gospels," in *The Expositor's Greek Testament*, 1:64.

[66]Carson, "Matthew," p. 63.

"In the first group, the Davidic throne is established; in the second group, the throne is cast down and deported to Babylon; in the third group, the throne is confirmed in the coming of the Messiah. Further, a basic covenant is set forth in each of these three periods: the Abrahamic covenant in the first (vv. 2-5), the Davidic covenant in the second (vv. 6-11), and the New Covenant [anticipated] in the third (vv. 12-16)."[67]

"In David the family [of Abraham] rose to royal power . . . At the captivity it lost it again. In Christ it regained it."[68]

Moreover, in each period covered by each section, God gave Israel an important covenant: the Abrahamic (Gen. 15), the Davidic (2 Sam. 7), and the New (Jer. 31).[69] All came to fruition in the person and work of Jesus Christ.

Generally, Matthew's genealogy shows that Jesus had the right to rule over Israel, since He was a descendant of David through Joseph. Legally, He was Joseph's son. Specifically, this section of the Gospel strongly implies that Jesus was the promised Messiah.

The differences with Jesus' genealogy in Luke 3:23-38 are a problem that no one has been able to solve adequately. The problem is that Joseph's ancestors in Matthew's genealogy are different from his ancestors in Luke's genealogy, especially from Joseph to King David. The theory that many scholars subscribe to now is this: Matthew gave the legal line of descent from David, stating who was the heir to the throne in each case, and Luke gave the actual descendants of David in the branch of David's family to which Joseph belonged.[70]

The reason for Matthew's genealogy is to show that Jesus of Nazareth was in the royal line of David and was qualified to be Israel's promised Messiah. This is, apparently, the genealogy of Jesus' earthly father, Joseph, that traces his *legal* ancestry. Luke's genealogy evidently traces Joseph's *blood* line. Joseph adopted Jesus as his son (1:25). This made Jesus legally eligible to serve as Israel's king. He was also genetically descended from David through Mary, but Matthew presented Joseph's ancestors because they were the former kings of Israel. This genealogy shows Jesus' right to rule as the King of the Jews and His genuine humanity.

B. THE KING'S BIRTH 1:18-25

The birth narrative that follows shows Jesus' genuine deity. The first sentence in this pericope (section) serves as a title for the section, as the sentence in verse 1 did for 1:1-17. Matthew recorded the supernatural birth of Jesus to demonstrate further His qualification as Israel's Messiah. He wanted to show that Mary could not have become pregnant by another man. These verses show how Jesus came to be the heir of Joseph and thus qualified to be Israel's King.

"Matthew ultimately is arguing that Jesus recapitulates the pattern of Israel's experience while also presenting him as Israel's hope."[71]

1:18-19   Jewish law regarded an engaged couple as virtually married.[72] Usually women married at about 13 or 14 years of age,[73] and their husbands were often several years older. Normally a one-year period of waiting followed the betrothal before the consummation of the marriage. During that year, the couple could only break their engagement with a divorce.

". . . a betrothed girl was a widow if her *fiance* died (Kethub. i.2), and this whether the man had 'taken' her into his house or not. After betrothal, therefore, but before marriage, the man was legally 'husband' . . ."[74]

Joseph, being a "righteous" (Gr. *dikaios*) man, could hardly let his fiancée's pregnancy pass without action, since it implied that she had been unfaithful and had violated the Mosaic Law. Joseph had three choices concerning how to proceed. First, he could expose Mary publicly as unfaithful. In this case she might suffer stoning, though that was rare in the first century.[75] Probably she would have suffered the shame of a public divorce (Deut. 22:23-24). A second option was to grant her a private divorce, in which case Joseph needed only to hand her a written certificate in the presence of two witnesses (cf. Num. 5:11-31).[76] His third option was to remain engaged and not divorce Mary, but this alternative appeared to Joseph to require him to

[67]*The Nelson Study Bible*, p. 1576.
[68]Allen, p. 2.
[69]Johnson, cited by Toussaint, p. 41.
[70]See I. Howard Marshall, *The Gospel of Luke: A Commentary on the Greek Text*, pp. 157-65, for further discussion and advocates of this and other views.
[71]Bock, *Jesus according . . .*, p. 64.
[72]See Edersheim, *Sketches of . . .*, p. 148.
[73]France, p. 50.
[74]M'Neile, pp. 6-7.
[75]Carson, "Matthew," p. 75.
[76]Edersheim, *The Life . . .*, 1:154.

break the Mosaic Law (Lev. 20:10). He decided to divorce her privately. This preserved his righteousness (i.e., his conformity to the Law) and allowed him to demonstrate compassion.

1:20-21   The appearance of an "angel of the Lord" . . . "in a dream" would have impressed Matthew's original Jewish readers that this revelation was indeed from God (cf. Gen. 16:7-14; 22:11-18; Exod. 3:2—4:16; et al.). The writer stressed the divine nature of this intervention four times in the prologue (1:20, 24; 2:13, 19).

The angel's address, "Joseph, son of David" (v. 20), gave Joseph a clue concerning the significance of the announcement he was about to receive. It connects with verse 1 and the genealogy in the narrative. The theme of the Davidic Messiah continues. Joseph was probably afraid of the consequences of his decision to divorce Mary.

The virgin birth is technically the virgin conception. Mary was a virgin—not only when she gave birth to Jesus, but also when the Holy Spirit conceived Him in her womb. But the idea that Mary remained a virgin for the rest of her life, the Roman Catholic doctrine of the perpetual virginity of Mary, has no support in the text. Nothing in Scripture suggests that Mary bore Jesus' half brothers and sisters supernaturally. This doctrine has gained credence because it contributes to the veneration of Mary.

The angel announced God's sovereign prerogative in naming the child (v. 21). God named His "Son." Joseph simply carried out the will of God by giving Jesus "His name" at the appropriate time (v. 25). As mentioned above, the name "Jesus" means "Yahweh saves" or "Yahweh is salvation." "Jesus" was one of the most common names in Israel at this time, so Jesus was often described more specifically as "Jesus of Nazareth."[77] The angel explained the appropriateness of this name: JESUS (cf. Ps. 130:8). The Jews anticipated a Messiah who would be both a political savior *and* a redeemer from sin.[78]

> "There was much Jewish expectation of a Messiah who would 'redeem' Israel from Roman tyranny and even purify his people, whether by fiat or appeal to law (e.g., Pss Sol 17). But there was no expectation that the Davidic Messiah would give his own life as a ransom (20:28) to save his people from their sins. The verb 'save' can refer to deliverance from physical danger (8:25), disease (9:21-22), or even death (24:22); in the NT it commonly refers to the comprehensive salvation inaugurated by Jesus that will be consummated at his return. Here it focuses on what is central, viz., salvation from sins; for in the biblical perspective sin is the basic (if not always the immediate) cause of all other calamities. This verse therefore orients the reader to the fundamental purpose of Jesus' coming and the essential nature of the reign he inaugurates as King Messiah, heir of David's throne . . ."[79]

"The single most fundamental character trait ascribed to Jesus is the power to save . . ."[80]

1:22-25   The phrase *plerothe to hrethen* ("what was spoken . . . fulfilled" [NASB] or "to fulfill what . . . had said" [NIV]) occurs often in Matthew's Gospel (2:15, 17, 23; 4:14; 8:17; 12:17; 13:35; 21:4; 27:9; cf. 26:56). It indicates a fulfillment of Old Testament prophecy.

Matthew worded this verse very carefully. He distinguished the source of the prophecy—God—from the instrument through whom He gave it—the prophet. For Matthew, the prophecy of Isaiah was God's Word (cf. 2 Pet. 1:21). The New Testament writers consistently shared this high view of inspiration (cf. 2 Tim. 3:16).

The prophecy Matthew said Jesus fulfilled comes from Isaiah 7:14 (v. 23). It is a difficult one to understand.[81]

The first problem concerns the meaning of "virgin" (Gr. *parthenos*). This noun usually refers to a literal virgin in the Greek Bible.[82] One exception occurs in Genesis 34:3 in the Septuagint. It always has this meaning in the Greek New Testament. That Matthew intended it to mean virgin appears clear for two reasons. First, virgin is the standard meaning of the word and, second, the context supports this meaning (vv. 18, 20, 25).

A second problem is the meaning of the Hebrew word translated "virgin" (*'alma*) in Isaiah 7:14. It means an unmarried young woman of marriageable age. Thus the Hebrew word has overtones of virginity. Every use of this word in the Hebrew Old Testament either requires or permits the meaning "virgin" (Gen. 24:43; Exod. 2:8; Ps. 68:25 [26]; Prov. 30:19; Song of

---

[77]France, p. 34.

[78]Gustaf Dalman, *The Words of Jesus*, p. 297.

[79]Carson, "Matthew," p. 76.

[80]Kingsbury, p. 12.

[81]See Homer A. Kent Jr., "Matthew's Use of the Old Testament," *Bibliotheca Sacra* 121:481 (January-March 1964):34-43; and Donald A. Hagner, *Matthew 1—13*, pp. 20-21.

[82]M'Neile, p. 9; Carson, "Matthew," p. 78.

Sol. 1:3; 6:8; Isa. 7:14).[83] That is why the Septuagint translators rendered 'alma "virgin" in Isaiah 7:14. Matthew's interpretation of this word as virgin harmonizes with the Septuagint translators' understanding.

A third problem is, what did this prophecy mean in Isaiah's day? At the risk of oversimplification, there are three basic solutions to this problem.

First, Isaiah predicted that an unmarried woman of marriageable age, at the time of the prophecy, would "bear" a "child" whom she would "name Immanuel." This happened in Isaiah's day. Jesus *also* fulfilled this prophecy, in the sense that a real virgin bore Him, and He was "God with us." This is a typological view, in which the child born in Isaiah's day was a sign or type (a divinely intended illustration) of the Child born in Joseph's day. I prefer this view.[84]

A second interpretation sees Isaiah predicting the virgin birth of a boy named Immanuel in his day. A virgin did bear a son named Immanuel in Isaiah's day, advocates of this view claim. Jesus *also* fulfilled the prophecy, since His mother was a virgin when she bore Him, and He was "God with us." This is a double fulfillment view. The problem with it is that it requires two virgin births, one in Isaiah's day and Jesus' birth.

A third view is that Isaiah predicted the birth of Jesus exclusively. He meant nothing about any woman in his day giving birth. Jesus alone fulfilled this prophecy. There was no fulfillment in Isaiah's day. This is a single fulfillment view. The main problem with it is that according to this view, Ahaz received no sign—but only a prophecy. Signs in Scripture were fairly immediate visible assurances that what God had predicted would indeed happen.[85]

Some question exists about the sense in which "Immanuel" was Jesus' name (and the name of a son born in Isaiah's day), since the New Testament writers never referred to Him as Immanuel. There is also no record of a son born in Isaiah's day of that name. Even though it was not one of Jesus' proper names, it accurately described who He was (cf. John 1:14, 18; Matt. 28:20). The same may be true of the son born in Isaiah's day. Some believe this person was one of Isaiah's sons, or the son of King Ahaz, who could have been King Hezekiah, or someone else. My guess is that Isaiah's son Maher-shalal-hash-baz was the initial fulfillment and that "Immanuel" may have been his secondary name.

"He [Jesus] is Emmanuel, and as such Jehovah the Saviour, so that in reality both names have the same meaning."[86]

"The key passages 1:23 and 28:20 . . . stand in a reciprocal relationship to each other . . . . Strategically located at the beginning and the end of Matthew's story, these two passages 'enclose' it. In combination, they reveal the message of Matthew's story: *In the person of Jesus Messiah, his Son, God has drawn near to abide to the end of time with his people, the church, thus inaugurating the eschatological age of salvation.*"[87]

The angel's instructions caused Joseph to change his mind. He decided not to divorce Mary privately, but to continue their engagement and eventually consummate it (v. 24). Matthew left no doubt about the virginal conception of Jesus, by adding that Joseph did not have sexual relations with Mary until after Jesus' birth (v. 25).[88] When Joseph named the child, he was taking "Jesus," which was a common name,[89] Jesus as his son.

"In other words, Jesus, born of Mary but not fathered by Joseph, is legitimately Son of David because Joseph son of David adopts him into his line."[90]

Adoption in Israel was informal rather than formal (cf. Gen. 15:2; 17:12-13; 48:5; Exod. 2:10; 1 Kings 11:20; Esth. 2:7; Luke 2:23).

---

[83]Willis J. Beecher, *The Prophets and the Promise*, p. 334, footnote; Toussaint, p. 45. This is a complete list of its occurrences in the Old Testament.

[84]See also Toussaint, p. 46, and many commentaries on Isaiah.

[85]For further discussion, see Carson, "Matthew," pp. 78-80. There are also many books on the subject of the virgin birth. One of the best of these is J. Gresham Machen, *The Virgin Birth of Christ*.

[86]Arno C. Gaebelein, *The Gospel of Matthew, An Exposition*, 1:37.

[87]Kingsbury, pp. 41-42. Italics his.

[88]See James P. Sweeney, "Modern and Ancient Controversies over the Virgin Birth of Jesus," *Bibliotheca Sacra* 160:638 (April-June 2003):142-58.

[89]See Flavius Josephus, *The Life of Flavius Josephus*.

[90]Kingsbury, p. 47.

Was Jesus' virgin birth theologically necessary, or was it only a fulfillment of prophecy? If parents (specifically fathers) transmit sinfulness to their children in some literal, physical way (i.e., genetically, hereditarily, etc.), the virgin birth was necessary to guard Jesus from transmitted sin. However, there is no clear revelation that fathers pass down their sinfulness as they pass down other characteristics. Theologians debate the subject of whether God imputes sin to every individual at birth, or if our parents pass it on to us (creationism vs. traducianism). My view is that fathers do not pass down sinfulness physically. Human nature is not necessarily sinful, though every human—except Jesus—has a sinful human nature, that in some way connects to our parents.

Matthew stressed the virgin birth of Jesus in this section. God, rather than Joseph, was Jesus' true father, making Him the literal Son of God (cf. 2 Sam. 7:14).

In this first chapter, the writer stressed the person of Jesus Christ as being both human (vv. 1-17) and divine (vv. 18-25).

"If Matthew i:1-17 were all that could be said of His birth, He might then *have had* a legal right to the throne, but He could never have been He who was to redeem and save from sin. But the second half before us shows Him to be truly the long promised One, the One of whom Moses and the prophets spake, to whom all the past manifestations of God in the earth and the types, pointed."[91]

Matthew presented three proofs that Jesus was the Christ in chapter 1: His genealogy, His virgin birth, and His fulfillment of prophecy.

C. THE KING'S CHILDHOOD CH. 2

There is nothing in chapter 2 that describes Jesus Himself. Therefore Matthew's purpose was not simply to give the reader information about Jesus' childhood. Rather, he stressed the reception that the Messiah received having entered the world. The rulers were hostile, the Jewish religious leaders were indifferent, but the Gentiles welcomed and worshipped Him. These proved to be typical responses throughout Jesus' ministry, as Matthew's Gospel reveals. This literary device of presenting implication and then realization is common in the first Gospel. Also in this chapter there are several references to the fulfillment of Old Testament prophecies (vv. 5-6, 15, 17-18, 23). Matthew wanted to continue to prove that Jesus was the promised Messiah who fulfilled what the prophets had predicted. In chapter 1, the emphasis is more on how Jesus' identity fulfilled prophecy, but in chapter 2, it is more on how Jesus' geographical connections fulfilled prophecy. To prove that Jesus was the Christ, Matthew had to show that Jesus was born where the Old Testament said Messiah would be born. Another purpose of this chapter was to show God's providential care of His Son.

1. The prophecy about Bethlehem 2:1-12

The Old Testament not only predicted *how* Messiah would be born (1:18-25) but *where* He would be born (2:1-12).

2:1-2

"In the 708th year from the foundation of Rome (46 B.C. by Christian reckoning) Julius Caesar established the Julian Calendar, beginning the year with January 1st. But it was not until the sixth century A.D. that Dionysius Exiguus, a Scythian monk living in Rome, who was confirming the Easter cycle, originated the system of reckoning time from the birth of Christ. Gradually this usage spread, being adopted in England by the Synod of Whitby in 664, until it gained universal acceptance. In 1582 Pope Gregory XIII reformed the Julian calendar. However, more accurate knowledge shows that the earlier reckonings of the time of Christ's birth were in error by several years. Thus it is now agreed that the birth of Christ should be placed c. 6-4 B.C."[92]

When did the Magi visit Jesus in Bethlehem?[93] There are several factors that point to a time about a year after Jesus' birth. First, Matthew described Jesus as a "child" (Gr. *paidion*, v. 11), not an "infant" (Gr. *brephos*, cf. Luke 2:27). Second, Jesus' family was residing in a house (v. 11), not beside a manger (cf. Luke 2:1-20). Third, Herod's edict to destroy all the male children two years old and under (v. 16) suggests that Jesus fell within this age span. Fourth, Joseph and Mary brought the offering of poor people to the temple when they dedicated Jesus about 40 days after His birth (Luke 2:24). After receiving the Magi's gifts, they could have presented the normal offering (cf. Lev. 12). Fifth, Joseph and Mary's decision to return to Judea from Egypt (v. 22) implies that Judea is where they had lived before they took refuge in Egypt.

Matthew carefully identified the "Bethlehem of Judea," in contrast to the Bethlehem in Zebulun (Josh. 19:15), as the birthplace of Jesus. This was important because the prophecy of Messiah's birthplace was specifically Bethlehem of Judah, the hometown of King David (v. 6; Mic. 5:2).

---

[91]Gaebelein, 1:27.

[92]*The New Scofield . . .*, pp. 992-93. See also Edersheim, *The Life . . .*, 2:704-5.

[93]For the geographical locations of places that Matthew referred to, see the map "Palestine in the Time of Jesus" at the end of these notes.

"Herod the Great, as he is now called, was born in 73 B.C. and was named king of Judea by the Roman Senate in 40 B.C. By 37 B.C. he had crushed, with the help of Roman forces, all opposition to his rule. Son of the Idumean Antipater, he was wealthy, politically gifted, intensely loyal, an excellent administrator, and clever enough to remain in the good graces of successive Roman emperors. His famine relief was superb and his building projects (including the temple, begun 20 B.C.) admired even by his foes. But he loved power, inflicted incredibly heavy taxes on the people, and resented the fact that many Jews considered him a usurper. In his last years, suffering an illness that compounded his paranoia, he turned to cruelty and in fits of rage and jealousy killed close associates, his wife Mariamne (of Jewish descent from the Maccabeans), and at least two of his sons . . ."[94]

"Herod was not only an Idumaean in race and a Jew in religion, but he was a heathen in practice and a monster in character."[95]

". . . the Jews had borne more calamities from Herod, in a few years, than had their forefathers during all that interval of time that had passed since they had come out of Babylon, and returned home . . ."[96]

"Behold" (Gr. *idou*) is a Hebraic expression that Matthew used to point out the wise men. They are the focus of his attention in this pericope.

It is not easy to identify the Magi (from the Gr. *magoi*) precisely. The Greek word from which we get "magi" comes from a Persian word that means experts regarding the stars. Centuries before Christ's time, they were a priestly caste of Chaldeans who could interpret dreams (cf. Dan. 1:20; 2:2; 4:7; 5:7). Later the term broadened to include men interested in dreams, magic, astrology, and the future. Some of these were honest inquirers after the truth, but others were charlatans (cf. Acts 8:9; 13:6, 8). The Magi who came to Jerusalem came from the East. Jerusalem at this time covered about 300 acres, and its population at non-feast times was between 200,000 and 250,000 people.[97] Probably the Magi came from Babylon, which for centuries had been a center for the study of the stars.[98] Babylon had also been the home of Daniel, who had been in command of former Magi in Babylonia (Dan. 2:48), and who had written of the death of Messiah (Dan. 9:24-27). The oldest opinion is that the Magi came from Arabia rather than Persia.[99] Magi had such a dubious reputation in Jewish and Christian circles, that it is unlikely that Matthew would have mentioned their testimony if it were not true.[100]

"The tradition that the Magi were kings can be traced as far back as Tertullian (died c. 225). It probably developed under the influence of OT passages that say kings will come and worship Messiah (cf. Pss 68:29, 31; 72:10-11; Isa. 49:7; 60:1-6). The theory that there were *three* 'wise men' is probably a deduction from the *three* gifts (2:11). By the end of the sixth century, the wise men were named: Melkon (later Melchior), Balthasar, and Gasper. Matthew gives no names. His *magoi* come to Jerusalem (which, like Bethlehem, has strong Davidic connections [2 Sam 5:5-9]), arriving, apparently . . ., from the east— possibly from Babylon, where a sizable Jewish settlement wielded considerable influence, but possibly from Persia or from the Arabian desert. The more distant Babylon may be supported by the travel time apparently required . . ."[101]

The Magi's question (v. 2) was not, "Where is He who has been born *to become* King of the Jews?" but, "Where is He who has been born King of the Jews?" Jesus' status as Israel's king did not come to Him later in His life. He was born with it (cf. 27:37). In this respect, He was superior to Herod, who was *not* born a king and saw the young Child as a threat to his throne. The only other occurrences of the title "king of the Jews" in Matthew are in 27:11, 29, and 37 where Gentiles used these words to mock Jesus.

---

[94]Carson, "Matthew," p. 84. See also Flavius Josephus, *Antiquities of the Jews*, books 14-18; idem, *The Wars of the Jews*, 1:10-33; and S. Perowne, *The Life and Times of Herod the Great*.

[95]*Unger's Bible Dictionary*, 1957 ed., s.v. "Herod," by S. L. Bowman.

[96]Idem, *The Wars . . .*, 2:6:2.

[97]Edersheim, 1:116-17.

[98]Richard C. H. Lenski, *The Interpretation of St. Matthew's Gospel*, p. 57; Allen, pp. 11-12.

[99]Tony T. Maalouf, "Were the Magi from Persia or Arabia?" *Bibliotheca Sacra* 156:624 (October-December 1999):423-42.

[100]France, p. 65.

[101]Carson, "Matthew," p. 85.

What Jesus' "star" was remains problematic. Some scholars have suggested a conjunction of the planets Jupiter and Saturn in the constellation of Pisces.[102] Others believed it was a supernova (a star that explodes and emits unusual light for several weeks or months), a comet, or some other planetary conjunctions or groupings. Still others believed it was a supernatural creation. Whatever it was, it was this same "star" that guided the Magi to Jesus' house in Bethlehem, or at least to Bethlehem (v. 9). The presence of the definite Greek article with "star" in verse 9 points to the same star mentioned in verse 2. It seems to me that it would be very unlikely that a planetary conjunction or other natural "star" could have given the wise men such specific guidance.

"Could it be that 'the star' which the Magi saw and which led them to a specific house was the Shekinah glory of God? That same glory had led the children of Israel through the wilderness for 40 years as a pillar of fire and cloud. Perhaps this was what they saw in the East, and for want of a better term they called it a 'star.'"[103]

Perhaps the Magi connected Balaam's messianic prophecy of a star that would rise out of Judah (Num. 24:17) with the Jewish King. Balaam evidently originated in the East (Num. 23:7). The Jews in Jesus' day regarded Balaam's oracle as messianic.[104] Interestingly, Balaam, like the wise men, experienced pressure from a king who was intent on destroying God's people, but he, and they, refused to cooperate.

The Magi's statement that they intended to "worship" the new King does not necessarily mean that they regarded Him as divine. They may have meant that they wanted to pay Him their respects. However, in view of chapter 1, we know that the new King was worthy of true worship. "Worship" (Gr. *proskyneo*) occurs 13 times in Matthew and is something the writer stressed. Apparently the Magi recognized the King as Israel's Messiah. "King of the Jews" was the Gentile way of saying "Messiah."[105] The Messiah was indeed the King of the Jews.

2:3-6   This news "troubled" Herod, because he was very aware of the Jews' desire to throw off the Roman yoke, and his own rule in particular. Remember Pharaoh's fear for his throne that also led to infanticide. Herod was an Edomite, a descendant of Esau, and the prospect of a Jewish Messiah's appearance was one he could not ignore. The rest of Jerusalem's citizens also became disturbed, because they realized that this news from the Magi might lead Herod to take further cruel action *against them*. This is exactly what happened (v. 16). Already we begin to see the opposition of the people of Jerusalem to Jesus that would eventually result in His crucifixion.

Herod assembled Israel's leaders to investigate the Magi's announcement further (v. 4). The chief priests were mainly Sadducees at this time, and most of the scribes ("teachers of the law," NIV) were Pharisees. The chief priests included the high priest and his associates. The high priest obtained his position by appointment from Rome. The scribes were the official interpreters and communicators of the law to the people, their "lawyers." Since these two groups of leaders did not get along, Herod may have had meetings with each group separately.

"The scribes were so called because it was their office to make copies of the Scriptures, to classify and teach the precepts of the oral law . . ., and to keep careful count of every letter in the O.T. writings. Such an office was necessary in a religion of law and precept, and was an O.T. function (2 Sam. 8:17; 20:25; 1 Ki. 4:3; Jer. 8:8; 36:10, 12, 26). To this legitimate work the scribes added a record of rabbinical decisions on questions of ritual (*Halachoth*); the new code resulting from those decisions (*Mishna*); the Hebrew sacred legends (*Gemara*, forming with the *Mishna*, the *Talmud*); commentaries on the O.T. (*Midrashim*); reasonings upon these (*Hagada*); and finally, mystical interpretations which found in Scripture meanings other than the grammatical, lexical, and obvious ones (the *Kabbala*), not unlike the allegorical method of Origen. In our Lord's time, the Pharisees considered it orthodox to receive this mass of writing which had been superimposed upon and had obscured the Scripture."[106]

[102]Edersheim, *The Life* . . ., 1:212-13.

[103]Barbieri, p. 22. Cf. Walvoord, p. 23; J. Dwight Pentecost, *The Words and Works of Jesus Christ*, p. 67.

[104]Carson, "Matthew," p. 86.

[105]France, p. 61.

[106]*The New Scofield* . . ., p. 993. See also *The New Bible Dictionary*, 1962 ed., s.v. "Talmud and Midrash," by Charles E. Feinberg; Edersheim, *The Life* . . ., 1:93-94; idem, *Sketches of* . . ., pp. 226-38; and Josephus, *Antiquities of* . . ., 13:10:6.

The Jews of Jesus' day regarded the *Halekhah* (from *halakh*, "to go," i.e., The Rule of the Spiritual Road) as having greater authority than the Hebrew Scriptures.[107]

Josephus wrote the following about influence of the Pharisees during the Inter-testamental Period:

". . . but they that were the worst disposed to him [John Hyrcanus] were the Pharisees, who are one of the sects of the Jews, as we have informed you already. These have so great power over the multitude, that when they say anything against the king or against the high priest, they are presently believed."[108]

Notice that Herod perceived the King, whom the Magi had spoken of, as "the Messiah" (v. 4). Some of the Jews—particularly the Essenes, whom Herod did not consult, but not the Sadducees and Pharisees—were expecting a Messiah to appear soon because of Daniel 9:24-27.[109] Daniel had been a "wise man" in the East also.

"Matthew adroitly answers Jewish unbelief concerning Jesus Christ by quoting their own official body to the effect that the prophecy of His birth in Bethlehem was literal, that the Messiah was to be an individual, not the entire Jewish nation, and that their Messiah was to be a King who would rule over them."[110]

"In the original context of Micah 5:2, the prophet is speaking prophetically and prophesying that whenever the Messiah is born, He will be born in Bethlehem of Judah. That is the *literal* meaning of Micah 5:2. When a literal prophecy is fulfilled in the New Testament, it is quoted as a *literal fulfillment*. Many prophecies fall into this category . . ."[111]

Another writer called this, literal prophecy plus literal fulfillment.[112]

Matthew's rendering of the Micah 5:2 prophecy adds the fact that the "Ruler" would "shepherd" the Israelites. This statement, from 2 Samuel 5:2, originally referred to David. Thus Matthew again showed the connection between the prophecies of Messiah and the Davidic line, a connection he also made in chapter 1. Perhaps the religious leaders put these passages together in their quotation.[113] Such seems to have been the case. The quotation is free, not verbatim from either the Hebrew or the Greek (Septuagint) texts.

2:7-8   Evidently Herod summoned the Magi "secretly" to avoid arousing undue interest in their visit among Israel's religious leaders (v. 7). He wanted to know when "the star" had "appeared," so he could determine the age of the child King.

Under a pretext of desire to "worship" the new King, Herod sent the Magi to Bethlehem as his representatives, with orders to report what they found to him. His hypocritical humility deceived the wise men. He must have sensed this, since he sent no escort with them but trusted them to return to him.

It is remarkable that the chief priests and scribes apparently made no effort to check out Jesus' birth as the Magi did.

"It is strange how much the scribes knew, and what little use they made of it."[114]

Their apathy contrasts with the Magi's curiosity and with Herod's fear. It continued into Jesus' ministry until it turned into antagonism.

". . . the conflict on which the plot of Matthew's story turns is that between Jesus and Israel, especially the religious leaders."[115]

---

[107]Edersheim, *The Life . . .*, 1:11.

[108]Josephus, *Antiquities of . . .*, 13:10:5.

[109]Ibid., 13:5:9; 20:8:8; and idem, *The Wars of the Jews*, 4:3:9. For Josephus' descriptions of these "three sects of philosophy" peculiar to the Jews, see his *Antiquities of . . .*, 18:1:3-5; and *The Wars . . .*, 2:8:2-14.

[110]Walvoord, p. 22.

[111]Arnold G. Fruchtenbaum, *Israelology: The Missing Link in Systematic Theology*, p. 843.

[112]David L. Cooper, *Messiah: His Historical Appearance*, pp. 174-75.

[113]See Edersheim, *The Life . . .*, 2:710-41, for a list of Old Testament passages messianically applied in ancient rabbinic writings, and talmudic discussion on the Messiah.

[114]Richard Glover, *A Teacher's Commentary of the Gospel of Matthew*, p. 14.

[115]Kingsbury, p. 8.

"Except for Jesus himself, the religious leaders are the ones who influence most the development of the plot of Matthew's story."[116]

2:9-12   Perhaps "the" star (v. 2), whatever it was, was so bright that the wise men could see it as they traveled in daylight. Travel at night was common to avoid the heat, so they may have made the five-mile trip south to Bethlehem at night. Nevertheless this would have been winter, so they probably traveled during daylight hours.[117]

The star may have identified Bethlehem as the town where Jesus abode, and the Magi may have obtained His exact location from the residents. On the other hand, the star may have identified "the" very "house" where Joseph and Mary dwelt. This seems more likely in view of verse 11. God supernaturally guided the seekers so they found the Messiah. God's provision gave them "great joy" (v. 10; cf. Luke 2:10).

The reaction of the wise men to discovering "the Child" and "His mother" was to bow and worship Him. Notice that they did not worship Mary, nor did they worship Jesus through Mary.

It was customary in the ancient Near East to present gifts when approaching a superior (cf. Gen. 43:11; 1 Sam. 9:7-8; 1 Kings 10:2). The wise men produced these from their "treasures" or coffers. The expensive gifts reflected the great honor the Magi bestowed on the Christ Child. The "gold" probably financed Joseph and Mary's trip to Egypt (vv. 14-21). "Frankincense" is a gum obtained from the resin of certain trees that was particularly fragrant. "Myrrh" was also a sap-like substance that came from a tree that grew in Arabia. People used it as a spice, and as a perfume, often for embalming as well as for other applications. Many commentators, ancient and modern, have seen symbolic significance in these three gifts. Some have said "gold" suggests royalty while others have seen deity. Some say "incense" represents deity, while others believe it better represents perfect humanity. Most expositors view "myrrh" as prefiguring Jesus' death and burial. It is unlikely that the Magi saw this significance, but Matthew may have intended his readers to see it. This act by Gentile leaders also prefigures the wealth that the Old Testament prophets said the Gentiles would one day present to Israel's Messiah (Ps. 72:10-11, 15; Isa. 60:5, 11; 61:6; 66:20; Zeph. 3:10; Hag. 2:7-8). This will occur in the fullest sense at the Second Coming of Christ.

God supernaturally intervened to keep the Magi from returning to Herod, who would have then been able, from them, to target Jesus precisely. Dreams were a common method of divine guidance during the Old Testament economy in which Jesus lived (cf. Num. 12:6).

Several contrasts in this section reveal Matthew's emphases. Herod, the wicked Idumean usurper king, contrasts with Jesus, the born righteous King of Israel. The great distance from which the Magi traveled to visit Jesus, contrasts with the short distance Israel's leaders *would have* had to travel to see Him. The genuine worship of the wise men contrasts with the feigned worship of Herod, and the total lack of worship from the chief priests and scribes. The Gentile Magi's sensitivity and responsiveness to divine guidance also contrast with the insensitivity and unresponsiveness of Israel's leaders.

"The first to worship the King in Matthew's Gospel are Gentiles, an implication of the last command of the Messiah. The supernatural stellar manifestations attest the divine character of the person of Jesus. Matthew also notes the fact that the Magi who worship the Messiah of Israel are forced to take refuge from Bethlehem. This, too, is a hint of the future antagonism of Israel to their King."[118]

". . . he [Matthew] contrasts the eagerness of the Magi to worship Jesus, despite their limited knowledge, with the apathy of the Jewish leaders and the hostility of Herod's court—all of whom had the Scriptures to inform them. Formal knowledge of the Scriptures, Matthew implies, does not in itself lead to knowing who Jesus is . . ."[119]

"Even though Israel is cognizant of the prophecies, they are blind to spiritual realities. The King of Israel is worshiped by Gentiles, while His own people do not bother to own Him as their King. The condition of Israel is clearly implied in the early verses of Matthew's Gospel. They are cold and indifferent."[120]

---

[116]Ibid., p. 18.

[117]Harold W. Hoehner, *Chronological Aspects of the Life of Christ*, pp. 25-26.

[118]Toussaint, p. 51.

[119]Carson, "Matthew," p. 86.

[120]Toussaint, p. 52

"The Gentile wise men worship the King of the Jews; the Jews are apathetic; and Herod is concerned only for his throne. Herod's interest in his own political well-being marks the attitude of the governmental authorities throughout the remainder of the Gospel."[121]

2. The prophecies about Egypt 2:13-18

Matthew continued to stress God's predictions about, and His protection of, His Messiah—to help his readers recognize Jesus as the promised King.

2:13   For the second time in two chapters, we read that "an angel" from "the Lord appeared" with a message for "Joseph" (cf. 1:20). This indicates that the message had unusual importance.

The order of the words "the Child and His mother" is unusual. Normally the parent would receive mention before the child. This order draws attention again to the centrality of Jesus in the narrative.

"Egypt" was a natural place of refuge at this time. Its border was just 75 miles from Bethlehem, though the nearest town was about 150 miles, and it provided escape from Herod's hatred. Herod had no authority there. Furthermore, there was a large Jewish population there, as well as a substitute for the Jerusalem temple.[122]

Joseph learned that he was to remain in Egypt until God directed him elsewhere, which happened when Herod died. Again the sovereignty of God stands out.

"In obeying at once this command from God and the other commands that follow, Joseph's righteousness (1:19) casts Herod's wickedness in ever sharper relief."[123]

In many respects, Jesus recapitulated Moses' life and experiences. Moses had also been the target of the ruler of his day, who sought to destroy him and all the other male Hebrew babies by ordering them slain (Exod. 1:15-22). Matthew wanted his readers to see Jesus as a "second Moses," as well as the "true Israel."

2:14-15   Herod died in 4 B.C.[124] Josephus recorded that he died a horrible death, his body rotting away and consumed by worms.[125] He was buried in the Herodium, one of the palace fortresses that he had constructed not far from Bethlehem.[126] His grandson, Herod Agrippa, later suffered a similar fate (Acts 12:23).

As noted, Matthew frequently used the fulfillment of Old Testament prophecies to show that Jesus was the Christ. Verse 15 contains another fulfillment. This one is difficult to understand, however, because in Hosea 11:1 the prophet did not predict anything. He simply described the Israelites' Exodus from Egypt as the departure of God's son (cf. Exod. 4:22). Old Testament writers frequently used the term "son" to describe Israel in its relationship to God. What did Matthew mean when he wrote that Jesus' departure from Egypt fulfilled Hosea's words (Hos. 11:1)? Matthew's quotation is from the Hebrew text.

Matthew did not say that Jesus was fulfilling a *prophecy*. Another significant factor is the meaning of the word "fulfill" (Gr. *pleroo*). It has a broader meaning than simply "to make complete." It essentially means "to establish completely."[127] In the case of predictive prophecy, the complete establishment of what the prophet predicted occurred when what he predicted happened. In the case of prophetic utterances that dealt with the past or present, the complete establishment of what the prophet said took place when another event that was similar happened. This is the sense in which Jesus' departure from Egypt fulfilled Hosea's prophecy (cf. James 2:21-23). Jesus was *the* Son of God (2:15; 3:17; 4:3, 6; 8:29; 11:27; 14:33; 16:16; 17:5; 26:63; 27:40, 43, 54). The history of "Israel," the "son of God" in a different sense, anticipated the life of *Messiah*.[128] To state the same thing another way, Jesus was the "typological recapitulation of Israel."[129] Another writer called this "literal [event] plus typical [fulfillment]."[130] Still another referred to it as "literal prophecy plus a typical import."[131]

---

[121]Ibid., p. 53.

[122]France, p. 79.

[123]Kingsbury, p. 49.

[124]Hoehner, p. 13.

[125]Josephus, *Antiquities of . . .*, 17:6:5; idem, *The Wars . . .*, 1:33:5-7.

[126]Ibid., 1:33:9.

[127]Hermann Cremer, *Biblico-Theological Lexicon of New Testament Greek*, p. 500.

[128]Plummer, p. 19.

[129]Carson, "Matthew," p. 91.

[130]Fruchtenbaum, pp. 843-44.

"There were similarities between the nation and the Son. Israel was God's chosen 'son' by adoption (Ex. 4:22), and Jesus is the Messiah, God's Son. In both cases the descent into Egypt was to escape danger, and the return was important to the nation's providential history."[132]

". . . Matthew looked back and carefully drew analogies between the events of the nation's history and the historical incidents in the life of Jesus."[133]

2:16-18   Some critical scholars discounted Matthew's account of Herod's slaughter of the Bethlehem children because there is no extrabiblical confirmation of it. However, Bethlehem was small, and many other biblically significant events have no secular confirmation, including Jesus' crucifixion. One writer estimated that this purge would have affected only about 20 children.[134] He believed that the total population of Bethlehem at this time was under 1,000. Compared to some of Herod's other atrocities this one was minor.[135]

"The New Testament account of the murder of all the little children at Bethlehem (Matt. ii. 16), in hope of destroying among them the royal scion of David, is thoroughly in character with all that we know of Herod and his reign."[136]

"Emperor Augustus reportedly said it was better to be Herod's sow than his son, for his sow had a better chance of surviving in a Jewish community. In the Greek language, as in English, there is only one letter difference between the words 'sow' (*hyos*) and 'son' (*hyios*)."[137]

"The selfsame character traits Herod exhibits in chapter 2, the [religious] leaders will exhibit later in the story. To enumerate the most obvious of these, Herod shows himself to be 'spiritually blind' (2:3), 'fearful' (2:3), 'conspiratorial' (2:7), 'guileful' and 'mendacious' (2:8), 'murderous' (2:13, 16), 'wrathful' (2:16; cf. 21:15), and 'apprehensive of the future' (2:16)."[138]

Matthew again claimed that another event surrounding Jesus' birth fulfilled prophecy (v. 17). Matthew is the only New Testament writer who quoted "Jeremiah" (31:15; cf. 16:14; 27:9). This quotation is evidently also from the Hebrew text. Incidentally, Matthew only quoted Isaiah and Jeremiah by name of all the prophets he quoted.

"Matthew is not simply meditating on Old Testament texts, but claiming that in what has happened they find fulfillment. If the events are legendary [rather than historical], the argument is futile."[139]

It is not clear whether Jeremiah was referring to the deportation of the northern tribes in 722 B.C., or to the Babylonian Captivity in 586 B.C. Since he dealt primarily with the second of these events in his ministry, he probably did so here too. Poetically, he presented "Rachel" as the idealized "mother" of the Jews, "mourning" from her grave because "her children" were going into captivity. Since Rachel died on the way to Bethlehem (Gen. 35:16, 19), mention of her ties in nicely with the events of Jesus' early childhood near Bethlehem.

"In the original context, Jeremiah is speaking of an event soon to come as the Babylonian Captivity begins. As the Jewish young men were being taken into captivity, they went by the town of Ramah. Not too far from Ramah is where Rachel was buried and she was the symbol of Jewish motherhood. As the young men were marched toward Babylon, the Jewish mothers of Ramah came out weeping for sons they will never see again. Jeremiah pictured the scene as Rachel weeping for her children. This is the *literal* meaning of Jeremiah 31:15. The New Testament cannot change or reinterpret what this verse means in

[131]Cooper, pp. 175-76.

[132]Barbieri, p. 22.

[133]Tracy L. Howard, "The Use of Hosea 11:1 in Matthew 2:15: An Alternative Solution," *Bibliotheca Sacra* 143:572 (October-December 1986):325. This article evaluated several other proposed solutions to this difficult citation. See also G. K. Beale, "The Use of Hosea 11:1 in Matthew 2:15: One More Time," *Journal of the Evangelical Theological Society* 55:4 (December 2012):697-715.

[134]France, p. 85.

[135]See Edersheim, *The Life* . . ., 1:127. See Josephus, *Antiquities of* . . ., 15:1:2; 15:3:3, 9; 15:6:2; 15:7:4, 8, 10; 15:8:4; 15:10:4; 16:8:4; 16:10:4; 16:11:7; 17:2:4; 17: 6:4, 6; 17:7:1; and idem, *The Wars* . . ., 1:178; 1:22:1, 4, 5; 1:24:8; 1:27:6; and 1:33:4 and 6, for the records of some of those that he executed.

[136]Edersheim, *Sketches of* . . ., p. 51.

[137]Barbieri, p. 23.

[138]Kingsbury, p. 117.

[139]R. T. France, "Herod and the Children of Bethlehem," *Novum Testamentum* 21 (1979):120.

that context, nor does it try to do so. In this category [of fulfilled prophecy], there is a New Testament event that has one point of similarity with the Old Testament event. The verse is quoted as an *application*. The one point of similarity between Ramah and Bethlehem is that once again Jewish mothers are weeping for sons they will never see again and so the Old Testament passage is applied to the New Testament event. Otherwise, everything else is different."[140]

Cooper called this "literal prophecy plus an application."[141] Bailey saw three points of comparison between the two situations: in both of them a Gentile king was threatening the future of Israel (cf. 2:13), children were involved, and the future restoration of Israel was nevertheless secure (cf. Jer. 31:31-37).[142]

Matthew evidently used Jeremiah 31:15, because it presented hope to the Israelites, that Israel would return to the land—even though they wept at the nation's departure. The context of Jeremiah's words is hope. Matthew used the Jeremiah passage to give his readers hope, that despite the tears of the Bethlehem mothers, Messiah had escaped from Herod and would return to reign ultimately.[143]

"Here Jesus does not, as in v. 15, recapitulate an event from Israel's history. The Exile sent Israel into captivity and thereby called forth tears. But here the tears are not for him who goes into 'exile' but because of the children who stay behind and are slaughtered. Why, then, refer to the Exile at all? Help comes from observing the broader context of both Jeremiah and Matthew. Jeremiah 31:9, 20 refers to Israel = Ephraim as God's dear son and also introduces the new covenant (31:31-34) the Lord will make with his people. Therefore the tears associated with Exile (31:15) will end. Matthew has already made the Exile a turning point in his thought (1:11-12), for at that time the Davidic line was dethroned. The tears of the Exile are now being 'fulfilled'—i.e., the tears begun in Jeremiah's day are climaxed and ended by the tears of the mothers of Bethlehem. The heir to David's throne has come, the Exile is over, the true Son of God has arrived, and he will introduce the new covenant (26:28) promised by Jeremiah."[144]

3. The prophecies about Nazareth 2:19-23 (cf. Luke 2:39)

Matthew concluded his selective account of the events in Jesus' childhood, that demonstrated His messiahship, and illustrated various reactions to Him with Jesus' return to Israel.

2:19-20   Herod the Great died in 4 B.C. Josephus wrote of his condition shortly before his death as follows:

". . . Herod's distemper greatly increased upon him after a severe manner, and this by God's judgment upon him for his sins: for a fire glowed in him slowly, which did not so much appear to the touch outwardly as it augmented his pains inwardly; for it brought upon him a vehement appetite to eating, which he could not avoid to supply with one sort of food or other. His entrails were also exulcerated, and the chief violence of his pain lay on his colon; an aqueous and transparent liquor also settled itself about his feet, and a like matter afflicted him at the bottom of his belly. Nay, farther, his privy member was putrified, and produced worms; and when he sat upright he had a difficulty of breathing, which was very loathsome, on account of the stench of his breath, and the quickness of its returns; he had also convulsions in all parts of his body, which increased his strength to an insufferable degree."[145]

God's sovereign initiative is again the subject of Matthew's record. This is the fourth "dream" and the third mention of the "angel of the Lord" appearing "to Joseph" in the prologue. The phrase "the land of Israel" occurs only here in the New Testament. Evidently Matthew used it since it recalls the promises and blessings God gave Jacob and his descendants.[146]

---

[140]Fruchtenbaum, p. 844.

[141]Cooper, p. 176.

[142]Bailey, p. 8.

[143]Robert H. Gundry, *The Use of the Old Testament in St. Matthew's Gospel, with Special Reference to the Messianic Hope*, p. 210; R. V. G. Tasker, *The Gospel According to St. Matthew: An Introduction and Commentary*, pp. 43-44.

[144]Carson, "Matthew," p. 95.

[145]Josephus, *Antiquities of . . .*, 17:6:5.

[146]Toussaint, p. 56.

2:21-23   Joseph obediently responded to the Lord's command. However, before he could do so, news reached him that Herod the Great's son, "Archelaus," had begun to rule as ethnarch "over Judea," Samaria, and Idumea. The rest of Herod the Great's kingdom went to his sons Antipas, who ruled as tetrarch over Galilee and Perea (4 B.C. - A.D. 39), and Philip. "Tetrarch" means Philip ruled over one-fourth of the kingdom of his father, Herod the Great. Philip became tetrarch of Iturea, Trachonitis, and some other territories (4 B.C. - A.D. 34).[147] The title "ethnarch" was a more honorable title than "tetrarch." It meant ruler over a people. It was also a title inferior to "king," however.

> "One of the first acts of Archelaus was to murder some three thousand people in the temple because some of their number had memorialized some martyrs put to death by Herod. Like father, like son."[148]

Archelaus proved to be a bad ruler. Caesar Augustus banished him for his poor record in A.D. 6.[149] Philip was the best ruler among Herod the Great's sons.

Evidently God "warned" Joseph not to return to Archelaus' territory. Joseph chose to settle in "Nazareth" in "Galilee" instead, on the northern border of Zebulun, undoubtedly guided there by God. This had been his and Mary's residence before Jesus' birth (13:53-58; Luke 1:26-27; 2:39). Matthew noted that this move was another fulfillment of prophecy (v. 23). Nazareth stood 70 miles north of Bethlehem, and archaeological evidence points to a population of about 480 at the beginning of the first century A.D.[150] It was the location of the Roman garrison in northern Galilee.[151]

> ". . . the ancient *Via Maris* [Sea Highway] led through Nazareth, and thence either by Cana, or else along the northern shoulder of Mount Tabor, to the Lake of Gennesaret—each of these roads soon uniting with the Upper Galilean. Hence, although the stream of commerce between Acco and the East was divided into three channels, yet, as one of these passed through Nazareth, the quiet little town was not a stagnant pool of rustic seclusion. . . . But, on the other hand, Nazareth was also one of the great centers of Jewish Temple-life. . . . The Priests of the 'course' which was to be on duty always gathered in certain towns, whence they went up in company to Jerusalem, while those of their number who were unable to go spent the week in fasting and prayer. . . . Thus, to take a wider view, a double symbolic significance attached to Nazareth, since through it passed alike those who carried on the traffic of the world, and those who ministered in the Temple."[152]

Careful attention to the terms Matthew used to describe this fulfillment helps us understand how Jesus fulfilled Scripture. First, Matthew said the prophecy came through "prophets," not *a* prophet. This is the only place in the first Gospel that he said this. Second, Matthew did not say that the prophets "said" or "wrote" the prediction. He said "what was said or spoken" through them happened. In other words, Matthew was quoting indirectly, freely.[153]

There is no Old Testament passage that predicted that the Messiah would come from Nazareth or that people would call Him "a Nazarene." How then could Matthew say that Jesus fulfilled Scripture by living there? The most probable explanation seems to be that Nazareth was an especially *despised* town—in the *despised* region of Galilee—in Jesus' day (John 1:46; 7:42, 52). Several of the Old Testament prophets predicted that people would "despise" the Messiah (Ps. 22:6-8, 13; 69:8, 20-21; Isa. 11:1; 42:1-4; 49:7; 53:2-3, 8; Dan. 9:26). Matthew often returned to this theme of Jesus being despised (8:20; 11:16-19; 15:7-8). The writer appears to be giving the substance of several Old Testament passages here, rather than quoting any one of them. There may also be an allusion to the *naser* ("branch") in Isaiah 11:1 that the rabbis in Jesus' day regarded as messianic.[154] In that passage, David's heir appears to be emerging from a lowly, obscure place. One writer gave evidence that the Targums, as well as the New Testament writers, exegeted the Old Testament messianically.[155]

---

[147]Cf. Josephus, *Antiquities of . . .*, 17:11:4; idem, *The Wars . . .*, 2:6:3.

[148]Walvoord, p. 24. See also Edersheim, *The Life . . .*, 1:220.

[149]Carson, "Matthew," p. 96.

[150]France, *The Gospel . . .*, p. 91.

[151]*The Nelson . . .*, pp. 1579, 1580.

[152]Edersheim, *The Life . . .*, 1:147-48.

[153]W. Barnes Tatum Jr., "Matthew 2.23," *The Bible Translator* 27 (1976):135-37.

[154]*The New Scofield . . .*, p. 994; Wiersbe, 1:16.

[155]See Michael B. Shepherd, "Targums, The New Testament, and Biblical Theology of the Messiah," *Journal of the Evangelical Theological Society* 51:1 (March 2008):45-58.

"In the first century, *Nazarenes* were people despised and rejected and the term was used to reproach and to shame (John 1:46). The prophets did teach that the Messiah would be a despised and rejected individual (*e.g.* Isa 53:3) and this is summarized by the term, *Nazarene*."[156]

Fruchtenbaum called this type of prophetic fulfillment "summation."[157] Cooper preferred to call it "literal prophecy plus a summation."[158]

"Jesus is King Messiah, Son of God, Son of David; but he was a branch from a royal line hacked down to a stump and reared in surroundings guaranteed to win him scorn. Jesus the Messiah, Matthew is telling us, did not introduce his kingdom with outward show or present himself with the pomp of an earthly monarch. In accord with prophecy he came as the despised Servant of the Lord."[159]

Less satisfying explanations of this prophecy and its fulfillment are the following. First, some connect "Nazarene" with "Nazirite" (cf. Judg. 13:5). However, Jesus was never a Nazirite (11:19). Furthermore the etymologies of these words do not connect. Second, some believe that the Hebrew word translated "branch" (*naser*), in Isaiah 11:1, sounds enough like "Nazareth" to justify a connection. The problem with this view is that the Hebrew word and the town of Nazareth have nothing in common except similar sounding names. Also *naser* occurs in only one passage, but Matthew quoted the "prophets." Third, some writers have posited a pre-Christian sect and suggested that Matthew referred to this. There is no evidence to support this theory. Fourth, some believe Matthew was making a pun by connecting the names Nazareth and Nazarene. If this were true, how could he claim a fulfillment of prophecy? Fifth, some think the writer referred to prophecies not recorded in Scripture, but known to, and accepted by, his original readers. Matthew gave no clue that this unusual meaning is what he intended. Furthermore, later readers would not only reject such an authority, but would charge Matthew with fabricating such a source to support his argument.

Matthew chapter 2 advances the writer's argument significantly by making three major points.

"The first relates to the Gentiles. The Magi come from the East and worship the King of the Jews. A glimmering foreview of all the nations of the earth being blessed in Abraham is seen in this act. . . . The second point Matthew makes concerns the Jews. They are shown to be unconcerned and indifferent to any report concerning Him. Finally, Matthew, by his use of the Old Testament, proves that Jesus is the promised Messiah. He is the fulfillment of all that is anticipated in their Scriptures. These three things form the basis of Matthew's Gospel. Jesus is presented as the Messiah prophesied and promised in the Old Testament. The Jews reject Him. Because of this rejection the King turns to the Gentiles and the kingdom program for the Jews is postponed.

"Chapter one declares the theanthropic character of the person of the Messiah. The reception which is to be given the claims of the Messiah is set forth in chapter two. Matthew three begins the narrative of the historical account of the presentation of Israel's Messiah to that nation."[160]

"Matthew 1—2 serves as a finely wrought prologue for every major theme in the Gospel."[161]

Chapters 1 and 2 show the reader who Jesus *was*, His identity, including the reactions of various groups of people. The rest of the book continues to clarify Jesus' identity and shows what Jesus *said* and *did*, and the reactions of various groups of people. The reactions of these groups and individuals become instructive for us in knowing how to respond to Jesus and how not to respond to Him.

D. THE KING'S PREPARATION 3:1—4:11

Matthew passed over Jesus' childhood quickly to relate His preparation for presentation to Israel as her King. He recorded three events that prepared Jesus for His ministry: the ministry of Jesus' forerunner, John the Baptist (3:1-12), Jesus' baptism (3:13-17), and Jesus' temptation (4:1-11). The major point is that Jesus is the true Son of God. John the Baptist witnessed that Jesus was the prophesied coming Son of God. Matthew's account of Jesus' baptism emphasizes heaven's (God's) attestation of Jesus as God's Son. The Spirit descended on Jesus to *empower* the King for service, and the voice from heaven *validated* Jesus as God's Son. The record of Jesus' temptation shows that He overcame temptation and so was qualified personally to be the perfect Son of God, not just *a* son of God in the traditional kingly sense. All the former "sons" of God (kings of Israel) had fallen before temptation.

---

[156]Fruchtenbaum, p. 845.

[157]Ibid.

[158]Cooper, pp. 177-78.

[159]Carson, "Matthew," p. 97.

[160]Toussaint, pp. 57-58.

[161]Carson, "Matthew," p. 73.

"The material of this section of the Gospel is particularly important since the baptism of Jesus serves as the occasion of his special anointing by the Holy Spirit for the ministry that follows, but it is also Christologically significant in that his divine Sonship is confirmed and the non-triumphalist nature of the present phase of that Sonship is indicated (3:17c and 4:1-11). Thus Matthew provides information that is vitally important to an understanding of the narrative that follows: what Jesus does in his ministry he does by the power of the Spirit; yet Jesus will not act in the manner of a triumphalist messiah, in accordance with popular expectation, but in his own unique way, in obedience to the will of his Father."[162]

Matthew presented four witnesses to Jesus' messiahship in this section: John the Baptist (3:1-15), the Holy Spirit (3:16), the Father (3:17), and Satan (4:1-11). A fifth witness follows in 4:12-15, namely, Jesus' ministry.

1. Jesus' forerunner 3:1-12 (cf. Mark 1:2-8; Luke 3:3-18)

It was common when Jesus lived, for forerunners to precede important individuals, in order to prepare the way for their arrival. For example, when a king would visit a town in his realm, his emissaries would go before him to announce his visit. They would make sure the town was in good condition to receive him. Sometimes his servants even had to do minor roadwork to smooth the highway the king would be taking as he approached his destination.[163] John not only prepared the way for Jesus, but also announced Him as an important person and implied His royalty. John preceded Jesus in His birth, in His public appearance, and in His death.

"As Jesus' forerunner, John foreshadows in his person and work the person and work of Jesus. Both John and Jesus are the agents of God sent by God (11:10; 10:40). Both belong to the time of fulfillment (3:3; 1:23). Both have the same message to proclaim (3:2; 4:17). Both enter into conflict with Israel: in the case of the crowds, a favorable reception ultimately gives way to repudiation; in the case of the leaders, the opposition is implacable from the outset (3:7-10; 9:3). Both John and Jesus are 'delivered up' to their enemies (4:12; 10:4). And both are made to die violently and shamefully (14:3-12; 27:37)."[164]

3:1-2   John appeared "in those days" (v. 1). This phrase is a general term that says little about specific time but identifies what follows as historical. It is a common transitional statement in Matthew's narrative.[165] John's ministry, as Matthew described it here, occurred just before the beginning of Jesus' public ministry, approximately 30 years after the events of chapter 2.

"John" became a popular name among the Jews following the heroic career of John Hyrcanus (died 106 B.C.). There are four or five Johns in the New Testament. This one received the surname "the Baptist" because of his practice of baptizing repentant Jews (v. 6).

John was a herald with a message to proclaim. He appears on the scene suddenly and mysteriously, much like Elijah, whose ministry John mirrored (cf. 1 Kings 17:1).[166] "Preaching" is literally heralding (Gr. *kerysso*).

"In the New Testament the verb does not mean 'to give an informative or hortatory or edifying discourse expressed in beautifully arranged words with a melodious voice; it means to proclaim an event' . . ."[167]

The event John proclaimed was the imminent arrival of God's kingdom.

The scene of John's ministry was "the wilderness of Judea." This loosely defined area lay mainly to the west and somewhat north of the Dead Sea. John evidently conducted his ministry there because of its rough conditions that were suitable to his appeal for repentance. In Israel's history, the wilderness forever reminded the Jews of their 40-year sojourn under extreme conditions and God giving them the Law of Moses. They associated it with a place of separation unto God, testing for refinement, and new beginnings. In John's day, the wilderness spawned many movements that challenged Israel's leadership.[168] This may explain why John chose to minister there.

John called for the people to "repent" (v. 2).

"Contrary to popular thinking, repent does not mean to be sorry. The Greek word *metanoeo* means '. . . to change one's mind or purpose . . .'[169] In the New Testament it '. . . indicates a complete change of

[162]Hagner, p. 43.

[163]Walvoord, p. 29.

[164]Kingsbury, p. 49.

[165]Robertson, *A Grammar* . . ., p. 708.

[166]See Edersheim, *The Life* . . ., 2:706-9, on rabbinic traditions about Elijah.

[167]A. M. Hunter, *The Message of the New Testament*, p. 24.

[168]Josephus, *The Wars* . . ., 2:13:4-5.

[169]Footnote 74: G. A. Abbott-Smith, *A Manual Greek Lexicon of the New Testament*, p. 287.

attitude, spiritual and moral, towards God.'[170] The primary meaning involves a turning to God which may indeed make a person sorry for his sins, but that sorrow is a by-product and not the repentance itself. . . . In a word, John's command to the people of Israel was for them to turn from their sins to God in anticipation of their Messiah."[171]

The Jews needed to change their thinking, because most of them believed that they would enter the Messiah's kingdom, simply because they were the children of Abraham (v. 9). John was attacking established religious concepts of his day and those who taught them. He demanded evidence of genuine repentance instead of mere complacency, hypocrisy, and superficiality (cf. v. 8).

John also announced that "the kingdom of heaven" (lit. the heavens) was "at hand." What was this kingdom? Students of this question have offered three basic answers.

First, some believe that "the kingdom" began with Jesus' ministry, and will continue until His second coming, which will mean the end of the world, in their view. They view the kingdom as spiritual, namely, as God's rule over the hearts and lives of believers in Jesus. This kingdom is spiritual in contrast to physical and earthly. Advocates do not believe Jesus will return to earth to set up an earthly, physical kingdom that will resume the Davidic kingdom of the Old Testament. They believe that the promises in the Old Testament—of Israel's restoration under Messiah—are being fulfilled in a spiritual sense in the experience of Christians. For example, promises of Israel's return to her land will find fulfillment in the church's entrance into heaven. Most advocates of this view believe that the church has replaced Israel, and that God has no special future for Israel *as Israel*. The kingdom that Jesus inaugurated, they believe, is *already* present. This is the typical amillennial (no millennium) understanding of the kingdom.

Second, some believe that "the kingdom" that Jesus preached will be entirely earthly. They hold that it is the resumption of the Davidic kingdom, which ended with the Babylonian exile and will resume when Jesus returns to earth at His second coming. Then He will establish this kingdom, which will continue for 1,000 years (the Millennium). The present inter-advent age is not the kingdom, nor is the kingdom the Church Age. There is no present form of this kingdom, according to this view. The kingdom Jesus preached is *not yet* from our perspective in history. This is the view of some premillennialists, mainly some dispensationalists.

Many who hold this second view acknowledge that though the kingdom Jesus announced will be an earthly kingdom, there is another kingdom that has existed throughout history. It is God's sovereign rule over all. Since He has ruled, is ruling, and will forever reign over all, we can speak of this universal rule as His kingdom. However, it is not the restored Davidic kingdom that Jesus announced as being at hand.

Third, some interpreters have concluded that the kingdom Jesus announced was both *already* present, in one form, *and not yet* present in another form. They believe there is a present spiritual form of the kingdom now (as in view one above), and a future physical form of the kingdom (as in view two above). Some advocates of this view believe that God has a future for Israel *as Israel* (the physical descendants of Jacob). The church has not replaced Israel in God's plans. This is the view of "progressive dispensationalists."[172] Other advocates of this view believe that the church *does* replace Israel. God's promises to Israel will find fulfillment in the church. These are mainly "historic premillennialists" (or "replacement theologians"). This group believes in a physical, earthly kingdom but for the church, not Israel.

Many dispensationalists are uncomfortable with the idea that the kingdom is already and not yet, in view of how they interpret kingdom passages. Specifically, they are uncomfortable with the idea that the church is the "already" stage of the kingdom. They prefer to view the church as an entity distinct from the kingdom, an intercalation or something inserted in the divine timeline between the Old Testament kingdom of David and the messianic kingdom. They make much of the terminology used to distinguish the church and the kingdom. Most in this group of interpreters see some form of God's kingdom in existence now, however, whether the universal rule of God or a mystery form of the coming kingdom.

Among dispensationalists, some hold that there were two kingdoms that Jesus preached: the "kingdom of God" and the "kingdom of heaven."[173] The former term, they say, refers to a smaller kingdom that includes only genuine believers, and is cosmic and universal in scope. The latter term, they say, refers to a larger kingdom that includes all who profess to be

---

[170]Footnote 75: J. H. Moulton and G. Milligan, *The Vocabulary of the Greek Testament*, p. 403.

[171]Toussaint, pp. 60-61.

[172]See Appendix 2 "The Kingdoms of God," and Appendix 3 "Views of the Messianic Kingdom," at the end of these notes.

[173]Lewis Sperry Chafer, *Systematic Theology*, 5:316; 7:223-24; John F. Walvoord, *The Millennial Kingdom*, p. 171; idem, "The Kingdom of Heaven," *Bibliotheca Sacra* 124:495 (July-September 1967):203; C. I. Scofield, ed., *The Scofield Reference Bible*, p. 1003.

believers, and is limited to the earth. This distinction has been shown to be invalid. One cannot make this distinction on the basis of how the New Testament writers used these terms.

"Most recent advocates of a distinction acknowledge that the two expressions are 'often used synonymously,' yet are to be distinguished in certain contexts.[174] Others who would generally be identified with dispensationalism agree with most non-dispensationalists that no distinction between these expressions is intended by the biblical writers.[175] Matthew's use of 'the kingdom of heaven' is to be explained as a Semitic idiom probably resulting from the Jewish reverence for the name of God and the tendency to use 'heaven' or 'heavens' as a substitute.[176] So, although some dispensationalists still distinguish the two terms in some passages, we agree with Ryrie that this issue is not a determinative feature of dispensationalism."[177]

Dispensationalists who are not "progressives" believe that the kingdom that John, Jesus (4:17), and His disciples (10:7) announced and offered the Jews was exactly the same kingdom that the Old Testament prophets predicted. Because the Jews rejected their King and His kingdom, God "postponed" the kingdom until a future time when Israel will accept her Messiah, namely, at His second advent (cf. Zech. 12:10-14). The word "postponed" does not imply that Jewish rejection of the Messiah took God by surprise. It views the coming of the kingdom from man's perspective. This view, I believe, best harmonizes the normal meaning of the Old Testament kingdom prophecies and Jesus' teachings.[178] Similarly, because the generation of Jews that left Egypt in the Exodus refused to trust and obey God at Kadesh Barnea, God postponed the nation's entrance into the Promised Land for 38 years. As God postponed Israel's entrance into the Promised Land because of Jewish unbelief, so He postponed Israel's entrance into the messianic kingdom because of Jewish unbelief.

There is good evidence that the kingdom that John and Jesus spoke about was the earthly eschatological kingdom that the Old Testament prophets foretold. First, the fact that John, Jesus, and Jesus' disciples did not explain what it was, but simply announced that it was near, indicates that they referred to a kingdom known to their hearers.[179] Second, Jesus restricted the proclamation about the kingdom to Jews (10:5-6). If the kingdom was spiritual, why was this necessary? Moreover, the inauguration of the kingdom predicted in the Old Testament depended on the Jews receiving it (Zech. 12:1-14; 13:7-9; Mal. 4:5-6). Third, Jesus' disciples expected the beginning of an earthly kingdom (20:20-21; Acts 1:6). They did so after they had listened to Jesus' teaching about the kingdom for a long time. Fourth, this kingdom cannot be the church, since God had not yet revealed the existence of the church, let alone established it (16:18). It cannot be God's universal reign over the hearts of mankind, since that had existed since creation.

". . . if the Kingdom, announced as 'at hand' by the Lord, had been exclusively a 'spiritual kingdom,' or as some have defined it, 'the rule of God in the heart,' such an announcement would have had no special significance whatever to Israel, for such a rule of God had always been recognized among the people of God [cf. Ps. 37:31; 103:19]."[180]

Therefore, we conclude that when John spoke of "the kingdom of heaven" (v. 2), he meant the earthly kingdom over which Messiah would rule, which the Old Testament prophets predicted.

"Only the premillennial interpretation of the concept of the kingdom allows a literal interpretation of both Old Testament and New Testament prophecies relating to the future kingdom"[181]

It is particularly important to distinguish "the church" from "the kingdom." The kingdom, whether described as "of heaven" or "of God," always refers to the earthly reign of Messiah as predicted in the Old Testament. The church will play a part in the kingdom, but they are separate entities. Progressive dispensationalists argue that the church is the *first phase* of the messianic kingdom, the "already" phase, in contrast to the eschatological, "not yet," phase. Matthew maintained the distinction between "the kingdom" and "the church" throughout his Gospel, as did the other New Testament writers.

---

[174]Footnote 20: *The New Scofield Reference Bible*, pp. 994, 1002.

[175]Footnote 21: Eric Sauer, *The Triumph of the Crucified*, p. 23; Toussaint, pp. 65-68.

[176]Footnote 22: Dalman, pp. 91-93. See also Edersheim, *The Life . . .*, 1:267.

[177]Robert L. Saucy, *The Case for Progressive Dispensationalism*, p. 19. His reference to (Charles C.) Ryrie is from *Dispensationalism Today*, pp. 170-71.

[178]See Alva J. McClain, *The Greatness of the Kingdom*, pp. 274-76.

[179]George N. D. Peters, *The Theocratic Kingdom of Our Lord Jesus, the Christ, as Covenanted in the Old Testament and Presented in the New Testament*, 1:195.

[180]McClain, p. 303.

[181]Walvoord, *Matthew: . . .*, p. 31.

What did John mean when he announced that the kingdom was "at hand" (v. 2)? The Greek verb *eggizo* means "to draw near," not "to be here" (cf. 21:1).[182] All that was necessary for the kingdom to be there was Israel's acceptance of her King (11:14). The kingdom was near because the King was present. Amillennialists, historic premillennialists, and progressive dispensationalists believe John meant that the kingdom was about to begin, which, they say, it did when Jesus began to minister.

"If Israel had accepted its Messiah, the earthly kingdom would have been inaugurated by the King."[183]

This statement may seem to some to render Christ's work on the cross unnecessary, but this is incorrect. Had the Jews accepted their Messiah when He offered the kingdom to them, He still would have died on the cross and experienced resurrection and ascension. He could not have been the Messiah without doing so, in fulfillment of many Old Testament prophecies (Ps. 22; Isa. 53; Dan. 9; Zech. 13). Then the prophecies concerning the seven years of Jacob's trouble would have been fulfilled (Jer. 30:7; Dan. 12:1; 9:26-27). Next, Messiah would have returned to set up His kingdom (Isa. 60:1-3; 66:18; Hab. 2:14; cf. Zech. 12:10; 13:6).

Since the Jews rejected Jesus' offer of the kingdom—was His offer genuine? Had God not already determined that Israel would reject her Messiah? Jesus' offer of the kingdom was just as genuine as any gospel offer of salvation to someone who rejects it.

"Those who cavil at the idea of an offer which is certain to be rejected betray an ignorance, not only of Biblical history (cf. Isa. 6:8-10 and Ezek. 2:3-7), but also of the important place of the legal proffer in the realm of jurisprudence."[184]

3:3   "This is the one OT citation of Matthew's own eleven direct OT quotations that is not introduced by a fulfillment formula . . . Instead he introduces it with a Pesher formula (e.g., Acts 2:16 . . .) that can only be understood as identifying the Baptist in an eschatological, prophecy-and-fulfillment framework with the one of whom Isaiah (40:3) spoke."[185]

In Isaiah 40:3, "the voice" exhorts the people to prepare for God's coming while He is bringing Israel back from her dispersion. The prophet then proceeded to describe the blessings that would follow her return. Matthew identified Yahweh in Isaiah 40:3 with Jesus in Matthew 3:3. This equates "the kingdom of God" to "the kingdom of Jesus." While this is not an implicit statement of Jesus' deity, it certainly presents Jesus as more than just Yahweh's representative.

3:4-6   In his dress and in "his food," as well as in his habitat and in his message, "John" associated himself with the poor and the prophets—particularly Elijah (cf. 2 Kings 1:8; Zech. 13:4; Mal. 4:5).

"In view of the considerable Jewish interest in the eschatological role of Elijah (see on 11:14 and 17:10-11) it is likely that John's clothing was deliberately adopted to promote this image."[186]

Likewise, John may have selected his venue for ministry because of its associations with Elijah. Poor people ate "locusts" (Lev. 11:22), and such a diet was compatible with that of a Nazirite. John called for the people to get right with God, because the appearing of their Messiah was imminent. Elijah had called the Israelites back to God at the time of their most serious apostasy. John called them back to God on the eve of their greatest opportunity. He was the first prophet from God in approximately 400 years.

Many people responded to John because they perceived that he was a genuine prophet with a message from God (v. 5).

Baptism represented purification to the Jews. Ceremonial washings were part of the Mosaic system of worship (Exod. 19; Lev. 15; Num. 19). When a Gentile became a proselyte to Judaism, he or she underwent baptism. But John "baptized" Jews. John's baptism carried these connotations of cleansing with it, but it was different. In the other types of ceremonial cleansing, the person washed himself or herself. John, on the other hand, baptized other people. He probably received the name "John the Baptist" or "Baptizer" for this reason.[187]

---

[182]William L. Lane, *The Gospel according to Mark*, p. 65, n. 93; A. J. Mattill Jr., *Luke and the Last Things: A Perspective for the Understanding of Lukan Thought*, pp. 70-77.

[183]Toussaint, p. 63.

[184]McClain, p. 344.

[185]Carson, "Matthew," p. 101.

[186]France, The Gospel . . ., p. 106.

[187]Ethelbert Stauffer, *New Testament Theology*, p. 22.

John's baptism did not make a person a member of the church, the body of Christ, since the church had not yet come into existence (16:18). It simply gave public testimony to that Jewish person's repentance and commitment to live a holy life.

Lenski, a Lutheran commentator, believed that John baptized by effusion (pouring) rather than by immersion.[188] It is impossible to identify the method of baptism John used from what the Gospels tell us. However, extrabiblical sources indicate that Jewish proselyte baptism took place in large tanks (Heb. *mikvah*) in which the person undergoing baptism stood.[189] The issue boils down to whether one takes the word "baptism" in its primary sense of *submersion*, or in its secondary sense of *initiation*.[190] Likewise, it is unclear whether the confession involved public or private acts.

3:7-10   This verse contains Matthew's first reference to the "Pharisees" ("separate ones") and the "Sadducees" ("righteous ones"). Significantly, John was antagonistic toward them because they were hypocritical, a trait that marks them throughout the Gospels. Matthew lumped them together here because they were Israel's leaders.

"After the ministry of the postexilic prophets ceased, godly men called *Chasidim* (saints) arose who sought to keep alive reverence for the law among the descendants of the Jews who returned from the Babylonian captivity. This movement degenerated into the Pharisaism of our Lord's day—a letter-strictness which overlaid the law with traditional interpretations held to have been communicated by the LORD to Moses as oral explanations of equal authority with the law itself (cp. Mt. 15:2-3; Mk. 7:8-13; Gal. 1:14). . . .

"The Sadducees were a Jewish sect that denied the existence of angels or other spirits, and all miracles, especially the resurrection of the body. They were the religious rationalists of the time (Mk. 12:18-23; Acts 23:8), and were strongly entrenched in the Sanhedrin and priesthood (Acts 4:1-2; 5:17). The Sadducees are identified with no affirmative doctrine, but were mere deniers of the supernatural."[191]

"The course of our investigations has shown, that neither Pharisees nor Sadducees were a sect, in the sense of separating from Temple or Synagogue; and also that the Jewish people as such were not divided between Pharisees and Sadducees. The small number of professed Pharisees (six thousand) at the time of Herod [Josephus, *Antiquities of* . . . 17:2:4], the representations of the New Testament, and even the curious circumstance that Philo never once mentions the name of Pharisee, confirm the result of our historical inquiries, that the Pharisees were first an 'order,' then gave the name to a party, and finally represented a direction of theological thought."[192]

"Vipers" is a word Isaiah used to describe God's enemies (Isa. 14:29; 30:6). John's use of it associates him with the former prophets and reflects his prophetic authority.

"The first major appearance of the religious leaders in Matthew's story occurs in conjunction with the ministry of John the Baptist (3:7-10). The importance of their appearance here has to do with the fact that John is the forerunner of Jesus. As such, the attitude that John assumes toward the leaders is predictive of the attitude that Jesus will assume toward them."[193]

John's question (v. 7) amounted to, "Who suggested to you that you would escape the coming wrath?"[194] The behavior of the Pharisees and Sadducees should have demonstrated the genuineness of their professed repentance, but it did not. "Fruit" is what people produce—that other people see—that indicates their spiritual condition (13:21; cf. Mark 4:19; Luke 8:14; John 15:1-6). The fruits of "repentance" were absent in the case of these leaders. There was no external evidence that they desired to draw near to God in anticipation of Messiah's appearance.

Many of the Jews in the inter-testamental period believed that if one was a descendant of "Abraham," he would automatically enter Messiah's kingdom.[195] They counted on the patriarch's righteousness as sufficient for themselves (cf. Rom. 4).

---

[188]Lenski, p. 101.

[189]See Edersheim, *The Life* . . ., 2:745-49; *A Dictionary of Christ and the Gospels*, s.v. "Baptism," by Marcus Dodds.

[190]Walvoord, *Matthew:* . . ., p. 31.

[191]*The New Scofield* . . ., p. 995.

[192]Edersheim, *Sketches of* . . ., p. 244.

[193]Kingsbury, p. 117.

[194]Carson, "Matthew," p. 103.

[195]Edersheim, *The Life* . . ., 1:271.

However, God had often pruned back the unrighteous in Israel and preserved a remnant in its history. As Matthew continued to point out in his Gospel, many of the Jews refused to humble themselves before God and instead trusted in their own righteousness. The Pharisees and Sadducees were doing that here. Josephus, himself a Pharisee,[196] placed the origin of both of these groups in the time of Jonathan, the son of Judas Maccabee (160-143 B.C.).[197]

John's reference to "stones" (v. 9) was a play on words with "children" in both the Hebrew and Aramaic languages. If stones could become God's children, certainly Gentiles could.

Verse 10 gives the reason the Jews needed to repent. Divine judgment would precede the establishment of Messiah's kingdom (cf. Isa. 1:27; 4:4; 5:16; 13:6-19; 42:1; Jer. 33:14-16; Dan. 7:26-27). The Jews connected the concepts of repentance and the messianic age closely in their thinking.[198] John announced that this judgment was imminent (vv. 10-12). *Any* "tree (better than "every" tree) that does not bear good fruit," regardless of its roots, will suffer destruction. Probably John had individuals and the nation of Israel in mind.

The reference to "fire" in verse 10 pictures the judgment and destruction of those who fail to repent (cf. "wrath," v. 7, and "winnowing fork," v. 13). For individuals, this judgment would involve eternal destruction (v. 12), assuming there was no later repentance. For the nation, it would involve the postponement of the kingdom and its attendant blessings.

3:11   John baptized in water "in connection with" repentance.[199] However, the One coming after him, the King, would "baptize . . . with the Holy Spirit (cf. Joel 2:28-29) and fire" (cf. Mal. 3:2-5). The Malachi prophecy speaks of fire as a refining or purifying agent, not as an instrument of destruction. Both prophecies involve the nation of Israel as a whole primarily.

Are these two different baptisms or one? This is a very difficult question to answer because the arguments on both sides are strong.[200] In both interpretations, *baptism* connotes both immersion, in the metaphorical sense of placing into something, and initiation.

The construction of the statement in the Greek text favors one baptism. Usually one entity is in view when one article precedes two nouns joined by a conjunction.[201] This would mean that the one baptism Jesus would perform would be with the Holy Spirit and fire together. Some interpreters believe that this prophecy was fulfilled on the day of Pentecost (Acts 2:3-4). However, since the church was a mystery announced first by our Lord (Matt. 16:18), and then explained more fully by subsequent apostles and prophets (Eph. 3:5; Col. 1:25-26), it seems to me that the baptism that John referred to was the one that will take place in the future day of the Lord. There is no indication that John the Baptist knew anything about the church.

The fire in Malachi's prophecy probably refers to purification and judgment. The purification emphasis is in harmony with Malachi's use. This has led many scholars to conclude that the fire baptism that John predicted is not the one at Pentecost.[202] They, and I, believe that the time when Jesus will baptize with the Holy Spirit and fire to fulfill these prophecies concerning Israel is yet future from our viewpoint in history. It will happen at His second advent. It would have happened at His first advent if Israel had accepted Him. Jesus' baptism of His disciples on the day of Pentecost was a similar baptism, but it was not the fulfillment of these prophecies, since they involved Israel and "the day of the Lord" specifically (cf. John 14:17; Acts 2; 1 Cor. 12:13).[203]

The context, which speaks of blessing for the repentant but judgment for the unrepentant, tends to favor two baptisms (vv. 8-10, 12; cf. Acts 1:5; 11:16). In this case, the "fire" would refer primarily, if not exclusively, to judgment.[204] The baptism "with the Holy Spirit" would refer to Spirit baptism that will happen when Israel accepts her Messiah (Isa. 44:3; Joel 2:28-32). A foretaste of that baptism occurred on the day of Pentecost (Acts 2). The baptism "with fire" would refer to Jesus' judgment of unrepentant Israel (cf. v. 12). After Israel's rejection of Jesus, it became clear that this national judgment will happen primarily at His second coming. This fiery judgment might also refer to unrepentant individuals when they reach the end of their lives.

[196]Josephus, *The Life . . .*, , par. 2.

[197]See Edersheim, *The Life . . .*, 1:96.

[198]C. G. Montefiore, "Rabbinic Conceptions of Repentance," *Jewish Quarterly Review* 16 (January 1904):211.

[199]Carson, "Matthew," p. 104.

[200]See Hagner, pp. 51-52.

[201]Robertson, *A Grammar . . .*, p. 566.

[202]E.g., Edersheim, *The Life . . .*, 1:272; M'Neile, p. 29; Toussaint, p. 70; Carson, "Matthew," p. 105; and James Morison, *A Practical Commentary on the Gospel According to St. Matthew*, p. 36. See also John Proctor, "Fire in God's House: Influence of Malachi 3 in the NT," *Journal of the Evangelical Theological Society* 36:1 (March 1993):12-13.

[203]See Renald E. Showers, *Maranatha: Our Lord, Come! A Definitive Study of the Rapture of the Church*, pp. 30-40, for an excellent discussion of "the day of the Lord."

[204]Those who favor this view include Walvoord, *Matthew: . . .*, p. 32; Barbieri, p. 25; and Wiersbe, 1:17.

All things considered, it seems probable that John was referring to one baptism that will find complete fulfillment at Jesus' second coming.

The rabbis taught that, even if one was a slave, loosening another person's sandal was beneath the dignity of a Jew.[205] So by saying he was unworthy to unloose ("remove") Jesus' "sandals," John meant that he was unworthy of even the most humiliating service of Jesus.

3:12   John metaphorically described God separating the true and the false, the repentant and the unrepentant, in a future judgment. This thorough judgment will result in the preservation of the believing Israelites and the destruction of the unbelieving (cf. 25:31-46). The "barn" probably refers to the kingdom, and the "unquenchable fire" to the endless duration and the agonizing nature of this punishment.

"'Unquenchable fire' is not just metaphor: fearful reality underlies Messiah's separation of grain from chaff. The 'nearness' of the kingdom therefore calls for repentance (v. 2)."[206]

What then was the essential message of Messiah's forerunner?

"John preached *both* a personal salvation, involving the remission of sins (Mark 1:4), *and* a national salvation, involving the establishment of the millennial kingdom with Israel delivered out of the hand of their enemies (Matt. 3:2; Luke 1:71-75)."[207]

2. Jesus' baptism 3:13-17 (cf. Mark 1:9-11; Luke 3:21-23)

Jesus' baptism was the occasion at which His messiahship became obvious publicly. Matthew recorded this event as he did to convince his readers further of Jesus' messianic qualifications. Thus John's baptism had two purposes: to prepare Israel for her Messiah (3:1-12) and to prepare the Messiah for Israel (3:13-17; cf. John 1:31).

3:13-14   John hesitated to baptize Jesus because he believed that Jesus did not need to repent. John evidently suggested that it was more appropriate that Jesus baptize him, than that he baptize Jesus, because he knew that Jesus was more righteous than he was. It is unlikely that John meant that he wanted the Spirit and fire baptism of Jesus. John did not know that Jesus was the Messiah until after he had baptized Him (John 1:31-34).

Jericho *   ✝ Place of Jesus' baptism (?)
Mt. of Temptation? ∧
Jerusalem *   ∧

JUDEA

THE BEGINNING OF JESUS' MINISTRY

25 miles

3:15   John agreed to baptize Jesus, only after Jesus convinced him that by baptizing Him, both of them would "fulfill all righteousness." What did Jesus mean?

An important prerequisite to understanding Jesus' words is an understanding of the meaning of "righteousness." Matthew's use of this word is different from Paul's. Paul used it mainly to describe a right standing before God, positional righteousness. Matthew used it to describe conformity to God's will, *ethical* righteousness.[208] Ethical righteousness is the display of conduct in one's actions that is right in God's eyes. It does not deal with getting saved but responding to God's grace. In Matthew, a righteous person is one who lives in harmony with the will of God (cf. 1:19). Ethical righteousness is a major theme of the Old Testament, and it was a matter that concerned the Jews in Jesus' day, especially the Pharisees.

Jesus understood that it was God's will for John to baptize Him. There is no Old Testament prophecy that states that Messiah would undergo water baptism, but there is prophecy that Messiah would submit Himself to God (Isa. 42:1; 53; et al.). That spirit of submissiveness to God's will is primarily what John's baptism identified in those who submitted to it. Consequently it was appropriate for Jesus to undergo John's baptism, and John consented to baptize Him. In doing so, Jesus authenticated John's ministry and identified Himself with the godly remnant within Israel.

[205] The rabbinic writing *Mekilta de Rabbi Ishmael, Nezikin 1* on Exod. 21:2, cited by Bock, *Jesus according . . .*, p. 83.
[206] Carson, "Matthew," p. 105.
[207] S. Lewis Johnson Jr., "The Message of John the Baptist." *Bibliotheca Sacra* 113:449 (January 1956):36. See also Toussaint, p. 69.
[208] Benno Przybylski, *Righteousness in Matthew and His World of Thought*, pp. 91-94.

"The King, because of His baptism, is now bound up with His subjects."[209]

"Jesus' baptism in the Jordan stands as a counterpart of Israel's crossing of the Red Sea at the onset of the Exodus. Thus Jesus transversed the Jordan and then, like Israel, spent a period of time in the wilderness. Jesus, another Moses, on whom the Spirit had been placed (Isa. 63:10-14), would lead the way."[210]

"Jesus fulfilled the Scripture by replicating in His own life the patterns of God's historical relations with Israel and by accomplishing in His own history the predicted events of prophecy."[211]

It is significant that Matthew did not describe Jesus' baptism. His emphasis was on the two revelatory events that followed it (cf. 2:1-23).

3:16-17   The Greek text stresses the fact that Jesus' departure from the water and God's attestation of Him as the Messiah occurred at the same time. The NIV translation gives this sense better than the NASB.

The person who "saw the Spirit of God descending" was evidently Jesus. Jesus is the person in the immediately preceding context. John the Evangelist recorded that John the Baptist also saw this (John 1:32), but evidently no one but Jesus heard the Father's voice. In fact, the baptism of Jesus appears to have been a private affair with no one present but John and Jesus. The phrase "the heavens were opened" or "heaven was opened" recalls instances of people receiving visions from God. In them they saw things unseen by other mortals (e.g., Isa. 64:1; Ezek. 1:1; cf. Acts 7:56; Rev. 4:1; 19:11). The phrase implies that new revelation will follow to and through Jesus. What Jesus saw was the Holy Spirit in the form of "a dove," not in a dove-like fashion, descending on Him (cf. Luke 3:22). This is the first explicit identification of the Holy Spirit with a dove in Scripture. It was an appropriate symbol because of its beauty, heavenly origin, freedom, sensitivity, purity, and peaceful nature.

"The descent of the Spirit upon Jesus denotes the divine act whereby God empowers him to accomplish the messianic ministry he is shortly to begin (4:17). Such empowerment, of course, is not to be construed as Jesus' initial endowment with the Spirit, for he was conceived by the Spirit. Instead, it specifies in what way Jesus proves to be the mightier One John had said he would be (3:11). It also serves as the reference point for understanding the 'authority' with which Jesus discharges his public ministry. Empowered by God's Spirit, Jesus speaks as the mouthpiece of God (7:28-29) and acts as the instrument of God (12:28)."[212]

In Isaiah 42:1, the prophet predicted that God would put His Spirit on His Servant. That happened at Jesus' baptism. Matthew's account shows fulfillment, though the writer did not draw attention to it as such here. When God's Spirit came on individuals in the Old Testament, He empowered them for divine service. That was the purpose of Jesus' anointing as well (Luke 4:14; 5:17; cf. Luke 24:49).

An audible revelation followed the visual one (v. 17). The "voice" from heaven could be none other than God's. After 400 years without prophetic revelation, God broke the silence. He spoke from heaven to humankind again. Matthew recorded God's words as a general announcement (cf. 17:5). The other evangelists wrote that God said, "You are my beloved Son" (Mark 1:11; Luke 3:22). Evidently the accounts in Mark and Luke contain the actual words God used, the *ipisissima verba*, whereas Matthew gave a free quotation of God's words, the *ipisissima vox*. These Latin terms mean essentially "own words" and "own voice" respectively. As used in New Testament studies, the former phrase indicates a verbatim quotation and the latter a free quotation. The former refers to the words the speaker in the narrative used and the latter to the words of the writer who interpreted the speaker's words. Matthew probably gave a free quotation because he used what happened at Jesus' baptism as evidence of His messiahship.

"Had the crowds heard the voice from heaven, it is inexplicable why one segment of the public does not at least entertain the idea that Jesus is the Son of God. And had John heard the voice from heaven, it is odd that his question of 11:2-3 contains no hint of this. On the contrary, it reflects the selfsame view of Jesus that John had expressed prior to the baptism, namely, that Jesus is the Coming One (3:11-12)."[213]

---

[209]Toussaint, p. 73.

[210]Don B. Garlington, "Jesus, the Unique Son of God: Tested and Faithful," *Bibliotheca Sacra* 151:603 (July-September 1994):287.

[211]Craig A. Blaising, "The Fulfillment of the Biblical Covenants," in *Progressive Dispensationalism*, p. 195.

[212]Kingsbury, p. 52.

[213]Ibid., p. 51.

The words God spoke identified Jesus as the Messiah promised in the Old Testament. The term "Son of God" was one that God used of David's descendant who would follow him on Israel's throne (2 Sam. 7:13-14; Ps. 2:7; 89:26-29; cf. Matt. 1:20; 2:15; 4:3, 6). God's commendation also linked Jesus with the Suffering Servant at the commencement of His ministry (Isa. 42:1; 53). The Beloved One is equivalent to the One with whom the Father was "well pleased" (Isa. 42:1). Genesis 22:2 may also be behind this announcement since that verse describes Isaac as Abraham's beloved only son (cf. Ps. 2:7; Isa. 42:1). Consequently, "Son of God" is a messianic title.[214] Notice the involvement of all three members of the Trinity in Jesus' baptism. This indicates its importance.

"For the first time the Trinity, foreshadowed in many ways in the O.T., is clearly manifested."[215]

In this one statement at the beginning of Jesus' ministry, God presented Him as the Davidic Messiah, the Son of God, the representative of the people, and the Suffering Servant. Matthew had presented Jesus in all of these roles previously, but now God the Father confirmed His identity.

". . . God's baptismal declaration at 3:17 reveals itself to be climactic within the context of 1:1—4:16 because this is the place where God's understanding of Jesus as his Son ceases to be of the nature of private information available only to the reader and becomes instead an element within the story that henceforth influences the shape of events. To illustrate this, notice how the words Satan speaks in 4:3, 6 ('If you are the Son of God . . .') pick up directly on the declaration God makes in the baptismal pericope ('This is my beloved Son . . .')."[216]

"Because Matthew so constructs his story that God's evaluative point of view is normative, the reader knows that in hearing God enunciate his understanding of Jesus, he or she has heard the normative understanding of Jesus, the one in terms of which all other understandings are to be judged. In Matthew's story, God himself dictates that Jesus is preeminently the Son of God."[217]

"He did not *become* Son of God at His baptism, as certain heretical teachers in the early Church maintained; but it was then that He was appointed to a work which He alone could perform, because of His unique relationship with His Father."[218]

Matthew passed over all the incidents of Jesus' childhood, including His appearance at the temple (Luke 2:41-50), because his interests were selective and apologetic rather than merely historical. He introduced Jesus as the messianic King of Israel who fulfilled Old Testament prophecy and received divine confirmation from God with an audible pronouncement from heaven (cf. Exod. 20:1).[219]

In chapter 1, Matthew stressed the glories of Messiah's person. In chapter 2, he gave a preview of the reception He would receive as Israel's Messiah. In chapter 3, he introduced the beginning of His ministry with accounts of His earthly forerunner's heralding and His heavenly Father's approbation.

3. Jesus' temptation 4:1-11 (cf. Mark 1:12-13; Luke 4:1-13)

". . . Jesus' testing in the wilderness of Judea is one of the most significant indicators of His uniqueness. In fact it may not be stretching the point to say that the very purpose of the temptation narratives is to underscore His uniqueness."[220]

Jesus' genealogy and virgin birth prove His legal human qualification as Israel's King. His baptism was the occasion of His divine approval. His temptation demonstrated His moral fitness to reign. The natural question a thoughtful reader of Matthew's Gospel might ask after reading God's attestation of His Son (3:17) is: Was He really that good? Jesus' three temptations prove that He was.

"By the end of the baptismal pericope, the Jesus of Matthew's story stands before the reader preeminently as the Son of God who has been empowered with the Spirit of God. So identified, Jesus is led by the Spirit into the desert to engage the devil, or

[214]Allen, p. 29.

[215]*The New Scofield* . . ., p. 995.

[216]Kingsbury, p. 44, and footnote 2.

[217]Ibid., p. 52.

[218]Tasker, p. 50.

[219]See S. Lewis Johnson Jr., "The Baptism of Christ," *Bibliotheca Sacra* 123:491 (July-September 1966):220-29.

[220]Garlington, p. 285.

Satan, in conflict in the place of his abode (4:1-11). . . . Ultimately, the substance of each test has to do with Jesus' devotion, or obedience, to God. The intent of Satan in each test is to entice Jesus to break faith with God, his Father, and thus disavow his divine sonship. Should Satan succeed at this, he succeeds in effect in destroying Jesus. In testing Jesus, Satan cunningly adopts God's evaluative point of view according to which Jesus is his Son (4:3, 6)."[221]

4:1-2   The same "Spirit" who brought Jesus into the world (1:20), and demonstrated God's approval of Him (3:16), now "led" Him "into the wilderness" for tempting by Satan.

"The [Greek word *peirazo*] means 'to try' or 'to make proof of,' and when ascribed to God in His dealings with people, it means no more than this (see Gen. 22:1). But for the most part in Scripture, the word is used in a negative sense, and means to entice, solicit, or provoke to sin. Hence the name given to the wicked one in this passage is 'the tempter' (4:3). Accordingly 'to be tempted' here is to be understood both ways. The Spirit conducted Jesus into the wilderness to try His faith, but the agent in this trial was the wicked one, whose object was to seduce Jesus away from His allegiance to God. This was temptation in the bad sense of the term. Yet Jesus did not give in to temptation; He passed the test (see 2 Cor. 5:21; Heb. 7:26)."[222]

"Just as God led Israel out of Egypt and through the waters and into the desert (Num 20.5; 1 *Bas* 12.6; Ps 80.1 LXX; etc., all using *anagein* ['to lead up']), so does the Spirit of God lead Jesus into the desert after he is baptized."[223]

"According to Hosea 2:14-23, the wilderness was the place of Israel's original sonship, where God had loved His people. Yet because they had forsaken Yahweh their Father, a 'renewal' of the exodus into the desert was necessary for the restoration of Israel's status as the 'son' of God. In this new exodus, God's power and help would be experienced again in a renewed trek into the wilderness."[224]

The wilderness of Judea (3:1) is the traditional site. Israel had, of course, experienced temptation in another wilderness for 40 years. The number 40 frequently has connections with sin and testing in the Old Testament (cf. Gen. 7:4, 12; Num. 14:33; 32:13; Deut. 9:25; 25:3; Ps. 95:10; Jon. 3:4). Jesus experienced temptation in the wilderness at the end of 40 days and nights.

The Greek word translated "tempted" (*peirazo*) means "to test" in either a good or bad sense. Here God's objective was to demonstrate the character of His Son by exposing Him to Satan's tests (cf. 2 Sam. 24:1; Job 1:6—2:7). Scripture consistently teaches that God does not test (Gr. *peirazo*) anyone (James 1:13). Nevertheless He does allow people to experience testing that comes from the world, the flesh, and the devil (1 John 2:15-17; Rom. 7:18-24; 1 Pet. 5:8).[225] God evidently led Jesus into the wilderness to demonstrate the obedience of this Son compared with the disobedience of His son Israel (2:15; cf. Exod. 4:22; Deut. 8:3, 5). God tested both His sons "to prove their obedience and loyalty in preparation for their appointed work."[226]

Fasting in Scripture was for a spiritual reason, namely, to forego a physical need to give attention to a more important spiritual need.[227] During this fast Jesus ate nothing but presumably drank water (cf. Luke 4:2). Moses and Elijah, two of God's most significant servants in the Old Testament, likewise fasted for 40 days and nights (Exod. 34:28; Deut. 9:9; 1 Kings 19:8). Jesus' fast would have connected Him with these servants of the Lord in the minds of Matthew's Jewish readers, as it does in ours.

4:3-4   Satan attacked Jesus when He was vulnerable physically. The form of Satan's question in the Greek text indicates that Satan was assuming that Jesus was "the Son of God" (3:17). It is a first class conditional clause.

"The temptation, to have force, must be assumed as true. The devil knew it to be true. He accepts that fact as a working hypothesis in the temptation."[228]

---

[221]Kingsbury, p. 55.

[222]*The Nelson . . .*, p. 1581.

[223]W. D. Davies and D. C. Allison, *A Critical and Exegetical Commentary on the Gospel according to Saint Matthew*, 1:354. Cf. Deut. 8:2, 16.

[224]Garlington, p. 287.

[225]See Sydney H. T. Page, "Satan: God's Servant," *Journal of the Evangelical Theological Society* 50:3 (September 2007):449-65.

[226]Carson, "Matthew," p. 112.

[227]On the practice of fasting, see Kent D. Berghuis, "A Biblical Perspective on Fasting," *Bibliotheca Sacra* 158:629 (January-March 2001):86-103.

[228]Robertson, *A Grammar . . .*, p. 1009.

This temptation was not for Jesus to doubt that He was God's Son. It was to suggest that, as the Son of God, Jesus surely had the power and right to satisfy His own needs independent of His Father. Satan urged Jesus to use His Sonship in a way that was inconsistent with His mission (cf. 26:53-54; 27:40). God had intended Israel's hunger in the wilderness to teach her that hearing and obeying God's Word is the most important thing in life (Deut. 8:2-3). Israel demanded bread in the wilderness but died. Jesus forewent bread in submission to His Father's will and lived.

"The impact of Satan's temptation is that Jesus, like Adam first and Israel later, had a justifiable grievance against God and therefore ought to voice His complaint by 'murmuring' (Exod. 16; Num. 11) and ought to provide for Himself the basic necessity of life, namely, bread. Satan, in other words, sought to make Jesus groundlessly anxious about His physical needs and thus to provoke Him to demand the food He craved (cf. Ps. 78:18). In short, the devil's aim was to persuade Jesus to repeat the apostasy of Adam and Israel. Satan wanted to break Jesus' perfect trust in His Father's good care and thereby to alter the course of salvation-history."[229]

The wilderness of Judea contains many limestone rocks of all sizes and shapes. Many of them look like the loaves and rolls of bread that the Jews prepared and ate daily.

Jesus' response to Satan's suggestion (v. 4) reflected His total commitment to follow God's will as revealed in His Word. He quoted the Septuagint translation of Deuteronomy 8:3. Its application originally was to Israel, but Jesus applied it to everyone and particularly Himself. By applying this passage to Himself, Jesus put Himself in the category of a true "man" (Gr. *anthropos*).

Jesus faced Satan as a man, not as God. He did not use His own divine powers to overcome the enemy, which is just what Satan tempted Him to do. Rather, He used the spiritual resources that are available to all people, including us, namely: the Word of God and the power of the Holy Spirit (v. 1). It is for this reason that He is an example for us of one who successfully endured temptation, and it is this victory that qualified Him to become our high priest (Heb. 2:10; 3:1-2).

"Matthew here shows that Jesus is not God only, but an unique theanthropic person, *personally* qualified to be King of Israel."[230]

Everyone needs to recognize and acknowledge his or her total dependence on God and His Word. Jesus' real food, what sustained Him above all else, was His commitment to do the will of His Father (John 4:34).

In this first temptation, Satan's aim was to seduce Jesus into using His God-given power and authority independently of His Father's will. Jesus had subjected Himself to His Father's will because of His mission (cf. Phil. 2:8). It was uniquely a personal temptation: it tested Jesus' person.

"Obedience to God's will takes priority over self-gratification, even over the apparently essential provision of food."[231]

4:5-7   The setting for the second temptation was Jerusalem, perhaps in a vision that Satan gave Jesus. Matthew referred to Jerusalem with a favorite Jewish term, "the holy city" (cf. Neh. 11:1; Isa. 48:2; Dan. 9:24; Matt. 4:5; 27:53). This suggests that the temptation would have national rather than solely individual implications. Satan took Him to a high point of the temple complex (Gr. *hieron*), not necessarily the topmost peak of the sanctuary. The Greek word is *pterygion*, which can be translated "little wing" or "high corner." The temple complex towered over the Kidron Valley far below.[232] Some of the Jewish rabbis taught that when Messiah came to deliver Israel, He would appear on the temple roof (cf. Mal. 3:1; John 6:30).[233]

"Jerusalem was considered the 'center of the nations, with lands around her,' the 'center of the world,' whose inhabitants 'dwell at the center of the earth' (Ezek. 5:5; 38:12; . . .). Thus when Jesus stood on the pinnacle of the temple, He was, theologically speaking, at the center of the world. From that vantage point the Messiah most naturally could claim the nations as His own and rule them with a rod of iron . . ."[234]

---

[229]Garlington, p. 297. Cf. Davies and Allison, 1:362.

[230]Toussaint, p. 76.

[231]France, *The Gospel . . .*, p. 131.

[232]Josephus, *Antiquities of. . .*, 15:11:5.

[233]Edersheim, *The Life . . .*, 1:293.

[234]Garlington, p. 299. Cf. Davies and Allison, 1:365; and T. L. Donaldson, *Jesus on the Mountain: A Study in Matthean Theology*, pp. 59-61.

Again the devil granted that Jesus was the Son of God. Satan's words replicate the Septuagint version of Psalm 91:11-12, appealing to the authority that Jesus used, namely: God's Word (v. 4). He omitted the words "to guard you in all your ways." Many expositors have assumed that Satan wanted to trick Jesus with this omission, but his free method of quoting was very common. Many New Testament writers quoted the Old Testament in the same loose way.

Probably Satan wanted Jesus to demonstrate His trust in God in a spectacular way to challenge God's faithfulness. He misapplied the Scripture he quoted. The Psalms passage refers to anyone who trusts in God. That certainly applied to Jesus. The verses promise that the angels will uphold such a person as a nurse does a baby (cf. Num. 11:12; Deut. 1:31; Isa. 49:22; Heb. 1:14). God had revealed Himself most particularly at the temple throughout Israel's history. Therefore what better place could there have been to demonstrate the Son of God's confidence in His Father's promise?

Jesus refused Satan's suggestion (v. 7) because the Scriptures prohibited putting God to a test, not because He questioned God's faithfulness to His promise. Satan tempted Jesus to test God. Satan was tempting Jesus to act as if God was there to serve Him, rather than the other way around. Israel had faced the same test and had failed (Exod. 17:2-7; cf. Num. 20:1-13). It is wrong to demand that God prove Himself faithful to His promises by giving us what He has promised *on our terms*. The proper procedure is simply to trust and obey God (Deut. 6:16-17).

"Testing is not trusting."[235]

Jesus refused to allow Satan to *apply* a valid promise so it contradicted another teaching in God's Word. "On the other hand" or "also" (Gr. *palin*) has the sense of "not contradicting but qualifying."[236] Jesus as a man, voluntarily under the authority of God's Word, proved to be faithful to its spirit as well as to its letter.

4:8-10   The "very high mountain" to which Satan took Jesus next is traditionally near Jericho, but its exact location is not important. It simply provided a vantage point from which Satan could point out other kingdoms that surrounded Israel.

"The placement of Jesus on the mountain of temptation, where He refused to acknowledge the devil's 'authority,' is deliberately juxtaposed to the mountain (Matt. 28:16) of 'the great commission,' on which He later affirmed that all 'authority' in heaven and on earth had been granted to Him (28:18)."[237]

Luke's wording suggests that Satan presented "all the kingdoms of the world" to Jesus *in a vision* (Luke 4:5). It is hard to tell if Jesus' temptations involved physical transportation or visionary transportation, but my preference is visionary transportation. This temptation would have universal significance, not just personal and national significance, as the first and second temptations did.

Satan offered to "give" Jesus immediate dominion and control over all the kingdoms of the world, and the "glory" connected with reigning over them (v. 9)—something that God would give Him eventually as the Messiah.[238] In the will of God, Jesus would achieve universal rule (Ps. 2), but only as the Suffering Servant who would have to endure the Cross first.

God's divine authentication of His Son (3:16-17) drew attention to both Jesus' Davidic messiahship and His Suffering Servant role. This temptation consisted of an opportunity for Jesus to obtain the benefits of messiahship without having to experience its unpleasant elements. To get this, however, Jesus would have to change His allegiance from God to Satan. This involved idolatry, putting someone or something in the place that God deserves. Later, Peter suggested the same shortcut to Jesus, and received a sharp rebuke as Satan's spokesman for doing so (16:23).

This was a legitimate offer. Satan had the ability, under the sovereign authority of God, to give Jesus what he promised, namely, power and glory (cf. 12:25-28; Luke 10:18; Eph. 2:2). Israel, God's other son, had formerly faced the same temptation to avoid God's uncomfortable will by departing from it, and had failed (Num. 13—14). This third temptation, like the other two, tested Jesus' total loyalty to His Father and His Father's will. Had Jesus taken Satan's bait, He would have been Satan's slave, albeit, perhaps, a world ruler.

"Jesus was in effect tempted to subscribe to the diabolical doctrine that the end justifies the means; that, so long as He obtained universal sovereignty in the end, it mattered not how that sovereignty was reached . . ."[239]

---

[235]J. W. Shepard, *The Christ of the Gospels*, p. 78.

[236]Bruce, 1:90.

[237]Garlington, pp. 301-2.

[238]See ibid., p. 290.

For a third time, Jesus responded by quoting Scripture to His adversary (v. 10). He banished Satan with the divine command to worship and to serve God alone (Deut. 6:13).

When Satan tempts us to doubt, deny, disobey, or disregard God's Word, we should do what Jesus did. Instead of *listening* to Satan, we should *speak* to him, reiterating what God has said.

4:11   Having resisted Satan's attacks successfully, the enemy departed temporarily (cf. James 4:7). God sent messengers ("angels") to assist His faithful Son (cf. 1 Kings 19:4-8). The Father rewarded the Son with divine assistance and further opportunity for service, because Jesus had remained faithful to Him. This is God's normal method.

Many have observed that Satan followed the same pattern of temptation with Jesus that he had used with Eve (Gen. 3). First, he appealed to the lust of the flesh, the desire to *do* something apart from God's will. Second, he appealed to the lust of the eyes, the desire to *have* something apart from God's will. Third, he appealed to the pride of life, the desire to *be* something apart from God's will (cf. 1 John 2:16).

"Approaching Jesus three times in Matthew's story, Satan urges him to place concern for self above allegiance to God."[240]

"Each temptation challenges Jesus' faithfulness. Will he provide for himself independently of God's direction and draw on his power in self-interest (bread)? Will he insist that God protect him by putting God to the test of his protection of the Son (temple)? Will the Son defect from the Father and worship someone else for his own gain (kingdoms)? In each text [sic] Jesus stresses his loyalty to the Father as he cites Deuteronomy."[241]

"All three of the tests are variations of the one great temptation to remove His Messianic vocation from the guidance of His Father and make it simply a political calling."[242]

Each of Jesus' three temptations related to His messiahship: the first to Him personally, the second to the Jews, and the third to all the nations (cf. 1:1). The twin themes of Jesus' royal kingship and His suffering servanthood, which combined in the name Immanuel, "God with us" (1:23), were in tension in the temptation. They remained in tension and created conflict in Jesus' ministry as it unfolded.

"In the first temptation Jesus does *not deny* that He is hungry and able to make bread; in the second, He does *not deny* that He is the Son of God, and under special protection; and in the third, He does *not deny* the Kingdom or dominion which is to be given to Him, but only rejects *the mode* by which it is to be obtained. As observed, if such a Kingdom is not covenanted, predicted, and intended, the temptation would not have any force."[243]

"In this pericope [4:1-11] we encounter a theme that is vital in the theology of the Gospels. The goal of obedience to the Father is accomplished, not by triumphant self-assertion, not by the exercise of power and authority, but paradoxically by the way of humility, service, and suffering. Therein lies true greatness (cf. 20:26-28). In fulfilling his commission by obedience to the will of the Father, Jesus demonstrates the rightness of the great commandment (Deut 6:5) as well as his own submission to it."[244]

"Just as the first Adam met Satan, so the Last Adam met the enemy (1 Cor. 15:45). Adam met Satan in a beautiful Garden, but Jesus met him in a terrible wilderness. Adam had everything he needed, but Jesus was hungry after forty days of fasting. Adam lost the battle and plunged humanity into sin and death. But Jesus won the battle and went on to defeat Satan in more battles, culminating in His final victory on the cross (John 12:31; Co. 2:15)."[245]

Since Jesus was both God and man, was it possible for Him to sin? Most evangelical theologians have concluded that He could not since God cannot sin. They believe He was impeccable (incapable of sinning). If so, was His temptation genuine? Most have responded yes.[246]

Henri Nouwen helpfully discussed Jesus' three temptations in relation to leadership in ministry. He saw them as temptations to relevance, popularity, and power, and he suggested prayer, ministry, and being led as antidotes.[247]

---

[239]Tasker, p. 54.

[240]Kingsbury, p. 55.

[241]Bock, *Jesus according . . .*, p. 90.

[242]S. Lewis Johnson Jr., "The Temptation of Christ," *Bibliotheca Sacra* 123:492 (October-December 1996):345.

[243]Peters, 1:700.

[244]Hagner, p. 70.

[245]Wiersbe, 1:18.

[246]See Joseph G. Sahl, "The Impeccability of Jesus Christ," *Bibliotheca Sacra* 140:557 (January-March 1983):11-20; and the major theologies.

[247]Henri J. M. Nouwen, *In the Name of Jesus: Reflections on Christian Leadership*.

In the first major section of his Gospel, Matthew showed that Jesus had all the qualifications to be Israel's Messiah—legally, scripturally, and morally. He was now ready to relate Jesus' presentation of Himself to Israel as her King.

II. THE AUTHORITY OF THE KING 4:12—7:29

Having introduced the King, Matthew next demonstrated the authority of the King. This section includes a narrative introduction to Jesus' teaching and then His teaching on the subject of His kingdom.

A. THE BEGINNING OF JESUS' MINISTRY 4:12-25

Matthew gave much prominence to Jesus' teachings in his Gospel. The first of these is the so-called Sermon on the Mount (chs. 5—7). To prepare the reader for this discourse, the writer gave a brief introduction to Jesus' ministry (4:12-25). In it, Matthew provided a résumé of His work, highlighting the authority of Israel's King: the setting of Jesus' ministry (Capernaum), Jesus' essential message ("Repent . . ."), Jesus' call of four disciples, and a summary of Jesus' ministry.

1. The setting of Jesus' ministry 4:12-16

Comparison of John's Gospel and Matthew's, shows that Jesus ministered for about a year before John the Baptist's arrest. John had criticized Herod Antipas for having an adulterous relationship with his brother Philip's wife (14:3-4; Mark 1:14; Luke 3:19-20). Jesus ministered first in Galilee (John 1:19—2:12) and then in Judea (John 2:13—3:21). Then He returned to Galilee by way of Samaria (John 3:22—4:42). Why did Matthew begin his account of Jesus' ministry with John's arrest? John's arrest by Herod signaled the beginning of a new phase of Jesus' ministry. The forerunner's work was now complete. It was time for the King to appear publicly.

"In royal protocol the King does not make His appearance in public until the forerunner has finished his work. Matthew, emphasizing the official and regal character of Jesus, follows this procedure exactly."[248]

4:12-13   The word "withdrew" (NASB) or "returned" (NIV; Gr. *anachoreo*) is significant. Evidently Jesus wanted to get away from Israel's religious leaders in Jerusalem who opposed John (John 4:1-3; 5:1-16). It is unlikely that Herod Antipas would have imprisoned John if the religious authorities had supported John. Matthew used the same Greek word, *paredothe* ("to be taken into custody"), later when he described Jesus' arrest (26:15, 16, 21, 23, 25; 27:3, 4). The religious leaders evidently played a significant role in both arrests.

To Matthew, "Galilee" had great significance for two reasons. First, it was the place where Isaiah had predicted Messiah would minister (Isa. 9:1). Second, since it was an area where many Gentiles lived, it corroborated Messiah's influence over the nations as well as Israel.

Jesus moved the base of His ministry from "Nazareth" to "Capernaum" (v. 13). Matthew described it as he did in view of the prophecy that Jesus' residence there fulfilled (vv. 15-16). This town stood on the northwest shore of the Sea of Galilee (14:34). It was the town where Peter, Andrew, James, and John (the fishermen) and Matthew (the tax collector) worked (8:14; 9:9). Estimates of its population in the first century range from 1,000 to 15,000.[249]

"If Joseph settled in Nazareth after the return from Egypt (2:22-23), Jesus now leaves Nazareth and moves to Capernaum (4:12-13), which becomes 'his own city' (9:1). He is thus poised to begin his public ministry."[250]

4:14-16   Jesus' move to Capernaum fulfilled Isaiah 9:1, part of a section of Isaiah's prophecy that describes Immanuel's coming. Matthew's quotation of this passage was a free one. Its point was that "light" had "dawned" in a dark part of Palestine. By New Testament times, the old tribal divisions had little actual relevance.[251] When Isaiah prophesied, Galilee was under the oppressive threat of the Assyrians. He predicted that Messiah would liberate the people living there. When Matthew wrote, Galilee was under Roman oppression. The "darkness" was also symbolic of the absence of religious, political, and cultural advantages available to Jews who lived in Jerusalem. "Dawned" (Gr. *aneteilen*) suggests that the light of Messiah's ministry would first shine brightly in Galilee (cf. John 1:9; 12:46).[252]

---

[248]Toussaint, p. 81. Cf. Johnson, "The Argument . . .," p. 146.

[249]See France, *The Gospel* . . ., p. 141.

[250]Kinsgbury, p. 57.

[251]France, *The Gospel* . . ., p. 141.

[252]Barnabas Lindars, *New Testament Apologetic*, p. 198.

". . . From of old the Messiah was promised to 'Galilee of the Gentiles' (*ton ethnon*), a foreshadowing of the commission to 'all nations' (*panta ta ethne*, 28:19). Moreover, if the messianic light dawns on the darkest places, then Messiah's salvation can only be a bestowal of grace—namely, that Jesus came to call, not the righteous, but sinners (9:13)."[253]

Whereas Galilee was a dark place in one sense, in another sense Jerusalem was even darker. There, hostility to Jesus was much greater, but in Galilee the people heard Jesus gladly.

"Matthew's story of Jesus' life and ministry possesses a clearly defined beginning, middle, and end and hence falls into three parts: (I) The Presentation of Jesus (1:1—4:16); (II) The Ministry of Jesus to Israel and Israel's Repudiation of Jesus (4:17—16:20); and (III) The Journey of Jesus to Jerusalem and His Suffering, Death, and Resurrection (16:21—28:20). In the first part, Matthew presents Jesus as the Davidic Messiah-King, the royal Son of God (1:1—4:16). To show that Jesus is preeminently the Son of God, Matthew depicts God as announcing within the world of the story that Jesus is his Son (3:17). As the Son of God, Jesus stands forth as the supreme agent of God who authoritatively espouses God's evaluative point of view."[254]

The divisions of the Gospel that I have used in these notes are theological more than narrative.

2. Jesus' essential message 4:17 (cf. Mark 1:14-15; Luke 4:14-15)

The clause "From that time Jesus" (Gr. *apo tote epxato Iesous*) is very significant in Matthew's Gospel. The writer used it only twice, here and in 16:21, and in both instances it indicates a major change in Jesus' ministry.[255] Here it signals the beginning of Jesus' public preaching that the kingdom was "at hand." Until now, His ministry had been to selected individuals and groups, which John's Gospel records. Jesus "went public" after John had ended his ministry of preparing Israel for her Messiah. Here Jesus took up exactly the same message that John had been preaching (cf. 3:2). It is exactly the same statement in the Greek text. The better translations have also rendered these sentences identically. In 16:21, having been rejected by Israel, Jesus announced His approaching passion and resurrection. The verb "to begin" (*erxato*) indicates the beginning of an action that continues, or it describes a new phase in the narrative, wherever it occurs.[256]

Jesus used the same words as John, and He, too, offered no explanation of their meaning. Clearly, Jesus' concept of "the kingdom" was the same as that of the Old Testament prophets and John. Some commentators claim that John's concept of the kingdom was eschatological but Jesus' was soteriological.[257] However, there is no basis for this distinction in the text. Both John and Jesus viewed the kingdom as having both soteriological and eschatological elements.

Alva McClain listed and explained five different answers that Bible scholars have given to the questions: "Was this Kingdom identical with the Kingdom of Old Testament prophecy? Or was it something different?"

"First, the *Liberal-Social* view: that Christ took over from the Old Testament prophets their ethical and social ideals of the kingdom, excluding almost wholly the eschatological element, and made these ideals the program of a present kingdom which it is the responsibility of His followers to establish in human society on earth here and now. . . .

"Second, the *Critical-Eschatological* view: that Jesus at first embraced fully the eschatological ideas of the Old Testament prophets regarding the Kingdom, and to some extent the current Jewish ideas; but later in the face of opposition He changed His message; or, at least, there are conflicting elements in the gospel records. . . .

"Third, the *Spiritualizing-Anti-millennial* view: that our Lord appropriated certain spiritual elements from the Old Testament prophetical picture, either omitted or spiritualized the physical elements (excepting the physical details involved in the Messiah's first coming!), and then added some original ideas of His own. . . .

"Fourth, the *Dual-Kingdom* view: that Christ at His first coming offered to Israel and established on earth a purely spiritual kingdom; and that at His second coming He will establish on earth a literal Millennial Kingdom. . . .

[253]Carson, "Matthew," p. 117. See Gene R. Smillie, "'Even the Dogs': Gentiles in the Gospel of Matthew," *Journal of the Evangelical Theological Society* 45:1 (March 2002):73-97.
[254]Kingsbury, p. 161.
[255]See ibid., p. 40; and Tasker, p. 57.
[256]M'Neile, p. 45.
[257]E.g., Shepard, pp. 62, 123.

"Fifth, the *One-Kingdom Millennial* view: that the Kingdom announced by our Lord and offered to the nation of Israel at His first coming was identical with the Mediatorial Kingdom of Old Testament prophecy, and will be established on earth at the second coming of the King. . . ."[258]

McClain then proceeded to prove from Scripture that view five above is the correct one.[259]

Now the King began announcing the nearness of the earthly kingdom of Messiah, and He urged His subjects to prepare themselves spiritually.

"The kingdom being at hand meant that it was being offered in the person of the prophesied King, but it did not mean that it would be immediately fulfilled."[260]

"Christ came to found a Kingdom, not a School; to institute a fellowship, not to propound a system."[261]

Normative (traditional) dispensationalists—such as Walvoord, Pentecost, Toussaint, Barbieri, Bailey, and myself—believe that the kingdom was postponed due to Jewish rejection of the Messiah. Progressive dispensationalists believe that it began with Jesus' earthly ministry, and continues through the church, but that it will also have a future manifestation in the Millennium.[262]

Matthew wrote "kingdom of heaven," whereas Mark and Luke usually wrote "kingdom of God" in the parallel passages. This was probably because Matthew wrote to Jews who used the word "heaven" instead of "God" to avoid unduly familiarizing the ear with the sacred name.[263] The phrase "of heaven" does not mean that it is a mystical or spiritual kingdom, as opposed to a physical, earthly kingdom. It means that this kingdom is sent from God who is in heaven.

3. The call of four disciples 4:18-22 (cf. Mark 1:16-20; Luke 5:1-11)

The calling of these four men shows Jesus' authority over people. The response of these disciples was appropriate in view of their summons by the King. They obeyed "immediately" (vv. 20, 22). From here on in the Gospel of Matthew, we will not read stories about Jesus alone; He is always with His disciples, until they desert Him in the garden of Gethsemane (26:56).

4:18-20   The Hebrews referred to lakes as "seas." The "Sea of Galilee" got its name from its district.[264] Its other name, the Sea of "Gennesaret," came from the plain to the northwest of the lake (Luke 5:1) and from a town on that plain: Gennesaret. The name "Gennesaret" connects to the Hebrew work *kinnor*, meaning "harp." In the Old Testament this body of water was called the Sea of Chinnereth because of its harp-like shape.[265] Sometimes people referred to the lake as the Sea of Tiberias. Tiberias was the Hellenistic city that Herod built on its west-southwest shore. This sea was approximately 12 miles long and 9 miles wide at its longest and broadest points. It supported a thriving fishing industry in Jesus' day, with nine towns on its western shore, plus others elsewhere. Simon and Andrew had moved from their hometown of Bethsaida (lit. "Fishtown," John 1:44) to Capernaum (Mark 1:21, 29).

Simon's nickname was Peter ("Rocky"). "Simon" was one of the most common names in first-century Palestine.[266] The "net" (Gr. *amphibleston*, used only here in the New Testament) that Simon and Andrew were "casting" into the lake was a circular one. It was a common tool of Galilean fishermen. Fishing was a major industry in Galilee.

Jesus' command (not invitation), "Follow Me" (v. 19), was a summons to leave their occupations, and literally follow Jesus wherever He would take them as His trainees (cf. 1 Kings 19:19-21).

"The expression 'Follow Me' would be readily understood, as implying a call to become the *permanent* disciple of a teacher. (Talmudic tractate *Erubhin* 30 a) Similarly, it was not only the practice of the Rabbis, but regarded as one of the most sacred duties, for a Master to gather around him a circle of disciples.

---

[258]McClain, pp. 274-75.

[259]Ibid., pp. 276-303. See also James Orr, "The Kingdom of God, of Heaven," in *A Dictionary of the Bible*, edited by James Hastings, 2:849.

[260]Walvoord, *Matthew: . . .*, p. 38. See also Peters, 1:364-65; McClain, p. 304; L. Berkhof, *The Kingdom of God*, p. 19, footnote; Stanley D. Toussaint, "The Contingency of the Coming of the Kingdom," in *Integrity of Heart, Skillfulness of Hands*, pp. 222-37; and *The New Scofield . . .*, p. 996.

[261]Edersheim, *The Life . . .*, 1:528.

[262]E.g., Robert L. Saucy, "The Presence of the Kingdom and the Life of the Church," *Bibliotheca Sacra* 145:577 (January-March 1988):30-46.

[263]Edersheim, *The Life . . .*, 1:267.

[264]See the map "Palestine in the Time of Jesus" at the end of these notes to locate the places mentioned in this stage of Jesus' ministry.

[265]See *The New Bible Dictionary*, 1962 ed., s.v. "Chinnereth," by R. F. Hosking.

[266]France, *The Gospel . . .*, p. 146.

(Talmudic tractates *Pirqey Abhoth* 1. 1; and *Sanhedrin* 91 b) Thus, neither Peter and Andrew, nor the sons of Zebedee, could have misunderstood the call of Christ, or even regarded it as strange."[267]

Etiquette required a rabbi's disciples to walk behind him.[268] The phrase "fishers of men" recalls Jeremiah 16:16. There Yahweh sent "fishermen" to gather Israelites for the Exile. Here Jesus called fishermen to announce the end of Israel's spiritual exile (cf. 1:11-12; 2:17-18) and to prepare for His messianic reign. Later, after experiencing rejection by Israel, Jesus re-commissioned these men for duty in the inter-advent age (28:18-20; John 21:15-23).

This message appeared on a church marquee: "Be fishers of men. You catch 'em. He'll clean 'em." That is the proper order.

Evidently Jesus had called Simon, Andrew, Philip, and Nathanael earlier (John 1:35-51). Probably they had returned to Galilee and resumed their former work.[269] This would partially explain their quick response to Jesus here (v. 20). Furthermore, Jesus had changed water into wine in Cana, which was not far away (John 2:1-11). If the miracle of Luke 5:1-11 occurred the night before this calling, we have another reason they followed Jesus "immediately." Matthew's interest was not in *why* these men responded as they did, but *how* authoritatively Jesus called them, and how they responded. They recognized Jesus' authority and left all to follow Him.

Disciples of other rabbis normally continued their trades, but Jesus wanted His disciples to be with Him fulltime (Luke 9:61). Also, in contrast to the rabbinic model, Jesus chose His disciples; typically the disciple chose the rabbi he would follow. Furthermore, Jesus called His disciples to follow *Him*, not to follow the Law or teaching in abstraction.

4:21-22   "James" and "John" were evidently repairing (Gr. *katartizo*) their nets after a night of fishing (cf. 1 Cor. 1:10; 2 Cor. 13:11).

"In the Synoptics, unlike Paul's epistles, Jesus' call is not necessarily effectual. But in this instance it was immediately obeyed."[270]

The disciples "left . . . their father" as well as their fishing (v. 22).

"The twelve arrived at their final intimate relation to Jesus only by degrees, three stages in the history of their fellowship with Him being distinguishable. In the first stage they were simply believers in Him as the Christ, and His occasional companions at convenient, particularly festive, seasons [e.g., John 2:1-11].

"In the second stage, fellowship with Christ assumed the form of an uninterrupted attendance on His person, involving entire, or at least habitual abandonment of secular occupations [Matt. 4:22; Mark 1:20; Luke 5:11].

"The twelve enter on the last and highest stage of discipleship when they were chosen by their Master from the mass of His followers, and formed into a select band, to be trained for the great work of the apostleship [Mark 3:13-15; Luke 6:12-13]."[271]

"The call of God through Jesus is sovereign and absolute in its authority; the response of those who are called is to be both immediate and absolute, involving a complete break with old loyalties. The actual shape of this break with the past will undoubtedly vary from individual to individual, but that there must be a fundamental, radical reorientation of a person's priorities is taken for granted."[272]

4. A summary of Jesus' ministry 4:23-25 (cf. Mark 1:35-39; Luke 4:42-44)

This brief résumé (cf. 9:35-38) stresses the varied activities and the geographical and ethnic extent of Jesus' ministry at this time. It sets the stage for the discourse to follow (chs. 5—7) implying that this is but a sample of Jesus' teaching (cf. 9:35).

---

[267]Edersheim, *The Life . . .*, 1:474.

[268]Idem, *The Temple*, p. 147.

[269]Cf. Lenski, p. 171.

[270]Carson, "Matthew," p. 120.

[271]A. B. Bruce, *The Training of the Twelve*, pp. 11-12.

[272]Hagner, p. 78.

"Galilee" (v. 23) covered an area of about 2,800 square miles (roughly 70 by 40 miles), and contained approximately 3,000,000 people who lived in 204 cities and villages.[273] As an itinerant preacher, Jesus engaged in three primary activities: *teaching* His disciples, *preaching* good news to the multitudes, and *healing* many who were infirm. This verse helps the reader identify Jesus' main activities during most of His earthly ministry. Matthew never used the verb *didasko* ("teach") of the disciples until after Jesus had departed from them. He presented Jesus as *the* Teacher during His earthly ministry. This is also Matthew's first of only four uses of *euangelion* ("gospel," "good news," cf. 9:35; 24:14; 26:13). His ministry was to the Jewish people. This is clear, first, since he preached in the Jewish synagogues of Galilee. Second, He preached a Jewish message, the good news about the messianic kingdom. Third, he practiced His healing among the Jews. The Greek word *laos* ("people") refers specifically to "the people," that is, the Jews.[274] Matthew was hyperbolizing when he wrote that Jesus healed "all who were ill"; He could not have healed every single individual, though His healing ministry was extensive (cf. "all Galilee").

"Syria" (v. 24), to the Jews in Galilee, meant the area to the north. However, the Roman province of Syria covered all of Palestine except Galilee, which was then under Herod Antipas' administration. Regardless of the way Matthew intended us to understand "Syria," Jesus' popularity spread far north. Matthew described the painfully diseased people who sought Jesus out in three categories. There were those whom demons oppressed. Others had ailments that resulted in mental and physical imbalances that demons did not induce. Still others suffered paralyses of various kinds. Jesus' miracles dealt with "incurable" afflictions, not just trivial maladies (cf. Isa. 35:5-6).

> ". . . both Scripture and Jewish tradition take sickness as resulting directly or indirectly from living in a fallen world . . . . The Messianic Age would end such grief (Isa. 11:1-5; 35:5-6). Therefore Jesus' miracles, dealing with every kind of ailment, not only herald the kingdom but show that God has pledged himself to deal with sin at a basic level (cf. 1:21; 8:17)."[275]

> "I use the word *Miracle* to mean an interference with Nature by supernatural power."[276]

When Matthew wrote that multitudes "followed" Jesus, he did not mean that they were all thoroughly committed disciples, as the text will show. Some were undoubtedly ardent disciples, but others were simply needy or curious individuals who followed Jesus temporarily. These people came from all over "Galilee, Decapolis" (the area to the east of Galilee as far north as Damascus and as far south as Philadelphia), "Jerusalem, Judea," and east of ("beyond") "the Jordan" River. Many of these had to be Gentiles. Matthew made no reference to Jesus ministering in Samaria or to Samaritans.

> "While Jesus begins His ministry with the Jews only, His fame becomes so widespread that both Jews and Gentiles respond. This is clearly a foreview of the kingdom. The King is present with both Jews and Gentiles being blessed, the Gentiles coming to the Jewish Messiah for blessing (Zechariah 2:10-12; 8:18-23; Isaiah 2:1-4)."[277]

This section (vv. 12-25) constitutes a fitting introduction to the discourse that follows. The King had summoned disciples to follow Him, and huge crowds were seeking Him out, anticipating great supernatural blessings from His hand. He had appealed mainly to the Jews, but multitudes of Gentiles were seeking Him and experiencing His blessing, too. No case was too difficult for Him.

> "The evangelist wants us quickly to sense the great excitement surrounding Jesus at the beginning of his ministry, where he began to preach 'the good news of the kingdom,' before presenting him in more detail as the master teacher (chaps. 5—7) and charismatic healer (chaps. 8—9)."[278]

B. JESUS' REVELATIONS CONCERNING PARTICIPATION IN HIS KINGDOM, CHS. 5—7

The Sermon on the Mount is the first of five major discourses that Matthew included in his Gospel. Each one follows a narrative section, and each ends with the same formula statement concerning Jesus' authority (cf. 7:28-29).

There are four features of all five of Jesus' major discourses to His disciples, that Matthew recorded, that are worthy of note.

First, they did not provoke conflict between Jesus and the religious leaders.

Second, the reason for this is that Jesus gave them to His disciples and the crowds, not to the religious leaders.

By the way, the Gospels use the word "disciple" in a slightly different way than many Christians do today. We usually think of disciples of Jesus as people who have believed in Jesus and who are going on in their walk with Him. The Gospel evangelists used "disciple" to refer to people who

---

[273]Josephus, *The Wars* . . ., 3:3:2.

[274]M'Neile, p. 47.

[275]Carson, "Matthew," pp. 121-22.

[276]C. S. Lewis, *Miracles*, p. 15.

[277]Toussaint, *Behold the* . . ., p. 85.

[278]Hagner, p. 81.

were learning from Jesus, before they came to faith in Him, as well as after they did. In the process of increasing insight into who Jesus was, and increasing belief in Him, many of Jesus' disciples experienced regeneration. The Gospels do not focus on the moment of regeneration for disciples. Instead, they focus on the identity of Jesus, and they encourage increasing faith in Him. The emphasis is more linear than punctiliar. The Greek word translated "disciple" is *mathetes*, which means simply "learner" or "pupil."

Third, Matthew recorded Jesus' discourses in such a way that Jesus appears to be speaking past His original audience (cf. 5:11; 6:17-18; 10:18, 22, 42; 13:18-23, 38; 18:15-20; chs. 24—25). Matthew related Jesus' teaching to include future, as well as original, disciples. This draws the reader into Jesus' teaching. What He taught has relevance for us as well as for the Twelve. Jesus was teaching all His disciples—of every era—when He taught these things.

Fourth, Matthew presented Jesus as the Prophet whom Moses predicted in Deuteronomy 18:18. As such, Jesus not only corrected some false teaching of His day, and clarified God's original intention in the Mosaic Law, but He also replaced the Old Covenant with the New Covenant. Some of Jesus' teaching contradicted and contravened Moses' teaching (cf. Heb. 1:1-2). For example, He declared all food clean.

The Sermon on the Mount has probably attracted more attention than any discourse in history. The amount of material in print on this sermon reflects its popularity and significance. It has resulted in the publication of thousands of books and articles.

> "His [Jesus'] first great speech, the Sermon on the Mount (chaps. 5—7), is the example par excellence of his teaching."[279]

> ". . . it were difficult to say which brings greater astonishment (though of opposite kind): a first reading of the 'Sermon on the Mount,' or that of any section of the Talmud.

> "He who has thirsted and quenched his thirst at the living fount of Christ's Teaching, can never again stoop to seek drink at the broken cisterns of Rabbinism."[280]

However, there is still much debate about its interpretation. A brief review of the basic interpretations of this discourse follows.[281]

Especially in former years, many interpreters believed that the purpose of the Sermon was to enable people to know what God required, so that by obeying they might obtain salvation. One writer articulated this *soteriological* interpretation this way.

> "The Kingdom of God, like the Kingdom of Science, makes no other preliminary demand from those who would enter it than that it should be treated experimentally and practically as a working hypothesis. 'This do and thou shalt live.'"[282]

> "The Faith of the Fellowship of the Kingdom would be expressed in its Creed-Prayer, the Lord's Prayer. No other affirmation of faith would be required. To pray that Creed-Prayer daily from the heart would be the prime expression of loyal membership. The duties of membership would be the daily striving to obey the Two Great Commandments and to realize in character and conduct the ideals of the Seven Beatitudes: the seeking of each member to be in his environment 'the salt of the earth' and 'the light of the world:' and the endeavour to promote by every means in his power the coming of the Kingdom of God among mankind. Membership of the Fellowship would be open to all men and women—whether Christians, Jews, Mohammedans, or members of any religion or of no religion at all—who desired to be loyal to the Kingdom of God and discharge its duties."[283]

There are two main reasons most interpreters now reject this interpretation. First, it contradicts the many passages of Scripture that present salvation as something impossible to attain by good works (e.g., Eph. 2:8-9). Second, the extremely high standards that Jesus taught in the Sermon make the attaining of these requirements impossible for anyone and everyone, except Jesus.

A second approach to the Sermon is the *sociological* view, that sees it not as a guide to personal salvation, but to the salvation of society.

> "What would happen in the world if the element of fair play as enunciated in the Golden Rule—'Do unto others as you would that men should do unto you'—were put into practice in the various relationships of life? . . . What a difference all this would

---

[279]Kingsbury, p. 106.

[280]Edersheim, *The Life* . . ., 1:525, 526.

[281]See Toussaint, *Behold the* . . ., pp. 86-94; John A. Martin, "Dispensational Approaches to the Sermon on the Mount," in *Essays in Honor of J. Dwight Pentecost*, pp. 35-48; and W. S. Kissinger, *The Sermon on the Mount: A History of Interpretation and Bibliography*.

[282]H. D. A. Major, *Basic Christianity*, p. 48.

[283]Ibid., pp. 67-68.

make, and how far we would be on the road to a new and better day in private, in public, in business, and in international relationships!"[284]

There are two main problems with this view. First, it assumes that people can improve their society simply by applying the principles that Jesus taught in the Sermon. History has shown that this is impossible without someone to establish and administer such a society worldwide. Second, this view stresses the social dimension of Jesus' teaching to the exclusion of the personal dimension, which Jesus also emphasized.

Still others believe that Jesus gave the Sermon primarily to convict His hearers about their sins. They believe His purpose was also to make them realize that their only hope of salvation and participation in His kingdom was God's grace. One might call this view the *penitential* approach.

> "Thus what we have here in the Sermon on the Mount, is the climax of law, the completeness of the letter, the letter which killeth; and because it is so much more searching and thorough than the Ten Commandments, therefore does it kill all the more effectually. . . . The hard demand of the letter is here in the closest possible connexion [*sic*] with the promise of the Spirit."[285]

The main problem with this view is that it fails to recognize that the primary listeners to this sermon were Jesus' disciples (5:1-2). While not all of them believed in Him, most of them did. This seems clear, since He called them the "salt of the earth" and the "light of the world" (5:13-14). Moreover, He taught them to address God in prayer as their Father (6:9; cf. 6:26). He also credited them with serving God already (6:24-34). Certainly the Sermon convicted those who heard it of their sins, but it seems to have had a larger purpose than this.

A fourth view holds that the Sermon contains Jesus' ethical teaching for the church. This is the *ecclesiastical* interpretation to the Sermon.

> "It is a religious system of living which portrays how transformed Christians *ought* to live in the world."[286]

The problem with this view is that the New Testament presents the church as an entity distinct from the kingdom. Nothing in the context warrants concluding that Jesus taught His disciples about the church here. Everything points to Him teaching about the kingdom. Even though there are some parallels between Jesus' teaching here and the apostles' teaching in the epistles, this similarity does not prove church teaching. There are also similarities between the Old Covenant and the New Covenant, nine of the Ten Commandments, for example. However, this similarity does not prove that the two covenants are the same.

A fifth view sees the Sermon as applying to the earthly messianic kingdom exclusively. This is the *millennial* view.

> "In our exegesis of the three chapters, . . . we shall always in every part look upon the sermon on the mount as the proclamation of the King concerning the Kingdom. The Kingdom is not the church, nor is the state of the earth in righteousness, governed and possessed by the meek, brought about by the agency of the church. It is the millennial earth and the Kingdom to come, in which Jerusalem will be the city of a great King. . . . While we have in the Old Testament the outward manifestations of the Kingdom of the heavens as it will be set up in the earth in a future day, we have here the inner manifestation, the principles of it."[287]

The main problem with this view is Jesus' frequent references to conditions that are incongruous with the messianic kingdom proclaimed by the Old Testament prophets. For example, Jesus said that His disciples will experience persecution for His sake (5:11-12). Wickedness abounds (5:13-16). The disciples should pray for the coming of the kingdom (6:10). False prophets pose a major threat to Jesus' disciples (7:15). Some who hold this view relegate these conditions to the Tribulation period.[288] However, if the Sermon is the constitution of the messianic kingdom, as advocates of this view claim, it is very unusual that so much of it deals with conditions that will mark the Tribulation period. Some who hold this view also believe Jesus taught that to enter the kingdom, one must live up to the standards that Jesus presented in the Sermon.[289] If this were the requirement, no one would be able to enter it. The standards of the Sermon on the Mount are even higher than those of the Ten Commandments.

The sixth view is that the Sermon presents ethical instructions for Jesus' disciples that apply from the time Jesus gave them until the beginning of the kingdom. This is the *interim* approach to interpreting the Sermon.

---

[284]F. K. Stamm, *Seeing the Multitudes*, pp. 68-69.

[285]Charles Gore, *The Sermon on the Mount*, p. 4-5.

[286]Thomas. S. Kepler, *Jesus' Design for Living*, p. 12. See also C. F. Hogg and J. B. Watson, *On the Sermon on the Mount*, p. 19; and A. M. Hunter, *A Pattern for Life: An Exposition of the Sermon on the Mount*, p. 122.

[287]Gaebelein, 1:10. See also Kelly, pp. 103-6; William L. Pettingill, *Simple Studies in Matthew*, p. 58; Lewis Sperry Chafer, "The Teachings of Christ Incarnate," *Bibliotheca Sacra* 108 (October 1951):410; idem, *Systematic Theology*, 4:177-78; D. K. Campbell, "Interpretation and Exposition of the Sermon on the Mount," (Th.D. dissertation, Dallas Theological Seminary, 1953); and Ryrie, *Dispensationalism Today*, pp. 106-8.

[288]E.g., Donald Grey Barnhouse, *His Own Received Him Not, But . . .*, p. 47; and Campbell, p. 66.

[289]E.g., Lewis Sperry Chafer, *Systematic Theology*, 5:111.

"The sermon is *primarily* addressed to disciples exhorting them to a righteous life in view of the coming kingdom. Those who were not genuine disciples were warned concerning the danger of their hypocrisy and unbelief. They are enjoined to enter the narrow gate and to walk the narrow way. This is included in the discourse, but it is only the *secondary* application of the sermon."[290]

Several factors commend this view. First, it fits best into the historical situation that provided the context for the giving of the Sermon. John and then Jesus had announced that the kingdom was at hand. Jesus next instructed His disciples about preparing for its inauguration.

Second, the message of the Sermon also anticipates the inauguration of the kingdom. This is obvious in the attitude that pervades the discourse (cf. 5:12, 19-20, 46; 6:1-2, 4-6, 10, 18; 7:19-23). Moreover there is prediction about persecution and false prophets arising (5:11-12; 7:15-18). The abundant use of the future tense also anticipates the coming of the kingdom (5:4-9, 19-20; 6:4, 6, 14-15, 18, 33; 7:2, 7, 11, 16, 20-22).

Third, this view recognizes that the primary recipients of the Sermon were Jesus' disciples whom He taught (5:1-2, 19; 7:29). They were salt and light (5:13-16), God was their Father (5:9, 16, 45, 48; 6:1, 4, 6, 8-9, 14-15, 18, 26, 32; 7:11, 21), and righteousness was to characterize their lives (5:19—7:12). Jesus had much to say about service (5:10-12, 13-16, 19-20, 21-48; 6:1-18, 19-34; 7:1-12, 15-23, 24-27) and rewards (5:12, 19, 46; 6:1-2; 5, 16) in the Sermon. Probably many of these disciples had been John's disciples who had left the forerunner to follow the King (cf. John 3:22-30; 4:1-2; 6:66). Jesus was instructing His disciples concerning their duties for the rest of their lives. However, Jesus also had words for the multitudes, especially toward the end of the Sermon, the people that did not fall into the category of being His disciples (5:1-2; cf. 7:13, 21-23, 24-27).

Fourth, the subject matter of the Sermon favors the interim interpretation. The Sermon dealt with the good fruit resulting from repentance that Jesus' disciples should manifest (cf. 3:8, 10). The only thing Matthew recorded that John preached and that Jesus repeated in this Sermon is, "Every tree that does not bear good fruit is cut down and thrown into the fire" (7:19). Jesus, too, wanted His hearers to bring forth fruit worthy of repentance, and He described that fruit in this address.

Many students of the New Testament have noted the similarity between Jesus' teaching in the Sermon on the Mount and James' epistle.[291] James also stressed the importance of believers producing fruit, godly character, and good works (James 2:14-26). All the New Testament epistles present high standards for believers to maintain (cf. Phil. 3:12; Col. 3:13; 1 Pet. 1:15; 1 John 2:1). These flow naturally out of Jesus' instruction. Only with the Holy Spirit's enablement and the believer's dependence on the Lord can we live up to these standards.

1. The setting of the Sermon on the Mount 5:1-2 (cf. Luke 6:17-19)

The "multitudes" or "crowds" consisted of the people Matthew just mentioned in 4:23-25. They comprised a larger group than the "disciples."

The disciples were not just the Twelve, but many others who followed Jesus and sought to learn from Him. Essentially "disciple" means learner. They did not all continue to follow Him (John 6:66). Not all of them were genuine believers, Judas Iscariot being the notable example. The term "disciples" in the Gospels is a large one that includes all who chose to follow Jesus, for some time, anyway (Luke 6:17). We should not equate "believer" in the New Testament sense with "disciple" in the Gospels, as some expositors have done.[292]

"To say that 'every Christian is a disciple' seems to contradict the teaching of the New Testament. In fact, one could be a disciple and not be a Christian at all! John describes men who were disciples first and who then placed their faith in Christ (Jn. 2:11). . . . This alone alerts us to the fact that Jesus did not always equate being a 'disciple' with being a Christian."[293]

Customarily rabbis (teachers) "sat down" to instruct their disciples (cf. 13:2; 23:2; 24:3; Luke 4:20).[294] This posture implied Jesus' authority.[295] The exact location of the "mountain" Matthew referred to is unknown, though probably it was in Galilee, near the Sea of Galilee, and perhaps near Capernaum. There are no real mountains nearby, but plenty of hills.

"There is probably a deliberate attempt on the evangelist's part to liken Jesus to Moses, especially insofar as he is about to present the definitive interpretation of Torah, just as Moses, according to the Pharisees, had given the interpretation of Torah on Sinai to be handed on orally."[296]

---

[290]Toussaint, *Behold the . . .*, p. 94. See also Albert Schweitzer, *The Quest of the Historical Jesus*, p. 354; Walvoord, *Matthew: . . .*, pp. 44-46; Saucy, p. 18; Barbieri, p. 28; and Hagner, p. 83.

[291]See Virgil V. Porter Jr., "The Sermon on the Mount in the Book of James," *Bibliotheca Sacra* 162:647 (July-September 2005):344-60, and 162:648 (October-December 2005):470-82.

[292]E.g., John Calvin, *Institutes of the Christian Religion*, 3:2:6; and John F. MacArthur, *The Gospel According to Jesus*, p. 196. For a critique of MacArthur's book, see Darrell L. Bock, "A Review of *The Gospel According to Jesus*," *Bibliotheca Sacra* 146:581 (January-March 1989):21-40.

[293]Joseph C. Dillow, *The Reign of the Servant Kings*, p. 151. Cf. pp. 150-56.

[294]*A Dictionary of New Testament Theology*, s.v. "*kathemai*," by R. T. France, 3:589.

[295]Tasker, p. 59.

[296]Hagner, p. 86.

The phrase "opening His mouth He began to teach them" (v. 2; NASB) or "He began to teach them" (NIV) is a New Testament idiom (cf. 13:35; Acts 8:35; 10:34; 18:14). It has Old Testament roots (Job 3:1; 33:2; Dan. 10:16) and introduces an important utterance wherever it occurs.

There is some difference between preaching (Gr. kerysso; 4:17) and teaching (Gr. didasko; 5:2) as the Gospel writers used these terms (cf. Acts 28:23, 31). Generally, preaching involved a wider audience, and teaching was to a narrower, more committed one, in this case the disciples.

2. The subjects of Jesus' kingdom 5:3-16

Their condition 5:3-10 (cf. Luke 6:20-26)

This pericope describes the character of the kingdom's subjects and their rewards in the kingdom.

Kingsbury identified the theme of this Sermon as "greater righteousness" and divided it as follows: (I) On Those Who Practice the Greater Righteousness (5:3-16); (II) On Practicing the Greater Righteousness toward the Neighbor (5:17-45); (III) On Practicing the Greater Righteousness before God (6:1-18); (IV) On Practicing the Greater Righteousness in Other Areas of Life (6:19—7:12); and (V) Injunctions on Practicing the Greater Righteousness (7:13-27).[297] The Book of Romans deals with the theme of God's righteousness and how people can share in it.

> "Looked at as a whole . . . the Beatitudes become a moral sketch of the type of person who is ready to possess, or rule over, God's Kingdom in company with the Lord Jesus Christ."[298]

Jesus described the character of those who will receive blessings in the kingdom as rewards from eight perspectives. He introduced each one with a pronouncement of blessedness. This form of expression goes back to the wisdom literature of the Old Testament, particularly the Psalms (cf. Ps. 1:1; 32:1-2; 84:4-5; 144:15; Prov. 3:13; Dan. 12:12). The Beatitudes (vv. 3-10) may describe the fulfillment of Isaiah 61:1-3.[299] They describe and commend the good life.[300]

The English word "beatitude" comes from the Latin word for "blessed," beatus. The Greek word translated "blessed," makarios, refers to a happy condition.

> "The special feature of the group makarios, makarizein, makarismos in the NT is that it refers overwhelmingly to the distinctive religious joy which accrues to man from his share in the salvation of the kingdom of God."[301]

> "It [makarios] describes a state not of inner feeling on the part of those to whom it is applied, but of blessedness from an ideal point of view in the judgment of others."[302]

Blessedness is happiness because of divine favor.[303] The other Greek word translated "blessed," eulogetos, connotes the reception of praise and usually describes God.

> ". . . the kingdom is presupposed as something given by God. The kingdom is declared as a reality apart from any human achievement. Thus the beatitudes are, above all, predicated upon the experience of the grace of God. The recipients are just that, those who receive the good news."[304]

The "for" (Gr. hoti) in each beatitude explains why the person is a blessed individual. "Because" would be a good translation. They are blessed now because they will participate in the kingdom. The basis for each blessing is the fulfillment of something about the kingdom that God promised in the Old Testament.[305]

[297]Kingsbury, p. 112. See also idem, "The Place, Structure, and Meaning of the Sermon on the Mount within Matthew," Interpretation 41 (1987):131-43; Robert A. Guelich, The Sermon on the Mount: A Foundation for Understanding; and Hagner, pp. 83-84.

[298]Zane C. Hodges, "Possessing the Kingdom," The KERUGMA Message 2:2 (Winter 1992):5.

[299]See Bock, Jesus according . . ., pp. 128-29; and Robert A. Guelich, "The Matthean Beatitudes: 'Entrance-Requirements' or Eschatological Blessings?" Journal of Biblical Literature 95 (1973):433.

[300]France, The Gospel . . ., p. 161.

[301]Theological Dictionary of the New Testament, s.v. "makarios," by F. Hauck, 4:367.

[302]Allen, p. 39.

[303]C. G. Montefiore, The Synoptic Gospels, 2:30.

[304]Hagner, p. 96.

[305]See Vernon C. Grounds, "Mountain Manifesto," Bibliotheca Sacra 128:510 (April-June 1971):135-41.

The Beatitudes deal with four attitudes—toward ourselves (v. 3), toward our sins (vv. 4-6), toward God (vv. 7-9), and toward the world (v. 10, and vv. 11-16). They proceed from the inside out; they start with attitudes and move to actions that are opposed, the normal course of spirituality.

5:3   The "poor in spirit" are those who recognize their natural unworthiness to stand in God's presence, and who depend utterly on Him for His mercy and grace (cf. Ps. 37:14; 40:17; 69:28-29, 32-33; Prov. 16:19; 29:23; Isa. 61:1). They do not trust in their own goodness or possessions for God's acceptance. The Jews regarded material prosperity as an indication of divine approval, since many of the blessings God promised the righteous under the Old Covenant were material. However, the "poor in spirit" does not regard these things as signs of intrinsic righteousness, but confesses his or her total unworthiness. The "poor in spirit" acknowledges his or her lack of personal righteousness. This condition, as all the others the Beatitudes identify, describes those who have repented and are broken (3:2; 4:17).

> "'Poverty in spirit' is not speaking of weakness of character ('mean-spiritedness') but rather of a person's relationship with God. It is a positive spiritual orientation, the converse of the arrogant self-confidence which not only rides roughshod over the interests of other people but more importantly causes a person to treat God as irrelevant."[306]

Such a person can have joy in his or her humility because an attitude of personal unworthiness is necessary to enter the kingdom. This kingdom does not go primarily to the materially wealthy, but to those who admit their spiritual bankruptcy. One cannot purchase citizenship in this kingdom with money as people could purchase Roman citizenship, for example. What qualifies a person for citizenship is that person's attitude toward his or her intrinsic righteousness.

One writer believed that Jesus was not talking about entering the kingdom but possessing it (i.e., it will be theirs in the sense that the poor in spirit will reign over it with Jesus [cf. Rev. 3:21]).[307]

The first and last beatitudes give the reason for blessedness: "for theirs is the kingdom of heaven" (cf. v. 10). This phrase forms an *inclusio* or envelope that surrounds the remaining beatitudes. The *inclusio* is a literary device that provides unity. Speakers and writers used it, and still use it, to indicate that everything within the two uses of this term refers to the entity mentioned. Here that entity is the kingdom of heaven. In other words, this literary form shows that all the beatitudes deal with the kingdom of heaven.

5:4   "Those who mourn" do so because they sense their spiritual bankruptcy (v. 4). The Old Testament revealed that spiritual poverty results from sin. True repentance produces contrite tears—more than jubilant rejoicing—because the kingdom is near. The godly remnant in Jesus' day, that responded to the call of John and of Jesus, wept because of Israel's national humiliation, as well as because of personal sin (cf. Ezra 10:6; Ps. 51:4; 119:136; Ezek. 9:4; Dan. 9:19-20). It is this mourning over sin that resulted in personal and national humiliation that Jesus referred to here.

The promised blessing in this beatitude is future comfort for those who now mourn. The prophets connected Messiah's appearing with the comfort of His people (Isa. 40:1; 66:1-3, 13). All sorrow over personal and national humiliation because of sin will end when the King sets up His kingdom and the repentant enter into it.

5:5   A "gentle" or "meek" person is not only gentle in his or her dealings with others (11:29; 21:5; James 3:13). Such a person is unpretentious (1 Pet. 3:4, 14-15), self-controlled, and free from malice and vengefulness. This quality looks at a person's dealings with other people. A person might acknowledge his or her spiritual bankruptcy and mourn because of sin, but to respond meekly when other people regard us as sinful is something else. Meekness then is the natural and appropriate expression of genuine humility toward others.

Inheriting the Promised Land was the hope of the godly in Israel during the wilderness wanderings (Deut. 4:1; 16:20; cf. Isa. 57:13; 60:21). Inheriting is the privilege of faithful heirs (cf. 25:34). He or she can "inherit" because of who that person is, due to the relationship with the one bestowing the inheritance. Inheriting is a concept that the apostles wrote about and clarified (e.g., 1 Cor. 6:9; 15:50; Gal. 5:21; Eph. 5:5; Col. 3:23-24; Heb. 9:15; 12:23; 1 Pet. 1:3-4; et al.). Inheriting is not always the same as entering. A person can enter another's house, for example, without inheriting it. The Old Testament concept of inheriting involved not only entering, but also becoming an owner of, what one entered. In this beatitude Jesus was saying more than that the meek will enter the kingdom. They will also enter into it as an inheritance and possess it.[308] A major theme in the Sermon on the Mount is the believing disciple's rewards (cf. v. 12; 6:2, 4-6, 18).[309]

[306]France, *The Gospel* . . ., p. 165.

[307]Hodges, "Possessing the Kingdom," *The KERUGMA Message* 1:1 (May-June 1991):1-2.

[308]Ibid., 1:2 (July-August 1991):1-2.

[309]See Dillow, p. 67.

"The earth" is what the meek can joyfully anticipate inheriting. The Old Testament concept of the messianic kingdom was earthly. Messiah would rule over Israel and the nations on the earth (Ps. 2:8-9; 37:9, 11, 29). Eventually the kingdom of Messiah will move to the new earth (21:1). This means Jesus' meek disciples can anticipate receiving possession of some of the earth during His messianic reign (cf. 25:14-30; Luke 19:11-27). They will, of course, be subject to the King then.

5:6   As mentioned previously, Matthew always used the term "righteousness" in the sense of personal fidelity to God and His will (3:15; cf. Ps. 42:2; 63:1; Amos 8:11-14). He never used it of imputed righteousness: justification. Therefore, the righteousness that the blessed "hunger and thirst for" is not salvation. It is personal holiness and, extending this desire more broadly, the desire that holiness may prevail among all people (cf. 6:10). When believers bewail their own, and society's sinfulness, and pray that God will send a revival to clean things up, they demonstrate a hunger and thirst for righteousness.

The encouraging promise of Jesus is that such people will eventually receive the answer to their prayers. Messiah will establish righteousness in the world when He sets up His kingdom (Isa. 45:8; 61:10-11; 62:1-2; Jer. 23:16; 33:14-16; Dan. 9:24).

5:7   A "merciful" person forgives the guilty and has compassion on the needy and the suffering. A meek person acknowledges to others that he or she is sinful, but a merciful person has compassion on others because they are sinful.[310] Notice that Jesus did not specify a situation or situations in which the merciful person displays mercy because he or she is characteristically merciful. The promise applies in many different situations.

The blessing of "the merciful" is that they will "receive mercy" from God. Jesus did not mean that people can earn God's mercy for salvation by being merciful to others. He meant that God will deal mercifully with people who have dealt mercifully with their fellowmen (cf. 6:12-15; 9:13; 12:7; 18:33-34). There are many Old Testament texts that speak of Messiah dealing mercifully with the merciful (e.g., Isa. 49:10, 13; 54:8, 10; 60:10; Zech. 10:6).

5:8   The "pure in heart" are those who are single-minded in their devotion to God, and therefore morally pure inwardly. Inner moral purity is an important theme in Matthew and in the Old Testament (cf. Deut. 10:16; 30:6; 1 Sam. 15:22; Ps. 24:3-4; 51:6, 10; Isa. 1:10-17; Jer. 4:4; 7:3-7; 9:25-26). Likewise, freedom from hypocrisy is also prominent (cf. Ps. 24:4; 51:4-17; Prov. 22:11; Matt. 6:22, 33). Jesus probably implied both ideas here.

The "pure in heart" can look forward to seeing God in the person of Messiah when He reigns on the earth (Ps. 24:3-4; Isa. 33:17; 35:2; 40:5). Messiah would be single-minded in His devotion to God and morally pure. Thus there will be a correspondence and fellowship between the King and those of His subjects who share His character. No one has seen God in His pure essence without some type of filter. The body of Jesus was such a filter. Seeing God is a synonym for having intimate knowledge of and acquaintance with Him (John 14; 1 John 1:1-4).

5:9   "Peacemakers" likewise replicate the work of the Prince of Peace (Isa. 9:6-7). Jesus, through His life and ministry, made peace between God and man, and between man and man. Isaiah predicted this of Messiah (Isa. 52:7). True disciples of Jesus make peace as they herald the gospel that brings people into a peaceful relationship with God and with one another.

People who seek to make peace behave as true "sons of God." God called Israel His "son" (Deut. 14:1; Hos. 1:10), and He charged the Israelites with bringing their Gentile neighbors into a peaceful relationship with Himself (Exod. 19:5-6). Whereas Israel failed largely in her calling, the Son of God, Messiah, succeeded completely. Those who follow Christ faithfully will demonstrate concern for the peace of humanity by leading people to Him.

5:10   Persecution is as much a mark of discipleship as peacemaking. The world does not give up its hates and self-centered living easily. This brings opposition on disciples of Christ. Righteous people, those whose conduct is right in God's eyes, become targets of the unrighteous (cf. John 15:18-25; Acts 14:22; 2 Tim. 3:12; 1 Pet. 4:13-14). Jesus, the perfectly righteous One, suffered more than any other righteous person has suffered. The Old Testament prophets foretold this, calling Him the Suffering Servant of the Lord (cf. Isa. 52:13—53:12).

Even though Jesus' disciples suffer as they anticipate the kingdom, they can find joy in knowing that the kingdom will eventually be theirs. It will provide release from the persecution of God-haters when the "Man of Sorrows" reigns. This second explicit reference to "the kingdom of heaven" concludes the *inclusio* begun in verse 3 and signals an end to the Beatitudes (vv. 3-10).

---

[310]John R. W. Stott, *The Message of the Sermon on the Mount*, p. 48.

"The ordinary Jew of Christ's day looked only at the physical benefits of the kingdom which he thought would naturally be bestowed on every Israelite. The amillennialist of today, on the other hand, denies the physical existence of the promised Jewish kingdom by 'spiritualizing' its material blessings. The beatitudes of the King indicate that it is not an either-or proposition, but the kingdom includes both physical and spiritual blessings. A careful study of the beatitudes displays the fact that the kingdom is a physical earthly kingdom with spiritual blessings founded on divine principles."[311]

Their calling 5:11-16

Jesus proceeded to clarify His disciples' calling and ministry in the world to encourage them to endure persecution and to fulfill God's purpose for them.

"Some might think that verses 11-12 constitute the concluding Beatitude, since these verses begin with the words 'blessed are you". But it is noteworthy that only here in the Beatitudes do we meet a verb in the second person (i.e., 'blessed are *you*'). In addition there are 36 (Greek) words in this Beatitude compared to a maximum of 12 words (verse 10) in the preceding eight Beatitudes. It is reasonable to conclude that verses 3-10 are a self-contained introduction to the Sermon, while verses 11-12 commence the body of the Sermon."[312]

5:11-12   These two verses expand and clarify the last beatitude (v. 10; cf. 6:12, 14-15) and provide a transition to what follows.

Verse 11 broadens the persecution to include insult and slander. It also identifies Jesus with righteousness.

"This confirms that the righteousness of life that is in view is in imitation of Jesus. Simultaneously, it so identifies the disciple of Jesus with the practice of Jesus' righteousness that there is no place for professed allegiance to Jesus that is not full of righteousness."[313]

The prophets experienced persecution because they followed God faithfully. Now Jesus said His disciples would suffer similar persecution because they followed Him (cf. Dan. 9:24-27). His hearers could not help concluding that He was putting Himself on a par with God. They also realized that they themselves would be the objects of persecution.

This persecution should cause the disciples to "rejoice" rather than despair (cf. James 1:2-4). Their "reward" for faithfully enduring would be great when the kingdom began. This fact also shows the greatness of Jesus. These are the first claims to messiahship that Jesus made that Matthew recorded in his Gospel.

The phrase "in heaven" (v. 12) probably means throughout eternity. Kingdom reward (v. 10) would continue forever. Some believe it means that God prepares the reward in heaven now for future manifestation.[314] This promise should be an incentive for Christ's disciples to view their opposition by the ungodly as temporary and to realize that their reward for persevering faithfully will be eternal (cf. 1 Pet. 1:3-9). Jesus' words about eternal rewards open and close the New Testament (cf. Rev. 22:12).

"Unlike many modern Christians, Matthew is not coy about the 'reward' that awaits those who are faithful to their calling."[315]

". . . because the eye of our mind is too blind to be moved solely by the beauty of the good, our most merciful Father out of his great kindness has willed to attract us by sweetness of rewards to love and seek after him.[316]

"One of the curious features of Jesus' great speeches is that they contain sayings that seemingly are without relevance for the characters in the story to whom they are addressed. Time and again, Jesus touches on matters that are alien to the immediate situation of the crowds or the disciples. This peculiar phenomenon—that Jesus speaks past his stipulated audience at places in his speeches—compels one to ask whether Jesus is not to be construed as addressing some person(s) other than simply the crowds or the disciples in the story. . . .

---

[311]Toussaint, *Behold the . . .*, p. 97.

[312]Hodges, 2:2 (Spring 1992):1.

[313]D. A. Carson, *The Sermon on the Mount*, p. 28.

[314]Dalman, pp. 206-8.

[315]France, *The Gospel . . .*, p. 172. Cf. idem, *Matthew: Evangelist and Teacher*, pp. 268-70.

[316]Calvin, 2:8:4.

"If in his great speeches Jesus periodically speaks past his story-audience of crowds or disciples, whom in addition to the latter is he addressing in these instances? From a literary-critical standpoint, he is addressing the implied reader(s)."[317]

5:13   Verses 13-16 have been called the epilogue to the Beatitudes, and have been compared to the prologue to the Ten Commandments (Exod. 20:3-6).[318]

By placing "you" (Gr. *hymeis*) in the emphatic position in the Greek text, Jesus was stressing the unique calling of His disciples (cf. v. 14). "Salt" was important in the ancient Near East because it flavored food, retarded decay in food, and in small doses fertilized land.[319] Jesus implied by this metaphor that His disciples could positively affect the world (Gr. *kosmos*, the inhabited earth, i.e., humankind).[320] They had the opportunity through their lives and witness to bring blessing to others and to retard the natural decay that sin produces in life. As salt thrown out on the earth, they could also produce fruit to God. Some critics have wondered how salt could lose its saltiness ("become tasteless"), since sodium chloride is a stable compound that does not break down.

"But most salt in the ancient world derived from salt marshes or the like, rather than by evaporation of salt water, and therefore contained many impurities. The actual salt, being more soluble than the impurities, could be leached out, leaving a residue so dilute it was of little worth."[321]

The most obvious characteristic of salt is that it is different from the medium into which its user places it. Jesus' disciples likewise are to be different from the world. As salt is an antiseptic, so the disciples are to be a moral disinfectant in a sin-infested world. This requires virtue, however, that comes only through divine grace and self-discipline.[322]

In modern Israel, weak salt still often ends up scattered on the soil that tops flat-roofed houses, which the residents sometimes use as patios. There it hardens the soil and so prevents leaks.[323] In biblical times, salt that had leached out, and lost its saltiness, was used for coating pathways.[324] God will use disciples, either as vessels unto honor or as vessels unto dishonor (cf. Rom. 9:21; 2 Tim. 2:20).

5:14-16   "Light" is a common symbol in the Bible. It represents purity, truth, knowledge, divine revelation, and God's presence—all in contrast to their opposites. The Israelites thought of themselves as lights in a dark world (Isa. 42:6; Rom. 2:19). However, the Old Testament spoke of Messiah as the true light of the world (Isa. 42:6; 49:6; cf. Matt. 4:16; John 8:12; 9:5; 12:35; 1 John 1:7). Jesus' disciples are lights in the derived sense, as the moon is a light but only because it reflects the light of the sun (cf. Eph. 5:8-9; Phil. 2:15).

The "city set on a hill" (v. 14) may refer to messianic prophecy concerning God lifting up Zion and causing the nations to stream to it (Isa. 2:2-5; et al.). Since God will make the capital of the messianic kingdom prominent, it is inappropriate for the citizens of that city to assume a low profile in the world before its inauguration (cf. Luke 11:33). Verse 15 is an early example of Jesus teaching with parables in Matthew's Gospel.[325]

The disciples must therefore manifest "good works," the outward demonstration or testimony to the righteousness that is within them (v. 16). Even though the light may provoke persecution (vv. 10-12), they must reflect the light of God. For the first time in Matthew, Jesus referred to God as the "Father" of His disciples (cf. vv. 45, 48; 6:1, 4, 6, 8-9, 14-15, 18, 26, 32; 7:11, 21).

"If salt (v. 13) exercises the negative function of delaying decay and warns disciples of the danger of compromise and conformity to the world, then light (vv. 14-16) speaks positively of illuminating a sin-darkened world and warns against a withdrawal from the world that does not lead others to glorify the Father in heaven."[326]

---

[317]Kingsbury, *Matthew as . . .*, pp. 107, 109. For other examples of this phenomenon in Matthew, see 6:16-18; 7:15-23; 10:18, 22, 41-42; 13:18-23, 38; 18:15-20; 24:3—25:46.

[318]Edersheim, *The Life . . .*, 1:529.

[319]Eugene P. Deatrick, "Salt, Soil, Savor," *Biblical Archaeologist* 25 (1962):44-45.

[320]See Don Garlington, "'The Salt of the Earth' in Covenantal Perspective," *Journal of the Evangelical Theological Society* 54:4 (December 2011):715-48.

[321]Carson, "Matthew," p. 138.

[322]Tasker, p. 63.

[323]Deatrick, p. 47.

[324]*The Nelson . . .*, p. 1583.

[325]See Appendix 4, a chart of "The Parables of Jesus," at the end of these notes.

[326]Carson, "Matthew," p. 140.

"Flight into the invisible is a denial of the call. A community of Jesus which seeks to hide itself has ceased to follow him."[327]

The introduction of "good works" (v. 16) leads on to further exposition of that theme in 5:17—7:12.

3. The importance of true righteousness 5:17—7:12

Jesus had just been speaking about the importance of His disciples demonstrating their righteousness publicly with their good works (v. 16). Now He dealt with the more fundamental question of what true righteousness is. This was important to clarify, since the religious leaders of His day misinterpreted righteousness and good works.

"The kinds of good deeds that enable light to be seen as light are now to be elaborated in the course of the sermon that follows. They are shown to be nothing other than the faithful living out of the commandments, the righteousness of the Torah as interpreted by Jesus."[328]

Righteousness and the Scriptures 5:17-48

In His discussion of righteousness (character and conduct that conforms to the will of God), Jesus went back to the revelation of God's will, namely: God's Word, the Old Testament.

Jesus' view of the Old Testament 5:17-20

It was natural for Jesus to explain His view of the Old Testament, since He would shortly proceed to interpret it to His hearers.

5:17   Some of the Jews may have already concluded that Jesus was a radical who was discarding the teachings of the Old Testament, their law. Many others would begin to do so soon. Jesus prepared them for the incongruity between His teaching, and their leaders' interpretations of the law, by explaining His relationship to the Old Testament.

"It seems likely that here Jesus is dealing with the charge of being antinomian since his controversies suggested an approach to the law that was different from traditional thinking. His reply shows that he seeks a standard that looks at the law from an internal, not an external, perspective."[329]

The terms "the Law" and "the Prophets" refer to two of the three major divisions of the Hebrew Bible, the third being "the Psalms" (Luke 24:44). "The Law and the Prophets" was evidently the most common way Jews referred to the Old Testament in Jesus' day (cf. 7:12; 11:13; 22:40; Luke 16:16; John 1:45; Acts 13:15; 28:23; Rom. 3:21). Jesus introduced the subject of Scripture interpretation in this verse with this phrase. In 7:12 He concluded the subject with the same phrase. Thus the phrase "the Law and the Prophets" forms another *inclusio* within the body of the Sermon on the Mount and identifies the main subject that it encloses.

Much debate has centered on what Jesus meant when He said He came "to fulfill" the Old Testament.[330] The first question is: Was Jesus referring to Himself when He said, "I came . . . to fulfill," or was He referring to His teaching? Did *He* fulfill the law, or did *His teaching* fulfill it? Since the contrast is "to abolish" the law, it seems probable that Jesus meant His teaching fulfilled the law. He did not intend that what He taught the people would replace the teaching of the Old Testament, but that it would fulfill (Gr. *pleroo*) or establish it completely. Of course, Jesus did fulfill Old Testament prophecy about Messiah, but that does not appear to be the primary subject in view here. The issue seems to be His teaching.

Some interpreters conclude that Jesus meant He came to fulfill (keep) the moral law (the Ten Commandments), but that He abolished Israel's civil and ceremonial laws.[331] However, there is no basis for this distinction in this text or in any other New Testament text. Others believe that He meant He came to fill out its meaning, to expound its full significance that until then remained obscure.[332] This view rests on an unusual meaning of *pleroo*, and it seems inconsistent with Jesus' comment about

---

[327]Dietrich Bonhoeffer, *The Cost of Discipleship*, p. 106.

[328]Hagner, p. 102.

[329]Bock, *Jesus according . . .*, p. 131.

[330]See John A. Martin, "Christ, the Fulfillment of the Law in the Sermon on the Mount," in *Dispensationalism, Israel and the Church*, pp. 248-63.

[331]E.g., Craig L. Blomberg, *Matthew*, pp. 103-5; Eugene H. Merrill, "Deuteronomy, New Testament Faith, and the Christian Life," in *Integrity of Heart, Skillfulness of Hands*, p. 22; and David Wenham, "Jesus and the Law: an Exegesis on Matthew 5:17-20," *Themelios* 4:3 (April 1979):92-26.

[332]E.g., Lenski, p. 199-201.

the jot and tittle in verse 18. Still others believe Jesus meant that He came to extend the demands of the Old Testament law to new lengths.[333] This interpretation is improbable because the extension of law does not involve its abolition. Another view is that Jesus meant He was introducing what the Law pointed toward, either by direct prediction or by typology.[334]

Probably Jesus meant that He came to establish the Old Testament fully, to add His authoritative approval to it. This view harmonizes with Matthew's use of *pleroo* elsewhere (cf. 2:15). This does not mean He taught that the Mosaic Law remained in force for His disciples. He taught that it did not (Mark 7:19).[335] Rather, here, Jesus authenticated the Old Testament as the inspired Word of God.[336] He wanted His hearers to understand that what He taught them in no way contradicted Old Testament revelation.

The purpose of the Mosaic Law was revelatory and regulatory, but not redemptive. That is, it revealed what God wanted people to know, and it regulated the life of the Israelites. But God never intended that people should view it as a way to earn salvation, namely: by keeping it perfectly. He gave it to a redeemed people: to Israelites who had been redeemed from bondage in Egypt.

"He [Jesus] disregarded the oral tradition, which they [the Pharisees] held to be equal in authority to the written Law; and He interpreted the written Law according to its spirit, and not, as they did, according to the rigid letter. He did not keep the weekly fasts, nor observe the elaborated distinctions between clean and unclean, and He consorted with outcasts and sinners. He neglected the traditional modes of teaching, and preached in a way of His own. Above all, He spoke as if He Himself were an authority, independent of the Law."[337]

There is good evidence that the Jewish leaders regarded the traditional laws, as not just having equal authority with the Old Testament, but having greater authority.[338]

"It is not obvious at first sight what Christ means by 'fulfilling (*plerosai*) the Law.' He does not mean taking the written Law as it stands, and literally obeying it. That is what he condemns, not as wrong, but as wholly inadequate. He means rather starting with it as it stands, and bringing it on to completeness; working out the spirit of it; getting at the comprehensive principles which underlie the narrowness of the letter. These Messiah sets forth as the essence of the revelation made by God through the Law and Prophets."[339]

5:18   The phrase "truly I say to you" (NASB) or "I tell you the truth" (NIV) indicates that what follows is extremely important. This is the first occurrence in Matthew of this phrase, which appears 30 times in this Gospel, 13 times in Mark, six times in Luke, and 25 times in John. It always conveys the personal authority of the person who utters it.[340] "Until heaven and earth pass away" is a vivid way of saying as long as this world lasts. The AV "jot," also translated "smallest letter" (NASB, NIV), refers to *yod*, the smallest letter of the Hebrew alphabet. The "tittle" (AV) or "smallest stroke" (NASB) or "least stroke" (NIV) is not as easy to identify. The best possibility seems to be that it refers to a small stroke on one Hebrew letter (a serif) that distinguished it from a similarly shaped letter.[341] In any case, Jesus meant that He upheld the entire Old Testament, down to the smallest features of the Hebrew letters that the writers used as they composed the original documents.

"The words of our Lord, as reported both by St. Matthew (Matt. v. 18) and by St. Luke (Luke xvi. 17), also prove that the copy of the Old Testament from which He had drawn was not only in the original Hebrew, but written, like our modern copies, in the so-called Assyrian, and not in the ancient Hebrew-Pheonician characters."[342]

[333]E.g., Wolfgang Trilling, *Das wahre Israel: Studien zur Theologie des Matthaus-Evangeliums*, pp. 174-79.

[334]France, *The Gospel . . .*, p. 182.

[335]See Hal Harless, "The Cessation of the Mosaic Covenant," *Bibliotheca Sacra* 160:639 (July-September 2003):349-66.

[336]Cf. Stephen Westerholm, "The Law in the Sermon on the Mount: Matt 5:17-48," *Criswell Theological Review* 6:1 (Fall 1992):43-56.

[337]Plummer, p. 75.

[338]Edersheim, *The Life . . .*, 1:97-98.

[339]Plummer, p. 76.

[340]France, *The Gospel . . .*, p. 184.

[341]See Carson, "Matthew," p. 145, for other less likely possibilities.

[342]Edersheim, *Sketches of . . .*, p. 118.

This verse is a strong testimony to the verbal inspiration of Scripture. That is, divine inspiration extends to the words, even the letters, in the original texts. Verses 17-19 also argue for the plenary inspiration of Scripture, the view that inspiration extends to all parts of the Old Testament. God inspired all of it, down to the very words the writers used. In verse 18, "the Law" refers to the whole Old Testament, not just the Mosaic Law or the Pentateuch (cf. v. 17). This is clear from the context.

God will preserve His Law until everything in it has happened as prophesied. It is as permanent as heaven and earth (cf. 24:35).

5:19   The Jewish rabbis had graded the Old Testament commands according to which ones they believed were more authoritative and which ones less, the heavy and the light.[343] Jesus corrected this view. He taught that all were equally authoritative. He warned His hearers against following their leaders' practice. Greatness in His kingdom depended on maintaining a high view of Scripture. This verse distinguishes different ranks within the messianic kingdom. Some individuals will have a higher standing than others. Everyone will not be equal. Notice that there will be people in the kingdom whose view of Scripture will not be the same as before they entered the kingdom. All will be righteous, but their obedience to and attitude toward Scripture will vary.

5:20   Many interpreters regard this verse as the key verse in Sermon on the Mount. "I say to you" is a claim to having authority (cf. 7:29). The relativistic view of the "scribes and Pharisees" led them to accept some Scriptural injunctions and to reject others (cf. 15:5-6).[344] This resulted in selective obedience that produced only superficial righteousness (only external conformity to the revealed will of God). That type of "righteousness," Jesus declared, would not be adequate for admission into the kingdom. The phrase "enter the kingdom" occurs seven other times in the New Testament (7:21; 18:3; 19:23, 24; Mark 9:47; John 3:5; Acts 14:22). The condition for entering—in every case—is faith alone. Selective obedience does not demonstrate a proper faith attitude to God, the attitude John and Jesus called for when they said, "Repent."

> "I have always felt that Matthew 5:20 was the key to this important sermon . . . The main theme is true righteousness. The religious leaders had an artificial, external righteousness based on Law. But the righteousness Jesus described is a true and vital righteousness that begins internally, in the heart. The Pharisees were concerned about the minute details of conduct, but they neglected the major matter of *character*. Conduct flows out of character."[345]

This pericope deals with various attitudes toward the Law: destroying it or fulfilling it (v. 17), and doing it and teaching it (v. 19).

Jesus proceeded to clarify exactly what the law did require in verses 21-48.[346] He selected six subjects. He was not contrasting His interpretation with Moses' teaching, but with the interpretation of the scribes and Pharisees. He was expounding the meaning of the text that God originally intended. He was doing Bible exposition.

God's will concerning murder 5:21-26

5:21   In each of these six cases, Jesus first related the popular understanding of the Old Testament, the view advocated by the religious teachers of His day. In this verse He introduced it by saying, "You have heard that the ancients were told" (NASB). This was an expression that the rabbis of Jesus' day used when they referred to the teachings of the Old Testament.[347]

Jesus quoted the sixth commandment and combined it with Leviticus 19:17. The "court" in view was the civil court in Israel.

5:22   Jesus contrasted His correct interpretation with the false common understanding of this command. His, "But I say to you" (vv. 22, 28, 32, 34, 39, 44) was not a common rabbinic saying, though it did have some parallels in rabbinic Judaism.[348] It expressed an authority that surprised His hearers (cf. 7:29). Thus Jesus "fulfilled" or established the meaning of the passages to which He referred (v. 17).[349]

---

[343]M'Neile, p. 59.

[344]For a good brief introduction to the scribes and the Pharisees, see France, *The Gospel . . .*, p. 189.

[345]Wiersbe, 1:21.

[346]William M. McPheeters, "Christ As an Interpreter of Scripture," *The Bible Student* 1 (April 1900):223-29.

[347]D. Daube, *The New Testament and Rabbinic Judaism*, p. 55.

[348]Hagner, p. 111.

[349]See Roger D. Congdon, "Did Jesus Sustain the Law in Matthew 5?" *Bibliotheca Sacra* 135:538 (April-June 1978):125.

"Jesus implicitly claimed deity in at least twelve ways. He claimed three divine rights: (1) to judge mankind, (2) to forgive sins, and (3) to grant eternal life. He declared that (4) his presence was God's presence as well as the presence of God's kingdom and that (5) the attitude people took toward him would determine their eternal destiny. He (6) identified his actions with God's actions, (7) taught the truth on his own authority, and (8) performed miracles on his own authority. He (9) appeared to receive worship or obeisance. He (10) assumed that his life was a pattern for others, a 'divinely authoritative form of life.' He (11) applied to himself OT texts that describe God and (12) in several parables indirectly identified himself with a father or king who represents God."[350]

When God gave the sixth commandment, He did not just want people to refrain from murdering one another. He wanted them to refrain from the hatred that leads to murder. Murder is only the external manifestation of the internal problem. The scribes and Pharisees dealt only with the external act. Jesus showed that God's concern ran much deeper. Refraining from homicide does not constitute a person righteous in God's sight. Inappropriate anger renders one subject to judgment at God's heavenly court "since no human court is competent to try a case of inward anger."[351]

Jesus often used the term "brother" in the sense of a brother disciple. The term usually occurs on Jesus' lips in the first Gospel, and Matthew recorded Him using it extensively. The relationship is an extension of the fact that God is the Father of believing disciples. Thus all believers are brothers in the spiritual sense. The early church's use of the term reflects that of Jesus.

"Raca" is the transliteration of the Aramaic reka. It means "imbecile," "numbskull," or "blockhead."[352] The "supreme court" (NASB) or "Sanhedrin" (NIV; Gr. synedrion) probably refers to God's highest court in view of the context, not the Jewish Sanhedrin of Jesus' day. The scribes and Pharisees taught that a person who referred to someone as a "Raca" was in danger of being sued for libel before the Sanhedrin.[353] "Fool" (Gr. mores) is another similar term that a person who felt hatred for even his brother might use. He, too, would be in danger of divine judgment. Jesus said the offender is "guilty" enough to suffer eternal judgment, not that he will. Whether he will suffer eternal judgment or not depends on his relationship to God. There does not seem to be any gradation or progression in these three instances of anger. Jesus simply presented three possible instances with an assortment of terms, and assured His hearers that in all these cases, there was a violation of God's will that could incur severe divine torment (cf. 3:12).

The word "hell" translates the Greek geenna, which is a transliteration of the Hebrew ge hinnom or "Valley of Hinnom." This was the valley south of Jerusalem, where a fire burned continually, consuming the city's refuse. This place became an illustration of the place where the wicked will suffer eternal torment.[354] Matthew recorded 11 references to it.

Jesus' demonstrations of anger were appropriate for Him since He was God, and God gets angry. His anger was always righteous, unlike the anger that arises from unjustified hatred. It is possible for humans to be angry and not sin (Eph. 4:26). Here Jesus was addressing unjustifiable anger that can lead to murder (cf. Col. 3:8).

5:23-24   Jesus gave two illustrations of anger, one involving temple worship (vv. 23-24), and the other, legal action (vv. 25-26). Both deal with situations in which the hearer is the cause of another person's anger rather than the offended party. Why did Jesus construct the illustrations this way? Perhaps He did so because we are more likely to remember situations, in which we have had some grievance against another person, than those in which we have simply offended another. Moreover, Jesus' disciples should be as sensitive about not making other people hate them, as they are about potentially hating others.

The offerer would present his offering at the brazen altar in the temple courtyard. It is more important to lift the load of hate from another brother's heart than to engage in a formal act of worship. Ritual worship was very important to the scribes and Pharisees, and to all the Jews, but Jesus put internal purity first, even the internal purity of another person (cf. 1 Sam. 16:7). Reconciliation, also, is more important than worship, in that it must come first.

"The most prominent object in the Court of the Priests was the immense altar of unhewn stones, a square of not less than 48 feet, and, inclusive of 'the horns,' 15 feet high. All around it a 'circuit' ran for the use of the ministering priests, who, as a rule, always passed round by the right, and retired by the left. As this

[350]Daniel Doriani, "The Deity of Christ in the Synoptic Gospels," Journal of the Evangelical Theological Society 37:3 (September 1994):339-40.
[351]Stott, p. 85.
[352]Carson, "Matthew," p. 149.
[353]The Nelson . . ., p. 1584.
[354]See Hans Scharen, "Gehenna in the Synoptics," Bibliotheca Sacra 149:595 (July-September 1992):324-37; 149:596 (October-December 1992):454-57.

'circuit' was raised 9 feet from the ground, and 1½ feet high, while the 'horns' measured 1½ feet in height, the priests would have only to reach 3 feet to the top of the altar, and 4½ feet to that of each 'horn.' An inclined plane, 48 feet long by 24 wide, into which about the middle two smaller 'descents' merged, led up to the 'circuit' from the south."[355]

5:25-26   The second illustration stresses the importance of making things right quickly. Two men walking together to the court where their disagreement would receive judicial arbitration should try to settle their grievance out of court (cf. 1 Cor. 6:1-11). The offender should remove the occasion for the other man's anger and hatred quickly. Otherwise the judge might make things difficult for both of them. The mention of going from judge to officer to prison pictures the red tape and complications involved in not settling out of court. Likewise, God will make it difficult for haters, and those who provoke hate in others, if they come before Him with unresolved interpersonal disagreements. Malicious anger is evil, and God's judgment is certain. Therefore, disciples must do everything they can to end inappropriate anger quickly (cf. Eph. 4:26).

God's will concerning adultery 5:27-30

5:27-28   Jesus proceeded to clarify God's intended meaning in the seventh commandment (Exod. 20:14; Deut. 5:18). The rabbis in Jesus' day tended to look at "adultery" as wrong because it involved stealing another man's wife. They viewed it as an external act.[356] Jesus, on the other hand, saw it as wrong because it made the lustful individual impure morally, an internal condition. The Greek word *gyn* can mean either wife or woman. Certainly the spirit of the command would prohibit lusting after any woman, not just a married woman. Fantasized immorality is just as sinful to God as physical immorality (cf. Exod. 20:17). The fact that fornication that takes place in the brain has fewer bad consequences than fornication that takes place on a bed does not mitigate this truth.

> "A man who gazes at a woman with the purpose of wanting her sexually has mentally committed adultery."[357]

5:29-30   As before (vv. 23-26), two illustrations aid our understanding. The eye is the member of the body initially responsible for luring us into an immoral thought or deed (cf. Num. 15:39; Prov. 21:4; Ezek. 6:9; 18:12; 20:8). The "right eye" is the best eye, the common metaphorical use of the "right" anything. A literal interpretation of this verse would have Jesus crippling every member of the human race. Should not one pluck out his left eye as well? Furthermore, disposing of the eye would not remove the real cause of the offense, a lustful heart. Clearly this is a hyperbolic statement designed to make a point by overstatement. The early church father Origen took it literally and castrated himself. Jesus' point was that His disciples must deal radically with sin. We must avoid temptation at all costs. Clearly this is not a condition for salvation but for discipleship.[358]

The reference to cutting off the "right hand" (v. 30) is also metaphorical, but how symbolic is it? Some take the "right hand" as a euphemism for the penis (cf. Isa. 57:8).[359] This view has the context in its favor. Others take the right hand literally and view it as the instrument of stealing another man's wife. "Hell" is Gehenna, the final place of punishment for all the wicked.[360] Its mention here does not imply that believers can go there. It represents the worst possible destiny. It, too, is hyperbole. The loss of any body part is preferable to the loss of the whole person, is the point.

> "Imagination is a God-given gift; but if it is fed dirt by the eye, it will be dirty. All sin, not least sexual sin, begins with the imagination. Therefore what feeds the imagination is of maximum importance in the pursuit of kingdom righteousness (compare Phil 4:8). Not everyone reacts the same way to all objects. But if (vv. 28-29) your eye is causing you to sin, gouge it out; or at very least, don't look . . .!"[361]

God's will concerning divorce 5:31-32

Not only is lust the moral equivalent of adultery, but so is divorce. The connective *de* ("and," NASB) that begins verse 31 ties this section in very closely with the one that precedes (vv. 27-30). In Israel, a man divorced his wife simply by giving her a written statement indicating that he

[355]Alfred Edersheim, *The Temple*, pp. 54-55.

[356]Carson, "Matthew," p. 151.

[357]*The Nelson . . .*, p. 1584.

[358]See Robert N. Wilkin, "Self-Sacrifice and Kingdom Entrance: Matthew 5:29-30," *The Grace Evangelical Society News* 4:8 (August 1989):2; 4:9 (September 1989):2-3.

[359]Brown, Driver, and Briggs, *A Hebrew and English Lexicon of the Old Testament*, s.v. "yad," p. 390; S. T. Lachs, "Some Textual Observations on the Sermon on the Mount," *Jewish Quarterly Review* 69 (1978):108-9.

[360]Scharen, p. 337.

[361]Carson, "Matthew," p. 151.

divorced her (cf. Deut. 24:1-4). It was a domestic matter, not something that went through the courts, and it was quite common. In most cases, a divorced woman would remarry, to another man, often for her own security. Jesus said that divorcing a woman virtually amounted to causing her to commit adultery since she would normally remarry. Likewise, any man who married a divorced woman committed adultery with her, because in God's eyes she was still married to her first husband. Jesus' explanation would have helped his hearers realize the ramifications of a decision that many of them viewed as insignificant, namely, divorcing one's wife. Women did not have the right to divorce their husbands in ancient Israel. Josephus, writing about the divorce of Salome, Herod the Great's sister, and her husband, Costobarus, commented on the Jewish divorce custom:

"But some time afterward, when Salome happened to quarrel with Costobarus, she sent him a bill of divorce, and dissolved her marriage with him, though this was not according to the Jewish laws; for with us it is lawful for a husband to do so; but a wife, if she departs from her husband, cannot of herself be married to another, unless her former husband put her away."[362]

We could add the exception clause to the last part of verse 32, since that seems to have been Jesus' intention (cf. Mark 10:12). He probably did not repeat it because He did not want to stress the exceptional case, but to focus on the seriousness of the husband's decision to divorce his wife. Jesus had more to say about divorce in 19:3-9 (cf. Mark 10:11-12; Luke16:18).

". . . Jesus introduces the new and shocking idea that even properly divorced people who marry a second time may be thought of as committing adultery. The OT, allowing divorce, does not regard those who remarry as committing adultery. . . . Marriage was meant to establish a permanent relationship between a man and a woman, and divorce should therefore not be considered an option for the disciples of the kingdom."[363]

Some interpreters limit fornication ("unchastity," "immorality," Gr. *porneia*) to unfaithfulness during the betrothal period, the year between a Jewish couple's engagement and the consummation of their marriage.[364] The problem with this view is that *porneia* has a broader range of meaning than this.[365]

God's will concerning oaths 5:33-37

5:33   Jesus next gave a condensation of several commands in the Old Testament that prohibited taking an oath, invoking the Lord's name to guarantee the oath, and then breaking it (Exod. 20:7; Lev. 19:12; Num. 30:2; Deut. 5:11; 6:3; 23:21-23). God has always intended simple truthfulness in speech as well as lifelong marriage. The rabbis had developed an elaborate stratification of oaths. They taught that swearing by God's name was binding, but swearing by heaven and earth was not binding. Swearing *toward* Jerusalem was binding, but swearing *by* Jerusalem was not. In some cases they even tried to deceive others by appealing to various authorities in their oaths.[366] Jesus was not talking about "cursing" here, but using oaths to affirm that what one said was true.

5:34-36   Jesus cut through all the casuistry by saying that if oaths that God intended to guarantee truthfulness in speech become the instruments of deceit, His disciples avoid them. Again, Jesus got below the external act to the real issue at stake, that had been God's concern from the beginning. His point was that people should not lie under *any* circumstances.

Jesus explained that whatever a person may appeal to in an oath has some connection with God. Therefore any oath is an appeal to God indirectly if not directly. To say that one could swear by one's own "head," for example, and then break his vow, because he did not mention God's name, was shortsighted.

". . . what is called 'promise' among men is called 'vow' with respect to God."[367]

Calvin noted that several passages of Scripture indicate that calling on God as witness, to confirm the truth of one's word, was a sort of divine worship (e.g., Isa. 19:18; 65:16; Jer. 12:16). Curses that contain manifest insults to God should not be regarded as oaths. It was wrong to swear falsely by (to "profane") His name (Lev. 19:12), to use His name in true but needless oaths, and to substitute God's servants in place of Him, thus transferring His glory to them (Exod. 23:13). God not only permitted the use of oaths under the Law, but He commanded their use in case of necessity (Exod. 22:10-11).[368]

---

[362]Josephus, *Antiquities of . . .*, 15:7:10.

[363]Hagner, p. 125.

[364]For discussion of this view, see David W. Jones, "The Betrothal View of Divorce and Remarriage," *Bibliotheca Sacra* 165:657 (January-March 2008):68-85.

[365]See Appendix 5 "What ends a marriage in God's sight?" at the end of these notes.

[366]Hogg and Watson, p. 54.

[367]Calvin, 4:13:1.

[368]Ibid., 2:8:23-26.

"To men of sound judgment there can then be no doubt that the Lord in that passage [i.e., Matt. 5:33-37] disapproved only of those oaths forbidden by the law [cf. James 5:12]. For he, who in his life gave an example of the perfection that he taught, did not shrink from oaths whenever circumstances required. And the disciples, who we may be sure obeyed their Master in all things, followed the same example. Who would dare say that Paul would have sworn if the taking of oaths had been utterly forbidden? But when circumstances demanded it, he swore without any hesitation, sometimes even adding a curse [Rom. 1:9; II Cor. 1:23]."[369]

5:37   Jesus' "yes, yes," and "no, no," is not the exact terminology He wanted His disciple to use. If He meant that, He would be doing just what He was correcting the rabbis for doing. Rather, it means a simple "yes" or "no." The NIV translation gives the sense: "Simply let your 'Yes' be 'Yes,' and your 'No,' 'No.'" The "evil" at the end of the verse may either be a reference to the devil, or it may mean that to go beyond Jesus' teaching on this point involves evil.

Some very conscientious believers have taken Jesus' words literally and have refused to take an oath of any kind, even in court. However, Jesus' point was the importance of truthfulness. He probably would not have objected to the use of oaths as a formality in legal proceedings.

"They [oaths in court or oaths of political allegiance] should not be needed, but in practice they serve a remedial purpose in a world where the ethics of the kingdom of heaven are not always followed. Refusal to take a required oath can in such circumstances convey quite the wrong impression."[370]

The Bible records that God Himself swore oaths, not because He sometimes lies or could possibly lie, but to impress His truthfulness on people (Gen. 9:9-11; Luke 1:73). Jesus testified under oath (26:63-64), as did Paul (Rom. 1:9; 2 Cor. 1:23; 1 Thess. 2:5, 10).

"It must be frankly admitted that here Jesus formally contravenes OT law: what it permits or commands (Deut. 6:13), he forbids. But if his interpretation of the direction in which the law points is authoritative, then his teaching fulfills it."[371]

God's will concerning retaliation 5:38-42

5:38   Retaliation was common in the ancient Near East. Frequently it led to vendettas in which escalating vengeance continued for generations. Israel's "law of retaliation" (Lat. *lex talionis*) limited retaliation to no more than equal compensation (Exod. 21:24; Lev. 24:19-20; Deut. 19:21). The Jews tended to view the law of retaliation as God's permission to take vengeance. That was never God's intention (cf. Lev. 19:18). He simply wanted to protect them from excessive vengeance and to curb vendettas. In some situations the Jews could pay to avoid the vengeance of their brethren (Exod. 21:26-27). By the first century, monetary reparations had replaced physical maiming as the penalty for physical injury.[372] As God had permitted divorce because of the hardness of man's heart, so He permitted a certain amount of retaliation under the Mosaic Law. However, His intention was that His people would avoid divorce and retaliation entirely. He wanted us to love one another and to put the welfare of others before our own.

5:39a   Jesus first expounded God's intention regarding retaliation. Essentially He said: When evil people do you wrong, do not resist them. "Resist" (Gr. *anthistemi*) means to defend oneself, to take aggressive action against someone, as the following verses illustrate. When evil people do bad things to us, Jesus' disciples should accept the injustice without taking revenge.[373] Implicit in this view are Old Testament promises that God will take care of the righteous. Therefore, to accept injustice without retaliating expresses trust that God will faithfully care for His own. The Old Testament taught that the Jews were to leave vengeance to God (Lev. 19:17-18; Deut. 32:35; Ps. 94:1; Prov. 20:22; 24:29). Discerning Jews realized this in Jesus' day.[374] Paul resisted (Gr. *antistemi*) Peter (Gal. 2:11) out of love for the gospel and his fellow believers, not out of selfishness. We should stand up for what is right and for the rights of others, but we should trust God to stand up for us.

[369]Ibid., 2:8:27.

[370]France, *The Gospel* . . ., p. 216.

[371]Carson, "Matthew," p. 154.

[372]Craig Keener, *Matthew*, p. 127.

[373]Stott, p. 105.

[374]Plummer, p. 85.

Jesus' purpose in the Sermon on the Mount was threefold: to reinforce the Law's timeless revelatory authority (e.g., 5:18-19), to refocus its original meaning (e.g., 5:21-22), and to replace its temporary regulatory provisions (e.g., 5:38-39). By doing these things, Jesus "fulfilled" (established) the Law.

5:39b-42   Jesus gave four illustrations to clarify what He meant. In the first (v. 39b), a disciple suffers an unjustified physical attack on his or her person. What is that one to do? He or she should not injure the aggressor in return but should absorb the injury and the insult. He should even be ready to accept the same attack again. In Jesus' illustration the disciple gets slapped on the right cheek. Under normal conditions this would come from the back of a right-handed person's right hand. Such a slap was an insult more than an injury. However, we should probably not make too much of that point. The point is that disciples should accept insult and injury without retaliating. In Jesus' "honor-shame" culture, such a sacrifice was perhaps greater than it is for us today in the West. As previously (e.g. vv. 29-30), Jesus was probably speaking somewhat hyperbolically.

Second, if someone wanted to extract as much as the disciple's undergarment for some real or imagined offense, the disciple was to part with it willingly (v. 40). The disciple should not resist the evil antagonist's action. Moreover, he or she should be ready and willing to part with his or her outer garment as well. Under Mosaic Law, a person's outer cloak was something he or she had an almost inalienable right to retain (Exod. 22:26-27; Deut. 24:13). This is another example of hyperbole. Jesus did not intend His disciples to walk around naked, but to be generous—even toward enemies—even if it meant parting with essential possessions.

The third illustration requires some background knowledge of customs in New Testament times to appreciate (v. 41). The Romans sometimes commandeered civilians to carry the luggage of military personnel, but the civilian did not have to carry the luggage for more than one Roman mile.[375] This imposition exasperated and infuriated many a proud Jew. Again, the disciple is not only to refrain from retaliating, but even to refrain from resisting this personal injustice. Jesus advocated going an extra mile. The disciple is to respond to unjustified demands by giving even more than the adversary asks, and he or she is to return good for evil.

"The Rabbis had a proverb to match, lively and piquant enough, but certainly lacking the gravity of this, and which never could have fallen from the same lips: *If thy neighbor call thee an ass, put a packsaddle on thy back*; do not, that is, withdraw thyself from the wrong, but rather go forward to meet it."[376]

Fourth, Jesus told His disciples to give what others request of them, assuming it is within their power to do so (v. 41). This applies to loans as well as gifts (cf. Exod. 22:25; Lev. 25:37; Deut. 23:19). A willing and generous spirit is implicit in this command (cf. Deut. 15:7-11; Ps. 37:26; 112:5). This does not mean we should give all our money away to individuals and institutions that ask for our financial assistance (cf. Prov. 11:15; 17:18; 22:26). The scene in view in all these illustrations, and in all of this teaching, is one individual dealing with another individual. Personal wrongs are in view, not social or governmental crimes.[377]

". . . Jesus is here talking to his disciples, and speaking of personal relations: he is not laying down moral directives for states and nations, and such issues as the work of police or the question of a defensive war are simply not in his mind."[378]

There is a progression in these illustrations, from simply not resisting, to giving generously to people who make demands that tempt us to retaliate against them. Love must be the disciple's governing principle, not selfishness.[379]

Some conscientious believers have taken Jesus' instructions about resisting aggression literally, and refuse to defend themselves in any situation, either as pacifists or as advocates of non-resistance. However, the spirit of the law, which Jesus clarified, did not advocate turning oneself into a doormat. It stressed meeting hatred with positive love rather than hatred. Though Jesus allowed His enemies to lead Him as a lamb to the slaughter, He did not cave in to every hostile attack from the scribes and Pharisees. Likewise, Paul claimed his Roman citizenship rather than suffering prolonged attack by the Jews. Disciples may stand up for their rights, but when they are taken advantage of, they should always respond in love.

---

[375]W. Hatch, *Essays in Biblical Greek*, pp. 37-38.

[376]Richard C. Trench, *On the Lessons in Proverbs*, p. 60.

[377]See Hagner, p. 131.

[378]Hunter, *A Pattern . . .*, pp. 57-58.

[379]See G. Campbell Morgan, *The Gospel According to Matthew*, p. 58.

God's will concerning love 5:43-47 (cf. Luke 6:27-36)

5:43   Jesus quoted the Old Testament again (Lev. 19:18), but this time He added a corollary that the rabbis, not Moses, provided. Nowhere does the Old Testament advocate hating one's enemies. However, this seemed to many of the Jewish religious teachers to be the natural opposite of loving one's neighbors.[380]

5:44-47   Jesus answered the popular teaching by going back to the Old Testament that commanded love for enemies (Exod. 23:4-5). "Love" (Gr. *agapao*) here probably includes emotion, as well as action, in view of Jesus' previous emphasis on motives.

> "To love one's enemies, though it must result in doing them good (Luke 6:32-33) and praying for them (Matt. 5:44), cannot justly be restricted to activities devoid of any concern, sentiment, or emotion. Like the English verb 'to love,' *agapao* ranges widely from debased and selfish actions to generous, warm, costly self-sacrifice for another's good. There is no reason to think the verb here in Matthew does not include emotion as well as action."[381]

> The word "enemies" also has a wide meaning, and includes any individuals who elicit anger, hatred, and retaliation from the disciple. Jesus seems to have be correcting the common interpretation of the command to love one's neighbor as an implicit license to hate one's enemies.[382]

> Prayer for someone's welfare is one specific manifestation of love for that person.

> "Jesus seems to have prayed for his tormentors actually while the iron spikes were being driven through his hands and feet; indeed the imperfect tense suggests that he kept praying, kept repeating his entreaty, 'Father, forgive them; for they know not what they do' (Luke 23:34). If the cruel torture of crucifixion could not silence our Lord's prayer for his enemies, what pain, pride, prejudice or sloth could justify the silencing of ours?"[383]

> Some liberal interpreters have concluded that Jesus meant that we become God's sons by loving and praying for friend and foe alike. However, consistent with other Scriptural revelation, Jesus did not mean His disciples can earn their salvation (v. 45). Rather, by loving and praying for our enemies, we show that we are God's sons because we do what He does.

> "They *show* their parentage by their moral resemblance to the God who is Love . . ."[384]

> Theologians refer to the blessings God bestows on His enemies, as well as on His children, as "common grace." Disciples, as their Father, should do good to all people as well as to their brethren (Gal. 6:10).

> Loving one's enemies is something God will reward (v. 46). This should be an added inducement to love the antagonistic. Tax gatherers were local Jews who collected taxes from their countrymen for the Romans. Matthew was one of them. The whole Roman system of collecting taxes was very corrupt, and strict Jews viewed these "tax collectors" as both traitorous and unclean, because of their close association with Gentiles. They were among the most despised people in Palestine. However, even they, Jesus said, loved those who loved them.

> Proper salutations were an evidence of courtesy and respect.[385] However, if Jesus' disciples only gave them to their brethren, they did no more than the Gentiles, most of whom were pagans.

Jesus' summary of His disciples' duty 5:48

This verse summarizes all of Jesus' teaching about the Old Testament's demands (vv. 21-47). It puts in epigrammatic form the essential nature of the "greater righteousness" of verse 20 that Jesus illustrated above. "Therefore" identifies a conclusion.

"Perfect" (Gr. *teleios*) often occurs in a relative sense in the New Testament, and translators sometimes render it "mature" (e.g., 1 Cor. 14:20; Eph. 4:13; Heb. 5:14; 6:1). However it also means perfect. In this context it refers to perfect regarding conformity to God's requirements, which

---

[380]Morison, p. 83.

[381]Carson, "Matthew," p. 158.

[382]David A. Hubbard, *Proverbs*, p. 240.

[383]Stott, p. 119. Cf. Acts 7:60.

[384]Plummer, p. 88.

[385]Carson, "Matthew," p. 159.

Jesus just clarified. He wanted His disciples to press on to perfect righteousness, a goal that no sinful human can attain but toward which all should move (cf. v. 3; 6:12). They should not view righteousness as simply external, as the scribes and Pharisees did, but they should pursue inner moral purity and love. This is only appropriate since their heavenly Father is indeed perfect.

> "Perfection here refers to uprightness and sincerity of character with the thought of maturity in godliness or attaining the goal of conformity to the character of God. While sinless perfection is impossible, godliness, in its biblical concept, is attainable."[386]

Good children in the ancient East normally imitated their fathers. Jesus advocated the same of His disciples. In giving this summary command, Jesus was alluding to Leviticus 19:2, which He modified slightly in view of Deuteronomy 18:13.

> "In Jesus' perspective, the debates concerning law and tradition are all to be resolved by the proper application of one basic principle, or better, of a single attitude of the heart, namely, utter devotion to God and radical love of the neighbor (5:48; 22:37-40)."[387]

While we are definitely to strive for perfection in our conformity to the will of God (cf. 1 Pet. 1:15-16), we must beware of the perils associated with perfectionism. Striving for an unattainable goal is difficult for anyone, but it is particularly frustrating for people with obsessive-compulsive personalities, people who tend to be perfectionists. In one sense a perfectionist is someone who strives for perfection, but in another sense it is someone who is obsessed with perfection. Such a person, for example, constantly cleans up his or her environment, straightens things that are not exactly straight, and corrects people for even minor mistakes. This type of striving for perfection is not godly. God is not constantly "on the backs" of people who are less than perfect, and we should not be either—whether on other people or on ourselves. In fact, He gives us a great deal of "space" and is patient with us, allowing us to correct our own mistakes before He steps in to do so (cf. 1 Cor. 11:31). It is possible for us, as disciples of Jesus, to become so obsessed with our own holiness that we shift our focus from Christ to ourselves. Rather, we should keep our eyes on Jesus (Heb. 12:1-3) more than on ourselves and on being perfect.

Righteousness and the Father 6:1-18

Jesus moved from correcting popular misinterpretations of selected Old Testament texts that speak of righteous conduct (5:17-48), to correcting popular misconceptions about righteous conduct. He moved from ethical distinctions to the practice of religion. Throughout this entire section, proper motivation for actions is a constant emphasis.

A basic principle 6:1

"Righteousness" means what is in harmony with the will of God, and righteous deeds are those that are pleasing to Him. Jesus warned His disciples about the possibility of doing good deeds for the wrong reason, as He began His teaching about righteous behavior. If one does what God approves to obtain human approval, that one will not receive a reward for his good deed from God. Notice again that disciples' rewards will vary. Some disciples will receive more reward from God than others. Disciples should practice good works publicly (5:16), but they should not draw special attention to them.

The rabbis considered almsgiving, prayer, and fasting as the three chief acts of Jewish piety.[388] Jesus dealt with each of these aspects of worship similarly. He first warned His disciples not to do the act for man's praise. Then He assured them that if they disregarded His warning, they would get human praise but nothing more. Third, He taught them how to do the act for God alone, secretly (not for public applause). Finally, He assured them that the Father who sees in secret would reward their righteous act openly.

Alms-giving 6:2-4

Alms were gifts of money to the needy. What Jesus said on this subject is applicable to all types of giving.

Interpreters have understood the practice of sounding a trumpet to announce alms-giving metaphorically and literally. Metaphorically it would mean that Jesus was using a figure of speech to picture showy giving, something like "blowing your own horn." However, His description seems to have had a custom behind it. There is historic evidence that during this period, the Jewish priests blew trumpets in the Temple when they collected funds for some special need.[389] Alternatively, this may be a reference to the horn-shaped collection receptacles in the Temple that noisily

---

[386]Walvoord, *Matthew: . . .*, p. 51.

[387]Kingsbury, *Matthew as . . .*, p. 63.

[388]C. G. Montefiore and H. Loewe, *A Rabbinic Anthology*, pp. 412-39; G. F. Moore, *Judaism in the First Centuries of the Christian Era*, 2:162-79.

[389]David Hill, *The Gospel of Matthew*, p. 133.

announced contributions that people tossed into them.[390] However, Jesus mentioned the synagogues and streets, not the Temple. Probably Jesus referred to the blowing of trumpets in the streets that announced fasts that included alms-giving.[391]

The idea of not letting the "left hand" know what the "right hand" does pictures secrecy (cf. 25:35-40). The way to avoid hypocrisy is to let no other people know when we give. We can carry this to the extreme, of course, but Jesus' point was that we should not draw attention to ourselves when we give. Hypocrisy does not just involve giving an impression that is incorrect, such as that one gives alms when he really does not. It also involves deceiving oneself even if one deceives no one else. A third kind of hypocrisy involves deceiving oneself and others into thinking that what one does is for a certain purpose when it is really for a different purpose. This seems to be the type of hypocrisy in view here.

"They were not giving, but *buying*. They wanted the praise of men, they paid for it."[392]

"The hypocrites are not identified here, but Matthew 23 clearly indicates that they are the scribes and Pharisees (Matthew 23:13, 14, 15, 23, 25, 27, 29). A clearer illustration of a facet of Matthew's style can hardly be found. First he intimates a fact, then he builds on it, and finally he establishes it. Here the intimation concerns the hypocrisy of the scribes and Pharisees."[393]

"As 'leaders,' the religious leaders evince their evilness most prominently by showing themselves to be 'hypocritical.' Hypocrisy in Matthew's story is the opposite of being 'perfect.' To be perfect is to be wholehearted, or single-hearted, in the devotion with which one serves God (5:48; Deut. 18:13). To be hypocritical is to be 'divided' in one's fealty to God. Hypocrisy, then, is a form of inner incongruity, to wit: paying honor to God with the lips while the heart is far from him (15:7-8); making pronouncements about what is right while not practicing them (23:3c); and appearing outwardly to be righteous while being inwardly full of lawlessness (23:28)."[394]

Praying 6:5-15 (cf. Luke 11:1-13)

6:5-6   Jesus assumed that His disciples would "pray," as He assumed they would give alms (v. 2) and fast (v. 16). Again He warned against ostentatious worship. The synagogues and streets were public places where people could practice their righteousness with an audience. The motive is what matters most. Obviously, Jesus was not condemning public prayer *per se* (cf. 15:36; 18:19-20; 1 Tim. 2:8). Praying out loud was common among the Jews, though one could still pray out loud in a private place.[395]

"The public versus private antithesis is a good test of one's motives; the person who prays more in public than in private reveals that he is less interested in God's approval than in human praise."[396]

Jesus alluded to the Septuagint version of Isaiah 26:20 where the private room is a bedroom (cf. 2 Kings 4:33). Any private setting will do. Jesus was not discouraging public praying, but praying in order to be admired for it.

6:7-8   Jesus digressed briefly to give a further warning about repetitious prayer (vv. 7-8) and a positive example of proper prayer (vv. 9-15). Jesus' disciples can fall into prayer practices that characterize the pagans. Jesus Himself prayed long prayers (Luke 6:12), and He repeated Himself in prayer (26:44). These practices were not the objects of His criticism. He was attacking the idea that the length of a prayer makes it efficacious. Pagan prayer commonly relies on length and "repetition" for effectiveness, the sheer quantity of "words."

". . . Christ does not forbid us to persist in prayers, long, often, or with much feeling, but requires that we should not be confident in our ability to wrest something from God by beating upon his ears with a garrulous flow of talk, as if he could be persuaded as men are."[397]

Jesus' disciples do not need to inform their omniscient "Father" of their "need" in prayer. He already knows what they are. Why pray then? Jesus did not answer that question here. Essentially we pray for the same reasons children speak to their parents: to share concerns, to have fellowship, to obtain help, and to express gratitude, among other reasons.

---

[390]Alfred Edersheim, *The Temple*, p. 26; J. Jeremias, *Jerusalem in the Time of Jesus*, p. 170, n. 73.

[391]Adolf Buchler, "St. Mathew vi 1-6 and Other Allied Passages," *Journal of Theological Studies* 10 (1909):266-70.

[392]Davies and Allison, 1:582.

[393]Toussaint, *Behold the . . .*, p. 107.

[394]Kingsbury, *Matthew as . . .*, p. 20.

[395]France, *The Gospel . . .*, p. 238.

[396]Carson, "Matthew," p,. 165.

[397]Calvin, 3:20:29.

6:9-13   Jesus gave His disciples a model prayer commonly known as "The Lord's Prayer." It was not His prayer in the sense that He prayed it, but it *was* His prayer in the sense that He taught it. He introduced the model as such. Here is a way to pray that is neither too long, ostentatious, nor unnecessarily repetitious.

One of Jesus' unique emphases, as I have already mentioned, was that His disciples should think of God as their heavenly "Father." It was not characteristic of believers to address God as their Father until Jesus taught them to do so.[398]

"Only fifteen times was God referred to as the Father in the Old Testament. Where it does occur, it is used of the nation Israel or to the king of Israel. Never was God called the Father of an individual or of human beings in general (though isolated instances occur in second temple Judaism, Sirach 51:10). In the New Testament numerous references to God as Father can be found."[399]

"The overwhelming tendency in Jewish circles was to multiply titles ascribing sovereignty, lordship, glory, grace, and the like to God . . ."[400]

"Our" Father indicates that Jesus expected His disciples to pray this prayer, fully aware of their group context, as being a part of His disciples. Private use of this prayer is all right, but the context in which Jesus taught it was corporate, so He gave a corporate address. The "our" does not include Himself, since it is part of Jesus' teaching His followers concerning how to pray.

"From this fact [i.e., that Jesus said "our" Father] we are warned how great a feeling of brotherly love ought to be among us, since by the same right of mercy and free liberality we are equally children of such a father."[401]

The way we think of God as we pray to Him is very important. In prayer, we should remember that He is a loving Father who will respond as such to His children. Some modern individuals advocate thinking of God as our Mother. However, this runs contrary to what Jesus taught, and to the thousands of references to God that God has given us in the masculine gender—in both Testaments. God is not a sexual being. Nevertheless He is more like a father to us than a mother. Thinking of Him primarily as a mother will result in some distortion in our concept of God. It will also result in some confusion in our thinking about how God relates to us and how we should relate to Him.[402] Thinking of God as our Father will also remind us of our privileged access into His presence, and of our need to treat Him respectfully.

"In heaven" reminds us of His transcendence and sovereignty. Our address to God in prayer does more to prepare us for proper praying than it does to secure the desired response from Him.[403]

The first three petitions deal with God, and the last three with us. This pattern indicates that disciples should have more concern for God than we do for ourselves. We should put His interests first in our praying, as in all our living. All the petitions have some connection with the kingdom. The first three deal with the coming of the kingdom, and the last three are appeals in view of the coming kingdom.[404]

The first petition (v. 9c) is that everyone would hold God's name (His reputation, everything about Him) in reverence. He is already holy. We do not need to pray that He will become more holy. What is necessary is that His creatures everywhere recognize and acknowledge His holiness. This petition focuses on God's *reputation*. People need to *hallow* it, to treat it as special. By praying these words we affirm God's holiness.

God's reputation and the kingdom had close connections in the Old Testament (Isa. 29:23; Ezek. 36:23).

"In one respect His name is profaned when His people are ill-treated. The sin of the nation which brought about the captivity had caused a profanation of the Name, Is. 43:25; 49:11; Ezk. 36:20-23. By their

---

[398]J. Jeremias, *The Prayers of Jesus*, p. 11.

[399]Mark L. Bailey, "A Biblical Theology of Paul's Pastoral Epistles," in *A Biblical Theology of the New Testament*, p. 342. Cf. H. F. D. Sparks, "The Doctrine of the Divine Fatherhood of God in the Gospels," in *Studies in the Gospels: Essays in Memory of R. H. Lightfoot*, pp. 241-62; and James Barr, "Abba Isn't Daddy," *Journal of Theological Studies* 39 (1988):28-47.

[400]Carson, "Matthew," p. 169.

[401]Calvin, 3:20:38.

[402]See Aida Besançon Spencer, "Father-Ruler: The Meaning of the Metaphor 'Father' for God in the Bible," *Journal of the Evangelical Theological Society* 39:3 (September 1996):433-42.

[403]Stott, p. 146.

[404]Toussaint, *Behold the . . .*, p. 107.

restoration His name was to be sanctified. But this sanctification was only a foreshadowing of a still future consummation. Only when the 'kingdom' came would God's name be wholly sanctified in the final redemption of His people from reproach."[405]

The second petition (v. 10a) is that the messianic "kingdom" will indeed "come" quickly (cf. Mark 15:43; 1 Cor. 16:22; Rev. 11:17). It was appropriate for Jesus' first disciples to pray this petition, since the establishment of the kingdom was imminent. It is also appropriate for modern disciples to pray it, since the inauguration of that kingdom will begin the righteous rule of Messiah on the earth, which every believer should anticipate eagerly. This kingdom has not yet begun. If it had, Jesus' disciples would not need to pray for it to come. Christ will rule over His kingdom, the Davidic kingdom, from the earth, and He is now in heaven.[406] This petition focuses on God's *kingdom*. People need to *prepare* for it.

"Those who maintain that for Jesus himself the kingdom of God had already come in his own person and ministry inevitably treat this second petition of the Lord's prayer in a rather cavalier fashion. It must be interpreted, they say, in line with other sayings of Jesus. Why? And what other sayings? When all the evidence in the sayings of Jesus for 'realized eschatology' is thoroughly tested, it boils down to the *ephthasen eph humas* ['has come upon you'] of Matt. 12:28 and Luke 11:20. Why should that determine the interpretation of Matt. 6:10 and Luke 11:2? Why should a difficult, obscure saying establish the meaning of one that is clear and unambiguous? Why not interpret the *ephthasen* ['has come,' 12:28] by the *elthato* ['come,' 6:10]; or rather, since neither can be eliminated on valid critical grounds, why not seek an interpretation that does equal justice to both?"[407]

"Jesus' conception of God's kingdom is not simply that of the universal sovereignty of God, which may or may not be accepted by men but is always there. That is the basis of his conception, but he combines with it the eschatological idea of the kingdom which is still to come. In other words, what Jesus means by the kingdom of God includes what the rabbinic literature calls the coming age."[408]

These are accurate and interesting conclusions coming from a non-dispensationalist.

The third petition (v. 10b-c) is a request that what God wants to happen on earth will indeed transpire "on earth," as it now does "in heaven." That condition will take place most fully when Christ sets up His kingdom on the earth. However, this should be the desire of every disciple in the inter-advent age while Jesus is still in heaven. Nothing better can happen than whatever God's will involves (Rom. 12:1). God's "will" (Gr. *thelema*) includes His righteous demands (7:21; 12:50; cf. Ps. 40:8), as well as His determination to cause and permit certain events in history (18:14; 26:42; cf. Acts 21:14). This petition focuses on God's *will*. People need to *do* it.

"This difference [between God's heavenly universal rule and His earthly millennial rule] arises out of the fact that rebellion and sin exist upon the earth, sin which is to be dealt with in a way not known in any other spot in the universe, not even among the angels which sinned. It is here that the great purpose of what I have named the Mediatorial Kingdom appears: On the basis of mediatorial redemption it must 'come' to put down at last all rebellion with its evil results, thus finally bringing the Kingdom and will of God on earth as it is in heaven."[409]

The remaining petitions (vv. 11-13) focus on the disciples' needs. Notice the "Thy," "Thy," "Thy," in verses 9 and 10 and the "us," "us," "us," in verses 11-13. Some believers have concluded that prayer should not include anything selfish, so they do not make personal petitions. However, Jesus commanded His disciples to bring their personal needs to God in prayer. The first three petitions stand alone, but the last three have connecting "ands" that bind them together. We need all three of these things equally; we cannot get along without any of them.

The "bread" in view (v. 11) probably refers to all our food, and even all our physical needs.[410] Bread has this larger significance in the Bible (cf. Prov. 30:8; Mark 3:20; Acts 6:1; 2 Thess. 3:12; James 2:15). Even today we speak of bread as

---

[405]Allen, p. 58.

[406]See McClain, pp. 34-35; 147-60; and Adolph Saphir, *The Lord's Prayer*, p. 173.

[407]Millar Burrows, "Thy Kingdom Come," *Journal of Biblical Literature* 74 (January 1955):4-5.

[408]Ibid., p. 8.

[409]McClain, p. 35.

[410]Calvin, 3:20:44; Walvoord, *Matthew: . . .*, p. 53.

"the staff of life." "Daily bread" refers to the necessities of life, not its luxuries. This is a prayer for our needs, not our greeds. The request is for God to supply our needs day by day (cf. Exod. 16:4-5; Ps. 104:14-15, 27-28; Prov. 30:8). The expression "this day [or today] our daily bread" reflects first century life in which workers received their pay daily. It also reminds disciples that we only live one day at a time, and each day we are dependent on God to sustain us. Asking God to provide our needs does not free us from the responsibility of working, however (cf. vv. 25-34; 2 Thess 3:10). God satisfies our needs partially by giving us the ability and the opportunity to earn a living. Ultimately everything comes from Him. Having to live from hand to mouth, and one day at a time, can be a blessing if it reminds us of our total dependence on God. This is especially true since we live in a world that glorifies self-sufficiency.

The fifth petition requests forgiveness from debts (v. 12). "Debts" (Gr. *opheilemata*) probably translates the Aramaic word *hoba* that was a common synonym for sins.[411] Viewing sins as debts was thoroughly Jewish (cf. Ps. 51:4).[412]

"He calls sins 'debts' because we owe penalty for them, and we could in no way satisfy it unless we were released by this forgiveness."[413]

The second clause in the sentence does not mean that we must earn God's forgiveness with our own. Our forgiveness of others demonstrates our felt need of forgiveness. The person who does not forgive a brother's offenses does not appreciate how much he himself needs forgiveness.

"Once our eyes have been opened to see the enormity of our offense against God, the injuries which others have done to us appear by comparison extremely trifling. If, on the other hand, we have an exaggerated view of the offenses of others, it proves that we have minimized our own."[414]

Some Christians have wondered why we should ask for God's forgiveness, since the New Testament clearly reveals that God forgives all sins—past, present, and future—when He justifies us (Acts 10:43; Eph. 1:7; Col. 1:14). That is judicial or forensic forgiveness. However, as forgiven believers we need to ask for forgiveness to restore fellowship with God (cf. 1 John 1:9). *Forensic* forgiveness brings us into God's family. *Family* forgiveness keeps our fellowship with God intimate within God's family.

"Personal fellowship with God is in view in these verses (not salvation from sin). One cannot walk in fellowship with God if he refuses to forgive others."[415]

Some interpreters view verse 13 as containing one petition, while others believe Jesus intended two. Probably one is correct, in view of the close connection of the ideas. They are really two sides of one coin.

"Temptation" is the Greek *peirasmos* and means "testing." It refers not so much to solicitation to evil, as to trials that test the character. God does not test (*peirasmos*) anyone (James 1:13-14). Why then do we need to pray that He will not lead us into testing? Even though God is not the instrumental cause of our testing, He does permit us to experience temptation from the world, the flesh, and the devil (cf. 4:1; Gen. 22:1; Deut. 8:2). Therefore, this petition is a request that He would minimize the occasions of our testing that could result in our sinning. It articulates the repentant disciple's felt weakness to stand up under severe trials, in view of his or her sinfulness (cf. Prov. 30:7-9).[416]

"But" introduces the alternative. "Deliver us" could mean "spare us from" or "deliver us out of." The meaning depends on what "evil" means. Is this a reference to evil generally or to the evil one, Satan? When the Greek preposition *apo* ("from") follows "deliver," it usually refers to deliverance from people. When *ek* ("from") follows it, it always refers to deliverance from things.[417] Here *apo* occurs. Also, the adjective "evil" has an article modifying it in the Greek text, which indicates that it is to be taken as a substantive: "the evil one." God does not always deliver us from evil, but He does deliver us from the evil one.[418]

[411] Carson, "Matthew," p. 172.
[412] M'Neile, p. 80.
[413] Calvin, 3:20:45.
[414] Stott, pp. 149-50. Cf. Matt. 18:21-35.
[415] Barbieri, p. 32.
[416] Rick W. Byargeon, "Echoes of Wisdom in the Lord's Prayer (Matt 6:9-13)," *Journal of the Evangelical Theological Society* 41:3 (September 1998):353-65.
[417] J. B. Bauer, "Libera nos a malo," *Verbum Domini* 34 (1965):12-15.
[418] See Page, pp. 458-59.

"It makes very little difference whether we understand by the word 'evil' the devil or sin."[419]

However, the Old Testament predicted that a time of great evil would precede the establishment of the kingdom (Jer. 30). Some commentators, including non-premillenarians, have understood the evil in this petition as a reference to Satanic opposition that will come to its full force before the kingdom begins.[420] God later revealed through Paul that Christians will not go through this Tribulation (1 Thess. 1:10; 4:13-18; et al.). Consequently, we do not need to pray for deliverance from *it*, but from other occasions of testing.

Some have seen a veiled reference to the Trinity in these last three petitions. The Father provides our bread through His creation and providence, the Son's atonement secures our forgiveness, and the Spirit's enablement assures our spiritual victory.

The final doxology appears in many ancient manuscripts, but there is so much variation in it that it was probably not originally a part of Matthew's Gospel. Evidently, pious scribes added it later to make the prayer liturgically complete. They apparently adapted the wording of David's prayer in 1 Chronicles 29:11.[421]

"In the Temple [in Jesus' day] the people never responded to the prayers by an *Amen*, but always with this benediction, 'Blessed be the name of the glory of His kingdom for ever!' [Footnote 4:] Thus the words in our Authorised [*sic*] Version, Matt. vi. 13, 'For Thine is the kingdom, and the power, and the glory, for ever. Amen,' which are wanting in all the most ancient MSS., are only the common Temple-formula of response, and as such may have found their way into the text. The word 'Amen' was in reality a solemn asseveration or a mode of oath."[422]

6:14-15   These verses explain the thought of the fifth petition (v. 12) more fully. Repetition stresses the importance of forgiving one another if we want God's forgiveness (cf. 18:23-35). Our horizontal relationships with other people must be correct before our vertical relationship with God can be.

"Prayer is straightforward and simple for those who have experienced the grace of the kingdom in Christ. In prayer the disciple does not try to coerce or manipulate God. There are no magical words or formulae, nor does an abundance of words count with God. Short, direct, and sincere prayers are adequate."[423]

"The sample prayer, it can be concluded, is given in the context of the coming kingdom. The first three requests are petitions for the coming of the kingdom. The last three are for the needs of the disciples in the interim preceding the establishment of the kingdom."[424]

Fasting 6:16-18

6:16   Fasting in Israel involved going without food to engage in a spiritual exercise, usually prayer, with greater concentration. Fasting fostered and indicated self-humiliation before God, and confession often accompanied it (Neh. 9:1-2; Ps. 35:13; Isa. 58:3, 5; Dan. 9:2-20; 10:2-3; Jon. 3:5; Acts 9:9). People who felt anguish, danger, or desperation, gave up eating temporarily in order to present some special petition to the Lord in prayer (Exod. 24:18; Judg. 20:26; 2 Sam. 1:12; 2 Chron. 20:3; Ezra 8:21-23; Esth. 4:16; Matt. 4:1-2; Acts 13:1-3; 14:23). Some pious believers fasted regularly (Luke 2:37). The Pharisees fasted twice a week (Luke 18:12). God only commanded the Israelites to fast on one day of the year, the Day of Atonement (Lev. 16:29-31; 23:27-32; Num. 29:7). However, during the Exile the Israelites instituted additional regular fasts (Zech. 7:3-5; 8:19). Fasting occurred in the early church and seems to have been a normal part of Christian self-discipline (1 Cor. 9:24-27; Phil. 3:19; 1 Pet. 4:3). Hypocritical fasting occurred in Israel long before Jesus' day (Isa. 58:1-7; Jer. 14:12; Zech. 7:5-6), but the Pharisees were notorious for it.

"Fasting emphasized the denial of the flesh, but the Pharisees were glorifying their flesh by drawing attention to themselves."[425]

[419]Calvin, 3:20:46.

[420]E.g., Theodore H. Robinson, *The Gospel of Matthew*, p. 52; M'Neile, p. 81; and T. Herbert Bindley, "Eschatology in the Lord's Prayer," *The Expositor* 17 (October 1919):319-20.

[421]See also Thomas L. Constable, "The Lord's Prayer," in *Giving Ourselves to Prayer*, compiled by Dan R. Crawford (Terre Haute, Ind.: PrayerShop Publishing, 2005), pp. 70-75.

[422]Edersheim, *The Temple*, p. 155.

[423]Hagner, p. 152.

[424]Toussaint, *Behold the . . .*, p. 112.

[425]Barbieri, p. 32.

Jesus' point in this verse was that His disciples should avoid drawing attention to themselves when they fasted. He did not question the genuine contrition of some who fasted, but He pointed out that the hypocrites wanted the admiration of other people even more than they wanted God's attention. Since that is what they really wanted, that is all they would get.

6:17-18   Jesus assumed His disciples would fast as He assumed they would give alms and pray. He said nothing to discourage them from fasting (cf. 9:14-17). He only condemned ostentatious fasting. To avoid any temptation to pander to the adulation of onlookers, Jesus counseled His disciples to do nothing that would attract attention to the fact that they were fasting when they fasted. Again, the Father who sees the worship that His children offer "in secret" will "reward" them.

The three major acts of Jewish worship—alms-giving, prayer, and fasting—were only representative of many other acts of worship that Jesus' disciples performed. His teaching in this section of the Sermon (6:1-18) stressed lessons they should apply more broadly. In His teaching about each of these three practices, Jesus first warned His disciples not to do the act for man's praise. Then He assured them that if they disregarded His warning, they would get human praise, but nothing more. Third, He taught them how to do the act secretly. Finally, He assured them that the Father who sees in secret would reward their righteous act openly. He thereby explained what it means to seek first the kingdom and its righteousness (6:33).

Righteousness and the world 6:19—7:12

Thus far in the Sermon, Jesus urged His disciples to base their understanding of the righteousness God requires on the revelation of Scripture, not the traditional interpretations of their leaders (5:17-48). Then He clarified that true righteousness involved genuine worship of the Father, not hypocritical, ostentatious worship (6:1-18). Next, He revealed what true righteousness involves as the disciple lives in the world. He dealt with four key relationships: the disciple's relationship to wealth (6:19-34), to his or her brethren (7:1-5), to his or her antagonists (7:6), and to God (7:7-12).

The disciple's relationship to wealth 6:19-34 (cf. Luke 12:13-34)

Having made several references to treasure in heaven, Jesus now turned to focus on wealth. In the first part of chapter 6, His main emphasis was on sincerity. In this part of the chapter, it is on single-mindedness.

6:19-21   In view of the imminence of the kingdom, Jesus' disciples should "stop laying up treasures on earth."[426] Jesus called for a break with their former practice. Money is not intrinsically evil. The wise person works hard and makes financial provision for lean times (Prov. 6:6-8). Believers have a responsibility to provide for their needy relatives (1 Tim. 5:8) and to be generous with others in need (Prov. 13:22; 2 Cor. 12:14). We can enjoy what God has given us (1 Tim. 4:3-4; 6:17). What Jesus forbade here was selfishness. Misers hoard more than they need (James 5:2-3). Materialists always want more. It is the *love* of money that is a root of all kinds of evil (1 Tim. 6:10).

"What Jesus precludes here is the accumulation of massive amounts of treasure as a life goal."[427]

It is foolish to accumulate great quantities of goods because they are perishable. "Moth(s)" eat clothing, a major form of wealth in the ancient Near East. "Rust" (Gr. *brosis*) refers to the destructive force of rats and mildew, not just the corrosion that eats metal.[428] "Thieves" can carry off just about anything in one way or another.

The "treasures in heaven" Jesus spoke of were the rewards God will give His faithful followers (5:12, 30, 46; 6:6, 15; cf. 10:42; 18:5; 25:40; 2 Cor. 4:17; 1 Tim. 6:13-19). They are the product of truly good works. These are secure in heaven, and God will dispense them to the faithful at His appointed time (cf. 1 Pet. 1:4).

The thing that a person values most highly ("treasure") inevitably occupies the center of his or her "heart." The heart is the center of the personality, and it controls the intellect, emotions, and will.[429]

"If honour is reckoned the supreme good, the minds of men must be wholly occupied with ambition: if money, covetousness will immediately predominate: if pleasure, it will be impossible to prevent men from sinking into brutal indulgence."[430]

On the other hand, if a person values eternal riches most highly, he or she will pursue kingdom values (cf. Col. 3:1-2; Rev. 14:13). Some Christians believe that it is always carnal to desire and to work for eternal rewards, but Jesus commanded us to

---

[426]Nigel Turner, *Syntax*, p. 76.

[427]Bock, *Jesus according* . . ., p. 142.

[428]Carson, "Matthew," p. 177.

[429]*A Dictionary of New Testament Theology*, s.v. "*kardia*," by T. Sorg, 2:180-84.

[430]John Calvin, *Commentary on a Harmony of the Evangelists, Matthew, Mark, and Luke*, 1:334.

do precisely that (cf. 1 Cor. 3:11-15; 2 Cor. 5:10). Serving the Lord to obtain a reward to glorify oneself is obviously wrong, but to serve Him to obtain a reward that one may lay at His feet as an act of worship is not (cf. Rev. 4:10).

> "What does it mean to lay up treasures in heaven? It means to use *all that we have* for the glory of God. It means to 'hang loose' when it comes to the material things of life. It also means measuring life by the true riches of the kingdom and not by the false riches of this world."[431]

6:22-23   The body finds its way through life with the aid of the eye. In that sense, "the eye is the lamp of the body" (cf. Luke 11:34-36). A "clear" or good "eye" admits "light" into the body, but a "bad . . . eye" leaves the body in "darkness." Evidently Jesus meant the eye is similar to the heart (v. 21). The heart fixed on God (Ps. 199:10) is similar to the eye fixed on God's law (Ps. 119:18, 148).

> "Eyes are the expression of the soul, not its intake, although certainly the two ideas are related. What Jesus stresses in this saying is that a good eye acts in a healthy way. It is the sign of a healthy soul."[432]

A "bad eye" is a miserly eye (Prov. 28:22). Jesus was speaking metaphorically. He probably meant that the person who is stingy and selfish cannot really see where he is going but is morally and spiritually blind (cf. vv. 19-21).[433] However, He may have meant that the person who is double-minded, dividing his loyalties between God and money, will have no clear vision but will lack direction (cf. v. 24).[434] Metaphorically, the body represents the whole person. The lack of light within is the dark vision that the bad eye with divided loyalties, a selfish attitude, provides.

6:24   The choice between "two masters" is what is depicted by the choice between two treasures and the choice between two visions. "Mammon" is the transliteration of the emphatic form of the Aramaic word *mamona*, meaning "wealth" or "property." The root word *mn*, in both Hebrew and Aramaic, indicates something in which one places confidence. Here Jesus personified it and set it over against God as a competing object of confidence. Jesus presented God and Mammon as two slave owners, masters.

> ". . . single ownership and fulltime service are of the essence of slavery."[435]

A person might be able to work for two different employers at the same time. However, God and Mammon are not employers but slave owners. Each demands single-minded devotion. To give either anything less is to provide no true service at all.

> "Attempts at divided loyalty betray, not partial commitment to discipleship, but deep-seated commitment to idolatry."[436]

> "The principle of materialism is in inevitable conflict with the kingship of God."[437]

6:25   "Therefore" draws a conclusion from what has preceded (vv. 19-24). Since God has given us "life" and a "body," He will certainly also provide what we need to maintain them (cf. Luke 12:22-31; Phil. 4:6-7; Heb. 13:5; 1 Pet. 5:7). This argument is *a fortiori*, or *qal wahomer*, "How much more . . .?" It is wrong, therefore, for a disciple to fret (worry) about such things. He or she should simply trust and obey God, and get on with fulfilling one's divinely revealed calling in life (cf. 28:19-20).

6:26-27   If we fret constantly about having enough "food" and "clothing," we show that we have not yet learned a very basic lesson that nature teaches us: God provides for His creatures' needs. Furthermore, God is the heavenly Father of believers. Consequently He will take special care of them. This argument is *a minori ad maius*, "From the lesser to the greater." This does not mean we can disregard work, but it does mean we should disregard worry.

Fretting cannot lengthen life any more than it can put food on the table or clothes on the back (v. 27). Worry really shortens life.

---

[431]Wiersbe, 1:28.

[432]Bock, *Jesus according* . . ., p. 143.

[433]Carson, "Matthew," p. 178.

[434]Floyd V. Filson, *A Commentary on the Gospel According to St. Matthew*, p. 100.

[435]Tasker, p. 76.

[436]Carson, "Matthew," p. 179.

[437]France, *The Gospel* . . ., p. 263.

6:28-30   The "lilies of the field" were probably the wild crocuses that bloom so abundantly in Galilee during the spring. However, Jesus probably intended them to represent all the wildflowers. His point was that God is so good that He covers the ground with beautiful wildflowers that have no productive value and only last a short time.

"Once dried, grass became an important fuel source in wood-poor Palestine."[438]
God's providential grace should not make the disciple lazy, but confident that He will similarly provide for His children's needs. God often dresses the simplest field more beautifully than Israel's wealthiest king could adorn himself. Therefore, anxiety about the essentials of life really demonstrates lack of ("little") "faith" in God.

6:31-32   Since God provides so bountifully for His own, it is not only foolish but pagan to fret about the basic necessities of life. The fretting disciple lives as an unbeliever (Gentile) who disbelieves and disregards God. Such a person devotes too much of his or her attention to the accumulation of material goods, and disregards the more important things in life.

"The key to avoiding anxiety is to make the kingdom one's priority (v 33)."[439]

6:33   Rather than pursuing material things, the disciple should replace this with a pursuit having much greater significance. Seeking the kingdom involves pursuing the things about the kingdom for which Jesus taught His disciples to pray, namely: God's honor, His reign, and His will (vv. 9-10). This is one of only five places in Matthew where we read "kingdom of God" rather than "kingdom of heaven" (cf. 12:28; 19:24; 21:31, 43). In each case, the context requires a more personal reference to "God," rather than a more oblique reference to "heaven." Seeking God's righteousness means pursuing righteousness in life in submission to God's will (cf. 5:6, 10, 20; 6:1). It does not mean seeking justification, in view of Jesus' use of "righteousness" in the context.

"In the end, just as there are only two kinds of piety, the self-centered and the God-centered, so there are only two kinds of ambition: one can be ambitious either for oneself or for God. There is no third alternative."[440]

The "things" God will add are the necessities of life that He provides providentially, about which Jesus warned His disciples not to fret (5:45; 6:11). Here, God promises to meet the needs of those who commit themselves to seeking the furtherance of His "kingdom" and "righteousness."

In view of this promise, how can we explain the fact that some animals, plants, and committed believers have perished for lack of food? There is a wider sphere of context in which this promise operates. We all live in a fallen world where the effects of sin pervade every aspect of life. Sometimes the godly, through no fault of their own, get caught up in the consequences of sin and perish. Jesus did not elaborate this dimension of life, here, but assumed it as something His hearers would have known and understood.

6:34   Since we have such a promise, backed up by the testimony of divine providence, we should not fret "about tomorrow." Today has enough "trouble" or evil for us to deal with. Moreover, the trouble we anticipate tomorrow may never materialize. God provides only enough grace so we can deal with life one day at a time. Tomorrow He will provide enough grace (help) for what we will face then.

To summarize, the disciple's relationship to wealth should be one of trust in God and to have a single-minded commitment to the affairs of His kingdom and righteousness. It should not be hoarding or pursuing wealth for its own sake. God, not Mammon, should be the magnet of the believer's life. The fruit of such an attitude will be freedom from anxiety about daily material needs.

"It is impossible to be a partially committed or part-time disciple; it is impossible to serve two masters, whether one of them be wealth or anything else, when the other master is meant to be God."[441]

The disciple's relationship to brethren 7:1-5 (cf. Luke 6:37-42)

Jesus first laid down a principle (v. 1). Then He justified this principle theologically (v. 2). Finally, He provided an illustration (vv. 3-5).

7:1   Jesus taught His disciples not to be judgmental or censorious of one another, in view of the high standards He was clarifying (cf. Rom. 14:10-13; James 4:11-12). He did not mean that they should accept everything and everyone uncritically (cf. vv. 5-6,

---

[438]Guelich, The Sermon . . ., p. 340.
[439]Hagner, p. 166.
[440]Stott, p. 172.
[441]Hagner, p. 160.

15-20; John 7:24; 1 Cor. 5:5; Gal. 1:8-9; 6:1; Phil. 3:2; 1 John 4:1). Neither did He mean, obviously, that parents, church leaders, and civil authorities are wrong if they pass judgment on those under their care. He meant that His disciples should not do God's job of passing judgment—for Him—when He has not authorized them to do so. They really could not, since no one but God knows all the facts that motivate people to do as they do. The disciple who usurps God's place will have to answer to Him for doing so. One poll indicated that this is currently the most popularly quoted verse from the Bible.

7:2   The thought here is similar to that in 6:14-15. The person who judges others very critically will experience a similarly rigorous examination from God (cf. 18:23-35). There is a word play in the verse in the Greek text that suggests Jesus may have been quoting a popular proverb.[442]

7:3-5   The "speck" (Gr. *karphos*) could be a speck of any foreign matter. The "log" or "plank" (Gr. *dokos*) refers to a large piece of wood. Jesus again used hyperbole to stress the folly of criticizing someone else. This act reveals a much greater problem in the critic's life, namely: a censorious spirit.

> Such a person is a hypocrite and his actions carry him away. He does not deceive others as much as he deceives himself. Other people may realize that his criticism is unjustifiable, but he does not. A proper attitude is important in judging oneself and other people (1 Cor. 11:31; Gal. 6:1). Censorious critics are not helpful. That is what Jesus warned against here (cf. Luke 6:39-42).

> "The disciples of the King are to be critical of self but not of their brethren. The group is to be noted for their bond of unity, which is indicated by a lack of criticism. This is fitting, since the kingdom is characterized by peace. (Isaiah 9:7)."[443]

The disciple's relationship to antagonists 7:6

Jesus' disciples had a responsibility to pass their knowledge of the kingdom on to others so they, too, could prepare for it. Jesus gave them directions about this responsibility in this verse. This exhortation balances the one He just gave (vv. 1-5). The disciples could be too naive and fail to be discerning (cf. 5:43-47).

Pigs ("swine") were typically unclean, wild, vicious animals. Likewise, most "dogs" were not domestic pets but unclean, wild, despised creatures. This verse contains a chiastic construction. The dogs "turn and tear to pieces" those who give them special gifts, and the pigs "trample" under foot the "pearls" thrown before them (cf. Prov. 11:22). "What is holy" and the "pearls" in this illustration evidently represent the good news announcing the kingdom. The pigs and dogs probably do not represent all Gentiles, but people of any race who react to the good news by rejecting and turning against those who bring it to them (cf. 10:14; 15:14).[444] One example of this type of person is Herod Antipas, who heard John the Baptist gladly (Mark 6:20), but then beheaded him (14:1-12; Mark 6:14-28; Luke 9:7-9). Later when Christ stood before Herod, He said nothing to him (Luke 23:8-9). Such enemies should be left alone (cf. 2 Cor. 6:14-18).

> "As with other parts of Jesus' teaching, the point is not an absolute prohibition, because then the disciple could not share the gospel with those who are not responsive. Rather, the point is that the disciple is not obligated to share with those who are hard-hearted."[445]

The disciple's relationship to God 7:7-12

This section of verses brings the main body of the Sermon to a climactic conclusion.

7:7-8   In view of such hard opposition, Jesus' disciples need to pray for God's help. He will always respond positively to their words, though others may reject them (v. 6). Still, their petitions must be for His glory rather than for selfish ends (cf. James 4:2-3). All that the disciple needs to serve Jesus Christ successfully is available for the asking.

> "Jesus' disciples will pray ('ask') with earnest sincerity ('seek') and active, diligent pursuit of God's way ('knock'). Like a human father, the heavenly Father uses these means to teach his children courtesy, persistence, and diligence. If the child prevails with a thoughtful father, it is because the father has molded the child to his way."[446]

---

[442]Carson, "Matthew," p. 184.

[443]Toussaint, *Behold the . . .*, p. 113.

[444]Cf. Calvin, *Commentary on . . .*, 1:349.

[445]Bock, *Jesus according . . .*, p. 146. Cf. Prov. 9:8; 23:9.

[446]Carson, "Matthew," p. 186.

The force of each present imperative verb is *iterative*.[447] We could translate them: "Keep on asking, keep on seeking, keep on knocking" (cf. Luke 11:9-10). However, no matter the level of intensity with which we seek God's help, He will respond to every one of His disciples who calls to Him.

7:9-11   In verses 9 and 10, Jesus put the matter of verses 7-8 in two other ways. Even though parents are "evil" (i.e., self-centered sinners), they do not typically give their children disappointing or dangerous counterfeits, in response to requests for what is wholesome and nutritious. Much more will the heavenly "Father," who is pure goodness, "give . . . gifts" that are truly "good" to His "children" who request them (cf. Jer. 29:13; Luke 11:11-13; James 1:5-8). This is another *a fortiori* argument (cf. 6:26). Jesus' disciples are in view as the "children" praying here (cf. 5:45). The good things they request have direct connection with the kingdom, things such as ability to follow God faithfully in spite of opposition (cf. Acts 4:29). God has ordained that we ask for the good gifts we need, because this is the way He trains us, not because He is unaware or unconcerned about our needs (cf. 6:8).

> "What is fundamentally at stake is man's picture of God. God must not be thought of as a reluctant stranger who can be cajoled or bullied into bestowing his gifts (6:7-8), as a malicious tyrant who takes vicious glee in the tricks he plays (vv. 9-10), or even as an indulgent grandfather who provides everything requested of him. He is the heavenly Father, the God of the kingdom, who graciously and willingly bestows the good gifts of the kingdom in answer to prayer."[448]

There are 14 references to rewards in the Sermon on the Mount (5:12, 46; 6:1, 2, 4, 5, 6, 16, 18, 19, 20, 21, 33; 7:11). While the desire for an eternal reward may not be the highest motivation for serving Christ, Jesus held it out as one motivation, as did other New Testament writers.[449]

7:12   The recurrence of "the Law and the Prophets" here takes us back to 5:17, the beginning of the body of the Sermon. As pointed out previously, this phrase forms an *inclusio*. Everything Jesus said between 5:17 and 7:12 was essentially an exposition of Old Testament revelation. Consequently the "therefore" in this verse probably summarizes the entire section (5:17—7:12).

> The "golden rule" sums up the teaching of the Old Testament (cf. Exod. 23:4; Lev. 19:18; Deut. 15:7-8; Prov. 24:17; 25:21; Luke 6:31). The title "golden rule" traditionally comes from "the Roman Emperor Alexander Severus (A.D. 222-35), who, though not a Christian, was reputedly so impressed by the comprehensiveness of this maxim of Jesus . . . that he had it inscribed in gold on the wall of his chamber."[450]

Rather than giving scores of specific commands to govern individual behavior during the inter-advent era, as the Old Covenant did for the Mosaic era, Jesus gave this principle. It provides a rule we can use in thousands of specific cases to determine what righteousness looks like. Doing to others what we would want them to do to us is what "the Law and the Prophets" taught. This behavior fulfills them (cf. 5:17). This behavior is the will of God, and that is why Jesus' disciples should do it.

4. The false alternatives 7:13-27

To clarify the essential choices that His disciples needed to make, Jesus laid out four pairs of alternatives. Their choices would prepare them to continue to get ready for the coming kingdom. Each of the four alternatives is a warning of catastrophic proportions. They all focus on future judgment and the kingdom. This section constitutes the conclusion to the Sermon on the Mount.

The two paths 7:13-14

The Old Testament contains several references to diverging ways that force the traveler to choose between two paths (e.g., Deut. 30:15, 19; Ps. 1; Jer. 21:8). The AV translation "straight" is a bit misleading. That translation reflected the Latin *strictum* meaning narrow, and it probably contributed to the common idea of "the straight and narrow." However, the Greek word *stene* clearly means "narrow" as contrasted with broad. The word "small" (v. 14, Gr. *tethlimmene*) relates closely to the Greek word *thlipsis*, meaning "tribulation." Thus, Jesus was saying that the narrow restricting gate has connections with persecution, a major theme in Matthew's Gospel (cf. 5:10-12, 44; 10:16-39; 11:11-12; 24:4-13; Acts 14:22).[451]

---

[447]Tasker, p. 80.

[448]Carson, "Matthew," p. 187.

[449]See Joe L. Wall, *Going for the Gold*.

[450]France, *The Gospel . . .*, p. 284.

[451]See also A. J. Mattill Jr., "'The Way of Tribulation,'" *Journal of Biblical Literature* 98 (1979):531-46.

The "narrow" road "leads to life," namely, life in the kingdom (cf. vv. 21-22). The "broad" road "leads to destruction," namely, death and hell (cf. 25:34, 46; John 17:12; Rom. 9:22: Phil. 1:28; 3:19; 1 Tim. 6:9; Heb. 10:39; 2 Pet. 2:1, 3; 3:16; Rev. 17:8, 11). Few will enter the kingdom compared with the many who will perish. Jesus clearly did not believe in the doctrine of universalism that is growing in popularity today, the belief that everyone will eventually end up in heaven (cf. John 14:6). Entrance through the narrow gate onto the narrow way will eventually lead a person into the kingdom. The beginning of a life of discipleship (the gate) and the process of discipleship (the way) are both restrictive and both involve persecution.

> "*Gate* is mentioned for the benefit of those who were not true followers; *way* is mentioned as a definition of the life of the disciples of Jesus. This is why Matthew uses the word 'gate' (*pule*) while Luke employs the word 'door' (*thura*, Luke 13:24). Luke is concerned primarily with salvation. Here the King desires subjects for His kingdom, so He uses a word which implies a path is to be followed after entrance into life."[452]

Only a "few" people would find the way "to life" (v. 14). As we noted earlier, Israel's leaders were lethargic about seeking the Messiah (2:7-8). Many of the Jews were evidently not seeking the kingdom either.

The two trees 7:15-20 (cf. Luke 6:43-44)

7:15   Jesus here sounded a warning, that the Old Testament prophets also gave, about "false prophets" (cf. Deut. 13; 18; Jer. 6:13-15; 8:8-12; Ezek. 13; 22:27; Zeph 3:4). He did not explain exactly what they would teach, only that they would deceptively misrepresent divine revelation. This covers a wide spectrum of false teachers. Their motive was ultimately self-serving, and the end of their victims would be destruction. These characteristics are implicit in Jesus' description of them. The scribes and Pharisees manned a narrow gate, but it was not the gate that led to the narrow way leading to life.

7:16-20   "Fruit" in the natural world, as well as metaphorically, represents what the plant or person produces. It is what other people see (or sample or taste) that leads them to conclude something about the nature and identity of what bears the fruit. "Fruits" are the best indicator of this nature. In false teachers, "fruits" represent their doctrines and deeds (cf. Jer. 23:9-15). Jesus said His disciples would be able to recognize false prophets "by their fruits": their teachings and their actions. Sometimes the true character of a person remains hidden for some time. People regard their good works as an indication of righteous character. However, eventually the true nature of the person becomes apparent, and it becomes clear that one's seemingly good fruits were destructive.

> Prophets true to God's Word produce righteous conduct, but false prophets who disregard God's Word produce unrighteous conduct (v. 17).

> A poisonous plant will yield poisonous fruit. It cannot produce healthful fruit. Likewise a "good tree," such as an apple tree, bears "good," nutritious "fruit" (v. 18). The "bad fruit" may look good, but it is bad nonetheless (v. 16). A false prophet can only produce bad works, even though his works may appear good, superficially or temporarily.

> Some interpreters of this passage take Jesus' teaching further than He went with it. They say it is impossible for a genuine believer to do bad works. This cannot be true in view of the hundreds of commands, exhortations, and warnings that Jesus and the prophets and apostles gave to believers in both Testaments. It is possible for a believer to do bad works (e.g., 16:23; Tit. 2:11-13; 3:8; 1 John 1:9). That they will not is the teaching of *sinless perfection*. Other interpreters say that some bad works are inevitable for the believer, but bad works will not habitually characterize the life of a true believer. This quickly turns into a question of how many bad works (would prove someone is unsaved)—which the New Testament does not answer. Rather, the New Testament writers present some people who have departed from God's will for a long time as believers (e.g., 1 Tim. 1:20; 2 Tim. 2:17-18). The point Jesus was making, in verse 18, was simply that false prophets do what is bad, and people who follow God faithfully typically do what is good. How disciples of Jesus live was very important to Him.

> The end of "every tree that does not bear good fruit" is "the fire" (v. 19). Likewise the false prophet who does bad works, even though they look good, suffers destructive judgment (cf. 3:10).

> The words and works of a prophet eventually reveal his true character, just as surely as the fruit of a tree reveals its identity (v. 20). Of these two criteria, words and works, works are the more reliable indicator of character.

Jesus was evidently dealing with typical false prophets in this section. He did not go into the case of a believer who deliberately distorts God's Word. Typically, a false prophet rejects God's Word because he is an unbeliever. However, even in the Old Testament, there were a few true prophets who lied about God's Word (e.g., 1 Kings 13:18).

---

[452]Toussaint, *Behold the . . .*, p. 116.

The two claims 7:21-23 (cf. Luke 6:46)

Verses 15-20 deal with false prophets, but verses 21-23 deal with false followers. The repeated cry of these false disciples reveals their fervency.

> "In Jesus' day it is doubtful whether 'Lord' when used to address him meant more than 'teacher' or 'sir.' But in the postresurrection period, it becomes an appellation of worship and a confession of Jesus' deity."[453]

Obedience to the Father's will determines entrance into the millennial "kingdom," not professed admiration for Jesus. This is the first occurrence of the phrase "My Father" in Matthew. By using it, Jesus was implicitly claiming to be the authoritative revealer of God. During Jesus' ministry, doing the will of God boiled down to believing that Jesus was the Messiah and responding appropriately (John 6:29).[454] Note that entrance into the kingdom was still future; the kingdom was not yet present. Judgment will precede entrance into the kingdom.

Jesus claimed to be the eschatological Judge (cf. John 6). This was one of Messiah's functions (e.g., Ps. 2). "That day" (v. 22) is the day Jesus will judge false professors. It is almost a technical term for the messianic age (cf. Isa. 2:11, 17; 4:2; 10:20; Jer. 49:22; Zech. 14:6, 20-21). "In your name" means as your representatives and claiming your authority. Obviously it was possible for false disciples to "prophesy," exorcise "demons," and "perform miracles" in Jesus' name (e.g., Judas Iscariot). The authority of His name (reputation) enabled them to do so, not their own righteousness or relationship to Him. Many onlookers undoubtedly viewed these works as good fruit and evidence of righteous character. However, these were cases of tares that looked like wheat (cf. 13:24-30).

Jesus Himself would sentence the hypocrites to depart from His presence (v. 23).[455] Thus Jesus claimed again that He is the Judge who will determine who will enter the kingdom and who will not. This was a decidedly messianic function. The quotation from Psalm 6:8 puts Jesus in the place of the sufferer whom God has vindicated, and He now tells those who have done Him evil to depart from His presence. Moreover, He will say He never knew these false professors. Many people deal with holy things daily yet have no personal acquaintance with God because they are hypocrites. It is their failure to bow before divine law, the will of God, that renders them practitioners of lawlessness—and guilty.

The two builders 7:24-27 (cf. Luke 6:47-49)

Verses 21-23 contrast those who say one thing but do another. Verses 24-27 contrast hearing and doing (cf James 1:22-25; 2:14-20).[456] The will of Jesus' Father (v. 21) now becomes "these words of mine" (v. 24). As throughout this section (vv. 13-27), Jesus was looking at a life in its entirety.

> "The two ways illustrate the *start* of the life of faith; the two trees illustrate the *growth* and results of the life of faith here and now; and the two houses illustrate the *end* of this life of faith, when God shall call everything to judgment."[457]

Each house in Jesus' illustration looks secure. However, severe testing reveals the true quality of the builders' work (cf. 13:21; Prov. 10:25; 12:7; 14:11; Isa. 28:16-17). Torrential downpours were and are common in Israel. Wise men build to withstand anything. The wise person is a theme in Matthew (cf. 10:16; 24:45; 25:2, 4, 8-9). The "wise" person is one who puts Jesus' "words" into practice. Thus the final reckoning will expose the true convictions of the pseudo-disciple.

Jesus later compared Himself to foundation rock (16:18; cf. Isa. 28:16; 1 Cor. 3:11; 1 Pet. 2:6-8). That idea was probably implicit here.

Verses 16-20 have led some people to judge the reality of a person's salvation from his or her works. All that Jesus said before (vv. 1-5), and following those verses, should discourage us from doing this. False prophets eventually give evidence that they are not faithful prophets. However, it is impossible for onlookers to determine the salvation of professing believers (vv. 21-23) and those who simply receive the gospel without making any public response to it (vv. 24-27). Their real condition will only become clear when Jesus judges them. He is their Judge, and we must leave their judgment in His hands (v. 1).

Jesus' point in this section (vv. 13-27) was that entrance into the kingdom and discipleship as a follower of the King are unpopular, and they involve persecution. Many more people will profess to be disciples than really are. The acid test is obedience to the revealed will of God.

> "So the sermon ends with a challenge not to ignore responding to Jesus and his teaching. Jesus is a figure who is not placing his teaching forward because it is a recommended way of life. He represents far more than that. His teaching is a call to an allegiance that means the difference between life and death, between blessing and woe. Jesus is more than a prophet."[458]

[453]Carson, "Matthew," p. 192.

[454]See Robern N. Wilkin, "Not Everyone Who Says 'Lord, Lord' Will Enter the Kingdom: Matthew 7:21-23," *The Grace Evangelical Society News* 3:12 (December 1988):2-3.

[455]See Karl E. Pagenkemper, "Rejection Imagery in the Synoptic Parables," *Bibliotheca Sacra* 153:610 (April-June 1996):189-90.

[456]Stott, p. 208.

[457]Wiersbe, 1:31.

5. The response of the audience 7:28-29

Each conclusion to each of the five major discourses in Matthew begins with the same formula statement: literally "and it happened" (Gr. *kai egeneto*) followed by a finite verb. It is, therefore, "a self-conscious stylistic device that establishes a structural turning point."[459] Each conclusion is also transitional and prepares for the next section.

We learn for the first time that, even though Jesus was teaching His disciples (5:1-2), multitudes were listening in to what He taught them. Probably for this reason, the end of the Sermon contains more material that is suitable for a general audience. France believed that all the discourses in Matthew are anthologies of Jesus' teachings on various occasions—that Matthew compiled into discourses—rather than single discourses that Jesus delivered on individual occasions.[460] This is a minority opinion, but it is probably true that the Gospel writers edited Jesus' teachings to some extent.

Jesus' "teaching" included both His content and His delivery. What impressed the crowds was Jesus' "authority" when He taught. This is the first occurrence of another theme that Matthew stressed (8:9; 9:6, 8; 10:1; 21:23-24, 27; 28:18). Jesus' authority was essentially different in that He claimed to be the Messiah. He not only claimed to interpret the Word of God, as other contemporary teachers did, but He claimed to fulfill it as well (5:17). He would be the One who would determine entrance into the kingdom (v. 21), and He would judge humankind eventually (v. 23). He also claimed that His teaching amounted to God's Word (vv. 24, 26). Therefore the authoritative note in His teaching was not primarily His sincerity, or His oratorical style, or His lack of reference to earlier authorities. It was who He was. He claimed to be *the* authoritative Interpreter of the Word of God (i.e., with the authority of the predicted Prophet, the Messiah)!

> "In the final analysis . . . what Jesus says about the law applies to it as something being authoritatively reinterpreted by his teaching. It is not the Mosaic law in and of itself that has normative and abiding character for disciples, but the Mosaic law as it has passed through the crucible of Jesus' teaching."[461]

To summarize this sermon, Jesus began by describing the character of the kingdom's subjects (5:1-10). He then explained their calling (5:11-16). Next, He specified their conduct (5:17—7:12). Finally, He clarified their choices and commitments (7:13-27).

Scholars have noted many parallels between Jesus' teaching in the Sermon on the Mount and Rabbinic instruction, probably more than in any other part of the New Testament. The similarities, however, lie in form of expression, subject matter, and turn of words, but definitely not in spirit.[462] The authority and power of His teaching, as Matthew ironically pointed out, was "not as their scribes."

> "The King has proclaimed the nearness of the kingdom and has authenticated that message with great signs. With people flocking to Him He instructs His disciples concerning the character of those who shall inherit the kingdom. The kingdom, though earthly, is founded on righteousness. Thus the theme of His message is righteousness."[463]

Jesus proceeded to demonstrate His authority by performing powerful miracles that liberated captives from their bondage, signs that the Old Testament prophets said Messiah would perform.

> "Throughout the rest of his story, Matthew makes it exceedingly plain that, whether directly or indirectly, the issue of authority underlies all the controversies Jesus has with the religious leaders and that it is therefore pivotal to his entire conflict with them."[464]

III. THE MANIFESTATION OF THE KING 8:1—11:1

> "Matthew has laid the foundational structure for his argument in chapters one through seven. The genealogy and birth have attested to the legal qualifications of the Messiah as they are stated in the Old Testament. Not only so, but in His birth great and fundamental prophecies have been fulfilled. The King, according to protocol, has a forerunner preceding Him in His appearance on the scene of Israel's history. The moral qualities of Jesus have been authenticated by His baptism and temptation. The King Himself then commences His ministry of proclaiming the nearness of the kingdom and authenticates it with great miracles. To instruct His disciples as to the true character of righteousness which is to distinguish Him, He draws

---

[458]Bock, *Jesus according . . .*, pp. 152-53. For a good exposition of the Sermon on the Mount, see Dallas Willard, *The Divine Conspiracy*.

[459]Carson, "Matthew," p. 195. Cf. Kingsbury, *Matthew as . . .*, p. 105.

[460]France, *The Gospel . . .*, pp. 8-10.

[461]Kingsbury, *Matthew as . . .*, p. 65. Cf. 5:17-18, 21-48; 22:37-40; 24:35; 28:20.

[462]See Edersheim, *The Life . . .*, 1:531-41.

[463]Toussaint, *Behold the . . .*, p. 119.

[464]Kingsbury, *Matthew as . . .*, p. 125.

them apart on the mountain. After Matthew has recorded the Sermon on the Mount, he goes on to relate the King's presentation to Israel (Matthew 8:1—11:1)."[465]

A. DEMONSTRATIONS OF THE KING'S POWER 8:1—9:34

Matthew described Jesus' ministry as consisting of teaching, preaching, and healing in 4:23. Chapters 5—7 record what He taught His disciples: principles of the kingdom. We have the essence of His preaching ministry in 4:17. Now in 8:1—9:34 we see His healing ministry. He demonstrated authority over human beings, unseen spiritual powers, and the world of nature. Matthew showed that Jesus' ability proves that He is the divine Messiah. He possessed the "power to banish from the earth the consequences of sin and to control the elements of nature".[466] The King authenticated His claims by performing messianic signs. In view of these things, the Jews should have acknowledged Him as their Messiah.

"The purpose of Matthew in these two chapters [8 and 9] is to offer the credentials of the Messiah as predicted in the Old Testament."[467]

Matthew did not record Jesus' miracles in strict chronological order. The harmonies of the Gospels make this clear.[468] His order is more thematic. He also selected miracles that highlight the gracious character of Jesus' signs. As Moses' plagues authenticated his ministry to the Israelites of his day, so Jesus' miracles should have convinced the Israelites of His day that He was the Messiah. Moses' plagues were primarily destructive, whereas Jesus' miracles were primarily constructive. Jesus' miracles were more like Elisha's than Moses' in this respect.

Matthew recorded 10 instances of Jesus healing in this section of his book (cf. the 10 plagues in Egypt), half of all the miracles that Matthew recorded. Some regard 8:16-17 as a miracle distinct from the previous healings in chapter 8, resulting in 10 miracles. Others regard 8:16-17 as a summary of the preceding miracles, resulting in 9 miracles. Both explanations have merit, since 8:16-17 records other miracles, but it does not narrate one specific miraculous healing.

Matthew presented these miracles in three groups and broke the three groups up with two discussions (narrative sections) concerning His authority. The first group of miracles involves healings (8:1-17), the second, demonstrations of power (8:23—9:8), and the third, acts of restoration (9:18-34). Together the section presents "a slice of life" out of Jesus' overall ministry.[469]

Miracles of healing 8:1-17		Demonstrations of power 8:23—9:8		Acts of Restoration 9:18-34
	Jesus' authority over His disciples 8:18-22		Jesus' authority over His critics 9:9-17	

"The provision of interludes on discipleship in order to divide the nine stories into three groups of three is also closely parallel to the arrangement of the parables of ch. 13 into groups of three with intervening explanatory material, an arrangement which is equally peculiar to Matthew [among the Gospel writers]."[470]

1. Jesus' ability to heal 8:1-17

This first group of four miracle events apparently all happened on the same day (v. 16).[471]

---

[465]Toussaint, Behold the . . ., p. 121.

[466]The New Scofield . . ., p. 1003.

[467]Walvoord, Matthew: . . ., p. 63.

[468]See, for example, Appendix 1 "A Harmony of the Gospels" at the end of these notes, or Robertson, A Harmony . . .; or, for the Greek text, Burton and Goodspeed, A Harmony . . .

[469]D. J. Weaver, Matthew's Missionary Discourse, p. 67.

[470]France, The Gospel . . ., p. 302.

[471]See Appendix 6 "The Miracles of Jesus" at the end of these notes for a chart.

The cleansing of a leprous Jew 8:1-4 (cf. Mark 1:40-45; Luke 5:12-16)

8:1   This verse is transitional (cf. 5:1). Great crowds continued to follow Jesus after He delivered the Sermon on the Mount, as they had before.

8:2-3   Matthew typically used the phrase *kai idou* ("and behold," not translated in the NIV) to mark the beginning of a new section, not to indicate the next event chronologically.

The exact nature of biblical leprosy is unknown. Apparently it included what we call leprosy today, Hansen's disease, but it involved other skin diseases too (cf. Lev. 13—14).[472] A leper not only had some loathsome skin disease that made him repulsive to others, but he also was ritually unclean because of his illness. This precluded contact with other people and participation in temple worship. The Jews regarded leprosy as a curse from God (Num. 12:10, 12; Job 18:13), and healings were rare (Num. 12:10-15; 2 Kings 5:9-14). The Jews thought that healing a leper was as difficult as raising the dead (2 Kings 5:7, 14).

"Leprosy is viewed in the Old Testament not so much as a type of sin as of the uncleanness and separation that sin produces."[473]

The "leper" in this story knelt (Gr. *prosekynei*) before Jesus. The same word describes worshippers in the New Testament. However, Matthew probably simply described him as kneeling, in order to leave his readers to draw their own conclusions about Jesus' worthiness to receive worship (cf. 7:22-23).

The man had great faith in Jesus' ability to heal him. Evidently he had heard about and perhaps seen others whom Jesus had healed (4:24). His only reservation was Jesus' willingness to use His power to heal him. The leper probably supposed that a Jewish teacher like Jesus would probably not want to have anything to do with him, since to do so would render Jesus ritually unclean.

"The phrase *if You are willing* is important because it indicates genuine faith. It does not necessarily mean that if one simply believes, God *will* do something, but that He *can* do it (see Dan. 3:17)."[474]

"In most cases . . . the purpose of the minor characters [in Matthew's story] is to function as foils for the disciples."[475]

Probably the crowd gasped when Jesus graciously extended His hand and touched the unclean leper. Lepers had to avoid all contact with other people, but Jesus compassionately reached out to him in his helpless condition. Jesus expressed His willingness with His word, and He expressed His power with His touch.

"Whatever remedies, medical, magical, or sympathetic, Rabbinic writings may indicate for various kinds of disease, leprosy is not included in the catalogue. They left aside what even the Old Testament marked as moral death, by enjoining those so stricken to avoid all contact with the living, and even to bear the appearance of mourners.

"In truth, the possibility of any cure through human agency was never contemplated by the Jews."[476]

"There is a sense in which leprosy is an archetypal fruit of the original fall of humanity. It leaves its victims in a most pitiable state: ostracized, helpless, hopeless, despairing. The cursed leper, like fallen humanity, has no options until he encounters the messianic king who will make all things new. . . . As Jesus reached out to the leper, God in Jesus has reached out to all victims of sin."[477]

---

[472]*A Dictionary of New Testament Theology*, s.v. "Leprosy," by R. K. Harrison, 2:363-66; Rebecca A. and E. Eugene Baillie, "Biblical Leprosy as Compared to Present-Day Leprosy," *Christian Medical Society Journal* 14:3 (Fall 1983):27-29.

[473]Pentecost, *The Words . . .*, p. 148.

[474]*The Nelson . . .*, p. 1588.

[475]Kingsbury, *Matthew as . . .*, p. 27.

[476]Edersheim, *The Life . . .*, 1:491, 492.

[477]Hagner, p. 200.

"When Jesus touched the leper, He contracted the leper's defilement; *but He also conveyed His health!* Is this not what He did for us on the cross when He was made sin for us? (2 Cor. 5:21)"[478]

8:4   Why did Jesus tell the cleansed leper to "tell no one" about his cleansing? Probably Jesus did not want the news of this cleansing broadcast widely because it would have attracted multitudes whose sole interest would have been to obtain physical healing.[479] In other words, He wanted to limit His physical ministry's appeal, since He came to provide much more than just physical healing.[480] A corollary of this view is that, by keeping quiet, the leper would have retarded the opposition of Jesus' enemies who were hostile to Him and who resented His popularity.

More significant is why Jesus told the man to present himself to the priests at the temple in Jerusalem. Jesus was encouraging the man to obey the Mosaic Law concerning the cleansing of lepers (Lev. 14:2; cf. Talmudic tractate Negaim 14). However, by sending him there to do that, Jesus was notifying the religious authorities in Israel that someone with messianic power was ministering in Galilee. Since no leper had received cleansing since Elisha had cleansed Naaman the Aramean, the priests should have wanted to investigate Jesus. (Moses had previously cleansed Miriam's leprosy [Num. 12:10-15].)

"Jesus in effect was presenting His 'calling card' to the priests, for they would have to investigate His claims."[481]

This investigation by Israel's leaders—who, we have observed, were surprisingly uninterested in Messiah's birth—was something Jesus initiated by sending the leper to the temple with his offering. When the priests examined the cleansed leper closely, they would have had to certify that Jesus had genuinely healed the man. Their certification should have convinced everyone in Israel of Jesus' power.

Matthew evidently recorded this miracle to show that Jesus' ability to heal leprosy marked Him as the Messiah to all who would pay attention in Israel.

"By recounting Jesus' response to the most feared and ostracized medical condition of his day, Matthew has thus laid an impressive foundation for this collection of stories which demonstrate both Jesus' unique healing power and his willingness to challenge the taboos of society in the interests of human compassion."[482]

The healing of a centurion's servant 8:5-13 (cf. Luke 7:1-10)

8:5   Centurions were Roman military officers, each of whom controlled 100 men, therefore the name "centurion." They were the military backbone of the Roman Empire. Interestingly, every reference to a centurion in the New Testament is a positive one. These centurions were, according to the biblical record, fair-minded men whom the Jews respected. "Capernaum" was an important garrison town in Jesus' day. Probably most of the soldiers under this centurion's command were Phoenician and Syrian Gentiles.[483]

8:6-7   Matthew recorded that the centurion's address to Jesus (lit. "lord") was polite, though he probably did not intend it as a title of deity.[484] The Greek word that the centurion used to describe his servant, *pais*, usually means "servant," though it can mean "son" (cf. John 4:51). This servant could have been the centurion's personal aide. Matthew did not record the cause of his paralysis. Perhaps reports of Jesus' healing of another official's son led this centurion to approach Jesus (John 4). Here was one Gentile asking Jesus to come and heal another Gentile. Evidently the centurion sent his request through messengers (Luke 7:3). This is one of only two miracles in which Jesus healed someone from a distance in Matthew's Gospel (cf. 15:21-28). Both involved Jesus healing *Gentiles*, whom He initially rebuffed, but later commended for their unusually great faith in Him.

It is possible to translate Jesus' response as a question: "Shall *I* [emphatic] come and heal him?" This translation has the advantage of providing a reason for Jesus emphasizing "I," namely, to focus attention on Jesus' person. Jesus would not have hesitated to go to the centurion because of ritual uncleanness, as Peter later did (Acts 10); He had already touched a leper (v.

[478]Wiersbe, 1:33.
[479]Tasker, p. 87.
[480]Ned B. Stonehouse, *The Witness of Matthew and Mark to Christ*, p. 62.
[481]Barbieri, p. 37.
[482]France, *The Gospel . . .*, p. 306.
[483]Carson, "Matthew," p. 200.
[484]See my comment on "lord" at 7:21.

3). Jesus' lack of concern about remaining ritually clean shows that He was replacing some laws in the Mosaic Code (cf. Deut. 18:18; Mark 7:19).

8:8-9   The centurion confessed that he felt unfit, Levitically speaking, to entertain Jesus in his home (cf. 5:3). John the Baptist had also expressed a similar feeling of unworthiness (3:14). The basis for the centurion's feeling of unworthiness (Gr. *hikanos*) was his own perception of how Jews regarded Gentile dwellings, plus the "authority" that he believed Jesus possessed. He believed Jesus had sufficient authority to simply speak and He could heal his servant (cf. John 4:46-53).

All authority in the Roman Empire belonged to the emperor, who delegated authority to others under his command. The Roman Republic ended about 30 B.C., and from then on, beginning with Caesar Augustus, the emperors enjoyed more authority under the Roman Empire. When the centurion gave a command it carried all the authority of the emperor, and people obeyed him. A soldier who might disobey an order the centurion gave was really disobeying the emperor. The centurion realized that Jesus also operated under a similar system. Jesus was *under* God's authority, but He also *wielded* God's authority. When Jesus spoke, God spoke. To defy Jesus was to defy God. Jesus' word, therefore, must carry God's authority to heal sickness. The centurion confessed that Jesus' authority was God's authority, and Jesus' word was God's word. The centurion believed that Jesus *could* heal His servant, not that He *would* heal him. We cannot know God's will in such matters, but we must believe that He is able to do anything.

8:10   Jesus expressed astonishment at this Gentile's great faith in Him. The Greek verb *thaumazo*, "to be amazed," usually describes the reaction of people to Jesus in Matthew (cf. 8:27; 9:33; 15:31; 21:20; 22:22; 27:14). This is the only time it describes Jesus' reaction to someone.

"*'Wonder'* cannot apply to God, for it arises out of what is new and unexpected: but it might exist in Christ, for he had clothed himself with our flesh, and with human affections."[485]

The introductory clause "I say to you" or "I tell you" alerted Jesus' disciples that He was about to say something very important on His personal authority (cf. 5:22). The greatness of the centurion's faith was due to his perception of Jesus' relationship to God. It was not that he believed Jesus could heal from a remote distance. Moreover the centurion was a Gentile who evidently lacked the knowledge of Old Testament revelation about Messiah. No Jew that Jesus had met had shown such insight into His person and authority.

Evidently, one of the reasons Matthew stressed the uniqueness of the centurion's faith so strongly, was that he wanted to show the shift in Jesus' ministry from Jews to all people (cf. 1:1, 3-5; 2:1-12; 3:9-10; 4:15-16; 28:18-20).

"This incident is a preview of the great insight which came later through another centurion's faith, 'Then to the Gentiles God has granted repentance unto life' (Acts 11:18)."[486]

8:11-12   Again Jesus introduced a solemn truth (cf. v. 10). He then referred to the messianic banquet prophesied in Isaiah 25:6-9 (cf. Isa. 65:13-14). There God revealed that Gentiles from all parts of the world will join the Jewish patriarchs "in the kingdom." The Old Testament has much to say about the participants in the kingdom. God would gather Israel from all parts of the earth (Ps. 107:3; Isa. 43:5-6; 49:12), but Gentiles from all quarters of the world would also worship God in the kingdom (Isa. 45:6; 59:19; Mal. 1:11). The Gentiles would come specifically to Jerusalem (Isa. 2:2-3; 60:3-4; Mic. 4:1-2; Zech. 8:20-23). As mentioned previously, in Jesus' day the Jews had chosen to view themselves as uniquely privileged because of the patriarchs. This led them to write the Gentiles out of the kingdom, despite these prophecies.

"The Jew expected that the Gentile would be put to shame by the sight of the Jews in bliss."[487]

The "sons [or subjects] of the kingdom" (v. 12) are the Jews who saw themselves as the patriarchs' descendants. They thought they had a right to the kingdom because of their ancestors' righteousness (cf. 3:9-10). Jesus turned the tables by announcing that many of the sons of the kingdom would not participate in it, but many Gentiles would. Many "sons of the kingdom" would find themselves outside the banquet ("into the outer darkness"). The terms "weeping" and "gnashing of teeth" (cf. 13:42, 50; 22:13; 24:51; 25:30; Luke 13:28) were common descriptions of Gehenna, hell (4 Ezra 7:93; 1 Enoch 63:10; Psalms of Solomon 14:9; Wisdom of Solomon 17:21).[488] (The works just cited in parentheses were Old Testament

---

[485]Calvin, *Commentary on . . .*, 1:382.

[486]R. T. France, "Exegesis in Practice: Two Samples," in *New Testament Interpretation*, p. 260.

[487]Plummer, p. 127.

[488]See Pagenkemper, pp. 183-86.

apocryphal books that the Jews viewed as generally reliable and helpful but not inspired.) This interpretation finds confirmation in the expression "outer darkness," another image of rejection (cf. 22:13; 25:30).[489]

"The idea of the Messianic Banquet as at once the seal and the symbol of the new era was a common feature in apocalyptic writings and an extremely popular subject of discussion, thought, and expectation."[490]

The Greek text has the definite article "the" before "weeping" and before "gnashing." This stresses the horror of the scene.[491] The terms in Rabbinic usage picture sorrow and anger respectively.[492]

Jesus shocked His hearers by announcing three facts about the kingdom. First, not all Jews would participate in it. Second, many Gentiles would. Third, entrance depended on faith in Jesus, not on ancestry, the faith that the centurion demonstrated.

". . . the locus of the people of God would not always be the Jewish race. If these verses do not quite authorize the Gentile mission, they open the door to it and prepare for the Great Commission (28:18-20) and Ephesians 3."[493]

8:13   A similar statement by Jesus helps us understand what He meant, when He said here that He would do for the centurion "as" (Gr. *hos*) he had believed (cf. 15:28). Jesus did not grant his request because the centurion had great faith, or in proportion to his amount of faith. He did so in harmony with what the centurion expected. Jesus did for him what he expected Jesus would do for him.

"It is . . . interesting to observe that the Gentile follows the Jew in the sequence of healing events. This is in accord with Matthew's plan of presenting Jesus first as Son of David and then as Son of Abraham."[494]

This healing marked Jesus as the Messiah who was under God's authority.

The healing of Peter's mother-in-law 8:14-15 (cf. Mark 1:29-31; Luke 4:38-39)

Peter and his family were evidently living in Capernaum when Jesus performed this miracle (4:13). People considered "fever" a disease in Jesus' day, rather than a symptom of a disease (cf. John 4:52; Acts 28:8).

"The Talmud gives this disease precisely the same name (*Eshatha Tsemirta*), 'burning fever,' and prescribes for it a magical remedy, of which the principal part is to tie a knife wholly of iron by a braid of hair to a thornbush, and to repeat on successive days Exod. iii. 2, 3, then ver. 4, and finally ver. 5, after which the bush is to be cut down, while a certain magical formula is pronounced. (Tractate *Shabbath* 37 a)"[495]

Jesus healed "Peter's mother-in-law" with a touch. His touch did not defile the healer, but it healed the defiled (cf. v. 3). Matthew consistently stressed Jesus' authority in this brief pericope. He probably mentioned the fact that, when Jesus healed the woman she *immediately* began to serve Him, in order to illustrate the instantaneous effectiveness of Jesus' power (cf. v. 26). Usually a fever leaves the body weak, but Jesus overcame that here.[496]

"Some see great significance in Matthew's deliberate rearrangement of these miracles. Since Matthew did not follow the chronological order, it seems he intended to illustrate the plan of his Gospel. Accordingly, the first miracle shows Christ ministering to the Jews. His mighty works bore testimony to His person, but His testimony was rejected. Consequently, He turns to the Gentiles, who manifest great faith in Him. Later, He returns to the Jews, represented by the mother-in-law of the apostle to the Jews. He heals her and all who come to Him. This third picture is that of the millennium, when the King restores Israel and blesses all the nations."[497]

[489]Ibid., pp. 186-88.
[490]Bindley, p. 317. Cf. William Barclay, *The Gospel of Matthew*, 1:309.
[491]Turner, p. 173.
[492]Edersheim, *The Life . . .*, 1:550-51.
[493]Carson, "Matthew," p. 203.
[494]Toussaint, *Behold the . . .*, p. 124.
[495]Edersheim, *The Life . . .*, 1:486.
[496]Barbieri, p. 37.
[497]Toussaint, *Behold the . . .*, p. 125.

This miracle shows Jesus' power to heal people fully, instantaneously, and completely. It also showcases His *compassion*, since the object of His grace was a woman. The Pharisees considered lepers, Gentiles, and women as outcasts, but Jesus showed mercy to them all. By healing a leper who was a social outcast, a Gentile, and finally a woman, Jesus was extending His grace to people the Jews either excluded or ignored as unimportant. Jewish narrowness did not bind Jesus any more than disease and uncleanness contaminated Him.[498]

"He began with the unfit persons for whom there was no provision in the economy of the nation."[499]

The healing of many Galileans 8:16-17 (cf. Mark 1:32-34; Luke 4:40-41)

That evening many other people brought their afflicted friends and relatives to Jesus for healing. In the Jewish inter-testamental literature, the writers spoke of demons as responsible for making people ill.[500] Jesus "cast out many" demonic "spirits," "and healed" many ("all") "who were ill." He had power over *every* affliction: "all who were ill" (v. 16).

Matthew noted that Jesus' healings fulfilled messianic prophecy (Isa. 53:4). Matthew's citation from Isaiah actually summarized all the healings in this chapter so far. He interpreted Isaiah freely as predicting the vicarious sufferings of Messiah. This was in accord with Isaiah's prophecy concerning Messiah that appears in Isaiah 53. The Old Testament taught that all sickness is the direct or indirect result of sin (cf. 9:5). Messiah would remove infirmities and diseases by dying as a substitute sacrifice for sin. He would deal with the fruit by dealing with the root. Jesus' healing ministry laid the foundation for His destroying (triumphing over, conquering) sickness by His death. Therefore it was appropriate for Matthew to quote Isaiah 53:4 here. Jesus' healing ministry also previewed kingdom conditions (cf. Isa. 33:24; 57:19).

"Thus the healings during Jesus' ministry can be understood not only as the foretaste of the kingdom [in which there will be little sickness] but also as the fruit of Jesus' death."[501]

For Matthew, Jesus' healing ministry pointed to the Cross. The healings were signs that signified more than the average observer might have understood. Matthew recorded that Jesus healed all types of people. Likewise when He died, Jesus gave His life as a ransom for many (20:28). Jesus' ministry of destroying sin, in death, was an extension of the authority that He demonstrated in His ministry of destroying (triumphing over, conquering) sickness during His life. Many scholars believe that the Jews of Jesus' day did not understand Isaiah 53 as messianic prophecy. Joachim Jeremias is one exception. Whether they did or not, they should have.

". . . it is to cast Jesus' activity of healing in the mold of 'serving' that Matthew informs the reader in a formula-quotation that Jesus, through healing, fulfills the words of the Servant Song of Isaiah: 'He took our infirmities and bore our diseases' (8:16-17; Isa. 53:4). In healing, Jesus Son of God assumes the role of the servant of God and ministers to Israel by restoring persons to health or freeing them from their afflictions (11:5). Through serving in this fashion, Jesus 'saves' (9:22)."[502]

Some Christians believe that Isaiah 53:4 and Matthew 8:16-17 teach that Jesus' death made it possible for people today to experience physical healing now by placing faith in Jesus. Most students of these and similar passages have concluded that the healing which Jesus' death provides believers today will come when they receive their resurrection bodies, not necessarily before then.[503] This conclusion finds support in the revelation about the purpose of periods of healing that the Bible records. Many Christians today fall into the same trap the Corinthian believers fell into when they demanded future blessings now (cf. 1 Cor. 4:6-13).[504]

This summary pericope stresses Jesus' power over every human affliction.

Jesus' *therapeutic* miracles, involving physical healings, presented Jesus to the *crowds* as the compassionate Servant of the Lord—and illustrated His *Messiahship* (18:17; 9:22). His *non-therapeutic* miracles, involving nature, presented Jesus to the *disciples* as having all authority—and illustrated His *deity*. Belief in Jesus' Messiahship was normally preliminary to belief in His deity. His disciples needed to learn this so they would rely on *His* authority for their ministries in the future.

[498]Walvoord, *Matthew: . . .*, p. 65.

[499]Morgan, *The Gospel . . .*, p. 82.

[500]Carson, "Matthew," p. 205.

[501]Ibid., p. 206.

[502]Kingsbury, *Matthew as . . .*, p. 68.

[503]See Hagner, p. 211.

[504]See. A. C. Thistleton, "Realized Eschatology at Corinth," *New Testament Studies* 24 (1977):510-26.

2. Jesus' authority over His disciples 8:18-22 (cf. Luke 9:57-62)

Matthew evidently inserted these teachings about Jesus' authority because they show the nature of Jesus' ministry and the kind of disciples He requires. The King has power over people, not just sickness. He can direct others as His servants, and they need to respond to Him as their King.

Jesus' demands regarding possessions 8:18-20

8:18-19   Verse 18 gives the occasion for the scribe's statement in verse 19 (cf. Mark 4:35). "The other side" of the lake (from Capernaum) would have been the eastern side. There was only so much room in the boat, and the "scribe" wanted to get in with other disciples. At this time in Jesus' ministry there were many more than just 12 disciples, though the Twelve were an inner circle. As mentioned above, the word "disciple" does not necessarily identify fully committed followers or even believers (cf. 5:1; 8:21). This scribe, a teacher of the law, looked to Jesus as his "teacher." He wanted to learn from Him. He said that he was willing to "follow" Him anywhere to do so.

> ". . . the designations 'rabbi' and 'teacher' attribute to the person so addressed human respect but nothing more. Hence, in addressing Jesus as 'teacher,' the religious leaders accord Jesus the honor they would accord any teacher, but this is the extent of it. To their mind Jesus' station is not that of the Messiah Son of God, his authority is not divine, and they in no sense follow him or have faith in him."[505]

> Some scholars believe that Matthew consistently denigrated the scribes in his Gospel.[506] I do not believe he did this (cf. 13:52; 23:34), but Matthew's references to the scribes are usually negative. Matthew seems to present everyone who came to Jesus without prejudice. The issue to Matthew was how various people responded to Jesus.

8:20   Jesus' reply did not encourage or discourage the scribe. It simply helped him count the cost of following Him as a disciple. Jesus was very busy traveling from one place to another as an itinerant preacher and teacher. His healing ministry complicated His life because it attracted crowds that placed additional demands on Him. He had no regular home, as most people did, but traveled all over the region. The scribe needed to understand this if he wanted to keep up with Jesus. We should not interpret Jesus' statement to mean that He was penniless and could not afford shelter at night (cf. Luke 8:1-3). His ministry simply kept Him on the move.

> "When the object of faith left the earth, and His presence became spiritual, all occasion for such nomadic discipleship was done away."[507]

> Jesus called Himself "the Son of Man." This expression occurs 81 times in the Gospels, 69 times in the Synoptics, and 30 times in Matthew.[508] In every instance except two, it was a term Jesus used of Himself. In those two instances, it is a term used by others who were quoting Jesus (Luke 24:7; John 12:34). Though it occurs in several Old Testament passages, as well as in apocryphal Jewish literature, its use in Daniel 7:13-14 is messianic. There, "one like a son of man" approaches the Ancient of Days and receives "authority, glory, and sovereign power." He also receives "an everlasting dominion that will not pass away," in which "all peoples, nations, and men of every language" worship Him. By using this title, Jesus was claiming to be the divine Messiah.

> "It is His name as the representative Man, in the sense of 1 Cor. 15:45-47, as Son of David is distinctively His Jewish name, and Son of God His divine name. Our Lord constantly uses this term as implying that His mission (e.g. Mt. 11:19; Lk. 19:10), His death and resurrection (e.g. Mt. 12:40; 20:18; 26:2), and His second coming (e.g. Mt. 24:37-44; Lk. 12:40) transcend in scope and result all merely Jewish limitations."[509]

> However, most of Jesus' hearers probably did not associate this title with a messianic claim when they first heard it. Many of them were probably not well enough acquainted with Daniel 7:13-14 to understand its meaning. Many who *did* understand its significance held a concept of Messiah that the rabbis had distorted. Furthermore, other Old Testament references to the "son of man" were not messianic. For example, David used the term to refer to man generically (Ps. 8:4). Asaph used it to describe

---

[505]Kingsbury, *Matthew as . . .*, p. 64. Cf. 9:11; 12:38; 17:24; 19:16; 22:16, 24, 36; 26:25, 49. See Gunther Bornkamm, "End-Expectation and Church in Matthew," in *Tradition and Interpretation in Matthew*, pp. 41-43.

[506]E.g., W. F. Albright and C. S. Mann, *Matthew*.

[507]Bruce, *The Training . . .*, p. 18.

[508]For a good introduction to the meaning of this term, see Hagner's excursus, pp. 214-15, or Carson's excursus in "Matthew," pp. 209-13.

[509]*The New Scofield . . .*, p. 1004.

Israel (Ps. 80:17). In the Book of Ezekiel, it is a favorite term God used when He addressed Ezekiel personally, in order to stress the prophet's humanity.

God used this term many times in the Old Testament to stress the difference between frail mortal man and God Himself.[510] Jesus' use of the title combined both the messianic and mortal aspects. He was both the Messiah King and the Suffering Servant of the Lord. Some who heard Him use this title probably did not know what it meant. Others understood Jesus' claim to messiahship, and others thought He was simply referring to Himself in a humble way.

". . . 'the Son of man' is not of the nature of a Christological title the purpose of which is to inform the reader of 'who Jesus is.' Instead, it is a self-designation that is also a technical term, and it describes Jesus as 'the man,' or 'the human being' ('this man,' or 'this human being') (earthly, suffering, vindicated). It is 'in public' or with a view to the 'public,' or 'world' (Jews and Gentiles but especially opponents), that Jesus refers to himself as 'the Son of man' ('this man'). Through his use of this self-reference, Jesus calls attention, for one thing, to the divine authority that he ('this man') exercises now and will also exercise in the future and, for another thing, to the opposition that he ('this man') must face. And should the question be raised as to who 'this man' Jesus is, the answer is, as Peter correctly confesses, that he is the Son of God (16:13, 16)."[511]

"It seems that the reason why Jesus found this title convenient is that, having no ready-made titular connotations in current usage, it could be applied across the whole range of his uniquely paradoxical mission of humiliation and vindication, of death and glory, which could not be fitted into any preexisting model. Like his parables, the title 'the Son of Man' came with an air of enigma, challenging the hearer to think new thoughts rather than to slot Jesus into a ready-made pigeonhole."[512]

In 8:20 "the Son of Man" occurs in a context that stresses Jesus' humanity. The scribe would have understood Jesus to mean that if he followed Jesus, he could anticipate a humble, even uncomfortable, existence. He should also have understood, since he was a teacher of the Old Testament, that Jesus was claiming to be Israel's Messiah.

Anyone who wants to follow Jesus closely as a disciple must be willing to give up many of the normal comforts of life. Following Him involves embarking on a God-given mission in life. Going where He directs, and doing what He commands, must take precedence over enjoying the normal comforts of life whenever these conflict. Discipleship is difficult.

Jesus' demands regarding parents 8:21-22

The first potential disciple was too quick and presumptuous when he promised wholehearted allegiance. This second potential disciple was too hesitant in committing to wholehearted allegiance.

Evidently this disciple made his request as Jesus prepared to depart for the next place of ministry (v. 18). He apparently meant that he wanted some time off from following Jesus in order to attend to family matters. Some students of this passage have concluded that the disciple's father had not yet died, and that he was asking for an indefinite leave of absence from Jesus' company.[513] Others believe that he had already died.[514] In either case, the disciple wanted to drop out temporarily.

Jesus' reply urged the disciple to keep following Him, and not to suspend his commitment to Jesus. He should put his commitment to Jesus even before his commitment to honor his parents (Exod. 20:12). When following Jesus and other commitments *conflict*, the disciple must always follow Jesus even though his or her other commitments are legitimate. Jesus was testing this man's priorities. Which was more important to him: following Jesus and participating in whatever Jesus' will for him might involve, or abandoning Jesus—even temporarily—for some less important purpose? His was not a choice between something good and something evil, but between something good and something better (cf. 10:37).

Jesus continued by encouraging the disciple to let "the dead . . . bury their own dead." Apparently He meant, let the spiritually dead (i.e., those who have no interest in following Jesus) bury the physically dead. There are many worthy activities in life that a true disciple of Jesus must forgo because he or she has a higher calling and higher demands on him or her. Forgoing these activities may bring criticism on the disciple from the spiritually insensitive, but that is part of the price of discipleship (cf. 7:13-27). Jesus called for commitment to Himself without reservation. The person and mission of the King deserve nothing less.

[510]John Bowker, "The Son of Man," *Journal of Theological Studies* 28 (1977):19-48.

[511]Kingsbury, *Matthew as . . .*, p. 103. This author wrote a lucid chapter on "Jesus' Use of 'the Son of Man,'" pp. 95-103.

[512]France, *The Gospel . . .*, p. 327.

[513]E.g., T. M. Donn, "'Let the Dead Bury Their Dead' (Mt. viii. 22, Lk. ix. 60)," *Expository Times* 61 (September 1950):384; *The Nelson . . .*, p. 1589; et al.

[514]Edersheim, *The Life . . .*, 2:133.

"It is better to preach the Gospel and give life to the spiritually dead than to wait for your father to die and bury him."[515]

"A disciple's business is with life, not with death."[516]

Christians must be willing to forsake all things and all people to follow Jesus faithfully. Jesus did not mean that we must give away all our possessions and break contact with our families. He meant that when we have to choose between following Him, and retaining our possessions or putting our families first, our allegiance to Him and His will must be primary. When these conflict, we must put Him first.

3. Jesus' supernatural power 8:23—9:8

Matthew's first group of miracles (vv. 1-17) demonstrated that Jesus possessed the messianic power (authority) to heal physical ailments. His second group (8:23—9:8) shows even greater powers over the fallen creation, namely, over nature, demons, and sin. All the beneficiaries of these miracles needed peace, and Jesus met their need.

"The miracles Jesus performs in Matthew's story divide themselves rather neatly into two groups: *(a)* therapeutic miracles (miracles of healing), in which the sick are returned to health or the possessed are freed of demons (cf. esp. chaps. 8—9); and *(b)* nontherapeutic miracles, which have to do with exercising power over the forces of nature. . . .

"The nontherapeutic miracles are less uniform in structure and differ in thematic [purpose from the therapeutic miracles]. Here the focus is on Jesus and the disciples, and the characteristic feature is that Jesus reveals, in the midst of situations in which the disciples exhibit 'little faith,' his awesome authority. . . . The reason Jesus gives the disciples these startling revelations is to bring them to realize that such authority as he exercises he makes available to them through the avenue of faith. In the later situation of their worldwide mission, failure on the part of the disciples to avail themselves of the authority Jesus would impart to them will be to run the risk of failing at their tasks (28:18-20; chaps. 24—25)."[517]

Jesus' stilling of a storm 8:23-27 (cf. Mark 4:36-41; Luke 8:22-25)

Even though Jesus sometimes enjoyed less shelter than the animals and birds (v. 20), He was not subject to nature. It was subject to Him.

8:23-25   It is difficult to know how much Matthew may have intended to convey with his comment that the "disciples followed" Jesus "into the boat." Perhaps it just describes their physical movements. Perhaps he meant that it symbolizes the disciples' proper response to Jesus in view of verses 18-22.

The Sea of Galilee was, and still is, infamous for its sudden and violent storms (Gr. *seismos*). They occur because of geographical conditions. The water is 600 feet below sea level, and the land to the east is considerably higher. As warm air rises from the lake it creates a vacuum that the air on the west rushes in to fill. This brings strong winds on the lake with little warning.

On the occasion Matthew described, the waves were so high that they kept spilling over into the boat. Evidently Jesus was asleep from weariness and because He realized that the time for His death had not yet arrived. He apparently lay in an area of the boat where the disciples had given Him some privacy. The word Matthew used to describe the boat (*ploion*) could fit a boat of many different sizes. However, it is probable that this was a fishing boat that carried at least a dozen or more people, plus fish, across the lake. Matthew probably would have used a different word if it were a larger boat.

"If the first-century-A.D. boat recovered from the mud of the northwest shore of the lake of Galilee in 1986 (now preserved in the Yigal Allon Center at Ginosar) is typical of the normal working boats of the period, its dimensions (8.20 meters long by 2.35 wide [about 26 and a half feet by 7 and a half feet]) would suggest that the boat might be overcrowded with more than thirteen people."[518]

In spite of the storm, Jesus continued to sleep. Finally, the disciples realized their inability to cope with their situation and called on Jesus to help ("save") them. They obviously thought He could do something to help, at least bail or at most perform a miracle. They had seen Him perform many miracles. However, their reaction to His help reveals that they did not really appreciate who He was.

[515]Wiersbe, 1:34.

[516]France, *The Gospel* . . ., p. 330.

[517]Kingsbury, *Matthew as* . . ., p. 69.

[518]France, *The Gospel* . . ., p. 336.

Compare the story of Jonah, who also had to be awakened during a storm at sea. However, rather than praying for God's help, as the sailors called on Jonah to do, Jesus used His own authority to still the sea. A greater than Jonah was here (12:41).

8:26-27   Jesus did not rebuke His disciples for disturbing Him but for failing to trust Him as they should have. He said they had "little faith" (Gr. *oligopistos*). Wherever Matthew used this word in his Gospel, it always reflects a failure to see below the surface of things.[519] Faith in Messiah and fear are mutually exclusive. Therefore the disciples should not have been "timid" (NASB) or "afraid" (NIV). Even though the disciples believed Jesus could help them, they did not grasp that He was the Messiah who would die a sacrificial death for their sins. How could the divine Messiah whom God had sent die in a storm before He had finished His messianic work? It was impossible.

> "The life of discipleship is susceptible to bouts of little faith. Such little faith is not to be condoned. Nevertheless, Jesus does not abandon his disciples at such times but stands ever ready with his saving power to sustain them so they can in fact discharge the mission he has entrusted to them."[520]

The disciples expected help, but they were unprepared for the kind of deliverance Jesus provided. It was a much greater salvation than they hoped for. "The sea . . . became perfectly calm."

> "His disciples who were seasoned fishermen had been through storms on this sea that had suddenly ceased. But after the wind would pass, the waves would continue to chop for a while."[521]

Jesus' ability to calm the wind and water with a word made it clear that He had greater powers than these disciples had witnessed previously. This is the first nature miracle that Matthew recorded Jesus doing. "What kind of a man is this?" they asked." Who was He? The reader of Matthew's Gospel knows better than the disciples did. He is the virgin-born Messiah, God with us, come to provide salvation and to set up His kingdom. While the disciples were "men" (v. 27), Jesus was a different type of man, the God-man.[522] Psalms 65:5-6; 89:8-9; 104:7; and 107:23-30 attribute the stilling of seas to God (cf. Jon. 1-2). Psalm 89:25 predicted that the ideal king would be able to do this.

The Israelites viewed the sea as an enemy they could not control. Throughout the Old Testament it epitomizes what is wild, hostile, and foreboding. It stood for their foes in some of their literature. Jesus' miracle also taught this secondary lesson. Here was a man exercising dominion over the sea, which God had appointed to man before the Fall (Gen. 1:28). Jesus must be the Second Adam (cf. Rom. 5:12-17).

> "The incident is related, not primarily for the sake of recording a miracle, but as an instance of the subduing of the power of evil, which was one of the signs of the nearness of the Kingdom; see xii. 28."[523]

In this incident, Matthew again presented Jesus as man and God. As man, He slept in the boat. As God, he calmed the sea (cf. 4:1-4; 12:22-32). As man, He suffers; but as God, He rules. The pericope indicates Jesus' power to fulfill the prophecies of Isaiah 30:23-24; 35:1-7; 41:17-18; 51:3; 55:13; Joel 3:18; Ezekiel 36:29-38; and Zechariah 10:1. He has all power over nature.

Jesus' deliverance of a demoniac in Gadara 8:28-34 (cf. Mark 5:1-20; Luke 8:26-39)

The central theme of this incident is Jesus' authority over evil spirits. Though Matthew previously mentioned Jesus' reputation as an exorcist (4:24; 8:16), this is the first of five exorcisms that he narrated (cf. 9:32-33; 12:22; 15:21-28; 17:14-20).

8:28   Gadara was the regional capital of the Decapolis area that lay southeast of the Sea of Galilee. Its population was strongly Gentile. This may account for the presence of "many swine" there (v. 30). The Gadara region stretched west to the Sea of Galilee. This was "the country of the Gadarenes." Other, less probable locations, are the village of "Kheras," near the eastern shore of the Sea of Galilee, and "Gerasa," about 30 miles southeast of the Sea.

Mark and Luke mentioned only one man, but Matthew said there were "two" (Mark 5:2; Luke 8:27). Mark and Luke evidently mentioned the more prominent one. Perhaps Matthew mentioned both of them because the testimony of two witnesses was valid in Jewish courts, and he wrote for Jews originally.

---

[519]Carson, "Matthew," p. 216.

[520]Kingsbury, *Matthew as . . .*, p. 135.

[521]Barbieri, p. 39.

[522]Plummer, p. 131.

[523]M'Neile, p. 111.

The Jews believed that demonic spirits could and did take over the bodies and personalities of certain individuals. Matthew reflected this view of the spirit world. A literal reading of Scripture leads to the same conclusion.[524] Demons are fallen angels who are Satan's agents.

These demoniacs lived lives of terror among tombs, away from other people, in a place that rendered them ritually unclean in Judaism.

8:29   The demoniacs hated and feared Jesus. They recognized Him as Messiah, calling Him by the messianic title "Son of God" (cf. 3:17; 16:16; Luke 4:41). The disciples in the boat did not know who He was, but the demoniacs taught them. The demoniacs may have known Jesus from some previous contact (cf. Acts 19:15), or perhaps the demons had asked the first question through the demoniacs (cf. v. 31).

Their second question revealed their knowledge that Jesus would judge them one day. This was a messianic function. Evidently Jesus will cast them into the lake of fire when He sends Satan there (Rev. 20:10).[525] When Jesus cast out demons, He was exercising this eschatological prerogative early. These demons asked if He planned to judge ("torment") them right then and there. He had cast out other demons recently (4:24; 8:16). "Here" probably refers to the earth, where demons have a measure of freedom to operate, rather than to that particular locale.

8:30-31   The presence of so many pigs may have been due to Jewish disobedience to the Mosaic Law, since for Jews pigs where unclean. However, this is unlikely, since the Jewish leaders were very particular about such flagrant violations of the Law. Probably they belonged to Gentiles, who lived in large numbers in the Decapolis where this story took place.

The demons may have requested asylum in the swine because they hated the creatures and or because they wanted to stir up trouble for Jesus. Demons do not like to be homeless (12:43-45). Exorcized evil spirits sometimes expressed their rage with acts of violence and vengefulness (cf. 17:14-20). What happened to the demons? Matthew did not tell us. Probably he wanted to impress us with Jesus' power over them, not detract us by making them the central feature of the incident. Perhaps they went to the lake of fire.

"We can construct a 'statement of faith' from the words of the demons. (Demons do have faith; see James 2:19.) They believed in the existence of God and the deity of Christ, as well as the reality of future judgment. They also believed in prayer. They knew Christ had the power to send them into the swine."[526]

8:32-34   Why did Jesus allow the demons to enter the swine, destroy the herd, and cause the owners considerable loss? Some commentators solve this puzzle by saying the owners were disobedient Jews whom Jesus judged. That is possible, but the answers to these questions were outside Matthew's field of interest. They are probably part of the larger scheme of things involving why God allows evil. As God, Jesus owned everything and could do with His own as He pleased. These details do, however, clarify the reality of the exorcism and the destructive effect of the demons.

We can observe from the reaction of the citizens that "they preferred pigs to persons, swine to the Savior."[527] They valued the material above the spiritual. This is the first instance in Matthew of open opposition to the Messiah. Matthew will show it building from here to the Cross. The pigs' stampede also testified to Jesus' deliverance of the demoniacs.

"This dramatic incident is most revealing. It shows what *Satan* does for a man: robs him of sanity and self-control; fills him with fears; robs him of the joys of home and friends; and (if possible) condemns him to an eternity of judgment. It also reveals what *society* does for a man in need: restrains him, isolates him, threatens him, but society is unable to change him. See, then, what Jesus Christ can do for a man whose whole life—within and without—is bondage and battle. What Jesus did for these two demoniacs, He will do for anyone else who needs Him."[528]

This incident shows Jesus fulfilling such kingdom prophecies as Daniel 7:25-27; 8:23-25; 11:36—12:3; and Zechariah 3:1-2. As Messiah, He is the Judge of the spirit world as well as humankind, the supernatural world as well as the natural world. He has all power over demons as well as nature (vv. 23-27). This is a story about power, not about mission.

---

[524]See Edersheim, *The Life . . .*, appendix 16, for differences between Jewish and New Testament views of demon possession.

[525]Walvoord, *Matthew: . . .*, p. 67.

[526]Wiersbe, 1:34.

[527]Carson, "Matthew," p. 219.

[528]Wiersbe, 1:34.

Jesus' healing and forgiveness of a paralytic 9:1-8 (cf. Mark 2:1-12; Luke 5:17-26)

The incident that follows occurred before the one in 8:28-34. Matthew placed it in his Gospel here for thematic reasons. It is another evidence of Jesus' supernatural power, but in a different realm.

9:1   Jesus arrived back in Capernaum ("His own city"), having traveled there by boat. This is another transitional verse that sets the stage for what follows.

9:2   Jesus saw the faith of the men who were carrying their "paralytic" friend.

"The reason the reader is provided with inside views of characters is to shape his or her attitude toward them."[529]

The evidence of their "faith" was that they "brought" him to Jesus for healing. However, Jesus spoke only to the paralytic. The term "son" (Gr. *teknon*) is an affectionate one that older people often used when speaking to the younger. What Jesus said implied a close connection between this man's sin and his sickness (cf. 8:17; Ps. 103:3; Isa. 33:24), and He implied that sin was the worse condition. Forgiveness of sins is basic to healing. Jesus told him that his sins were forgiven (right at that moment), not previously. He used the present tense that here has punctiliar force.[530] Punctiliar action is action that is regarded as happening at a particular point in time.

9:3   Some of the teachers of the law ("scribes") who were standing by took offense at what Jesus said. He was claiming to forgive sins, but God alone can forgive sins, since He is the One people sin against (Ps. 51:4; Isa. 43:25; 44:22). They called Jesus' words blasphemy because they viewed them as a slanderous affront to God. This is the first instance of this charge in Matthew, but it will become a prominent theme.

9:4   Jesus probably knew what they were thinking simply because He knew them, though some interpret this statement as expressing divine insight. Jesus did not need supernatural power to perceive the typical attitude of the scribes. What they were "thinking" was "evil" because it involved a denial of His messiahship, the very thing His words were claiming.

9:5-7   Jesus' question in verse 5 was rhetorical. His critics believed it was easier to say, "Get up and walk," because only God can forgive sins. Jesus had claimed to do the more difficult thing from their viewpoint, namely, to forgive sins. Jesus responded ironically in verse 6. He would do the easier thing. From the scribes' perspective, since Jesus had blasphemed God, He could not heal the paralytic, since God does not respond to sinners (John 9:31). By healing the paralytic, Jesus showed that He had not blasphemed God. He *could indeed* forgive sins.

Jesus again used the term "Son of Man" for Himself (v. 6). His critics should have sensed the messianic claim that Jesus' use of this title implied, since they knew the Old Testament well. The Judge had come to earth with authority to forgive sins (cf. 1:21, 23).[531]

Finally, Jesus not only healed the paralytic, but also assured him that God had forgiven his sins. He also refuted the scribes' charge of blasphemy.

9:8   The response of the observing crowd was appropriate in view of Jesus' action. People should respect and admire the One who can forgive sins. Here was a manifestation of God before them. They "glorified God" because they saw a man exercising divine authority. Unfortunately they failed to perceive that Jesus was their divine Messiah.

Readers of Matthew's Gospel, however, perceive that this was the promised King come to rule "on earth" (cf. v. 6). The King had come to save His people from their sins. The kingdom of David's Son was at hand.

"This is one of the most significant signs Jesus performs relative to the kingdom program. It shows that He is capable of forgiving sins *on earth*."[532]

---

[529]Kingsbury, *Matthew as . . .*, p. 37.

[530]Ernest de Witt Burton, *Syntax of the Moods and Tenses in NT Greek*, p. 9; Turner, p. 64.

[531]See Morna D. Hooker, *The Son of Man in Mark*, pp. 81-93.

[532]Toussaint, *Behold the . . .*, p. 129.

This miracle proves that Jesus could forgive sins and so produce the conditions prophesied in Isaiah 33:24; 40:1-2; 44:21-22; and 60:20-21. He has power over the spiritual world, as well as the supernatural world and the natural world. The three miracles in this section (8:23—9:8) show that Jesus could establish the kingdom because He had the authority to do so. He demonstrated authority over nature, the angelic world, and sin.

4. Jesus' authority over His critics 9:9-17

Matthew returned to the subject of Jesus' authority over people (cf. 8:18-22). In 8:18-22, Jesus directed those who came to Him voluntarily as disciples. Here, He explained the basis for His conduct to those who criticized Him. This is another section that contains discipleship lessons. In the former section, Jesus dealt with their persons, but in this one He dealt with their work.

The question of company 9:9-13 (cf. Mark 2:13-17; Luke 5:27-32)

The main point of this pericope is: Jesus' *response* to the Pharisees' criticism that Jesus and His disciples kept company with tax collectors and sinners.

9:9   This incident probably took place in or near Capernaum. The tax office (NASB), or the "tax collector's booth" (NIV), would have been a room close to the border between the territories of Philip and Herod Antipas. There Matthew sat to collect customs and excise taxes. Capernaum stood on the caravan route between Egypt and the East. Matthew thus occupied a lucrative post.

"It was the very busiest road in Palestine, on which the publican Levi Matthew sat at the receipt of 'custom,' when our Lord called him to the fellowship of the Gospel . . ."[533]

As mentioned before, the Jews despised tax collectors because they were notoriously corrupt, and they worked for the occupying Romans—extracting money from their own countrymen (cf. 5:46).[534]

Jesus proceeded to do the unthinkable. He called a social pariah to become one of His disciples. Matthew was a sinner and an associate of sinners in the eyes of the Jews.

"The pericope on the call of Matthew (9:9) illustrates yet another aspect of discipleship, to wit: the broad spectrum of those whom Jesus summons to follow him. . . . Matthew . . . is a toll-collector. As such, he is looked upon by the Jewish society of Matthew's story as no better than a robber and one whose testimony would not be honored in a Jewish court of law. . . . Not only the upright are called by Jesus, but also the despised."[535]

"The eye of Jesus was single as well as omniscient: He looked on the heart, and had respect solely to spiritual fitness."[536]

"Since Jesus' mission is predicated upon mercy and not merit, no one is despicable enough by the standards of society to be outside his concern and invitation."[537]

Jews frequently had two names, and Matthew's other name was *Levi* (Mark 2:14; Luke 5:27). "Matthew" may derive from Mattaniah (1 Chron. 9:15), meaning "gift of God," or it may come from the Hebrew *emet* meaning "faithful." Perhaps because of its meaning Matthew preferred to use "Matthew" in his Gospel rather than "Levi." Matthew's response to Jesus' call to follow Him was immediate.

9:10-11   Matthew's own account of the feast that he threw for Jesus that followed his calling is brief, and it focuses on the controversy with the Pharisees that occurred then. Matthew had friends who were also "tax collectors" (cf. 5:46). "Sinners" is a term the Pharisees used to describe people who broke their severe rules of conduct (Pharisaic Halakoth). "Eating with" these people put "Jesus and His disciples" in danger of ceremonial defilement, but the spiritual need of these people was more important to Jesus than ritual cleanliness.

[533]Edersheim, *Sketches of . . .*, p. 42.

[534]W. H. Griffith Thomas, *Outline Studies of the Gospel of Matthew*, p. 129.

[535]Kingsbury, *Matthew as . . .*, p. 135.

[536]Bruce, *The Training . .*, p. 19.

[537]Hagner, p. 240.

"In the ancient world generally a shared meal was a clear sign of identification, and for a Jewish religious teacher to share a meal with such people was scandalous, let alone to do so in the 'unclean' house of a tax collector."[538]

The Pharisees' question, addressed to Jesus' disciples, was really a subtle accusation against Him (v. 11). A teacher would normally keep all the religious traditions, as well as the Mosaic Law, to provide the best example for his disciples. The Pharisees despised Jesus for the company He kept, which implied that He had a lax view of the Law. Note that the Pharisees now become critics of Jesus, as the scribes had earlier (v. 3). Opposition mounts.

9:12-13   Jesus Himself responded to the Pharisees' question. He said that He went to the tax collectors and sinners because they were sinners. They had a spiritual illness and needed spiritual healing. Note that Jesus did not go to these people because they received Him warmly, but because they needed Him greatly. In the Old Testament, God taught His people that He was their "Physician" who could heal their diseases (e.g., Exod. 15:26; Deut. 32:39; 2 Kings 20:5; Ps. 103:3). The prophets also predicted that Messiah would bring healing to the nation (Isa. 19:22; 30:26; Jer. 30:17).

The phrase "go and learn" was a rabbinic one that indicated that the Pharisees needed to study the text further.[539] Jesus referred them to Hosea 6:6. God had revealed through Hosea, that the apostates of his day had lost the heart of temple worship, even though they continued to practice its rituals. Jesus implied that the Pharisees had done the same thing. They were preserving the external practices of worship carefully, but they had failed to maintain its essential heart. Their attitude toward the tax collectors and sinners showed this. God, on the other hand, cares more for the spiritual wholeness of people than He does about flawless worship.

Jesus did not mean that the tax collectors and sinners needed Him but the Pharisees did not. His quotation put the Pharisees in the same category as the apostates of Hosea's day. They needed Him, too, even though they believed they were righteous enough (cf. Phil 3:6).

The last part of verse 13 defines Jesus' ministry of preparing people for the coming kingdom. "Compassion" (NASB) or "mercy" (NIV, Heb. *hesed*) was what characterized His mission. He came to "call" (Gr. *kalesai*) or "invite" people to repentance and salvation. Paul's used this Greek work in the sense of efficacious calling, but that is not how Jesus used it. If someone does not see himself or herself as a sinner, that person will have no part in the kingdom.

Disciples of Jesus should be need-oriented, as Jesus was. Meeting the needs of needy individuals, regardless of who they may be, was very important to Jesus. Christians should give priority to the needs of people over forms of worship.

The question of fasting 9:14-17 (cf. Mark 2:18-22; Luke 5:33-39)

The Pharisees criticized Jesus' conduct in the previous pericope. Now John's disciples criticized the conduct of Jesus' disciples and, by implication, Jesus.

9:14   The people who questioned Jesus here were "disciples of John" (the Baptist) who had not left John to follow Jesus. They, as well as the Pharisees, observed the regular fasts that the Mosaic Law did not require. During the Exile—and subsequently—the Jews had made several of these fasts customary (cf. Zech. 7). The strict Pharisees even fasted twice a week—on Thursdays and Mondays—during the weeks between Passover and Pentecost, and between the Feast of Tabernacles and the Feast of Dedication. They believed that on a Thursday Moses had gone up into Mount Sinai, and that on a Monday he had come down, after receiving the Law the second time.[540]

9:15   Jesus responded with three illustrations. John the Baptist had described himself as the "best man" and Jesus as the "bridegroom" (John 3:29). Jesus extended John's figure and described His disciples as the "friends" (attendants, NASB) of the bridegroom." They were so joyful that they could not fast because they were with Him.[541]

The Old Testament used the groom figure to describe God (Ps. 45; Isa. 54:5-6; 62:4-5; Hos. 2:16-20). The Jews also used it of Messiah's coming and the messianic banquet (22:2; 25:1; 2 Cor. 11:2; Eph. 5:23-32; Rev. 19:7, 9; 21:2). When Jesus applied this figure to Himself, He was claiming to be the Messiah, and He was claiming that the kingdom banquet was imminent.

"As the *Physician*, He came to bring spiritual health to sick sinners. As the *Bridegroom*, He came to give spiritual joy."[542]

---

[538]France, *The Gospel . . .*, p. 353.

[539]Carson, "Matthew," p. 225.

[540]Edersheim, *The Temple*, p. 197.

[541]See Richard D. Patterson, "Metaphors of Marriage as Expressions of Divine-Human Relations," *Journal of the Evangelical Theological Society* 51:4 (December 2008):689-702.

When Jesus returned to heaven following His ascension, His friends did indeed "fast" (Acts 13:3; 14:23; 27:9). This is the first hint that Jesus would be "taken away" (a violent and unwanted removal) from His disciples, but that theme will become more dominant soon (cf. 16:21).

9:16-17   The meaning of the second illustration is clear enough (v. 16). The third may need some comment (v. 17). Old wine containers made out of animal skins eventually became hard and brittle. "New wine," that continued to expand as it fermented, would "burst" the inflexible "old wineskins." "New (fresh) wineskins" were still elastic enough to stretch with the expanding new wine.

The point of these two illustrations was that Jesus could not patch or pour His new ministry into old Judaism. The Greek word translated "old" (vv. 16, 17) is *palaios* and means not only old but worn out by use. Judaism had become inflexible due to the accumulation of centuries of non-biblical traditions. Jesus was going to bring in a kingdom that did not fit the preconceptions of most of His contemporaries. They misunderstood and misapplied the Old Testament, and particularly the messianic and kingdom prophecies. Jesus' ministry did not fit into the traditional ideas of Judaism. Moreover, it was wrong to expect that His disciples would fit into these molds. Jesus used two different Greek words for "new" in verse 17. *Neos* means recent in time, and *kainos* means a new kind. The messianic kingdom would be new both in time and in kind.

In the second and third illustrations, which advance the revelation of the first, the old cloth and wineskins perish. Jesus' kingdom would terminate Judaism, which had served its purpose.

John the Baptist belonged to the old order. His disciples, therefore, should have left him and joined the Groom. Unless they did, they would not participate in the kingdom (cf. Acts 19:1-7).

"In his characteristic style Matthew here hints that another new age will be brought in if the kingdom comes or not. This may be the first intimation of the church age in Matthew's Gospel."[543]

The point of this incident in Matthew's story seems to be: Disciples of Jesus need to recognize that following Him will involve new methods of serving God. The old Jewish forms passed away with the coming of Jesus, and His disciples now serve under a new covenant with new structures and styles of ministry, compared to the old order. This is a dispensational distinction that even non-dispensationalists recognize.

5. Jesus' ability to restore 9:18-34

The two groups of miracles that Matthew presented so far demonstrated Jesus' ability to heal (8:1-17), and His authority to perform miracles with supernatural power (8:23—9:8). This last cluster demonstrates His ability to restore. These miracles show that Jesus can restore all things, as the prophets predicted the Son of David would do. Furthermore, He can do this in spite of opposition.

The raising of Jairus' daughter and the healing of a woman with a hemorrhage 9:18-26 (cf. Mark 5:21-43; Luke 8:40-56)

9:18-19   This incident evidently happened shortly after Jesus and His disciples returned from Gadara on the east side of the lake (cf. Mark 5:21-22; Luke 8:40-41). The name of this Capernaum synagogue ruler was Jairus (Mark 5:22). He was a Jew who enjoyed considerable prestige in his community. It is noteworthy that someone of his standing believed in Jesus. This ruler humbly knelt before Jesus with a request (cf. 2:2; 8:2). According to Matthew, he announced that his "daughter" had "just died." Mark and Luke have him saying that she was near death. Since she died before Jesus reached her, Matthew evidently condensed the story to present at the outset what was true before Jesus reached his house.[544]

The ruler had probably seen or heard of Jesus' acts of healing with a touch (e.g., 8:2, 15). However, his faith was not as strong as the centurion's who believed that Jesus could heal with a word (8:5-13). Jesus arose from reclining at the table and proceeded to follow the ruler to his house. Here is another instance where the verb *akoloutheo*, "to follow," does not imply discipleship (cf. 8:23). Context must determine its meaning, not the word itself.

9:20-21   A "hemorrhage" is an uncontrolled bleeding. This woman had suffered with one somewhere in her body for 12 years. Many commentators assume it had some connection with her reproductive system. In any case, bleeding rendered a Jewish person ritually unclean (cf. Lev. 15:19-33). She should have kept away from other people, and not touched them, since by doing so she made them unclean. However, hope of healing led her to push her way through the crowd so that she might "touch" Jesus ("His garment"). She apparently believed that since Jesus' touch healed people, if she touched Him she would get the same

[542]Wiersbe, 1:35.
[543]Toussaint, *Behold the . . .*, p. 132.
[544]Carson, "Matthew," p. 230.

result. "The fringe of" Jesus' "cloak" (v. 20) was probably one of the four tassels that the Jews wore on the four corners of their cloaks to remind them to obey God's commands (Num. 15:37-41; Deut. 22:12; cf. Matt. 23:5).

9:22   Jesus encouraged the woman and commended her "faith" (i.e., her trust in Him). It was her faith that was significant; it "made" her "well." Her touching Jesus' garment simply expressed her faith. Faith in Jesus is one of the themes Matthew stressed in his Gospel. It is not the strength of one's faith that saves him or her, but faith in a *strong Savior*.

The Greek word translated "made you well" or "healed you" is *sozo*, which the translators often rendered as "save." The context here clarifies that Jesus was talking about the woman's faith resulting in her physical deliverance, not necessarily in her eternal salvation. Salvation is a broad concept in the Old and New Testaments. The context determines what aspect of deliverance is in view in every use of the verb *sozo* and the noun *soteria*, "salvation."[545]

"The association of the language of 'salvation' with faith perhaps also allows Matthew's readers, if so inclined, to find in this story a parable of spiritual salvation."[546]

Why did Matthew include this miracle within the account of the healing of Jairus' daughter? I suspect the answer is the common theme of life. The woman's life was gradually ebbing away. Her hemorrhage symbolized this, since blood represents life (cf. Lev. 17:11). Jesus stopped her dying and restored her life. His instantaneous healing contrasts with her long-term illness. In the case of Jairus' daughter, who was already dead, Jesus restored her, as well, to life. Both incidents show His power over death.

9:23-26   Perhaps Matthew, of all the Gospel writers who recorded this incident, mentioned the "flute players," because he wanted to stress Jesus' complete reversal of this situation. Even the poorest Jews hired flute players to play at funerals.[547] Their funerals were also occasions of almost unrestrained wailing and despair ("noisy disorder"), which verse 23 reflects.

The "crowd" ridiculed Jesus by "laughing" at His statement (v. 24). They thought He was both wrong and late in arriving, too late. They apparently thought He was trying to cover up His mistake and would soon make a fool of Himself by exposing His only limited healing power. However, "sleep" is a common euphemism for *death* (Dan. 12:2; John 11:11; Acts 7:60; 1 Cor. 15:6, 18; 1 Thess. 4:13-15; 2 Pet. 3:4), and it was also so in Jesus' day.[548]

Jesus touched another unclean person. His touch, rather than defiling Him, *restored life* to the girl. Other prophets and apostles also raised the dead (1 Kings 17:17-24; 2 Kings 4:17-37; Acts 9:36-42). However, Jesus claimed to be more than a prophet. This miracle showed He had supernatural power over man's last enemy: Death. The Old Testament prophets predicted that Messiah would restore life (Isa. 65:17-20; Dan. 12:2).

"The raising of the dead to life is a basic symbolism of the gospel (e.g., Rom 4:17; Eph 2:1, 5; Col 2:13). What Jesus did for the dead girl he has done for all in the Church who have experienced new life. There is too, beyond this life, the Church's confidence that Jesus will literally raise the dead (cf. 1 Thess 4:16; 1 Cor 15:22-23)."[549]

Matthew recorded that everyone heard about this incident (v. 26). Consequently many people faced the choice of believing that Jesus was the Messiah or rejecting Him.

"We must learn to trust Christ and His promises no matter how we feel, no matter what others say, and no matter how the circumstances may look."[550]

Jesus' power to bring life where there was death stands out in this double instance of restoration—two witnesses—for the benefit of Jewish readers especially.

"It is interesting that Jairus and this woman—two opposite people—met at the feet of Jesus. Jairus was a leading Jewish man; she was an anonymous woman with no prestige or resources. He was a synagogue leader, while her affliction kept her from worship. Jairus came pleading for his daughter; the woman came with a need of her own. The girl had been healthy for 12 years, and then died; the woman had been ill for 12 years and was now made whole. Jairus' need was public—all knew it; but

---

[545]For a very helpful discussion of key Old and New Testament passages containing these Greek words, see Dillow, pp. 111-33.

[546]France, *The Gospel . . .*, p. 361.

[547]Mishnah *Kethuboth* 4:4.

[548]Edersheim, *The Life . . .*, 1:630.

[549]Hagner, p. 250.

[550]Wiersbe, 1:35.

the woman's need was private—only Jesus understood. Both Jairus and the woman trusted Christ, and He met their needs."[551]

The healing of two blind men 9:27-31

Another instance of double restoration shows Jesus' ability to restore sight where there had been blindness.

9:27-28   This is the first time in Matthew's Gospel that someone called Jesus the "Son of David" (cf. 1:1; 12:23; 15:22; 20:30, 31; 21:9, 15). This was a messianic title, and the blind men's use of it undoubtedly expressed their belief that Jesus was the Messiah. The Gospel writers recorded that Jesus healed at least six blind men, and each case was different (cf. John 9; Mark 8:22-26; Matt. 20:29-34, Mark 10:46-52, and Luke 18:35-43). Blindness was a common ailment in Jesus' day, but the Gospel evangelists also used it to illustrate lack of spiritual perception.

> "The use of the Davidic title in address to Jesus is less extraordinary than some think: in Palestine, in the time of Jesus, there was an intense messianic expectation."[552]

Ironically, these "two" physically "blind men" saw who Jesus was more clearly than most of their seeing contemporaries. Isaiah had prophesied that Messiah would open the eyes of the blind (Isa. 29:18; 35:5-6). Frequently in the Synoptics, the desperately needy individuals cried out to Jesus, calling Him the "Son of David."[553] There seems to be a relationship between the depth of a person's felt need and his or her willingness to believe in Jesus.

Probably Jesus did not heal these men outdoors for at least two reasons. He had already done two miracles outdoors, before many witnesses that day, and may have wanted to keep the crowd under control (cf. v. 30). Second, by bringing the blind men indoors, He heightened their faith, since it involved waiting longer for a cure. Jesus' question furthered this aim (v. 28). It also clarified that their cries for help came from confidence in Him, rather than just out of desperation, and it focused their faith on Jesus specifically, and not only God generally.

9:29-31   Perhaps Jesus "touched" the "eyes" of the blind men, in order to help them associate Him with their healing, as well as because He was compassionate. However, it was primarily Jesus' word, not just His touch, that resulted in their healing (cf. Gen. 1). "According to your faith" does not mean "in proportion to your faith" but "because you believed" (cf. v. 22). This is the only time in the first Gospel that Matthew presented faith as a condition for healing.

Jesus "sternly warned" them against telling anyone about the miracle, probably because these blind men had identified Jesus as the Son of David. The verb *embrimaomai* occurs only five times in the New Testament (Mark 1:43; 14:5; John 11:33, 38). Jesus wanted to avoid the masses of people that would have dogged His steps and hindered Him from fulfilling His mission (cf. 8:4). He wanted people to hear about Him and face the issue of His messiahship, but too much publicity would be counterproductive. Unfortunately, but understandably, these beneficiaries of Messiah's grace disobeyed Him, and broadcast what He had done for them widely, "throughout all that land." They should have simply joined the band of disciples and continued to follow Jesus faithfully.

This incident shows that some people in Galilee, besides the Twelve, were concluding that Jesus was the Messiah.[554] The emphasis in the incident is on Jesus' ability to restore sight where once there was blindness.

The casting out of a spirit that caused dumbness 9:32-34

Not only could Jesus bring life out of death, and sight out of blindness, but He could also enable people to speak who could not previously do so. Each of these physical healings has metaphorical implications: eternal spiritual life, understanding and insight, and witness.

9:32-33   The Greek word translated "dumb" (NASB, *kophos*) refers to deaf people, mutes, and people who were both deaf and dumb. This man's condition was the result of demonic influence, though that was not the cause in all such cases (cf. Mark 7:32-33). The crowd's reaction here climaxes their reaction in this entire section of the text. Here was Someone with more power than anyone who had ever appeared before. Messiah would heal the dumb (Isa. 35:5-6). The natural conclusion was that Jesus was the Messiah.

---

[551]Ibid.

[552]Hill, p. 180.

[553]Dennis C. Duling, "The Therapeutic Son of David: An Element in Matthew's Christological Apologetic," *New Testament Studies* 24 (1978):392-410.

[554]Plummer, p. 143; Samuel J. Andrews, *The Life of Our Lord Upon the Earth*, p. 307.

9:34   The reaction of the Pharisees contrasts with that of the crowd in the sharpest possible terms. They attributed Jesus' power to Satan, not God. They concluded that He came from Satan rather than from God. Instead of being the Messiah, He must be a satanic counterfeit. Notice that the Pharisees did not deny the authenticity of Jesus' miracles. They could not do that. They accepted them as supernatural acts. However, they ascribed them to demonic rather than divine power.

This testimony to Jesus' authority comes at the end of a collection of stories about demonstrations of Jesus' power (8:1—9:34). Matthew probably intended the reader to understand that this was the common reaction to all these miracles.[555] This reaction continued, and culminated in the Pharisees' accusation in 12:24: "This man cast out demons only by Beelzebul the ruler of the demons."

This testimony contrasts, too, with the opinion of the Gentile centurion (8:5-13), who saw that Jesus' operated under God's authority. This is one evidence of a chiastic structure in chapters 8 and 9, which I shall comment on further below.

The incident illustrates Jesus' ability to enable people to speak who could not formerly do so. This was important in people confessing Jesus as the Son of God and the disciples bearing witness to Jesus. It also illustrates Jesus' compassion for needy people.

One of the main themes in this section (8:1—9:34) is the spreading of Jesus' fame. This resulted in an increasing number to people concluding that Jesus was the Messiah. It also resulted in increasing opposition from Jesus' enemies, Israel's religious leaders, and even some of John the Baptist's disciples. However, some religious leaders believed in Jesus, Jairus being one. Opposition to Jesus was mounting among those who suffered economically, because of His ministry, as well as those who suffered religiously. Matthew's primary purpose, however, was to present Jesus as the promised Messiah who could establish God's kingdom on earth.

All of this material also prepares the reader for the next events: Jesus' self-disclosure to His disciples in His second major discourse (ch. 10).

Chapters 8—9 seem to be a chiasm focusing the reader's attention on Jesus' power to overcome Satan (8:28-34).

A   Jesus' power to heal (8:1-17; three incidents and a summary [8:16-17])
    B   Jesus' authority over His disciples' persons (8:18-22; two lessons)
        C   Jesus' supernatural power (8:23—9:8; three incidents with victory over Satan in the middle)
    B'   Jesus' authority over His disciples' work (9:9-17; two lessons)
A'   Jesus' power to restore (9:18-38; three incidents and a summary [9:35-38])

B. DECLARATIONS OF THE KING'S PRESENCE 9:35—11:1

The heart of this section contains Jesus' charge to His disciples to proclaim the nearness of the kingdom (ch. 10): Jesus' Mission Discourse. Matthew prefaced this charge with a demonstration of the King's power, as he prefaced the Sermon on the Mount by authenticating the King's qualifications (cf. 4:23; 9:35). However, there are also some significant dissimilarities between these sections of the Gospel. Before the Sermon on the Mount, Jesus separated from the multitudes (5:1), but here He has compassion on them (9:36). Then He ministered to His disciples, but now He sends His disciples to minister to the multitudes in Israel. The Sermon on the Mount was basic to the disciples' understanding of the kingdom. This discourse is foundational to their proclaiming the kingdom. Jesus had already begun to deal with discipleship issues (chs. 5—7; 8:18-22; 9:9-17). Now He gave them more attention.

1. Jesus' compassion 9:35-38 (cf. Mark 6:6)

This section summarizes the previous incidents that deal primarily with healing, and prepares for Jesus' second discourse to His disciples. It is transitional, providing a bridge from the condition of the people that chapter 9 revealed, to what the King determined to do about that condition (cf. 4:23-25). Jesus' work was so extensive that He needed many more workers to assist Him.

9:35   This verse summarizes the heart of Jesus' ministry in Galilee. It also provides the rationale for the new phase of His ministry through the Twelve. At this time, there were about 240 cities and villages in Galilee.[556]

9:36   Until now, Matthew presented the crowds as those Galileans who listened to and observed Jesus with wonder. Now they become the objects of Jesus' concern. His "compassion for" the multitudes recalls Ezekiel's description of God's compassion for Israel (Ezek. 34). "Distressed" (NASB) really means "harassed" (NIV). It pictures the Jews bullied and oppressed by their religious leaders. They were "downcast" (NASB) because they were "helpless" (NIV). No one was able to deliver them. They

---

[555]France, *The Gospel . . .*, p. 369.

[556]Josephus, *The Life . . .*, par. 45.

lacked effective leadership, as "sheep without a shepherd" (cf. Num. 27:17; 1 Kings 22:17; 2 Chron. 18:16; Isa. 53:6; Ezek. 34:23-24; 37:24). The Old Testament describes both God and Messiah as Shepherds of their people (cf. 2:6; 10:6, 16; 15:24; 25:31-46; 26:31).

9:37-38   Jesus' figure of speech in addressing His disciples, however, was an agricultural one. He wanted to infuse His compassion for the multitudes into them. Jesus viewed Israel as a field composed of numerous stalks of grain. They needed gathering for safe-keeping in the barns of the kingdom. They would die where they were, and the nation would suffer ruin if "workers" did not bring them in soon. Unfortunately there were not enough workers to do this massive task. Consequently Jesus commanded His disciples to beseech God, the Lord of the harvest, to provide additional laborers for "His harvest."

The picture is of imminent change. A change was coming, whether or not the Israelites accepted their Messiah. It would either be beneficial or detrimental to the nation. An adequate number of workers was one factor that would determine the way the change would go. Evidently Matthew expected his readers to understand "disciples" as *all* who were in a learning relationship to Jesus, at that point in time, rather than just the Twelve. That is the way he used the term so far in this Gospel (cf. 10:1).

"In the early period of their discipleship hearing and seeing seem to have been the main occupation of the twelve."[557]

2. Jesus' commissioning of 12 disciples 10:1-4 (cf. Mark 6:7; Luke 9:1-2)

10:1   This is Matthew's first reference to Jesus' 12 disciples, though here He implied their previous identity as a group. He "summoned" (Gr. *proskaleo*) these men as a king commands His subjects. He who had all "authority" now delegated some of it to this select group of disciples. Perhaps Jesus chose 12 close disciples because Israel consisted of 12 tribes.

"As soon as he [Jesus] remarked that number, every Jew of any spiritual penetration must have scented 'a Messianic programme.'"[558]

If Israel had accepted Jesus, these 12 disciples probably would have become Israel's leaders in the messianic kingdom. As it turned out, they became leaders of the church.

Until now, there is no evidence that Jesus' disciples could cast out demons and heal the sick. This was new power He delegated to them for the mission on which He would shortly send them. This ability is a clear demonstration of Jesus' unique greatness.

"This was without a precedent in Jewish history. Not even Moses or Elijah had given miraculous powers to their disciples. Elijah had been allowed to transmit his powers to Elisha, but only when he himself was removed from the earth."[559]

10:2-4   The 12 special disciples now received the title "apostles." This noun, *apostolos* in Greek, comes from the verb *apostello* meaning "to send." This was not a technical term until Jesus made it such. It continued to refer generally to people sent out with the Christian message,, such as Barnabas (Acts 14:4, 14; Rom. 16:7; 1 Cor. 12:28-29; 2 Cor. 8:23; Phil. 2:25). It referred to any messenger (John 13:16) and even to Jesus (Heb. 3:1). Paul became an apostle who received his commission directly from the Lord, as the 12 special disciples had. This is the only place Matthew used the word "apostle." He probably used it here because Jesus proceeded to prepare to send these 12 men on a special mission to the Israelites (vv. 5-42).

[557]Bruce, *The Training* . . ., p. 41.

[558]Hunter, *The Message* . . ., p. 62.

[559]Plummer, p. 147.

Lists of the 12 Apostles occur in Mark 3:16-19; Luke 6:13-16; and Acts 1:13, as well as here. Comparing the four lists, we note that there appear to have been three groups of four disciples each. Peter, Philip, and James the son of Alphaeus seem to have been the leaders of these groups.

	Matt. 10:2-4	Mark 3:16-19	Luke 6:14-16	Acts 1:13
1.	Simon Peter	Simon Peter	Simon Peter	Peter
2.	Andrew	James	Andrew	John
3.	James	John	James	James
4.	John	Andrew	John	Andrew
5.	Philip	Philip	Philip	Philip
6.	Bartholomew	Bartholomew	Bartholomew	Thomas
7.	Thomas	Matthew	Matthew	Bartholomew
8.	Matthew	Thomas	Thomas	Matthew
9.	James, son of Alphaeus	James, son of Alphaeus	James, son of Alphaeus	James, son of Alphaeus
10.	Thaddaeus	Thaddaeus	Judas, son or brother of James	Judas, son or brother of James
11.	Simon the Cananaean	Simon the Cananaean	Simon the Zealot	Simon the Zealot
12.	Judas Iscariot	Judas Iscariot	Judas Iscariot	

Peter's name occurs first, here, as in all the other lists, probably because he was the "first among equals." Matthew may also have listed him first because he became the leading apostle to the Jews.[560] James' name occurs before his brother John's, probably because James was older. Matthew described himself humbly as "the tax-gatherer."

"Thaddaeus" and "Judas the son (or brother) of James," seem to be two names for the same man, and "Simon the Cananaean" seems to have been the same person as "Simon the Zealot." The Zealots constituted a political party in Israel, centered in Galilee, that sought to throw off the Roman yoke.[561] However, "Zealot" did not become a technical term for a member of this revolutionary group until the time of the Jewish Wars (A.D. 68-70).[562] So "Zealot" here probably refers to Simon's reputation for religious zeal.[563] "Cananaean" is the Aramaic form of "Zealot" and does not refer to the land of Canaan.

"Iscariot" may mean "of Kerioth," the name of two Palestinian villages, or "the dyer," his possible occupation. It may be a transliteration of the Latin *sicarius*, a Zealot-like movement.[564] Some scholars believe it means "false one" and comes from the Aramaic *seqar* meaning "falsehood."[565] The names "Andrew" and "Philip" are Greek and probably reflect the more Hellenistic flavor of their hometown, Bethsaida, on the east side of the Jordan River (John 1:44).

These men became Jesus' main agents in carrying out His mission, though "Judas," of course, proved to be a hypocritical disciple. Probably Matthew described the Twelve in pairs because they went out in pairs (Mark 6:7).[566]

---

[560]Toussaint, *Behold the . . .*, p. 138.

[561]See Edersheim, *The Life . . .*, 1:237.

[562]Cf. Josephus, *The Wars . . .*, 4:3:9, 13, 14; 4:4:5-7; 4:5:1, 5; and 7:8:1.

[563]France, *The Gospel . . .*, p. 378.

[564]Carson, "Matthew," p. 239, listed six possible meanings.

[565]Earle E. Ellis, *The Gospel of Luke*, p. 110; Marshall, p. 240.

[566]Tasker, p. 106.

3. Jesus' charge concerning His apostles' mission 10:5-42

Matthew proceeded to record Jesus' second major discourse in his Gospel: the Mission Discourse. It contains the instructions Jesus gave the 12 Apostles before He sent them out to proclaim the nearness of the messianic kingdom.

"If the Sermon on the Mount was appropriately delivered on the occasion when the apostolic company was formed, this discourse on the apostolic vocation was not less appropriate when the members of that company first put their hands to the work unto which they had been called."[567]

Kingsbury saw the theme of this speech as "the mission of the disciples to Israel" and outlined it as follows: (I) On Being Sent to the Lost Sheep of the House of Israel (10:5b-15); (II) On Responding to Persecution (10:16-23); and (III) On Bearing Witness Fearlessly (10:34-42).[568] Whereas there is much instruction on serving Jesus here, there is also quite a bit of emphasis on persecution.

"Before Jesus sent His ambassadors out to minister, He preached an 'ordination sermon' to encourage and prepare them. In this sermon, the King had something to say to *all* of His servants—past, present, and future. Unless we recognize this fact, the message of this chapter will seem hopelessly confused."[569]

"It is evidential of its authenticity, and deserves special notice, that this Discourse, while so un-Jewish in spirit, is more than any other, even more than that on the Mount, Jewish in its forms of thought and modes of expression."[570]

This observation suggests that this mission was uniquely Jewish. Yet, as in the Sermon on the Mount, Jesus spoke beyond His immediate audience with later disciples also in mind. This seems clear as we compare this instruction with later teaching on the conduct of Christ's disciples in the present age.

The scope of their mission 10:5-8

Jesus first explained the sphere and nature of the apostles' temporary ministry to Israel.

10:5-6   The apostles were to limit their ministry to the Jews living in Galilee. They were not to go north or east into Gentile territory, or south where the Samaritans predominated. The "Samaritans" were only partially Jewish by race. They were the descendants of the poorest of the Jews, whom the Assyrians left in the Promised Land when they took the Northern Kingdom into captivity, and the Gentiles whom the Assyrians imported. On religion, they only accepted the Pentateuch as authoritative. This is Matthew's only reference to the Samaritans.

The apostles were to go specifically to "the lost sheep of the house of Israel," a term that described all the Jews (Isa. 53:6; Jer. 50:6; Ezek. 34). The designation highlights the needy character of the Jews. Jesus sent them to the Jews exclusively to do three things. They would announce the appearance of a Jewish Messiah, announce a Jewish kingdom, and provide signs—to Jews who required them—as proof of divine authorization. Jesus did not need the additional opposition that would come from Gentiles and Samaritans. He would have to deal with enough of that from the Jews. His kingdom would be a universal one, but at this stage of His ministry, Jesus wanted to offer it to the Jews first. We have already noted that Jesus had restricted His ministry primarily, but not exclusively, to Jews (8:1-13). He was the King of the Jews.

10:7-8   The apostles were to herald the same message that John (3:2) and Jesus proclaimed (4:17, 23; 9:35). They were to be itinerant preachers, as these men had been.[571] The absence of "repent" here should not be a problem since, as we have pointed out, repentance was not a separate step in preparation but a way of describing adequate preparation.

"If the Jewish nation could be brought to repentance, the new age would dawn; see Ac. iii. 19f., Jo. iv. 22."[572]

"The kingdom of heaven" was "at hand," namely, imminent. It had not yet begun. The powers the apostles had would impress their Jewish hearers with God's authentication of their message (cf. 12:28). That was the purpose of signs throughout the Old and New Testaments.[573]

---

[567]Bruce, *The Training . . .*, p. 110.

[568]Kingsbury, *Matthew as . . .*, p. 112.

[569]Wiersbe, 1:36.

[570]Edersheim, *The Life . . .*, 1:641. See ibid., 1:641-53, for many parallels.

[571]Cf. Plummer, p. 149.

[572]M'Neile, p. 134.

[573]See Thomas R. Edgar, "The Cessation of the Sign Gifts," *Bibliotheca Sacra* 145:580 (October-December 1988):371-86.

Matthew had not mentioned raising the "dead" and cleansing "lepers" previously (v. 1). The disciples were to offer their services free of charge because the good news they had received had not cost them anything.

The provisions for their mission 10:9-15 (cf. Mark 6:8-11; Luke 9:3-5)

Jesus explained further how the 12 Apostles were to conduct themselves on their mission.

10:9-10   They were not to take enough money with them to sustain them while they ministered. "Acquire" (NASB, Gr. *ktesesthe*) can mean "take along" (NIV, Mark 6:9) or "procure" while they ministered (Acts 1:18; 8:20; 22:28). Probably Jesus did not want them to accumulate money as they ministered, or to take along enough money to sustain them. They were not to take an extra tunic ("two coats"), either. In other words, they were to travel lightly and to remain unencumbered by material possessions. As a general principle, those who minister spiritual things have a right to expect physical recompense in return (Deut. 25:4; 1 Cor. 9:4-18; 1 Tim. 5:17-18). That is the principle Jesus wanted to teach His disciples. Itinerant philosophers and teachers typically expected board, room, and a fee from their hearers.[574]

10:11-15   They were to stay with "worthy" hosts, not necessarily in the most convenient or luxurious accommodations. A worthy person would be one who welcomed a representative of Jesus and the kingdom message. He or she would be the opposite of the "dogs" and "pigs" Jesus earlier told His disciples to avoid (7:6). By this time, there were probably people in most Galilean villages who had been in the crowds and observed Jesus. His sympathizers would have been the most willing hosts for His disciples.

The "greeting" the disciple was to give his host was the normal greeting of the day ("Peace"). If his host proved to be unworthy by not continuing to welcome the disciple, he was to leave that house and stay somewhere else. By withdrawing personally, the disciple would withdraw a *blessing* from that house, namely, his presence as a representative of Jesus. The apostles were to do to towns as they did to households.

"A pious Jew, on leaving Gentile territory, might remove from his feet and clothes all dust of the pagan land now being left behind . . . thus dissociating himself from the pollution of those lands and the judgment in store for them. For the disciples to do this to Jewish homes and towns would be a symbolic way of saying that the emissaries of Messiah now view those places as pagan, polluted, and liable to judgment (cf. Acts 13:51; 18:6)."[575]

More awful "judgment" awaited the inhabitants of the Jewish towns that rejected Messiah, than the judgment coming on the wicked residents of "Sodom and Gomorrah," that had already experienced divine destruction (Gen. 19). This statement implies that there will be degrees of judgment and torment for the lost (cf. 11:22, 24). The unbelievers of Sodom and Gomorrah will receive their sentence at the great white throne judgment (Rev. 20:11-15). The unbelieving Jews of Jesus' day would also stand before Jesus then. One's eternal destiny then, as now, depended on his or her relationship to Jesus, and that was evident in his attitude toward one of His emissaries (cf. v. 40; 25:40, 45). In that culture, people treated a person's official representative as they would treat the one he represented. The apostles could anticipate opposition and rejection, as Jesus experienced, and as the Old Testament prophets had as well.

The perils of their mission 10:16-25

Jesus proceeded to elaborate on the dangers the apostles would face and how they should deal with them.

In His descriptions of the opposition His disciples would experience, Jesus looked beyond His death to the time of tribulation that would follow. Then, the disciples would have the same message—and the same power—as they did when He sent them out here. The narrow road leading to the kingdom led through a period of tribulation and persecution for the disciples. They did not understand that Jesus would have to die and experience resurrection before the kingdom began, even though this is what the Old Testament revealed. Jesus was beginning to prepare them and their successors for these events and the persecution they would experience as His followers. If Israel had accepted her Messiah, He still would have had to die, rise from the grave, and ascend into heaven. Seven years of tribulation would have followed. Then Jesus would have returned to the earth and set up His kingdom. As it happened, Israel rejected Jesus, so the period of Tribulation, His return, and the kingdom are all still future.

"The King performed His ministry according to the Old Testament Messianic calendar of events. According to the Hebrew Scriptures the Messiah, after He appeared, was to suffer, die, and be raised again (Daniel 9:26; Psalm 22; Isaiah 53:1-11;

---

[574]France, *The Gospel . . .*, p. 384.

[575]Carson, "Matthew," p. 246.

Psalm 16:10). Following the death and resurrection of Christ there was to be a time of trouble (Daniel 9:26-27; Jeremiah 30:4-6). The Messiah was then to return to the earth to end this tribulation and to judge the world (Daniel 7:9-13, 16-26; 9:27; 12:1; Zechariah 14:1-5). Finally, the Messiah as King would establish His kingdom with Israel as the head nation (Daniel 7:11-27; 12:1-2; Isaiah 53:11-12; Zechariah 14:6-11, 20-21)."[576]

Part of the tribulation that Jesus prepared His disciples for took place when the Romans destroyed Jerusalem and scattered the Jews all over the world, in A.D. 70. Yet the destruction of Jerusalem then was not the full extent of the tribulation the prophets foretold for Israel. This becomes clear as one compares the prophesied tribulation for the Jews with the events that surrounded the destruction of Jerusalem.

10:16   Jesus pictured His defenseless disciples in a dangerous environment. The Shepherd was sending His "sheep" into a wolf pack. They needed, therefore, to be as "shrewd as serpents," a proverbial way of saying *prudent*. People sometimes think of snakes as shrewd because they are silent, dangerous, and because of how they move. The disciples' shrewdness must not be cunning (sinister or dishonest) though, for they needed to be "innocent" as well. Either characteristic without the other is dangerous. Innocence without prudence becomes naiveté.

The disciples were to be both prudent and innocent toward the objects of their ministry. "Doves" are peaceful, retiring birds; they leave when other birds challenge or oppose them rather than fighting. This is how the disciples were to behave. They needed to be shrewd by avoiding conflicts and attacks where possible, but when these came they were to withdraw to other households and other towns. These figures were common in Rabbinic teaching. But the rabbis normally used the sheep and doves as figures of Israel, and the wolves and serpents as representing the Gentiles.[577]

10:17   "But" (Gr. *de*) does not introduce a contrast here; it shows how the disciples should apply the warning Jesus just gave them. Opposition would come from the Jews. The courts in view could be either civil or religious. This is the only occurrence of the plural "courts" or "local councils" (Gr. *synedria*) in the New Testament. The responsibility of these courts was to preserve the peace. The scourging in view would be the result of judicial action, not mob violence.[578]

10:18   This prediction has caused problems for many interpreters, since there is no indication that the disciples appeared before governors and kings during the mission that followed. As mentioned above, Jesus was evidently looking beyond their immediate mission, to what His disciples would experience after His death, resurrection, and ascension.[579]

10:19-20   Jesus promised that the Holy Spirit, called here "the Spirit of your Father," would enable the disciples to respond to their accusers. Some lazy preachers have misappropriated this promise, but it applies to disciples who must answer charges leveled against them for their testimonies. Jesus had not yet revealed the Spirit's relationship to these men after His departure into heaven (John 14—16). Here He simply assured them of the Spirit's help. Several of the apostles' speeches in Acts reflect this divine provision.

10:21-22   The disciples would find themselves opposed by everyone without distinction, including their own family members, not just rulers. In spite of such widespread and malicious persecution, the disciple must endure patiently to the end. "The end" refers to the end of this period of intense persecution, namely, the Tribulation (cf. 24:13). The Second Coming of the Son of Man will end it (v. 23). The promise of salvation ("will be saved") for "the one" who remains faithful (endures "to the end"), does not refer to eternal salvation, here, since that depends on faith alone in Jesus. It is *deliverance* from the period of intense persecution that is in view. Entrance into the millennial kingdom would constitute salvation for these future persecuted disciples.

Thus, this verse does not say that all genuine believers will inevitably persevere in their faith and good works.[580] Rather, it says that those who do during the Tribulation, can expect God to deliver them at its end. Jesus was not speaking about eternal salvation but temporal deliverance. Temporal deliverance depended on faithful perseverance. Whereas "the end" has specific reference to the end of the Tribulation in 24:13, here it probably has the more general meaning of "as long as may be necessary."

If the Jews had accepted Jesus, these 12 disciples would have taken the message of the kingdom throughout Israel during the Tribulation period that would have followed Jesus' death, resurrection, and ascension. Before they could finish their task, Jesus would have returned from heaven. Those of them who persevered faithfully would have experienced deliverance from

---

[576]Toussaint, *Behold the . . .*, p. 140.

[577]Edersheim, *The Life . . .*, 1:645.

[578]Douglas R. A. Hare, *The Theme of Jewish Persecution of Christians in the Gospel According to St. Matthew*, p. 104.

[579]Hagner, p. 262.

[580]E.g., John Murray, *Redemption—Accomplished and Applied*, p. 152; et al.

further persecution by entering the kingdom following His return. But since the Jews rejected Jesus, God postponed the kingdom for at least 2,000 years. During the Tribulation period yet future, the 144,000 Jewish disciples of Jesus living in Palestine—and elsewhere in the world—will be preparing people for Jesus' return to set up His kingdom (Rev. 7:1-8; 14:1-5). Those who remain faithful, and withstand persecution, will be saved from further persecution by Jesus' return to the earth to set up His kingdom.

"If those who fight under earthly commanders, and are uncertain as to the issue of the battle, are carried forward even to death by steadiness of purpose, shall those who are certain of victory hesitate to abide by the cause of Christ to the very last?"[581]

10:23   Jesus promised that He would return for His disciples before they had finished preaching the kingdom throughout "the cities of Israel." If Israel had accepted Jesus as her Messiah, this would have happened at the end of seven years of persecution following Jesus' death, resurrection, and ascension. Since Israel rejected her Messiah, it will happen at the end of the Tribulation, yet future from our perspective in history (Dan. 7:13). Obviously it did not happen after the destruction of Jerusalem in A.D. 70.

Commentators have offered many other explanations of this verse. There is great diversity of opinion concerning what Jesus meant, mainly because people have failed to take Jesus' offer of Himself—and the messianic kingdom—literally. Some interpreters believe that Jesus simply meant He would return to the Twelve before they completed the mission He sent them on in this passage. The problem with this view is that there is no indication in the text that that happened. Others interpret the "Son of Man *coming*" as a reference to the public identification of Jesus as the Messiah. However, that is not what Jesus said, and it is not what happened. Some believe Jesus made a mistake, and what He predicted did not happen. Obviously this view reflects a low view of Jesus' person. Still others believe that Jesus was predicting the destruction of Jerusalem, but this hardly fits the Old Testament prophecies or the context of this verse. Carson summarized seven views, and preferred one that equates the coming of the Son of Man with the coming of the kingdom. He viewed "the end" as the destruction of Jerusalem.[582]

"What was proclaimed here was more fully demonstrated in the apostles' lives after the day of Pentecost (Acts 2) in the spread of the gospel in the church (e.g., Acts 4:1-13; 5:17-18, 40; 7:54-60). But these words will find their fullest manifestation in the days of the Tribulation when the gospel will be carried throughout the entire world before Jesus Christ returns in power and glory to establish His kingdom on the earth (Matt. 24:14)."[583]

10:24-25   Jesus' point was that persecution should not surprise His disciples. They had seen the scribes and Pharisees, and even John's disciples, oppose Jesus. They could expect the same treatment.

Beelzebul was Satan, the head of the household of demons (12:24-27). The word "Beelzebul" probably came from the Hebrew *baal zebul*, meaning "Prince Baal." Baal was the chief Canaanite deity, and the Jews regarded him as the personification of all that was evil and satanic. The "house" in view is Israel. Jesus as Messiah was "the head of" that "household." However, His critics charged Him with being Satan (cf. 9:34). Therefore, the disciples could expect similar slander from their enemies.

"We believe, that the expression 'Master of the house' looked back to the claims which Jesus had made on His first purification of the Temple [John 2:16]. We almost seem to hear the coarse Rabbinic witticism in its play on the word *Beelzebul*. For, *Zebhul*, . . . means in Rabbinic language, not any ordinary dwelling, but specifically the Temple, and *Beel-Zebul* would be the Master of the Temple.' On he other hand, *Zibbul* . . . means sacrificing to idols; and hence *Beel-zebul* would, in that sense, be equivalent to 'lord' or 'chief of idolatrous sacrificing'—the worst and chiefest of demons, who presided over, and incited to, idolatry. 'The Lord of the Temple' . . . was to them 'the chief of idolatrous worship,' the Representative of God that of the worst of demons: Beelzebul was Beelzibbul!"[584]

---

[581]Calvin, *Commentary on . . .*, 1:456.

[582]Carson, "Matthew," pp. 250-53.

[583]Barbieri, p. 42.

[584]Edersheim, *The Life . . .*, 1:648.

The attitudes of the disciples 10:26-39 (cf. Luke 12:1-12)

Even though Jesus' disciples would encounter hostile opposition, they should fear God more than their antagonists.

10:26-27   The basis for confidence, in the face of persecution, is an understanding that whatever is presently "hidden" will eventually come out into the open. This proverbial statement applies to the truth about Jesus (the gospel) that the fearful disciple might seek to keep hidden for fear of opposition. It also applies to the disciple who might himself want to hide instead of letting his light shine. It applies also to the preceding teaching about persecution.

What Jesus told His disciples privately would eventually become public knowledge, so they should declare it publicly. In Palestine, common flat-roofed houses were good places from which to make public addresses.

"Good news is not meant to be kept under wraps, however little some people may wish to hear it."[585]

10:28   It also helps to conquer "fear," if the disciple will remember that the worst a human adversary can do, does not compare with the worst God can do. Jesus was not implying that true believers might go to hell if they do not remain faithful to God. His point was, that God has power over the disciple after he dies, whereas human adversaries can do nothing beyond killing the disciple's body. The believer needs to remember that he or she will stand before God one day to give an account of his or her stewardship. "Destroy" here does not mean annihilation, but ruination. The same Greek verb appears in 9:17, and describes ruined wineskins. Walvoord took "him who is able to destroy both soul and body in hell" as a reference to Satan.[586]

10:29-31   Third, the same God who will not permit a sparrow to "fall to the ground," will certainly take care of His faithful servants. The Jews were very familiar of this illustration.[587] The poor in Israel ate many "sparrows," since they only cost a fraction of a day's wage ("a cent"; Gr. *assarion*, a small-value coin).[588] The mention of the disciples' heavenly "Father" (v. 29) stresses His care—that extends to the numbering of his or her "hairs." Often people think that God cares only for the big things in life and is unconcerned about the details. Jesus taught the opposite. God's concern with details should give us confidence that He controls the larger affairs of life.

"Indeed, the principal purpose of Biblical history is to teach that the Lord watches over the ways of the saints with such great diligence that they do not even stumble over a stone [cf. Ps. 91:12]."[589]

10:32-33   Disciples of Jesus must acknowledge Him publicly. One cannot fulfill the basic requirements of a disciple privately (cf. 5:13-16). Again, the terms "believer" and "disciple" are not synonymous. In the context, confessing Jesus means acknowledging Him faithfully in spite of persecution to do otherwise. Jesus will acknowledge faithful disciples as such to His Father. He will not give this reward to unfaithful disciples who cave in to pressure to deny Him. Obviously, Jesus believed it is possible for believers to be unfaithful. Notice that the blessing of Jesus' commendation will go to anyone (i.e., any disciple) who confesses Him publicly. Jesus probably looked at the whole course of the disciple's life as He made this statement. One act of unfaithfulness does not disqualify a disciple from Jesus' commendation (e.g., Peter). An example of Jesus confessing a faithful disciple before others is His testimony concerning John the Baptist's greatness (11:11; Luke 7:28).

The view that this passage teaches that a believer may lose his or her salvation—if he or she fails to confess, or denies Jesus—cannot be correct. Elsewhere Jesus taught that believers will never lose their salvation (cf. John 10:28-29). This is the consistent revelation of the rest of the New Testament (e.g., John 10:28-29; Rom. 8:31-39; et al.). Jesus was speaking here of rewards, not salvation.[590]

10:34-36   Jesus meant that His immediate purpose would entail conflict, even though Messiah would ultimately bring "peace" (Isa. 11; Luke 2:14). People would divide over whether Jesus was the Messiah.

Micah 7:6 refers to rebellion that happened during King Ahaz's reign. It pointed to a greater division in Jesus' day. In both cases, the root of the conflict involved righteousness and unrighteousness.

---

[585]France, *The Gospel . . .*, pp. 402-3.

[586]Walvoord, *Matthew: . . .*, p. 77.

[587]Edersheim, *The Life . . .*, 1:649.

[588]Adolf Deissmann, *Light from the Ancient East*, pp. 272-75.

[589]Calvin, *Institutes of . . .*, 1:17:6.

[590]See also Robert N. Wilkin, "Is Confessing Christ a Condition of Salvation?" *The Grace Evangelical Society News* 9:4 (July-August 1994):2-3.

"Feud between members of a family is also mentioned in the Talmud as a sign of the coming of the Messianic age."[591]

Jesus spoke of the consequences of His first coming in terms that sounded like they were His main purpose in coming. But He came to bring this kind of conflict only in an *indirect* sense. By expressing Himself in this way, Jesus demonstrated His Christological and eschatological awareness. These conditions will prevail before Jesus' second coming. too.

10:37-39   Jesus taught that people must love one another, but they must love Him more. This is a remarkable claim that shows what great importance Jesus placed on the supreme allegiance of His disciples. Taking one's "cross" does not mean tolerating some unpleasant situation in one's life for Jesus' sake. It means dying to self, namely: putting Jesus first. In this sense every disciple bears the same cross. Jesus' reference to crucifixion, His first in Matthew, would have helped His disciples realize that their calling would involve pain and shame.

Those who find (i.e., preserve) their lives now will forfeit them later. Conversely, the disciple who loses his or her life (Gr. *psyche*) by martyrdom or by self-denial now, "will find (preserve) it" in the next stage of his or her existence. This is true in a twofold sense. The person who lives for the present loses the real purpose of life.[592] He or she also loses the reward for faithful living.

"There is an absolutism in the call to Jesus and the kingdom that can seem unattractive, if not unendurable. But this is only half the story, for the rewards are beyond calculation."[593]

This entire section (vv. 26-39) contrasts the present with the future. For the 12 Apostles: their present ministry, self-denial, and consequential persecution, involved identifying themselves publicly as Jesus' disciples. It involved calling on the Jews to repent: because the kingdom was near at hand, and the King had arrived! For modern disciples: our present ministry, self-denial, and consequential persecution, likewise involve identifying ourselves publicly as Jesus' disciples. They also involve urging people to believe in Him. In both groups, those who are faithful to their calling will receive God's commendation when they stand before Him. Old Testament saints will stand before God when He judges Israel at Jesus' second coming (Dan. 12:1-2). Modern Christians will stand before the judgment seat of Christ (2 Cor. 5:10; 1 Cor. 3:10-15). Those who are unfaithful will not receive some of the commendation, joy, and reward that could have been theirs had they remained faithful.

This discourse (ch. 10) covers the whole period during which disciples of Jesus will minister, from Jesus' day until the establishment of the messianic kingdom. It begins with the duty of the 12 Apostles, but then broadens to include all subsequent disciples before the establishment of the kingdom. The scope of the Mission Discourse and the Sermon on the Mount are the same: the interim between Jesus' first and second advents.

The reward for hospitality 10:40-42

These verses bring Jesus' teaching to a positive and encouraging conclusion. Jesus had given His disciples severe warnings. Now He gave them great encouragement.

10:40   By receiving His disciples, those to whom the disciples would go would show that they welcomed Jesus. Because they received Jesus, they would also receive God. How a person receives an agent shows his or her attitude toward the agent's master, and toward all that the agent represents.

10:41   "A prophet" is one who speaks for another. The disciples served as prophets when they announced Jesus' message. Jesus Himself was a prophet since He spoke for God. The one who received the disciple would "receive a prophet's reward" from God, suitable to the one who had entertained one of God's representatives. Likewise, the disciples were righteous men who represented another righteous Man: Jesus. God would give those who received the disciples, as ("in the name of") "righteous" men, a "reward" in keeping with what a righteous man deserves (cf. 5:20; John 13:20).

10:42   The "little ones," in view of the context, probably refer to the persecuted disciples who remain faithful to the Lord. Anyone who assists "one of" them—by giving him or her "even a cup of" refreshing "cold water"—will receive a reward from God. That person can even give the cup of cold water "in the name of" (on behalf of) a follower of Jesus, not in the name of Jesus Himself. The point is that no act of kindness for one of Jesus' suffering disciples will pass without (or "lose") God's "reward."

---

[591]Montefiore, *The Synoptic . . .*, 2:152.

[592]William Hendriksen, *New Testament Commentary, Exposition of the Gospel According to Matthew*, p. 477.

[593]Hagner, p. 293.

"Keep in mind that the theme of this last section is discipleship, not sonship. We become the children of God through faith in Christ; we are disciples as we faithfully follow Him and obey His will. Sonship does not change, but discipleship does change as we walk with Christ. There is great need today for faithful disciples, believers who will learn from Christ and live for Him."[594]

This Mission Discourse (ch. 10) is instruction for Jesus' disciples in view of their ministry to call people to prepare for the kingdom. Jesus gave the 12 Apostles specific direction about where they should go and to whom they should minister. However, He broadened His instruction, in view of mounting opposition, by giving guidance to disciples who would succeed the Twelve. Their ministry was essentially the same as that of the apostles.

The scope of this discourse, as the scope of the Sermon on the Mount, is the entire inter-advent age, the time between the two advents of Christ to the earth, including the time of His earthly ministry, the Church Age, and the Tribulation period. Both discourses prepare Jesus' disciples during this period for service before His kingdom on the earth begins and when it does begin.

Jesus did not reveal here that Israel's rejection of Him would result in a long gap between His first and second advents. That gap is irrelevant to the instruction and its meaning. Christian disciples today need to do essentially what the Twelve were to do, but to a different audience and region (28:19-20). Jesus explained those changes after His firm rejection by the Jews.

Whereas some of what Jesus told the Twelve to do on this occasion applied only to them, many things that He told them apply to modern disciples as well. These lessons include: preach the gospel, help people, live simply, move on if you are rejected, use wisdom and discernment, expect persecution, do not be afraid, remain faithful to God, and remember your reward.

"These two words, Care not, Fear not, are the soul and marrow of all that was said by way of prelude to the first missionary enterprise, and we may add, to all which might follow. For here Jesus speaks to all ages and to all times, telling the Church in what spirit all her missionary enterprises must be undertaken and carried on, that they may have His blessing."[595]

4. Jesus' continuation of His work 11:1 (cf. Mark 6:12-13; Luke 9:6)

Here is another of Matthew's formulas that ended a discourse (cf. 7:28-29; 13:53; 19:1; 26:1). Matthew had no concern for recording what happened when the Twelve went out having received Jesus' "instructions." He passed over their ministry in silence and resumed narration of Jesus' ministry.

"The motif that dominates Matthew's story throughout 4:17—11:1 is Jesus' ministry to Israel of teaching, preaching, and healing (4:23; 9:35; 11:1)."[596]

IV. THE OPPOSITION TO THE KING 11:2—13:53

To review, Matthew introduced the King of the Jews, then demonstrated His authority, and then explained His manifestation in Israel. Matthew proceeded next to record Israel's opposition to Him and rejection of Him. Chapters 11—13 record Israel's rejection of her Messiah and its consequences. Opposition continued to build, but Jesus announced new revelation in view of hardened unbelief.

"The Evangelist has carefully presented the credentials of the king in relationship to His birth, His baptism, His temptation, His righteous doctrine, and His supernatural power. Israel has heard the message of the nearness of the kingdom from John the Baptist, the King Himself, and His disciples. Great miracles have authenticated the call to repentance. Now Israel must make a decision."[597]

"Thematically the three chapters (11—13) are held together by the rising tide of disappointment in and opposition to the kingdom of God that was resulting from Jesus' ministry. He was not turning out to be the kind of Messiah the people had expected."[598]

[594]Wiersbe, 1:40.
[595]Bruce, The Training . . ., p. 111.
[596]Kingsbury, Matthew as . . ., p. 72.
[597]Toussaint, Behold the . . ., p. 147.
[598]Carson, "Matthew," p. 260.

A. EVIDENCES OF ISRAEL'S REJECTION OF JESUS 11:2-30

Matthew presented three evidences of opposition to Jesus that indicated rejection of Him: John the Baptist's questions about the King's identity, the Jews' indifference to the King's message, and their refusal to respond to the King's invitation.

1. Questions from the King's forerunner 11:2-19

This section illustrates how deeply seated Israel's disenchantment with Jesus was.

The confusion of the King's forerunner 11:2-6 (cf. Luke 7:18-23)

Even John the Baptist had doubts about whether Jesus was really the promised Messiah.

> "Matthew includes the record of this interrogation for at least two reasons. First, the questioning of Jesus by John, a representative of the best in Israel, points up the misconception of Israel as to the program of the Messiah and His method. He had heard of the works of Jesus (Matthew 11:2), and they certainly appeared to be Messianic. However, Jesus did not suddenly assert His authority and judge the people as John probably had thought He would (Matthew 3:10-12). Because of this misconception he began to doubt. Perhaps his being in prison, a place which was certainly incongruous for the herald of the King, reinforced his doubts. . . .

> "The second purpose of these few verses (Matthew 11:2-6) is to reaffirm the concept that the works of Jesus prove His Messiahship."[599]

11:2-3   Herod Antipas had "imprisoned" John in the fortress of Machaerus, east of the Dead Sea (cf. 4:12; 14:3-5).[600] There John heard about Jesus' ministry. Matthew wrote that John "heard" about "the works" of "the Christ." This is the only place in Matthew where the name "Christ" standing alone refers to Jesus.[601] Matthew evidently referred to Jesus this way here to underscore the fact that Jesus was the Christ, the Greek term for Messiah. John had doubts about that, but Matthew presented Jesus as the Messiah in unequivocal terms. The "works" of Jesus would include His teachings and all of His activities, not just His miracles.

> John sent Jesus a question through some of John's disciples. This use of "disciples" is another proof that this word does not necessarily mean believers in Jesus. These disciples were still following John. They had not begun to follow Jesus. John questioned whether Jesus was "the Coming (Expected) One" after all (Ps. 40:7; 118:26; Isa. 59:20). "The Coming One" was a messianic title.[602] John had previously announced Jesus as the coming One (3:11), but Jesus did not quite fit John's ideas of what Messiah would do. He was bringing blessing to many but judgment to none (cf. 3:10-12).[603]

>> "The prophetic infirmity of querulousness [complaining in a petulant or whining manner] and the prison air had got the better of his judgment and his heart, and he was in the truculent humor of Jonah, who was displeased with God, not because He was too stern, but rather because He was to gracious, too ready to forgive."[604]

>> "The same questions of the ultimate triumph of God undoubtedly face everyone in suffering for Christ's sake. If our God is omnipotent, why does He permit the righteous to suffer? The answer, of course, is that the time of God's judgment has not yet come but that the final triumph is certain."[605]

> An old interpretation of John's question is that he asked it for his disciples' sake, but he himself never doubted Jesus' identity. There is nothing in the text to support this view. Rather John, like Elijah, seems to have become discouraged (cf. v. 14). Probably this happened because Jesus did not begin to judge sinners immediately.

---

[599] Toussaint, *Behold the . . .*, p. 148.

[600] Josephus, *Antiquities of. . .*, 18:5:2. See idem, *The Wars . . .*, 7:6:2, for a description of this fortress.

[601] Henry Alford, *The Greek Testament*, 1:114.

[602] Lenski, p. 425.

[603] See James D. G. Dunn, *Jesus and the Spirit*, pp. 55-62.

[604] Bruce, *The Training . . .*, pp. 49-50.

[605] Walvoord, *Matthew: . . .*, p. 80.

11:4-6   Jesus sent a summary of His ministry back to John. He used the language of Isaiah's prophecies to assure His forerunner that He really was the Messiah (Isa. 35:5-6; 61:1; cf. Isa. 26:19; 29:18-19). It is interesting that all of these Isaiah passages contain some reference to judgment. Thus Jesus assured John that He *was* the Coming One, and He implied that He would fulfill the judgment prophecies, though He had not done so yet.

Verse 6 may contain an allusion to Isaiah 8:13-14. It is a gentle warning against allowing Jesus' ministry to become an obstacle to belief and a reason for rejecting Jesus. It assumes that John and his disciples began well, but it warned them against reading the evidence of Jesus' miracles incorrectly. The little beatitude in verse 6 commends those who believe God is working without demanding undue proof (cf. John 20:29).[606]

"It is well to note that if John had an erroneous concept of the kingdom, this would have been the logical time for Christ to have corrected it. But He did no such thing."[607]

The commendation of the King's forerunner 11:7-11 (cf. Luke 7:24-28)

John had borne witness to Jesus, and now Jesus bore witness to John. In doing so, Jesus pointed to Himself as the person who would bring in the kingdom.

11:7-8   As John's disciples were leaving, Jesus took the opportunity "to speak to the crowds about John." Reeds of cane grass grew abundantly along the Jordan River banks. "A reed" blown "by the wind" represents a person easily swayed by public opinion or circumstances. The multitudes certainly did not go into the Judean wilderness to view such a common sight. They did not "go out to see . . . a man dressed in soft," even effeminate clothes (Gr. *malakos*) either. Such people lived in "kings' palaces." Jesus probably alluded derogatorily to King Herod, who had imprisoned John. Herod wore soft garments, but John wore rough garments (cf. 3:4-6).

By replying this way, Jesus was allaying public suspicion that John's question might have arisen from a vacillating character or undisciplined weakness. John's question did not arise from a deficient character, but from misunderstanding concerning Messiah's ministry. Jesus was defending John.

11:9-11   The people had gone out into the wilderness to hear John because they believed he was "a prophet." Jesus affirmed that identification. He was the first true prophet who had appeared in hundreds of years. However, John was an unusual prophet. He was not only a spokesman from and for God, as the other prophets were, but he was also the fulfillment of prophecy himself. He was the one predicted to prepare for Messiah's appearing.

The passage Jesus quoted is Malachi 3:1, and His quotation reflects an allusion to Exodus 23:20. The changes Jesus made in His quotation had the effect of making Yahweh address Messiah (cf. Ps. 110:1). This harmonizes with the spirit of Malachi's context (cf. 4:5-6). By quoting this passage, Jesus was affirming His identity as Messiah.[608] He viewed John as potentially fulfilling the prophecy about Elijah preparing the way for Yahweh and the day of the Lord. Whether John really would have fulfilled it depended on Israel's acceptance of her Messiah then (cf. v. 14). In either case, John fulfilled the *spirit of the prophecy*, because he came in the spirit and power of Elijah.

Jesus called "John the Baptist" the greatest human being because he served as the immediate forerunner of Messiah. This was a ministry no other prophet enjoyed. Yet, Jesus added, anyone in "the kingdom" will be "greater than" John. Perhaps Jesus supported John so strongly, too, because some of the Jews may have questioned John's commitment to the Messiah.[609]

Scholars have offered many different explanations of the last part of verse 11. Some translate "the least" as "the younger," and believe Jesus was contrasting Himself, as younger than John, with John, who was older.[610] However, this is an unusual and unnecessary translation. Others believe that even the least in the kingdom will be able to point unambiguously to Jesus as the Messiah, but John's testimony to Jesus' messiahship was not persuading many who heard it.[611] The best explanation, I believe, is that John at that time only anticipated the kingdom, whereas participants will be *in it*, thus "greater."

---

[606]France, *The Gospel . . .*, p. 425.

[607]Toussaint, *Behold the . . .*, p. 148. Cf. McClain, pp. 301-2.

[608]R. T. France, *Jesus and the Old Testament*, p. 155.

[609]*The Nelson . . .*, p. 1594.

[610]E.g., Fenton, p. 179.

[611]E.g., Carson, "Matthew," p. 265.

"... possession of a place in the kingdom is more important than being the greatest of the prophets."[612]

Jesus did not mean that John would fail to participate in the kingdom. All true prophets will be in it (Luke 13:28). He was simply contrasting participants and announcers of the kingdom.

The identification of the King's forerunner 11:12-15

This section further explains John the Baptist's crucial place in God's kingdom program.

11:12-13   These verses record Jesus' description of the condition of the kingdom when He spoke these words. "From the days of John the Baptist until now" began when John began to minister, and extended to the time Jesus uttered the words Matthew recorded here. What does "suffers violence" mean? If the Greek verb *biazetai* is a deponent middle tense, it could mean that disciples must enter the kingdom through violent effort.[613] This seems to introduce a foreign element into Jesus' teaching on discipleship. Entrance into the kingdom depends on faith in Jesus as the Messiah. The deponent middle could also mean that the kingdom has been forcefully advancing, but it had not swept away all opposition, as John had been expecting.[614] However, the image of an irresistibly advancing kingdom seems foreign to Matthew's portrayal of Jesus' ministry thus far. Mounting opposition suggests that the kingdom was encountering severe resistance.

Probably the verb *biazetai* is in the passive tense. "The kingdom of heaven suffers violence" because evil men take it violently. Perhaps Jesus meant that men were snatching the kingdom from God and forcing its coming.[615] This is impossible, since Israel was not forcing the kingdom to come. The Jews were unwilling to receive it when Jesus offered it. Perhaps Jesus meant that some Jews, such as Barabbas, where trying to bring in the kingdom by political revolution.[616] This is unlikely, since Jesus made no other reference to this happening in the context. Probably Jesus meant that the religious leaders of His day were trying to bring in the kingdom in their own, carnal way, while refusing to accept God's way that John and Jesus announced.[617]

This view explains satisfactorily Jesus' reference to the period from the beginning of John's ministry to when He spoke. Ever since John began his ministry of announcing Messiah, the Jewish religious leaders had opposed him. Moreover, in 23:13, Jesus accused the scribes and Pharisees of trying to seize the reins of kingdom power from Messiah, to lead the kingdom as they wanted it to go. They also snatched (took "by force") the kingdom from the people by rejecting, and eventually crucifying, the Messiah. The imprisonment of John was another evidence of violent antagonism against the kingdom, but that opposition came from Herod Antipas. John and Jesus both eventually died at the hands of these violent men.

Jesus described the imminent kingdom as in grave danger because of His enemies. The Old Testament ("all the") "prophets" had predicted the Messiah, "until John," but when John began his ministry, the time of fulfillment began. That was a unique time that the law and the prophets had foretold (v. 13).[618]

11:14-15   In the previous two verses, Jesus spoke of the imminent kingdom. It was encountering severe opposition. In these two verses, He discussed the potential beginning of the kingdom.

The messianic kingdom would come if the Jews would accept it. In the Greek text, the conditional particle (*ei*) assumes for the sake of the argument that they would receive it. Assuming they would, John would fulfill Malachi's prophecy about Elijah being Messiah's forerunner (Mal. 4:5-6).

"There is scarcely a passage in Scripture which shows more clearly that the kingdom was being offered to Israel at this time."[619]

All amillenarians and some premillenarians, namely, covenant (historic) premillenarians and progressive dispensationalists, believe that the kingdom really began with Jesus' preaching.[620] They interpret this conditional statement as follows. They say

[612]Marshall, p. 296.

[613]J. N. Darby, *Synopsis of the Books of the Bible*, 3:59.

[614]Carson, "Matthew," p. 267.

[615]Schweitzer, p. 357.

[616]Robinson, p. 102.

[617]Toussaint, *Behold the . . .*, pp. 151-52; Walvoord, *Matthew: . . .*, p. 82.

[618]See Edersheim, *The Life . . .*, 2:764-66, for discussion of how the Jews understood the Law in Jesus' day.

[619]Toussaint, *Behold the . . .*, p. 153.

Jesus was acknowledging that it was difficult to accept the fact that John was the fulfillment of the prophecies about Elijah. They take "it" as referring to Jesus' statement about John rather than the kingdom. Since both antecedents are in the context, the interpretation hinges on one's conclusion about whether the kingdom really did begin with Jesus' preaching, or if it is still future. I favor the second alternative, in view of the Old Testament prophecies about the kingdom, and how Matthew presented Jesus' concept of the kingdom. Jesus viewed the messianic kingdom as future and earthly, not present and future. In saying this, I do not deny that in one sense, God rules over His own now. However, this is a heavenly rule, a rule from heaven. The Old Testament prophets predicted that Messiah would rule on the earth. This earthly rule of God over His own is still future. This is the kingdom that John announced, and Jesus offered, to Israel.

Jesus did not say that John was Elijah. That depended on Israel's repenting and accepting Jesus as the Messiah. John fulfilled Isaiah 40:3 and Malachi 3:1, prophecies about Messiah's forerunner, but not Malachi 4:5-6, the prophecy about the forerunner turning the people's hearts to God, since Israel rejected Jesus.

". . . John the Baptist stands in fulfillment of the promise of Malachi concerning the coming of Elijah, but only in the sense that he announced the coming of Christ."[621]

Who will fulfill Malachi 4:5-6, and when? Perhaps Elijah himself will be one of the two witnesses who will prepare the Israelites for Messiah's second coming (Rev. 11:1-14). Since John could have fulfilled the prophecy of Elijah, I tend to think that Elijah need not return to earth personally for this ministry.[622] Probably the two witnesses will be two contemporary believers in the Tribulation, who will turn the people's hearts to God, as Elijah did in his day.

Verse 15 underlines the great significance of what Jesus had just stated.

The dissatisfaction with the King and His forerunner 11:16-19 (cf. Luke 7:29-35)

Jesus proceeded to describe the Jews' reaction to John and Himself more fully to clarify their opposition.

11:16-17   The "generation" Jesus spoke of consisted of the Jews to whom He offered the kingdom (cf. vv. 20-24; 12:39, 41-42, 45; 16:4; 17:17; 23:36; 24:34). This use of "generation" refers to a group or circle of His countrymen (cf. Prov. 30:11-14). Jesus must have observed "children" playing the marriage and funeral games He referred to here, and He used them to illustrate the childish reaction of most of His adult contemporaries. The point was that the people found fault with whatever Jesus did. He did not behave or teach in harmony with what *they* wanted Him to do, or as *they* expected that Messiah would do. His concept of the kingdom was different from theirs. They wanted a King who would fit into and agree with their traditional understanding of the Messiah. Consequently they rejected Him.

11:18-19   Even though John lived as an ascetic, as some of the Old Testament prophets did, most of the Jews rejected him and even charged him with "demon" possession. Jesus ate and drank with "sinners," and many of the people criticized Him for lack of moderation, and concluded that He despised the Law. If they had understood John, they would have understood Jesus.

Jesus concluded with a proverb that justified John's and His lifestyles. The Jews had criticized both John and Jesus for the ways they lived. Jesus' point was: the good "deeds" that John and Jesus did "vindicated" their choices to live as they did. Who could justifiably criticize them, since they went about doing good? "Wisdom" in the Old Testament is almost a synonym for *God* in many places. Jesus claimed that He and John were living wisely, under God's control, by behaving as they did. The Jews could make childish criticisms, but the lifestyles of John and Jesus argued for their credibility.

In spite of John's doubts, Jesus supported and affirmed His forerunner to his disciples and his critics. John's message was correct—even if he had developed some misgivings about it.

2. Indifference to the King's message 11:20-24

One indication of Israel's opposition to her King was the antagonism she displayed toward John and Jesus' methods (vv. 2-19). Another was her indifference to Jesus' message. Jesus and His disciples had preached and healed throughout Galilee. However, most of the people did not repent. Therefore Jesus pronounced judgment on their cities that had witnessed many mighty miracles. Jesus had the residents of the cities in view when He spoke of the cities.

---

[620]E.g., Carson, "Matthew," p. 268, a premillenarian.

[621]Merrill, "Deuteronomy . . .," p. 30.

[622]Walvoord, *Matthew: . . .*, p. 82.

"Those who really wish to know their Bibles should see that we are in new country from this verse forward. Draw a thick black line between the nineteenth and the twentieth verses. There is a great divide here. Truth flows down to opposite oceans from this point. We are face to face with a new aspect of the work of Christ. The Lord Jesus was henceforth a different Man in His action and in His speech. The One Who was the meek and lowly Jesus was about to exhibit His strong wrath in no uncertain way."[623]

11:20   The Greek word *oneidizein*, translated "reproach" (NASB) and "denounce" (NIV), is a strong word that conveys deep indignation (cf. 5:11; 27:44). Jesus did not denounce these cities because they actively opposed His ministry. He did so because the residents refused "to repent," in spite of the many "miracles" that Jesus and His disciples had performed there (cf. 3:2; 4:17). The verb "to be done" (Gr. *egenonto*) looks at Jesus' Galilean ministry as completed (cf. v. 21).[624]

11:21-22   *Ouai* can mean "woe," a word announcing doom, or "alas," meaning "pity." Both ideas are appropriate here. Isaiah used the Hebrew equivalent 22 times. "Chorazin" stood about two miles northwest of Capernaum. This "Bethsaida" was probably the one on the northeast coast of the Sea of Galilee, on the east side of the Jordan River (cf. Mark 6:45; 8:22; Luke 9:10; John 1:44; 12:21). "Tyre and Sidon" lay on the Mediterranean coast to the north. The Old Testament prophets often denounced Tyre and Sidon for their Baal worship. "Sackcloth and ashes" were common ancient Near Eastern accouterments to mourning.

               The Greek word *dunamis* ("miracle" or "power") is one of four that the Gospel writers used to describe Jesus' miracles (cf. Mark 6:2, 5, 14; 9:39; Acts 13:10). This one emphasizes the mighty power of God that His miracles displayed. The other three Greek words are *teras*, meaning "wonder," which underscores the extraordinary character of His miracles (cf. 24:24; Mark 13:22; John 4:48); *ergon*, meaning "works," which describes both Christ's miracles and His ordinary deeds of mercy (cf. John 5:20, 36; 7:3; 10:25); and *semeion*, meaning "sign," which indicates that His miracles were to teach spiritual truth (cf. John 2:11; 4:54; 6:2; 11:47).[625]

               Jesus' statement reveals that as God, He knew what the people of Tyre and Sidon would have done, had they received the amount of witness the Jewish cities had enjoyed. It also indicates that the reception of special revelation is a privilege, not a right. Furthermore when God judges, He will take into account the opportunity people have had. There are degrees of punishment in hell, as there are degrees of felicity in heaven (v. 41; 23:13; Luke 12:47-48; Rom. 1:20—2:16).[626]

11:23-24   "Capernaum" was Jesus' base, and He performed many "miracles" there, half of the 10 recorded in this section of the Gospel (4:13; 8:5-17; 9:2-8, 18-33). It, like wicked Babylon, would suffer eternal damnation (Isa. 14:15). "Hades" is the place of the dead (cf. 5:22; 16:18). In view of the tower of Babel and the Exile, the Jews regarded Babylon as the worst of all cities. "Sodom" likewise was infamous for its wickedness (cf. 10:15). Jesus probably used the second person singular as a rhetorical device to address these cities. He addressed His audience with the plural "you" (vv. 22, 24).

                    "Anyone who visits the ruins of Capernaum today and sees the pitiful remains of what was once a beautiful city, can realize the literalness with which this prophecy has been fulfilled. Significantly, Tiberias, not far away, was not condemned and is not in ruins."[627]

               These towns had rejected Jesus and His ministry by their indifference. The citizens followed Him and appreciated His healing ministry, but they did not respond to His message.

                    "They perhaps took a languid interest in His miracles and teaching; but His beneficence never touched their hearts, and His doctrine produced no change in their lives."[628]

               "This passage vividly illustrates the simple truth that the greater the revelation, the greater the accountability."[629]

It was not just the hardhearted religious leaders who did not accept their King, but the majority of the common people rejected Him as well.[630]

---

[623]Barnhouse, p. 77.

[624]M'Neile, p. 159.

[625]Ryrie, *The Miracles . . .*, p. 10.

[626]Carson, "Matthew," p. 273.

[627]Walvoord, *Matthew: . . .*, pp. 83-84.

[628]Plummer, p. 165.

[629]Hagner, p. 314. Cf. Rom. 2:12-16.

[630]See McClain, p. 309-10.

3. The King's invitation to the repentant 11:25-30

This invitation is a sign of Israel's rejection of her King, since with it, Jesus invited those who had believed in Him, to separate from unbelieving Israel, and to follow Him. In verses 20-24, Jesus addressed the condemned; but in verses 25-30, He spoke to the accepted. This section is a Christological high point in the Gospel.

11:25-26   Matthew's connective "at that time" is loosely historical and tightly thematic.[631] Jesus' titles for God are appropriate in view of His prayer. "Father" focuses on Jesus' sonship, and prepares for verse 27, whereas "Lord of heaven and earth" stresses God's sovereignty, and prepares for verses 25-26. "These things" refer to the significance of Jesus' miracles, the imminence of the messianic kingdom, and the implications of Jesus' teaching.

> "As elaborated in the context, it [this revelation] concerns in greatest measure two matters. The one matter is the mysteries of the Kingdom of Heaven (13:11). And the other is insight into Jesus' identity as the Son of God (14:33; 16:16)."[632]

> The "wise and prudent [or learned]" are the self-sufficient Jews who rejected Jesus because they felt no need for what He offered. The "babes [or little children]" are the dependent who received Jesus' teaching as needy individuals. Israel was not humble but proud. Consequently she could not understand the things that Jesus revealed to her.

> It was God's good pleasure to hide truth from some and reveal it to others. This may make God appear arbitrary and unfair. However, Scripture reveals that God owes man nothing. God is not unjust because He hides truth from some while revealing it to others. Hiding things from some is an evidence of God's judgment, not His justice. That He extends mercy to any is amazing. That He extends it to those who are inadequate and totally dependent is even more incredible. Furthermore, because He hides truth from those who reject it, means that He shows mercy to them because He will judge all people by their response to the truth they have.

> Jesus delighted in the fact that His Father revealed and concealed truth as He did (v. 26). Jesus delighted in whatever God did. His disciples should do likewise.

> "It is often in a person's prayers that his truest thoughts about himself come to the surface. For this reason the thanksgiving of Jesus here recorded is one of the most precious pieces of spiritual autobiography found in the Synoptic Gospels."[633]

11:27   Here is another of Jesus' claims to being the Son of God.[634] Jesus claimed to be the exclusive revealer of God's message that the "babes" received. Jesus has authority over those to whom He reveals God the Father. Reciprocal knowledge with God the Father assumes a special type of sonship. It reflects relationship more than intellectual attainment. The only way people can "know the Father" is through the Son (cf. John 14:6). Similarly, there are some things about the Son that only the Father knows (e.g., the date and hour of His return). Some of what the Son has chosen to reveal concerns the kingdom.

11:28   This invitation recalls Jeremiah 31:25, where Yahweh offered His people "rest" in the New Covenant. The "weary" are those who have struggled long and toiled hard. The "heavy-laden" are those who stagger under excessive burdens.

> "The one [term] implies toil, the other endurance. The one refers to the weary search for truth and for relief from a troubled conscience; the other refers to the heavy load of observances that give no relief, and perhaps also the sorrow of life, which, apart from the consolations of a true faith, are so crushing."[635]

> Jesus, the revealer of God, invites those who feel their need for help that they cannot obtain by themselves, to "come to" Him (cf. 5:3; Rev. 22:17). Israel's spiritual leaders had loaded the people with unscriptural burdens that were too heavy to bear. The "rest" in view involves kingdom rest (cf. Heb. 4), but it is a present reality too.

> Throughout Israel's history, God held out the promise of rest if His people would trust and obey Him. The Promised Land was to be the scene of this rest. However, when Israel entered Canaan under Joshua's leadership, she enjoyed rest there only partially due to limited trust and obedience. As her history progressed, she lost much rest through disobedience. Now Jesus,

---

[631]Carson, "Matthew," p. 274.

[632]Kingsbury, *Matthew as . . .*, p. 137.

[633]Tasker, p. 121.

[634]Cf. Plummer, p. 168.

[635]Ibid., p. 170.

as her Messiah, promised that the rest she had longed for for centuries could be hers—if she humbly came to Him. He provided this rest for anyone in Israel who came to Him in humble trust.[636] He will provide this rest for Israel—in the future—in the Promised Land. This will take place when He returns to earth to establish His kingdom.

11:29-30   The "yoke" that farmers put on their oxen is a metaphor for the discipline of discipleship. This is not the yoke of the Mosaic Law, but the yoke of discipleship to Jesus. Learning from Him involves assimilating what He reveals, not just imitating Him or learning from His experience.

Jesus is not only the authoritative revealer. He is also the humble Servant of the Lord. He deals gently with the weak (cf. 18:1-10; 19:13-15). Jesus quoted Jeremiah 6:16, a passage that pointed to Him. The yoke of discipleship may involve persecution, but it "is easy" (good and comfortable). His "burden is light" compared to the loads Israel's religious leaders imposed on their disciples.

"... this voluntary making of the yoke as heavy as possible, the taking on themselves as many obligations as possible, was the ideal of Rabbinic piety."[637]

"... what makes the difference is what sort of master one is serving."[638]

Israel's unbelief is a strong theme in this chapter. We can see it in John's question (vv. 1-15), in Jesus' generation (vv. 16-19), in the cities of Galilee (vv. 20-24), and in the proud wise (vv. 25-30).[639]

B. SPECIFIC INSTANCES OF ISRAEL'S REJECTION OF JESUS CH. 12

Matthew has shown that opposition to Jesus came from two main sources: the animosity of the religious leaders, and the indifference of the common Israelites. In this chapter he presented five instances in which opposition manifested itself and increased. In each situation the approach to Jesus was negative, but Jesus responded positively.[640]

"Central to the plot of Matthew's story is the element of conflict. The principal conflict pits Israel against Jesus, and the death of Jesus constitutes the primary resolution of this conflict. On another level, Jesus also struggles with the disciples. Here the conflict is to bring them to understanding, or to enable them to overcome their 'little faith,' or to invite them to avail themselves of the great authority Jesus has given them, or, above all, to lead them to comprehend that the essence of discipleship is servanthood."[641]

This chapter records where the tide turned in Jesus' ministry. Here opposition became rejection. Chapter 12 is the climax of the rejection motif so far in Matthew's Gospel.

1. Conflict over Sabbath observance 12:1-21

The first two instances of conflict that Matthew recorded arose over Sabbath observance. Sabbath observance was very important to the Jews.[642] The Sabbath was a uniquely Israelite institution that commemorated the creation of the cosmos and the creation of Israel. Jewish rules of conduct concerning the Sabbath had become very detailed by Jesus' day.

The Sabbath and legal observance 12:1-8 (cf. Mark 2:23-28; Luke 6:1-5)

The immediate connection between this section and what precedes is twofold. The first is the theme of rising opposition (11:2—13:53), and the second is the heavy yoke of Pharisaic tradition that made the Israelites weary and heavy laden (11:28-30). The aim of the Sabbath was to provide rest, which Jesus said those who took His yoke upon themselves would find. It was not to provide a burden, which the Pharisees had made it by their traditions.

---

[636]Feinberg, p. 66.

[637]Edersheim, *The Life* . . ., 2:144.

[638]France, *The Gospel* . . ., p. 450.

[639]Morgan, *The Gospel* . . ., p. 111.

[640]Toussaint, *Behold the* . . ., p. 158.

[641]Kingsbury, *Matthew as* . . ., p. 9.

[642]See Edersheim, *The Life* . . ., 2:777-87, for discussion of the ordinances and law of the Sabbath as laid down in the Mishnah and the Jerusalem Talmud.

Matthew recorded that Pharisaic opposition began when Jesus forgave sins (9:1-8). It increased when Jesus associated with tax collectors and sinners (9:9-13). Now it boiled over because Jesus did not observe the Pharisees' legalistic traditions.[643]

> ". . . the leaders (Pharisees), in charging the disciples with breaking the law by plucking grain on the sabbath and hence working, do what they heretofore have not done: they engage Jesus himself in direct debate (12:1-8)."[644]

12:1   "At that time" does not mean immediately after that but at approximately that time (cf. 9:3, 11, 14, 34; 10:25; 11:19). The Mosaic Law permitted the Israelites to do what the disciples did, namely, pluck a few ears of grain "and eat" as they passed through a field (Deut. 23:25).

12:2   The Pharisees criticized Jesus' disciples for doing what was unlawful under Pharisaic tradition, namely, "reaping" on the Sabbath.[645] The Mishnah listed 39 categories of activity that qualified as work on the Sabbath.

> "The Mishnah includes Sabbath-desecration among those most heinous crimes for which a man was to be stoned."[646]

12:3-4   Jesus responded to the Pharisees' question with another, in common rabbinic style (cf. v. 5; 19:4; 21:16, 42; 22:31). The record of the incident He cited is in 1 Samuel 21:1-6, and the law governing the use of consecrated bread is in Exodus 25:30 and Leviticus 24:5-9. "The house of God" that David "entered" was the tabernacle that then stood at Nob. "David" and his men "ate . . . consecrated bread" that only the priests had a right to eat.

> The event to which Jesus referred may have occurred on a Sabbath day, though that is not certain (cf. 1 Sam. 21:5-6). That factor is inconsequential, as is the fact that David ate after lying to the priests. Another inconsequential feature is that David's men were very hungry, but Jesus' disciples were evidently not. Jesus drew this illustration from a time in David's life when Israel's leadership was rejecting him. The Son of David was now experiencing similar rejection.

> David ate even though it was unlawful for him to do so, yet the Old Testament did not condemn him for his act. Therefore the Pharisees should not condemn Jesus' disciples for doing something Scripture did not condemn David's men for doing. Jesus was arguing that His authority should override the Law more than their view of the Sabbath should.

> Jesus' disciples were not breaking any Old Testament command concerning Sabbath observance. These laws aimed primarily at prohibiting regular work on the Sabbath. The Old Testament set aside a regulation in the Law for David and his men in the sense that it did not condemn them for what they did (cf. 2 Chron. 30:18-20). Who David *was*, was the important factor in this concession. He was the Lord's anointed who occupied a special place in Israel. If anyone had a right to do what David did, David did. Could not Jesus then set aside a Pharisaic law that had no basis in the Old Testament for Himself and His men? By arguing this way, Jesus was claiming that He was at least as important as David was. The parallels between David and Jesus make Jesus' veiled claim to being the Son of David obvious.

12:5-6   Jesus' second argument came from Numbers 28:9-10. Technically, the priests broke the "Sabbath" every week, by changing the consecrated bread, and by offering the burnt offerings the Law specified for that day. However, "the Law" considered the priests guiltless ("innocent") for doing this "work" on the Sabbath.

> Jesus claimed that "something greater than the temple" was present. He used the neuter, "something," to refer to His authority, because He wanted to stress a quality about the temple—its authority—that He as an individual shared with the temple.[647] What is "greater" than the temple as a symbol of authority is Messiah, a superior authority. Another point of comparison was that God came to meet with His people, both in the temple and in Immanuel.

> In Jesus' argument, the temple was greater than the Sabbath. However, now something greater than the temple was there, namely Messiah, and specifically, His authority. Consequently Messiah takes precedence over the Sabbath. The Pharisees not only mishandled the Law, but they also failed to perceive who Jesus was. As the temple's authority shielded the priests from guilt, so Jesus' authority as Messiah shielded His disciples from guilt. Jesus was not comparing but contrasting the priests' authority and His authority.

---

[643]Morgan, *The Gospel* . . ., p. 124.

[644]Kingsbury, *Matthew as* . . ., p. 73.

[645]Mishnah *Shabbath* 7:2.

[646]Edersheim, *The Life* . . ., 2:52. Mishnah *Shabbath* 7:4.

[647]Turner, p. 21.

"In truth, the reason why David was blameless in eating the shew-bread was the same as that which made the Sabbath-labour of the priests lawful. The Sabbath-Law was not one merely of rest, but of rest for worship. The Service of the Lord was the object in view. The priests worked on the Sabbath, because this service was the object of the Sabbath; and David was allowed to eat of the shew-bread, not because there was danger to life from starvation, but because he pleaded that he was on the service of the Lord and needed this provision. The disciples, when following the Lord, were similarly on the service of the Lord; ministering to Him was more than ministering in the Temple, for He was greater than the Temple."[648]

12:7-8   Jesus again criticized the Pharisees for failing to understand the Scriptures (cf. v. 3), and He quoted Hosea 6:6 again (cf. 9:13). Previously Jesus had cited this verse to show the Pharisees that they failed to recognize their own need. Now He used it to show them that they failed to recognize Him. The Jews in Hosea's day relied on mere ritual to satisfy God. The Pharisees were doing the same thing. They had not grasped the real significance of the Law, as their criticism of Jesus' disciples demonstrated. Jesus accused the accusers, and declared the disciples "innocent."

"Note that Jesus appealed to prophet [vv. 3-4], priest [vv. 5-6], and king [v. 7]; for He is Prophet, Priest, and King. Note too the three 'greater' statements that He made: as the *Priest*, He is 'greater than the temple' (Matt. 12:6); as *Prophet*, He is 'greater than Jonah' (Matt. 12:41); and as *King*, He is 'greater than Solomon' (Matt. 12:42)."[649]

As "Son of Man," *this man Jesus* was "Lord of the Sabbath." That is, His authority was greater than the authority that God had granted the Sabbath to have over His people. Jesus had the authority to do anything He wished with the Sabbath. Significantly, He abolished its observance when He terminated the whole Mosaic Code—even as the temple effectively abolished it for the priests within the Mosaic system.

"We are free while we are doing anything for Christ; God loves mercy, and demands not sacrifice; His sacrifice is the service of Christ, in heart, and life, and work. We are not free to do anything we please; but we are free to do anything needful or helpful, while we are doing any service to Christ."[650]

The Old Testament did not condemn David because he ate the priests' bread, even though David broke the law involving ritual worship. Therefore the Pharisees should not condemn Jesus because He violated their tradition. By comparing Himself to David, Jesus implied that He, too, was the Lord's Anointed. Like David, Jesus was the Lord's Anointed who was doing God's will while He was being opposed by Israel's leadership. By contrasting the Mosaic Law with the Pharisees' tradition, Jesus exposed their confusion of tradition with Law and their misplaced priorities. They taught that ritual law was as important as moral law. *How* people worship is never as important as *that* they worship. The Pharisees' hearts were not right with God, even though they were scrupulous about *how* they worshipped God.

This is the first of seven incidents, that the Gospel evangelists recorded, in which Jesus came into conflict with the Jewish religious leaders over Sabbath observance. The chart below lists them in probable chronological order.

SABBATH CONTROVERSIES				
Event	Matthew	Mark	Luke	John
The disciples plucked ears of grain in Galilee.	12:1-8	2:23-28	6:1-5	
Jesus healed a paralytic at the Pool of Siloam in Jerusalem.				5:1-18
Jesus healed a man with a withered hand in Capernaum.	12:9-14	3:1-6	6:6-11	
Jesus referred to the Jews circumcising on the Sabbath.				7:22-23
Jesus healed a man born blind in Jerusalem.				9:1-34
Jesus healed a woman bent over in Judea.			13:10-17	
Jesus healed a man with dropsy in Perea.			14:1-6	

---

[648]Edersheim, *The Life . . .*, 2:58.

[649]Wiersbe, 1:42.

[650]Edersheim, *The Life . . .*, 2:59.

The healing of a man with a withered hand 12:9-14 (cf. Mark 3:1-6; Luke 6:6-11)

In the previous encounter, Jesus appealed to Scripture, but in this one He did not. In that one, His *disciples* were the targets of Pharisaic criticism, but in this one *He* was.

12:9-10	The Pharisees believed that it was permissible to give medical assistance "on the Sabbath" only if a sick person's life was in danger.[651] They also permitted midwifery and circumcision on the Sabbath.[652]

12:11-13   This is the third time in Matthew that Jesus argued for the superiority of human life over animal life (cf. 6:26; 10:31). His argument presupposed the special creation of man (Gen. 1—2). Jesus assumed, apparently with good reason, that the Pharisees would "lift . . . a sheep" out of "a pit" on the Sabbath. His argument was again *qal wahomer* (from the light to the heavy, cf. vv. 5-6). Neither the sheep in the illustration, nor the man in the synagogue, was in mortal danger. Jesus cut through the Pharisaic distinctions—about how much help one could give—to the more basic issue of doing good.

Jesus again healed with a word (9:1-8). The healing confirmed the power of His word, a power that God demonstrated in creation and that marked Jesus as God's agent. This miracle confirmed again Jesus' lordship over the Sabbath (v. 8) and His authority to forgive sins (9:1-8). Notice that Matthew made no reference to the healed man's faith. It may have played no part in this miracle, or Matthew simply may have made no mention of it. Matthew wanted to focus attention on Jesus and the Pharisees, not on the man.

12:14   The Pharisees would not have put someone to death simply because he broke one of their traditional laws. They wanted to kill Jesus because they understood Him to be making messianic claims that they rejected. "Counseled together" (NASB) or "plotted" (NIV, Gr. *sumboulion elabon*) means the Pharisees had reached a definite decision.

"The phrase means to come to a conclusion, rather than to deliberate whether or not."[653]

This verse takes the official rejection of Messiah further than it has gone before in Matthew. It is "the culminating point of the opposition of the Jewish religious authorities."[654]

"Given this narrative comment, the reader knows that the leaders' repudiation of Jesus has now become irreversible."[655]

Not only should human *need* take precedence over ritual worship (vv. 1-8), but human *welfare* should also take precedence over ritual worship (vv. 9-14).

Scriptural vindication of Jesus' ministry 12:15-21 (cf. Mark 3:7-12)

Matthew concluded the two accounts of the Pharisees' conflict with Jesus over Sabbath observance. He did so with a summary of His ministry that shows He fulfilled messianic prophecy and was indeed the Messiah. Jesus' tranquility and gentleness in this pericope contrast with the Pharisees' hatred in the former one.

12:15-17   Jesus "withdrew" when opposition became intense, before His time to go to the cross had arrived (cf. 4:12; 14:13; 15:21).

"This is the pattern of His ministry until His final and open rejection in chapters twenty-one to twenty-seven—opposition, withdrawal, and continued ministry."[656]

He had instructed His disciples to follow a similar procedure (10:11-14, 23-24). He withdrew specifically to avoid open conflict with the Pharisees.[657] His extensive ministry continued (cf. 4:23; 8:16; 9:35), as did His encouragements to those He healed to keep quiet about what had happened to them—but with no greater cooperation (cf. 8:4; 9:30). His conduct fulfilled Scripture.

12:18-21   Matthew recently selected material that presented Jesus as the Son of God, the Son of David, and God Himself. Now he pointed out again that Jesus' conduct proved Him to be the prophesied Suffering Servant of the Lord. The citation is from Isaiah 42:1-4. This is the longest Old Testament quotation in the first Gospel.

---

[651]Mishnah *Yoma* 8:6.

[652]Mishnah *Shabbath* 18:3; 19:2.

[653]Plummer, p. 175.

[654]M'Neile, p. 171.

[655]Kingsbury, *Matthew as . . .*, p. 73.

[656]Toussaint, *Behold the . . .*, p. 161.

[657]John Henry Bennetch, "Matthew: An Apologetic," *Bibliotheca Sacra* 103 (October 1946):480.

". . . by inserting this quotation here Matthew helps his readers to put the confrontation in context: it is not of the Messiah's choosing."[658]

The Greek word *pais* translated "servant" can also mean "son." However, the Hebrew word that it translates means "servant." Matthew recorded "whom I have chosen" rather than "whom I uphold" in Isaiah 42:1, evidently to stress God's election and love of Jesus (cf. 3:16-17; 17:5). Jesus performed His miracles with the power of the "Spirit" whom the Father had poured out "upon Him." These miracles extended even to Gentiles. Note the presence of the Trinity in this Old Testament passage.

Isaiah predicted that Messiah would minister with gentleness and humility (v. 19). He would not present Himself arrogantly or brashly. He would be very compassionate (v. 20). He would not advance His own program by stepping on others. He would bring salvation, finally, to the harassed and helpless (9:36), as well as to the weary and burdened (11:28), without crushing the weak.[659] This concept of Messiah was much more gentle than the one Jesus' contemporaries held. They expected Him to crush all opposition. He would, however, bring justice to pass. In Matthew, "justice" (Gr. *krisis*) means fast-approaching judgment, not simply justice as opposed to injustice.[660] Justice in the kingdom is in view. Consequently the Gentiles would put their trust in Him (v. 21).

"In the face of rejection by the nation of Israel Matthew, by Messianic prophecies, prepares his Jewish reader for the proclamation of a universal Savior."[661]

This Old Testament quotation helps the reader to see how many of the characteristics of Jesus and His ministry, that Matthew has presented, fit the pattern of messianic prophecy. It also sets the stage for other things that Matthew recorded that demonstrated Jesus' messiahship.

2. Conflict over Jesus' power 12:22-37 (cf. Mark 3:19-30; Luke 11:14-26)

The Pharisees moved beyond debate to personal abuse and character assassination in this pericope.

"We come now to a crucial turning point in the relationship between the Pharisees, the nation, and Christ."[662]

Jesus' miracle and the response 12:22-24

12:22   "Then" (Gr. *tote*) does not demand a close chronological connection with what precedes (cf. 2:7; 11:20). The Greek text describes the man's afflictions in terms that show that his demon possession produced his blindness and dumbness. The miracle itself did not interest Matthew as much as the confrontation that it produced.

12:23-24   The astonishment of the crowd prompted their question. It expected a negative answer. Literally they said, "This cannot be the Son of David, can it?" They raised the faint possibility that Jesus might be the Messiah, but primarily their question reflected their amazed unbelief. The Jews expected Messiah to perform miracles (v. 38), but other things about Jesus, for example His servant characteristics, led them to conclude that He was not the "Son of David."

The Pharisees again attributed Jesus' power to Satan ("Beelzebul"; cf. 10:25). This time their accusation created an open breach between themselves and Jesus.

"Three times before Matthew 12 the kingdom was said to be near (3:2; 4:17; 10:7). Then after Jesus' opponents accused Him of casting out demons by the power of Satan (12:24-32; Mark 3:22-30; Luke 11:14-26), the nearness of the kingdom is never mentioned again in the Gospels."[663]

John's Gospel, by the way, makes no reference to the nearness of God's kingdom. By the time John wrote, probably late in the first century A.D., it was clear that the messianic kingdom had been postponed.

---

[658]France, *The Gospel . . .*, pp. 468-69.

[659]Carson, "Matthew," pp. 286-87.

[660]M'Neile, p. 172.

[661]Toussaint, *Behold the . . .*, p. 161.

[662]Pentecost, *The Words . . .*, p. 205.

[663]Stanley D. Toussaint and Jay A. Quine, "No, Not Yet: The Contingency of God's Promised Kingdom," *Bibliotheca Sacra* 164:654 (April-June 2007):138.

Jesus' reply in view of the response 12:25-37

12:25-26   Probably Jesus' knew His critics' "thoughts" as anyone else who had suffered such an attack would (cf. 9:4). Alternatively, this may be a statement of Jesus' omniscience. Any "kingdom," "city," or "household" that experiences internal conflict, will destroy itself eventually if the strife continues. This holds true for the domain over which "Satan" rules, as well. For Satan to cast out demons would amount to his casting out himself, since the demons do his work.

12:27   The Pharisees' "sons" cast out demons occasionally. These "sons" were probably their disciples, or less likely, the Jews more generally. In either case, some Jews in Jesus' day could cast out demons (cf. Acts 19:13). If the Pharisees asserted that Jesus cast out demons by Satan's power, they would have to admit that their sons did so by the same power, something they would have denied.

12:28   The "Spirit of God" stands in stark contrast to Beelzebul. Matthew probably used "kingdom of God" here, rather than "kingdom of heaven," in order to connect the kingdom with the Spirit.

> "References to the Spirit occur only twelve times altogether in Matthew's gospel, with one-third of them in chapter 12. As might be expected in a gospel concerned to interpret the significance of the life and ministry of Jesus, most of the references describe the work of the Spirit in relation to Him."[664]

> Jesus was claiming that He received His power from God's "Spirit" (cf. v. 18), a clear messianic claim.[665] The kingdom was imminent because the King was present.

> "Upon" you does not mean the kingdom had somehow entered the Jews or overtaken them, and they were now in it. Jesus was addressing the Pharisees, and He did not mean the kingdom had entered them, of all people, but that it had "suddenly arrived" and was "among" them with His Messianic presence. Moreover, Jesus' concept of the kingdom was an earthly physical one. Furthermore, everywhere else Jesus spoke of people entering the kingdom, not the kingdom entering them.[666]

12:29   Jesus encouraged the Pharisees to look at the same issue another way. Only a stronger person can bind a homeowner and ransack his house (cf. Isa. 49:24-25). On a deeper level, Jesus was speaking of Himself binding Satan and spoiling his house by casting out demons (cf. Mark 3:27; Luke 11:21-22). Thus, Jesus was claiming a superior power to Satan, that could only be divine. Jesus will really bind Satan for 1,000 years when the kingdom begins (Rev. 20:2). Jewish pseudepigraphal literature predicted that Messiah would do this (Assumption of Moses 10:1). The pseudepigrapha (lit. false writings) is a large body of Jewish writings that are not in the Old Testatment, or in what Protestants refer to as the Apocrypha. These books date from ca. 200 B.C. to ca. A.D. 100.

12:30   Jesus' point in this statement was that there can be no neutrality in one's relationship to Him. Those who do not side with Jesus side with Satan. This put the Pharisees in undesirable company. The Old Testament viewed man's judgment as a harvest that God would conduct. Jesus claimed that He would be the harvesting Judge. Jesus' statement here would have rebuked the Pharisees and warned the undecided in the crowd. Apparently the Pharisees were not only refusing to come to Jesus themselves, but were even scattering the disciples that Jesus was gathering.

12:31-32   Jesus followed up His statement about the impossibility of being neutral (v. 30) with this further warning. The "therefore" (Gr. *dia touto*) indicates this relationship. "Blasphemy" involves extreme slander (cf. 9:3). God would forgive "any sin," including extreme slander of Jesus, when a person trusted in Jesus. However, He would not forgive "blasphemy against the Holy Spirit."

> Blasphemy against the Holy Spirit, in view of the context (vv. 24-28), involved attributing Jesus' works to Satan rather than to the Spirit. The sin was not a matter of speech; the words spoken simply reflected the attitude of the heart. God would not forgive this sin because the person who committed it in Jesus' day was thereby strongly rejecting Jesus as the Messiah.[667] Even today, the only sin one can commit that God will not forgive, and that will result in his or her eternal damnation, is rejection of Jesus Christ (cf. John 3:18). Attributing Jesus' works to Satan was blasphemy of the Spirit in Jesus' day and this resulted in damnation.

---

[664]Lowery, pp. 31-32.

[665]See Mark R. Saucy, "Miracles and Jesus' Proclamation of the Kingdom of God," *Bibliotheca Sacra* 153:611 (July-September 1996):281-307.

[666]H. D. A. Major, T. W. Manson, and C. J. Wright, *The Mission and Message of Jesus*, p. 596.

[667]See McClain, p. 315.

Can a person commit this sin today? One can reject Jesus Christ, but one cannot blaspheme the Spirit in the same sense in which Jesus' contemporaries could. To do so, one would have to observe Jesus doing His works and at the same time attribute them to Satan.[668] One could say, therefore, that blasphemy against the Spirit was an unforgivable sin during Jesus' earthly ministry. The unforgivable sin at any time since Jesus began His earthly ministry to the present day is rejection of Jesus Christ.

Speaking "a word against" is the same as blasphemy. Extreme slander of Jesus was forgivable in His day, provided it did not go as far as attributing His works to Satan. That constituted blasphemy of the Holy Spirit. Jesus gave this warning to the professedly neutral person who might attribute His works to Satan (v. 30). Such a person needed to realize that, even though he or she was not speaking against Jesus, that one could potentially be doing something with much graver consequences.

"Given Matthew's christological interests and the unique and central position held by Jesus throughout the Gospel, one may understandably be surprised that Matthew has not said the reverse of what stands in the text, i.e., that blasphemy against the Spirit is forgivable but not that against the Son of Man. The gravity of the blasphemy against the Spirit, however, depends upon the Holy Spirit as the fundamental dynamic that stands behind and makes possible the entire messianic ministry of Jesus itself . . ."[669]

12:33   Jesus proceeded to point out that conduct typically reflects character (vv. 33-37; cf. 7:16-19). To have "good fruit" one must "make the tree good," for example by cultivating, grafting, fertilizing, etc. If one makes a tree rotten by neglect and abuse, for example, one will get "bad fruit." A good tree produces good fruit, and a bad tree yields bad fruit. Jesus' works were good, so He must be good.

12:34-35   Everywhere else in Matthew where the "brood of vipers" figure occurs, it refers to the Pharisees and other religious leaders (3:7; 23:33). That is undoubtedly whom Jesus addressed here, too. The figure pictures deadly antagonists. Jesus' point was that a person's character determines what he or she says and does. The mouth usually reveals what is in the heart. The Pharisees' extreme slander of Jesus revealed their rejection of Him. They needed a change of attitude toward Him, not just a change in their speech about Him.

It is going beyond what Jesus said, to interpret this statement as meaning that no true believer will ever say or do what is contrary to the nature of a believer to say or do. All good people say and do some things that are good and some things that are bad. Likewise, all bad people say and do some things that are good and some things that are bad. We are not exactly like the trees in this illustration.

12:36-37   Jesus did not want His critics to gain any satisfaction from what He had just said. Their externally righteous appearance did not excuse them from speaking as they did. Rather, people's "words" are what God will use to judge them eventually. The "careless" word is the word spoken without deliberation. One might think it insignificant, except that it reveals character. "Every word" spoken reflects the heart's overflow, and God knows about it. Therefore words are very important (cf. Eph. 5:3-4, 12; Col. 3:17; James 1:19; 3:1-12).

Verse 37 sounds as though it may have been proverbial, or perhaps Jesus made it a proverb here. The context clarifies that the justification and condemnation in view deal with God passing judgment on everyone. Obviously, Jesus did not mean that if a person was able to say all the right words, he or she could deceive God and win salvation by clever speech. The basis of justification and condemnation is character, but "words" reveal character, so *they* become the instruments by which God judges.

Jesus' critics thought they were assessing Him when they said He did His works by Satan's power (v. 24). Jesus pointed out that they were really assessing themselves. They thought they were judging Him with their words, but really God would judge them with their words.

The break between Jesus and the religious leaders was now final. They charged Jesus with doing miracles with Satan's power rather than God's power. Jesus refuted their charge and warned them about the seriousness of this sin, but they still rejected Him.

"It is worth noting that in Mt. the breach between Jesus and the authorities is not definite until the Beelzebub charge."[670]

---

[668]Cf. Barbieri, p. 46.

[669]Hagner, p. 348.

[670]M. Kiddle, "The Conflict Between the Disciples, the Jews, and the Gentiles in St. Matthew's Gospel," *The Journal of Theological Studies* 36 (January 1935):37.

"This incident, then, marked the great turning point in the life of Christ. From this point on to the cross the nation is viewed in the Gospels as having rejected Christ as Messiah. The unofficial rejection by the leaders would become official when finalized at the cross."[671]

3. Conflict over Jesus' sign 12:38-45

The fourth incident, and the third type of conflict, concerned a sign that Jesus' critics requested.

"The Pharisees and teachers of the law knew full well that Jesus was claiming to be the heaven-sent Messiah. They were familiar with the multitude of miracles He had already performed to authenticate His person. But now they came to challenge Him and request a sign that would prove to them He was what He claimed to be."[672]

12:38 Matthew's connective again was weak. This incident was not a continuation of the preceding controversy chronologically, but thematically. Some of the scribes and Pharisees asked Jesus to perform "a sign," not just a miracle. He had performed many miracles, and they had concluded that they were satanic (v. 24). A sign was an immediate tangible assurance that something prophesied would surely happen. They requested a particular type of miracle. Evidently they believed Jesus could not produce one and that His failure would discredit Him.

12:39-40 The "evil and adulterous generation" was the larger group of unbelieving Jews that the scribes and Pharisees represented. Adultery is a common Old Testament metaphor for spiritual apostasy, departure from God (Isa. 50:1; 57:3; Jer. 3:8; 13:27; 31:32; Ezek 16:15, 32, 35-42; Hos. 2:1-7; 3:1; 7:13-16). God had granted signs in the past to strengthen the weak faith of believers such as Abraham, Joshua, and Gideon. Jesus refused to give His critics one, since they wanted a sign to trap Him, rather than to bolster weak faith.

"The sign of Jonah" was not a sign for the scribes and Pharisees. It became a sign to believers in Him later. The sign of Jonah means the sign that Jonah himself was to the Ninevites. He signified one whom God had delivered from certain death.[673] Jesus' use of "Son of Man" stressed His suffering role (cf. 8:20). The "heart" of the earth may recall Jonah 2:3 (cf. Ps. 46:2). This is a reference to Jesus' burial. Jesus was saying that His deliverance from death in the grave, which would be similar to Jonah's deliverance, only greater, would prove His claims. As the Jews reckoned time, three days and three nights meant three full days or any parts of three days.[674] Jesus was in the grave for parts of three days.

12:41 The Pharisees believed, correctly, that judgment followed resurrection.[675] Jesus followed His comments about resurrection in verse 40 with instruction about "judgment" in verse 41.

His critics' condemnation would be greater than that of the Ninevites, because the Ninevites "repented" at Jonah's preaching, but the scribes and Pharisees would not repent at Jesus' preaching. Jesus did not mean that the believing Ninevites and the unbelieving Jews of Jesus' day would appear before God at the same time. That is clear because the Ninevites would not condemn the Jews, but God would. Jesus meant that the believing Ninevites could testify against the unbelieving Jews when each group appeared before God for "judgment."

The "something greater than Jonah" was, again, the authority of Messiah. The sign Jesus promised did not meet His critics' demand, since they did not need weak faith strengthened. It was a sign that He provided for His own disciples. By refusing to respond to Jesus' message, the scribes and Pharisees showed themselves to be worse sinners than the Gentile Ninevites.

"Jesus is greater than Jonah in many ways. He is greater in His person, for Jonah was a mere man. He was greater in His obedience, for Jonah disobeyed God and was chastened. Jesus actually died, while Jonah's 'grave' was in the belly of the great fish. Jesus arose from the dead under His own power. Jonah ministered only to one city [according to the Book of Jonah], while Jesus gave His life for the whole world. Certainly Jesus was greater in His love, for Jonah did not love the people of Nineveh—he wanted them to die. Jonah's message saved Nineveh from judgment; he was a messenger of the wrath of God. Jesus' message was that of grace and salvation."[676]

---

[671]Pentecost, The Words . . ., p. 208.

[672]Ibid.

[673]Eugene H. Merrill, "The Sign of Jonah," Journal of the Evangelical Theological Society 23 (1980):23-30.

[674]Carson, "Matthew," p. 296.

[675]F. W. Green, ed., The Gospel According to Saint Matthew in the Revised Version, p. 183.

[676]Wiersbe, 1:43.

12:42   By referring to "Jonah" the same way He referred to the "Queen of the South," Jesus strongly supported the view that Jonah was a historical person. The "Queen of the South" was the "Queen of Sheba" (1 Kings 10:1-13). She came from the southern end of the Arabian Peninsula, that for the Jews, was the "ends of the earth" (cf. Jer. 6:20; Joel 3:8). She visited Jerusalem because of reports about Solomon's great "wisdom" that had reached her ears. The "something greater than Solomon" was Messiah, the embodiment of divine wisdom. The queen would join the Ninevites in condemning the unbelievers of Jesus' day, because they failed to acknowledge One with greater wisdom than Solomon's, as well as One with a greater message than Jonah's. Jesus was greater than Solomon in His wisdom, wealth, and works.

In both of Jesus' comparisons: Gentiles responded, and Jews did not. Such had been the case in Jesus' ministry so far, and this would continue. The proud scribes and Pharisees undoubtedly resented Jesus comparing them unfavorably with Gentiles.

"It is a tragic feature in the history of Israel that the nation rejected their deliverers the first time, but accepted them the second time. This was true with Joseph, Moses, David, the prophets (Matt. 23:29), and Jesus Christ."[677]

"Temple and priesthood, prophet, king, and wise man—something greater is now here."[678]

12:43-45   The point of these verses that describe demon possession goes back to Jesus' warning about the peril of being neutral toward Him (v. 30). A demon cast out of a person initially goes through arid "places seeking rest." This statement affirms the Jewish belief that demons prefer dry places (Tobit 8:3; cf. Rev. 18:2).[679] Eventually they seek to inhabit human bodies, through which they can do more damage.

Jesus implied the possibility of demonic repossession (v. 44). The demon's "house" is a human body in Jesus' story. The demon returns to the person it had left, discovering that he or she is still receptive to the demon's presence, because no superior power occupies that person. Consequently the demon invites "seven other" demons—a full complement ("more wicked than itself")—and they take up residence in the person.

Jesus compared the unbelieving Jews of His day to the demon-possessed person. John the Baptist and Jesus had purified the lives of many in Galilee by calling them to repentance, but not all of them had embraced Jesus in faith. Jesus had cast demons out of many people, but they did not all believe that He was the Messiah. This neutral condition left them vulnerable to an even worse invasion from Satan, to say nothing about judgment from God. These neutral individuals represented the nation as a whole.

Many Christians believe that Jesus' teaching here gives evidence that demons cannot possess a true believer. That may be so, but demons can afflict believers greatly. Believers are no more immune against attack from Satan, and his demons, than they are against attacks from the world and the flesh. The line between demon possession and demon affliction is a thin one that is very hard to identify.

Jesus' critics already had plenty of evidence as to who He was. They did not need to see more miracles that proved Jesus' Messiahship. Instead, He gave them a different kind of sign, one that would vindicate His claims after He rose from the dead.

4. Conflict over Jesus' kin 12:46-50 (cf. Mark 3:31-35; Luke 8:19-21)

A very subtle form of opposition arose from Jesus' physical family members. It provided an opportunity for Jesus to explain true relationship to Messiah and to affirm His disciples.

12:46-47   Jesus' "brothers" were evidently His physical half-brothers, the sons of Mary. Some Roman Catholics, desiring to maintain their "perpetual virginity of Mary" doctrine, and some Protestants, have argued that they were Jesus' brothers but the sons of Joseph by a previous marriage.[680] If they were, the oldest of these brothers would have been the legal heir to David's throne.

12:48-50   Jesus' question did not depreciate His physical "mother and brothers." His answer showed that He simply gave priority to His heavenly Father and doing His will (cf. 10:37). Spiritual relationship takes precedence over physical relationship (cf. 8:18-23). This underlines the importance of believing in Jesus and giving Him first place. Jesus' disciples become His adopted, spiritual

---

[677]Ibid., 1:44.

[678]France, *The Gospel . . .*, p. 493.

[679]Cf. Tasker, p. 133. See Edersheim, *The Life . . .*, 2:748-63, and 2:770-76, for the Jewish views of angels and demons.

[680]E.g., John McHugh, *The Mother of Jesus in the New Testament*, pp. 200-202; B. F. Westcott, *The Gospel According to St. John*, p. 116.

family. Note that the word "whoever," referring to those who do the will of God by believing on His Son, left the possibility of salvation open to anyone (cf. 11:28-30).

These verses have strong Christological implications. They also reveal more about the spiritual family that was forming around Jesus. In spite of rising opposition, God's purposes through Messiah were advancing (cf. vv. 18, 20).

C. ADAPTATIONS BECAUSE OF ISRAEL'S REJECTION OF JESUS 13:1-53

"The die is cast. The religious leaders have openly declared their opposition to their Messiah. The people of Israel are amazed at the power of Jesus and His speech, but they fail to recognize Him as their King. Not seeing the Messiahship of Jesus in His words and works, they have separated the fruit from the tree. Because of this opposition and spiritual apathy, the King adapts His teaching method and the doctrine concerning the coming of the kingdom to the situation."[681]

Jesus had occasionally used parables to illustrate His teaching (e.g., 5:15; 7:3-5, 13-14, 15-20, 21-27, 35; 9:15-17; 11:16-17; 12:25, 29, 43-45). Rising opposition led Him to use them more.[682] Now He began to use parables to reveal new truth about the kingdom.[683] Chapter 13 contains Jesus' third major discourse in Matthew, His Parables about the Kingdom.[684] Matthew presented the first two discourses as uninterrupted monologues by Jesus, except for a question and answer at 18:21-22. He interrupted this third discourse frequently with narrative introductions.

John and Jesus had previously announced that the kingdom was at hand. *Jesus stopped saying that when Israel's rejection of Him was firm* (i.e., after chapter 12). Instead, He began to reveal new truth about the kingdom, because of Israel's rejection of Him and His rejection of the nation. This new truth, revelation not previously given, was a mystery. The term "mystery," as it occurs in the New Testament, refers to newly revealed truth. It has nothing to do with spookiness. God had previously not revealed it, but now He did.

Kingsbury perceived the theme of this speech as "instruction in the secrets of the Kingdom" and outlined it as follows: (I) On the Secrets of the Kingdom as Being Revealed to the Disciples But Not to Israel (13:3-35); and (II) On the Secrets of the Kingdom as Urging Disciples to Obey Without Reserve the Will of God (13:36-52).[685]

As elsewhere in Matthew, references to the kingdom indicate the future messianic (millennial) kingdom. However, Jesus taught some things here about the unseen growth and development of the kingdom, in the *inter-advent age*, that precede the establishment of that kingdom. The scope of this discourse, as is true of the former two major discourses in Matthew, is the whole inter-advent age.

Matthew presented this discourse in a chiastic (crossing) structure.[686] This structure is common in the Old Testament and in other Jewish writings. It enhances the unity of the discourse and focuses attention on the central element as what is most important. A diagram of this structure follows.

A   The introduction vv. 1-2
   B   The first parable to the crowds vv. 3-9
      C   An explanatory interlude: purpose and explanation vv. 10-23
         D   Three more parables to the crowd vv. 24-33
            E   An explanatory interlude: fulfillment and explanation vv. 34-43
         D'   Three parables to the disciples vv. 44-48
      C'   An explanatory interlude: explanation and response vv. 49-51
   B'   The last parable to the disciples v. 52
A'   The conclusion v. 53

This structural analysis reveals that the discourse consists of two sections of four parables each, the first four to the multitudes and the last four to the disciples. In each section, one parable stands out from the others. In the first group it is the first parable, and in the second group it is the last one. The central section between the two groups of parables explains the function of the parables and explains one of them.

"Modern readers are so used to thinking of parables as helpful illustrative stories that they find it hard to grasp the message of this chapter that parables do not explain. To some they may convey enlightenment, but for others they may only deepen confusion. The difference lies in the hearer's ability to rise to the challenge. Far from giving explanations, parables themselves

[681]Toussaint, *Behold the . . .*, p. 168.

[682]See Appendix 4, a chart of "The Parables of Jesus," at the end of these notes.

[683]See Mark L. Bailey, "Guidelines for Interpreting Jesus' Parables," *Bibliotheca Sacra* 155:617 (January-March 1998):29-38.

[684]See J. Dwight Pentecost, *Thy Kingdom Come*, pp. 215-45; idem, *The Parables of Jesus*.

[685]Kingsbury, *Matthew as . . .*, p. 112.

[686]David Wenham, "The Structure of Matthew XIII," *New Testament Studies* 25 (1979):516-22.

need to be explained, and three are given detailed explanations in this chapter (vv. 18-23, 37-43, 49-50). But that explanation is not given to everyone, but only to the disciples (vv. 10 and 36), and Matthew not only makes the point explicit in v. 34 (only parables for the crowds, not explanations), but also confirms it by a formula quotation in v. 35: parables are 'hidden things.' In this way the medium (parables) is itself integral to the message it conveys (the secrets of the kingdom of heaven)."[687]

"Perhaps no other mode of teaching was so common among the Jews as that by Parables. Only in their case, they were almost entirely illustrations of what had been said or taught; while, in the case of Christ, they served as the foundation for His teaching."[688]

1. The setting 13:1-3a (cf. Mark 4:1-2; Luke 8:4)

Matthew linked this parabolic teaching with the controversy in chapter 12 by using the phrase "on that day" (NASB) or "that same day" (NIV, Gr. *en te hemera ekeine*). These parables were a response to Israel's rejection of her King.

Jesus sat down by the Sea of Galilee to teach the people in typical rabbinic fashion (cf. 5:1-2). In response to the large "crowd" that assembled to listen to Him, Jesus "sat" in a "boat" where more people could hear Him more easily. He proceeded to address this crowd, most of whom had rejected Him (cf. 11:16-24).

Jesus proceeded to tell four parables to the crowd assembled before Him (vv. 3b-9, 24-30, 31-32, 33). He did not interpret the meaning of these parables to the crowd. They would have to figure them out on their own, and disbelief in Jesus as the Messiah clouded their understanding.

Matthew prefaced Jesus' first parable by introducing what follows as parabolic teaching. The Greek word *parabole* is a noun, and *paraballo* is the verb, meaning "to throw beside." The noun means, "a placing of one thing by the side of another, juxtaposition, as of ships in battle."[689] Metaphorically it means "a comparing, comparison of one thing with another, likeness, similitude."[690] The Septuagint translates the Hebrew word *masal* with *parabole* 28 of its 33 occurrences in the Old Testament. The word *masal* refers to proverbs, maxims, similes, allegories, fables, comparisons, riddles, taunts, and stories embodying some truth. Thus it has a wide range of meanings. The New Testament uses of *parabole* likewise reflect a wide range of meanings, though essentially a parable involves a comparison. Most parables are extended similes or metaphors.

". . . in the Synoptic Gospels a parable denotes an extended comparison between nature or life and the things involving the spiritual life and God's dealings with men."[691]

"So understood, a *parabole* is an utterance which does not carry its meaning on the surface, and which thus demands thought and perception if the hearer is to benefit from it."[692]

Jesus deliberately "spoke . . . in parables" to conceal truth from the unbelieving crowds (vv. 11-15; cf. 7:6). Why did He speak to them in parables if He did not want them to understand what He said? He did so because a parable might be the instrument God would use to enlighten some who had not yet firmly rejected Him, but were still open-minded (cf. 11:25-26). By concealing the truth from His unbelieving critics, Jesus was showing them grace.

"They were saved from the guilt of rejecting the truth, for they were not allowed to recognize it."[693]

Jesus also taught in parables because the Old Testament predicted that Messiah would speak in veiled language (v. 35; cf. Ps. 78:2).

As will become clear, Jesus was instructing His disciples about what would happen since Israel had rejected Him. God would postpone the messianic kingdom until a later time. If Jesus had told the multitudes that the kingdom would not begin immediately, the people would have turned against Him in even greater numbers. Most of the Jews could not bring themselves to believe that Jesus was the Messiah. It would be even more difficult for them to accept a postponement of the kingdom. Significantly, Jesus' teaching about the postponement of the kingdom followed Israel's rejection of Him as her King.[694]

---

[687]France, *The Gospel . . .*, p. 500.

[688]Edersheim, *The Life . . .*, 1:581.

[689]Thayer, *A Greek-English Lexicon of the New Testament*, s.v. "*parabole*," p. 479.

[690]Ibid.

[691]Toussaint, *Behold the . . .*, p. 169.

[692]France, *The Gospel . . .*, p. 502.

[693]Plummer, p. 188.

[694]See Mark Saucy, "The Kingdom-of-God Sayings in Matthew," *Bibliotheca Sacra* 151:602 (April-June 1994):175-97.

"The seven parables of ch. 13, called by our Lord 'mysteries of the kingdom of heaven' (v. 11), taken together describe the result of the presence of the Gospel in the world during the present age, that is, the time of seed-sowing which began with our Lord's personal ministry and will end with the 'harvest' (vv. 40-43). The result is the mingled tares and wheat, good fish and bad, in the sphere of Christian profession. It is Christendom."[695]

2. Parables addressed to the multitudes 13:3b-33

Jesus spoke four parables to the multitudes, and provided some instruction to His disciples about how to interpret them.

The parable of the soils 13:3b-9 (cf. Mark 4:3-9; Luke 8:5-8)

The first parable is an introduction to those that follow, and the last one is a conclusion and application of the whole series.[696] Both emphasize God's Word.

"Modern interpretation of the parable has increasingly recognized this implication of the literary form of this particular parable, over against the dogmatic assertion of earlier NT scholarship, following Adolf Jülicher, that a parable has only a single point and that all the rest is mere narrative scenery, which must not be 'allegorized' to determine what each detail means. In this cast the way the story is constructed demands that the detail be noticed, and to interpret those details individually is not arbitrary 'allegorization' but a responsible recognition of the way Jesus constructed the story."[697]

13:3b-7   The focus in the first parable is on the *soils*, rather than on "the sower." Some seeds fell beside the path that was hard from traffic (v. 4). They lay on the surface where birds saw them and devoured them before they could germinate. Other seeds fell where the topsoil was thin (vv. 5-6). Their roots could not penetrate the limestone underneath to obtain necessary moisture from the subsoil. When the hot weather set in, the seeds germinated quickly but did not have the necessary resources to sustain continued growth. Consequently they died. A third group of seeds fell among "the thorns" that grew along the edges of the field (v. 7). These thorn bushes robbed the young plants of light and nourishment, so they died too.

"The figure marks a new beginning. To labor in God's vineyard (Israel, Isa. 5:1-7) is one thing; to go forth sowing the seed of the Word in a field which is the world, quite another (cp. Mt. 10:5)."[698]

13:8-9   Some seed also fell on good ground and produced "a crop." Even "a hundredfold" return was not outstanding.[699] The same sower and seed produced no crop, some crop, or much crop—depending on the soil.

"This fourth soil cautions us not to expect identical levels of fruitfulness in all people, since believers grow spiritually at different rates."[700]

Jesus' final statement means the parable needs careful consideration and interpretation (v. 9). Jesus interpreted it to His disciples later in verses 18-23.[701]

The first interlude about understanding the parables 13:10-23

This pericope falls into two parts: Jesus' explanation of why He taught with parables (vv. 10-17), and His explanation of the first parable (vv. 18-23).

The purpose of the parables 13:10-17 (cf. Mark 4:10-12; Luke 8:9-10)

13:10   The disciples wanted to know "why" Jesus was teaching "in parables." This was not the clearest form of communication. Evidently the disciples asked this question when Jesus had finished giving the parables to the crowd (cf. Mark 4:10). The plural "parables" suggests this. Matthew apparently rearranged the material Jesus presented, to help his readers understand the reasons for Jesus' use of parables at this point, since their enigmatic character raises questions in our minds.

---

[695]*The New Scofield . . .*, p. 1013.

[696]Stanley D. Toussaint, "The Introductory and Concluding Parables of Matthew Thirteen," *Bibliotheca Sacra* 121:484 (October-December 1964):351-55.

[697]France, *The Gospel . . .*, p. 503.

[698]*The New Scofield . . .*, p. 1013. See also McClain, pp. 324-25.

[699]Carson, "Matthew," p. 305.

[700]Bailey, in *The New . . .*, p. 25.

[701]See idem, "The Parable of the Sower and the Soils," *Bibliotheca Sacra* 155:618 (April-June 1998):172-88.

13:11-12   Jesus explained that He was teaching in parables, because He wanted to give new revelation ("mysteries") concerning "the kingdom" to His disciples, but not to the multitudes (cf. 7:6). Therefore He presented this truth in a veiled way. The word "mysteries" (Gr. *mysterion*, secrets) comes from the Old Testament and the Hebrew word *raz* (Dan. 2:18, 19, 27, 28, 29, 30, 47 [twice]; 4:9). It refers to what God knows will happen in the future. "Mysteries" are "secrets," namely, divine plans for the future that He reveals to His elect. Paul defined a mystery in Colossians 1:26 where he wrote, "the mystery which has been hidden from the past ages and generations, but has now been manifested to His saints."

> "A 'mystery' in Scripture is a previously hidden truth now divinely revealed. This chapter shows clearly for the first time, that there will be an interval between Christ's first and second advents (vv. 17, 35; cp. 1 Pet. 1:10-12)."[702]

Jesus was revealing some of God's plans concerning the future of the messianic kingdom, but He was not allowing the unbelieving multitudes to understand these plans.

> "Whenever, then, the fewness of believers disturbs us, let the converse come to mind, that only those to whom it is given can comprehend the mysteries of God [Matt. 13:11]."[703]

Some have interpreted these parables as revealing "the coming of the Kingdom into history in advance of its apocalyptic manifestation."[704] This is the view of covenant premillenarians and progressive dispensationalists. Others believe Jesus revealed information about the kingdom in view of its postponement.[705] This is the interpretation of normative dispensationalists.

> ". . . the very outskirts of the subject already force the conclusion that those mysteries refer not to the nature of the kingdom, but to the manner of its establishment, the means employed, the preparation for it, the time for its manifestation, and such related subjects."[706]

The Bible student must determine which of these two views is correct, on the basis of the meaning of the parables, and from all that Matthew has recorded about the kingdom.

Some dispensational writers believe the parables in Matthew 13 deal with the period between the first and second advents of Messiah, exclusively.[707] Some of these believe that there is no connection between these parables and Old Testament teaching.[708] Other dispensationalists believe these parables describe the inter-advent period culminating in the messianic kingdom. This is the interpretation I prefer, and it is quite similar to the preceding view. It seems to me that since Jesus consistently used the same terms for the kingdom in chapter 13 that He did elsewhere in Matthew, He was referring to the same entity. Nothing in the chapter makes this interpretation unnatural. Another option is that these parables describe only the messianic (millennial) kingdom.[709]

Verse 12 repeats a proverbial truth (cf. 25:29). It encourages gratitude for spiritual blessings and warns against taking these for granted. The believing disciples had access into the kingdom by faith in Jesus Christ. God would give them greater understanding that would result in abundance of blessing. However, the unbeliever would not only fail to receive further revelation, but God would remove the privilege of becoming a subject in the kingdom from him or her.

13:13   Jesus restated His reason for using parables, in terms of human perception, rather than divine intention (cf. vv. 11-12). The unbelievers were not able to understand what He had to reveal, since they had refused to accept more basic revelation, namely, about Jesus and the imminence of the kingdom. The parables do not just convey information. They challenge for a response. The unbelievers had not responded to the challenge Jesus had already given them. Until they did, they were in no condition to receive more truth.

---

[702]*The New Scofield . . .*, p. 1014.

[703]Calvin, *Institutes of . . .*, 1:7:5.

[704]George E. Ladd, *The Presence of the Future: The Eschatology of Biblical Realism*, p. 222; cf. p. 225. See also Carson, "Matthew," p. 307.

[705]Toussaint, pp. 171-72.

[706]Peters, 1:142.

[707]E.g., Walvoord, *Matthew: . . .*, p. 97-107; Barbieri, p. 50-51; and Pentecost, *The Words . . .*, p. 214.

[708]E.g., Gaebelein, 1:263-64; Barnhouse, pp. 169-70; Kelly, pp. 265-66; E. Schuyler English, *Studies in the Gospel According to Matthew*, pp. 91-92; and Ada R. Habershon, *The Study of the Parables*, pp. 112, 118-19.

[709]E.g., Toussaint, *Behold the . . .*, pp. 175-76; and Ronald N. Glass, "The Parables of the Kingdom: A Paradigm for Consistent Dispensational Hermeneutics," paper presented at the meeting of the Evangelical Theological Society, Lisle, Illinois, 18 November 1994.

"The giving of these parables, therefore, must be regarded as a *divine judgment* upon the nation of Israel."[710]

13:14-15   Jesus quoted Isaiah 6:9-10, where God told His prophet that widespread unbelief, and consequent divine heart-hardening, would be what he would experience in his ministry. The context of the Isaiah passage explained that Israel's hardness would continue until the land lay in ruins. The Exile was not the complete fulfillment of this prophecy. The hardhearted condition was still present in Jesus' day and, we might add, even today. Most Jews will remain generally unresponsive until their land is desolate in the Tribulation, but they will turn to the Lord when He returns to earth at His Second Coming (Zech. 12:10-14; Rom. 11:25-26). The word "lest" (NASB) or "otherwise" (NIV), in the middle of verse 15, probably indicates God's judicial hardening of the Jews' hearts (cf. 2 Thess. 2:11).

13:16-17   The believing disciples were "blessed" for this reason. They saw not only what their unbelieving contemporaries could not see, but what many prophets and righteous people of bygone years longed to see—but could not. Jesus referred to Old Testament prophets and believers who wanted more revelation about the kingdom than they had. Jesus' claim, to being able to reveal more than the Old Testament prophets knew, was a claim to being more than a prophet. Only God could do what He claimed to be doing.

> ". . . in Rabbinic opinion revelation of God's mysteries would only be granted to those who were righteous or learned."[711]

As the unbelievers in Jesus' day were the spiritual descendants of the unbelievers in Isaiah's day, so the disciples were the sons of the prophets. Likewise, Jesus was the Son of God.

The explanation of the parable of the soils 13:18-23 (cf. Mark 4:13-20; Luke 8:11-15)

Jesus interpreted His first parable to help His disciples understand both it and the others that followed (cf. Mark 4:13).

13:18   Since former prophets and righteous people wanted to know this revelation, and since the unbelieving could not understand it, the disciples needed to listen to it carefully.

13:19   Some people heard Jesus' preaching about the kingdom, but, like hard soil, the truth did not penetrate them. Satan ("the evil one") snatched the message away before they really understood it. The four soil types represent four *kinds of reception* people gave to the preaching about the kingdom.

13:20-21   The second type of soil stands for those whose initial response to the message Jesus preached was enthusiastic reception ("joy"). This reception gave hope for much fruit to follow. However, external pressures inhibit growth, and because they do not have an adequate rooting in the truth, they soon fade and wither (cf. 5:29). These people are disciples who begin well, but fail to continue to follow the Lord faithfully. Whether they are saved or lost is beside the point. However, some expositors have restricted the meaning to either saved or lost disciples.[712]

> "It is important to understand the explanation of the parable of the soils in its context and with the purpose of the original parable particularly in mind. The key issue is responsiveness or non-responsiveness to the message of the kingdom."[713]

13:22   This disciple (soil "among thorns") allows the other concerns of life to crowd out his commitment to Jesus. He permits the competing concerns of life to take precedence over his spiritual development (cf. 19:16-22). The present life, rather than the life to come, and present treasure, rather than future treasure, capture his affections. They are deceitful because they can drain spiritual vitality before the person realizes what is happening to him or her.

13:23   The "good soil" stands for the person who understands the message about the kingdom, when he or she hears it, and responds appropriately to it. This would involve believing in Jesus. Such a person eventually becomes spiritually productive, though the degree of productivity varies (cf. 20:1-15). However, Jesus commended all who received the message of the

---

[710]McClain, p. 322.

[711]Edersheim, *The Life* . . ., 1:597.

[712]E.g., Robert N. Wilkin, "The Parable of the Four Soils: Do the Middle Two Soils Represent Believers or Unbelievers? (Matthew 13:20-21)," *The Grace Evangelical Society News* 3:8 (August-September 1988):2.

[713]Hagner, p. 381.

kingdom, and believed it, regardless of their measure of productivity. The "fruit" in view probably represents increasing understanding of, and proper response to, divine revelation, in view of the context.

If the disciples understood this parable, they could understand the others that followed.

> "The principle taught by the parable is this: reception of the word of the kingdom in one's heart produces more understanding and revelation of the kingdom."[714]

The parable of the weeds 13:24-30

> "Between these two parables [the parable of the soils, vv. 2-23, and the parable of the homeowner, v. 52] are six parables that reveal new truths about God's kingdom. Jesus called them 'the mysteries of the kingdom of heaven' (v. 11). These new truths revealed that a new age would intervene before the millennial kingdom would come; this new age is the present church-age dispensation. Because Israel refused to accept Jesus as their Messiah, a drastic change was made in God's prophetic program. Whereas the kingdom had been proclaimed as near, now a formerly unpredicted period of time would intervene before the kingdom would come. These parables contain truths not seen in the Old Testament."[715]

> "The parable of the sower shows that though the kingdom will now make its way amid hard hearts, competing pressures, and even failure, it will produce an abundant crop. But one might ask whether Messiah's people should immediately separate the crop from the weeds; and this next parable answers the question negatively: there will be a delay in separation until the harvest."[716]

The second and seventh parables both deal with judgment.

13:24   Jesus told the crowds another parable. He literally said, "The kingdom of heaven *has become like* . . ." Matthew used the aorist passive tense, *homoiothe*. This is very significant because it indicates a change in the kingdom program. The change was a result of Israel's rejection of Jesus. In all these parables, Jesus did not mean that any single person or object in the parable symbolized the kingdom. The narrative itself communicated truth about the kingdom.

> "The parable of the wheat and tares is not a description of the world, but of that which professes to be the kingdom [i.e., Christendom]."[717]

13:25-26   The farmer's "enemy" maliciously "sowed" weeds ("tares") that looked like the "wheat." This weed was evidently bearded darnel (Lat. *lolium temulentum*), a plant that looks very much like wheat when the plants are young. The roots would intertwine with those of the wheat, but when the two plants reached maturity it would be clear which was which. The enemy thoroughly distributed the darnel seed among the young wheat. As the plants grew, it "became evident" to the field owner's servants what the enemy had done.

13:27   The function of the slaves in the parable is simply to get information from the owner.

13:28-30   The farmer "landowner" recognized that "an enemy" was responsible for the weeds, but he instructed his servants to allow the weeds "to grow" among the wheat "until the harvest." Then he would separate them. Evidently there were many weeds. "The reapers" would "gather" the weeds first and "burn them." Then they would harvest "the wheat."

> The new truth about the present age that this parable revealed is that good and evil people will co-exist in it (e.g., Judas Iscariot among Jesus' disciples; cf. vv. 47-49). In contrast, the Old Testament prophets said that in the coming messianic kingdom, righteousness will prevail and God will judge sin swiftly (cf. Isa. 11:1-5; 16:5; 32:1; 54:14; 60:17-18; Jer. 33:14-15).

Jesus interpreted this parable to His disciples later (vv. 36-43). He previously used the Old Testament figure of harvest to refer to *judgment* (9:37-38). In this case, the wheat and the weeds must both be people who face judgment in the future.[718]

---

[714]Toussaint, *Behold the* . . ., p. 179.

[715]Idem and Quine, p. 139.

[716]Carson, "Matthew," pp. 315-16.

[717]*The New Scofield* . . ., p. 1015.

[718]See Mark L. Bailey, "The Parable of the Tares," *Bibliotheca Sacra* 155:619 (July-September 1998):266-79.

The parable of the mustard seed 13:31-32 (cf. Mark 4:30-32; Luke 13:18-19)

This third, and the fourth parable, both deal with the growth of the present form of the kingdom.

The "mustard seed" was so small that the Jews used it proverbially to represent a very small thing (cf. 17:20).[719] When mature, the mustard plant stood 10 to 12 feet tall as "the largest of garden plants" (NIV).[720] Consequently it became a perch for "birds." Several Old Testament passages use a tree with birds flocking to its branches to illustrate a kingdom that people perceive as great (Judg. 9:15; Ps. 104:12; Ezek. 17:22-24; 31:3-14; Dan. 4:7-23). The birds evidently represent those who seek shelter in the kingdom.

The Jews correctly believed that the messianic kingdom would be very large. Why did Jesus choose the mustard plant since it did not become as large as some other plants? Evidently He did so because of the small beginning of the mustard plant. The contrast between an unusually small beginning and a large mature plant is the point of this parable.[721] Jesus' ministry began despicably small in the eyes of many Jews. Nevertheless, from this small beginning would come the worldwide kingdom predicted in the Old Testament.[722]

The parable of the yeast hidden in meal 13:33 (cf. Luke 13:20-21)

This parable stresses the extensive ultimate condition and consequences, of the kingdom, that would be out of all proportion to its insignificant beginnings.

> "Whereas the parable of the mustard seed answers the question of whether the phase of the kingdom planted by Jesus would survive, the parable of the leavening process answers how."[723]

Some interpreters have understood yeast as a metaphorical reference to evil.[724] However, not all uses of yeast in the Old Testament carry this symbolic meaning (e.g., Lev. 7:13; 23:15-18).[725]

This parable stresses the hidden internal change taking place in the kingdom, between its inception in Jesus' ministry, and its final form when the kingdom will cover the earth in the Millennium (cf. 5:13).

> "The kingdom of heaven may be initially insignificant, but it is pervasive."[726]

> ". . . the Kingdom of God, when received within, would seem like leaven hid, but would gradually pervade, assimilate, and transform the whole of our common life."[727]

> "The manifestation of the presence of the kingdom in some form in the Church age is clearly taught in the parables of the mustard seed and the leaven . . ."[728]

This fact led J. Dwight Pentecost to call the inter-advent age the mystery form of the kingdom.[729]

The fact that "a woman" put the "leaven" in the meal is probably an insignificant detail of the parable, as is the amount of flour. Three satas of flour (about three-fifths of a bushel) is the amount of flour that a housewife baked into bread for an average family.[730]

---

[719]Mishnah *Niddah* 5:2.

[720]Cf. Lenski, p. 528.

[721]Cf. N. A. Dahl, *Jesus in the Memory of the Early Church*, pp. 155-56.

[722]See Mark L. Bailey, "The Parable of the Mustard Seed," *Bibliotheca Sacra* 155:620 (October-December 1998):449-59.

[723]Idem, "The Parable of the Leavening Process," *Bibliotheca Sacra* 156:621 (January-March 1999):62.

[724]E.g., Toussaint, *Behold the . . .*, p. 182; Walvoord, *Matthew: . . .*, p. 103; and *The New Scofield . . .*, p. 1015.

[725]Cf. Barbieri, p. 51.

[726]France, *The Gospel . . .*, p. 528.

[727]Edersheim, *The Life . . .*, 1:594.

[728]Gerry Breshears, "The Body of Christ: Prophet, Priest, or King?" *Journal of the Evangelical Theological Society* 37:1 (March 1994):9.

[729]J. Dwight Pentecost, *Things to Come*, pp. 142-44.

[730]Idem, *The Words . . .*, p. 218.

"Practical applications of this parable to present readers can include the following. First, believers should depend on what God is doing through His Spirit in the present age. Second, Christians should be suspicious of any man-made, externally influenced institutional structures that say they are the manifestation of God's kingdom. Third, believers must be cautious about setting dates and presuming the arrival of the kingdom since the parable gives no hint as to when the permeation ends. Fourth, Jesus' followers can be confident that regardless of any current perspectives, the kingdom of God has a glorious future."[731]

3. The function of these parables 13:34-43

This section, like the other two interludes in the discourse (vv. 10-23, 49-51), has two parts. The first is an explanation about parables generally (vv. 34-35), and the second is an explanation of one parable in particular (vv. 36-43).

The fulfillment of prophecy 13:34-35 (cf. Mark 4:33-34)

13:34   Matthew stressed the importance of parables in Jesus' teaching. This verse is a chiasm in the Greek text with "parables" in the middle. Jesus constantly used parables in His spoken ministry to the multitudes following His rejection (cf. v. 3a).

> "Jesus deliberately adopted the parabolic method of teaching at a particular stage in His ministry for the purpose of withholding further truth about Himself and the kingdom of heaven from the crowds, who had proved themselves to be deaf to His claims and irresponsive to His demands. Hitherto, He had used parables as illustrations, whose meaning was self-evident from the context in which they were spoken (e.g., vi. 24-27). From now onwards, when addressing the unbelieving multitude he speaks only in parables (34), which He interprets to His disciples in private."[732]

13:35   The writer claimed that this portion of Jesus' ministry fulfilled Asaph's statement in Psalm 78:2. Asaph wrote that he would explain to his readers aspects of Israel's history that had been previously unknown. He then proceeded to use Israel's history to teach the Israelites how consistently rebellious they had been toward God, and how just and merciful God had been with them. He taught these lessons by using "parables," by comparing various things. By comparing various incidents in Israel's history, he revealed things previously unclear. Stephen used the same technique in Acts 7.

> Jesus did the same thing when He taught the multitudes using parables. He revealed to the people some things that they had not previously understood. Jesus was not teaching entirely new things any more than Asaph was in Psalm 78. He put things together that taught the crowds new lessons. Jesus *concealed* some truth by using parables, but with them He also *revealed* some truth to the multitudes. This is the point of Matthew's quotation of Asaph here. Jesus was bringing together pieces of previous revelation about the kingdom, and by combining these, was teaching the people new things about the kingdom. He was throwing new light on the kingdom with His comparisons (parables). Thus, while these parables were mysteries, new revelations, they contained some elements that God has previously revealed.

The explanation of the parable of the weeds 13:36-43

Matthew separated the explanation of this parable from its telling in the text (vv. 24-30). He evidently did this to separate more clearly, for the reader, the parables Jesus spoke to the multitudes from the parables He told His disciples.

13:36   Jesus now removed Himself from "the crowds" by reentering "the house," evidently in Capernaum, from which He had departed to teach the multitudes (v. 1). There he explained three of the parables (vv. 10-23, 37-43, 49-50) and taught His disciples four more (vv. 44-48, 52). Jesus' disciples were not different from the crowd because they immediately understood the parables. They were different because they persisted in asking Jesus to help them understand the parables, whereas the crowds showed less interest. Why did Jesus continue to teach His believing disciples by parables rather than with straightforward explanations? Evidently so many people were following Jesus that whenever He spoke, except in private to His disciples, a mixed audience heard Him.

13:37-39   Jesus identified Himself as both the sower and the director of the harvest. He took these Old Testament figures for God and applied them to Himself.[733] "The field" is "the world" where the sowing takes place, but the wheat (good seed) and "the tares" represent true and professing-only believers.

[731]Bailey, "The Parable . . . Leavening . . .," p. 71.

[732]Tasker, pp. 134-35.

[733]See Philip B. Payne, "Jesus' Implicit Claim to Deity in His Parables," *Trinity Journal* 2NS:1 (Spring 1981):3-23.

"This brief statement presupposes a mission beyond Israel (cf. 10:16-18; 28:18-20) and confirms that the narrower command of 10:5-6 is related exclusively to the mission of the Twelve during the period of Jesus' earthly ministry."[734]

Notice particularly that the field is not the church. The identification of the field as the church was common in the writings of some early church fathers and in those of some Reformers, and it is quite popular with many modern critical, evangelical, and even dispensational scholars. I think it is incorrect, since the kingdom predicted in the Old Testament is distinctly different from the church. This parable does not teach that there will be a mixture of good and evil in the "true" church, true believers and professing-only believers. The terms "world," "church," and "kingdom" are all distinct in the New Testament.

The "good seed" represents the "sons of the kingdom," namely, those destined for the kingdom, not those presently in the kingdom. The messianic kingdom has not yet begun. Compare 8:12, where the sons of the kingdom are Jewish unbelievers, namely, Jews who should have been destined for the kingdom but were unbelievers of Jesus. The weeds are "sons of the evil one," i.e., sons of Satan (cf. John 8:44; 1 John 5:19).

"Not all unbelievers are called children of the devil; only those who have willfully rejected the light are so designated (cp. v. 38; Jn. 8:38-44)."[735]

The "devil" is the "enemy," the "harvest" is the "end of the age" (9:37; cf. Jer. 51:33; Hos. 6:11; Joel 3:13), and the harvesters ("reapers") are "angels" (24:30-31; 25:31; cf. 18:10; Luke 15:7; Heb. 1:14; 1 Pet. 1:12). Obviously several elements in this parable have significance. However, note that many others do not (e.g., the conversation between the man and his servants, the servants' sleep, the order of the sowing, etc.).

"This condition of the kingdom was never revealed in the Old Testament, which spoke of a kingdom of righteousness in which evil would be overcome."[736]

The "end of the age" refers to the end of the *present age*, that will culminate in Jesus' Second Coming and a judgment of living unbelievers (cf. vv. 40, 49; 24:3).

13:40-42   The unbelievers who are born in Jesus' messianic (millennial) kingdom, which will begin when He returns to earth at His Second Coming, will continue to live in that earthly kingdom. I put the word "millennial" in parentheses because God did not reveal the 1,000-year length of the kingdom until Revelation 20. However, at the end of the kingdom, at the end of the 1,000-year reign, Jesus will separate the unbelievers from the believers (cf. Zeph. 1:3). The unbelievers will then perish eternally (Rev. 20:15; cf. Matt. 3:11; 5:22; 8:12; 13:50; Jer. 29:22).[737]

13:43   In contrast to the unbelievers, the believers ("the righteous") will continue to glorify God ("shine forth as the sun") forever (5:13-16; cf. Dan 12:3). "The kingdom of their Father" is probably a synonym for the kingdom of the Son (v. 41), in the sense that the kingdom belongs to both the Father and the Son. However, when the messianic (millennial) kingdom ends, the rule of the Son and the Father will continue forever in the new heaven and the new earth (Rev. 21—22). The Messiah's reign on this earth will be the first phase of His reign, that will continue on the new earth forever.

This parable describes an order of events that is the same as what Jesus presented elsewhere as occurring at His Second Coming (cf. 24:37-41; Luke 17:26-37). This order of events is the opposite of what He said would happen at the Rapture. At the Rapture, Christ will remove all believers from the earth and unbelievers will remain on the earth (John 14:2-3; cf. 1 Thess. 4:17). At the Second Coming, unbelievers will be removed from the earth in judgment, while believers will remain on the earth to enter the millennial kingdom. Thus, the Rapture does not take place at the same time as the Second Coming, which posttribulationists believe.[738]

[734]Carson, "Matthew," p. 325.

[735]*The New Scofield . . .*, p. 1015.

[736]Barbieri, p. 50.

[737]See Pagenkemper, pp. 181-83.

[738]See Showers, pp. 176-91, for an extended discussion of the passages that indicate the differences between the Rapture and the coming of Christ with His holy angels, i.e, the Second Coming.

4. Parables addressed to the disciples 13:44-52

The first and second parables in this group are quite similar, as was true of the third and fourth parables in the preceding group. This is a further reflection of the chiastic structure of this section (vv. 1-53). These fifth and sixth parables, among the eight, both deal with the value of participating in the kingdom.

The parable of the hidden treasure 13:44

"The kingdom" (of heaven on earth) lay concealed in history for hundreds of years, perhaps from the Exile to the time of Jesus. Toussaint believed Jesus meant from the time of Rehoboam to Jesus.[739] When the Jews in Jesus' day stumbled on it, the believers among them recognized its worth and were eager to make any sacrifice necessary for it. The point of the parable to Jesus' disciples was that they should be willing to pay any price to have a significant part in the kingdom.

Some interpreters believe the person who "hid" and then paid a great price for the "treasure" was Jesus, the price being His own life.[740] This seems unlikely to me, since in all these parables the focus seems to be on the disciples more than on Jesus. They should pay the price.

The parable of the pearl 13:45-46

The same basic point recurs in this parable. The difference between this parable, and the last, is that here the person who finds the treasure is looking for it, whereas in the previous parable the discovery was accidental. In Jesus' day, there were Jews who were looking for the kingdom and Messiah (11:3), and those who were not (e.g., the religious leaders who did not accompany the wise men to Bethlehem). For both types of people, the ultimate price of complete discipleship was not too much to pay for participation in the kingdom. Jesus was not teaching that entrance into the kingdom depended on self-sacrifice; entrance depended on faith in Him. The amount and kind of one's inheritance in the kingdom, however, depended on commitment to Messiah (cf. 5:5; 8:18-22; 25:34).

Some people view "the pearl of great value," as well as the hidden treasure, as references to Jesus.[741] Others believe they refer to the church.[742] I think they refer primarily to the kingdom. Several dispensational interpreters believe the treasure in the field (or land) represents Israel—and that the pearl, taken from the sea, represents the Gentiles.[743]

> "Like the treasure, the kingdom is the source of highest joy, and, as seen in the pearl, the kingdom should be deemed as the most precious possession."[744]

The parable of the dragnet 13:47-48

This parable has a meaning similar to the parable of the weeds (vv. 24-30), which is its opposite in the chiastic structure of the discourse. However, the focus here is on the judgment at the end of the kingdom, rather than the mixed citizens of the kingdom. In both parables there are "good" and "bad" elements, believers and unbelievers. Jesus will separate these individuals at the end of His messianic (millennial) reign. They will all fall into one of two categories: "the good" (believers) or "the bad" (unbelievers).

The Greek word for "dragnet," *sagene*, occurs only here in the New Testament. It describes a large net that fishermen drew to shore between two boats. Sometimes they tied one end to the shore and the other end to a boat. Then they would sweep an area of the lake with it, possible a half mile long, drawing as many fish as possible to the shore with it.[745] Then they would separate the fish that they could sell from those that they could not.

The second interlude about understanding the parables 13:49-51

As with the previous interlude (13:10-23), in this interlude there is an explanation of one parable (vv. 49-50), and then a word about understanding all the parables (v. 51; cf. vv. 10-23, 34-43).

---

[739]Toussaint, *Behold the . . .*, p. 183.

[740]E.g., Ibid., p. 184; and Robert N. Wilkin, "A Great Buy!" *The Grace Evangelical Society News* 6:9 (September 1991):2.

[741]E.g., Richard C. Trench, *Notes on the Parables of Our Lord*, pp. 102-10.

[742]E.g., Walvoord, *Matthew: . . .*, p. 105; Toussaint, *Behold the . . .*, p. 184; and *The New Scofield . . .*, p. 1016.

[743]E.g., Pentecost, *The Words . . .*, p. 218.

[744]Mark L. Bailey, "The Parables of the Hidden Treasure and of the Pearl Merchant," *Bibliotheca Sacra* 156:622 (April-June 1999):189.

[745]Lenski, p. 547.

The explanation of the parable of the dragnet 13:49-50

Jesus interpreted the meaning of the previous parable without waiting for His disciples to ask Him to do so. The picture seems to be of judgment at the end of the messianic (millennial) kingdom (cf. vv. 41-42). Many other premillennial interpreters believed the judgment in view is the one before the establishment of the kingdom.[746] Later, Matthew recorded that Jesus told two more parables about this judgment at the beginning of the Millennium. The parable of the ten virgins (25:1-13) stressed the need for readiness for this judgment. The parable of the sheep and the goats (25:31-46) identified the basis for the judgment.

In the parable of the dragnet, the point was the sorting out of righteous and wicked individuals that will happen then. "The angels" will assist Jesus in this process. "The wicked" will go to eternal destruction (cf. v. 42), but "the righteous" will continue on in Messiah's kingdom, which will then move from the present earth to the new earth.

"The fear motive is often condemned by modern Christians, but the Book of Matthew shows Jesus was not opposed to using it properly."[747]

The importance of understanding the parables 13:51

Jesus' question here marks the conclusion to His explanation of the miracles that the disciples' question in verse 36 requested. "All these things" probably refers to everything that Jesus had said to the disciples. The disciples claimed to understand what Jesus had said, and presumably they did understand somewhat, at least superficially (cf. 15:16).

"Matthew contains a total of seven parables, the first and longest of which has to do with Jesus' parabolic method. The rest of the parables have to do with the kingdom of heaven. Every one of the six stresses the hiddenness of the kingdom. It is like treasure hidden in a field, like yeast hidden in dough, like good seed hidden in soil. But we have become bottom-line conscious in the institutional Church and in parachurch organizations. We cannot raise money to support our ministries unless we can quote statistics concerning how successful we are. We have to be able to measure results. We want to evaluate the harvest day after day after day so that we can use the information in our fund-raising endeavors. And we forget that the real impact of the Church of Jesus Christ in the world is immeasurable. We will only know what it is at the harvest, which is the end of the age."[748]

The parable of the homeowner 13:52

Commentators often omit this verse from discussions of the parables in this discourse. Some do not consider it one of the parables of the kingdom.[749] However, it contains a parable, as should be clear from the content of the verse itself, and from the literary structure of the discourse.

Jesus drew a comparison between a "scribe" instructed about the kingdom and the owner of a house ("head of a household"). In view of what follows, the "scribe" portrayed seems to be one who received instruction about the kingdom and believed it. He is a believing "disciple." As with the owner of a house, this type of scribe brings "new and old" things "out of his" storeroom or "treasure" (Gr. *thesauros*). The owner of the house in the parable brings things out of his storeroom to use them beneficially. The storeroom from which the disciple-scribe brings these things is evidently his heart or understanding (i.e., his very being). He brings out *new* understanding concerning the kingdom that Jesus had taught him, as well as *old* understanding about the kingdom, that the Old Testament taught him. The new did not displace the old but supplemented it. Jesus was comparing His believing disciples to this believing scribe. They had just said they understood what Jesus had taught them (v. 51). Therefore they had a responsibility to teach others what they now understood. Every disciple must become a scribe, a teacher of the law, because he or she understands things that require communicating to others (cf. 10:27; 28:19; Heb. 5:12).

"The first two parables relate to planting. The parable of the sower speaks of different responses to the message of the kingdom. The parable of the tares explains the origins of the conflict between the sons of the kingdom and the sons of the enemy and announces that a final separation of the two groups will take place when Jesus, the Son of Man, will return at the end of the age. The second pair of parables utilizes the analogy of growth. The mustard seed reveals the extent of the rapid international growth of the kingdom of heaven, and the leavening process addresses the internal and invisible dynamic of that growth. The next two parables (the treasure and the pearl merchant) address the value of the kingdom. Whether one is looking or not looking, no sacrifice is too great for the kingdom. The final set of parables reveals the disciples' dual responsibilities. The dragnet teaches that evangelism without discrimination should be done in view of Jesus' discriminating

---

[746]E.g., Toussaint, *Behold the . . .*, p. 184; Walvoord, *Matthew: . . .*, p. 106; and Showers, p. 178.

[747]Mark L. Bailey, "The Parables of the Dragnet and of the Householder," *Bibliotheca Sacra* 156:623 (July-September 1999):290.

[748]Richard C. Halverson, "God and Caesar," *Journal of the Evangelical Theological Society* 37:1 (March 1994):127.

[749]E.g., Ibid., p. 107; Walvoord, *Matthew: . . .*, p. 97; and Hagner, pp. 362-64.

judgment at the end of the age. The householder encourages the teaching of both the older and newer truths of the kingdom of heaven by the disciples of the kingdom."[750]

THE LESSONS OF JESUS' KINGDOM PARABLES IN MATTHEW 13	
Soils	God's Word will be sown and predictable results will follow culminating in the earthly kingdom.
Tares	There will be counterfeit believers in the inter-advent kingdom whom God will judge eventually.
Mustard seed	The kingdom will grow from a small beginning to become a large entity.
Leaven	The present form of the kingdom will become increasingly influential.
Treasure	Participation in the kingdom is worth paying any price for.
Pearl	Those seeking the kingdom will find it worth any sacrifice.
Dragnet	The kingdom will include universal harvesting followed by judgment.
Householder	The kingdom will involve new revelation as well as old.

"As we survey the parables, then, we find that in view of Israel's rejection of the person of Christ, He foresaw the postponement of the millennial form of the kingdom. He announced the introduction of a new form of the kingdom, one that will span the period from Israel's rejection of Christ until Israel's future reception of Christ at the Second Advent."[751]

"What is certain in the teaching of these difficult parables is that the present age, viewed from the standpoint of the Kingdom, is a time of *preparation*."[752]

5. The departure 13:53

Matthew leaves the reader with the impression, from this concluding transition, as well as from the structure of the discourse—that Jesus related all the preceding parables at one time. This was apparently the case, though He may have repeated some of them at various other times as well. Jesus now left Capernaum and traveled to Nazareth (v. 54).

The clause "and it came about that when Jesus had finished" signals the end of the discourse and the end of another major section of this Gospel. Matthew carefully traced the course of opposition to the King in this section. Israel's rejection of Jesus was so clear that the King began to tailor His teaching more specifically to unbelievers and to believers.

"Thematically the three chapters (11—13) are held together by the rising tide of disappointment in and opposition to the kingdom of God that was resulting from Jesus' ministry. He was not turning out to be the kind of Messiah the people had expected. Even John the Baptist had doubts (vv. 2-19), and the Galilean cities that were sites of most of Jesus' miracles hardened themselves in unbelief (vv. 20-24). The nature of Jesus' person and ministry were 'hidden' (an important word) from the wise, despite the most open and compassionate of invitations (vv. 28-30). Conflicts with Jewish leaders began to intensify (12:1-45), while people still misunderstood the most basic elements of Jesus' teaching and authority (12:46-50)."[753]

However, Jesus' enemies had not checkmated Him. The kingdom would still come. Matthew 13 provides assurance of that fact. Jesus added new revelation to old, about the kingdom—in this chapter—to appeal further to the crowds, and to prepare His disciples for what lay ahead. He did not teach about the church in this chapter, though He did describe conditions that would exist in the Church Age, which is part of the inter-advent era. The new revelation that there would be a "church" did not come until chapter 16. He *did* give further revelation here concerning the coming messianic kingdom (ch. 13).[754]

---

[750]Bailey, "The Parables of the Dragnet . . .," p. 296. For a summary of the major themes in these parables and a list of applicational principles, see idem, "The Doctrine of the Kingdom in Matthew 13," *Bibliotheca Sacra* 156:624 (October-December 1999):443-51.

[751]Pentecost, *The Words* . . ., p. 219.

[752]McClain, p. 441.

[753]Carson, "Matthew," p. 260.

[754]See Bailey, in *The New* . . ., pp. 29-30, for a list of 25 major truths taught in Matthew 13.

V. THE REACTIONS OF THE KING 13:54—19:2

Matthew recorded increasing polarization in this section. Jesus expanded His ministry, but as He did so opposition became even more intense. The Jewish leaders became increasingly hostile. Consequently Jesus spent more time preparing His disciples. Jesus revealed Himself more clearly to His disciples, but they only understood some of what He told them. They strongly rejected other things He said. The inevitability of a final confrontation between Jesus and His critics became increasingly clear. The general movement in this section is Jesus withdrawing from Israel's leaders (13:54—16:12) and preparing His disciples for His passion (16:13—19:2).

A. OPPOSITION, INSTRUCTION, AND HEALING 13:54—16:12

This section records the course that Jesus' ministry took because of Israel's rejection of Him. Opposition from several quarters led Him to withdraw to safer places, where He continued to minister to Jews and Gentiles, and to prepare His disciples for what lay ahead.

1. The opposition of the Nazarenes and Romans 13:54—14:12

The theme of opposition continues from the Parables about the Kingdom. Jesus' reaction to opposition by Israel's leaders was to withdraw (cf. 10:23). Matthew recorded Him doing this twice in this section. The first instance of opposition came from the people among whom Jesus had grown up in Nazareth (13:54-58). The second came from the Roman leadership of the area in which Jesus was ministering (14:1-12). Both sections show that opposition to Jesus was intense, from the Jewish common people to the Roman nobility.

The opposition of the Nazarenes 13:54-58 (cf. Mark 6:1-6)

13:54   Jesus' "hometown" was Nazareth (Luke 4:16). The local "synagogue" attendees wondered where Jesus obtained His authority. The "wisdom" in His teaching and the power ("powers") in His miracles demonstrated remarkable authority, but "where" did He get these? Did they come from God—or elsewhere (12:24)?

This is the last of Matthew's references to Jesus "teaching" in a "synagogue" (from the Greek meaning, "gathering together").[755] From now on, Jesus appears increasingly outside the structures of traditional Judaism.[756]

13:55-57a   The words of Jesus' critics reveal wounded pride. They did not like His having wisdom and power superior to theirs, since they had the same background. Their questions reveal denial of His Messiahship. By referring to Joseph as "the carpenter," and to Jesus as "the carpenter's son," they were implying that Jesus should have followed in His earthly father's footsteps. The definite article before "carpenter" suggests that there may have been only one carpenter in Nazareth. Carpenters did all types of work with wood and stone. Jesus was more of a builder, or construction worker, than a carpenter in the modern usage.[757]

In one sense, these questions were legitimate. However, the people of Nazareth rejected Jesus' claim to being a prophet (v. 57b). They "took offense" at Him in the sense that His claim caused them to stumble. It was their reaction to His claim, however, not the claim itself, that stumbled them.

"(Incidentally, their questions render impossible the fanciful miracles ascribed to Jesus' childhood by the apocryphal gospels.)"[758]

We must be careful not to confuse Jesus' half-"brothers"—"James," "Simon," and "Judas"—with the disciples who had the same names. There is no evidence that Jesus' half-brothers believed on Him until after His resurrection. His brother James eventually became the leader of the Jerusalem church (Acts 11).

13:57b-58   Usually a person enjoys a better reception at home than anywhere else, except if he has attained an exalted position, in which case the opposite is often true. Jesus could "not do many miracles there," because to do so would have been contrary to His mission. He did miracles in order to create and to strengthen faith in Himself. When settled unbelief reigned, there was no point in doing miracles.

The point of this section is to show that even those who knew Jesus best refused to believe on Him.

"Jesus led a perfect life and still had family members and friends who struggled to believe. Sometimes those most difficult to reach are those who know us best."[759]

---

[755]See Edersheim, Sketches of . . ., ch. xvi: "Synagogues: Their Origin, Structure, and Outward Arrangements."

[756]France, The Gospel . . ., p. 547.

[757]Ken M. Campbell, "What Was Jesus' Occupation?" Journal of the Evangelical Theological Society 48:3 (September 2005):501-19; France, The Gospel . . ., p. 549.

[758]Carson, "Matthew," p. 336.

The opposition of Herod and his friends 14:1-12 (cf. Mark 6:14-29; Luke 9:7-9)

14:1-2   "At that time" is again a loose connective not intended to communicate chronological sequence necessarily. Herod Antipas ("Herod the tetrarch") lived primarily at Tiberias on the west shore of Lake Galilee.[760] However, if all the events described in this story happened on one day, as seems likely, they must have taken place at Herod's residence at the Machaerus fortress, in southern Perea east of the Jordan River.[761] Antipas ruled over Galilee and Perea from 4 B.C. to A.D. 39, namely, during Jesus' entire earthly life.

Word about Jesus' ministry reached him easily there (cf. Luke 8:3). Herod had previously beheaded John for criticizing his morality (vv. 3-12). Herod could do this because John had ministered within Herod's jurisdiction of Perea (John 1:28). Public opinion evidently encouraged Herod to conclude that Jesus was "John the Baptist" who had come back to life (cf. Mark 6:14; Luke 9:7). He attributed Jesus' miracles to the supposedly resurrected John.

"The idea of a ghostly or even physical return of someone who has had a special influence, especially if that influence has been prematurely cut off by violent death, is found in various cultures (think of Elijah, Nero, King Arthur, Elvis)."[762]

14:3-5   The Synoptic writers ascribed moral and religious motives to Herod for executing John (cf. Mark 6:16-29; Luke 3:19-20). Josephus wrote that Herod beheaded John for political reasons.[763] Probably both reasons led Herod to act as he did.[764]

Herod Antipas had two brothers named Philip. The one Matthew referred to here was Herod Philip I. The other brother named Philip was Herod Philip II, tetrarch of Iturea and Trachonitis. Philip I was Herod Antipas' half-brother. Therefore, Antipas' marriage to Philip's wife "Herodias" was incestuous (cf. Lev. 18:16; 20:21). Evidently John had repeatedly rebuked Antipas since the verb in verse 4 can read, "he used to say [repeatedly]." Herodias was also Antipas' niece, but this would have been no problem for John since the law did not forbid uncles marrying their nieces. Combining the Synoptic accounts, Antipas appears to have been a weak man controlled by a wicked and ruthless wife, Herodias. Interestingly John, the latter-day Elijah, faced the modern counterparts of King Ahab and Queen Jezebel in Antipas and Herodias. Unfortunately Herodias succeeded where Jezebel had failed.

14:6-8   The day of celebration may have been "Herod's birthday" or the anniversary of his accession to the throne (Gr. *genesia*).[765] Herodias' daughter, by her previous marriage to Philip I, was Salome, who was then between 12 and 14 years old.[766] The popular idea that her dance was sensuous does not come from the text but from the reputation of the Herodians for low morals and from the low status of dancing girls.[767] Antipas was only a petty monarch, but he acted like one of the powerful Persian kings (cf. Esth. 5:3, 6; 7:2).

14:9-11   Antipas was wrong to give his "oath," which he evidently repeated more than once (vv. 7, 9), and he was wrong to keep it. He feared losing face with "his dinner guests." The Romans practiced decapitation. That form of execution was not Jewish. Likewise, the Romans executed certain prisoners without a trial, whereas Jewish law required one.[768] The gore of this scene testifies to the hardhearted condition of the Roman royal family and their courtiers. As the last of the Old Testament prophets, John suffered a martyr's death, as did many of his predecessors.

"Death, the temporary end of physical life, is not the worst enemy of humanity. Alienation from God is. And thus those who murdered John are far more pitiable than is John himself."[769]

14:12   Matthew's notation that Jesus heard about John's death unites John and Jesus against this political enemy. It also suggests that John's disciples still had high regard for Jesus (cf. 11:2-6). As Herod had heard the news about Jesus (v. 1), now Jesus heard the news about John.

---

[759]Bailey, in *The New . . .*, p. 30.

[760]Carson, "Matthew," p. 337.

[761]See Harold W. Hoehner, *Herod Antipas*, pp. 146-48; and Josephus, *Antiquities of . . .*, 18:5:2.

[762]France, *The Gospel . . .*, p. 553.

[763]Josephus, *Antiquities of . . .*, 18:5:2.

[764]Hoehner, *Herod Antipas*, pp. 124-49.

[765]Edersheim, *The Life . . .*, 1:672.

[766]Hoehner, *Herod Antipas*, pp. 151-56.

[767]Carson, "Matthew," p. 338.

[768]Ibid., p. 339.

[769]Donald A. Hagner, *Matthew 14—28*, p. 413.

Herod's testimony to the supernatural character of Jesus' miracles is important in Matthew's unfolding theme of people's perceptions of the King. Likewise the forerunner's unjust execution at the hands of hardhearted Roman officials foreshadows the fate of the King.[770] Matthew evidently recorded these verses to show how Roman political leaders viewed the King and His forerunner. Opposition against Him was intense, mainly for religious and moral reasons.

> "Matthew so connected the ministries of these two men that what happened to one was viewed as having a direct effect on the other. Herod, by rejecting the King's forerunner, was rejecting the King who followed him."[771]

2. The withdrawal to Bethsaida 14:13-33

Having experienced strong rejection from the common people and from the nation's political leaders, Jesus withdrew to train His disciples further. In view of the coming conflict, they needed stronger faith in Him. Jesus cultivated their faith with two miracles.

Jesus' feeding of the 5,000 14:13-21 (cf. Mark 6:30-44; Luke 9:10-17; John 6:1-13)

Matthew's record of this miracle, which all four Gospels contain, stresses Jesus' power to create, His compassion, and the disciples' responsibility to minister to multitudes as Jesus' representatives. It also previews the kingdom banquet (cf. 8:11). The simple meal that Jesus provided on this occasion, in a wholesome setting, contrasts with Herod's lavish feast, in a degenerate setting, just described.[772]

14:13-14   Since verses 3-12 are an excursus, the opening words of this pericope must refer to Herod's response to Jesus' ministry. When Jesus heard that, "He withdrew" from Herod's territory and his animosity (cf. 12:15). Evidently Jesus believed that Herod Antipas would also oppose Him, just as he had opposed His forerunner. As previously (12:15) and later (15:21), Jesus withdrew from a place of danger and confrontation.

> However, Jesus could not escape the crowds that followed Him wherever He went. The lonely place where Jesus retreated was evidently near Bethsaida Julias on Galilee's northeast shore (Luke 9:10). Jesus traveled there from Capernaum by boat, but the crowds beat "Him there on foot," having learned where He was going. They walked east along the northern coast of the Sea of Galilee. Matthew again noted the great "compassion" of the King (cf. 9:36).

14:15-17   In view of the context (v. 23), and the meaning of "evening" (Gr. *opsios*), the time must have been late afternoon.[773] There were several small towns within walking distance of this region where the people could have bought their own suppers.

> Jesus directions (v. 16) turned the disciples' attention to their own resources. By urging them to consider these, Jesus was leading them to recognize their personal inadequacy—and to appeal to Him as the *only* adequate resource (cf. John 2:1-11). There is nothing in the text or context that suggests the number of the loaves and fishes had symbolic significance, though many of the commentators have thought so.

14:18-21   Jesus' acts of looking heavenward, thanking God, and then breaking the loaves, were normal for the head of any Jewish household.[774] Jesus then performed the miracle, namely, creating enough bread and fish to feed the assembled throng. With 5,000 men present, the total size of the crowd may have been 10,000 to 20,000. Counting only the males had Old Testament precedent (cf. Exod. 12:37). Everyone had enough to eat and felt "satisfied" (v. 20). Jesus' provision was so abundant that there were 12 large wicker "baskets," "full" of scraps "left over," even after many thousands had eaten all they wanted. Evidently each of the 12 disciples had a large basket (Gr. *kophinos*) and circulated among the crowd until his basket was full (cf. John 6:12-13).

> "This sign was very important to three groups—the disciples, the believing remnant, and the wonder-watching unbelievers. From now on the miracles are primarily for the benefit of the disciples in that they are designed to instruct them. But in addition they confirm the faith of those who believe and the unbelief of the unbelieving masses. That they are for the disciples' training is seen in the fact that the rejection of the Lord is evident. The cities in which He had performed most of His mighty works had already indicated their apathy and opposition. He had left the masses so that He could be apart with the disciples."[775]

Jesus' training of the disciples is evident in His questioning them and His using them as His agents.

---

[770]Plummer, p. 201.

[771]Barbieri, p. 53.

[772]See Edersheim, *The Life . . .*, 1:677.

[773]See ibid., 1:681.

[774]Moore, 2:216-17.

[775]Toussaint, *Behold the . . .*, p. 190.

"The significance of this miracle was intended primarily for the disciples. Jesus was illustrating the kind of ministry they would have after His departure. They would be involved in feeding people, but with spiritual food. The source for their feeding would be the Lord Himself. When their supply ran out, as with the bread and fish, they would need to return to the Lord for more. He would supply them, but the feeding would be done through them."[776]

The Jews had a traditional belief that when Messiah came, He would feed the people with bread from heaven as Moses had done (Deut. 18:15).[777] Elisha also had miraculously fed 100 men (2 Kings 4:42-44). This miracle proved Jesus' ability to provide for Israel as her King. Also it probably reminded the spiritually perceptive, in the crowd, of the messianic banquet that the Old Testament predicted Messiah would provide (Ps. 132:15; cf. Matt. 6:11).

Jesus' walking on the water 14:22-33 (cf. Mark 6:45-52; John 6:14-21)

Jesus proceeded to do a second miracle to deepen His disciples' faith in Him even more.

14:22   As soon as the people had finished eating, Jesus "immediately compelled" (Gr. *eutheos enagkasen*) His disciples to enter a boat and depart for the other side of the lake. There appear to have been several reasons for His unusual action. First, this miracle appears to have refueled the enthusiasm of some in the crowd to draft Jesus and to force Him to lead the nation (cf. John 6:15). Perhaps Jesus wanted to spare His disciples from this attractive temptation.[778] Second, Jesus wanted to get away to pray (v. 23). Third, He wanted to prepare to get some rest (Mark 6:31-32). Fourth, He had an important lesson to teach them.

". . . there are two kinds of storms: storms of *correction*, when God disciplines us; and storms of *perfection*, when God helps us to grow. Jonah was in a storm because he disobeyed God and had to be corrected. The disciples were in a storm because they obeyed Christ and had to be perfected."[779]

Evidently Jesus sent the disciples up the eastern Galilee coast toward Bethsaida Julias with orders to wait for Him, but not beyond a certain time (John 6:17).[780] He planned to travel north by foot. They proceeded west across the lake by boat when He did not appear by the prearranged deadline.

14:23-24   After dismissing the crowd, Jesus walked up the mountainside (NIV) "to pray." There are no real mountains in this part of the Galilee coastline, but there are hills that slope down to the lake. He evidently stayed there longer than He had led the disciples to conclude that He would. Perhaps He prayed about the crowd's attempts to make Him king (John 6:15), among other things.

The word "evening," as the Jews used it, covers a period from late afternoon to shortly after sunset (cf. v. 15). Obviously it was now late in that evening period. By this time, the boat the disciples were in was quite "a long distance" out from the shore (v. 24). A storm had arisen, and the winds were blowing from the west, evidently forcing them away from the northern shore, and impeding their progress to the west.

14:25-27   The Jews divided the night, from sunset to sunrise, into three watches (Judg. 7:19; Lam. 2:19). The Romans, however, divided it into four. Matthew used the Roman division of watches. "The fourth watch of the night" was between 3:00 and 6:00 a.m. Jesus had spent most of the night *praying*, and the disciples had spent most of the night *rowing*.

Some translators rendered the Greek word *phantasma* as "ghost," but it means an apparition, i.e., an optical illusion or distorted appearance (cf. Mark 6:49). The disciples saw Jesus, but to them His appearance resembled that of a ghost. Perhaps rain or fog was responsible as well as poor light. They may have believed the popular superstition that evil spirits lived in the sea and that those who had drowned haunted the water.[781]

Jesus' response centered on, "It is I." Note the chiasm of His response. The disciples could take courage and not fear because Jesus was there. The words, "I am," were a term Jesus used to claim deity (cf. Exod. 3:14; Isa. 43:10; 51:12). The fourth Gospel stressed Jesus' use of this term especially. The disciples may not have realized this claim in the terror of the moment, but later they undoubtedly saw the significance of what He had said more clearly.

[776]Barbieri, p. 54.

[777]Plummer, p. 206.

[778]Lenski, p. 568.

[779]Wiersbe, 1:51.

[780]Leon Morris, *The Gospel According to John*, pp. 348-49.

[781]France, *The Gospel . . .*, p. 569.

"Fear is unwarranted where Jesus is present [cf. 1:23; 28:20]."[782]

Before the Fall, God had ordained that man rule over the sea (Gen. 1:28). Here Jesus was doing precisely that; He was fulfilling God's purpose for humankind. This action gave testimony to His being the Second Adam (cf. 8:27; Rom. 5:12-17), the Man who succeeded where Adam had failed. The Old Testament speaks of God walking on or through the sea (Job 9:8; Ps. 77:19; Isa. 43:16; cf. Ps. 18:16; 144:7).

14:28   This is the first of three occasions in which Matthew recorded that Peter received special treatment (cf. 16:13-23; 17:24-27).

"The Evangelist here presents Peter in all of his impetuosity mixed with his great devotion. In keeping with Matthew's style of writing, these traits, which are first mentioned here, characterize Peter throughout the remainder of the Gospel. More significant is the fact that the place of preeminence among the apostles which Peter here assumes is never lost in the rest of Matthew's Gospel."[783]

"The man who said, 'Bid me come to Thee,' was just the man to say, 'Lord, I am ready to go with Thee both into prison and to death.' . . . The scene on the lake was but a foreshadowing or rehearsal of Peter's fall."[784]

It seems almost incredible that Peter could have believed he would walk on water. However, the disciples had already done many mighty miracles because Jesus had given them the power to do so (cf. 10:1). We could translate the first class condition rendered "if it is you" as "since it is you." Peter evidently wanted to be as close to Jesus as he possibly could, as often as possible (cf. John 21:7).

14:29-31   With remarkable trust, Peter climbed over the side of the boat and began walking "on the water." He, too, in obedience to Jesus' command, was able to fulfill man's destiny by subduing the sea. He was doing well until he became more concerned about the waves than about Jesus. "Seeing the wind" is a figure of speech (synecdoche) for seeing the storm.[785] His distressing circumstances distracted his attention and weakened his faith in Jesus. Jesus rebuked him for his weak ("little") "faith," even though it was stronger than that of the other disciples who remained in the boat. Jesus used this rebuke to help Peter and the other disciples see that consistent confidence in Himself was absolutely necessary. Peter became both a good example and a bad one. Jesus rescued him—as God had rescued many others from watery graves (cf. Ps. 18:16; 69:1-3; 144:7; Jon. 2:10).

14:32-33   The stilling of "the wind" is not the climax of the story. The disciples' worship of Jesus is. This is the first time they addressed Jesus with His full title: "God's Son" or "the Son of God" (16:16; 26:63; 27:40, 43, 54; cf. 3:17; 4:3, 6). This was a new high for the disciples in their appreciation of Jesus' person.

"Retrospectively, the disciples, in making this confession, are giving answer to the earlier question they had raised in an equally perilous situation at sea: 'What sort of man is this, that even wind and sea obey him?' (8:27)."[786]

In view of their later lapses, the disciples evidently understood this title in the Messianic sense, but their understanding was still not very mature (cf. Mark 6:52). Perhaps, too, their confession here arose from the drama of the moment, whereas later they may have forgotten what they had spoken so truly about Jesus.

"Several important lessons can be learned from this account. (a) Courage comes from knowing that Jesus is present. (b) The answer to fear is faith, and faith is best placed in the One who is identified as the 'I Am.' (c) Doubt is an evidence of a divided mind. (d) Confessing Jesus' divine sonship is evidence of faith."[787]

---

[782]Hagner, *Matthew 14—28*, p. 425.

[783]Toussaint, *Behold the* . . ., pp. 191-92.

[784]Bruce, *The Training* . . ., p. 134.

[785]See Appendix 7 at the end of these notes for a list of the more common figures of speech in the Bible and their meanings.

[786]Kingsbury, *Matthew as* . . ., p. 74.

[787]Bailey, in *The New* . . ., p. 31.

3. The public ministry at Gennesaret 14:34-36 (cf. Mark 6:53-56)

This short section summarizes Jesus' public ministry at this stage of His ministry. It shows that even though Jesus was withdrawing from unbelievers (13:54—14:12), and giving special attention to the training of His disciples (14:13-33), He still had time to minister to people who were in need.

"Gennesaret" was a plain on the northwest coast of the Sea of Galilee. There was also a village called Gennesaret on this coastal plain, probably very close to the modern town of Ginosar. The crowds recognized Jesus instantly when He got out of the boat, and they "brought . . . all" types of needy people "to Him" for healing (cf. 3:5; 4:24). The woman with the hemorrhage had also obtained healing from Jesus after touching the "fringe of His cloak" (9:20-22). Now many others pressed on Him with similar faith and found healing (v. 36). The faith of these people contrasts with the faith of the disciples in the boat that was much greater.

These few verses do three things. They show the continuing broad appeal of Jesus' ministry (cf. 4:23-25; 8:16; 9:35-36). They show that Jesus continued to minister to the multitudes, even though He concentrated His ministry on His disciples. Third, Jesus showed no concern with becoming ritually unclean through His contacts with the common people. He made people clean, rather than becoming unclean Himself from these contacts. This last feature sets the stage for the confrontation over clean and unclean in the next section (15:1-20).

4. The opposition of the Pharisees and scribes 15:1-20 (cf. Mark 7:1-23; John 7:1)

Matthew recorded another round of opposition, withdrawal and disciple training, and public ministry (ch. 15). This is his last substantial group of events in Jesus' Galilean ministry. The writer's repetition of this pattern highlights the chief features of this stage of Jesus' ministry. This second round also reveals growth in each area of ministry. There is greater opposition, greater faith, and greater help for the multitudes than Matthew recorded previously.

This controversy with the Pharisees and scribes is sharper and more theological than Jesus' earlier confrontations with these critics. Note that these Pharisees and scribes had come from Jerusalem (v. 1). Jesus also explained His view of the law more clearly than before.

The charge and Jesus' response 15:1-9

15:1   These "Pharisees and scribes" came "from Jerusalem" to question Jesus. They appear to have had more official authority than the local Galilean religious leaders who opposed Jesus earlier. Jesus' great popularity makes such a delegation understandable to the reader.

15:2   The critics again raised a question about the behavior of Jesus' disciples, not His own behavior (cf. 9:14). They did not do so because Jesus behaved differently than His disciples, who followed His example and teaching. They did so because they could attack Him less directly than if they had questioned His personal conduct. In view of Jesus' popularity, they may have chosen this approach because it was safer, not because it was more respectful.

The critics objected to the disciples' disregard for the traditions of the elders, not to their disregard for the Mosaic Law. These traditions were the rabbinic interpretations of Old Testament law that had accumulated over the centuries, the Halakah. In Jesus' day most of these traditions were not yet in written form, but later the rabbis compiled them into the Mishnah (A.D. 135-200). For the Pharisees, these traditions carried almost as much authority, if not more authority, than the law itself.[788]

The disciples' hand-washing was only a specific example of the larger charge. One entire tractate in the Mishnah dealt with proper hand-washing procedures for ceremonial purposes.[789] There were even requirements for proper hand-washing before meals, since the ritual cleanliness of food was such an important matter to the Jews.

15:3-6   Jesus responded with a counterattack. He made a basic distinction between God's commandments and the Jews' traditions. He charged His critics with breaking the former to keep the latter.

". . . the ordinances of the Scribes were declared more precious, and of more binding importance than those of Holy scripture itself."[790]

In verse 4, Jesus quoted Exodus 20:12 and 21:17. "Curses" (NIV) is too strong. "Speaks evil of" (NASB) is better since the Greek verb *kakologeo* means "to insult."

---

[788]Moore, 1:251-62.

[789]Mishnah, *Yadaim*.

[790]Edersheim, *The Life* . . ., 2:15.

The Pharisees and scribes, however, had evaded the spirit of the command, namely, that children should take responsibility for their needy parents. The "you" is emphatic in the Greek text. *Halakic* (rabbinic) tradition said that if someone vowed to give something to God, he should not break his vow. Jesus said the law taught a more fundamental duty. To withhold from one's parents what one could give to "help" them, because of what the rabbis taught, was greedy hypocrisy. The error was not so much using the money for oneself or donating it for a good cause, but failing to give it to the needy parent.

Jesus had taught His disciples to put commitment to Him before family responsibilities (8:21-22; 10:38). He was the Messiah, and as such He had a right to demand such a strong commitment. The traditions of the Jews did not carry that much authority. Moreover, the situation Jesus had addressed previously involved family members opposing His disciples, not His disciples opposing their family members (cf. 10:37-39).

15:7-9   Chronologically, this is the first time Jesus called the Pharisees and teachers of the law "hypocrites." Their hypocrisy consisted of making a show of commitment to God, while at the same time giving human "tradition" (v. 6) precedence over God's Word.

Isaiah addressed the words that Jesus quoted to Jerusalem Jews, who sometimes allowed external acts of worship to vitiate principle. Rather than continuing God's will, the Jews' traditions perpetuated the spirit of the hypocrites in Isaiah's day. The context of the Isaiah quotation is a criticism of the Jews for displacing heartfelt worship with mere ritual. Isaiah branded this type of religion "vain." The hypocrites in his day had substituted their own teachings for God's. Jesus' application of this quotation to the Pharisees and law teachers of His day, therefore, condemned their entire worship of God, not just their carefully observed traditions.

Jesus' preaching and teaching about man's heart 15:10-20

15:10-11   Jesus had been responding to the question of His critics so far. Now He taught the assembled crowds the same lesson, and at the same time gave a direct answer to the Pharisees and scribes. He responded with a parable (v. 15). He did not utter this one to veil truth from the crowds, however. He urged them to hear and understand what He said (v. 10). This parable (proverb, epigram) was a comparison for the sake of clarification. Yet some did not understand what Jesus said (vv. 15-16).

Jesus was speaking of ceremonial (ritual) defilement when He said that eating certain foods does not make one unclean.[791] This was a radical statement that went beyond even the Mosaic Law. Mark noted that when He said this Jesus declared all food clean (Mark 7:19). As Messiah, Jesus was terminating the dietary distinction between clean and unclean foods that was such a large part of the Mosaic system of worship (cf. Acts 10:15; Rom. 14:14-18; 1 Cor. 10:31; 1 Tim. 4:4; Titus 1:15). Matthew's concern, however, was not to highlight this termination but to stress the point of Jesus' teaching. The point was, that to God, "what proceeds" from the heart ("out of the mouth") is more important than "what enters the mouth." Motives and attitudes are more significant than food and drink.

15:12-14   Mark recorded that this interchange between the disciples and Jesus happened in a house after they had retired there from the public confrontation that preceded (Mark 7:17). Jesus' disciples, as all the Jews, held the Pharisees and teachers of the law in high regard. Since Jesus' words had "offended" His critics, the disciples wanted to know why He had said them. Jesus proceeded to disillusion His disciples regarding the reliability of His critics' spiritual leadership. If there was any doubt in the reader's mind that the religious leaders had turned against Jesus, the disciples' statement in verse 12 should end it.

First, Jesus compared the non-elect, including the unbelieving Pharisees and scribes, to plants that God had not planted (cf. 13:24-30, 36-43). There are several passages in the Old Testament that compare Israel to a plant that God had planted (e.g., Ps. 1:3; Isa. 60:21). Isaiah also described God uprooting rebellious Israel as a farmer pulls up a worthless plant (Isa. 5:1-7). Jesus meant that God would uproot the Pharisees and scribes, and other unbelievers, because they were not people that He had planted. Furthermore, they were worthless as leaders. This would have been a shocking revelation to the disciples. Jesus had previously hinted at this (3:9; 8:11-12), but now, since they had definitely rejected Him, He made the point clear.

Jesus told the disciples to leave the critics "alone," even as He had said God would leave the weeds along that the enemy had planted in the field (13:28-29). Some of the Jews considered themselves guides of the spiritually blind (cf. Rom. 2:19). These Pharisees and scribes apparently did, since they knew the law and understood its traditional interpretations. However, Jesus disputed their claim. To Him they were "blind guides of the blind." They failed to comprehend the real meaning of the Scriptures they took so much pride in understanding. A tragic end awaits the blind guides, as well as those whom they guide. The critics' rejection of Jesus was only one indication of their spiritual blindness.

15:15-16   Peter again took the leadership among the disciples (cf. 14:28). Jesus' answer to Peter's request for an explanation of the parable (vv. 17-20) identifies the parable as His statement on defilement in verse 11. Jesus again rebuked the disciples for failing to understand what He meant (cf. 14:31). The unbelieving multitudes were understandably ignorant, but Jesus'

---

[791] Carson, "Matthew," p. 350.

believing disciples should have known better. Jesus had taught them the priority of reality over ritual before (3:9; 12:1-21). Jesus' rebuke was probably also a pedagogical device. It would have made the disciples try their best in the future to understand what He was teaching, so they could avoid further rebukes.

15:17-20   Jesus contrasted tangible food with intangible thoughts. Matthew's list of the heart's products follows the order of the Ten Commandments essentially. Jesus' point was this: what a person *is* determines what he or she *does and says* (cf. 12:34-35; Rom. 14:14, 17; 1 Cor. 8:8; Heb. 9:10). Note that Jesus presupposed the biblical revelation that "the heart" (the seat of thought and will) is evil (cf. 7:11). True religion must deal with people's basic nature and not just with externals. The Pharisees and scribes had become so preoccupied with the externals that they failed to deal with what is more basic and important, namely: a *genuine* relationship with God. Jesus had more concern about human nature than the form of worship. He came to seek and to save the lost (1:21; cf. 6:1-33; 12:34-35).

In this pericope, Jesus rejected the Pharisees and scribes as Israel's authentic interpreters of the Old Testament. He claimed that role for *Himself!* This was a theological issue that ultimately led to Jesus' arrest and crucifixion.

"The occupation with the outward religious ceremony, instead of inner transformation of the heart, has all too often attended all forms of religion and has plagued the church as well as it has Judaism. How many Christians in church history have been executed for difference of opinion on the meaning of the Lord's Supper elements or the mode of baptism or for failure to bow to church authority? The heart of man, which is so incurably religious, is also incurably evil, apart from the grace of God."[792]

5. The withdrawal to Tyre and Sidon 15:21-28 (cf. Mark 7:24-30)

As previously occurred, opposition led Jesus to withdraw and train His disciples (cf. 14:13-33). However, this time He did not just withdraw from Galilee, but from Jewish territory altogether. The response of the Canaanite woman to Jesus, in this story, contrasts with that of the Jerusalem Pharisees and scribes in the preceding pericope. She was a Gentile, with no pretensions about knowing the law, but she came to Jesus in humble belief, trusting only in His grace. She received Jesus' commendation, whereas the critics had received His censure. This incident helped the disciples know how to deal with people who believed in Jesus, even Gentiles.

"This section at the close of the Galilean phase of Matthew's story thus marks a decisive break from the previous pattern of Jesus' ministry, a deliberate extension of the mission of the Messiah of Israel to the surrounding non-Jewish peoples. The whole new approach is a practical enactment of Jesus' radical attitude toward Jewish purity laws which has just been declared in vv. 11-20; he and his good news will recognize no such restriction of the grace of God."[793]

15:21   Matthew used the key word "withdrew" many times (cf. 2:12, 22; 4:12; 12:15; 14:13). "Tyre and Sidon" stood on the Mediterranean coast, about 30 and 50 miles north of Galilee respectively. This was pagan Gentile territory. This was not a mission to preach the kingdom in this Gentile region. Jesus was simply getting away with His disciples for a rest.

15:22   Matthew introduced this extraordinary story with an extraordinary word, "Behold," which the NIV version omits. By describing this woman as "a Canaanite," the writer drew attention to the fact that she was a descendant of Israel's ancient enemies. She "came out . . . from that region" in the sense that she left her home environs to meet Jesus. Her use of "Lord" may have been only respectful.[794] However, by calling Him the "Son of David," she clearly expressed belief that He was Israel's promised Messiah who would heal His people (cf. 9:27; 12:23).

"She plainly reveals that she has knowledge of the Messianic hopes of Israel and had heard that they were being connected with Jesus as the promised great descendant of King David."[795]

15:23-24   The disciples probably wanted Jesus to heal the woman's daughter so she would stop bothering them. Jesus had previously healed many demon-possessed people (4:24; 8:16, 28, 33; 9:32; 12:22). However, He declined to do so here because His mission was to the Jews. "The lost sheep of the house of Israel" probably means "the lost sheep which is the house of Israel," rather than the lost sheep who are a part of the house of Israel (cf. 10:6).

"He still claims the place of the King who shall shepherd Israel (Matthew 2:6; 2 Samuel 5:2)."[796]

[792]Walvoord, *Matthew: . . .*, pp. 117-18.
[793]France, *The Gospel . . .*, p. 588.
[794]See my note on 8:2.
[795]Lenski, p. 594.
[796]Toussaint, *Behold the . . .*, p. 195.

"A good teacher may sometimes aim to draw out a pupil's best insight by a deliberate challenge which does not necessarily represent the teacher's own view—even if the phrase 'devil's advocate' may not be quite appropriate to this context!"[797]

15:25 This woman's desperate feeling of helplessness, and her confidence in Jesus' ability to meet her need, are obvious in her posture and her words. Matthew used the imperfect tense to describe her kneeling, making her action even more vivid. She did not just kneel and stand, but she was (stayed) kneeling (in a bowed position) "before Him." This was the attitude of a humble suppliant.

15:26 Jesus again clarified the difference between Jews and Gentiles, in order to challenge her. Parents normally feed their children first. The house dogs get whatever might remain. God, of course, was the Person providing the spiritual Bread of Life to His chosen people (the children's bread), and "the dogs" were the Gentiles, as the Jews regarded them popularly.

15:27 In her reply the woman said, "for even," not "but even" (Gr. *kai gar*). This is an important distinction to make, because she was not challenging what Jesus had said. She acknowledged the truthfulness of what He said, and then appealed to Him on the basis of its implications. Her words reveal great faith and spiritual wisdom. She did not ask for help because her case made her an exception, or because she believed she had a right to Jesus' help. She did not argue about God's justice in seeking the Jews first. She simply threw herself on Jesus' mercy without pleading any merit.

> ". . . she is confident that even if she is not entitled to sit down as a guest at the Messiah's table, Gentile 'dog' that she is, yet at least she may be allowed to receive a crumb of the uncovenanted mercies of God."[798]

She used the diminutive form of "dogs" (Gr. *kynaria*) probably because small house dogs are even more dependent than large street dogs. She also used the diminutive form of "crumbs" (Gr. *psichion*) that expressed her unworthiness to receive a large blessing.

> "The metaphor which Christ had used as a reason for rejecting her petition she turns into a reason for granting it."[799]

She bowed to God's will regarding Jewish priority, but she also believed that God would extend His grace to believing Gentiles (cf. Rom. 9—11).

> "The Canaanite woman was a source of unending wonder and comfort to Luther because she had the audacity to argue with Christ."[800]

15:28 "O" before "woman," also not translated in the NIV, makes this an emotional address.[801] Jesus responded emotionally to her trust; it moved Him deeply. The woman's "faith" was "great" because it revealed humble submission to God's will, and it expressed confidence in His Messiah to do what only God could do. Jesus "healed" the girl with His word, and immediately she became well (cf. 8:13; 9:22).

Jesus had healed Gentiles before, but this was the first time He healed one in Gentile territory. Both people whom Jesus commended for their great faith in Matthew were Gentiles, this Canaanite woman and the Roman centurion (8:5-13). In each case, Jesus initially expressed reluctance to heal because they were Gentiles. In both cases, Jesus provided healing for an acquaintance of theirs from a distance, and He said their faith was greater than that of any Jew. In the case of the centurion, Jesus responded fairly quickly to the request, but in this one He played "hard to get." So of the two cases, the woman appears to have had greater faith than even the centurion.

In the spiritual sense, Gentiles were "far off" until Calvary, when Jesus reconciled them. Then they enjoyed equal footing with Jews in the church (Eph. 2—3).

---

[797]France, *The Gospel . . .*, p. 591.

[798]Tasker, p. 152.

[799]Plummer, p. 217.

[800]Roland H. Bainton, *Here I Stand*, p. 284.

[801]F. Blass and A. Debrunner, *A Greek Grammar of the New Testament and Other Early Christian Literature*, § 146 (1b).

This miracle was another important lesson for the disciples. The Jews had priority in God's kingdom program. However, God would deliver Gentiles who also came to Him in humble dependence, relying only on His power and mercy for salvation.

> "In this miracle of mercy there is a clear foreview of Gentile blessing which fits the pattern established in Matthew 1:1 and Romans 15:8-9. The actions of Christ show that He was a minister of the circumcision for the truth of God, for confirmation of the promises made unto the fathers and that the Gentiles might glorify God for His mercy."[802]

6. The public ministry to Gentiles 15:29-39

Matthew again recorded a summary of Jesus' general healing ministry (cf. 4:23-25; 9:35-38; 12:15-21; 14:34-36) following opposition (13:54—14:12; 15:1-20) and discipleship training (14:13-33; 15:21-28). Opposition and discipleship training did not occupy His attention so exclusively that He had no time to heal the multitudes compassionately.

Jesus' healing ministry 15:29-31 (cf. Mark 7:31-37)

Jesus departed from the region around Tyre and Sidon (v. 21) and returned to the "Sea of Galilee." There are several clues in the verses that follow that enable the reader to see that Jesus went to the eastern (Gentile) side of the lake (cf. Mark 7:31). Again, "large crowds" brought their sick to Jesus for healing. He performed these acts of healing freely ("and He healed them," the "many" who were "brought"). The reference to the people glorifying "the God of Israel" is one clue that the people were mainly Gentiles. They saw a connection between Jesus and the God of Israel. The Decapolis region east of the Sea of Galilee was strongly Gentile in population.

Why did Jesus so freely heal Gentiles, here, when in the previous section He showed such reticence to do so? Undoubtedly, He said what He did to the Canaanite woman for the benefit of His disciples. and to give her an opportunity to demonstrate her great faith *before them*.

Jesus' feeding of the 4,000 15:32-39 (cf. Mark 8:1-10)

Jesus had previously fed 5,000 men, but that was near the northeast coast of Lake Galilee, where the people were mainly Jews (14:13-21). Now He fed 4,000 men on the east coast of Lake Galilee, where the people were mainly Gentiles.

Feeding the 5,000	Feeding the 4,000
Primarily Jews	Primarily Gentiles
In Galilee near Bethsaida	In the Decapolis
Five loaves and two fish	Seven loaves and a few fish
12 baskets of scraps	7 baskets of scraps
People with Jesus one day	People with Jesus three days
Spring season	Summer season
Jews tried to make Jesus king	No popular response

15:32-33   Matthew again called attention to Jesus' "compassion" (v. 32; cf. 9:36). Evidently the crowds had not gone home at nightfall, but had slept on the hillsides to be close to Jesus. This presents a picture of huge crowds standing in line—for days at a time—to obtain Jesus' help. Some of them were becoming physically weak from lack of food.

The disciples' question amazes the reader, since Jesus had recently fed 5,000 men—plus women and children. Probably the fact that the crowd was predominantly *Gentile* led the disciples to conclude that Jesus would not do the same for them that He had done for the Jews. This may have been especially true in view of what He had said to the Canaanite woman about Jewish priority in God's kingdom program. If they thought of "the feeding of the 5,000" as a *foretaste* of the kingdom banquet, they probably would have thought that it was a uniquely Jewish experience. Or perhaps since Jesus rebuked the crowd for just wanting food after the feeding of the 5,000, the disciples did not consider that He would duplicate the miracle (cf. John 6:26). Undoubtedly the disciples' limited faith was also a factor (cf. 16:5-12).

15:34-39   Matthew wrote that this time the disciples gathered the remaining scraps in a different type of basket. The Greek word *spyridas* describes baskets made of rushes that the Gentiles used to carry fish and other food (cf. Acts 9:25). In 14:20, the

[802]Toussaint, *Behold the* . . ., p. 196.

disciples had used *kophinous*, baskets the Jews used to carry kosher food, at least in Rome.[803] This is another clue that the audience here was mainly Gentile.

Possibly there is some significance in the number of baskets of fragments the disciples collected. If "12" in 14:20 represents the 12 tribes of Israel, these "seven" baskets may stand for the mark of a creative act of God, as in the seven days of creation. However, this symbolism is highly tenuous.

As before, everyone got enough to eat ("and were satisfied"). Matthew again only recorded the number of the males present, in keeping with Jewish thinking. Perhaps the total crowd numbered between 8,000 and 16,000 people.

The site of "Magadan" is unknown (v. 39). Probably it was on the west side of the lake, the Jewish side, since conflict with the Pharisees and Sadducees followed. Some commentators believe Magadan is the same as Magdala, an area just north of Tiberias on Galilee's western shore.[804] Some conjecture that this was the hometown of Mary Magdalene.

This incident would have impressed the disciples with God's graciousness in dealing with the Gentiles. His kingdom plan definitely included them, albeit in a secondary role. Their role as disciples would include ministry to the Gentiles as well as to Jews. They had the same ministry responsibilities to both ethnic groups.

"If Jesus' aphorism about the children and the dogs merely reveals *priority* in feeding, then it is hard to resist the conclusion that in the feeding of the four thousand Jesus is showing that blessing for the Gentiles is beginning to dawn."[805]

The fact that *Moses* and *Elisha* each performed two feeding miracles should have elevated Jesus to a status, at least equal with *them*, in the people's minds (cf. Exod. 16; Num. 11; 2 Kings 4:1-7, 38-44). Unfortunately most of the people, both Jews and Gentiles, continued to come to Jesus only to obtain physical help.

7. The opposition of the Pharisees and Sadducees 16:1-12

Back in Jewish territory, Jesus faced another attack from Israel's religious leaders.

The renewed demand for a sign 16:1-4 (cf. Mark 8:11-12)

16:1   Matthew introduced "*the* Pharisees and Sadducees" with one definite article in the Greek text. Such a construction implies that they acted together. That is remarkable, since they were political and theological enemies (cf. Acts 23:6-10). However, a common opponent sometimes transforms enemies into allies (cf. Luke 23:12; Ps. 2:2). Representatives of both parties constituted the Sanhedrin, the highest Jewish governing body in Israel (cf. Acts 23:6). This delegation, evidently from Jerusalem, represented the most official group of religious leaders that Matthew reported coming to Jesus thus far.

These men came specifically to test Jesus (Gr. *peipazontes*), to demonstrate who He was by subjecting Him to a trial that they had contrived (cf. 4:1, 7). The scribes and Pharisees had asked Jesus for a sign earlier (12:38). Now the Pharisees and Sadducees asked Him to produce "a sign from heaven." The Jews believed that demons could do signs on earth, but only God could produce a sign out of heaven.[806] The Jews typically looked for signs as divine authentication that God was indeed working through people who professed to speak for Him (cf. 1 Cor. 1:22).

16:2-3   Jesus suggested that His critics did not need a special sign since many things pointed to His being the Messiah. They could read "the sky" well enough to predict what the "weather" would be like soon. However, they could not read what was happening in their midst well enough to know that their Messiah had appeared. The proof that they could not discern the signs of the times was that they asked for a sign.

"It is surprising that in a wide variety of different fields of knowledge human beings can be so knowledgeable and perceptive, yet in the realm of the knowledge of God exist in such darkness. The explanation of the latter sad state is not to be found in a lack of intellectual ability—no more for the Pharisees and Sadducees than for today. The evidence is there, examinable and understandable for those

[803]A. E. J. Rawlinson, *The Gospel According to St. Mark*, p. 87.

[804]E.g., Walvoord, *Matthew: . . .*, p. 120.

[805]Carson, "Matthew," p. 357.

[806]Alford, 1:169.

who are open to it and who welcome it. The issue in the knowledge of God is not intellect but receptivity."[807]

What were "the signs of the times" that Israel's religious leaders failed to read? John the Baptist's appearance and preaching were two. John had told these leaders that *he* was the fulfillment of Isaiah's prophecy of Messiah's forerunner (Isa. 40:3; Matt. 3:1-12).[808] Jesus had also identified John as the forerunner (11:14). Jesus' works were another sign that the King had arrived, and Jesus had pointed this out (12:28). Finally, the prophecy of Daniel's 69 weeks should have alerted these students of the Old Testament to the fact that Messiah's appearance was near (Dan. 9:25-26; cf. John 5:30-47; 8:12-20).

16:4   Jesus refused to give His critics the sign they wanted. The only "sign" they would get would be "the sign of Jonah" when Jesus rose from the dead (cf. 12:38-42).

> "The only sign to Nineveh was Jonah's solemn warning of near judgment, and his call to repentance—and the only sign now, or rather 'unto this generation no sign,' [Mark 8:12] was the warning cry of judgment and the loving call to repentance."[809]

> "Miracles will give confirmation where there is faith, but not where there is willful unbelief."[810]

Jesus withdrew again in response to opposition. However, this time Matthew used a stronger word (*kataleipo*) meaning "to forsake or abandon." Jesus turned His back on these religious leaders because they were hopeless and incorrigible.[811] This was to be Jesus' last and most important withdrawal from Galilee before His final trip south to Jerusalem (19:1). He remained outside Galilee through 17:20, when He returned there from the North.

Jesus' teaching about the doctrine of the Pharisees and Sadducees 16:5-12 (cf. Mark 8:13-26)

16:5-7   The NIV translation of verse 5 is clearer than that of the NASB. "When they went across the lake" pictures what follows as happening either during the journey, probably by boat, or after it. Jesus was still thinking about the preceding conflict with the Pharisees and Sadducees, but the disciples were thinking about food. "Leaven" or yeast is primarily an illustration of something small that inevitably spreads and has a large effect (cf. 13:33). Often it stands for the spread of something evil, as it does here (cf. Exod. 34:25; Lev. 2:11; 1 Cor. 5:6-8). The disciples may not have understood what Jesus meant because they were thinking in literal terms, but He was speaking metaphorically. Perhaps they were still thinking about Jesus' instructions for their mission in 10:9-11.[812] Another possibility follows.

> "They thought the words of Christ implied, that in His view they had not *forgotten* to bring bread, but purposely omitted to do so, in order, like the Pharisees and Sadducees, to 'seek of Him a sign' of His divine Messiahship—nay, to oblige Him to show such—that of miraculous provision in their want. The mere suspicion showed what was in their minds, and pointed to their danger. This explains how, in His reply, Jesus reproved them, not for utter want of discernment, but only for 'little faith.'"[813]

The pervasive influence of both the Pharisees and the Sadducees was worldly-mindedness.[814] Perhaps this was what Jesus was warning His disciples to avoid. They apparently believed that He meant that they should not buy bread from people belonging to either of these sects.

16:8-12   Jesus' rebuke probably arose from the disciples' failure to believe that He could provide bread for them—in spite of their having witnessed two feeding miracles. This was a serious mistake for them (cf. 6:30).

> "The miracles Jesus performs, unlike the signs the Pharisees demand, do not compel faith; but those with faith will perceive their significance."[815]

---

[807]Hagner, *Matthew 14—28*, p. 456.

[808]For the Jewish understanding of Isaiah 40:3, see Edersheim, *The Life . . .*, 2:744.

[809]Ibid., 2:70.

[810]Wiersbe, 1:56.

[811]Plummer, p. 221.

[812]France, *The Gospel . . .*, p. 609.

[813]Edersheim, *The Life . . .*, 2:71.

[814]Bruce, *The Training . . .*, p. 159.

[815]Carson, "Matthew," p. 363.

The disciples did not perceive their significance, namely, that Jesus was the Messiah who could and would provide for His people. In this, their attitude was not much different from that of the Pharisees and Sadducees.

Jesus did not explain His metaphor to the disciples, but, as a good teacher, He repeated it forcing them to think more deeply about its meaning. Matthew provided the interpretation for his readers (v. 12). Though the Pharisees and Sadducees differed on several points of theology, they held certain beliefs in common. Specifically, the "teaching of the Pharisees and Sadducees," that Jesus warned His disciples about, was the skepticism toward divine revelation that resulted in failure to accept Messiah. These critics tried to fit the King and His kingdom into their preconceptions and preferences, rather than accepting Him as the Old Testament presented Him.

This section of the Gospel (13:54—16:12) emphasizes the continuing and mounting opposition to the King. Matthew recorded Jesus withdrawing from this opposition twice (14:13; 15:21). In both instances He proceeded to train His disciples. The first time He ministered to Jews, and the second time He ministered to Gentiles. Opposition arose from the Jewish people (13:54-58), from the Romans (14:1-12), and most strongly from the religious leaders within Judaism (15:1-9; 16:1-4). The rejection of this last group finally became so firm that Jesus abandoned them (16:4). From now on, He concentrated on preparing His disciples for what lay ahead of them because of Israel's rejection of Her King.

B. JESUS' INSTRUCTION OF HIS DISCIPLES AROUND GALILEE 16:13—19:2

Almost as a fugitive from His enemies, Jesus took His disciples to the far northern extremity of Jewish influence, the most northerly place Jesus visited. At this place, as far from Jerusalem and Jesus' opponents as possible, Jesus proceeded to give them important revelation concerning what lay ahead for Him and them. Here, Peter would make the great confession of the true identity of Jesus, whereas in Jerusalem to the south, the Jews would deny His identity. In this safe haven, Jesus revealed to the Twelve more about His person, His program, and His principles as Israel's rejected King.

1. Instruction about the King's person 16:13-17 (cf. Mark 8:27-29; Luke 9:18-20)

16:13 The "district of Caesarea Philippi" lay 25 miles north of Galilee. Its inhabitants were mainly Gentiles. Herod Philip II, the tetrarch of the region, had enlarged a smaller town on the site at the foot of Mt. Hermon: Paneas. The town's elevation was 1,150 feet above sea level. He renamed it "Caesarea" in honor of Caesar, and it became known as "Caesarea Philippi," in distinction from the Caesarea on the Mediterranean coast, Caesarea Sebaste (also known as Caesarea Palaestinae and Caesarea Meritima).[816]

Since Jesus had previously used the title "Son of Man" of Himself, His question must have meant: "Who do people say that I am?" The disciples answered accordingly.

"He [Jesus] wished them [the Twelve] to be fairly committed to the doctrine of His *Messiahship* before proceeding to speak in plain terms on the unwelcome theme of His *death*."[817]

16:14 There were many different opinions about who Jesus was. Some, including Herod Antipas, believed He was the resurrected "John the Baptist" (14:2). Others believed He was the fulfillment of the "Elijah" prophecy, namely, the forerunner of the Messiah (Mal. 4:5-6; cf. Matt. 3:1-3; 11:9-10; 17:10-13). Some concluded that Jesus was the resurrected "Jeremiah," probably because of similarities between the men and their ministries. For example, both men were quite critical of Israel generally, and both combined authority and suffering in their ministries.[818] Still other Jews thought Jesus was some other resurrected prophet. It is interesting that the disciples did not answer that some said Jesus was the Messiah. That opinion was not a popular one, reflecting the widespread unbelief in Israel.

"What we must recognize is that christological confession was not cut and dried, black or white. It was possible to address Jesus with some messianic title without complete conviction, or while still holding some major misconceptions about the nature of his messiahship, and therefore stopping short of unqualified allegiance or outright confession."[819]

16:15-16 The "you" in verse 15 is in the emphatic first position in the Greek text, and it is plural. Peter responded, therefore, partly as spokesman for the disciples, again (cf. 15:15). Peter said he believed Jesus was "the Christ," the Messiah that the Old

[816]Josephus, *Antiquities of . . .*, 18:2:1.

[817]Bruce, *The Training . . .*, p. 164.

[818]See Gary E. Yates, "Intertextuality and the Portrayal of Jeremiah the Prophet," *Bibliotheca Sacra* 170:679 (July-September 2013):286-303.

[819]Carson, "Matthew," p. 365.

Testament prophesied, the hope of Israel (cf. 1:1). Matthew's only use of Peter's full name here, "Simon Peter," highlights the significance of the disciple's declaration.

Peter further defined Jesus as "the Son of the living God." This is a more definite identification of Jesus as deity than "God's Son" or "a son of God" (14:33). Those title forms leave a question open about the sense in which Jesus was God's Son. The Jews often described their God as the living God, the contrast being with dead idols. By referring to God in this way, Peter left no doubt about which "God" was the Father of Jesus. He was the one *true* God. Since Jesus was the Son of God, He was the Messiah, the King over the long anticipated earthly kingdom (cf. 2 Sam. 7:14; Isa. 9:6; Jer. 23:5-6; Mic. 5:2). Peter expressed belief that Jesus was both Messiah and God. Jesus had just referred to Himself as the "Son of Man" (v. 13), but Peter viewed Him as the "Son of God."

"In the region of Caesarea Philippi, a center for the worship of Pan (as it had been previously of the Canaanite Baal), the title ["Son of the living God"] would have a special resonance as marking out the true God from all other gods."[820]

This was probably not the first time that the idea that Jesus was the Messiah had entered Peter's mind. The disciples followed Jesus hoping that He was the Messiah (John 1:41, 45, 49). However, as we have seen, the disciples gained a growing awareness and conviction that Jesus really was the Messiah (cf. 14:33). Their appreciation of the implications of His messiahship would continue to grow as long as they lived, though Jesus' resurrection resulted in their taking a giant step forward in this understanding. Peter's great confession here was an important benchmark in their understanding and faith.

"Matthew shows that whereas the public in Israel does not receive Jesus and wrongly conceives of him as being a prophet, Peter, as spokesman for the disciples, confesses Jesus aright to be the Son of God and so reveals that the disciples' evaluative point of view concerning Jesus' identity is in alignment with that of God [cf. 3:17; 17:5]."[821]

16:17   "Blessed" (Gr. *makarios*) identifies someone whom God has singularly favored and who, therefore, enjoys happiness (cf. 5:3-11). It is not the announcement of some special benediction or blessing on Peter for answering as he did.[822] However, verse 19 does reveal that Peter would receive a reward for his confession. "Barjonas" is a Greek transliteration of the Hebrew *bar yonah* meaning "son of Jonah" (short for Yohanan). This address stressed Peter's human nature. Jesus only used this full name for Peter when He had something very important to say to him (cf. John 1:42; 21:15).

Peter gained this insight about Jesus, that he had just expressed, because God had given it to him (cf. 11:27; cf. John 6:44). It did not come from Peter himself. "Flesh and blood" was a Hebrew idiom for man as a mortal being (cf. 1 Cor 15:50; Gal. 1:16; Eph. 6:12; Heb. 2:14).[823] Jesus perceived that Peter's confession came from God-given insight. However, not all such statements about Jesus did, or do, necessarily (cf. 21:9; 27:54).

2. Instruction about the King's program 16:18—17:13

Jesus proceeded immediately to build on the disciples' faith. They were now ready for more information. He gave them new revelation concerning what lay ahead so they would be ready for it.

Revelation about the church 16:18-20

16:18   "I say to you" (cf. 5:18, 20, 22, 28, 32, 34, 39, 44; 8:10) may imply that Jesus would continue the revelation the Father had begun. However, the phrase occurs elsewhere when that contrast is not in view. Undoubtedly, it means at least that Jesus was about to teach the disciples some important truth. Peter had made his declaration, and now Jesus would make His declaration.

Jesus drew attention to Peter's name because He was about to make a pun on it. The English name "Peter" is a transliteration of the Greek name *Petros*. *Petros* translates the Aramaic word *kepa*. This word transliterated into Greek is *Kephas* from which we get "Cephas" in English (John 1:42; et al.). The Aramaic word *kepa* was a rare name in Jesus' day (cf. 4:18). It means "rock." Peter's nickname was "Rocky." *Petros* commonly meant "stone" in pre-Christian Greek, but *kepa*, which underlies the Greek, means "(massive) rock."[824] It is incorrect to say that the name "Peter" describes a small stone.

[820]France, *The Gospel . . .*, p. 619.
[821]Kingsbury, *Matthew as . . .*, p. 75.
[822]Morgan, *The Gospel . . .*, p. 210.
[823]M'Neile, p. 240.
[824]Carson, "Matthew," p. 367.

There are three main views about the identity of "this rock." The first is that Jesus meant Peter was the rock.[825] Peter's name meant "rock," so this identity seems natural in the context. Moreover, Peter's confession of Jesus as the Messiah and Jesus' subsequent confirmation of his confession also point in that direction. Peter became the leading disciple in the early church (Acts 1-12), a third argument for this view.

However, Jesus used two different words for "Peter" and "rock." Matthew recorded the Aramaic distinction in Greek. If Jesus had wanted to identify Peter as the rock on which He would build the church, the clearest way to do this would have been to use the same word. Second, while Peter's confession triggered Jesus' comment about building His church on a rock, it did not place Peter in a privileged position among the disciples. Jesus never treated Peter as though he occupied a favored position in the church because he made this confession. Third, the New Testament writers never connected Peter's leadership in the early church with his confession. That rested on divine election, Jesus' command to strengthen his brethren (Luke 22:32), and Peter's personality.

A second view is that Jesus meant the truth that Peter confessed, namely, that Jesus is the Messiah and God, was the rock.[826] This position has in its favor the different words Jesus used for "rock" and the definite "this" before "rock" as identifying something in the immediately preceding context. Furthermore, other New Testament references to the foundation of the church could refer to the truth concerning Jesus' person and work (Rom. 9:33; Eph. 2:20; 1 Pet. 2:5-8).

Nevertheless, calling "the truth about Jesus" a "rock," when Jesus had just called Peter a "rock," seems unnecessarily confusing. The addition of "this" only compounds the confusion. Also, the other New Testament passages that refer to the foundation of the church never identify that foundation as the truth about Jesus. They point to something else.

This leads us to the third and what I believe is the best solution to this problem. Many interpreters believe that Jesus Himself is the Rock in view.[827] The Old Testament prophets likened Messiah to a Stone (Ps. 118:22; Isa. 28:16), and Jesus claimed to be that Stone (21:42). Peter himself identified Jesus as that Stone (Acts 4:10-12; 1 Pet. 2:5-8), as Paul did (Rom. 9:32-33; 1 Cor. 3:11; 10:4; Eph. 2:20). Second, this interpretation explains the use of two different though related words for "rock." Third, this view accounts for the use of "this" since Jesus was present when He said these words. Fourth, the Old Testament used the figure of a Rock to describe God (Deut. 32:4, 15, 18, 30, 31, 37; 2 Sam. 22:2; Ps. 18:2, 31, 46; 28:1). Since Peter had just confessed that Jesus was God, it would have been natural for Jesus to use this figure of God to picture Himself.

Critics of this view point out that this interpretation makes Jesus mix His metaphors. Jesus becomes the foundation of the church and the builder of the church. However, the New Testament refers explicitly to Jesus as the church's foundation elsewhere (Rom. 9:33; 1 Cor. 3:11; 1 Pet. 2:5-8), and Jesus referred to Himself as the church's builder here. Second, Paul's statement that God builds the church on the apostles and prophets has ruled Jesus out as the foundation for some interpreters (Eph. 2:20). However, the apostles and prophets were the foundation in a secondary sense, Jesus being the chief rock (cornerstone) around which they also provided a foundation (cf. 1 Cor. 3:10-11). Third, Peter's prominence among the disciples, and in the early church, seems (to some) to argue against Jesus being the foundation in view. Still, Peter was only the first among equals. His leadership in the church was not essentially different from that of the other apostles, as the New Testament writers present it.

The next key word in this important verse is "church." The only occurrences of this word (Gr. *ekklesia*) in all four Gospels are here and in 18:17.[828] The Greek word refers to an assembly of people called out for a particular purpose. It comes from the verb *ekkaleo*, "to call out from." The Septuagint translators used it of Israel (Deut. 4:10; Josh. 9:2; Judg. 20:2; et al.; cf. Acts 7:38).[829] In the New Testament it also refers to an assembly of citizens with no religious significance (Acts 19:39).[830] However, Jesus used it here with a new meaning.

". . . *ekklesia* was the only possible word to express the Christian body as distinct from Jews. . . . He had just ended His public ministry in Galilee, had taken the disciples on a long journey alone, and was about to go to Jerusalem with the avowed intention of being killed; no moment was more suitable for preparing His

---

[825]E.g., Plummer, pp. 228-29; Carson, "Matthew," p. 468; France, *The Gospel . . .*, p. 621-22; Edwin W. Rice, *People's Commentary on the Gospel of Matthew*, pp. 168-69; and most Roman Catholic interpreters.

[826]E.g., M'Neile, p. 241; Tasker, p. 158; Edersheim, *Sketches of . . .*, pp. 12, 22; and Toussaint, *Behold the . . .*, p. 202.

[827]E.g., Calvin, *Institutes of . . .*, 4:6:3, 6; Morgan, *The Gospel . . .*, p. 211; Walvoord, *Matthew: . . .*, p. 123; Lenski, p. 626; Barbieri, p. 57; and Wiersbe, 1:57.

[828]See Benjamin L. Merkle, "The Meaning of '*Ekklesia* in Matthew 16:18 and 18:17," *Bibliotheca Sacra* 167:667 (July-September 2010):281-91.

[829]See M'Neile, p. 241.

[830]See Marvin R. Vincent, *Word Studies in the New Testament*, 1:93.

followers to become a new body, isolated both from the masses and from the civil and religious authorities."[831]

Jesus used the term *ekklesia* to refer to a new entity that was yet to come into existence. He said He would build it in the future. He would not yet establish His kingdom on earth, but He would "build" His "church."

"The word *build* is also significant because it implies the gradual erection of the church under the symbolism of living stones being built upon Christ, the foundation stone, as indicated in 1 Peter 2:4-8. This was to be the purpose of God *before* the second coming, in contrast to the millennial kingdom, which would follow the second coming."[832]

Furthermore, Jesus claimed the church as His own in a unique sense by calling it "My church." Jesus revealed the existence of this new organism here for the first time in history. There is no Old Testament revelation of its existence. Jesus brought it into being because Israel had rejected her Messiah, and consequently God would postpone the kingdom of God on earth. In the meantime, Jesus would construct an entirely new entity. He Himself would be both its foundation and its builder.

Jesus' "church" is not the same as His "kingdom." It is interesting that even some scholars who were not dispensationalists acknowledged this.[833] Jesus would create a new entity (on the day of Pentecost), but He only postponed the kingdom, which will come into being at His second coming after He has taken the church to heaven (John 14:1-3). "Christians" (believers living in the Church Age) will return with Jesus Christ at His Second Coming, and will participate in His messianic kingdom on the earth in glorified bodies (cf. 1 Thess. 4:17).

"Gates" in biblical usage refer to fortifications (Gen. 22:17; Ps. 127:5). "Hades" is the place of departed spirits (cf. 5:22; 11:23). Together these terms refer to death and dying (Job 17:16; 38:17; Ps. 9:13; 107:18; Isa. 38:10).[834] Jesus meant that the powers of death, Satan, and his minions—doing their most powerful work of opposing life—would not prevail over the church. The church cannot die. This statement anticipated Jesus' resurrection, as well as the resurrection and translation of church saints. Even Jesus' death would not prevent Him from building the church. Jesus' church would be a living church, just as Yahweh was the living God (cf. v. 16).

This is all that Jesus revealed about the church here. He simply introduced this new revelation to the disciples as a farmer plants a seed. All of their thinking had been about the kingdom. To say more about the church now would have confused them unnecessarily. Jesus would provide more revelation about the church later (ch. 18; John 14—16).

16:19   Jesus resumed talking about "the kingdom." When Peter first heard these words, he probably thought that when Jesus established His kingdom, he would receive an important position of authority in it. That is indeed what Jesus promised. The kingdom in view is the same messianic (millennial) kingdom that Jesus had been talking about since He began His public ministry. It is not the church. Peter did not receive a reward of *power* over the other disciples in the church for his confession of Jesus as the divine Messiah, though he did enjoy *honor* among them (cf. Acts 2:14; 4:8; 15:7).[835] His blessing was not superiority authority in the *church*, but a position of authority in the *kingdom* (equal with the other apostles; cf. 19:27-28). Jesus' reintroduction of the subject of the kingdom here helped the disciples understand that the church would not replace the kingdom.

"We must . . . be careful not to identify the *ekklesia* with the kingdom. There is nothing here to suggest such identification. . . . To S. Peter were to be given the keys of the kingdom. The kingdom is here, as elsewhere in this Gospel, the kingdom to be inaugurated when the Son of Man came upon the clouds of heaven. . . . The *ekklesia*, on the other hand, was the society of Christ's disciples, who were to wait for it, and who would enter into it when it came. The Church was built upon the truth of the divine Sonship. It was to proclaim the coming kingdom. In that kingdom Peter should hold the keys which conferred authority."[836]

[831]M'Neile, pp. 241-42.
[832]Walvoord, *Matthew: . . .*, p. 124.
[833]E.g., Carson, "Matthew," p. 369; and Plummer, p. 230.
[834]See Jack P. Lewis, "'The Gates of Hell Shall Not Prevail Against It' (Matt 16:18): A Study of the History of Interpretation," *Journal of the Evangelical Theological Society* 38:3 (September 1996):349-67.
[835]Calvin, *Institutes of . . .*, 4:6:5.
[836]Allen, p. 177.

Shortly after this event, Jesus told the other disciples that they too had the power to "bind" and "loose" (18:18). He gave this revelation in the context of teaching on church discipline. So evidently all the disciples, who became apostles in the church, shared Peter's authority in the kingdom.

The Roman Catholic Church, following Augustine, equates the (Roman Catholic) church with the kingdom. Protestants who follow Augustine in this matter, namely, amillennialists, as well as many premillennialists (covenant or historic premillennialists and progressive dispensationalists) also equate the church and the kingdom, at least to some extent. Most normative dispensationalists acknowledge that there is presently a mystery form of the kingdom of which the church is a part, but that is not the messianic millennial kingdom.

The "keys" in view probably represent Peter's authority to admit or refuse admission to the kingdom. They may also signify his authority to make appropriate provision for the household.[837] In Acts we see him opening the door to the church for Jews (Acts 2), Samaritans (Acts 8), and Gentiles (Acts 10). All who enter the church will eventually enter the messianic kingdom, so Peter began to exercise this authority when the church came into existence. However, the church is not the kingdom. Jesus' prerogative as Judge is in view here (cf. 3:11-12; John 5:22, 30; Rev. 19:21). Probably the keys stand for the judicial authority that chief stewards of monarchs exercised in the ancient world (Isa. 22:15, 22; cf. Rev. 1:18; 3:7).[838] They could permit people to enter the monarch's presence or give them access to certain areas and privileges. As the Judge of all humanity, Jesus gave this authority to Peter. Of course, some of the other Apostles exercised it too (18:18; Acts 14:27).

"The traditional portrayal of Peter as porter at the pearly gates depends on misunderstanding 'the kingdom of heaven' here as a designation of the afterlife rather than denoting God's rule among his people on earth."[839]

The next problem in this verse is the binding and loosing. First, what is the proper translation of the Greek text? The best evidence points to the NASB translation: "Whatever you shall bind on earth shall have been bound in heaven, and whatever you shall loose on earth shall have been loosed in heaven."[840] The "whatever" seems to include people and privileges, in view of how the Old Testament described the stewards' use of keys.

The rabbis of Jesus' day often spoke of binding and loosing in the sense of forbidding and permitting.[841] So Jesus could have meant that whatever Peter forbade to be done on earth would have already have been forbidden in heaven, because Peter would be speaking for God and announcing God's will. Whatever he permitted to be done on earth would have already been permitted in heaven for the same reason. The problem with this view is that from this time on, Peter did not always say and do the right thing (Gal. 2:11). Roman Catholics appeal to this interpretation to argue that when Peter, and his supposed successors, the popes, speak *ex cathedra*—they are using the keys of the kingdom.

Josephus interpreted binding and loosing as punishing and absolving, not for declaring actions lawful or unlawful.[842] We see Peter exercising these powers in the Book of Acts: he punished Ananias and Sapphira (Acts 5:1-11), and absolved Cornelius (i.e., declared him acceptable to God when Cornelius placed his trust in Jesus Christ; Acts 11:17).

"These two powers—the legislative [i.e., binding and loosing] and judicial [i.e., remitting and retaining]—which belonged to the Rabbinic office, Christ now transferred, and that not in their pretension, but in their reality, to His Apostles: the first here to Peter as their Representative, the second after His Resurrection to the Church [John 20:23]."[843]

Later, Jesus told His disciples: "If you forgive the sins of any, their sins have been forgiven them; if you retain the sins of any, they have been retained" (John 20:23). These words seem to explain what binding and loosing mean (cf. 2 Cor. 5:18; 10:6).[844]

Another, less likely view, is that this was a promise that Peter will fulfill only in the messianic kingdom.

[837]U. Luz, *Matthew 8—20*, p. 364.

[838]Vincent, 1:96.

[839]France, *The Gospel . . .*, p. 625.

[840]See Carson, "Matthew," pp. 370-72; or Toussaint, *Behold the . . .*, pp. 206-7; for explanation of the syntactical arguments leading to this conclusion.

[841]Edersheim, *The Life . . .*, 2:85; Wiersbe, 1:59.

[842]Josephus, *The Wars . . .*, 1:5:2; and see the footnote there.

[843]Edersheim, *The Life . . .*, 2:85.

[844]Calvin, *Institutes of . . .*, 4:6:3; 4:11:1-2.

".. . the verse is a promise to Peter of a place of authority in the future earthly kingdom. With this promise the Lord gives Peter the basis of the decisions which he shall make. Peter is to discern what is the mind of God and then judge accordingly."[845]

Peter may determine God's will in particular instances of rendering judgment in the messianic kingdom. Perhaps he will consult the Scriptures or get a direct word from Jesus who will be on earth reigning then. Then he will announce his decision. With his announcement, Peter will give or withhold whatever may be involved in the judgment, but he will really be announcing what the divine authority has already decided. Peter did some of this in the early history of the church (cf. Acts 5:1-11; 8:20-24). All the disciples will have similar judicial functions in the kingdom (19:27-28). Furthermore, all Christians will have some judicial function in the kingdom (1 Cor. 6:2-3).

16:20   Jesus' warning in this verse seems to run contrary to His purpose to manifest Himself as the Messiah to Israel for her acceptance (cf. Mark 8:30; Luke 9:21). Jesus wanted His disciples to keep a "messianic secret," namely, that He was the Messiah. Jesus was not trying to conceal His true identity, but He was controlling how people would respond to Him (cf. 12:38-39; 16:4). If the disciples had broadcast the fact that Jesus of Nazareth was the Messiah, some people would have tried to draft Jesus as a political liberator. However, Jesus wanted people to come to believe on Him because of the words He spoke and the works He performed (cf. 11:4, 25-26). These were the tools God had ordained to give people divine insight into Jesus' identity (11:27), as Peter had experienced (v. 17).

"Contrary to common misappropriation of the messianic secret, it was not Jesus' purpose to conceal his messianic identity. It was his purpose to set before Israel symbol-charged acts and words implying a persistent question: Who do you say that I am?"[846]

Jesus wanted His disciples to stay within the means and limits that He had imposed on Himself for His self-disclosure. They should not appeal for people's acceptance of Jesus because of nationalistic zeal, or misguided messianic expectations, but because of faith rooted in understanding. Jesus' popularity on a superficial level could short-circuit the Cross. After Jesus' death and resurrection, the disciples could take a more unrestrained approach to calling people to repentance and faith (cf. 10:27). The disciples apparently grasped the danger of people accepting Jesus for superficial reasons, but they did not understand the threat of short-circuiting the Cross, as the next section shows.[847]

"Why this prohibition? Because although the disciples correctly understand who Jesus is, they do not as yet know that central to Jesus' divine sonship is death on the cross. Hence, they are in no position at this point to go and make disciples of all nations."[848]

"In the second part of his story (4:17—16:20), Matthew tells of Jesus' ministry to Israel (4:17—11:1) and of Israel's repudiation of Jesus (11:2—16:20). Sent to Israel, Jesus teaches, preaches, and heals (4:23; 9:35; 11:1). He also calls disciples, and commissions them to a ministry in Israel modeled on his own (4:17—11:1). Israel's response to Jesus, however, is one of repudiation (11:2—16:20). Still, even as Israel repudiates him, it wonders and speculates about who he is. Wrongly, the religious leaders think of him as one who acts in collusion with Satan (9:34; 12:24), and the Jewish public imagines him to be a prophet (16:13-14; 21:46). In stark contrast to Israel, the disciples, as the recipients of divine revelation, are led by Jesus to think about him as God 'thinks' about him, namely, as the Messiah Son of God (16:15-17; 14:33). Nevertheless, because the disciples do not know at this point in the story that the central purpose of Jesus' mission is death, Jesus commands them to silence concerning his identity (16:20)."[849]

Revelation about Jesus' death and resurrection 16:21-27

This is the second aspect of His program that Jesus proceeded to explain to His believing disciples, the first being His creation of the church. He told them about His coming passion and then about His resurrection.

---

[845]Toussaint, Behold the . . ., p. 207.

[846]Ben F. Meyer, The Aims of Jesus, p. 350, footnote 59; cf. pp. 250, 309-10, footnotes 119-20.

[847]Carson, "Matthew," p. 375.

[848]Kingsbury, Matthew as . . ., p. 75.

[849]Ibid., pp. 161-62.

Jesus' passion 16:21-23 (cf. Mark 8:31-33; Luke 9:22)

16:21   This is only the second time in his Gospel that Matthew used the phrase *apo tote erxato*, "from that time" (cf. 26:16). The first time was in 4:17, where Jesus began to present Himself to Israel as her Messiah. Here it announces Jesus' preparation of His disciples for the Cross, because of Israel's rejection, and His disciples' acceptance of Him as the divine Messiah. Thus the evangelist signaled a significant turning point in Jesus' ministry.

Jesus had hinted at His death earlier (9:15; 10:38; 12:40). However, this is the first time He discussed it with His disciples. He began "to show" or "to explain" (Gr. *deikeyo*) these things with His actions as well as His words, not just "to teach" (Gr. *didasko*) them.

Jesus said that He "must" (Gr. *dei*) go to Jerusalem. He had to do this because it was God's will for Messiah to "suffer" and die, as well as to experience resurrection.[850] He had to do these things to fulfill prophecy (Isa. 53; cf. Acts 2:22-36). Jerusalem had been the site of the martyrdom of numerous Old Testament prophets (cf. 23:37).

". . . Jesus reveals to his disciples, in all he says and in all he does beginning with 16:21, that God has ordained that he should go to Jerusalem to suffer, and that his way of suffering is a summons to them also to go the way of suffering (i.e., the way of servanthood) (cf. 20:28). In other words, Matthew alerts the reader through the key passages 16:21 and 16:24 that suffering, defined as servanthood, is the essence of discipleship and that Jesus will show the disciples in what he says and does that this is in fact the case."[851]

Jesus identified three groups that would be responsible for His sufferings and death there: the "elders," the "chief priests," and the "scribes" (cf. 27:41). Together these groups constituted the Sanhedrin, Israel's supreme religious body. One definite article describes all three groups and binds them together in a single entity in the Greek text (cf. 16:1, 6). This would be Israel's final and formal official rejection of her Messiah.[852] Jesus' announcement implied that a trial would take place.[853] However, Jesus also announced that He would arise from the dead on the third day (cf. 12:40; Ps. 16:10-11; 118:17-18, 22; Isa. 52:13-15; 53:10-12).

Here, as in the following two announcements of Jesus' death (17:22-23; 20:18-19), the accompanying announcement of Jesus' resurrection made no impression on the disciples. Apparently the thought of His dying so upset them that they did not hear the rest of what He had to say to them.

Verse 21 "prepares the reader already for the resolution of Jesus' conflict with Israel in at least two respects: (*a*) It underscores the fact that there are three principals involved in Jesus' passion, namely, God (*dei*: 'it is necessary'), Jesus, and the religious leaders. And (*b*) it reminds the reader that while all three desire the death of Jesus, the objective the leaders pursue is destructive (12:14), whereas that intended by God and Jesus is to save (1:21)."[854]

16:22   Peter obviously understood that Jesus was predicting His death. He "began to rebuke" Jesus privately for thinking such a thing, but Jesus cut him off (v. 23). Apparently Peter's understanding of Messiah did not include a Suffering Servant, which almost everyone in Israel rejected as well.

"Like many modern readers of the Bible, Peter did not want to accept what did not agree with his hopes and ambitions."[855]

Peter used a very strong negative expression meaning "Never, Lord!" The Greek expression is *ou me*, and it is comparatively rare in the New Testament. Peter followed up his great confession (v. 16) with a great contradiction.

---

[850]Lenski, p. 634.

[851]Kingsbury, *Matthew as* . . ., p. 140.

[852]Toussaint, *Behold the* . . ., p. 208.

[853]M'Neile, p. 244.

[854]Kingsbury, *Matthew as* . . ., p. 77.

[855]Walvoord, *Matthew:* . . ., p. 125.

"Peter's strong will and warm heart linked to his ignorance produce a shocking bit of arrogance. He confesses that Jesus is the Messiah and then speaks in a way implying that he knows more of God's will than the Messiah himself."[856]

16:23   Evidently Jesus turned to confront Peter face to face. "Get behind Me, Satan" probably means: "Do not stand in My way as a stumbling block." Jesus had used similar language when rebuking Satan himself (4:10). "Satan" means "adversary." Jesus viewed Peter's comment as coming from Satan ultimately.

"It does not matter how one interprets the rebuke to Peter. Jesus' main point is one that demands a response from his audience. Whether he said, 'Get out of my sight!' [NIV], 'Get behind me!' [AV], or 'Follow after me!'[857], he intended to focus his attention on the necessity of unconditional obedience in discipleship."[858]

Jesus had recently called Peter a rock. Now He called him a different type of rock, a rock that causes someone to stumble (Gr. *skandalon*). Satan had offered Jesus messiahship without suffering (4:8-9), and now Peter was suggesting the same thing. These were both appeals to Jesus' humanity. The idea of a suffering Messiah caused Peter to stumble here, and after Jesus' resurrection the same concept caused many Jews to stumble (cf. 1 Cor. 1:23).

Peter was not thinking God's thoughts but man's. When he confessed that Jesus was the Messiah earlier (v. 16), he was thinking God's thoughts. Now he was thinking not only without regard to revelation, but in opposition to revelation, as Satan does. The contrast between verses 13-20 and verses 21-23 clearly shows that the disciples' understanding was a matter of growth. As they accepted what they came to understand progressively by divine illumination, their faith also grew.

The cost and reward of discipleship 16:24-27 (cf. Mark 8:34-38; Luke 9:23-26)

Jesus proceeded to clarify the way of discipleship. He had just explained what was involved in messiahship, and now He explained what is involved in discipleship. In view of Jesus' death, His disciples, as well as He, would have to die to self. However, they could rejoice in the assurance that the kingdom would come eventually. Glory would follow suffering. Interestingly, this was one of Peter's main emphases in his first epistle. He learned this lesson well.

16:24   Discipleship would require self-denial in the most fundamental areas of individuality. What Jesus said applies to anyone who really wants to follow Him. The Jews had renounced Jesus, but His disciples must renounce themselves (cf. 10:33; Rom 14:7-9; 15:2-3). The Romans customarily compelled someone condemned to crucifixion to carry at least part of his own cross. This act gave public testimony to his being under and submissive to the rule he had opposed. This was both a punishment and a humiliation. Likewise, Jesus' disciples must publicly declare their submission to the One whom they formerly rebelled against.[859]

Jesus did not explicitly identify the method of His death until later (20:19), but the disciples understood, at least initially, what Jesus meant about the price they would have to pay.

"Death to self is not so much a prerequisite of discipleship to Jesus as a continuing characteristic of it . . ."[860]

"(I once met a lady who told me her asthma was the cross she had to bear!)"[861]

Asthma, or another similar affliction, is not the type of cross that Jesus had in mind. Self-denial, as Jesus taught it, does not involve denying oneself things, as much as it involves denying one's own authority over his or her life (cf. 4:19; John 12:23-26). This is the great challenge. The three verbs in this challenge are significant. The first two, "deny" and "take up," are aorist imperatives indicating a decisive action. The last one, "follow," is a present imperative indicating a continuing action.

16:25-26   Verses 25, 26, and 27 all begin with "for" (Gr. *gar*). Jesus was arguing logically. Verse 25 restates the idea that Jesus previously expressed in 10:28. The Greek word translated "life" is *psyche*, translated some other places in the New Testament

[856]Carson, "Matthew," p. 377.

[857]Footnote: Gundry, *Matthew . . .*, p. 338.

[858]Dennis C. Stoutenburg, "'Out of my sight!', 'Get behind me!', or 'Follow after me!': There Is No Choice in God's Kingdom," *Journal of the Evangelical Theological Society* 36:1 (March 1993):178.

[859]Barbieri, p. 59.

[860]Carson, "Matthew," p. 379.

[861]Wiersbe, 1:60.

"soul." It means the whole person (cf. James 1:21; 5:20). Jesus was not talking about one's eternal salvation.[862] The point of Jesus' statement is that living for oneself now will result in a leaner life later, whereas denying oneself now for Jesus' sake will result in a fuller life later. It pays to serve Jesus, but payday will come later. As the next verse explains, the *later* in view for these disciples was the inauguration of the kingdom.

Two rhetorical questions show the folly of earning great material wealth at the expense of one's very "life" (*psyche*, v. 26). Life in the physical sense is not all that Jesus meant. As He used the word, it includes one's existence, his or her *entire being*.

"For the world, there is immediate gain but ultimate loss: for the disciple, there is immediate loss but ultimate gain."[863]

16:27   God's future judgment of His disciples, as well as Jesus' example, should be an inducement to deny self, identify with Christ, and follow Him (v. 24; cf. 10:24-25). This verse teaches both eschatology and Christology. Jesus will come with "the glory of His Father" when He returns to earth at His Second Coming (Rev. 19:11-16). Jesus is the "Son of Man" (Dan. 7:13) who will come with the same glory that God enjoys. The "angels" will enhance His glory, and assist Him in gathering people for judgment (13:41; 24:31; 25:31-32; Luke 9:26). The angels are under Jesus' authority. Then He will reward each person "according to his deeds" (conduct). Conduct demonstrates character. Again Jesus referred to the disciples' rewards (cf. 5:12; et al.). The prospect of reward should motivate Jesus' disciples to deny self and follow Him. The disciple who does so simply to obtain a reward has not really denied himself. Rewards are precisely that: rewards.

The rewards in view seem to be opportunities to glorify God by serving Him (cf. 25:14-30; Luke 19:11-27). The disciple will have greater or smaller opportunities to do so during the millennial kingdom, and forever after, in proportion to his or her faithfulness on earth now. The New Testament writers spoke of these rewards symbolically as "crowns" elsewhere (cf. 1 Cor. 9:25; Phil. 4:1; 1 Thess. 2:19; 2 Tim. 4:8; James 1:12; 1 Pet. 5:4; Rev. 2:10; 3:11). It is perfectly proper to serve Jesus Christ to gain a reward if our motives are correct (6:19-21). We will one day lay our crowns at the feet of our Savior. The crown is an expression of a life of faithful service that we performed out of gratitude for God's grace to us (cf. Rev. 4:4, 10).[864]

Both Jesus and Paul urged us to lay up treasure in heaven, to make investments that will yield eternal rewards (6:19-21; Luke 12:31-34; 1 Tim. 6:18-19). It is perfectly legitimate to remind people of the consequences of their actions to motivate them to do what is right. That is precisely what Jesus was doing with His disciples here.

"By including this discussion here Matthew once more emphasized the program of the Messiah as it is based on Daniel's prophecy. The Messiah must first be cut off (Daniel 9:26), a period of intense trouble begins at a later time (Daniel 9:27), and finally the Son of Man comes in glory to judge the world (Daniel 7:13-14). Thus the disciples must endure suffering, and when the Son of Man comes in His glory, they will be rewarded."[865]

"In the third part of this story (16:21—28:20), Matthew describes Jesus' journey to Jerusalem and his suffering, death, and resurrection (16:21; 17:22-23; 20:17-19). Jesus' first act is to tell his disciples that God has ordained that he should go to Jerusalem and there be made by the religious leaders to suffer and die (16:21). On hearing this, Peter rejects out of hand the idea that such a fate should ever befall Jesus (16:22), and Jesus reprimands Peter for thinking the things not of God, but of humans (16:23). Then, too, Peter's inability to comprehend that death is the essence of Jesus' ministry is only part of the malady afflicting the disciples: they are also incapable of perceiving that servanthood is the essence of discipleship (16:24)."[866]

More revelation about the kingdom 16:28—17:13

Jesus proceeded to reveal the kingdom to His inner circle of disciples: to strengthen their faith, and to prepare them for the trials of their faith that lay ahead of them.

---

[862]See Dillow, pp. 116-18.

[863]Walvoord, *Matthew: . . .*, p. 126.

[864]For a helpful introduction to the study of the Christian's rewards, see Zane C. Hodges, *Grace in Eclipse*.

[865]Toussaint, *Behold the . . .*, p. 208.

[866]Kingsbury, *Matthew as . . .*, p. 162.

The announcement of the kingdom's appearing 16:28 (cf. Mark 9:1; Luke 9:27)

Jesus revealed next that "some of" the disciples whom He addressed would not die until they saw Him "coming in His kingdom." This prediction may at first appear to be very similar to the one in 10:23. However, that verse refers to something else, namely, Jesus' reunion with His disciples following their preaching tour in Galilee.

This verse (v. 28) cannot mean that Jesus returned to set up the messianic kingdom during the lifetime of these disciples, since that did not happen. Neither does it mean that Jesus had already set up the kingdom when He spoke these words, as some writers have believed.[867] What Jesus predicted would happen in the future rules this out. Some interpreters have taken Jesus' words as a reference to His resurrection and ascension. However, Jesus spoke of those events elsewhere as His "departure," not His "coming" (John 16:7). Moreover, such a view interprets the kingdom in a heavenly sense, rather than in the earthly sense, in which the Old Testament writers consistently spoke of it.

Most amillennial, and some premillennial interpreters, confuse the eternal heavenly rule of God with the millennial earthly rule of Messiah. Some take the kingdom as entirely heavenly, and others take it as both heavenly and earthly. Among the latter group are those who believe the kingdom is operating in a heavenly form now but will become an earthly kingdom later. A popular name for this view is the "now, not yet" view. This view often involves confusing the church with the kingdom.[868] This is the view that progressive dispensationalists hold as well.

Other interpreters believe that Jesus was speaking about the day of Pentecost.[869] However, the Son of Man did not come then. The Holy Spirit did. Furthermore, the kingdom did not begin then. The church did. Still others hold that the destruction of Jerusalem is in view.[870] The only link with that event is judgment.

Jesus appears to have been predicting the *preview* of His coming to establish His kingdom, which He gave Peter, James, and John in the Transfiguration (17:1-8).[871] The Transfiguration follows this prediction immediately in all three of the Gospels that record it (cf. Mark 9:1-8; Luke 9:27-36). Moreover Matthew, Mark, and Luke all linked Jesus' prediction and the Transfiguration with connectives. Matthew and Mark used "and" (Gr. *de*) while Luke used "and . . . it came about" (Gr. *egeneto de*). Peter, one of the witnesses of the Transfiguration, interpreted it as a preview of the kingdom (2 Pet. 1:16-18). Finally, Jesus' "truly I say to you" or "I tell you the truth" (v. 28), separates His prediction of the establishment of the kingdom (v. 27), from His prediction of the vision of the kingdom (v. 28). Jesus' reference to some "who" would "not taste death" until they saw the kingdom may seem strange at first, but in the context Jesus had been speaking of dying (vv. 24-26).

Jesus had just announced that He was going to build His church (16:18), so what would happen to the promised kingdom? Here He clarified that the kingdom would still come (cf. 6:10).

The preview of the kingdom 17:1-8 (cf. Mark 9:2-8; Luke 9:28-36)

The Transfiguration confirmed three important facts. First, it confirmed to the disciples that the kingdom was indeed future. Second, it confirmed to them that Jesus was indeed the divine Messiah in three ways. The alteration of Jesus' appearance revealed that He was more than a human teacher. His association with Moses and Elijah demonstrated His messianic role. And the voice from heaven declared that He is the Son of God.[872] Third, it confirmed to them that Messiah had to suffer.

17:1   The Synoptic evangelists rarely mentioned exact periods of time. Consequently there was probably a good reason Matthew did so here. Probably he did so to show that what happened on the mountain fulfilled what Jesus predicted would happen in 16:28. The reference provides a sturdy link between the two events: prediction and fulfillment.

"Peter, James, and John" constituted Jesus' handpicked inner circle of disciples (cf. 26:37; Mark 5:37). They were evidently the best prepared and most receptive of the Twelve to receive this revelation, not the best loved, since Jesus loved all His disciples equally. Interestingly, when Moses ascended Mt. Sinai he took with him three companions: Aaron, Nadab, and Abihu (Exod. 24:1).

The mountain where the Transfiguration happened is traditionally Mt. Tabor, a 1,900-foot hill that rises conspicuously at the east end of the Jezreel Valley. However, Josephus wrote that there was a walled fortress on its summit then.[873] This fact throws doubt on the traditional identification. Other scholars have suggested Mt. Hermon as the site. It was close to Caesarea

[867]E.g., C. H. Dodd, *The Parables of the Kingdom*, pp. 53-54.

[868]E.g., Ladd, et al.

[869]Morgan, *The Gospel . . .*, p. 221.

[870]Richard C. Trench, *Studies in the Gospels*, p. 198.

[871]Walvoord, *Matthew: . . .*, p. 126; Toussaint, *Behold the . . .*, pp. 209-10.

[872]France, *The Gospel . . .*, p. 642-43.

[873]Josephus, *The Wars . . .*, 2:20:6; 4:1:8.

Philippi, and it was 9,232 feet high.[874] This was probably the location. Another suggestion is Mt. Miron, the highest mountain in Israel between Caesarea Philippi and Capernaum at 3,926 feet (cf. vv. 22, 24).[875] A fourth possibility is Mt. Arbel on the west side of the Sea of Galilee. It is a high mountain from which the whole of the Sea of Galilee is visible.

Fortunately we do not have to identify the mountain to understand the text. It is significant that the Transfiguration happened on a mountain, however. Moses and Elijah both had intimate encounters with God on mountains, probably Mt. Sinai in both cases (Exod. 19; 24; 1 Kings 19). A close encounter with God is what Jesus' three disciples had, too. These were very special revelatory events in all three instances. The location of these "mountain top experiences" also ensured privacy.

17:2   Jesus underwent a metamorphosis. The Greek word that Matthew used is *metamorphoo* meaning "to transform or change in form." It was not just His appearance that changed, but His essential form became different.[876] Probably Jesus assumed His post-resurrection body that was similar to, but somewhat different from, His pre-resurrection body (cf. 2 Pet. 1:16-18; Rev. 1:16).

Matthew's statement that Jesus "was transfigured before" the disciples indicates that the transformation was for their benefit. Jesus' "face shone like the sun," as Moses' face had, and "His garments became as white as light" because they radiated God's glory (cf. Exod. 34:29-30). Moses, however, reflected God's glory whereas Jesus radiated His own glory.

"... wherever *leukos* [white] is used here or elsewhere in the New Testament in connection with clothing it always has reference either to that of angels (beings surrounded with glory), or else to the garments of the saints who enter into a glorified state in heaven."[877]

This vision of Jesus would have strengthened the disciples' faith that He was the Messiah. It would also have helped them understand that the sufferings He said He would experience would not be final (16:21). They would see Him glorified "coming in His kingdom" (16:28).

17:3   "Behold" again introduced something amazing (cf. 1:20; 2:13; et al.). Matthew probably mentioned "Moses" first, because to the Jews he was the more important figure. Moses was the model for the eschatological Prophet whom God would raise up, specifically, Messiah (Deut. 18:18). "Elijah" was the prophesied forerunner of Messiah (Mal. 4:5-6; cf. Matt. 3:1-3; 11:7-10; 17:9-13). Both prophets had unusual ends. Perhaps Moses represented those who will be in the kingdom who had died, and Elijah those whom God had translated.[878] The disciples may represent those there who had not died.[879]

Both Moses and Elijah played key roles in God's plan for Israel. Moses established the (Mosaic) covenant under which Israel proceeded to live, and Elijah led the people back to that covenant and God after their worst apostasy. Both experienced a vision of God's glory on a mountain. Both experienced rejection by Israel (Acts 7:35, 37; 1 Kings 19:1-9; cf. Matt. 17:12). Moses was the greatest figure associated with the Law, and Elijah was arguably the greatest of the Old Testament prophets. The disciples would later learn that Jesus was greater than either of these great men (vv. 5, 8). However, now the disciples saw Moses and Elijah talking with Jesus.

"The abiding validity of the Law and the Prophets as 'fulfilled' by Christ (Mt. v. 17) is symbolized by the harmonious converse which He holds with their representatives, Moses and Elijah."[880]

17:4   In addressing Jesus, Peter called Him "Lord," a title of general respect (cf. 7:21; et al.). That title would later take on the idea of unqualified supremacy when applied to Jesus, but Peter's appreciation of Jesus was probably not mature enough to recognize that yet. The proof of this is Peter's rebuke of Jesus (16:22), and his putting Jesus on a par with Moses and Elijah here.

Peter did not speak because someone had spoken to him. In countries with monarchies, it was and is often customary for subjects to speak to the monarch, in his or her presence, only if the monarch first initiates conversation. He evidently spoke because he perceived the greatness of the occasion, and he wanted to offer a suggestion. The "tabernacles" (Gr. *skenas*)

[874]E.g., Edersheim, *The Life . . .*, 2:96.

[875]Walter L. Leifeld, "Theological Motifs in the Transfiguration Narrative," in *New Dimensions in New Testament Study*, p. 167, footnote 27.

[876]Lenski, pp. 651-51.

[877]Joseph B. Bernardin, "The Transfiguration," *Journal of Biblical Theology* 52 (October 1933):185.

[878]Walvoord, *Matthew: . . .*, p. 130.

[879]Barbieri, p. 59.

[880]M'Neile, p. 251.

Peter suggested erecting were temporary structures that the Jews pitched for the Feast of Tabernacles every year. This was a seven-day feast that looked forward to the time when Israel would dwell in permanent peace and rest in the Promised Land (Lev. 23:42-43). It anticipated kingdom conditions. Probably Peter meant that since the messianic age was apparently going to begin soon, he should make booths for Jesus, Moses, and Elijah—subject to Jesus' approval.

17:5   The "cloud" was "bright," Matthew said. This was undoubtedly the *shekinah* glory of God. God had hidden Himself in a cloud through which He spoke to the Israelites on Mt. Sinai (Exod. 19:16). He led the Israelites with it after the Exodus (Exod. 13:21-22), and it manifested His glory to His people in the wilderness (Exod. 16:10; 24:15-18; 40:34-38). The prophets predicted that Messiah would come with clouds to set up His kingdom, and that clouds would overshadow the kingdom (Ps. 97:2; Isa. 4:5; Dan. 7:13).[881] If the three disciples remembered these passages, they would have seen another reason to believe that Jesus was the Messiah. The presence of the "bright cloud" should have reminded them of the closeness of God's presence, and linked Jesus *with God* in their thinking.

The cloud may have "overshadowed" (NASB) or "enveloped" (NIV) them. The Greek word *epeskiasen* permits either translation (cf. Exod. 40:35). However, Luke wrote that they entered into the cloud (Luke 9:34). The voice from the cloud essentially repeated what the voice from heaven had said at Jesus' baptism (3:17). It confirmed Jesus' identity as both God's Son and His Suffering Servant (cf. Ps. 2:7; Isa. 42:1). Thus the voice from the cloud, God's voice, identified Jesus as superior to Moses and Elijah. Previously the voice from heaven (3:16-17) was for Jesus' benefit, but now it was for the benefit of Peter, James, and John.

The words "Hear Him" or "Listen to Him"—with Moses present—indicated that Jesus was the prophet greater than Moses whom Moses predicted would come (Deut. 18:15-18; cf. Acts 3:22-23; 7:37). God had said through Moses of that prophet, "You shall listen to Him" (Deut. 18:15). Jesus was the climax of biblical revelation, and now people should listen to what He said (cf. Heb. 1:1-2).

"The voice is that of God, and for the second time [cf. 3:17] God bursts into the world of Matthew's story as 'actor' and expresses his evaluative point of view concerning Jesus' identity."[882]

"The injunction to hear Jesus is an exhortation . . . that the disciples are to attend carefully to Jesus' words regarding the necessity both of his own going the way of suffering (16:21) and of their emulating him (16:24)."[883]

17:6-8   This revelation had the same effect on Peter, James, and John that the revelation God gave the Israelites at Sinai did (Exod. 20:18-21; Deut. 4:33; Heb. 12:18-21), and that the revelation God gave Daniel had on him (cf. Dan. 10:8-12). When people see the glory of God revealed, and realize that they are in *His* presence, they feel terror. The Transfiguration was mainly for the disciples' benefit. Jesus brought the three disciples to the mountaintop, the Transfiguration happened before them, and the voice spoke to them. The disciples did not understand the significance of all they saw immediately. However, it was a revelation that God continued to help them understand, especially after the Resurrection (cf. 2 Pet. 1:16-19). Immediately it did give them a deeper conviction that Jesus was the Messiah.[884]

"The purpose of the transfiguration was primarily confirmation. It confirmed several vital facts. One of these was the reality of a future kingdom. The very fact that the transfiguration took place attests this. The presence of Old Testament saints on earth with Christ in a glorified state is the greatest possible verification of the kingdom promises in the Old Testament. The reality of this kingdom is also evident from the connection of the transfiguration with the promise of Matthew 16:27-28. The Son of Man was going to come one day to judge the world and establish His kingdom (Matthew 16:27). As an earnest of the coming of the kingdom three disciples were permitted to see the Son of Man in His kingdom (Matthew 16:28). This is exactly the manner in which Peter uses the transfiguration (2 Peter 1:16-21)."[885]

Why did Jesus let only Peter, James, and John witness His transfiguration? Perhaps they were further along in their faith than the other disciples. They were, after all, the core group of His disciples. Perhaps it was to avoid further misunderstanding among the disciples as a whole (cf. v. 9).

---

[881]See Richard D. Patterson, "The Imagery of Clouds in the Scriptures," *Bibliotheca Sacra* 165:657 (January-March 2008):13-27.

[882]Kingsbury, *Matthew as . . .*, p. 79.

[883]Ibid., p. 140.

[884]See James A. Penner, "Revelation and Discipleship in Matthew's Transfiguration Account," *Bibliotheca Sacra* 152:606 (April-June 1995):201-10.

[885]Toussaint, *Behold the . . .*, pp. 210-11. See also S. Lewis Johnson Jr., "The Transfiguration of Christ," *Bibliotheca Sacra* 124:494 (April-June 1967):133-43.

The clarification of the kingdom's herald 17:9-13 (cf. Mark 9:9-13; Luke 9:36)

17:9   This is the last of five times Matthew recorded Jesus telling His disciples to keep silent (cf. 8:4; 9:30; 12:16; 16:20). This time He told them that they could tell others after His resurrection, since this is the first time He told them to keep quiet after He had revealed that He would rise again. The proclamation of the King and the kingdom would begin again after the Resurrection. Temporary silence was important because of popular political views of Messiah, and because the signal proof of Jesus' messiahship would be His resurrection, the sign of Jonah.

17:10   The disciples in view seem to be Peter, James, and John (cf. v. 14). It seems unlikely that the disciples viewed Elijah's appearance in the Transfiguration as the fulfillment of Malachi 4:5-6. If they did, their question would have been: "Why did Messiah appear before Elijah, when the scribes taught the reverse order of appearances?" Moreover, Elijah's appearance in the Transfiguration did not turn the hearts of the people back to God.

Peter, James, and John's question evidently arose over an apparent inconsistency involving Jesus' announcement of His death. Elijah's appearance on the mountain probably triggered it. Elijah was to come and turn the hearts of the people back to God before Messiah appeared (Mal. 4:5-6). If that restoration happened, how could Jesus die at the hands of Israel's leaders (16:21)? The disciples were struggling to understand how Messiah's death could fit into what they believed about the forerunner's ministry.

Notice that from the Transfiguration onward, these disciples had no further doubts about Jesus' messiahship.

17:11-12   Jesus confirmed the scribes' teaching about "Elijah coming," but He said another factor needed consideration. John the Baptist's ministry had been a success as far as it had gone (cf. 3:5-6; 14:5), but he had "restored all things" to only a limited degree. The scribes perceived the ministry of Messiah's forerunner correctly, but they did not realize that John the Baptist had been that forerunner (11:10). Elijah had already come in John the Baptist. However, Israel's leaders had rejected him, and he had died without accomplishing the complete restoration of Israel. John had not completely fulfilled his mission because he died while doing so. Likewise, Jesus would die at His enemies' hands without fulfilling His mission of establishing the kingdom. John had restored all things as much as he could, and yet died. Jesus, too, would fulfill His mission as much as He could, and yet die. This was the answer to the disciples' question.

"A suffering Forerunner is to be followed by a suffering Messiah."[886]

"In other words, just as the messianic forerunner's coming had two phases: John the Baptizer (one to suffer and die), and Elijah the Prophet (one of restoration and glory), so also would the Messiah's coming. The response to the forerunner foreshadowed the response to the Messiah and necessitated the postponement of the fulfillment specifically promised to national Israel."[887]

God predicted through Malachi that a Jewish revival would precede Messiah's kingdom (Mal. 4:5-6), and the revival did not come. Consequently that revival and the kingdom must still be future.

17:13   The disciples now understood that John the Baptist initially fulfilled the prophecy about Elijah returning. However, their continuing problems with Jesus' death seem to indicate that they did not really understand that He had to die. This incident reveals another step of understanding that the disciples took, but it was only a small step.

3. Instruction about the King's principles 17:14-27

Jesus' instruction of His disciples in view of the King's coming death and resurrection and the kingdom's postponement continued. Jesus had taught them about His person (16:13-17) and His program (16:18—17:13). He now taught them principles that clarified His work and His person further.

The exorcism of an epileptic boy 17:14-21 (cf. Mark 9:14-29; Luke 9:37-43a)

The term "exorcism" means the action of exorcizing or expelling an evil spirit by adjuration or the performance of certain rites. In Jesus' case, this involved His authoritatively commanding a demon or demons to depart, with no appeal to a higher authority or to incantations—which are common in exorcisms that other people perform.

"The contrast between the glory of the Transfiguration and Jesus' disciples' tawdry unbelief (see v. 17) is part of the mounting tension that magnifies Jesus' uniqueness as he moves closer to his passion and resurrection."[888]

[886]Plummer, p. 240.

[887]J. Randall Price, "Prophetic Postponement in Daniel 9 and Other Texts," in *Issues in Dispensationalism*, p. 134.

[888]Carson, "Matthew," p. 390.

It also recalls Moses' experience of descending Mt. Sinai only to find the Israelites failing by worshipping the golden calf (Exod. 32:15-20).

17:14-16   The Greek word *gonypeteo*, translated "falling on his knees" or "knelt," suggests humility and entreaty, not necessarily worship (cf. 27:29; Mark 1:40; 10:17). Likewise "Lord" was perhaps only a respectful address (cf. 8:2). The young man's epilepsy was evidently a result of demon possession (v. 18). The impotent disciples were some of, or all of, the nine who did not go up the mountain for the Transfiguration.

There are many instances of the disciples' failures in this section of Matthew (cf. 14:16-21, 26-27, 28-31; 15:16, 23, 33; 16:5, 22; 17:4, 10-11). Earlier they had great miraculous powers (10:1, 8). However, their power was not their own; it came from Jesus. As Jesus progressively trained the disciples, He also withdrew some of their power to teach them that it came from Him and related to their trust in Him (14:26-17, 31; 15:5, 8).

"The sovereign authority of Jesus the Messiah in healing and exorcism is unique; his disciples can draw on it only by faith, and that is what they have failed to do in this case."[889]

17:17-18   Jesus' rebuke recalls Moses' words to Israel in Deuteronomy 32:5 and 20. Unbelief characterized the "generation" of Jews that had rejected Jesus, and now it marked His disciples to a lesser extent. Their failure to believe stemmed from moral failure to recognize the truth, rather than from lack of evidence, as the combination of "perverse" and "unbelieving" makes clear (cf. Phil. 2:15). The disciples, too, were slow to believe, slower than they should have been. Jesus' two rhetorical questions expressed frustration and criticism.

"Jesus has accepted that he will be rejected by the official leadership of Israel (16:21), but to find himself let down even by his own disciples evokes a rare moment of human emotion on the part of the Son of God."[890]

17:19-21   The "we" in the disciples' question is in the emphatic position in the Greek text. The problem, as Jesus explained, was their weak faith (Gr. *oligopistia*). It was not the quantity of their faith that was deficient but its quality (strength). In spite of the revelation of Jesus that they had received, the disciples had not responded to it with trust as they should have done. They had some faith in Jesus, but it should have been stronger.

"Much earlier, Jesus had endowed the disciples with authority to exorcise demons as part of their mission to Israel (10:1, 8). Consequently, he expects them to draw on this authority. But if they approach the tasks of their mission forgetful of their empowerment and encumbered by a crisis of trust, they render themselves ineffectual."[891]

". . . the expression, 'small as a mustard-seed,' had become proverbial, and was used, not only by our Lord, but frequently by the Rabbis, to indicate the smallest amount . . ."[892]

Removing mountains is a proverbial figure of speech for overcoming great difficulties (cf. Isa. 40:4; 49:11; 54:10; Matt. 21:21-22; Mark 11:23; Luke 17:6; 1 Cor. 13:2). In this context, the difficulties in view involved exercising the authority that Jesus had delegated to them to heal people. The disciples were treating the gift of healing that Jesus had given them as a magical ability that worked regardless of their faith in Him. Now they learned that their power depended on proper response to revelation, namely, dependent confidence in Jesus to work through them to heal. Continual dependence on Jesus, rather than simply belief in who He is, constitutes strong faith (cf. Mark 6:5-6).

"Nothing is impossible for the disciple of Jesus who with faith works within the established will of God. It is therefore the case that not every failure in the performance or reception of healing is the result solely of insufficient faith."[893]

Verse 21 does not occur in several important ancient manuscripts. Evidently copyists assimilated it from Mark 9:29: "And He said to them, 'This kind cannot come out by anything but prayer.'"

The lesson of this miracle for the disciples was that simple belief that Jesus is the King may be adequate when a person first realizes who Jesus is. It can even result in spectacular miracles. However, with the privilege of added revelation about the

[889]France, *The Gospel* . . ., p. 659.

[890]Ibid., p. 661.

[891]Kingsbury, *Matthew as* . . ., p. 141.

[892]Edersheim, *The Life* . . ., 1:592-93.

[893]Hagner, *Matthew 14—28*, p. 506.

person and work of Jesus comes increased responsibility to trust totally in Him. Failure to do this weakens faith and restricts Jesus' work through the disciple (cf. John 15:5).

Understanding Jesus' death and resurrection 17:22-23 (cf. Mark 9:30-32; Luke 9:43-45)

Jesus next gave His disciples His second clear announcement of His passion (cf. 16:21-24). The reference to it in 17:12 was only a passing one. He had alluded to it in veiled terms before He articulated it clearly (cf. 9:15; 10:38; 12:40).

17:22   Matthew's reference to time was general. All the disciples were again with Jesus "in Galilee." Jesus introduced the subject of His passion again, which the Transfiguration and the events that had followed it had interrupted.

Jesus' statement was direct, but it was also somewhat ambiguous. The Greek word *paradidosthai* means either "to hand over" or "to betray" depending on the context, which is no help here. Furthermore, this verb is in the passive tense, so the perpetrator of this action, whomever it would be, remained hidden. In typical fashion Jesus gave His disciples more information, but He did not give them all He could have. More information would have created questions and problems that He did not want them to face yet. This is the first time Matthew recorded Jesus announcing that He would be betrayed. The Son of *Man* would be betrayed into the hands of *men*.

17:23   The disciples' response shows that they understood and did not like to hear what lay ahead. They grasped Jesus' death but did not yet understand His resurrection. It was not until after Jesus arose from the dead that they understood the Resurrection. Had they understood His resurrection now, they would not have been sorrowful.

Appreciating Jesus' sonship 17:24-27

"This story is a nut with a dry, hard shell, but a very sweet kernel."[894]

"The present incident supplies, in truth, an admirable illustration of the doctrine taught in the discourse on humility."[895]

17:24   The "two-drachma *tax*" was a Jewish tax that every male Jew between 20 and 50 years of age had to pay toward the maintenance of the temple and its services (Exod. 30:13). There was no two-drachma coin in circulation at this time, so two adults often went together and paid one shekel that was worth four drachmas.[896]

17:25-26   Jesus turned this inquiry from the tax collector into a teaching situation for Peter—and presumably the other disciples. In His lesson's illustration, Jesus changed the tax from a religious one to a civil one to make His point clearer. The principle is the same in both cases, but it was easier to illustrate in the civil arena of life.

Jesus' point was that as the "sons" of "kings" are exempt from the taxes their fathers impose, so He was exempt from the taxes His Father imposed. He meant the temple tax. The temple really belonged to God (Mal. 3:1). Jesus was teaching Peter the implications of His deity. He was not teaching Peter to fulfill his civic responsibility.

17:27   Even though He was "exempt" (v. 26), Jesus would pay the tax, because He did "not" want to "offend" anyone needlessly (cf. 5:29). Failure to pay the tax would create unnecessary problems. Because Peter was one of Jesus' disciples and one of God's children through faith in Jesus, he also had no obligation to pay the temple tax (cf. 12:1-8). Paul later followed Jesus' example of not giving offense in a similar situation (1 Cor. 8:13; 9:12, 22), as all God's children should.

God had clearly declared Jesus His Son in the Transfiguration (v. 5), as well as at Jesus' baptism. Yet Jesus' glory remained veiled as He moved toward the Cross. This established a pattern for His disciples (cf. 18:1-5). Since the sons of God are exempt from maintaining the temple and its service, the end of this system of worship appeared to be approaching, as it was. Here is another indication that Jesus ended the Mosaic Law (15:11). Again the disciples failed to grasp the major significance of these things—until after the Resurrection.

What an impression this miracle must have made on Peter—as a fisherman—and on his fellow fishermen disciples! Imagine, not only catching a fish but a fish with money in its mouth. This was one of many miracles that Jesus performed for Peter. He healed Peter's mother-in-law (1:29-34), helped him catch fish (Luke 5:1-9), enabled him to walk on water (14:22-33), healed Malchus' ear (26:47-56), and delivered him from prison (Acts 12). No wonder Peter could write, "Casting all your anxiety upon Him, because He cares for you" (1 Pet. 5:7).

---

[894]Bruce, *The Training . . .*, p. 222.
[895]Ibid., p. 223.
[896]Carson, "Matthew," p. 393. Cf. Josephus, *Antiquities of . . .*, 3:8:2; 18:9:1; and Mishnah *Shekalim*.

Jesus alone could obtain the stater ("shekel") as He did. Again the sinless Man fulfilled the command of the Adamic Covenant to exercise dominion over the fish of the sea (cf. 8:27; 14:25). Even though He was free from the Law's demands, being God's Son, He submitted to them and miraculously provided for His disciples to do so. This demonstration of humility and power is even more impressive following as it does an announcement of Jesus' passion.

Far from the feelings of pride, pretension, and self-assertion that the disciples manifested, by discussing who would be the greatest in Christ's kingdom, Jesus Himself humbly paid a tax that He really did not owe. He did not owe it, in the sense that He was Lord over the whole system that this tax supported. His humility further manifested itself in that, being Lord of land and sea, He made Himself subject to one of its creatures—a fish. Furthermore, He took no offense at having to pay this tax, and He was careful to give no offense to those to whom it was due.

"It [this story] teaches the children of the kingdom not to murmur because the world does not recognize their status and dignity."[897]

Jesus continued to teach His disciples the importance of following the examples that He provided for them in the next section (ch. 18).

4. Instructions about the King's personal representatives ch. 18

Chapter 18 contains the fourth major discourse that Matthew recorded (cf. chs. 5—7; ch. 10; 13:1-53; chs. 24—25): His Discipleship Discourse. This discourse continues Jesus' instruction of His disciples that He began in 17:14. Instead of focusing on Jesus, the Lord's teaching focused on the disciples and their responsibilities as His representatives. The theme of this discourse is humility. The theme of the Sermon on the Mount was righteousness. The theme of the Mission Discourse in chapter 10 was ministry. The theme of the Kingdom Discourse in chapter 13 was the kingdom, and the theme of the Olivet Discourse would be the Second Coming. Like the other discourses, the scope of this one is also the inter-advent age.

Kingsbury called the theme of this speech "life within the community of the church" and outlined it as follows: (I) On True Greatness as Consisting in Humbling Oneself so as to Serve the Neighbor (18:1-14); and (II) On Gaining and Forgiving the Errant Disciple (18:15-35).[898]

Apart from the second question (v. 18), this discourse proceeds as a unit of teaching similar to the first discourse (chs. 5—7) and the second discourse (ch. 10), but not the third discourse (ch. 13).

"The theme of this discourse is not so much individual discipleship (though several of the examples and instructions are expressed in the singular) as the corporate life of those who are joined by their common commitment as disciples, with special attention being given to the strains and tensions to which such a life is exposed through self-concern and lack of care for fellow disciples, through bad examples and errant behavior, and through an unwillingness to forgive as we have been forgiven."[899]

The introduction of the theme of humility 18:1-4 (cf. Mark 9:33-36; Luke 9:46-47)

18:1-2   The writer introduced and concluded this discourse, as he did the others, with statements suggesting that Jesus delivered this address on one specific occasion (cf. 5:1; 7:28-29). The last two discourses in Matthew were responses to questions from the disciples (v. 1; cf. 24:1-3).

"At that time" probably means "in that stage of Jesus' ministry" (cf. 10:19; 26:45). The preceding revelations about the King and the kingdom led the disciples, probably the Twelve, to express interest in "who" would be "greatest in the kingdom" (cf. Mark 9:33-38; Luke 9:46-48). Perhaps Peter's leadership among the disciples, and Peter, James, and John's privilege of seeing Jesus transfigured, made this one of their growing concerns. Jesus had taught that there would be distinctions in the kingdom (5:19; 10:32-33). If Jesus gave this teaching in Peter's house, the "child" may have been Peter's (cf. 17:25; Mark 9:33), but this is only a possibility.

In any case, what Jesus did in setting "a child" forward—as an example for adults to follow—was shocking in His day. People of the ancient Near East regarded children as inferior to adults. Children did not receive the consideration that adults enjoyed until they reached adult status. They were taught to look to adults as examples to follow. Now Jesus turned the tables and urged His disciples to follow the example of a child. To do so would require humility indeed.

---

[897]Bruce, The Training . . ., p. 228.

[898]Kingsbury, Matthew as . . ., p. 112.

[899]France, The Gospel . . ., p. 672.

18:3-4 Jesus announced His revolutionary words with a solemn introductory formula (cf. 5:18). He said it was necessary that His disciples change and "become" as little "children." The word "converted" in the NASB is misleading. Jesus was not speaking about "getting saved." Childlikeness was necessary for entrance into the messianic kingdom. Children have many characteristics that distinguish them from adults, but because of the disciples' concern with position in the kingdom and the teaching that follows, humility is clearly in view. Young children have little concern about their personal prestige and position in relation to other people.

"The feature of child-nature which forms the special point of comparison is its unpretentiousness. . . . A king's child will play without scruple with a beggar's, thereby unconsciously asserting the insignificance of the things in which men differ, compared with the things that are common to all."[900]

In one sense the disciples had already humbled themselves as children when they believed on Jesus. This gave them access to the kingdom. However, in another sense, they had abandoned that attitude when they became concerned about their status in the kingdom. They needed to return to their former childlike attitude. Similarly, they had exercised great power through simple faith in Jesus, but as time passed, they got away from depending on Him, lost their power, and needed to return to dependent faith. Peter, for example, had made a great confession of faith in Jesus, but shortly after that he regressed and failed to submit to Jesus.

Verse 3 also clarifies that the kingdom was still future when Jesus said these words.[901] The disciple who humbled himself as a little child would be the "greatest in the kingdom." Greatness in the kingdom was what these disciples wanted (v. 1). Jesus had previously commended childlike characteristics to His disciples (5:3; 11:25).

Since Jesus was speaking to disciples who believed on Him (16:16), it appears that He used the polar expressions "not enter the kingdom" and "greatest in the kingdom" to clarify His point. His point was the importance of humility. Jesus had previously said that if the disciple's eye caused him to stumble he should gouge it out (v. 9; cf. 5:29). That was a similar extreme statement (hyperbole) made to clarify a point.

The seriousness of impeding the progress of a disciple 18:5-14 (cf. Mark 9:37-50; Luke 9:48-50)

The major sub-theme of this discourse is offenses (Gr. *skandalon*, stumbling blocks). The humble disciple will be careful not to put a stumbling block in the path of another disciple as that one proceeds toward the kingdom.

18:5-6 The "child" in view in these verses is not a literal child, but the disciple who has humbled himself or herself, and in so doing has become childlike (vv. 3-4). Jesus was speaking of receiving a humble disciple of His in verse 5. (Jesus taught the importance of receiving a little child in Mark 9:36-37 and Luke 9:48.) Whoever does this "in Jesus' name" welcomes the disciple because he or she is one of Jesus' disciples, not because that one is personally superior, influential, or prominent. The person who welcomes one of Jesus' humble disciples, simply for Jesus' sake, virtually welcomes Jesus Himself (cf. 10:42). In this context, as well as in chapter 10, Jesus was speaking of welcoming in the sense of extending hospitality—with its accompanying encouragement and support. "To receive" (Gr. *dekomai*) means to receive into fellowship.[902]

The antithesis, in verse 6, involves *not* welcoming a disciple, i.e., rejecting or ignoring him. Withholding supportive encouragement would cause a disciple to stumble in the sense that it would make it harder for him to do his work. Jesus was not speaking of causing the disciple to stumble by leading him or her into apostasy. The contrast makes this clear. Discouraging the disciple amounts to rejecting the Master. Consequently, drowning at sea would be better for the offender than having to face Jesus' condemnation in hell for rejecting Him (vv. 8-9). Again, hyperbole presents the consequences as extremely bad. "Little ones who believe in Me" (v. 6) defines the disciples in view. This is the only place in the Synoptics where "believe in Me" occurs. This phrase is very common in John's writings.

Drowning was a Greek and Roman method of execution, but not a Jewish one.[903] The type of "millstone" in view was a large ("heavy") one that a donkey would rotate, not the small hand millstone that every Palestinian woman used to prepare her flour.[904] Drowning in this way would be horrible, but it would be "better" than perishing in the lake of fire (v. 8).

[900]Bruce, *The Training* . . ., pp. 201-2.
[901]Cf. Montefiore, *The Synoptic* . . ., 2:247.
[902]Thayer, s.v. "*dekomai*," p. 130.
[903]Carson, "Matthew," p. 398.
[904]Edersheim, *The Life* . . ., 2:120.

18:7   Jesus pronounced "woe" on "the world" because it is the source of opposition to Him and His disciples, and the source of much "stumbling" and many "stumbling blocks." The NIV translation may be a little misleading here. "Woe" announces judgment (cf. 11:21; 23:13-32). It is inevitable that the world will reject Jesus' disciples, but God will hold those who do reject them responsible (cf. Isa. 10:5-12; Acts 4:27-28).

18:8-9   Jesus next warned His disciples about the possibility of their doing what the world does, namely, making it difficult for another disciple to fulfill his or her mission for Jesus. In the context, one's competitive pride of position might cause another disciple to stumble (v. 1). The illustrations Jesus used recall 5:29-30, where He also urged His disciples to discipline their thoughts and motives.

The point of this section was the seriousness of rejecting or opposing Jesus' disciples in their work of carrying out His will. It is as serious as child abuse.

18:10-11   Jesus warned His disciples not to look down on His followers who were very humbly following Him. The Twelve were in danger of using worldly standards to measure and give value to their fellow disciples, as we are today (cf. 5:3). Judas Iscariot was one disciple who failed to heed this warning.

Many interpreters believe that the last part of verse 10 teaches that God has guardian angels who take special care of small children. However, the context of verse 10 is not talking about small children, but disciples who need to be as humble as small children. Furthermore, the "angels" in this passage are "continually" beholding God's "face in heaven," not watching the movements of small children on earth. Evidently the angels in view are the supernatural messengers (the normal meaning of "angels") who assist God's people (Heb. 1:14). This seems to me to be more likely—than that they are the spirits of believers after death who constantly behold God's face (cf. Acts 12:15).[905] Another view is that they are the spirits of children who have died.[906] Are there guardian angels for children? I like to think there are, because of God's concern for children (e.g., 19:14-15), but I cannot point to a verse that teaches this explicitly.

The Jews believed that only the most knowledgeable of the angels beheld God's face, while the rest remained outside awaiting His bidding.[907] Jesus taught that the angels responsible for believers all have access to Him, because of God's love for His own.

Verse 11 does not appear in the earliest ancient copies of Matthew's Gospel. Probably scribes influenced by Luke 19:10 included it here in later versions of the text.

18:12-13   Having taught the importance of humility, Jesus now illustrated it with a parable. Jesus taught the same parable on a different occasion to teach a slightly different lesson (Luke 15:4-7). His purpose there was evangelistic, whereas His purpose here is pastoral.

The shepherd in the story is God (v. 14). The sheep are those who follow Him, namely, Jesus' disciples (cf. 10:6; 15:24). God has concern for every one of His sheep and seeks to restore those of them that wander away from Him. He has such great concern for the wayward, that when they return to Him, "He rejoices more" than over those who did not wander away. This does not mean that God loves His wayward sheep more than He loves His faithful sheep. It means that when wayward sheep return to Him it gives Him special joy.

Since God has such great concern for His disciples who go astray, His disciples should be very careful not to do anything that would cause one of His sheep to go astray.[908]

Notice again Jesus' identification of Himself and God in this parable. Jesus' disciples are God's sheep. Therefore Jesus and God are one.

18:14   This verse concludes the argument of the discourse thus far. The heavenly "Father" does not want a single "one" of Jesus' humble disciples to wander away—from his calling in life—because someone has discouraged, rejected, or opposed him. Moreover, He does not want His disciples, of all people, to be responsible for this. "Perish" in this context does not mean loss of salvation, but the ultimate result of failing to achieve God's goal for him or her as a disciple, namely: a wasted life.

---

[905]B. B. Warfield, *Selected Shorter Writings*, 1:253-66.

[906]Thomas, p. 268.

[907]Edersheim, *The Life . . .*, 2:122.

[908]Plummer, p. 252.

The restoration of a wayward disciple 18:15-20

Jesus proceeded to explain what a humble disciple should do when a brother or sister disciple has wandered from the Shepherd and the sheep.

18:15   By using the term "brother" Jesus encouraged a humble approach. The disciples should deal with each other as brothers rather than as superiors and inferiors (cf. 1 Tim. 5:1-2). Contextually the sin in view is probably despising a brother or sister. However, Jesus did not specify what it was, but He implied that it was any sin that takes the disciple away from the Shepherd. Jesus commanded His disciples to "go" to such a person and reprove ("show him his fault") him "in private." The disciple must take the initiative and confront (cf. Gal. 6:1).

". . . if it is hard to accept a rebuke, even a private one, it is harder still to administer one in loving humility."[909]

"The possession of humility is proven not by passively waiting for one to beg forgiveness and then granting it. Rather, it is manifested by actively seeking out the erring brother and attempting to make him penitent."[910]

The verb "reprove" or "show him his fault" (Gr. *elencho*) means "to convict" in the sense of producing an awareness of guilt, not in the sense of lording it over someone (cf. 1 Cor. 9:19-22; 1 Pet. 3:1). The objective should be the erring brother or sister's restoration, not the initiator's glorification (cf. Luke 17:3-4; 2 Thess. 3:14-15; James 5:19-20). This approach was one that the Mosaic Law had taught, too (Lev. 19:17), and that the Rabbis also supported.[911]

"Sin, of whatever form, is not to be tolerated within the disciple community, but is to be dealt with when it is noticed. But this is to be done with sensitivity and with a minimum of publicity."[912]

18:16   The Mosaic Law had also advocated the second step that Jesus taught (Deut. 19:15). However, Jesus broadened the field of civil law that the Deuteronomy passage covered, to include any sin about which a disciple might need rebuke. Jesus was not perpetuating the whole Mosaic Law. He was simply carrying over these provisions in the Law that He declared were now binding on His disciples.

Probably the function of the "witnesses" is to witness to the erring disciple's reaction to the confrontation. This seems to have been the purpose in the Deuteronomy passage. Their presence would be an added inducement to return to the fold of the faithful. These seem to be witnesses to the confrontation, not to the sin. If the brother or sister proved unrepentant, and the initiator needed to take the third step (v. 17), witnesses to the confrontation might be necessary.

18:17   The third step, if necessary, is to report the situation to the "church." This is the second reference to *ekklesia* in Matthew, and the only other occurrence of this word in the four Gospels. As I pointed out above (cf. 16:18), this word means "a called out assembly of people." Jesus probably used it in a wide sense here. We have noted that the terms "lord," "disciple," "apostle," and others came to have more specific meanings as God's kingdom plan unfolded. Jesus predicted the existence of the church, the body of Christ, in 16:18. However, the disciples undoubtedly understood Him to mean just His band of disciples. Jesus was talking about "the assembly of His disciples" that He was calling out of the world to represent Him, that He knew would become a large body. He knew this would be the church as we know it, but the disciples must have thought He only meant themselves in a collective sense. Perhaps they thought He was referring to a Jewish assembly, a synagogue.[913]

Jesus revealed almost nothing about the church in the Gospels, as the absence of references to it in these books indicates. The disciples were struggling to grasp Jesus' deity, His suffering servant role, and His passion. Jesus did not confuse them with much revelation about the form that their corporate identity would take following His ascension. He did not even do that after His resurrection (Acts 1:6-8). That revelation came through His apostles after His ascension. We have it in Acts and the Epistles.

When Jesus said, "Tell it to the church (assembly)," the disciples probably heard, "Tell it to all the other disciples, not just the two or three witnesses." Applying this command today becomes more difficult because the number of the disciples is

[909]Carson, "Matthew," p. 402.
[910]Toussaint, *Behold the . . .*, p. 217.
[911]Edersheim, *The Life . . .*, 2:123.
[912]France, *The Gospel . . .*, p. 692.
[913]Walvoord, *Matthew: . . .*, p. 137.

incalculable and they live around the globe. In most situations the scope of public announcement would be a local church congregation, the particular collection of disciples of which the wayward brother is a part.

If the erring disciple does not respond to the church's encouragement to return to the Shepherd, Jesus said the disciples should treat such a person as "a Gentile and a tax collector." This does not mean the disciples should receive him or her warmly, as Jesus received such people (8:1-11; 9:9-13; 15:21-28). The context, as well as the New Testament parallels to this exhortation, shows that Jesus had exclusion in mind (cf. Rom. 16:17; 2 Thess. 3:14). Jesus probably used Gentiles and tax collectors as examples, because the Jews typically withdrew from them. That is what He wanted His disciples to do regarding the erring brother or sister. A. B. Bruce explained his understanding of the difference between "Gentile" and "tax-gatherer" this way:

"The idea is, that the persistently impenitent offender is to become at length to the person he has offended, and to the whole church, one with whom is to be held nor religious, and as little as possible social fellowship. The religious aspect of excommunication is pointed at by the expression 'as an heathen man,' and the social side of it is expressed in the second clause of the sentence, 'and a publican.'"[914]

The "you" in the Greek text is singular, indicating that the initiator is a single individual, and the sphere of life Jesus had in mind throughout this section was interpersonal relations (cf. v. 15)

"He cannot be treated as a spiritual brother, for he has forfeited that position. He can only be treated as one outside the church, not hated, but not held in close fellowship."[915]

Neither Jesus nor the apostles specified the exact form this discipline should take (e.g., excommunication, exclusion from the Lord's Supper, social isolation, withheld table fellowship, etc.). France argued that since the sphere of life in view is interpersonal relationships, the guilty party should only suffer isolation from the initiator of action, not the whole community of believers.[916] However, it seems that if the whole church gets involved in reproving the offender, some sort of communal, as well as individual, punishment would be involved. Consequently I assume that Jesus intended the disciples involved in such situations to make these determinations on the basis of all the facts in each particular case. However, it seems to be going too far to put the offender in a situation in which it would become impossible for him or her to repent and experience restoration later. The objective of all discipline is ultimately restoration, not exclusion.[917]

"Such unseemly mixtures of the godly and the godless are too common phenomena in these days. And the reason is not far to seek. It is not indifference to morality, for that is not generally a characteristic of the church in our time. It is the desire to multiply members. The various religious bodies value members still more than morality or high-toned Christian virtue, and they fear lest by discipline they may lose one or two names from their communion roll. The fear is not without justification. Fugitives from discipline are always sure of an open door and a hearty welcome in some quarter. This is one of the many curses entailed upon us by the greatest of all scandals, religious division. One who has become, or is in danger of becoming, as a heathen man and a publican to one ecclesiastical body, has a good chance of becoming a saint or an angel in another."[918]

18:18   This verse is identical to 16:19. There Jesus was talking specifically about the messianic kingdom. Here He was speaking more generally about how His disciples should conduct themselves in humility. The "whatever" again seems to include people and privileges, in view of how the Old Testament describes the stewards' use of keys. The disciples would determine God's will in each particular instance of rendering judgment in the church. Hopefully they would consult the Scriptures and pray to do this. Then they would announce their decision. With their announcement they would give or withhold whatever the judgment might involve, but they would really be announcing what God, the divine authority, had already decided. Their decision would be God's will for the person being disciplined, assuming they had obtained the will of God before announcing it.[919]

---

[914]Bruce, The Training . . ., p. 208.

[915]Wiersbe, 1:66.

[916]France, The Gospel . . ., pp. 690-94.

[917]See Calvin, Institutes of . . ., 4:12:2-11; J. Carl Laney, "The Biblical Practice of Church Discipline," Bibliotheca Sacra 143:572 (October-December 1986):353-64; and Ted G. Kitchens, "Perimeters of Corrective Church Discipline," Bibliotheca Sacra 148:590 (April-June 1991):201-13.

[918]Bruce, The Training . . ., pp. 213-14.

[919]See Craig S. Keener, "Exegetical Insight," in William D. Mounce, Basics of Biblical Greek: Grammar, p. 115.

"To Peter the King promised authority in the kingdom, assuring him of guidance in the use of that authority. Now the Lord instructs His disciples concerning the subject of discipline in the church and also promises divine direction in their decisions."[920]

18:19-20   It should be obvious from the context that this promise does not refer to whatever two or three disciples agree to ask God for in prayer. The Bible contains many promises concerning prayer (cf. 7:7-8; 21:22; John 14:13-14; 15:7-8, 16; 1 John 5:14-15; et al.), but this is not one of them.

In the context, "anything" refers to any judicial decision involving an erring disciple that the other disciples may make corporately. God has always stood behind His judicial representatives on earth when they carry out His will (cf. Ps. 82:1). This is a wonderful promise. God will back up with His power and authority any decision involving the corporate discipline of an erring brother or sister that His disciples may make after determining His will.[921]

"The meeting, supposed to be convened in Christ's name, need not therefore be one of church officers assembled for the transaction of ecclesiastical business: it may be a meeting, in a church or in a cottage, purely for the purposes of worship. The promise avails for all persons, all subjects of prayer, all places, and all times; for all truly Christian assemblies great and small."[922]

"He did not wish His church to consist of a collection of clubs having no intercommunion with each other, any more than He desired it to be a monster hotel, receiving and harboring all comers, no questions being asked."[923]

Here again (v. 20) Jesus takes God's place as "God with us" (1:23; 2:6; 3:3; 11:4-6, 7-8; cf. 28:20). This statement implies a future time when Jesus would not be physically present with His disciples, the inter-advent age, specifically the period following His ascension and preceding His return. Jesus anticipated His ascension.

One writer argued that verses 18-20 are the center of a structural and theological chiasm that embraces 17:22—20:19.[924] This thesis seems a bit stretched to me.

The importance of forgiving a disciple 18:21-35

From a discussion of discipline, Jesus proceeded to stress the importance of forgiveness. Sometimes zealous disciples spend too much time studying church discipline and too little time studying the importance of forgiveness.

18:21-22   Jesus had been talking about excluding rather than forgiving (v. 17). This led Peter to ask how often he as a disciple should forgive an erring brother before he stopped forgiving. The rabbis taught that a Jew should forgive a repeated sin three times, but after that there need be no more forgiveness (Amos 1:3; 2:6).[925] Peter suggested "seven times," and probably felt very magnanimous doing so. Seven was a round number, sometimes regarded as a perfect number, obviously exceeding what the scribes taught (cf. Lev. 26:21; Deut. 28:25; Ps. 79:12; Prov. 24:16; Luke 17:4).

Jesus' response alluded to Genesis 4:24, where the ungodly Lamech said: "If Cain is avenged sevenfold, then Lamech seventy-sevenfold." Lamech claimed to have taken even more revenge on the man who struck him than God had taken on Cain for killing his brother Abel. Jesus turned Lamech's bad example around, and urged His disciples to practice generous forgiveness when their brothers hurt them.

The NASB has Jesus saying "seventy times seven," whereas the NIV translators wrote "seventy-seven times." Probably the NIV is correct since Jesus quoted the Septuagint of Genesis 4:24 exactly here, and it has "seventy-seven times." Even though the difference between these two translations is great numerically, it is not a very important difference. Jesus was not

[920]Toussaint, *Behold the* . . ., p. 218.

[921]See C. Samuel Storms, *Reaching God's Ear*, pp. 254-58.

[922]Bruce, *The Training* . . ., pp. 214-15.

[923]Ibid., p. 215.

[924]David McClister, "'Where Two or Three Are Gathered Together': Literary Structure as a Key to Meaning in Matt 17:22—20:19," *Journal of the Evangelical Theological Society* 39:4 (December 1996):549-58.

[925]Carson, "Matthew," p. 405; Lenski, p. 708.

specifying a maximum number of times His disciples should forgive their brothers. Neither was He wiping out what He had just taught about confronting an erring brother (vv. 15-20). His point was that disciples who are humble should not limit the number of times they forgive one another, or limit the frequency with which they forgive each other. The following parable of the unmerciful servant clarified this point.

18:23   Since Jesus required His disciples to forgive this way, the kingdom had become similar to what He proceeded to describe, not the king in the parable but the whole parable scene. The whole parable taught a certain type of interpersonal relationship based on forgiveness. This parable illustrates kingdom conditions, conditions that will prevail when Jesus establishes His kingdom. Jesus was not saying the kingdom was in existence then, any more than He was saying that the conditions He described were already in existence. He argued that kingdom conditions should be those that the King's disciples should seek to follow in their lives now, since they already live under the King's authority (cf. chs. 5—7; esp. 6:12, 14-15).

The whole parable deals with repeated personal forgiveness and the reason for it. The King had already forgiven them much more than they could ever forgive their fellow disciples.

Immediately Jesus put the disciples in the position of servants (Gr. *douloi*) of a great King—who is God. This is one of the relationships that disciples have with God that they must never forget. They are His servants as well as His sons.

18:24-27   This servant had great authority under an even greater king (cf. v. 1). However, he had amassed a debt of such huge proportions that he could not possibly repay it. A talent was a measure of weight equivalent to 75 pounds. The exact, or even the relative buying power of 10,000 talents of silver, is really secondary to the point Jesus was making, namely, that the debt was impossible to repay. Depending on the current price of silver, the slave owed the equivalent of many millions of dollars. There was no way he could begin to pay off such a debt.

"Ten thousand (*myria*, hence our 'myriad') is the largest numeral for which a Greek term exists, and the talent is the largest known amount of money. When the two are combined, the effect is like our 'zillions.'"[926]

The king "commanded" that the servant sell everything he had, to compensate him, even though what he could pay amounted to a mere fraction of what he owed. The servant pleaded for time ("Have patience with me"), promising to "repay everything," an obvious impossibility in view of the amount of the debt. Moved by compassion for the hopeless servant, the lord (master) graciously cancelled ("forgave him") the entire "debt."

The Greek word for "debt" in verse 27 is *daneion* and really means "loan." Evidently the king decided to write off the indebtedness as a bad loan rather than view it as embezzlement, another indication of his grace.

18:28-31   The reaction of the forgiven servant was appalling. He proceeded to try to collect a debt from a "fellow slave," and even resorted to physical violence (tried to "choke" him) to obtain it. A denarius was a day's wage for a common laborer or a foot soldier.[927] Therefore the debt owed was substantial, but compared with the debt the king had forgiven the creditor servant it was trivial.

Both debtors appealed to their respective creditors similarly (vv. 26, 29). Yet the servant creditor remained unmoved, hardhearted. He "threw" his fellow servant into the debtor's "prison until he" could extract the full amount of his debt from him. Other servants of the king, who were aware of the situation and deeply distressed by it, reported everything to their lord "in detail" (Gr. *diesaphesan*).

18:32-34   The king called the wicked servant into his presence and reminded him of the merciful treatment that he had received. It is interesting that the word he used for "debt" here is the usual word for debt, not "loan" as in verse 27. He took a different view of the servant's debt now. Instead of forgiving him, the king turned the unforgiving servant over to the "torturers" (Gr. *basanistais*, cf. vv. 6, 8-9). The servant would experience torture until he repaid his total debt, which he could never do. In other words his torment would be endless.

18:35   Jesus drew the crucial comparisons in applying the parable to His disciples. He pictured God as forgiving graciously, yet punishing ruthlessly. God cannot forgive those who are devoid of compassion and mercy because He is so full of these qualities Himself. Jesus did not mean that people can earn God's forgiveness by forgiving one another (cf. 6:12, 14-15). Those whom God has forgiven must "forgive"—as God has forgiven them—from the "heart." This demonstrates true humility.

---

[926]France, *The Gospel . . .*, p. 706.
[927]Tobit 5:14; Tacitus *Annales* 1:17.

The idea of God delivering His servants, the disciples, over to endless torment has disturbed many readers of this parable. Some have concluded that Jesus meant a disciple can lose his salvation "if" he "does not forgive." This makes salvation dependent on good works rather than belief in Jesus. Another possibility is that Jesus was using an impossible situation, endless torment, to warn His disciples. If the disciples knew it was an impossible situation, the warning would lose much of its force. Perhaps He meant that a disciple who does not genuinely forgive gives evidence that he or she has never really received God's forgiveness.[928] That person may be a disciple, but he or she is not a believer (cf. Judas Iscariot). However, many genuine believers do not forgive their brethren as they should. Perhaps the punishment takes place in this life, not after death, and amounts to divine discipline (v. 14).[929] Another possibility is that Jesus had in mind a loss of eternal reward. Or perhaps this is simply another case of hyperbole to drive home a point.

Jesus concluded this discourse on humility, as He had begun it, with a reference to entering the kingdom (v. 3). Humility is necessary to enter the kingdom because it involves humbly receiving a gift of pardon from God (v. 27). However, humility must continue to characterize the disciple. Not only must a disciple live before God as a humble child (v. 4); he or she must also be careful to avoid putting a stumbling block in the path of another disciple (vv. 5-14). Furthermore, he or she must humbly seek to restore a wayward fellow disciple (vv. 15-20). Forgiving fellow disciples— wholeheartedly and completely—is likewise important for humble disciples (vv. 21-35).

"His [Jesus'] message to the disciples is that loving concern for the neighbor and the spirit of forgiveness are to be the hallmarks of the community of believers in whose midst he, the Son of God, will ever be present."[930]

5. The transition from Galilee to Judea 19:1-2 (cf. Mark 10:1)

Matthew marked the end of Jesus' discourse on humility (ch. 18) and reported Jesus' departure from Galilee for Judea. This is the first time in Matthew's Gospel that Jesus moved into Judea for ministry. Until now all of Jesus' public ministry following His baptism and temptation was in Galilee and its surrounding Gentile areas. Now Jesus began to move toward Judea, Jerusalem, and the Cross.

Evidently Jesus departed from Capernaum and journeyed through Samaria, or perhaps around Samaria,[931] and into Judea to Jerusalem. Then He proceeded east across the Jordan River into Perea northeast of the Dead Sea. From there He went to Jerusalem again. Then leaving Jerusalem, Jesus visited Ephraim, traveled farther north into Samaria, headed east into Perea, and returned to Jerusalem. The following ministry took place during this last loop in Perea and Judea.[932] Great multitudes continued to follow Him, and He continued to heal many people. Jesus did not abandon His ministry to the masses, even though the nation had rejected Him as her Messiah (cf. 22:39).

"Even as He journeys to Jerusalem to suffer and die, He manifests His royal benevolence in healing those who come to Him."[933]

These verses conclude a major section of Matthew's Gospel (13:54—19:2). This section has highlighted Jesus' reaction to Israel's rejection of Him. Jesus continued to experience opposition from the ordinary Israelites, from the Roman leadership of the area, and from the religious leaders within Israel. His reaction was to withdraw and to concentrate on preparing His disciples for what lay ahead of them in view of His rejection. However, He also continued to minister to the needs of the masses, primarily the Jews, because He had compassion on them.

VI. THE OFFICIAL PRESENTATION AND REJECTION OF THE KING 19:3—25:46

This section of the Gospel continues Jesus' instruction of His disciples in preparation for their future (19:3—20:34). Then Jesus presented Himself formally to Israel as her King with His triumphal entry (21:1-17). This resulted in strong rejection by Israel's leaders (21:18—22:46). Consequently Jesus pronounced His rejection of Israel (ch. 23). Finally He revealed to His disciples that He would return to Israel later and establish the kingdom (chs. 24—25).

Throughout this entire section, the Jewish leaders' opposition to Jesus continues to mount in intensity, and it becomes more focused on Him. Reconciliation becomes impossible. Jesus revealed increasingly more about Himself and His mission to His disciples, and stressed the future inauguration of the kingdom. Between these two poles of opposition and inauguration, God's grace emerges even more powerfully than we have seen it so far. Matthew never used the word "grace" (Gr. *karis*), but its presence is obvious in this Gospel (cf. 19:21-22; 20:1-16).

---

[928]Pentecost, *The Parables* . . ., p. 67.

[929]Walvoord, *Matthew:* . . ., p. 140.

[930]Kingsbury, *Matthew as* . . ., p. 79. Cf. vv. 6, 10, 20, 21-22.

[931]France, *The Gospel* . . ., p. 709.

[932]Hoehner, *Chronological Aspects* . . ., pp. 62-63.

[933]Toussaint, *Behold the* . . ., p. 220.

". . . despite the gross rejection of Jesus, the chronic unbelief of opponents, crowds, and disciples alike, and the judgment that threatens both within history and at the End, grace triumphs and calls out a messianic people who bow to Jesus' lordship and eagerly await his return."[934]

A. JESUS' INSTRUCTION OF HIS DISCIPLES AROUND JUDEA 19:3—20:34

The primary emphasis in this section of Matthew's Gospel is Jesus' instruction of His disciples to prepare them for the future. Specifically, He emphasized the importance of the first becoming last and the last first: humble servanthood (cf. 19:30; 20:16).

1. Instruction about marriage 19:3-12 (cf. Mark 10:2-12)

Matthew evidently included this instruction because the marriage relationships of Jesus' disciples were important factors in their effective ministries. Jesus clarified God's will for His disciples, which was different from the common perception of His day. He dealt with the single state, as well as the essence of marriage, and the subjects of divorce and remarriage.

19:3
The Pharisees again approached Jesus to trap Him (cf. 12:2, 14, 38; 15:1; 16:1; 22:15, 34-35). This time they posed a question about "divorce." In 5:31-32, Jesus had taught the sanctity of marriage in the context of kingdom righteousness. Here the Pharisees asked Him what divorces were legitimate. Perhaps they hoped Jesus would oppose Herod as John had done, and suffer a similar fate. The Machaerus fortress, where Herod Antipas had imprisoned and beheaded John, was nearby, located east of the north part of the Dead Sea. Undoubtedly the Pharisees hoped Jesus would say something that they could use against Him.

Both the NASB and NIV translations have rendered the Pharisees' question well. They wanted to know if Jesus believed a man could "divorce his wife for any" and every "reason." The Mosaic Law did not permit wives to divorce their husbands.

There was great variety of opinion on this controversial subject among the Jews. Most of them believed that divorce was "lawful" for Jews, though not for Gentiles, but they disagreed as to its grounds.[935] The Qumran community believed that divorce was not legitimate for any reason.[936] In mainstream Judaism there were two dominant views, both of which held that divorce was permissible for "something indecent" (Deut. 24:1). Rabbi Shammai and his school of followers believed the indecency was some gross indecency, though not necessarily adultery. Rabbi Hillel and his school interpreted the indecency more broadly, to include practically any offense that a wife might have committed, real or imagined by the husband. This even included a wife not cooking her husband's meal to his liking.[937] One of Hillel's disciples, Rabbi Akiba, permitted a man to divorce his wife if a prettier woman caught his eye.[938] Josephus was a divorced Pharisee, and he believed in divorce "for any causes whatsoever."[939] In many Pharisaic circles "the frequency of divorce was an open scandal."[940]

19:4-6
Jesus' opponents based their thinking on divorce on Deuteronomy 24:1-4, where Moses permitted divorce. Jesus went back to Genesis 1 and 2 as expressing God's original intention for marriage: no divorce. He argued that the original principle takes precedence over the exception to the principle.

Jesus' citation of Genesis 1:27 and 2:24 shows that He believed that marriage unites a man and a woman in a unified "one flesh" relationship.

"The union is depicted in the vivid metaphor of Genesis as one of 'gluing' or 'welding'—it would be hard to imagine a more powerful metaphor of permanent attachment. In the Genesis context the 'one flesh' image derives from the creation of the woman out of the man's side to be 'bone of my bones and flesh of my flesh' (Gen 2:21-23); in marriage that original unity is restored."[941]

---

[934]Carson, "Matthew," pp. 410-11.

[935]Edersheim, The Life . . ., 2:332-33.

[936]J. R. Mueller, "The Temple Scroll and the Gospel Divorce Texts," Revue de Qumran 38 (1980):247-56.

[937]For a fuller discussion of the two major views, see Edersheim, The Life . . ., 2:333-34.

[938]Mishnah Gittin 9:10.

[939]Josephus, Antiquities of . . ., 4:8:23.

[940]Hill, p. 280.

[941]France, The Gospel . . ., p. 717.

"One flesh" expresses the fact that when a man and a woman marry, they become whole, as Adam was a whole person before God created Eve from his side. It is a way of saying that, as unmarried individuals, Adam and Eve were each lacking something, but when God brought them together in marriage they became whole.

God was the Creator in view (v. 4), though Jesus did not draw attention to that point (cf. John 1:3; Col. 1:16). The phrase "for this cause" (v. 5) in Genesis 2:23-24 refers to becoming one flesh. Eve became related to Adam in the most intimate sense when they married. Having been taken from Adam and made from his rib, Eve became "one flesh" with him when God joined them in marriage. When a man and a woman marry, they become "one flesh," a whole entity, thus reestablishing the intimate type of union that existed between Adam and Eve.

". . . the 'one flesh' in every marriage between a man and a woman is a reenactment of and testimony to the very structure of humanity as God created it."[942]

Note, too, that it is the union of *a man and a woman* that Jesus affirmed as constituting marriage, not same sex marriages.

In view of this union, Jesus concluded, a husband and wife are no longer two but one (v. 6). God has united them in a "one flesh" relationship by marriage. Since God has done this, separating them by divorce is not only unnatural but rebellion against God. Essentially Jesus allied Himself with the prophet Malachi, as well as Moses, rather than with any of the rabbis. Malachi had revealed that God hates divorce (Mal. 2:16).

". . . the argument here is expressed not in terms of what cannot happen, but of what *must* not happen: the verb is an imperative, *'let* not man separate.' To break up a marriage is to usurp the function of God by whose creative order it was set up, and who has decreed that it shall be a permanent 'one flesh' union."[943]

Jesus focused on the God-ordained and supernaturally created unity of the married couple. The rabbis stressed the error of divorce as involving taking another man's wife. Jesus appealed to the principle. He went back to fundamental biblical revelation, in this case Creation. He argued that marriage rests on how God made human beings, not just the sanctity of a covenantal relationship between the husband and the wife. This covenantal relationship is what some evangelical books on marriage stress primarily. Marriage does not break down simply because one partner breaks the covenant with his or her spouse. God unites the husband and wife in a new relationship when they marry, that continues regardless of marital unfaithfulness.

In summary, Jesus gave three reasons why married couples should remain married: First, the Creator determines what is the ideal in marriage, and since He created one male and one female originally, He intended only one mate for each. Second, God ordained marriage as the strongest bond in all human interpersonal relationships, so it should not be broken. Third, the basic element in marriage is a covenant or contract that the husband and wife make with each other (cf. Mal. 2:14), and that contract involves becoming "one flesh" (i.e., physical intimacy).[944]

19:7   Jesus had not yet answered the Pharisees' question about how one should take the Mosaic Law on this subject, so they asked Him this question. Granting Jesus' view of marriage, why did Moses allow divorce? In the Deuteronomy 24:1-4 passage to which the Pharisees referred, God showed more concern about prohibiting the remarriage of the divorced woman and her first husband than the reason for granting the divorce. However, the Pharisees took the passage as a "command" (Gr. *entellomai*) to "divorce" one's wife for any indecency. God intended it as only a permission to divorce, as the passage itself shows.

19:8   Jesus explained that the concession in the Mosaic Law was just that, a concession. It did not reflect the will of God in creation but the hardness of the human heart. Divorce was not a part of God's creation ordinance any more than sin was. However, He "permitted" divorce, as He permitted sin.

"Moses regulated, but thereby conceded, the practice of divorce; both were with a view to (*pros*) the nation's (*hymon*) hardness of heart: since they persist in falling short of the ideal of Eden, let it at least be within limits."[945]

[942]Carson, "Matthew," p. 412.
[943]France, *The Gospel* . . ., p. 718.
[944]*The Nelson* . . ., p. 1608.
[945]M'Neile, p. 273.

The divorce option that God granted the Israelites testifies to man's sinfulness. Therefore one should always view divorce as evidence of sin, specifically hardness of heart. He or she should never view it as simply a morally neutral option that God granted, the correctness or incorrectness of which depended on the definition of the indecency. The Pharisees' fundamental attitude toward the issue was wrong. They were looking for grounds for divorce. Jesus was stressing the inviolability of the marriage relationship.

Notice in passing that Jesus never associated Himself with the sin in the discussion. He consistently spoke of the peoples' sin as *their* sin or *your* sin, never as *our* sin (cf. 6:14-15). This is a fine point that reveals Jesus' awareness that He was sinless.

What was the indecency for which Moses permitted divorce? It was not adultery, since the penalty for that was death, not divorce (Deut. 22:22). However, it is debatable whether the Israelites enforced the death penalty for adultery.[946] It could not be suspicion of adultery, either, since there was a specified procedure for handling those cases (Num. 5:5-31). Probably it was any gross immoral behavior short of adultery, namely, fornication, which includes all types of prohibited sexual behavior. Even though divorce was widespread and easy to obtain in the ancient Near East, and in Israel, the Israelites took marriage somewhat more seriously than their pagan neighbors did.

19:9 Jesus introduced His position on this subject with words that stressed His authority: "I say to you" (cf. 5:18, 20, 22, 28, 32, 34, 39, 44; 8:10; 16:18, 28). His was the true view because it came from Him who came to fulfill the Law. Matthew recorded only Jesus' words concerning a man who "divorces his wife," probably because in Judaism wives could not divorce their husbands. However, Mark recorded Jesus saying that the same thing holds true for a woman who divorces her husband (Mark 10:12). Mark wrote originally for a Roman audience. Wives could divorce their husbands under Roman law. Matthew's original readers lived under Jewish law, which did not permit wives to divorce their husbands.

There are four problems in this verse that account for its difficulty. First, what does the exception clause include? The best textual evidence points to the short clause that appears in both the NASB and the NIV translations, "except for immorality" or "except for marital unfaithfulness."[947]

Second, what is the meaning of *porneia* ("immorality" NASB, "marital unfaithfulness" NIV, "fornication" AV) in the exception clause? Some interpreters believe it refers to incest.[948] Paul used this word to describe prostitution in 1 Corinthians 6:13 and 16. Others believe *porneia* refers only to premarital sex. If a man discovered that his fiancé was not a virgin when he married her, he could divorce her.[949]

Even though the Jews considered a man and a woman to be husband and wife during their engagement period, they were not really married. Consequently, to consider this as grounds for divorce seems to require a redefinition of marriage that most interpreters resist. Furthermore, Deuteronomy 24:1 indicates that the couple is living together, which in Jewish culture would have meant that they were truly married, and not just engaged.

Still others define *porneia* as adultery.[950] However, the normal Greek word for adultery is *moicheia*, which Matthew used back to back with *porneia* previously (15:19). Therefore they must not mean the same thing. It also seems unlikely that *porneia* refers to *spiritual* adultery, in view of 1 Corinthians 7:12.

The best solution seems to be that *porneia* is a broad term that covers many different sexual sins that lie outside God's will. This conclusion rests on the meaning of the word.[951] These sexual sins, called "fornication," would include: homosexuality, bestiality, premarital sex, extramarital sex, incest, adultery, prostitution, and perhaps others. Essentially it refers to any sexual intercourse that God forbids (i.e., with any creature other than one's spouse).

A third problem in this verse is: Why did Matthew alone of all the Synoptic evangelists include this exception clause, here and in 5:32, when the others excluded it? To answer this question, we must also answer the fourth question, namely: What does this clause mean?

---

[946]See Henry McKeating, "Sanctions Against Adultery in Ancient Israelite Society," *Journal for the Study of the Old Testament* 11 (1979):57-72.

[947]Bruce M. Metzger, *A Textual Commentary on the Greek New Testament*, pp. 47-48.

[948]E.g., J. A. Fitzmyer, "The Matthean Divorce Texts and Some New Palestinian Evidence," *Theological Studies* 37 (1976):208-11.

[949]E.g., Mark Geldard, "Jesus' Teaching on Divorce," *Churchman* 92 (1978):134-43.

[950]E.g., T. V. Fleming, "Christ and Divorce," *Theological Studies* 24 (1963):109; and Toussaint, *Behold the . . .*, p. 225.

[951]*Theological Dictionary of the New Testament*, s.v. "*porne . . .*," by F. Hauck and S. Schulz, 6:579-95. See also Joseph Jensen, "Does *porneia* Mean Fornication? A Critique of Bruce Malina," *Novum Testamentum* 20 (1978):161-84.

Some scholars believe that Matthew simply added the clause himself, to make what Jesus *really* said stronger. They assume that what Mark wrote represents what Jesus *really* said. This view reflects a low view of Scripture, since it makes Matthew distort Jesus' words.

Another answer is that the exception clause does not express an exception. This view requires interpreting the Greek preposition *epi* ("except") as "in addition to" or "apart from." However, when *me* ("not") introduces *epi*, it always introduces an exception elsewhere in the Greek New Testament.

Another similar answer is that the exception is an exception to the whole proposition, not just to the verb "divorces."[952] In this case the *porneia* is not involved. We might translate the clause as follows to give the sense: "Whoever divorces his wife, quite apart from the matter of fornication, and marries another—commits adultery." Thus in this view, as in the one above, there is no real exception. The main problem with this view, as with the one above, is its unusual handling of the Greek text. One has to read in things that are not there.

A fourth view is that when Jesus used the Greek verb *apolyo* ("divorces"), He really meant "separates from," and thus permitted separation but not divorce.[953] Following this logic, there can be no remarriage, since a divorce has not taken place. However, in verse 3, *apolyo* clearly means "divorce," so to give it a different meaning in verse 9 seems arbitrary without some compelling reason to do so.

Other interpreters believe Jesus meant that in some cases divorce is not adulterous, rather than that in some cases divorce is not morally wrong.[954] In the case of *porneia* the husband does not make her adulterous; she is already adulterous. However, the text does not say he makes her "adulterous" or "an adulteress"; it says he makes her *commit adultery*. If the woman had committed *porneia*, divorce and remarriage would not make her adulterous. However, divorce and remarriage would make her commit adultery. The major flaw in this view is that in verse 9, it is the man who commits adultery, not his wife.

Probably it is best to interpret *porneia* and the exception clause as they appear normally in our English texts. Jesus meant that whoever divorces his wife, except for some gross sexual sin, and then remarries someone else—commits adultery (cf. 5:32).

> "On any understanding of what Jesus says . . ., he agrees with neither Shammai nor Hillel; for even though the school of Shammai was stricter than Hillel, it permitted remarriage when the divorce was not in accordance with its own Halakah (rules of conduct) (M[ishnah] *Eduyoth* 4:7-10); and if Jesus restricts grounds for divorce to sexual indecency . . ., then he differs fundamentally from Shammai. Jesus cuts his own swath in these verses . . ."[955]

Divorce and remarriage always involve evil (Mal. 2:16). However, just as Moses permitted divorce because of the hardness of man's heart, so did Jesus. Yet, whereas Moses was indefinite about the indecency that constituted grounds for a divorce, Jesus specified the indecency as gross sexual sin—fornication.[956]

Why then did Mark and Luke omit the exception clause? Probably they did so simply because it expresses an exception to the rule, and they wanted to stress the main point of Jesus' words without dealing with the exceptional situation. Since Matthew wrote for Jews primarily, he probably felt, under the Spirit's inspiration, that he needed to include the exception clause for the following reason. The subject of how to deal with divorce cases involving marital unfaithfulness was of particular interest to the Jews, in view of Old Testament and rabbinic teaching on this subject. Mark and Luke wrote primarily for Gentiles, so they simply omitted the exception clause.[957]

19:10-12   Some scholars, who believe that Jesus meant to discourage remarriage in verse 9, interpret the disciples' statement in verse 10 as evidence that they understood Him in this light.[958] If a person has to remain unmarried after he divorces, it would be better if he never married in the first place. However, this is probably not what Jesus meant in verse 9. The evidence for this is His reference to "eunuchs" in verse 12, as well as the inferiority of this view as explained above.

---

[952]Bruce Vawter, "The Divorce Clauses in Mt 5, 32 and 19, 9," *Catholic Biblical Quarterly* 16 (1959):155-67; idem, "Divorce and the New Testament," *Catholic Biblical Quarterly* 39 (1977):528-48.

[953]G. J. Wenham, "May Divorced Christians Remarry?" *Churchman* 95 (1981):150-61. See Tim Crater, "Bill Gothard's View of the Exception Clause," *Journal of Pastoral Practice* 4 (1980):5-12.

[954]John J. Kilgallen, "To What Are the Matthean Exception-Texts [5, 32 and 19, 9] an Exception?" *Biblica* 61 (1980):102-5.

[955]Carson, "Matthew," p. 411.

[956]See Craig L. Blomberg, "Marriage, Divorce, Remarriage, and Celibacy: An Exegesis of Matthew 19:3-12," *Trinity Journal* 11NS (1990):161-96.

[957]See Appendix 5 "What ends a marriage in God's sight?" at the end of these notes.

[958]E.g., Francis J. Moloney, "Matthew 19, 3-12 and Celibacy. A Redactional and Form-Critical Study," *Journal for the Study of the New Testament* 2 (1979):42-60.

Probably the disciples expressed regret because Jesus had come down more conservatively than even Rabbi Shammai, the more conservative of the leading rabbis. Jesus conceded divorce only for sexual indecency, as Shammai did, but He was even more conservative than Shammai on the subject of remarriage. He encouraged the disciples not to remarry after a divorce not involving sexual indecency, whereas Shammai permitted it. His encouragement lay in His clarification that marriage constitutes a very binding relationship (vv. 4-6). The disciples thought that if they could not divorce and remarry, which both Hillel and Shammai permitted, they would be better off remaining single.

Jesus responded that not everyone can live by the strict verdict that the disciples had just passed in verse 10, namely, never marrying. He did not mean that it is impossible to live with the standards He imposed in verses 4-9. If He meant the latter, He eviscerated all that He had just taught. Some could live by the strict verdict that the disciples suggested, namely, eunuchs whom God graciously enables to live unmarried.

Jesus identified three types of eunuchs (v. 12). Some eunuchs were born impotent or without normal sexual drive and therefore remained unmarried. Other eunuchs were eunuchs because others had castrated them, most notably those eunuchs who served in government positions where they had frequent access to royal women. Still other eunuchs were those who had chosen an unmarried life for themselves so they could serve God more effectively. Thus in answer to the disciples' suggestion that Jesus' encouragement to remain unmarried presented an unreasonably high standard (v. 10), Jesus pointed out that many people can live unmarried. He was one who did. For those so gifted by God, it is better not to marry. Those who can accept this counsel should do so.

However, neither Jesus nor the apostles viewed celibacy as an intrinsically holier state than marriage (1 Tim. 4:1-3; Heb. 13:4; cf. 1 Cor. 9:5). They viewed it as a special calling that God has given some of His servants so they can be more useful in His service. Eunuchs could not participate in Israel's public worship (Lev. 22:24; Deut. 23:1). However, they can participate in the kingdom and, we might add, in the church (Acts 8:26-40; 1 Cor. 7:7-9). Evidently there were some in Jesus' day who had foregone marriage in anticipation of the kingdom. Perhaps John the Baptist was one, and maybe some of Jesus' disciples had given up plans to marry in order to follow Him (cf. v. 27). Jesus was definitely one of the "eunuchs for the kingdom's sake."

To summarize, Jesus held a very high view of marriage. When a man and a woman marry, God creates a union that is as strong as the union that bound Adam and Eve together before God created Eve from Adam's side. Man should not separate what God has united (cf. Rom. 7:1-3). However, even though God hates divorce, He permits it in cases where gross sexual indecency (fornication) has entered the marriage. Similarly, God hates sin, but He permits it and gave instructions about how to manage it. Jesus urged His disciples not to divorce (cf. 1 Cor. 7:10), and if they divorced He urged them not to remarry (cf. 1 Cor. 7:8, 11, 27). However, He did not go so far as prohibiting remarriage (cf. 1 Cor. 7:9, 28). He encouraged them to realize that living unmarried after a divorce is a realistic possibility for many people, but He conceded it was not possible for all (cf. 1 Cor. 7:9). A primary consideration should be how one could most effectively carry on his or her work of preparing for the kingdom (cf. 1 Cor. 7:32-34).

Matthew did not record the Pharisees' reaction to this teaching. His primary concern was the teaching itself. He only cited the Pharisees' participation because it illustrated their continuing antagonism, a major theme in his Gospel, and because it provided the setting for Jesus' authoritative teaching.

2. Instruction about childlikeness 19:13-15 (cf. Mark 10:13-16; Luke 18:15-17)

Another incident occurred that provided another opportunity for Jesus to emphasize the importance of childlike characteristics in His disciples (cf. ch 18). Instruction about children follows instruction about marriage.

19:13   It was customary for people to bring their children to rabbis for blessings.[959] The Old Testament reflects this practice (Gen. 48:14; Num. 27:18; cf. Acts 6:6; 13:3). "The disciples rebuked" those who "brought" the "children" to Jesus for doing so (Mark 10:13; Luke 18:15). The evangelists did not reveal why the disciples did this. However, the fact that they did it shows their need for Jesus' exhortation that followed. They were not behaving with humility as Jesus had previously taught them to do (ch. 18; esp. v. 5). Moreover, Jesus' teaching about the sanctity of marriage (vv. 4-6) did not affect how they viewed children. The Jews cherished their children, but viewed them primarily as needing to listen, to learn, and to be respectful.

19:14-15   Jesus welcomed the children. This attitude was harmonious with His attitude toward all the humble, dependent, needy, trusting, and vulnerable people who came to Him. Furthermore, children coming to Him symbolized people with the characteristics of children coming to Him. Jesus did not want to discourage anyone like them from coming to Him. He did not say "the kingdom" belonged to children, but to people who are similar to children ("to such as these"). Children provided an excellent object lesson that Jesus used to illustrate the qualities necessary for entering and serving in the kingdom.

---

[959]Carson, "Matthew," p. 420.

The difference between this lesson, and the one in chapter 18, is that there the focus was on the childlike quality of humility that is so important in a disciple. Here Jesus broadened the lesson to include other childlike characteristics, all of which are important.

3. Instruction about wealth 19:16—20:16

Again someone approached Jesus with a question that provided an opportunity for Jesus to give His disciples important teaching (cf. v.3). This man's social standing was far from that of a child, and he provides a negative example of childlikeness. Previously the disciples did not welcome children (v. 13), but here they can hardly believe that Jesus would not welcome this man of wealth (v. 25).

The encounter with the rich young ruler 19:16-22 (cf. Mark 10:17-22; Luke 18:18-23)

19:16-17   A rich young man asked Jesus "what" he needed to do to "obtain eternal life." Luke 18:18 identifies him as a ruler. Matthew presented him as a rather typical obsessive-compulsive personality who probably never knew when to stop working.

The term "eternal life" occurs here for the first time in Matthew's Gospel (cf. Dan. 12:2, LXX). However, the concept of eternal life occurs in 7:14. Eternal life is life that continues forever in God's presence, as opposed to eternal damnation apart from God's presence (7:13; cf. 25:46).

The young man's idea of how one obtains eternal life was far from what Jesus had been preaching and even recently illustrating (vv. 13-15). He demonstrated the antithesis of childlike faith and humility. He thought he had to perform some particular act of righteousness in addition to keeping the Mosaic Law (v. 20). He wanted Jesus to tell him what that act was. He was a performance-oriented person.

Jesus' question in verse 17 did not imply that He was unable to answer the young man's question, or that He was not good enough to give an answer.[960] It implied that His questioner had an improper understanding of goodness. Jesus went on to explain that only God "is good" enough to obtain eternal life by performing some good deed. No one else is good enough to gain it that way. Jesus did not discuss His own relationship to God here. However, by answering this, Jesus implied that He was God or at least spoke for God. The young man had asked Jesus questions about goodness that only God could adequately answer.

The last part of verse 17 does not mean that Jesus believed a person can earn eternal life by obeying God's commandments. Obedience to God's commandments is a good preparation for entering into life. However, obedience apart from faith will not do.

19:18-20   The rabbis had added so many commands to those in the Mosaic Law, that the young man did not know which "commandments" Jesus meant. Jesus listed the sixth, seventh, eighth, ninth, and fifth commandments, in that order, plus part of "the greatest commandment" (Lev. 19:18). All of these commandments deal with observable behavior.

"Jesus did not introduce the Law to show the young man how to be saved, but to show him that *he needed to be saved* [cf. James 1:22-25]."[961]

The fact that the young man claimed to have "kept all" of them, reveals the superficiality of his understanding of God's demands (cf. 5:20; Phil. 3:6). Moreover, having apparently lived an upright life, he still had no assurance that he possessed eternal life. This is always the case when a person seeks to earn eternal life by his or her goodness. One can never be sure he or she has done enough. This young man may have been rich materially, but he was lacking what was more important, namely, the assurance of his salvation.

19:21-22   By referring to being "complete," Jesus was referring to the young man's statement that he felt incomplete (v. 20; cf. v. 16), that he needed to do something more to assure his eternal life. Jesus did not mean that the young man had eternal life and just needed to do a little more, to put the icing on the cake (cf. 23:8-12). Earlier Jesus had told his disciples that *perfection*, the same Greek word translated "complete" here, came from following Him (5:48). He repeated the same thing here.

What this young man needed to do was to become a disciple of Jesus, to start following Him and learning from Him. God's will did not just involve keeping commandments. It also involved following Jesus. If he did that, he would learn how a person obtains eternal life: not by good deeds, but by faith in Jesus. To follow Jesus, this rich young man would need to "sell" his "possessions." He could not accompany Jesus as he needed to without disposing of things that would have distracted him

[960]See B. B. Warfield, "Jesus' Alleged Confession of Sin," *Princeton Theological Review* 12 (1914):127-228.
[961]Wiersbe, 1:72.

(cf. 8:19-22). Such a material sacrifice to follow Jesus would gain a reward eventually (cf. v. 29; 6:19-21). Jesus was assuming the young man would become a believer after he became a disciple.

> "So attached was he to his great wealth that he was unwilling to part with it. Such is the insidiousness of riches that, as Bengel notes, 'If the Lord had said, Thou art rich, and art too fond of thy riches, the young man would have denied it.' He had to be confronted with all the force of a radical alternative."[962]

The young man was not willing to part with his possessions to follow Jesus. He was willing to keep the whole Mosaic Law, and even to do additional good works, but submitting to Jesus was something else. Jesus had put His finger on the crucial decision this young man had to make when He told him to dispose of his possessions. Would he value his possessions, or following Jesus to learn more about eternal life, more highly? His decision revealed his values (cf. 6:24).

> "His real problem was lack of faith in Christ, whom he considered a good Teacher but who apparently was not to be regarded as one who had the right to demand that he give up all in order to follow Him."[963]

This passage does not teach that salvation is by works. Jesus did not tell the young man that he would obtain eternal life by doing some good thing, but neither did He rebuke him for the good things that he had done. He made it very clear that what he needed to do was to follow Jesus so he could come to faith in Jesus.

This passage does not teach that a person must surrender all to Jesus *before* he or she can obtain eternal life, either. Jesus never made this a condition for salvation. He made giving away possessions here a condition for discipleship, not salvation. We have seen a consistent order in Matthew's Gospel that holds true in all the Gospels. First, Jesus called a person to follow Him, that is, to begin learning from Him as a disciple. Second, He called His disciples to believe on Him as the God-man. Third, He called His believing disciples to continue following Him and believing on Him because He had an important job for them to do.

The teaching concerning riches 19:23-30 (cf. Mark 10:23-31; Luke 18:24-30)

19:23-24   "Truly I say to you" or "I tell you the truth" introduces another very important statement (cf. 5:18; et al.). Jesus evidently referred to a literal "camel" and a literal sewing "needle" (Gr. *rhaphidos*) here. His statement appears to have been a common proverbial expression for something impossible. I have not been able to find any basis for the view that "the eye of the needle" was a small gate, as some commentators have suggested. Jesus presented an impossible situation.

> "We should recognize that by the standards of first-century Palestine, most upper-middle-class Westerners and those on the Pacific rim would be considered wealthy. For all such persons the questions of wealth, discipleship, and the poor cannot be side-stepped if following Christ and his teaching means anything at all."[964]

Probably Jesus referred to "the kingdom of *God*" in verse 24 for the sake of variety, since He had just spoken of "the kingdom of *heaven*" in verse 23. Also, by using God's name, He stressed God's personal authority. He proceeded to contrast two kings: God and Mammon. While some interpreters take the kingdom of God and the kingdom of heaven as two different kingdoms, usage argues for their being synonymous.[965]

19:25-26   The disciples' amazement was due to the Jewish belief that wealth signified God's favor. "Saved" is a synonym for entering the kingdom (v. 24) or obtaining eternal life (v. 16, cf. Mark 9:43-47). The antecedent of "this" in verse 26 is salvation (v. 25). In other words, man cannot save himself (cf. v. 21). Nevertheless God can save him, and He can do anything else. Jesus characteristically pointed the disciples away from man's work to God's work. Joseph of Arimathea was exceptional in that he was both rich and a disciple (26:57).

19:27-28   Jesus' statement encouraged Peter to ask a question. It may have occurred to him when Jesus told the rich young man that if he followed Him he would receive treasure in heaven (v. 21). Peter asked Jesus what those who had made this sacrifice could expect to receive.

> Jesus assured the disciples very definitely—"Truly I say to you"—that God would reward them for leaving what they had left and following Him (v. 28). The "regeneration" or "renewal" (Gr. *palingenesia*) refers to the establishment of the messianic

---

[962]Hagner, *Matthew 14—28*, p. 559. See also Calvin, *Institutes of . . .*, 4:13:13.

[963]Walvoord, *Matthew: . . .*, p. 145. See Alan P. Stanley, "The Rich Young Ruler and Salvation," *Bibliotheca Sacra* 163:649 (January-March 2006):46-62.

[964]Hagner, *Matthew 14—28*, p. 562.

[965]See my comments on 3:1-2.

kingdom (Isa. 2:2-4; 4:2-6; 11:1-11; 32:16-18; 35:1-2; 65:17; 66:22; cf. Acts 3:21; Rom. 8:18-23). Then "the Son of Man will sit on His glorious throne" (lit. throne of glory, cf. 25:31; Dan. 7:13-14). This is a very clear messianic claim. Jesus equated Himself with the Son of Man, the judge of humanity (Dan. 7:13). Moreover, the 12 disciples will then "sit upon 12 thrones, judging the 12 tribes of Israel" (cf. Isa. 1:26; Dan. 7:22).

"In the O.T. *krinein* [to judge] often means 'govern' (e.g. Ps. ix. 4, 8)."[966]

Since there were 12 chief disciples or apostles (10:2-4), it seems clear that Jesus had these individuals in mind. "Israel" always means Israel, the physical descendants of Jacob (Israel), whenever this term appears in the New Testament. The reward of these disciples, for forsaking all and following Jesus, would be sharing judgment and rule with the great Judge, Jesus, in His kingdom (Ps. 2). This judgment will take place and this rule will begin on earth when Jesus returns at the Second Coming (25:31-46).

"This is clearly a picture of the millennial earth, not heaven. Late in Christ's ministry, He supports the concept that the kingdom, while postponed as far as human expectation is concerned, is nevertheless certain of fulfillment following His second coming."[967]

How much the rich young man gave up to retain his "much property" (cf. vv. 21-22)!

"The Lord thus confirms the promise He had already given to Peter (Matthew 16:19) and enlarges it to include all of the apostles. They are to be rulers over Israel in the kingdom."[968]

There is a vast difference between earning salvation with works and receiving a reward for works. Salvation is always apart from human works, but rewards are always in response to human works.

19:29   Not only the 12 Apostles, but every self-sacrificing disciple, will receive a reward for his or her sacrifice.[969] Jesus meant here that "everyone" who makes a sacrifice to follow Him will receive *much more than* he or she sacrificed—as a reward! He did not mean that if one sacrifices one house he or she will receive 100 houses, much less 100 mothers or 100 fathers, etc. If a disciple leaves a parent to follow Jesus, he or she will find many more people who will be as a parent to him or her in the kingdom. God is no man's debtor.

". . . the promise will be found to hold good with the regularity of a law, if we do not confine our view to the individual life, but include successive generations."[970]

Additionally, that person "will inherit eternal life." That is, he or she will enter into the enjoyment of his or her eternal life in the kingdom, as *heirs* for whom their heavenly Father has prepared many blessings.

"We must remember that eternal life in the Bible is not a static entity, a mere gift of regeneration that does not continue to grow and blossom. No, it is a dynamic relationship with Christ Himself [cf. John 10:10; 17:3]."[971]

Other passages that present eternal life as something the believer must work to *inherit* are 19:16; Mark 10:17, 30; Luke 10:25; 18:18, 30; John 12:25-26; Romans 2:7; 6:22; and Galatians 6:8. Eternal life is quantitative as well as qualitative.

19:30   This proverbial saying expresses the reversals that will take place when the King begins to reign in the kingdom. The "first" and "last" are positions representing greatness and lowliness, respectively. The rich young man and the disciples are cases in point. The young man was rich then, but would not have received many blessings in the kingdom if he was a believer in Jesus. The disciples, on the other hand, had given up everything to follow Jesus, but they will have a great wealth of blessings in the kingdom.

This statement introduces the parable of the workers and their compensation (20:1-15). Jesus repeated it at the end of the parable but in reverse order (20:16). This structure shows that the parable illustrates the point stated in this verse. Here He

---

[966]M'Neile, I 282.

[967]Walvoord, *Matthew: . . .*, p. 146. See also David K. Lowery, "Evidence from Matthew," in *A Case for Premillennialism: A New Consensus*, p. 180.

[968]Toussaint, *Behold the . . .*, p. 229.

[969]See also Calvin, *Institutes of . . .*, 3:25:10.

[970]Bruce, *The Training . . .*, p. 269.

[971]Dillow, p. 136.

evidently meant that many (not all) of those in the first rank of priority then—for example, the rich, the famous, and the comfortable disciples—will be last in the kingdom. Their reward will be small because they were not willing to sacrifice themselves to follow Jesus wholeheartedly. Conversely, those whom the world regarded with contempt, because of the sacrifices they made to follow Jesus, will receive great honor in the kingdom for making those sacrifices.

"The principle taught in this account is that neither poverty or [*sic*] wealth guarantees eternal life. . . .

". . . what guarantees eternal life is following Christ (in faith), and what guarantees eternal rewards is living according to His commands (obedience)."[972]

The parable of the workers in the vineyard 20:1-16

This parable explains why the last will become first. It begins with a well-known scene but then introduces surprising elements to make a powerful point.

"Jesus deliberately and cleverly led the listeners along by degrees until they understood that if God's generosity was to be represented by a man, such a man would be different from any man ever encountered."[973]

"Any union leader worth their salt would protest at such employment practices. Anyone who took this parable as a practical basis for employment would soon be out of business."[974]

20:1-2   Jesus introduced this parable as He did the other kingdom parables in chapter 13 (cf. 13:24, 31, 33, et al.). This is how conditions will be in the messianic kingdom. One "denarius" was the normal day's wage for a day laborer in Jesus' day (cf. 18:28).[975] The "vineyard" is a common figure for Israel in the Old Testament (Isa. 3:14; 5:1-2; Jer. 12:10; et al.).

20:3-7   The "third hour" would be about 9:00 a.m., the "sixth hour" about noon, and the "eleventh hour" about 5:00 p.m. The "market place" would have been the central square of the town where day laborers obtained work and pay. The "landowner" did not promise a particular wage, only that He would deal justly with the laborers. Jesus did not explain why the landowner kept hiring more workers throughout the day. That was an irrelevant detail in His story. All the workers trusted the landowner to give them what was fair at the end of the day.

> "The day laborer did not have even the minimal security which a slave had in belonging to one master. There was no social welfare program on which an unemployed man could fall back, and no trade unions to protect a worker's rights. An employer could literally 'do what he chose with what belonged to him' (v. 15)."[976]

20:8-12   The "evening" was the time of reckoning for the workers (cf. Lev. 19:13). The order in which the landowner's foreman paid the workers ("last to the first") may imply that he took greater pleasure in rewarding those hired last.[977] In view of what he paid those hired late in the day, those who began working earlier *expected* to receive more than they had hoped for. They grumbled against him because he had been "generous" (v. 15) to the latecomers and only just with them. They cited their hard working conditions as justification for their grievance. Their error was that they had served for the pay they would receive, whereas those who served for only one hour did so simply trusting in the grace of their employer. The difference lay in their motivation. We can see the same differences in the motives of Jacob and Abraham, the Pharisee and the woman who anointed Jesus (Luke 7:36-50), and the elder and younger brothers in the parable of the prodigal son (Luke 15:11-32).

20:13-15   "Friend" is only a mild term of rebuke in this context. The landowner pointed out that he had not cheated those whom he hired earlier in the day. He had paid the wage they agreed to. It was his business if he wanted to pay the latecomers more than they deserved. The evil or "envious eye" (v. 15) is an idiom depicting jealousy (cf. 6:23; Deut. 15:9; 1 Sam. 18:9).

The landowner's rhetorical questions explained that he had distributed the wages as he had because he was gracious and "generous," as well as just (cf. Luke 15:11-32; Rom. 4:4-6; 11:6).

---

[972]Bailey, in *The New* . . ., p. 39.

[973]Norman A. Huffman, "Atypical Features in the Parables of Jesus," *Journal of Biblical Literature* 97 (1978):209.

[974]France, *The Gospel* . . ., p. 748.

[975]Edersheim, *The Life* . . ., 2:417.

[976]France., *The Gospel* . . ., p. 749.

[977]Bruce, *The Training* . . ., p. 276.

Some interpreters understand the laborers hired early in the morning to represent the Israelites, since the owner made an agreement (covenant, promises) with them. Those hired later did not have this guarantee, so they represent the Gentiles.[978]

20:16   The point of the parable was that God will graciously do more, for some of those who work for Him, than His justice demands. His servants should serve Him while trusting in His grace and goodness toward them, rather than calculating how much He owes them for their service.

> "The first are in danger of becoming the last when self-denial is reduced to a system, and practiced ascetically, not for Christ's sake, but for one's own sake."[979]

In view of the context, the 12 disciples correspond to the workers hired at the beginning of the day, the beginning of Jesus' public ministry. Those hired later correspond to other people who became Jesus' disciples later in His ministry. One of these people might have been the rich young man, if he had become a disciple (19:16-22). Peter's question about what the Twelve would receive (19:27) had implied that they should receive a greater reward, since their sacrifice had been, and later would be, greater. This parable taught him that God would give him a just reward for his sacrificial labor for Jesus. Nonetheless, God had the right to give just as great a reward to those whose service was not as long. This parable taught the disciples not to think of heavenly rewards in terms of justice, getting in proportion to what they deserved. They should think of them in terms of grace, any reward being an act of God's grace. Even those hired early in the day received a reward, and the landowner had been gracious and generous in hiring them and not others.

Modern disciples of Jesus should view heavenly rewards in the same way. The only reason we will receive any reward is that God has called us to be His workers. We can count on God dealing with us justly, graciously, and generously whether we serve God all our lives, or only a short time, having become His disciples later in life.

> "The parable is emphasizing a right attitude in service."[980]

This parable does not teach that God will reward all His disciples equally. Other parables also teach that He will not (e.g., 25:14-30). The point of this one is that God will reward all His disciples justly, graciously, and generously. In some cases, "the last" called will be among "the first" in rank of blessing. Conversely, in some cases, those whom God called early in their lives may not receive as much reward as those called later in life.

Jesus was probably hinting at more in this parable. At least we can draw the following applications from it. Disciples in Jesus' day would not necessarily receive more reward than disciples whom God calls to serve Him just before the day of laboring ends, before His second coming. Neither would Jewish disciples necessarily receive more than Gentile disciples, whom God would call later in His program of preparation for the kingdom (cf. 1 Cor. 6:2; Rev. 2:26).

4. Instruction about Jesus' passion 20:17-19 (cf. Mark 10:32-34; Luke 18:31-34)

There is a theological connection between this section and the former one. The death of Jesus provided the basis for God's gracious dealings with believers in His Son. This connection is clear to Matthew's readers because Matthew selected his material as he did, but the disciples probably did not see it when Jesus revealed it.

20:17   Matthew's reference to Jesus going "up to Jerusalem" reminds the reader of the climax toward which the conflict between the religious leaders and Jesus was heading. Of course, Jerusalem was "up" topographically from most places in Israel, but the idea of "going up" there was metaphorical as well, since Jerusalem was the center of national life. The rejection of Messiah is, of course, one of the main themes in Matthew's Gospel. The writer did not say that Jesus had begun "moving toward" Jerusalem, only that He was preparing His disciples further for that next important step.

20:18-19   Jesus was taking His disciples up to Jerusalem for the Passover celebration there. While there, the Son of Man would somehow be "delivered" over "to the chief priests and scribes," His antagonistic opponents. This implied a betrayal (cf. 17:22). They would "condemn Him to death." This implied legal proceedings. He would fall under the control of the "Gentiles," who would ridicule ("mock"), torture ("scourge"), and "crucify" Him. The Romans were the only Gentiles with authority to crucify; the Jews did not have this power under Roman rule. Three days later Jesus would "be raised up" to life.

This was Jesus' third and most specific prediction of His death (16:21; 17:22-23; cf. 12:40; 16:4; 17:9). He mentioned for the first time the mode of His death—crucifixion—and the Gentiles' part in it. Jesus' ability to predict His own death was another indication of His messiahship. His

---

[978]E.g., *The Nelson . . .*, p. 1610.

[979]Bruce, *The Training . . .*, p. 279.

[980]Wiersbe, 1:73.

willingness to proceed toward Jerusalem, in view of what lay before Him, shows that He was the Suffering Servant—obedient even to death on a cross.

> "These three passion-predictions are the counterpart to the major summary-passages found in the second part of Matthew's story (4:23; 9:35; 11:1). The function they serve is at least twofold. On the one hand, they invite the reader to view the whole of Jesus' life story following 16:21 from the single, overriding perspective of his passion and resurrection. On the other hand, they also invite the reader to construe the interaction of Jesus with the disciples throughout 16:21—28:20 as controlled by Jesus' concern to inculcate in them his understanding of discipleship as servanthood (16:24-25; 20:25-28)."[981]

5. Instruction about serving 20:20-28 (cf. Mark 10:35-45)

This pericope shows that the disciples did not understand what Jesus had said (cf. Luke 18:34).

> "Despite Jesus' repeated predictions of his passion, two disciples and their mother are still thinking about privilege, status, and power."[982]

> "The natural human concern with status and importance is clearly one of the most fundamental instincts which must be unlearned by those who belong to God's kingdom."[983]

20:20   Evidently James and John approached Jesus with their "mother," who voiced the request for them (cf. Mark 10:35). The reason they took this approach was not significant to the Gospel writers, though it suggests some reticence on the part of James and John. Evidently they believed Jesus would be more favorable to their mother's request than to theirs, perhaps because Jesus had been teaching them to be humble. Their kneeling ("bowing down") implied respect but not necessarily worship.

20:21   The request evidently grew out of what Jesus had said about the Son of Man sitting on His throne of glory, and the disciples judging the 12 tribes of Israel (19:28). The "right" and "left" side positions alongside Jesus suggest positions of prestige and power in His kingdom. Note that the disciples viewed the messianic kingdom as still future. The fact that they would make this request shortly after Jesus had again announced His death, shows how little they understood about His death preceding the establishment of the kingdom. They did not understand the need for the Cross, much less Jesus' resurrection, ascension, and the inter-advent period.

20:22   The disciples and their mother did not realize that the Cross must precede the crown. To share the crown they would have to share the Cross. Since they did not know what that involved for Jesus, they could hardly appreciate what it would mean for them (cf. 5:10-12; 10:37-39). The "cup" in Old Testament figurative usage sometimes refers to blessing (Ps. 16:5; 23:5; 116:13). Sometimes it is a metaphor for *judgment* or *retribution* (cf. Ps. 75:8; Isa. 51:17-18; Jer. 25:15-28; Ezek. 23:31-34). It also pictures *suffering* (Isa. 51:17-23; Lam. 4:21). Jesus used this figure, the cup, to represent the *divine judgment* that He would have to undergo to pay for the sins of humanity—and its accompanying *suffering*. The disciples evidently thought that all He meant was popular rejection.

20:23   Jesus answered the disciples on their own terms. They *would* experience suffering and rejection. James would become the first apostolic martyr (Acts 12:2) and John would suffer exile (Rev. 1:9), but Jesus would not be the one to determine who will sit on His right and left in the kingdom. The Father, under whose authority Jesus served, had already determined that (cf. Mark 10:40).

20:24-27   James and John's request evidently offended the other "ten" disciples—because they were hoping for those positions. Greatness in the kingdom was still much on their minds, despite Jesus' teaching on humility and childlikeness (cf. 18:10).

> "The fact that the other disciples were angered at James and John shows that they were in heart and spirit no better than the two brothers. . . . They all wanted the first place."[984]

Jesus proceeded to contrast greatness in the pagan Gentile world with greatness in His kingdom. He did not criticize the abuse of power that is so common in pagan governments. Rather, He explained that the power structure that exists in pagan

[981]Kingsbury, *Matthew as . . .*, p. 78.

[982]Carson, "Matthew," p. 430.

[983]France, *The Gospel . . .*, p. 755.

[984]W. A. Criswell, *Expository Notes on the Gospel of Matthew*, p. 117.

governments would be absent in His kingdom. In pagan governments, people who promote themselves over others often get positions of leadership. However, in Jesus' kingdom, those who place themselves under others will get those positions. In pagan governments, individuals are great who have others serving them, but in Jesus' kingdom, those who serve others will be great. To make His point even clearer, Jesus used "servant" (Gr. *diakonos*) in verse 26, and then "slave" (Gr. *doulos*) in verse 27.

20:28   Jesus presented Himself, "the Son of Man," as the supreme example of a slave to others. He would even lay down "His life" in the service of others, not just helping them, but dying in their place (cf. Isa. 53). As Messiah, Jesus had every right to expect service from others, but instead He served others.

> "To be great is to be the servant (*diakonos*) of many; to be first is to be the bond-servant (*doulos*) of many; to be supreme is to give one's life for many."[985]

The Greek word *lytron* ("ransom") was a term used frequently in non-biblical Greek to describe the purchase price for freeing a slave.[986] This word connotes a purchase price whenever it occurs in the New Testament.[987] "For" (Gr. *anti*) indicates the substitute nature of Jesus' death.[988] The "many" for whom He would die could be either the elect, or all of mankind (cf. Isa. 52:13—53:12).

> "A theology of 'limited atonement' is far from the intention of the passage and would be anachronistic in this context."[989]

Other passages seem to favor the interpretation that by His death, Jesus made all people savable. However, only the elect experience salvation and enter the kingdom (e.g., John 3:16; Eph. 1:4-7). Only One would die, but many would benefit from His death. This is one of the great Christological and soteriological verses in the Bible. It is also the first time that Jesus explained to His disciples the reason He would die.

> "The implication of the cumulative evidence is that Jesus explicitly referred to himself as Isaiah's Suffering Servant . . . and interpreted his own death in that light . . ."[990]

6. An illustration of illumination 20:29-34 (cf. Mark 10:46-52; Luke 18:35-43)

Even on the way to give His life a ransom for many, Jesus continued to serve, as this pericope shows. Rather than delivering Himself from the fate He foresaw, He mercifully and compassionately delivered others from their afflictions.

20:29   Jesus and His disciples left "Jericho," at the north end of the Dead Sea, and proceeded west, up the Judean wilderness road toward Jerusalem for the Passover feast (cf. v. 17). Jericho was the last town that travelers to Jerusalem would go through after crossing the Jordan River from Perea. Great crowds continued to follow Jesus, undoubtedly to benefit from His healing ministry. The road was probably full of Jews, many from Galilee, making their way to Jerusalem for the feast.

20:30   Probably the "blind men" were begging (cf. Mark 10:46). Mark mentioned just one beggar, probably the more prominent of the "two." Matthew may have mentioned both to provide two witnesses for his original Jewish readers. They cried out to Jesus for help, appealing to Him as the "Son of David" for "mercy" (cf. 9:27; 21:9). This title expressed their belief that Jesus was the Messiah.[991] They wanted Jesus to heal them (v. 33).

20:31-34   Matthew's version of this healing stresses Jesus' "compassion," which overcame the opposition of the crowds to provide healing for these men (cf. 19:13-15). When Jesus previously healed two blind men *in Galilee*, He commanded them to tell no one about the healing. He did not do that here, because it was now unnecessary to conceal His identity. Jesus would soon publicly proclaim His messiahship in the Triumphal Entry (21:1-11). The healed "blind men" immediately "followed" Jesus. This was the proper response for people who had come to see who Jesus was. These believers in His messiahship became disciples.

---

[985]Plummer, p. 280.

[986]Deissmann, pp. 331-32; A.T. Robertson, *Word Pictures in the New Testament*, 1:163.

[987]Leon Morris, *The Apostolic Preaching of the Cross*, pp. 29-38.

[988]Robertson, *A Grammar . . .*, p. 573.

[989]France, *The Gospel . . .*, p. 763.

[990]Carson, "Matthew," p. 434.

[991]Morison, p. 365.

It is significant that these men, though physically blind, were spiritually perceptive regarding Jesus' identity. The other disciples had recently demonstrated their own spiritual imperceptibility (vv. 17-23). Jesus had taught them that insight into messianic truth came only from divine revelation (16:17).

> "The 'sight' of these blind men discloses the 'blindness' of Israel's sight."[992]

> "The giving of sight to the blind is a dramatic miracle that points to the dawning of the era of messianic fulfillment. The Son of David is present among his people. And as he compassionately delivers them from their literal darkness, so he continues on his way to Jerusalem, where in his sacrificial death he will deliver all of humanity from an even greater darkness—that of the bondage to sin and death. . . . This healing pericope thus may be seen as the gospel in a microcosm."[993]

This was the last public miracle the evangelists recorded Jesus doing before His death. Even though the nation as a whole rejected Jesus, individuals continued to believe that He was the Messiah. The postponement of the kingdom did not rule out personal salvation for anyone who believed. They would enter the messianic kingdom by resurrection at the Second Coming (Isa. 26:19; Dan. 12:2). For this reason Jesus continued to present Himself to Israel as her Messiah in the Triumphal Entry. This miracle is a prelude to that presentation in Matthew's Gospel.

B. Jesus' Presentation of Himself to Israel as her King 21:1-17

Jesus came to Jerusalem to present Himself formally to the leaders of Israel as the nation's Messiah. He did this when He entered Jerusalem, as Isaiah and Zechariah predicted Messiah would appear.

> "Jesus entered Jerusalem for the last time in a manner which showed that He was none other than the Messiah, the Son of David, who was coming to Sion to claim the city as His own."[994]

The events Matthew recorded in chapters 21—28 happened within six days. John recorded that Jesus arrived in Bethany six days before Passover, evidently the Saturday evening before Passion Week (John 12:1-10). Jesus had previously traveled from Jericho, eventually arriving in a town called Ephraim, from which He then went to Bethany (cf. Luke 19:1-28; John 11:55-57). Jesus apparently stayed in Bethany until Monday when He entered Jerusalem.[995] After that, He seems to have gone back and forth between Bethany and Jerusalem throughout the week (21:17).

Matthew continued to tell his story by presenting groups of three, as he did in previous chapters: three symbolic actions (21:1-22), three polemical parables (21:28—22:14), and three hostile questions and responses (22:15-40).

1. Jesus' preparation for the presentation 21:1-7 (cf. Mark 11:1-7; Luke 19:29-35; John 12:12-16)

21:1-2   Jesus and his disciples traveled the 17 miles from Jericho to Bethany along the Roman road. They climbed about 3,000 feet in elevation between those towns. "Bethphage" ("house of figs") lay slightly farther west than Bethany, also on the southeast slope of the "Mount of Olives." It no longer exists, and its exact location is unknown, but it had messianic connotations (Zech. 14:4; cf. Ezek. 11:23; 43:1-5). It may have been the name of that district, as well as the name of a little village close to Jerusalem where the district began.[996] When Jesus approached Bethphage, He instructed "two disciples" to go into that village and "bring" a "donkey" and its "colt" to Him. Most people, except the wealthy, walked everywhere in first-century Palestine.[997] This is the only record of Jesus riding an animal. He was preparing to recreate the return of King David to Jerusalem in peace and humility (2 Sam. 19—20), and the entrance of Solomon into Jerusalem for his enthronement (1 Kings 1:38-40; cf. Gen. 49:10-11). On each of these occasions, a king rode either a donkey or a mule.

21:3   This is the only place in Matthew's Gospel where Jesus used the title "Lord" (Gr. *kyrios*) of Himself. In every other place it refers to Yahweh. Even though "lord" was a respectful address, used this way it became a title of authority. Probably Jesus had previously made arrangements with the owner to use the animals. Now the disciples went to pick them up, and when questioned, explained that they were taking them to "the Lord," who needed them (Mark 11:5-6; Luke 19:33-34). Evidently the owner was a believer in Jesus.

[992]Kingsbury, *Matthew as . . .*, p. 80.

[993]Hagner, *Matthew 14—28*, p. 588.

[994]Tasker, p.197.

[995]Hoehner, *Chronological Aspects . . .*, p. 91.

[996]Edersheim, *The Life . . .*, 2:364.

[997]France, *The Gospel . . .*, p. 775.

"The careful preparation which the Lord makes indicates His sovereignty. That which is about to transpire is no accident."[998]

21:4-5   It is possible that Jesus spoke these words. However, it is probable that Matthew added them, as he did for other fulfillment passages in his Gospel (1:22; et al.). The first two lines of the quotation are from Isaiah 62:11, and the last two cite Zechariah 9:9. "Zion" is a poetic name for Jerusalem, often used of the city under Messiah's rule during the kingdom.[999] Jerusalem belonged to Messiah (5:35). Matthew omitted quoting the part of Zechariah 9:9 that speaks of Messiah bringing national salvation to Israel. Jesus would not do that yet because of Israel's rejection.

"Here was the King's final and official offer of Himself, in accord with the prophecy of Zech. 9:9."[1000]

Rulers rode donkeys in Israel during times of peace (Judg. 5:10; 1 Kings 1:33). This was a sign of their humble service of the people. Warriors rode horses. Jesus was preparing to declare His messiahship by fulfilling this messianic prophecy. By coming in peace, He was extending grace rather than judgment to the city. He was coming as a servant now. He would return as a conquering King riding on a war horse later (cf. Rev. 19:11).

Jesus rode on the "colt" (a young male donkey), not on its mother, the donkey (Mark 11:2; Luke 19:30). It would have been remarkable that Jesus was able to control a presumably unbroken animal, moving through an excited crowd with an unfamiliar burden on its back. This was just one more demonstration that Jesus was the Messiah who was the master of nature (cf. 8:23-27; 14:22-32). Surely He could bring peace to Israel if He could calm the young colt (Isa. 11:1-10).

"Matthew could hardly make the presentation of the royalty of Jesus more explicit."[1001]

Toussaint titled his commentary on Matthew "Behold The King" because he believed these words are the theme of Matthew's Jewish Gospel.

21:6-7   The disciples ran their errand, returned to Jesus, and spread their outer garments on both animals. Both the donkey and the colt entered Jerusalem. The "them" on which Jesus sat were the garments, not both animals.

This deliberate preparation for a citywide reception contrasts with Jesus' former approach to ministry. Before, He had deliberately *not* drawn attention to Himself, but now He prepared to do so. He had formerly withdrawn from the antagonistic hierarchy, but now He organized a parade that they could not miss.[1002]

2. Jesus' entrance into Jerusalem 21:8-11 (cf. Mark 11:8-11a; Luke 19:36-44; John 12:17-19)

21:8   The large company of pilgrims, mainly from Galilee, were acknowledging Jesus as a King by "spreading" their coats on "the road" before Him (cf. 2 Kings 9:13). Likewise, throwing small "branches from the trees" before Him symbolized the same thing (cf. 1 Macc. 13:51; 2 Macc. 10:7).[1003]

"A Galilean was essentially a foreigner in Jerusalem, and Jesus' entourage, being made up of Galileans, would normally stand out as distinctive among the Jerusalem crowd."[1004]

21:9   This crowd of non-Jerusalemites both preceded Jesus and followed Him as He approached Jerusalem.

"Apparently the Galilean pilgrims accompanying Jesus and the Jerusalem crowd coming out to greet him formed a procession of praise."[1005]

Undoubtedly, word of Jesus' coming had preceded him, so the people of Jerusalem were anticipating His arrival. Since Jesus was an obedient Jew, He visited Jerusalem for the three required feasts annually. The Synoptic writers gave no hint of this, but John mentioned ministry that Jesus had in Jerusalem during these visits. Therefore many people who lived in Jerusalem had seen and heard Him before He entered Jerusalem in the Triumphal Entry. The population of Jerusalem, which covered

[998]Toussaint, *Behold the* . . ., p. 237.
[999]Walvoord, *Matthew:* . . ., p. 155.
[1000]*The New Scofield* . . ., p. 1027.
[1001]Toussaint, *Behold the* . . ., p. 238.
[1002]Morgan, *The Gospel* . . ., p. 249.
[1003]Edersheim, *The Life* . . ., 2:372.
[1004]France, *The Gospel* . . ., p. 771.
[1005]Carson, "Matthew, p. 439.

only about 300 acres, normally numbered between 200,000 and 250,000. But during the feasts, this number swelled to nearly 3,000,000.[1006]

The people's words of praise came from Psalm 118:25-26. The Jews used this psalm at the Passover as part of "the great Hallel" (Pss. 113—18) and at the feasts of Tabernacles and Dedication. "Hosanna" transliterates the Hebrew word for "Save us now!" (cf. 2 Sam. 14:4; 2 Kings 6:26). It had become an acclamation through usage (cf. Rev. 7:10).[1007] "Son of David" is the messianic title that stressed the kingly role that Messiah would play. "He who comes in the name of the Lord" is likewise a messianic reference (23:39; cf. 3:11; 11:3; Ps. 118:26).[1008] "Hosanna in the highest" probably meant "Glory to God in the highest" (Luke 2:14).[1009] Quoting this passage voiced praise to God for sending the Messiah, and cried out to Him for deliverance.

"The enthusiastic multitudes thus acclaim Jesus as being blessed by Jehovah, not merely with a verbal benediction, but, as Jehovah always blesses, with the gifts and the treasures implied in the benedictory words; and they acclaim him as coming and bringing all these blessings to them and to their capital and their nation."[1010]

However the people, like the disciples, did not understand Messiah's role as the Suffering Servant who would have to die. Also, they did not appreciate the universal scope of the kingdom, as contrasted with its national scope.

21:10-11   Jesus probably entered Jerusalem through the sheep gate (St. Stephen's gate, a name given to it after Stephen's martyrdom; cf. Acts 7:58). This gate pierced the eastern city wall to the north of the temple enclosure. Worshippers brought sheep into the city through this gate for sacrificing because it was the closest gate to the temple. It was fitting that the Lamb of God should enter Jerusalem through this gate. Jesus' entrance into Jerusalem became the popular topic of conversation (cf. 2:3). The residents wondered who He really was. Most people who knew about Jesus, described Him as a "prophet from Nazareth," whose arena of ministry had been mainly "Galilee" (cf. 2:23; 16:14; 21:46). This description reflects popular disbelief that He was the Messiah.[1011]

Matthew stated that Jesus' entry "stirred" up the whole "city" (cf. 2:3). At that time, a Herodian king no longer ruled Judea. Rome ruled it directly through a prefect.[1012] The arrival of a Jewish king, from Galilee of all places, would therefore have caused great concern among Jerusalem's residents. How would the Romans react?

"The significance of the triumphal entry is tremendous in this Gospel. To Matthew it is the final and official presentation of Jesus to Israel as its Messiah. This is evident for several reasons. The first is the manner in which Christ acts throughout this whole course of events. He deliberately makes very careful preparations to fulfill every detail of the prophecy of Zechariah 9:9. In addition He planned His movements with understanding of their significance. . . .

"A second indication of the fact that Jesus presented Himself to Israel is seen in that the people recognized it as such. . . .[1013]

"A third proof that the Lord presented Himself as the King of Israel is seen in the parables which the Messiah gives following this event. . . .

"A fourth indication . . . is the time in which it occurred. Sir Robert Anderson has shown that the entry of Christ into Jerusalem occurred on the very day that the sixty-ninth week of Daniel's prophecy had run out.[1014] This is the exact time in which the Messiah was to come (Daniel 9:25).

[1006]Edersheim, The Life . . ., 1:116-17.

[1007]Gundry, The Use . . ., pp. 41-43; Dalman, p. 221.

[1008]Carr, p. 242.

[1009]Carson, "Matthew," p. 439.

[1010]Lenski, p. 809.

[1011]See Kingsbury, Matthew as . . ., pp. 80-81.

[1012]France, The Gospel . . ., p. 781.

[1013]Footnote 48: Johnson, "The Argument . . .," p. 151.

[1014]Footnote 50: Robert Anderson, The Coming Prince, pp. 127-28.

"Because Israel refused to accept the King when He was presented in exact fulfillment of their Scripture, their unbelief was confirmed beyond the shadow of a doubt. The reception which was given the King was without genuine faith and understanding. However, it did give a brief glimpse of that which will characterize the King's reception when He appears to Israel for a second time."[1015]

3. Jesus' entrance into the temple 21:12-17 (cf. Mark 11:11b, 15-18; Luke 19:45-48)

Matthew stressed Jesus' cleansing of the temple as the work of David's Son (vv. 9, 15). This activity had great messianic significance.[1016]

21:12   The Mosaic Law required that the Jews pay a half-shekel temple tax, which they paid in temple coinage (cf. 17:24-27). To accommodate out of town pilgrims, the religious leaders set up currency exchange tables in the large temple courtyard. There people with Greek and Roman money could obtain the required Tyrian currency. The religious leaders also accommodated worshippers by selling animals used in the offerings of Judaism there. Thus the temple courtyard had come to resemble an outdoor market. Probably greedy merchants cheated their buyers if they could, especially during the feasts when pilgrims from far away crowded the temple area. However, it was that Sadducean priests permitted merchants to conduct business in the Court of the Gentiles, rather than how the merchants conducted their business, that provoked Jesus' wrath.

> "If one bought his animals here, had his money exchanged here, these would be accepted; otherwise he might have trouble on that score."[1017]

Jesus entered the temple area (Gr. *hieron*) and proceeded to destroy the market (cf. Zech. 14:21). The whole Temple area, in Jesus day, probably occupied an elongated square about 925 by 950 feet.[1018] There were actually four courtyards in the temple area: the Court of the Gentiles (that anyone could enter), the Court of the Women (that only clean Jewish men and women could enter), the Court of Israel (that only clean Jewish men could enter), and the Court of the Priests (that only clean Jewish priests could enter).[1019]

21:13   Jesus explained why He was doing what He did to the authorities. He quoted Scripture here, similarly to the way He did in replying to Satan (4:1-10). First, He referred to Isaiah 56:7, a passage in which Isaiah looked forward to a time when the temple would be "a house of prayer." Significantly, Matthew omitted "for all the peoples" from Isaiah's statement, focusing his readers' attention on Israel as still the target of Jesus' ministry. Second, Jesus referred to Jeremiah 7:11, a condemnation of superstitious reverence for the temple while the people dishonored it.

> "No matter what they do even by violating the sanctity of their Temple, they imagine that their adherence to this Temple will protect and shield them from any penalty."[1020]

In the context of Jeremiah's prophecy (Jer. 7:9-11), the "robbers" in view were nationalist rebels. That is also the meaning of the Greek word *lestai* that Jesus used here. Rather than being a house for prayer, Israel's leaders had turned it into a stronghold of Jewish nationalism that dishonored the temple while they maintained a superstitious respect for it.[1021]

> ". . . for Jesus to raise the claim through his cleansing of the temple that the temple has, under the custody of the religious leaders, become a 'den of robbers' and that his purification of it from the desecration of merchants is its restoration to rightful use as Israel's house of prayer and worship, is for him to mount a massive assault on the authority and integrity of the religious leaders (21:12-13)."[1022]

By coming to the temple and purifying it, Jesus was making another messianic claim (cf. Mal. 3:1-4). However, the nation's rejection of her Messiah frustrated the cleansing of the temple, and precluded the fulfillment of the blessing following purification (Mal. 3:5-6). This prophecy will finally find fulfillment when Messiah comes the second time.

[1015]Toussaint, *Behold the . . .*, pp. 241-42. See S. Lewis Johnson Jr., "The Triumphal Entry of Christ," *Bibliotheca Sacra* 124:495 (July-September 1967):218-29.

[1016]See the diagrams of Jerusalem and Herod's Temple at the end of these notes.

[1017]Lenski, p. 813.

[1018]Edersheim, *The Temple*, p. 38.

[1019]See Flavius Josephus, *Against Apion*, 2:8.

[1020]Lenski, p. 816.

[1021]For some insights into the temple environment to which Jesus alluded, see Karen K. Maticich, "Reflections on Tractate Shekalim," *Exegesis and Exposition* 3:1 (Fall 1988):58-60.

[1022]Kingsbury, *Matthew as . . .*, p. 81.

21:14   This is the last reference to Jesus' healing ministry in Matthew's Gospel. The healing probably happened in the Court of the Gentiles. Some of these "blind and lame" people could not participate fully in worship activities at the temple (cf. 2 Sam. 5:6-8, where David excluded the blind and lame). However, Jesus made it possible for them to do so by healing them (cf. Acts 3:2). Jesus therefore cleansed both the temple and those who came to it. One greater than the temple had arrived (12:6). The authorities would later question His authority to do this cleansing (v. 23).

21:15-16   The popular response to Jesus' actions aggravated the chief priests and teachers of the law further. The wonderful things that Jesus was doing had messianic implications, and the people realized this.

Jesus introduced the Psalm 8:2 quotation with a rebuke. Surely these experts in the Old Testament should have seen the messianic implications of what Jesus was doing, and heard the words people were using as they responded to Him (cf. 12:3; 19:4; 21:42; 22:31). This psalm describes the "praise" that people, even little "children," will give to God for the conditions that will prevail during the messianic kingdom. Ancient Near Eastern mothers often nursed their babies long after the children learned to talk, sometimes for as long as three years following their births.

Jesus' rebuke provided a basis for the children's continuing praise, and temporarily stifled the leaders' criticism. It also declared His deity, since Jesus accepted praise reserved only for God. Moreover, it reinforced the truth that the humble and childlike often perceive spiritual truth more clearly than the sophisticated, though they are often unaware of its full significance (cf. 19:13-15).

"The 'Magi' (2:1) and the 'centurion' (8:5) serve as foils for Israel: the faith of these Gentiles contrasts with the unbelief of Israel (2:1-12; 8:5-13). The 'two blind men' (9:27), the 'Canaanite woman' (15:22), the other 'two blind men' (20:30), and the 'children' in the temple (21:15) also serve as foils for Israel: these 'no-accounts' see and confess what Israel cannot, namely, that Jesus is its Davidic Messiah."[1023]

21:17   Jesus' withdrawal "to Bethany" each evening during the festival season was probably for practical reasons. Jerusalem was full of pilgrims, and Jesus had dear friends in Bethany, namely, Mary, Martha, and Lazarus. Joachim Jeremias estimated the normal population of Jerusalem at this time as about 30,000, but during Passover about 180,000.[1024]

C. Israel's Rejection of Her King 21:18—22:46

This section of Matthew's Gospel presents Israel's formal rejection of her Messiah. Jesus had made a formal presentation of Himself to the nation's populace and leadership in the messianic capital with His triumphal entry (21:1-17). Jesus' earlier rejection had taken place in rural Galilee (ch. 12). Now Matthew recorded Israel's response.[1025]

1. The sign of Jesus' rejection of Israel 21:18-22 (cf. Mark 11:12-14, 19-25; Luke 21:37-38)

The Triumphal Entry happened on Monday. The cursing of the fig tree took place on Tuesday, and the disciples' mention of its withering followed on Wednesday (cf. Mark 11:1-14).[1026]

21:18-19   Jesus passed the "lone fig tree" somewhere between Bethany and Jerusalem.

"Fig leaves appear about the same time as the fruit or a little after [normally in April]. The green figs are edible, though sufficiently disagreeable as not usually to be eaten till June. Thus the leaves normally point to every prospect of fruit, even if not fully ripe. Sometimes, however, the green figs fall off and leave nothing but leaves."[1027]

The "leaves only" on this tree suggested that it had borne fruit, since fig trees bore fruit before the leaves came out, but it had not. Jesus saw an opportunity to teach His disciples an important truth using this tree as an object lesson. He cursed the tree to teach them the lesson, not because it failed to produce fruit.

[1023]Ibid., pp. 26-27. See also p. 81.

[1024]Jeremias, Jerusalem in . . ., pp. 77-84.

[1025]For more light on the connections that unite this pericope with the previous one, see Mark Moulton, "Jesus' Goal for Temple and Tree: A Thematic Revisit of Matt 21:12-22," Journal of the Evangelical Theological Society 41:4 (December 1998):561-72.

[1026]Hoehner, Chronological Aspects . . ., p. 91.

[1027]Carson, "Matthew," p. 444.

Most interpreters of this pericope have seen Jesus' cursing of the fig tree as closely related to the context, namely, the cleansing of the temple and Jesus' denunciation of Israel's leaders. Many see the fig tree as a symbol of the whole nation of Israel not bearing the fruit of repentance (cf. Jer. 8:13; Hos. 9:10, 16; Luke 13:6-9).[1028] The problem with this view is that Jesus did not abandon Israel forever for rejecting Him (Rom. 11). A similar view takes the fig tree as representing the generation of Jews who rejected Jesus.[1029] God would judge them by withholding the kingdom from them. This is the best view from my viewpoint. A third view is that the fig tree illustrates a segment within Jesus' generation of Jews, namely, the hypocrites within the nation who made a show of bearing fruit but did not (cf. 6:2, 5, 16; 7:5; 15:7; 22:18; 23:1-39).[1030] They were barren spiritually. These were the temple merchants and the chief priests and scribes, but not the children, or the blind and the lame. However, Jesus cursed the whole tree and nation, not just the parts in it that proved unfruitful.

The idea that Jesus cursed a helpless fig tree for no fault of its own has bothered some people. However, Jesus also cast demons out of people and into pigs that drowned in the sea (8:28-34). This really demonstrates Jesus' compassion for people as distinct from the animal and plant forms of life. Humankind was God's special creation, and Jesus' recognition of this superior form of life shows that He did not regard all life as equally valuable. In the destruction of the swine, Jesus warned people of Satan's destructive power. In the cursing of the fig tree, He warned them of God's judgment for lack of fruit (cf. 3:8, 10; 7:16-20; 12:33; 13:8).

"One of the Old Testament images of God's judgment on Israel was the picture of the land being unable to bear figs (Jer. 8:13; Mic. 7:1-6)."[1031]

21:20-22   Mark separated the cursing of the tree, from the disciples' discovery that it had withered, by one day (Mark 11:13, 20). Matthew simply combined both events into one story without saying anything that would make Mark's account incompatible.

Jesus' response has led some commentators to conclude that, what He was teaching with the cursing of the fig tree was simply the importance of faith, not God's judgment on Israel.[1032] However, this seems unlikely to me in view of the preceding context and the symbolism of the fig tree. It seems to me that Jesus was teaching both lessons. The disciples' amazement that the fig tree had withered so quickly led Jesus to comment on that lesson but not on the other. He used the miracle to teach them a lesson on the power of believing prayer.

Jesus had exercised faith in God when He cursed the tree. God had rewarded Jesus' trust by killing the tree. Jesus pointed out that trust in God can have amazing consequences. The hyperbolic figure of casting a "mountain . . . into the sea" was one that Jesus had used before to illustrate the power of faith (17:20). There His point was that even a little faith can accomplish great feats. Here His point was that His disciples should believe God rather than disbelieve Him. The disciples had been observing many doubters in those who did not believe that Jesus was the Messiah, in spite of the evidence that God had given them, and they themselves had struggled with doubt. Jesus was urging them to have full confidence in Him as the Messiah, with the promise that *that* kind of faith can accomplish supernatural feats (cf. Acts 3:6-7).[1033]

". . . belief in the NT is never reduced to forcing oneself to 'believe' what he does not really believe. Instead, it is related to genuine trust in God and obedience to and discernment of his will . . ."[1034]

Jesus may have been teaching a deeper lesson with His reference to the mountain cast into the sea. A mountain in the Bible sometimes stands for a kingdom (Ps. 30:7; Isa. 2:2; 41:15; Jer. 51:25; Dan. 2:35, 44; cf. Rev. 8:8; 16:20; 17:9). The sea likewise has the metaphorical meaning of the Gentile nations (Deut. 33:19; Ps. 72:8; 114:3, 5; Isa. 11:11; 60:5). Perhaps with this illustration Jesus was anticipating the coming of His kingdom that would destroy Gentile world dominion (cf. 6:10; Dan. 2:44-45).

Verse 22 assumes what Jesus taught elsewhere about prayer, namely, that God will grant the petitions of His people when they are in harmony with His will (6:9-13; 7:7-11; cf. John 14:13-14; 15:16; 16:23-24; 1 John 5:14-15). His point was that when

[1028]E.g., Bruce, "The Synoptic . . .," 1:264; Tasker, p. 201; and Lenski, p. 825.

[1029]E.g., Toussaint, *Behold the . . .*, p. 245; and Barbieri, p. 69.

[1030]E.g., Carson, "Matthew," p. 445.

[1031]Bailey, in *The New . . .*, p. 43. Cf. Jer. 24:1-10; Hos. 9:10, 16-17; Mic. 7:1-6.

[1032]E.g., Walvoord, *Matthew: . . .*, p. 159-60.

[1033]See David DeGraaf, "Some Doubts about Doubt: The New Testament Use of *Diakrino*," *Journal of the Evangelical Theological Society* 48:8 (December 2005):733-55.

[1034]Carson, "Matthew," p. 446.

we pray, we should believe that God *can* do anything we request, and that He *will* do what is consistent with His will and what He has promised to do.[1035]

2. Rejection by the chief priests and the elders 21:23—22:14 (cf. Mark 11:27—12:12; Luke 20:1-19)

The cursing of the fig tree happened as Jesus and the disciples walked from Bethany to Jerusalem on Tuesday. The disciples' exclamation about the withered tree and Jesus' lesson followed on Wednesday. Jesus and His disciples proceeded into Jerusalem where confrontations with three groups erupted in the temple courtyard that day.

The issue of authority 21:23-27

Israel's religious leaders approached Jesus, asking that He show them His credentials authorizing Him to disrupt the buying and selling in the courtyard and to heal people.

> "Two incidents about authority (21:23-27 and 22:41-46) serve as 'bookends' to three parables (21:28—22:14) and three controversial dialogues with the Pharisees and Herodians, the Sadducees, and the Pharisees (22:15-40)."[1036]

21:23   Jesus taught in "the temple" courtyard, or perhaps under one of the colonnades that surrounded it. The "chief priests" were high officials in the temple. At this time in Israel's history the Roman authorities appointed these leaders (cf. 2:4). They constituted part of the Sanhedrin, the ruling council in Judaism. The "elders" were evidently non-priests who represented leading families in Israel. They also had representation on the Sanhedrin.[1037] Matthew described these men in terms of their status, not their party affiliation. His point was that these were high-ranking leaders of Israel.

They inquired about Jesus' authority to drive out the moneychangers and merchants, heal the sick, and teach the people. They were the people with authority to control what happened in the temple area. Authority (Gr. *exousia*) is the right, and the power that goes with the right, to do something.[1038] They wanted to know "what authority" Jesus had, and "who" had given Him "this authority" to do what He did, since they had not. The validity of Jesus' authority depended on its source.[1039] Their question indicated their opposition to what He did.

> ". . . at the time of our Lord, no one would have ventured authoritatively to teach without proper Rabbinic authorisation [*sic*]. . . . 'who gave Thee this authority to do these things?' seems clearly to point to their contention, that the power which Jesus wielded was delegated to Him by none other than Beelzebul."[1040]

> "The real issue in the passage concerns not information about the authority of Jesus but the unbelief and unreceptivity of the Jewish leadership. The latter knew well enough that Jesus would have claimed divine authority for his doings in the temple area. Their question thus reflects not an inquisitive openness but an already established rejection of Jesus and the attempt to gain evidence that could later be used against him."[1041]

21:24-26   Jesus responded to their question with one of His own. This was common rabbinic debate technique (cf. 15:3; 22:20).[1042] By referring to John's baptism, Jesus meant everything associated with his baptism: his whole message and ministry. Since John was Jesus' forerunner, the leaders' response to John's ministry would answer their own question about Jesus' authority. If they answered that John's ministry was from heaven, they would have had to acknowledge that Jesus received His authority from God, since that is what John announced.[1043] If they answered that John's ministry was from men, lacking divine authentication, they knew the people would rise up against them, because the people regarded John as a prophet from God. The leaders refused to commit themselves, knowing that whatever they said would bring bad consequences for them. They wanted to avoid losing face.

[1035]See Thomas L. Constable, *Talking to God: What the Bible Teaches about Prayer*, pp. 170-76.

[1036]Bailey, in *The New . . .*, p. 44.

[1037]Jeremias, *Jerusalem in . . .*, pp. 222-32.

[1038]Lenski, p. 826.

[1039]Bruce, "The Synoptic . . .," 1:265.

[1040]Edersheim, *The Life . . .*, 2:382, 283.

[1041]Hagner, *Matthew 14—28*, p. 610.

[1042]Plummer, p. 293.

[1043]Allen, pp. 225-26.

Edersheim wrote that the Temple enclosure could have contained as many as 210,000 people at one time. This is about twice the capacity of the Coliseum in Rome.[1044] During the Passover season, close to this number were probably present. Thus the chief priests and elders could well have felt intimidated by the masses.

Any honest seeker among the leaders would have understood and accepted Jesus' answer to the leaders' question. However, most of the leaders simply wanted to get rid of Jesus, having previously rejected Him. Jesus pointed out, with His question, that their rejection of Him grew out of an earlier rejection of John.

21:27   The leaders' equivocation gave Jesus a reason to refuse them a direct answer without losing face. Why did He not give them one? They had refused earlier revelation through John. Having refused that revelation, they had no right to ask for more. They were incompetent to judge Jesus' authority, since they misunderstood the Old Testament and rejected the ministry of John. That was tragic, since these were the men charged with evaluating the claims of those who said they spoke for God. They were ineffective spiritual leaders because they refused to judge fairly.[1045]

> "Jesus' subtle answers to the religious leaders' challenge concerning His authority continued for several chapters even after it initially seemed that He had stopped. Without reading on, one would miss the answers Jesus actually did give, namely, that He is the Son of the Father, and that He demonstrated His authority conclusively when challenged to debate by those who considered themselves authorities."[1046]

Matthew used this confrontation over Jesus' authority to introduce three parables. He typically used events to introduce teaching in this Gospel. All three parables deal with these religious leaders. They focus on their failure to respond to God's call, and the consequences of this failure for the future of the Israelites.

The parable of the two sons 21:28-32

This first parable condemned the conduct of these leaders. It showed that they condemned themselves by judging Jesus as they did.

21:28   Jesus evidently launched into this parable immediately. His introductory question, unique in Matthew, continued the rabbinic dialogue. The "first" son was the older of the two (v. 30). The "vineyard," again, referred to Israel, in view of Old Testament usage (cf. 20:1-15).

21:29-31   The ancient Greek texts of these verses contain variations that have resulted in different translations. The NASB (1971 ed.) has the older son saying yes but doing nothing. The younger son says no but repents and goes. The younger son does the father's will. The NIV has the older son saying no but then repenting and going. The younger son says yes but does not go. The older son does the father's will. Probably the interpretation of the parable influenced early copyists. The better reading appears to be the one represented in the NASB.[1047]

> This is the first time Jesus applied one of His parables directly to Israel's leaders (v. 31). He introduced this application with His usual solemn introduction (cf. 5:16; et al.). Both the NASB and the NIV have translated the last verb in this sentence poorly. The Greek verb *proago* ("get into . . . before" or "entering . . . ahead of") here means "enter instead of."[1048]

The "tax collectors and prostitutes" were the dregs of Jewish society. Jesus undoubtedly shocked His listeners when He made this statement. The scum of society, though it originally said "no" to God, repented at the preaching of John and Jesus, and thereby *did* God's will (cf. 8:11-12). Consequently these people would enter the kingdom (by resurrection). However, the religious leaders affirmed their willingness to do God's will, but refused to do so by rejecting Jesus. They would not enter the kingdom.

Note that Jesus described both groups as "sons" of the father in the parable. All the Jews, those with a privileged position and those with none, enjoyed being "sons" of God in the sense that God had chosen Israel as His "son" (cf. Hos. 11:1). The leaders could still believe in Jesus and enter the kingdom. Individual salvation was still possible, even though national rejection was strong.

[1044] Edersheim, *The Temple*, pp. 68-69.

[1045] Carr, p. 246.

[1046] Gene R. Smillie, "Jesus' Response to the Question of His Authority in Matthew 21," *Bibliotheca Sacra* 162:648 (October-December 2005):469.

[1047] Metzger, pp. 55-56.

[1048] *Theological Dictionary of the New Testament*, s.v. "*telones*," by Otto Michel, 8:105, footnote 158. See also J. Jeremias, *The Parables of Jesus*, p. 102, footnote 54.

21:32   This verse links the parable with Jesus' earlier words about the leaders' response to John and His authority (vv. 23-27). John had come preaching what was right, "the way of righteousness." Israel's leaders had not responded positively to his message. Even the repentance of Israel's most despised citizens did not change their minds. It should have.

The parable of the wicked tenant farmers 21:33-46

Jesus proceeded immediately to tell another parable. Luke wrote that Jesus addressed it to the crowds in the temple courtyard (Luke 20:9). The chief priests and elders continued to listen (vv. 45-46).

21:33-34   Jesus alluded to Isaiah 5:1-7 and Psalm 80:8-16, where the "vineyard" is Israel and the "landowner" is God. The care the landowner took with his vineyard shows God's concern for Israel. He had a right to expect that it would be a fruitful vineyard and yield much fruit. The tenants ("vine-growers") to whom the landowner entrusted his vineyard represent Israel's leaders. The "harvest time" (lit. the season of the fruits) stands for the time when God could expect to obtain some reward for His investment in Israel. The "slaves" (Gr. douloi) are God's faithful servants the prophets. In Jesus' society, slaves were not necessarily on a low social level; many of them held important positions in their owners' households.[1049]

21:35-37   Israel's leaders had beaten and killed various prophets (cf. 1 Kings 18:4, 13; 22:24; 2 Chron. 24:21-22; Jer. 20:1-2; 26:20-23; 37:15). Sending "his son" might seem foolhardy in view of the tenants' former behavior.[1050] However, this act showed the landowner's patience, and his hope that the tenants would respond properly to the representative with the greatest authority.

"The contrast is between what men would do and what God had done."[1051]

21:38-40   Israel's leaders did not reject Jesus because it was not clear who He was, but because they refused to submit to His authority (23:37). Jesus had announced to His disciples that the Jewish leaders would kill Him (16:21; 17:23; 20:18). Now He announced this to the leaders themselves and the people.

21:41   The hearers who answered may have been the leaders, but since Jesus identified the guilty in the parable clearly, they were probably the people standing around listening. They easily anticipated God's action. He would depose the leaders and bring them to a miserable end. Then God would turn over the care of His "vineyard" to "other tenants," who would deliver the desired fruit at the appointed time. These refer to the prophets, apostles, and servants of God who would represent Him after Jesus' death, resurrection, and ascension.

21:42   Every time Jesus said, "Did you never read?"—He was stressing that the Scriptures pointed to Him (cf. 12:3, 5; 19:4; 21:16; 22:31; Mark 12:10). In these instances He also referred to well known texts, but He used them in unexpected ways. Jesus changed the figure from a vineyard to a building. This quotation is from Psalm 118:22-23. It probably originally described David, Jesus' ancestor and type. All of Israel's leaders, including Samuel and Saul, had originally rejected David—but God chose him and made him the capstone (or "chief corner [stone]") of the nation. Likewise God had chosen Israel, a nation that the other world leaders despised. However, God would make Israel the capstone of the nations when He established the kingdom.

Similarly, in Jesus' day, Israel's leaders had rejected after trial (Gr. apodokimazo) the Son of David, but God would make Him the capstone (or "chief corner [stone]") of His building. Jesus' history recapitulated the history of both Israel and David. Earthly leaders were rejecting Him, but God would exalt Him over all eventually. This reversal of fortunes is a phenomenon that onlookers marvel at as they observe it. Jesus made another strong messianic claim when He applied this passage to Himself.

21:43   This verse continues to explain the parable of the wicked tenant farmers. Because Israel's leaders had failed in "producing the fruit" that God desired, and had slain His Son, He would remove responsibility and privilege from them, and give these to another "nation" or "people" (Gr. ethnei). What God did was transfer the responsibility for preparing for the kingdom from Israel, and give it to a different group, namely, the church (cf. Acts 13:46; 18:5-6; Rom. 10:19; 1 Pet. 2:9). David Turner argued that those who received the responsibility were the faithful Jewish remnant represented by Jesus' apostles.[1052] This is a very similar view since Jesus' apostles became the core of the church.

"Matthew 21:43 could be the key verse in the entire argument of Matthew."[1053]

[1049]France, The Gospel . . ., p. 812.

[1050]Lenski, p. 835.

[1051]Walvoord, Matthew: . . ., p. 162.

[1052]David L. Turner, "Matthew 21:43 and the Future of Israel," Bibliotheca Sacra 159:633 (January-March 2002):46-61.

[1053]Bailey, in The New . . ., p. 45.

The unusual term "kingdom of God," rather than Matthew's customary "kingdom of heaven," probably stresses the fact that the kingdom belongs to God, not the leaders of Israel.

Jesus did not mean that God would remove the kingdom from Israel forever (cf. Rom. 11:26-27). When Jesus returns to the earth and establishes His kingdom, Israel will have the most prominent place in it (Gen. 12; 15; 2 Sam. 7; Jer. 31).

"For the first time the King speaks openly and clearly to someone outside of the circle of the disciples about a new age. This is full proof that the kingdom was no longer near at hand."[1054]

21:44   The capstone, the top stone on a wall or parapet around a flat-roofed building, could and did become a stumbling block to some. Many Jews similarly tripped over Jesus' identity and plunged to their destruction. Likewise a capstone could fall on someone below and crush him or her. These are allusions to Isaiah 8:14-15 and Daniel 2:35, 44-45. Jesus was a "dangerous person," as well as God's chosen representative and the occupier of God's choice position in His building, Israel. Jesus was claiming to be the Judge; He would crush those on whom He fell.

21:45-46   The meaning of Jesus' words was clear to Israel's leaders who heard Him. Matthew probably described them as "chief priests," who were mostly Sadducees, "and Pharisees," because these were the two leading parties within Judaism. Together, these two groups stood for all the Jewish authorities who opposed Jesus.

Rather than fearing Jesus, whom they "understood" claimed to be the instrument of their final judgment, these leaders feared the multitudes—whose power over them was much less. Rather than submitting to Him in belief, they tried "to seize Him." Thus they triggered the very situation that Jesus had warned them about, namely, His death at their hands. Their actions confirmed their rejection of Jesus and their consequent blindness.

The parable of the royal wedding banquet 22:1-14

The three parables in this series are similar to three concentric circles in their scope. The scope of the parable of the two sons encompassed Israel's leaders (21:28-32). The parable of the wicked tenant farmers exposed the leaders' lack of responsibility, and their guilt, to the people listening in, as well as to the leaders themselves (21:33-46). This last parable is the broadest of the three. It condemned the contempt with which Israel as a whole had treated God's grace to her.

22:1   Early editions of the NASB and the NKJV say, "Jesus answered." This was Matthew's way of introducing what Jesus said (cf. 11:25). It does not mean that what Jesus said was a response to a particular question someone had asked Him. Newer editions and the NIV have "spoke." Jesus responded to the leaders' desires (cf. 21:45-46). The antecedent of "them" was the Jewish leaders, but there were many other Jews in the temple courtyard listening to the dialogue.

22:2-3   Jesus said the kingdom was similar to what the following story illustrated (cf. 13:24, 31, 33, 44, 45, 47; 20:1). The "king" represents God the Father. "His son," the bridegroom (cf. 9:15; 25:1), is Messiah. The "wedding feast" is the messianic banquet that will take place on earth at the beginning of the kingdom (8:11-12; 25:1; cf. Ps. 132:15; Isa. 25:6-8; 65:13-14; Rev. 21:2). As in the previous parable, the "slaves" (Gr. douloi) of the king are His prophets (21:34-36).[1055] They announced the coming of the banquet and urged those whom God invited to it, the Jews, to prepare for it. However, most of those who heard about it did not respond to the call to prepare for it. Several writers have taken this invitation as corresponding to the ministries of John the Baptist and Jesus.[1056]

22:4-5   The fact that the king repeated his invitation, and urged those who had previously shown no interest in attending, demonstrates his grace and compassion. This was customary practice in the ancient Near East.[1057] The Greek word translated "dinner" (ariston) usually refers to the first of two meals that the Jews ate each day, most commonly near mid-morning. This was the first of many meals that the guests at this banquet would enjoy, since wedding feasts usually lasted a week or so in the ancient Near East (cf. v. 13).[1058] The king emphasized the imminency of the feast, as "he sent out" his servants again. This is, of course, what John and Jesus had been preaching as they urged the Jews to get ready for the

---

[1054]Toussaint, Behold the . . ., p. 252. See also idem, "The Contingency . . ., pp. 234-35; and idem and Quine, p. 140.

[1055]Pentecost, The Parables . . ., pp. 139-40.

[1056]E.g., Morgan, The Gospel . . ., p. 263; Walvoord, Matthew: . . ., p. 165; and Toussaint, Behold the . . ., p. 254.

[1057]Goebel, The Parables of Jesus, p. 351.

[1058]Edwin M. Yamauchi, "Cultural Aspects of Marriage in the Ancient World," Bibliotheca Sacra 135:539 (July-September 1978):241-52. See also Paul E. Robertson, "First-Century Jewish Marriage Customs," Biblical Illustrator 13:1 (Fall 1986):33-36.

kingdom. Some scholars took this invitation as one that the apostles issued after Jesus' ascension—that resulted in the destruction of Jerusalem in A.D. 70.[1059]

> "A very important fact revealed in the parable is the fact that the offer of the kingdom was a genuine one. The kingdom in all of its reality was as prepared and near as was the feast of the parable."[1060]

The wedding feast is not the kingdom, however. It is the celebration at the beginning of the kingdom, the marriage supper of the Lamb (Rev. 19:9).

The people whom the slaves of the king invited showed more interest in their own possessions and activities than they did in the banquet (John 1:12). They refused the invitation of their king, that was both an honor and a command.

22:6-7   Some of those invited not only refused the gracious invitation, but abused and even murdered the king's servants. "Enraged" at their conduct, the king "sent his armies," "destroyed" the "murderers," and burned down "their city" (cf. 21:38-41). Burning down an enemy's city was a common fate of rebels in the ancient East (cf. 2 Chron. 36:19; Nah. 3:14-15). Here Jesus implied it would happen to Jerusalem again. It did happen, in A.D. 70, when the Roman emperor Titus finally overcame the Jewish rebels and scattered them from Palestine. This was Jesus' first prediction of the destruction of Jerusalem.

22:8-10   The king did not begin the wedding feast yet. He sent out more slaves to invite anyone to attend. The original guests "were not worthy" because they disregarded the king's invitations. They failed to respond to his invitation to come freely. The king sent His slaves out into the "main highways" (NASB, Gr. *tas diexodous ton hodon*, lit. "street corners," NIV, places where people congregated) to invite everyone to the feast (cf. 8:11; 21:43). His "slaves went out into the streets" and "gathered" everyone who would come, both the "evil" and the "good" in the sight of men. Finally the "wedding hall" was full of "guests."

> "The calling of other guests now (still going on) takes the place of the first invitation—a new exigency and preparation being evolved—and the supper, until these guests are obtained . . . *is postponed* to the Second Advent."[1061]

The majority of the Jews were not worthy to attend the messianic banquet at the beginning of the kingdom, because they rejected God's gracious offer of entrance by faith in His Son. Therefore, God's slaves would go out into the whole world ("all the streets"), to invite as many as would accept the invitation to come, Jews ("good") and Gentiles ("evil") alike (28:19). Jesus predicted that many, not just Jews but also Gentiles, would respond—so that when the kingdom began, the great banquet hall would be as full as God intended.

22:11-13   The "man" who did not wear the proper wedding garment was unprepared for the banquet. In that culture, the proper wedding garment was just clean clothes.[1062] He was there, whether evil or good (v. 10), because he had accepted the king's gracious invitation. However, he was subject to the king's scrutiny. The king addressed his guest as a "friend." He asked how he had obtained admission without the proper (clean) garment. The man was "speechless" due to embarrassment. Then the king gave orders to his servants (Gr. *diakonois*) to "bind" the man, "hand and foot" like a prisoner, and to "throw him" out of the banquet hall. They would throw him into the "outer darkness" (NASB) or "outside, into the darkness" (NIV). The place where he would go would be a place of "weeping and gnashing of teeth."

It is probably significant that Jesus referred to the king's slaves (Gr. *douloi*, vv. 3, 4, 6, 8, 10) as heralding the kingdom, but He said the king's servants (Gr. *diakonoi*, v. 13) evicted the unworthy guest. Evidently the slaves refer to the prophets and the servants to the angels.

These verses have spawned several different interpretations. One view is that the man who tries to participate in the banquet but gets evicted represents those whom God will exclude in the judgment that will take place before the kingdom begins.[1063] This view takes the man evicted as representing a Jew who hopes to gain entrance to the kingdom because he is a Jew. Since he does not have the proper clothing, the robe of righteousness, he cannot enter the kingdom. The lesson Jesus wanted to teach was that individual faith in Him, not nationality, was necessary for entrance. This view seems best to me.

[1059] E.g., Morgan, *The Gospel* . . ., p. 263; Walvoord, *Matthew:* . . ., p. 165; and Toussaint, *Behold the* . . ., p. 254.
[1060] Ibid., p. 255.
[1061] Peters, 1:379.
[1062] France, *The Gospel* . . ., pp. 826-27.
[1063] Toussaint, *Behold the* . . ., pp. 254-55.

"Christ revealed that unless they prepared themselves to be judged acceptable by the host, they would be excluded from the kingdom when it was instituted."[1064]

A second view is that the man was at the banquet because he was a believer in Jesus. There the king, upon careful examination, discovered that he did not have the prerequisite righteousness. Therefore the king excluded him from the kingdom. In other words, he withdrew the man's salvation. The problem with this view is that it involves the withdrawing (loss) of salvation. This view is untenable, in view of Scripture promises that once God gives the gift of eternal life, He *never* withdraws it (John 10:28-29; Rom. 8:31-39).

A third view is that the loss of salvation is not in view, but the loss of eternal reward (inheritance) is. The man has eternal life. The wedding garment does not represent salvation, but good works, with which the believer should clothe himself in response to the demands God has on his or her life.

"There is no suggestion here of punishment or torment. The presence of remorse, in the form of weeping and gnashing of teeth, does not in any way require this inference. Indeed, what we actually see in the image itself is a man soundly 'trussed up' out on the darkened grounds of the king's private estate, while the banquet hall glows with light and reverberates with the joys of those inside. That is what we actually see. *And that is all!*"[1065]

However, the term "weeping and gnashing of teeth," as Jesus used it elsewhere, seems to describe *hell*, the place where unbelievers go (cf. 8:12; 13:42, 50; 24:51; 25:30; Luke 13:28). This term was a common description of Gehenna, hell (4 Ezra 7:93; 1 Enoch 63:10; Psalms of Solomon 14:9; Wisdom of Solomon 17:21). The works just cited in parentheses are Hebrew pseudepigraphal and apocryphal books.[1066]

22:14   Jesus concluded the parable with a pithy statement that explained it (cf. 18:7). Not all whom God has invited to the kingdom will participate in the sharing of rulership authority and special rewards. Only those who respond to God's call and prepare themselves by trusting in Jesus will.

"Finally, the parable teaches that a general call does not constitute or guarantee election (verse fourteen). The Israelites took great pride in the fact that they as a nation possessed the kingdom promises. But this of itself did not mean each Jew was elected to it. Entrance was an individual responsibility, and that is what Christ is emphasizing in the last portion of the parable."[1067]

"Ironically, the 'chosen people' show in their refusal of the invitation that they are *not* all among the 'elect' but only among the 'called.'"[1068]

"While the invitation is broad, those actually chosen for blessing are few."[1069]

The point of these three parables is quite clear. God would judge Israel's leaders because they had rejected Jesus, their Messiah. He would postpone the kingdom and allow anyone to enter it—not only the Jews, as many of them thought.[1070] The prophets had predicted that Gentiles would participate in the kingdom; this was not new revelation. However the Jews, because of national pride, had come to believe that being a Jew was all the qualification one needed to enter the kingdom. Jesus taught them that receiving God's gracious invitation, and preparing oneself by trusting in Him, was the essential requirement for participation.

3. Rejection by the Pharisees and the Herodians 22:15-22 (cf. Mark 12:13-17; Luke 20:20-26)

The dialogue continued in the temple courtyard. Israel's leaders proceeded to confront Jesus, three times, attempting to show that He was no better than any other rabbi. Jesus responded with great wisdom, silenced His accusers with another question of His own, and disclosed His identity again in a veiled way.

[1064]Pentecost, *The Parables* . . ., p. 142.

[1065]Hodges, *Grace in* . . ., p. 89. See also Dillow, pp. 344-53.

[1066]For Rabbinic parallels to this parable, see Edersheim, *The Life* . . ., 2:425-30.

[1067]Toussaint, *Behold the* . . ., p. 256.

[1068]Hagner, *Matthew 14—28*, p. 632.

[1069]Walvoord, *Matthew:* . . ., p. 165.

[1070]See Toussaint and Quine, pp. 140-41.

"Jesus was going to die as the Lamb of God, and it was necessary for the lamb to be examined before Passover (Ex. 12:3-6). If any blemish whatsoever was found on the lamb, it could not be sacrificed. Jesus was examined publicly by His enemies, and they could find no fault in Him."[1071]

22:15-16a   The Pharisees wanted to ensnare or entrap (Gr. *pagideuo*) Jesus by their question. Clearly their purpose was not simply to get Jesus' opinion on a controversial issue. It was to alienate Him from a major portion of the Jewish population, or to get Him to lay Himself open to a charge of treason, depending on His answer, and to lose face.

The Pharisees had come into existence during the Babylonian exile. The word "Pharisee" means "separate one." During the Exile, the Jews were in danger of assimilation by the Gentiles. The Pharisaic party was started because the Jews wanted to maintain their distinctiveness from their pagan neighbors. This was a good thing then. However, as time passed and the Jews returned to the Promised Land, the Pharisees' separation became too much of a good thing. It resulted in isolation as those Jews built up traditions designed, not just to keep the Mosaic Law, but to enforce the rabbis' interpretations of the Law. The result was what we have seen in this Gospel, namely, Pharisaic devotion to the traditions of the elders that surpassed devotion to the Word of God.

The Herodians constituted a party within Judaism that favored cooperation with the Herods, who ruled Israel under Rome's authority. They supported the reigning Herods and their pro-Roman policies. The Romans had deposed the Herod who ruled over Judea in A.D. 6, but Herods ruled other parts of Palestine.[1072] This position compromised Jewish independence and distinctiveness in the minds of many Jews, including the Pharisees. Consequently it was very unusual that representatives from these two competing groups would unite in opposing Jesus. They rarely united on any subject, but both parties viewed Jesus as a threat to their individual interests.

22:16b-17   The unholy alliance introduced its question with a flattering preamble. The leaders credited Jesus with being a "teacher" or rabbi. Moreover, they said they believed He spoke the truth, and taught God's will truthfully ("in truth," honestly and faithfully). If Jesus failed to reply to their question after such an introduction, He would appear to be trying to hide something, perhaps because of pressure He felt. His integrity would be open to question.

Their question was theological, since all such issues involved God's will in Israel. They wanted to know how Jesus felt about their Roman overlords. Paying the "poll-tax," or head tax, was a kind of litmus test of one's feelings toward Rome, as one's attitude toward paying taxes has indicated one's attitude toward government throughout history. This was a particularly volatile issue in Israel since it was a theocracy. The poll tax was not objectionable because it was large. Really it was quite small. However, it was almost universal, covering women between the ages of 12 and 65, and men between 14 and 65. "Caesar," the family name of Julius Caesar, had become a title for Roman rulers by this time. The Roman emperor then was Tiberius. The accusers phrased their question to elicit a "yes or no" answer from Jesus. They thought that either answer would embroil Him in controversy.

"The poll tax had been among the taxes imposed on Judea following the imposition of direct Roman rule in A.D. 6, not long before, and had been fiercely resented by patriotic Jews, resulting in a serious revolt led by Judas (Josephus, *War* 2.117-18; *Ant.* 18.4-10). That revolt was the inspiration for the later Zealot movement which led to the war of independence beginning in A.D. 66 and so to the fall of Jerusalem and the destruction of its temple in A.D. 70."[1073]

22:18-20   Jesus refused to give the "yes or no" answer they wanted. Instead, He initially pointed out, for the benefit of the crowd standing around, that they were "testing" Him (Gr. *peirazo*, to demonstrate intrinsic quality by testing, cf. 4:1; 16:1). This was a more gracious word than the one Matthew used to describe their real intent (v. 15). Their question did not intimidate Jesus, even though He "perceived their malice," but He saw it as an opportunity to reveal His identity. They were "hypocrites" in that they came under a pretense of great respect, but they really had little respect for Him.

Jesus chose to answer on His own terms, not theirs. The coin that most people used to pay their Roman "poll-tax" was "a denarius," the value of which was one day's wage for a workingman or soldier. This coin bore the image of the emperor and the inscription "Tiberius Caesar, son of the divine Augustus" on one side and "*pontifex maximus*" on the other. The Jews understood "*pontifex maximus*" (lit. chief bridge-builder) in the sense of "high priest." Both inscriptions were offensive to the Jews.[1074]

[1071]Wiersbe, 1:79.

[1072]France, *The Gospel . . .*, p. 832.

[1073]Ibid., p. 829.

[1074]Carson, "Matthew," p. 459.

The fact that Jesus asked someone to "show" Him a denarius has led some readers to conclude that He was extremely poor. Others believe He did this because He and His disciples shared a common purse. Still others believe He was using a pedagogical technique. Whatever His reason may have been, we should probably not make much of it since Matthew did not.

22:21-22   Jesus' answer accorded with the Old Testament teaching that people should "render" (give over, pay) taxes to those over them, even pagans, because rulers ultimately owe their positions to God (Prov. 8:15; Dan. 2:21, 37-38; cf. Rom. 13:1-7; 1 Pet. 2:13-17). He did not side with the Zealots, a party that sought the violent overthrow of Rome, or with any other group that wanted Messiah to bring immediate political independence to Israel.

"The questioners had said *dounai* ["to give"] (v. 17), as though of a gift which might be withheld; the Lord replies with *apo dote* ["render to"], the payment of a rightful due."[1075]

However, Jesus also advocated rendering "to God" what belonged to Him. As the coin bore the emperor's image, and so testified to his ownership of it, so human beings bear God's image, and so testify to His ownership of them. God has an even more fundamental claim on people than Caesar did. The Jews should acknowledge Caesar's claim by paying their taxes, but what is more important: they should acknowledge God's claim by obeying Him. This was a condemnation of Israel's leaders, who were not obeying God, as well as an exhortation to all the people to follow God's will. For them, that involved believing in and following Jesus.

This incident shows Jesus' great wisdom and authority, the intensity of the leaders' opposition to Him, and how Jesus prepared His disciples for what lay ahead of them (cf. Rom. 13; 1 Pet. 2:11-17).

4. Rejection by the Sadducees 22:23-33 (cf. Mark 12:18-27; Luke 20:27-40)

Sometime later that day, another group of leaders approached Jesus with a different question—but with the same purpose: to trap Him in a theological controversy that would destroy His reputation.

22:23   The Pharisees believed in resurrection from the dead (Isa. 26:19; Dan. 12:2). The Sadducees did not, because they could not find it explicitly taught in the Pentateuch.[1076] They believed that both the material and the immaterial parts of man perish at death (cf. Acts 23:8).[1077] There was much diverse opinion concerning death and the afterlife in Jesus' day.[1078]

22:24-28   The Sadducees, like the Pharisees, approached Jesus with hypocritical respect, calling Him "teacher" (cf. v. 16). They had evidently learned to appreciate Jesus' high regard for the Old Testament, because they came to Him with a question of biblical interpretation (Deut. 25:5-6). This is only the second recorded time that Jesus had come into public conflict with the Sadducees (cf. Matt. 16:1).

Levirate marriage was an ancient Near Eastern custom that antedated the Mosaic Law (Gen. 38:8). The Law incorporated it and regulated it. This law encouraged the younger brother to marry his deceased brother's widow and have children by her. People considered the first child born to be the older brother's heir, and that child would perpetuate his name in Israel. Customarily a widower was expected to wait over three festivals before he remarried, a widow three months, and a pregnant or nursing mother two years.[1079]

This was an unlikely question for Sadducees to ask, since they did not believe in resurrection. Probably they knew that Jesus believed in resurrection, and wanted to create what they thought was an impossible situation, in order to embarrass Him.

"It was probably an old conundrum that they had used to the discomfiture of the Pharisees."[1080]

The case they posited could have been a real one or, more likely, a hypothetical one. Their question presupposed that life the other side of the grave will be exactly as it is this side, in terms of human relationships. Since the woman had had "seven" husbands, "whose wife" would "she be . . . in the resurrection," or would she be guilty of incest? For the Sadducees, belief in resurrection created insuperable problems. They probably wondered: Would Jesus deny the resurrection, and thus circumvent the problem, but alienate Himself even further from the Pharisees?

[1075]M'Neile, pp. 319-20.

[1076]Edersheim, *Sketches of . . .*, p. 241.

[1077]Josephus, *Antiquities of . . .*, 18:1:3-4; idem, *The Wars . . .*, 2:8:14.

[1078]Cf. G. W. E. Nickelsburg, *Resurrection, Immortality and Eternal Life in Intertestamental Judaism*.

[1079]Edersheim, *Sketches of . . .*, p. 156.

[1080]Robertson, *Word Pictures . . .*, 1:176.

22:29-30   The Sadducees did not understand "the Scriptures"—because the Scriptures taught resurrection (e.g., Ps. 16; et al.). They did not understand God's "power"—because they assumed that life after resurrection, in heaven, would be the same as it is now. They assumed that the resurrection would just involve an awakening, not a transformation. God is able to raise people to a form of existence unlike what we experience now (cf. 1 Cor. 15:35-49).

In the resurrection form of existence, sexual relationships will be different from what they are now. Jesus was speaking of the resurrection life, not a particular resurrection event, as is clear from the Greek preposition *en* ("in," v. 30, not "at," NIV). Marriage relationships as we now know them will not exist after our resurrection. Jesus' reference to the "angels" was an additional correction of their theology, since the Sadducees also denied the existence of angels (Acts. 23:8).

Jesus did not say that in the resurrection state, all memory of our former existence and relationships will end. This is a conclusion some interpreters have drawn without warrant. Neither did He say that we will become angels. We will not be. We will be *like* the angels.

"The greatness of the changes at the Resurrection (cf. 1 Cor 15:44; Phil 3:21; 1 John 3:1-2) will doubtless make the wife of even seven brothers (vv. 24-27) capable of loving all and the object of the love of all—as a good mother today loves all her children and is loved by them."[1081]

22:31-32   Jesus returned to what Scripture teaches (v. 29). He introduced His clarification with a customary rebuke: "Have you not read?" (cf. 21:42; et al.). The passage He cited, Exodus 3:6, came from the Pentateuch, a part of the Hebrew Bible that the Sadducees treated with great respect.

God described Himself to Moses as then being "the God" of "Abraham, . . . Isaac, and . . . Jacob." He was *still their God*, even though they had died hundreds of years earlier. This statement implied the continuing bodily existence of the patriarchs. The logical conclusion is that if God will fulfill His promise to continue to be the God of the patriarchs, He must some day raise them from the dead. Thus Jesus showed that the Pentateuch, the abbreviated canon of the Sadducees, clearly implied the reality of a future resurrection.

"The argument is not linguistic: 'I am the God of Abraham' would be a perfectly intelligible way for God to identify himself as the God whom Abraham worshiped long ago. The argument is based rather on the nature of God's relationship with his human followers: the covenant by which he binds himself to them is too strong to be terminated by their death."[1082]

22:33   Matthew closed his account of this encounter by recording the reaction of the multitude, not the reaction of the Sadducees. Probably few of the Sadducees changed their theology as a result of this conversation, since they continued to oppose Jesus. However, the reaction of the crowd shows that Jesus' teaching had a powerful impact. To the unprejudiced observer, Jesus' arguments, authority, and understanding of the Old Testament were astonishing. Matthew undoubtedly hoped this would be the reaction of his readers too.

This pericope reveals the intensity of the opposition to Jesus that existed among Israel's leaders. This was the third group to try to trap Him in one day. It also shows the guilt of Israel's leaders, since they did not understand either the Scriptures or God's power—*but should have*. Jesus had spoken of people entering the kingdom after death (v. 10). For them to do this, there would have to be a resurrection. Jesus also confirmed the belief that the patriarchs would live in the kingdom by what He said. Thus Jesus' teaching about resurrection answered questions about participation in the kingdom because of its postponement. Not many in Jesus' immediate audience may have understood this, but Matthew's readers could.

5. Rejection by the Pharisees 22:34-46

This pericope contains two parts. First, a representative of the Pharisees asked Jesus a question (vv. 34-40). Then Jesus asked the Pharisees a question (vv. 41-46).

A Pharisee's question of Jesus 22:34-40 (cf. Mark 12:28-34)

22:34   "The Pharisees" learned that "Jesus had silenced the Sadducees." In other words, they learned that the Sadducees would no longer oppose Him publicly. Consequently the Pharisees decided to renew their attack against Him.

[1081]Carson, "Matthew," pp.461-62.

[1082]France, *The Gospel* . . ., p. 840.

22:35-36   The NASB describes the Pharisees' spokesman as "a lawyer." The Greek word *nomikos* means "expert in the law" (NIV). He would have been a teacher of the Old Testament who was particularly learned in both theology and law. He subjected Jesus to a test (Gr. *peirazon*) to prove His quality.

He, too, addressed Jesus with hypocritical respect as "teacher," though as the discussions with Jesus progressed this day His opponents' respect for Him undoubtedly increased. The Pharisee asked Jesus another controversial question to which various Scripture experts gave various answers.

"The scene is like an ordination council where the candidate is doing so well that some of the most learned ministers ask him questions they themselves have been unable to answer—in the hope of tripping him up or of finding answers."[1083]

The rabbis documented 613 commandments in the Mosaic Law, 248 positive and 365 negative. Since no one could possibly keep them all, they divided them into "heavy" (more important) and "light" (less important). The Pharisees taught that the Jews needed to give attention to all the laws but particularly the "heavy" ones. This Pharisee was asking which of the "heavy" ones Jesus considered the "heaviest."

22:37-39   To answer, Jesus quoted Deuteronomy 6:5 and then Leviticus 19:18. The terms "heart," "soul," and "mind" are not completely distinct, watertight categories. They overlap somewhat and together cover the whole person. Taken together, the meaning is that we should "love . . . God" preeminently and unreservedly.

"Jesus loves God with his whole heart, for he is blameless in his fealty to God (4:1-11). Jesus loves God with his whole soul, for he is prepared to surrender his life should God so will (26:36-46). And Jesus loves God with his whole mind, for he lays claim for himself neither to the prerogatives of worldly power [cf. 20:25, 28; 21:5] nor to the security of family, home, and possessions (8:20; 12:50)."[1084]

The "and" in verse 38 is explicative. The one command is great because it is primary.

"The second" greatest command is similar to the first in character and quality (v. 39). It also deals with love (cf. 1 Cor. 12:13). We should "love" our fellow man ("neighbor") unselfishly (cf. 1 John 3:17-18).

"A simple reading of Leviticus 19:18 . . . divulges that the command pertained to loving others, not oneself. The 'as yourself' part of the command only furnishes a comparison of how Jesus' disciples are to love others."[1085]

The writer just quoted went on to discuss why it is inappropriate hermeneutically to argue from this command that one needs to learn to love himself or herself before he or she can love someone else.

22:40   The rest of the Old Testament ("whole Law and the Prophets") hangs from or flows out of "these two commandments." All the other laws deal with specific applications of one or the other of these two commands. The prophets consistently stressed the importance of heart reality with God and genuine love for one's neighbor. Without these two commandments the Old Testament lacks unifying summaries. These are the most important commandments, but they are not the only ones.

"Mark includes the clause '. . . is much more than all burnt offerings and sacrifices' (Mark 12:33). Matthew omits this since it might offend his [unsaved] Jewish reader, and the point is well made without it."[1086]

This declaration prepared for Jesus' denunciation of the religious leaders in 23:1-36.

"Jesus had now answered three difficult questions. He had dealt with the relationship between religion and government, between this life and the next life, and between God and our neighbors. These are fundamental relationships, and we cannot ignore our Lord's teachings. But there is a question more fundamental than these, and Jesus asked it of His enemies."[1087]

[1083]Ibid., p. 464.

[1084]Kingsbury, *Matthew as . . .*, p. 12.

[1085]Robert L. Thomas, *Evangelical Hermeneutics*, p. 130.

[1086]Toussaint, *Behold the . . .*, p. 259.

[1087]Wiersbe, 1:82.

Jesus' question of the Pharisees 22:41-46 (cf. Mark 12:35-37; Luke 20:41-44)

22:41-42   Having received several questions from His critics, Jesus now turned the tables and asked the Pharisees one. He wanted them to explain what the Scriptures taught about Messiah. This would face them and the crowd with "who" He really was. The real issue was Christological—not taxes, resurrection, or even the greatest commandment.

Jesus broached the subject of Messiah's identity by asking "whose son" He was (v. 42). This was perhaps "the most familiar subject in their theology, that of the descent of Messiah."[1088] The Pharisees gave a standard correct answer based on Old Testament passages (2 Sam. 7:13-14; Isa. 11:1, 10; Jer. 23:5). He was David's son or descendant (cf. 1:1; 9:27-28; et al.). However, it was not the full answer.

Jesus had previously asked His disciples a similar question about His identity (16:13, 15). Peter, speaking for the disciples, had given the proper full answer (16:16). That response led to commendation (16:17-21). The Pharisees' improper response here led to condemnation (ch. 23). Everything hinges on one's view of Jesus.

22:43-45   Jesus pointed out that the Pharisees' answer contained a problem. "How" could Messiah be David's "son" if "David" called Him his "Lord"? Jesus referred to Psalm 110, the most frequently quoted Old Testament chapter in the New Testament. This was a psalm that David wrote, as is clear from the superscription. Jesus regarded it as He regarded all the Old Testament, namely, inspired by the Holy Spirit (v. 43; cf. Acts 4:25; Heb. 3:7; 9:8; 10:15; 1 Pet. 1:21). Jesus assumed that Psalm 110 was Davidic and Messianic, and the Pharisees agreed. He referred to the psalm's inspiration here to reinforce its correctness in the minds of His hearers. David had not made a mistake when he wrote this. The "right hand" is the position of highest honor and authority (cf. 19:28).

There is good evidence that almost all Jews in Jesus' day regarded Psalm 110 as messianic.[1089] Jesus' point was that Messiah was not just David's descendant, but He was God's Son also. This is a point that Matthew stressed throughout his Gospel (chs. 1—2; 3:17; 8:20; 17:5; et al.). Jesus was bringing together the concepts that Messiah was the human son of David and the divine Son of God.[1090]

Moreover, this quotation also shows the preexistence of Messiah. David's Lord was alive when David lived. Furthermore it reveals plurality within the Godhead. One divine person spoke to another.

The psalm pictured Messiah at God's "right hand" while His enemies were hostile to Him. However, Messiah would crush that hostility eventually. This is precisely the eschatological picture that has been unfolding throughout this Gospel. Rejected by His own, Jesus would return to the Father, but He would return later to earth to establish His kingdom. The Jewish rabbis after Jesus' time interpreted David's lord as Abraham, not Messiah.[1091]

22:46   This question silenced the public criticism of Jesus' critics permanently. The confrontation had ended. His enemies could not escape the logical consistency of Jesus' biblical arguments. Rather than submitting to His authority, as they should have (cf. 21:23), they plotted His destruction.

"Defeated in debate, the leaders withdraw from Jesus in the temple, just as Satan, also defeated by Jesus in debate, had earlier withdrawn from him (4:11)."[1092]

Verse 46 finishes off this entire sub-section of the Gospel (21:23—22:46). Israel had rejected her King. Jesus had predicted this rejection (21:18-22). It resulted from the series of confrontations with Israel's leaders that happened on a single Wednesday in the temple courtyard. Now the King would formally reject the nation, but not permanently in view of the promises to the patriarchs.

D. THE KING'S REJECTION OF ISRAEL CH. 23

Israel's rejection of Jesus as her King was now unmistakably clear. Her various groups of leaders had consistently refused to accept Him.

". . . it seems that for Matthew the Pharisees particularly exemplify all that is wrong with Jerusalem's current leadership."[1093]

[1088]Edersheim, The Life . . ., 2:405.

[1089]David M. Hay, Glory at the Right Hand: Psalm 110 in Early Christianity, pp. 11-33.

[1090]See Kingsbury, Matthew as . . ., p. 82.

[1091]France, The Gospel . . ., p. 851.

[1092]Kingsbury, Matthew as . . ., p. 7.

[1093]France, The Gospel . . ., pp. 853-54.

The leaders' rejection was a rejection of Jesus' person (22:42). It contrasts sharply with the disciples' confession that Jesus was the Messiah and the Son of God (16:16). Consequently Jesus announced His rejection of that generation of unbelieving Israelites. Note the parallels between this situation and that of the Israelites at Kadesh Barnea (Num. 13—14). That generation would not experience the blessing of participating in the inauguration of the promised messianic kingdom. Jesus' strong language reflects the seriousness of their error and its dire consequences. It also reflects the conventions of ancient polemic.[1094]

Chapter 23 contains a discourse that Jesus delivered the same day His critics assailed Him: Wednesday. However, most students of Matthew's Gospel have not regarded this discourse as one of the major ones in the book. The primary reason for this is it lacks the structural marker by which the writer highlighted the other major discourses. That marker is the characteristic discourse ending (cf. 7:28-29). Rather, chapter 23 appears to be the climax of the confrontations that preceded it (21:23—22:46). The content of this discourse is mainly negative and condemnatory, and its target was a specific group. That it is not part of the discourse in chapters 24 and 25 is clear, because Jesus addressed different audiences.

"As Matthew began his rehearsal of Jesus' ministry at 4:17, he depicted Jesus as becoming successively involved with three major groups, each of which functions as a character in his story: the *disciples* (4:18-22); the *crowds*, together with the disciples (4:25; 5:1-2); and the religious *leaders* (9:2-13). As an indication that only the climax of his story (i.e., the passion of Jesus) still remains to be narrated, Matthew now depicts Jesus' involvement with each of these same three groups as being successively terminated in a reverse order to the initial one, that is to say, in an order that is chiastic in nature. For example, by reducing the religious *leaders* in open debate to silence, Jesus forces their withdrawal from the scene (22:46). With the leaders gone, Jesus publicly addresses the *crowds* in the temple, together with the disciples (23:1). And leaving the temple, Jesus delivers his eschatological discourse to the *disciples* alone (24:1-3). Through the use of this chiastic pattern, Matthew signals the reader that the culmination of his story is at hand."[1095]

"The attitude attacked in this chapter is a religion of externals, a matter of ever more detailed attention to rules and regulations while failing to discern God's priorities."[1096]

1. Jesus' admonition of the multitudes and His disciples 23:1-12 (cf. Mark 12:38-39; Luke 20:45-46)

23:1   As we have seen, there were three groups of people present in the temple courtyard. These were: the "disciples" of Jesus, His critics, namely, the various groups of Israel's "leaders," and "the crowds" of ordinary Israelites. Jesus now turned from addressing the Pharisees (22:41), and proceeded to speak to the multitudes and His disciples primarily.

Jesus had begun to criticize the Pharisees and scribes to their faces about one year earlier (15:7). Later He warned His disciples to beware of the teachings of the Pharisees and the Sadducees (16:5-12). Now He denounced these enemies publicly. He did so because the decision the masses and His disciples now faced was whether to follow Jesus or Israel's established religious leaders. They could not do both.

23:2   "The scribes" were the official teachers of the Old Testament. "The Pharisees" were a theological party within Judaism. Jesus was addressing two different, though somewhat overlapping, groups when He made this distinction. Some scribes were Pharisees, but not all Pharisees were scribes. The first title addressed the role of some of the leaders and the second the theological beliefs of some of them. A modern illustration might be "preachers" and "evangelicals." Not all preachers are evangelicals, though some are. Likewise, not all evangelicals are preachers, though some are.

According to Old Testament figurative usage, a person who sat on a predecessor's seat was that person's successor (Exod. 11:5; 12:29; 1 Kings 1:35, 46; 2:12; 16:11; 2 Kings 15:12; Ps. 132:12). When Jesus said the scribes and Pharisees had "seated themselves" on Moses' "chair," He meant they viewed themselves as Moses' legal successors, possessing his authority. This is indeed how they viewed themselves.[1097] Jewish synagogues typically had a stone seat at the front where the authoritative teacher sat.[1098] Accordingly, most rabbis sat when they taught. The NASB translation "have seated themselves" hints at the irony that follows in the first part of verse 3. They presumed to be Moses' successors, with *his* authority.

[1094]See L. T. Johnson, "The New Testament's Anti-Jewish Slander and Conventions of Ancient Rhetoric," *Journal of Biblical Literature* 108 (1989):419-41.

[1095]Kingsbury, *Matthew as . . .*, p. 84.

[1096]France, *The Gospel . . .*, p. 855.

[1097]Mishnah *Sanhedrin* 11:3.

[1098]E. L. Sukenik, *Ancient Synagogues in Palestine and Greece*, pp. 57-61.

23:3-4   Jesus' statement in the first part of verse 3 seems to contradict what He said earlier about how the other Jews should respond to the teaching of the scribes and Pharisees (15:7-14; 16:5-12). Assuming the consistency of Jesus' teaching, we should understand His words here as ironical.[1099] Another view sees Jesus affirming the authority of the Pharisees in principle, since they taught the Torah, but not endorsing all their teachings (*halakhah,* legal interpretations of Scripture).[1100] The first, preferable interpretation allows the Greek aorist verb *ekathisan* ("to sit," v. 2) to have its natural force. This view also explains the chiasm in verses 2-4, in which the first two statements constitute irony, and the second two give non-ironical advice.

A   The leaders presumed to take on Moses' teaching authority. v. 2
    B   Do what they say. v. 3a
    B'   Do not do what they do. v. 3b
A'   Their teaching merely binds people. v. 4

Jesus continued to use irony in this address (vv. 23-28).

Both the School of Hillel and the School of Shammai increased the burden of responsibility on the Jews by adding to the Law.[1101]

23:5-7   Jesus proceeded to identify more of these leaders' practices that the crowds and His disciples should not copy (cf. 6:1-18). "Phylacteries" were small boxes of leather or parchment in which the Jews placed copies of four Old Testament texts written on vellum (fine parchment, customarily Exod. 13:1-10, 11-16; Deut. 6:4-9; and 11:13-21). They then tied these onto their foreheads and or forearms with straps to fulfill Exodus 13:9 and 16, and Deuteronomy 6:8 and 11:18. God probably intended the Jews to interpret these commands figuratively, but the superficial religious leaders took them literally. The Greek word translated "phylacteries" (*totapot,* lit. "frontlets") occurs only here in the New Testament. It had pagan associations, and Jesus' use of it here implied that the Jews were using these little boxes as good luck charms.[1102] Furthermore, they made them so big that other Jews would be sure to notice their "piety."[1103]

In addition, the hypocritical leaders would "lengthen the tassels" they wore on the corners of their garments (v. 5). God had commanded the wearing of these tassels to remind His people of their holy and royal calling (Num. 15:37-41; Deut. 22:12). All the Jews wore these tassels, including Jesus (9:20; 14:36). However, the religious leaders characteristically wore long ones to imply great piety and to attract the admiration of the common people.

The leaders wanted to sit as close to the law scrolls as possible in the synagogues. These were the "chief seats" (v. 6). The title "rabbi" meant "my teacher" or "my master." It was originally just a title of respect. However, eventually the term became a title expressing great veneration. The leaders in Jesus' day wanted the title because it set them off as distinctive and superior to others. Modern people who take this view of an advanced academic degree or a title fall into the same error.

23:8-10   These verses applied to all the Jews, but particularly the disciples (cf. v. 1). By placing "you" in the emphatic first position when He spoke to the disciples, Jesus was implying that they would take the position of leadership over God's people that the critics currently occupied (cf. 13:52). They were not to love it when people called them "Rabbi," because they had but *one* Teacher (Gr. *didaskalos*), namely, Jesus. They were to regard themselves as on the same brotherly level, as learners, rather than as masters over the unlearned.

The term "fathers" (v. 9) probably referred to their fathers in the faith, the spiritual predecessors of the present generation (cf. 2 Kings 2:12). Apparently the fathers in view were dead. The change in tense of the Greek verbs between verses 8, 9, and 10 seems to suggest this. If this is true, the person who now addresses a Roman Catholic priest, for example, as "father" is probably using this term in a slightly different sense than the Jews used it in Jesus' day (cf. 1 Cor. 4:15; 1 John 2:13-14). If a modern Christian uses the term with the idea that the "father" is his or her spiritual superior, however, he or she would be guilty of doing what Jesus forbade here.

The only person worthy of the title of "Teacher" in the ultimate sense is Messiah. He is the only "One" who can sit in Moses' seat, and continue to interpret and reveal the will of God correctly and authoritatively (cf. 1:1; 16:16; 22:41-46). Jesus used a third Greek word for "teacher" here, namely, *kathegetes*. He probably did so to connect it with other key words in this section

---

[1099]J. Jeremias, *New Testament Theology,* Part I, *The Proclamation of Jesus,* p. 210.

[1100]See Noel S. Rabbinowitz, "Matthew 23:2-4: Does Jesus Recognize the Authority of the Pharisees and Does He Endorse their *Halakhah?*" *Journal of the Evangelical Theological Society* 46:3 (September 2003):423-47.

[1101]Edersheim, *The Life . . .,* 2:407.

[1102]*Zondervan Pictorial Encyclopedia of the Bible,* s.v. "phylactery," by J. Arthur Thompson, 4:786-87.

[1103]See Edersheim, *Sketches of . . .,* pp 220-24.

having to do with authoritative teaching: *ekathisan* ("they sat down," v. 2) and *kathedra* ("seat," v. 2). Thus He employed the rhetorical device of homophony (similar sounding words).

"Jesus' enemies, the certified teachers of Israel, could not answer basic biblical questions about the Messiah. Now he, Jesus the Messiah, declares in the wake of that travesty that he himself is the only one qualified to sit in Moses' seat—to succeed him as authoritative Teacher of God's will and mind."[1104]

It would be incorrect to conclude, from this teaching, that Jesus discouraged all recognition of distinctions between leaders and their roles among His servants. The apostles, for example, had authority in the church that surpassed that of ordinary Christians. Elders and deacons continue to exercise divinely recognized authority in the church, and God has commanded us to respect these individuals (1 Cor. 16:15-16; Heb. 13:7, 17). What Jesus was condemning was, seeking and giving honor that transcends what is appropriate—since believers are all brethren, since God is our true spiritual Father, and since Jesus is our real teacher and leader. The teachers and leaders of God's people must remember that they are always fellow learners with the saints. They are still children of the heavenly Father, and they are always subject to Jesus Christ.

". . . the risen Christ is as displeased with those in his church who demand unquestioning submission to themselves and their opinions and confuse a reputation for showy piety with godly surrender to his teaching as he ever was with any Pharisee."[1105]

23:11-12   In concluding these warnings, Jesus returned to the subject of *humility* that He had stressed with His disciples earlier (cf. 18:4; 20:20-28). Jesus taught His disciples to be servants of others, not lords over them.

"Leadership positions should never be a goal in and of themselves, but should always be viewed as opportunities to serve others."[1106]

The reversal of fortunes that Jesus predicted here will happen when the kingdom begins. Jesus Himself was the greatest example of what He taught here (cf. 20:26-28; Phil. 2:5-11).

2. Jesus' indictment of the scribes and the Pharisees 23:13-36 (cf. Mark 12:40; Luke 20:47)

Jesus now directed His attention toward the scribes and the Pharisees in the temple courtyard (cf. v. 1). He proceeded to announce a scathing indictment of them in seven parts. Compare the six woes of Isaiah 5:8-23 and the five woes of Habakkuk 2:6-20. He introduced each indictment with the word "woe." Jesus spoke *of* the scribes and Pharisees, but He spoke *to* the crowds and His disciples.

"No passage in the Bible is more biting, more pointed, and more severe than this pronouncement of Christ upon the Pharisees. It is significant that He singled them out, as opposed to the Sadducees, who were more liberal, and the Herodians, who were the politicians. The Pharisees, while attempting to honor the Word of God and manifesting an extreme form of religious observance, were actually the farthest from God."[1107]

Essentially Jesus was criticizing them for their hypocrisy.[1108] As the theme of the Sermon on the Mount was righteousness, the theme of these woes is hypocrisy. There is a common strong emphasis in both addresses on the leaders' failure to understand and submit to the Scriptures. Jesus gave both addresses to contrast the true meaning of Scripture with the Pharisees' interpretation and application of it. The Pharisees professed to teach the Scriptures accurately but did not do so. They were therefore hypocrites.

The literary structure of these woes is chiastic.

A   Rejection of the kingdom v. 13
    B   Effects on others being more harm than good v. 15
        C   Misguided use of Scripture affecting conduct vv. 16-22
            D   Failure to understand Scripture vv. 23-24
        C'   Misguided use of Scripture affecting character vv. 25-26
    B'   Effects on others frustrating the desired result vv. 27-28
A'   Rejection of the kingdom's heralds vv. 29-36

[1104]Carson, "Matthew," p. 475.

[1105]Ibid.

[1106]Barbieri, p. 74.

[1107]Walvoord, *Matthew: . . .*, pp. 171-72.

[1108]See Andrew R. Simmonds, "'Woe to you . . . Hypocrites!' Re-reading Matthew 23:13-36," *Bibliotheca Sacra* 166:663 (July-September 2009):336-49.

The first woe 23:13[-14]

"But" introduces the transition from the words to the disciples that preceded (vv. 1-12). The scribes and Pharisees had taken the exact opposite position on Jesus' person than the disciples had. Consequently their futures would be radically different (cf. 16:17-28; 19:27-29).

"Woe" can be a mild exclamation of compassion (24:19), a strong expression of condemnation (11:21), or both (18:17; 26:24). In this address condemnation is in view, as is clear from what Jesus said. However, we should not interpret this word as connoting vindictiveness or spitefulness here. Rather it is a judicial announcement of condemnation from Messiah, the Judge.

> "Every one of the seven 'woes' is an exclamation like the 'blessed' in the Beatitudes. It does not state a wish but a fact. It is not a curse that calls down calamity but a calm, true judgment and verdict rendered by the supreme Judge himself. Hence six of these judgments have the evidence attached by means of a causal *hoti* [because] clause which furnishes the full reason for the verdict 'woe;' and in the remaining judgment (v. 16) the varied form of expression does the same by means of an apposition."[1109]

These leaders were hypocrites because they professed to teach God's will, but they kept people from entering the kingdom when it was God's will for His people to enter then. They kept people from entering the kingdom: by not preparing to enter it themselves and by discouraging others from doing so (cf. 18:6-7; 22:41-46).

Some interpreters believe the syntax of verse 13 assumes that the kingdom had already begun.[1110] However, the basis for this conclusion is the presupposition that it had begun, more than the requirements of the Greek syntax. The syntax requires that we understand the substantival participle *tous eiserchomenous* ("those entering") and the present finite verb *oude . . . aphiete* ("nor . . . do you permit") as describing action happening simultaneous with the speaker's words. Both actions can and do describe what the leaders were doing in anticipation of the kingdom's beginning. Jesus consistently referred to the messianic kingdom as future, not as present. The King's presence does not equate with the kingdom's presence.

Most of the best and earliest copies of Matthew's Gospel available to us omit verse 14. Some of the manuscripts that do contain it place it before verse 13, and others place it after. Perhaps scribes inserted it later, since it occurs in the parallel passages (Mark 12:40; Luke 20:47).

The second woe 23:15

The scribes and Pharisees were very zealous to get Jews to subscribe to their doctrinal convictions. Some commentators stress that the Pharisees made disciples to Judaism. This may have been true, but their chief offense was bringing Jews under their corrupt theology.[1111] Jesus did not criticize them for their zeal. He criticized them because of what they taught their converts and the effect that this "conversion" had on their converts.

As noted previously, what marked the teaching of these leaders was that they gave the oral traditional interpretations and teachings of the rabbis at least the same authority as the Old Testament, if not more authority. Practically, they twisted the Old Testament when it did not harmonize with the accepted teachings of the rabbis (cf. 5:21-48).

The converts to Pharisaism became more zealous for the traditions of the fathers than their teachers were. This is often the result of conversion. Students sometimes take the views of their teachers further than their teachers do. The dynamic nature of the Pharisees' view of the authority of the fathers' interpretations increased this problem. When a person believes that Scriptural authority extends beyond the statements of Scripture, there is no limit to what else may be authoritative. The Pharisees' interpretation of Messiah locked Jesus out of His role as Interpreter.

The proselytes were the sons "of hell" (Gehenna) in the sense that they belonged to hell and would go there eventually (cf. 8:12; 13:38). Rather than leading them to heaven, the Pharisees and teachers of the law led them to hell. Gehenna represented the place of eternal damnation, the lake of fire (cf. 25:51). Hades is the temporary abode of the wicked, from which God will raise them for judgment at the great white throne, and then final damnation in the lake of fire (Rev. 20:11-15).

The third woe 23:16-22

Jesus had dealt with the subject of taking oaths in the Sermon on the Mount (5:33-37). He had called His critics "blind guides" before, too (15:14). Here is a specific example of what Jesus condemned in the second woe (v. 15). By differentiating between what was binding in their oaths and what was not, the Pharisees and teachers of the law were encouraging evasive oaths that amounted to lying. Jesus' point was that people should tell the truth. Jesus condemned His critics for mishandling the Scriptures that they claimed to defend and expound.

[1109]Lenski, p. 903.

[1110]E.g., Carson, "Matthew," pp. 477-78.

[1111]See Irena Levinskaya, *The Book of Acts in Its Diaspora Setting*, pp. 36-46.

Verses 20-22 provide the rationale for 5:33-37. Whenever a Jew took an oath, he connected it in some way with God. All their oaths were therefore binding. Jesus disallowed all evasive oaths and viewed them as untruthful speech.

The fourth woe 23:23-24

The Mosaic Law required the Israelites to tithe grain, wine, and oil (Deut. 14:22-29). How far they had to take this was a matter of debate. Jesus did not discourage scrupulous observance of this law. He directed His condemnation to the leaders' failure to observe more important, "weightier" commands in the Law, while dickering over which specific plants, spices, and seeds to tithe. He went back to Micah 6:8 for the three primary duties that God requires: "justice and mercy and faithfulness." He probably chose the gnat (Gr. *qalma*) and the camel (Gr. *gamla*) as examples because of their sizes and their similar sounding names.

> "It is usually the case that legalists are sticklers for details, but blind to great principles. This crowd thought nothing of condemning an innocent man, yet they were afraid to enter Pilate's judgment hall lest they be defiled (John 18:28)."[1112]

This judgment constitutes the center of the chiasm and the most important failure of the scribes and Pharisees. They were distorting the will of God as He had revealed it in Scripture (cf. 9:9-13; 12:1-14). This distortion resulted in erroneous doctrine (woes 3 and 5), which resulted in disastrous practice (woes 2 and 6), which resulted in kingdom postponement (woes 1 and 7).

It is important to recognize that Scripture reveals God's will, and that we should never elevate the authority of human interpretations to the level of Scripture itself. However, it is also important to recognize that within Scripture, some commands are more important than others, and that we should observe these distinctions and not confuse them. This involves wisdom and balance in interpretation and application.

Modern teachers and preachers of God's Word can commit many of the errors that marked the Pharisees. However, we need to remember that the Pharisees did not believe that Jesus was the divine Messiah.

The fifth woe 23:25-26

Jesus condemned characteristic Pharisaic superficiality with this metaphor. The vessels represent the Pharisees and those they taught. The Jews were to be clean vessels that God could use to bring spiritual nourishment and refreshment to others. The Pharisees taught the importance of being ritually clean by observing the dietary and cleansing ordinances of the Law. Nevertheless they neglected internal purity. The Pharisees were erring in their emphases. They put too much importance on minor matters, especially ritual and external matters, and not enough on major matters, especially those involving spiritual reality. The singular "Pharisee" is probably a generic reference to all Pharisees (v. 26).

The sixth woe 23:27-28

The Jerusalem Jews whitewashed grave markers just before Passover to alert pilgrims to their presence.[1113] They did this so these strangers would not unknowingly touch one, become unclean, and therefore be ineligible to participate in the feast.[1114] It was not so much the whitewashing that made them attractive as it was the monuments themselves that were attractive. Jesus compared these "whitewashed" monuments ("tombs") to the Pharisees. Both appeared attractive ("beautiful on the outside"), but both also contaminated people who contacted them (i.e., through their teaching, which "inwardly" was: "full of hypocrisy and lawlessness"). Pharisaic contamination precluded participation in the blessings that Passover anticipated, namely, kingdom blessings.

Jesus' mention of "lawlessness" is significant (v. 28). The Pharisees prided themselves on punctilious observance of the Law (Gr. *nomos*). Ironically, their failure to understand and apply the Law correctly made them lawless (Gr. *anomia*) in Jesus' view. *Anomia* is a general word for wickedness in the New Testament. Jesus implied that the Pharisees' whole approach to the Law was in fact *wicked*.

The seventh woe 23:29-36

23:29-30   By building the "monuments" to "the prophets" and other "righteous" people that their forefathers had martyred, the Pharisees were saying that they would not have killed them if they had been alive then. These construction projects constituted professions of their own spiritual superiority as well as honors for the dead. The Christian who naively thinks he or she would not have committed the mistakes that the early disciples of Jesus did makes the same assumption of superiority.

[1112]Wiersbe, 1:85.

[1113]Edersheim, *The Temple*, pp. 216-17.

[1114]Mishnah *Shekalim* 1:1; Mishnah *Kelim* 1:4; Mishnah *Moed Katan* 1:2; Mishnah *Masser Sheni* 5:1.

23:31 "Consequently" refers to the Pharisees' acknowledgment of themselves as "the sons of those who murdered the prophets" (v. 30), not to their tomb-building (v. 29). The Pharisees were the descendants of those who killed the prophets more than they knew, not just physically but also spiritually. They were plotting to kill the greatest Prophet (21:38-39, 46).

23:32 The Old Testament idea behind this verse is that God will tolerate only so much sin. Then He will act in judgment (cf. Gen. 6:3, 7; 15:16; cf. 1 Thess. 2:14-16). Here Jesus meant that Israel had committed many sins—and incurred much guilt—by murdering the prophets. When the Pharisees killed Jesus and His disciples (cf. v. 34), the cup of God's wrath would be full, and He would respond in wrath. The destruction of Jerusalem, and the worldwide dispersion of the Jews—resulted—in A.D. 70.

23:33 Jesus repeated the epithets He had used before to announce His critics' condemnation (cf. 3:7; 12:34). They would perish in "hell" for their failure to accept Jesus (cf. 5:22; 23:15).

> "There is today only one proper Christian use of the woe saying of this pericope. It is found not primarily in the application of the passage to the historical Pharisees, and even less to modern Judaism as a religion, but in the application of the passage to members of the church. Hypocrisy is the real enemy of this pericope, not the scribes, the Pharisees, or the Jews. If, on the model of this pericope, a bitter woe is to be pronounced against anyone today, it must be directed *solely* against hypocrisy in the church (cf. 1 Peter 2:1)."[1115]

23:34 The antecedent of "therefore" (Gr. *dia touto*) is the Jews' execution of the prophets that God had sent them in the past (vv. 29-30; cf. 22:3-10). Because the Jews had rejected the former prophets, Jesus would send them additional "prophets," "wise men," and teachers ("scribes"). These men the Jews would also reject, filling up the measure of their guilt to the full. This is probably a reference to the witnesses that followed Jesus and appealed to the Jews to believe in Him (Acts 3:19-21; 7:2-53; cf. Matt. 5:10-12; 9:37-38; 28:18-20).

> Jesus would not yet establish His kingdom, because Israel rejected Him as her Messiah. However, in this verse Jesus revealed that God would punish the generation of Israelites that rejected Him, and the apostles who would follow Him, in an additional way. This included the destruction of Jerusalem and the dispersion of the Jews from the Promised Land. Jesus clarified these events in the Olivet Discourse that follows (chs. 24—25).

> Since the Jews did not have the authority to "crucify" people, we should probably understand Jesus' reference to them crucifying some of these witnesses in a causative sense. They would cause others, notably the Romans, to crucify them (cf. 10:24-25).

23:35 Jesus was not saying that the Jews who rejected Him were responsible for the deaths of all the righteous martyrs throughout biblical history. They simply were the ones who would add the last measure of guilt that would result in the outpouring of God's wrath for all those murders.

> "In the case of the Jews, the limit of misbehavior had been almost reached, and with the murder of the Messiah and His Apostles would be transgressed."[1116]

> "Abel" was the first righteous person murdered that Scripture records (Gen. 4:8). We do not know exactly when "Zechariah" the prophet, "the son of Berechiah," died, but he began prophesying as a young man in 520 B.C., and delivered some prophecies in 518 B.C. He may have been the last martyr in Old Testament history.[1117] However, according to Jewish tradition, *this* Zechariah died peacefully at an advanced age.[1118]

> Many students of this problem believe that the Zechariah to whom Jesus referred was the priest whom the Jews stoned in the temple courtyard (2 Chron. 24:20-22). That man died hundreds of years earlier than Zechariah the prophet. Jesus seems to have been summarizing all the righteous people the Jews had slain throughout Old Testament history. Zechariah the son of Jehoiada was the last martyr in the last book of the Hebrew Bible, so Jesus may have been saying the equivalent of "all the martyrs from Genesis to Revelation."

> Nevertheless, *that* "Zechariah" was the son of *Jehoiada*, not Berechiah, and Jesus mentioned *Berechiah* as the father of the "Zechariah" He meant (cf. 2 Chron. 24:22). Berechiah may have been the actual father of this martyr, and the writer of

[1115]Hagner, *Matthew 14-28*, p. 673.
[1116]Plummer, p. 320-21.
[1117]See Gleason L. Archer Jr., *A Survey of Old Testament Introduction*, p. 425.
[1118]*Lives of the Prophets* 15:6.

2 Chronicles may have designated him as the son of his famous grandfather, Jehoiada. It seems less probable that Zechariah's father had two separate names: Berechiah and Jehoiada. The fact that Abel's name begins with the letter "A" and Zechariah's name with the letter "Z" is simply coincidence. "Z" is not the last letter in either the Hebrew or the Greek alphabet.

23:36   With a strong assertion of certainty, Jesus predicted that God's judgment would "fall" (v. 35) on the "generation" of Jews that rejected Him. This is Jesus' formal, culminating rejection of Israel for rejecting Him as her Messiah. "These things" refer to the outpouring of God's wrath just revealed (vv. 33, 35). That generation would lose the privilege of witnessing Messiah's establishment of the kingdom, and the privilege of being the first to enter it by faith in Jesus. Instead they would suffer the destruction of their capital city and the scattering of their population from the Promised Land (in A.D. 70). The whole generation would suffer because the leaders acted for the people, and the people did not abandon their leaders to embrace Jesus as their Messiah (cf. Num. 13—14).

> "The perversity of the religious leaders of Israel does not excuse the people of Israel. They were guilty of willfully following blind guides."[1119]

> However, notice that it is only *that* "generation" that Jesus so cursed. It was not the entire Jewish race.[1120] God is not finished with Israel (Rom. 11:1). He postponed the kingdom. He did not cancel it.

Jesus' mention of the suffering of the present generation led Him to lament the coming condition of Jerusalem (vv. 37-39).

3. Jesus' lamentation over Jerusalem 23:37-39 (cf. Luke 13:34-35)

This lamentation should help us realize that the judgment Jesus just announced—in such strong language—was not something that delighted Him. It broke His heart. This is also clear in that He personalized the people in Jerusalem in these verses; Jesus spoke of the city as many people ("your children"), not as an impersonal thing (symbolized by the brood of "chicks"). He also spoke here as Israel's Savior (symbolized by the "hen" protecting "her chicks under her wings"), not just a prophet but God Himself. These three verses are Jesus' last public words to the Israelite multitudes that the evangelists recorded.

> "Jesus' lament over Jerusalem revealed that He made a legitimate offer of the kingdom to Israel and that it was His desired will that they would respond. As a result of their having rejected such a contingent offer, their house was destroyed. . . . The time from His rejection to His return is the 'mystery' phase of the kingdom, as described in Matthew 13. The final phase of that period is outlined in chapters 24—25."[1121]

Most dispensationalists view the "kingdom" as having two phases. Normative (traditional) dispensationalists often refer to the present inter-advent age as the mystery phase of the kingdom, and the future millennial age as the messianic kingdom. Progressive dispensationalists refer to the present inter-advent age as the "already" phase of the messianic kingdom, and the future millennial age as the "not yet" phase of the messianic kingdom. A few dispensationalists deny any present phase of the kingdom.[1122]

23:37   "Jerusalem" was the city of David and the city of peace. It was the city God had chosen: to reveal Himself to Israel through the temple; and to be the capital of His kingdom on earth. However, *It* or *She* (personified) had murdered the prophets God had sent to His people with His messages. Stoning was the penalty for the worst crimes in Israel, including false prophecy. The people had used this form of execution on those who faithfully brought God's Word to them. Jesus' words recall His ancestor David's sorrow over the death of his son Absalom (2 Sam. 18:33; 19:4). The repetition of "Jerusalem" reveals the strong emotion that Jesus felt (cf. Luke 10:41; Acts 9:4).

> Many times during His ministry, Jesus had sought to gather and shelter Jerusalem, used here by synecdoche to represent the whole nation. Synecdoche is a figure of speech in which one part stands for the whole or the whole stands for one of its parts. He wanted the people to take refuge in Him as chicks do under their mother hen, physically, and as God's people had done under God's care, spiritually (cf. Deut. 32:11; Ps. 17:8; 36:7; 91:4; Jer. 48:40). In spite of God's loving initiatives, Israel had willfully rejected Him—repeatedly. Jesus' identification with God is very clear in this verse (cf. Ezek. 18:32). Jeremiah prefigured Jesus, as he sadly described Jerusalem's destruction by the Babylonians in the Book of Lamentations.

23:38   The "house" in view is probably the temple (cf. 1 Kings 9:7-8). Other views are that it refers to the city, the Davidic dynasty, the nation, or all of the above. Jesus had formerly claimed the temple as His own house (5:35; 17:25-26; 21:12-16). Now He

---

[1119]Toussaint, *Behold the . . .*, p. 263.

[1120]For defense of the view that "this generation" refers to wicked people of all time, see Susan M. Rieske, "What Is the Meaning of 'This Generation' in Matthew 23:36?" *Bibliotheca Sacra* 165:658 (April-June 2008):209-26.

[1121]Bailey, in *The New . . .*, p. 49.

[1122]E.g., Toussaint, *Behold the . . .*, pp. 175-80.

spoke of it as their ("your") "house," the house of prayer that they had converted into a den of thieves (21:13). Jesus and God would leave the temple "desolate" by removing Jesus' presence from it. Instead of it becoming the focal point of worship during the messianic kingdom, it would be devoid of Immanuel—"God with us"—until He returns to it (1:23; cf. Jer. 12:7; 22:5; Ezek. 43:1-5). Instead of bringing promised rest and blessing to Israel, Messiah would leave her desolate, uninhabited.

23:39   Jesus quoted Psalm 118:26 (cf. 21:9). He was referring to His return to the temple in power and great glory, when He returns at His Second Coming, not to some return to the temple before His ascension. The negative is very strong in the Greek text (*ou me*). When He returns, all will acknowledge Him instead of rejecting Him (cf. Zech. 12:10). Moreover, He will come in judgment (cf. 24:30-31; Phil. 2:9-11; Rev. 1:7).

> "It is extremely important for one to note that Christ's rejection of Israel is not an eternal one. The word 'until' (*eos*) of verse thirty-nine together with the following statement affirms the fact that Christ will come again to a repentant nation to establish the promised millennial kingdom."[1123]

Having said His good-bye to the temple, Jesus left its courtyard where He had spent a busy Wednesday teaching (21:18—23:46).

> "Surprisingly, Jesus' teaching occasions less conflict in Matthew's story than one would expect. The reason is that the religious leaders are the recipients of none of the great discourses of Jesus [chs. 5—7; 10; 13; 18; 24—25], and even Jesus' speech of woes is not delivered to the scribes and Pharisees but to the disciples and the crowds (chap. 23). It is in certain of the debates Jesus has with the religious leaders that his teaching generates conflict."[1124]

E. THE KING'S REVELATIONS CONCERNING THE FUTURE CHS. 24—25

We now come to the fifth and final major discourse in Matthew's Gospel, the Olivet Discourse. Its theme is the kingdom, specifically, events leading up to the establishment of the messianic kingdom.

1. The setting of these revelations 24:1-3 (cf. Mark 13:1-4; Luke 21:5-7)

24:1   The connective "and" (NASB, Gr. *kai*) ties what follows to Jesus' preceding denunciation of the generation of Jews that rejected Him and the divine judgment that would follow (23:36-39). However, the "apocalyptic" or "eschatological" discourse that He proceeded to give was not merely an extension of the address in chapter 23. This is clear because the setting, audience, and major themes changed. There is some continuity of subject matter, but not enough to justify viewing chapters 23—25 as one discourse.

> Jesus and His disciples were about to leave the temple complex (Gr. *hieron*) and proceed east toward Bethany, where Jesus was spending His nights during the Passover season. However, before they left the temple area, the disciples commented to Jesus about the magnificent temple buildings (cf. Mark 13:1; Luke 21:5).[1125]

> "They still focus on the temple, on which Jesus has pronounced doom, since the true center of the relation between God and man has shifted to himself. In chapter 23 Jesus has already insisted that what Israel does with him, not the temple, determines the fate of the temple and of Israel nationally."[1126]

24:2   "All these things," which Jesus pointed out to the disciples, were the buildings that they had just pointed out to Him. He then prefaced an important revelation with a characteristic emphatic introduction: "Truly I say to you," or "I tell you the truth." Jesus forecast the destruction of the temple complex, that Herod the Great had begun building about 20 B.C., which was not complete until A.D. 64.[1127] He used Old Testament language (Jer. 26:6, 18; Mic. 3:12; cf. 23:38; 26:61; Luke 23:28-31).

> "This statement is given with great force because of the aorist passive subjunctive of the verb 'to leave' with the double negative *ou me* (translated 'not')."[1128]

[1123]Ibid., pp. 265-66. Cf. Lowery, "Evidence from . . .," p. 180.

[1124]Kingsbury, *Matthew as . . .*, p. 63.

[1125]See Josephus, *Antiquities of . . .*, 15:11:1-7; and idem, *The Wars . . .*, 1:21:1, for his descriptions of the temple.

[1126]Carson, "Matthew," p. 496.

[1127]See Josephus, *The Wars . . .*, 5:4 and 5, for descriptions of Jerusalem and the temple just before the Romans destroyed them.

[1128]Toussaint, *Behold the . . .*, p. 268.

"The temple was made of huge stones, some of them many tons in size, carved out in the stone quarries underneath the city of Jerusalem. Such large stones could be dislodged only through deliberate force. The sad fulfillment was to come in A.D. 70, only six years after the temple was completed, when the Roman soldiers deliberately destroyed the temple, prying off stones one by one and casting them into the valley below."[1129]

". . . the Roman destruction of Herod's temple in A.D. 70 was so complete that all that now remains is part of the substructure of the temple precincts, not of the temple buildings themselves."[1130]

". . . the precise location of the sanctuary is still unknown today."[1131]

"It may be, as Jewish tradition has it, that ever since the Babylonish captivity the 'Ark of the Covenant' lies buried and concealed underneath the wood-court at the north-eastern angle of the Court of the Women."[1132]

24:3   The "Mount of Olives" stands directly east of the temple area, on the eastern side of the Kidron Valley that separates Mt. Olivet from Mt. Zion. The site of this discourse has given it its name: the Olivet Discourse. It was an appropriate place for Jesus to give a discourse dealing with His return. The Mount of Olives is where Zechariah predicted that Messiah would stand to judge the nations and establish His kingdom (Zech. 14:4). This prophecy is foundational to the discourse that follows.

The word "privately," as Matthew and Mark used it, set the disciples apart from the crowds. Mark wrote that Peter, James, John, and Andrew asked Jesus the question (Mark 13:3). Whether He gave the answer only to them, which seems improbable, or to all "the disciples," He did not give it to the multitudes. This was further revelation for their believing ears only. Luke did not mention the disciples as the recipients of this teaching, but implied that a larger audience heard it (Luke 21:5-7). However, this appears to have been deliberate by Luke, to show that this teaching had significance for all the people.

The disciples probably asked Jesus two questions, though some interpreters believe that they asked only one.

"To the disciples, the devastation of the city and the coming of the Messiah were part of one event. The disciple's [sic] questions should probably be taken as one question, though the fulfillment would come in stages."[1133]

The question first was, "When will these things be?" The second question had two parts, as is clear from the Greek construction of the sentence. It linked two nouns, "coming" (Gr. parousias) and "end" (Gr. synteleias), with a single article, "the" (Gr. to), and the conjunction "and" (Gr. kai). The second question was, "What will be the sign of your coming and of the end of the age?" By asking the question this way, we know that the disciples believed Jesus' coming (23:39) would end the present age and introduce the messianic age.[1134] The first question dealt with the time of the destruction of the temple. The second one dealt with the sign that would signal Jesus' second coming and the end of the age.

What did the disciples mean when they asked Jesus about the sign of His coming? This is the first occurrence of parousia ("coming") in Matthew's Gospel (cf. vv. 27, 37, 39). In classical non-biblical Greek, this word meant "presence," and later "arrival" or "coming," the first stage of being present.[1135] In the New Testament, parousia does not always have eschatological overtones (e.g., 2 Cor. 7:6; 10:10). In the second and third centuries A.D., writers used it to describe the visit of a king or other important official.[1136] In view of Jesus' recent statement that the Israelites would not see Him again until they would say, "Blessed is He who comes in the name of the Lord," it was undoubtedly to that coming that the disciples referred (23:39). They wanted to know when He would return to the temple having been accepted, rather than rejected by the nation. Specifically, they wanted to know what would signal His return, what would be the harbinger of His advent.

[1129]Walvoord, Matthew: . . ., p. 180.

[1130]France, The Gospel . . ., p. 888.

[1131]The Nelson . . ., p. 1620.

[1132]Edersheim, The Temple, p. 60.

[1133]The Nelson . . ., p. 1620.

[1134]See Edersheim, The Life . . ., 2:434-45, for an explanation of the Jewish expectation connected with the advent of the Messiah.

[1135]Abbott-Smith, p. 347.

[1136]M'Neile, p. 345.

What did they mean by "the end of the age?" Jesus had used this phrase before (13:39, 40, 49; cf. 28:20). By "the end of the age" Jesus meant the end of the present age that will consummate in His Second Coming and a judgment of living unbelievers (cf. Jer. 29:22; 51:33; Dan. 3:6; Hos. 6:11; Joel 3:13; Zeph. 1:3). This will occur just before the messianic kingdom begins. The disciples used the phrase "the end of the age" as Jesus and the Old Testament prophets spoke of it. They understood that Jesus meant the present age, the one before the messianic age began, since in their question they associated it with Jesus' return to the temple.

Both of the disciples' questions, occurring as they did together, suggest that the disciples associated the destruction of the temple with Jesus' return to it and the end of the present age.[1137] The Old Testament taught that several eschatological events would happen in the following order. First, Jerusalem would suffer destruction (Zech. 14:1-2; cf. Matt. 24:2). Second, Messiah would come and end the present age (Zech. 14:3-8; cf. Matt. 23:39). Third, Messiah would set up His kingdom (Zech. 14:3-11). The disciples wanted to know when in the future the destruction of the temple, Jesus' return to it, and the end of the present age would occur. They probably did not ask Him when He would inaugurate His kingdom, because they knew this would happen right after He returned to the temple and ended the present age.

"Matthew's gospel does not answer the first question, which relates to the destruction of Jerusalem in A.D. 70. This is given more in detail in Luke, while Matthew and Mark answer the second and third questions, which actually refer to Christ's coming and the end of the age as one and the same event. Matthew's account of the Olivet discourse records that portion of Christ's answer that relates to His future kingdom and how it will be brought in, which is one of the major purposes of the gospel."[1138]

2. Jesus' warning about deception 24:4-6 (cf. Mark 13:5-7; Luke 21:8-9)

Jesus began the Olivet Discourse by warning His disciples about the possibility of their concluding wrongly that He had returned or was just about to return. Kingsbury divided this speech on the "last times" as follows: (I) On Understanding Aright the Signs of the End (24:4-35); (II) On Being on the Alert for Jesus' Coming at the Consummation of the Age (24:36—25:30); and (III) On the Second Coming of Jesus and the Final Judgment (25:31-46).[1139]

24:4-5   The destruction of Jerusalem, and other similar catastrophes, would not indicate that Messiah's coming and the end of the present age were just around the corner—as Zechariah's prophecy seemed to indicate. The future appearance of people who claimed to be the Messiah should not deceive the disciples into concluding that He had arrived, either. Those who would "come in" Messiah's "name" refers to those who would come claiming to be Messiah, not those who would come as Jesus' representatives.

24:6   The presence of "wars and rumors of wars" should likewise not mislead the disciples into thinking that the prophesied destruction of Jerusalem was near (cf. Rev. 6:3-4). Wars and rumors of wars would come, but they would not necessarily be the fulfillment of the prophecies about Messiah's destroying His enemies when He returns (Zech. 14:2-5). The disciples should not let the presence of wars and rumors of wars deceive them into thinking that Messiah's return to reign was imminent.

"Verses 4-6 may describe the first part of Daniel's seventieth week (see Dan. 9:25-27), but possibly they present a general picture of the present age."[1140]

3. Jesus' general description of the future 24:7-14 (cf. Mark 13:8-13; Luke 21:10-19)

Jesus proceeded to give His disciples a general picture of conditions just before He will return to end the present age and inaugurate His kingdom.

24:7-8   Wars, "famines," and "earthquakes" will anticipate the end of the present age (cf. Rev. 6:1-8; 8:5-13; 9:13-21; 16:2-21).

"The horrors described are not local disturbances, but are spread over the known world; nations and kingdoms are in hostility with one another."[1141]

[1137]Bruce, "The Synoptic . . .," 1:289.

[1138]Walvoord, *Matthew: . . .*, p. 182.

[1139]Kingsbury, *Matthew as . . .*, p. 112.

[1140]*The Nelson . . .*, p. 1621.

[1141]M'Neile, p. 346.

The Jews believed that a seven-year period of time will immediately precede Messiah's coming to rule the world.

"Our Rabbis taught: In the seven-year cycle at the end of which the son of David will come . . . at the conclusion of the septennate the son of David will come."[1142]

"The idea became entrenched that the coming of the Messiah will be preceded by greatly increased suffering . . . This will last seven years. And then, unexpectedly, the Messiah will come."[1143]

"A prominent feature of Jewish eschatology, as represented especially by the rabbinic literature, was the time of trouble preceding Messiah's coming. It was called 'the birth pangs of the Messiah,' sometimes more briefly translated as 'the Messianic woes.'"[1144]

The phrase "birth pains" had its origin in Old Testament passages that describe the period of distress preceding the messianic age, namely, the Tribulation (Isa. 13:8; 26:17; Jer. 4:31; 6:24; Mic. 4:9-10; cf. 1 Thess. 5:3).

"'Birth pangs' are a favorite metaphor for the tribulations God's judgment brings upon man."[1145]

The "birth pangs" Jesus spoke about here will be a period seven years long immediately before Messiah returns to establish His kingdom.[1146] This corresponds to "Daniel's seventieth week" (Dan. 9:26-27). The beginning of "birth pangs" is the beginning of this Tribulation. Some interpreters believed verses 4-8 describe the first half of the Tribulation and verses 9-14 the last half.[1147] I think this is correct. Others believed verses 4-14 describe the beginning of the Tribulation, verses 15-22, the middle of it, and verses 23-44 the end of it.[1148]

"Just as the first labor pangs of a pregnant woman indicate the nearness of the birth of a child, so these great signs anticipate the end of the age and the beginning of a new one."[1149]

The 70th Week of Daniel 9 Seven Years The Tribulation	
	Great Tribulation Time of Jacob's Trouble
Beginning of Birth Pangs	Hard-Labor Birth Pangs
First Half	Second Half

"The effect of these verses [6-8], then, is not to curb enthusiasm for the Lord's return but to warn against false claimants and an expectation of a premature return based on misconstrued signs."[1150]

"A comparison of Christ's description of the beginning of birth pangs in Matthew 24:5-7 with the first four seals of Revelation 6:1-8 indicates that the beginning of birth pangs and the first four seals are the same thing.

1142 *The Babylonian Talmud*, p. 654.

1143 Raphael Patai, *The Messianic Texts*, pp. 95-96.

1144 Millar Burrows, *Burrows on the Dead Sea Scrolls*, pp. 343-44.

1145 *Theological Dictionary of the Old Testament*, s.v. "Chebel," by H. J. Fabry, 4:191.

1146 See Showers, pp. 23-24.

1147 E.g., Pentecost, *Thy Kingdom . . .*, pp. 250-52; and Bailey, in *The New . . .*, pp. 49-50.

1148 E.g., Wiersbe, 1:87-89.

1149 Toussaint, *Behold the . . .*, p. 271.

1150 Carson, "Matthew," p. 498.

"Beginning of birth pangs (Mt. 24)	First Four seals (Rev. 6)
1. False messiahs who will mislead many (v. 5)	1. First seal: Rider on white horse, a false messiah (v. 2)
2. Wars, rumors of wars, nation rising against nation (vv. 6-7)	2. Second seal: Rider on red horse takes away peace from earth (vv. 3-4)
3. Famines (v. 7)	3. Third Seal: Rider on black horse holds balances, represents famine (vv. 5-6)
4. Death through famine, pestilences, and earthquakes (v. 7)	4. Fourth seal: Rider on pale horse, represents death through famine, pestilence, and wild beasts (vv. 7-8)

"In addition, immediately after His description of the beginning of birth pangs, Christ referred to the killing of those associated with Him (Mt. 24:9). Parallel to this, the fifth seal refers to people killed because of their testimony (Rev. 6:9-11)."[1151]

The sixth seal seems also to fall within this period.

24:9-13   In the context, "all these things" (v. 8) described in these verses, will happen during the period of "birth pains," namely, during the Tribulation. However, what follows seems to locate these events in the last half of the Tribulation. During the "birth pains," the disciples would experience persecution and martyrdom. The "you" extends beyond Jesus' immediate disciples, and includes disciples living in the future when these things will happen. Jesus was again speaking beyond His immediate audience.

The word "tribulation" or "persecuted" (Gr. thlipsis, or "distress") is a key word in this passage, occurring three times (vv. 9, 21, 29; cf. 13:21). These are all the occurrences of the word in Matthew's Gospel. The outstanding characteristic of this time will be thlipsis.[1152] This persecution will lead many disciples to turn away from the faith (cf. Dan. 11:35). They will even "hate one another" (v. 10). The deceiving influence of "false prophets," as well as the persecution the disciples will experience, will cause many to turn from the faith (to "fall away," v. 10; cf. 7:15-23; 13:21). Those disciples who hate one another will do so because wickedness will abound, and the "love" of many of them (for the Savior, the truth, and or one another) "will grow cold" (v. 12).

Though the term "disciple" is a broader one than "believer," it seems clear that Jesus meant some believers would be deceived, turn from the faith, and even hate other believers. There is no other revelation in Scripture that would preclude this interpretation, and much that warns believers about this possibility (e.g., 1 Tim. 4; 2 Tim. 3). There is much revelation, however, that precludes the view that those who will turn from the faith will lose their salvation (e.g., John 10:28-29; Rom. 8:31-39).

In contrast to those who prove unfaithful, those who persevere and endure the temptations of that period will experience deliverance (v. 13). Their deliverance, unfortunately referred to as being "saved" by the majority of the English translations, will happen when and because Messiah will return at "the end" of the Tribulation. Jesus did not mean that perseverance results in eternal salvation. Only faith in Him does that. He will end the persecution of His disciples and thereby deliver them from this distress. Another view is that "the end" refers to the end of the faithful disciple's life.[1153] However, the main subject of the promise seems to be the time (period) of testing, not the disciple's life.

"It is a promise that those who are faithful to the end, in the midst of the tribulation persecutions of Antichrist, will be abundantly rewarded with joint rulership with Christ in His coming kingdom."[1154]

[1151]Showers, p. 25.

[1152]For other uses of the Greek word skandalisthesontas, "to turn away from," in Matthew, see 5:29; 13:21, 57.

[1153]See I. Howard Marshall, Kept by the Power of God, p. 74.

[1154]Dillow, p. 384.

24:14   Another characteristic of this second half of the Tribulation period, is that during those years, the good news ("gospel") concerning the coming of the messianic kingdom will reach the ears of virtually everyone on earth. "And" ties this verse into the period in view in verses 9-13. The "gospel of the kingdom" is the same good news that John the Baptist, Jesus, and the disciples had preached, namely, that the kingdom was imminent (3:2; 4:17). Later revelation informs us that the 144,000 Jewish missionaries, whom God will protect during the Tribulation, will provide the leadership in this worldwide gospel proclamation (Rev. 7:1-8; 14:1-5). Undoubtedly the message will be similar to the message that John, Jesus, and the original disciples preached. They preached that people should get ready for the inauguration of the messianic kingdom by believing in the King: Jesus. Undoubtedly, too, some people will believe and others will not.

> "For those who accept the message, entrance into the kingdom awaits. But eternal damnation accrues to those who refuse the gospel of the kingdom."[1155]

> "This is not exactly the same message the church is proclaiming today. The message preached today in the Church Age and the message proclaimed in the Tribulation period calls for turning to the Savior for salvation. However, in the Tribulation the message will stress the coming kingdom, and those who then turn to the Savior for salvation will be allowed entrance into the kingdom."[1156]

> "This verse does not teach that the Gospel of God's grace must be spread to every nation today before Jesus can return for His church. It is the Lord's return *at the end of the age* that is in view here."[1157]

In answering the disciples' second question, Jesus explained that there would be many signs of His coming and the end of the present age. Wars, rumors of wars, famines, and earthquakes would be relatively common occurrences (vv. 6-8). The signs would include the worldwide persecution of His disciples, the apostasy of some, the success of false prophets, and increased lawlessness (wickedness). The love of some disciples would cool, but others would persevere faithfully as the gospel would extend to every part of the earth (vv. 9-14). Then the end (of the Tribulation) would come (v. 14; cf. v. 3).

> "In general, these signs have been at least partially fulfilled in the present age and have characterized the period between the first and second coming of Christ."[1158]

However, we should expect complete fulfillment in the future. Revelation 6—18 gives further information concerning this time.

4. The abomination of desolation 24:15-22 (cf. Mark 13:14-20)

Having given a general description of conditions preceding His return and the end of the present age, Jesus next described one particular event that would be the greatest sign of all.

24:15   "Therefore" or "So" (Gr. *oun*) ties this pericope very closely to the preceding one. It does not indicate, however, that what follows in the text will follow chronologically what Jesus just finished describing, namely the end of the Tribulation. In view of Daniel's chronology, it seems to occur in the middle of the seven-year Tribulation.

> The "abomination of desolation," or "the abomination characterized by desolation," is a term Daniel used in Daniel 8:13; 9:27; 11:31; and 12:11. It describes something that—because of its abominable character—causes the godly to desert the temple on its account.[1159] In Daniel 11:31, the prophet referred to Antiochus Epiphanes as an abomination that caused desolation. Antiochus proved to be this *abomination* when he erected an altar to Zeus over the brazen altar in Jerusalem, and proceeded to offer a swine on it. In the Bible, the Greek word translated "abomination" (*bdeluyma*) describes something particularly detestable to God that He rejects.[1160] It often refers to heathen gods and the articles connected with idolatry.[1161] In the contexts of Daniel's references it designates an idol set up in the temple.

> Jesus urged the reader of Daniel's references to the abomination of desolation, particularly the ones dealing with a future abomination of desolation (Dan. 9:27; 12:11), to understand their true meaning. Jesus further stressed the importance and

[1155]Toussaint, *Behold the . . .*, p. 272.

[1156]Barbieri, p. 77.

[1157]Wiersbe, 1:87.

[1158]Walvoord, *Matthew: . . .*, p. 183.

[1159]C. E. B. Cranfield, "St. Mark 13," *Scottish Journal of Theology* 6 (July 1953):298-99.

[1160]Toussaint, *Behold the . . .*, p. 273.

[1161]Cranfield, p. 298.

validity of these prophecies by referring to Daniel as "the prophet." Matthew's inclusion of the phrases "the abomination of desolation," which Luke omitted, and "the holy place," which Mark and Luke omitted, were appropriate in view of his Jewish audience.

Daniel 9:24-27 predicted that from the time someone issued a decree allowing the Jews to rebuild Jerusalem until the coming of Israel's Messiah, 69 weeks (lit. sevens) of years would elapse. This 483-year period began when King Artaxerxes issued his decree, and it ended when Jesus entered Jerusalem in the Triumphal Entry (21:8-11). Because Israel refused to accept Jesus as her King, the events that Daniel prophesied to happen in the seventieth week (i.e., the remaining seven years in his 70-week prophecy) would not follow immediately. What Daniel predicted would happen in those seven years was unique national distress for Israel (Dan. 12:1; cf. Jer. 30:7). It would commence when a wicked ruler signs a covenant with Israel (Dan. 9:27). After three and a half years, the ruler would break the covenant and terminate worship in the temple. He would end temple worship by setting up an abominable idol there (cf. 2 Thess. 2:4; Rev. 13:14-15).

Some interpreters have concluded that we should not take Daniel's prophecy of the seventieth week literally and or as still future. Some of them believe the abomination of desolation refers to the Zealots' conduct in the temple before the Romans' destroyed it in A.D. 70.[1162] This view seems unlikely since the Zealots did not introduce idolatry into the temple. This view seems to water down the force of "abomination." Another view is that when the Romans brought their standards bearing the image of Caesar into the temple and offered sacrifices to their gods they set up the abomination that Daniel predicted.[1163] The main problem with this view is that Jesus told the Jews living in Jerusalem and Judea to flee when the abomination appeared in the temple (vv. 16-20). However, when the Romans finally desecrated the temple in A.D. 70, most of the Jews had already left Jerusalem and Judea. Thus Jesus' warning would have been meaningless.

". . . there is reasonably good tradition that Christians abandoned the city, perhaps in A.D. 68, about halfway through the siege."[1164]

There are several reasons why the abomination of desolation must be a future event in God's eschatological program. First, verse 15 is in a context of verses that describes events that have not yet happened (vv. 14-21; cf. v. 29). Second, Daniel's seventieth week, with its unique trouble, has not yet happened. Third, Mark described Jesus saying that the abomination of desolation would stand (masculine participle *estekota*) *as a person who set himself up as God* in the temple (Mark 13:14). This has not happened since Jesus made this prophecy. Fourth, other later revelation points to the future Antichrist as the abomination of desolation (2 Thess. 2:3-4; Rev. 13:11-18).[1165]

"An interesting parenthesis occurs at the end of Matthew 24:15—'whoso readeth, let him understand.' This statement indicates that what Jesus was teaching would have greater significance for people reading Matthew's Gospel in the latter days."[1166]

24:16-20   When the abomination of desolation appears, the Jews living in Jerusalem and Judea should "flee" immediately (cf. Luke 17:31; Rev. 12:14). His influence would extend far beyond Jerusalem. They must seek refuge in places ("mountains") where they can escape his persecution. They must not even take time to retrieve possessions from their houses as they flee. It will be like when a house is on fire: the residents should escape to save their lives, giving no thought to possessions left behind (cf. Gen. 19:17). "Pregnant" women and "nursing" mothers will have a hard time because their physical conditions will limit their mobility. Weather would make flight harder in the "winter," and observant Jews would seek to discourage travel "on" the "Sabbath."

When the temple was destroyed in A.D. 70, many of the Christians fled and hid in the clefts of Petra. But the final fulfillment of this prophecy lies in the future. Then everyone in "Judea" will have to "flee to the mountains."

24:21   Jesus explained the reason for such hasty retreat. "A tribulation" much greater than any the world has ever seen or ever will see would be about to break on the Jews. This description fits the Old Testament previews of the Great Tribulation: the last three and a half years of the Tribulation (Rev. 11:2; 13:5).
Again, the term "Tribulation" refers to the future seven-year period of distress, Daniel's seventieth week (Jer. 30:7; Dan. 9:26). The term "Great Tribulation" refers to the last half, or the second "three and one-half years" of that seven-year period (Matt. 24:15-22), which Jeremiah called "the time of Jacob's trouble" (Jer. 30:6-7). During the first half of the Tribulation, Israel will

[1162]E.g., Alford, 1:239; and Lenski, p. 938.
[1163]E.g., J. Marcellus Kik, *Matthew Twenty-Four, An Exposition*, p. 45; Carson, "Matthew," p. 500; Morison, pp. 467-68; Shepard, p. 517; and Vincent, 1:128.
[1164]Carson, "Matthew," p. 501.
[1165]Toussaint, *Behold the . . .*, pp. 274-75.
[1166]Wiersbe, 1:88.

enjoy the protection of Antichrist's covenant (Dan. 9:27), but during the second half, after Antichrist breaks his covenant with Israel, she will experience unprecedented persecution (Dan. 9:27).

The description in this verse is not a fitting description of the destruction of Jerusalem in A.D. 70, as bad as that was. Certainly the Nazi holocaust in which an estimated six million Jews perished, and other purges in which added multitudes have died, have been worse times than the destruction of Jerusalem. Yet the Great Tribulation will be the worst of all times for the Jews. The coming distress will be unprecedented in its suffering (cf. Dan. 12:1; Rev. 7:14).

"In a century that has seen two world wars, now lives under the threat of extinction by nuclear holocaust, and has had more Christian martyrs than in all the previous nineteen centuries put together, Jesus' prediction does not seem farfetched. But the age will not run its course; it will be cut short."[1167]

24:22   Unless God ends (Gr. *ekolobothesan*, "to terminate or cut off") the Tribulation, no living thing will remain alive.

"This does not mean that the period will be less than three-and-a-half years, but that it will be definitely terminated suddenly by the second coming of Christ."[1168]

The antecedent of "those days" is the days Jesus just described in verses 15-21: the days of the Tribulation. Jesus will shorten them a little out of compassion. Later revelation of this period in the Book of Revelation helps us appreciate the truth of Jesus' statement here (cf. Rev. 6—18). Not just people, but all forms of life (Gr. *pasa sarx*, lit. "all flesh") will experience drastic cutbacks during the Great Tribulation (cf. Rev. 6:7-8; 16:13-21). Antichrist will target the Jews and then Jews who believe in Jesus particularly (Rev. 12:13-17), but great multitudes of people will perish because of the distress that he brings. The "elect" are believers (cf. 20:16; 22:14; 24:22, 24, 31).

Many interpreters, however, take this verse as describing the present age rather than a future tribulation.[1169] This is the typical amillenarian and postmillenarian interpretation, though some premillenarians, such as Carson, also hold it. Weighing the distress of the present age against that of the Tribulation, I must conclude that verse 22 and this whole passage describes the future Tribulation, not the present age.

"This entire paragraph [vv. 15-22] relates only to Jews, for no Christian believer would worry about breaking a Sabbath law."[1170]

5. The second coming of the King 24:23-31 (cf. Mark 13:21-27; Luke 21:25-28)

Jesus proceeded to explain to His disciples that His coming would terminate the Tribulation.

24:23-24   "Then" means "at that time," namely, at the end of the Tribulation (v. 2). Jesus warned the disciples about people who would claim that Messiah had returned toward the end of the Tribulation, before He actually would return. People professing to be the Messiah ("false christs"), and others claiming to be prophets ("false prophets"), "will arise" and "mislead" many people, because of their ability to perform impressive miracles (cf. v. 11; 7:21-23; 16:1; Luke 17:23-24; Rev. 13:15). Evidently Satan will enable them to perform these "great signs and wonders."

"While false Christs and false prophets have always been in evidence, they will be especially prominent at the end of the age in Satan's final attempt to turn people from faith in Christ."[1171]

"If possible" (Gr. *ei dynaton*, v. 24) means the false prophets will hope to mislead the elect living in the Tribulation. It does not mean that the elect will inevitably remain true to the faith. Jesus had already said that some of His disciples would abandon the truth under persecution (vv. 10-11; cf. 26:31). However, the elect will not lose their salvation.

24:25   Jesus reminded His disciples that He had forewarned them about these impostors (cf. Mark 13:1-37; Luke 21:5-36). They would need to be very careful so they will not dupe them.

[1167]Carson, "Matthew," pp. 502-3.

[1168]Walvoord, *Matthew: . . .*, p. 188. Cf. Pentecost, *Thy Kingdom . . .*, p. 253; and Showers, pp. 50-54.

[1169]E.g., Louis Berkhof, *Systematic Theology*, pp. 696-707.

[1170]Wiersbe, 1:88.

[1171]Walvoord, *Matthew: . . .*, p. 189.

The disciples Jesus addressed undoubtedly thought they would be alive when these things happened. However, that was not to be the case, and Jesus said nothing to mislead them. He was teaching disciples of His in the years to come, as well as those sitting in His presence in this discourse, and in His other discourses.

24:26-27   Jesus' point in these verses was that His coming would be obvious to all, rather than obscure. When He comes, everyone will know it. Consequently, the disciples would not need to fear missing the event, and they should not react to every rumor that announced it was happening. His coming will be as obvious as a flash of "lightning" that covers the heavens (Zech. 9:14). It will be a public event, not something private that only the disciples or some small group would witness.

24:28   This appears to have been a well-known proverbial saying (cf. Luke 17:37; Job 39:30). One view of its meaning is that Jesus meant that the false Messiahs and the false prophets were similar to vultures (vv. 24, 26). They would be trying to pick the corpse of a dead Israel clean, for their own advantage, when Jesus returned.[1172] This is a possibility in view of the context. Another view is that the corpse refers to Christ, and the vultures are God's children gathered to feed on Him.[1173] However, the idea of feeding on Christ is foreign to the context, and the comparison of Him to carrion is unappealing. Other interpreters take Jesus' illustration to mean "signs as visible and indicative [as vultures gathering to a carcass] will herald the reality of the Parousia."[1174] Another writer paraphrased the verse as follows to give another interpretation.

> ". . . just as when life has abandoned a body, and it becomes a corpse, the vultures immediately swoop down upon it; so when the world has become rotten with evil, the Son of Man and His angels will come to execute the divine judgment."[1175]

The Greek word translated "vultures," *aetoi*, also means "eagles," but eagles rarely search out carrion. Still another view is that the figure emphasizes the swiftness of Messiah's coming.[1176] However, the repulsive character of vultures and carrion suggest more than just a swift coming. Furthermore, vultures do not always arrive and devour carrion swiftly. The view that appeals most to me is that Israel is the corpse and the vultures represent Israel's hostile enemies. Where moral corruption exists, divine judgment falls (cf. Job 39:27-30).[1177] Jesus' point was that there will be terrible carnage when He comes in judgment.

24:29   This verse and the following two give a positive description of Messiah's coming. "But" (NASB, Gr. *de*) introduces the contrast from the negative warning that preceded. At the very end of the Tribulation there will be signs in the sky. "The sun" and "the moon" will darken and "the stars will fall from the sky" (Isa. 13:9-10; 34:4; Ezek. 32:7; Joel 2:31; 3:15; Amos 8:9; Hag. 2:6; Zech. 14:6; Rev. 6:12-14). This is probably the language of appearance. The "powers of the heavens" (NASB) or the "heavenly bodies" (NIV) probably is a collective reference to the sun, moon, and stars.[1178] However, the descriptions of the Tribulation in the Book of Revelation suggest that God may fulfill these predictions literally.

24:30   What is "the sign of the Son of Man"? One very old interpretation is that it is a display of the cross in the sky.[1179] This view has seemed fanciful to most interpreters. A popular view is that it will be a light and or a cloud, similar to or perhaps identical with the Shekinah, that will surround Jesus when He comes.[1180] This seems most probable to me, since Jesus evidently was referring to Daniel 7:13 when He said these words. Furthermore, when Jesus ascended to heaven in a cloud, an angel told His disciples that He would return the same way (Acts 1:11). The clouds symbolize the heavenly origin and character of the King (cf. 17:5).[1181] A third view is that the sign will be Christ *Himself*.[1182] In this case, the appearance of Christ would signify coming judgment. This may be the correct view.

Zechariah prophesied that all the tribes of Israel in the land would mourn in repentance (Zech. 12:12). Jesus identified this prediction with His coming, and broadened it to include "all the tribes of the earth." Probably the unsaved "will mourn" because of the judgment they anticipate.

[1172]Lenski, p. 946; Toussaint, *Behold the . . .*, p. 276; Pentecost, *Thy Kingdom . . .*, p. 254.

[1173]Calvin, *Commentary on . . .*, 3:143-44.

[1174]Hill, p. 322.

[1175]Paul J. Levertoff, *St. Matthew (Revised Version)*, p. 79. Cf. Walvoord, *Matthew: . . .*, p. 190.

[1176]T. W. Manson, *The Sayings of Jesus*, p. 147.

[1177]*The New Scofield . . .*, p. 1034.

[1178]M'Neile, p. 352.

[1179]Alford, 1:243.

[1180]M'Neile, p. 352; English, p. 177; Gaebelein, 2:209; Pentecost, *The Words . . .*, p. 404.

[1181]Plummer, p. 336.

[1182]Allen, pp. 258-59; Darby, 3:125; Kelly, p. 27; Lenski, p. 948; *The Nelson . . .*, p. 1622.

24:31 Jesus explained another event that will happen when He returns at the end of the Tribulation. The passage He referred to was Isaiah 27:12-13. There Israel is in view, so Jesus must have been speaking about the gathering of Israelites again to the Promised Land at His Second Coming. The four winds refer to the four compass points. This regathering will involve judgment (13:39, 41; 24:40-41; 25:31; 2 Thess. 1:7-8). Jesus had previously spoken of the angels' role of assisting Him at this time (13:41; cf. 16:27). This regathering will set the stage for Messiah's worldwide reign.

God summoned the Israelites to march and to worship using trumpets during the wilderness wanderings and in the land (Exod. 19:16; 20:18; Jer. 4:5; et al.). This is not the same trumpet that will call Christians to heaven at the Rapture (1 Cor. 15:52; 1 Thess. 4:16). Other trumpets will sound announcing various other events in the future (cf. Rev. 8:2, 6, 13; 9:14; 11:15; et al.).

Events in the Church Age, between Pentecost and the Rapture, are not in view in the Olivet Discourse. This is the typical pretribulational interpretation of the discourse.[1183] The whole discourse deals with the return of Messiah to establish His kingdom on the earth and the things leading up to that. Jesus mentioned no sign, in this discourse, involving anything in the Church Age. The signs begin in the Tribulation when Christians will have gone to be with the Lord. Jesus' first reference to the Rapture was in the Upper Room Discourse (John 14:1-3), which He gave after the Olivet Discourse.[1184] Turner compared and contrasted four main evangelical views of this passage: the futurist, the preterist, the traditional preterist-futurist, and the revised preterist-futurist.[1185] He preferred the third of these, and I take the first.

"Those accepting the posttribulational view, that the rapture of the church and the second coming of Christ occur at the same time, tend to ignore the details of this discourse in the same fashion as the amillenarians do."[1186]

The reference to Jesus gathering the elect "from the sky" may indicate that the resurrected dead and raptured Christians are also in view.[1187] They will accompany Him when He returns to reign on the earth (cf. Col. 3:4). Some interpreters believe the reference to "the sky" simply describes the whole world in different words, and that only Jews are in view in this verse. Some feel this may include Old Testament saints who have died.[1188] I think it includes Christians and Old Testament saints and possibly angels.

This concludes Jesus' answer to the disciples' question about the sign of His coming and the end of the present age (v. 3). Other important passages of Scripture dealing with the Second Coming are the following: Deuteronomy 30:3; Psalm 2; Isaiah 63:1-6; Daniel 2:44-45; Romans 11:26; 1 Thessalonians 3:13; 5:1-4; 2 Thessalonians 1:7—2:12; 2 Peter 2:1—3:17; Jude 14-15; and Revelation 1:7; 19:11-21.[1189]

[1183]See Bruce A Ware, "Is the Church in View in Matthew 24—25?" *Bibliotheca Sacra* 138:550 (April-June 1981):158-72.,

[1184]See Thomas R. Edgar, "An Exegesis of Rapture Passages," in *Issues in Dispensationalism*, pp. 217-21; and Paul D. Feinberg, "Dispensational Theology and the Rapture," in ibid., pp. 235-44.

[1185]David L. Turner, "The Structure and Sequence of Matthew 24:1-41: Interaction with Evangelical Treatments," *Grace Theological Journal* 10:1 (Spring 1989):3-27. For a refutation of the preterist interpretation, see Stanley D. Toussaint, "A Critique of the Preterist View of the Olivet Discourse," *Bibliotheca Sacra* 161:644 (October-December 2004):469-90.

[1186]Walvoord, *Matthew: . . .*, p. 181. E.g., Morgan.

[1187]Walvoord, *Matthew: . . .*, p. 190.

[1188]Toussaint, *Behold the . . .*, pp. 277-78; Carson, "Matthew," p. 506; Barbieri, p. 78.

[1189]For parallels between the eschatology of Matthew 24 and that of the *Didache*, see William C. Varner, "The *Didache* 'Apocalypse' and Matthew 24," *Bibliotheca Sacra* 165:659 (July-September 2008):309-22.

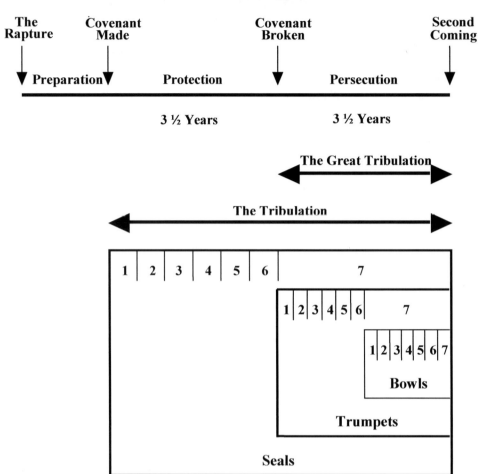

6. The responsibilities of the disciples 24:32—25:30

Next, Jesus exhorted His disciples on the basis of this revelation concerning the future. He taught them using seven parables.

The importance of vigilance 24:32-44

Jesus told His disciples four parables advocating vigilance in view of the time of His return. These stories were illustrations of His main points in the Olivet Discourse.

The parable of the fig tree 24:32-36 (cf. Mark 13:28-32; Luke 21:29-33)

This parable stresses the importance of the signs signaling Jesus' return.

24:32-33   The lesson (Gr. *parabole*, lit. parable) "of the fig tree" is quite simple. As the appearance of "tender" twigs and "leaves" on "the fig tree" indicate the nearness of "summer," so the appearance of the signs Jesus explained would indicate that His coming is near.

A popular interpretation of this parable equates modern Israel's presence in the Promised Land with the budding of the fig tree.[1190] This view may be placing too much emphasis on the identification of the fig tree with the modern State of Israel (cf. Jer. 24:1-8; 29:17). On the other hand, this could be at least part of what Jesus intended. Many commentators take this parable as describing the destruction of Jerusalem.[1191] As mentioned before, this is probably not correct.

24:34   Jesus first stressed the importance of what He would say.

[1190]Gaebelien, 2:213-14; Kelly, p. 451.

[1191]E.g., Morgan, *The Gospel* . . ., p. 286; Allen, p. 259; and Tasker, p. 227.

What did He mean by "this generation?" Many interpreters have concluded that Jesus meant the generation of disciples to whom He spoke (cf. 11:16; 12:39, 41-42, 45; 16:4; 17:17; 23:36). Some within this group of interpreters have concluded that because these signs did not occur before that generation of disciples died, Jesus made a mistake.[1192] This solution is unacceptable in view of who Jesus was. Other interpreters in this group have concluded that since these signs did not appear during the lifetime of that generation of disciples, Jesus must have been speaking metaphorically, not literally.[1193] They say the destruction of Jerusalem fulfilled what Jesus predicted. This solution is also unacceptable, because there is nothing in the text to indicate that Jesus meant that the disciples should understand the signs non-literally. Moreover, numerous similar prophecies concerning Messiah's first coming happened literally.

Perhaps Jesus meant that the generation of disciples that saw the future signs would also witness His return.[1194] However, the demonstrative pronoun "this" (Gr. *aute*) seems to stress the generation Jesus was addressing. Even so, this pronoun could refer to the end times rather than to that generation.[1195] I prefer this view.

Other interpreters have noted that "generation" (Gr. *genea*) can refer to a race of people, not just to one generation (cf. 16:4; Phil. 2:15).[1196] They conclude that Jesus meant the Jewish race would not end before all these signs had attained fulfillment.[1197] This is a possible solution, but it seems unusual that Jesus would introduce the continuing existence of the Jewish race to confirm the fulfillment of these signs.

Another view has focused attention on the words "take place" or "have happened" (Gr. *genetai*) that occur in all three synoptic accounts. The Greek word meant "to begin" or "to have a beginning." Advocates affirm that Jesus meant that the fulfillment of "all these things" would begin in the generation of His present disciples (cf. v. 33), but complete fulfillment would not come until later.[1198] However, Jesus said "all" those things would begin during that generation. It is possible that "all" those things would begin during that generation if one interprets "all those things" as *the signs as a whole* (cf. v. 32). The earliest signs then would correspond to the branches of the fig tree becoming tender. This would be the first evidence of fulfillment shaping up. "This generation" then "represents an evil class of people who will oppose Jesus' disciples until the day He returns."[1199]

24:35   Jesus further stressed the certainty of what the signs anticipated with these words. He claimed that His predictions had the same authority and eternal validity as God's words (cf. Ps. 119:89-90; Isa. 40:6-8).

24:36   The certainty of fulfillment should not lead the disciples to conclude that they could predict the time of fulfillment exactly. Jesus explained that *only* the heavenly "Father" knew precisely when the Son would return (cf. Acts 1:7).

"This verse becomes the main proposition which is developed from this point to Matthew 25:30."[1200]

Watchful preparation is necessary, since "no one knows" the "day" or the "hour" when Jesus will return. We do not know the year or the month, either. The alternative to preparing would be living life as usual without regard to the King's return. Jesus deliberately discouraged His disciples from setting dates.

Jesus' self-confessed ignorance has created a problem for some readers. How could He be God and not know everything? The answer is part of the problem of God becoming man, the Incarnation. Jesus voluntarily limited Himself, and limitation of His knowledge was part of His humiliation (Luke 2:52; Phil. 2:7).[1201]

[1192]E.g., M'Neile, p. 355.

[1193]E.g., Kik, pp. 10-12; and Plummer, p. 338.

[1194]Carl Armerding, *The Olivet Discourse*, p. 44; Charles Lee Feinberg, *Israel in the Last Days: The Olivet Discourse*, p. 22; Toussaint, *Behold the . . .*, pp. 279-80; Barbieri, p. 78; Bailey, in *The New . . .*, pp. 51-52.

[1195]George Benedict Winer, *Grammar of the Idiom of the New Testament*, p. 157.

[1196]Cremer, pp. 148-49.

[1197]E.g., English, p. 179; and Gaebelein, 2:214-15.

[1198]E.g., Cranfield, "St. Mark 13," *Scottish Journal of Theology* 7 (July 1954):291; C. E. Stowe, "The Eschatology of Christ, With Special Reference to the Discourse in Matt. XXIV. and XXV.," *Bibliotheca Sacra* 7 (July 1850):471; Mark L. Hitchcock, "A Critique of the Preterist View of 'Soon' and 'Near' in Revelation," *Bibliotheca Sacra* 163:652 (October-December 2006):467-78.

[1199]Neil D. Nelson Jr., "'This Generation' in Matt 24:34: A Literary Critical Perspective," *Journal of the Evangelical Theological Society* 38:3 (September 1996):385. See also Lawrence A. DeBruyn, "Preterism and 'This Generation,'" *Bibliotheca Sacra* 167:666 (April-June 2010):180-200.

[1200]Toussaint, *Behold the . . .*, p. 280.

[1201]See Appendix 8 "The Incarnation of God the Son" at the end of these notes.

"John's Gospel, the one of the four Gospels most clearly insisting on Jesus' deity, also insists with equal vigor on Jesus' dependence on and obedience to his Father—a dependence reaching even to his knowledge of the divine. How NT insistence on Jesus' deity is to be combined with NT insistence on his ignorance and dependence is a matter of profound importance to the church; and attempts to jettison one truth for the sake of preserving the other must be avoided."[1202]

The parable of Noah's days 24:37-39 (cf. Luke 17:26-27)

This parable clarifies verse 36, as the introductory "for" (Gr. *gar*) indicates. The previous parable stressed the signs leading up to Jesus' return, but this one stresses the responses to those signs and their consequences. Life will be progressing as usual when the King returns to judge. Similarly, life was progressing as usual in Noah's day, just before God broke in on humankind with judgment (cf. 1 Pet. 3:20-21). Despite upheavals, people will continue their normal pursuits. Ignorance and disregard of the Bible will be widespread then.

"The special point of the analogy is not that the generation that was swept away by the Flood was exceptionally wicked; none of the occupations mentioned are sinful; but that it was so absorbed in its worldly pursuits that it paid no attention to solemn warnings."[1203]

Jesus' disciples need to maintain constant vigilance, because the daily grind, including distress and persecution, will tend to lull them into dangerous complacency. It is normal for even remarkable signs of an impending change to have no effect on people. For example, when meteorologists announce the coming of a hurricane or tornado, there are always some people in its path who refuse to seek safety.

The parables of one taken and one left behind 24:40-41 (cf. Luke 17:34-35)

Having explained the importance of the signs leading up to His return and the responses to those signs, Jesus next explained the respective consequences of the two responses.

Many Christians who have read these verses have assumed that they describe believers, taken to heaven at the Rapture, and unbelievers left behind to enter the Tribulation. However, the context is dealing with the Second Coming of Christ, not the Rapture. The sequence of events will be: Jesus' ascension, the Church Age (beginning on Pentecost and ending with the Rapture), the Tribulation, the Second Coming, and the beginning of the messianic kingdom.

"It will be a taking away judicially and in judgment. The ones left will enjoy the blessings of Christ's reign on earth, just as Noah and his family were left to continue life on earth. This is the opposite of the rapture, where those who are left go into the judgment of the Great Tribulation."[1204]

"Jesus was not referring to the Rapture of the church in Matthew 24. When that event takes place, all the saved will be removed from the earth to meet Christ in the air, and all the unsaved will be left on the earth. Thus, the Rapture will occur in reverse of the order of things in the days of Noah and, therefore, the reverse of the order at Jesus' coming immediately after the Great Tribulation."[1205]

Some interpreters have made a case for this being a reference to the Rapture, because Jesus used two different words for "take" in the context. In verse 39, the Greek verb is *airo*, whereas in verses 40 and 41, He used *paralambano*. The argument is that *paralambano* is a word that describes Jesus taking His own to Himself. However, it also occurs in a bad sense (4:5, 8). Probably Jesus used *paralambano* because it more graphically pictures sweeping away as in a flood.[1206]

Perhaps Jesus used two illustrations to show that: neither gender, nor occupation, nor close relationship, will prevent the separation for judgment (cf. 10:35-36). Typically two women—often sisters, a mother and a daughter, or two servants—sat opposite each other turning the small hand mill between them.[1207]

[1202]Carson, "Matthew," p. 508. For further discussion, see idem, *Divine Sovereignty and Human Responsibility*, pp. 146-60.

[1203]Plummer, p. 340.

[1204]Feinberg, *Israel in . . .*, p. 27.

[1205]Showers, p. 180. See also Gerald B. Stanton, *Kept from the Hour*, pp. 51-65.

[1206]Morison, p. 489.

[1207]Carson, "Matthew," p. 509.

An exhortation to watchfulness 24:42 (cf. Mark 13:33-37; Luke 21:34-36)

This verse applies all that Jesus said beginning in verse 32. Jesus' disciples need to remain watchful because the exact time of the King's return is unknown, even though signs of His coming will indicate His approach.

The parable of the watchful homeowner 24:43-44

Jesus concluded His instructions concerning the importance of vigilance, in view of His return, by giving a parable urging watchfulness.

The introductory "but" connects this illustration with the former one and identifies a contrast. Jesus is like a "thief" in only one respect, namely, that other people will not expect His coming. The point of this parable is that: if a homeowner knows the general time when a thief will break in, he will prepare accordingly. The signs of the times during the Tribulation that Jesus revealed (vv. 5-22) will enable believers to know the general time He will return. Consequently believers in the Tribulation should prepare themselves.

"The death-day of the world needs to be hid for the purposes of providence as much as the dying-day of individuals."[1208]

This concludes the emphasis on vigilance that marks the first part of Jesus' instructions to His disciples, anticipating His return and the end of the present age.

"Jesus used Noah to warn that men will not know *the day*, and He used the picture of the burglar to warn that they will not know *the hour*."[1209]

It seems clear, then, that Jesus was speaking of His Second Coming and of the Tribulation signs that would precede it, as well as about the coming destruction of Jerusalem in A.D. 70. This was His intended meaning, and understanding what He said this way is the proper *interpretation* of His words, I believe. However, Christians living in the Church Age can *apply* this passage to our situation, because what we face now is similar to the one that Tribulation saints will face in the future. We, too, look forward to a return of the Lord (at the Rapture) that will be preceded by increasing trouble for believers (e.g., 1 Tim. 4; 2 Tim. 3). It is as important for us to be watchful as it will be for saints living during the Tribulation.

The importance of prudence and faithfulness 24:45—25:30

Jesus continued instructing His disciples, but now stressed the importance of prudence and faithfulness, as He prepared them for His return. There are three parables in this section. All of them refer to two types of disciples, the faithful and the unfaithful.[1210]

The parable of the two servants 24:45-51 (cf. Luke 12:42-48)

This parable illustrates the two attitudes that people *during the Tribulation* will have regarding Jesus' return.

24:45-47   The servants (Gr. *douloi*) are Jesus' disciples, to whom He has entrusted the responsibility of managing His affairs during His absence from the earth. Some servants will be "faithful and sensible" (prudent, cf. 7:24; 10:16). They will carry out God's will for them, including feeding the world the gospel, which dispensing food represents in the parable. When Jesus returns, these faithful servants will be "blessed" (i.e., the objects of God's favor who are consequently happy, cf. 5:3). Moreover, Jesus will promote them to positions of greater responsibility in the kingdom that He will establish.

"The reward of faithfulness is to be trusted with higher responsibilities; cf. xxv. 21, 23, Lk. xvi. 10a. Since the parable deals with the Parousia, the words apply to higher activities in the age to come."[1211]

24:48-51   Other disciples may conclude that Jesus' delay indicates a postponement of His appearing. This conclusion may lead to their abusing their fellow disciples and their carousing. Jesus' return will surprise such disciples who will not be ready for it. The fate of such unfaithful and unwise servants will be tragic. Jesus will "cut" them to "pieces"—a graphic and hyperbolic description of personal destruction (v. 51; cf. 1 Sam. 15:33; Heb. 11:37).[1212] Their lot will be "with the hypocrites," those whom Jesus predicted would experience God's most severe judgment (cf. 6:2, 5, 16; 16:3; 23:13-29). Furthermore they will eventually go to hell.

[1208]Bruce, *The Training . . .*, p. 338.
[1209]Wiersbe, 1:90.
[1210]See Dillow, pp. 385-96.
[1211]M'Neile, p. 358.
[1212]See Pagenkemper, pp. 191-94.

"Invariably throughout Matthew this phrase [weeping and gnashing of teeth] refers to the retribution of those who are judged before the millennial kingdom is established (Matthew 8:12; 13:42, 50; 22:13; 25:30)."[1213]

These unfaithful servants must be disciples of Jesus during the Tribulation who are not genuine believers. There will be some people who claim to be followers of Jesus in the Tribulation, but who have not trusted in Him for salvation. There were many such in Jesus' day, and there are many today.

In this parable the good servant was both prudent and faithful (v. 45). Jesus next gave the parable of the 10 virgins to illustrate prudence, and then He gave the parable of the talents to illustrate faithfulness.[1214]

"This [next] part of the Olivet Discourse [i.e., ch. 25] goes beyond the 'sign' questions of the disciples (24:3) and presents our Lord's return in three aspects: (1) as testing profession, vv. 1-13; (2) as testing service, vv. 14-30; and (3) as testing individual Gentiles, vv. 31-46."[1215]

The parable of the 10 virgins 25:1-13

This parable helps disciples understand what it means to await the King's return with prudence.

". . . the point is simply that readiness, whatever form it takes, is not something that can be achieved by a last-minute adjustment. It depends on long-term provision, and if that has been made, the wise disciple can sleep secure in the knowledge that everything is ready."[1216]

25:1   The introductory "then" ties this parable to the subject of the preceding instruction, namely, the Second Coming of the Son of Man. The beginning of "the kingdom of heaven" is in view. It will be similar to what the following story describes.

Jesus probably chose "10 virgins" for His illustration because such a number was customary for marriages of His day.[1217] The number probably does not have symbolic significance. Likewise that the women were "virgins" (Gr. *parthenos*, cf. 1:23), probably has no other significance than that they were young women who were friends of the bride and groom. Their virginity is not a factor in the parable. The "lamps" (Gr. *lampas*) could have been either torches or smaller lamps with wicks. "To meet" (Gr. *hypantesis*) connotes an official welcome of a visiting dignitary.[1218]

Most premillennial commentators have taken these virgins as representing Jews during the Tribulation. However, some argued that they stand for Christians in the present age.[1219] The arguments in favor of the second view are, primarily, what the passage does not contain, such as: the title "Son of Man," the phrase "times or seasons," and Old Testament quotations. However, arguments from silence are never strong, and they are unconvincing here. The better explanation is that this parable deals with the same time and people as the immediately preceding and following parables do. The ten virgins represent Jewish disciples in the Tribulation waiting for the coming of the King. That is not to say, however, that the principle of watchfulness that this parable teaches is not applicable to Christian disciples who await the Lord's return for them at the Rapture.

Some background information concerning weddings in the ancient Near East is helpful in understanding this parable.[1220] First, the parents arranged the marriage with the consent of the bride and groom. Second, the couple passed an engagement period of many months in which it would become clear, hopefully, that the bride was a virgin. Third, on the day of the wedding the groom would go to the bride's house to claim his bride from her parents. His friends would accompany him. Fourth, the marriage ceremony would take place at the bride's home. Fifth, on the evening of the day of the wedding, the groom would take his bride home. This involved a nighttime procession through the streets. Sixth, the bride and groom would consummate their marriage at the groom's home the night of the wedding ceremony. Seventh, there would be a banquet that would often last as long as seven days. This often took place at the groom's home.

[1213]Toussaint, *Behold the* . . ., p. 282.

[1214]M'Neile, p. 359.

[1215]*The New Scofield* . . ., p. 1035.

[1216]France, *The Gospel* . . ., p. 947.

[1217]Edersheim, *The Life* . . ., 2:455; idem, *Sketches of* . . ., p. 155.

[1218]M'Neile, p. 360.

[1219]E.g., Gaebelein, 2:225-36. Cf. Carr, p. 275; and Plummer, p. 343.

[1220]See Yamauchi, 241-52; Jeremias, *The Parables* . . ., pp. 173-74; and Trench, *Notes on* . . ., pp. 200-201.

The scene in this parable is at night, when the bride's friends are waiting to welcome the couple, and to enter the groom's house where the banquet will begin shortly. All ten of the virgins knew that the groom's appearing would be soon.

25:2-5   The "five prudent (Gr. *phronimoi*, cf. 7:24; 10:16; 24:45) virgins" represent Jewish disciples who not only anticipated Jesus' arrival but also prepared for it (cf. 3:2: 4:17). The five foolish virgins anticipated it but did not prepare for it. Preparedness is what separated the wise from the foolish.

> "Perhaps their spiritual condition will be analogous to the Jews at the Lord's first coming. With eyes only for the physical benefits of the kingdom, the foolish Jews fail to prepare themselves spiritually for its coming."[1221]

Both groups of young women fell asleep. This period of delay corresponds to the time between the first signs of Jesus' coming and His appearance. Jesus did not praise or blame the virgins for sleeping. Only the wise virgins "took oil" with them (v. 4).

The foolish ones evidently just lit their torches or wicks without oil.[1222] The symbolism of oil is probably significant since it often represents the Holy Spirit in Scripture (e.g., 1 Sam. 16:13). If so, those with oil might be believers, and those without oil, unbelievers.

25:6-9   "Midnight" probably also has significance, since it is often the time of *judgment* in Scripture (e.g., Exod. 11:4). When someone announced the arrival of the groom, the "virgins" all woke up and "trimmed their lamps." However, the lamps of the foolish soon began to go out (present tense in the Greek text). The preparations of the wise virgins did the unwise no good. The time to prepare had passed.

Though Jesus did not go into this, the bride in the parable must be the church, the bride of Christ (cf. 2 Cor. 11:2). The church will be in heaven with Jesus, during the Tribulation, having gone there at the Rapture (1 Thess. 4:13-17). Christians will return to earth with Jesus at His Second Coming, and will evidently have some part in the judgment that will begin the kingdom (vv. 31-46; cf. 1 Cor. 6:2).

25:10-12   Shortly after the announcement went out, the groom arrived (cf. 24:27, 39, 50). There was not enough time for the foolish virgins to obtain oil then. The wise virgins entered the wedding feast, and someone "shut . . . the door" into the banquet hall (cf. vv. 34-40). There was no more opportunity for the foolish to enter. Their pathetic cries were of no avail (cf. 7:21-23; 23:37). The groom's refusal to admit them was not the result of callous rejection in spite of their desire to enter the feast. Rather, he refused to admit them because they had failed to prepare adequately.

> "The closed door, which to those who were ready meant security and untold bliss, to the others meant banishment and untold gloom."[1223]

These verses picture the judgment of Jews that will happen at the end of the Tribulation and before the establishment of the messianic kingdom.

25:13   This is the lesson the disciples were to learn from this parable. Disciples need to prepare for Messiah's appearing as well as to anticipate that event. Jesus was not calling for alertness in this parable, remaining awake when others sleep, as important as that is. He was calling for preparation. Preparing involves trusting in Jesus as the Messiah. Many Jews in Jesus' day were anticipating the appearance of Messiah and the inauguration of the kingdom. However, they did not prepare, even though John the Baptist, Jesus, and Jesus' disciples urged them to. Those who did, became believing disciples of Jesus. Once again, the same two types of Jews will exist during the Tribulation, before Messiah appears the second time. The prudent disciple is the one who makes the necessary preparation by trusting in Jesus.[1224]

The parable of the talents 25:14-30

The other important quality that will make a servant blessed when Jesus returns, in addition to prudence, is faithfulness (cf. 24:45-46). This parable explains what Jesus regards as faithfulness. Essentially it involves using what God has entrusted to one to advance His interests in the world. It involves making a spiritual profit with the deposit God has entrusted to each disciple (cf. James 2:14-26). The parable of the ten virgins speaks of salvation, but this one emphasizes the importance of rewards and judgment.

[1221]Toussaint, *Behold the . . .*, p. 285.

[1222]Robertson, *Word Pictures . . .*, 1:196.

[1223]Plummer, p. 346. Cf. Pagenkemper, pp. 188-89.

[1224]See J. Gregory Sheryl, "Can the Date of Jesus' Return Be Known?" *Bibliotheca Sacra* 169:673 (January-March 2012):20-32, for a review of date-setters through history.

25:14	"For" links the following parable with the lesson expressed in verse 13. The antecedent of "it" is the kingdom of heaven (v. 1).

"Probably this parable is so tightly associated with the last one as to share its introduction . . ."[1225]

Thus, the point of the parable of the 10 virgins, and the parable of the talents, is the same. The difference is a matter of emphasis. The emphasis of the first one is the importance of spiritual preparation, whereas the emphasis of the second is the importance of spiritual service. The second parable deals with the period of waiting, that the first parable only mentioned in passing. Both parables deal primarily with the judgment of Jews at the end of the Tribulation, though both apply to Christians today, as does the whole Olivet Discourse.

Some slaves (Gr. *douloi*) in the ancient biblical world enjoyed considerable responsibility and authority. In the parable, the man taking the journey turned over his money to three of his slaves. They understood that they could share in the profits if they managed well what they had received.

25:15	In New Testament times, a talent (Gr. *talanton*) was a unit of exchange. Its value depended on the type of metal that was in view—gold, silver, or copper. The talents in this parable may have been silver, though this is not important. The Greek word *argyrion* in verse 18 can mean either "money" or "silver." Originally, a talent was a measure of weight, between 58 and 80 pounds.[1226] Many translators and commentators use "75 pounds" as a convenient working amount. Later the talent was a coin worth about 6,000 denarii. The earning power of a talent coin was therefore the equivalent of about 16 and a half years wages for a working man or a foot soldier. By any calculation, the worth of the talents entrusted to the slaves in this parable was great. "Five talents" might amount to considerably more than a lifetime of earnings.

This master distributed his resources according to his evaluation of the ability of each slave. As always, greater privilege brings greater responsibility.

Probably we should understand the talents to represent all the working capital that God entrusts to His disciples. To limit the significance of talents to either: spiritual gifts, natural abilities, the gospel, opportunities for service, money, or whatever—limits the scope of what Jesus probably intended. All of these things constitute what God has given His servants to use for His glory.

"This capacity for work lies not within our own power; but it *is* in our power to use for Christ whatever we may have."[1227]

These slaves represent Jews living during the Tribulation, not Christians living in the Church Age, though this parable is applicable to us as well. Tribulation Jews will have unparalleled opportunities to serve Jesus Christ. The opportunity to herald the gospel to the ends of the earth will be one of these great privileges. Many disciples then (144,000 missionaries; Rev. 7; 14) will probably have the opportunity to present the gospel to thousands, and perhaps millions of individuals, using the technology of their day.

25:16-18	"Immediately," the slaves entrusted with "five" and "two talents" began to put their money to use for their master. This shows their faithfulness to their duty to make money for him. They traded with the money in some way, and they made a profit. The other slave, however, was unwilling to work and to risk. By burying the money, he showed that he valued safety above all else. Burying his talent was even much safer than putting it in a savings account. Before the days of modern banking, many people buried money in the ground for safekeeping.

The slaves of God who have a heart for God and His coming kingdom will sense their privilege, seize their opportunities, and serve God to the maximum extent of their ability in the Tribulation. Those who have no real concern about preparing people for the coming King will do nothing with their opportunities. Their own safety will be more important to them than working to prepare for the arrival of the King. Being a good steward involves taking some risks.

25:19-23	Jesus' mention of "a long time" passing probably suggests the time between His ascension and His second coming (cf. 24:48; 25:5). Thus, while the slaves in view are those living during the Tribulation, with which the whole Olivet Discourse deals, the parable has meaning for all of Jesus' disciples who anticipate the kingdom. This is true of all of Jesus' discourses in Matthew.

The first slave received a verbal commendation from his master, increased responsibility under his master, and joy with his master (v. 21; cf. 24:46; John 15:11). He would exercise his increased responsibility and enjoy his joy in the kingdom and, I assume, beyond it when the earthly messianic kingdom moves to new heavens and a new earth (Rev. 21:1—22:5). The second slave received the same verbal commendation as the first slave, and he received increased responsibility and joy

---

[1225]Carson, "Matthew," p. 515.

[1226]Walter Bauer, *A Greek-English Lexicon of the New Testament and Other Early Christian Literature*, s.v. "talanton," p. 803.

[1227]Edersheim, *The Life . . .*, 2:460.

commensurate with his God-given capacity (v. 23). Since we can do nothing except by God's grace (cf. John 15:5), these rewards—like all similar rewards—are really due to God's grace, rather than to the servants' faithfulness, which His grace enables (cf. 1 Cor. 4:7).

"You don't 'retire' from being a disciple."[1228]

25:24-25   When the third slave said his master was a "hard" (Gr. *skleros*) man, he meant that he exploited the labor of others, namely, this slave and his fellow slaves (cf. John 6:60; Acts 26:14; James 3:4; Jude 15). This slave evidently felt that his master would not share many of the rewards of his labor with him, if he proved successful, but would punish him severely if he failed. The fact that he had received less than the other slaves should not have made him resentful, if it did, since even he had a great opportunity. He ignored his responsibility to his master and his obligation to discharge his duty. Moreover, he showed no love for his master, whom he blamed, attempting thereby to cover up his own failure.[1229]

"Grace never condones irresponsibility; even those given less are obligated to use and develop what they have."[1230]

25:26-27   Rather than commending this slave, his master gave him a scathing condemnation. Instead of being "good and faithful," he was "wicked" and "lazy." To be lazy is to be unfaithful. The master used the slave's own words to condemn him (vv. 24-25). If the master really was hard and grasping, the slave should have known he was in for trouble if he proved unfaithful. At least he should have put his master's money into the hands of bankers. That would have been a fairly safe and easy way to manage it, and it would have earned some "interest." The Jews were not to charge fellow Jews interest on loans, but they could charge Gentiles interest (Deut. 23:19-20).

". . . risk is at the heart of discipleship (10:39; 16:25-26); by playing safe the cautious slave has achieved nothing, and it is his timidity and lack of enterprise . . . which is condemned. Schweizer, 473, pertinently describes his attitude as representing 'a religion concerned only with not doing anything wrong.'"[1231]

25:28-30   Rather than giving this servant increased responsibility, the master took back "the talent" he had entrusted to him. Rather than blessing him with the joy of fellowship with the master, the slave had to depart from his master's presence. Verse 29 expresses a kingdom principle that Jesus had formerly explained (13:12; cf. 21:43). The master removed the slave's opportunity to serve him further. He declared him "worthless" (v. 30) because he had failed to do his master's will with what the master gave him to use. This resulted in the loss of his resources, rejection by the master ("throw out the worthless slave"), banishment from his presence ("outer darkness"), tears ("weeping"), and "gnashing of teeth."

Does the unfaithful slave represent a believing or an unbelieving Jew in the Tribulation? In view of the punishment he received, he must be an unbeliever (cf. 13:12).[1232] Everywhere else in Matthew's Gospel where the phrase "weeping and gnashing of teeth" occurs, it refers to the final condition of unbelievers (8:12; 13:42, 50; 22:13; 24:51). The "darkness" outside (v. 30) contrasts with the "joy" inside the messianic banquet and kingdom (vv. 21, 23).

"The last three parables give practical instructions in the light of the King's coming to judge and to reign. The principle which underlies each is the same one which was given in the Sermon on the Mount (Matthew 7:16-21). The fruit of faithfulness and preparedness would indicate the character of those living in the days before His coming. In each parable, character is manifested by works. This thought forms the key to the following passage which deals with the judgment of the nations (Matthew 25:31-46)."[1233]

This concludes the section of the Olivet Discourse in which Jesus taught His disciples their responsibilities in view of His coming and the end of the present age (24:32—25:30). He stressed the importance of vigilance with four parables (24:32-44), and the importance of prudence and faithfulness with three parables (24:43—25:30). Modern Christians should cultivate all these qualities as disciples of Christ who anticipate His "any moment" coming for us at the Rapture.

[1228]France, *The Gospel . . .*, pp. 954-55.
[1229]Carson, "Matthew," p. 517.
[1230]Ibid.
[1231]France, *The Gospel . . .*, p. 956. He quoted the English translation of E. Schweizer, *The Good News according to Matthew*.
[1232]Darby, 3:131; Pagenkemper, pp. 194-98.
[1233]Toussaint, *Behold the . . .*, p. 288.

7. The King's judgment of the nations 25:31-46

Jesus concluded the Olivet Discourse with further revelation about the judgment that will take place at the end of the present age when He returns. He had referred to it often in the discourse, but now He made it a special subject of explanation. This judgment will occur when the King returns to earth at the end of the Tribulation to set up His kingdom.[1234]

As we have seen, Matthew stressed judgment in his Gospel (3:12; 6:2, 5, 16; 7:24-27; 13:30, 48-49; 18:23-34; 20:1-16; 21:33-41; 22:1-14; 24:45-51; 25:1-12, 14-30). This is not unusual, since the Old Testament predicted that judgment would precede the messianic kingdom, and Matthew emphasized the kingdom. It is not surprising, therefore, that Jesus concluded this discourse that reveals events leading up to the inauguration of the kingdom, by explaining the judgment that will precede it.

The New Testament teaches that there will be two distinct judgments relative to the kingdom. Many scholars believe there will only be one general judgment at the end.[1235] Most of these are amillenarians, but some premillenarians believe this as well.[1236] One of these judgments will occur just before the messianic kingdom begins, and another will follow at its end. The one at the end is the great white throne judgment, when God will send all unbelievers to hell (Rev. 20:11-15).

Some differences between these two judgments indicate their distinctness. First, the first judgment will not involve a resurrection of unbelievers, but will deal with unbelievers alive then on the earth. The word "nations" (i.e., Gentiles, Gr. *ethne*) never refers to the dead elsewhere in Scripture.[1237] The second judgment will involve a resurrection of unbelievers. Second, the first judgment will involve three different kinds of people: the sheep, the goats, and Jesus' brethren. The second will involve the wicked (Rev. 20:13-15), and possibly the righteous who have died during the Millennium. Third, the first will result in some inheriting the kingdom and others getting eternal punishment, but the second will result in the wicked judged going into the lake of fire. Fourth, the first happens at the beginning of the messianic (millennial) kingdom, but the second happens at its end.[1238]

This pericope rounds off Jesus' instructions about the future, in a similar way to how 10:40-42 completes Jesus' charge concerning His apostles' mission to Israel (10:5-42). It is the parable of the sheep and the goats. Some writers have argued that this is not a parable.[1239] However, most interpreters have dealt with this section as a parable, in the looser sense of a lesson.

25:31	This verse fixes the time of the judgment described in the following verses at the beginning of Jesus' messianic reign (cf. Dan. 7:9-14, 22-27). Nowhere in this discourse did Jesus explicitly identify Himself as "the Son of Man." However, since He used that title in answer to the disciples' questions in verse 3, the inference is inescapable (cf. Zech. 14:5; Joel 3:1-12). Jesus becomes the eschatological Judge that the Old Testament identified as God. Jesus again referred to His coming with "His" heavenly "glory" and "all the angels" (16:27; 24:30; cf. 1 Thess. 4:16; 2 Thess. 1:8). Jesus "will sit on His glorious" earthly "throne" as Judge and King (cf. 28:18; 1 Cor. 15:25; Heb. 12:2).
25:32-33	Usually "the nations" (Gr. *ta ethne*) refers to Gentiles—as distinguished from Jews (e.g., Luke 21:24; Acts 14:16).[1240] Because of this, some interpreters believe the judgment of verses 31-46 is a judgment of Gentiles only.[1241] However, the phrase "all the nations" is often more inclusive, referring to all people, including the Jews (cf. Rom. 16:26; Rev. 15:4). Here it probably refers to all people living on earth when Jesus establishes His kingdom (cf. 28:19; Mark 13:10). Everyone will have heard the gospel of the kingdom preached during the Tribulation (24:14). In Jesus' day, shepherds separated "the sheep" from "the goats" in their flocks, for various reasons, at various times (cf. Ezek. 34:17). Also, sheep and goats in the Middle East look more alike than they do in some other parts of the world.[1242] The "right" often signified the place of favor, and "the left" the place of comparative disfavor, in biblical and Jewish literature.[1243]
25:34	The identification of "the King" with "the Son of Man" (v. 31) recalls Daniel 7:13-14, where the Son of Man approaches the Ancient of Days (God the Father) to receive a kingdom. The purpose of Jesus separating humanity into two groups at the beginning of the kingdom is to determine whom He will admit to the kingdom, and whom He will exclude (cf. vv. 41, 46). The

---

[1234]See Eugene W. Pond, "The Background and Timing of the Judgment of the Sheep and Goats," *Bibliotheca Sacra* 159:634 (April-June 2002):201-20.

[1235]E.g., Kik, pp. 92-97; Lenski, pp. 986-88; Tasker, p. 238; M'Neile, p. 369; France, *The Gospel . . .*, p. 959; and Shepard, pp. 528-29.

[1236]E.g., Alford, 1:254.

[1237]Peters, 2:374.

[1238]Cf. Toussaint, *Behold the . . .*, pp. 288-89.

[1239]E.g., Walvoord, *Matthew: . . .*, p. 200; and Carson, "Matthew," p. 518.

[1240]Abbott-Smith, pp. 129-30; Thayer, *A Greek-English . . .*, p. 168; Vincent, 1:135.

[1241]E.g., Barbieri, p. 80; Bailey, in *The New . . .*, p. 53; and Eugene W. Pond, "Who Are the Sheep and Goats in Matthew 25:31-46?" *Bibliotheca Sacra* 159:635 (July-September 2002):288-301.

[1242]Bailey, in *The New . . .*, p. 54.

[1243]J. M. Court, "Right and Left: The Implications for Matthew 25.31-46," *New Testament Studies* 31 (1985):223-29.

Father blesses (Gr. *eulogemenoi*, cf. 21:9; 23:39) some by allowing them to enter the kingdom. They now enter into their *inheritance*, a term that presupposes relationship with the Father. The inheritance involves the blessings God will give them in the kingdom, that will vary, depending on their service during the Tribulation (cf. vv. 14-23, 28-29).

Jesus' description of "the kingdom" as what God has "prepared . . . from the foundation of the world" is significant. The rule of Messiah on the earth over all humankind has been part of God's plan since creation. This shows its central place in God's program for humanity. Its establishment will be the fulfillment of many promises and covenants that God gave to Adam and Eve (Gen. 3:15), to Abraham (Gen. 12; 15; 17; 21), to David (2 Sam. 7:12-16), and to the nation of Israel (Ezek. 34:20-31; Jer. 31:31-40; Zech. 10:5-12).[1244]

25:35-40   Jesus clarified the basis for judgment then. It would be the reception or rejection of the "King" as divinely seen in people's reception or rejection of the King's "brothers." The King's "brothers" are probably His faithful disciples who fulfill His will by preaching the gospel of the kingdom during the Tribulation (cf. 12:48-49; 28:10; Isa. 58:7). Most of these will be Jews, including the 144,000, though some may be Gentile converts as well (cf. Rev. 7:1-8; 14:1-5). They will have become believers following the Rapture, since all believers alive on the earth just before the Rapture will have already gone to be with Jesus.[1245] Other interpreters have variously identified these brethren as: all the needy of the world,[1246] all Jews,[1247] or Christian apostles and missionaries.[1248]

> "Those described here are people who have lived through the great tribulation, a time of unparalleled anti-Semitism, when the majority of Jews in the land will be killed. Under these circumstances, if a Gentile befriends a Jew to the extent of feeding and clothing and visiting him, it could only mean that he is a believer in Jesus Christ and recognizes the Jews as the chosen people."[1249]

> "The least of" Jesus' "brothers" are probably Jewish Tribulation martyrs.[1250]

25:41-45   Jesus will banish the goats and send them "into the eternal fire" (cf. 13:24-30, 31-43, 47-50; Rev. 14:11; 19:15). Jesus' descriptions of hell were familiar to the Jews of His day (cf. 3:10, 12; 5:22; 7:19; 13:40, 42, 50; 18:8-9; Jude 7; Rev. 20:10-15). Only the righteous will enter the kingdom (v. 34). The fact that the goats will address Jesus as "Lord" (v. 44) does not show they are believers, since everyone will acknowledge Him as Lord then (cf. Phil. 2:11).

> The sheep and the goats will express surprise, but not because they anticipated a different fate. They will express surprise because of the evidence upon which Jesus will judge their condition, namely: their treatment of His brethren. Normally a person's works demonstrate his faith or lack of it.

> "The King's messengers, immediately before He appears in glory, will go forth preaching the gospel of the kingdom everywhere; and when the King takes His throne, those that received the gospel of the kingdom among the nations are recognized as 'sheep,' and the despisers perish as 'goats.'"[1251]

25:46   The goats (unbelievers) will go "into eternal punishment" in hell eventually, instead of entering the messianic kingdom (cf. 7:21-23; 13:40-43). This is the only place in Scripture where the term "eternal punishment" appears. Some interpreters believe that "eternal" here does not mean "everlasting" but pertaining to the age to come, which is eternal.[1252] They favor understanding Jesus to mean that the lost will suffer annihilation. This view is sometimes called "conditional immortality."[1253]

[1244]Peters, 2:375.

[1245]Toussaint, *Behold the . . .*, pp. 290-91; Feinberg, *Israel in . . .*, p. 46; Allen, p. 265; Gaebelein, 2:246-47; Darby, 3:133; Hodges, "Possessing the . . .," 1:3 (November-December 1991):1, 4; and 2:1 (Spring 1992):1, 4.

[1246]E.g., David R. Catchpole, "The Poor on Earth and the Son of Man in Heaven: A Re-appraisal of Matthew xxv. 31-46," *Bulletin of the John Rylands Library* 61 (1978-79):355-97.

[1247]E.g., Walvoord, *Matthew: . . .*, p. 201; Barbieri, p. 81; and Donald Grey Barnhouse, *Romans. Vol. I: Man's Ruin. God's Wrath*, 2:38-39.

[1248]E.g., J. R. Michaels, "Apostolic Hardships and Righteous Gentiles," *Journal of Biblical Literature* 84 (1965):27-37; and Peters, 2:376.

[1249]Walvoord, *Matthew: . . .*, p. 202.

[1250]See Eugene W. Pond, "Who Are 'the Least' of Jesus' Brothers in Matthew 25:40?" *Bibliotheca Sacra* 159:636 (October-December 2002):436-48.

[1251]Kelly, p. 485.

[1252]E.g., France, *The Gospel . . .*, pp. 966-67.

[1253]See Robert A. Peterson, "A Traditionalist Response to John Stott's Arguments for Annihilationism," *Journal of the Evangelical Theological Society* 37:4 (December 1994):553-68; idem, "Does the Bible Teach Annihilationism?" *Bibliotheca Sacra* 156:621 (January-March 1999):13-27; Millard J. Erickson, "Is Hell Forever?" *Bibliotheca Sacra* (July-September 1995):259-72; and Bruce W. Davidson, "Reasonable Damnation: How Jonathan Edwards Argued for the Rationality of Hell," *Journal of the Evangelical Theological Society* 38:1 (March 1995):47-56.

"*Everlasting* and *eternal* are used to describe both torment and *life*, indicating that one will last as long as the other. In fact, 'everlasting' is used of God in Rom. 16:26."[1254]

"At the time of Christ the punishment of the wicked was certainly regarded as of eternal duration."[1255]

Immediately these unbelievers will enter Hades, the place of departed spirits, until God resurrects them at the end of the millennium and sends them to hell (cf. Rev. 20:11-15). The sheep (believers) will enter the kingdom, which will be the first stage of their ceaseless life with God. Whereas eternal life begins when a person trusts Jesus Christ, the first stage of life in the King's presence for these believers will be the messianic kingdom. Elsewhere, God revealed that there are degrees of happiness and responsibility in the kingdom (vv. 14-30; cf. 1 Cor. 3:10-15), and degrees of punishment in hell (11:22; Luke 12:47-48). Jesus described the sheep as "righteous."

"This whole discourse again reflects the Lord's emphasis on righteousness [cf. the Sermon on the Mount]. It is a righteousness founded in faith in God which in turn, by God's grace, empowers the whole man to live a new and righteous life."[1256]

Does this passage (25:31-46) teach us anything about the time of the Rapture?

"Although the question of whether Christ will come for His church before the tribulation (the pretribulational view) or at the time of His second coming to earth (the posttribulational view) is not dealt with in this passage, the implications are clearly in favor of the pretribulational view. If the rapture and translation of the church occur while Christ is coming from heaven to earth in His second coming to set up His kingdom, and the church meets the Lord in the air, it is obvious that this very act would separate all the saved from the unsaved. Under these circumstances, no judgment of the nations would be necessary subsequent to the second coming of Christ, because the sheep and the goats would already be separated."[1257]

Thus ends the Olivet Discourse. Revelation 6—20 provides further exposition of Jesus' teaching in the Olivet Discourse.[1258]

"Taken as a whole, the Olivet discourse is one of the great prophetic utterances of Scripture and provides facts nowhere else given in quite the same way. In it, Christ, the greatest of the prophets and the master Teacher, described the end of the age as the climax of the troubles of earth in a great tribulation. The time of unprecedented trouble will be terminated by the second coming of Christ. The saved and the unsaved will be separated, and only the saved will enter the millennial kingdom. This is the final word, which Matthew brings in answer to the leading question of this first gospel, concerning the fulfillment of the prophecies of the Old Testament of a glorious kingdom on earth. Matthew states clearly that while Christ, in His first coming, suffered and died and was rejected as both King and Saviour by His own people, He will come again and, in triumph, will bring in the prophesied kingdom literally, just as the Old Testament prophecies had anticipated. There is postponement but not annulment of the great prophecies of the kingdom on earth."[1259]

[1254] *The Nelson . . .*, p. 1625.

[1255] Edersheim, *The Life . . .*, 2:440. See ibid., 2:791-96, on eternal punishment according to the rabbis and the New Testament.

[1256] Toussaint, *Behold the . . .*, pp. 291-92.

[1257] Walvoord, *Matthew: . . .*, p. 203. See also Paul D. Feinberg, "Dispensational Theology . . .," pp. 229-35.

[1258] For other expositions of the whole Olivet Discourse, see Walvoord, "Christ's Olivet Discourse on the End of the Age," *Bibliotheca Sacra* 128:510 (April-June 1971):109-16; 128:511 (July-September 1971):206-14; 128:512 (October-December 1971):316-26; 129:513 (January-March 1972):20-32; 129:514 (April-June 1972):99-105; 129:515 (July-September 1972):206-10; 129:516 (October-December 1972):307-15; and Pentecost, *Thy Kingdom . . .*, pp. 247-62.

[1259] Walvoord, *Matthew: . . .*, p. 204.

The Biblical Forecast for the Future

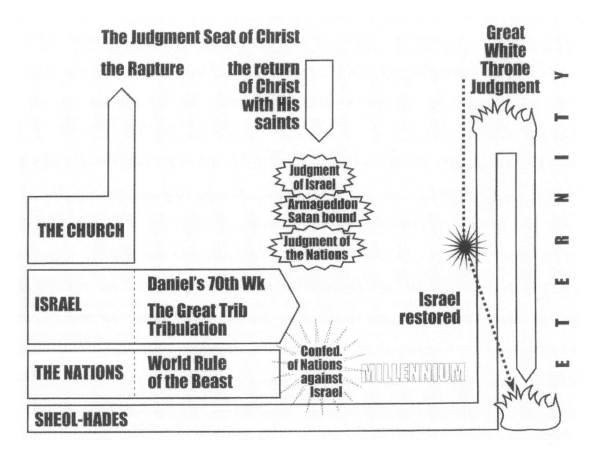

In one sense 25:46 is the climax of Matthew's argument in this Gospel.[1260]

> "He has at this point accomplished his main purposes in presenting the credentials of the King and the kingdom program of the Jews. The King has shown Himself by His words and His works to be Israel's Messiah. Because Israel refused to accept Him as their King, the kingdom is taken from them and given to a nation bringing forth fruit worthy of repentance. However, this situation will exist only until the Son of Man comes in His glory. At that time, all unrighteousness will be vindicated and Christ shall reign as Israel's King over the nations of the earth."[1261]

VII. THE CRUCIFIXION AND RESURRECTION OF THE KING CHS. 26—28

The key phrase in Matthew's Gospel "And it came about that when Jesus had finished" (26:1) indicates another major transition (cf. 7:28; 11:1; 13:53; 19:1). As usual, it occurs at the end of a major address. In this case, it introduces the final and longest continuous narrative section that reaches its climax with another address, in this case a very brief but important one (28:18-20). The Great Commission was the King's final speech that set the final course for His disciples during the age between Jesus' two advents. The record of Jesus' crucifixion and resurrection should motivate the modern reader to fulfill the Great Commission. It is in view of what Jesus did for us that we should make disciples of Him all over the world.

> "As the culmination of Matthew's story, the passion account also constitutes the decisive stage in Jesus' conflict with Israel (chaps. 26—28).[1262] Here the resolution of this conflict works itself out in dramatic detail."[1263]

The narrative section consists of two parts, the crucifixion (chs. 26—27) and the resurrection of the King (28:1-15).

[1260] Kiddle, p. 44.

[1261] Toussaint, *Behold the . . .*, p. 292.

[1262] Footnote 10: For a more detailed treatment of the passion account in Matthew, see Frank J. Matera, *Passion Narratives and Gospel Theologies: Interpreting the Synoptics through Their Passion Stories*, chs. 4-6; and Donald Senior, *The Passion of Jesus in the Gospel of Matthew*.

[1263] Kingsbury, *Matthew as . . .*, p. 84.

"Relentlessly the events of the King's life move toward His death on the cross. He has completed His public manifestation to Israel and the nation has rejected Him. In addition, the disciples have been instructed concerning the rejection of Israel and the spiritual basis of entrance into the earthly kingdom. All that remains is the work of the Messiah to provide the means whereby those who exercise faith in Him may enter His kingdom. This work, the death and resurrection of the King, is recounted very succinctly by Matthew. In a large part Matthew's argument is accomplished, and these last events form a fitting conclusion to his book since Jesus here moves through defeat unto victory."[1264]

A. THE KING'S CRUCIFIXION CHS. 26—27

Matthew reported Jesus crucifixion in five scenes: the preparations for it, Jesus' arrest, His trials, the crucifixion itself, and His burial.

1. Preparations for Jesus' crucifixion 26:1-46

There were several events that led up to Jesus' arrest. Matthew did not present them in strict chronological order but in a logical narrative order.

Jesus' fourth passion prediction and the plot to betray Him 26:1-5 (cf. Mark 14:1-2; Luke 22:1-2)

These verses record the fourth major prediction of Jesus' death that He gave His disciples (cf. 16:21; 17:22-23; 20:18-19). Matthew just finished recording Jesus' claim to judge humankind (25:31-46). Now he wrote that the Judge would suffer condemnation from the condemned. Jesus had warned His enemies about the consequences of hypocrisy (23:12-31). Now we learn that they were paying no heed to His warning, but were hypocritically proceeding to crucify Him. This irony points out Jesus' sovereign control over the affairs that led to His death, and it is an example of masterful narrative composition.

26:1-2   Jesus evidently said these words sometime on Wednesday, the same day as His controversy with the religious leaders (21:23—23:39) and the Olivet Discourse (chs. 24—25). Jesus predicted that His enemies would deliver Him up to die by "crucifixion" in two days. The connection between Jesus' death and the Passover would emerge more clearly when Jesus celebrated that feast with His disciples the next day. Thursday, then, was a day of rest for Jesus, during which He prepared for His great agony on Friday.

26:3-5   Opposition to Jesus had been rising for some time (cf. 12:14; 21:45-46). Matthew's narration of this plot's advance toward its climax, following Jesus' prediction (v. 2), has the effect of showing that His enemies' conspiracy was ultimately a result of Jesus' sovereign authority. He was not a powerless pawn under their control. He was really orchestrating His own passion.

"The chief priests and the elders" represented the clerical and lay members of the Sanhedrin, respectively (cf. 21:23). At that time in history, Rome appointed Israel's "high priest," but typically someone bought the office.[1265] Annas had been the high priest until A.D. 15, when the Romans deposed him and set up his son Eleazar in his place. Eleazar served for about two years (A.D. 16-17), until the Romans replaced him with Joseph Caiaphas in A.D. 18. "Caiaphas" held the office until his death in A.D. 36.[1266] His unusually long tenure reflects his political skill and his acceptability to the Roman prefects.

The Old Testament regarded the high priest as high priest until his death. Consequently the Jews still viewed Annas as the high priest. This probably explains why Matthew and John spoke of Caiaphas as the high priest (John 11:49), but Luke said Annas was the high priest (Luke 3:2; Acts 4:6). Annas was Caiaphas' father-in-law, and he continued to exercise much power—even after the Romans forced him out of office.

The Jewish leaders plotted to execute an innocent man in the very place where justice should have been strongest. *The spiritual leader* of Israel—"the high priest"—took a leading role in this travesty! Matthew's original Jewish readers could not help marveling at this injustice. However, "the chief priests and elders" were representatives of the people, so the people shared part of the blame. The leaders resorted to deceit, because they could not trap Jesus with questions and turn the crowds against Him, or take Him by force.

"In portraying the leaders throughout the passion, Matthew orchestrates numerous variations both on this theme of 'deception' and on the related theme of 'self-deception.'"[1267]

[1264]Toussaint, Behold the . . ., p. 295.
[1265]Edersheim, *The Temple*, p. 94. See Josephus, *Antiquities of . . .*, 20:8:5: footnote, and 20:10:1, for lists of all of Israel's high priests.
[1266]Carson, "Matthew," p. 524. Compare the list of high priests from the accession of Herod the Great to the destruction of Jerusalem in Edersheim, *The Life . . .*, 2:702.
[1267]Kingsbury, *Matthew as . . .*, p. 123.

Jerusalem's population swelled with pilgrims during Passover season. Since Jesus had a large following, especially among the Galileans, the leaders realized they had to plan to do away with Him secretly, and carefully, lest popular sentiment turn against them.[1268] They did not know how to solve their problem—until Judas volunteered to hand Jesus over to them privately.

Jesus' anointing for burial 26:6-13 (cf. Mark 14:3-9; John 12:1-8)

26:6-7   This event evidently happened on the previous Saturday evening "in Bethany" (John 12:1).[1269] The reference to two days before the Passover in verse 2 dates the plot to seize Jesus, not the anointing in Simon's house.[1270] Apparently Jesus spent the evening of that Saturday in "the home of Simon," a healed "leper," with His disciples and other guests. John recorded that Lazarus was there, his sister Martha helped with the serving, and their sister Mary was the woman who broke the vial and anointed Jesus' head (and feet, John 12:2-3). Perhaps Matthew did not mention them by name in order to keep Jesus central in his story. John further recorded that the pound of perfume cost 300 denarii, about one year's wages for a working man (John 12:3, 5). Matthew and Mark just said it was "very" expensive ("costly"). The perfume was *nard* that probably came from India.[1271]

26:8-9   Evidently Judas Iscariot led the disciples' criticism of Mary's act (John 12:4). According to the Gospel records, every time Mary tried to do something for Jesus she was misunderstood.[1272] The disciples failed to appreciate the significance of what Mary was doing, and that such an anointing was appropriate, in view of Jesus' identity as "the Lord's Anointed" and His impending death (cf. 16:21-28; 17:22-23; 20:18-19). Regardless of Judas' true motive, the other disciples felt that Mary's gift was inappropriate since so many poor people could have profited from it. They did not realize that the sacrifice Jesus was about to make would solve the basic need of every poor person throughout all of history. Their objection was not evil but wrong, due to lack of understanding. Mary does not seem to have understood that Jesus was going to die any more than the disciples. She evidently made her great sacrifice simply because she loved Jesus.

26:10-11   Jesus probably overheard His disciples talking, though His awareness of their thoughts could have been supernatural (cf. 16:8). Jesus regarded the disciples' outspoken criticism of Mary as a "bother" to her. This beautiful thing that Mary did, which Jesus called "a good deed," was scornfully named "this waste" by the disciples. The disciples would "always have the poor" (people), whom they could help with good deeds, but they would not have the incarnate Son of Man with them much longer.

"The disciples' concern for the poor is by no means incorrect. In this one instance, however, the timing was wrong."[1273]

"Implicitly, the distinction Jesus makes is a high christological claim, for it not only shows that he foresees his impending departure but also that he himself, who is truly 'gentle and humble in heart' (11:29), *deserves* this lavish outpouring of love and expense.

"Jesus is the poor, righteous Sufferer par excellence; and the opportunity to help him in any way will soon be gone forever [cf. Ps. 41]."[1274]

26:12   Normally friends of the deceased would "prepare" the body "for burial" after death, but that was impossible in the case of criminals.[1275] Mary may not have understood the full significance of what she was doing, but Jesus used the situation to remind His disciples of His coming crucifixion.

26:13   The "gospel" or *good news* to which Jesus referred was probably the good news about His death, namely, that it is the basis for salvation (v. 12). This is probably not a reference to the gospel of the kingdom. In either case, Mary's act has become a part of the gospel story in the larger sense, because the Holy Spirit preserved the record of it in Scripture. Jesus introduced this prediction with His characteristic phrase that highlighted something especially important: "Truly I say to you" or "I tell you the truth."

[1268]Cf. Josephus, *Antiquities of . . .*, 20:5:1-3, for evidence that many tumults and seditions arose during the Jewish festivals.

[1269]Hoehner, *Chronological Aspects . . .*, p. 91.

[1270]M'Neile, p. 373; Hendricksen, p. 898; Taylor, p. 527.

[1271]Carson, "Matthew," p. 526.

[1272]Wiersbe, 1:95.

[1273]Hagner, *Matthew 14—28*, p. 759.

[1274]Carson, "Matthew," p. 527.

[1275]D. Daube, "The Anointing at Bethany and Jesus' Burial," *Anglican Theological Review* 32 (1950):187-88.

The agreement to betray Jesus 26:14-16 (cf. Mark 14:10-11; Luke 22:3-6)

Here the word "then" probably identifies a logical connection with what preceded.[1276] Evidently "Judas Iscariot" made these plans the same day that Jesus predicted His crucifixion in two days, namely, on Wednesday (vv. 1-5). None of the evangelists recorded Judas' motives for betraying Jesus, but Judas may have taken offense at Jesus' rebuke on the previous Saturday evening (vv. 10-13). Perhaps the fact that Jesus permitted Mary's extravagant act without rebuke convinced him that Jesus was not the Messiah.[1277] This may have been part of his motivation. The "chief priests" were the clerical leaders of Israel. They were able to do Jesus in.

The "30 pieces of silver" they agreed to pay Judas was a paltry sum (in contrast to the "high price" at which Mary evaluated Jesus, v. 9), and fulfilled Zechariah 11:12. The amount constituted a month's wages, if the silver pieces were denarii, which seems likely.[1278] Matthew did not refer to this as a fulfillment of prophecy here, but he did later in 27:9-10. Nevertheless he was careful to make the verbal correspondence with the Zechariah passage close here.[1279] This was the price an Israelite had to pay his neighbor if his ox accidentally gored his neighbor's slave to death (Exod. 21:32). This small amount of money shows the light esteem with which the chief priests and Judas regarded Jesus (cf. Isa. 53:3).

> "... tragically, Judas, in selling his services to the chief priests to betray Jesus, unwittingly acts in a manner that is the exact opposite of 'servanthood': Jesus is the servant par excellence, for he delivers himself to death in order that others might gain life; by contrast, Judas delivers Jesus to death in order that he might gain advantage for himself . . ."[1280]

Jesus' last Passover 26:17-30

In this section Matthew emphasized the preparations for the Passover meal, Jesus' prediction of His betrayal, and the institution of the Lord's Supper.

Preparations for the Passover 26:17-19 (cf. Mark 14:12-16; Luke 22:7-13)

26:17   The first day of the Feast of Unleavened Bread would have been Thursday, the fourteenth of Nisan (cf. Exod. 12:18).[1281] The Jews commonly spoke of "Passover and the Feast of Unleavened Bread," combined, as the "Feast of Unleavened Bread," or simply, "Unleavened Bread."[1282]

> "It was probably after the early meal, and when the eating of leaven had ceased, that Jesus began preparations for the Paschal Supper."[1283]

26:18-19   "The city" was Jerusalem. The identity of the "certain man" to whom Jesus referred His disciples, Peter and John (Luke 22:8), was not important enough for any of the evangelists to record. Obviously Jesus was planning this Passover meal carefully (cf. 21:2-3). To the disciples and the man responsible for the room, the "time" to which Jesus referred was the time of the Passover. Later the disciples realized that by "My time," Jesus meant His time of suffering, when He would culminate His mission—the Passion. They complied with Jesus' instructions. Perhaps Jesus kept the location of the Passover secret so Judas could not inform the religious leaders.

Jesus' prediction of His betrayal 26:20-25 (cf. Mark 14:17-21; Luke 22:14-16, 21-30; John 13:21-30)

26:20-22   This Passover would have taken place on Thursday evening. I have dealt with the problems involving the harmonization of John 13:1, 27; 18:28; 19:14, and 36—with the observance of the Passover that the Synoptic evangelists recorded—in my notes on the Gospel of John. The Jews did not eat the Passover meal until after sundown. Those of them living in Palestine ate it in Jerusalem or not at all.[1284] This fact helps us understand that a large number of pilgrims would have been in Jerusalem then. The Rabbis insisted that at least some of the Passover be eaten in a recumbent position, since this was the

---

[1276]Plummer, p. 356; M'Neile, p. 376.

[1277]Walvoord, *Matthew: . . .*, p. 209.

[1278]France, *The Gospel . . .*, p. 979.

[1279]Charles C. Torrey, "The Foundry of the Second Temple at Jerusalem," *Journal of Biblical Literature* 55 (December 1936):249.

[1280]Kingsbury, *Matthew as . . .*, p. 143.

[1281]For detailed discussions of the chronology of these last days, see Hoehner, *Chronological Aspects . . .*, pp. 81-93; Carson, "Matthew," pp. 528-32; and France, *The Gospel . . .*, pp. 980-85.

[1282]Josephus, *Antiquities of . . .*, 2:15:1.

[1283]Edersheim, *The Life . . .*, 2:480.

[1284]Carson, "Matthew," p. 534.

position in which free men ate. Slaves, on the other hand, ate standing.[1285] Sometime during the meal, Jesus announced that one of the Twelve would "betray" Him to His enemies. As the significance of this new prediction sank in, each of the disciples present asked Jesus if it was himself. The form of the question in the Greek text expected a negative reply: "Surely not I, Lord?"

26:23   Jesus' answer did not identify the betrayer specifically. His response meant that the betrayer was someone who had already "dipped his hand" into the same "bowl" as Jesus had, namely, one of the Twelve, someone close to Jesus. This reply stressed the heinousness of the betrayal and the graciousness of Jesus.

> "The whole incident must be interpreted as a gracious attempt on the part of Jesus to make Judas realize his terrible sin and turn from it before it was too late."[1286]

> If this was the main course of the meal, the bowl would have contained herbs and a fruit purée, that everyone would have been scooping out with bread to eat with the lamb.

> "Toward midafternoon of Thursday, 14 Nisan, the lambs (one per 'household'—a convenient group of perhaps ten or twelve people) would be brought to the temple court where the priests sacrificed them. The priests took the blood and passed it in basins along a line till it was poured out at the foot of the altar. They also burned the lambs' fat on the altar of burnt offerings. The singing of the *Hallel* (Pss 113—18) accompanied these steps.

> "After sunset (i.e., now 15 Nisan), the 'household' would gather in a home to eat the Passover lamb, which by this time would have been roasted with bitter herbs. The head of the household began the meal with the thanksgiving for that feast day (the Passover *Kiddush*) and for the wine, praying over the first of four cups. A preliminary course of greens and bitter herbs was, apparently, followed by the Passover *haggadah*—in which a boy would ask the meaning of all this, and the head of the household would explain the symbols in terms of the Exodus (cf. M[ishnah] *Pesahim* 10:4-5)—and the singing of the first part of the *Hallel* (Ps 113 or Pss 113—14). Though the precise order is disputed, apparently a second cup of wine introduced the main course, which was followed by a third cup known as the 'cup of blessing,' accompanied by another prayer of thanksgiving. The participants then sang the rest of the *Hallel* (Pss 114—18 or 115—18) and probably drank a fourth cup of wine."[1287]

26:24   The "Son of Man" title here combines Jesus' messianic and Suffering Servant roles almost equally, as is clear from the context. Likewise Jesus' "woe" here expressed a combination of compassion and condemnation (cf. 18:17). Jesus did not identify the Old Testament prophecy that He had in mind. It may have been Isaiah 53:7-9, Daniel 9:26, or a combination of passages such as those dealing with the Passover lamb. The fact that God sovereignly planned for Messiah to die does not mitigate Judas' human responsibility in betraying Him. Jesus' death resulted in salvation for many, but it meant personal and eternal ruin for Judas.

26:25   Judas' hypocritical question, which Matthew only among the evangelists recorded, stresses again the awfulness of Judas' action in betraying Jesus. Probably Judas felt pressure to repeat the question the other disciples had asked, or else he would give himself away by his silence. "Rabbi" was a respectful title. The other disciples had called Jesus "Lord" (v. 22). Perhaps the different title suggested that Judas viewed Jesus differently from the other disciples.[1288] Jesus' reply was sufficiently vague to lead the other disciples to conclude that Judas was not guilty—and Judas himself, to wonder if Jesus had found him out. "You said it, not I," gives the sense of Jesus' response. The Greek text reads "*su eipas*."[1289] The NIV translation, "Yes, it is you," is too strong. Jesus later said the identical words to Pilate (v. 64). Judas then left the room (John 13:30).

Jesus' institution of the Lord's Supper 26:26-30 (cf. Mark 14:22-25; Luke 22:17-20; 1 Cor. 11:23-26)

26:26   "And" introduces the second thing Matthew recorded that happened, as Jesus and His disciples were eating the Passover meal, the first being Jesus' announcement about His betrayer (v. 21). Jesus "took bread" (Gr. *artos*, 4:4; 6:11; 15:2, 26),

---

[1285]Edersheim, *The Temple*, p. 234.

[1286]Walvoord, *Matthew: . . .*, p. 213.

[1287]Carson, "Matthew," p. 533.

[1288]Lenski, p. 1019.

[1289]Cf. Carr, p. 290; M'Neile, p. 381; Plummer, p. 361.

specifically the unleavened bread on the table before Him (cf. Exod. 12:15; 13:3, 7; Deut. 16:3), and then gave thanks to God ("a blessing"). A traditional prayer that many Jews used when thanking God for food was, "Blessed are you, O Lord our God, King of the universe, who brings forth bread from the earth." Perhaps Jesus said some such words. He then "broke" the bread into parts, distributed it among "the disciples," and instructed them to "eat" it, with the words: "This is My body."

The words "This is My body" were not part of the Passover ritual. Jesus' actions of breaking the bread, and then distributing it, were both significant. His body, like the bread, would be broken, though His bones were not, and His disciples would need to partake of Him personally. Jesus was linking His sacrifice with redemption history when He instituted this rite during the Passover meal. The Israelites associated their redemption from Egypt with eating the Passover meal. Now, Jesus' disciples were to associate their redemption with Jesus' death, symbolized in this similar meal.

There have been various interpretations of what Jesus meant when He said, "This is My body." There are four main views. Roman Catholics take it as a literal statement meaning the bread really becomes the body of Christ, and the contents of the cup literally become the blood of Christ. This is true when duly authorized representatives of the church conduct the service properly. This is the *transubstantiation* view. Adherents believe God transfers the body and blood of Christ into the substance of the elements. This view holds that the bread and wine *really* become the physical body and blood of Christ.[1290]

A second view is not quite so literal. It is the *consubstantiation* view and, as the word implies, its advocates see the body and blood of Christ as present "in, with, and under" the elements. Christ is really present, though not physically present, according to this Lutheran view.[1291]

The third major view is the *spiritual presence* view that Presbyterians, and other followers of Calvin's teaching on the Lord's Supper, hold. For them the spiritual presence of Christ is in the elements and, as in the former views, God ministers grace to the communicant in a concrete way through participation.[1292]

"Now, if anyone should ask me how this takes place, I shall not be ashamed to confess that it is a secret too lofty for either my mind to comprehend or my words to declare."[1293]

The fourth view is the *memorial* view. Advocates believe that when Jesus said: "This is My body," He meant: "This represents My body." In other words, they understand His statement as completely metaphorical (cf. 13:19-23, 36-39; John 15:1). A metaphor is a comparison, in which one thing is likened to a different thing by being spoken of as if it *were* that other thing (e.g., "All the world is a stage."). Advocates view the elements as pictures or emblems of the body and blood of Christ. In contrast to the preceding views, this one does not see Christ present—*in any special sense*—in the elements. Ulrich Zwingli, the Swiss reformer, promoted this view. Today most of the churches from the Anabaptist branch of Protestantism (i.e., Baptists, Methodists, Mennonites, independent Bible churches, Evangelical Free churches, et al.) hold this interpretation.[1294] I believe this view best represents the total revelation concerning the Lord's Supper in Scripture.

Some Christian groups refer to the Lord's Supper as one of the "sacraments."[1295] They mean the elements minister grace to the participant in a more direct and physical way than those who speak of it as an "ordinance," assuming they are using these terms properly. An ordinance or sacrament is a rite the Lord commanded His followers to observe.

26:27   *This* "cup" was probably the *third* cup drunk in the Passover meal, namely, the "cup of blessing." It contained wine diluted with water. This diluted wine was what the Jews usually drank with their meals.[1296] Jesus then gave "thanks" again. The Greek word *eucharistesas* ("gave thanks") is a cognate of *euchariste* ("thanksgiving") from which we get the English word "Eucharist," another name for the Lord's Supper.

[1290]See Calvin, *Institutes of . . .*, 4:17:14 for refutation.

[1291]Lenski, pp. 1026-31.

[1292]Calvin, *Institutes . . .*, 4:17:1-3.

[1293]Ibid., 4:17:32.

[1294]See Albert H. Newman, *A Manual of Church History*, 2:312-13. For more information on these views, see articles on the Lord's Supper and synonymous terms in Bible encyclopaedias.

[1295]E.g., Calvin, *Institutes of . . .*, 4:19:1-2.

[1296] See Robert Stein, "Wine-Drinking in New Testament Times," *Christianity Today* 19:19 (June 20, 1975):9-11; Norman Geisler, "A Christian Perspective on Wine-Drinking," *Bibliotheca Sacra* 139:553 (January-March 1982):46-56.

"... to this day, in every Jewish home, at a certain part of the Paschal service—just after the 'third cup,' or the 'cup of blessing,' has been drunk—the door is opened to admit Elijah the prophet as forerunner of the Messiah, while appropriate passages are at the same time read which foretell the destruction of all heathen nations (Ps. 79:6; 69:25; Lam. 3:66). It is a remarkable coincidence that, in instituting His own Supper, the Lord Jesus connected the symbol, not of judgment, but of His dying love, with this 'third cup.'"[1297]

Jesus commanded "all" of His disciples to "drink from" the cup. They had to personally appropriate what symbolized His blood, as they had to personally appropriate what symbolized His body. Together, these elements represented *Jesus Himself*.

"... he [Jesus] ordained the cup separately from the bread in order to teach us that he suffices for drink no less than for food."[1298]

The Eleven learned to appreciate the larger significance of these things after His resurrection (cf. 1 Cor. 11:23-28).

26:28   Jesus revealed that the sacrificial death He was about to die would ratify (make valid) "a covenant" (Gr. *diatheke*) with His people. Similarly, the sacrificial death of animals had originally ratified the Abrahamic and Mosaic Covenants with Abraham and Moses (Gen. Gen. 15:9-10; Exod. 24:8). In all cases, blood symbolized the life of the substitute sacrifice (cf. Lev. 17:11). Jeremiah had prophesied that God would make a New Covenant with His people in the future (Jer. 31:31-34; 32:37-40; cf. Exod. 24:8; Luke 22:20). When Jesus died, His blood ratified that covenant. This upper room meal memorialized the ratification of that covenant. Messiah saved His people from their sins by His sacrificial death (cf. 1:21). The resulting relationship between God and His people is a covenant relationship.

"It appears, then, that Jesus understands the covenant he is introducing to be the fulfillment of Jeremiah's prophecies and the antitype of the Sinai covenant [cf. Exod. 24:8]. His sacrifice is thus foretold both in redemption history and in the prophetic word. The Exodus becomes a 'type' of a new and greater deliverance; and as the people of God in the OT prospectively celebrated in the first Passover their escape from Egypt, anticipating their arrival in the Promised Land, so the people of God here prospectively celebrate their deliverance from sin and bondage, anticipating the coming kingdom ..."[1299]

The Greek preposition translated "on behalf of" or "for" is *peri*. Mark used the preposition *hyper*, also translated "on behalf of" or "for" (Mark 14:24). Both Greek words imply substitution, though the force of *peri* is more on the fact that Jesus died for us. The force of *hyper* is that He died both for us and in our place.[1300] The "many" for whom Christ died includes everyone (cf. 20:28; Isa. 53:11-12). Evidently Jesus used "many" in its Semitic sense to contrast with His one all-sufficient sacrifice (cf. Rom. 5:15-19; Heb. 9:26-28; 10:10, 12, 14).[1301] Jesus' death provides the basis for God to forgive sinners. The phrase "for forgiveness of sins" goes back to Jeremiah 31:34, where forgiveness of sins is one of the blessings of the New Covenant. There are many allusions to the Suffering Servant in this verse (cf. Isa. 42:6; 49:8; 52:13—53:12).

Jeremiah predicted that God would make a New Covenant "with the house of Israel and with the house of Judah" (Jer. 31:31). This is a reference to the nation of Israel. Therefore the New Covenant would be a covenant with Israel particularly (but not exclusively). Jeremiah and Ezekiel predicted many blessings that would come to Israel under the New Covenant. The Jews would experience regeneration (Jer. 31:33), forgiveness of sins (Jer. 31:34), other spiritual blessings (Jer. 31:33-34; 32:38-40), and regathering as a nation (Jer. 32:37). Jeremiah also prophesied that this covenant would be everlasting (Jer. 32:40), and that Israel would enjoy safety and prosperity in the Promised Land (Jer. 32:37; Ezek. 34:25-31). Ezekiel added that God would dwell forever with Israel in His sanctuary (Ezek. 37:26-28).

Even though Jesus ratified the New Covenant when He died on the cross, the blessings that will come to Israel did not begin then. They will begin when Jesus returns and establishes His kingdom on the earth. However, the church enters into some of the blessing of the New Covenant now.[1302] The Apostle Paul wrote of Christians serving under the New Covenant (2 Cor. 3:1—6:10; Gal. 4:21-31; cf. 1 Cor. 11:25). The writer of the Epistle to the Hebrews also spoke to Christians of presently enjoying benefits of the New Covenant (Heb. 7:1—10:18).

[1297]Edersheim, *The Temple*, p. 230.

[1298]Calvin, *Institutes of . . .*, 4:17:47.

[1299]Carson, "Matthew," p. 538.

[1300]Richard C. Trench, *Synonyms of the New Testament*, p. 291.

[1301]See *Theological Dictionary of the New Testament*, s.v. "*polloi*," by J. Jeremias, 6:543-45.

[1302]Cf. Kelly, p. 491; Scofield, *The Scofield . . .*, pp. 1297-98, footnote 1.

The New Covenant is similar to a "last will and testament." When Jesus died, the provisions of His will went into effect. Immediately all people began to benefit from His death. For example, the forgiveness of sins and the possession of the Holy Spirit become the inheritance of everyone who trusts in Him, Jew and Gentile alike. However, those provisions of Jesus' "will" having to do with Israel as His particular focus of blessing, will not take effect until the nation turns to Him in repentance at His Second Coming. Thus the church partakes in the benefits of the New Covenant, even though God made it with Israel particularly.

"The church's relationship to the new covenant is parallel in certain respects to its connection with the kingdom promises of Israel. The church is constituted, blessed, and directed by the same Person who shall bring about the literal Jewish kingdom. It also will reign with Christ during the millennial age. In a parallel manner, the church participates in the benefits of the new covenant. Therefore, in instituting the new covenant, Christ makes provisions for this covenant to include the present program of the church as well as the future age of Israel."[1303]

Amillenarians and postmillenarians view the relationship of the church to the New Covenant differently. They believe the church replaces Israel in God's plan.[1304] The only way they can explain how the church fulfills all the promises in Jeremiah and Ezekiel is to take them non-literally. Yet the Apostle Paul revealed that God is not finished with "Israel"; it has a future in God's plan (Rom. 11:26). It is very helpful to remember that every reference to Israel in the New Testament can and does refer to the physical descendants of Jacob.

Some premillenarians believe that the church has no relationship to the New Covenant that Jeremiah and Ezekiel prophesied.[1305] They see two new covenants, one with Israel that Jesus will ratify when He returns, and one with the church that He ratified when He died. Most premillenarians, including myself, reject this view because everything said about the New Covenant can be explained adequately with only one New Covenant.

26:29   As the first Passover looked forward to deliverance and settlement in the Promised Land, so the Lord's Supper looked forward to deliverance and settlement in the promised kingdom. Disciples are to observe the Lord's Supper only until He returns (1 Cor. 11:26). Then we will enjoy the messianic banquet together with our Savior and King (Isa. 25:6; cf. Matt. 8:11). Probably Jesus spoke these words after drinking the third cup of the Passover ritual.

"The four cups were meant to correspond to the fourfold promise of Exodus 6:6-7. The third cup, the 'cup of blessing' used by Jesus in the words of institution, is thus associated with redemption (Exod. 6:6); but the fourth cup corresponds to the promise 'I will take you as my own people, and I will be your God' (Exod. 6:7; . . .). Thus Jesus is simultaneously pledging that he will drink the 'bitter cup' immediately ahead of him and vowing not to drink the cup of consummation, the cup that promises the divine presence, till the kingdom in all its fullness has been ushered in. Then he will drink the cup with his people."[1306]

By referring to drinking the wine ("fruit of the vine") "anew" (Gr. *kainon*, i.e., new in a qualitatively different way), Jesus meant that He and the disciples anticipated suffering and death, but in the future they would experience the joy of the messianic banquet and "kingdom."[1307]

This verse shows that Jesus' death was very near.[1308] It also reveals that God has a definite eschatological program.[1309] Jesus wanted His disciples to labor for Him in the present age, joyfully anticipating reunion with Him in the kingdom.[1310]

26:30   What Jesus and the disciples sang was undoubtedly the last part of the *Hallel* (Ps. 114—118 or 115—118; cf. Mark 14:26; Luke 22:39; John 18:1). The Jews customarily sang this antiphonally: with the leader, in this case Jesus, singing the first lines, and the other participants responding with "Hallelujah!" What Jesus sang included a commitment to keep His vows

---

[1303]Toussaint, *Behold the . . .*, p. 303.

[1304]E.g., Carr, p. 291.

[1305]E.g., Darby, 3:281; Chafer, *Systematic Theology*, 4:325; L. Laurenson, *Messiah, the Prince*, pp. 187-88; and John R. Master, "The New Covenant," in *Issues in Dispensationalism*, pp. 93-110.

[1306]Carson, "Matthew," p. 539.

[1307]Plummer, p. 365.

[1308]M'Neile, p. 383.

[1309]Allen, p. 277.

[1310]Toussaint, *Behold the . . .*, p. 303.

(Ps. 116:12-13). Another section of the *Hallel* referred to Messiah's appearing (Ps. 118:25-26). It can be edifying to read these psalms, while thinking of Jesus singing them in the upper room with His disciples.

"The disciples in the immediacy of the moment could not have begun to realize the significance of what Jesus was saying and doing. This they would first do after the resurrection. But by the time Matthew's readers read this account, the Eucharist had long since become a fixed component in their worship; hence they read the narrative with fuller understanding."[1311]

Jesus' prediction of the disciples' abandonment and denial 26:31-35 (cf. Mark 14:27-31; Luke 22:31-38; John 13:31-38)

Jesus evidently gave this prediction before He and His disciples left the upper room (cf. Luke 21:31-38; John 13:36-38). Matthew and Mark probably placed it where they did, in their Gospels, to stress the gravity of the disciples' defection and Peter's denial.[1312] Matthew presented Jesus as knowing exactly what lay ahead of Him. He was not a victim of fate, but He deliberately approached His death as a willing Sacrifice, and prepared His disciples carefully for the trauma of that event.

26:31   "Then" (Gr. *tote*) here expresses a logical, rather than a temporal, connection with what precedes. Jesus emphasized that the disciples would desert Him very soon, that very "night." They would find Him to be a source of stumbling (Gr. *skandalon*, cf. 11:6). Jesus' arrest would trip them up, and they would temporarily stop following Him faithfully. They still did not understand that the Messiah must die. By quoting Zechariah 13:7 freely, Jesus was telling them again that He would die, and that their scattering from Him was something within God's sovereign plan. This did not excuse their failure, but it prepared them for it and helped them recover after it.

In Zechariah 13:1-6, the prophet spoke of a day when, because of prevailing apostasy, "the Shepherd" would be cut down and His followers would be scattered. The "sheep" in the prophecy are the Jews, many of whom would depart from the Shepherd, but a third of whom would remain. The disciples constituted the core of this remnant that Zechariah predicted God would bless in the future (Zech. 13:7-9).

26:32   Jesus assured the disciples that He would meet them in Galilee after His resurrection. Following as it does the announcement of their abandoning Him, this promise assured them that He would not abandon them. Jesus would precede them "to Galilee," where He would be waiting for them when they arrived (cf. John 21).

26:33-35   Peter was ready to suffer martyrdom with Jesus, but he was unprepared for Jesus' voluntary self-sacrifice. Despite Peter's claim, Jesus explained that his defection was only hours away. The crowing of cocks signals the morning. Peter refused to accept the possibility that he would deny Jesus. The language he used, the rare subjunctive of the Greek verb *dei* ("if I *must*"), may imply that he really did not think Jesus was going to die.[1313]

Jesus' prayer to His Father in Gethsemane 26:36-46 (cf. Mark 14:32-42; Luke 22:40-46)

This pericope illustrates the importance of facing temptation with vigilance and prayer. What is more important, it reveals Jesus' attitude toward what He was about to do. Until now, Jesus seems to have been anticipating His death with calm control and great courage. Here He appears under deep emotional stress. These attitudes harmonize with His being both the Son of God and the Servant who came to give His life a ransom for many (1:21; 20:28). Martyrs can face death bravely, but voluntary self-sacrifice demands greater strength. Moreover, Jesus knew that God would forsake Him when He died, because He would bear the punishment for (God's wrath against) the sins of humanity. As Jesus' death was unique, so was His anguish as He anticipated it.

26:36-37   Having left the upper room, traditionally located on the southern part of Mt. Zion, west of the City of David (Old Jerusalem), Jesus took His disciples east, out of Jerusalem, and across the Kidron Valley to the western slope of Mt. Olivet.[1314]

"The streets could scarcely be said to be deserted, for, from many a house shone the festive lamp, and many a company may still have been gathered; and everywhere was the bustle of preparation for going up to the Temple, the gates of which were thrown open at midnight."[1315]

[1311]Hagner, *Matthew 14—28*, p. 775.

[1312]Carson, "Matthew," p. 540.

[1313]Ibid., p. 542.

[1314]See the diagram of Jerusalem in New Testament Times at the end of these notes.

[1315]Edersheim, *The Life . . .*, 2:533.

The word "Gethsemane" means "oil press." This olive press was in an olive grove where Jesus and His disciples had been before (John 18:1-2). Peter and the disciples had just boasted of their strength, whereas Jesus told them they were weak (vv. 31-35). In contrast, Jesus sensed His own weakness, and thus made plans to gain strength from His Father.[1316] This section of the text is full of contrasts involving strength and weakness (cf. 2 Cor. 12:9-10).

Jesus left most of the disciples in one part of the olive orchard, and took Peter, James, and John with Him to another area (cf. 17:1; Mark 5:37; Luke 8:51). There He began to release some of the emotions that He had held in check thus far. He became grieved or sorrowful (Gr. *lypeisthai*); and distressed or troubled (Gr. *ademonein*). The second Greek word implies, "a restless, distracted, shrinking from some trouble, or thought of trouble, which nevertheless cannot be escaped."[1317]

"No man, in sinful and mortal flesh, can understand the conflict in the holy soul of Jesus who had never experienced the slightest shadow of sin and had never known any barrier between Himself and the Father."[1318]

26:38   The "soul" here (Gr. *psyche*) represents the whole person. Jesus meant that He felt sorrowful, painful grief (*agony* affecting His mind, will, emotions, and body) so deeply that He felt that it would almost kill Him ("to the point of death").[1319] He did not mean that He was so sad He wished He were dead. Jesus' words recall the refrain of Psalms 42:5, 11 and 43:5, which He probably had in mind. He shared these feelings with the chosen three disciples, in order to encourage them to "watch" and "pray" with Him.

26:39   Jesus' prostrate posture ("on His face") reflected the intense anguish He felt. He addressed God as "My Father" (cf. 6:9). This title stresses the intimacy that Jesus felt with God (cf. Mark 14:36). This is the only time, according to the Gospels, that Jesus addressed God this way. In view of the limits that His incarnation involved, Jesus may not have known if another way to provide redemption existed (cf. 24:36), though this seems unlikely.

"We are here in full view of the deepest mystery of our faith: the two Natures in One Person. Both Natures spake [*sic*] here, and the 'if it be possible' of St. Matthew and St. Mark is in St. Luke 'if Thou be willing.'"[1320]

In one sense God can do anything, but in another sense He binds Himself to certain courses of action because of His own purposes. Jesus was asking for a release ("let this . . . pass"), "if possible," from having to undergo the outpouring of God's wrath ("this cup") for humankind's sins on the cross (cf. 4:1-11; 16:21-23).[1321] Notwithstanding, He wanted something more than that. Above all else, He wanted His Father's "will" to happen. He was submitting to suffering and death, if this was the only way to provide salvation, but He requested another solution "if possible." The "cup" is an Old Testament figure for suffering and death under the wrath of God (cf. v. 27; 20:22-23; Ps. 11:6; 75:7-8; Isa. 51:17, 22; Jer. 25:15-16, 27-29; et al.).[1322]

This is an excellent model prayer when we do not know the will of God specifically. We can request our preference, as Jesus did, but we should also submit our preference to the will of God, whatever that may be (cf. 6:10). That God may overrule our wants does not make prayer meaningless, because sometimes our preferences will be within God's will. However, He may not give us what we want without our requesting it, so we still must ask to receive (cf. James 4:2). If our preference is outside God's will, His denying our request will be a positive answer to our prayer, if we want His will above all else.

26:40-41   Jesus returned to the inner circle of disciples only to find them "sleeping." He wakened them and addressed His question to Peter as the disciples' representative. His question contained a plural "you" in the Greek text. "One hour" may be a round number, but it is undoubtedly approximate. Jesus urged them to remain spiritually alert (cf. 24:32-44), and to continue "praying" for strength to withstand the "temptation" that He had told them was coming (vv. 31-35). Even though Jesus had told them they would deny Him, their failure could have been even greater. Therefore prayer for God's sustaining grace in temptation was necessary.

One of the evidences of Jesus' greatness and His compassion, is that even in the face of the Cross, He still thought of His disciples in their lesser trials—and encouraged them.

[1316]Plummer, p. 368.

[1317]M'Neile, p. 389.

[1318]Walvoord, *Matthew: . . .*, p. 218.

[1319]Taylor, p. 553.

[1320]Edersheim, *The Life . . .*, 2:540.

[1321]See Hagner, *Matthew 14—28*, p. 785.

[1322]See C. E. B. Cranfield, "The Cup Metaphor in Mark xiv. 36 and Parallels," *Expository Times* 59 (1947-48):137-38.

The contrast between "the flesh" and "the spirit" is not between the sinful human nature and the Holy Spirit (as in Gal. 5:17), but between man's volitional strength and his physical weakness (cf. v. 35). We often want to do the right thing but find that we need supernatural assistance to accomplish it (cf. Rom. 7:15-25).

26:42-44   Jesus' repetition of His request illustrates persistence in prayer, not vain repetition. Persistence expresses the intensity with which we feel the need to have our petition met, and it shows our faith in God's ability to meet our need. Vain repetition relies on the simple repetition of words to supposedly wear God down so that He will give what we want.

Jesus' again illustrated the importance of submission to the Father's will for His disciples. He had taught them the importance of this attitude earlier (6:10). By submitting to God's will, Jesus learned obedience (Heb. 5:7-9).[1323]

"In the first garden 'Not your will but mine' changed Paradise to desert and brought man from Eden to Gethsemane. Now 'Not my will but yours' brings anguish to the man who prays it but transforms the desert into the kingdom and brings man from Gethsemane to the gates of glory."[1324]

"After three assaults had the tempter left Him in the wilderness; after the threefold conflict in the Garden he was vanquished."[1325]

26:45-46   Jesus' statement, translated as a question in the NASB and NIV versions, though more properly as a statement in the AV ("Sleep on now, and take your rest"), reflected the irony of the moment (cf. 23:2-3).[1326] Time that the disciples should have spent praying was past. Jesus' arrest and their temptation were at hand. Sadly, they might as well "sleep on."

The irony continues. The Son of Man's betrayer was about to hand over *Him who is the Messiah* to sinners. Jesus probably saw and heard the group that Judas led, making its way across the Kidron Valley, and up the Mount of Olives, to Gethsemane.

"His hour is come, and He is anxious to fulfill all that is required of Him."[1327]

Jesus had prayed: and now met His temptation with strength and dignity, and He overcame it. The disciples had slept: and now met theirs with weakness and fear, and they fell before it.

2. The arrest of Jesus 26:47-56 (cf. Mark 14:43-52; Luke 22:47-53; John 18:2-12)

26:47   The reader, who has been aware of Jesus' submissiveness to lay down His life voluntarily, may view the large armed mob as unnecessary. However, the religious leaders had feared the reaction of the people if they arrested Jesus. The people who accompanied Judas probably did not come along only to arrest Jesus, but also to restrain His disciples and other sympathizers. They probably thought they were going to have to contend with at least 11 frightened and belligerent disciples. Evidently everyone in this mob was either Jewish, from the Sanhedrin, or Roman (John 18:12).

26:48-50   Judas needed to identify Jesus because it was dark and because, even though many people knew about Jesus, far fewer had really seen Him up close. Judas turned the symbol of friendship, a kiss, into a symbol of hypocritical betrayal with his action. His greeting signal was to target Jesus, not to show affection and honor Him. Judas "kissed" Jesus repeatedly, loudly, and effusively (Gr. *katephilesen*).

Jesus' greeting, "Friend," was not intimate but gracious. Jesus' following words have been translated either as a statement or a question. As a statement, they reflect Jesus' sovereign control in this situation: "Do what you came for." As a question, they offer an ironic rebuke: "Why do you come?" Of course, Jesus knew why Judas had come.

26:51-54   John identified the aggressor as Peter and the wounded man as Malchus (John 18:10). Some have taken the description of this man, "the slave (servant) of the high priest," as indicating that he may have been the commander of the soldiers.[1328] Perhaps the other evangelists did not record Peter and Malchus' names to focus attention on Jesus. His control of this situation, even though He was the One being arrested, is an obvious emphasis by Matthew. Peter's response was predictable in view of his earlier protestations (vv. 33-35). Peter's courage was admirable, if misdirected. He rushed in to defend Jesus.

[1323]See S. Lewis Johnson Jr., "The Agony of Christ," *Bibliotheca Sacra* 124:496 (October-December 1967):303-13.

[1324]Carson, "Matthew," p. 545.

[1325]Edersheim, *The Life . . .*, 2:541.

[1326]C. F. D. Moule, *An Idiom Book of New Testament Greek*, p. 161.

[1327]Plummer, p. 372.

[1328]E.g., France, *The Gospel . . .*, p. 1013.

However, Jesus' prohibition of violence and His submission to arrest made Peter look foolish. Evidently the disciples had brought two swords with them in view of Jesus' predictions (Luke 22:38). Probably Judas' guards did not arrest Peter because Jesus restrained him.

> "Peter had argued with the Word, denied the Word, and disobeyed the Word (when he went to sleep). Now he ran ahead of the Word."[1329]

Jesus' words to Peter in verse 52 showed that violence in defense of Himself was not proper. Jesus did not mean that violence in any situation is wrong.[1330] Jesus had at His disposal more than six thousand ("12 legions") of "angels" to assist Him, plus each of His 11 faithful disciples (v. 53). He did not need Peter's help.

> "It is characteristic of this gospel that the authority and kingly majesty of Jesus should be suggested at a moment when every hope seemed to have perished."[1331]

It was necessary for Jesus to experience arrest to fulfill many "Scriptures," including all those that pertained to His death and resurrection. Jesus again voiced His commitment to the Father's will (v. 54; cf. vv. 39, 42).

26:55-56   The mob did not need to arrest Jesus secretly and violently at night. They could have found Him easily any day during the Passover season teaching in the temple courtyard. Their nighttime arrest made Jesus look like a dangerous criminal. Jesus pointed out that their time and manner of arresting Him said more about them than about Him. They were the threatening ones, not He.

> "The Lord not only reprimands His disciple, but He also reproves the crowd which is taking Him. Even in His arrest Jesus is King."[1332]

> "The characterization of the crowds [in Matthew's story] develops along two lines: through their interaction with Jesus; and through their being contrasted with their leaders. Until Jesus' arrest, the reader's attitude toward the crowds is largely one of approval and sympathy."[1333]

> "On balance, then, the Jewish crowds are 'well-disposed' toward Jesus but 'without faith' in him. In being without faith in Jesus, they contrast with the disciples. And in being well-disposed toward Jesus, they contrast with their leaders."[1334]

Matthew again pointed out that all these events fulfilled Scripture, a point of particular interest to his Jewish readers (v. 56). It was imperative that Messiah fulfill prophecy. The writers of the Old Testament Scriptures were prophets, God's authoritative representatives. By fleeing, the disciples fulfilled one of these prophecies, as Jesus had predicted (cf. v. 31; Zech. 13:7).

3. The trials of Jesus 26:57—27:26

Matthew stressed Jesus' righteousness for his readers by highlighting the injustice of His trials.

> "The breaches in law are so numerous as to be unbelievable . . ."[1335]

> ". . . even the ordinary legal rules were disregarded in the following particulars: (a) The examination by Annas without witnesses. (b) The trial by night. (c) The sentence on the first day of trial. (d) The trial of a capital charge on the day before the Sabbath. (e) The suborning of witnesses. (f) The direct interrogation by the High Priest."[1336]

France noted that these rules applied later, as reflected in the Mishnah (at the end of the second century A.D.), so not all of them may have been in force when Jesus was tried.[1337]

[1329]Wiersbe, 1:98.

[1330]See Hagner, Matthew 14—28, p. 791.

[1331]Carr, p. 295.

[1332]Toussaint, Behold the . . ., p. 306.

[1333]Kingsbury, Matthew as . . ., p. 24.

[1334]Ibid., p. 25.

[1335]Carson, "Matthew," p. 549.

[1336]Carr, p. 297.

It may be helpful to take a brief overview of Jesus' trials, since none of the Gospel evangelists gives the complete picture. There were essentially two trials, one Jewish and one Roman. The Jewish trial, really a preliminary hearing, began when Annas informally examined Jesus late Thursday night (John 18:12-14, 19-23). During this examination, members of the Sanhedrin were evidently assembling. His accusers then brought Jesus before Caiaphas and the Sanhedrin, who decided He was guilty of blasphemy (Matt. 26:57-68; Mark 14:53-65). At sunrise on Friday, the Sanhedrin decided to send Jesus to Pilate for trial (Matt. 27:1-2; Luke 22:66-71). The Roman trial began with Jesus appearing before Pilate (Matt. 27:11-14; John 18:28-38a). Pilate then sent Jesus to Herod for interrogation (Luke 23:6-12). Finally, Herod sent Jesus back to Pilate for a second examination (Matt. 27:15-31; John 18:38b—19:16). The trials were over and Jesus was at Golgotha by mid-morning, about 9:00 a.m. (Mark 15:25).

The trial before the Sanhedrin 26:57-68 (cf. Mark 14:53-65; Luke 22:54, 63-65)

Matthew omitted Jesus' hearing before Annas (John 18:12-14, 19-23). Quite possibly, Annas lived in one wing of the same building in which the Sanhedrin met.[1338]

> "This is the point at which Jesus' death is sealed; all that follows involving the Roman prefect is only the formal implementation
> of a verdict already decided by the Jewish authorities."[1339]

26:57   Josephus wrote that the building in which the Sanhedrin normally met, the "chamber of hewn stone," stood close to the western wall of the temple enclosure.[1340] Part of this western wall is the modern Wailing Wall where Jews go daily to pray. The exact location of this chamber is presently unknown. However, this meeting of the Sanhedrin took place in Caiaphas' house or palace, the location of which is also debated (Luke 22:54).[1341] While Annas examined Jesus, the Sanhedrin members assembled.

As mentioned earlier, "Caiaphas" was the official "high priest" then. He would have presided over the Sanhedrin. He was probably a Sadducee. The Sadducees held the power in Israel then. The "scribes" were the official teachers of the law, and the "elders" were the lay representatives of the people. The "chief priests," mainly Sadducees, were also present (v. 59). These were the three groups that composed Israel's chief ruling body.

26:58   All the disciples had fled and left Jesus (v. 56; cf. Mark 14:54; Luke 22:54; John 18:15-18), "but Peter" followed "at a" safe "distance," as Jesus' guards led Him across the Kidron Valley, into Jerusalem, and into the high priest's house. This house contained an open courtyard in the middle, which was typical. Peter positioned himself inconspicuously, he thought, near a fire in "the courtyard," to observe what would happen (cf. John 18:15-16). A church now stands over the traditional site on Mt. Zion: the church of St. Peter in Gallicantu, or St. Peter at the Crowing of the Cock.

26:59-63a   The phrase "whole Council" or "whole Sanhedrin" need not mean that all 70 members plus the high priest were present, since only 23 constituted a quorum (cf. Luke 23:50-51).[1342] Perhaps Matthew meant that representatives from all parts of the Sanhedrin were present. The chief priests were also the legal experts, so they evidently took the lead in conducting the trial. Matthew wrote that they tried to get "false testimony against Jesus." This does not mean they looked for liars, but they looked for witnesses who would validate their conviction that Jesus was a lawbreaker. To do that, the witnesses would have to give "false testimony."

The Mosaic Law required at least two witnesses in cases of capital offense. The lawyers had to interview several people ("false witnesses") before they finally found "two" of them that would agree on a charge against Jesus. This was another way that Matthew stressed Jesus' innocence. Interpreting with wooden literalism, one might take Jesus' words as a threat to desecrate the temple, but Jesus had spoken metaphorically (John 2:19-21). He had meant that He was the true temple, the place where people met God and where God met them. Most ancient Near Eastern people regarded the desecration of a temple as a capital offense, and the Jews shared this viewpoint (cf. Jer. 26:1-19). Jesus had not, as far as the Gospel records go, said that He would or could destroy the temple. He had only said it would be destroyed. Nor had He said that He would rebuild the temple.

Even though the religious leaders oppressed and afflicted Jesus, He did not open His mouth. He "kept silent," like a lamb going to the slaughter and as a sheep before its shearers (v. 63a; cf. Isa. 53:7).

[1337]France, The Gospel . . ., p. 1019.

[1338]Carson, "Matthew," pp. 552-53.

[1339]France, The Gospel . . ., p. 1016.

[1340]Josephus, Antiquities of . . ., 5:4:2.

[1341]See the diagram of Jerusalem in New Testament Times at the end of these notes.

[1342]Carson, "Matthew," p. 553.

26:63b   Frustrated by Jesus' silence, "the high priest" tried to cut through to the basic issue. Did Jesus claim to be the Messiah ("the Christ") or not?

> "In terms of the plot of Matthew's story, this unexpected query raises the problem as to the source from which the high priest has even gotten the idea to question Jesus about being the Son of God. This source is Jesus himself and his narration of the parable of the wicked husbandmen [21:33-45]. As the presiding officer of the Sanhedrin, the high priest has knowledge of the claim to divine sonship which Jesus made in telling his parable to the chief priests and the elders. At the trial, therefore, the high priest seizes on Jesus' own claim . . . and hurls it back at Jesus as a weapon by which to destroy him."[1343]

> Caiaphas demanded that Jesus answer under oath "by the living God." "Son of God" was an equivalent title with "Messiah" (cf. 2:15; 3:17; 11:27; 16:13-20). If Jesus refused to answer, He would break an oath imposed on Him legally by the high priest. If He denied the charge, He would have had no further influence even though the Sanhedrin might acquit Him. If He affirmed the charge, He would appear to be an impostor given the presuppositions of the Sanhedrin. From their viewpoint, the Messiah would not allow others to imprison Him and put His life in jeopardy.

26:64   Jesus gave the same answer to Caiaphas that He had given to Judas (v. 25). It was "affirmative in content, and reluctant or circumlocutory in formulation."[1344] Caiaphas took it as a yes (v. 65). Jesus then proceeded to expand or qualify His response, because the religious leaders' concept of Messiah was inadequate. Jesus claimed to be the Messiah, but not the "Messiah" that Caiaphas and his cronies had in mind.

> Jesus alluded to Psalm 110:1 and Daniel 7:13, to show that He was not a political Messiah in the popular mold. He was a Messiah who would *receive a kingdom from the Ancient of Days*, and return to reign in great "power" and honor. This was one of Jesus' clearest claims of messiahship (cf. 16:27; 23:39; 24:30-31; 26:29). It constituted both a revelation and a threat to Israel's leaders. From now on, Jesus claimed, His hearers would not see Him as He stood before them then. In the future, they would see Him as the Messiah and their Judge.

26:65-66 Rending one's garments expressed indignation or grief (cf. 2 Kings 18:37). It became a traditional response to blasphemy (cf. Acts 14:14).[1345] However, it was illegal for the high priest to rend his garments (Lev. 21:10). The punishment for "blasphemy" in the Mosaic Law was death (Lev. 24:16). At that time, blasphemy consisted of claiming for oneself a unique association with God, reflected in "sitting at God's right hand," not only misusing God's name.[1346] It also included speaking against the temple and Israel's leaders.[1347]

26:67-68 Jesus' messianic claims did not impress or intimidate His accusers. They proceeded to humiliate Him for what they considered to be His false pretensions. Jesus' passive acceptance of these indignities only reinforced their assumption and encouraged them to be even more hostile (cf. Isa. 53:7). Mark and Luke recorded that they blindfolded Jesus (Mark 14:65; Luke 22:64). Perhaps Matthew's omission of this fact suggests that the leaders, and or their servants, "beat" Jesus so badly that He could not see who was doing the beating, even if they *had not* blindfolded Him (cf. Isa. 52:14). If He was the Messiah, He should have been able to tell ("prophesy" in the sense of revealing something unknown) "who hit" Him. Whether or not Jesus was limited in this knowledge is not the point: when the abusers stand before Jesus some day, when He is their Judge, the person(s) who hit Him will have to answer a question from *Him*: What is your defense for hating Me?

> "It is a remarkable fact, that when the Lord Jesus and when His martyr Stephen were before the Sanhedrim [*sic*; Acts 7:58], the procedure was in each case in direct contravention of all the rules of Rabbinical criminal law."[1348]

[1343]Kingsbury, *Matthew as . . .*, p. 87.

[1344]David R. Catchpole, "The Answer of Jesus to Caiaphas (Matt. xxvi. 64)," *New Testament Studies* 17 (1970-71):226.

[1345]Mishnah *Sanhedrin* 7:5.

[1346]See Darrell L. Bock, *Blasphemy and Exaltation in Judaism and the Final Examination of Jesus*, pp. 30-183.

[1347]Ibid., pp. 111-12, 206-9.

[1348]Edersheim, *The Temple*, p. 67. See also Laurna L. Berg, "The Illegalities of Jesus' Religious and Civil Trials," *Bibliotheca Sacra* 161:643 (July-September 2004):330-42; and *The New Scofield . . .*, p. 1042.

Peter's denials of Jesus 26:69-75 (cf. Mark 14:66-72; Luke 22:55-62; John 18:15-18, 25-27)

All four evangelists recorded three denials, but the details differ slightly.

26:69-70   Peter was warming himself near the fire "in the" center of the "courtyard" (Mark 14:66-67; Luke 22:55; John 18:18). The servant girl's words expressed both curiosity and accusation. She referred to Jesus derogatorily as "the Galilean" (cf. Mark 14:67). Residents of Judea, and especially Jerusalem, regarded Galileans as inferior to themselves because Galilee was mainly rural. Evidently several people overheard her comment and may have joined in her questioning. Peter "*denied it* before them all," replying with words similar to a formal *legal oath*.[1349]

26:71-72   Peter withdrew "to the gateway" leading from the street into the courtyard, perhaps because that area was darker and there were fewer people there. There "another" (servant) girl pointed him out to others standing about, as one who had been with Jesus "of Nazareth," another derogatory slur in view of the bad reputation of Nazareth (cf. 2:23). Peter denied her accusation, this time with a stronger oath. Matthew did not mean that Peter used profanity, but he invoked a curse on himself if he was lying. He appealed to something sacred to confirm his truthfulness (cf. 5:33-34; 23:16-22).

26:73-75   A third person, one of the high priest's servants who was a relative of the man whose ear Peter had cut off in Gethsemane (John 18:26), approached Peter with some "bystanders" about an hour later (Luke 22:59). *They* accusingly asked Peter, again, if he was not one of Jesus' disciples, since he was a Galilean. Galileans had an accent that gave them away (much like a Texan or Boston or New York accent does in America).[1350] This shows how thoroughly the residents of Jerusalem connected Jesus' ministry with Galilee, since it was the site of most of His activity. Most, if not all, of His disciples were Galileans. The one who may not have been was Judas Iscariot, if "Iscariot" refers to the town of Kerioth in Judah. Peter denied that he knew Jesus a third time, using more oaths to confirm his testimony. He may have even cursed Jesus.[1351] "Immediately a rooster crowed." Peter heard it and "remembered" Jesus' prediction that he would deny Jesus before the rooster crowed (v. 34). Peter left the courtyard and "wept bitterly" over his cowardice and failure (cf. 2 Cor. 7:10). This is Matthew's last reference to Peter.

Matthew probably recorded this incident because it illustrates Jesus' ability to foretell the future, a messianic characteristic. It also reveals the weakness of the disciples, whom Jesus had taken such pains to prepare for His passion—but without apparent success. Their concept of the Messiah and the kingdom was still largely that of most people in Israel then, though they had come to recognize Jesus as God. Only Jesus' resurrection would clarify their understanding of His messiahship and kingdom program.

> "The reader is invited to choose between two models of how the man of God behaves under pressure, the one who escapes death but with his spiritual reputation in tatters and the one who will be killed only to live again in triumph; so the reader is reminded that 'anyone who finds their life will lose it, and anyone who loses their life will find it' (10:39; 16:25)."[1352]

The formal decision of the Sanhedrin 27:1-2 (cf. Mark 15:1; Luke 22:66-71)

Matthew's narrative directs the reader's attention from the courtyard back to the Sanhedrin's council chamber (v. 68). Josephus wrote that the Jews' law forbade them from putting to death anyone without a condemnation by the Sanhedrin.[1353]

The "chief priests and elders" had to decide how they would present Jesus' case "to Pilate" to secure the verdict they wanted from him. The title "governor" is a general one. Really Pilate was a prefect (procurator) whom Tiberius Caesar had appointed in A.D. 26 to succeed his predecessor, Valerius Gratus.[1354] Judea and Samaria had become one Roman province in A.D. 6, that Pilate now governed (in A.D. 33). Normally he lived in Caesarea, but during the Jewish feasts he often came to Jerusalem and stayed in Herod's former palace, because Jerusalem became a potential trouble spot then.[1355] The site of Herod's palace was what is now known as the Citadel, south of the Jaffa Gate. "Pontius" was his family name.

[1349]Cf. Mishnah *Shebuoth* 8:3.

[1350]Hoehner, *Herod Antipas*, pp. 61-64; France, *The Gospel . . .*, p. 1033.

[1351]France, *The Gospel . . .*, p. 1034.

[1352]Ibid., p. 1017.

[1353]Josephus, *Antiquities of . . .*, 14:9:3.

[1354]*Zondervan Pictorial Encyclopedia of the Bible*, s.v. "Pilate, Pontius," by J. G. Vos, 4:790-93. For a list of the procurators of Judea, see Edersheim, *The Life . . .*, 2:702. Cf. Josephus, *Antiquities of . . .*, 18:2:2; and idem, *The Wars . . .*, 2:9:2-4.

[1355]Cf. ibid., 2:12:1; and idem, *Antiquities of . . .*, 18:3:1.

The suicide of Judas 27:3-10 (cf. Acts 1:18-19)

"Peter has sinned by words, under the pressure of the moment, and for him there can be a new start; Judas has sinned in deed, in a premeditated, settled course of action which has now borne fruit which, too late, he wishes he could have undone."[1356]

27:3 Judas evidently "felt remorse" because he realized that he had "condemned" an innocent man to death. His remorse (Gr. *metamelomai*) resulted in a kind of repentance (Gr. *metanoeo*), but it was not complete enough. The first of these two Greek words does not indicate "sorrow for moral obliquity and sin against God, but annoyance at the consequences of an act or course of acts, and chagrin at not having known better."[1357] Judas was sorry for what he had done, and tried to make amends, but he never believed that Jesus was the Son of God (cf. Acts 1:16-19).

27:4 Judas' testimony to Jesus' innocence is an important part of Matthew's witness that Jesus was the Messiah. The response of the Sanhedrin members likewise proved their guilt. It should have meant something to them that Judas said that Jesus was innocent. Judas betrayed "innocent blood," and they condemned innocent blood.[1358] They were wrong in thinking they could avoid responsibility for Jesus' death because of Judas' guilt in betraying Him.

"They are 'guileful' and 'callous,' purchasing the services of Judas to betray Jesus yet leaving Judas to his own devices in coming to terms with his burden of guilt (26:14-16; 27:3-4)."[1359]

27:5-8 Judas "threw" the 30 "pieces of silver" that he had received for betraying Jesus "into the temple sanctuary." Perhaps Judas thought he could atone for his sin to some extent with this gift. Then he went out "and hanged himself" (cf. 2 Sam. 17:23 LXX). Many scholars believe this was in the region of *gehenna*, the city dump of Jerusalem, near the confluence of the Kidron and Hinnom valleys south of the city.

The chief priests properly refused to receive the silver "into the temple treasury" (cf. Deut. 23:18). Here again, they appear scrupulous about ritual observance of the Law, while at the same time they failed to defend what is more important, namely, the innocence of Jesus (cf. 12:9-14; 15:1-9; 23:23: 28:12-13). They decided to use the money for a public project, a graveyard for foreigners. The place they bought had evidently been an area of land from which potters obtained their clay, but which by now had become depleted.

The account of Judas' death in Acts 1:18-19 is slightly different, but it is easy to harmonize the two stories. The chief priests "bought" the cemetery "with" Judas' ("the") "money" (v. 7). Judas evidently hanged himself, and then the corpse apparently fell to the ground and burst open. Perhaps the branch from which he hanged himself broke, or his body may have fallen when it began to decompose. The place of his suicide could have received the name "Field of Blood" before or after Judas' death. If it was before, Judas may have chosen to kill himself on the field that his money had purchased. It seems more likely, however, that the Sanhedrin purchased the field sometime after the events of this night.

27:9-10 This difficult fulfillment seems to be a quotation from Zechariah 11:12-13, but Matthew attributed it to Jeremiah. Probably Matthew was referring to Jeremiah 19:1-13, which he condensed using mainly the phraseology of Zechariah 11:12-13 because of its similarity to Judas' situation.[1360] See Mark 1:2-3 and 2 Chronicles 36:21 for other examples of this type of fulfillment involving the fusing of sources. Matthew named only Isaiah and Jeremiah as sources of his quotations (2:17; 3:3; 4:14; 8:17; 12:17; 13:14; 15:7; 17:9); he left his other prophetic sources unspecified. He also attributed one allusion to Daniel (24:15).

"Joining two quotations from two Old Testament books and assigning them to one (in this case, Jeremiah) was also done in Mark 1:2-3, in which Isaiah 40:3 and Malachi 3:1 are quoted but are assigned to Isaiah. This follows the custom of mentioning the more notable prophet first."[1361]

Another possibility is that the prophecy was spoken by Jeremiah but recorded by Zechariah.[1362]

[1356]France, *The Gospel . . .*, pp. 1039-40.

[1357]Vincent, 1:117.

[1358]Carson, "Matthew," p. 561.

[1359]Kingsbury, *Matthew as . . .*, pp. 22-23.

[1360]See Douglas J. Moo, "The Use of the Old Testament in the Passion Texts of the Gospels," (Ph.D. dissertation, University of St. Andrews, 1979), pp. 191-210; and Gundry, *The Use . . .*, pp. 122-27.

[1361]Bailey, in *The New . . .*, p. 59.

[1362]*The Nelson . . .*, p. 1630.

A different explanation of this problem is that Jeremiah was the first book in the prophets division of the Hebrew Old Testament. Jesus quoted Zechariah as from Jeremiah because the Book of Zechariah was in the section of the Hebrew Bible that began with the Book of Jeremiah.[1363] However, it is uncertain that the Book of Jeremiah occupied this leading position in the third division of the Hebrew Bible in Matthew's day.[1364] A similar explanation is that the name "Jeremiah" stood for the collection of prophetic writings in which the Book of Zechariah was found.

In Jeremiah 19, Israel's rulers had forsaken God and made Jerusalem a place for foreign gods. The valley where the prophet delivered his prophecy and where he smashed the vessel, received the name "Valley of Slaughter," symbolic of Judah and Jerusalem's ruin. Similarly, in Matthew 26—27, the rejection of Jesus led to the polluting of a field that is symbolic of death and the destruction of Israel, which foreigners were about to "bury." In Zechariah 11, and in Matthew 26—27, the people of Israel reject God's Shepherd and value him at the price of a slave. In both passages, someone throws the money into the temple, and eventually someone else uses it to buy something that pollutes.

". . . what we find in Matthew, including vv. 9-10, is not *identification* of the text *with* an event but *fulfillment* of the text *in* an event, based on a broad typology governing how both Jesus and Matthew read the OT . . ."[1365]

This understanding of the fulfillment also explains the changes Matthew made in the texts which he said fulfilled the events involving Judas. Matthew saw in Jeremiah 19 and Zechariah 11, not just several verbal parallels, but a pattern of apostasy and rejection that found its ultimate fulfillment in Jesus.[1366]

The trial before Pilate 27:11-26 (cf. Mark 15:2-15; Luke 23:3-25; John 18:33—19:16)

Pilate was a cruel ruler who made little attempt to understand the Jews whom he hated.[1367] He had treated them unfairly and brutally on many occasions, but recently Caesar had rebuked him severely.[1368] This probably accounts for the fairly docile attitude he displayed toward the Sanhedrin in the Gospel accounts. He wanted to avoid another rebuke from Caesar. However, his relations with the Jews continued to deteriorate until A.D. 39, when Caesar removed him from office and banished him.

After describing Pilate's severity with his Jewish subjects, Josephus wrote the following about Jesus:

"Now, there was about this time Jesus, a wise man, if it be lawful to call him a man, for he was a doer of wonderful works—a teacher of such men as receive the truth with pleasure. He drew over to him both many of the Jews, and many of the Gentiles. He was [the] Christ; and when Pilate, at the suggestion of the principal men amongst us, had condemned him to the cross, those that loved him at the first did not forsake him, for he appeared to them alive again the third day, as the divine prophets had foretold these and ten thousand other wonderful things concerning him; and the tribe of Christians, so named from him, are not extinct at this day."[1369]

In the Gospels, Pilate seems to be on Jesus' side, but he probably only *appeared* favorable to Jesus because he hated the Sanhedrin that opposed Him. Pilate may have also dealt with Jesus as he did, because Jesus posed no threat whatsoever to him from his viewpoint. Conviction by both the Sanhedrin and Pilate were necessary to condemn Jesus. These inveterate enemies united against Him.[1370]

27:11   The location of this trial is uncertain. It probably took place in Herod's former palace (cf. v. 2). Another less probable site is the Antonia Fortress. This fortress was the site of Peter's later imprisonment and miraculous release (Acts 12:3-11), and Paul's defense before the people of Jerusalem and his imprisonment (Acts 21:27—23:30). Herod the Great had rebuilt this fortress and renamed it—its former name was Baris (the Citadel)—in honor of his friend Caesar Antonius.[1371]

[1363]Lenski, pp. 1082-83; Walvoord, *Matthew: . . .*, p. 227.
[1364]See *The New Scofield . . .*, p. 1041.
[1365]Carson, "Matthew," p. 565.
[1366]See also Charles Lee Feinberg, *God Remembers, A Study of Zechariah*, pp. 167-69.
[1367]Hoehner, *Herod Antipas*, pp. 172-83.
[1368]Idem, *Chronological Aspects . . .*, pp. 105-14.
[1369]Josephus, *Antiquities of . . .*, 18:3:3.
[1370]See also *The New Bible Dictionary*, 1962 ed., s.v. "Pilate," by D. H. Wheaton.
[1371]Josephus, *Antiquities of . . .*, 15:8:5; 15:11:4; idem, *The Wars . . .*, 5:5:8.

Pilate's question grew out of Jesus' claim to be Israel's Messiah (26:64), that the Sanhedrin undoubtedly reported to Pilate (cf. 2:2). This was a political charge, whereas the charge that Caiaphas had brought against Jesus had been religious (26:61, 63). Jesus responded to Pilate's question with the same affirmative, but qualified, statement that He had formerly given Judas (26:25) and the Sanhedrin (26:64). He *was* "the King of the Jews" (cf. 2:2), but not in the way that Pilate would have thought of such a person. Only non-Jews used this title of Jesus. Herod the Great had been the last official king of the Jews, before the Romans had assumed sovereign control of them. Jesus was not some military rebel bent on throwing off Rome's yoke using armed forces. Once again, Matthew recorded Jesus' claim to be the Messiah.

27:12-14   Having responded to the charge against Him, Jesus made no further attempt to defend or clear Himself (cf. 26:63). Pilate could hardly believe that Jesus would not try to defend Himself. Obviously Jesus was not trying to avoid the Cross (cf. Isa. 53:7). Such an attitude led Pilate to conclude that Jesus was either foolish or crazy.

Only Luke reported that now Pilate sent Jesus to Herod Antipas for questioning (Luke 23:6-12). Herod then returned Jesus to Pilate.

27:15   Evidently it had become traditional for Pilate "to release . . . one" Jewish "prisoner," that he had taken, as a favor to the Jews each Passover. He probably did this to improve relations with his subjects on a politically important occasion.

27:16   Barabbas' name means "son of the father." Jesus, of course, was the true *Son of the Father*. The Greek word translated "notorious" (*episemos*) really means eminent or outstanding (cf. Rom. 16:7). He was a famous prisoner, but not necessarily one that the Jews regarded as an undesirable character, as portrayed in some movies. On the contrary, he had evidently been leading an insurrection against the Roman government as a freedom fighter (cf. Mark 15:7; Luke 23:19; John 18:40). His guerrilla actions were fairly common then.[1372] Many of the Jews would have viewed Barabbas as a hero rather than as a villain. He was more of a messianic figure, in the minds of most Jews, than Jesus was.

Possibly the two men crucified with Jesus were Barabbas' partners. Matthew used the same Greek word to describe them as the other evangelists used to describe Barabbas (i.e., *lestes*, "rebels" or "insurrectionists," v. 38). All three were better men than common robbers; they were more like Robin Hood's men.

Jesus really took the place of one rebel, Barabbas, because the people preferred the one who tried to overthrow Rome's power, to the Messiah that God had provided for them. This shows their insistence on having a "messiah" of their own design (cf. 1 Sam. 8:5, 19-20).

27:17-18   The "them" (NASB) or "crowd" (NIV) is the multitude of common people (v. 15; cf. Mark 15:8). Pilate saw that the Sanhedrin was trying to get him to eliminate someone they saw as a threat to their own authority, namely, Jesus. He knew the Sanhedrin had no special desire to advance the welfare of Rome. Pilate undoubtedly knew that Jesus enjoyed great popularity among many of the Jewish people (cf. 21:1-16), and that their leaders envied Him. Therefore he appealed to the people to let him know which prisoner they wanted him "to release." He undoubtedly thought the crowd would request Jesus, thus giving him a reason to humiliate the Sanhedrin by releasing Jesus. He may have mistakenly concluded that the residents of Jerusalem supported Jesus because of His notoriety in Jerusalem at that time. However, it was actually the Galileans who were Jesus' main supporters. The people of Jerusalem seem to have willingly followed the lead of the Sanhedrin in *willfully* rejecting Jesus.

27:19   Pilate's "wife" interrupted him as he sat "on the judgment seat," about to render a verdict in Jesus' case. Matthew probably recorded this incident because it is another indication of Jesus' innocence. Many of the Romans considered dreams a means of divine guidance (cf. 1:20).[1373] In this case, God did guide her to testify to Jesus' righteousness.

> "Tradition has given her the name *Procula*; an Apocryphal Gospel describes her as a convert to Judaism [i.e., The Gospel according to Nicodemus, ch. 2]; while the Greek Church has actually placed her in the Catalogue of Saints."[1374]

> "Pilate's 'wife' (27:19) serves as a foil for Pilate himself: her warning to Pilate not to have anything to do with that innocent man (Jesus) contrasts with Pilate's decision to accede to the Jewish demand that Jesus be put to death. 'Barabbas' (27:15-26) serves as foil for Jesus; a notorious prisoner is set free, whereas an innocent man is delivered up to be crucified."[1375]

[1372]Josephus, *Antiquities of . . .*, 18:1:1.

[1373]France, *The Gospel . . .*, p. 1055.

[1374]Edersheim, *The Life . . .*, 2:569.

[1375]Kingsbury, *Matthew as . . .*, p. 27.

| 27:20-21 | The Sanhedrin members "persuaded the crowd(s)" to insist that Pilate release Barabbas and crucify Jesus (cf. Mark 15:11). Initially this may seem incredible, but both Jesus and Barabbas were popular with the crowd. Pilate seemed to the people to be favoring Jesus' release, but their religious leaders favored Barabbas' release. It was quite natural that the Jerusalemites would side with their leaders against Pilate, given such a choice, especially since Jesus was a "foreign" Galilean. The Sanhedrin had previously sowed doubts about Jesus in the people's minds by circulating reports that He had blasphemed. To many of them, He was now a heretic. Jesus Himself had not even attempted what Barabbas had attempted, namely: to overthrow Rome's authority over Israel. This may have been another reason the people wanted Barabbas released. |

| 27:22-23 | Pilate tried to reverse his tactical error by asking more questions, but mob sentiment against him and his choice became stronger with each question he asked the crowd. First, Pilate offered a milder sentence for Jesus, but the crowd would have none of it (v. 22). Second, he attested Jesus' innocence, but the crowd's original answer had become a mob chant that the governor apparently could not change or silence. |

> "One can almost picture this scene, somewhat like a football stadium in which the crowd shouts 'Defense!' Their cheer was 'Crucify, crucify!'"[1376]

> The Jews wanted Pilate to "crucify" Jesus, rather than to punish Him another way, because: for the Jews, a person hanging on a tree was a demonstration that he was under God's curse (Deut. 21:23).

| 27:24 | Washing one's hands to symbolize one's innocence was a Jewish custom, not a Roman custom (cf. Deut 21:6; Ps. 26:6).[1377] Probably Pilate did this to show contempt for the Jews, as well as to relieve his conscience by publicly declaring himself "innocent of this Man's blood." Pilate could wash his hands with a clear conscience because he had tried to release Jesus, but the Jews would not allow him to do so. This is not saying he was innocent of guilt, but he undoubtedly felt justified in doing what he did. Pilate delivered Jesus up for crucifixion out of cowardice and fear of the Jews whom he despised. He could no more pass his personal responsibility for Jesus' death off on the people, than the chief priests and elders could avoid their responsibility for it by blaming Judas (v. 4). |

| 27:25 | The people's response was not new (2 Sam. 1:16; 3:28; cf. Acts 18:6; 20:26). "All the people" in the context refers to the crowd present, not just the Sanhedrin or the whole Jewish nation. This phrase did not cover the Jews who believed on Jesus, but unbelieving Israel. Therefore it is inappropriate to use this verse to justify anti-Semitism.[1378] |

> "The viciousness of their anger could hardly be described more graphically than by this horrible utterance."[1379]

> "Owing to the leaders' abject repudiation of Jesus, they unwittingly effect, not the salvation of Israel as they had anticipated, but just the opposite, Israel's demise as God's special people: they bring a curse upon themselves and the people (27:25); they provoke the destruction of Jerusalem (22:7); and they unknowingly make themselves responsible for the transfer of God's Rule to another nation, the church, which becomes God's end-time people (21:43; 16:18; 13:38)."[1380]

| 27:26 | Under Mosaic Law, the Jews could not scourge someone with more than 40 lashes (Deut. 25:3; cf. 2 Cor 11:24). However here, the Romans—not the Jews—were scourging Jesus. *They* had no limit on the number of lashes they could impose on a prisoner. They customarily used a leather whip with pieces of bone and or metal embedded in the thongs, a *flagellum*. Scourging with this whip often turned human flesh into pulp and exposed the bones and internal organs.[1381] People frequently died from this type of flogging. The Romans used it to weaken prisoners before crucifixion. This scourging fulfilled Jesus' words in 20:19. After this violent and bloody brutality, Pilate sent Jesus to die like a condemned criminal, by crucifixion (cf. Isa. 53:6, 12). |

> "Judas yielded to *the devil* in his great sin (John 13:2, 27); Peter yielded to *the flesh* when he denied his Lord; but Pilate yielded to *the world* and listened to the crowd."[1382]

[1376]Barbieri, p. 87.

[1377]Carson, "Matthew," p. 570.

[1378]See Hagner, *Matthew 14—28*, p. 828; France, *The Gospel . . .*, pp. 1057-58.

[1379]Toussaint, *Behold the . . .*, pp. 310-11.

[1380]Kingsbury, *Matthew as . . .*, p. 124. Cf. Edersheim, *The Life . . .*, 2:578.

[1381]Josephus, *The Wars . . .*, 2:21:5; 6:5:3.

[1382]Wiersbe, 1:101.

Matthew's account of the trial before Pilate makes Jesus' innocence clear.[1383] As in the religious trial, Jesus stood before an unjust judge whose personal prejudices guided him rather than justice. The self-sacrifice of the Suffering Servant also comes through in this trial. No one took Jesus' life from Him as a martyr. He laid it down for others in self-sacrifice.

4. The crucifixion of Jesus 27:27-56

Matthew narrated the crucifixion of Jesus by emphasizing the Roman soldiers' abuse of Jesus, the Jews' mockery of Jesus, His actual death, and the events that immediately followed His death.

The soldiers' abuse of Jesus 27:27-31 (cf. Mark 15:16-20; John 19:16-17a)

27:27   The "soldiers" in view were probably "Pilate's" troops. The "Praetorium," or courtyard, probably refers to the one in Herod's palace near the Jaffa Gate or, less likely, the one in the Antonia Fortress. All "the soldiers" of "the cohort" present ("the whole *Roman* cohort") evidently "took Jesus into the Praetorium," i.e., the Praetorium's central courtyard. A cohort consisted of 600 soldiers. These soldiers would have been auxiliaries drawn from the non-Jewish population of surrounding areas, since there was no Roman legion stationed in Palestine at this time.[1384]

27:28-31   The Sanhedrin and or its servants had abused Jesus as a false Messiah (26:67-68). Now Pilate's soldiers abused Him as a false king. Ironically, Jesus was everything He was mocked for being: Messiah and King of Israel. The "scarlet robe" (Gr. *chlamys*) they put on Jesus (v. 28) was probably the reddish purple cloak that Roman military and civil officials wore. Perhaps the thorny spikes that the soldiers wove into a circle ("crown of thorns") resembled the one on Tiberius Caesar's head, on Roman coins, that consisted of palm branches. The imperfect tense of the Greek verb translated "beat" means they beat Jesus on the head repeatedly (cf. Isa. 52:14). Typically, four soldiers plus a centurion accompanied a condemned prisoner to his crucifixion. The criminal normally carried the crossbeam, to which the soldiers would later nail his hands (cf. John 19:17, 23).[1385]

This pericope shows sinners at their worst, mocking and brutalizing the very Person who was laying His life down as a sacrifice for their sins (cf. 20:19).

> "Few incidents in history more clearly illustrate the brutality in the desperately wicked heart of man than that which was inflicted on Jesus the Son of God."[1386]

> "The ultimate explanation of the cross is neither Jewish hostility nor Roman injustice, but the declared purpose of God."[1387]

The crucifixion and mockery of Jesus 27:32-44 (cf. Mark 15:21-32; Luke 23:26-43; John 19:17b-27)

> "The overenthusiastic attempts to draw out the physical horror of crucifixion which disfigure some Christian preaching (and at least one recent movie) find no echo in the gospels. Perhaps the original readers were too familiar with both the torture and the shame of crucifixion to need any help in envisaging what it really meant. At any rate, the narrative focus in these verses is rather on the surrounding events and the people involved (Simon, the soldiers, the bandits), together with the ironical placard over Jesus' head which sums up the Roman dismissal of his claims."[1388]

Matthew's emphasis in his account of Jesus' crucifixion was on the mocking of the onlookers.

27:32   Jesus was able to carry the crossbeam of His cross until He passed through the city gate (cf. Mark 15:21; John 19:17). Normally crucifixions took place outside the city wall (cf. Lev. 24:14; Num. 15:35-36; 1 Kings 21:13; Acts 7:58). This location symbolized added rejection (cf. Heb. 13:13).

              Simon's name was Jewish. He came from the town of "Cyrene" on the Mediterranean coast of North Africa (cf. Acts 2:10; 6:9; 11:20; 13:1). The Roman soldiers forced him to carry Jesus' cross. Perhaps Matthew mentioned this because it is another piece of irony. Jesus was really bearing Simon's cross by dying in his place. The reader understands this, but at the time,

---

[1383]See R. Larry Overstreet, "Roman Law and the Trial of Jesus," *Bibliotheca Sacra* 135:540 (October-December 1978):323-32.

[1384]France, *The Gospel . . .*, p. 1062.

[1385]Carson, "Matthew," p. 573.

[1386]Walvoord, *Matthew: . . .*, p. 231.

[1387]France, *The Gospel . . .*, p. 1060.

[1388]Ibid., p. 1064.

things looked completely the opposite to onlookers. Another reason Matthew may have mentioned "Simon of Cyrene" by name, is that he may have been well known among the early Christians. Ironically, *Simon Peter* should have been present to help Jesus, in view of his previous boasts (26:33, 35), but a different "Simon" had to take his place.

The Muslim teaching that Simon took Jesus' place, and died on the cross in His stead, evidently rests on the teaching of Basilides, a second century Gnostic heretic.[1389]

27:33   The word "Golgotha" is a Greek transliteration of the Aramaic *gulgolta* meaning "skull." "Calvary" comes from the Latin *calva*, "skull." Its exact location is unknown. It was evidently north of the old city wall, probably not far from the site of the present Church of the Holy Sepulcher (cf. John 19:20). Edersheim believed that the site was very close to the present Damascus Gate.[1390] Gordon's Calvary, which is not far from the Damascus Gate, does not enjoy much support as a site from scholars any more.[1391] The traditional *Via Dolorosa* ("the way of sorrow"), the route from Jesus' trial to the site of His crucifixion, rests on the assumption that Jesus' trial before Pilate took place in the Antonia Fortress.

27:34   Evidently some women offered Jesus some wine to drink, to which they had added myrrh to decrease His pain (Mark 15:23).[1392] Jesus refused it after tasting it, because He chose to endure the cross fully conscious. Matthew wrote "gall" because of the myrrh's bitter taste, and to make the fulfillment of Psalm 69:20-21 clearer. Another view is that the soldiers offered the drink to Jesus, but it seems uncharacteristic that they would have tried to lessen His sufferings.

27:35   The Romans normally tied or nailed the victim to the crossbeam of his cross. In Jesus' case they did the latter. They would then hoist the crossbeam and the prisoner up onto the upright member of the cross. Next they would fasten the crucified person's feet to the upright, by tying with a rope, or nailing them with a large spike. The Romans constructed crosses in various shapes: an X, a T, or, as in Jesus' case, the traditional T with the upright extending above the crossbeam (v. 37). Sometimes the victim was only a few inches off the ground, but Jesus appears to have been a few feet higher (v. 48; John 19:29). Normally the Romans crucified their victims naked. The executioners took the criminal's clothes for themselves. In Jesus' case, they cast "lots" for His robe ("garments"), fulfilling Psalm 22:18 (cf. John 19:23-24). This happened in the late morning on Friday (Mark 15:25; John 19:14).

"In the case of Jesus we have reason to think that, while the mode of punishment to which He was subjected was un-Jewish [i.e., crucifixion], every concession would be made to Jewish custom, and hence we thankfully believe that on the Cross He was spared the indignity of exposure. Such would have been truly un-Jewish."[1393]

Muslims believe that God took Jesus to heaven before He died, and that He will come back to earth to finish His work. They believe that it was Judas who died on the cross.

"Crucifixion was unspeakably painful and degrading. Whether tied or nailed to the cross, the victim endured countless paroxysms as he pulled with his arms and pushed with his legs to keep his chest cavity open for breathing and then collapsed in exhaustion until the demand for oxygen demanded renewed paroxysms. The scourging, the loss of blood, the shock from the pain, all produced agony that could go on for days, ending at last by suffocation, cardiac arrest, or loss of blood. When there was reason to hasten death, the execution squad would smash the victim's legs. Death followed almost immediately, either from shock or from collapse that cut off breathing."[1394]

The Romans reserved crucifixion for the worst criminals from the lowest classes of society. Roman citizens were exempt from crucifixion unless Caesar himself ordered it. For the Jews, crucifixion was even more horrible because it symbolized a person dying under God's curse (Deut. 21:23). Israel's leaders hung up those who had died under God's curse for others to see and learn from. Jesus bore God's curse for the sins of humankind, so that people would not have to experience that curse.

[1389]See Iraneus, *Against Heresies* 2:24:4; and J. M. Robinson, ed., *The Nag Hammadi Library in English*, p. 332.

[1390]Edersheim, *The Life . . .*, 2:585.

[1391]See Andre Parrot, *Golgotha and the Chruch of the Holy Sepulchre*, pp. 59-65.

[1392]Babylonian Talmud *Sanhedrin* 43a.

[1393]Edersheim, *The Life . . .*, 2:584.

[1394]Carson, "Matthew," p. 574. Cf. M. Hengel, *Crucifixion*; J. A. Fitzmyer, "Crucifixion in Ancient Palestine, Qumran Literature, and the New Testament," *Catholic Biblical Quarterly* 40 (1978):493-513; and Edwin A. Blum, "Jesus and JAMA," Christian Medical Society Journal 17:4 (Fall 1986):4-11, which contains drawings of a Roman scourging, a Roman cross, the placement of the nails in Jesus' hands and feet, how Jesus would have hung on the cross, and the piercing of His side.

| 27:36 | This verse is unique to the first Gospel. Sometimes people took criminals down from their crosses to prevent them from dying. The solders guarded Jesus to prevent this from happening. Jesus really did die; no one rescued Him. |

27:36   This verse is unique to the first Gospel. Sometimes people took criminals down from their crosses to prevent them from dying. The solders guarded Jesus to prevent this from happening. Jesus really did die; no one rescued Him.

27:37   Often the Romans wrote the charge against the crucified criminal on a white tablet with red or black ink and attached it to his cross. Pilate had Jesus' charge written in Aramaic, Greek, and Latin (John 19:20). He meant it to be insulting to the Jews. The title "King of the Jews" meant "Messiah" to the Jews. Pilate meant that Jesus was a messianic pretender, but of course He was indeed the Messiah. Pilate ironically stated what Matthew wanted his readers to understand, that Jesus was the Messiah that the Old Testament had predicted: Son of God and Suffering Servant.

"'This is Jesus the King of the Jews' is actually the theme of the book, though it here is used in sheer derision."[1395]

The full accusation, compiled by comparing the various Gospel accounts, was evidently "This is Jesus of Nazareth, the King of the Jews" (cf. Mark 15:26; Luke 23:38; John 19:19).

"In one sense, this title proved to be the first 'Gospel tract' ever written."[1396]

I regard this verse as the key verse in Matthew's Gospel because it states concisely Matthew's message.

27:38   The "two" men crucified with Jesus were guerrilla freedom fighters, not simply "robbers" (Gr. *lestai*, cf. v. 16). Jesus, the true Messiah, hung between two men who wanted to bring in Israel's kingdom through violent action against Israel's enemies— contrary to God's will. Matthew may have had Isaiah 53:12 in mind when he wrote this verse.

27:39-40   The Romans crucified people publicly to be an example to others. Evidently the site of Jesus' crucifixion was beside a road. Israel's leaders had charged Jesus with being a blasphemer because of His claim to be the One they would see seated at God's right hand (26:64). Matthew pointed out that the people passing by were really the ones "hurling abuse" (lit. blaspheming), since they charged Jesus unjustly (cf. 9:3:12:31; 26:65). Their derision fulfilled prophecy (Ps. 22:7; 109:25; Lam. 2:15). These blasphemers continued to question Jesus' identity (cf. 26:63). Like Satan, they tempted Him to prove who He was by demonstrating His identity in a way contrary to God's will (cf. 4:3, 6). Here Matthew showed the Jews mocking Jesus as the Romans had done earlier (vv. 27-31).

27:41   The "chief priests," "scribes," and "elders" represented all segments of the Sanhedrin (cf. 21:23; 26:59). They all mocked Jesus, probably with words that Jesus heard.

27:42   The reference to His saving others probably goes back to Jesus' healing ministry. The religious leaders intended to throw doubt on Jesus' healing ministry by claiming that He could not even heal His own condition. Perhaps these Jerusalemites were also recalling Jesus' triumphal entry and the cries of His mainly Galilean followers: "Save us now!" (21:9, 15). Of course, Jesus could have saved Himself from His suffering on the cross, but He could not have done so and provided salvation for humankind. In one sense the religious leaders spoke the truth.

The critics continued to point out Jesus' apparent helplessness. They implied that their failure to believe on Jesus was His fault. They promised to "believe in Him" if He would "come down" off "the cross." If He had done so, there would have been no salvation for anyone (cf. 1:21; 8:16-17; 20:28; 26:26-29; 28:18-20). They may also have been ridiculing the belief of the simple Galileans who had become His disciples.

27:43   The leaders were probably unwittingly quoting Psalm 22:8 (cf. John 11:51-52). They meant that God's failure to rescue Jesus proved that God *did not delight* in Him. Jesus' claims to be God's Son were therefore pretentious in their sight. God would identify His Son by delivering Him from death, but not in the way the religious leaders supposed. Presently God had to abandon His Son (cf. Ps. 2).

27:44   The insurrectionists crucified with Jesus joined the others who mocked Him (cf. Isa. 53:12). Matthew did not record that anyone spoke in His defense.

This section presents many different groups and individuals mocking Jesus: the Roman soldiers, the mob, the Jewish leaders, and the insurrectionists. The picture is of the Suffering Servant totally forsaken, misunderstood, and rejected by everyone. Yet through all this, Jesus fulfilled the prophecies about Messiah.

[1395]Toussaint, *Behold the . . .*, p. 312.

[1396]Wiersbe, 1:102-3.

"As the leaders see it, Jesus threatens the overthrow of law and tradition and the destruction of the nation (12:1-14; 15:12; 21:43). In claiming to be the Son of God and the decisive figure in the history of salvation [cf. 21:33-42; 26:63-64], Jesus makes himself guilty of blasphemy against God and is deserving of death (26:65-66). Accordingly, in effecting the death of Jesus, the leaders understand themselves to be purging Israel of the error with which a false messiah would pervert the nation (27:63-64). The irony, however, is that in abjectly repudiating Jesus, the leaders achieve the opposite of what they had intended: far from purging Israel from error, they plunge it into fatal error, for they make both themselves and the people responsible for the death of the one who is in fact the Son of God and through whom God proffers salvation to Israel; unwittingly, therefore, the leaders make themselves responsible for Israel's [temporary] loss of its privileged place among the nations as God's chosen people (15:13-14; 21:37-43; 22:7; 27:20-25)."[1397]

The death of Jesus 27:45-50 (cf. Mark 15:33-37; Luke 23:44-46; John 19:28-30)

Matthew now turned his spotlight away from the observers of Jesus to Jesus Himself.

27:45   The "land" (Gr. *ge*) of Palestine became abnormally dark from noon until 3:00 p.m. This was quite clearly an abnormal, literal darkening of the sky. It could not have resulted from a solar eclipse since the Passover was celebrated at full moon.[1398] Matthew's use of *ge* probably implies Israel as well. Darkness in Scripture often represents judgment and or tragedy (cf. Amos 8:9-10). Compare the three *days* of darkness in Egypt (Exod. 10:21-23) and the three *hours* of darkness here. Matthew's description of the setting "conveys a strong sense of impending disaster."[1399] This was a judgment on Israel and its people, but it was also a judgment on Jesus. His cry of desolation came out of this darkness (v. 46). This was a time of judgment on Jesus for the sins of all humanity.

27:46   Jesus cried out the words of Psalm 22:1 because His Father was abandoning Him. It was out of a similar sense of abandonment that David originally wrote the words of this psalm.

". . . the psalm expresses the spiritual desolation of a man who continues to trust and to appeal to God in spite of the fact that his ungodly opponents mock and persecute him with impunity."[1400]

Separation from the Father must have been the worst part of the Cross for Jesus who had never before experienced anything but intimate fellowship with His Father. Jesus became the center of God's judgment on mankind's sin (cf. Rom. 3:21-26; 2 Cor. 5:21).[1401]

"Here Jesus was bearing the sins of the whole world, and even God the Father had to turn away as Jesus bore the curse and identified Himself with the sins of the whole world. When Jesus actually died, He commended Himself back into the Father's hands."[1402]

The NASB has "*Eli, Eli,*" a transliteration of the Hebrew words that mean "My God, my God." The NIV has "*Eloi, Eloi,*" the Aramaic words that mean the same thing. Probably the NIV is correct here. Jesus evidently quoted these words in Aramaic (cf. Mark 15:34). The remaining words "*lama sabachthani*" are Aramaic. Matthew translated Jesus' Aramaic words into Greek, or perhaps a later copyist made the change.

By comparing the Gospel accounts we know that Jesus spoke seven times while hanging on the cross. First, He said, "Father, forgive them" (Luke 23:34). Second, He told one of the insurrectionists crucified with Him, "Today you shall be with me in paradise" (Luke 23:43). Third, He told His mother, "Woman, behold your son," and He told John, "Behold, your mother" (John 19:26-27). Fourth, He cried, "My God, my God, why have you forsaken me?" (Matt. 27:46; Mark 15:34). Fifth, He said, "I thirst" (John 19:28). Sixth, He exclaimed, "It is finished" (John 19:30). Seventh, He cried, "Father, into your hands I commend my spirit" (Matt. 27:50; Luke 23:46).

27:47   This statement, made by "some" onlookers "standing there," reflects a belief that "Elijah," whom God took to heaven without dying, would come to rescue the righteous from their distress. There is no biblical basis for this idea, though later Jews held it.[1403] Perhaps it had some connection with the prophecy about Elijah's return to herald Messiah's appearing.

[1397]Kingsbury, *Matthew as . . .*, p. 162.

[1398]F. F. Bruce, *Jesus and Christian Origins outside the New Testament*, pp. 29-30.

[1399]Kingsbury, *Matthew as . . .*, p. 28.

[1400]France, *The Gospel . . .*, p. 1076.

[1401]See S. Lewis Johnson Jr., "The Death of Christ," *Bibliotheca Sacra* 125:497 (January-March 1968):10-19.

[1402]Walvoord, *Matthew: . . .*, pp. 234-35.

[1403]*Theological Dictionary of the New Testament*, s.v. "El(e)ias," by J. Jeremias, 2:930.

27:48-49   Evidently one of the soldiers took another opportunity to mock Jesus further (cf. v. 34). The Greek word translated "sour wine" or "wine vinegar" is *oxos* and means "vinegar." It probably describes the wine that the soldiers strengthened with vinegar and drank themselves. By giving this to Jesus they really lengthened His sufferings. It was a profession of compassion to offer Jesus the drink, but it did Him no favor (cf. Ps. 69:21). "But" (Gr. *de*) in the NASB in verse 49 is too strong a translation. Including the phrase "Leave Him alone now" (NIV) gives the sense of verse 49. The soldiers wanted to see what the result of Jesus' drinking the vinegar would be. With false piety, the soldiers sarcastically said they would wait to see if Elijah would come to rescue Jesus.

27:50   Forsaken by everyone, including His Father, Jesus again cried out loudly in His agony (cf. John 19:30). This was His sixth utterance on the cross. Then followed His seventh and final statement: "Father, into Your hands I commit My spirit" (Luke 23:46; cf. Ps. 31:6). Shortly thereafter, He dismissed "His spirit" (i.e., what animated His life, Gr. *pneuma*). Matthew's description of the moment of Jesus' death shows that Jesus had sovereign control over His own life (cf. John 10:18). Jesus manifested His kingly authority even with His dying breath. He did not commit suicide as Judas had done, but He laid down His life in self-sacrifice for the sins of humankind (cf. 20:28).

> "The Greek words used here and in Jn. 19:30 are unique in the N.T. In fifteen other Bible verses, 'gave up the spirit,' or 'yielded up the spirit,' is used to translate a single Hebrew or Greek word meaning *breathe out* or *expire*. This is true of the description of the death of Jesus in Mk. 15:37, 39 and Lk. 23:46. But in Mt. 27:50 and Jn. 19:30 alone these expressions translate a Greek phrase of two words, meaning *give over the spirit* or *deliver up the spirit*. The death of Jesus was different from that of any other man. No one could take His life from Him except as He was willing to permit it (Jn. 10:18). Christ chose to die so that we might live."[1404]

The immediate results of Jesus' death 27:51-56 (cf. Mark 15:38-41; Luke 23:45, 47-49)

27:51a   The inner "veil" of the temple is probably in view here, the one separating the holy place from the most holy place (cf. Heb. 4:16; 6:19-20; 9:11-28; 10:19-22).[1405]

> "According to Jewish Tradition, there were, indeed, two Veils before the entrance to the Most Holy Place (Yoma v. 1). . . . one Veil hung on the side of the Holy, the other on that of the Most Holy Place. . . . The Veils before the Most Holy Place were 40 cubits (60 feet) long, and 20 (30 feet) wide, of the thickness of the palm of the hand . . ."[1406]

> "A wooden partition separated the Most Holy from the Holy Place; and over the door hung the veil which was 'rent in twain from the top to the bottom' when the way into the holiest of all was opened on Golgotha."[1407]

> "The Rabbis speak of two veils, and say that the high-priest went in by the southern edge of the first veil, then walked along till he reached the northern corner of the second veil, by which he entered the Most Holy Place."[1408]

The tearing happened at 3:00 p.m., the time of the evening incense offering. A priest would normally have been standing in the holy place offering incense when it tore (cf. Luke 1:8-10). Some early non-biblical Jewish sources also report unusual phenomena in the temple 40 years before its destruction in A.D. 70, one of which is the temple curtain tearing.[1409]

> "The fact that this occurred from top to bottom signified that God is the One who ripped the thick curtain. It was not torn from the bottom by men ripping it."[1410]

[1404]*The New Scofield . . .*, pp. 1043-44.

[1405]France, *The Gospel . . .*, pp. 1079-80.

[1406]Edersheim, *The Life . . .*, 2:611; idem, *Sketches of . . .*, p. 197.

[1407]Idem, *The Temple*, p. 58.

[1408]Ibid., f. 3.

[1409]See Robert L. Plummer, "Something Awry in the Temple? The Rending of the Temple Veil and Early Jewish Sources that Report Unusual Phenomena in the Temple around AD 30," *Journal of the Evangelical Theological Society* 48:2 (June 2005):301-16.

[1410]Barbieri, p. 90.

This was a supernatural act that symbolized the opening of access to God and the termination of the Mosaic system of worship. This event marked the end of the old Mosaic Covenant and the beginning to the New Covenant (cf. 26:26-29). Jesus Himself now replaced the temple (cf. 26:61). He also became the Great High Priest of His people. The rent veil also prefigured the physical destruction of the temple, a necessary corollary to its spiritual uselessness from then on.

27:51b-53   Earthquakes often accompanied divine judgment and the manifestation of God's glory in the Old Testament (1 Kings 19:11; Isa. 29:6; Jer. 10:10; Ezek. 26:18).[1411] This one may have been responsible for the rending of the temple veil, the splitting of the rocks, and the opening of the tombs. The temple stood on a geological fault that has caused minor damage throughout history.[1412] The supernatural occurrences that accompanied Jesus' crucifixion hinted at its spiritual implications.

One writer suggested that the sentence begun in verse 51 should really end with "were opened" or "broke open" in verse 52.[1413] There were no punctuation marks in the original Greek text. Thus the two events that accompanied the earthquake were: the rending of the temple veil and the splitting of the rocks. These first two things happened when Jesus died.

The resurrection of the saints (lit. holy people), that Matthew described, happened later when Jesus arose from the dead. This explanation obviates the problem of people coming out of their graves when Jesus died but not showing themselves until He arose. Matthew did not answer many questions that we would like answers to, such as what type of bodies they had, and whether they died again or went directly to heaven. They were Old Testament saints. I suspect that they experienced the same type of resurrection that Lazarus did. Perhaps Matthew mentioned their resurrections here, to help us appreciate the fact that Jesus' death provided the basis for the resurrection of believers who died before the Cross as well as after it. Maybe he placed it here also to avoid breaking the narrative flow of chapter 28, and to connect Jesus' death immediately with resurrection.[1414] The King had authority over life and death.

"This event is nowhere explained in the Scriptures but seems to be a fulfillment of the feast of the first fruits of harvest mentioned in Leviticus 23:10-14. On that occasion, as a token of the coming harvest, the people would bring a handful of grain to the priest. The resurrection of these saints, occurring after Jesus Himself was raised, is a token of the coming harvest when all the saints will be raised."[1415]

27:54   What the "centurion" and the other soldiers meant, when they called Jesus "the Son of God," depends somewhat on who they were and what their background was. The centurion was a Roman soldier responsible for 100 men, not that *that many* guarded Jesus at the Cross. The other soldiers may have been Romans from outside Palestine, or possibly Gentile residents of the land who served in the army. They probably meant that Jesus was a divine being in a pagan sense ("a son of a god" rather than "The Son of God"). If so, they spoke more truly than they knew. The darkness, earthquake, and Jesus' manner of dying convinced these hardened soldiers that this was no ordinary execution. They seem to have reacted superstitiously and fearfully. Matthew recorded the centurion's comment as another ironical testimony to Jesus' messianic identity. Here *Gentiles* testified to the identity of Israel's Messiah—whom the Jews had rejected!

"In declaring Jesus to be the Son of God, the Roman soldiers 'think' about him as God 'thinks' about him [cf. 3:17; 17:5; 16:23]. Accordingly, their evaluative point of view concerning Jesus' identity can be seen to be in alignment with that of God. . . .

"Two consequences flow from this. The first is that the soldiers acclamation becomes the place in Matthew's plot where Jesus is, for the first time, both correctly and publicly affirmed by humans to be the Son of God. And the second consequence is that, as a result of the soldiers' acclamation, the way is in principle now open for the task of 'going and making disciples of all nations.' Or, to put it differently, one could also say that the way is now open for the task of making the salvation Jesus has accomplished in his death owing to his conflict with Israel redound to the benefit of all humankind. Then, too, since the Roman soldiers are themselves Gentiles, they attest in this way as well that the time for embarking upon the universal mission is at hand."[1416]

[1411]See R. J. Bauckham, "The Eschatological Earthquake in the Apocalypse of John," *Novum Testamentum* 19 (1977):224-33.

[1412]D. Baly, *The Geography of the Bible*, p. 25.

[1413]J. W. Wenham, "When Were the Saints Raised?" *Journal of Theological Studies* 32 (1981):150-52.

[1414]Carson, "Matthew," p. 582.

[1415]Walvoord, *Matthew: . . .*, p. 236.

[1416]Kingsbury, *Matthew as . . .*, p. 90.

Other confessions that Jesus is God's Son appear in 3:17; 4:3, 6; 8:29; 11:25-27; 14:33; 16:16; 17:5; 21:37-39; 22:42-45; and 24:36.

27:55-56   Why did Matthew include reference to the "women" who observed the crucifixion? Even though Jewish society did not regard women equally with men, their witness of Jesus' death would have added some credibility to Matthew's account (cf. 1 Cor. 1:27-31). As Mary, who seemed to understand and believe something of what Jesus had said about dying (26:6-13), they did not abandon Him as most of His unfaithful male disciples had done. The only believing disciples who did not abandon Him appear to have been a few powerless women, who could not help Him but only observed His sufferings from afar, and John (John 19:26-27). These women were the last at the cross and the first at the tomb (cf. 28:1), indicating their devotion to Jesus, whom they "had followed" in and "from Galilee," and whom they had ministered to financially (Luke 8:2-3). Thus one reason for this mention of the women appears to be to bridge Jesus' crucifixion and His resurrection. The women Matthew chose to identify by name were probably those whom his original readers knew best by the names he used to describe them. The following chart attempts to harmonize the references in the Gospels that identify the women who observed Jesus on the cross.

SOME WOMEN WHO OBSERVED THE CRUCIFIXION		
Matthew 27:56	**Mark 15:40**	**John 19:25**
Mary Magdalene	Mary Magdalene	Mary Magdalene
		Jesus' mother (Mary)
Mary the mother of James and Joseph =	Mary the mother of James the Less and Joses =	Mary the wife of Clopas
Mother of Zebedee's sons =	Salome =	Jesus' mother's sister

5. The burial of Jesus 27:57-66

Matthew emphasized two things about Jesus' burial: the fulfillment of prophecy, and the impossibility of the theory that someone stole Jesus' body.

The placing of Jesus in the tomb 27:57-61 (cf. Mark 15:42-47; Luke 23:50-56; John 19:31-42)

Normally the Romans let the bodies of crucified criminals rot on their crosses without burial. If family members wanted to bury a crucified loved one, they had to apply for permission to do so. The Romans usually granted these requests, with the exception of criminals who had committed high treason. The Jews, however, did not want dead corpses to remain unburied overnight (Deut. 21:22-23).

27:57   "Evening" would have been late afternoon. The next day, a Sabbath, began at sundown, which would have occurred about 6:00 p.m. at this time of year in Palestine. Hoehner calculated that this was the evening of Friday, April 3, A.D. 33.[1417]

The location of Joseph's home is uncertain. It may have been Ramathaim-zophim, located about 20 miles northwest of Jerusalem.[1418] Joseph was a member of the Sanhedrin who had not consented to Jesus' death (Luke 23:51). Matthew only mentioned that he was a "rich . . . disciple" of Jesus (cf. Isa. 53:9-12). In the Greek text, the word translated "rich" is in the emphatic position in the sentence. Matthew apparently wanted to stress the fulfillment of Isaiah 53:9: "His grave was assigned to be with wicked men, yet with a rich man in His death." Evidently Joseph was a follower *from a distance*, since John wrote that he was a secret disciple for fear of the Jews (John 19:38). Matthew noted that even a member of the ruling body that condemned Jesus believed on Him, another testimony that He was indeed the Messiah.

27:58-60   Joseph was bold enough to "ask" Pilate "for Jesus' body." The fact that Pilate allowed Joseph to bury Jesus' body shows that the governor did not think Jesus was guilty of treason. Joseph prepared the body of Jesus for burial with the help of Nicodemus (John 19:39), and perhaps other friends and or servants.

Matthew did not mention how these men wrapped Jesus' body for burial, but simply stated that the "clean linen cloth" (Gr. *sindon*) they used was expensive. This reflected their respect for Jesus.

[1417]Hoehner, *Chronological Aspects* . . ., p. 143.

[1418]France, *The Gospel* . . ., p. 1089.

Joseph's "new tomb," a sign of his wealth, was probably near the present Church of the Holy Sepulcher. This area had been a stone quarry centuries earlier, out of whose walls the Jews had cut tombs.[1419] Joseph had prepared this tomb for himself, but now he put Jesus in his place. This was an extravagant act of devotion (cf. 26:6-13). It was impossible (humanly speaking) for Jesus to escape from a tomb "hewn out" of solid massive rock (Gr. *petra*, cf. 16:18), even if He had been alive when placed in it. Matthew built a strong case for the reality of Jesus' resurrection, as he did for the virgin birth of Jesus.

> "Tombs were of various kinds. Many were sealed with some sort of boulder wedged into place to discourage wild animals and grave robbers. But an expensive tomb consisted of an antechamber hewn out of the rock face, with a low passage (cf. 'bent over,' John 20:5, 11) leading into the burial chamber that was sealed with a cut, disk-shaped stone that rolled in a slot cut into the rock. The slot was on an incline, making the grave easy to seal but difficult to open: several men might be needed to roll the stone back up the incline."[1420]

27:61   The Romans did not permit friends to mourn the deaths of criminals they executed. However, the women mentioned here witnessed Jesus' burial, along with Joseph and Nicodemus (cf. 1 Cor. 15:4). Matthew's notation of what they saw prepares for 28:1.

The guarding of Jesus' tomb 27:62-66

Matthew's Gospel is the only one that includes this pericope. It is a witness to the falsehood of the chief priests and elders' claim that someone stole Jesus' body (28:11-15).

27:62   The day to which Matthew referred was the Sabbath. He probably referred to it as he did ("the day after the preparation") to avoid the confusion that often arises when describing the Sabbaths associated with feasts. The Sanhedrin members could confer with Pilate if they did not have to travel more than a Sabbath day's journey, and if they did not have to enter his residence (cf. John 18:28). However, they could hardly do everything else they did without violating the Sabbath, something they hypocritically had charged Jesus with doing.

27:63-64   Jesus was in the tomb only about 36 hours, but because these hours spanned across parts of three consecutive days, the Jews reckoned the period as three days long (cf. 12:40). The fact that Jesus' prediction of His resurrection had reached the ears of these men reflects badly on the disciples' lack of faith. They should have understood and believed that Jesus would arise, since knowledge of His prediction of this event was so widespread. These Sanhedrin members did not believe Jesus would rise. They wanted to guard against any plot that His disciples might concoct alleging that He arose. The Jews needed Pilate's approval for any military action.

> Jesus' first "deception" from their viewpoint was His messiahship, and His "last" (second) was His claim that He would rise from the dead. The falsely pious chief priests and Pharisees pretended to want to protect the people from deception. Matthew viewed their action as self-deception designed to deceive others ("blind leading the blind"). They had formerly accused Jesus, as here, of being a "deceiver" (26:4).

27:65-66   Pilate refused to assign his own troops to guard Jesus' tomb, but he allowed the Jewish leaders to use their temple guards for this purpose (cf. 28:11). Pilate's reply was probably cynical. These men had feared Jesus when He was alive, and now they feared His disciples after He was dead. Pilate did not think the chance that Jesus' disciples would steal His body was very great. The chief priests and Pharisees secured the tomb by posting their guards at the site, and by putting an official wax "seal on the stone" door (cf. Ps. 2:4).

This pericope stresses the corruptness of Israel's rulers and their willful rejection of Jesus.[1421] It also shows that Jesus was definitely dead.

> "The incongruous, ironical result is that the opponents took Jesus' words about rising from the dead more seriously than did the disciples."[1422]

[1419]Carson, "Matthew," p. 584.
[1420]Ibid. See also Edersheim, *Sketches of . . .*, p. 171.
[1421]Toussaint, *Behold the . . .*, p. 314.
[1422]Hagner, *Matthew 14—28*, p. 864.

B. THE KING'S RESURRECTION CH. 28

The resurrection is central to Christian theology (cf. 1 Cor. 15:12-19). However, the Gospel evangelists did not deal with the theological implications of the resurrection, but simply recorded the facts. The Apostle Paul wrote much to help us appreciate the significance of this great event (cf. Rom. 4:24-25; 6:4; 8:34; 10:9; 1 Cor. 15; 2 Cor. 5:1-10, 15; Phil. 3:10-11; Col. 2:12-13; 3:1-4; 1 Thess. 4:14).

"The history of the Life of Christ upon earth closes with a Miracle as great as that of its inception."[1423]

1. The empty tomb 28:1-7 (cf. Mark 16:1-8; Luke 24:1-8; John 20:1)

28:1   The NASB translation of the Greek preposition *opse* as "late" is misleading. The word can also mean "after," and it makes better sense if translated as such here.[1424] The women waited until "after the Sabbath" to go to Jesus' tomb (cf. Mark 16:1-2). They went early Sunday morning. The "other Mary" was Mary the mother of James and Joseph (27:56). Mark added that Salome also accompanied them (Mark 16:1). Salome was evidently the name of the mother of Zebedee's sons. The "and" (Gr. *kai*) in Mark 16:1 is probably assensive, meaning "even." Apparently they did not know that the Sanhedrin had posted a guard at the tomb. They evidently went there to remember Jesus but also to anoint Jesus' corpse (Mark 16:1). They must not have known that it had been sealed, either.

28:2-4   A second "earthquake" (divine intervention) had occurred (cf. 27:51). The relationship between the earthquake, the descent of the angel, and the rolling away of the stone is indefinite in the text. All of these events have supernatural connotations. An angel had announced the Incarnation, and now an angel announced the Resurrection (1:20-23; cf. 18:10).[1425] The angel rolled the stone away to admit the witnesses, not to allow Jesus to escape (cf. John 20:26). The guards experienced the earthquake and observed the angel, who appeared as a young man (Mark 16:5). It was seeing the angel—whose appearance was also "like lightning," which evidently terrified them so greatly—that Matthew could describe them as appearing "like dead men" (vv. 3-4). Perhaps they fainted "dead away," as in a deep sleep or coma.

28:5-7   The "angel" calmed the women's fear, caused by the shock of observing the scene, by speaking to them (cf. Mark 16:2-7; Luke 24:1-8; John 20:1). Of all the possible reasons for the tomb being open and empty that the women could have imagined, the angel clarified the one true explanation. "Jesus" had "risen" from the grave! The angel reminded them that Jesus had predicted His resurrection (cf. 16:21; 17:23; 20:18-19). He then invited them to "come" and "see" where He had lain, and to "go" and "tell" the other "disciples" that He had "risen from the dead." They should go "quickly" because this was the greatest news of all time. Jesus would confirm His resurrection with a personal appearance in Galilee shortly (cf. 26:32). He would arrive in "Galilee" before they did, and meet them there.

> "Earlier in Matthew's story, Jesus twice said to the disciples that 'whoever loses his life will find it [10:39; 16:25],' and on the cross Jesus held fast to God in trust even as he relinquished his life (27:46, 50). In raising Jesus from the dead, God certifies the truth of Jesus' words and the efficacy of his trust, which is to say that God vindicates Jesus: God resolves Jesus' conflict with Israel by showing that Jesus is in the right."[1426]

Who Moved the Stone? is a classic apologetic on the subject of the resurrection of Jesus Christ. Frank Morison, whose real name was Albert Henry Ross, was a skeptical British journalist when he began his research, but it convinced him of the historicity of the resurrection, and he became a Christian. This book presents a careful study of the last seven days of Jesus' pre-crucifixion ministry.[1427]

2. Jesus' appearance to the women 28:8-10

All the Gospels mention the fact that women were the first people to see Jesus alive. This is a proof that the resurrection was real. In that culture the witness of women was not regarded very highly.[1428] Thus, if the evangelists fabricated the resurrection, they certainly would not have written that women witnessed it first.

> "The crowning events of the resurrection narrative are the appearances of the risen Jesus first to the women and then to his disciples, i.e., the eleven. The empty tomb, for all of its impressiveness and importance, is not sufficient evidence in itself for

---

[1423]Edershiem, *The Life . . .*, 2:621.

[1424]Moule, p. 86.

[1425]Plummer, p. 417.

[1426]Kingsbury, *Matthew as . . .*, pp. 90-91.

[1427]Frank Morison, *Who Moved the Stone?*

[1428]Craig S. Keener, *A Commentary on the Gospel of Matthew*, pp. 698-99, especially footnote 282.

the resurrection of Jesus. What alone can be decisive is reliable eyewitness testimony that Jesus had been raised from the dead."[1429]

28:8-9   Jesus' sudden appearance must have given the women the shock of their lives (cf. Mark 16:8). He gave them a customary salutation (Gr. *chariete*, cf. 26:49). They kneeled at and grabbed "His feet," and "worshipped Him" (cf. v. 17). Grasping someone's feet was a recognized act of supplication and homage (Mark 5:22; 7:25; Luke 17:16).

28:10   Jesus calmed the women's fears as the angel had done, and He repeated the instructions that the angel had given them. Jesus' "brethren" were His disciples (12:48-50; 18:15; 23:8; 25:40; cf. 5:22-24; 7:3-5; 18:21, 35).

> "Why, then, Matthew's record of a resurrection appearance in Galilee? The answer surely lies in the combination of two themes that have permeated the entire Gospel. First, the Messiah emerges from a despised area . . . and first sheds his light on a despised people . . .; for the kingdom of heaven belongs to the poor in spirit (5:3). For this reason, too, the risen Jesus first appears to women whose value as witnesses among Jews is worthless . . . Second, 'Galilee of the Gentiles' (4:15) is compatible with the growing theme of Gentile mission in this Gospel . . . and prepares for the Great Commission (28:18-20)."[1430]

3. The attempted cover-up 28:11-15

This brief account finishes off Matthew's story of the guard in 27:62-66.

28:11   "Some" of the guards left the others at the tomb and "reported" the earthquake, the angel, and the empty tomb "to the chief priests." That they reported to the priests strongly suggests that they were Jewish temple guards rather than Roman guards (cf. 27:65). If they had been Roman guards and had reported to their Roman superiors, they probably would have lost their lives for falling asleep on duty (cf. Acts 12:19; 16:27-28).

28:12-14   The action of these Sanhedrin members proves that their promise to believe in Jesus if He would come down from the cross was hypocritical (cf. 27:42; Luke 24:13-32). They continued to show more concern for their own reputations and what was expedient than for the truth.

> Their devised story was a weak one that a critic might easily discredit. If the guards had been asleep, they could not have known of the theft. If one of them was awake, why did he not sound an alarm? It was also incredible that the disciples, who had abandoned Jesus out of fear, would have summoned enough courage to risk opening the guarded tomb. Moreover, if the Sanhedrin had any evidence against the disciples, they surely would have prosecuted them, but they did not.

> Molesting graves was sometimes punishable with death in the ancient Near East.[1431] Consequently Jesus' enemies resorted to bribery to shut the mouths of the soldiers, and later Pilate, if necessary. Previously they had been willing to pay Judas money to protect their interests (26:15).

28:15   Matthew explained that this was the origin of the Jewish explanation of the empty tomb that persisted to the time of his writing, whenever that may have been.

> "Justin, *Dial[logus]*. 108, tells us that this charge was still being actively propagated in the middle of the second century; it was an obvious countermove to Christian claims of Jesus' resurrection."[1432]

> Justin was an early Christian writer.

"The reason for Matthew's diligence in approaching the resurrection in such an apologetic manner is evident since so much is dependent upon the resurrection of the Messiah. It authenticated His person. To the nation of Israel, His resurrection was the sign of the prophet Jonah (Matthew 12:38-39) attesting the fact that Jesus was the Messiah. The reason Matthew says nothing about the ascension is bound up in this point. If Jesus is the Messiah, then an account of the ascension is both unnecessary and self-evident to the Israelite. He would yet come in clouds of glory. What mattered to Matthew was that Jesus was Israel's Messiah and the resurrection proved that fact; therefore he goes no further. Second, the resurrection validated

---

[1429]Hagner, *Matthew 14—28*, p. 874. Cf. p. 878.

[1430]Carson, "Matthew," p. 590. See Zane C. Hodges, "Form-Criticism and the Resurrection Accounts," *Bibliotheca Sacra* 124:496 (October-December 1967):339-48.

[1431]Cf. Bruce M. Metzger, "The Nazareth Inscription Once Again," in *Jesus und Paulus*, pp. 221-38.

[1432]France, *The Gospel . . .*, p. 1093.

Christ's prophecies concerning His rising from the dead (Matthew 16:21; 17:22-23; 20:17-19). Finally, the message of the King involving the character of the kingdom, the offer of the kingdom, and the offer's withdrawal are all involved in the resurrection, for the resurrection verifies the truthfulness of all that Christ ever spoke."[1433]

4. The King's final instructions to His disciples 28:16-20 (cf. Mark 16:15-18; 1 Cor. 15:6)

Whereas the chief priests used bribe money to commission the soldiers to spread lies, the resurrected Jesus used the promise of His power and presence to commission His disciples to spread the gospel.[1434] This is the final address that Matthew recorded Jesus giving. As usual, he used a narrative to lead up to the address. In this case the narrative consisted of the crucifixion and resurrection of Jesus. Therefore this address is the climax of these events in Matthew's structure of his Gospel. It is also climactic because of its position at the very end of the Gospel and because of its content. It recapitulates many of Matthew's themes, and it ends the story of Jesus where it began: in Galilee.[1435]

". . . to demonstrate that Jesus, in enduring the humiliation of the cross, did not die as a false messiah but as the Son who did his Father's will (21:37-39), God vindicates Jesus by raising him from the dead (28:5-6). Consequently, when Jesus appears to the disciples on the mountain in Galilee (28:16-17), it is as the crucified Son of God whom God has vindicated through resurrection (28:5c-6). Although some disciples show, in doubting, that they are yet weak of faith (28:17; 14:32), they all see on the person of Jesus that crucifixion, or suffering sonship, was the essence of his ministry (21:42). Correlatively, they also grasp at last that servanthood is the essence of discipleship (16:24; 20:25-28). As ones, therefore, who comprehend, in line with God's evaluative point of view (17:5), not only who Jesus is but also what he was about and what it means to be his followers, the disciples receive from Jesus the Great Commission and embark on a mission to all the nations (28:18-20; chaps. 24—25)."[1436]

28:16   "But" (NASB) is too strong a contrast for the Greek word *de* that occurs here and means "then" (NIV). However, the action of "the Eleven" contrasts with the action of the guards (v. 15). We do not know "the mountain" to which Jesus had directed them, and to which they went (cf. 26:32; 28:7, 10). "Galilee," of course, was where Jesus began His ministry, and it had Gentile connotations because of the presence and proximity of many Gentiles. What Jesus would tell His disciples in Galilee would continue His ministry and teaching that they had already experienced.

28:17   When the Eleven finally "saw" Jesus, "they worshipped Him." Yet some of them still had unresolved questions about how they should respond to Him. The word "doubted" (Gr. *edistasan*) means "hesitated" (cf. 14:31).[1437] Apparently Jesus' resurrection did not immediately dispel all the questions that remained in the minds of His disciples. Perhaps, also, some of them still felt embarrassed about deserting Him and wondered how He would deal with them.

28:18   Jesus proceeded to address the Eleven. Matthew did not record them saying anything, which focuses our attention fully on Jesus' words. Notice the repetition of "all" in verses 18-20: all authority, all nations, all things, and all the days. Matthew stressed the "authority" of Jesus throughout his Gospel (7:29; 10:1, 7-8; 11:27; 22:43-44; 24:35).

"Not merely power or might (*dunamis*), such as a great conqueror might claim, but '*authority*' (*exousia*), as something which is His by right, conferred upon Him by One who has the right to bestow it (Rev. ii. 27)."[1438]

God restricted Jesus' authority before His resurrection because of His role as the Suffering Servant. Following His resurrection, God broadened the sphere in which Jesus exercised authority (cf. 4:8-10). He became the One through whom God now mediates "all authority" (cf. Dan. 7:14; Phil. 2:5-11). This was Jesus' great claim.

"By raising Jesus from the dead and investing him with all authority, God vindicates Jesus and thus decides the conflict in his favor (28:5-6, 18)."[1439]

[1433]Toussaint, *Behold the . . .*, pp. 316-17.

[1434]Carson, "Matthew," p. 590.

[1435]See France, *The Gospel . . .*, pp.2-5, for further explanation of the geographical plan of Matthew's Gospel.

[1436]Kingsbury, *Matthew as . . .*, pp. 162-63.

[1437]I. P. Ellis, "'But some doubted,'" *New Testament Studies* 14 (1967-68):574-80.

[1438]Plummer, p. 428.

[1439]Kingsbury, *Matthew as . . .*, p. 8.

28:19   Jesus' disciples should "go . . . and make disciples" because Jesus now has universal authority. He gave them a new universal mission in keeping with His new universal authority. Previously He had limited their work to Israel (10:1-8; cf. 15:24). Now He sent them *into all the world*. They could go confidently, knowing that Jesus has sovereign control over everything "in heaven and on earth" (cf. Rom. 8:28). Note the similarity between the original cultural mandate to be fruitful, multiply, and fill the earth (Gen. 1:28; 9:1) and this new mandate for believers.

In the Greek text, there is one imperative verb, "make disciples" (Gr. *matheteusate*), modified by three participles, "going," "baptizing," and "teaching."[1440] This does not mean that we should make disciples wherever we may happen to go. The participle "going" is not just circumstantial, but it has some imperatival force.[1441] In other words, Jesus commanded His disciple to reach out to unreached people to make disciples, not just to make disciples among those with whom they happened to come in contact.

Making disciples involves bringing people into relationship with Jesus as pupils to Teacher. It involves getting them to take His yoke of instruction upon themselves as authoritative (11:29), accepting His words as true, and submitting to His will as what is right. A good disciple is one who listens, understands, and obeys Jesus' instructions (12:46-50). Disciples of Jesus must duplicate themselves in others.[1442]

The "all nations" (Gr. *panta ta ethne*) in view are all tribes, nations, and peoples, including Israel (cf. Gen. 12:3; 18:18; 22:18).[1443] The phrase does not mean Gentiles exclusive of Jews. Matthew hinted at the Gentiles' inclusion in God's plan to bless humanity throughout his Gospel (1:1; 2:1-12; 4:15-16; 8:5-13; 10:18; 13:38; 24:14; et al.). Jesus' disciples should make disciples among all people without distinction.

"Baptizing" and "teaching" are to characterize making disciples. Baptizing is to be into "the name" of the triune God (cf. 1 Cor. 12:4-6; 2 Cor. 13:14; Eph. 4:4-6; 2 Thess. 2:13-14; 1 Pet. 1:2; Rev. 1:4-6). The "into" (Gr. *eis*) suggests coming into relationship with God as a disciple. Baptism indicates both coming into covenant relationship with God, and pledging submission to His Lordship.[1444] Obviously water baptism rather than Spirit baptism is in view (cf. 3:6, 11, 13-17).

This baptism differs from John the Baptist's baptism. This one is universal, whereas John's baptism was for Israelites. This baptism rests on the finished work of Jesus Christ, but John's baptism prepared people for Jesus' person and work.[1445]

Jesus placed Himself on a level with the Father and the Holy Spirit.

"It is one thing for Jesus to speak about his relationship with God as Son with Father (notably 11:27; 24:36; 26:63-64) and to draw attention to the close links between himself and the Holy Spirit (12:28, 31-32), but for 'the Son' to take his place as the middle member, between the Father and the Holy Spirit, in a threefold depiction of the object of the disciple's allegiance is extraordinary."[1446]

"The Trinity of God is confessedly a great mystery, something wholly beyond the possibility of complete explanation. But we can guard against error by holding fast to the facts of divine revelation: that (1) with respect to His *Being* or essence, God is one; (2) with respect to His *Personality*, God is three; and (3) we must neither divide the essence, nor confuse the Persons."[1447]

The early Christians evidently did not understand the words "in the name of the Father and the Son and the Holy Spirit" as a baptismal formula that they needed to use whenever they baptized someone (cf. Acts 2:38; 8:16; 10:48; 19:5; Rom. 6:3). Jesus apparently meant that His disciples were to connect others with the triune God of the Bible in baptism.

"What, then, did Christ mean when he commanded that Baptism should be in the name of the Father, and of the Son, and of the Holy Spirit, except that we ought with one faith to believe in the Father, the Son, and the Spirit? What else is this than to testify clearly that the Father, Son, and Spirit are one God?"[1448]

[1440]See Robert D. Culver, "What Is the Church's Commission? Some Exegetical Issues In Matthew 28:16-20," *Bibliotheca Sacra* 125:499 (July-September 1968):239-53.

[1441]Cleon Rogers, "The Great Commission," *Bibliotheca Sacra* 130:519 (July-September 1973):258-67.

[1442]See James G. Samra, "A Biblical View of Discipleship," *Bibliotheca Sacra* 160:638 (April-June 2003):219-34.

[1443]John P. Meier, "Nations or Gentiles in Matthew 28:19," *Catholic Biblical Quarterly* 39 (1977):94-102.

[1444]G. R. Beasley-Murray, *Baptism in the New Testament*, pp. 90-92.

[1445]Lenski, p. 1178.

[1446]France, *The Gospel . . .*, p. 1118.

[1447]The New Scofield . . ., p. 1046.

[1448]Calvin, *Institutes of . . .*, 1:13:16.

Jesus did not specify a mode of baptism, though immersion was common in Judaism and is consistent with the meaning of the Greek word *baptizo*, "to immerse or submerge." His command to baptize disciples seems to rule out baptism for infants and others who cannot consciously understand and agree with what baptism signifies.

28:20	Discipling also involves "teaching" followers everything ("all") that Jesus "commanded" His disciples. Notice that the content is not the Old Testament law but Jesus' commands. This does not mean that the Old Testament is unimportant. Jesus validated the whole Old Testament during His ministry (5:17-20). However, the focus now becomes *Jesus* as the Source of revelation, rather than secondary sources such as the Old Testament prophets (cf. Heb. 1:1-4). Likewise, the revelation of the rest of the New Testament came through Jesus and is therefore also authoritative (Acts 1:1-2). "All" of this teaching remains authoritative forever (24:35).

Disciples must not just *understand* what Jesus has commanded, as foundational as that is. They must also *obey* it.

". . . Matthew uses this command to weave the final thread of his argument. The purpose of his Gospel was to prove to Israel that Jesus is the Messiah. The inquiring Jew would ask, 'If Jesus is our King, where is our kingdom?' Matthew has indicated that the kingdom was offered to Israel, rejected by them, and postponed by God. At the present time and until the end of the tribulation the kingdom is being offered to the Gentiles (Romans 11). Therefore, the disciples are to disciple all nations. At the end of the age the kingdom of Israel will be inaugurated by the return of Israel's King."[1449]

This Gospel ends not with a command but with a promise, or rather a fact. Jesus will "always" be "with" His disciples as they carry out His will. This is His great commitment. Immanuel is still "God with us" (1:23; cf. 18:20). The expression "to the end of the age" (Gr. *pasas tes hemeras*) literally means "the whole of every day."[1450] Jesus promised to be with us every day forever. It does not mean He will cease being with us when the present age ends and the messianic kingdom begins. Throughout the present age (Gr. *sunteleias tou aiovos*), Jesus' disciples are to carry out His Great Commission.[1451]

The Great Commission explains what Jesus has called His believing disciples to do between His departure from the earth and His return to establish His kingdom on earth (i.e., during the inter-advent age). That is why these verses are so important. Every Gospel writer recorded Jesus giving these marching orders, but they did not all record the same occasion when He did so. Jesus evidently gave this commission on at least three separate occasions. Mark and John recorded the first one (Mark 16:15-16; John 20:21-23). Matthew recorded the second one (28:19-20), and Luke recorded the third one (Luke 24:46-48; Acts 1:8). His purposes for us as His disciples could not be clearer.

Jesus began each of the preceding major sections of Matthew's Gospel with ministry, and concluded each with teaching. However, in this one He concluded with a command for His disciples to continue His ministry and teaching. Thus the book closes with the sense that the ministry and teaching of Jesus are ongoing.

[1449]Toussaint, *Behold the . . .*, p. 319.

[1450]Moule, p. 34.

[1451]See D. Edmond Hiebert, "An Expository Study of Matthew 28:16-20," *Bibliotheca Sacra* 149:595 (July-September 1992):338-54; and L. Legrand, "The Missionary Command of the Risen Lord Mt 28:16-20," *Indian Theological Studies* 24:1 (March 1987):5-28.

Appendix 1

A HARMONY OF THE GOSPELS					
	Date	Matthew	Mark	Luke	John
Introduction					
The sources of the Gospels				1:1-4	
The pre-existence and incarnation of Jesus					1:1-18
The genealogies of Jesus		1:1-17		3:23-38	
Events before the beginning of Jesus' public ministry					
The announcement of John the Baptist's birth				1:5-25	
The announcement of Jesus' birth to Mary				1:26-56	
The birth and early life of John the Baptist				1:57-80	
The announcement of Jesus' birth to Joseph		1:18-25			
The birth of Jesus	Winter of 5-4 B.C.			2:1-7	
The announcement to the shepherds				2:8-20	
Jesus' circumcision				2:21	
Jesus' presentation in the temple				2:22-38	
The visit of the wise men		2:1-12			
The holy family's trip to Egypt		2:13-18			
The holy family's return to Nazareth		2:19-23		2:39	
Jesus' childhood				2:40	
The holy family's trip to Jerusalem	Passover, April 29, 9 A.D.			2:41-50	
Jesus' youth in Nazareth				2:51-52	
The beginning of John the Baptist's ministry	29 A.D.			3:1-2	
John's message		3:1-6	1:1-6	3:3-6	
John's preaching		3:7-12	1:7-8	3:7-18	
The beginning of Jesus' public ministry					
Jesus' baptism	Summer or fall of 29 A.D.	3:13-17	1:9-11	3:21-22	
Jesus' temptation		4:1-11	1:12-13	4:1-13	
John the Baptist's testimony about Jesus					1:19-28
John's identification of Jesus as the Messiah					1:29-34
Jesus' first disciples					1:35-51
Jesus' early Galilean ministry					
Jesus' first miracle at Cana					2:1-11
Jesus' initial visit to Capernaum					2:12
Jesus' first visit to Jerusalem					
Jesus' first cleansing of the temple	April 7, 30 A.D.				2:13-22
Initial response to Jesus in Jerusalem					2:23-25
Jesus' conversation with Nicodemus					3:1-15
Jesus' mission and its consequences					3:16-21
The parallel ministries of Jesus and John the Baptist					3:22-30
The explanation of Jesus' preeminence					3:31-36
Jesus' reasons for leaving Judea		4:12	1:14	3:19-20; 4:14	4:1-4
Jesus' ministry in Samaria					
Jesus' conversation with the Samaritan woman					4:5-26

A Harmony of the Gospels	Date	Matthew	Mark	Luke	John
Jesus' explanation of evangelistic ministry					4:27-38
The response to Jesus in Samaria					4:39-42
Jesus' major Galilean ministry					
Jesus' arrival in Galilee					4:43-45
A synopsis of Jesus' teaching		4:17	1:14-15	4:14-15	
The healing of an official's son					4:46-54
Jesus' first rejection in Nazareth				4:16-30	
Jesus' move to Capernaum		4:13-16		4:31a	
Jesus' call of four disciples		4:18-22	1:16-20	5:1-11	
Jesus' healing of a demoniac in Capernaum			1:21-28	4:31b-37	
Jesus' healing of Peter's mother-in-law in Capernaum		8:14-15	1:29-31	4:38-39	
Jesus' healing of many other Galileans		8:16-17	1:32-34	4:40-41	
Jesus' first tour of Galilee		4:23-25	1:35-39	4:42-44	
Jesus' healing of a leprous Jew		8:1-4	1:40-45	5:12-16	
Jesus' healing and forgiveness of a paralytic		9:1-8	2:1-12	5:17-26	
Jesus' call of Matthew		9:9-13	2:13-17	5:27-32	
Jesus' defense of His disciples for not fasting		9:14-17	2:18-22	5:33-39	
Jesus' second visit to Jerusalem					
Jesus' healing of the paralytic at the Bethesda pool in Jerusalem					5:1-9
The antagonism of the Jewish authorities					5:10-18
The Son's equality with the Father					5:19-29
The Father's witness to the Son					5:30-47
Jesus' resumption of His Galilean ministry					
Jesus' defense of His disciples for plucking grain		12:1-8	2:23-28	6:1-5	
Jesus' healing of a man with a withered hand		12:9-14	3:1-6	6:6-11	
Jesus' teaching and healing by the Sea of Galilee		12:15-21	3:7-12		
Jesus' selection of the Twelve			3:13-19	6:12-16	
The Sermon on the Mount		5:1—7:29		6:17-49	
Jesus' healing of a centurion's servant		8:5-13		7:1-10	
Jesus' raising of a widow's son				7:11-17	
John the Baptist's inquiry		11:2-19		7:18-35	
Jesus' woes on the Galilean cities		11:20-30			
Jesus' anointing in Simon the Pharisee's house				7:36-50	
Jesus' second tour of Galilee				8:1-3	
The controversy about Jesus' connection with Beelzebul		12:22-37	3:20-30		
The Jewish leaders' demand for a sign		12:38-45			
The visit of Jesus' family members		12:46-50	3:31-35	8:19-21	
Kingdom parables Jesus taught by the Sea of Galilee		13:1-53	4:1-34	8:4-18	
Jesus' stilling of the Sea of Galilee		8:18, 23-27	4:35-41	8:22-25	
Jesus' healing of a demoniac in Gadara		8:28-34	5:1-20	8:26-39	
Jesus' healings of a woman and Jairus' daughter		9:18-26	5:21-43	8:40-56	
Jesus' healing of two blind men		9:27-31			

A Harmony of the Gospels					
	Date	Matthew	Mark	Luke	John
Jesus' healing of a dumb demoniac		9:32-34			
Jesus' last visit to Nazareth		13:54-58	6:1-6a		
Jesus' third tour of Galilee		9:35—10:4	6:6b-7	9:1-2	
The Twelve's tour of Galilee two by two		10:5—11:1	6:8-13, 30	9:3-6, 10a	
Herod's curiosity about Jesus		14:1-3	6:14-16	9:7-9	
The earlier death of John the Baptist	31 or 32 A.D.	14:4-12	6:17-29		
The training of the Twelve around Galilee					
The feeding of the 5000		14:13-21	6:31-44	9:10b-17	6:1-14
Jesus' withdrawal for prayer		14:22-23	6:45-46		6:15
Jesus' walking on the water		14:24-33	6:47-52		6:16-21
Jesus' reception at Gennesaret		14:34-36	6:53-56		
The bread of life discourse					6:22-59
Responses to the bread of life discourse					6:60—7:1
Jesus' defense of His disciples for eating with unwashed hands		15:1-20	7:1-23		
Jesus' healing of the Phoenician girl		15:21-28	7:24-30		
Jesus' healing of a deaf man in the Decapolis region			7:31-37		
Jesus' healing of many near the Sea of Galilee		15:29-31			
The feeding of the 4000		15:32-39	8:1-10		
The sign of Jonah		16:1-4	8:11-13		
Jesus' rebuke of His disciples' dullness		16:5-12	8:14-21		
Jesus' healing of a blind man near Bethsaida			8:22-26		
Peter's confession of faith		16:13-20	8:27-30	9:18-21	
Jesus' first prediction of His death and resurrection		16:21-26	8:31-37	9:22-25	
Jesus' prediction of His coming in glory		16:27-28	8:38—9:1	9:26-27	
The Transfiguration		17:1-8	9:2-8	9:28-36	
The question of Elijah's return		17:9-13	9:9-13		
Jesus' healing of an epileptic boy		17:14-20	9:14-29	9:37-43a	
Jesus' second prediction of His death and resurrection		17:22-23	9:30-32	9:43b-45	
Jesus' lesson on paying taxes		17:24-27			
Jesus' teaching on greatness in the kingdom		18:1-5	9:33-37	9:46-48	
Jesus' teaching about stumbling others		18:6-14	9:38-50	9:49-50	
Jesus' teaching about forgiving others		18:15-35			
Jesus' teaching about forsaking all as disciples		8:19-22		9:57-62	
The brothers of Jesus' counsel to display Himself in Jerusalem					7:2-9
Jesus trip to Jerusalem through Samaria				9:51-56	7:10
Jesus' later Judean ministry					
The controversy surrounding Jesus					7:11-13
Jesus' ministry at the feast of Tabernacles	September 10-17, 32 A.D.				7:14-44
The Jewish leaders' unbelief					7:45-52
The woman caught in adultery					7:53—8:11
Jesus' light of the world discourse					8:12-20
The Pharisees' attempt to stone Jesus					8:21-59

	A Harmony of the Gospels				
	Date	Matthew	Mark	Luke	John
Jesus' healing of the man born blind					9:1-41
Jesus' good Shepherd discourse					10:1-21
The tour of the Seventy two by two				10:1-24	
The parable of the good Samaritan				10:25-37	
Jesus' meal in Mary and Martha's home				10:38-42	
The Lord's Prayer				11:1-4	
The parable of the shameless friend				11:5-13	
The second charge of Jesus' collusion with Satan				11:14-36	
Jesus' condemnation of the Pharisees				11:37-54	
Jesus' teaching about stewardship				12:1-59	
The parable of the barren fig tree				13:1-9	
Jesus' healing of the woman bent double				13:10-17	
Parables of the kingdom repeated				13:18-21	
The confrontation at the feast of Dedication	December 18, 32 A.D.				10:22-39
Jesus' withdrawal to Perea					10:40-42
Jesus' later Perean ministry					
Jesus' teaching about the narrow way				13:22-35	
Jesus' healing of a man with dropsy				14:1-6	
Jesus' teaching about participants in the kingdom				14:7-24	
Jesus' teaching on the cost of discipleship				14:25-35	
The parables of three lost things				15:1-32	
Three parables about stewardship				16:1—17:10	
Jesus' raising of Lazarus					11:1-54
Jesus' healing of 10 lepers				17:11-19	
Jesus' teaching about His return				17:20-37	
The parable of the persistent widow				18:1-8	
The parable of the Pharisee and the tax collector				18:9-14	
Jesus' departure from Galilee and entrance into Judea		19:1-2	10:1		
Jesus' teaching on divorce		19:3-12	10:2-12		
Jesus' reception of the children		19:13-15	10:13-16	18:15-17	
The rich young ruler's encounter with Jesus		19:16-30	10:17-31	18:18-30	
The parable of the laborers in the vineyard		20:1-16			
Jesus' third announcement of His death and resurrection		20:17-19	10:32-34	18:31-34	
James and John's desire for prominence		20:20-28	10:35-45		
The healing of blind men near Jericho		20:29-34	10:46-52	18:35-43	
Jesus' visit with Zachaeus				19:1-10	
The parable of the minas				19:11-27	
Jesus' final public ministry in Jerusalem					
Jesus' arrival in Bethany	Saturday, March 28, 33 A.D.				11:55-57
Mary's anointing of Jesus' feet		26:6-13	14:3-9		12:1-11
The Triumphal Entry	Monday, March 30, 33 A.D.	21:1-11, 14-17	11:1-11	19:28-44	12:12-19
Jesus' cursing of the fig tree	Tuesday, March 31, 33 A.D.	21:18-19a	11:12-14		
Jesus' second cleansing of the temple		21:12-13	11:15-18	19:45-48	

	A Harmony of the Gospels				
	Date	**Matthew**	**Mark**	**Luke**	**John**
The disciples' discovery of the withered fig tree	Wednesday, April 1, 33 A.D.	21:19b-22	11:19-25		
Jesus' kernel of wheat teaching					12:20-50
The Sanhedrin's challenge of Jesus' authority		21:23—22:14	11:27—12:12	20:1-19	
The question of paying taxes to Caesar		22:15-22	12:13-17	20:20-26	
The Sadducees' question about the resurrection		22:23-33	12:18-27	20:27-40	
The question about the greatest commandment		22:34-40	12:28-34		
Jesus' question about David' Lord		22:41-46	12:35-37	20:41-44	
Jesus final denunciation of Israel's religious leaders		23:1-39	12:38-40	20:45-47	
The widow who gave all she had			12:41-44	21:1-4	
Jesus' preparation of the Twelve for the future					
The Olivet Discourse		24:1—25:46	13:1-37	21:5-36	
Jesus' practices during this week				21:37-38	
Jesus' prediction of His crucifixion in two days	Thursday, April 2, 33 A.D.	26:1-5	14:1-2	22:1-2	
Judas' agreement to betray Jesus		26:14-16	14:10-11	22:3-6	
Preparations for the Passover meal		26:17-19	14:12-16	22:7-13	
The beginning of the Passover meal		26:20	14:17	22:14-16, 24-30	
Jesus' washing of the Twelve's feet					13:1-20
Jesus' identification of His betrayer		26:21-25	14:18-21	22:21-23	13:21-30
Jesus' giving of the new commandment					13:31-35
Jesus' prediction of Peter's denial		26:31-35	14:27-31	22:31-34	13:36-38
Jesus' instruction to prepare for mission				23:35-38	
Jesus' institution of the Lord's Supper		26:26-29	14:22-25	22:17-20	
The Upper Room Discourse					14:1—16:33
Jesus' high priestly prayer					17:1-26
Jesus' departure for Mt. Olivet		26:30	14:26	22:39	18:1
Jesus' agony in Gethsemane		26:36-46	14:32-42	22:40-46	
Jesus' passion ministry					
Jesus' arrest	Friday, April 3, 33 A.D.	26:47-56	14:43-52	22:47-53	18:2-14
Jesus' interrogation by Annas					18:19-24
Jesus' interrogation by Caiaphas		26:57-68	14:53-65	22:54-65	18:15-18, 25-27
Jesus' condemnation by the Sanhedrin		27:1	15:1a	22:66-71	
Judas' remorse and suicide		27:3-10			
Jesus' first appearance before Pilate		27:2, 11-14	15:1b-5	23:1-7	18:28-38a
Jesus' appearance before Herod				23:8-12	
Jesus' second appearance before Pilate		27:15-26	15:6-15	23:13-25	18:38b—19:16
The Roman soldiers' severe beating of Jesus		27:27-31	15:16-20		
Jesus' journey to Golgotha		27:32-34	15:21-23	23:26-32	19:17
Jesus' first three hours on the cross		27:35-44	15:24-32	23:33-43	19:18-27
Jesus' second three hours on the cross		27:45-50	15:33-37	23:44-45a, 46	19:28-30
The phenomena accompanying Jesus' death		27:51-56	15:38-41	23:45b, 47-49	

	A Harmony of the Gospels				
	Date	Matthew	Mark	Luke	John
The treatment of Jesus' body after His death					19:31-37
Jesus' burial		27:57-60	15:42-46	23:50-54	19:38-42
The women's visit to Jesus' tomb		27:61-66	15:47	23:55-56	
Jesus' resurrection and post-resurrection appearances					
The earthquake and the angel's removal of the stone	Sunday, April 5, 33 A.D.	28:2-4			
The women's return to Jesus' tomb		28:1, 5-7	16:1-8	24:1-8	20:1
The women's report of the empty tomb to the disciples		28:8		24:9-11	20:2
Peter and John's visit to the tomb				24:12	20:3-9
Jesus' appearance to Mary Magdalene			16:9-11		20:10-18
Jesus' appearance to other women		28:9-10			
The guards' report of the empty tomb		28:11-15			
Jesus' appearance to Peter				24:34b	
Jesus' appearance to the disciples walking to Emmaus			16:12-13	24:13-34a, 35	
Jesus' appearance to the disciple when Thomas was absent			16:14-18	24:36-43	20:19-23
Jesus' appearance to the disciples when Thomas was present	Sunday, April 12, 33 A.D.				20:24-31
Jesus' appearance to seven disciples at the Sea of Galilee	Between April 12 and May 14, 33 A.D.				21:1-24
Jesus' appearance to the Eleven on a mountain in Galilee		28:16-20			
Jesus' last appearance and Ascension	Thursday, May 14, 33 A.D.		16:19-20	24:44-53	
Conclusion					
The scope of the Gospels					20:25

Appendix 2

THE KINGDOMS OF GOD

TRADITIONAL DISPENSATIONALISM

The Sovereign Rule of God

1011 B.C.

Davidic Kingdom

586 B.C.

First Advent

Ascension

Church

Mystery Form
of the Kingdom

Second Advent

Messianic Kingdom

PROGRESSIVE DISPENSATIONALISM AND
COVENANT PREMILLENNIALISM

The Sovereign Rule of God

1011 B.C.

Davidic Kingdom

586 B.C.

First Advent

Ascension

Church

Second Advent

Messianic Kingdom

Appendix 3

Views of the Messianic Kingdom

View	Has it begun?	How many stages?	Jesus' location	Jesus' agent
Non-millennial	Yes	One	Heaven or the New Earth	Church
Covenant Premillennial	Yes	Two	Heaven (already) and Earth (not yet)	Church and Church
Progressive Dispensational	Yes	Two	Heaven (already) and Earth (not yet)	Church and Israel
Traditional Dispensational	No	One	Earth	Israel

Appendix 4
The Parables of Jesus (in probable chronological order)

	Matthew	Mark	Luke	John
The physician			4:23	
The lamp	5:15	4:21-25	8:16; 11:33	
The blind guide	7:3-5		6:39-42	
The two trees	7:15-20		6:43-44	
The two paths	7:13-14			
The two men	12:35		6:45	
The two builders	7:21-27		6:46-49	
The friends of the bridegroom	9:15	2:19-20	5:34-35	
The new patch and the old garment	9:16	2:21	5:36	
The new wine and the old wineskins	9:17	2:22	5:37-38	
The children in the market	11:16-17		7:31-32	
The two debtors			7:41-42	
The divided house	12:25	3:24-25		
The strong man's house	12:29	3:27	11:21-22	
The empty house	12:43-45			
The soils	13:3b-9, 18-23	4:3-20	8:5-15	
The seed growing by itself		4:26-29		
The weeds	13:24-30, 36-42			
The mustard seed	13:31-32	4:30-32	13:18-19	
The yeast hidden in meal	13:33		13:20-21	
The hidden treasure	13:44			
The pearl	13:45-46			
The dragnet	13:47-50			
The homeowner	13:52			
The unforgiving servant	18:21-35			
The good Samaritan			10:30-37	
The shameless friend			11:5-8	
The rich fool			12:16-21	
The faithful servants			12:36-38	
The two servants	24:45-51		12:42-48	
The barren fig tree			13:6-9	
The seats at the wedding feast			14:7-11	
The great banquet			14:15-24	
The tower builder			14:28-30	
The king going to battle			14:31-33	
The lost sheep	18:12-14		15:4-7	
The lost coin			15:8-10	
The prodigal son			15:11-32	
The shrewd manager			16:1-9	
The rich man and Lazarus			16:19-31	
The unworthy servant			17:7-10	
The one taken and the one left	24:40-42		17:34-35	
The persistent widow			18:1-8	
The Pharisee and the tax collector			18:9-14	
The laborers in the vineyard	20:1-16			
The minas			19:11-27	
The two sons	21:28-32			
The wicked tenant farmers	21:33-46	12:1-12	20:9-19	
The royal wedding banquet	22:1-14			
The fig tree	24:32-34	13:28-30	21:29-31	
The doorkeeper		13:34-37		
The watchful homeowner	24:43-44			
The ten virgins	25:1-13			
The talents	25:14-30			
The sheep and the goats	25:31-46			

Appendix 5

What ends a marriage in God's sight?

<u>Jesus' teaching</u>

Matthew 5:27-32
1. Adultery is a sin. v. 27 (Exod. 20:14; Deut. 5:18)
2. Lusting after someone sexually is a form of adultery, so it's sin. v. 28
3. Therefore, Jesus' disciples need to deal with sexual temptations seriously. vv. 29-30
4. Moses allowed the Israelites to divorce. v. 31
5. People who divorce and then remarry someone else commit adultery. v. 32
6. But, remarriage by the innocent party in a divorce doesn't result in adultery if the guilty party was sexually unfaithful. v. 32
7. (Marital unfaithfulness, Gr. *pornea*, means having sexual intercourse with anyone other than one's spouse.)
8. Summary: Divorce is permissible, but it's never God's best (Mal. 2:16).

Matthew 19:9
(Same as points 5 - 7 above.)

Mark 10:11-12; Luke 16:18
(Same as point 5 above.)

<u>Paul's teaching</u>

1 Cor. 7:11-16
1. Christians who divorce have two options: remain unmarried or be reconciled. vv. 11-12
2. Christians who are married to non-Christians shouldn't initiate a divorce. v. 13
3. Christians who are married to non-Christians shouldn't refuse to grant a divorce if their mate insists on getting one. vv. 14-16

1 Cor. 7:39-40
1. Only death ends a marriage in God's sight (not adultery, marital unfaithfulness, or a divorce). v. 39
2. Widows and widowers are free to remarry other Christians. v. 39
3. But they may be happier if they remain unmarried. v. 40

Appendix 6

The Miracles of Jesus
(in probable chronological order)

Key: **N** = nature miracles (9); **H** = healings (21); **E** = exorcisms (6); **R** = raising the dead (3)

Event	Place	Matthew	Mark	Luke	John
Changing water into wine - **N**	Cana (Galilee)				2:1-11
Healing an official's son - **H**	Capernaum (Galilee)				4:46-54
Providing a large catch of fish - **N**	Sea of Galilee			5:1-11	
Healing a demoniac - **E**	Capernaum (Galilee)		1:21-28	4:31-37	
Healing Peter's mother-in-law - **H**	Capernaum (Galilee)	8:14-15	1:29-31	4:38-39	
Healing many others - **H**	Capernaum (Galilee)	8:16-17	1:32-34	4:40-41	
Healing a leprous Jew - **H**	Galilee	8:1-4	1:40-45	5:12-16	
Healing and forgiving a paralytic - **H**	Capernaum (Galilee)	9:1-8	2:1-12	5:17-26	
Healing a paralytic - **H**	Pool of Bethesda, Jerusalem (Judea)				5:1-9
Healing a man with a withered hand - **H**	Galilee	12:9-14	3:1-6	6:6-11	
Healing many others - **H**	Galilee	12:15	3:10-11		
Healing a centurion's servant - **H**	Capernaum (Galilee)	8:5-13		7:1-10	
Raising a widow's son - **R**	Nain (Galilee)			7:11-17	
Healing a dumb and blind demoniac - **E**	Galilee	12:22-24			
Stilling a storm - **N**	Sea of Galilee	8:23-27	4:35-41	8:22-25	
Healing a demoniac - **E**	Gadara (Decapolis)	8:28-34	5:1-20	8:26-39	
Healing a woman with a hemorrhage - **H**	Galilee	9:20-22	5:25-34	8:43-48	
Raising Jairus' daughter - **R**	Galilee	9:23-26	5:35-43	8:49-56	
Healing two blind men - **H**	Capernaum (Galilee)	9:27-31			
Healing a dumb demoniac - **E**	Capernaum (Galilee)	9:32-34			
Feeding over 5000 people - **N**	Near Bethsaida (Galilee)	14:13-21	6:31-44	9:10b-17	6:1-14
Walking on water - **N**	Sea of Galilee	14:22-33	6:45-52		6:15-21
Healing a Phoenician girl - **H**	Phoenicia	15:21-28	7:24-30		
Healing a deaf man with a speech impediment - **H**	Decapolis		7:31-37		
Healing many others - **H**	Near the Sea of Galilee	15:29-31			
Feeding over 4000 people - **N**	Decapolis	15:32-38	8:1-9		
Healing a blind man - **H**	Near Bethsaida (Galilee)		8:22-26		
Healing an epileptic boy - **E**	Galilee	17:14-20	9:14-29	9:37-43a	
Placing money in a fish's mouth - **N**	Capernaum (Galilee)	17:24-27			
Healing a man born blind - **H**	Jerusalem (Judea)				9:1-7
Healing a dumb demoniac - **E**	Judea			11:14-15	
Healing a woman bent double - **H**	Judea			13:10-17	
Healing a man with dropsy - **H**	Perea			14:1-6	
Raising Lazarus - **R**	Bethany (Judea)				11:1-44
Healing ten lepers - **H**	Samaria			17:11-19	
Healing two blind men - **H**	Near Jericho (Judea)	20:29-34	10:46-52	18:35-43	
Killing a fig tree - **N**	Near Jerusalem (Judea)	21:18-22	11:12-14, 19-25		
Restoring Malchus' ear - **H**	Near Jerusalem (Judea)			22:49-51	
Providing a large catch of fish - **N**	Sea of Galilee				21:1-13

Appendix 7

Some Figures of Speech in Scripture			
Figure		**Definition**	**Example**
Hendiadys		the expression of a single complex idea by joining two substantives with "and" rather than by using an adjective and a substantive	"the sacrifice and service of your faith" = the sacrificial service of your faith
Hyperbole		overstatement for the sake of emphasis	cut off your hand if it causes you to stumble = deal radically with instruments of temptation
Litotes		the statement of a negative to stress its positive opposite	"no small thing" = a very large thing
Merism		the identification of two extremes to represent the whole	"heaven and earth" = the universe
Metaphor		a comparison in which one thing is likened to a different thing by being spoken of as if it were that other	"All the world is a stage."
Metonymy		the use of the name of one thing for that of another asssociated with or suggested by it	"Jerusalem" = Israel; "the White House has decided" = "the President has decided"
Oxymoron		the joining of contradictory or incongruous terms to make a point	"an hour is coming and now is" = what will characterize the future is present even now
Personification		attributing the qualities of a person to an inanimate object	"the stones would cry out"
Polarization		expressing the extremes to highlight the difference between them	"as far as the east is from the west" = a very great distance
Simile		a comparison in which one thing is likened to a different thing by the use of "like," "as," etc.	a heart as big as a whale
Synecdoche		the use of the whole to represent a part of it, or the use of a part to represent the whole	"all the world" = all the Roman world, or "bread" = "food"

Appendix 8

The Incarnation of God the Son

There are several aspects of the incarnation of God the Son that merit clarification.

First, God the Son existed throughout eternity. The incarnation was not the beginning of His existence (John 1:1-3; Col. 1:15-17).

Second, when the Son became incarnate He took upon Himself full humanity. He became a man in every essential respect. Specifically, He didn't just take a human body, but He also took a human personality (emotions, intellect, and will), soul (the capacity to interact with other humans), and spirit (the capacity to interact with God). He was fully human in the non-material aspects of humanity, not just the material (physical) aspects. Every human being, including Jesus Christ, possesses both material (physical) characteristics and immaterial (spiritual) characteristics. Both are essential to humanity.

Third, the incarnation does *not* mean Jesus took a *sinful* human nature when He became a man. Sin is not an essential part of being human. God created man without sin, and then Adam and Eve chose to sin. Sin has affected all human beings since the fall, but being sinful is not an essential part of being human. Sin is, in a sense, foreign to humanity. It's a stain that has discolored every aspect of every person (total depravity). That Jesus was not sinful is clear from two facts.

> First, He committed no sins (1 Pet. 2:22). This includes thoughts as well as actions, omissions as well as commissions, little sins as well as big sins. In no way did Jesus ever deviate from God's will for human beings.

> Second, He did not inherit a sinful nature from His human father, as all other human beings do, since He was conceived by the Holy Spirit (Matt. 1:23; Luke 1:35). The virgin birth of Jesus guarantees His sinless human nature.

Fourth, whereas Jesus assumed a human body and a human nature at His birth, He has never and will never cease to be fully human as well as fully divine. When Jesus Christ returns to the earth at His second coming, He will have a human body and a human nature, as He did when He ascended into heaven (Acts 1:11). We will see Jesus as His disciples saw Him one day. And He will remain that way throughout eternity. Today there is a Man in heaven for us.

Fifth, the body that Jesus was born with is not the same kind of body that He arose from the dead with. He was born with a mortal body (i.e., one that could die), but He was raised with an immortal body (i.e., one that cannot and will never die). There are sufficient similarities between these bodies that His disciples recognized Jesus after His resurrection, but there are some dissimilarities so they had trouble, occasionally, recognizing Him.

Sixth, in the incarnation Jesus did not cease to be fully God. What Jesus "emptied Himself" of when He became a human (Phil. 2:7) was not His deity. It was the glory that He had enjoyed with the Father and the Spirit before the incarnation. Rather than retaining this glory, the Son of God assumed the limitations of humanity (sin apart). Furthermore, He became a servant among humans, which extended to dying for the sins of humanity in the most horribly agonizing and humiliating way possible (i.e., by crucifixion).

Seventh, during Jesus earthly ministry He sometimes demonstrated the qualities of full humanity and sometimes the qualities of full deity. For example, see the chart on the next page:

As a man Jesus . . .	As God Jesus . . .
Became weary.	Invited the weary to find rest in Him.
Became hungry.	Presented Himself as the bread of life.
Became thirsty.	Claimed to be the water of life.
Suffered great agony.	Was impervious to suffering and healed the afflictions of others.
Grew in favor with God and man.	Is the same yesterday, today, and forever.
Experienced temptation.	Could not experience temptation.
Said He didn't know some things.	Is omniscient.
Was present in only one place at a time.	Is omnipresent.
Operated in the power of the Holy Spirit.	Operated in His own power and authority.
Said the Father was greater than He.	Claimed that He and the Father are equal.
Prayed.	Received and answered the prayers of others.
Wept at the tomb of the dead.	Raised the dead.
Asked who people said He was.	Knew what people were thinking.
Asked why God had forsaken Him.	Claimed that God was always with Him.
Died.	Is eternal and gives eternal life to those who trust Him.
Was God's ideal man.	Is man's ideal God.

These are some of the paradoxes involved in the dual divine-human natures of Christ following His incarnation. It's because of these paradoxes that we sometimes have difficulty understanding the accounts of Jesus' words and works in the Gospels. He was like no other person, not because He was not fully human but because he was also fully God.

As God, the incarnate Christ reveals God and deserves our worship and service. As man, He reveals what God intended humans to be, and He provides the perfect example of how we should live as human beings.

End Maps

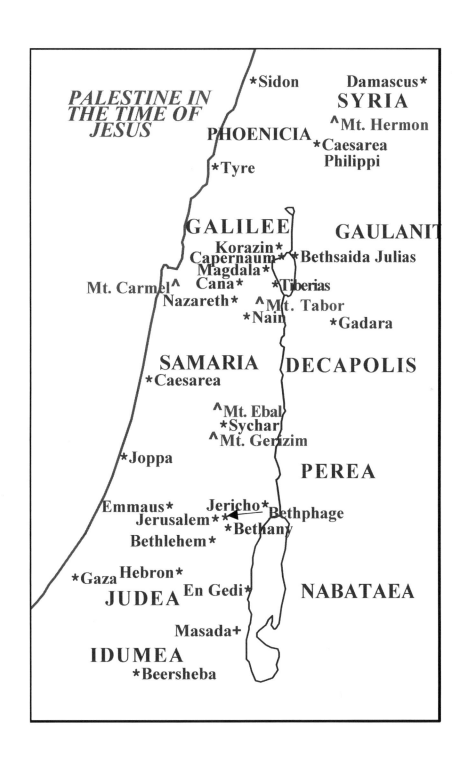

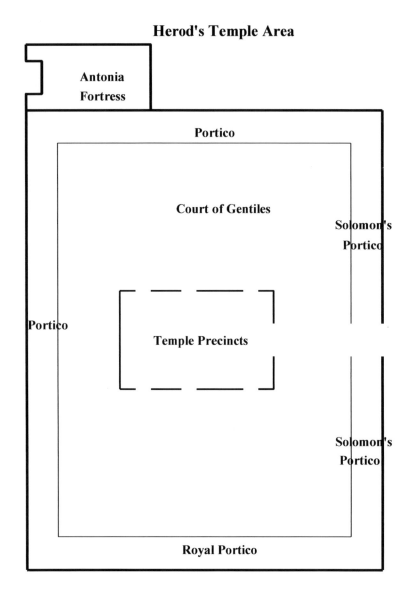

Herod's Temple Area

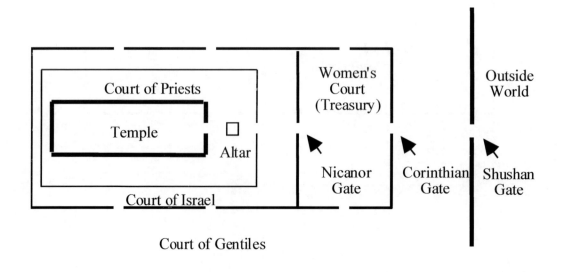

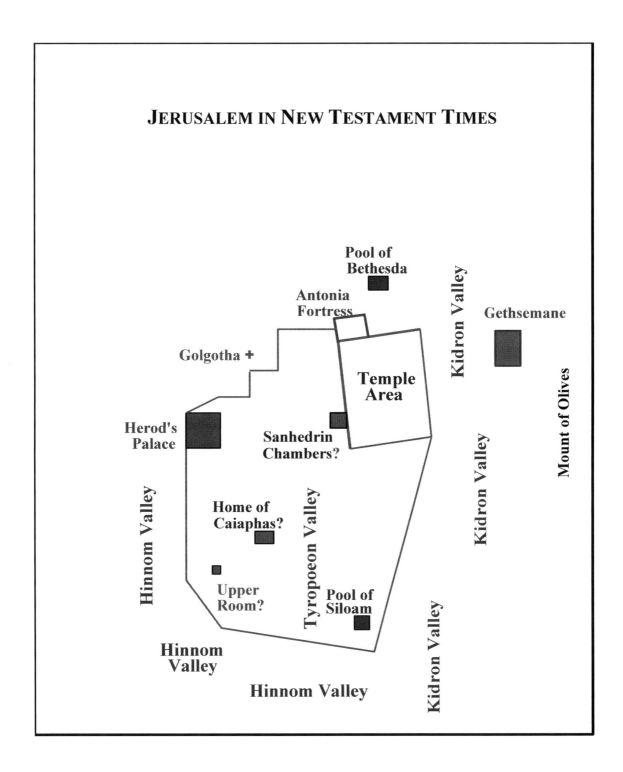

JERUSALEM IN NEW TESTAMENT TIMES

Pool of Bethesda

Antonia Fortress

Golgotha +

Kidron Valley

Gethsemane

Temple Area

Herod's Palace

Sanhedrin Chambers?

Mount of Olives

Kidron Valley

Hinnom Valley

Home of Caiaphas?

Tyropoeon Valley

Upper Room?

Pool of Siloam

Kidron Valley

Hinnom Valley

Hinnom Valley

Bibliography

Abbott-Smith, G. A. *A Manual Greek Lexicon of the New Testament*. Edinburgh: T. & T. Clark, 1937.

Albright, W. F., and C. S Mann. *Matthew*. The Anchor Bible series. Garden City, N.Y.: Doubleday, 1971.

Alford, Henry. *The Greek Testament*. 4 vols. Reprint ed. Grand Rapids: Baker Book House, n. d.

Allen, Willoughby C. *A Critical and Exegetical Commentary on the Gospel According to S. Matthew*. 3rd ed. International Critical Commentary on the Holy Scriptures of the Old and New Testaments series. Edinburgh: T. & T. Clark, 1912.

Anderson, Robert. *The Coming Prince*. Grand Rapids: Kregel Publications, 1975.

Andrews, Samuel J. *The Life of Our Lord Upon the Earth*. New York: Charles Scribner's Sons, 1891.

Archer, Gleason L., Jr. *A Survey of Old Testament Introduction*. 1964; revised ed., Chicago: Moody Press, 1974.

Armerding, Carl. *The Olivet Discourse*. Findlay, Ohio: Dunham Publishing Co., n. d.

The Babylonian Talmud. London: Soncino Press, 1935.

Bailey, Mark L. "A Biblical Theology of Paul's Pastoral Epistles." in *A Biblical Theology of the New Testament*, pp. 333-67. Edited by Roy B. Zuck. Chicago: Moody Press, 1994.

_____. "Dispensational Definitions of the Kingdom." In *Integrity of Heart, Skillfulness of Hands*, pp. 201-21. Edited by Charles H. Dyer and Roy B. Zuck. Grand Rapids: Baker Book House, 1994.

_____. "The Doctrine of the Kingdom in Matthew 13." *Bibliotheca Sacra* 156:624 (October-December 1999):443-51.

_____. "Guidelines for Interpreting Jesus' Parables." *Bibliotheca Sacra* 155:617 (January-March 1998):29-38.

_____. "The Parable of the Leavening Process." *Bibliotheca Sacra* 156:621 (January-March 1999):61-71.

_____. "The Parable of the Mustard Seed." *Bibliotheca Sacra* 155:620 (October-December 1998):449-59.

_____. "The Parable of the Sower and the Soils." *Bibliotheca Sacra* 155:618 (April-June 1998):172-88.

_____. "The Parable of the Tares." *Bibliotheca Sacra* 155:619 (July-September 1998):266-79.

_____. "The Parables of the Dragnet and of the Householder." *Bibliotheca Sacra* 156:623 (July-September 1999):282-96.

_____. "The Parables of the Hidden Treasure and of the Pearl Merchant." *Bibliotheca Sacra* 156:622 (April-June 1999):175-89.

Bailey, Mark L., and Thomas L Constable. *The New Testament Explorer*. Nashville: Word Publishing, 1999. Reissued as *Nelson's New Testament Survey*. Nashville: Thomas Nelson Publishers, 1999.

Baillie, Rebecca A., and E. Eugene Baillie. "Biblical Leprosy as Compared to Present-Day Leprosy." *Christian Medical Society Journal* 14:3 (Fall 1983):27-29.

Bainton, Roland H. *Here I Stand: A Life of Martin Luther*. Nashville: Abingdon Press, 1950. Reprint ed., New York: Mentor Books, 1955.

Baly, D. *The Geography of the Bible*. New York: Harper and Row, 1974.

Barbieri, Louis A., Jr. "Matthew." In *The Bible Knowledge Commentary: New Testament*, pp. 13-94. Edited by John F. Walvoord and Roy B. Zuck. Wheaton: Scripture Press Publications, Victor Books, 1983.

Barclay, William. *The Gospel of Matthew*. 2 vols. Edinburgh: Saint Andrew Press, 1956.

Barnhouse, Donald Grey. *His Own Received Him Not, But . . .* New York: Fleming H. Revell Co., 1933.

_____. *Romans. Vol. I: Man's Ruin. God's Wrath*. Grand Rapids: Wm. B. Eerdmans Publishing Co., 1952.

Barr, James. "Abba Isn't Daddy." *Journal of Theological Studies* 39 (1988):28-47.

Bauckham, R. J. "The Eschatological Earthquake in the Apocalypse of John." *Novum Testamentum* 19 (1977):224-33.

Bauer, J. B. "Libera nos a malo." *Verbum Domini* 34 (1965):12-15.

Bauer, Walter. *A Greek-English Lexicon of the New Testament*. Translated and revised by William F. Arndt, F. Wilbur Gingrich, and Frederick W. Danker. 2nd ed. Chicago: University of Chicago Press, 1958.

Beale, G. K. "The Use of Hosea 11:1 in Matthew 2:15: One More Time." *Journal of the Evangelical Theological Society* 55:4 (December 2012):697-715.

Beasley-Murray, G. R. *Baptism in the New Testament*. London: Macmillan, 1954.

Bennetch, John Henry. "Matthew: An Apologetic." *Bibliotheca Sacra* 103 (October 1946):477-84.

Berg, Laurna L. "The Illegalities of Jesus' Religious and Civil Trials." *Bibliotheca Sacra* 161:643 (July-September 2004):330-42.

Berghuis, Kent D. "A Biblical Perspective on Fasting." *Bibliotheca Sacra* 158:629 (January-March 2001):86-103.

Berkhof, Louis. *The Kingdom of God: The Development of the Idea of the Kingdom, Especially Since the Eighteenth Century*. Grand Rapids: Wm. B. Eerdmans Publishing Co., 1951.

_____. *Systematic Theology*. 4th ed. Grand Rapids: Wm. B. Eerdmans Publishing Co., 1941.

Bernardin, Joseph B. "The Transfiguration." *Journal of Biblical Theology* 52 (October 1933):181-89.

Bindley, T. Herbert. "Eschatology in the Lord's Prayer." *The Expositor* 17 (October 1919):315-20.

Blaising, Craig A. "The Fulfillment of the Biblical Covenants." In *Progressive Dispensationalism*, pp. 174-211. By Craig A. Blaising and Darrell L. Bock. Wheaton: Victor Books, 1993.

Blass, F., and A Debrunner. *A Greek Grammar of the New Testament and Other Early Christian Literature*. Translated and revised by Robert W. Funk. Cambridge: University Press, 1961.

Blinzler, J. *The Trial of Jesus: The Jewish and Roman Proceedings against Jesus Christ Described and Assessed from the Oldest Accounts*. English translation. Cork, Ire.: Mercier, 1959.

Blomberg, Craig L. "Degrees of Reward in the Kingdom of Heaven?" *Journal of the Evangelical Theological Society* 35:2 (June 1992):159-72.

_____. "Marriage, Divorce, Remarriage, and Celibacy: An Exegesis of Matthew 19:3-12." *Trinity Journal* 11NS (1990):161-96.

_____. *Matthew*. New American Commentary series. Nashville: Broadman Press, 1992.

Blum, Edwin A. "Jesus and JAMA." *Christian Medical Society Journal* 17:4 (Fall 1986):4-11.

Bock, Darrell L. *Blasphemy and Exaltation in Judaism and the Final Examination of Jesus: A Philological-Historical Study of the Key Jewish Themes Impacting Mark 14:61-64.* Wissenschaftliche Untersuchungen zum Neuen Testament, number 106. Tübingen, Germ.: Mohr Siebeck, 1998.

_____."A Review of *The Gospel According to Jesus*." *Bibliotheca Sacra* 146:581 (January-March 1989):21-40.

_____. *Jesus according to Scripture: Restoring the Portrait from the Gospels.* Grand Rapids: Baker Book House; and Leicester, England: Apollos, 2002.

Bonhoeffer, Dietrich. *The Cost of Discipleship.* 6th ed. London: SCM, 1959.

Bornkamm, Gunther. "End-Expectation and Church in Matthew." In *Tradition and Interpretation in Matthew*, pp. 15-51. Edited by Gunther Bornkamm, Gerhard Barth, and H. J. Held. Translated by P. Scott. London: SCM Press, 1963.

_____. "The Stilling of the Storm in Matthew." In *Tradition and Interpretation in Matthew*, pp. 52-57. Edited by Gunther Bornkamm, Gerhard Barth, and H. J. Held. Translated by P. Scott. London: SCM Press, 1963.

Bowker, John. "The Son of Man." *Journal of Theological Studies* 28 (1977):19-48.

Breshears, Gerry. "The Body of Christ: Prophet, Priest, or King?" *Journal of the Evangelical Theological Society* 37:1 (March 1994):3-26.

Brown, Raymond. *The Birth of the Messiah.* Garden City, N.Y.: Doubleday, 1977.

Bruce, Alexander Balmain. "The Synoptic Gospels." In *The Expositor's Greek Testament.* Edited by W. Robertson Nicoll. Grand Rapids: Wm. B. Eerdmans Publishing Co., 1910.

_____. *The Training of the Twelve.* 8th ed. N. c.: A. C. Armstrong and Son, 1894; reprint ed. Grand Rapids: Kregel Publications, 1971.

Bruce, Frederick F. *Jesus and Christian Origins outside the New Testament.* London: Hodder & Stoughton, 1974.

Buchler, Adolf. "St. Mathew vi 1-6 and Other Allied Passages." *Journal of Theological Studies* 10 (1909):266-70.

Burrows, Millar. *Burrows on the Dead Sea Scrolls.* Grand Rapids: Baker Book House, 1978.

_____. "Thy Kingdom Come." *Journal of Biblical Literature* 74 (January 1955):1-8.

Burton, Ernest de Witt. *Syntax of the Moods and Tenses in NT Greek.* Edinburgh: T. & T. Clark, 1894.

Burton, Ernest DeWitt, and Edgar Johnson Goodspeed. *A Harmony of the Synoptic Gospels in Greek.* 2nd ed. Chicago: University of Chicago Press, 1947.

Byargeon, Rick W. "Echoes of Wisdom in the Lord's Prayer (Matt 6:9-13)." *Journal of the Evangelical Theological Society* 41:3 (September 1998):353-65.

Calvin, John. *Commentary on a Harmony of the Evangelists, Matthew, Mark, and Luke.* 3 vols. Translated by William Pringle. Edinburgh: The Calvin Translation Society, 1845.

_____. *Institutes of the Christian Religion.* The Library of Christian Classics series, volumes 20 and 21. Edited by John T. McNeill. Translated by Ford Lewis Battles. Philadelphia: Westminster Press, 1960.

Campbell, Donald K. "Interpretation and Exposition of the Sermon on the Mount." Th.D. dissertation, Dallas Theological Seminary, 1953.

Campbell, Ken M. "What Was Jesus' Occupation?" *Journal of the Evangelical Theological Society* 48:3 (September 2005):501-19.

Carr, A. *The Gospel According To St. Matthew.* Cambridge: University Press, 1913.

Carson, Donald A. *Divine Sovereignty and Human Responsibility.* Atlanta: John Knox Press, 1981.

_____. "Matthew." In *Matthew-Luke.* Vol. 8 of *The Expositor's Bible Commentary.* 12 vols. Edited by Frank E. Gaebelein and J. D. Douglas. Grand Rapids: Zondervan Publishing House, 1984.

_____. "Redaction Criticism: On the Legitimacy and Illegitimacy of a Literary Tool." In *Scripture and Truth*, pp. 119-42. Edited by D. A. Carson and J. D. Woodbridge. Grand Rapids: Zondervan Publishing House, 1983.

_____. *The Sermon on the Mount.* Grand Rapids: Baker Book House, 1978.

Carson, Donald A., and Douglas J. Moo. *An Introduction to the New Testament.* 2nd ed. Grand Rapids: Zondervan, 2005.

Catchpole, David R. "The Answer of Jesus to Caiaphas (Matt. xxvi. 64)." *New Testament Studies* 17 (1970-71):213-26.

_____. "The Poor on Earth and the Son of Man in Heaven: A Re-appraisal of Matthew xxv. 31-46." *Bulletin of the John Rylands Library* 61 (1978-79):355-97.

Chafer, Lewis Sperry. *Systematic Theology.* 8 vols. Dallas: Dallas Seminary Press, 1947.

_____. "The Teachings of Christ Incarnate." *Bibliotheca Sacra* 108 (October 1951):389-413.

Congdon, Roger D. "Did Jesus Sustain the Law in Matthew 5?" *Bibliotheca Sacra* 135:538 (April-June 1978):117-25.

Constable, Thomas L. "The Lord's Prayer." In *Giving Ourselves to Prayer: An Acts 6:4 Primer for Ministry*, pp. 70-75. Compiled by Dan R. Crawford. Terre Haute, Ind.: PrayerShop Publishing, 2005, pp. 70-75.

_____. *Talking to God: What the Bible Teaches about Prayer.* Grand Rapids: Baker Book House, 1995; reprint ed., Eugene, Oreg.: Wipf & Stock Publishers, 2005.

Cooper, David L. *Messiah: His Historical Appearance.* Los Angeles: Biblical Research Society, 1958.

Court, J. M. "Right and Left: The Implications for Matthew 25.31-46." *New Testament Studies* 31 (1985):223-33.

Cranfield, C. E. B. "The Cup Metaphor in Mark xiv. 36 and Parallels." *Expository Times* 59 (1947-48):137-38.

_____. "St. Mark 13." *Scottish Journal of Theology* 6 (April 1953):165-96; (July 1953):287-303; 7 (April 1954):284-303.

Crater, Tim. "Bill Gothard's View of the Exception Clause." *Journal of Pastoral Practice* 4 (1980):5-12.

Cremer, Hermann. *Biblico-Theological Lexicon of New Testament Greek.* Translated by William Urwick. 4th English ed. Edinburgh: T. & T. Clark, 1895.

Criswell, W. A. *Expository Notes on the Gospel of Matthew.* Grand Rapids: Zondervan Publishing House, 1961.

Culver, Robert D. "What Is the Church's Commission? Some Exegetical Issues In Matthew 28:16-20." *Bibliotheca Sacra* 125:499 (July-September 1968):239-53.

Cunningham, Scott, and Darrell L Bock. "Is Matthew Midrash?" *Bibliotheca Sacra* 144:574 (April-June 1987):157-80.

Dahl, N. A. *Jesus in the Memory of the Early Church.* Minneapolis: Augsburg, 1976.

Dalman, Gustaf H.. *The Words of Jesus.* Translated by D. M. Kay. Edinburgh: T. & T. Clark, 1909.

Darby, John Nelson. *Synopsis of the Books of the Bible.* 5 vols. Revised ed. New York: Loizeaux Brothers Publishers, 1942.

Daube, D. "The Anointing at Bethany and Jesus' Burial." *Anglican Theological Review* 32 (1950):187-88.

_____. *The New Testament and Rabbinic Judaism.* London: Athlone, 1956.

Davidson, Bruce W. "Reasonable Damnation: How Jonathan Edwards Argued for the Rationality of Hell." *Journal of the Evangelical Theological Society* 38:1 (March 1995):47-56.

Davies, W. D., and D. C. Allison. *A Critical and Exegetical Commentary on the Gospel according to Saint Matthew.* International Critical Commentary series. 2 vols. Edinburgh: T. & T. Clark, 1988.

Deatrick, Eugene P. "Salt, Soil, Savor." *Biblical Archaeologist* 25 (1962):41-48.

DeBruyn, Lawrence A. "Preterism and 'This Generation,'" *Bibliotheca Sacra* 167:666 (April-June 2010):180-200.

DeGraaf, David. "Some Doubts about Doubt: The New Testament Use of *Diakrino.*" *Journal of the Evangelical Theological Society* 48:8 (December 2005):733-55.

Deissmann, Adolf. *Light from the Ancient East.* Translated by Lionel R. M. Strachan. London: Hodder and Stoughton, 1927.

Derickson, Gary W. "Matthew's Chiastic Structure and Its Dispensational Implications." *Bibliotheca Sacra* 163:652 (October-December 2006):423-37.

A Dictionary of the Bible. Edited by James Hastings. 1958 ed. S.v. "Kingdom of God, of Heaven," by James Orr.

A Dictionary of Christ and the Gospels. Edited by James Hastings. S.v. "Baptism," by Marcus Dodds.

_____. S.v. "Genealogies of Jesus Christ," by P. M. Barnard.

A Dictionary of New Testament Theology. Edited by Colin Brown. S.v. "*kardia,*" by T. Sorg.

_____. S.v. "*kathemai,*" by R. T. France.

_____. S.v. "Leprosy," by R. K. Harrison.

Dillow, Joseph C. *The Reign of the Servant Kings.* Miami Springs, Fla.: Schoettle Publishing Co., 1992.

Dodd, C. H. *The Parables of the Kingdom.* London: Nisbet, 1936.

Donaldson, T. L. *Jesus on the Mountain: A Study in Matthean Theology.* Sheffield: JSOT, 1985.

Donn, T. M. "'Let the Dead Bury Their Dead' (Mt. viii. 22, Lk. ix. 60)." *Expository Times* 61 (September 1950):384.

Doriani, Daniel. "The Deity of Christ in the Synoptic Gospels." *Journal of the Evangelical Theological Society* 37:3 (September 1994):333-50.

Duling, Dennis C. "The Therapeutic Son of David: An Element in Matthew's Christological Apologetic." *New Testament Studies* 24 (1978):392-410.

Dunn, James D. G. *Jesus and the Spirit: A Study of the Religious and Charismatic Experience of Jesus and the First Christians as Reflected in the New Testament.* London: SCM, 1975.

Dyer, Charles H. "Do the Synoptics Depend on Each Other?" *Bibliotheca Sacra* 138:551 (July-September 1981):230-44.

The Ecclesiastical History of Eusebius Pamphilus. Twin Brooks series. Popular ed. Grand Rapids: Baker Book House, 1974.

Edersheim, Alfred. *The Life and Times of Jesus the Messiah.* 2 vols. Grand Rapids: Wm. B. Eerdmans Publishing Co., 1971.

_____. *Sketches of Jewish Social Life in the Days of Christ.* Reprint ed. Grand Rapids: Wm. B. Eerdmans Publishing Co., 1974.

_____. *The Temple: Its Ministry and Services As They Were at the Time of Jesus Christ.* Reprint ed. Grand Rapids: Wm. B. Eerdmans Publishing Co., 1972.

Edgar, Thomas R. "The Cessation of the Sign Gifts." *Bibliotheca Sacra* 145:580 (October-December 1988):371-86.

_____. "An Exegesis of Rapture Passages." In *Issues in Dispensationalism,* pp. 203-23. Edited by Wesley R. Willis and John R. Master. Chicago: Moody Press, 1994.

Ellis, Earle E. *The Gospel of Luke.* New Century Bible series. New York: Thomas Nelson Publishers, 1966.

Ellis, I. P. "'But some doubted.'" *New Testament Studies* 14 (1967-68):574-80.

English, E. Schuyler. *Studies in the Gospel According to Matthew.* New York: Fleming H. Revell Co., 1935.

Erickson, Millard J. "Is Hell Forever?" *Bibliotheca Sacra* (July-September 1995):259-72.

Farmer, William Reuben. *The Synoptic Problem.* New York: Macmillan, 1964.

Feinberg, Charles Lee. *God Remembers, A Study of Zechariah.* 4th ed. Portland, Oreg.: Multnomal Press, 1979.

_____. *Israel in the Last Days: The Olivet Discourse.* Altadena, Calif.: Emeth Publications, 1953.

_____. *Premillennialism or Amillennialism?* Wheaton: Van Kampen Press, 1954.

Feinberg, Paul D. "Dispensational Theology and the Rapture." In *Issues in Dispensationalism,* pp. 225-45. Edited by Wesley R. Willis and John R. Master. Chicago: Moody Press, 1994.

Fenton, J. C. *Saint Matthew.* Westminster Pelican Commentaries series. Philadelphia: Westminster Press, 1978.

Filson, Floyd V. *A Commentary on the Gospel According to St. Matthew.* London: Adam & Charles Black, 1960.

Fitzmyer, J. A. "Crucifixion in Ancient Palestine, Qumran Literature, and the New Testament." *Catholic Biblical Quarterly* 40 (1978):493-513.

_____. "The Matthean Divorce Texts and Some New Palestinian Evidence." *Theological Studies* 37 (1976):208-11.

Fleming, T. V. "Christ and Divorce." *Theological Studies* 24 (1963):109.

France, R. T. "Exegesis in Practice: Two Samples." In *New Testament Interpretation,* pp. 252-81. Edited by I. Howard Marshall. Exeter: Paternoster Press, 1977.

_____. *The Gospel of Matthew*. The New International Commentary on the New Testament series. Grand Rapids: Wm. B. Eerdmans Publishing Co., 2007.

_____. "Herod and the Children of Bethlehem," *Novum Testamentum* 21 (1979):98-120.

_____. *Jesus and the Old Testament: His Application of Old Testament Passages to Himself and His Mission*. London: Tyndale House Publishers, 1971.

_____. *Matthew: Evangelist and Teacher*. Exeter, U.K.: Paternoster Press, 1989.

Franzmann, Martin L. *Follow Me: Discipleship According to Saint Matthew*. St. Louis: Concordia, 1961.

Freed, Edwin D. "The Women in Matthew's Genealogy." *Journal for the Study of the New Testament* 29 (1987):3-19.

Fruchtenbaum, Arnold G. *Israelology: The Missing Link in Systematic Theology*. Tustin, Calif.: Ariel Ministries Press, 1989.

Gaebelein, Arno C. *The Gospel of Matthew, An Exposition*. 2 vols. in 1. Neptune, N.J.: Loizeaux Brothers, 1910.

Garlington, Don B. "Jesus, the Unique Son of God: Tested and Faithful." *Bibliotheca Sacra* 151:603 (July-September 1994):284-308.

_____. "'The Salt of the Earth' in Covenantal Perspective." *Journal of the Evangelical Theological Society* 54:4 (December 2011):715-48.

Geisler, Norman L. "A Christian Perspective on Wine-Drinking." *Bibliotheca Sacra* 139:553 (January-March 1982):46-56.

Geisler, Norman L., and William E Nix. *A General Introduction to the Bible*. Chicago: Moody Press, 1968.

Geldard, Mark. "Jesus' Teaching on Divorce." *Churchman* 92 (1978):134-43.

Glass, Ronald N. "The Parables of the Kingdom: A Paradigm for Consistent Dispensational Hermeneutics." Paper presented at the meeting of the Evangelical Theological Society, Lisle, Illinois, 18 November 1994.

Glover, Richard. *A Teacher's Commentary of the Gospel of Matthew*. Grand Rapids: Zondervan Publishing House, 1956.

Goebel, Siegfried. *The Parables of Jesus*. Translated by Professor Banks. Edinburgh: T. & T. Clark, 1913.

Gore, Charles. *The Sermon on the Mount*. London: John Murray, 1896.

A Greek-English Lexicon of the New Testament. By C. G. Wilke. Revised by C. L. Wilibald Grimm. Translated, revised and enlarged by Joseph Henry Thayer, 1889.

Green, F. W., ed. *The Gospel According to Saint Matthew in the Revised Version*. The Clarendon Bible series. Oxford: Clarendon Press, 1936.

Grounds, Vernon C. "Mountain Manifesto." *Bibliotheca Sacra* 128:510 (April-June 1971):135-41.

Guelich, Robert A. "The Matthean Beatitudes: 'Entrance-Requirements' or Eschatological Blessings?" *Journal of Biblical Literature* 95 (1973):415-34.

_____. *The Sermon on the Mount: A Foundation for Understanding*. Waco: Word Books, 1982.

Gundry, Robert H. *Matthew: A Commentary on His Literary and Theological Art*. Grand Rapids: Wm. B. Eerdmans Publishing Co., 1982.

_____. *The Use of the Old Testament in St. Matthew's Gospel, with Special Reference to the Messianic Hope*. Leiden, Netherlands: Brill, 1975.

Habershon, Ada R. *The Study of the Parables*. Grand Rapids: Kregel Publications, 1904.

Hagner, Donald A. *Matthew 1—13*. Word Biblical Commentary series. Dallas: Word Books, 1993.

_____. *Matthew 14—28*. Word Biblical Commentary series. Dallas: Word Books, 1995.

Halverson, Richard C. "God and Caesar." *Journal of the Evangelical Theological Society* 37:1 (March 1994):125-29.

Hare, Douglas R. A. *The Theme of Jewish Persecution of Christians in the Gospel According to St. Matthew*. Cambridge: University Press, 1967.

Harless, Hal. "The Cessation of the Mosaic Covenant." *Bibliotheca Sacra* 160:639 (July-September 2003):349-66.

Hatch, W. *Essays in Biblical Greek*. Oxford: Clarendon Press, 1889.

Hay, David M. *Glory at the Right Hand: Psalm 110 in Early Christianity*. Nashville: Abingdon, 1973.

A Hebrew and English Lexicon of the Old Testament. By William Gesenius. Translated by Edward Robinson. Edited by Francis Brown, S. R. Driver, and Charles A. Briggs, 1906.

Hendriksen, William. *New Testament Commentary, Exposition of the Gospel According to Matthew*. Grand Rapids: Baker Book House, 1973.

Hengel, G. *Crucifixion*. London: SCM, 1977.

Hiebert, D. Edmond. "An Expository Study of Matthew 28:16-20." *Bibliotheca Sacra* 149:595 (July-September 1992):338-54.

Hill, David. *The Gospel of Matthew*. Grand Rapids: Wm. B. Eerdmans Publishing Co., 1972.

Hitchcock, Mark L. "A Critique of the Preterist View of 'Soon' and 'Near' in Revelation." *Bibliotheca Sacra* 163:652 (October-December 2006):467-78.

Hodges, Zane C. "Form-Criticism and the Resurrection Accounts." *Bibliotheca Sacra* 124:496 (October-December 1967):339-48.

_____. *Grace in Eclipse*. Dallas: Redencion Viva, 1981.

_____. "Possessing the Kingdom." *The KERUGMA Message* 1:1 (May-June 1991):1-2; 1:2 (July-August 1991):1-2; 1:3 (November-December 1991):1, 4; 2:1 (Spring 1992):1, 4; 2:2 (Winter 1992):1, 5-6.

Hoehner, Harold W. *Chronological Aspects of the Life of Christ*. Contemporary Evangelical Perspectives series. Grand Rapids: Zondervan Publishing House, 1977.

_____. *Herod Antipas*. Cambridge: University Press, 1972.

Hogg, C. F., and J. B Watson. *On the Sermon on the Mount*. 2nd ed. London: Pickering and Inglis, 1934.

Hooker, Morna D. *The Son of Man in Mark*. London: SPCK, 1967.

Howard, Tracy L. "The Use of Hosea 11:1 in Matthew 2:15: An Alternative Solution." *Bibliotheca Sacra* 143:572 (October-December 1986):314-28.

Hubbard, David A. *Proverbs*. The Preacher's Commentary series. Nashville: Thomas Nelson Publishers, 1989.

Huffman, Norman A. "Atypical Features in the Parables of Jesus." *Journal of Biblical Literature* 97 (1978):207-20.

Hunter, Archibald M. *The Message of the New Testament*. Philadelphia: Wesminster Press, 1944.

_____. *A Pattern for Life: An Exposition of the Sermon on the Mount*. Rev. ed. Philadelphia: Westminster Press, 1966.

Hutchison, John C. "Women, Gentiles, and the Messianic Mission in Matthew's Genealogy." *Bibliotheca Sacra* 158:630 (April-June 2001):152-64.

Irenaeus. *Against Heresies*. Vol. 1 of *The Ante-Nicene Fathers*. 10 vols. Edinburgh: T. & T. Clark, and Grand Rapids: Wm. B. Eerdmans Publishing Co., 1989.

Jensen, Joseph. "Does *porneia* Mean Fornication? A Critique of Bruce Malina." *Novum Testamentum* 20 (1978):161-84.

Jeremias, Joachim. *Jerusalem in the Time of Jesus*. 3rd ed. Translated by F. H. and C. H. Cave. London: SCM, 1962.

_____. *New Testament Theology*. Part I. *The Proclamation of Jesus*. Translated by John Bowden. London: SCM, 1971.

_____. *The Parables of Jesus*. Translated by S. H. Hooke. London: SCM, 1963.

_____. *The Prayers of Jesus*. Translated by John Bowden and Christoph Burchard. London: SCM, 1967.

Johnson, L. T. "The New Testament's Anti-Jewish Slander and Conventions of Ancient Rhetoric." *Journal of Biblical Literature* 108 (1989):419-41.

Johnson, M. D. *The Purpose of Biblical Genealogies*. 2nd ed. Cambridge: Cambridge University Press, 1988.

Johnson, S. Lewis, Jr. "The Agony of Christ." *Bibliotheca Sacra* 124:496 (October-December 1967):303-13.

_____. "The Argument of Matthew," *Bibliotheca Sacra* 112:446 (April 1955):143-53.

_____. "The Baptism of Christ." *Bibliotheca Sacra* 123:491 (July-September 1966):220-29.

_____. "The Death of Christ." *Bibliotheca Sacra* 125:497 (January-March 1968):10-19.

_____. "The Message of John the Baptist." *Bibliotheca Sacra* 113:449 (January 1956):30-36.

_____. "The Temptation of Christ." *Bibliotheca Sacra* 123:492 (October-December 1996):342-52.

_____. "The Transfiguration of Christ." *Bibliotheca Sacra* 124:494 (April-June 1967):133-43.

_____. "The Triumphal Entry of Christ." *Bibliotheca Sacra* 124:495 (July-September 1967):218-29.

Jones, David W. "The Betrothal View of Divorce and Remarriage." *Bibliotheca Sacra* 165:657 (January-March 2008):68-85.

Josephus, Flavius. *The Works of Flavius Josephus*. Translated by William Whiston. London: T. Nelson and Sons, 1866; reprint ed. Peabody, Mass.: Hendrickson Publishers, 1988.

Keener, Craig. *A Commentary on the Gospel of Matthew*. Grand Rapids: Wm. B. Eerdmans Publishing Co., 1999.

_____. *Matthew*. IVP New Testament Commentary series. Downers Grove, Ill.: InterVarsity Press, 1997.

Kelly, William. *Lectures on the Gospel of Matthew*. New York: Loizeaux Brothers, n. d.

Kent, Homer A., Jr. "Matthew's Use of the Old Testament." *Bibliotheca Sacra* 121:481 (January-March 1964):34-43.

Kepler, Thomas. S. *Jesus' Design for Living*. New York: Abingdon Press, 1955.

Kiddle, M. "The Conflict Between the Disciples, the Jews, and the Gentiles in St. Matthew's Gospel." *The Journal of Theological Studies* 36 (January 1935):33-44.

Kik, J. Marcellus. *Matthew Twenty-Four, An Exposition*. Swengel, Pa.: Bible Truth Depot, n. d.

Kilgallen, John J. "To What Are the Matthean Exception-Texts [5, 32 and 19, 9] an Exception?" *Biblica* 61 (1980):102-5.

Kingsbury, Jack Dean. *Matthew as Story*. 2nd ed. Philadelphia: Fortress Press, 1988.

_____. "The Place, Structure, and Meaning of the Sermon on the Mount within Matthew." *Interpretation* 41 (1987):131-43.

Kissinger, W. S. *The Sermon on the Mount: A History of Interpretation and Bibliography*. Metuchen, N.J.: Scarecrow & ATLA, 1975.

Kitchens, Ted G. "Perimeters of Corrective Church Discipline." *Bibliotheca Sacra* 148:590 (April-June 1991):201-13.

Lachs, S. T. "Some Textual Observations on the Sermon on the Mount." *Jewish Quarterly Review* 69 (1978):98-111.

Ladd, George E. *The Presence of the Future: The Eschatology of Biblical Realism*. Grand Rapids: Wm. B. Eerdmans Publishing Co., 1974.

Lane, William L. *The Gospel according to Mark*. New International Commentary on the New Testament series. Grand Rapids: Wm. B. Eerdmans Publishing Co., 1975.

Laney, J. Carl. "The Biblical Practice of Church Discipline." *Bibliotheca Sacra* 143:572 (October-December 1986):353-64.

Larson, Mark J. "Three Centuries of Objections to Biblical Miracles." *Bibliotheca Sacra* 160:637 (January-March 2003):77-100.

Laurenson, L. *Messiah, the Prince*. New York: Loizeaux Brothers, 1924.

Legrand, L. "The Missionary Command of the Risen Lord Mt 28:16-20." *Indian Theological Studies* 24:1 (March 1987):5-28.

Leifeld, Walter L. "Theological Motifs in the Transfiguration Narrative." In *New Dimensions in New Testament Study*, pp. 162-79. Edited by Richard N. Longenecker and Merrill C. Tenney. Grand Rapids: Zondervan Publishing House, 1974.

Lenski, Richard C. H. *The Interpretation of St. Matthew's Gospel*. Minneapolis: Wartburg Press, 1943.

Levertoff, Paul J. *St. Matthew (Revised Version)*. London: Thomas Murby & Co., 1940.

Levinskaya, Irena. *The Book of Acts in Its Diaspora Setting*. Vol. 5 of *The Book of Acts in Its First Century Setting*, edited by Bruce W. Winter. Grand Rapids: Wm. B. Eerdmans Publishing Co., and Carlisle, England: Paternoster Press, 1996.

Lewis, Clive Staples. *Miracles: A Preliminary Study*. London: Geoffrey Bles, The Centenary Press, 1947.

Lewis, Jack P. "'The Gates of Hell Shall Not Prevail Against It' (Matt 16:18): A Study of the History of Interpretation." *Journal of the Evangelical Theological Society* 38:3 (September 1996):349-67.

Lindars, Barnabas. *New Testament Apologetic*. London: SCM, 1961.

Lowery, David K. "Evidence from Matthew." In *A Case for Premillennialism: A New Consensus*, pp. 165-80. Edited by Donald K. Campbell and Jeffrey L. Townsend. Chicago: Moody Press, 1992.

_____. "A Theology of Matthew." In *A Biblical Theology of the New Testament*, pp. 19-63. Edited by Roy B. Zuck. Chicago: Moody Press, 1994.

Luz, U. *Matthew 8—20: A Commentary*. Hermeneia series. Minneapolis: Fortress Press, 2001.

Maalouf, Tony T. "Were the Magi from Persia or Arabia?" *Bibliotheca Sacra* 156:624 (October-December 1999):423-42.

MacArthur, John F., Jr. *The Gospel According to Jesus*. Grand Rapids: Zondervan Publishing House, Academie Books, 1988.

Machen, J. Gresham. *The Virgin Birth of Christ*. London: Marshall, Morgan & Scott, 1930.

Major, H. D. A. *Basic Christianity*. Oxford: Basil Blackwell, 1944.

Major, H. D. A.; T. W. Manson; and C. J. Wright. *The Mission and Message of Jesus*. New York: E. P. Dutton and Co., Inc., 1938.

Manson, T. W. *The Sayings of Jesus*. London: SCM, 1949.

Marshall, I. Howard. *The Gospel of Luke: A Commentary on the Greek Text*. New International Greek Testament Commentary series. Exeter, England: Paternoster Press, 1978.

_____. *Kept by the Power of God*. Minneapolis: Bethany House Publishers, 1969.

Martin, John A. "Christ, the End of the Law in the Sermon on the Mount." In *Dispensationalism, Israel and the Church: The Search for Definition*, pp. 248-63. Edited by Craig A. Blaising and Darrell L. Bock. Grand Rapids: Zondervan Publishing House, 1992.

_____. "Dispensational Approaches to the Sermon on the Mount." In *Essays in Honor of J. Dwight Pentecost*, pp. 35-48. Edited by Stanley D. Toussaint and Charles H. Dyer. Chicago: Moody Press, 1986.

Marx, Werner G. "Money Matters in Matthew." *Bibliotheca Sacra* 136:542 (April-June 1979):148-57.

Master, John R. "The New Covenant." In *Issues in Dispensationalism*, pp. 93-110. Edited by Wesley R. Willis and John R. Master. Chicago: Moody Press, 1994.

Matera, Frank J. *Passion Narratives and Gospel Theologies: Interpreting the Synoptics through Their Passion Stories*. Theological Inquiries series. New York: Paulist Press, 1986.

Maticich, Karen Kristine. "Reflections on Tractate Shekalim." *Exegesis and Exposition* 3:1 (Fall 1988):58-60.

Mattill, A. J., Jr. *Luke and the Last Things: A Perspective for the Understanding of Lukan Thought*. Dillsboro, N.C.: Western North Carolina Press, 1979.

_____. "'The Way of Tribulation.'" *Journal of Biblical Literature* 98 (1979):531-46.

McClain, Alva J. *The Greatness of the Kingdom, An Inductive Study of the Kingdom of God*. Winona Lake, Ind.: BMH Books, 1959; Chicago: Moody Press, 1968.

McClister, David. "'Where Two or Three Are Gathered Together': Literary Structure as a Key to Meaning in Matt 17:22—20:19." *Journal of the Evangelical Theological Society* 39:4 (December 1996):549-58.

McHugh, John. *The Mother of Jesus in the New Testament*. Garden City, N.Y.: Doubleday, 1975.

McKeating, Henry. "Sanctions Against Adultery in Ancient Israelite Society." *Journal for the Study of the Old Testament* 11 (1979):57-72.

McPheeters, William M. "Christ As an Interpreter of Scripture." *The Bible Student* 1 (April 1900):223-29.

Meier, John P. "Nations or Gentiles in Matthew 28:19." *Catholic Biblical Quarterly* 39 (1977):94-102.

Merkle, Benjamin L. "The Meaning of 'Ekklesia in Matthew 16:18 and 18:17." *Bibliotheca Sacra* 167:667 (July-September 2010):281-91.

Merrill, Eugene H. "The Book of Ruth: Narration and Shared Themes." *Bibliotheca Sacra* 142:566 (April-June 1985):130-41.

_____. "Deuteronomy, New Testament Faith, and the Christian Life." In *Integrity of Heart, Skillfulness of Hands*, pp. 19-33. Edited by Charles H. Dyer and Roy B. Zuck. Grand Rapids: Baker Book House, 1994.

_____. *Kingdom of Priests: A History of Old Testament Israel*. Grand Rapids: Baker Book House, 1987.

_____. "The Sign of Jonah." *Journal of the Evangelical Theological Society* 23 (1980):23-30.

Metzger, Bruce M. "The Nazareth Inscription Once Again." In *Jesus und Paulus*, pp. 221-38. Edited by E. Earle Ellis and Max Wilcox. Gottingen: Vandenhoeck und Ruprecht, 1975.

_____. *A Textual Commentary on the Greek New Testament*. London: United Bible Societies, 1971.

Meyer, Ben F. *The Aims of Jesus*. London: SCM Press, 1979.

Michaels, J. R. "Apostolic Hardships and Righteous Gentiles." *Journal of Biblical Literature* 84 (1965):27-37.

Miller, Earl. *The Kingdom of God and the Kingdom of Heaven*. Meadville, Pa.: By the Author, 1950.

The Mishnah. Translated by Herbert Danby. London: Oxford University Press, 1933.

M'Neile, Alan Hugh. *The Gospel According to St. Matthew*. London: Macmillan & Co., 1915.

Moloney, Francis J. "Matthew 19, 3-12 and Celibacy. A Redactional and Form-Critical Study." *Journal for the Study of the New Testament* 2 (1979):42-60.

Montefiore, C. G. "Rabbinic Conceptions of Repentance." *Jewish Quarterly Review* 16 (January 1904):209-57.

_____. *The Synoptic Gospels*. 2 vols. Rev. ed. New York: KTAV, 1968.

Montefiore, C. G., and H. A Loewe. *Rabbinic Anthology*. London: Macmillan, 1938.

Moo, Douglas J. "The Use of the Old Testament in the Passion Texts of the Gospels." Ph.D. dissertation, University of St. Andrews, 1979.

Moore, G. F. *Judaism in the First Centuries of the Christian Era*. 3 vols. Cambridge, Mass.: Harvard University Press, 1927-30.

Morgan, G. Campbell. *The Gospel According to Matthew*. New York: Fleming H. Revell Co., 1929.

_____. *Living Messages of the Books of the Bible*. 2 vols. New York: Fleming H. Revell Co., 1912.

Morison, Frank [Albert Henry Ross]. *Who Moved the Stone?* London: Faber and Faber, 1930. Reprint ed. Grand Rapids: Zondervan Publishing House, Lamplighter Books, 1976.

Morison, James. *A Practical Commentary on the Gospel According to St. Matthew*. Boston: N. J. Bartlett & Co., 1884.

Morris, Leon. *The Apostolic Preaching of the Cross*. London: Tyndale Press, 1965.

_____. *The Gospel According to John*. New International Commentary on the New Testament series. Grand Rapids: Wm. B. Eerdmans Publishing Co., 1971.

Moule, C. F. D. *An Idiom Book of New Testament Greek*. 2nd ed. London: Cambridge University Press, 1959.

Moulton, James Hope, and George Milligan. *The Vocabulary of the Greek Testament*. Grand Rapids: Wm. B. Eerdmans Publishing Co., 1930.

Moulton, Mark. "Jesus' Goal for Temple and Tree: A Thematic Revisit of Matt 21:12-22." *Journal of the Evangelical Theological Society* 41:4 (December 1998):561-72.

Mounce, William D. *Basics of Biblical Greek: Grammar*. Grand Rapids: Zondervan Publishing House, 1993.

Mueller, James R. "The Temple Scroll and the Gospel Divorce Texts." *Revue de Qumran* 38 (1980):247-56.

Murray, John. *Redemption—Accomplished and Applied*. Grand Rapids: Wm. B. Eerdmans Publishing Co., 1955.

Nelson, Neil D., Jr. "'This Generation' in Matt 24:34: A Literary Critical Perspective." *Journal of the Evangelical Theological Society* 38:3 (September 1996):369-85.

The Nelson Study Bible. Edited by Earl D. Radmacher. Nashville: Thomas Nelson Publishers, 1997.

Neufeld, Edmund K. "The Gospel in the Gospels: Answering the Question 'What Must I Do To Be Saved?' from the Synoptics." *Journal of the Evangelical Theological Society* 51:2 (June 2008):267-96.

The New Bible Dictionary. 1962 ed. S.v. "Chinnereth," by R. F. Hosking.

_____. S.v. "Pilate," by D. H. Wheaton.

_____. S.v. "Talmud and Midrash," by Charles E. Feinberg.

The New Scofield Reference Bible. Edited by Frank E. Gaebelein, William Culbertson, et al. New York: Oxford University Press, 1967.

Newman, Albert H. *A Manual of Church History*. 2 vols. Chicago: American Baptist Press, 1931.

Nickelsburg, G. W. E. *Resurrection, Immortality and Eternal Life in Intertestamental Judaism*. Cambridge, Mass.: Harvard University Press, 1972.

Nouwen, Henri J. M. *In the Name of Jesus: Reflections on Christian Leadership*. New York: Crossroad, 1994.

Overstreet, R. Larry. "Roman Law and the Trial of Jesus." *Bibliotheca Sacra* 135:540 (October-December 1978):323-32.

Page, Sydney H. T. "Satan: God's Servant." *Journal of the Evangelical Theological Society* 50:3 (September 2007):449-65.

Pagenkemper, Karl E. "Rejection Imagery in the Synoptic Parables." *Bibliotheca Sacra* 153:610 (April-June 1996):179-98; 611 (July-September 1996):308-31.

Parrot, Andre. *Golgotha and the Chruch of the Holy Sepulchre*. Translated by E. Hudson. London: SCM, 1957.

Patai, Raphael. *The Messianic Texts*. Detroit: Wayne State University Press, 1979.

Patterson, Richard D. "The Imagery of Clouds in the Scriptures." *Bibliotheca Sacra* 165:657 (January-March 2008):13-27.

_____. "Metaphors of Marriage as Expressions of Divine-Human Relations." *Journal of the Evangelical Theological Society* 51:4 (December 2008):689-702.

Payne, Philip B. "Jesus' Implicit Claim to Deity in His Parables." *Trinity Journal* 2NS:1 (Spring 1981):3-23.

Penner, James A. "Revelation and Discipleship in Matthew's Transfiguration Account." *Bibliotheca Sacra* 152:606 (April-June 1995):201-10.

Pentecost, J. Dwight. "The Biblical Covenants and the Birth Narratives." In *Walvoord: A Tribute*, pp. 257-70. Edited by Donald K. Campbell. Chicago: Moody Press, 1982.

_____. *The Parables of Jesus*. Grand Rapids: Zondervan Publishing House, 1982.

_____. *Things to Come: A Study in Biblical Eschatology*. Findlay, Ohio: Dunham Publishing Company, 1958.

_____. *Thy Kingdom Come*. Wheaton: Scripture Press Publications, Victor Books, 1990.

_____. *The Words and Works of Jesus Christ*. Grand Rapids: Zondervan Publishing House, 1981.

Perowne, S. *The Life and Times of Herod the Great*. London: Hodder and Stoughton, 1956.

Peters, George N. D. *The Theocratic Kingdom of Our Lord Jesus, the Christ, as Covenanted in the Old Testament and Presented in the New Testament*. 3 vols. New York: Funk and Wagnalls, 1884; reprint ed., Grand Rapids: Kregel Publications, 1972.

Peterson, Robert A. "Does the Bible Teach Annihilationism?" *Bibliotheca Sacra* 156:621 (January-March 1999):13-27.

_____. "A Traditionalist Response to John Stott's Arguments for Annihilationism." *Journal of the Evangelical Theological Society* 37:4 (December 1994):553-68.

Pettingill, William L. *Simple Studies in Matthew*. Findlay, Ohio: Dunham Publishing Co., n. d.

Plummer, Alfred. *An Exegetical Commentary on the Gospel According to S. Matthew*. Grand Rapids: Wm. B. Eerdmans Publishing Co., 1953.

Plummer, Robert L. "Something Awry in the Temple? The Rending of the Temple Veil and Early Jewish Sources that Report Unusual Phenomena in the Temple around AD 30." *Journal of the Evangelical Theological Society* 48:2 (June 2005):301-16.

Pond, Eugene W. "The Background and Timing of the Judgment of the Sheep and Goats." *Bibliotheca Sacra* 159:634 (April-June 2002):201-20.

_____. "Who Are 'the Least' of Jesus' Brothers in Matthew 25:40?" *Bibliotheca Sacra* 159:636 (October-December 2002):436-48.

_____. "Who Are the Sheep and Goats in Matthew 25:31-46?" *Bibliotheca Sacra* 159:635 (July-September 2002):288-301.

Porter, Virgil V., Jr. "The Sermon on the Mount in the Book of James, Part 1." *Bibliotheca Sacra* 162:647 (July-September 2005):344-60.

_____. "The Sermon on the Mount in the Book of James, Part 2." *Bibliotheca Sacra* 162:648 (October-December 2005):470-82.

Price, J. Randall. "Prophetic Postponement in Daniel 9 and Other Texts." In *Issues in Dispensationalism*, pp. 133-65. Edited by Wesley R. Willis and John R. Master. Chicago: Moody Press, 1994.

Proctor, John. "Fire in God's House: Influence of Malachi 3 in the NT." *Journal of the Evangelical Theological Society* 36:1 (March 1993):9-14.

Przybylski, Benno. *Righteousness in Matthew and His World of Thought*. Cambridge: University Press, 1980.

Rabbinowitz, Noel S. "Matthew 23:2-4: Does Jesus Recognize the Authority of the Pharisees and Does He Endorse their *Halakhah?*" *Journal of the Evangelical Theological Society* 46:3 (September 2003):423-47.

Rawlinson, A. E. J. *The Gospel According to St. Mark*. 5th ed. London: Methuen, 1942.

Rice, Edwin W. *People's Commentary on the Gospel of Matthew*. Philadelphia: American Sunday School Union, 1887.

Rieske, Susan M. "What Is the Meaning of 'This Generation' in Matthew 23:36?" *Bibliotheca Sacra* 165:658 (April-June 2008):209-26.

Robertson, Archibald T. *A Grammar of the Greek New Testament in the Light of Historical Research*. Nashville: Broadman Press, 1934.

_____. *A Harmony of the Gospels for Students of the Life of Christ*. New York: Harper & Row, 1922.

_____. *Word Pictures in the New Testament*. 6 vols. Nashville: Broadman Press, 1930.

Robertson, Paul E. "First-Century Jewish Marriage Customs." *Biblical Illustrator* 13:1 (Fall 1986):33-36.

Robinson, J. M., ed. *The Nag Hammadi Library in English*. New York: Harper and Row, 1977.

Robinson, Theodore H. *The Gospel of Matthew*. Moffatt New Testament Commentary series. London: Hodder and Stoughton, 1928.

Rogers, Cleon. "The Great Commission." *Bibliotheca Sacra* 130:519 (July-September 1973):258-67.

Ryrie, Charles C. *Dispensationalism Today*. Chicago: Moody Press, 1965.

_____. *The Miracles of our Lord*. Dubuque, Iowa: ECS Ministries, 2005.

Sahl, Joseph G. "The Impeccability of Jesus Christ." *Bibliotheca Sacra* 140:557 (January-March 1983):11-20.

Samra, James G. "A Biblical View of Discipleship." *Bibliotheca Sacra* 160:638 (April-June 2003):219-34.

Saucy, Mark. "The Kingdom-of-God Sayings in Matthew." *Bibliotheca Sacra* 151:602 (April-June 1994):175-97.

_____. "Miracles and Jesus' Proclamation of the Kingdom of God." *Bibliotheca Sacra* 153:611 (July-September 1996):281-307.

Saphir, Adolph. *The Lord's Prayer*. Harrisburg, Pa.: Christian Alliance Publishing Co., n.d.

Saucy, Robert L. *The Case for Progressive Dispensationalism*. Grand Rapids: Zondervan Publishing House, 1993.

_____. "The Presence of the Kingdom and the Life of the Church." *Bibliotheca Sacra* 145:577 (January-March 1988):30-46.

Sauer, Erich. *The Triumph of the Crucified*. Translated by G. H. Lang. Grand Rapids: Wm. B. Eerdmans Publishing Co., 1951.

Scharen, Hans. "Gehenna in the Synoptics." *Bibliotheca Sacra* 149:595 (July-September 1992):324-37; 149:596 (October-December 1992):454-70.

Schweitzer, Albert. *The Quest of the Historical Jesus*. Translated by W. Montgomery. New York: Macmillan Co., 1961.

Schweizer, E. *The Good News according to Matthew*. English translation. London: SPCK, 1976. German original: *Das Evangelium nach Matthäus*. Das Neue Testament Deutsch series, number 2. Göttingen, Germ.: Vandenhoeck & Ruprecht, 1973.

Scofield, C. I., ed. *The Scofield Reference Bible*. New York: Oxford University Press, 1917.

Scroggie, W. Graham. *A Guide to the Gospels*. Old Tappan, N.J.: Fleming H. Revell Co., 1975.

Senior, Donald. *The Passion of Jesus in the Gospel of Matthew*. Wilmington, Del.: Michael Glazier, 1985.

Shepard, J. W. *The Christ of the Gospels*. Grand Rapids: Wm. B. Eerdmans Publishing Co., 1939.

Shepherd, Michael B. "Targums, The New Testament, and Biblical Theology of the Messiah." *Journal of the Evangelical Theological Society* 51:1 (March 2008):45-58.

Sheryl, J. Gregory. "Can the Date of Jesus' Return Be Known?" *Bibliotheca Sacra* 169:673 (January-March 2012):20-32.

Showers, Renald E. *Maranatha: Our Lord, Come! A Definitive Study of the Rapture of the Church*. Bellmawr, N.J.: Friends of Israel Gospel Ministry, 1995.

Simmonds, Andrew R. "'Woe to you . . . Hypocrites!' Re-reading Matthew 23:13-36." *Bibliotheca Sacra* 166:663 (July-September 2009):336-49.

Smillie, Gene R. "'Even the Dogs': Gentiles in the Gospel of Matthew." *Journal of the Evangelical Theological Society* 45:1 (March 2002):73-97.

_____. "Jesus' Response to the Question of His Authority in Matthew 21." *Bibliotheca Sacra* 162:648 (October-December 2005):459-69.

Sparks, H. F. D. "The Doctrine of the Divine Fatherhood of God in the Gospels." In *Studies in the Gospels: Essays in Memory of R. H. Lightfoot*, pp. 241-62. Edited by D. E. Nineham. Oxford: Blackwell, 1955.

Spencer, Aída Besançon. "Father-Ruler: The Meaning of the Metaphor 'Father' for God in the Bible." *Journal of the Evangelical Theological Society* 39:3 (September 1996):433-42.

Stamm, Frederick Keller. *Seeing the Multitudes*. New York: Harper & Brothers, 1943.

Stanley, Alan P. "The Rich Young Ruler and Salvation." *Bibliotheca Sacra* 163:649 (January-March 2006):46-62.

Stanton, Gerald B. *Kept from the Hour*. Fourth ed. Miami Springs, Fla.: Schoettle Publishing Co., 1991.

Stauffer, Ethelbert. *New Testament Theology*. Translated by John Marsh. London: SCM Press, 1955.

Stein, Robert H. "Wine-Drinking in New Testament Times." *Christianity Today* 19:19 (June 20, 1975):9-11.

Stonehouse, Ned B. *The Witness of Matthew and Mark to Christ*. Grand Rapids: Wm. B. Eerdmans Publishing Co., 1944.

Storms, C. Samuel. *Reaching God's Ear*. Wheaton: Tyndale House Publishers, 1988.

Stott, John R. W. *The Message of the Sermon on the Mount*. Downers Grove, Ill.: InterVarsity Press, 1978.

Stoutenburg, Dennis C. "'Out of my sight!', 'Get behind me!', or 'Follow after me!': There Is No Choice in God's Kingdom." *Journal of the Evangelical Theological Society* 36:1 (March 1993):173-78.

Stowe, C. E. "The Eschatology of Christ, With Special Reference to the Discourse in Matt. XXIV. and XXV." *Bibliotheca Sacra* 7 (July 1850):452-78.

Sukenik, E. L. *Ancient Synagogues in Palestine and Greece*. London: Oxford University Press, 1934.

Sweeney, James P. "Modern and Ancient Controversies over the Virgin Birth of Jesus." *Bibliotheca Sacra* 160:638 (April-June 2003):142-58.

Tasker, R. V. G. *The Gospel According to St. Matthew: An Introduction and Commentary*. Tyndale New Testament Commentaries series. Grand Rapids: Wm. B. Eerdmans Publishing Co., 1961.

Tatum, W. Barnes, Jr. "Matthew 2.23." *The Bible Translator* 27 (1976):135-38.

Taylor, Vincent. *The Gospel According to St. Mark*. London: Macmillan, 1952.

Tenney, Merrill C. *The Genius of the Gospels*. Grand Rapids: Wm. B. Eerdmans Publishing Co., 1951.

Theological Dictionary of the New Testament. Edited by Gerhard Kittel. S.v. "El(e)ias," by Joachim Jeremias.

_____. S.v. "*makarios*," by F. Hauck.

_____. S.v. "*polloi*," by Joachim Jeremias.

_____. S.v. "*porne . . .*," by F. Hauck and S. Schulz.

_____. S.v. "*telones*," by Otto Michel.

Theological Dictionary of the Old Testament. Edited by G. Johannes Botterweck and Helmer Ringgren. Translated by David E. Green. S.v. "Chebel," by H. J. Fabry.

Thiessen, Henry C. *Introduction to the New Testament*. Grand Rapids: Wm. B. Eerdmans Publishing Co., 1943.

Thistleton, A. C. "Realized Eschatology at Corinth." *New Testament Studies* 24 (1977):510-26.

Thomas, Robert L. *Evangelical Hermeneutics: The New Versus the Old*. Grand Rapids: Kregel Publications, 2002.

Thomas, W. H. Griffith. *Outline Studies of the Gospel of Matthew*. Grand Rapids: William B. Eerdmans Publishing Co., 1961.

Torrey, Charles C. "The Foundry of the Second Temple at Jerusalem." *Journal of Biblical Literature* 55 (December 1936):247-60.

Toussaint, Stanley D. *Behold the King: A Study of Matthew*. Portland, Oreg.: Multnomah Press, 1980.

_____. "The Contingency of the Coming of the Kingdom." In *Integrity of Heart, Skillfulness of Hands*, pp. 222-37. Edited by Charles H. Dyer and Roy B. Zuck. Grand Rapids: Baker Book House, 1994.

_____. "A Critique of the Preterist View of the Olivet Discourse." *Bibliotheca Sacra* 161:644 (October-December 2004):469-90.

_____. "The Introductory and Concluding Parables of Matthew Thirteen." *Bibliotheca Sacra* 121:484 (October-December 1964):351-55.

Toussaint, Stanley D., and Jay A. Quine. "No, Not Yet: The Contingency of God's Promised Kingdom." *Bibliotheca Sacra* 164:654 (April-June 2007):131-47.

Trench, Richard Chenevix. *Notes on the Parables of Our Lord*. New York: Appleton, 1851.

_____. *On the Lessons in Proverbs*. New York: Redfield, 1853.

_____. *Studies in the Gospels*. 3rd ed. Grand Rapids: Baker Book House, 1979.

_____. *Synonyms of the New Testament*. New ed. London: Kegan Paul, Trench, Trubner & Co. Ltd., 1915.

Trilling, Wolfgang. *Das wahre Israel: Studien zur Theologie des Matthaus-Evangeliums*. Munchen, Germany: Kosel, 1964.

Turner, David L. "Matthew 21:43 and the Future of Israel." *Bibliotheca Sacra* 159:633 (January-March 2002):46-61.

_____. "Matthew among the Dispensationalists." *Journal of the Evangelical Theological Society* 53:4 (December 2010):697-716.

_____. "The Structure and Sequence of Matthew 24:1-41: Interaction with Evangelical Treatments." *Grace Theological Journal* 10:1 (Spring 1989):3-27.

Turner, Nigel. *Syntax*. Vol. 3 of J. H. Moulton. *A Grammar of New Testament Greek*. Edinburgh: T. & T. Clark, 1963.

Unger's Bible Dictionary. 1957 ed. S.v. "Herod," by S. L. Bowman.

Varner, William C. "The *Didache* 'Apocalypse' and Matthew 24." *Bibliotheca Sacra* 165:659 (July-September 2008):309-22.

Vawter, Bruce. "Divorce and the New Testament." *Catholic Biblical Quarterly* 39 (1977):528-48.

_____. "The Divorce Clauses in Mt 5, 32 and 19, 9." *Catholic Biblical Quarterly* 16 (1959):155-67.

Vincent, Marvin R. *Word Studies in the New Testament*. 4 vols. New York: Charles Scribner's Sons, 1887; reprint ed., Grand Rapids: Wm. B. Eerdmans Publishing Co., 1946.

Wall, Joe L. *Going for the Gold*. Chicago: Moody Press, 1991.

Walvoord, John F. "Christ's Olivet Discourse on the End of the Age." *Bibliotheca Sacra* 128:510 (April-June 1971):109-16; 128:511 (July-September 1971):206-14; 128:512 (October-December 1971):316-26; 129:513 (January-March 1972):20-32; 129:514 (April-June 1972):99-105; 129:515 (July-September 1972):206-10; 129:516 (October-December 1972):307-15.

_____. "The Kingdom of Heaven." *Bibliotheca Sacra* 124:495 (July-September 1967):195-205.

_____. *Matthew: Thy Kingdom Come*. Chicago: Moody Press, 1974.

_____. *The Millennial Kingdom*. Findlay, Ohio: Dunham Publishing Co., 1959.

Ware, Bruce A "Is the Church in View in Matthew 24—25?" *Bibliotheca Sacra* 138:550 (April-June 1981):158-72.

Warfield, Benjamin B. "Jesus' Alleged Confession of Sin." *Princeton Theological Review* 12 (1914):127-228.

_____. *Selected Shorter Writings*. 2 vols. Edited by John E. Meeter. Nutley, N.J.: Presbyterian and Reformed, 1970.

Weaver, D. J. *Matthew's Missionary Discourse: A Literary-Critical Analysis*. Journal for the Study of the New Testament series, number 38. Sheffield, U.K.: Sheffield Academic Press, 1990.

Wenham, David. "Jesus and the Law: an Exegesis on Matthew 5:17-20." *Themelios* 4:3 (April 1979):92-26.

_____. "The Structure of Matthew XIII." *New Testament Studies* 25 (1979):516-22.

Wenham, G. J. "May Divorced Christians Remarry?" *Churchman* 95 (1981):150-61.

Wenham, J. W. "When Were the Saints Raised?" *Journal of Theological Studies* 32 (1981):150-52.

Westcott, Brooke Foss. *The Gospel According to St. John: The Authorised Version with Introduction and Notes*. 1880. London: James Clarke & Co., Ltd., 1958..

Westerholm, Stephen. "The Law in the Sermon on the Mount: Matt 5:17-48." *Criswell Theological Review* 6:1 (Fall 1992):43-56.

Wiersbe, Warren W. *The Bible Expositon Commentary*. 2 vols. Wheaton: Scripture Press, Victory Books, 1989.

Wilkin, Robert N. "A Great Buy!" *The Grace Evangelical Society News* 6:9 (September 1991):2.

_____. "Is Confessing Christ a Condition of Salvation?" *The Grace Evangelical Society News* 9:4 (July-August 1994):2-3.

_____. "Not Everyone Who Says 'Lord, Lord' Will Enter the Kingdom: Matthew 7:21-23." *The Grace Evangelical Society News* 3:12 (December 1988):2-3.

_____. "The Parable of the Four Soils: Do the Middle Two Soils Represent Believers or Unbelievers? (Matthew 13:20-21)." *The Grace Evangelical Society News* 3:8 (August-September 1988):2.

_____. "Self-Sacrifice and Kingdom Entrance: Matthew 5:29-30." *The Grace Evangelical Society News* 4:8 (August 1989):2; 4:9 (September 1989):2-3.

Willard, Dallas. *The Divine Conspiracy: Rediscovering Our Hidden Life with Christ*. San Francisco: HarperSanFrancisco, 1998.

Winer, George Benedict. *Grammar of the Idiom of the New Testament*. Translated from the 7th German ed. by J. Henry Thayer. Philadelphia: Smith, English, & Co., 1874.

Yamauchi, Edwin M. "Cultural Aspects of Marriage in the Ancient World." *Bibliotheca Sacra* 135:539 (July-September 1978):241-52.

Yates, Gary E. "Intertextuality and the Portrayal of Jeremiah the Prophet." *Bibliotheca Sacra* 170:679 (July-September 2013):286-303.

Zondervan Pictorial Encyclopedia of the Bible. Edited by Merrill C. Tenney. S.v. "phylactery," by J. Arthur Thompson.

_____. S.v. "Pilate, Pontius," by J. G. Vos.

Constable's Notes
on Mark

Introduction

WRITER

The writer did not identify himself by name anywhere in this Gospel. This is true of all four Gospels.

> "The title, 'According to Mark' (. . . [*kata Markon*]), was probably added when the canonical gospels were collected and there was need to distinguish Mark's version of the gospel from the others. The gospel titles are generally thought to have been added in the second century but may have been added much earlier. Certainly we may say that the title indicates that by A.D. 125 or so an important segment of the early church thought that a person named Mark wrote the second gospel."[1]

There are many statements of the early church fathers that identify the "John Mark" who is frequently mentioned in the New Testament as the writer.

The earliest reference of this type is in Eusebius' *Ecclesiastical History* (ca. A.D. 326).[2] Eusebius quoted Papius' *Exegesis of the Lord's Oracles* (ca. A.D. 140), a work now lost. Papius quoted "the Elder," probably the Apostle John, who said the following things about this Gospel: Mark wrote it, though he was not a disciple of Jesus during Jesus' ministry or an eyewitness of Jesus' ministry. He accompanied the Apostle Peter and listened to his preaching. He based his Gospel on the eyewitness account and spoken ministry of Peter. Mark did not write his Gospel in strict orderly sequence, meaning either chronological order[3] or rhetorical and artistic order[4], but he recorded accurately what Peter remembered of Jesus' words and deeds. He considered himself an interpreter of Peter's content. By this, "the Elder" probably meant that Mark recorded the teaching of Peter for the church, though not necessarily verbatim, as Peter expressed himself.[5] Finally, "the Elder" said that Mark's account is wholly reliable.

Another important source of the tradition that Mark wrote this Gospel is the Anti-Marcionite Prologue to Mark (A.D. 160-180). It also stated that Mark received his information from Peter. Moreover, it recorded that Mark wrote after Peter died, and that he wrote this Gospel in Italy.[6] Irenaeus (ca. A.D. 180-185), another early church father, noted that Mark wrote after Peter and Paul had died.[7] Other early tradition documenting these facts comes from Justin Martyr (ca. A.D. 150-160), Clement of Alexandria (ca. A.D. 195), Tertullian (ca. A.D. 200), the Muratorian Canon (ca. A.D. 200), and Origen (ca. A.D. 230). This testimony dates from the end of the second century. Furthermore it comes from three different centers of early Christianity: Asia Minor (modern Turkey), Rome (in Italy), and Alexandria (in Egypt). Thus there is strong external evidence that Mark wrote this Gospel.

The Mark in view is the "John Mark" mentioned frequently in the New Testament (Acts 12:12, 25; 13:5, 13; 15:36-39; Col. 4:10; Phile. 24; 2 Tim. 4:11; 1 Pet. 5:13; et al.). He was evidently a relative of Barnabas, and he accompanied Barnabas and Paul on their first missionary journey, but left these apostles when they reached Perga. Mark became useful to Paul during Paul's second Roman imprisonment, and was also with Peter when Peter was in Rome. Peter described him as his "son," probably his protégé.[8]

It seems unlikely that the early church would have accepted this Gospel as authoritative, since its writer was a secondary figure, without having convincing proof that Mark wrote it. Perhaps Luke showed special interest in John Mark, in Acts, because he was the writer of this Gospel, more than because he caused a breach between Paul and Barnabas.[9]

> "It is evident that he [Mark] was a charismatically endowed teacher and evangelist. . . . A careful reading of the Gospel will serve to introduce the author as a theologian of the first rank who never forgot that his primary intention was the strengthening of the people of God in a time of fiery ordeal."[10]

---

[1] Donald A. Carson and Douglas J. Moo, *An Introduction to the New Testament*, p. 172. See ibid, pp. 726-43 for a brief discussion of the formation of the New Testament canon.

[2] *The Ecclesiastical History of Eusebius Pamphilus*, 3:39:15.

[3] Martin Hengel, "Literary, Theological, and Historical Problems in the Gospel of Mark," in *Studies in the Gospel of Mark*, p. 48.

[4] Robert A. Guelich, *Mark 1—8:26*, p. xxvii.

[5] Richard C. H. Lenski, *The Interpretation of St. Mark's Gospel*, p. 12.

[6] The Anti-Marcionite Prologue.

[7] *Against Heresies*, 3:1:2.

[8] For a table comparing Peter's address in Acts 10:36-40 and the structure of Mark's Gospel, see Carson and Moo, p. 193.

[9] A. E. J. Rawlinson, *The Gospel According to St. Mark*, p. xxxi.

[10] William L. Lane, *The Gospel according to Mark*, p. 23.

Date

The earliest Mark could have written, if the testimonies of the Anti-Marcionite Prologue and Irenaeus are correct, was after the death of Peter and Paul. The most probable dates of Peter's martyrdom in Rome are A.D. 64-67. Paul probably died as a martyr there in A.D. 67-68. However, Clement of Alexandria and Origen both placed the composition of this Gospel during Peter's lifetime. This may mean that Mark wrote shortly before Peter died. Perhaps Mark began his Gospel during Peter's last years in Rome and completed it after Peter's death.

The latest that Mark could have written his Gospel was probably A.D. 70, when Titus destroyed Jerusalem. Many scholars believe that since no Gospel writer referred to that event, which fulfilled prophecy, they all must have written before it. To summarize, Mark probably wrote this Gospel sometime between A.D. 63 and 70.

Origin and Destination

Most of the early Christian tradition says Mark wrote in Italy, and specifically in Rome.[11] This external testimony finds support in the internal evidence of the Gospel itself. Many indications in the text point to Mark's having written for Gentile readers originally, particularly Romans. He explained Jewish customs that would have been strange to Gentile readers (e.g., 7:2-4; 15:42). He translated Aramaic words that would have been unfamiliar to Gentiles (3:17; 5:41; 7:11, 34; 15:22). Compared to Matthew and Luke he used many Latinisms and Latin loan words, indicating Roman influence. He showed special interest in persecution and martyrdom, which would have been of special interest to Roman readers when he wrote (e.g., 8:34-38; 13:9-13). Christians were then suffering persecution in Rome, and in various other places throughout the empire, especially after Nero began to persecute Christians in A.D. 65. For Romans, death by crucifixion was enough to disqualify Jesus as the Savior, and much of what Mark emphasized showed that He did not deserve crucifixion.[12] Finally, the early circulation and widespread acceptance of this Gospel among Christians suggest that it originated from, and went to, a powerful and influential church.[13]

Characteristics

Linguistically, Mark used a relatively limited vocabulary when he wrote this Gospel. For example, he used only about 80 words that occur nowhere else in the Greek New Testament, compared with Luke's Gospel that contains about 250 such words. Another unique feature is that Mark also liked to transliterate Latin words into Greek. However, the Aramaic language also influenced Mark's Greek. He evidently translated into Greek many of Peter's stories that Peter had recounted in Aramaic. The result was at times a rather rough and ungrammatical Greek wording, compared with Luke, who had a much more polished style of writing. However, Mark used a forceful, fresh, and vigorous style of writing. This comes through in his frequent use of the historical present tense that expresses action as happening at once. It is also obvious in his frequent use (41 times) of the Greek adverb *euthys* translated "immediately."[14] The resulting effect is that as one reads Mark's Gospel, one feels that he or she is reading a reporter's eyewitness account of the events.

> "Though primarily engaged in an oral rather than a written ministry, D. L. Moody was in certain respects a modern equivalent to Mark as a communicator of the gospel. His command of English was seemingly less than perfect and there were moments when he may have wounded the grammatical sensibilities of some of the more literate members of his audiences, but this inability never significantly hindered him in communicating the gospel with great effectiveness. In a similar way, Mark's occasional literary lapses have been no handicap to his communication in this gospel in which he skillfully set forth the life and ministry of Jesus."[15]

> "The evidence points to Mark's being not a creative literary artist but an extremely honest and conscientious compiler."[16]

Mark addressed his readers directly (e.g., 2:10; 7:19), through Jesus' words (e.g., 13:37), and with the use of rhetorical questions addressed to them (e.g., 4:41). This gives the reader the exciting feeling that he or she is interacting with the story personally. It also impresses the reader with the need for him or her to respond to what the story is presenting. Specifically, Mark wanted his readers to believe that Jesus is the Messiah and the Son of God, and to follow Him.

Historically, Mark recorded many intimate details that only an eyewitness could have observed, which he evidently obtained from Peter (e.g., 1:27, 41, 43; 2:12; 3:5; 7:34; 9:5-6, 10; 10:24, 32). He stressed Jesus' acts and gave a prominent place to His miracles in this Gospel.[17] Matthew, on the other hand, stressed Jesus' discourses, His teachings about His kingdom. Mark recorded a smaller proportion of Jesus' words, and a greater

---

[11]Irenaeus, and Clement of Alexandria.

[12]Robert H. Gundry, *Mark*, p. 1045.

[13]Walter W. Wessel, "Mark," in *Matthew-Luke*, vol. 8 of *The Expositor's Bible Commentary*, p. 609.

[14]See Rodney J. Decker, "The Use of *euthys* ('immediately') in Mark," *Journal of Ministry and Theology* 1:1 (Spring 1997):90-121.

[15]David K. Lowery, "A Theology of Mark," in *A Biblical Theology of the New Testament*, p. 67.

[16]Cranfield, p. 16.

[17]See Appendix 6 "The Miracles of Jesus" in my notes on Matthew for a chart of all the miracles recorded in the Gospels.

proportion of His works, than Matthew did. Jesus comes through in Mark's Gospel as a *Man of action*. Mark emphasized Jesus' role as the "Servant of the Lord."

> "Mark's story of Jesus is one of swift action and high drama. Only twice, in chapters 4 and 13, does Jesus pause to deliver extended discourses."[18]

Candor also marks this Gospel. Mark did not glorify the disciples, but recorded them doing unflattering things such as criticizing Jesus. He also described the hostility of Jesus' family members toward Him. He stressed the human reactions and emotions of Jesus.

All four Gospels are primarily narrative literature in their genre. Cranfield distinguished four different kinds of narrative material in Mark's Gospel:

> "(i) Narratives the wealth of detail and vividness of which suggest direct derivation from the reminiscence of an eyewitness. . . . (ii) Narratives which by their rounded form and lack of vivid details give the impression of being units of oral tradition which have been worn smooth by frequent repetition. . . . (iii) Narratives which, though based on tradition, do not seem to be actual units of oral tradition, but rather to have been constructed by Mark himself . . . (iv) Brief summary statements indicating in general terms what was happening during a certain period . . ."[19]

Theologically, this Gospel presents a high Christology beginning with the introduction of Jesus as "the Son of God" (1:1). Mark revealed Jesus' preference for the title "Son of Man," which He used to describe Himself frequently.

Purpose

These characteristics help us understand Mark's purpose for writing, which he did not state directly. Mark's purpose was not just to give his readers a biographical or historical account of Jesus' life. He had a more practical purpose. The biographical material he chose to include and omit suggests that he wanted to enable his Christian readers to endure suffering and persecution for their faith effectively. To do this, he recorded much about Jesus' sufferings. About one third of this Gospel deals with the passion of Jesus.

> "Mark's Gospel has been called a Passion story with a long introduction."[20]

Moreover, there are many other references to suffering throughout the book (e.g., 1:12-13; 3:21-22, 30-35; 8:34-38; 10:30, 33-34, 45; 13:8, 11-13). Clearly, Mark implied that faithfulness and obedience as a disciple of Jesus will inevitably result in opposition, suffering, and perhaps death. This emphasis would have ministered to the original readers who were undergoing persecution for their faith. It is a perennial need in pastoral ministry. It is interesting that the theme of suffering is strong in Peter's first epistle, too. Evidently this was a subject that lay heavily on Peter's heart. Mark also wanted his Gentile Christian readers to be good servants of God and other people. Therefore he devoted much attention to Jesus' training of the Twelve for service.

Mark had a theological (Christological) as well as a pastoral (discipleship) purpose in writing. It was to stress the true humanity of the Son of God. Whereas Matthew presented Jesus as the Messiah, Mark showed that He was the human servant of God who suffered as no other person has suffered. Mark stressed Jesus' complete obedience to His Father's will. This emphasis makes Jesus an example for all disciples to follow (10:45). One wonders if Mark presented Jesus as he did, in order to balance a tendency that existed in the early church, by Docetists and others, to think of Jesus as divine but not fully human.

> "Whereas a parenetic [exhorting] purpose with regard to Christian discipleship would explain only one small element in the contents of Mark and even then would misconstrue that element, an apologetic purpose with regard to the Cross provides a comprehensive explanation of all elements and, more especially, of the ways in which those elements are presented. Fitting together to form an apology for the Cross are not only the authority and radicalism of Jesus' teaching but also the fulfillment of his predictions, not only his power-packed miracles and exorcisms but also the supernatural manner and accompaniments of his death, not only his attraction of crowds but also his burial by a pious and brave member of the Sanhedrin, not only his baptismal approval by the Father and enduement with the Spirit but also his resurrection."[21]

---

[18]J. D. Kingsbury, *Conflict in Mark: Jesus, Authorities, Disciples*, p. 1.

[19]Cranfield, p. 11.

[20]*The Nelson Study Bible*, p. 1665.

[21]Gundry, p. 1026.

Mark's position among the Gospels

It is common today for scholars to hold *Markan* priority. This is the view that Mark wrote his Gospel first and the other Gospel evangelists wrote after he did. This view has become popular since the nineteenth century. Before that, most biblical scholars believed that Matthew wrote his Gospel first. Since then, many scholars have concluded that Mark was one of the two primary sources that the other Synoptic Gospel writers used, the other being Q.[22] There is presently no definitive solution to this problem of which came first, though by far the majority of scholars favor Mark.

Scholars favoring Markan priority base their view on the fact that: Mark contains about 90 percent of what is in Matthew and about 40 percent of what is in Luke. Matthew and Luke usually follow Mark's order of events, and they rarely agree against the content of Mark when they all deal with the same subject. Matthew and Luke also often repeat Mark's wording, and they sometimes interpret and tone down some of Mark's statements. Normally, Mark's accounts are fuller than Matthew and Luke's, suggesting that they may have edited his work.

However, sometimes Matthew and Luke agree against Mark in a particular account. Luke omitted a large section of Mark's material, including all of what is in Mark 6:45—8:26. Moreover, in view of the likelihood that Mark wrote in the 60s, if he wrote first, Matthew and Luke may have written after the fall of Jerusalem. This seems unlikely, because although that event fulfilled prophecy, neither writer cited the fulfillment as such.[23]

All things considered, I favor *Matthean* priority. This view is currently enjoying a resurgence in popularity. William Farmer has been a leader among those who hold Markan priority.[24] However, this debate is not crucial to the interpretation of the text.

Outline

I.   Introduction 1:1-13

      A.   The title of the book 1:1

      B.   Jesus' preparation for ministry 1:2-13

            1.   The ministry of John the Baptist 1:2-8
            2.   The baptism of Jesus 1:9-11
            3.   The temptation of Jesus 1:12-13

II.   The Servant's early Galilean ministry 1:14—3:6

      A.   The beginning of Jesus' ministry 1:14-20

            1.   The message of the Servant 1:14-15
            2.   The first disciples of the Servant 1:16-20

      B.   Early demonstrations of the Servant's authority 1:21-34

            1.   Jesus' teaching and healing in the Capernaum synagogue 1:21-28
            2.   The healing of Peter's mother-in-law 1:29-31
             3.   Jesus' healing of many Galileans after sundown 1:32-34

      C.   Jesus' early ministry throughout Galilee 1:35-45

            1.   The first preaching tour of Galilee 1:35-39
            2.   The cleansing of a leprous Jew 1:40-45

      D.   Jesus' initial conflict with the religious leaders 2:1—3:6

            1.   The healing and forgiveness of a paralytic 2:1-12
            2.   The call of Levi and his feast 2:13-17
            3.   The religious leaders' question about fasting 2:18-22
            4.   The controversies about Sabbath observance 2:23—3:6

---

[22]See my note on the introduction to Matthew for a fuller discussion of Q.

[23]John D. Grassmick, "Mark," in *The Bible Knowledge Commentary: New Testament*, p. 98. For fuller discussion, see the commentaries and works on Bible introduction.

[24]William R. Farmer, *The Synoptic Problem*. See also C. E. B. Cranfield, *The Gospel According to St. Mark*, pp. 6-7, for a summary of arguments for Markan priority.

III.   The Servant's later Galilean ministry 3:7—6:6a

    A.   The broadening of Jesus' ministry 3:7-19

        1.   Jesus' ministry to the multitudes 3:7-12
        2.   Jesus' selection of 12 disciples 3:13-19

    B.   The increasing rejection of Jesus and its result 3:20—4:34

        1.   The increasing rejection of Jesus 3:20-35
        2.   Jesus' teaching in parables 4:1-34

    C.   Jesus' demonstrations of power and the Nazarenes' rejection 4:35—6:6a

        1.   The demonstrations of Jesus' power 4:35—5:43
        2.   Jesus rejection by the Nazarenes 6:1-6a

IV.   The Servant's self-revelation to the disciples 6:6b—8:30

    A.   The mission of the Twelve 6:6b-30

        1.   The sending of the Twelve 6:6b-13
        2.   The failure of Antipas to understand Jesus' identity 6:14-29
        3.   The return of the Twelve 6:30

    B.   The first cycle of self-revelation to the disciples 6:31—7:37
        1.   The feeding of the 5,000 6:31-44
        2.   Jesus' walking on the water and the return to Galilee 6:45-56
        3.   The controversy with the Pharisees and scribes over defilement 7:1-23
        4.   Jesus' teaching about bread and the exorcism of a Phoenician girl 7:24-30
        5.   The healing of a deaf man with a speech impediment 7:31-36
        6.   The preliminary confession of faith 7:37

    C.   The second cycle of self-revelation to the disciples 8:1-30
        1.   The feeding of the 4,000 8:1-9
        2.   The return to Galilee 8:10
        3.   Conflict with the Pharisees over signs 8:11-13
        4.   Jesus' teaching about the yeast of the Pharisees and Herod 8:14-21
        5.   The healing of a blind man near Bethsaida 8:22-26
        6.   Peter's confession of faith 8:27-30

V.   The Servant's journey to Jerusalem 8:31—10:52

    A.   The first passion prediction and its lessons 8:31—9:29

        1.   The first major prophecy of Jesus' passion 8:31-33
        2.   The requirements of discipleship 8:34—9:1
        3.   The Transfiguration 9:2-8
        4.   The coming of Elijah 9:9-13
        5.   The exorcism of an epileptic boy 9:14-29

    B.   The second passion prediction and its lessons 9:30—10:31

        1.   The second major prophecy of Jesus' passion 9:30-32
        2.   The pitfalls of discipleship 9:33-50
        3.   Lessons concerning self-sacrifice 10:1-31

    C.   The third passion prediction and its lessons 10:32-52

        1.   The third major prophecy of Jesus' passion 10:32-34
        2.   Jesus' teaching about serving 10:35-45
        3.   The healing of a blind man near Jericho 10:46-52

VI.   The Servant's ministry in Jerusalem chs. 11—13

    A.   Jesus' formal presentation to Israel 11:1-26

        1.   The Triumphal Entry 11:1-11
        2.   Jesus' judgment on unbelieving Israel 11:12-26

    B.   Jesus' teaching in the temple 11:27—12:44

        1.   The controversy over Jesus' authority 11:27—12:12
        2.   The controversy over Jesus' teaching 12:13-37
        3.   Jesus' condemnation of hypocrisy and commendation of reality 12:38-44

    C.   Jesus' teaching on Mt. Olivet ch. 13

        1.   The setting 13:1-4
        2.   Warnings against deception 13:5-8
        3.   Warnings about personal danger during deceptions 13:9-13
        4.   The coming crisis 13:14-23
        5.   The second coming of the Son of Man 13:24-27
        6.   The time of Jesus' return 13:28-32
        7.   The concluding exhortation 13:33-37

VII.   The Servant's passion ministry chs. 14—15

    A.   The Servant's anticipation of suffering 14:1-52

        1.   Jesus' sufferings because of betrayal 14:1-11
        2.   Jesus' sufferings because of desertion 14:12-52

    B.   The Servant's endurance of suffering 14:53—15:47

        1.   Jesus' Jewish trial 14:53—15:1
        2.   Jesus' Roman trial 15:2-20
        3.   Jesus' crucifixion, death, and burial 15:21-47

VIII.   The Servant's resurrection ch. 16

    A.   The announcement of Jesus' resurrection 16:1-8

    B.   The appearances and ascension of Jesus 16:9-20

        1.   Three post-resurrection appearances 16:9-18
        2.   Jesus' ascension 16:19-20

Carson and Moo divided the book a bit differently, as follows.[25]

I. Preliminaries to the ministry 1:1-13
    Transition 1:14-15
II. First part of the Galilean ministry 1:16—3:6
    Transition 3:7-12
III. Second part of the Galilean ministry 3:13—5:43
    Transition 6:1-6
IV. The concluding phase of the Galilean ministry 6:7—8:26
    Transition 8:27-30
V. The way of glory and suffering 8:31—10:45
    Transition 10:46-52
VI. Final ministry in Jerusalem 11:1—13:37
    Transition 14:1-2
VII.   The passion and empty tomb narratives 14:3—16:8

---

[25]See Carson and Moo, pp. 169-72.

Message

Matthew presents Jesus in the purple and gold of royalty. Mark portrays Him in the brown and green of a servant who has come to do His Father's will.

The message of the book is similar to Matthew's message. A concise statement of it appears in 1:14-15: "After John had been taken into custody, Jesus came into Galilee, preaching the gospel of God, and saying, 'The time is fulfilled, and the kingdom of God is at hand; repent and believe in the gospel.'" Jesus proclaimed this good news during most of His earthly ministry.

Another verse that is key to understanding the message of this Gospel is 10:45: "For even the Son of Man did not come to be served, but to serve, and to give His life a ransom for many." This verse provides the unique emphasis of the book, Jesus' role as a servant, and a general outline of its contents.

First, the Son of Man came. That is the Incarnation. The Son of Man was God incarnate in human nature. His identity is a major theme in this Gospel, as it is in all the Gospels.

Second, the Son of Man did not come to be ministered unto, but to minister. That is service. This Gospel also has much to teach disciples about service to God and to our fellow men.

Third, the Son of Man came to give His life a ransom for many. That is His sufferings. Mark's Gospel stresses the sufferings of the Suffering Servant of the Lord. Mark is the Gospel of the Servant of God.

Jesus was, of course, by nature the Son of God. He is, and always has been, equal with the Father, because He shares the same divine nature with the Father. However in the Incarnation, Jesus became the Servant of God.

The hope for a divine Servant of God was an Old Testament revelation. Isaiah had more to say about the Servant of the Lord than any other Old Testament prophet, though many other prophets spoke of Him too.

In the New Testament, the Apostle Paul expounded the significance of Jesus becoming the Servant of God more than any other writer. His great Kenosis passage, in Philippians 2, helps us grasp what it meant for the Son of God to become the Servant of God. In the Incarnation, Jesus limited Himself. He did not cease to be God, but He poured Himself into the nature and body of a man. This limited His divine powers. Moreover, He submitted Himself to a mission that the Father prescribed for Him that constrained His divine freedom. Mark presents Jesus as a real man who was also God in the role of a servant.

Consider first the *nature* of Jesus' service.

The second person of the Trinity became a servant to create a gospel, to provide good news for human beings. This good news is that Jesus has provided salvation for humankind. To provide salvation, the eternal Son became a servant. Whenever the Bible speaks of Jesus as a servant it is always talking about His providing salvation.

Mark began by citing Isaiah, who predicted the Servant of God (1:3; cf. Isa. 40:3). The quotation from Malachi in verse 2 is only introductory. This is very significant because Mark, unlike Matthew, rarely quoted from the Old Testament. Isaiah pictured One who would come to accomplish God's purpose of providing final salvation. His picture of the Servant became more distinct and detailed, like a portrait under construction, until in chapter 53, Isaiah depicted the Servant's awful sufferings. This chapter is the great background for the second Gospel, as Psalm 110 lies behind the first Gospel.

The picture of the Servant suffering on the Cross is the last in a series of pictures that Mark has given us. He also shows the Servant suffering in His struggle against the forces of Satan and his demons. Another picture is of the Servant suffering the opposition of Israel's religious leaders. Another one is of the Servant suffering the dullness and misunderstanding of His own disciples. These are all major themes in Mark's Gospel that have in common the view of Jesus as the Suffering Servant.

Turning to the Apostle Paul's theological exposition of the Suffering Servant theme in Scripture, we note that he picked up another of Mark's emphases. Mark did not just present Jesus as the Suffering Servant as an interesting theological revelation. He showed what that means for disciples of the Suffering Servant. We need to adopt the same attitude that Jesus had (Phil. 2:5). Disciples of the Suffering Servant should expect and prepare for the same experiences He encountered. We need to have the same graciousness, humility, and love that He did. The Son of God emptied Himself to become a servant of God and man. We must also sacrifice ourselves for the same purpose.

Isaiah revealed that the central meaning of the Servant's mission was to provide salvation through self-sacrifice (Isa. 53). Paul also revealed that the Son became a servant to provide salvation through self-sacrifice (Phil. 2). The sense in which the Son of God became the Servant of the Lord is that He created a gospel by providing salvation from the slavery of sin.

When Jesus began His public ministry, He announced, "The time is fulfilled" (1:15). The person whom Isaiah and the other prophets had predicted had now arrived. God had drawn near by becoming a man. He had drawn near in the form of a humble servant. He was heading for the Cross. He would conquer what had ruined man and nature. He would provide good news for humankind, and He would return one day to establish His righteous kingdom over all the earth in grace and glory. The Cross was the focal point of Jesus' service.

"Jesus" was His human name. "Messiah" was the title that described His role, though most people misunderstood it. "Son of God" was the title that represented His deity. These three are primary in Mark's Gospel.

In addition to the *nature* of Jesus service, we also need to consider what Mark teaches about the *characteristics* of Jesus' service.

Jesus' sympathy with sinners stands out in this Gospel. Mark recorded no word of severity coming from Jesus' lips for sinners. Jesus reserved His severity for hypocrites, those who pretended to be righteous but were really unrighteous. He was hard on them because they ruined the lives of other people.

Sympathy comes from suffering. We have sympathy for someone who is undergoing some painful experience that we have gone through. It is hard to sympathize with someone whose experience is foreign to us.

Sympathy comes from suffering, and it manifests itself in sacrifice. It involves bearing one another's burdens. Jesus' sympathy for us sinners arose from sharing our sufferings, and it became obvious when He sacrificed Himself for us. If there was ever anyone who bore the burdens of others, it was Jesus (10:45).

Consider, also, the *result* of Jesus' service. It is the gospel. Reference to the gospel opens and closes this book (1:1; 16:20). The gospel is the good news that Jesus Christ died for our sins according to the Scriptures, that He was buried, and that He was resurrected on the third day according to the Scriptures (1 Cor. 15:3-4).

When Jesus arose from the dead, His disciples were fearful, and they refused to believe that He was alive. Jesus' strongest words of criticism of them occur in 16:14: "He reproached them for their unbelief and hardness of heart, because they had not believed those who had seen Him after He had risen." This is the climax of the theme of the disciples' unbelief that runs through this Gospel. Look what He said to them immediately after that in 16:15: "Go into all the world and preach the gospel to all creation." He sent them out to proclaim the good news of salvation accomplished to every creature. The resurrection of the Servant is the great proof of the acceptability of His service, and it demands the service of His disciples.

The abiding appeal of this book is, "Repent and believe the gospel" (1:15). Repenting is preliminary. Believing is the essential call.

Jesus did not preach that people should believe *into* the gospel (Gr. *eis*), nor that they should believe *close to* the gospel (Gr. *apo*). He called them to rest *in* the gospel (Gr. *en*). The gospel is a sphere of rest. We can have confidence in the gospel, put our trust in it, and rest in it.

The unbelievers in Mark's Gospel refused to rest in the reality that Jesus was not just a human Messiah come to deliver Israel from Rome, but the divine Son of God. The disciples had little rest in their spirits, because they still could not overcome the limited traditional misconceptions of Messiah's role in history, even though they believed that Jesus was God's Son.

The application of this Gospel to the church as a whole is: "Believe the gospel." As the disciples not only believed, but also struggled to believe, so the church needs to have a continuing and growing confidence in the gospel of Jesus Christ, the "Servant of God."

It is a message of pardon and of power. Peter had to learn that it was a message of pardon after his triple denial of Jesus. All the disciples had to learn that it is a message of power after they refused to believe that God had raised Jesus back to life.

When the church loses its confidence in the gospel, its service becomes weak. If we doubt the power of the gospel, we have no message for people who are the servants of sin. The measure of our confidence in the gospel will be the measure of our effectiveness as God's servants.

How can we have greater confidence in the gospel? It is not primarily by studying or trying or experiencing. It is mainly by the illuminating work of God's Holy Spirit in our hearts. Jesus' disciples were blind until God opened their eyes, first to Jesus' true identity, and then to see Jesus' central place in time and history. They huddled in unbelief following the resurrection, until the Holy Spirit illuminated their understanding about the significance of the resurrection. Then they went everywhere proclaiming the gospel (16:20).

Mark calls on individual disciples of Jesus to believe in this gospel, to rest in it for pardon from sin and for power for service. He tells the story of the perfect Servant of God, whose perfect and perfected service is procuring a perfect salvation. God's Son became a *servant* to get near people, to help them, and to lift them up. *That* is the good news which people need to hear; that "good news" gospel message is what is meant in the phrase "preach the *gospel*."[26]

[26]Adapted from G. Campbell Morgan, *Living Messages of the Books of the Bible*, 2:1:25-39.

Exposition

I. INTRODUCTION 1:1-13

This opening section of the book sets the stage for the presentation of Jesus Christ as the unique Servant of the Lord. Mark omitted references to Jesus' birth and youth.[27] These subjects are irrelevant when presenting the life of a servant.

> "The accent falls upon the disclosure that Jesus is the Messiah, the very Son of God, whose mission is to affirm his sonship in the wilderness. His encounter with Satan provides the background for the delineation of the conflict between the Son of God and the forces of Satan which is so prominent an element in the Marcan narrative of Jesus' ministry."[28]

A. THE TITLE OF THE BOOK 1:1 (CF. LUKE 3:1-2)

Mark may have intended this sentence to introduce the ministry of John the Baptist, since that is what follows immediately (vv. 4-8). It could also refer to the inception of Jesus' public ministry and therefore be a title of the Gospel's introduction (1:1-13). It seems more probable, however, that this verse is a title for the whole book. It summarizes Mark's whole Gospel. Incidentally, the New Testament never uses the word "Gospel" to describe a book of the Bible. That is a more recent use of the word.

> "The term 'gospel' or 'evangel' was not a word first coined among the Christians. On the contrary, the concept was significant both in pagan and Jewish culture. Among the Romans it meant 'joyful tidings' and was associated with the cult of the emperor, whose birthday, attainment to majority and accession to power were celebrated as festival occasions for the whole world. The reports of such festivals were called 'evangels' in the inscriptions and papyri of the Imperial Age."[29]

Possibly Mark began his Gospel as he did ("the beginning") in order to recall the opening verse of Genesis. The good news about Jesus Christ provides a "beginning" of as great a significance as the creation of the cosmos. When Jesus came to earth and began His ministry, God created something new. This Gospel presents a *new beginning*, in which God revealed "good news about Jesus Christ." Thus this title might be a clue to the divine origin of the second Gospel.

> "In Galatians 4:4-6, Paul viewed the gospel story as in two parts, God's sending 'his Son' and the sending of 'the Spirit of his Son.' Mark covers the first of these two sendings. The full apostolic message also included the sending of the Holy Spirit. But the story of the sending of the Son of God had its historical beginning with the coming of John the forerunner."[30]

The word "gospel" is the modern equivalent of the old English "god-spel" meaning good news. The Greek word is *euangelion*. The gospel is the "good news" that God has provided eternal salvation through the ministry of Jesus Christ (cf. Isa. 40:9; 41:27; 52:7; 61:1-3; Rom. 1:16). This term is important in the theological emphasis of Mark's narrative (cf. 1:14-15; 8:35; 10:29; 13:9-10; 14:9).

> "'The Gospel is neither a discussion nor a debate,' said Dr. Paul S. Rees. 'It is an announcement!'"[31]

The word "gospel" also had a pagan background associated with the emperor cult. The birth of an heir to the throne, his coming of age, and his accession to office were announced as "good news"—"gospel," *euangelion*. The early Christians, therefore, connected the "gospel" of Jesus Christ with the "gospel" of the *true* ruler of *God's* kingdom.[32]

The word "gospel" also describes a certain type of literature, a literary genre. Gospel literature is not just history or biography. It is "preaching materials, designed to tell the story of God's saving action in the life, ministry, death and resurrection of Jesus of Nazareth."[33] Mark's Gospel contains the good news that the early Christians preached (cf. Acts 2:36).[34]

> "Mark does not write as a disinterested historian. He writes as a preacher conveying God's good news of salvation by emphasizing Jesus' saving ministry . . . Mark also writes as a theologian, arranging and interpreting the tradition to meet the needs of his hearers."[35]

---

[27]See Appendix 1 "A Harmony of the Gospels" at the end of my notes on Matthew.

[28]Lane, p. 40.

[29]Ibid., pp. 42-43.

[30]D. Edmond Hiebert, *Mark: A Portrait of the Servant*, p. 27

[31]Warren W. Wiersbe, *The Bible Exposition Commentary*, 1:110.

[32]Cranfield, p. 36.

[33]R. P. Martin, *Mark: Evangelist and Theologian*, p. 21.

[34]C. F. D. Moule, *The Gospel According to Mark*, p. 8.

"Jesus Christ" is the subject of this gospel (objective genitive). He is also the source of it (subjective genitive). Probably the former meaning is what Mark had in mind here. He seems to have wanted to provide an account of Jesus' ministry, so his readers could have a factual basis for their understanding of the gospel they had believed.

"Jesus" is the Greek form of the Hebrew "Joshua," meaning "Yahweh is salvation" or "salvation of Yahweh." "Christ" transliterates the Greek word *kristos*, which means "anointed." The Hebrew word for "anointed" is *masiah*, from which we get "Messiah." By the time Mark wrote his Gospel, "Jesus Christ" had become a proper name, not a name (Jesus) and a title (Christ), the original meanings of these words. However, Mark intended "Christ" to have its full titular meaning as well (cf. 8:29; 12:35; 14:61; 15:32). "Jesus" was a common name among the Jews until the beginning of the second century A.D., when the Jews stopped using it, because they hated Jesus of Nazareth, and Gentiles stopped using it, out of respect for Him.[36]

Mark further identified Jesus Christ as the "Son of God." This title does not appear in some important early manuscripts of Mark, but it is probably legitimate.[37] It expresses Jesus' unique relationship to God and identifies an important theme in the second Gospel (cf. 1:11; 3:11; 5:7; 9:7; 12:6; 13:32; 14:36, 61; 15:39). The title does not necessarily imply divinity, or preexistence in heaven, since it sometimes describes human beings (e.g., 2 Sam. 7:14; Ps. 2:7). Nevertheless, as modifying Jesus here, the title is messianic, but it connotes a subordinate relationship to God. Mark presented Jesus as the *Servant of God*—particularly—in this book. Rather than recording a nativity narrative that showed that Jesus was the Son of God, Mark simply stated that fact with this title.[38]

> ". . . from the start the narrator of Mark's story establishes with the reader a relationship of confidence by divulging the secret of Jesus' identity long before it becomes known to characters in the story, for the first line is an aside to the reader revealing that Jesus is the anointed one, the son of God. This technique puts the reader on the inside, among those who know, and enables the reader to understand more than many of the characters in the drama understand. This technique is an important foundation in this story which is concerned with what is hidden and what is secret."[39]

> "The Gospel is not a mystery story in which the identity of the main character has to be guessed; from the outset it is made clear who this is—the Son of God."[40]

Taken together: "Jesus," "Christ," and "Son of God" present Jesus as a Man who was God's special agent, but who was also fully divine.

> "The superscription refers to Jesus as 'the anointed one, the son of God.' At the end of the first half of the story, Peter acknowledges Jesus as 'the anointed one' [8:29] and at the end of Jesus' life the centurion identifies Jesus as 'son of God' [15:39]. The first half of the gospel emphasizes the authority of Jesus to do acts of power. The second half emphasizes the suffering of Jesus in filial obedience to God. Although the characterization of Jesus is consistent throughout, there appears, nevertheless, a clear development in the portrayal of Jesus from one half of the gospel to the next. In the first step, he serves with power; in the second, he serves as the one who suffers. Throughout the style and the structure of episodes the two-step progressions prepare the reader to be drawn more readily into seeing this larger second step and accepting this clearer, more precise understanding of Jesus."[41]

> "In the gospel story he narrates, Mark tells, of course, of Jesus. Intertwined with the story of Jesus, however, are two other story lines: that of the religious authorities and that of the disciples."[42]

B. JESUS' PREPARATION FOR MINISTRY 1:2-13

Mark proceeded to record three events that the reader needs to understand in order to appreciate Jesus' ministry correctly. They are: John the Baptist's ministry, Jesus' baptism, and Jesus' temptation. Two words that recur throughout this section of the text are key to understanding Mark's emphasis: "desert" and "the Spirit."[43]

---

[35]Wessel, p. 611.

[36]Cranfield, p. 37.

[37]See Carson and Moo, p. 187.

[38]See Herbert W. Bateman IV, "Defining the Titles 'Christ' and 'Son of God' in Mark's Narrative Presentation of Jesus," *Journal of the Evangelical Theological Society* 50:3 (September 2007):537-59.

[39]David M. Rhoads and Donald M. Michie, *Mark as Story: An Introduction to the Narrative of a Gospel*, p. 41.

[40]E. Best, *The Temptation and the Passion*, p. 168.

[41]Rhoads and Michie, pp. 48-49.

[42]Kingsbury, p. vii.

[43]See Frank J. Matera, "The Prologue as the Interpretive Key to Mark's Gospel," *Journal for the Study of the New Testament* 34 (October 1988):3-20.

1. The ministry of John the Baptist 1:2-8 (cf. Matt. 3:1-6, 11-12; Luke 3:3-6; 15-18)

The writer pointed out that the ministry of Jesus' forerunner fulfilled prophecy. It made a significant impact on those whom John contacted.[44] Then Mark recorded the essence of John's message.

1:2-3   Mark began with a quotation from the Old Testament. A proper understanding of Jesus' ministry requires an understanding of prophecy concerning Messiah. He literally wrote: "It stands written" (perfect tense in the Greek text). The early Christians believed that the Old Testament was God's authoritative Word.

This quotation is a blend of words taken from the Septuagint version of Exodus 23:20, Malachi 3:1, and Isaiah 40:3. Mark shaped this quotation to stress the messianic emphasis in these Old Testament passages. He probably introduced this quotation by referring to Isaiah, because the Isaiah part contains the main point he wanted to stress (v. 3), or perhaps because Isaiah was the more prominent of the prophets he quoted.

The *desert* ("wilderness"), where God met with His people, was a significant Old Testament motif. Messiah would come out of the desert. "The Lord" proved to be Jesus. Mark's introduction of the word "way" (Gr. *hodos*, lit. road or highway) begins one of his themes, namely, the path through life. This is what a disciple of Jesus must follow (cf. 8:27; 9:33; 10:17, 32, 52; 12:14).

This is the only time Mark quoted an Old Testament passage, except for when he quoted Jesus referring to the Old Testament. The quotation in 15:28 lacks ancient manuscript authority. What a contrast with Matthew!

> "The point of the whole quotation is that John's preparatory ministry, in fulfillment of prophecy, authenticated Jesus' Messiahship and prepared for the beginning of His official ministry as the Messiah."[45]

1:4   The "wilderness" or desert (Gr. *eremos*) where John ministered was dry and uninhabited. It was the wilderness of Judea west and north of the Dead Sea (Matt. 3:1).

John baptized people when they gave evidence of *repentance*. "A baptism of repentance" means a baptism characterized by repentance. The Jews whom John baptized not only changed their minds, the basic meaning of *metanoia*, but they also changed their behavior. This is the only occurrence of *metanoia* in Mark. The changes were for, and resulted in, "the forgiveness of sins." Change of behavior does not earn forgiveness, but change of behavior demonstrates genuine contrition that results in forgiveness. The unusual thing about John's baptism was that in his day, Gentiles baptized themselves when they converted to Judaism, and the Jews baptized themselves for ritual cleansing.

> "As Israel long ago had been separated from Egypt by a pilgrimage through the waters of the Red Sea, the nation is exhorted again to experience separation; the people are called to a second exodus in preparation for a new covenant with God."[46]

Peter's sermon in Acts 10:37 began at the same place as Mark's Gospel: with the ministry of John the Baptist. This is one hint of Peter's influence on the second Gospel.

1:5   Multitudes of Jews responded enthusiastically to John's ministry. Large crowds from southern Palestine and Jerusalem went to "the Jordan River," in response to his call to prepare for Messiah's appearance. Mark's use of "all" was hyperbolic. Every individual did not come out to John, but very many did. Those who did, confessed "their sins" by submitting to *baptism*. By allowing the forerunner of Messiah to baptize them, the Jews who submitted to his baptism were pledging to receive Messiah when He came.

1:6   This description of John would have identified him as a typical "holy man" of the ancient East who lived in the desert. His clothing was woven "camel's hair" held in place with "a leather belt" (cf. 2 Kings 1:8; cf. Mal. 4:5-6). This is how prophets typically dressed (cf. Zech. 13:4). His diet consisted of dried "locusts" and the "honey" of "wild" bees. This was clean food for the Jews (cf. Lev. 11:21-22). John may have been a lifelong Nazirite, or he may simply have lived an ascetic life out of devotion to God (Luke 1:15). His personal appearance and behavior, in addition to his divine anointing, must have encouraged the Jews who came to him to abandon self-indulgent living—in preparation for Messiah's appearing.

> "A careful comparison of the Qumran Covenanters with John the Baptist ... reveals differences so extensive as to make the possibility of contact unimportant."[47]

---

[44]For parallels between the ministries of John the Baptist and Elijah, See Alfred Edersheim, *The Life and Times of Jesus the Messiah*, 1:255-56.

[45]Hiebert, p. 29.

[46]Lane, p. 50.

[47]Ibid., p. 48.

"At last that solemn silence was broken by an appearance, a proclamation, a rite, and a ministry as startling as that of Elijah had been. In many respects, indeed, the two messengers and their times bore singular likeness. It was to a society secure, prosperous, and luxurious, yet in imminent danger of perishing from hidden, festering disease; and to a religious community which presented the appearance of hopeless perversion, and yet contained the germs of a possible regeneration, that both Elijah and John the Baptist came. Both suddenly appeared to threaten terrible judgment, but also to open unthought-of possibilities of good. And, as if to deepen still more the impression of this contrast, both appeared in a manner unexpected, and even antithetic to the habits of their contemporaries. John came suddenly out of the wilderness of Jueaea [sic], as Elijah from the wilds of Gilead; John bore the same strange ascetic appearance as his predecessor; the message of John was the counterpart of that of Elijah; his baptism that of Elijah's novel rite on Mount Carmel. And, as if to make complete the parallelism, with all of memory and hope which it awakened, even the more minute details surrounding the life of Elijah found their counterpart in that of John."[48]

1:7-8   Mark's synopsis of John's message is brief (cf. Matt. 3:7-10; Luke 3:10-14). It stresses the coming of the Mighty One who would baptize "with the Holy Spirit." John described the greatness of this One by contrasting himself with the Messiah. Slaves did not have to "untie" their masters' sandals, but John felt unworthy ("not fit") to do even this most menial task for Messiah. This emphasis on the humility of God's servants persists through this Gospel.

Another contrast is the baptisms of the two men (v. 8). This one foreshadows the superior ministry of the Coming One.

"The Baptist evidently meant that the great coming One would not merely cleanse with water but would bring to bear, like a deluge, the purging, purifying, judging presence of God himself."[49]

Jesus' baptism with the Holy Spirit probably looks forward to a baptism yet future from our viewpoint in history. In Matthew's and in Luke's account of this statement, John said Jesus would baptize "with the Holy Spirit and fire." The single article before two nouns in the Greek text implies a single baptism with Spirit and fire. While a similar baptism happened on the day of Pentecost (cf. Acts 1:5; 2:32-33), not all of what the prophets predicted would happen—when that baptism took place—actually transpired then (cf. Isa. 44:3; Joel 2:28-32). Consequently we anticipate a future baptism with the Spirit—and fire—that will fulfill these prophecies completely.

2. The baptism of Jesus 1:9-11 (cf. Matt. 3:13-17; Luke 3:21-23)

Mark next recorded two events that immediately preceded the beginning of Jesus' public ministry: His baptism and His temptation. The first of these events signaled His appearing as Messiah and His induction into that office. Mark simply recorded the fact of Jesus' baptism and two attendant events that confirmed that He was the Messiah.

1:9   The fact that Mark identified Jesus simply as "Jesus," may show that he wrote his Gospel to people already familiar with Him. Jesus did not come to John from Judea or Jerusalem (cf. v. 5), but "from Nazareth in Galilee," where He had grown up and was now living.[50] The obscurity of this little town is clear from the fact that neither the Old Testament, nor Josephus, nor the Talmud ever mentioned it.[51]

Jesus underwent John's baptism to identify with man and man's sin (cf. 2 Cor. 5:21). He did not do so because He needed to repent of personal sins. He had none! He also submitted to baptism because by doing so, He identified with the particular group of people that John was baptizing, namely: the Israelites. Jesus associated His baptism with His death (10:38; Luke 12:50). Consequently it is probably proper to conclude that He viewed His baptism as a public acceptance of His role as Israel's Suffering Servant, Messiah. Jesus was about 30 years old then (Luke 3:23).

1:10   This is the first of Mark's 42 uses of the Greek adverb *euthys* ("immediately") that give his narrative a feeling of rapidly moving action. Mark used this word more than the other three evangelists combined.

"As the story progresses, the frequency of the word 'immediately' drops off, but reappears later to reinforce how quickly the arrest and trial of Jesus take place. And the tempo varies. Whereas early in the narrative the action shifts rapidly from one location to another, the end of the journey slows to a day-by-day description of what happens in a single location, Jerusalem, and then an hour-by-hour depiction of the

---

[48]Edersheim, 1:255.
[49]Moule, p. 10.
[50]See the map "Places Mentioned in Mark's Gospel" at the end of these notes.
[51]For Josephus' description of Galilee, see *The Wars of the Jews*, 3:3:2-3.

crucifixion. Because the whole narrative moves toward Jerusalem and toward crucifixion, the slowing of the tempo greatly intensifies the experience of this event for the reader."[52]

Mark described "Jesus" *Himself* seeing "the heavens" opened ("being parted"), though at least John the Baptist saw this as well (John 1:32-34).

"Jesus' *seeing* the heavens being split and the Spirit descending into him makes him aware of receiving heavenly power. This awareness will lead him to use the power throughout the rest of Mark."[53]

Mark also used the vivid word *schizomenous*, meaning tearing or rending, to describe the heavens opening. This word recalls Isaiah 64:1, where the prophet called on God to rend the heavens and come down (cf. Ps. 18:9, 16-19; 144:5-8). God now answered Isaiah's prayer. The descent of the Spirit on Jesus constituted His anointing for ministry (cf. Luke 4:18; Acts 10:38). He was God's anointed servant ("Christ"; cf. David, another anointed of the Lord).

The "dove" is a bird that symbolizes the humble self-sacrifice that characterizes it. It was a bird that poor Israelites' offered in sacrifice to the Lord. The same spirit of humble self-sacrifice indwelt Jesus.

"The Spirit" coming upon Jesus here does not imply that Jesus had lacked Holy Spirit empowering previously. Here the Spirit came to empower Jesus specifically for His messianic ministry, which began now.

1:11   The Father's "voice from heaven" expressed approval of Jesus and His mission, in words recalling Genesis 22:2. What the voice said identified the speaker. God's words from heaven fused the concepts of King (Ps. 2:7) and Servant (Isa. 42:1). This combination constituted the unique sonship of Jesus.

"The first clause of the [Father's] declaration (with the verb in the present tense of the indicative mood) expresses an eternal and essential relationship. The second clause (the verb is in the aorist indicative) implies a past choice for the performance of a particular function in history."[54]

From this point on, the reader of Mark's Gospel knows God's authoritative evaluation of Jesus. This evaluation becomes the norm by which we judge the correctness or incorrectness of every other character's understanding of Him.

"If Mark refuses knowledge of Jesus' identity to human characters in the beginning and middle of his story, who, then, knows of his identity? The answer is Mark himself as narrator, the reader, and such supernatural beings as God, Satan, and demons."[55]

Jesus began His official role as the Messiah at His baptism (cf. 2 Sam. 7:12-16; Ps. 89:26; Heb. 1:5). He also began His official role as the Suffering Servant of the Lord then (cf. 8:31; 9:30-31; 10:32-34, 45; 15:33-39).

"Jesus' baptism did not change His divine status. He did not *become* the Son of God at His baptism (or at the transfiguration, 9:7). Rather, His baptism showed the far-reaching significance of His acceptance of His messianic vocation as the suffering Servant of the Lord as well as the Davidic Messiah. Because He is the Son of God, the One approved by the Father and empowered by the Spirit, He is the Messiah (not vice versa)."[56]

3. The temptation of Jesus 1:12-13 (cf. Matt. 4:1-11; Luke 4:1-13)

Jesus' temptation by Satan was another event that prepared the divine Servant for His ministry.[57] Mark's account is brief, and it stresses the great spiritual conflict that this temptation posed for Jesus. The writer omitted any reference to Jesus' feelings about the temptation. A servant's response to his trials is more important than his feelings about them. Jesus must have told His disciples about His temptation sometime after it occurred.

1:12   "Immediately" connects the temptation closely with the baptism. The same "Spirit" who came upon Jesus at His baptism, now "impelled" or drove (Gr. *ekballo*) Him "into the wilderness" for testing.[58] In the Old Testament, the Israelites associated inhabited and cultivated land with God's blessing, and wilderness with His curse. Jesus had submitted humbly to identification

---

[52]Rhoads and Michie, p. 45.

[53]Gundry, p. 48.

[54]Lane, p. 58.

[55]Kingsbury, p. 38.

[56]Grassmick, pp. 105-6.

[57]For comparison of Moses', Elijah's, and Jesus' 40-day periods of temptation, see Edersheim, 1:294.

[58]See Sydney H. T. Page, "Satan: God's Servant," *Journal of the Evangelical Theological Society* 50:3 (September 2007):449-65.

with humankind and Israel in particular. Now He experienced the consequences of that identification: temptation. Temptation is not an indication that one is out of God's will. It sometimes results from following the Spirit's leading.

> "Mark's expression does not mean that Jesus was forced out into the wilderness against His will but that He went with a strong sense of the Spirit's compulsion upon Him. Since the object of His Messianic mission was to 'destroy the works of the devil' (1 Jn 3:8), Jesus recognized that His acceptance of the Servant vocation made the encounter essential. It was the initiation of His mission to overthrow the devil. His miracle-working ministry of authority over demons was based on the victory won in this encounter."[59]

> "Mark makes evident that the wilderness in his story carries a dual significance: At times it is a hostile and threatening atmosphere, at other times it is a place of preparation."[60]

1:13   The traditional site of this temptation, dating back to the twelfth century A.D., is the *Mons Quarantania*, the "Hill of the Forty Days." It stands just west of Jericho. However, the exact location is unknown.

The Greek word *peirazo* means to put someone or something through a trial to demonstrate its character. God allowed Satan to tempt Jesus for two reasons: to show that He would not draw away from the Father's will, and to demonstrate His qualification for His mission. The name "Satan" is a transliteration of the Hebrew word *satan*, meaning "adversary."

By omitting reference to the three tempting offers that Satan posed, Mark focused the reader's attention on the fact that Jesus endured continuous testing for "40 days." He pointed out this continuing conflict throughout this Gospel (8:11, 32-33; 10:2; 12:15). Mark's unique reference to "the wild beasts" heightens the fierceness of the temptation. The Jews associated the wilderness with wild beasts and Satanic hostility (cf. Isa. 13:20-22; 34:8-15; Ps. 22:11-21; 91:11-13).

> ". . . in His exposure to the assaults of Satan, Jesus was 'Adam' as well as 'Israel.' Israel's sonship was modeled on Adam's, since God is the Creator-Father in both instances. The wilderness forges a link between the two, for it represents reverse imagery, especially with Mark's mention of the 'the wild beasts' (1:13). Opinion on the proper location of the animals is divided between the paradise and wilderness settings. However, it may be that the Gospels glance at the beasts both in Adam's mandate to rule the earth (Gen. 1:26-28) and in their association with satanic powers (Ps. 22:11-21; Ezek. 34:5, 8, 25; Luke 10:19), thus suggesting the chaos that threatens to (re)impose itself on the ordered world (e.g., Job 5:22; Ezek. 5:17; 14:21; . . .)."[61]

God's angelic servants "were ministering to" Jesus during His time of testing (cf. Heb. 1:14). God did not leave His Son alone, but provided grace to help in this time of need.

> "The presence of angels to sustain Jesus underlines the cosmic dimension of the temptation: Jesus' struggle with Satan is a clash between the kingdom of God and the kingdom of evil. In the temptation, then, Jesus Son of God shows what his ministry will be about: the binding of Satan and the inauguration of the end-time age of salvation (3:27)."[62]

> "The first Adam succumbed in an environment that was beautiful and friendly; the last Adam maintained His purity in an environment that was desolate and hostile."[63]

In the introduction to his Gospel, Mark stressed the humility and faithful service that Jesus rendered to God at the commencement of His public ministry. Jesus was fully human, yet at the same time He was fully approved by the Father and aided by the Spirit, and strengthened and encouraged by God's angelic helpers. He was also fully deity. Readers undergoing persecution for their faith can find great encouragement in this section, especially in Jesus' victory over temptation from Satan.

---

[59]Hiebert, p. 39.

[60]B. Dale Ellenburg, "A Review of Selected Narrative-Critical Conventions in Mark's Use of Miracle Material," *Journal of the Evangelical Theological Society* 38:2 (June 1995):175-76.

[61]Don B. Garlington, "Jesus, the Unique Son of God: Tested and Faithful," *Bibliotheca Sacra* 151:603 (July-September 1994):288-89. See also Guelich, p. 39.

[62]Kingsbury, p. 35.

[63]Hiebert, p. 40.

II. THE SERVANT'S EARLY GALILEAN MINISTRY 1:14—3:6

Mark omitted Jesus' year of early Judean ministry (John 1:15—4:42), as did the other Synoptic evangelists. He began his account of Jesus' ministry of service in Galilee, northern Israel (1:14—6:6a). Because of increasing opposition and rejection, Jesus made several withdrawals from Galilee followed by returns to this region. Mark recorded four of these (6:6b—8:30). Then Jesus left Galilee for Jerusalem. Mark recorded lessons on four important subjects pertinent to discipleship—that Jesus taught His disciples during this transition—for his readers' benefit (ch. 10). Next Jesus ministered in Jerusalem, and Mark selected three significant events there for inclusion in his story (chs. 11—13).

> "Four major characters stand out, as do two groups of minor characters: Jesus, the religious authorities, the disciples, the crowd, and those groups of minor characters who either exhibit faith or somehow exemplify what it means to serve."[64]

Examples of minor characters who model great faith in Jesus are the leper who requested cleansing (1:40-45), the friends of the paralytic (2:3-5), Jairus (5:21-24, 35-43), the woman with the hemorrhage (5:25-34), the Syrophoenician woman (7:25-30), the father of the demon possessed boy (9:14-29), and blind Bartimaeus (10:46-52). Those who model service are the woman who anointed Jesus for burial (i.e., Mary; 14:3-9), Simon of Cyrene (15:21), Joseph of Arimathea (15:42-46), and the women who visited Jesus' tomb to anoint His body (16:1).

Mark stressed Jesus' ministry as a servant in his Gospel. The rest of the book details how He served God and man. During the first part of Jesus' ministry, He laid down His life in service (1:14—13:37). His passion is the record of His laying down His life in self-sacrifice (chs. 14—16). Mark began his account of Jesus' service with an overview of selected events in Jesus' early Galilean ministry that were typical of His whole ministry (1:14—3:6). He first recorded four narratives, which took place in and around Capernaum, that provide the reader with a good idea of what Jesus' ministry looked like (1:14-38). Then Mark included a group of stories that show how hostility to Jesus was growing (2:1—3:6).

A. THE BEGINNING OF JESUS' MINISTRY 1:14-20

Mark introduced his readers to the message of the Servant (vv. 14-15) and the first disciples of the Servant (vv. 16-20).

1. The message of the Servant 1:14-15 (cf. Matt. 4:12, 17; Luke 4:14-15)

This topic sentence summarizes Jesus' whole ministry in Galilee. It identifies when it started, where it happened, and the essence of what Jesus' proclaimed that was the basis of His ministry.

1:14   Jesus began His Galilean ministry, the first major phase of His public ministry, after His forerunner had ended his ministry. Jesus' forerunner suffered a fate that prefigured what Jesus would experience (cf. 9:31; 14:18). Mark used the same root word in Greek to describe both men. The passive voice of the verb *paradidomi* ("taken into custody" or "put in prison," lit. delivered up) suggests God's sovereign control over both men's situations.

Probably Jesus chose "Galilee" as His site of ministry because the influence of hostile Pharisees and chief priests was less there than it was in Judea. Fewer Jews lived in Samaria as well, which lay between Judea and Galilee.[65]

> ". . . Jesus changes setting more than forty times in his travels throughout Galilee and into gentile territory."[66]

Jesus heralded the good news of God. The Greek construction permits two different translations: "the good news about God" and "the good news from God." Mark probably intended the second meaning because the next verse explains what the good news that God revealed through Jesus was. "Preaching" this "good news" was Jesus' characteristic activity, and it was foundational for all the other forms of His ministry.

1:15   Jesus' message consisted of two declarations and two commands. First, He declared that "the time" that God had predicted in the Old Testament had arrived (was "fulfilled"). He was referring to the end of the present age and the beginning of the messianic age, as His second declaration clarified (cf. Gal. 4:4; Heb. 1:2; 9:6-15).

The term "kingdom" (Gr. *basileia*), as it occurs with "the kingdom of God" in Scripture, does not just mean everything over which God exercises sovereign authority. The term "kingdom of God" occurs 14 times in Mark: 1:15; 4:11, 26, 30; 9:1, 47; 10:14, 15, 23, 24, 25, 12:34; 14:25; and 15:43. It means a particular worldwide kingdom over which He Himself will rule

[64]Kingsbury, p. 4.

[65]For Josephus' description of Samaria, see *The Wars . . .*, 3:3:4.

[66]Rhoads and Michie, p. 68.

directly.[67] Of course God *does* sovereignly rule over all, and over His people in a more particular sense (1 Chron. 29:12; Ps. 103:19-20). However, this is not the rule of God that the Old Testament prophets spoke of, when they described a descendant of David ruling over all the earth from Jerusalem. Many Old Testament passages predicted the coming of this kingdom (2 Sam. 7:8-17; Isa. 11:1-9; 24:23; Jer. 23:5-6; Dan. 2:34; Mic. 4:6-7; Zech. 9:9-10; 14:9; cf. Matt. 20:21; Mark 10:37; 11:10; 12:35-37; 15:43; Luke 1:31-33; 2:25, 38; Acts 1:6). Jesus' Jewish hearers knew exactly what He meant when He said the kingdom of God was at hand, or they should have if they did not. The presence of the King argued for the nearness of His kingdom, but it was still in the future (cf. 9:47-48).

> ". . . the identification of the kingdom of God with the Church made by Augustine, which has become deeply rooted in Christian thinking, is not true to the teaching of Jesus."[68]

The Jews needed to make a double response since the kingdom of God was at hand. They needed to "repent" and "believe." These two words call for successive actions, but the action is really one act that involves two steps taken almost simultaneously. Repenting involves turning from something, and believing involves embracing something else. For example, a drowning man who is clinging to a scrap of wood needs to do two things when a lifeguard reaches him. He needs to release the wood and entrust himself to the lifeguard.

When John the Baptist called the Jews to repent, he urged them to abandon their former hope of salvation because the Lifeguard was there to save them. When Jesus said, "Believe in the gospel," He meant, "Believe the good news that Messiah is here." Messiah was the subject of the gospel and the object of belief.

This is the only occurrence of the phrase "believe in [Gr. *en*] the gospel" in the New Testament. It points to the gospel as the basis of faith.

2. The first disciples of the Servant 1:16-20 (cf. Matt. 4:16-22; Luke 5:1-11)

The account of the calling of these first disciples clarifies that repenting and believing the gospel (v. 15) should result in abandoning one's former life to follow Jesus from then on. This is the appropriate response that Mark commended to his readers with these disciples' example.

1:16   The "Sea of Galilee" was the scene of a thriving fishing industry in Jesus' day.[69] "Simon and Andrew . . . were fishermen" by trade. Fishermen on this lake did not enjoy high social standing, but their work required skill. The Greek word for "net" describes a circular rope with a tent-shaped net attached. Fishermen threw this type of net out into the water, let it sink, and then drew the rope that closed the neck of the trap and secured the fish inside.

1:17-18   Simon (Peter) and Andrew had met Jesus previously (John 1:35-42). Mark stressed the urgency of Jesus' call and the immediacy of the disciples' response (cf. 1 Kings 19:19-21). Normally young men who wanted to learn from a rabbi sought one out, but Jesus called Simon and Andrew to participate in an urgent task with Him.

"Follow Me" meant "Come behind Me as a disciple." It was an invitation, but in view of who Jesus was, it had the force of a command. These men would have understood it as a call to become a *permanent* disciple of Jesus.[70] The figure of fishing people out of divine judgment comes from the Old Testament (Jer. 16:16; Ezek. 29:4-5, 38:4; Amos 4:2; Hab. 1:14-17). God was the fisher of men. Likewise, the sea had a metaphorical meaning of sin and death (Isa. 57:20-21). This illustration would have appealed to fishermen. Jesus was calling these men to assist Him in delivering people from divine judgment by taking the gospel to them. As with fishing, this calling would also involve hard work, self-sacrifice, and skill.

> "First, the call came *after* the open breach with, and initial persecution of, the Jewish authorities. It was, therefore, a call to fellowship in His peculiar relationship to the Synagogue. Secondly, it necessitated the abandonment of all their former occupations, and, indeed, of all earthly ties. (Matt. 4:20, 22) Thirdly, it was from the first, and clearly, marked as totally different from a call to such discipleship, as that of any other Master in Israel. It was not to learn more of doctrine, nor more fully to follow out a life-direction already taken, but to begin and to become, something quite new, of which their former occupation offered an emblem."[71]

---

[67] *Theological Dictionary of the New Testament*, s.v. "*basilia*," by K. L. Schmidt, 1:579-81.

[68] Cranfield, p. 67.

[69] For Josephus' description of this lake, see *The Wars . . .*, 3:10:7.

[70] Edersheim, 1:474.

[71] Ibid., 1:474-75.

"These words (whose originality stamps them as a genuine saying of Jesus) show that the great Founder of the faith desired not only to have disciples, but to have about Him men whom He might train to make disciples of others: to cast the net of divine truth into the sea of the world, and to land on the shores of the divine kingdom a great multitude of believing souls [cf. John 17:6]."[72]

"Jesus did not invent the term 'fishers of men.' In that day, it was a common description of philosophers and other teachers who 'captured men's minds' through teaching and persuasion."[73]

The brothers' response was admirably immediate (Gr. *euthys*). They began to follow Jesus by quitting their jobs as fishermen: "Immediately they left their nets and followed Him." Their commitment to Jesus increased as time passed. There is a strong emphasis on discipleship in the second Gospel. Evidently Simon and Andrew believed that Jesus was the Messiah, but they had much to learn about His full identity (cf. John 3:22-30).

"Precisely because Jesus has come fishing becomes necessary."[74]

1:19-20 Jesus then issued the same call to two similar brothers with the same response. All four men were evidently partners in the fishing business (cf. Luke 5:7, 10). "James" and "John" had also come to believe that Jesus was the Messiah (John 1:35-42). Mark recorded more about their decision to follow Jesus than he did about Simon and Andrew's. "James" (Jacob in Hebrew) and "John" broke family ties to follow Jesus. The mention of "hired men" suggests that their father "Zebedee" owned a prosperous business that James and John left. It also shows that these brothers did not leave their father all alone without help; they were not being irresponsible. The main point, however, is the immediacy of their response to Jesus. This reflects Jesus' great authority over people. James and John were Jesus' cousins (cf. Matt. 27:55-56; Mark 15:40; John 19:25). However, they did not yet know that He was also God.

"Noteworthy is that the call of each pair of brothers conforms to an identical pattern, to wit: (*a*) Underway, (*b*) Jesus sees the brothers, (*c*) calls them, and (*d*) immediately they go after him. By means of this pattern, Mark sets forth the nature and purpose of discipleship.

"The nature of discipleship is joining oneself to Jesus in total allegiance. . . .

"The purpose of discipleship is announced by Jesus in his call to Simon and Andrew: 'Come after me, and I shall make you become fishers of men' (1:17). Plainly, discipleship has 'mission work' as its purpose. Striking is the universal nature of the mission Jesus envisages."[75]

"Except perhaps for Judas, the disciples do not greatly influence the plot, or course of events, in Mark's story. . . .

"Though a group, the disciples plainly stand out as a single character.

". . . the many traits the disciples exhibit spring from two conflicting traits: The disciples are at once 'loyal' and 'uncomprehending.' On the one hand, the disciples are 'loyal': Jesus summons them to follow him and they immediately leave behind their former way of life and give him their total allegiance. On the other hand, the disciples are 'uncomprehending': Understanding fully neither the identity nor the destiny of Jesus and not at all the essential meaning of discipleship, they forsake Jesus during his passion."[76]

B. EARLY DEMONSTRATIONS OF THE SERVANT'S AUTHORITY IN CAPERNAUM 1:21-34

This section of the Gospel records three instances of ministry in Capernaum. These were Jesus' teaching and healing in the synagogue, His healing of Peter's mother-in-law, and His healing of many others. These events further demonstrated Jesus' authority. They all occurred on one day, or two days from the Jewish perspective in which a new day began at sunset. Mark implied that this was a typical day of ministry for Jesus.

[72]A. B. Bruce, *The Training of the Twelve*, pp. 12-13.
[73]Wiersbe, 1:112.
[74]Lane, p. 68.
[75]Kingsbury, pp. 90, 91.
[76]Ibid., pp. 8, 9.

1. Jesus' teaching and healing in the Capernaum synagogue 1:21-28 (cf. Luke 4:31-37)

1:21   "Capernaum" became Jesus' base of ministry in Galilee (cf. Luke 4:16-31). It stood on the Sea of Galilee's northwest shore and was the hub of the most populous district in Galilee. Archaeologists have done extensive restoration work there. They have reconstructed a synagogue that stood on that spot in the third and fourth centuries.

The synagogues came into existence during the Babylonian exile. The word originally described a group of people, but it later became associated with the building in which the people met. The word "church" has experienced a similar evolution. Customarily the leaders of a local synagogue would invite recognized visiting teachers to speak to the congregation. Mark referred to Jesus' teaching ministry frequently, but he did not record much of what Jesus taught. Jesus' actions were of more interest to him. This seems to reflect the active disposition of Peter, who influenced Mark's writing, and perhaps the active character of the Romans for whom Mark wrote.

> "What Jesus *says* discloses his understanding of himself and his purposes. What Jesus *does* reveals primarily the extent and nature of his authority from God. Both what Jesus does and says determine his values and the dynamics of his relations with other characters. They also show Jesus' integrity in living up to his values and commitments."[77]

1:22   Mark used a strong Greek word to describe the reaction of Jesus' hearers, though he did not record what Jesus taught. The word is *exeplessonto*, meaning that Jesus' words astounded or overwhelmed the people. A distinguishing feature of Mark's Gospel is his references to people's emotional reactions (cf. v. 27; 2:12; 5:20, 42; 6:2, 51; 7:37; 10:26; 11:18), even those of Jesus (6:6). It was Jesus' great authority that impressed them. He was, of course, not a mere scribe (teacher of the law) but a prophet, even the greatest Prophet ever to appear. Jesus proclaimed revelation directly from God, rather than just interpreting the former revelations that God had given to others, and reiterating the traditional rabbinic interpretations of the law.

> "They [the scribes] habitually established their views by long learned quotations from other rabbis. At best, they could only claim an authority derived from their understanding of the law. Their teaching was generally pedantic and dull, occupied with minute distinctions concerning Levitical regulations and petty legalistic requirements."[78]

> "Fundamentally . . . Mark presents Jesus' conflict with the religious authorities as one of authority: Does Jesus or does he not discharge his ministry as one authorized by God? As this conflict unfolds, it becomes progressively more intense, until it finally ends in Jesus' death."[79]

> "The narrator paints the authorities in a consistently negative light from their first mention as legal experts who teach without authority. The narrator builds their characterization on their opposition to Jesus. What the authorities say involves primarily questions which imply accusations or aim at trapping Jesus. As for what they do, they primarily work at plotting the destruction of Jesus. Neither Jesus nor the narrator says anything favorable about them. And the narrator's inside views on their thoughts and feelings regularly distance the reader from the authorities. Apart from attributing a few favorable attitudes to Herod and Pilate, the narrator depicts the authorities as thoroughly untrustworthy characters."[80]

1:23   An outburst from a man in the congregation interrupted the service. He was under the influence of a demonic spirit. The Jews spoke of demonic spirits as evil or "unclean" spirits. Mark used the terms "demon" and "unclean spirit" interchangeably. This is his first reference to demonic influence on human beings.[81] The man cried out with a strong emotional shriek (Gr. *anekraxen*).

> "Neither the New Testament, nor even Rabbinic literature, conveys the idea of permanent demonic indwelling, to which the later term 'possession' owes its origin."[82]

1:24   The man cried out, but it was really the demon speaking through him. This is clear because Jesus replied to the demon (v. 25). The words "What do we have to do with You?" represent a Hebrew idiom that spells conflict (cf. 5:7; Josh. 22:24; Judg. 11:12; 2 Sam. 16:10; 19:22). Today we might express the same thought by saying, "Why are You meddling with us? Mind Your own business!"

---

[77]Rhoads and Michie, p. 103.

[78]Hiebert, p. 52.

[79]Kingsbury, p. 67.

[80]Rhoads and Michie, p. 117.

[81]For additional information on demonic influence, see William M. Alexander, *Demonic Possession in the New Testament: Its Relations Historical, Medical, and Theological*; Merrill F. Unger, *Biblical Demonology: A Study of the Spiritual Forces Behind the Present World Unrest*, ch. 6; and idem., *Demons in the World Today*, ch. 6.

[82]Edersheim, 1:481.

The demon recognized Jesus, and it knew about His mission. It was common for the Jews to identify a person by his place of origin (cf. 10:47; 14:67; 16:6). In Jesus' case this was Nazareth. We could just as accurately translate the words rendered "Have you come to destroy us" as a statement of fact: "You have come to destroy us." In either case, the demon expressed dread. Clearly this demon recognized Jesus as its Judge. This showed Jesus' great authority.

By calling Jesus "the Holy One of God," the demon testified to His empowerment by the Holy Spirit—the Enemy of all unclean spirits. This title also probably implies belief in Jesus' deity. The title "Holy One" was a popular designation of God in the Old Testament. Isaiah called God the Holy One about 30 times (Isa. 1:4; 5:19, 24; et al.). Whereas people referred to Jesus as "Lord" (7:8), "Teacher" (9:17), "Son of David" (10:47-48), and "Master" (10:52), the demons called Him "the Holy One of God" (1:24), "the Son of God" (3:11) or "the Son of the Most High God" (5:7).

"These 'confessions' . . . can hardly be explained as testimonies wrested from the demons against their will. More probably they are to be understood as desperate attempts to get control of Jesus or to make him harmless, in accordance with the common idea of the time that by using the exactly correct name of a spirit one could gain the mastery over him."[83]

1:25-26   Jesus did not need a magical formula to exorcize this demon, as other exorcists of His day did.[84] He simply ordered it to be quiet and to leave the man. Jesus probably commanded the demon to "be muzzled" (Gr. *phimotheti*) because He desired to maintain control when the demon revealed His identity. The Jews might have mobbed Jesus because He fed and healed them. The Romans might have concluded that He was mobilizing an insurrection to overthrow the government, and could have arrested Him prematurely.

"At his trial we discover why Jesus hides his identity. Upon openly declaring who he is, the authorities condemn him to death for blasphemy. The dilemma for Jesus is this: how can he inaugurate God's rule, yet evade the efforts of the authorities to trap him? Many aspects of the secrecy motif are related to this problem."[85]

The malicious nature of the demon is evident in its treatment of the man.

Jesus' authority over demons showed that He had power as God's Servant to destroy the devil and his agents. Mark continued to stress Jesus' continuing conflict with demonic forces and power over them in his Gospel. This emphasis would have given his original suffering readers encouragement that Jesus' power could overcome any enemy that might assail them.

"We expect a servant to be *under authority* and to *take* orders, but God's Servant *exercises* authority and *gives* orders—even to demons—and His orders are obeyed."[86]

"To have allowed the defensive utterance of the demon to go unrebuked would have been to compromise the purpose for which Jesus came into the world, to confront Satan and strip him of his power. As such, this initial act of exorcism in the ministry of Jesus is programmatic of the sustained conflict with the demons which is a marked characteristic in the Marcan presentation of the gospel."[87]

1:27-28   The people's reaction to this exorcism was an important part of Mark's narrative. The witnesses expressed alarm, as well as amazement, at this unique demonstration of authority by word and by deed. This was the typical result of the "fishing" that Jesus and His disciples did.

The "authority" that the crowd referred to was probably prophetic authority.[88] Jesus spoke and did miracles like one of the former prophets. His "new teaching" was new in that prophetic authority marked His teaching, in contrast to the teaching of the inferior teachers of His day—and even the authorized rabbis. It was new in quality, not in time.[89]

"One surprise following close on another provoked wondering inquiry as to the whole phenomenon."[90]

---

[83]Cranfield, p. 77.

[84]Flavius Josephus, *Antiquities of the Jews*, 8:2:5.

[85]Rhoads and Michie, p. 84.

[86]Wiersbe, 1:111.

[87]Lane, p. 75.

[88]Cranfield, p. 74.

[89]Vincent Taylor, *The Gospel According to St. Mark*, p. 176.

[90]A. B. Bruce, "The Synoptic Gospels," in *The Expositor's Greek Testament*, 1:346.

The result of this miracle was that people all over that part of Galilee heard about Jesus.

> "Despite the fact that the crowd reacts to Jesus' teaching and healing with amazement, or astonishment, this is an expression not of understanding but of incomprehension.

> ". . . the crowd in Mark's story is at once 'well disposed' toward Jesus and 'without faith' in him. In being well disposed toward Jesus, the crowd stands in contrast to its leaders, the religious authorities. In being without faith in Jesus, the crowd stands in contrast to the disciples."[91]

This incident highlights the authority of Jesus that the worshippers in Capernaum first observed in His teaching, and then witnessed in His exorcism. The people should have concluded that only a great prophet of Yahweh could possess such authority. Jesus did not reveal who He was completely on this occasion, but He did give these practicing Jews enough revelation about Himself so they should have accepted it and asked for more. James Edwards clarified the divine authority of Jesus, as Mark recorded it in many places, that demonstrated His deity.[92]

2. The healing of Peter's mother-in-law 1:29-31 (cf. Matt. 8:14-15; Luke 4:38-39)

This incident, which happened immediately after the previous one, displays a different aspect of Jesus' authority: His power over physical sickness. In Jesus day, people regarded fever as a disease not necessarily related to other maladies.[93]

> "The Talmud gives this disease precisely the same name . . ., 'burning fever,' and prescribes for it a magical remedy, of which the principal part is to tie a knife wholly of iron by a braid of hair to a thornbush, and to repeat on successive days Exod. iii. 2, 3, then ver. 4, and finally ver. 5, after which the bush is to be cut down, while a certain magical formula is pronounced. (Shabb. 37a)."[94]

This account is full of detail, and it must have come to Mark through Peter, who had a special interest in this healing. Evidently "Simon and Andrew" shared this "house" with "Simon's mother-in-law" and perhaps other family members. Jesus' power resulted in instantaneous and complete recovery. The fact that Peter had a family helps us appreciate the sacrifice he made to follow Jesus. The result of this woman's healing was that she served.

> ". . . selfless also means an eager willingness to serve."[95]

Jesus' miracles can be divided into four groups: exorcisms, healings, raising the dead, and nature miracles.[96] Miracles occupy a large part of Mark's Gospel: 47 percent of the verses in chapters 1 through 10 deal with them directly or indirectly.[97]

3. Jesus' healing of many Galileans after sundown 1:32-34 (cf. Matt. 8:16-17; Luke 4:40-41)

This little pericope shows that the former two healings were not isolated cases. Jesus' power benefited "many" people ("the whole city"), who came to Peter's house after sundown ended the Sabbath, allowing the Jews to travel farther to obtain His help (cf. Exod. 20:10; Mark 3:1-5).

> "The two-step progression is the most pervasive stylistic feature in the gospel. It occurs in phrases, sentences, pairs of sentences, and the structure of episodes. It is a key to understanding many lines and episodes. A simple example is, 'When it was evening, after the sun set. . . .' The time reference, 'When it was evening,' is repeated in 'after the sun set.' However, this is no mere repetition, for the second part adds precision and clarifies the first part. Both parts comprise a two-step progressive description. The first part is important, yet the emphasis often lies on the second step which usually contains the more significant element. In this example, the second step refers to the setting sun, which denoted precisely the end of the Sabbath when people were again permitted to travel and could therefore seek out Jesus for healing."[98]

> "Jesus forces healing on no one. He does not seek people out to heal but heals only those who come to him. He initiates a healing only when he takes responsibility for healing on the Sabbath. And Jesus heals freely, with no strings attached to those healings. He does not demand that people believe he is the anointed one (none do) or even believe in the Jewish God. He

---

[91]Kingsbury, pp. 23, 24. Cf. 6:51-52.

[92]See James R. Edwards, "The Authority of Jesus in the Gospel of Mark," *Journal of the Evangelical Theological Society* 37:2 (June 1994):217-33.

[93]Lane, p. 77.

[94]Edersheim, 1:486.

[95]Charles C. Ryrie, *The Miracles of our Lord*, p. 39.

[96]See Appendix 6, in my notes on Matthew, for a list of them in probable chronological order.

[97]Cranfield, p. 82.

[98]Rhoads and Michie, p. 47. See pp. 47-49 for several other examples of this narrative device.

does not require a person to be morally good . . . . Jesus does not expect to gain personally from healing, for he never asks anyone he heals to follow him. Usually he orders them, often harshly, to keep quiet or go home. They proclaim or follow on their own, and Jesus does not consider either action a condition for healing."[99]

"What a symbol of this world's misery, need, and hope; what a symbol, also, of what the Christ really is as the Consoler in the world's manifold woe! Never, surely, was He more truly the Christ; nor is He in symbol more truly such to us and to all time, than when, in the stillness of that evening, under the starlit sky, He went through that suffering throng, laying His hands in the blessing of healing on every one of them, and casting out many devils. No picture of the Christ more dear to us, than this of the unlimited healing of whatever disease of body or soul. In its blessed indefiniteness it conveys the infinite potentiality of relief, whatever misery have fallen on us, or whatever care or sorrow oppress us."[100]

Jesus' healings demonstrate His compassion for people.

"No scene [*sic* is] more characteristic of the Christ than that on this autumn evening at Capernaum."[101]

Probably Jesus did not permit the demons to identify Him because this would have encouraged the people to think of Him as most of the Jews then thought of the Messiah. He wanted to avoid this stereotype as much as He could because it did not represent the type of Messiah He was. Notice the clear distinction between demonic influence and mere physical illness (cf. 6:13).

This section of the Gospel (1:21-34) shows Jesus doing miracles, both to identify Himself as God's Servant, and to authenticate His message (v. 15).

C. JESUS' EARLY MINISTRY THROUGHOUT GALILEE 1:35-45

Jesus made several preaching tours throughout Galilee. Mark summarized the first of these (vv. 35-39), and then related one especially significant event during that tour (vv. 40-45). This section continues to present Jesus as the "Servant of the Lord," who went about doing the messianic work that His Father had assigned to Him.

1. The first preaching tour of Galilee 1:35-39 (cf. Luke 4:42-44)

While these verses record the itinerant ministry of Jesus, Mark's emphasis was clearly on Jesus' spiritual preparation for that ministry. It highlighted His dependence on His Father.

1:35   Mark implied that these events happened the next day: "In the early morning." Many people would have slept late after such a busy day, but Jesus rose early, even before dawn, and went to a remote (Gr. *eremon*, v. 4, wilderness, cf. v. 12) place to pray (Gr. *proseucho*, the general word for prayer). This sacrificial act paints Jesus as consciously dependent on His Father for strength and direction for what lay ahead of Him (i.e., a servant; cf. Isa. 50:4). Secluded prayer also implies further conflict with Satan, since Satan had confronted Him in the wilderness previously. Prayerlessness typically manifests self-sufficiency, but prayerfulness reveals humility.

"Mark selectively portrayed Jesus at prayer on three crucial occasions, each in a setting of darkness and aloneness: near the beginning of his account (v. 35), near the middle (6:46), and near the end (14:32-42). All three were occasions when He was faced with the possibility of achieving His messianic mission in a more attractive, less costly way. But in each case He gained strength through prayer."[102]

In this case, the wave of popular support that Jesus had ridden the day before, threatened to carry Him into political leadership that might have washed out the Cross.

1:36-37   Simon and his companions—who they were is unimportant—did not understand Jesus' need for prayer. They seem to have had the common attitude, that when things are favorable, we do not need God's help. Their words implied annoyance. Apparently they felt Jesus was not taking advantage of His popularity to promote His mission. They did not realize that God directed Jesus' mission, not the responses of people. This is the first instance of Peter's impetuous leadership that Mark recorded.

[99]Ibid, p. 110.
[100]Edersheim, 1:487.
[101]Ibid., 1:486.
[102]Grassmick, p. 110.

"His [Jesus'] purpose is not to heal as many people as possible as a manifestation of the kingdom of God drawn near in his person, but to confront men with the demand for decision in the perspective of God's absolute claim upon their person."[103]

1:38-39   Peter viewed the healing ministry of Jesus as primary, as did many of his companions. Jesus viewed it as only a small part of His larger mission. He had "come out" from God to fulfill this mission. Peter encouraged Jesus to stay where He could not escape pressure to perform miracles (cf. John 7:3-5). Jesus chose to move on to other parts of "Galilee," where He could present the gospel (v. 14) and His claims (v. 15), since "that is what"—as He said—"I came out for."

Verse 39 summarizes this preaching tour throughout Galilee. It may have lasted several weeks or even months (cf. Matt. 4:23-25). Jesus centered His ministry during this time in the synagogues, because His mission was essentially religious rather than political or economic. His main activity was heralding (Gr. *kerysso*) the gospel, but He authenticated His preaching with miracles, the most dramatic of which were exorcisms.

Josephus wrote that Galilee, which contained much rich agricultural land, was full of cities and villages, not the least of which contained 15,000 inhabitants.[104] This figure may refer to the cities and their surrounding villages, however, because there is evidence that towns like Capernaum and Bethsaida, both on the Sea of Galilee, had only 2,000 to 3,000 inhabitants each.[105] Herod Philip II ("the tetrarch") elevated Bethsaida from the status of a village to that of a city, because of its increased population, and called it "Bethsaida Julius," in honor of Tiberius Caesar's daughter.[106] Each group of villages had its head city, and synagogues existed in these regional capitals.[107]

2. The cleansing of a leprous Jew 1:40-45 (cf. Matt. 8:1-4; Luke 5:12-16)

This pericope evidently describes one incident during the Galilean preaching tour just summarized. It provides a striking example of Jesus' supernatural power. This is only one of two healings of lepers that the Gospels record, though Jesus healed other lepers besides these (cf. Matt. 11:5). The other recorded incident involved Jesus cleansing 10 lepers in Samaria (cf. Luke 17:11-19). The only Old Testament instances of lepers experiencing healing involved Miriam (Num. 12:10-15) and Naaman the Syrian (2 Kings 5). This incident that Mark recorded was significant because it brought the religious leaders from Jerusalem into Galilee to investigate Jesus. This is the beginning of the hostility motif in Mark.

"Lepers were allowed to live unhampered wherever they chose, except in Jerusalem and cities which had been walled from antiquity. They could even attend the synagogue services if a screen was provided to isolate them from the rest of the congregation. In spite of these two provisions, however, leprosy brought deep physical and mental anguish for both the afflicted individual and the community in which or near which he lived."[108]

"If you are willing" (v. 40) expressed the leper's confidence in Jesus rather than doubt as to the Lord's willingness to heal him.[109]

Mark is the only evangelist who recorded that "compassion" moved Jesus to heal this pitiable man (v. 41). However, his version of this miracle stressed what the leper did after Jesus healed him. Jesus had "sternly warned" (Gr. *embrimaomai*) the cleansed leper not to tell anyone what Jesus had done for him (vv. 43-44; cf. vv. 25, 34; 3:12; 5:43; 7:36; 9:9). Only Mark used this strong word. It stresses the forcefulness and authority with which Jesus instructed and sent the cleansed leper to the priest.[110] Jesus wanted to avoid becoming known simply as a miracle worker, which might lead to pressure to avoid the Cross. However, the man disobeyed Jesus, even though he probably thought he had good reason to do so, namely, to bring praise to Jesus. His disobedience to Jesus' word frustrated His work rather than advancing it. Jesus needed to minister to people, but the leper's action forced Him to spend more time in uninhabited, solitary places (Gr. *eremon*, vv. 4, 35).

Perhaps Mark pointed this out to encourage his Christian readers to follow the Word of God carefully. Sometimes believers disobey God because we think our way will be better than His. It never is. Frequently it has the same result as this cleansed leper's disobedience. It retards God's mission rather than advancing it. The fact that this man was a cleansed leper makes believers' identification with him easy, since leprosy in the Bible is similar to sin, and believers are cleansed sinners.

---

[103]Lane, p. 82.

[104]Josephus, *The Wars . . .*, 3:3:2.

[105]Lane, p. 232.

[106]Josephus, *Antiquities of . . .*, 18:2:1.

[107]Lane., p. 83.

[108]Ibid., p. 85. See also Ryrie, pp. 43-44.

[109]Cranfield, p. 91.

[110]Gundry, p. 96.

The leper's disobedience did not destroy God's plan, but only created complications. The Galileans still kept seeking Jesus out (v. 45).[111]

> "We should learn some important spiritual lessons from this chapter. To begin with, if the Son of God came as a servant, then being a servant is the highest of all callings. We are never more like the Lord Jesus than when we are serving others. Second, God shares His authority with His servants. Only those who are *under* authority have the right to *exercise* authority. Finally, if you are going to be a servant, be sure you have compassion; because people will come to you for help and rarely ask if it is convenient!"[112]

D. JESUS' INITIAL CONFLICT WITH THE RELIGIOUS LEADERS 2:1—3:6

Mark next recorded five instances in which Israel's leaders opposed Jesus, evidently not in chronological order. These occurred during the Galilean ministry of Jesus. Mark appears to have grouped them so his readers would see that opposition from leaders, particularly religious leaders, was something Jesus had to contend with and overcome. His readers were probably facing similar opposition, and this section should encourage and help all Christians experiencing conflict because they are trying to fulfill God's mission for them.

Popularity with the masses led to problems with the magistrates. Opposition to Jesus intensifies throughout this section.

> "The five conflicts between Jesus and the authorities in Galilee show a concentric [chiastic] relationship of A, B, C, B[1], and A[1]. . . .

> ". . . this central episode [Jesus' teaching about fasting, 2:18-22] focuses on Jesus' response rather than on conflicts or actions, and Jesus' response illuminates all five of the episodes that make up the concentric pattern."[113]

> "Mark's story is one of conflict, and conflict is the force that propels the story forward. The major conflict is between Jesus and Israel, made up of the religious authorities and the Jewish crowd. Since the crowd does not turn against Jesus until his arrest, his antagonists are the authorities. . . .

> "The groups comprising the religious authorities are the Pharisees, the Sadducees, the Herodians, the chief priests, the scribes, and the elders."[114]

1. The healing and forgiveness of a paralytic 2:1-12 (cf. Matt. 9:1-8; Luke 5:17-26)

> ". . . as Rabbinism stood confessedly powerless in face of the living death of leprosy, so it had no word of forgiveness to speak to the conscience burdened with sin, nor yet word of welcome to the sinner. But this was the inmost meaning of the two events which the Gospel-history places next to the healing of the leper: the forgiveness of sins in the case of the paralytic, and the welcome to the chief of sinners in the call of Levi-Matthew."[115]

2:1-2   These two verses are an introduction to what follows. Mark frequently used summaries such as this one (cf. 1:14-15, 39; 2:13; 3:7-12, 23; 4:1, 33-34; 8:21-26, 31; 9:31; 10:1; 12:1). They are a characteristic of his literary style. "Several days afterward" translates a Jewish phrase that means "after a considerable interval."[116]

When Jesus returned "to Capernaum" after one of His preaching tours, it did not take news of His arrival long to circulate. Soon locals were mobbing Him. Jesus could not find a restful retreat even at home in Capernaum. He graciously used the opportunity to preach to them. Mark's account stresses Jesus' popularity.

2:3-4   "In order to understand the action these verses describe, it is necessary to visualize the layout of a typical Palestinian peasant's house. It was usually a small, one-room structure with a flat roof. Access to the roof was by means of an outside stairway. The roof itself was usually made of wooden beams with thatch and compacted earth in order to shed the rain. Sometimes tiles were laid between the beams and the thatch and earth placed over them."[117]

---

[111]See Joel F. Williams, "Discipleship and Minor Characters in Mark's Gospel," *Bibliotheca Sacra* 153:611 (July-September 1996):332-43; Kingsbury, pp. 24-27.

[112]Wiersbe, 1:114.

[113]Rhoads and Michie, p. 52. See pp. 52-53 for their full description of this narrative structure.

[114]Kingsbury, p. 63.

[115]Edersheim, 1:499.

[116]Ibid., 1:501.

[117]Wessel, p. 632.

Another possibility is that this was the roof of a porch that was attached to the house.[118] Mark's unusually detailed account pictures "four men" almost frantic to get their paralyzed friend to Jesus so Jesus would heal him. They must have been unconcerned about the damage they were doing to the house and the shower of dirt they sent raining down on everyone below.

2:5   The pains they took proved their "faith" in Jesus' ability and willingness to heal. Jesus responded by dealing with their friend's need better than they had expected. Sin is the root of all sickness, not that there is always a close correspondence between sinfulness and sickness (cf. Luke 13:1-3; John 9:2-3). Jesus authoritatively forgave the man's "sins" as only God could do, and so dealt with the ultimate cause of sickness. We might think that Jesus was only announcing God's forgiveness in view of their faith, as Nathan announced God's forgiveness of David (2 Sam. 12:13). But the scribes took Jesus' statement as blasphemy (v. 7).

> "We must admire several characteristics of these men, qualities that ought to mark us as 'fishers of men.' For one thing, they were deeply concerned about their friend and wanted to see him helped. They had the faith to believe that Jesus could and would meet his need. They did not simply 'pray about it,' but they put some feet to their prayers; and they did not permit the difficult circumstances to discourage them. They worked together and dared to do something different, and Jesus rewarded their efforts. How easy it would have been for them to say, 'Well, there is no sense trying to get to Jesus today! Maybe we can come back tomorrow.'"[119]

2:6-7   Jesus' claim to possess divine authority upset the teachers of the law who were present. The fact that they were sitting in that crowded house shows the respect the Jews gave them. No Old Testament prophet ever claimed personal authority to forgive sins, though Nathan had announced God's forgiveness to David (2 Sam. 12:13). The Jews believed even the Messiah could not forgive sins because the Old Testament never attributed that power to Him. Only "God" could do that (cf. Exod. 34:6-9; Ps. 103:3; 130:4; Isa. 43:25; 44:22; 48:11; Dan. 9:9; Mic. 7:18).[120] Consequently they regarded Jesus' claim as blasphemous. Later they condemned Jesus to death for what they considered blasphemy (14:61-64).

> "So from the very beginning of the story Jesus walks a tightrope—under constant threat—and must evade incriminating charges until the right time. His narrow escape from such a serious charge early in the story contributes significantly to the tension and suspense in this conflict."[121]

> "The main purpose of the miracles was to teach, to reveal. Christ used miracles to demonstrate his deity (Mark 2:7), to support his claims to being the messiah (Matthew 9:27), and to serve as illustrations of deeper spiritual truths (see John 6:32-35). But the miracles also remind us of the consequences of sin—sickness, blindness, death—and of the power of the Lord to do something about those consequences. That is why many of his physical cures illustrate so well the spiritual salvation he secured when he died and rose from the dead."[122]

2:8-9   Only God can heal and forgive sins. These actions are equally impossible to men. However, a person cannot verify his claim to forgive sins, but his claim to be able to heal paralysis is verifiable. The scribes therefore assumed that the claim to heal paralysis was the greater one. Jesus frequently used the rabbinic device of asking counter questions, especially when dealing with opponents (cf. 3:4; 11:30; 12:37).

2:10-11   Jesus chose to do what they considered harder to show that He could also do what they considered easier.

> "He did the miracle which they could see that they might know that he had done the other one that they could not see."[123]

This is Mark's first use of the title "Son of Man." He used it 14 times (cf. v. 28; 8:31, 38; 9:9, 12, 31; 10:33, 45; 13:26; 14:21 [twice], 41, 62). Scholars have debated the meaning of this title, but the best evidence points to Jesus meaning that He was the divine Messiah—the representative Man (cf. Dan. 7:13-14).[124]

[118]Edersheim, 1:504.
[119]Wiersbe, 1:115.
[120]Cf. Edwards, p. 222.
[121]Rhoads and Michie, p. 87.
[122]Ryrie, pp. 10-11.
[123]A. M. Hunter, *The Gospel According to Saint Mark*, p. 38.
[124]See Taylor, pp. 197-98, who also presented four other views.

"Jesus apparently chose this title for Himself because its use would not immediately associate Him in the thinking of the people with the undesirable connotations which had developed around the common term *Messiah*. Thus, His use of the term half concealed and half revealed His self-identification as the personal Messiah. While the term was recognized to have Messianic connections, the title *Son of man* would not force the people to make a premature decision concerning His identity in terms of their usual Messianic expectations. It would enable Him to connect His Messianic self-presentation with views more in harmony with His own Person and teaching."[125]

Jesus used the title "Son of Man" when He spoke of His sufferings and death (8:31; 9:9-13, 31; 10:33, 45; 14:21, 41). He also used it when speaking of His future return in glory (8:38; 13:26, 32; 14:62). Thus He used this title to blend the concepts of the Suffering Servant and the Messiah in His listeners' minds. It also connected and identified Him with mankind as the Son of Man. Still, He was the Man with "authority on earth to forgive sins," the Judge.

Verse 10 reads awkwardly. It begins with Jesus apparently addressing the scribes. Without finishing His sentence He turned to the paralytic and spoke to Him (v. 11). Some commentators have concluded that Jesus did not utter the first part of verse 10, but Mark inserted it in the narrative as a statement to his readers.[126] Those who hold this view usually point out that Mark did not record Jesus' revealing of Himself as the Son of Man to unbelievers before the Resurrection.[127] Advocates take verse 28 as another statement by Mark to his readers.

"The purpose of Mark's commentary is to make the community of believers aware that they have experienced the messianic forgiveness of the Son of Man."[128]

However, this type of editorial insertion is unusual in the Synoptics. Perhaps Jesus addressed the scribes and then let His comment to the paralytic, along with the miraculous healing, be the conclusion of His word to them.[129]

Jesus gave the paralytic a threefold command. "Rise" tested his faith. "Take up your pallet" required him to assume responsibility for himself that others had previously shouldered. "Go home" gave him direction that he needed.

"The pronouncement in v. 10 means that the One who has authority to forgive sins in heaven is present in the Son of Man to forgive sins 'on earth.'"[130]

2:12   The man responded to all three commands "immediately" and obediently.

Jesus' healing was complete and instantaneous. Everyone in the house witnessed the miracle including the religious leaders. They were amazed (Gr. *existasthai*, lit. "out of their minds," cf. 3:21; 5:42; 6:51). They had witnessed something that neither they nor anyone else had ever seen. No one had ever given evidence of forgiving the sins of someone else. This was a strong testimony to Jesus' deity. However, from the reaction of the observers, most of them apparently marveled at the physical miracle (even "glorifying God")—but did not *worship Jesus as God*.

"The pericope ends, then, with a recognition of his power as God-given. Mark's audience are [*sic* is] to infer that the Crucifixion will therefore be unjustified."[131]

2. The call of Levi and his feast 2:13-17 (cf. Matt. 9:13; Luke 5:27-32)

The call of Levi as one of Jesus' disciples was the setting for the second instance of opposition from the religious leaders that Mark recorded in this section.

"Having shown Jesus' authority to forgive sins (vv 1-12), Mark can appropriately introduce a story about Jesus' calling sinners."[132]

---

[125]Hiebert, p. 67.

[126]Cranfield, p. 100; Wessel, p. 633; Grassmick, pp. 112-13.

[127]E.g., Lane, pp. 96-98; and G. H. Boobyer, "Mark II, 10a and the Interpretation of the Healing of the Paralytic," *Harvard Theological Review* 47 (1954):115.

[128]Lane, p. 98.

[129]Taylor, p. 197; Hiebert, p. 67.

[130]Edwards, p. 223.

[131]Gundry, p. 115.

[132]Ibid., p. 123.

2:13   "Again" (Gr. *palin*) identifies this incident as a different occasion (cf. 1:16). Jesus had been in Capernaum, which was very close to the Sea of Galilee, but now He returned to the water's edge where He could teach the large crowds that followed Him (cf. 1:45; 2:13; 3:7, 13; 4:1; 5:21; et al.).

> "This action becomes meaningful when it is seen as part of a recurring pattern in Mark's Gospel. After a demonstration of the saving power of God, Jesus withdraws from the populace to a lonely region, whether the wilderness, the mountain or the sea. . . . Like the return to the wilderness, the move to the sea entails a deliberate entrance into the sphere of forces which manifest their hostility to God."[133]

2:14   "Levi" was this man's given name whereas Matthew ("gift of God," also Nathanael and Theodore) was a nickname. Matthew used the latter name for himself in his Gospel (Matt. 9:9; cf. Mark 3:18), but Mark and Luke spoke of him by his given name.

> ". . . in Galilee it was common to have two names—one the strictly Jewish, the other the Galilean. (Talmudic tractate *Gittin* 34 b)"[134]

> "It was not uncommon for a man to receive or assume a new name upon entering a new career."[135]

The Jews despised tax collectors because they worked for the Romans and because they often extorted money for Rome from their fellow Jews.[136] Levi worked for Herod Antipas since he lived in Capernaum. A major road passed through Capernaum connecting Damascus and the Mediterranean coast.

> "Capernaum was the first important place in Herod Antipas' territory that travellers from Herod Philip's territory or Decapolis would pass through, coming round the north end of the lake."[137]

The taxes Levi collected at his "tax booth" included: export and import fees, sales and custom taxes, and various tolls.[138] Levi gave up a lucrative business when he chose to follow Jesus. A fisherman might return to fishing, but a tax collector could not return to his job, since many people competed for this career—even though it involved social ostracism. Nonetheless, Levi responded immediately to Jesus' gracious and authoritative invitation to follow Him.

> "When a Jew entered the customs service he was regarded as an outcast from society: he was disqualified as a judge or a witness in a court session, was excommunicated from the synagogue, and in the eyes of the community his disgrace extended to his family."[139]

The fact that both Levi and James the Less had fathers named "Alphaeus" does not necessarily mean they were brothers. Apparently they were not. No Gospel writer linked them as they linked Simon and Andrew, or James and John. Furthermore Alphaeus was a fairly common name.

2:15-16   Eating a meal together meant something in Jesus' world that it does not mean today in the West. Hospitality was a sacred duty in the ancient Near East. When someone invited someone else to eat with him, he was extending a pledge of loyalty and protection to that person. To accept an invitation to dinner implied a willingness to become a close friend of the host. Jesus' acceptance of table fellowship with "sinners" (i.e., outcasts) conveyed by action the forgiveness that He gave verbally in 2:5.[140]

> "It was an offer of peace, trust, brotherhood and forgiveness; in short, sharing a table meant sharing life."[141]

This meal took place in Levi's house (Luke 5:29). Apparently he had a large house that accommodated the throng easily, which indicates that he had some wealth.

---

[133]Lane, p. 100.

[134]Edersheim, 1:514.

[135]Hiebert, p. 69.

[136]See. A. W. F. Blunt, *The Gospel According to Saint Mark*, pp. 155-56.

[137]Cranfield, p. 102.

[138]Guelich, p. 101.

[139]Lane, pp. 101-2.

[140]Guelich, p. 105.

[141]Joachim Jeremias, *New Testament Theology*, p. 115.

Normally the Jews of Jesus' day ate their meals *seated*. They only *reclined* on pillows or rugs when special guests were present or for festival meals.[142] Obviously Levi regarded Jesus' presence with him as a special occasion.

The antecedent of the "them" who followed Jesus is probably the "tax collectors and sinners," though it may be the disciples. The term "the scribes of the Pharisees" occurs nowhere else in the Gospels. These were teachers of the law who belonged to the sect of the Pharisees.

> "The Pharisees were progressive, a party among, though not of, the people. Their goal was that Israel should become the righteous nation of the covenant. To this end they taught compliance with the 'tradition of the elders,' an oral code of conduct effectively adapting the law of Moses to later times and changing demands."[143]

"Tax collectors" had a bad reputation because they were often dishonest.[144] The term "sinners" refers to Jews who did not follow the Pharisees' traditions, as well as worse sinners. Jesus' critics believed that He should not associate with such people if He had a genuine regard for the Old Testament, as they professed to have. To do so risked ceremonial defilement.

> ". . . the Talmud distinguishes two classes of 'publicans': the tax-gatherer in general (*Gabbai*), and the *Mokhes*, or *Mokhsa*, who was specially the *douanier* or custom-house official. Although both classes fall under the rabbinic ban, the *douanier*—such as Matthew was—is the object of chief execration."[145]

2:17 Self-righteous people such as these Pharisees saw no need for *true* righteousness, because they viewed themselves as already "righteous." However, the people the Pharisees labeled "sinners" represented real sinners, those lacking righteousness. Jesus said He spent time with sinners because they were the people who felt a need for what He had to offer, namely, spiritual healing. He was evidently modifying a well-known proverb. Jesus was using the terms "righteous" and "sinners" ironically here.

> "It would be true to say that this word of Jesus strikes the keynote of the Gospel. The new thing in Christianity is not the doctrine that God saves sinners. No Jew would have denied that. It is the assertion 'that God loves and saves them as sinners.' . . . This is the authentic and glorious doctrine of true Christianity in any age."[146]

> "The specific reference in verse 17 to Jesus' call of sinners to the Kingdom suggests that the basis of table-fellowship was *messianic forgiveness*, and the meal itself was an anticipation of the messianic banquet."[147]

This verse is a fine summary statement of Jesus' mission during His earthly ministry. It is one of only two sayings in Mark in which Jesus expressed His purpose in coming (cf. 10:45). Here He presented Himself as the Healer, a divine title in the Old Testament (Exod. 15:26).

> "Among the most striking of His answers or apologies to them who examined Him, were those in which He vindicated Himself for mixing with publicans and sinners. They are three in number, spoken on as many occasions: the first in connection with Matthew's feast [Matt. 9:12-13; Mark 2:17; Luke 5:31-32]; the second in the house of Simon the Pharisee [Luke 7:36]; and the third on an occasion not minutely defined, when certain scribes and Pharisees brought against Him the grave charge, 'This man receiveth sinners, and eateth with them.' [Luke 15:2]. . . . The first may be distinguished as the *professional* argument, and is to this effect: 'I frequent the haunts of sinners, because I am a *physician*, and they are sick and need healing. . . .' The second may be described as the *political* argument, its drift being this: 'It is good policy to be the friend of sinners who have much to be forgiven; for when they are restored to the paths of virtue and piety, how great is their love! . . .' The third may be denominated the argument from *natural instinct*,

[142]Idem, *The Eucharistic Words of Jesus*, pp. 48-49.

[143]Kingsbury, p. 63.

[144]J. R. Donahue, "Tax Collectors and Sinners: An Attempt at Identification," *Catholic Biblical Quarterly* 33 (1971):39-61.

[145]Edersheim, 1:515.

[146]Hunter, pp. 40-41.

[147]Lane, p. 106. Cf. Matt. 8:10-11; and Rev. 3:20; 19:6-9.

and runs thus: 'I receive sinners, and eat with them, and seek by these means their moral restoration, for the same reason which moves the shepherd to go after a lost sheep, leaving his unstrayed flock in the wilderness, viz. because it is natural to seek the lost, and to have more joy in finding things lost than in possessing things which never have been lost. . . .'"[148]

3. The religious leaders' question about fasting 2:18-22 (cf. Matt. 9:14-17; Luke 5:33-39)

The third objection the religious leaders voiced arose from the failure of Jesus' disciples to observe the traditional, not Scriptural, fast days that the Pharisees observed (cf. Lev. 16:29). Jesus' association with tax gatherers and sinners seemed to them to result in the neglect of devout practices. This incident shows that Jesus had the authority to overturn prevailing practices of piety and to turn the sorrow of fasting into the joy of feasting.[149]

2:18   We do not know why John the Baptist's disciples "were fasting." Perhaps it was because he was then in prison, or possibly it was an expression of repentance designed to hasten the coming of the kingdom. The Pharisees fasted twice a week, Mondays and Thursdays (cf. Luke 18:12).[150] The feast in Levi's house may have occurred on one of these days. Jesus' disciples were to fast (cf. Matt. 6:16-18), but they apparently did not observe the extra fasts that the Pharisees did.[151]

2:19-20   Jesus responded with a parable in which He is the "bridegroom" and His disciples are the friends ("attendants") "of the bridegroom" (cf. John 3:29). Jesus had come to unite with Israel, His bride, as her Messiah. The figure of Messiah as a bridegroom may have been unknown among the Jews at this time.[152] The wedding banquet seemed just a short time away. The prophets said it would occur after Messiah's death and resurrection and after the Tribulation. The bridegroom would have to leave His friends and His bride before the banquet. While they were still together, they could and did rejoice—not mourn, which fasting represented. Jewish custom exempted the friends of a bridegroom from certain religious obligations, including participating in the weekly fasts.[153] This was Jesus' first hint of His coming death in Mark's Gospel.[154]

2:21-22   Two more parables clarified why fasting was inappropriate for Jesus' disciples then.[155] Not only was the timing wrong, but the messianic age that Jesus would introduce would render the old traditional forms of Judaism obsolete. Judaism had become "old," and Jesus was going to set up a "new" form of God's kingdom on earth that would be similar to a new garment (cf. Heb. 8:13), the messianic kingdom.

A "garment" symbolized the covering of man's sinful condition in Old Testament usage (e.g., Gen. 3:21; Isa. 61:10). The Jews were to lay aside "the old garment" of the Mosaic dispensation, and put on "the new" of the messianic age. Judaism had also become rigid and inflexible because of the traditions that had encrusted it, like old goatskins that contained wine. Jesus' kingdom could not operate within those constraints. It would be a new and more flexible vehicle for bringing joy ("new wine") to humanity.

The first of these three parables may have been more relevant to John's disciples since they anticipated a coming change. Jesus may have directed the second and third parables more to the Pharisees, since they wanted to maintain the legalistic practices of Judaism that were now threadbare and inflexible.

4. The controversies about Sabbath observance 2:23—3:6

The remaining two instances of opposition from the religious leaders arose over and concerned Sabbath observance. In the first case, the Pharisees opposed Jesus for permitting His disciples to do something they considered sinful. In the second, they opposed Him for doing something Himself that they objected to.

---

[148]Bruce, *The Training* . . ., pp. 26-27.

[149]Gundry, p. 131.

[150]Wessel, p. 636.

[151]See George C. Gianoulis, "Did Jesus' Disciples Fast?" *Bibliotheca Sacra* 168:672 (October-December 2011):413-25.

[152]See Lane, p. 110.

[153]Hiebert, p. 74.

[154]Cranfield, p. 111.

[155]See Appendix 4 "The Parables of Jesus" at the end of my notes on Matthew for a full list of them.

Picking grain on the Sabbath 2:23-28 (cf. Matt. 12:1-8; Luke 6:1-5)

2:23-24 Jesus' disciples did something that the Mosaic Law permitted when they plucked the ears of wheat or barley (Deut. 23:25). However, by doing it on a Sabbath day, they violated a traditional Pharisaic interpretation of the law. The Pharisees taught that to do what the disciples did constituted reaping, threshing, and winnowing, and that was forbidden work on the Sabbath (Exod. 20:10).[156]

"This reference to growing corn is the only clear indication in the Synoptic Gospels (cf. vi. 39) that the Ministry covered at least a year. The incident must have happened in the few weeks after Passover, from April to the beginning of June."[157]

2:25-26 The incident Jesus referred to is in 1 Samuel 21:1-6. Mark was the only evangelist to mention that "Abiathar" was the "high priest" then. This seemingly contradicts the Old Testament since *Ahimelech*, the father of Abiathar, was the high priest then according to the writer of 1 Samuel. The best solution to this problem seems to be that Jesus referred to Abiathar because he was the better-known priest during David's reign. The phrase "in the time of" or "in the days of" probably means "during the lifetime of" rather than "during the high priesthood of."[158]

Jesus' point was this: David technically broke the *ritual* law by eating bread that only the priests were to eat. Nevertheless he could do so because David was on the Lord's service. As such, he could do things other Israelites, not on the Lord's service, could not do. Again, the offense was a matter of religious ritual, not a moral violation of the law, as the Pharisees were implying. Another example of violating the letter of the law to observe its spirit is King Hezekiah's granting the Israelites who were unclean permission to eat the Passover (2 Chron. 30:18-20). God did not object to that, either. Another explanation of David's action is that God permitted it because of the urgency of his situation, and that Jesus was claiming that His mission was equally urgent.[159] A third explanation follows.

"Rather, the drift of the argument is that the fact that scripture does not condemn David for his action shows that the rigidity with which the Pharisees interpreted the ritual law was not in accordance with scripture, and so was not a proper understanding of the Law itself."[160]

The Pharisees failed in two respects. First, they did not distinguish which laws were more important. Serving the Lord is more important than resting, and man is more important than the Sabbath.

"Human need is a higher law than religious ritual."[161]

Second, they did not recognize Jesus as the anointed Servant of the Lord that the Old Testament predicted would come: the Son of David. Mark did not mention, as Matthew did, that Jesus pointed out that One *greater than the temple* had come (Matt. 12:6). Mark's emphasis was not on Jesus as the King, as much as it was on Jesus as the Lord's anointed Servant. As God's anointed Servant, Jesus had the right to provide for His disciples' physical needs—even though that meant violating a tradition governing ritual worship.

2:27-28 The Pharisees made the Sabbath a straitjacket that inhibited the Jews, though the rabbis conceded that some life-saving activities superceded Sabbath observance.[162] Jesus pointed out that God gave the Sabbath as a good gift "for man." He designed it to free His people from ceaseless labor and to give them rest. Sabbath observance had to contain enough elasticity to assure the promotion of human welfare. Jesus' point was the following.

"Anyone could violate the Sabbath to meet a legitimate human need that keeping the Sabbath would leave unmet."[163]

"Since the Sabbath was made for man, He who is man's Lord . . . has authority to determine its law and use."[164]

---

[156]Mishnah *Shabbath* 7:2.

[157]Taylor, p. 216.

[158]James Morison, *A Practical Commentary on the Gospel According to St. Mark*, pp. 60-63, gave 10 possible solutions to this problem.

[159]Mark L. Bailey, in *The New Testament Explorer*, p. 72.

[160]Cranfield, p. 115.

[161]Ralph Earle, *The Gospel According to Mark*, p. 49.

[162]Edersheim, 2:57, 60-61; Gundry, p. 142.

[163]Ibid., p. 144.

Only Mark recorded, "The Sabbath was made for man, not man for the Sabbath" (v. 27). One of his concerns in this Gospel was the welfare of mankind.

Since in the Old Testament the Sabbath was the "Lord's Day" in a special sense, Mark's statement about Jesus in verse 28 identifies Him again for the reader as God.[165] Jesus had the right to determine how people should use the Sabbath. As mentioned previously, there is some question as to whether the words in this verse were those of Jesus or of Mark (cf. v. 10).

> ". . . the *exousia* [authority] of Jesus manifests itself *vis-a-vis* the rabbinic tradition, the religious hierarchy, and the temple tradition. Foremost here is Jesus' reinterpretation of the Sabbath . . ."[166]

> "With this word Mark drives home for his readers the theological point of the pericope. These things were written that they may understand Jesus' true dignity: he is the Lord of the Sabbath."[167]

One writer sought to prove that the New Testament teaches Sabbath observance for Christians.[168] I do not think it does (cf. Rom. 7:4; 10:4; 14:5; Gal. 4:10-11).

This is the first of seven incidents that the Gospel evangelists recorded in which Jesus came into conflict with the Jewish religious leaders over Sabbath observance. The chart below lists them in probable chronological order.

SABBATH CONTROVERSIES				
Event	**Matthew**	**Mark**	**Luke**	**John**
The disciples plucked ears of grain in Galilee.	12:1-8	2:23-28	6:1-5	
Jesus healed a paralytic at the Pool of Siloam in Jerusalem.				5:1-18
Jesus healed a man with a withered hand in Capernaum.	12:9-14	3:1-6	6:6-11	
Jesus referred to the Jews circumcising on the Sabbath.				7:22-23
Jesus healed a man born blind in Jerusalem.				9:1-34
Jesus healed a woman bent over in Judea.			13:10-17	
Jesus healed a man with dropsy in Perea.			14:1-6	

Healing on the Sabbath 3:1-6 (cf. Matt. 12:9-14; Luke 6:6-11)

The following incident demonstrated Jesus' sovereign authority over the Sabbath. This is the last in this series of conflict accounts in this part of this Gospel (cf. ch. 12). It provides the climax in this section of Mark's narrative.

3:1-2   This event happened on a different "Sabbath" than the one just described in 2:23-28 (cf. Luke 6:6). The location of the synagogue is unimportant. The Pharisees continued to watch Jesus in order to "accuse Him" (2:23; 3:6). Rather than honestly evaluating His claims, most of them looked for an opportunity to discredit Him. Here they found an opportunity to charge Him with a capital offense in Israel, namely, Sabbath violation (Exod. 31:14-17).

3:3-4   Rather than avoiding a conflict, Jesus provoked one. He did so to teach His critics a lesson. His question raised the issue of Sabbath observance from the level of what was legal to the level of what was moral. For Jesus not to heal the man would have been a violation of God's purpose for the Sabbath, namely, to bring blessing to people (cf. James 4:17). Moreover, by healing the man "on the Sabbath," Jesus was doing "good," whereas the Pharisees were doing "evil" by trying to trap Him. Mark alone wrote that the critics kept quiet, probably to clarify their guilt.

---

[164]Taylor, p. 219.

[165]See Daniel Doriani, "The Deity of Christ in the Synoptic Gospels," *Journal of the Evangelical Theological Society* 37:3 (September 1994):333-50.

[166]Edwards, p. 224.

[167]Lane, p. 120.

[168]Walter J. Chantry, "Does the New Testament Teach the Fourth Commandment?" *The Banner of Truth* 325 (October 1990):18-23.

3:5   Vainly Jesus was "looking around" for someone who would respond to His question (cf. v. 34; 5:32; 10:23; 11:11). This expression is unique to the second Gospel. Evidently Peter remembered Jesus' "lookings" around and communicated these to Mark as significant indications of His "looking" *for the proper response* from people.

This is the only place in the New Testament where a writer explicitly stated that Jesus was angry. This was a case of righteous indignation in the presence of unrepentant evil. "Hardness of heart" (Gr. *porosei*) can also mean "blindness" (cf. Rom. 11:25; Eph. 4:18).[169] This is also the only account of this miracle that records Jesus' compassion for the objects of His anger. The tenses of the Greek verbs indicate that Jesus was angry momentarily (aorist tense), but His attitude of compassion was persistent (present tense). References to Jesus' emotions are peculiar to Mark's Gospel. They show His humanity.

"Jesus' action was perfectly consistent with His love and mercy. As a true man, Jesus experienced normal human emotions, among them anger as well as grief at obstinate sin. In His reaction to the sullen refusal of the Pharisees to respond to the truth, the incarnate Christ revealed the character of our holy God."[170]

"Their opposition rested on a fundamental misunderstanding—an inability, or refusal, to see that Jesus was God's eschatological agent and that his sovereign freedom with regard to law and custom sprang from that fact."[171]

Since Jesus did not use anything but His word to heal the man, His enemies could not charge Him with performing work on the Sabbath. Jesus' beneficent creative work on this occasion recalls His work in creating the cosmos (Gen. 1). The Pharisees should have made the connection and worshipped Jesus as God.

"Thus when Jesus as Son of Man declares himself to be master of the Sabbath . . . he presumes the very authority by which the Sabbath was instituted by the Creator.

"This sovereign disposition toward the Sabbath is typical of Jesus' challenges to the rabbinic tradition as a whole. Such challenges are found primarily at the outset and conclusion of Mark, as if to signify that from beginning to end the antidote to the 'leaven of the Pharisees' (8:15) is the *exousia* [authority] of Jesus. He violates laws of purity by touching and cleansing a leper (1:40-45) and by association with sinners and tax collectors (2:13-17). He places in question the issue of purification by violating food prohibitions in fasting (2:18-22) and by eating with unwashed hands (7:1-23). He contravenes marriage laws in his teaching on divorce (10:1-12), and he openly denounces the scribes (12:38-40). In the question on the son of David he tacitly assumes supremacy over Israel's greatest king who, according to 2 Sam 7:14, would be the progenitor of the Messiah (12:35-37)."[172]

3:6   This verse is the climax of this whole confrontation section (2:1—3:6). Faced with the most convincing arguments and actions about Jesus' deity, the Pharisees chose to reject them. Furthermore, instead of simply leaving Jesus alone, they took steps to kill Him. As the gospel story unfolds, it becomes increasingly clear that Jesus' enemies opposed Him because He constituted a threat to their authority. That motivation is evident here, too, because "the Herodians" were supporters of Roman authority over Palestine. Together, the Pharisees and the Herodians "feared he might be an unsettling political influence in Palestine."[173] These two groups had little in common except their common enemy, Jesus.

This is Mark's first explicit reference to Jesus' death. Jesus' enemies had decided to "destroy Him." They only needed to plan how. In spite of their objections to Jesus working on the Sabbath, they did not mind plotting His death on that day. His words and works, from their viewpoint, undermined their whole approach to the Law, their outward "piety," and their actions.

This decision of Jesus' enemies to kill Him constitutes a turning point in Mark's narrative. It is a benchmark that affected Jesus' ministry from then on.

[169]Cranfield, p. 121.
[170]Hiebert, p. 81.
[171]D. E. Nineham, *Saint Mark*, p. 110.
[172]Edwards, p. 225.
[173]Wessel, p. 640.

III. THE SERVANT'S LATER GALILEAN MINISTRY 3:7—6:6A

There are some structural similarities between 1:14—3:6 and 3:7—6:6a in Mark's story. The beginnings and endings of these two sections are similar. The first section describes Jesus' ministry in Galilee before the religious leaders determined to kill Him, and the second shows His ministry after that decision. That decision is the basis for the division of Jesus' Galilean ministry into an earlier and a later stage.

A. THE BROADENING OF JESUS' MINISTRY 3:7-19

This section is similar to 1:14-20 in that it records a general description of Jesus' ministry (vv. 7-12) and His calling of more disciples (vv. 13-19).

1. Jesus' ministry to the multitudes 3:7-12 (cf. Matt. 12:15-21)

This pericope introduces Jesus' continuing ministry in Galilee following the religious leaders' decision to kill Him (cf. 1:14-15; 2:13). It provides much more detail than the parallel account in Matthew.

3:7-8   The "sea" to which Jesus "withdrew" was the Sea of Galilee. He went there rather than to the areas farther south, where it would have been easier for His enemies to harass Him. Jesus withdrew because of the religious leaders' plot to kill Him (Matt. 12:15).

Mark put the disciples in the emphatic first position in the Greek text. They shared Jesus' breach with the religious leaders. They would be the objects of His preparation for future ministry because of Jesus' coming death.

Mark described many people coming to Jesus from all over Jewish Palestine. "Jerusalem" was in "Judea" to the south.[174] "Idumea," named only here in the New Testament, was the old Edomite territory southeast of Judea. People also came from the east side of "the Jordan" River (Perea and the Decapolis), and from the Mediterranean coast to the northwest ("vicinity of Tyre and Sidon"). It is interesting that these locations form something of an outline of this Gospel. Jesus first ministered in Galilee (chs. 1—6), then in Tyre, Sidon, and the Decapolis (ch. 7), and finally in Jerusalem (chs. 10—16).[175] Notably absent were people from Samaria, the land of Jewish iconoclasts who separated from the other Jews.

3:9-10   Jesus addressed the crowds from a little "boat" (Gr. *ploiarion*, not a fishing boat) on the lake when they "pressed" too heavily upon Him. Apparently the disciples kept this little boat handy whenever Jesus spoke to the crowds from the shore. If He needed to step back from them, He would have a place of retreat. Mark probably mentioned this detail to stress the large numbers of people who followed Jesus. It also shows Jesus' willingness to adapt His presentation to the needs of His audience. Perhaps "the big fisherman," Peter, was responsible for this notation.

The multitudes seemed to have little interest in worshipping Jesus as God, but they were eager to receive the physical benefits of His ministry. These benefits Jesus graciously bestowed on them.

3:11-12   As before, Jesus continued to exorcize demons. He also continued to forbid them to reveal His identity. This would have encouraged the people to associate the title "Son of God" with the physical aspects of Jesus' ministry almost exclusively (cf. 1:34). Moreover, Jesus by this means retained more control over His self-revelation and the progress of His mission. Perhaps He also did not want the people to associate Him with these demons.

The idea that Jesus silenced the demons because they sought to control Him by using His name and thereby gaining power over Him seems improbable to me.[176] While conflict with demonic forces is definitely a theme in Mark's Gospel, the demons had no real power over Jesus simply from knowing His name. This was a pagan superstition.

> "The earliest confession of the Sonship seems to have come from evil spirits, who knew Jesus better than he [sic He] was known by His own disciples."[177]

---

[174]For Josephus' description of Judea, see *The Wars . . .*, 3:3:5.

[175]Eduard Schweizer, *The Good News According to Mark*, p. 79.

[176]Cf. Lane, p. 130.

[177]Henry B. Swete, *The Gospel According to St. Mark*, p. 57.

2. Jesus' selection of 12 disciples 3:13-19 (cf. Luke 6:12-16)

Jesus' selection of 12 disciples constituted an important advance in His ministry. These men would be the primary beneficiaries of His training for leadership to carry out His mission. The plot to take His life made the training of disciples imperative.

3:13   The exact location of this incident is uncertain. It was probably somewhere in Galilee, since this whole section describes Jesus' ministry there (1:14—6:6a). Jesus first called His disciples to join Him. Then, from that larger group, He selected 12 men as apostles (Luke 6:13). Evidently Jesus selected 12 apostles for leadership over Israel's 12 tribes in His messianic reign (Matt. 19:28). In view of Israel's rejection of Jesus, they became the nucleus of the church, which the New Testament never refers to as the "new Israel." This is a term that covenant theologians have applied to the church, which has created serious confusion in the minds of many Bible students.

> ". . . from a mountaintop, an imagery reminiscent of Yahweh's summons to Moses on Mount Sinai (Exod 19:20), Jesus sovereignly summons the Twelve into a new community (Mark 3:13-19) and to a mission that is founded on a relationship with himself ('in order that they might be with him,' v. 14). He confers his authority on the Twelve and sends them out with dominion over demons (6:7-13) and with freedom from the tradition of the elders (7:5-13)."[178]

> "In Mark's story world, the mountain connotes nearness to God and is therefore a place of divine-human communication and encounter. Atop a mountain, Jesus prays (6:46), is transfigured by God (9:2-8), and foretells the future (13:3-5)."[179]

Mark stressed that Jesus initiated this appointment, and the Twelve voluntarily responded (cf. Exod. 19:20). Perhaps he did this to remind his readers that God had chosen them as disciples; they had not sought this privilege. The response of these initial disciples provided a good example for all succeeding followers of Jesus.

3:14-15   "The Twelve" became a technical term for this group of disciples. Some early manuscripts add "whom also He named apostles" (cf. NIV). This was probably not in Mark's original Gospel. Probably a scribe inserted it having read Luke 6:13, the parallel passage, though some disagree.[180]

Jesus appointed these disciples for a twofold purpose: to "be with Him," and "to preach." The order is significant.

> "Fellowship with Him must precede preaching about Him."[181]

Jesus also gave these disciples the ability ("authority") "to cast out demons," along with preaching. The miracles would convince many of their hearers that God had sent them as His spokesmen. Mark probably mentioned exorcisms because this was the greatest demonstration of the disciples' authority, not the only one. This Gospel documents Jesus' training of the Twelve in these two basic areas particularly: being with Jesus and preaching.

---

[178]Edwards, p. 224.

[179]Kingsbury, p. 93.

[180]E.g., Christopher W. Skinner, "'Whom He Also Named Apostles': A Textual Problem in Mark 3:14," *Bibliotheca Sacra* 161:643 (July-September 2004):322-29.

[181]George Williams, *The Student's Commentary on the Holy Scriptures*, p. 734.

Constable's Notes

3:16-19   The following table shows the 12 disciples as they appear in the four lists that the Holy Spirit has given us in Scripture.

	Matt. 10:2-4	Mark 3:16-19	Luke 6:14-16	Acts 1:13
1.	Simon Peter	Simon Peter	Simon Peter	Peter
2.	Andrew	James	Andrew	John
3.	James	John	James	James
4.	John	Andrew	John	Andrew
5.	Philip	Philip	Philip	Philip
6.	Bartholomew	Bartholomew	Bartholomew	Thomas
7.	Thomas	Matthew	Matthew	Bartholomew
8.	Matthew	Thomas	Thomas	Matthew
9.	James, son of Alphaeus	James, son of Alphaeus	James, son of Alphaeus	James, son of Alphaeus
10.	Thaddaeus	Thaddaeus	Judas, son or brother of James	Judas, son or brother of James
11.	Simon the Cananaean	Simon the Cananaean	Simon the Zealot	Simon the Zealot
12.	Judas Iscariot	Judas Iscariot	Judas Iscariot	

All four lists contain three groups of four names each. The same individuals head each group, though there is variation within each group. Probably these groups constituted ministry teams that broke up into pairs when the Twelve preached apart from Jesus (6:7).

Mark never used the double name "Simon Peter." Peter ("Rocky") was Simon's second given name, his nickname. All the lists place Peter first, and they all put Judas Iscariot last, except for the Acts list that omits him.

> "Jesus *gave* Peter a new *name* because it was the Jewish custom to rename someone who had experienced a life-changing event. This renaming of the disciples has similarities to the renaming of Abram (Gen. 17:3-5) and of Saul (Acts 9[; 13:9])."[182]

"Boanerges" is a Hebrew word, but why Jesus called James and John "sons of thunder" is unknown. Perhaps they had an impetuous nature (cf. 9:38; Luke 9:54).

"Bartholomew" is not really a name, but a *patronym* meaning "son of Talmai (Ptolemy)." He may have had another name, but the disciples consistently referred to him as Bartholomew. Matthew's other name was Levi.

"James the son of Alphaeus" was also known as James the Less (or little, 15:40). "Thaddaeus" and "Judas, the son or brother of James" may have been the same person. Likewise, "Simon the Cananaean" was the same person as Simon the Zealot, "Cananaean" being the Aramaic form of "Zealot." The Zealots were a later political party bent on the overthrow of the Roman government, so it is unlikely that Simon was a member of this party. Probably the name "zealot" referred to Simon's personality, not his political affiliation. "Iscariot" is a name of origin, but the exact location of Judas' hometown is uncertain, though many believe it was a town in Judea named Kerioth. "Iscariot" means "man of Kerioth."[183]

> "It was a strange group of men our Lord chose to be his disciples. Four of them were fishermen, one a hated tax collector, another a member of a radical and violent political party [?]. Of six of them we know practically nothing. All were laymen. There was not a preacher or an expert in the Scriptures in the lot. Yet it was with these men that Jesus established his church and disseminated his Good News to the end of the earth."[184]

[182]*The Nelson . . .*, p. 1645.
[183]See *The New Bible Dictionary*, 1962 ed., s.v. "Judas Iscariot," by R. P. Martin.
[184]Wessel, p. 643.

"Learning, rank, wealth, refinement, freely given up to his [*sic*, Jesus'] service, He would not have despised; but He preferred devoted men who had none of these advantages to undevoted men who had them all. And with good reason; for it mattered little, except in the eyes of contemporary prejudice, what the social position or even the previous history of the twelve had been, provided they were spiritually qualified for the work to which they were called. What tells ultimately is, not what is without a man, but what is within."[185]

B. THE INCREASING REJECTION OF JESUS AND ITS RESULT 3:20—4:34

As Jesus' ministry expanded, so did rejection of Him as God's anointed Servant. Mark documented the increasing rejection that Jesus experienced (3:20-35), and then explained that Jesus taught the multitudes in parables as a result (4:1-34).

1. The increasing rejection of Jesus 3:20-35

Mark again returned to the opposition theme (cf. 2:1—3:6). He directed his readers back and forth between Jesus' acceptance on a superficial level by the multitudes, His disciples' growing commitment to Him, and the increasing hostility of the religious leaders. This structural pattern highlights the contrasts between the three groups.

In this section, Mark used a chiastic structure to show two different kinds of opposition that Jesus faced, which many of His disciples have faced as well. He used this "sandwich" structure elsewhere too (cf. 5:21-43; 6:7-31; 11:12-26; 14:1-11, 27-52). It focuses attention on the central part of the section (chiasm), in this case the serious charge that Satan controlled Jesus.

A   The opposition of family 3:20-21
    B   The opposition of enemies 3:22-30
A'   The opposition of family 3:31-35

The plan of Jesus' family 3:20-21

The picture the writer painted was of Jesus and His disciples in a house in Capernaum ("home"). Jews wanting healing or some other favor from Jesus barged right in through the door. There were so many of them that Jesus "could not even eat a meal," much less get some needed rest. The house was completely full of seekers. Probably more people thronged around outside the building, trying to get in through the doors and windows. The Servant of the Lord was constantly at work serving.

Jesus' family members heard about His extreme busyness. The Greek term translated "His own people" (NASB, lit. "those with Him") is an idiom meaning His family members, not just His friends.[186] They felt concern for His health. Perhaps they worried that He was not eating properly. They may even have concluded that His overworked condition had affected His mental stability. They decided to come to Capernaum from Nazareth and take charge of Him for His own good. The Greek word *kratesai* ("take custody" or "take charge") elsewhere describes arresting someone (cf. 6:17; 12:12; 14:1, 44, 46, 49, 51). Thus it appears that the best of intentions motivated Jesus' family. However, they misread the evidence. He was not too busy nor was He out of His mind (cf. Acts 26:24; 2 Cor. 5:13). He was simply carrying out His Father's will. Sometimes those who have concern for a disciple's welfare apply pressure to depart from God's will. This constitutes opposition, not assistance. Some readers of Mark's story who suffer persecution from family members for following Jesus can identify.

The unbelief of Jesus' enemies 3:22-30 (cf. Matt. 12:22-37; Luke 11:14-26)

Evidently it was between the time that Jesus' family left Nazareth to take custody of Him, and the time they arrived in Capernaum (v. 31), that this incident occurred. Mark's account is shorter than Matthew's, and stresses the nature of the mounting hostility of the religious leaders.

3:22   While well-meaning family opponents were coming from Nazareth, which lay to the west, hostile adversaries were moving up "from Jerusalem" to the south. "The scribes" (teachers of the law), who constituted an official delegation, had concluded that Satan ("Beelzebul, ruler of the demons") "possessed" Jesus and gave Him power to exorcize demons. They viewed Jesus as being allied with Satan.

> "In the Greek, the name is always *Beelzeboul*; the familiar 'Beelzebub' is from the [Latin] Vulgate. Some view the name as a derisive corruption of the title of the god of Ekron, Baal-zebub, 'the lord of flies,' to make it mean the lord of dung. More probably it means lord of the dwelling, that is, the dwelling of the evil spirits. This agrees with the reference to 'the strong man's house' in verse 27, as well as Christ's comment in Matthew 10:25, that as 'the master of the house,' He has been called Beelzebub."[187]

[185]Bruce, *The Training . . .*, p. 38.

[186]J. H. Moulton and G. Milligan, *The Vocabulary of the Greek Testament*, pp. 478-79.

[187]Hiebert, p. 92. See also Cranfield, p. 136.

3:23-27   Jesus replied to the charge against Him "with parables" (cf. Matt. 12:29; Luke 11:21-22). That is, He used comparisons. He pointed out that it was illogical for Him to "cast out" Satan's agents if He was one of Satan's agents. Satan would then be working against himself. Therefore, since Jesus was in fact destroying Satan's work, He must be stronger than Satan (v. 27).

> "It may be enough to say that 3:22-27 declares Jesus' ministry, without specifying the 'when,' to reflect the eschatological defeat of Satan as seen in his exorcisms."[188]

> "Jesus occasionally avoids indictment by talking in riddles."[189]

3:28-30   Jesus followed up His refutation with a solemn warning. The words "truly I say to you" or "I tell you the truth" occur 13 times in this Gospel, always on Jesus' lips. This phrase occurs 30 times in Matthew, six times in Luke, and 25 times in John (where the "truly" is always double). It denotes that Jesus was speaking out of His own authority. A comparable expression in the Old Testament is, "As I live, says the Lord."

> "His use of 'Amen' to introduce and endorse his own words is without analogy in the whole of Jewish literature and in the remainder of the NT. . . . 'Amen' denotes that his words are reliable and true because he is totally committed to do and speak the will of God. As such, the Amen-formulation is not only a highly significant characteristic of Jesus' speech, but a Christological affirmation: Jesus is the true witness of God."[190]

> "In light of the context this [sin] refers to an attitude (not an isolated act or utterance) of defiant hostility toward God that rejects His saving power toward man, expressed in the spirit-empowered person and work of Jesus. It is one's preference for darkness even though he has been exposed to light (cf. John 3:19). Such a persistent attitude of willful unbelief can harden into a condition in which repentance and forgiveness, both mediated by God's Spirit, become impossible. This person is guilty (*enochos*, 'liable to, in the grasp') of an eternal sin (sing., the ultimate sin because it remains forever unforgiven; cf. Matt. 12:32). Judas Iscariot (cf. Mark 3:29; 14:43-46) proved the reality of these words."[191]

We should not focus so exclusively on the exception to forgiveness that we fail to appreciate the breadth of forgiveness that Jesus offered here. "All sins" means all classes and types of sins, not all sins without exception. Jesus was not teaching universalism, the theory that everyone will go to heaven. "Blasphemy" is a type of sin, namely: speech that is hostile, malicious, injurious, and derogatory of God. This was the type of sin the scribes were committing.

The scribes were committing the unpardonable sin, because they attributed the power of Jesus' exorcisms to Satan rather than to the Holy Spirit (cf. 1:11-12).

> "Having rejected the testimony of the Father, the Son, and now the Spirit's miraculous authentication, nothing more could be done for the salvation of those religious leaders."[192]

> "Those who most particularly should heed the warning of this verse today are the theological teachers and the official leaders of the churches."[193]

This saying of Jesus has caused many people great anxiety throughout the history of the church. Many have wondered if they have committed the unpardonable sin. Concern that one may have committed it is a good indication that one probably has not. The way to avoid committing the unpardonable sin is to believe the testimony that the Holy Spirit has given about Jesus in Scripture, namely, that He is the Christ (i.e., the divine Messiah, cf. 1 John 5:1).

The interference of Jesus' family 3:31-35 (cf. Matt. 12:46-50; Luke 8:19-21)

3:31   "His mother" Mary, along with Jesus' half-brothers, finally "arrived" from Nazareth (cf. vv. 20-21). By inserting Jesus' conflict with the scribes in this story, Mark heightened the readers' suspense about the results of Jesus' conflict with His family. Perhaps the house where Jesus was present was so full of people that His family could not get in, but had to send word to Him that they had arrived. This approach reflects normal family relationships. Jesus' mother and brothers were not being rude,

---

[188]Guelich, p. 177.

[189]Rhoads and Michie, p. 85.

[190]Lane, p. 144.

[191]Grassmick, p. 117.

[192]Bailey, p. 74.

[193]Cranfield, p. 148.

but were expecting that Jesus would acknowledge their presence by respectfully coming out to meet them. They wanted to talk to Him privately and convince Him to restrain His activity.

3:32-34 The multitude "sitting around" Jesus evidently consisted of a group of His disciples (v. 34). Jesus' question focused on the quality of relationship with Himself. He meant: "Who are the sort of people who are My family?" Again Jesus looked around, but this time affectionately (cf. v. 5). He identified His disciples as those closest to Him. This would have been a startling statement for Jesus' hearers, because the Jews valued *natural* family relationships highly. Jesus was not repudiating family relationships (cf. 7:10-13). He was teaching the priority of *spiritual* over natural relationships.

3:35 Those who do God's "will," not just those who profess discipleship, constitute Jesus' spiritual family. The terms "brother and sister and mother" are figurative. "Father" is absent because Jesus had only one spiritual Father. His spiritual "mothers" were those believing female disciples who sustained Him in motherly ways. Jesus claimed the authority to redefine motherhood and sibling relationships: according to the doing of God's "will," rather than blood lineage (cf. 6:1-6).[194]

This pericope should be a great encouragement to any disciple who is suffering persecution for his or her faith. Such disciples were Mark's original readers. Some disciples suffer broken family relationships and even ostracism because of their commitment to do God's will. Some experience intense opposition from unbelievers who try to make their good works look bad. One reward for such sacrifices is an intimate relationship with Jesus Christ.

2. Jesus' teaching in parables 4:1-34

This is the first of three extended teaching sessions that Mark recorded (cf. 7:1-23; 13:3-37). Jesus' three parables in this section describe the character of the messianic kingdom.

Parables are illustrations that teach truth by comparisons (Gr. *parabole*, lit. "something thrown alongside," similitudes). Some are long stories, but others are short similes, metaphors, analogies, or proverbial sayings (cf. 2:19-20, 21, 22; 3:24-25, 27). The popular definition that a parable is an earthly story with a heavenly meaning, is essentially accurate as far as it goes. The use of parables for teaching was a common rabbinic device that Jesus adopted and used with great skill.

> "A parable begins innocently as *a picture* that arrests our attention and arouses our interest. But as we study the picture, it becomes *a mirror* in which we suddenly see ourselves. If we continue to look by faith, the mirror becomes *a window* through which we see God and His truth. How we respond to that truth will determine what further truth God will teach us."[195]

The setting 4:1-2 (cf. Matt. 13:1-3a; Luke 8:4)

Jesus may have taught these "parables" shortly after the incident Mark just finished recording (3:20-35; cf. Matt. 13:1). If so, this was a very busy day in Jesus' ministry. It may have included all the events in 3:19—4:41 (cf. Matt. 12:22—13:53; Luke 8:4-25). "Again" looks back to 3:7 and perhaps to 2:13. The "boat" (Gr. *ploion*) in which Jesus "sat" was a vessel larger than a rowboat (cf. 3:7), perhaps a fishing boat.

Matthew recorded Jesus giving two groups of parables on this occasion: four to the multitudes (Matt. 13:3b-35), and four to the disciples (Matt. 13:36-52). Mark recorded only Jesus' parables to the multitudes. Both evangelists recorded Jesus' explanations to His disciples, though what they recorded Him saying is not identical.

The parable of the soils 4:3-9 (cf. Matt. 13:3b-9; Luke 8:5-8)

Jesus introduced and concluded this parable with instructions that His hearers should give it careful consideration (vv. 3, 9, cf. v. 23). Mark's account of this parable is almost identical to Matthew's. It is the only parable that Jesus spoke this day that all three synoptic evangelists recorded. Probably Jesus taught this parable many times during His ministry as an itinerant preacher, and the disciples were familiar with it. It is also a key parable because it introduced elements that recur in the other parables Jesus taught that day, such as the seed.

Rhoads and Michie suggested that "the interpretation of the seed falling on 'rocky' ground suggests an opposite and ironic meaning of that name [i.e., Peter, "Rock"], unmistakably depicting Peter and the other disciples."[196]

[194]Edwards, p. 224.
[195]Wiersbe, 1:121.
[196]Rhoads and Michie, p. 128.

Jesus' explanations to His disciples 4:10-29

This section of Mark's account records Jesus' words to His disciples that the multitudes did not hear.

The purpose of the parables 4:10-12 (cf. Matt. 13:10-17; Luke 8:9-10)

4:10   Mark alone noted that those who asked Jesus to explain the parables included the Twelve plus other disciples (v. 10). Evidently their question concerned *why* Jesus was using parables to teach, as well as what they meant. Jesus could have been clearer, but He deliberately chose to speak enigmatically.

4:11-12   Jesus drew a distinction between those who accepted His teaching, such as the Twelve, and those who rejected it, such as the scribes and Pharisees. Those "outside" were those outside the circle of discipleship. God was giving those who welcomed Jesus' teaching new revelation about the coming messianic kingdom. He was withholding that revelation from those who rejected Him. The parables were the vehicle of that revelation. The Holy Spirit enabled the receptive to understand this enigmatic revelation, but He made it incomprehensible to the unbelieving. The parabolic method acted as a filter to separate those two types of people.

> ". . . just as Jesus predetermines his own death partly by healing on the Sabbath despite the Pharisees' watching him with murderous intent (see 3:1-6 with comments) and partly by choosing the betrayer (see 3:16-19 with comments), so also he predetermines his own death partly by speaking in parables."[197]

The religious teachers of Jesus' day used parables extensively, so Jesus' hearers were familiar with them. But the rabbis used them only to illustrate and clarify, not to conceal.[198]

> ". . . the three seed parables illustrate various aspects of the Kingdom of God by depicting God's sovereign rule at work in the present but in a way unexpected in Judaism (cf. Jeremias, *Parables*, 146-53)."[199]

God was doing through Jesus what He had done through Isaiah centuries earlier. Jesus' quotation of Isaiah 6:9-10 drew this comparison. One writer believed Jesus meant that most of the Jews were still in exile spiritually.[200] We might add that this is always the double effect of revelation (cf. 1 Cor. 2:6-16). God uses it to enlighten the receptive, but He also uses it to befuddle the unreceptive. Their inability to comprehend is a divine judgment for their unbelief (cf. Rom. 11:25-32). Further enlightenment requires positive reception of present revelation. This knowledge is very helpful for Jesus' disciples. It would have been an encouragement to Mark's original readers as they shared the gospel with others and noted the two responses, as it is to modern readers.

> "The judgment is a merciful one. The parable which the cold-hearted multitudes hear without understanding they remember, because of its penetrating and impressive form; and when their hearts become able to receive its meaning, the meaning will become clear to them. Meanwhile they are saved from the guilt of rejecting plain truth."[201]

> "Throughout the ministry we can see these two motives (revealing and veiling) at work. On the one hand, Jesus gathers the crowds about him and teaches them, sends out the Twelve to preach, and reveals the power and compassion of God by his miracles. God's self-revelation is not to be accomplished in a corner. On the other hand, Jesus teaches the crowds indirectly by means of parables, seeks to conceal his miracles, and forbids the demoniacs to declare his identity. The two motives, both of which are necessary to the divine purpose, are constantly in tension—a fact which explains some apparent inconsistencies (e.g. between the command *egeire eis to meson* ["Rise and come forward"] in iii. 3 and the frequent injunctions to silence)."[202]

> "God's self-revelation is veiled, in order that men may be left sufficient room in which to make a personal decision. A real turning to God or repentance (*epistrephein*) is made possible by the inward divine

[197]Gundry, p. 196.

[198]Edersheim, 1:580-81.

[199]Guelich, p. 206.

[200]Douglas S. McComiskey, "Exile and the Purpose of Jesus' Parables (Mark 4:10-12; Matt 13:10-17; Luke 8:9-10)," *Journal of the Evangelical Theological Society* 51:1 (March 2008):59-85.

[201]Alfred Plummer, "The Gospel According to St. Mark," in *The Cambridge Greek Testament*, p. 124.

[202]Cranfield, p. 157.

enabling of the Holy Spirit (*dedotai*), but would be rendered impossible by the external compulsion of a manifestation of the unveiled divine majesty. The revelation is veiled for the sake of man's freedom to believe."[203]

The explanation of the parable of the soils 4:13-20 (cf. Matt. 13:18-23; Luke 8:11-15)

4:13   Jesus believed that the disciples should have understood the parable of the soils. It is, after all, one of the easier ones to understand.

4:14-20   Jesus did not give His disciples several hermeneutical principles by which they could understand the parables. He gave them a sample interpretation as a pattern that they could apply in understanding other parables.

The "seed" represents "the word" or message of God that "the sower" proclaims. People make a negative or a positive response when they hear this message. They may make a negative response for any one of three reasons. Regardless of the reason, a negative response proves unproductive in their lives. A positive response, however, will produce spiritual fruit, but the fruit will be in varying amounts depending on various factors.

> "Each of the three fruitless hearts is influenced by a different enemy: the hard heart—the devil himself snatches the seed; the shallow heart—the flesh counterfeits religious feelings; the crowded heart—the things of the world smother the growth and prevent a harvest. These are the three great enemies of the Christian: the world, the flesh, and the devil (Eph. 2:1-3)."[204]

Some interpreters want to know which soils represent believers and which unbelievers. This was not Jesus' point in the parable. Both believers and unbelievers need to welcome the word gladly rather than allowing its enemies to make it unfruitful.

The "word" that Jesus was sowing was the good news concerning the coming messianic kingdom. The people He addressed gave these characteristic responses. However, these are typical responses that have marked the proclamation of God's Word throughout history, among believers and unbelievers alike. Mark's original readers would have found encouragement in this parable to receive the Word of God—as good soil—and to beware of the enemies that limit Christians' fruitfulness.

> "Words may be sound and lively enough, but it is up to each hearer to let them sink in and become fruitful. If he only hears without responding—without doing something about it and committing himself to their meaning—then the words are in danger of being lost, or of never coming to anything. The whole story thus becomes a parable about the learner's responsibility, and about the importance of learning with one's whole will and obedience, and not merely with one's head."[205]

"In summary, the good hearers welcome the word immediately, so that Satan cannot snatch it away. They welcome it deeply, so that persecution because of it cannot induce them to apostatize. They welcome it exclusively, so that other concerns do not stifle it. The understanding that results from this kind of reception goes beyond the intellectual to touch conduct, commitment, and devotion. . . . Thus the mystery turns out to be that God's rule is established, not by conquest, but by speaking; and that a person participates in God's rule, not by joining an army, but by hearing the message in right ways . . ."[206]

The parable of the lamp 4:21-25 (cf. Luke 8:16-18)

Jesus' statements in this pericope appear scattered throughout the other Gospels. Verse 21 occurs in Matthew 5:15 and in Luke 11:33. Verse 22 is in Matthew 10:26 and in Luke 12:2. Verse 24 appears in Matthew 7:2 and in Luke 6:38. Verse 25 is also in Matthew 13:12 and 25:29, in addition to Luke 19:26. This phenomenon does not mean that this pericope lacks authenticity. It means that Jesus frequently used these expressions at other times during His teaching ministry—not just here. He was an itinerant preacher, and itinerant preachers often use the same messages with the same or similar words with different audiences.

---

[203]Ibid., p. 158.
[204]Wiersbe, 1:123.
[205]Moule, p. 36.
[206]Gundry, pp. 206-7.

4:21 Jesus continued His address to the inquiring disciples (cf. vv. 10-20). The "lamp" would have been a small clay dish, with the edges pinched up to form a spout. A small piece of fabric typically hung over the spout from the body of the lamp serving as a wick. These household lamps usually held only a few teaspoons of oil, and rested on extensions of wood or plaster protruding from a wall. The "basket" was a common container that held about a peck (one-quarter bushel).

The lamp seems to represent the illumination that Jesus had just given about the purpose of the parables and the meaning of the parable of the soils. He did not want His disciples to conceal what He had just told them but to broadcast it. In His day, this involved revelation about the impending kingdom particularly. In the wider sphere of application, it would include all that God has revealed (cf. Ps. 119:105).

Another interpretation sees Jesus as the Light that His disciples were not to conceal.[207] Jesus elsewhere spoke of Himself as the Light of the world (John 8:12). Nevertheless in this context, the "light" seems to represent *revelation*. Light has both metaphorical meanings in Scripture.

4:22 The former verse expressed a parable. This one explained a literal reality. As a principle, people do not hide precious things forever. They only conceal them temporarily, and then they bring them out into view. If they remain hidden forever, they are virtually lost. People conceal them to protect them from others who would abuse and take them. For example, people who own expensive jewelry or art treasures may keep them locked up for safe keeping part of the time, but they display them publicly at other times. Keeping them locked up privately all the time is a misuse of their purpose.

The disciples should not conclude, that just because God had previously hidden the characteristics about the kingdom that Jesus was revealing, He wanted them to remain unknown. The time had come to proclaim them publicly.

> "The kingdom of God, as embodied in Jesus' Person and ministry, was now a veiled revelation to those without, but He intended that later it should receive a glorious manifestation through the ministry of His followers."[208]

4:23 What Jesus had told the multitudes (v. 9), He now repeated specifically for His disciples. They could "hear." They needed to use that ability by paying attention to what Jesus had just said.

4:24 The disciples needed to consider carefully what Jesus was telling them. The degree to which they paid attention to what He said, would be the degree to which they would profit from it. God would graciously bless attentive disciples with even greater benefit than the effort they expended in heeding His words. Their blessing would be disproportionately large.

4:25 If a person works hard to obtain something good, he or she normally receives other good things in addition. If a disciple pays attention to and assimilates the revelation God has given, God will increase his or her capacity to understand and appropriate more revelation. However, this principle works the other way, too. The person who does not use his or her ability to understand and respond to God's revelation, appropriately loses that ability. The disciples needed to use their understanding of Jesus and the kingdom—by proclaiming the gospel—or they would lose their ability and their understanding. This is a call for disciples to continue growing (cf. 2 Pet. 3:18, the key verse of that epistle, I believe).

The parable of the seed growing by itself 4:26-29

Since this parable supplements the parable of the soils, it appears that Jesus addressed it to the multitudes (cf. vv. 1-9). Mark is the only evangelist who recorded this part of the discourse. Each parable to the multitudes illuminated something about the messianic kingdom.

The identity of the man in the parable is secondary, though in view of the former parable, he represents Jesus and His disciples. The significant element is how the seed grows. In the former parable, the seed represented the good news about the kingdom, and it means the same thing here. The primary motif of the parable is the seed.[209]

The "seed" enters into the ground "and grows" mysteriously, without the continuing work of the sower. God causes it to grow. Farmers know the conditions that help or hinder plant growth, but they do not fully understand the growth process nor can they cause growth. Only God can do that. The earth itself appears to cause plants to grow automatically as they move through the various stages from germination to maturity. Jesus stressed this fact by putting the Greek word *automate* ("by itself") in the emphatic first position in the sentence. Finally the sower, who had played no visible role in the growth of the crop, returned to the field as its reaper. The same divine person who sows also reaps.

---

[207]E.g., Wessel, p. 652.
[208]Hiebert, p. 107.
[209]Guelich, p. 240.

This parable would have encouraged the disciples to realize that the preaching of Jesus and their own preaching, in anticipation of the kingdom, would bear fruit in time. God would cause the seed that they planted in the ears and minds of many to germinate into new life and to grow. Growth of the believing community would increase, though no one could really explain why it was growing except that God was responsible for it (cf. Matt. 16:18). Eventually there would be a harvest of the crop when God, the ultimate sower, saw that the time was right. Probably this refers to the end of the messianic kingdom. The parable bridges history, from the initial time of sowing in Jesus' day, culminating in the harvest at the end of the messianic (millennial) kingdom.

Another interpretation of this parable views it as describing growth within individual believers.[210] The problem with this view is the identity of the kingdom of God. Other interpreters see it as picturing the mysterious appearing of the messianic kingdom at the time of harvest.[211] However, the emphasis in the parable is on the growth of the seed, not the harvest of the crop. A third view takes the period of growth to be the inter-advent age, with the harvest occurring when Jesus returns to establish His kingdom on earth.[212] This view limits the parable to the "mystery form" of the kingdom. I find nothing in the text to justify interpreting "the kingdom" as the Old Testament predicted it, or simply as the mystery form of the kingdom. I believe that when Jesus said the kingdom of heaven (or God) was similar to something, what He described included the messianic (millennial) kingdom. It did not just represent the inter-advent age leading up to its beginning.

The parable of the mustard seed 4:30-32 (cf. Matt. 13:31-32; Luke 13:18-19)

The third and last parable that Mark recorded Jesus giving to the multitudes, stressed the contrast between the kingdom's insignificant beginnings and its final impressively large size. When Jesus came declaring that the kingdom of heaven was "at hand," He began preparations for the inauguration of the kingdom. He planted the seed. That beginning was a very inauspicious one. Even though Jesus had a popular following, He had few disciples who followed Him faithfully. Nonetheless this parable assured the multitudes that the kingdom would one day be impressively large. The Old Testament predicted that it would cover the earth and incorporate Gentiles as well as Jews (Ps. 2; Ezek. 17:22-24; 31:6; Dan. 4:12; et al.). The final form of the kingdom is at the end of the kingdom, not at its beginning when Jesus comes at His Second Coming to begin it. The parable describes the kingdom, not the church (all genuine Christians), and not Christendom (all professing Christians).

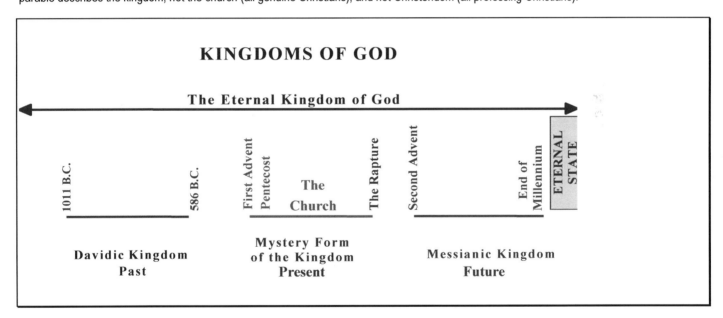

The beginnings of the kingdom were small and discouraging. Jesus experienced rejection and left this world as an apparent failure. Nevertheless God will eventually establish the kingdom that the Old Testament prophets and Jesus predicted—as a worldwide organization that will dominate all aspects of life. This hope encourages believers, especially believers who are suffering for their faith. We can press on knowing that our labor in spreading the gospel is not in vain.

"The example of the mustard seed should prevent us from judging the significance of results by the size of the beginnings."[213]

---

[210]E.g., R. A. Cole, *The Gospel According to Mark*, p. 151.

[211]E.g., Cranfield, p. 168; J. Jeremias, *The Parables of Jesus*, pp. 152-53; and Wessel, pp. 652-53.

[212]E.g., J. Dwight Pentecost, *The Parables of Jesus*, pp. 49, 53; and Grassmick, p. 121.

[213]Nineham, p. 144.

The summary conclusion 4:33-34 (cf. Matt. 13:34-35)

Some of the other parables Jesus taught included the following ones that Matthew recorded: He taught the parable of the weeds (Matt. 13:24-30, 36-43), and the parable of the yeast hidden in the meal (Matt. 13:33), to the multitudes. He also taught the parables of the hidden treasure (Matt. 13:44), the pearl (Matt. 13:45-46), the dragnet (Matt. 13:47-50), and the householder (Matt. 13:52) to the disciples.

Mark concluded his account of Jesus' kingdom parables by explaining Jesus' purpose and approach in teaching this way. These were only a few of the parables Jesus used to correct popular erroneous ideas about the kingdom. The parables were similar to bait for the multitudes. They kept them seeking what Jesus had to offer, which included revelation of Himself as the God-man. When seekers came to follow Jesus as disciples, He explained the true characteristics of His kingdom more clearly to prepare them for it. When Mark said that Jesus was not speaking to the people without parables, he meant that Jesus consistently spoke indirectly and in a veiled manner to them.[214]

The three parables Mark chose to record reveal three important facts about the kingdom. The parable of the soils shows that there will be a variety of responses to the good news about the kingdom. The parable of the seed growing by itself teaches that the good news will bring forth fruit by itself. The parable of the mustard seed reveals that though the word is small, it will eventually produce something very large and beneficial.

When we proclaim the gospel today, we are announcing good news about the kingdom. I do not mean that the gospel of the kingdom that John the Baptist, Jesus, and Jesus' first disciples preached is the same as the gospel of God's grace that we preach. They focused specifically on the Messiah's kingdom as imminent. We focus on trusting in the Messiah. Nevertheless, just as their gospel included the importance of trusting in the Messiah, so ours includes the importance of preparing for the messianic kingdom. At least it should. The coming messianic kingdom should be an important factor in the thinking, motivation, and proclamation of modern disciples of Jesus (cf. Matt 6:10).

C. JESUS' DEMONSTRATIONS OF POWER AND THE NAZARENES' REJECTION 4:35—6:6A

In spite of demonstrations of supernatural power, the multitudes continued to miss seeing who Jesus really was. Why? Because enlightenment comes only as a gift from God (Matt. 16:17). This section presents more evidence of Jesus' identity (4:35—5:43) and the failure of those who knew Him best to understand who He really was (6:1-6a).

1. The demonstrations of Jesus' power 4:35—5:43

There are four miracles in this section. Jesus authenticated His words (vv. 1-34) with His works (4:35—5:43). He demonstrated power over nature, demons, illness, and death. The purpose of these miracles was to demonstrate Jesus' ability to vanquish all powers that are hostile to God.[215]

The stilling of a storm 4:35-41 (cf. Matt. 8:18, 23-27; Luke 8:22-25)

Many unique features of Mark's narrative indicate that at least some of it came from an eyewitness's account: probably Peter. These include mention of "that day" (v. 35), "as He [Jesus] was" and the "other boats" (v. 36), the "stern" and the "cushion" (v. 38), and the rebuke, terror, and bewilderment of the disciples (vv. 38, 41).

4:35-36	Jesus and the disciples would have been crossing from the west to the east side of the lake (cf. 5:1). Fewer people lived on the east side. Evidently Jesus wanted to get away from the multitudes that had given Him no rest all that day (3:20—4:34) and before. Mark normally did not give precise time designations. Probably he did so here ("evening") to impress the reader with Jesus' extreme busyness that moved Him to withdraw temporarily.
4:37-38	The Sea of Galilee was susceptible to sudden violent storms because of its geography.

> "The atmosphere, for the most part, hangs still and heavy, but the cold currents, as they pass from the west, are sucked down in vortices of air, or by the narrow gorges that break upon the lake. Then arise those sudden storms for which the region is notorious."[216]

Jesus was probably sleeping on a seat, "in the stern" of the boat, that had a "cushion" on it. The fact that Jesus could sleep in such a storm shows His physical exhaustion, another indication of His full humanity. This is the only place where Matthew, Mark, and Luke recorded Jesus sleeping, though He slept at other times, of course.

---

[214]Cranfield, pp. 171-72.

[215]Lane, p. 173.

[216]G. A. Smith, *The Historical Geography of the Holy Land*, pp. 441-42.

Mark alone recorded the disciples' rebuke. It was inappropriate because of who Jesus was. However, the disciples did not yet fully appreciate who He was. They did not like the fact that Jesus appeared to be unconcerned about their safety. Note the contrast between the disciples' anxiety and Jesus' lack of concern.

> "It was a cry of distrust, but one often matched by believers today in difficult circumstances when they feel that the Lord has forsaken them."[217]

The disciples should not have been fearful. Jesus had told them that they were going to the other side; He implied that they would arrive there (v. 35). Second, He was with them; they would not die because He would not die before His time. Third, Jesus was sleeping peacefully and was not afraid of the storm. Fourth, He had demonstrated compassion for them and the multitudes many times.

4:39-40   Mark is the only evangelist who recorded the words Jesus spoke. Jesus addressed His creation as His *child* ("Hush, be still"), and it responded accordingly. The wind ceased and the waves calmed down.

> "In the calming of the storm (4:35-41) his 'rebuke' of the wind and 'muzzling' of the waves are phrased in the language of exorcism, recalling the power of God over chaos at creation. Both episodes are effected solely by the word."[218]

> "In Mark's story the sea is a place of chaos and destruction as well as of instruction and fellowship."[219]

Jesus expressed disappointment that the disciples had not demonstrated more mature faith (cf. 7:18; 8:17-18, 21, 32-33; 9:19). "Timid" (NASB, Gr. *deiloi*) means fearful. "No faith" meant no trust in Him on this occasion. They did not yet realize that Jesus was *God*—the One who controls nature (cf. Ps. 89:8-9; 104:5-9; 106:8-9; 107:23-32).

> ". . . Jesus anticipates comprehension on the part of the disciples and they exhibit a profound lack thereof. The upshot is that conflict erupts between Jesus and the disciples, and nowhere is this more apparent than in a series of three boat scenes and two feeding miracles, with the miracles interspersed among the boat scenes."[220]

4:41   The disciples now became even more "afraid" than they had been when the wind and waves were swamping their boat. The Greek words Mark used, *ephobethesan phobon*, describe respectful awe that people feel in the presence of supernatural power (cf. 16:8). They had seen Jesus perform many healings and exorcisms, but this was a new revelation of the extent of His authority. Still they did not understand who He really was, as is clear from their question.

This story should encourage all of Jesus' disciples with the knowledge that He can control the natural circumstances of life, including its storms, and keep them safe. This would have been an especially comforting revelation to Mark's original readers in their persecutions.

> "It is not surprising that in early Christian art the Church was depicted as a boat driven upon a perilous sea; with Jesus in the midst, there was nothing to fear."[221]

> "Assuredly, no narrative could be more consistent with the fundamental assumption that He is the God-Man."[222]

The deliverance of a demoniac in Gadara 5:1-20 (cf. Matt. 8:28-34; Luke 8:26-39)

Even though Mark had already reported that Jesus had exorcized many demons, this case was extraordinary.

> "Christ, Who had been charged by the Pharisees with being the embodiment and messenger of Satan [Matt. 12:24; Mark 3:22; Luke 11:15], is here face to face with the extreme manifestation of demoniac power and influence. It is once more, then, a Miracle in Parable which is about to take place. The question, which had been raised by the enemies, is about to be brought to the issue of a practical demonstration."[223]

---

[217]Hiebert, p. 115.
[218]Edwards, p. 223.
[219]Ellenburg, p. 175.
[220]Kingsbury, p. 97.
[221]Lane, p. 178.
[222]Edersheim, 1:600.
[223]Ibid., 1:609.

"This account, more graphically than any other in the Gospels, indicates that the function of demonic possession is to distort and destroy the image of God in man."[224]

5:1   Mark and Luke called this area "the country of the Gerasenes," but Matthew called it the country of the Gadarenes. Gergesa (also referred to as Gersa and Kersa) was a small village about midway on the eastern shore of the lake. Gadara was a larger town six miles southeast of the lake's southern end. This incident apparently happened somewhere near both towns on the southeast coast of the lake. Another town with a similar name, Gerasa (Jarash), stood 37 miles southeast of the lake, too far southeast to qualify as the site of this miracle.

> "At the site of Kersa the shore is level, and there are no tombs. But about a mile further south there is a fairly steep slope within forty yards from the shore, and about two miles from there cavern tombs are found which appear to have been used for dwellings."[225]

5:2-5   Mark gave many more details describing this man than either Matthew or Luke did. This reflects an eyewitness account and Mark's special interest in demonic activity. Matthew wrote that there were two men, but Mark and Luke mentioned only the more prominent of the two. Mark stressed this man's great physical strength that had progressively increased, evidently due to the demons' increasing hold on him. Now nothing could restrain him. The poor man was miserable in his condition.

5:6-7   The way the man related to Jesus shows that the demons within him recognized Jesus as someone superior to them. The demons controlled the man's physical movements and his words. They addressed Jesus as "Son of the Most High God"—recognizing His deity (Gen. 14:18-24; Num. 24:16; Isa. 14:14; Dan. 3:26; 4:2; cf. Mark 1:23-24). "Most High God" is a title used in the Old Testament, mainly by non-Israelites, to denote the God of Israel.[226] The fact that the man knelt before Jesus likewise shows that the demons regarded Jesus as their superior. The demons feared that Jesus would send them to their eternal judgment immediately, something only God could do (Rev. 20:1-3; cf. Matt. 8:29; Luke 8:31). The tormentor appealed ("I implore You") for deliverance from "torment."[227] Ironically, he appealed to Jesus for mercy *in God's name* ("by God"). He probably did this because he knew that Jesus was subject to His Father.

5:8   Jesus evidently addressed the leading demon. The Greek imperfect tense can mean that Jesus had been repeatedly commanding the demons to depart, as the NASB and NIV translations imply. However, it can also mean that something was about to follow. In this case, a translation such as the AV, "For He said unto him," is better. Apparently in verse 8, Mark gave us the reason for the demons' request in verse 7, even though Jesus did not allow the demons to depart until verse 13.

5:9   These verses resume the conversation from verse 7. A "legion" was 4,000 to 6,000 Roman soldiers.[228] Probably the leading demon used this as a round number to represent thousands of demons (cf. v. 13). The word "legion" also suggests their organization, strength, oppression, and authority over the man they influenced.[229] Probably Jesus asked this question for the disciples' benefit.

5:10   This verse also shows the superiority of Jesus' power (authority), which the demons recognized. It is unclear why the demons wanted to remain in that area of the "country."

5:11-13   Evidently the demons requested permission to enter the swine so they could destroy them. Jesus' permission resulted in everyone seeing the great destructive power and number of the demons, and that the man had experienced an amazing deliverance. Only Mark recorded the number of swine ("about 2,000"). As usual, Mark drew attention to Jesus' awesome power.

> "Few animals are so individually stubborn as swine, yet the rush was simultaneous."[230]

> "The story of the deliverance of a man becomes the story of the deliverance of a land."[231]

Some interpreters believe the owners of the swine were Jews who disregarded the Mosaic prohibition against eating pork (Lev. 11:7). Jesus would then have been punishing them by allowing their pigs to perish. However, this explanation is unlikely because of the demographics of the Decapolis region (mostly Gentile), of which this area was a part (cf. Matt. 8:31).

---

[224]Lane, p. 180.

[225]Ibid., p. 181.

[226]Cranfield, p. 177.

[227]R. Jamieson, A. R. Fausset, and D. Brown, *A Commentary Critical and Explanatory on the Old and New Testaments*, 2:70.

[228]Cranfield, p. 178.

[229]Hiebert, p. 120.

[230]Matthew B. Riddle, "The Gospel According to Mark," in *International Revision Commentary on the New Testament*, p. 60.

[231]Guelich, p. 283.

5:14-15	The "city" in view was probably Gergesa. The demoniac had formerly been a restless raving maniac, but now he was "sitting" peacefully ("in his right mind"). He had been shamelessly naked (Luke 8:27), but now he "clothed" himself. He had been out of control, but now he controlled his senses and himself. The people's fear arose, partially, from anticipating what Jesus might do with the great power that He obviously possessed.
5:16-17	Perhaps the people "implored" Jesus "to leave their" area, because they reasoned that if He dealt so severely with evil—He would eventually destroy them, too. Rather than turning *to* Him in worship, they turned *from* Him to the darkness they preferred (cf. John 1:11; 3:19). Mark's account implies that what happened to the pigs disturbed the local population, suggesting that economic loss played a part in their request.
5:18-19	Why did Jesus instruct the man to tell others about "what great things the Lord" had "done for" him, whereas He had told the cleansed leper not to tell anyone (1:44; cf. 5:43; 7:36)? Apparently there was little danger in this Gentile region that the people would create problems for Jesus' mission, as they *did* cause in Jewish territory. We need not understand Jesus' command as a permanent prohibition against the man's following Him. Perhaps this man rejoined Jesus and become a disciple after he bore witness locally. The synonymous use of the names "Lord" and "Jesus" shows that the man regarded Jesus as God (cf. v. 7; Luke 8:39).

Jesus' instructions to this man in a Gentile region would have helped Mark's original Gentile readers to know what was an appropriate response to His deliverance of them.

> "Though we are not tortured by the devil, yet he holds us as his slaves, till the Son of God delivers us from his tyranny. Naked, torn, and disfigured, we wander about, till he restores us to soundness of mind."[232]

5:20	The "Decapolis" was a league of 10 Greek cities, all but one of which stood on the east side of the lake. One of these towns was Gergesa. The others were Damascus, Kanatha, Scythopolis, Hippos, Raphana, Pella, Dion, Philadelphia, and Gadara.[233]

People marveled at the man's testimony. That was good as far as it went, but it should have led them to seek Jesus out. Perhaps some of them did.

> "Exemplary evangelism is not the point; rather, evangelism serves the Christological point that Jesus' act of power inspired the ex-demoniac to exceed by far the commission that Jesus gave him."[234]

Mark's account of this miracle stressed Jesus' divine power and authority, and these events presented a greater revelation of His person to the disciples than they had previously witnessed. It also provides a model of how disciples can express their gratitude to God for His saving work in their lives.

> "Furthermore, in the flow of Mark's narrative, this story must be read against the backdrop of the dispute between Jesus and the scribes over his exorcisms in 3:22-27. It vividly describes Jesus as the one in whom 'the Most High God's' sovereign rule was being established through the binding of the 'strong man' (3:27) who through Legion had so powerfully controlled a man that no one else could successfully bind with human fetters (5:3-5)."[235]

The raising of Jairus' daughter and the healing of a woman with a hemorrhage 5:21-43 (cf. Matt. 9:18-26; Luke 8:40-56)

This is one of the sections of Mark's Gospel that has a chiastic structure (cf. 3:22-30; 6:14-29; 11:15-19).

A   The appeal of Jairus for his daughter 5:21-24
     B   The healing of the woman with the hemorrhage 5:25-34
A'   The raising of Jairus' daughter to life 5:35-43

In this case, the delay caused by the healing of the woman created a greater problem that Jesus overcame easily. This account of a double miracle further revealed Jesus' identity to His disciples.

> "The healing of Jairus's daughter shows that Jesus is the Lord of life, and the healing of the woman with the problem of persistent bleeding shows that He is the Lord of health."[236]

---

[232]John Calvin, *Commentary on a Harmony of the Evangelists*, 2:436.

[233]J. McKee Adams, *Biblical Backgrounds*, pp. 150-160.

[234]Gundry, p. 255.

[235]Guelich, p. 289.

[236]Bailey, p. 76.

Some commentators believed that Mark did not follow a chronological order of events, but rearranged them to make his theological points.[237] However, all three synoptic evangelists recorded the events in the same order, so perhaps they occurred in this sequence.[238] Mark's account is the fullest of the three.

> "The stilling of the storm and the healing of the demonized were manifestations of the absolute power inherent in Christ; the recovery of the woman and the raising of Jairus' daughter, evidence of the absolute efficacy of faith."[239]

5:21   Having withdrawn from Galilee to the southeastern Decapolis region (4:35—5:20), Jesus and His disciples now returned to the northwestern side of the lake and to Galilee. Immediately, a multitude of Jews "gathered around Him" again.

5:22-24   "Synagogue rulers" were not priests, but lay leaders, who were responsible for the worship services and the synagogue's physical facilities. This honorary title also described distinguished members of the synagogue.[240] As such, "Jairus" (the Greek form of the Hebrew "Jair": "he will give light or awaken"; cf. Num. 32:41; Judg. 10:3) undoubtedly enjoyed much respect in his community. Most healing stories are anonymous, so perhaps Mark included Jairus' name because of its connection with Jesus' miracle of awakening the girl to life (cf. v. 39). "Laying hands on" a sick person for healing associated the power of the healer with the person needing deliverance (cf. 6:5; 7:32; 8:23, 25).

Upon returning to Galilee, Jesus immediately began to serve in response to this urgent emotional plea, but the thronging crowd slowed His progress.

5:25-28   Mark stressed the desperate condition of the woman by recording details of her history that the other evangelists passed over. Uncharacteristically, Mark described the woman's plight with a series of seven participles. She was, before she met Jesus, incurable. She had faith in Jesus' ability to heal her and a belief that she could obtain healing by touching His clothing (cf. 3:10; 6:56). She tried to remain unobtrusive, since her condition rendered her and all who contacted her ritually unclean (Lev. 15:25-27). Perhaps she had come from some distance, since apparently no one in the crowd recognized her, or objected to her being there.

5:29   As soon as (Gr. *euthys*, "immediately") she touched Jesus' garment, she knew that she was whole. The healing was instantaneous, but it happened without Jesus' conscious participation. Such was the power He had.

5:30   Just as quickly (Gr. *euthys*) Jesus perceived that "power . . . had gone" from Him.

> "The immediacy of his knowing, the omniscience with which Mark writes about it, the mention of Jesus' name, and its forward position all show the supernaturalness of Jesus' knowledge to be another point of emphasis."[241]

5:31-32   The harshness of the disciples' reply is unique to Mark. Luke wrote that Peter voiced it (Luke 8:45). Probably the disciples were eager to get Jesus to Jairus' house before it was too late. Yet Jesus wanted to speak to the woman, and to assure her that it was her *faith* in Him that had resulted in her healing, not merely her touch. He "looked around," searching the faces in the crowd to discover the person of faith.

> "His healing power did not work automatically, like a battery discharging its power when accidentally short-circuited. Jesus perceived in Himself, without any external suggestion, the significance of the woman's touch, and, actively willing to honor her faith, He was immediately conscious of His healing power going toward her. His power, the inherent ability to perform, was always under the control of His conscious volition. His consciousness of that power going forth from Him suggests that His healing ministries cost Jesus much spiritual energy. It would explain why He found it necessary at times to escape the crowds to find time for refreshing through fellowship with the Father."[242]

5:33-34   Jesus did not rebuke her, even though her faith in Him seems to have been mixed with superstition. Yet He wanted to speak to her, lest she conclude that *touching* Him was what cured her. His words were full of spiritual sensitivity and compassion.

---

[237]E.g., Hugh Anderson, *The Gospel of Mark*, p. 151; Lane, p. 189; and Wessel, p. 660.

[238]Cf. Cranfield, p. 182; Taylor, p. 289; and Hiebert, p. 125.

[239]Edersheim, 1:616.

[240]Cranfield, p. 183.

[241]Gundry, p. 270.

[242]Hiebert, pp. 129-30. Cf. Cranfield, p. 185.

She had nothing to fear from Him. Perhaps the woman was afraid because she had obtained Jesus' power surreptitiously (stealthily). Still, we have seen that a typical response to the revelation of Jesus' power was fear (cf. 4:41; 5:15).

This is the only place in the Gospels where Jesus called someone "daughter." The woman's faith in Jesus had not only resulted in her physical healing but also (a *double entendre*) brought her into His spiritual family (cf. Isa. 53:10; Mark 3:35; 7:26; 10:52). Her "faith" was the means whereby she obtained Jesus' help. It expressed belief that Jesus *could* heal her and hope that He *would*.

The phrase "Go in peace" (Heb. *shalom*) was a common way of saying "good-bye" among the Jews (cf. Judg. 18:6; 1 Sam. 1:17).

> Shalom ". . . means not just freedom from inward anxiety, but that *wholeness* or *completeness* of life that comes from being brought into a right relationship with God."[243]

It was God's will for this woman to experience healing. Jesus assured her that her healing was complete and permanent with these words: "your faith has made you well." She could now enjoy social interaction and participation in public worship, as well as physical health, since she was clean.

> "From Mark's perspective, the entire incident is a call for radical faith."[244]

5:35   If the disciples had been impatient (v. 31), how much more so must Jairus have been. How his heart must have broken when word reached him that his "daughter" had "died." The people who reported the death of Jairus' daughter regarded Jesus as an ordinary teacher or rabbi. They believed He could only help the living.

> "There is no hint of anyone taking it amiss that Jesus did not proceed as fast as He could to Jairus' house; or that He could have dealt with the haemorrhage [*sic*] after the more serious case of the child at death's door. . . . It is quite Palestinian still to do the things that need doing at the psychological juncture."[245]

5:36   Jairus had believed that Jesus could heal his daughter, and he had just observed the result of believing in Jesus (vv. 25-34). His faith, with Jesus' encouragement, enabled him to "believe" (keep believing) that Jesus could still help his daughter. Literally Jesus said, "Stop fearing; continue believing."

5:37   Jesus "allowed" only His inner circle of disciples "to accompany Him" to witness this miracle (cf. Deut. 17:6; Mark 9:2; 14:33). He probably did so to limit popular reaction to it. If the multitudes thronged to Jesus because He healed them, how much more would they seek His physical help if they knew He could raise the dead.

> "While raising the dead may be the greatest miracle from our perspective, this miracle comes in a series of miracles involving absolutely hopeless situations."[246]

5:38   Jesus dismissed one crowd, but found another one waiting for Him at Jairus' house.[247] As was customary, paid mourners were already at work: weeping, wailing, singing, playing flutes, and clapping their hands (cf. Jer. 9:17; Amos 5:16).[248] The Mishnah specified that even the poorest husband had to hire at least two flute players and one female to wail when his wife died.[249] Evidently the little girl's death was so expected that mourners were ready the moment she died.

5:39-40   Jesus meant that she was "asleep" *in death*. He was using the word "sleep" figuratively (cf. Matt. 9:24; John 11:11-14). He meant that though she was dead, her death would be no more permanent than sleep.[250] The observers present, however, took Jesus' words literally, and mocked the Great Physician for His apparent superficial diagnosis. Their reaction proves that the girl was dead. Jesus excluded them and allowed only those whom He wanted to witness the miracle to stay.

5:41   Apparently Jesus took "the hand" of the dead girl in order to associate His power with her healing in the witnesses' minds. He did not need to touch her to raise her. Elijah (1 Kings 17:17-23) and Elisha (2 Kings 4:18-37) had both raised children to life,

---

[243]Anderson, p. 154.

[244]Lane, p. 194.

[245]Eric F. F. Bishop, *Jesus of Palestine*, p. 137.

[246]Guelich, p. 301.

[247]Swete, p. 107.

[248]Cf. H. Van der Loos, *The Miracles of Jesus*, p. 568.

[249]Mishnah *Ketuboth* 4:4.

[250]Cranfield, p. 189.

but they had to exert considerably more effort, and spend more time doing so, than Jesus did. It was probably this healing that led many of the people to identify Jesus with Elijah (6:15). Touching a dead person resulted in ceremonial defilement, but Jesus overcame this with His power, that was both healing and cleansing.

Mark alone recorded Jesus' command in Aramaic and translated it for his Roman readers.

> "Mark gives the translation as a contrast with magical formulas so esoteric and nonsensical that they mock would-be translators . . ."[251]

In every instance of Jesus raising the dead in the Gospels, He addressed the dead person directly (cf. Luke 7:14; John 11:43).

> "It has been suggested that His very words were those used by the mother each morning to arouse her daughter from sleep."[252]

There is only one letter difference between Jesus' command here and the one Peter uttered when he restored Dorcas to life (Acts 9:40). Peter said, "*Tabitha kum!*" This shows that Jesus continued to exercise His power through Peter after His ascension (cf. Acts 1:1-2).

5:42   When Jesus restored life, recovery was instantaneous (Gr. *euthys*, twice in this verse), not gradual, as was also true with former prophets (cf. 1 Kings 17:19-20; 2 Kings 4:33). Perhaps Mark mentioned the girl's age because she was 12, and the woman whom Jesus had just healed had suffered with her affliction for 12 years (v. 25). The woman had begun living when she should have died from her incurable condition. The girl had died just when she should have begun living as a young woman. Jesus could—and did—deliver both from death. Everyone present expressed extreme amazement at Jesus' power (cf. 4:41). The Greek word, from *existemi*, literally means they were "out of their minds with great amazement."[253]

5:43   Jesus gave the observers two commands. First, He told them not to tell anyone about the miracle who did not need to know about it. Obviously many people outside the house would have discovered what had happened, but Jesus wanted to avoid all unnecessary publicity, at least immediately, so He could continue His ministry with maximum freedom of movement (cf. 1:43-45). He wanted those present to keep the event as private as possible.[254]

His second command revealed His continuing compassion for the girl in her need. It also clarified that He had restored her to physical life that needed sustaining. He had not resurrected her to a new form of life with an immortal body (cf. 1 Cor. 15:35-57).

This double miracle (the raising of Jairus' daughter and the healing of the bleeding woman) taught the disciples that Jesus not only had the power to control nature (4:35-41) and demonic spirits (5:1-20), but also death. These were important revelations to those who had exercised some faith in Him. They learned that Jesus was more than a man, and even more than the greatest of the prophets. Undoubtedly God used these revelations to enable the disciples to see that Jesus was the divine Messiah (8:29).

> "Faith involved more than simply believing Jesus could perform miracles. No one questioned that in Nazareth. They questioned how he could do what he was doing because of who they 'know' him to be. By implication, therefore, healing faith for Mark in these two stories means more than faith in a miracle worker. Both Jairus and the woman displayed faith that God was somehow at work in Jesus. Therefore, the evangelist uses these stories to underscore the role of faith and its corollary, the person of Jesus as seen in his ministry that highlights the role of faith in these stories."[255]

2. Jesus' rejection by the Nazarenes 6:1-6a (cf. Matt. 13:54-58)

Even though Jesus gave ample evidence that He was more than a mere man (4:35—5:43), those who knew Him best on the physical plane still refused to believe in Him (6:1-6a). This refusal led Jesus to turn increasingly from the multitudes to the training of His disciples (6:6b—8:30).

6:1   Mark mentioned the disciples' presence with Jesus, but Matthew omitted that detail. Mark evidently recorded this incident because it constituted another occasion of discipleship training, a particular concern of Mark's in this section of his Gospel. Jesus visited Nazareth as a rabbi preparing His disciples for their ministry. This was the second rejection in Nazareth that the

---

[251]Robert H. Gundry, *Mark*, p. 274.

[252]Hiebert, p. 136.

[253]Grassmick, p. 126.

[254]Cranfield, p. 191.

[255]Guelich, p. 305.

synoptic writers documented. The first one came when Jesus left Nazareth to establish His base of operations in Capernaum (Matt. 4:13; Luke 4:16-31).

6:2-3   The reaction of the people in this synagogue contrasts with that of Jairus, the ruler of another synagogue (5:22). Mark recorded three questions the observers in Nazareth raised. They wondered "*where*" Jesus got the teaching and the authority that He demonstrated. They asked each other *who* had given Him the "wisdom" He manifested, and they questioned *how* Jesus had obtained His ability to do "miracles." Obviously they had not concluded that they came from God. Their questions manifested unbelief and hostility. Their personal acquaintance with Jesus' family, and Jesus' former manner of life among them, made it hard for them to think of Him as anything more than a mere man. This is the only place in the New Testament where the writer referred to Jesus as a carpenter. A "carpenter" (Gr. *tekton*) worked with stone and metal, as well as wood.[256] Jesus' critics asked, rhetorically, whether Jesus was not just a common worker with His hands, as most of them were.

> "It was the common practice among the Jews to use the father's name, whether he were alive or dead. A
> man was called the son of his mother only when his father was unknown."[257]

Formerly the people of Nazareth had referred to Jesus as Joseph's son (Luke 4:22). Evidently they now called Him "the son of Mary" as a deliberate insult, implying that He was an illegitimate child (cf. Judg. 11:1-2; John 8:41; 9:29). The Jews did not speak insultingly about such a person's birth if they believed he lived a life pleasing to God, but if that person became an apostate, they spoke publicly and unreservedly about his illegitimate birth.[258] Consequently this appellation reflects the belief of the Nazarenes that Jesus was not virgin born and was displeasing to God.[259]

6:4   Jesus either quoted or invented a proverb to reply to their rejection. It expressed a principle, namely: familiarity breeds contempt. Jesus implied that He was "a prophet," which He was. The people of Nazareth could not even appreciate this aspect of Jesus' character, because they regarded Him as someone just like themselves.

6:5-6a   Mark stressed that Jesus performed miracles in response to faith. Here we see the other side of that coin. The Nazarenes' refusal to believe in Jesus resulted in His not being able to do many miracles among them. "Unbelief" limits God's working (cf. Acts 14:9-10).

> "The point of ouk edunato ["no miracle"] is not that Jesus was powerless apart from men's faith, but that in
> the absence of faith he could not work mighty works *in accordance with the purpose of his ministry*; for to
> have worked miracles where faith was absent would, in most cases anyway, have been merely to have
> aggravated men's guilt and hardened them against God."[260]

This is the only time Mark said that Jesus was amazed. He marveled that the unbelief of the Nazarenes was as strong as it was. This implies that their decision not to believe was in spite of evidence adequate to lead them to another conclusion. They were morally blameworthy for their unbelief.

> "The people of Nazareth represent Israel's blindness. Their refusal to believe in Jesus pictured what the disciples would soon
> experience (cf. 6:7-13) and what Mark's readers (then and now) would experience in the advance of the gospel."[261]

IV. THE SERVANT'S SELF-REVELATION TO THE DISCIPLES 6:6B—8:30

The increasing hostility of Israel's religious leaders, and the rejection by the multitudes (3:7—6:6a), led Jesus to concentrate increasingly on training His disciples. This section of Mark's Gospel shows how Jesus did that. While Jesus gave His disciples increasing responsibility for ministry (6:6b-30), the focus of Jesus' instruction was His own identity, which the disciples had great difficulty understanding (6:31—8:30).

> "After the 'beginning of the gospel' in 1:1-15, the first half of Mark's Gospel falls rather neatly into three major sections (1:16—
> 3:12; 3:13—6:6; 6:7—8:26). Each section opens with a story about the disciples (1:16-20; 3:1-19; and 6:7-13). Each section

---

[256]Ibid., p. 310.

[257]Hiebert, p. 139.

[258]See Ethelbert Stauffer, *Jesus and His Story*, pp. 207-8, cf. pp. 16-17.

[259]Cf. Cranfield, p. 195.

[260]Ibid., p. 197.

[261]Grassmick, p. 127.

winds down with a story about the negative response generated by Jesus' ministry (3:1-6; 6:1-6a; 8:14-21). And each section concludes with a summary statement that recalls for the reader the nature of Jesus' ministry (3:7-12; 6:6b; 8:22-26)."[262]

A. THE MISSION OF THE TWELVE 6:6B-30

This is another of Mark's "sandwich" or chiastic sections. The main event is Jesus' sending the Twelve on a preaching and healing mission that extended His own ministry. Within this story, between their departing and their returning, the writer inserted the story of John the Baptist's death. The main feature of that story that interested Mark was Herod Antipas' perception of who Jesus was. The identity of Jesus, which is the heart of this section, becomes the main subject of the sections that follow (6:31—8:30).

1. The sending of the Twelve 6:6b-13 (cf. Matt. 9:35—11:1; Luke 9:1-6)

Jesus continued to minister in Galilee. His ministry to the Twelve was an important part of His ministry. It prepared the disciples for further future service. It also anticipated His ministry through them following His ascension. This was the third tour of the Galilean villages that Mark reported (cf. 1:14, 39).

6:6b   This brief transitional statement introduces Jesus twofold ministry, personally and through His disciples. Mark's interest lay in the disciples' training, so he stressed that. Matthew gave a slightly longer explanation of Jesus' personal ministry (Matt. 9:35).

6:7   Jesus "summoned the Twelve" to Himself, and then sent them out as His official representatives (cf. 3:14). In Jesus' culture, a person who was sent (a messenger) was regarded exactly as the person who sent (the master).[263] Jesus was following Jewish custom and wisdom in sending the disciples out "in pairs," which Mark alone mentioned (cf. Deut. 17:6; 19:15; Eccles. 4:9-12). This was primarily to validate the truthfulness of their message by providing two witnesses (cf. Num. 35:30; Deut. 17:6). The Twelve were to preach the kingdom of God (Luke 9:2) and to perform miracles to authenticate their message for their Jewish audiences (Matt. 10:1; Luke 9:1-2). Mark only mentioned "authority over" demons, as it was the most powerful demonstration of Jesus' power at work through them. This was a mission that would prepare the Twelve for greater responsibility in Jesus' service later.

> "Jesus authorized the disciples to be his delegates with respect to both word and power. Their message and deeds were to be an extension of his own."[264]

6:8-9   The Twelve were to take with them no food, no luggage, and no money.

> "It was customary both in the east and the west to keep small change in one's girdle ["belt"]."[265]

They were not even to take the usual extra tunic—that Palestinians often used as a blanket at night. The Twelve were to rely on God to provide their needs, including the need for hospitable hosts. The urgency of their mission required light travel, and it prohibited elaborate preparations. They could take a walking stick ("staff"), and they would need "sandals," but they were not to take spares. Apparently Jesus stressed what *not* to take more than what *to* take, in order to deprive the disciples of any sense of self-sufficiency.[266]

Matthew's account reported Jesus forbidding shoes, whereas Mark said He permitted them (Matt. 10:10). Probably a spare pair of sandals was what Jesus forbade. Matthew 10:9-10 and Luke 9:3 forbid taking a staff, but Mark 6:8 allows one. One solution to this apparent contradiction may be that Jesus gave these instructions on more than one occasion.[267] Jesus was training His disciples to *serve*, not to lord it over others or to expect others to serve them.

> "The particular instructions apply literally only to this brief mission during Jesus' lifetime; but in principle, with the necessary modifications according to climate and other circumstances, they still hold for the

---

[262]Guelich, p. 316.

[263]Lane, pp. 206-7.

[264]Ibid., p. 206.

[265]Cranfield, p. 199.

[266]Guelich, p. 322.

[267]See Monte A. Shanks, "An Alternative Solution to an Alleged Contradiction in the Gospels," *Bibliotheca Sacra* 169:675 (July-September 2012):317-27.

continuing ministry of the Church. The service of the Word of God is still a matter of extreme urgency, calling for absolute self-dedication."[268]

6:10-11   The 12 disciples were normally to stay in the home of a hospitable host, as long as they remained in that particular town, rather than moving from house to house. This would minimize distractions and tend to preserve the good reputation of the disciple, whom others might consider greedy if he moved frequently. Moving to better accommodations for the sake of comfort would also bring shame on the former host.

The Jews customarily shook the dust off their clothes and sandals when they reentered Jewish territory from Gentile territory.[269]

"In the culture of the time the gospel was written, Jews made a distinction between Jewish and gentile territory. Jews considered their land to be holy and the gentile land unclean."[270]

Shaking dust off their feet symbolized the defiling effect of contact with pagans. When the Twelve did this, it implied that those who had refused their message were unbelieving, defiled, and subject to divine judgment (cf. Acts 13:51; 18:6).

"It was a visible sign of acceptance or rejection of the Master and the Father Who sent Him (Mt. x. 40, Lk. x. 16), and therefore an index of the relation in which the inhabitants as a whole stood to the eternal order."[271]

This act would cause those who rejected the message to reconsider their decision.

6:12-13   The Twelve were to do the same three things that Jesus did in His ministry (cf. 1:4, 14-15, 32-34, 39; 3:10). Their mission was an extension of His mission (cf. 16:15-20). Mark did not mention that Jesus sent them only to the Jews. Perhaps he wanted his readers to view themselves as carrying on Jesus' ministry as the Twelve did then (cf. Matt. 10:5-6). The Twelve learned that Jesus' power extended beyond His personal presence, and that God would work through them as He did through Jesus.

"Their coming to a village brought healing and salvation in the most comprehensive terms *because they were his representatives*. Jesus had commissioned them and they came in his name. What Jesus did in his own power as commissioned by God, the disciples did in his power."[272]

Mark alone mentioned the Twelve "anointing" people "with oil." People commonly applied oil for medicinal purposes in Jesus' day (cf. Luke 10:34; James 5:14).[273] This ritual also symbolized God coming on the anointed person, enabling that one to serve Him, and setting the anointed person apart for God's use. This, too, would have special significance for reader disciples who had experienced God's anointing with the Holy Spirit at conversion, and who had a similar ministry in their (and our) day.

This pericope shows Jesus continuing to train His disciples for the ministry that lay before them, and continuing to extend His own ministry of service through them. In their duties, the manner of their service, and their responses to the reactions to their ministry, they were to conduct themselves as the servants of the Servant.

"Hitherto they had been like young children in a family under the care of their parents, or like young birds in a nest sheltered by their mother's wing, and needing only to open their mouths wide in order to get them filled; now they were to become like boys leaving their father's house to serve an apprenticeship, or like fledglings leaving the warm nest in which they were nursed, to exercise their wings and seek food for themselves."[274]

"This participation of the Twelve in Jesus' ministry and its apparent success contributes greatly to the irony in Mark's portrait of the Twelve in this segment of the Gospel (6:7—8:26). On the one hand, it opens with this special mission whose success

[268]Cranfield, p. 200.
[269]Wessel, p. 667.
[270]Rhoads and Michie, p. 70.
[271]Plummer, p. 144.
[272]Lane, p. 209.
[273]Merrill F. Unger, "Divine Healing," *Bibliotheca Sacra* 128:511 (July-September 1971):236.
[274]Bruce, *The Training . . .*, p. 113.

reported in 6:30 apparently reached to Herod's court (6:14) and led to a relentless response by the crowds (6:31-33). On the other hand, the very Twelve who experienced a special calling and relationship with Jesus and now participate fully in this ministry are seen to lack understanding (6:52; 7:18; 8:14-21) and even reflect a 'hardened heart' (6:52; 8:17-18). This growing irony between the Twelve's special privilege and lack of understanding has its seed in the previous section (e.g., 4:11; cf. 4:13; 4:33-34; cf. 4:41)."[275]

2. The failure of Antipas to understand Jesus' identity 6:14-29

The writer of the second Gospel inserted this account into his narrative about the mission of the Twelve. It is similar to the filling in a sandwich (cf. v. 30). The incident probably happened during the mission of the Twelve just announced. It illustrates the mounting opposition to Jesus, and it provides helpful guidance for disciples of Jesus. Mark's is the fullest of the synoptic records at this point.

The varying opinions about Jesus' identity 6:14-16 (cf. Matt. 14:1-3; Luke 9:7-9)

6:14   "Herod" Antipas was not really a king, "king" being a popular designation rather than an official title in his case. He was the tetrarch (ruler of one of four [political] divisions) who was born in 20 B.C., and ruled over Galilee and Perea from 4 B.C. to A.D. 39, when he was banished to Gaul. Perea lay east of the Jordan River and south of the Decapolis. Its northern border was about halfway between the Sea of Galilee and the Dead Sea, and its southern border was about halfway between the northern and southern ends of the Dead Sea. The territory of Ammon lay east of Perea. Mark probably called Antipas a king because that is how the people in his territory spoke of him popularly.[276] It was natural for Mark, who was writing for Romans, to use this title since the Roman government used it to describe all eastern rulers.[277]

The antecedent of "it" (NASB) or "this" (NIV) seems to be the ministry of Jesus' disciples (vv. 7-13). Their ministry focused on the identity of Jesus, which is the subject of this pericope. Interestingly, Jesus sent them on this mission even though their own understanding of His identity was still partial. He wanted them to share what they knew then, even though they would understand more later.

Matthew recorded that Herod had heard "the report (news) concerning Jesus" (Matt. 14:1), and Luke wrote that he heard of "all that was happening" (Luke 9:7). These are complementary, not mutually exclusive descriptions. Herod heard about the ministry that Jesus was carrying on.

People were explaining Jesus' miraculous powers in several different ways. Mark mentioned three. Some said "John the Baptist" had "risen from the dead," and he was the person doing these miracles. John had not performed miracles before his death (John 10:41), so this view may have arisen from misinformation.

> "John was a forerunner of Jesus in his birth, ministry, and death. Also the way people identified John the Baptist was as varied as the way they identified Jesus."[278]

6:15-16   Perhaps the view that Jesus was "Elijah" owed its origin to John's description of Jesus as "the Coming One" (Mal. 3:1; 4:5; cf. Deut. 18:15-19). Some people concluded that Jesus was "a prophet" (like one of the Old Testament prophets) because of His preaching and miracle working powers. Herod's view that Jesus was John resurrected to life seems to have originated from his guilty conscience—since he had murdered John. Evidently Herod had not heard about Jesus before he killed John.

The death of Jesus' forerunner 6:17-29 (cf. Matt. 14:4-12)

Verses 17-29 are a flashback account, in which Mark explained how John had died. This is the only story in Mark's Gospel that does not concern Jesus directly.[279] Why did Mark include it? Perhaps he did so because John's death prefigured Jesus' violent end. Mark devoted 14 verses to John's death but only three to his ministry. He really gave two passion narratives: Jesus' and John's.[280]

> "Though not directly concerned with Jesus, it is yet relevant to the history of Jesus, the passion of the Forerunner being a pointer to the subsequent passion of the Messiah (cf. ii. 19f.). The parallels between vi. 17-29 and xv. 1-47 are interesting: e.g. Herod's fear of John as *aner dikaios kai hagios* ["a righteous and holy man"] (v. 20) and Pilate's attitude to Jesus (xv. 5, 14);

---

[275]Guelich, p. 324.

[276]Taylor, p. 308.

[277]Bruce, "The Synoptic . . .," 1:380.

[278]Bailey, p. 77.

[279]Taylor, p. 310.

[280]Lane, p. 215.

Herodias' implacable hatred of John and the Jewish leaders' implacable hatred of Jesus; Herod's and Pilate's yielding to pressure; the details of the burials of John and Jesus."[281]

Mark showed particular interest in what "King" Herod Antipas, and especially Herodias, did to John.[282] The main reason Mark included this pericope will emerge later (9:13).

6:17-18   Herod Philip I was in fact Herod Antipas' half-brother, not brother.[283] Herodias was the daughter of Aristobulus, the son of Herod the Great and Mariamne, and therefore the niece of Herod Antipas.[284] It was unlawful for Herod to marry Herodias because their "marriage" was incestuous; it was also adulterous—because Philip was still alive (cf. Lev. 18:16; 20:21)! Antipas had converted to Judaism, so he had placed himself under Mosaic Law.[285]

    "We behold in John an illustrious example of that moral courage, which all pious teachers ought to possess, not to hesitate to incur the wrath of the great and powerful, as often as it may be found necessary: for he, with whom there is acceptance of persons, does not honestly serve God."[286]

    "Not even the royal house was exempt from the call to radical repentance."[287]

6:19-20   Antipas' passion for Herodias conflicted with his respect for and interest in John. He wanted to maintain both relationships, and tension arose as a result.

    "Kingliness changed places: the subject did not fear the sovereign; the sovereign feared the subject."[288]

Antipas could live with this tension, but Herodias could not, so she sought to kill her rival. Antipas evidently protected John from Herodias, the latter day Jezebel. John was "righteous" in his relations with other people, and "holy" in his relationship to God. The perplexity the king felt undoubtedly arose over his conflicting affections for Herodias and John. Sometimes unrepentant sinners are curious about spiritual matters and spiritual people. This seems to have been true of Antipas. Probably the king and John conversed whenever Herod visited the Machaerus fortress, east of the Jordan River, where John was a prisoner. Its site in southern Perea, south of the north end of the Dead Sea, overlooked that sea. This was probably the site of this whole event.[289]

    "Herod was awed by the purity of John's character, feared him as the bad fear the good."[290]

6:21-23   Finally Herodias was able to trick her husband into getting rid of her nemesis. Salome was Herodias' daughter by Philip. She would have been in her mid-teens at this time, and her dance was undoubtedly lascivious.[291] The phrase "up to half of my kingdom" is figurative, meaning "at great personal sacrifice" (cf. Esth. 5:3; 7:2). Antipas could not have given away half of his kingdom because he lacked the authority to do so.

    "There is also a certain likeness between Esther's accomplishment of the destruction of Haman and Salome's of that of John. Perhaps the story of Salome reminded Mark of Esther, with the result that he used some of the language of LXX Esther."[292]

6:24-25   Women were not present at such banquets as observers. Consequently Salome had to leave the banquet hall to confer with her mother. The daughter apparently shared her mother's hatred for John the Baptist, rather than Herod's respect for him. She hurried back to Herod with her request before he might change his extravagant offer. Perhaps she asked for John's head "on a platter" to humiliate him further, comparing John to an animal—slain and prepared for dinner.

[281]Cranfield, pp. 208-9.

[282]For discussions of the differences between Mark and Josephus' accounts of John's death, see ibid., pp. 208-9; Taylor, pp. 310-11; or Lane, pp. 215-16.

[283]See ibid., p. 218, for a diagram of the Herodian family tree.

[284]Cranfield, p. 209.

[285]Hiebert, p. 149.

[286]Calvin, 2:222.

[287]Lane, p. 219.

[288]Morison, p. 152.

[289]Lane, p. 216; Harold W. Hoehner, *Herod Antipas*, pp. 146-48.

[290]Swete, p. 123.

[291]Lane, p. 221.

[292]Cranfield, p. 212.

6:26-28   The only other time Mark used the Greek word *perilupos*, translated "very sorry" or "greatly distressed," was in 14:34 where it describes Jesus' agony in Gethsemane. This rare usage shows the extent of Antipas' anxiety over the dilemma Salome's request created for him. His pride got him in trouble, as Pilate's did later. Both of these rulers sacrificed a righteous and holy man on the altar of their personal popularity.

The Greek word *spekoulatora*, translated "executioner," is a Latinism reflecting the Roman influence on Mark's Gospel. It refers to a bodyguard of Herod's. The fact that John's "head" finally went to Herodias shows that she was the person responsible for his death. However, her husband gave the order to execute him, so he was also culpable. In Jesus' case, the Jewish religious leaders called for His death, as Herodias had done, and Pilate, like Herod, gave the official order for execution.

6:29   The parallels between John's burial and Jesus' are also striking (cf. 15:42-47). John died alone; his disciples were not with him. The same was true of Jesus, with the exception of His disciple John and some of His female disciples. Herod gave John's disciples permission to bury John's corpse, as Pilate permitted Joseph of Arimathea to bury Jesus. The disciples of each man gave their teacher an honorable burial in a tomb.

This pericope shows that people who preach repentance, and point to Jesus as the Messiah, can expect: opposition, persecution, imprisonment, and perhaps a martyr's death. This is a comfort for disciples who suffer for their witness for Jesus. It does not relieve them of their suffering or hold out the hope of escape, but it does enable them to see that they are in the best of company. This is some encouragement. Historically martyrs have found strength in remembering that they are part of a large company who have shared the sufferings of their Savior.

3. The return of the Twelve 6:30 (cf. Luke 9:10)

This verse marks the conclusion of the apostolic mission of the Twelve that the writer introduced in verses 7-13. With that phase of Jesus' training of the Twelve completed, He moved on to the next stage.

This is the only time Mark called the Twelve "apostles" (Gr. *apostoloi*, lit. sent ones). There is not any good textual evidence for its presence in 3:14. The 12 apostles now returned to the One who had sent them out, and "reported to Him" regarding what had transpired. Mark used "apostles" in the general sense of authorized representatives or agents (cf. Acts 14:14; et al.), rather than as a technical title (cf. Eph. 2:20; et al.).

"This agent operates in the name of the one having given the authorization. Therefore, the term 'apostles' and their action of reporting to Jesus demonstrate the Twelve's dependent relationship to Jesus. Their mission was an extension of his mission."[293]

These men, with the exception of Judas Iscariot, later became the official "apostles." They evidently presented their report to Jesus somewhere in Galilee, possibly near Capernaum.

B. THE FIRST CYCLE OF SELF-REVELATION TO THE DISCIPLES 6:31—7:37

Mark arranged selected events in Jesus' training of His disciples to show how He brought them to a deeper understanding of who He was, and to a deeper commitment to Himself. Jesus led them through two similar series of experiences to teach them these lessons. He had to do it twice because the disciples where slow to learn.

1. The feeding of the 5,000 6:31-44 (cf. Matt. 14:13-21; Luke 9:11-17; John 6:1-13)

Mark's account of this miracle plays an important role in his Gospel. The unusually long introduction provides the setting for this miracle. It stresses Jesus' humanity, and the miracle itself demonstrates His deity. Mark later referred to this miracle twice (6:52; 8:17-21), showing that the disciples did not learn what they should have from it. This meal on the mountainside contrasts with the feast in Antipas' fortress that Mark just described (vv. 17-29). It shows the simplicity of Jesus' provision for a vast multitude—compared to Herod's sumptuous and selfish banquet, that resulted in the death of a righteous and holy man.[294] There is also an emphasis in this section of the Gospel on how Jesus cares for His own.

6:31   This verse does not appear in any of the other Gospels. Jesus provided "rest" for His busy servants, by leading them out to a lonely area of wilderness (Gr. *eremos*), where the crowds—that were now greater than ever—were not as likely to follow (cf. 1:35). This place was near Bethsaida Julius on the northeast side of the lake (cf. Luke 9:10; John 6:1). It is interesting that Mark did not record Jesus' evaluation of the disciples' work, but mentioned His *consideration* for them as workers.

"For continued effectiveness, every worker must now and then stop to take a breath and relax a little."[295]

[293]Guelich, pp. 338-39.
[294]Cf. ibid., p. 227.
[295]Hiebert, p. 156.

| 6:32-34 | "Many" people anticipated where Jesus was heading with His disciples in a large "boat," probably a fishing boat (Gr. *ploion*). They were able to skirt the northern end of the lake "on foot," and meet the boat when it landed. Instead of feeling frustrated, Jesus felt compassion for the multitudes. He saw them as sheep lacking a shepherd who would provide for their needs (cf. Num. 27:17; 1 Kings 22:17; 2 Chron. 18:16; Ezek. 34:5). As David had done, Jesus provided for His sheep in a remote wilderness area (John 10:1-21; cf. Ezek. 34:23-25). He began to teach them, and apparently did so for many hours (v. 35). Teaching was their greatest need, though healing was what they craved. |

> "The fact that we have six accounts of Jesus' feeding a multitude in the gospels (two in Mk, two parallels in Mt., one in Lk. And one in Jn) indicates that the early Church regarded the feeding(s) as being among the greatest and most luminous for faith of the mighty works of Jesus."[296]

| 6:35-36 | The disciples assumed that Jesus wanted the people to provide their own suppers. They reminded Jesus of the time ("already quite late") so He could dismiss them. Jesus had something else in mind. He wanted to teach the disciples and the multitudes to look to Him for their needs. He was the ultimate source of all they needed. |

> "The extended conversation of Jesus with his disciples concerning bread is the distinctive element in the Marcan account of the feeding of the multitude."[297]

Bread is the pervading motif of 6:14—8:30.[298]

| 6:37 | Jesus suggested that the disciples themselves feed the people, because He wanted them to realize their inability to do so. The word "you" is emphatic in the Greek text. Having admitted their inability, Jesus' ability would make a greater impression on them. It would teach them that He was different from them. The disciples' response shows that they had not yet learned to look to Jesus for all their needs. Instead of asking Him to provide what the people needed, they calculated the cost of the food and concluded that they could not afford to pay for it. "Two hundred denarii" was the equivalent of an entire year's wages for a day laborer (cf. Matt. 20:2). |

| 6:38 | Jesus asked them "how many loaves" of bread they had, because He would use what they had to feed the multitude. Normally Jesus uses what His disciples have to meet the needs of others. While the loaves were inadequate, they were still essential elements in this miracle. While disciples need to realize the inadequacy of their resources, they also need to understand that it is those resources, as inadequate as they are, that Jesus uses. The barley "loaves" in view were small and flat (cf. John 6:9). One person could eat several of them in one meal.[299] The "two *small* fish" (Gr. *opsaria*) were probably salted and dried, and were commonly eaten, bones and all, with bread as a relish.[300] |

| 6:39-40 | Mark alone noted the "green grass," thus dating this miracle in the late winter or early spring. John dated it more specifically as near Pentecost, which fell in late March or early April (John 6:4). Hoehner dated this Pentecost at April 13-14, A.D. 32.[301] In the summer, much of the grass turns brown in Palestine. |

The orderly division of the people at least facilitated the distribution of food. The Greek phrases *symposia symposia* (v. 39) and *prasiai prasiai* (v. 40) picture the people spread out on the hillside like several garden plots. This organization may reflect the student-teacher relationship that the rabbis fostered by seating their students in rows.[302] This seems farfetched to me. Another suggestion is that Jesus intended this arrangement to recall Israel camping in the wilderness (cf. Exod. 18:21).[303] The reader should then view Jesus as the second Moses, and the crowd as the new people of God.[304] This view has some attractive elements. However, most of those present were probably unbelievers.

| 6:41 | By praying, Jesus gave God thanks for ("blessed") the food and reminded the people that it came from Him. Giving thanks before meals was a common Jewish and early Christian practice. Jesus "blessed" God for giving the food. He did not bless the |

[296]Cranfield, p. 216.

[297]Lane, p. 228.

[298]Ibid., p. 210.

[299]Wessel, p. 673.

[300]Edersheim, 1:682.

[301]Harold W. Hoehner, *Chronological Aspects of the Life of Christ*, p. 143.

[302]P. Carrington, *According to Mark*, p. 136.

[303]Guelich, p. 341.

[304]Lane, pp. 229-30.

food itself. "Looking up toward heaven" further clarified that it was *God* to whom He was praying, though looking down while praying was customary. The bread was probably "finger-thick, plate-shaped 'loaves.'"[305]

Mark did not record how Jesus performed the miracle, though evidently the multiplication happened in Jesus' hands. He stressed that it was Jesus who did it. This was the most important point to him. Jesus met the needs of people in innumerable creative ways. It is important for disciples to focus on the source of the provision, God, rather than the means and methods He uses to provide. By thanking God for the food, and then providing it miraculously for the people, Jesus was presenting evidence that He was God. Thoughtful individuals in the crowd remembered God's miraculous provision of manna in the wilderness (John 6:14), and realized that Jesus was God's Servant who delivered what God provided; i.e., He was "a second Moses."

Jesus served the people through the disciples, who presented what He had provided to the multitudes. The disciples served as waiters. This is the work of servant disciples. This was another lesson in discipleship.

6:42-44   The abundance and adequacy of Jesus' provision were obvious in the amount of food scraps that remained uneaten. The "baskets" (Gr. *kophinoi*), "twelve full" ones, were large wicker types, though there was not much edible food left over. Some authorities believe *kophinoi* describes small baskets, but most believe they were large. Jesus provides generously, but He does not provide so extravagantly that there is needless waste.

> "It is possible to conclude that the leftovers gave each disciple enough food for his own use. When we put the will of God first, He will care for our needs (Matt. 6:33) and provide our daily bread."[306]

This miracle revealed the person of Jesus to the multitudes, but it was its effect on the disciples that Mark stressed. As noted, this miraculous event contained many lessons about discipleship, as well as revelations of Jesus' identity.

2. Jesus' walking on the water and the return to Galilee 6:45-56

Jesus now returned from the northeast coast of the lake to its northwest coast.

The walking on the water 6:45-52 (cf. Matt. 14:22-33; John 6:14-21)

This miracle followed the feeding of the 5,000 by just a few hours. Both miracles were important parts of Jesus' discipleship training program for the Twelve. Earlier Jesus had calmed the sea with a command from His *mouth* (4:35-41). Here, He used His *whole body* to walk on top of the sea.

6:45   The feeding of the 5,000 evidently happened on the northeast side of the Sea of Galilee, south of Bethsaida Julius. This town stood immediately east of the place where the Jordan River empties into the lake on its northern coast. Some of the town may have been on the western side of the Jordan.[307] Evidently Jesus sent His disciples to another Bethsaida, near Capernaum, by boat (cf. John 6:17). Peter, Andrew, and Philip were evidently from this other Bethsaida (John 1:45; 12:21), and Peter and Andrew's home was in Capernaum (Mark 1:29). So the two villages must have been very close together, perhaps even connected.[308] "The boat" was the one they had used to travel in earlier that day (v. 32). God had appeared to Israel from a mountain (Deut. 33:2; Hab. 3:3), and now Jesus appeared to His disciples after being on a mountain with God in prayer.[309]

6:46   This is the second of the three crises, all at night, that moved Jesus to pray, that Mark recorded (cf. 1:35; 14:32-36). Evidently the desire of the multitudes—to take Jesus by force to make Him king—drove Him to pray (Gr. *proseuchomai*, cf. John 6:15). This was another temptation to secure Israel's leadership without the Cross. References to Jesus praying always show His humanity and His dependence on His Father. The mountain contrasts with the shore where Jesus left the disciples.

> "As in 1:35, Jesus' praying may recommend him as a godly person, not a criminal worthy of crucifixion; but there is no indication that he prays for power to work miracles. According to Mark, that power already resides in Jesus."[310]

---

[305]Guelich, p. 342.
[306]*The Nelson* . . ., p. 1654.
[307]Hiebert, p. 164.
[308]Edersheim, 2:3-4.
[309]Guelich, p. 349.
[310]Gundry, p. 335.

6:47-48	The disciples had evidently reached Bethsaida Julius, but Jesus had not yet come to them (John 6:17). The disciples had then turned their boat toward Capernaum (cf. John 6:17). Perhaps Mark implied that Jesus had supernatural vision.[311] Others have suggested that it would have been easy for Jesus to see the disciples from His prayer site on the hilltop, since they would have been only a few miles from where He was praying. Perhaps the moon illuminated the lake. They were "in the middle of the lake (sea)," in the sense that they were quite far from the coastline. The "fourth watch of the night"—by Roman reckoning, which Mark followed—would have been between 3:00 and 6:00 a.m. (The Jews divided the night into three watches.[312]) Jesus intended to pass beside the disciples, perhaps to reassure them (cf. Exod. 33:19, 22; 34:6; 1 Kings 19:11; Mark 6:50).

"Mark relates that 'He would have passed by then [*sic*, them],' affecting strangeness, as we understand it, out of delicate consideration for their weakness. He knew what He would be taken for when first observed; and therefore He wished to attract their attention at a safe distance, fearing lest, by appearing among them at once, He might drive them distracted [insane]."[313]

Another explanation is that Jesus intended to pass by them because He wanted the disciples to call to Him for help.[314]

Even though Jesus had been praying, He had not forgotten or forsaken His disciples. He was probably praying for them.

". . . instead of a story about Jesus' rescue of his disciples who are distressed but not in danger (cf. 4:35-41), this is an epiphany story about Jesus' self-revelation to his own followers."[315]

"Whenever the master is absent from the disciples (or appears to be so, as in Ch. 4:35-41), they find themselves in distress. And each time they experience anguish it is because they lack faith (Chs. 4:35ff.; 6:45ff.; 9:14ff.)."[316]

6:49-50	Mark noted that "all" the disciples "saw" Jesus, and they all thought He was a phantom (Gr. *phantasma*). Jesus told them to "take courage" and stop fearing (cf. Isa. 41:10, 13-14; 43:1; 44:2). Some interpreters believe the reference to Jesus passing by them (v. 48) and His words, "It is I," indicate a theophany (cf. Exod. 3:14; 33:19, 22; 1 Kings 19:11; Isa. 41:4; 43:10; 51:12; 52:6). Undoubtedly the clause at least indicates self-identification.

". . . Jesus' walking on the water (6:45-52) connotes that Jesus treads where only God can walk [Job 9:8; cf. Ps. 77:19; Isa. 43:16] and designates Jesus by the same expression (*ego eime* [I am]) that is used for God's self-disclosure to Moses (Exod 3:14 LXX)."[317]

"Consequently, as the concluding story of the miracle collection, it provides the answer to the 'Who is this?' question posed by the disciples after Jesus stills the storm in the opening story of the collection (4:41)."[318]

6:51	Mark omitted the record of Peter walking on the water (Matt. 14:28-31). This seems unusual if Peter influenced Mark's writing. Perhaps Peter "was reluctant to picture himself in such a unique and spectacular incident."[319]

Another miracle happened (cf. 4:35-41). "The wind" died down ("stopped") as soon as Jesus stepped "into the boat." This "astonished" (Gr. *existanto*, cf. 2:12; 5:42) the disciples further.

6:52	Here is the reason the disciples reacted as they did in this series of miracles. Mark alone recorded it, probably as a result of Peter's preaching. The disciples had "not" learned ("gained any insight") from the feeding of the 5,000 ("the loaves")—that Jesus was God. Their collective mind was not open to this possibility.

---

[311]Ibid., p. 336.

[312]Cranfield, p. 226.

[313]Bruce, *The Training . . .*, p. 133.

[314]Ryrie, p. 111.

[315]Guelich., p. 350.

[316]Lane, p. 235.

[317]Edwards, p. 223.

[318]Guelich, p. 351.

[319]Hiebert, p. 167.

Healings near Gennesaret 6:53-56 (cf. Matt. 14:34-36)

Jesus returned to the northwest area of the Sea of Galilee coast from the predominantly Gentile area where He had been recently.

> ". . . the literal storm on the water was succeeded by a spiritual storm on the land, equally sudden and violent, and not less perilous to the souls of the twelve than the other had been to their bodies."[320]

6:53   "Gennesaret" was the name of both a town and the plain on which the town stood.[321] The region was the northwest coast of the lake. It was so prominent because of its agricultural richness that another name for the Sea of Galilee was the Sea of Gennesaret (Luke 5:1).[322] It was an area of dense population.

6:54-56   These verses summarize Jesus' ministry in many towns on many days before His next withdrawal to Phoenicia. Mark stressed the immense popularity of Jesus and His generous healing of multitudes of "sick" people. "Cured" (v. 56) is literally "saved" (Gr. *sozo*). The sick experienced deliverance from their infirmities and restoration to physical soundness. That is the salvation in view.

3. The controversy with the Pharisees and scribes over defilement 7:1-23 (cf. Matt. 15:1-20)

This confrontation played an important part in Jesus' decision to withdraw from Galilee again (v. 24; cf. 2:1—3:6). Along with mounting popularity (6:53-56) came increasing opposition from the Jewish religious leaders. This section is essentially another block of Jesus' teaching. It revealed Jesus further and continued the preparation of the disciples for what lay ahead of them. In Mark's narrative, the words "unclean" (vv. 2, 5, 15, 18, 20, 23) and "tradition" (vv. 3, 5, 8, 9, 13) are key.

The religious leaders' objection 7:1-5

7:1-2   For a second time, Mark recorded a delegation of religious leaders coming from Jerusalem to investigate Jesus (cf. 3:22). The writer clarified what "ceremonially impure" hands were—"that is, unwashed"—for his Gentile readers. The "scribes" and "Pharisees" were not objecting because the disciples were eating with dirty hands, but because they had not gone through the accepted purification rituals before eating with their hands.

7:3-4   These verses do not appear in Matthew's parallel account. They explain Pharisaic tradition for those unfamiliar with it, such as Mark's original Gentile readers. In Jesus' day, "the Jews" communicated "the traditions of the elders" *orally*, from generation to generation. About A.D. 200, the rabbis completed compiling these into the Mishnah, which became the basis for the Talmud (ca. A.D. 425). The Pharisees customarily washed themselves after visiting the marketplace, in order to rid themselves of the defilement that contact with Gentiles produced. Most Jews regarded breaking these traditions as sin.

> "Indeed, a Rabbi who had held this command in contempt was actually buried in excommunication."[323]

7:5   The critics asked Jesus for an explanation of His disciples' conduct because, as their teacher, He was responsible for them. They suspected that the disciples' failure to wash properly indicated that Jesus disregarded all the traditions of the elders. *Walking* is a Hebrew figure of speech meaning habitual conduct (e.g., Gen. 5:24; Ps. 1:1). It occurs frequently in John's Gospel and in Paul's epistles.

Jesus' teaching about the source of authority 7:6-13

In replying, Jesus did not explain or justify His disciples' conduct. Instead He addressed the issue of the source of religious authority (vv. 6-13) and the nature of defilement (vv. 14-23).

7:6-7   Jesus boldly called His critics "hypocrites." They professed to honor God with their behavior, but they really did not honor Him in their hearts. What "Isaiah" said about the hypocrites in his day fit these critics exactly. They stressed human "precepts" to the exclusion of principles.

> "Jesus calls the opponents 'hypocrites' (*hupokriton*), a word in classical Greek that means 'to play a part,' an 'actor.' It does not carry the moral overtone of fraud that our English word does today. Rather it refers to

---

[320]Bruce, *The Training . . .*, p. 130.

[321]For Josephus' description of the countryside, see *The Wars . . .*, 3:10:8.

[322]Cf. ibid., 3:10:8.

[323]Edersheim, 2:10.

the discrepancy in the behavior of one who unconsciously has alienated oneself from God, an 'ungodly' person . . , by one's actions . . ."[324]

7:8-9   Jesus differentiated the commands of God from the traditions of men. The rabbis had built a fence around the law—by erecting their "dos" and "don'ts"—to prevent the Israelites from breaking the law. However, rather than protecting it, their legalistic requirements distorted and even contradicted the law. This is always the problem that accompanies attempting to legislate obedience to God's Word. Legalism involves making laws that God has not made and treating them as equally authoritative as God's Word. The Pharisees had even abandoned God's commandments in favor of their oral traditions that came from men. Jesus rejected the authority of the oral law.

7:10-13   Jesus cited an example of how His critics used human traditions to "set aside" divine imperatives. They professed to honor "Moses," through whom God commanded the Israelites to "honor" their "parents," and threatened disobedience with death (Exod. 20:12; 21:17). Honoring parents manifests itself in financial support and practical care if necessary. Mark interpreted the word "*corban*," a gift devoted to God, for his Gentile readers.[325] This word is Greek, but it transliterates a Hebrew word that the Jews used when they dedicated something to God. Jewish tradition permitted people to declare something they owned as *dedicated to God*.[326] This did not mean that they had to give it to the priests, or even give up the use of it themselves. However, it freed them from giving it to someone else—even a needy parent.[327]

> "History reveals that the Jewish religious leaders came to honor their traditions far above the Word of God. Rabbi Eleazer said, 'He who expounds the Scriptures in opposition to the tradition has no share in the world to come.' The *Mishna*, a collection of Jewish traditions in the *Talmud*, records, 'It is a greater offense to teach anything contrary to the voice of the Rabbis than to contradict Scripture itself.' But before we criticize our Jewish friends, perhaps we should examine what influence 'the church fathers' are having in our own Christian churches. We also may be guilty of replacing God's truth with man's traditions."[328]

Jesus claimed the authority to reorder social relationships. He said a son's responsibility to provide for his parents superseded the legal option of *corban*.[329]

Note that Jesus equated what Moses said (v. 10) with the Word of God (v. 13). He also attributed Mosaic authorship to the Torah, something many liberal modern critics of the Bible deny. Jesus' enemies failed to recognize the difference between inspired and uninspired instruction. The "you" in verse 11 is in the emphatic first position in the Greek text, indicating a strong contrast between God's view and the critics'. They had not only rejected God's Word (v. 9), but they had even invalidated it, that is, robbed it of its authority (v. 12). Mark included Jesus' words that indicated this was only one example, of how these Pharisees and scribes had voided, by their traditions, the authority of what God had revealed (v. 13).

Jesus' teaching about the true nature of defilement 7:14-23

Jesus continued His response to the critics by focusing on the particular practice that they had objected to (v. 5). The question of what constituted defilement was very important. The Jews had wandered far from God's will in this matter because of their traditions.

7:14-15 [16]   What Jesus had to say was so important that He urged "the crowd" present to "listen" carefully to His words (cf. 4:3). His response so far had been to His critics primarily.

Verse 15 states the general principle. It clarifies what does not and what does cause uncleanness. Food does not, but thoughts do (cf. Isa. 29:13). Obviously Jesus was speaking morally and spiritually, not medically and physiologically. Jesus clarified the intent of the Mosaic laws regarding clean and unclean food (Lev. 11; Deut. 14). The Jew who ate unclean food became unclean because he or she disobeyed God's Word, not because the food made him or her unclean.

Verse 16 is of questionable authenticity. Later copyists may have added it as a result of reading 4:9 and or 4:23. It may be genuine since many early manuscripts contain it. Most modern translators have judged it a later addition to the text.

7:17   Jesus had finished His response to His critics and His teaching of the multitude. He went into "the house" nearby with His disciples. There they asked Him a question that indicated they had not understood what He meant. What He had said was

---

[324]Guelich, p. 366.

[325]See also Flavius Josephus, *Against Apion*, 1:22.

[326]See Guelich., p. 369, for an example.

[327]Cranfield, p. 237.

[328]Wiersbe, 1:134.

[329]Edwards, p. 224.

revolutionary when He said it. They probably could not believe that He really meant what He had said. In Mark's Gospel, a house was a common setting where Jesus taught His disciples privately (cf. 9:28, 33; 10:10).

7:18-19   The disciples had heard and seen enough to have been able to understand Jesus' meaning. Their "hardness of heart" is a prominent theme in 6:31—8:26 (cf. 6:52; 8:14-21).

Mark interpreted the significance of Jesus' teaching for his Gentile readers. Mark meant that Christians need not observe the dietary restrictions of the Mosaic Law (cf. Rom. 14:14; Gal. 2:11-17; Col. 2:20-22). This was a freedom that Jewish Christians struggled with for many years during the infancy of the church (cf. Acts 10; 11; 15). Later revelation clarified that Jesus terminated the entire Mosaic Law as a code (Rom. 10:4; et al.).

> "In vv 6-13 Jesus equated the Mosaic law [*sic* Law] with God's Word and scolded the Pharisees for nullifying God's Word with their tradition. Now Jesus himself is nullifying God's Word with regard to food. But it is the prerogative of Jesus as God's Son to change the Law. Such a change does not count as human tradition, for Jesus' word is divine."[330]

> "This statement ["Thus He declared all foods clean"] clearly has its eye on a situation such as developed in the Pauline mission churches in which questions of clean and unclean foods (cf. Acts 10:9-16; 11:5-10 and see Rom 14:13ff.) and idol-meats became live issues (as we know from I Cor 8:10). This chapter in Mark 7 is perhaps the most obvious declaration of Mark's purpose as a Christian living in the Graeco-Roman world who wishes to publicize the charter of Gentile freedom by recording in the plainest terms Jesus' detachment from Jewish ceremonial [*sic* ceremony] and to spell out in clear tones the application of this to his readers."[331]

If Peter did influence Mark's writing, it is interesting that the disciple who struggled with unwillingness to abandon the dietary laws should have spoken out so strongly for their termination. Mark apparently got the material for his Gospel mainly from Peter's sermons, as mentioned earlier. Thus it appears that Peter finally learned this lesson.

> "These ceremonial regulations in the law had a function as symbolically teaching the reality and importance of *moral* purity. They demanded an external separation which pointed to the need for an inner heart condition of separation unto God. But these external regulations in themselves did not convey the purity of heart to which they pointed. They were the shadow and not the substance (Heb. 10:1). When they found their fulfillment in Christ, these ceremonial foreshadowings became obsolete."[332]

7:20-23   Jesus repeated and became more specific so the disciples would understand Him. The list of sins proceeds from six actions to six attitudes (cf. Rom 1:29-31; Gal. 5:19-23). Matthew's record included only six sins. "Evil thoughts" are the ground out of which the evil actions and attitudes grow. The order in the text is true to life. Sin proceeds from the heart (human nature) to the thoughts (human mind) to actions (human deeds).

This controversy with the Pharisees and the scribes was a factor that led Jesus to withdraw from Galilee a third time (cf. 4:35-36; 6:31-32).

4. Jesus' teaching about bread and the exorcism of a Phoenician girl 7:24-30 (cf. Matt. 15:21-28)

Jesus increased His ministry to Gentiles as He experienced increasing rejection from the Jews. This third withdrawal from Galilee took Jesus outside Palestine for the first time. Mark also recorded Jesus doing more things outside of Galilee, and fewer things within Galilee, than the other evangelists. By pointing this out, Mark helped his readers realize that ministry to Gentiles was God's will, in view of Israel's final rejection of Jesus. One writer believed the point of this story was simply that Jesus could heal.[333] But this seems shortsighted. Mark included three events that occurred outside Palestine and one following Jesus' return.

There is a logical connection between this section and the one that precedes it (7:1-23). Jesus had explained why He did not observe the traditional separation from defiling associations. Now He illustrated that by going into Gentile territory. This contact would have rendered Him ceremonial unclean according to the Jews' traditions.

---

[330]Gundry, p. 356.

[331]Martin, p. 220.

[332]Hiebert, p. 181.

[333]R. S. Sugirtharajah, "The Syrophoenician Woman," *The Expository Times* 98:1 (October 1986):13-15.

7:24	Mark normally began a new paragraph with the Greek word *kai* ("and"). Here he used *de* ("and" or "now"). This difference indicates a significant change in the narrative. The hostility of Israel's leaders led Jesus to correct them "and" to leave Galilee for ministry elsewhere.

The New Testament writers often spoke of Phoenicia as "the land (region) of Tyre (and or Sidon)," because they were the two notable cities of the region. Tyre stood on the Mediterranean coast about 40 miles northwest of Capernaum. Jesus went there to be alone with the disciples. Nevertheless His fame accompanied Him, and He was not able to remain *incognito*. Josephus described the people of this region as follows:

"... they are known to have born [*sic*] the greatest ill will toward us ..."[334] |
| 7:25-26 | "Syrophoenician" combines the terms Syrian and Phoenician. Phoenicia was a part of the larger Roman province of Syria, which also included all of Palestine—Galilee, Samaria, Perea, Judea, Idumea, and other regions.[335] Other Phoenicians lived elsewhere, since they were a great seafaring and commercial people. For example, the Libyo-Phoenicians lived in North Africa.[336] "Syrophoenician" specifically distinguished the Phoenicians of Syria from the Carthaginians.[337]

The woman who heard about Jesus and sought Him out was a Gentile. A demon was afflicting her young daughter (cf. v. 30). Her persistent request for help demonstrated her faith in Jesus. She believed Jesus could heal her if He would do so. |
| 7:27-28 | Jesus probably conversed with the woman in the Greek language, which was common in that area. The woman conceded that the Jews had a prior claim on Jesus' ministry. Nonetheless if the little pet dogs (Gr. *kynarion*) get the table scraps, then she felt she had a right to a crumb from Jesus' table. She implied that the Gentiles need not wait to receive Jesus' blessings until a later time. They could feed when "the children" did, namely, during Jesus' ministry. A little Gentile blessing would not deprive the Jews of what God wanted them to have.

"The Gentiles are not called 'dogs' but 'doggies,' not outside scavengers, but household companions."[338]

"This 'title' of 'Lord' that consistently comes on the lips of 'believers' in Matthew occurs only this one time with confession overtones in Mark and sets the stage for Jesus' concluding remark and his offer of help to the woman."[339] |
| 7:29-30 | The woman's answer had revealed a quick wit and humility, but it was her persistent faith that Jesus rewarded (cf. Matt. 15:28).

"In contrast to the tradition of the elders Jesus [authoritatively] embraces the alienated of the Mosaic and rabbinic tradition: a leper (1:40-45), tax collectors and sinners (2:13-17), and even unclean Gentiles, including a Syrophoenician woman (7:24-30)."[340]

The woman's departure for home without Jesus also shows her faith. This is the only instance of Jesus healing from a distance—without a vocal command—that Mark recorded. As such, it demonstrates the great power of Jesus working for this woman's need. The healing was instantaneous, as usual. Perhaps one of the disciples accompanied the woman and reported what Mark wrote in verse 30. |

This incident would have sparked special interest for Gentile readers. It shows that Jesus rewards Gentile faith as well as Jewish faith. Jesus had come to deliver both Gentiles and Jews (10:45).

---

[334]Josephus, *Against Apion*, 1:13.
[335]*The Nelson . . .*, pp. 1656-57.
[336]Wessel, p. 682.
[337]Cranfield, p. 247.
[338]Plummer, p. 189.
[339]Guelich, p. 588.
[340]Edwards, p. 224.

5. The healing of a deaf man with a speech impediment 7:31-36

Mark was the only evangelist to record this miracle. He apparently included it in his Gospel because it is another instance of Jesus healing a Gentile. This particular miracle is also significant because it prefigured Jesus opening the spiritual ears of His disciples. From 6:31, the beginning of the second withdrawal and return, to 7:37, Jesus had been revealing Himself with increasing clarity to the disciples but with little response. A repetition of some of these lessons followed, culminating in the disciples' confession of Jesus as the divine Messiah (8:1-30).

7:31   Jesus took a circular route, first traveling north toward Sidon, which stood about 20 miles north of Tyre, and then eventually back to the east side of the Sea of Galilee. He penetrated deep into Gentile territory. The Decapolis region was also primarily Gentile (cf. 5:1-20). Evidently Jesus looped around northern Palestine and approached the Sea of Galilee from the north or east. This trip may have taken several weeks or even months.[341]

7:32   The Greek word describing this man's speech impediment, *mogilalos*, is a rare one. It occurs only here in the New Testament, and only in Isaiah 35:6 in the Septuagint version of the Old Testament. Its presence there is significant because Isaiah predicted that Messiah would loose the tongues of the dumb when He came (cf. v. 37).

"Defective speech usually results from defective hearing, both physically and spiritually."[342]

7:33   Jesus had personal contact with this man, as He did with so many others He healed, which Mark stressed. Jesus apparently did what He did to help the man place his trust in Himself.

"The laying on of hands would of itself have been sufficiently efficacious, and even, without moving a finger, he might have accomplished it by a single act of his will; but it is evident that he made abundant use of outward signs, when they were found to be advantageous. Thus, by touching the tongue with spittle, he intended to point out that the faculty of speech was communicated by himself alone; and by putting his fingers into the ears, he showed that it belonged to his office to pierce the ears of the deaf."[343]

Jesus may have spat on the ground first, and then "touched" the man's "tongue" with His finger. Both acts would have told the man that Jesus intended to do something about his tongue and mouth.

". . . spittle supposedly had a therapeutic function in both the Greco-Roman (e.g., Pliny, *Nat. Hist.* 28.4.7; Tacitus, *Hist.* 6.18; Suetonius, *Vesp.* 7) and the Jewish world (Str-B, 2:15-17)"[344]

7:34-35   "Looking up to heaven" and sighing were also acts intended to communicate with the man. By looking up, Jesus associated the coming healing with God. By sighing or groaning, He conveyed His compassion for the man and the fact that the healing involved spiritual warfare.[345] This was an unusually difficult miracle, and even Jesus had to take special measures to perform it. Jesus spoke in Aramaic since this was the language that was common in Palestine (cf. 5:41). Probably the man could read Jesus' lips. Jesus' healing was again instantaneous. Not only could the man now speak, but he spoke without any defect. Jesus' elaborate use of means to heal this man would have minimized the possibility of magic and focused attention on Him as the healer.

7:36   Another command to keep the miracle quiet went unheeded (cf. 1:44; 5:43).

"The conduct of the multitude is a good example of the way in which men treat Jesus, yielding him all homage, except obedience."[346]

"Jesus' role once known always draws a crowd in Mark."[347]

---

[341]Blunt, p. 192.

[342]Grassmick, p. 136.

[343]Calvin, 2:271-72. Cf. Gundry, p. 383.

[344]Guelich, p. 395. Str-B is H. L. Strack and P. Billerbeck, *Kommentar zum Neuen Testament aus Talmud und Midrasch*.

[345]Cranfield, p. 252.

[346]Ezra P. Gould, *A Critical and Exegetical Commentary on the Gospel According to St. Mark*, p. 139.

[347]Guelich, p. 397.

"The difficult conflicts . . . lie not with demons, for Jesus has authority from God to destroy them, nor does Jesus struggle much in conflict with nature, for Jesus has authority over it. The difficult conflicts arise with people, for Jesus has no authority to control them; people choose and nothing can be forced upon them. . . . He can successfully order a deaf-mute to hear and talk, but he cannot make him keep quiet or stop others from listening to him. Furthermore, he cannot make his disciples understand nor can he constrain the authorities to stop opposing him."[348]

6. The preliminary confession of faith 7:37 (cf. Matt. 15:29-31)

Mark expressed the crowd's amazement with a strong word that appears only here in the New Testament: *hyperperissos*. It means "extremely overwhelmed" (cf. 1:22; 6:2; 10:26; 11:18). Their statement that Jesus did everything "well" recalls Genesis 1:31, where Moses wrote that God saw that everything that He had created was good. The restoration of hearing to the deaf and speaking to the dumb was the work of God (cf. Isa. 35:3-6). Matthew recorded that Jesus healed many other people with various afflictions at this time (Matt. 15:29-31).

C. THE SECOND CYCLE OF SELF-REVELATION TO THE DISCIPLES 8:1-30

The disciples had not yet understood the lessons that Jesus sought to teach them. Mark constructed his Gospel to show that in His discipleship training, Jesus repeated His lessons in order to train the disciples. One writer noticed the following repetitive parallel structure in this section of the Gospel.[349]

6:31-44	Feeding of the multitude	8:1-9
6:45-56	Crossing of the sea and landing	8:10
7:1-23	Conflict with the Pharisees	8:11-13
7:24-30	Conversation about bread	8:14-21
7:31-36	Healing	8:22-26
7:37	Confession of faith	8:27-30

1. The feeding of the 4,000 8:1-9 (cf. Matt. 15:32-38)

This miracle repeated the lesson of the feeding of the 5,000—for the disciples who had not learned what they should have from the former miracle (vv. 17-21).[350]

"Mark clearly understood that there were two occasions when Jesus miraculously fed a multitude."[351]

8:1-3   Jesus and His disciples were still in the Decapolis region east of the lake. "Three days" had passed and the crowds were now hungry, having exhausted the provisions they had brought with them. Perhaps Jesus waited three days to see if the disciples would ask Him to feed this crowd as He had fed the former one (6:31-44). They did not. Jesus' "compassion" for the multitude led Him to articulate their plight. Even with this cue, the disciples did not ask Jesus to meet the need. Even the similar surroundings did not jog the disciples' memories.

8:4   Why did the disciples not catch on? Probably several months had passed since Jesus fed the 5,000. People tend to forget even great events. Moreover, depending on Jesus rather than relying on self is a very difficult lesson to learn, especially when one has a limited perception of who Jesus is. Furthermore, Jesus' occasional reluctance to perform miracles may have discouraged the disciples from asking Him for help.[352] Their question revealed their blindness. Rather than thinking about sending the crowds away, they despaired of finding enough bread to satisfy everyone in that wilderness (Gr. *eremon*, cf. 6:32). At least they referred their question to Jesus this time (cf. 6:37).

---

[348]Rhoads and Michie, p. 78.

[349]Lane, p. 269.

[350]See E. Schuyler English, "A Neglected Miracle," *Bibliotheca Sacra* 126:504 (October-December 1969):300-5.

[351]Lane, p. 272.

[352]Cranfield, p. 205.

8:5   Jesus asked them the same question He had voiced before He fed the 5,000 (6:38). Even this did not remind the disciples to trust Jesus to provide for their need.

8:6-7   Mark explained exactly what Jesus did, and with greater precision than Matthew did (Matt. 15:36). This reflects his typical interest in detail.

> "Comparing Jesus' prayers offered before these two feeding miracles shows that the first included the Jewish blessing of looking toward heaven (6:41), whereas the second was a simple thanksgiving (8:6)."[353]

8:8-9   Jesus' provision was again typically adequate, and abundant, but not excessive. The type of basket mentioned (Gr. *spuris*) was large enough to carry a man (cf. Acts 9:25).

Some critics of the Bible have argued that Matthew and Mark told the story of one miraculous feeding twice and made mistakes that account for the differences in the accounts.[354] However, the differences between the two stories are so great that most readers believe Jesus fed two different groups of people, on two separate occasions.

Another debatable point is whether this crowd was Gentile, since the location was primarily Gentile, and the former crowd was Jewish, in view of its location. Probably there were more Gentiles present on this occasion and more Jews on the other. This points to a mixture of Jews and Gentiles that Jesus helped and that believed on Him, prefiguring the mixed composition of the church and the kingdom.

2. The return to Galilee 8:10 (cf. Matt. 15:39)

Jesus and the disciples had returned to Galilee by boat after they had fed the 5,000 (6:45-56). They did the same thing after feeding the 4,000. The exact location of "Dalmanutha" is unknown, but it must have been near Magadan (Magdala?) on the west side of the lake (Matt. 15:39).

> "Magadan was the name of a town, while Dalmanutha in Aramaic meant 'the harbor.' Thus Dalmanutha was the harbor of Magadan and was located near Capernaum."[355]

3. Conflict with the Pharisees over signs 8:11-13 (cf. Matt. 16:1-4)

Matthew's account of this incident is fuller than Mark's. Probably Mark just summarized it, to parallel 7:1-23, and so advance his theme of discipleship training.

8:11   Matthew noted that the Sadducees accompanied the Pharisees (Matt. 15:1). They came out from Jerusalem again just to argue, not to learn. They asked Jesus to provide some confirmation of His divine authority and trustworthiness. They wanted an immediate, public, definitive proof that God was with Him (cf. 11:30). They had previously concluded that His power came from Satan (3:22). The miracles that Jesus performed did not convince them. They were not requesting another one of these, but a different type of verification—perhaps similar to those that God gave the Israelites at Mt. Sinai to authenticate Moses as His servant. They did this to subject Jesus to a trial (Gr. *peirazo*) that would reveal His true character. They hoped to expose Him as a phony.

> "'Sign' (*semeion*) consistently differs in Mark from 'wonders' or 'miracles' (*dunameis*). Nowhere in the Synoptics does 'sign' refer to a 'miracle' or is a miraculous event called a 'sign.' . . . They sought a 'sign' in the OT Jewish sense, a confirmation or authentication of Jesus' ministry."[356]

Probably the Pharisees wanted Jesus to give them indisputable proof that God confirmed Jesus' credibility.[357]

> "The Pharisees were progressive, a party among, though not of, the people. Their goal was that Israel should become the righteous nation of the covenant. To this end they taught compliance with the 'tradition of the elders,' an oral code of conduct effectively adapting the law of Moses to later times and changing demands."[358]

---

[353]Bailey, p. 80.
[354]E.g., Gould, p. 142.
[355]J. Dwight Pentecost, *The Words and Works of Jesus Christ*, pp. 246-47.
[356]Guelich, p. 413.
[357]Ibid., p. 414.
[358]Kingsbury, pp. 63-64.

8:12	The Greek word translated "sighing deeply" is *anastenazo*.

> "It describes Jesus' grief and disappointment when faced with the unbelief of those who, because of their spiritual privileges, ought to have been more responsive to him."[359]

"His spirit" refers to Jesus' human spirit. The contemporary Jews who opposed Jesus constituted the "generation" to which He referred. He refused to give the type of sign they requested, because the evidence that He had presented was more than adequate to convince an open-minded person. Jesus distinguished between miracles (Gr. *dynamis*) and signs (Gr. *semeion*) by using the second word here. He had given plenty of miracles to bolster faith. He would not give "a sign" to those bent on disbelieving. From this, Mark's readers were to learn that Jesus' miracles were ample proof of His deity.

8:13	Jesus again left the presence of unbelievers (cf. 4:35; 7:24). He acted in keeping with His pronounced judgment. He departed for the northeast coast of the lake. From now on, Jesus' ministry focused more on His disciples than on the public.

This incident was and is a lesson to disciples on the importance of accepting the evidence that Jesus has given concerning His supernatural person.

4. Jesus' teaching about the yeast of the Pharisees and Herod 8:14-21 (cf. Matt. 16:5-12)

This pericope parallels and recalls Jesus' teaching about the children's bread, when He cast the demon out of the Phoenician girl (7:24-30). In both cases, leavened bread metaphorically represented teaching. The Gentile woman wanted Jesus' teaching, and so presented a positive example for the disciples. The Jewish religious leaders rejected Jesus' teaching, and at the same time advanced the *false* teaching (leaven), which Jesus warned His disciples to avoid.

8:14	The "one loaf" of bread recalls the two miraculous feedings of the two crowds. A shortage of bread should have been no great concern to the disciples, in view of Jesus' supernatural powers.
8:15	Jesus used "the leaven" in the loaf of bread as an object lesson: to illustrate the pervasive corrupting teaching "of the Pharisees" and "of Herod." *Leaven* was a common metaphor for an invisible, pervasive, corrupting influence in both Jewish and Hellenistic circles.[360] The teaching of the Pharisees was that Jesus received His authority from Satan rather than from God (3:22; cf. 7:8-13). It was a denial of His role as God's anointed Servant, Messiah. The teaching of Herod Antipas, what he believed and articulated, was likewise that Jesus was not the Messiah. Herod told others that Jesus was just John the Baptist come back to life (6:14-16). The Pharisees and Herod, though so different from each other in many respects, promoted the same heretical view that Jesus was not the Messiah, much less divine. In short, this leaven was *unbelief*. This attitude, like leaven, had started to permeate the general population. Another view is that the yeast of the Pharisees was their hypocritical, self-righteous traditionalism; and the yeast of Herod was his spirit of imperial pride.[361] Still others view the yeast of the Pharisees as false and inconsistent piety, and the yeast of Herod as godlessness.[362]
8:16	The disciples' interest in the problem of lack of food sharply contrasts with Jesus' fervent concern over unbelief (cf. vv. 12, 15). Spiritual truth failed to impress them because they had minds that were not open to it (v. 17).
8:17-21	Jesus strongly rebuked His disciples for their lack of spiritual understanding (cf. Isa. 6:9-10; Jer. 5:21; Ezek. 12:2). In view of the two miraculous feedings they had witnessed, they should have understood who He was. They did "remember" the facts (vv. 19-20), but they did not "understand" their significance (v. 21). As God had provided bread abundantly for the Israelites in the wilderness, Jesus had provided bread abundantly for them in another wilderness. The conclusion should have been obvious. Jesus was the Prophet that Moses had predicted would come after him and supersede him. He was the divine Messiah.

> "His rebuke was not because of their failure to grasp the meaning of His warning (v. 15), but at their failure to understand the meaning of His presence with them."[363]

It was extremely important that the disciples perceive who Jesus was. Without that perception, they could not enter into a proper relationship with Him that was realistic and fulfilling. Jesus' use of questions forced them to interact with the implications of what they had heard and seen.

---

[359]Wessel, p. 688. Cf. Gundry, p. 402.

[360]Lane, p. 280; *The Nelson* . . ., p. 1658.

[361]Bailey, p. 80.

[362]E.g., Cranfield, p. 261.

[363]Grassmick, p. 138.

"In this way, Mark appears to say that being an 'insider,' even a 'disciple,' did not guarantee that one 'understood' or perceived the significance of Jesus and his ministry."[364]

The incident ends with a question but no answer. To paraphrase: "Do you *still* not understand—even after I explained it to you?" This was an indication that the disciples *even then* did not grasp what Jesus had explained. Mark leaves the reader hanging. The answer is of utmost importance. Peter finally verbalized it in verse 29. However, the reader of this Gospel already knows the answer because of what Mark previously wrote.

5. The healing of a blind man near Bethsaida 8:22-26

Mark is the only evangelist who recorded this miracle. It corresponds to the healing of the deaf man with the speech impediment (7:31-36), the only other miracle that Mark alone recorded. This is the only miracle in Mark that was not instantaneous; it happened gradually. Sight is a common metaphor for understanding. The disciples should have seen the deaf man as a picture of themselves, unable to comprehend what Jesus said. This blind man also represented them in their inability to understand what Jesus showed them (cf. v. 21). Jesus could and would make them whole, as He healed these two physically limited men.

8:22   As mentioned above, Bethsaida Julius stood on the northeast shore of the lake (cf. 6:45). Evidently friends of the "blind man" led him to Jesus.

8:23-24   "Our Lord's action here is significant. Having abandoned Bethsaida to judgment (Mt. 11:21-24), He would neither heal in that village nor permit further testimony to be borne there (v. 26). The probation of Bethsaida as a community was ended, but He would still show mercy to individuals."[365]

Jesus may have led the man out of Bethsaida so He could establish a personal relationship with him (cf. 5:35-43; 7:31-37), and or perhaps to avoid publicity (cf. v. 26). The man's willingness to follow Jesus demonstrated some faith. This was evidently one of only three miracles that Jesus did in private that Mark recorded. In all three cases, some disciples were present, as witnesses.

The English translations permit a rather unpleasant interpretation of what Jesus did, namely, spitting in the man's face and placing His hands on his head or shoulders. The Greek text encourages us to interpret the data differently. Probably Jesus applied a small quantity of His spittle to the man's eyes with His fingers. This action would have made it clear to the blind man that Jesus was restoring his vision. Perhaps the saliva told the man that this healing came out of Jesus' mouth (cf. Gen. 1:3, 6, et al.).

". . . the use of saliva was a well-known Jewish remedy for affections of the eyes."[366]

Jesus asked the man, "Do you see anything?" to get him to state what he saw for the disciples' benefit. Evidently the man had lost his vision; he appears not to have been blind from birth. He knew what "trees" looked like. Blindness from disease was and still is common in many Middle Eastern countries.

8:25   Why did Jesus heal the man gradually in stages? Perhaps He did so to show that He could heal in any manner He chose.[367] Perhaps the man was fearful, and Jesus healed him as He did to accommodate his needs.[368] Perhaps He did so to illustrate for the disciples that He chose to give spiritual perception one step at a time. Perhaps He wanted to present Himself as the Great Physician. Perhaps this was an unusually difficult miracle, so the method of healing magnified Jesus' power.[369] Probably Jesus had more than one reason.

"Is this miracle paradigmatic of Jesus' struggle with the disciples? Is Jesus' earthly ministry stage one, during which time Jesus must contend with the disciples who are at once committed to him but afflicted with incomprehension? Is the time following Easter stage two, when Jesus shall have led the disciples, like this man, to 'see everything clearly'?"[370]

---

[364]Guelich, p. 427.

[365]*The New Scofield Reference Bible*, p. 1059.

[366]Edersheim, 2:48.

[367]Calvin, 2:285.

[368]Alexander Maclaren, "St. Mark," in *Expositions of Holy Scripture*, 8:326.

[369]Gundry, p. 418.

[370]Kingsbury, p. 102.

Mark was careful to record that the man "looked intently" (NASB). Human responsibility played a part in this healing as does gaining spiritual understanding. Nevertheless it is God who is ultimately responsible for the perception. Perhaps Jesus healed the man's optic nerve completely at first, but, as with children, the man had to learn to focus on objects. So Jesus touched the man's eyes a second time, which gave him the ability to see clearly.[371]

> "The primary focus of this story, however, is on the man's total healing. The disciples show themselves to be in need of the second touch, and the story bespeaks their experiencing it. A time must come when they see all things distinctly."[372]

8:26   Probably Jesus gave this order to safeguard His mission (cf. 1:44-45; 5:43; 7:36). The man appears to have lived somewhere other than in Bethsaida.

> "Thus, 8:26 imposes no secrecy concerning the miracle or the means by which Jesus has effected it, much less a messianic secret (for his identity as the Christ has not entered the picture). Rather, this verse carries a demonstration of healing: the man can now see to go home without needing people to take him there as he did need them to bring him to Jesus (v. 22)."[373]

With this miracle, Jesus fulfilled another aspect of messianic prophecy. The divine Messiah would open blind eyes (Isa. 35:5-6). Old Testament writers claimed that it is God who gives sight to the blind (Ps. 146:8; Isa. 29:18). The conclusion should have been obvious: Jesus is the God-man.

6. Peter's confession of faith 8:27-30 (cf. Matt. 16:13-20; Luke 9:18-21)

The healing of the deaf man with the speech impediment resulted in a confession of Jesus' greatness that fell short of identifying Him as God (7:37). The healing of the blind man was the incident that God used to open the disciples' eyes to the biblical messianic identity of Jesus that Peter articulated.

Mark further highlighted the cause and effect relationship between these last two events by structuring the pericopes similarly. First, he presented the circumstances (vv. 22, 27). Second, he described partial sight and understanding (vv. 23-24, 28). Third, he recorded the giving of sight and understanding (vv. 25, 29). Fourth, he noted Jesus' command to remain silent (vv. 26, 30).[374]

> "Mark has placed at the center of his narrative the recognition that Jesus is the Messiah. The pivotal importance of this moment is indicated by the fact that already in the first line of the Gospel the evangelist designates Jesus as the Messiah. Yet between Ch. 1:1 and Ch. 8:29 there is no recognition of this fact in spite of a remarkable sequence of events which demanded a decision concerning Jesus' identity. . . .

> "The recognition that Jesus is the Messiah is thus the point of intersection toward which all the theological currents of the first half of the Gospel converge and from which the dynamic of the second half of the Gospel derives. In no other way could Mark more sharply indicate the historical and theological significance of the conversation in the neighborhood of Caesarea Philippi."[375]

8:27-28   Jesus and His disciples continued traveling north from Bethsaida toward "Caesarea Philippi," where Herod Philip lived, that stood about 25 miles away. The disciples confessed their belief that Jesus was Lord ("the Christ") near the place where the pagans confessed that Caesar was "Lord." Jesus asked the first question in verse 27, with a view toward asking the second question in verse 29. In Mark, Jesus' questions often led to new teaching (cf. 9:33; 12:24, 35). The popular answers to Jesus' first question all reflect an inadequate view of Him. They assigned Jesus a preparatory role, but failed to recognize His consummative role. Evidently few people believed that Jesus was the Messiah, so the disciples did not even mention that possibility.

8:29   Jesus stressed "you" when He asked this question. He wanted to know whom the disciples, in contrast to the multitudes, believed He was. "Peter" spoke for the disciples. The other disciples evidently agreed with his statement and made no objection. This is the first time in Mark that Peter acted as spokesman for the Twelve. Yet from this time on, Peter was the prominent representative of the other disciples. Peter's name appears twice before in Mark, and 16 times after this incident. It

---

[371]Pentecost, *The Words* . . ., p. 248.

[372]Guelich, p. 436.

[373]Gundry, p. 419.

[374]Wessel, p. 692.

[375]Lane, pp. 288, 289. Cf. Cranfield, p. 271.

occurs five times before this incident in Matthew and 18 times after, four times before in Luke and 16 times after, and four times before in John and 29 times after.[376]

> ". . . Peter's name, 'Rock,' is ironic, for he thinks he is like a rock. He happens to be the opposite of what his nickname suggests, for he falls asleep and later falls apart under the incriminating remarks of a maid of the High Priest."[377]

"Christ" is the English transliteration of the Greek *christos* that translates the Hebrew *masiah* meaning "anointed one." Originally this Hebrew term had a broad meaning and included anyone anointed by God, including priests, kings, and prophets. Later in the Old Testament it came to have the technical meaning of the divine Davidic king who would appear to deliver Israel and establish a worldwide kingdom (Ps. 110:1; Dan. 9:25-26). In Mark, Jesus rarely used this term Himself (cf. 9:41; 12:35; 13:21), and He never used it of Himself. Probably He avoided it because of its political connotations and the popular misunderstanding of it, but Jesus accepted the title when others applied it to Him (cf. 14:6-62; John 4:25-26).

> ". . . the title . . . was particularly fitted to express his true relation both to the OT and to the people of God. . . . the title, applied to Jesus, designates him as the true meaning and fulfillment of the long succession of Israel's anointed kings and priests, the King and Priest . . .; the Prophet anointed with the Spirit of God, who fulfills the long line of Israel's prophets, and the One in whom the life of the whole nation of Israel finds its fulfillment and meaning, in whom and for whose sake the people of Israel were, and the new Israel now is, the anointed people of God."[378]

The timing of this question in Jesus' ministry was very important. The disciples had believed that Jesus was the Messiah from the beginning of their contact with Him (John 1:41, 51). However, their understanding of the Messiah then was the traditional one of their day, namely, that of a political leader. The multitudes likewise failed to understand that Jesus was much more than that. The religious leaders were becoming increasingly antagonistic. The disciples were about to receive new revelation regarding Jesus that would have costly implications for them. Therefore it was necessary for them to confess Jesus' identity clearly and unmistakably now.

Why did Mark only record that Peter said, "You are the Messiah," rather than his complete statement, "You are the Messiah, the Son of the living God" (Matt. 16:16)? Mark's emphasis throughout his Gospel was on Jesus' humanity, as we have seen. By omitting the last part of Peter's statement, Mark did not mean that Peter failed to acknowledge Jesus' deity. This is precisely what Peter was confessing. However in Mark, the term "Messiah" includes the concept of deity, as it does in the Old Testament. Earlier when the disciples said they had found "the Messiah," before Jesus called them to be His disciples, they used the title in the popular way (John 1:41, 51). Mark did not record those statements. He presented the disciples using the term "Messiah" in its true biblical meaning for his Gentile readers.

> "For the Christians of Rome who read Mark, the confession 'You are the Messiah' was precisely their profession of faith . . ."[379]

Peter's confession constitutes a high-water mark in the disciples' understanding of, and commitment to, Jesus. They still had much to learn about the significance of Jesus being *the* Messiah that the Old Testament promised, and all of its implications. Nevertheless now, Jesus could build on their faith and commitment.

> ". . . Jesus' identity is progressively unveiled in three stages, though only from the standpoint of the reader. . . .
>
> "The first stage in the progressive disclosure of Jesus' identity is the confession of Peter on behalf of the disciples (8:27-30)."[380]

8:30   Probably Jesus instructed ("warned") the disciples "to tell no one about Him" for at least three reasons. First, such an announcement would have hindered His mission. Second, the disciples would not have been able to cope with the questions

---

[376]Hiebert, p. 203, footnote 3.

[377]Rhoads and Michie, p. 60.

[378]Cranfield, pp. 270-71. See Bateman, pp. 537-59.

[379]Lane, p. 292, n. 67. Cf. 1 John 5:1.

[380]Kingsbury, p. 43. Cf. 10:46—11:11 (and 12:35-37); and 11:12—15:39.

and opposition such an announcement would generate. They still held many popular misconceptions about Israel's Messiah that Jesus needed to correct. Jesus proceeded to continue preparing them so they could represent Him effectively. Third, Jesus wanted privacy for predicting His passion and resurrection.

"At the center of his Gospel Mark placed Peter's confession that Jesus is the Messiah. Up to this point the underlying question had been, 'Who is He?' After Peter's declaration on behalf of the Twelve, Mark's narrative is oriented toward the Cross and the Resurrection. From now on the underlying double question was, 'What kind of Messiah is He, and what does it mean to follow Him?' This crucial passage is the point to which the first half of the book leads and from which the second half proceeds."[381]

V. THE SERVANT'S JOURNEY TO JERUSALEM 8:31—10:52

Having comprehended Jesus' true identity, the disciples next turned south with Jesus and headed from Caesarea Philippi toward Jerusalem. This section of the Gospel traces that journey, and stresses Jesus' preparation of His disciples for His coming death and resurrection.

"It is no coincidence that the narrator frames the journey to Jerusalem with two healing stories about blindness [8:22-26; 10:46-52], for the journey surely seems dominated by Jesus' urgent efforts to deal with the disciples' blindness to the things of God."[382]

Mark structured his narrative around three predictions of Jesus' passion that He gave the disciples. Each unit begins with a prediction followed by the disciples' reaction. Then follow lessons that Jesus taught them about discipleship. Until now, Mark reported Jesus speaking in veiled terms (cf. 2:20; 4:33-34). From this point on, He spoke more clearly to both the disciples and the multitudes.

"This openness is theologically significant within the larger context of Jesus' messianic self-revelation in the Gospel of Mark. It points beyond Jesus' hiddenness, which reaches its climax on the cross, to his revealed glory. In the cross and resurrection of Jesus the secret of the Kingdom is thoroughly veiled as well as gloriously revealed. Mark exposes this tension, which is inherent in the gospel, through the reaction of the disciples to Jesus' sober teaching throughout Chs. 8:31—10:52."[383]

A. THE FIRST PASSION PREDICTION AND ITS LESSONS 8:31—9:29

In this section, Mark recorded Jesus' first clear prediction of His passion (8:31), the disciples' reaction to it (8:32-33), and several lessons on discipleship (8:34—9:29).

1. The first major prophecy of Jesus' passion 8:31-33 (cf. Matt. 16:21-23; Luke 9:22)

8:31   Jesus' clear revelation of His coming suffering, death, and resurrection resulted from Peter's confession of faith. The disciples were now ready to receive what would have been completely incomprehensible—if they still viewed Jesus then as only a political Messiah.

Jesus referred to Himself as "the Son of Man," a biblical messianic title (Dan. 7:13-14; cf. Mark 2:10, 28). This was by far the favorite term that Jesus used to describe Himself in the Gospels. It appears 81 times. In its Old Testament usage, this title presented Messiah as coming in glory—but also suffering and dying. This title was not as popular as "Messiah," so when Jesus used it, people unfamiliar with the Old Testament often did not know what He meant. "Son of Man" was also an idiom in Jesus' day, that most people would have understood as a circumlocution for "I"—adding to the curiosity when Jesus used it.[384]

Here Jesus revealed that the Son of Man "must" (Gr. *dei*) suffer, because of God's purpose. Most Jews of Jesus' day believed that Messiah would establish His kingdom without suffering and dying.

"The necessity arises, first, from the hostility of men; secondly, from the spiritual nature of his work, which made it impossible for him to oppose force to force; and thirdly from the providential purpose of God, who made the death of Jesus the central thing in redemption [Isa. 52:13—53:12]."[385]

[381]Grassmick, pp. 138-39.

[382]Rhoads and Michie, pp. 126-27.

[383]Lane, p. 294.

[384]Ibid., p. 297. See Cranfield, pp. 272-77, for a discussion of the views concerning its meaning and a bibliography.

[385]Gould, p. 153.

The three groups that would reject Jesus made up the Sanhedrin. The "elders" were its lay members. They were men of wealth and were the leaders of aristocratic families. The "chief priests" were the ranking priests and were mostly Sadducees. They occupied a hereditary office and supervised the temple and the sacrificial system. The chief priests included Annas, Caiaphas, and the leaders of the 24 divisions of the priesthood. The "scribes," or "teachers of the Law," were the approved interpreters of the Law, and they were mostly Pharisees. They were the theologians and lawyers of Judaism who were "experts" in Israel's "laws." Together these three groups formed a united front as opponents of Jesus.

Jesus also announced His resurrection "after three days." Mark's readers would have understood this phrase as synonymous with "on the third day" (cf. Hos. 6:1-2; Matt. 16:21; Luke 9:22).

> "Verse 31 is particularly important because it is the only explanation in Mark's Gospel of 'the messianic secret.' Jesus did not want his messiahship to be disclosed because it involved suffering, rejection, and death. Popular expectations of messiahship would have hindered, if not prevented, the accomplishment of his divinely ordained (*dei*, 'must') messianic mission."[386]

8:32   Until now, Jesus had only hinted at His sufferings (cf. 2:20; 4:33-34; 7:14-15, 17-23). The disciples were unprepared for this clear revelation that Messiah would suffer, die, and rise again. Peter understood it but refused to accept it. He could not reconcile this view of Messiah with the popular one. The word Mark chose to describe Peter's rebuke is a strong one (Gr. *epitimao*). It is the same one he used to describe Jesus silencing demons (cf. 1:25; 3:12). Peter reacted with "an air of conscious superiority."[387] He probably "took" Jesus "aside" to avoid appearing to rebuke the Lord in the presence of the other disciples.[388]

> "It is often assumed that the suggestion that the Messiah would suffer must have been shocking to Peter. Perhaps it was rather the suggestion that he would suffer after rejection by the authorities of Israel that called forth Peter's rebuke. The idea of the Messiah suffering a glorious martyrdom at the hand of Israel's foes may not have been altogether strange to him . . ."[389]

8:33   Jesus spoke His rebuke for the other disciples as well as for Peter. This indicates that Peter was speaking for them. Jesus addressed Peter as "Satan," because He recognized Satan as the ultimate (and immediate) source of Peter's suggestion (cf. Matt. 4:10). Peter's words had opposed God's will in favor of the popular messianic idea.

2. The requirements of discipleship 8:34—9:1 (cf. Matt. 16:24-28; Luke 9:23-27)

Jesus now proceeded to explain to His disciples that suffering would not only be His destiny but theirs too.

8:34   Jesus now addressed "the crowd," as well as "His disciples," because the requirements are the same for anyone who contemplates discipleship. Some in the crowd were thinking about becoming Jesus' disciples but had not yet made up their minds.

> "He stated two requirements which, like repent and believe (cf. 1:15), are bound together."[390]

One, a negative requirement, is self-denial, replacing one's own preferences and plans with God's priorities and program.[391]

> "To deny oneself is to disown, not just one's sins, but one's self, to turn away from the idolatry of self-centredness [*sic*]."[392]

The other, a positive requirement, is following Jesus faithfully and publicly—even though that would mean shame, suffering, and perhaps physical death (cf. 1:17-18; 2:14; 10:21, 52).

Four explanatory clarifications follow, each introduced by "for" (Gr. *gar*, vv. 35-38) plus an encouragement (v. 38). They are appropriate warnings for present disciples and those considering discipleship. For believers, they apply to the loss of reward,

---

[386]Wessel, p. 696. For further discussion of the "messianic secret," see Lowery, pp. 74-76.

[387]Swete, p. 180.

[388]Cranfield, p. 279.

[389]Ibid., p. 280.

[390]Grassmick, p. 140.

[391]See Michael P. Green, "The Meaning of Cross-Bearing," *Bibliotheca Sacra* 140:558 (April-June 1983):117-33.

[392]Cranfield, p. 281.

and for unbelievers, to the loss of eternal life, i.e., the salvation *they could have had*. Both types of people were in Jesus' audience when He said this.

8:35   Jesus used the word "life" (Gr. *psyche*) in two ways in this verse. The translation of this Greek word as "soul" here has caused some people to conclude that Jesus was only warning about the loss of salvation. He was not. In its first occurrence in each clause, "life" refers to one's physical life. In the second part of each clause, "it" means the essential person (the soul/spirit) that continues to exist beyond the grave. Likewise, "lose" has two meanings. In the first clause, "lose it" means the loss of *reward* for believers, and the loss of *salvation* for unbelievers. In the second clause, "loses his life" means loss of physical life—which can include physical suffering, loss of health and or well-being, or literal death.

Jesus meant that if a person wants to retain control of his or her life now, he or she will suffer the loss of something more valuable in the future. Conversely, if a person will relinquish control of his or her life to follow God's will faithfully, he or she will gain something of greater ultimate worth.[393]

"The calm assertion, 'for my sake,' reflects Christ's consciousness of His unique supremacy which justly claims the absolute allegiance of His disciples. *And the gospel's*, added only in Mark (cf. 10:29), points to the message which he accepts and propagates at the cost of himself. The two form two sides of one great reality. Christ is known to us only through the gospel, and our adherence to the gospel means our loyalty to Him."[394]

"In the second half of Mark 'the gospel' always denotes the message announced by the Church, of which Jesus is the content (Chs. 8:35; 10:29; 13:10; 14:9), precisely as in Ch. 1:1."[395]

8:36-37   The *psyche* in these verses means the essential person (soul/spirit). It is foolish to preserve one's comforts now, because by doing so one sacrifices something of much greater value—that God would otherwise give him or her. The "whole world" includes: earthly possessions, position, pleasure, and power—all that the world can provide. Verse 37 stresses the irrevocable nature of the choice.

8:38   "Whoever" means unbelievers or believers (cf. v. 34). For unbelievers living when the Son of Man returns to set up His kingdom, Jesus being "ashamed before" His "Father" will result in their loss of salvation. For believers living then, it will mean their loss of reward. This is the first explicit reference in Mark to Jesus' return in glory (though 4:21-22 and 30-32 contain veiled references). Being ashamed of Jesus, rejecting His claims, has serious consequences.

". . . this conflict between Jesus and the disciples on the way to Jerusalem exemplifies the clash between the values of the disciples and those of Jesus."[396]

". . . why should you deny yourself, take up your cross, and follow Jesus? (1) Because you will save your life for eternity even though you lose it now. Here is a savings account with better returns than you ever dreamed of (v 35). (2) because your life is much more valuable than the whole world; so do not be gulled into making a foolish deal (v 36). (3) because once you have lost your life, there is no buying it back, no matter how much you offer. The opportunity to invest in futures is now; do not let it slip by (v 37). (4) because when the tables are turned on this hostile world, when the glorious Son of man comes with the approval of God his Father and with the holy angels as his army, you will want to be on his side, not on the world's side [v. 38]."[397]

9:1   This verse is the positive truth about the coming kingdom, whereas 8:38 expressed the negative. It concludes Jesus' solemn warnings in this pericope on an encouraging note. Some standing in that mixed audience would not experience death before they saw a preview of the kingdom that the Son of Man would establish after He came in glory (8:38; cf. 2 Pet. 1:16-19). Those individuals were Peter, James, and John (vv. 2-8).

This pericope should warn unbelievers and believers alike. It is also an encouragement to become a disciple of Jesus and to follow Him faithfully. The choice involves eternal loss or gain. This section would have been a special encouragement for Mark's original readers who faced the choice of undergoing persecutions and trials for faithful commitment or abandoning their life of discipleship. Suffering and temporary loss would be Jesus' portion, and that would also be the destiny of His disciples. However, His faithful followers would eventually experience glory and blessing, as He would.

---

[393]See Narry F. Santos, "Jesus' Paradoxical Teaching in Mark 8:35; 9:35; and 10:43-44," *Bibliotheca Sacra* 157:625 (January-March 2000):15-25.

[394]Hiebert, p. 209.

[395]Lane, p. 309.

[396]Rhoads and Michie, p. 91.

[397]Gundry, pp. 439-40.

3. The Transfiguration 9:2-8 (cf. Matt. 17:1-8; Luke 9:28-36)

This event not only fulfilled Jesus' prediction in verse 1, but it also confirmed what Peter had confessed in 8:29. Despite Jesus' coming death (8:31-32), it assured His disciples of eventual glory (8:38). Jesus had just finished addressing a wide audience (8:34). Now He spoke to a very narrow one (v. 2).

"The transfiguration scene develops as a new 'Sinai' theophany with Jesus as the central figure."[398]

9:2-4   Mark's account is almost identical to Matthew's here. He added that Jesus' garments became whiter than any human "launderer" could make ("whiten") them. This reflects an eyewitness's testimony if nothing else. Perhaps the reference to six days followed by revelation should recall Exodus 24:15-16. Moses was on Mt. Sinai for six days and then God revealed Himself on the seventh. This is the most precise timeline in Mark's Gospel before the passion story. It also connects this fulfillment with Jesus' prediction in verse 1. In the Old Testament, the glory of God was represented with bright light. Mark placed Elijah in the prominent position before Moses (v. 4), probably because he was to be Messiah's forerunner (Mal. 3:1; 4:5).

9:5-6   Mark explained Peter's blunder in verse 5 in verse 6. He did it more fully than Luke did. Matthew did not give a reason for Peter's words. Again Peter opposed Jesus' sufferings and death, though he was not fully aware of what he was doing (cf. 8:32). He evidently believed that Jesus was going to set up His kingdom immediately (cf. Acts 1:6).

9:7-8   A "cloud" frequently pictured God's presence and protection in the Old Testament (e.g., Exod. 16:10; 19:9; 24:15-16; 33:1; 40:34-38; Num. 9:15-22; 1 Kings 8:10-11, Isa. 4:5). Probably the cloud enveloped and concealed Jesus, Moses, and Elijah, rather than simply overshadowing them.[399] The heavenly "voice" assured the disciples that, even though the Jews would reject Jesus and the Romans would execute Him, He was still pleasing to the Father (cf. 1:11).[400] It also helped these disciples understand Jesus' superiority over the greatest of God's former servants (cf. Deut. 18:15; Ps. 2:7; Isa. 42:1). They disappeared, but Jesus remained—indicating the end of their ministries, in contrast to Jesus' continuing ministry. Listening to Jesus in the fullest sense means obeying Him.

This revelation should encourage every disciple of Jesus. The Son of Man's humiliation will give way to His glorification. He will certainly return to earth and establish the kingdom that the biblical prophets predicted. The faithful disciple can anticipate a glorious future with Him as surely as the beloved Son could look forward to that kingdom (cf. 8:35).

4. The coming of Elijah 9:9-13 (cf. Matt. 17:9-13)

The appearance of Elijah on the mountain led to a discussion of his role as Messiah's forerunner. This conversation developed as the disciples followed Jesus down the mountain.

9:9   Jesus again commanded secrecy to avoid being mobbed (cf. vv. 15, 25; 1:34, 43-44; 3:11-12; 5:43; 7:36; 8:30). William Wrede developed the view that Jesus never claimed to be the Messiah and that the early church originated that idea.[401] Mark, he argued, invented incidents in which Jesus commanded secrecy about His messiahship to resolve this contradiction. Most conservative scholars have rejected this theory because the evidence for Jesus' messiahship is pervasive in all the Gospels.

               If the multitudes heard about this demonstration of Jesus' glory, it would only fuel the fires of popular messianic expectation that created pressure for Jesus to depart from God's will. This is the last command to maintain secrecy in this Gospel. It is also the only one with a time limit. The people the disciples would soon tell the transfiguration story to would only understand it after Jesus arose from the dead. With His resurrection behind them, they could appreciate the fact that He would return in glory to establish the messianic kingdom.

9:10   The Old Testament taught a resurrection of the dead (Ps. 16; Isa. 26:19; Dan. 12:2; cf. John 11:24), but the disciples could not harmonize that revelation with Jesus' statement that He would rise three days after He died (8:31). The whole idea of Messiah dying was incomprehensible to them.

9:11   Rather than asking for clarification about the resurrection issue, the disciples raised questions about the larger problem of Messiah dying. If Jesus was the Messiah and He would die, what did the scribes' teaching about Elijah being the forerunner of Messiah mean (Mal. 3:1-4; 4:5-6)? They taught that he would turn the hearts of the people back to God (cf. Mal. 4:6), but Elijah had not appeared and most of the people had not repented.

---

[398]Lane, p. 317.

[399]Cranfield, p. 292.

[400]Plummer, p. 215.

[401]William Wrede, *The Messianic Secret*. See Cranfield, pp. 78-79, for refutation of Wrede's theory.

9:12	Jesus affirmed the scribes' interpretation of the prophecy about Elijah. He went on to explain that that interpretation did not invalidate what He had just predicted about His own sufferings and shameful rejection (Ps. 22; Isa. 52:13—53:12).
9:13	The disciples thought Elijah still had to come, but Jesus explained that he had come. His enemies had done to him what the Old Testament recorded. Jesus was speaking of John the Baptist (Matt. 17:13). The Old Testament passage to which Jesus referred was 1 Kings 19:1-3 and 10. There Ahab, and especially Jezebel, swore to kill Elijah. They "wished" to execute him. This is exactly what "King" Herod Antipas, and especially Herodias, really did to John the Baptist. Now we see why Mark recorded the story of John's death (6:17-29). It was to show that John the Baptist fulfilled the prophecies about Elijah coming.

> "In this case Scripture had foretold the future not by prophecy but by a type. The fate intended for Elijah (I Kings xix. 2, 10) had overtaken John."[402]

Evidently Mark did not mention John the Baptist as the fulfillment of this prophecy, as Matthew did, because his identity is obvious to the careful reader. The fulfillment was not complete, however, because someone will come in the spirit and power of Elijah to prepare the way before Messiah's second coming (Mal. 4:5; cf. Rev. 11).

This discussion clarified for the disciples, and for Mark's readers, how Jesus' messiahship harmonized with Old Testament prophecy that seems to contradict it. Disciples of Jesus must have no doubts about His being the Son of Man, especially since they can anticipate testing through suffering for their faith. The importance of strong faith comes through in the next incident that Mark narrated.

5. The exorcism of an epileptic boy 9:14-29 (cf. Matt. 17:14-20; Luke 9:37-43a)

This is the last exorcism that Mark recorded. His narration of this story includes more detail than either Matthew or Luke's. The disciples' lack of glory in this story contrasts with Jesus' glory in the Transfiguration.

9:14-15	Mark did not explain the reason for the crowd's great amazement (Gr. *exethambethesan*) at seeing Jesus. Since Jesus had forbidden Peter, James, and John from speaking about the Transfiguration, it is unlikely that some glorious afterglow caused the crowd's reaction. Probably the nine disciples' failure to cast out the demon, followed by Jesus' personal appearance, produced their extreme response (cf. 10:32).
9:16-18	Perhaps Mark alone recorded Jesus' question, in order to stress His humanity. The result of the demons' activity again shows their destructive purpose (cf. 5:1-5). Jesus had given His disciples power to cast out demons (3:15), and they had done so successfully earlier (6:13). This boy showed the symptoms of epilepsy because of the demons' affliction.
9:19	The "unbelieving generation" included the father and the crowd. The nine disciples could not exorcize the demon because of their weak faith (cf. v. 29). Jesus' first rhetorical question expressed frustration that His presence with them had not resulted in greater faith (cf. 4:40; 6:50, 52; 8:17-21). His second question reveals the heavy load that their unbelief placed on Him (cf. 3:5; 8:12).

> "Mark probably wanted his own audience to take a warning against unbelief in Jesus, unbelief caused by the scandal of the Crucifixion."[403]

9:20-22	Mark's unique record of Jesus' third "How long?" question shows His compassion. A demon had afflicted the boy for several years. Evidently the failure of the nine disciples had weakened the father's confidence in Jesus to help his son.
9:23-24	The father thought the crucial question was whether Jesus could heal the boy. Jesus explained that it was really whether the father *could* believe that Jesus *could* heal him. This pinpointed the father's understanding of who Jesus was (cf. 1:40). The issue was not how strongly the father believed Jesus *would* heal his son.[404] This is an important distinction. Modern "faith healers" usually stress the amount of trust that the person coming for help has, rather than the *object* of that trust. Later, Jesus revealed that the disciples' failure to heal the boy resulted from lack of trust in Him, too (v. 29).

[402]Swete, p. 194.
[403]Gundry, p. 489.
[404]Cranfield, p. 303.

"One who has faith will set no limits to the power of God."[405]

"But the faith that has such mighty results will submit to the will of God in making its petitions. Faith-prompted prayer asks in harmony with the will of God."[406]

The father voiced his confidence in Jesus, imperfect as it was, and asked Jesus to strengthen his faith.

"He declares that he *believes* and yet acknowledges himself to have *unbelief*. These two statements may appear to contradict each other but there is none of us that does not experience both of them in himself."[407]

He was an unbelieving believer, namely, a believer whose faith was weak.

9:25-27   Jesus acted quickly to avoid greater publicity.

"Addressing the spirit as deaf as well as dumb heightens the difficulty of the exorcism which Jesus is performing and may carry some irony in that a deaf spirit should not be able to hear his command to come out—but he *makes* it hear."[408]

". . . the accumulation of the vocabulary of death and resurrection in verses 26-27, and the parallelism with the narrative of the raising of Jairus' daughter [5:39-42], suggest that Mark wished to allude to a death and resurrection. The dethroning of Satan is always a reversal of death and an affirmation of life."[409]

9:28-29   Evidently the nine disciples were ineffective, because they believed that the power to cast out demons, that Jesus had given them, was now inherent in (part of) themselves. It was not. It was still God's power, and it came directly from Him. Therefore they needed to acknowledge their dependence on *Him*, for power, in order to be successful.

"Experience can teach, but it cannot empower."[410]

Jesus' prayer life reflected even *His* dependence on the Father. Some cases require more spiritual power than others, and some demons are stronger than others (Matt. 12:45). Probably later copyists added "and fasting" because fasting often accompanied earnest prayer in the early church, as it did in Israel.[411]

This incident taught the disciples that they needed to serve God in constant conscious dependence on Him that expresses itself in prayer. "Prayer" is a discipline that reminds disciples of, and expresses their dependence on, God. It also reinforced their belief in Jesus as the Messiah, who would defeat Satan, and so is worthy of glory, as the Transfiguration witnessed.

B. THE SECOND PASSION PREDICTION AND ITS LESSONS 9:30—10:31

For a second time, Jesus told His disciples of His coming death and resurrection (cf. 8:31), and again they failed to understand what He meant (cf. 8:32-33). Jesus responded by teaching them additional lessons on discipleship (cf. 8:34—9:29).

1. The second major prophecy of Jesus' passion 9:30-32 (cf. Matt. 17:22-23; Luke 9:43-45)

Jesus and the disciples probably left the region of Caesarea Philippi and Mt. Hermon, or wherever they were now, and proceeded farther south toward Jerusalem through Galilee. In view of what lay ahead in Jerusalem, Jesus again prepared them by telling them that He would suffer execution and experience resurrection.

9:30   Jesus' public ministry in Galilee was over. He wanted to pass through that area without further distractions from the multitudes.

---

[405]Rawlinson, p. 124. See also Ryrie, p. 133.

[406]Hiebert, p. 223. Cf. John 14:13-14; 15:16; 16:23-24; and 1 John 5:11-15.

[407]Calvin, 2:325.

[408]Gundry, p. 491.

[409]Lane, p. 334.

[410]Ryrie, p. 134.

[411]Cranfield, p. 305.

9:31 Jesus was concentrating on teaching His disciples during this phase of His ministry. Here He revealed to them for the first time that someone would deliver Him up or hand Him over (Gr. *paradidotai*) to His enemies. Ultimately God did this, but Judas was the human agent that brought His will to pass. Probably there is an intended contrast between "Son of Man" and "men" in this verse.

"... in a fallen world men had become so hostile to God that when, as the culmination of his plans for their salvation, he sent to them the Man, their Saviour and ultimate model, they regarded and treated him as their worst enemy. Men and the Son of Man stood on opposite sides in God's eschatological battle against the powers of evil."[412]

Mark recorded Jesus saying that He would rise of His own power (active voice). Matthew said Jesus spoke of being raised (passive voice, Matt. 17:23). Probably Jesus said both things in the course of His teaching. This verse probably summarizes instruction that Jesus gave the disciples as they walked.[413]

9:32 The disciples did not understand because God withheld understanding from them (Luke 9:45). Initially, God may have appeared to be working at cross purposes with Himself, revealing through Jesus and concealing by hardening the disciples' hearts. The solution seems to be that God was working with the disciples as He had worked with the multitudes through Jesus' parables. If so, the disciples' ignorance was a result of divine blindness that their unbelief produced. Their willingness to remain in ignorance and not ask Jesus to clarify His statement is the evidence of their unbelief. Mark implied that all they gained from this revelation was a sense of sorrow (Matt. 17:23). Similarly, *we* manifest a form of unbelief, when we fail to seek clarification of biblical revelation that we find confusing.

2. The pitfalls of discipleship 9:33-50

Jesus next taught His disciples lessons dealing with the dangers that threatened their effectiveness as His disciples. These were the desire for greatness, the folly of a sectarian attitude, and failure in self-discipline. They would suffer as He would. Moreover their suffering would threaten their unity with Jesus and with one another.

"Jesus warned against the spirit of elitism that can exist within a ministry team and between ministry teams. The answer to elitism from within is to have a servant's heart, and the answer to elitism toward outsiders is to recognize the unity of the family of God that transcends smaller groups of ministry."[414]

The desire for greatness 9:33-37 (cf. Matt. 18:1-5; Luke 9:46-48)

9:33-34 Jesus returned "to Capernaum," evidently after several months of absence. This was His last recorded activity there. Rather than discussing Jesus' coming death and resurrection, the disciples had been arguing about their own futures in the kingdom. Their silence was probably a result of shame.

"'Does the favor shown to Peter, James, and John, in selecting them to be eye-witnesses of the prefigurement of the coming glory, imply a corresponding precedence in the kingdom itself?' The three disciples probably hoped it did; the other disciples hoped not, and so the dispute began."[415]

9:35 By seating Himself, Jesus assumed the traditional position of a rabbi. He taught them that greatness in His kingdom depends on sacrificial service. All three synoptic evangelists recorded His words, indicating the importance of this lesson.

"The spirit of service is the passport to eminence in the Kingdom of God, for it is the spirit of the Master Who Himself became *diakonos panton* ["servant of all"]."[416]

The Greek word for servant, *diakonos*, describes someone who serves willingly. It does not describe the servile status of such a person, which *doulos* (slave) suggests. The desire to excel need not be unspiritual (cf. 1 Tim. 3:1). However, it must include willingness to put the welfare of others before selfish interests.[417]

---

[412]Plummer, p. 222.

[413]Bruce, "The Synoptic . . .," 1:404.

[414]Bailey, p. 84.

[415]Bruce, *The Training* . . ., p. 200.

[416]Swete, p. 205.

[417]See Santos, pp. 20-23, 25.

9:36-37	"Just as by sitting he [Jesus] took the authoritative posture of a teacher, so he makes the child take the reverential posture of standing, as befits one who will turn out to represent all children who believe in Jesus (see v 42 . . .)."[418]

A child was the least significant person in Jewish and in Greco-Roman culture.[419] By using "a child" as His object lesson, Jesus was saying that service involves caring about people, even insignificant people such as children. The same Aramaic word means both "child" and "servant."[420]

"Jesus was one of the first ever to see how essentially precious any person is, particularly a young child. A concern for children was not invented by the welfare state: it goes back to the teaching of Jesus."[421]

Jesus proceeded to compare the humblest of His disciples to the child (cf. v. 42). This was the focus of Jesus' teaching that Matthew recorded (cf. Matt. 18:3-14).

The folly of a sectarian attitude 9:38-42 (cf. Matt. 18:6-7; Luke 9:49-50)

9:38	This is the only place where the synoptic writers mentioned John speaking out alone. John spoke for the other disciples in the house (v. 33).

Evidently the exorcist was a believer in Jesus, though not one of the Twelve, or possibly not even one who spent much time following Jesus around. He evidently commanded demons to leave the people they afflicted by using Jesus' name. The Twelve apparently did not mind that this man claimed Jesus' authority to exorcize demons. They objected to his actions because Jesus had not commissioned him to do so as He had the Twelve (3:14-15). Perhaps his success and the recent failure of the nine disciples irritated them further. In view of what Jesus had just said about receiving little children, John wondered if the Twelve had done right in rebuking the man. They had tried to protect Jesus' honor by rebuking him (cf. Num. 11:26-29).

"It is striking . . . that after each of the three major prophecies of the passion the evangelist inserts the response of one of the three disciple who were closest to Jesus: Peter (Ch. 8:32f.), John (Ch. 9:38), and James, with John (Ch. 10:35-37). Mark shows in this way that even the most privileged of the disciples failed to understand what the passion signified for their life and mission."[422]

"John is not now what he will be, but differs from his future self, as much as an orange in its second year differs from the same orange in its third final year of growth. The fruit of the Spirit will ultimately ripen in this disciple into something very sweet and beautiful; but meantime it is green, bitter, and fit only to set the teeth on edge."[423]

9:39-40	Jesus did not mind that the man was casting out demons by invoking His name. Since the man had such respect for Jesus, he would not "soon" speak against Him. By casting out demons, he showed that he was not against Jesus. Jesus expressed the opposite truth in Matthew 12:30: "He who is not with Me is against Me." There is no neutral ground regarding one's orientation to Jesus. Jesus' point was that the disciples should not view the exorcist as an antagonist—just because he was not part of their group. He was doing God's will and would not oppose them.

"Jesus avoided forcing men precipitously into a position in which they had to make a final decision about him and used delayed-action methods of teaching in order to give them as much time as possible in which to decide. So long as the critical point has not been reached the principle of Mk ix. 40 holds, and the attitude of the disciple toward those who have not yet decided is to be that of recognizing in the unbeliever of today the possible believer of tomorrow . . ."[424]

9:41	The connecting idea with what precedes is the "name." Not only would the exorcist receive God's blessing, but anyone who does anything to help another person using even the name of a disciple of Jesus would receive His reward. This help extends

[418]Gundry, p. 509.

[419]*Theological Dictionary of the New Testament*, s.v. "*pais*," by Albrecht Oepke, 5:639-52.

[420]Lane, p. 340.

[421]Moule, p. 75.

[422]Lane, p. 342.

[423]Bruce, *The Training . . .*, p. 231.

[424]Cranfield, p. 311.

to the almost insignificant act of giving "a cup of" cold "water" to some thirsty person. This act was much less helpful than delivering from demonic affliction.

This is one of the rare occasions when Jesus used the title "Messiah" of Himself. His use of it here makes the lesson even more forceful. The person giving the cup of cold water might have only a superficial understanding of Jesus. Nonetheless, if that person offered simple hospitality to one of Jesus' disciples—"because" he was a disciple of "Messiah"—that one would receive God's blessing.

9:42   This verse gives the other side of the idea just expressed. Anyone who discouraged a disciple of Jesus from following Him faithfully could expect severe treatment from God. Probably Jesus used the little child present to illustrate or represent a childlike disciple (vv. 36-37; cf. Matt. 18:3-14). Jesus referred to a large donkey-driven "millstone" (Gr. *mylos onikos*), not a small one that people turned by hand (Gr. *mylos*). The Romans had so drowned some insurrectionists in Galilee (cf. Acts 5:37), and a group of the Galileans had so dealt with some of Herod's supporters.[425] The disciples had probably heard about these events.

"This brief incident stands as a firm rebuke to the spirit of sectarianism. It condemns that exclusive attitude which insists that only those who carry on their work in harmony with our own views and practices can be accepted as really doing God's work. If they demonstrate that they are on God's side in the war with Satan, even though their views may be imperfect, they must not be condemned for such work or regarded with abhorrence."[426]

"Just as The Twelve's receiving and serving child-believers will counteract pretensions to grandeur, so the Twelve's letting the independent exorcist carry on his ministry apart from themselves will counteract those same pretensions."[427]

"In summary, the independent exorcist is not to be hindered, (1) because suspecting fellow believers outside one's close circle underestimates the number of people loyal to Jesus (v 39b); (2) because a sense of rivalry makes believers fail to recognize their friends (v 40); and (3) because receiving a messenger of the gospel brings salvation to a quondam [former] unbeliever (v 41), whereas causing even a child who believes in Jesus to sin brings judgment on the believer who causes the sin (v 42)."[428]

John evidently learned this lesson well, as evidenced by the frequent references to loving one another that appear in his writings.

Failure in self-discipline 9:43-50 (cf. Matt. 18:8-14)

Jesus' proceeded to elaborate on the importance of disciples dealing radically with sin in their lives. He had just warned about leading other disciples astray. Now He cautioned against being led astray oneself.

"Seducing simple souls is disastrously easy work; but still more easy is seducing oneself, by letting the body lead the spirit astray."[429]

9:43-48   Jesus compared the members of the human body to the agents of sinful activities. He did not want His disciples to perform *physical* surgery, but *spiritual* surgery, to excise the sin within themselves. The language is hyperbolic, but Jesus described real sins. The threefold repetition highlights the importance of the warning (cf. Rom. 6:12-13).

"It was not a Palestinian custom to refer to an abstract activity but to the specific member of the body which is responsible for it. For this reason Jesus speaks of the offending hand, foot and eye, all members which have highly important functions to fulfill."[430]

"As a surgeon does not hesitate to cut off a gangrenous hand to save a life, so evil and destructive practices, though precious to us as a very part of our lives, must be sacrificed to save the soul [person]."[431]

---

[425]Lane, p. 346; Suetonius, *De Vita Caesarum* 1:67; Josephus, *Antiquities of . . .*, 14:15:10.

[426]Hiebert, p. 231.

[427]Gundry, p. 510.

[428]Ibid., p. 513.

[429]Plummer, p. 226.

[430]Lane, pp. 347-48.

[431]Hiebert, p. 232.

"Hell" translates the Greek word *gehenna*, the transliteration of the Hebrew phrase *ge hinnom* (lit. "Valley of Hinnom"). This valley, just south of Jerusalem, is where apostate Jews formerly offered human sacrifices to the pagan god Molech (cf. Jer. 7:31; 19:5-6; 32:35). King Josiah terminated this practice and converted the site into a city dump where rubbish burned constantly (2 Kings 23:10). The fire never went out at Jerusalem's *gehenna*, and the worms that fed on the garbage never died off. "Unquenchable fire" must mean *eternal*.[432] External "fire" and internal "worms" are Old Testament pictures of destruction (cf. Isa. 66:24). Thus *gehenna* became a picture of the place of eternal punishment (Enoch 27:2; 90:26), not annihilation.[433] The word *gehenna* appears 12 times in the New Testament, and in all but one of these occurrences Jesus spoke it (i.e., James 3:6).

Disciples should take prompt and decisive action against anything that might lead them away from their allegiance to Jesus. Physical temptations come through the hands (what we do), the feet (where we go), and the eyes (what we see) primarily. Disciples who are believers will suffer the loss of rewards in the kingdom if they do not exercise self-discipline. Disciples who are unbelievers will experience eternal damnation if they fail to do so.

Verses 44 and 46 are absent in important early manuscripts. Probably scribes added them later to fill out the parallelism in the passage. They repeat verse 48.

9:49   This verse evidently alludes to Leviticus 2:13 (cf. Exod. 30:35; Ezek. 43:24). The "everyone" in view could refer to unbelievers who enter hell. Unbelievers are the immediate antecedent of this verse. As salt preserves food, so God will preserve them forever in torment.

A second interpretation is that "everyone" refers to believers living in a hostile world. Jesus' believing disciples were those to whom He addressed these words. As the Old Testament priests salted the animal sacrifices, so God will season His living sacrifices with fiery trials to purify their faith (cf. 1 Pet. 1:7; 4:12).[434]

A third interpretation is that "everyone" refers to every person, unbelievers and believers alike.[435] God will subject everyone to fiery trials. He does this to believers and unbelievers alike during their earthly lives (James 1:1-18). He will also do this to believers' works when they stand before the judgment seat of Christ (cf. Matt. 25:14-46; 1 Cor. 3:10-15). He will do this to unbelievers when they stand before Him at the great white throne judgment (Rev. 20:11-15). This seems to me to be the best interpretation. It takes "everyone" literally and is consistent with other revelation. The point is that everyone should realize that divine testing is an inevitable part of life.[436]

Since this verse appears only in Mark, it must have had special significance for the original readers. If they were Roman Christians, it would have encouraged them to realize that the fires of persecution were part of their calling. Everyone will experience trials (cf. James 1:1-18). We sometimes say that "into every life a little rain must fall." We could change that a little and say that "into every life a little salt of testing must fall."

9:50   Jesus continued to use "salt" as a figure for testing. He said that tests from God, as salt on food, are "good" for us. Salt preserves food, prevents decay, and enhances flavor. The trials that God allows people to experience should have similar beneficial effects on them (cf. James 1:2-4). However, if salt becomes bland, it will not achieve its desired results (cf. Matt. 5:13). Likewise if God's trials lose their bite—if we become insensible and unresponsive to the self-discipline that He is seeking to teach us, by hardening our hearts—these trials can cease to benefit us. Therefore we must "have salt in" ourselves, namely, accept the trials that God sends us that demand self-discipline, rather than rejecting them. Furthermore we must live peacefully "with one another," rather than becoming sectarian (v. 38) or self-seeking (v. 34).

Another less probable view, I think, of what Jesus meant by the figure of "salt" follows. This view connects with references in a more distant context.

> "It seems likely that the saltiness of the salt stands for that for which the disciples are to be prepared to lose their lives (viii. 35), and of which they are not to be ashamed (viii. 38), i.e. the gospel, Jesus' words, Jesus himself."[437]

This command concludes this section of instruction that deals with the enemies of disciple fidelity (9:33-50).

---

[432]Lenski, p. 408.

[433]See Robert A. Peterson, "Does the Bible Teach Annihilationism?" *Bibliotheca Sacra* 156:621 (January-March 1999):13-27.

[434]Hiebert, p. 234; Lane, p. 349; Lenski, pp. 410-11; Cranfield, pp. 315-16; Taylor, p. 413; Cole, p. 224.

[435]E.g., *The Nelson . . .*, p. 1661.

[436]H. A. W. Meyer, "Critical and Exegetical Hand-Book to the Gospels of Mark and Luke," in *Meyer's Critical and Exegetical Commentary on the New Testament*, pp. 120-23, listed 15 different interpretations.

[437]Cranfield, p. 316.

3. Lessons concerning self-sacrifice 10:1-31

Jesus gave this series of lessons south of Galilee in Perea and Judea, not in Galilee. Another contrast is the audience. He gave the preceding instruction to the disciples in a house, but He gave this teaching to the multitudes and the disciples in the open air.

The transition from Galilee to Judea 10:1 (cf. Matt. 19:1-2)

Though Mark did not record it, Jesus gave His disciples much additional instruction as they traveled from Capernaum in Galilee toward Jerusalem (cf. Matt. 8:19-22; 18:15-35; Luke 9:51—18:14; John 7:2—11:54). Evidently Jesus departed from Capernaum and journeyed through Samaria to Jerusalem. Then He proceeded east across the Jordan River into Perea, which lay east and north of the Dead Sea. From there He returned to Jerusalem again. Leaving Jerusalem Jesus visited the tribal territory of Ephraim, traveled farther north into Samaria, headed east into Perea, and returned to Jerusalem a third time. The following ministry took place during this last loop in Perea and Judea.[438]

Jesus' instruction about marriage 10:2-12 (cf. Matt. 19:3-12)

10:2   This teaching grew out of the Pharisees' attempt to trap Jesus. The incident occurred in Perea, Herod Antipas' territory. Perhaps the Pharisees wanted to get Jesus to explain His view of divorce because they suspected it was the same as John the Baptist's. John had lost his head literally because of his views on marriage. Probably Jesus' critics hoped that He would also antagonize the Roman ruler with His views. The form of their question implied they thought that Jesus was against divorce for any reason.

The Pharisees all believed that the Old Testament permitted Jewish men to divorce their wives and to remarry (Deut. 24:1-4). They disagreed among themselves on the grounds for divorce. Followers of Rabbi Shammai believed Moses meant the only ground was fornication: any sexual sin. Rabbi Hillel's disciples held that anything a wife did that displeased her husband constituted legitimate grounds for divorce.

10:3   Jesus responded in rabbinic fashion with another question. He asked the Pharisees what Moses, the authority whom they all professed to recognize, taught. Jesus sent them to God's Word, rather than debating traditional interpretations that the Pharisees treated as authoritative.

10:4-5   The Pharisees viewed Moses' permission as God's desire, but Jesus viewed it as a divine concession.

"A distinction has to be made between that which sets forth the absolute will of God, and those provisions which take account of men's actual sinfulness and are designed to limit and control its consequences. Whereas the Ten Commandments (in this connection Exod. xx. 14) and such passages as the verses quoted in vv. 6-8 represent God's absolute command, Deut. xxiv. 1 is a divine provision to deal with situations brought about by men's *sklerokardia* [hardness of heart] and to protect from its worst effects those who would suffer as a result of it. (Much that is contained in the O.T. falls within the category of such provisions.)"[439]

10:6-8   Jesus contrasted the Pharisee's view of marriage with God's view of it. God instituted marriage.

"In Gen 2:24, 'for this cause' did not refer to God's making the first human beings 'male a female,' but to God's making Eve out of Adam's rib. The reason for a man's leaving his father and mother, cleaving to his wife, and becoming one flesh with her was not sexual, then. It had to do with Eve's origin in Adam: since woman came from man, man should unite himself with woman to recapture their original unity."[440]

Marriage involves the union of a male and a female that results in a uniquely close relationship, a "one flesh" relationship. "One flesh" is a Semitic expression that means "one."[441] This relationship is closer than even the parent-child relationship. Furthermore it continues throughout the rest of the husband and wife's lives.

"The import of all this is that marriage from its very nature and from the divine institution by which it is constituted is ideally indissoluble. It is not a contract of temporary convenience and not a union that may be dissolved at will."[442]

[438]Hoehner, *Chronological Aspects . . .*, pp. 62-63.
[439]Cranfield, p. 319.
[440]Gundry, pp. 531-32.
[441]Wessel, p. 711.

"While the spiritual element is vitally important in marriage, the emphasis here is that marriage is a *physical* union: the two become one *flesh*, not one spirit. Since marriage is a physical union, only a physical cause can break it—either death (Rom. 7:1-3) or fornication (Matt. 5:32; 19:9)."[443]

10:9   Jesus drew a conclusion from what the Scriptures, that He just quoted, revealed. It is therefore wrong for man to break a bond that God has fashioned. Thus Jesus did not side with either school of rabbinic interpretation. He affirmed God's ideal in marriage, namely: no divorce.

10:10-12   The disciples wanted clarification of Jesus' view, so they asked Him for it in private. Mark recorded His straightforward reply. Neither husband nor wife should divorce their partner and remarry someone else. To do so constitutes committing adultery against the spouse.

             Verse 12 is unique in Mark. Under Roman law a wife could divorce her husband, but under Jewish law she could not.[444] There were exceptions, however, as in the case of Herodias who had divorced Philip to marry Antipas (6:17-18). Herod the Great's sister also divorced her husband.[445] Jesus viewed all divorce followed by remarriage as constituting adultery no matter who initiated it. Divorce is wrong, but divorce followed by remarriage is worse.

             "The new element in this teaching, which was totally unrecognized in the rabbinic courts, was the concept of a husband committing adultery against his former wife. According to rabbinic law a man could commit adultery against another married man by seducing his wife (Deut. 22:13-29) and a wife could commit adultery against her husband by infidelity, but a husband could not be said to commit adultery against his wife. . . . This sharp intensifying of the concept of adultery had the effect of elevating the status of the wife to the same dignity as her husband and placed the husband under an obligation of fidelity."[446]

             Mark's omission of the exception clause that Matthew included was also due to his audience (cf. Matt. 5:32; 19:9). He did not want to draw attention to the exceptional case because to do so would weaken the main point, namely, that people should not divorce. Divorce was very common in the Greco-Roman world. Apparently Matthew included Jesus' permission to divorce for fornication, because the subject of how to deal with divorce cases involving marital unfaithfulness was of particular interest to the Jews, his primary audience.

Jesus' instruction about childlikeness 10:13-16 (cf. Matt. 19:13-15; Luke 18:15-17)

The simple trust in Jesus, that the children in this pericope demonstrated, contrasts with the hostility of the Pharisees in the previous paragraph. Another thought connection is the progression from discussing marriage to discussing children.

10:13-14   Mark's account of this incident is very similar to Matthew's. However, Mark alone noted that Jesus became "indignant" when He learned that "the disciples" were discouraging those who "were bringing" the "children (Gr. *paidia*) to Him." This is another indication of the evangelist's interest in Jesus' humanity (cf. 1:25, 41, 43; 3:5; 7:34; 8:12; 9:19). Jesus had formerly commanded His disciples not to forbid the exorcist who cast out demons in Jesus' name (9:39). The disciples were abusing their authority by excluding some people from coming to Jesus: those outside their circle, and those regarded generally as unimportant.

10:15   This verse occurs in Mark and Luke (Luke 18:17), but Matthew recorded Jesus' similar statement on another occasion (Matt. 18:3). It expands Jesus' words in verse 14. Jesus' point was that people must receive things associated with "the kingdom of God" as children receive things, namely, with trust and dependence on Himself. Personal ability and effort do not determine one's reception of God's best gifts, but a proper orientation to Jesus does.

             "To receive the kingdom as a little child is to allow oneself to be given it, because one knows one cannot claim it as one's right or attempt to earn it."[447]

             "We tell the children to behave like adults, but Jesus tells the adults to model themselves after the children!"[448]

---

[442]John Murray, *Divorce*, p. 29.

[443]Wiersbe, 1:144.

[444]Nineham, p. 266, footnote.

[445]Josephus, *Antiquities of . . .*, 15:7:10.

[446]Lane, p. 357.

[447]Cranfield, p. 324.

[448]Wiersbe, 1:145.

10:16   Mark also wrote that Jesus "took" the children "in His arms" and blessed them fervently (Gr. *kateulogei*). This was the act of a father in Jewish life (cf. Gen. 27:38). This Greek word appears only here in the New Testament. The disciples viewed the children as individuals unworthy of Jesus' attention, but Jesus saw them as important in their own right and possessing important qualities that adults need to cultivate. Mark recorded eight times that Jesus touched someone, and in each case the effect was beneficial (cf. 1:41; 3:10; 5:28, 41; 6:56; 7:32; 8:22; 10:13).

> "This was the overflowing of Jesus' divine love for children. It was this experience that the disciples in their insensitivity were preventing the children from having and Jesus from giving! No wonder Jesus was indignant."[449]

Jesus' instruction about wealth 10:17-31

A question from a man in the crowd initiated this incident. Then Jesus proceeded to instruct His disciples following up the encounter. The position of this section in Mark's Gospel is significant. It occurs after Jesus' teaching about the importance of receiving the kingdom with trust and humility (vv. 13-16), and it precedes Jesus' third prediction of His passion (vv. 32-34). The young man thought he could obtain the kingdom with works and self-assertion, not as a little child. Jesus' following call to commitment set up His passion announcement.

The encounter with the rich young ruler 10:17-22 (cf. Matt. 19:16-22; Luke 18:18-23)

10:17   Mark tied this incident into what immediately preceded more closely than the other evangelists did. He wanted his readers to see this young man as expressing exactly the opposite of what Jesus had just taught His disciples. The "man" was a "rich" (v. 22) *young* (Matt. 19:20) *ruler* (Luke 18:18). His approach to Jesus was unusually earnest and respectful, but he viewed eternal life as something one must earn.

Matthew wrote that he asked what he should do to get or obtain (Gr. *scho*) eternal life, but Mark and Luke said that he used the term "inherit" (Gr. *kleponomeo*).

> "*kleponomeso* ["inherit"] reflects Jewish usage, which spoke of 'inheriting' eternal life."[450]

The man clearly did not believe that he had eternal life and wanted to learn what he needed to do to get it. Probably Matthew recorded the exact word he used (the *ipisissima verba*) and Mark and Luke interpreted what he meant (the *ipisissima vox*). It was important for Matthew to tell his original Jewish readers that the young man was talking about getting something that he did not possess. Mark and Luke wrote for Gentiles for whom "inheriting" clarified what was in the rich young ruler's mind. He was talking about getting something that he as a Jew thought that he had a right to obtain because of his ethnic relationship to Abraham.

> "In the rich young ruler's mind entering heaven, inheriting eternal life, and having eternal life were all the same thing, and all meant 'go to heaven when I die.' Jesus neither affirms or denies this equation here. He understands that the young man wants to know how to enter life, or enter the kingdom."[451]

10:18   The man had a superficial understanding of goodness. Jesus' response confronted the man with the implications of trying to do some good work to earn eternal life and calling Jesus "good." Was he ready to respond to Jesus' instructions as to God's Word?

10:19   The Old Testament taught that if a person kept the Mosaic Law he would live (Deut. 30:15-16). This was theoretically possible but practically impossible. Jesus reminded the man of what the law required by citing five commands in the second table of the Decalogue. The commands Jesus mentioned are easily verifiable in conduct. Mark alone recorded the prohibition against defrauding, which was evidently a particular type of stealing pertaining to the wealthy.[452]

10:20   The man's superficial understanding of God's standards became apparent in his claim that he had "kept all" those commandments from his "youth up." He regarded obedience simply as external conformity without internal purity (cf. Phil. 3:6). This was the natural implication and consequence of the Pharisees' teaching. At age 12, a Jewish boy became a "son of the covenant" (Heb. *bar miswah*, from which comes Bar Mitzvah). The Jews regarded themselves as responsible for their obedience to the Law from that age on.[453] It is probably that the man meant he had observed the Law from the age of 12.

---

[449]Wessel, p. 714.

[450]Cranfield, p. 327.

[451]Joseph C. Dillow, *The Reign of the Servant Kings*, p. 65. Cf. William E. Brown, "The New Testament Concept of the Believer's Inheritance" (Th.D. dissertation, Dallas Theological Seminary, 1984).

[452]Plummer, p. 239.

[453]Mishnah *Berachoth* 2:2.

"That man possesses the ability to fulfill the Commandments of God perfectly was so firmly believed by the Rabbis, that they spoke in all seriousness of people who had kept the whole Law from A to Z."[454]

10:21   Only Mark recorded that Jesus loved the rich young ruler when he replied as he did. Evidently the man had sincerely tried to earn eternal life by obeying the law. His superficial understanding of what God required was more his teachers' fault than his own.

Jesus put His finger on what kept this man from having eternal life. He expressed it in the terms that the man had been using, namely, doing something. He was trusting in his wealth, wealth he probably viewed as evidence that his good works made him acceptable to God. The Old Testament taught that God normally blessed the righteous with physical prosperity (e.g., Job 1:10; 42:10; Ps. 128:1-2; Isa. 3:10). He needed to abandon that essentially self-confident faith, and he needed to trust in and follow Jesus. He had also made wealth his god rather than God. His reluctance to part with it revealed his idolatry. By selling all he had, giving it to the poor, and following Jesus—he would confess his repudiation of confidence in self and affirm his trust in Jesus. Then he would "have treasure in heaven," something that would last forever.

Today many people consider themselves good because they have lived a moral life and have not committed gross sins. Some believe that all they need to do is a little more good and God will accept them. They fail to see that they are totally bankrupt spiritually and that even their good deeds are as filthy rags in God's sight. They need to cast themselves on God's mercy, trust in what He has done for them in Christ rather than in their own goodness, and begin following the One who loved them and gave Himself for them. Such was the case with the rich young ruler.

10:22   Abandoning his physical security and trusting in Jesus was too great a risk to take. The rich young ruler's wealth brought him sorrow instead of joy. This is the only time in the Gospels when someone called to follow Jesus did not do so.

Jesus' teaching concerning riches 10:23-31 (cf. Matt. 19:23-30; Luke 18:24-30)

Jesus used the previous incident to teach His disciples about riches. Matthew's account is the fullest.

10:23   The case of this unbeliever had important significance for Jesus' believing disciples. Rather than being a preview of divine eternal blessing, wealth could be a barrier to obtaining it. Jesus did not envy the rich, as most of His contemporaries did. He pitied them.[455] Wealth does not exclude a person from the kingdom, but it gives him a handicap.

"In the O.T. there are two main attitudes toward riches: one regarding them as the sign of God's favour, a reward for goodness, the other identifying the poor with the pious, the rich with the ungodly. Jesus' attitude to the rich, as shown in this verse, is startlingly fresh. He neither covets their wealth, not hates them. Instead he pities them—for the rich man is to be pitied because of his specially great temptations and the frightening handicap in relation to the kingdom of God under which he labours. It is so easy for him to feel a false security and rely on his possessions and become so taken up with them that he forgets what is infinitely more important."[456]

10:24   This verse is unique to Mark. The disciples' amazement arose from the popular belief that riches were a result of God's blessing for righteousness. They thought riches were an advantage, not a disadvantage in one's relationship with God. Only here in the Gospels did Jesus address the disciples as "children" (Gr. *tekna*). Their amazement revealed their spiritual immaturity.

The longer textual reading at the end of verse 24 gives the sense of Jesus' statement, but it was probably not a part of the Gospel originally. The shorter statement is perfectly true as it stands, and accounts partially for the disciples' second amazement (v. 26). Jesus' statement in verse 25 also helps us understand their added surprise.

10:25-26   One writer paraphrased Jesus' proverb as follows.

"It is easier to thread a needle with a great big camel than to get into the kingdom of God when you are bursting with riches."[457]

---

[454]Strack and Billerbeck, 1:814, quoted by Cranfield, p. 329.

[455]Hiebert, p. 249.

[456]Cranfield, p. 331.

[457]Moule, p. 80.

The camel was the largest beast of burden in Palestine. The needle Jesus referred to was a common sewing needle (Gr. *hraphis*). The disciples reacted with amazement because they thought that wealth indicated righteousness (cf. Job, Abraham, Solomon).

10:27   Jesus' point was that salvation is totally God's work (cf. Jon. 2:9; Eph. 2:8-9). It is humanly impossible to obtain it on the basis of achievement or merit. But God can enable anyone to realize his or her complete dependence on Him and turn to Him for salvation.

10:28   Peter, speaking for the other disciples, was still thinking in physical rather than spiritual terms. He turned the conversation back to the subject of giving up all to follow Jesus (v. 22). The rich young ruler had refused to forsake all and follow Jesus, but the disciples had done just that. "We" is emphatic in the Greek text. Mark did not record the rest of Peter's statement: "What then will there be for us?" (Matt. 19:27). Mark did not need to. The implication is clear enough from Peter's statement without his question.

10:29-30   Jesus graciously did not rebuke Peter's selfishness but rewarded his self-sacrifice with a promise. Disciples who follow Jesus wholeheartedly can anticipate three things. First, God will give them more in kind spiritually of what they have sacrificed physically. Second, they will receive persecution as Jesus' disciples. Only Mark mentioned this, undoubtedly for his original persecuted readers' benefit. Commitment to discipleship means "persecutions" as well as rewards. Third, faithful disciples will enjoy their eternal life to an extent that unfaithful disciples will not (cf. John 10:10; 17:3).[458]

> "God takes nothing away from a man without restoring it to him in a new and glorious form."[459]

The present age refers to the inter-advent era, and the age to come refers to the messianic kingdom.

10:31   The "first" in rank and position in this age, such as the rich young ruler, "will be last" in the next. Conversely, "the last" in this age, such as the Twelve apostles, will be "first" in the next. These words summarized Jesus' teaching on discipleship on that occasion and in this section of Mark's Gospel (vv. 1-31). This was a saying that Jesus used at other times as well during His ministry (cf. Matt. 20:16: Luke 13:30). Here, these words also warned Peter against looking for immediate physical rewards for his self-sacrifices (cf. Matt. 20:1-16).

All three of the lessons on discipleship, that Mark recorded in this section of his Gospel, dealt with self-sacrifice (10:1-31). The lessons that Jesus taught following His first passion prediction dealt mainly with future glory (8:31—9:29). Those He taught following His second passion prediction concerned present suffering primarily (9:30—10:31).

C. THE THIRD PASSION PREDICTION AND ITS LESSONS 10:32-52

This is the last time that Jesus, as He approached Jerusalem, told His disciples He would die and rise again. Each time, Jesus gave them more information than He had given before. The first time, the disciples reacted violently (8:32). The second time, they did not understand what He meant, and were afraid to ask Him for an explanation (9:32). Now, the third time, Mark recorded no reaction to Jesus' announcement, except that an argument about who would be the greatest in the kingdom followed immediately. Clearly the disciples did not comprehend what was coming, because they continued to focus increasingly on the coming physical kingdom and their roles in it. Nevertheless Jesus continued to teach them lessons of discipleship that they needed.

1. The third major prophecy of Jesus' passion 10:32-34 (cf. Matt. 20:17-19; Luke 18:31-34)

10:32   Jesus and His disciples were traveling to Jerusalem from somewhere in Perea or Judea. They had not yet passed through Jericho (vv. 46-52). Jesus' position "ahead of them," in typical rabbinic fashion, suggests His determination to go to Jerusalem in spite of His coming death there (cf. 14:28; 16:7). His attitude probably accounted for some of the disciples' amazement. Other disciples, following farther behind, were "fearful" because of what Jesus had said lay ahead there. Jesus turned to give the Twelve further information about His coming passion.

---

[458]See Dillow, pp. 135-36.
[459]Lane, p. 372.

10:33-34   The following chart shows the greater detail of this prediction and the fulfillment in the passion narrative—compared with the previous two predictions.[460]

		First prediction 8:31—9:29	Second prediction 9:30—10:31	Third prediction 10:32-52	Passion narrative 14:1—15:47
1.	Handing over to the Sanhedrin		9:31	10:33	14:53
2.	Condemnation by the Sanhedrin	8:31		10:33	14:64
3.	Handing over to the Romans			10:33	15:1
4.	Mocking, spitting, and scourging			10:34	14:64; 15:15, 16-20
5.	Execution	8:31	9:31	10:34	15:24, 37
6.	Resurrection	8:31; 9:9	9:31	10:34	16:1-8

Since there is such a remarkable correspondence between these predictions and their fulfillment in the passion narrative, some commentators believed Jesus could not have predicted them.[461] Still, even apart from His divine foresight, Jesus could have anticipated what awaited Him in Jerusalem. He knew the depth of the religious leaders' antagonism, and He understood the Old Testament prophecies of Messiah's career (cf. Ps. 22:6-8; Isa. 50:6; 52:13—53:12). The antecedent of "they" in verse 34 is probably "the Gentiles" in verse 33.

> "'Jerusalem' is a place of danger and condemnation to death [in Mark]. Jesus' enemies are at home here, and from here scribes and Pharisees come to Galilee to attack him and his disciples. And the 'Temple,' the house of God's presence and the seat of the religious authorities' power, is a place of intense conflict: Prior to his passion, Jesus' last great confrontation with the religious authorities occurs here."[462]

2. Jesus' teaching about serving 10:35-45 (cf. Matt. 20:20-28)

This pericope parallels 9:30-37. Both sections deal with true greatness, and both follow predictions of Jesus' passion. This second incident shows the disciples' lack of spiritual perception, and their selfishness, even more than the first one.

10:35-37   James and John's request seems almost incredible. They wanted Jesus to give them "whatever" they requested: *carte blanche*. When asked what that might be, they explained that they wanted the positions of highest honor in Jesus' messianic kingdom. The person who sat on a ruler's "right" hand side enjoyed the highest assigned position, and the person who sat on his "left," the second highest.[463] These brothers obviously believed that Jesus was the Messiah, and they thought He was going to establish His kingdom soon, probably when they reached Jerusalem.

Matthew wrote that their mother, Salome, the sister of Jesus' mother, voiced their request for them (Matt. 20:20). Mark put the words in their own mouths, because the request came from their hearts, even though Salome spoke them. Perhaps they thought their family connection with Jesus justified their request. James and John were Jesus' cousins (cf. Matt. 27:55-56; Mark 15:40; John 19:25). Frequently rulers appointed close family members to important government positions.

> "This narrative contains a bright mirror of human vanity; for it shows that proper and holy zeal is often accompanied by ambition. . . . They who are not satisfied with himself alone, but seek this or the other thing apart from him and his promises, wander egregiously from the right path."[464]

---

[460]Adapted from Taylor, p. 436.
[461]E.g., Nineham, p. 278.
[462]Kingsbury, p. 4.
[463]Josephus, *Antiquities of . . .*, 6:11:9. Cf. 1 Kings 2:19; and Ps. 110:1.
[464]Calvin, 2:417.

10:38-40 Those who share Jesus' honor in the kingdom must also share His sufferings in this age. The "cup" often is a symbol of trouble and suffering in the Old Testament (Ps. 75:8; Isa. 51:17; Jer. 25:15-28; 49:12; 51:7; Ezek. 23:31-34; Hab. 2:16; Zech. 12:2). Likewise baptism, being under water, pictures inundation with trouble (Job 22:11; Ps. 18:16; 69:1-2, 15; Isa. 43:2).

James and John confidently (and unwittingly) affirmed that they could endure all the trouble and suffering, that Jesus would have to endure, because they did not understood what He had predicted about His passion. In their desire for prominence, they were willing to promise Jesus anything. They would indeed experience a measure of suffering themselves, as Jesus' *disciples*, but not as much as Jesus would have to endure. James was the first apostle to experience martyrdom (Acts 12:2), and John may have been the last.[465]

"The Authorized Version suggests the idea that the bestowal of rewards in the kingdom is not in Christ's hands at all. That, however, is not what Jesus meant to say; but rather this, that though it is Christ's prerogative to assign to citizens their places in His kingdom, it is not in His power to dispose of places by partiality and patronage, or otherwise than in accordance with fixed principles of justice and the sovereign ordination of His Father."[466]

"Jesus' answer once again displays his supernatural knowledge."[467]

10:41-44 The jealous reaction of the other disciples shows that selfish ambition also motivated them.[468] Jesus had to repeat His teaching about greatness because the disciples had not learned its lesson (9:33-37).[469]

Rule and authority in the kingdom come by faithful and humble service in the present age.[470] The disciples needed to concentrate on present service rather than future honor. The godless world focuses on the benefits of position. Disciples of Jesus should concentrate on qualifying for honor. The godless ("rulers of the Gentiles") even exercise authority prematurely by "*lording* it over" others. Disciples should voluntarily place themselves under others to help them. A slave (Gr. *doulos*) was sometimes one who voluntarily sacrificed his or her rights to serve others (cf. Luke 22:24-30)—most slaves, however, were not voluntary servants. The Greek word signifies subjection, but not necessarily bondage.

Notice that Jesus did not rebuke the disciples for wanting to be great in the kingdom. This ambition is good. He corrected them for focusing on self-centered goals rather than on altruistic goals, and He clarified the method for obtaining greatness.

"The idea is this: earthly kingdoms are ruled by a class of persons who possess hereditary rank—the aristocracy, nobles, or princes. The governing class are those whose birthright it is to rule, and whose boast it is never to have been in a servile position, but always to have been served. In my kingdom, on the other hand, a man becomes a great one, and a ruler, by being first the servant of those over whom he is to bear rule."[471]

"Here is the paradox of the Kingdom of God. Instead of being lords, its great ones become servants, and its chiefs the bond-servants of all."[472]

10:45 Even the Son of Man had to follow the rule that Jesus just explained. He is the great example of it. His incarnation was not that of a potentate whom others had to serve, but that of a Servant who met the needs of others.

His service extended to giving "His life" as "a ransom" (Gr. *lytron*, cf. Matt. 20:28). In *koine* Greek (the common Greek of the New Testament world), this word often described the money paid for the release of slaves. In the New Testament, it has a narrower, more theological meaning, namely: *release* or *redemption*. The only two occurrences of this word in the New

---

[465]See Lane, p. 381, footnote 87.

[466]Bruce, *The Training . . .*, p. 286.

[467]Gundry, p. 577.

[468]Cf. Cole, p. 170.

[469]See Santos, pp. 23-25.

[470]See idem, "The Paradox of Authority and Servanthood in the Gospel of Mark," *Bibliotheca Sacra* 154:616 (October-December 1997):452-60.

[471]Bruce, *The Training . . .*, pp. 290-91.

[472]Gould, p. 202.

Testament are in Matthew 20:28 and Mark 10:45. The Exodus is the great Old Testament instance of this redemption and release.

"For" (Gr. *anti*), used in Mark only here, means "instead of" or "in place of," not "on behalf of," a clear reference to substitution (cf. Matt. 2:22; Luke 11:11; 1 Pet. 3:9).[473]

"Many" (lit. "the many") contrasts with the one life (Gr. *psychen*) of Jesus given as a payment (cf. 14:24). One Man's act affected many others (cf. Isa. 53:11-12). "Many" does not mean "some *in contrast to* all." While Jesus' death benefits *everyone* in one sense, and only *the elect* in another sense, that was not the point of Jesus' contrast here. Jesus took the place of everyone else by paying the penalty for their sins.

This verse is not only the climax of this pericope (vv. 35-41), but it is the key verse of Mark's Gospel. It summarizes the ministry of Jesus as the Suffering Servant of the Lord, Mark's particular emphasis.[474] Here it constituted another announcement of Jesus' coming death, but it added the purpose for His dying not previously revealed.

> "This verse contains the clearest statement of the object of Christ's coming found in the gospels. But this theological declaration was made to enforce a practical truth for everyday conduct."[475]

That John finally got the message is clear from what he wrote in 1 John 3:16: "He laid down His life for us, and we ought to lay down our lives for the brethren."

Contrasts between a Helper and a Servant	
A Helper	A Servant
A helper helps others when it is convenient.	A servant serves others even when it is inconvenient.
A helper helps people that he or she likes.	A servant serves even people that he or she dislikes.
A helper helps when he or she enjoys the work.	A servant serves even when he or she dislikes the work.
A helper helps with a view to obtaining personal satisfaction.	A servant serves even when he or she receives no personal satisfaction.
A helper helps with an attitude of assisting another.	A servant serves with an attitude of enabling another.

3. The healing of a blind man near Jericho 10:46-52 (cf. Matt. 20:29-34; Luke 18:35-43)

Mark probably included this incident in his Gospel because it illustrates how Jesus would open the spiritual eyes of His disciples that were still shut (cf. 8:22-26). This is the last healing miracle that Mark recorded.

> "This second account of the blind being healed (see 8:22-26 for the first account) concludes this central section of Mark (8:27—10:52) and serves as 'bookends' of this section. Recorded as they were and where they were may be suggestive of the trouble the spiritually blind disciples were having in grasping the need for the death of Christ and the need for faithfulness in taking a stand for Christ in the midst of opposition.

> "This passage is the only place in Mark where someone called Jesus 'Son of David.' That Jesus accepted this title and healed the man is evidence that He affirmed the truth that He is indeed the Messiah."[476]

10:46   "Jericho" stood about five miles west of the Jordan River and six miles north of the Dead Sea.

Scholars have attempted to harmonize this account with the other two in the Synoptics. A few believe that the accounts represent three separate events. Some believe there were two healings, one as Jesus entered Jericho (Luke 18:35) and another as He left Jericho (Matt. 20:29; Mark 10:46). Still others believe there was only one healing, and it happened

[473]Moulton and Milligan, p. 46; Cranfield, p. 343.
[474]See John C. Hutchison, "Servanthood: Jesus' Countercultural Call to Christian Leaders," *Bibliotheca Sacra* 166:661 (January-March 2009):53-69.
[475]Hiebert, p. 261.
[476]Bailey, p. 87.

somewhere between old Jericho and the new Jericho that Herod the Great had built one mile southwest of the old city.[477] I prefer this view since the three accounts are quite similar. Another view is that the beggars approached Jesus as He entered the city, but He healed them as He departed from it. The various descriptions of what happened argue against this theory.

Mark was the only evangelist to record the more prominent of the two beggars' names. This is in harmony with his interest in individuals and detail. Perhaps Mark's original readers knew Bartimaeus.

10:47-48   The two descriptions of Jesus in these verses reveal the faith of Bartimaeus. The crowds simply described Jesus as "the Nazarene." Bartimaeus had obviously heard about Jesus and had concluded that He was the Messiah. "Son of David" is a messianic title (cf. 11:9-10; 12:35-37; 2 Sam. 7:8-16; Isa. 11:1, 10; Jer. 23:5-6; Ezek. 34:23-24). Even though Bartimaeus lacked physical sight, he saw more clearly *who Jesus was* than the multitudes who could see. His cry for mercy from Jesus expressed the attitude of trust, humility, and dependence that Jesus had been teaching His disciples to maintain.

> "Presumably, Jesus did not silence the beggar (in contrast to Ch. 8:30) because he is at the threshold of Jerusalem where his messianic vocation must be fulfilled. The 'messianic secret' is relaxed because it must be made clear to all the people that Jesus goes to Jerusalem as the Messiah, and that he dies as the Messiah."[478]

10:49-50   Jesus responded again to the faith of a believer. Bartimaeus' response verified his belief that Jesus could help him. Mark's details emphasize Jesus' compassion and the beggar's conviction.

10:51-52   Jesus' question allowed Bartimaeus to articulate his faith, and through it Jesus made personal contact with him. "Rabboni" is an emphatic personal form of "rabbi," and means "my Lord and Master" (cf. John 20:16). Jesus healed him instantly with a word, attributing his healing to his faith. His faith was its means, not its cause. The Greek word translated "made well" or "healed" is *sesoken*, meaning "saved."

> "What was happening in the man's body was really, we may presume (ver. 47, 48), but the outward picture of what had happened in his soul."[479]

> "The second stage in the progressive disclosure of Jesus' identity [to the reader] centers on his Davidic sonship (10:46—11:11; 12:35-37). . .

> "What is noteworthy in this scene is that Bartimaeus, a person of great faith, appeals to Jesus as the Son of David. By granting Bartimaeus his request for sight, Jesus in effect accepts for himself the title Son of David. Moreover, he also shows how he fulfills the end-time expectations associated with David. He does so not by donning the helmet of a warrior king but by using his authority to heal and in this way to save."[480]

Bartimaeus responded appropriately, and "*began* following" Jesus "immediately," at least "on the road" to Jerusalem—if not as a disciple.

This incident sets the stage for the climax of Mark's story. Jesus had finished His journey from Galilee to Jerusalem. Some people, like Bartimaeus, were believing on and following Jesus. Others, like the religious leaders, did not believe. Conflict in Jerusalem was inevitable.

> "Bartimaeus pictured discipleship clearly. He recognized his inability, trusted Jesus as the One to give him God's gracious mercy, and when he could 'see' clearly he began to follow Jesus."[481]

VI. THE SERVANT'S MINISTRY IN JERUSALEM CHS. 11—13

The rest of Jesus' ministry, as Mark recorded it, took place in and around Jerusalem. Chapters 11—13 present Jesus' ministry before His passion. It consisted of Jesus' formal presentation to the nation (11:1-26), His teaching in the temple area (11:27—12:44), and His eschatological discourse to the disciples (ch. 13). Mark presented these events as occurring on three successive days. Jesus entered Jerusalem each morning and then withdrew to Bethany each evening (cf. 11:11-12, 19-20). Mark may have compressed these events and they may really have occurred during a

---

[477]E.g., Zane C. Hodges, "The Blind Men at Jericho," *Biblitheca Sacra* 122:488 (October-December 1965):319-30.

[478]Lane, p. 387.

[479]Morison, p. 301.

[480]Kingsbury, p. 45. Cf. 8:27-30; and 11:12—15:39.

[481]Grassmick, p. 155.

longer period of time, namely, between the feasts of Tabernacles and Passover.[482] However, all four evangelists give the impression that they all happened during one week (cf. John 12:1, 12-15), and this has been the interpretation of the church since the fourth century.[483]

A. JESUS' FORMAL PRESENTATION TO ISRAEL 11:1-26

Mark chose to record four events: the Triumphal Entry (11:1-11), the cursing of the fig tree (11:12-14), the cleansing of the temple (11:15-19), and the lesson of the cursed fig tree (11:20-25). These events happened on three successive days (Monday through Wednesday) as the writer noted.

1. The Triumphal Entry 11:1-11 (cf. Matt. 21:1-17; Luke 19:29-44; John 12:12-19)

This is only the second incident that all four evangelists recorded, the other being the feeding of the 5,000 (cf. 6:30-44). This fact reflects its importance. Mark's account of this event gives much detail, indicating its eyewitness source. It does not stress Jesus' messiahship greatly. Mark presented Jesus as a humble servant of God and the people.

11:1a   Mark described Jesus' approach from Jericho generally. He would have come to "Bethany" ("place of unripe figs"), and then Bethphage ("place of young figs"), traveling from the east. These villages stood on the southeastern slope of Mt. Olivet, approximately two miles east of Jerusalem. The Mount of Olives stands about 2,600 feet above sea level, just east of Jerusalem. The Kidron Valley separates it from the city. The heights of Mt. Olivet provide a splendid view of the temple area.

11:1b-3   The "village opposite" was evidently Bethphage, the one the disciples would have encountered after leaving Bethany for Jerusalem. The "colt" was a young donkey. The Mosaic Law specified that an animal devoted to a sacred purpose had to be one that had not been used for ordinary purposes (Num. 19:2; Deut. 21:3). Jesus told the disciples to bring both the colt and its mother to Him (Matt. 21:2). The "Lord" is simply a respectful title here, possibly referring to Jesus, whom the owner may have met previously or knew about. If the owner was a believer in Jesus, "Lord" may have had a deeper meaning for him. Other views are that the "Lord" here refers to God, or to the owner of the animal.[484] Nowhere else in his Gospel did Mark (or Matthew) use "Lord" as a name for Jesus.

             The colt was unbroken, and Jesus was able to ride on it comfortably. These facts suggested that Jesus was the sinless Man who was able to fulfill the Adamic Covenant mandate to subdue the animals (Gen. 1:28; cf. Matt. 17:27), the Second Adam.

11:4-6   The "bystanders" may have been, or at least included, the owner of the animals (Luke 19:33). Perhaps the synoptic writers recorded the disciples' obedience in such detail because the untying of the colt may have been a messianic sign (cf. Gen. 49:8-12). Pre-Christian Jewish texts interpreted Genesis 49:10 as messianic.[485]

11:7-8   The disciples made a saddle for Jesus from their outer garments. Jesus' decision to enter Jerusalem this way fulfilled the messianic prophecy in Zechariah 9:9. It also indicated that He entered as a servant ruler, not as a political conqueror. When Israel's rulers wanted to present themselves as servants of the people, they rode donkeys (e.g., Judg. 10:4; 12:14). When they entered as military leaders, they rode horses. Normally pilgrims to Jerusalem entered the city on foot.[486] Placing one's garment on the ground before someone was a sign of homage to royalty (cf. 2 Kings 9:12-13; 1 Macc. 13:51).

             "What is described is apparently a spontaneous expression of respect."[487]

11:9-10   The people hoped Jesus would be their Messiah. "Hosanna" is the transliteration of a Greek word that transliterated the Hebrew *hosi ah na* (lit. "O save us now," Ps. 118:25a). It was an exclamation of praise calling for deliverance.

             "Blessed is He who comes in the name of the Lord" is a quotation from Psalm 118:26, that was part of the liturgy the Jews used during the Passover. This was a common greeting for visitors to Jerusalem.[488] However, on this occasion it took on new meaning (cf. Gen. 49:10). It is likely, however, that the crowd was not identifying Jesus with the Messiah.[489] Other

---

[482]Lane, pp. 390-91.

[483]See Appendix 1, "A Harmony of the Gospels," at the end of my notes on Matthew for the events of Holy Week in chronological order.

[484]Cranfield, pp. 349-50; Taylor, p. 455.

[485]Lane, p. 395.

[486]Ibid., p. 393.

[487]Cranfield, p. 350.

[488]Wessel, p. 725.

[489]Cranfield, p. 351.

interpreters, however, believe that the use of these terms indicates that the multitude knew that Jesus was presenting Himself as the Messiah.[490]

The peoples' reference to the coming Davidic kingdom shows that they hoped for its establishment soon (2 Sam. 7:16; Amos 9:11-12). Some in the crowd acknowledged Jesus as the Son of David (Matt. 21:9).

"Hosanna in the highest" meant "O, You who live in heaven, save us now." This was a call to God to deliver His people. The chiastic structure of the peoples' words shows that they were chanting antiphonally, as was customary at Passover.

Someone who knew nothing about Jesus might have concluded from witnessing this procession that it was just a part of the traditional Passover celebration. Often when pilgrims caught sight of the temple for the first time, coming from the east over the Mount of Olives, they burst out in jubilant praise.[491] It did not provoke action from the Roman soldiers.

11:11   Having "entered Jerusalem," the crowd seems to have disbursed quickly, and Jesus proceeded to the temple area (Gr. *hieron*). He had been there many times before. He looked around and noted that the temple needed cleansing again (cf. John 2:13-22). Since the hour was "late"—the city gates closed at sunset—He departed "for Bethany" with the disciples to spend the night there.

"On the whole, it seems to be the most probable conclusion that the entry in this peculiar fashion into Jerusalem was deliberate on the part of our Lord, and was meant to suggest that, though He was indeed the Messiah and 'Son of David,' yet the Messiahship which He claimed was to be understood in a spiritual and non-political sense, in terms of the prophecy of Zechariah, rather than in terms of the 'Son of David' idea as interpreted by contemporary expectation (*e.g.*, in the Psalms of Solomon). The time had in fact come for our Lord to put forward His Messianic claims, and to make His appeal to Jerusalem in a deliberately Messianic capacity. He does so, however, in a manner which is suggestive rather than explicit, and which was so calculated as to afford the minimum of pretext for a charge of quasi-political agitation."[492]

"We conclude that Jesus' action in riding into Jerusalem was not an obvious and unambiguous assertion of his Messiahship and that neither the disciples nor the crowd were aware of its messianic meaning. . . . It seems clear that he intended to fulfill the prophecy of Zech. ix. 9, but to do so in circumstances so paradoxical as to make the meaning of his action hidden. It was a veiled assertion of his Messiahship, which would not be recognized at the time, though it would afterwards be luminous for his disciples. To them it would then be a confirmation of the truth of his Messiahship—they would know that the scripture had been fulfilled, though the fact had been unnoticed at the time, and that he had indeed come to Jerusalem as the true Messiah. But it would also be a token of the nature of his Messiahship; for the Zech. passage told of a King who should 'speak peace unto the nations', not a conquering nationalist Messiah. Moreover, his royal entry into Jerusalem was to be of a piece with the rest of his ministry, his majesty hidden under an outward appearance that was far from kingly."[493]

2. Jesus' condemnation of unbelieving Israel 11:12-26

This incident is the first part of another of Mark's interrupted stories (cf. 3:20-35; 5:21-43; 6:7-31). Its structure provides the key to its interpretation. First, Jesus cursed the fig tree. Then He cleansed the temple. Finally He came back to the fig tree with a lesson for the disciples. There is unity of subject matter in the whole section. The chiastic arrangement highlights the central element as being most revealing.

The cursing of the fig tree 11:12-14 (cf. Matt. 21:18-19)

Mark gave more precise time intervals than Matthew did. Matthew related the cursing of the fig tree (Matt. 21:18-19), and Jesus' lesson to the disciples the following day (Matt. 21:20-22), back to back.

11:12-13   The next day was Tuesday, which Hoehner dated as March 31, A.D. 33.[494] Apparently the events of "Palm Sunday" took place on a Monday. The incident that Mark recorded next, beginning in verse 12, occurred as Jesus and His disciples walked from Bethany to Jerusalem on Tuesday morning (Matt. 21:18). Normally, small, edible buds appeared on the fig trees in March, before the leaves did in April.[495] The lack of edible buds indicated that this tree would not bear figs later on, even though there were leaves on this tree. Mark explained that "it was not the season for figs"—for his non-Palestinian readers. Matthew did not add this explanation.

[490]E.g., Pentecost, *The Words . . .*, p. 373.

[491]Lane, p. 397.

[492]Rawlinson, p. 151.

[493]Cranfield, pp. 353-54.

[494]Hoehner, *Chronological Aspects . . .*, pp. 91, 143.

[495]Edersheim, 2:374; cf. *The Nelson . . .*, pp. 1666-67.

11:14   Jesus saw an opportunity to teach His disciples an important truth using this tree as an object lesson. Being a prophet, Jesus performed a symbolic act (cf. Isa. 20:1-6; Jer. 13:1-11; 19:1-13; Ezek. 4:1-15). He cursed the tree to teach them the lesson, not because it failed to produce fruit. The tree was a good illustration of the large unbelieving element within the nation of Israel. God had looked to that generation of Israelites for spiritual fruit, as Jesus had hoped to find physical fruit on the fig tree (Matt. 3:8; cf. Jer. 8:13; Hos. 9:10; Mic. 7:1; Nah. 3:12; Zech. 10:2). Israel's outward display of religious vitality was impressive, like the leaves on the tree, but it bore no spiritual fruit of righteousness. It was hypocritical (7:6; 11:15-19, 27—12:40).

> "Jesus was on the eve of spiritual conflict with a nation whose prime and patent fault was hypocrisy or false pretense, and here he finds a tree guilty of the same thing. It gives him his opportunity, without hurting anybody, to sit in judgment on the fault."[496]

> "In Mark's story world, hypocrisy exists where there is a discrepancy between appearance and underlying truth."[497]

This is the only destructive miracle that the Gospel writers attributed to Jesus, and it involved a tree. The healing of the Gadaran demoniac resulted in the destruction of pigs (5:13), but that miracle itself was positive in that it healed the man.

The cleansing of the temple 11:15-19 (cf. Matt. 21:12-13; Luke 19:45-48)

This was Jesus' second messianic act that constituted part of His formal presentation to Israel. The first was the Triumphal Entry (vv. 1-11).

11:15-16   A marketplace atmosphere existed in the court of the Gentiles, the outermost courtyard within the temple enclosure (Gr. *hieron*, cf. v. 17). During Passover season, pilgrims could buy sacrificial animals and change their money on the Mount of Olives, so there was no need to set up facilities to do these things in the temple courtyard—which Caiaphas had done.[498] Jesus' literal housecleaning represented His authority as Messiah to clean up the corrupt nation of Israel. Verse 16, unique in Mark, shows the extent to which Jesus went in purifying the temple. By doing this, Jesus was acting as a faithful servant of the Lord and demonstrating zeal for God's honor.

> "The court of the Gentiles should have been a place for praying, but it was instead a place for preying and paying."[499]

11:17   The Isaiah prophecy was a prediction yet unfulfilled, as well as a statement of God's perennial intent for the temple. From Jesus' mouth, it was also a prophecy of conditions in the messianic kingdom (cf. Zech. 14:21).

Mark added "for all the nations," which Matthew omitted from Isaiah 56:7. The phrase has special significance for Gentile readers. God permitted Gentiles to come and worship Him in the temple court of the Gentiles, indicating His desire to bring them into relationship with Himself.

The Jewish leaders, however, had made this practically impossible—by converting the only place Gentiles could pray in the temple complex into a market where fraud abounded. They had expelled the Gentile worshippers to make room for Jewish "robbers" (Gr. *lestes*), a term that referred to the swindling and extortion practiced there.

Jesus was claiming that the temple belonged to Him—rather than to the Jewish leaders—by cleaning it up! The quotation He cited from Isaiah presented the temple as God's "house." Thus Jesus was claiming to be God.

> "The third stage in the progressive disclosure of Jesus' identity [to the reader] focuses on the secret that he is the Son of God."[500]

11:18-19   Jesus' action and words had threatened the reputation and resources of the Sanhedrin members. They plotted to kill ("destroy") Him (cf. 3:6). The intensity of their hatred becomes clear later (11:27—12:37). Mark alone recorded that they "were afraid of" Jesus. The reason was the impact His teaching was having on the multitudes that gathered from all over the ancient world for Passover (cf. 1:22; 6:2; 7:37; 10:26). Jesus was acting like Israel's King and High Priest.

---

[496]Gould, pp. 211-12.

[497]Kingsbury, p. 15.

[498]Lane, pp. 403-4. See also V. Eppstein, "The Historicity of the Gospel Account of the Cleansing of the Temple," *Zeitschrift für die Neutestamentliche Wissenschaft* 55 (1964):42-58.

[499]Wiersbe, 1:151.

[500]Kingsbury, p. 46. Cf. 8:27-30; 10:46—11:11 and 12:35-37.

"And so we have reached Mark's main point: the awe-inspiring power of Jesus' teaching, backed up as it is by his strong actions. He strikes fear even in the hearts of the hierarchs who are trying to destroy him. In fact, they are trying to destroy him *because* they fear him, *because* he has a powerful hold on the crowd. He will be crucified, then, not because of any weakness in him. Quite oppositely, because of his power! Furthermore, the power for which he will be crucified is a power that he exerts for the benefit of all the nations, Gentiles as well as Jews. He uses his power for the sake of Mark's audience, that is to say, and at great cost to himself. So for his crucifixion Jesus deserves honor and worship, not scorn and ridicule."[501]

At evening, Jesus and the disciples again left Jerusalem and spent the night on Mt. Olivet (Luke 21:37), probably in Bethany (v. 11).

"If the Lord Jesus were to show up in our house of worship, what changes would He make?"[502]

The lesson of the withered fig tree 11:20-26 (cf. Matt. 21:19-22)

This is the third part of the incident centering on the cleansing of the temple (cf. vv. 12-14).

11:20-21   This event happened on Wednesday morning. "Withered from the roots" means that death was spreading through the tree, emanating from its sources of nourishment. The "roots" of the tree correspond to the religious leaders of the nation. The curse of *spiritual death* would spread from them to that whole generation of unbelieving Jews. Peter connected the judgment with Jesus' words. In parallel fashion, Jesus' pronouncement of judgment on that generation of Jews would have a similar effect.

11:22-23   Rather than explaining the symbolic significance of the cursing of the fig tree, Jesus proceeded to focus on the means by which the miracle happened. This was an important discipleship lesson that Jesus had taught before (cf. Matt. 6:13-14; 7:7; 17:20; 18:19; Luke 11:9; 17:6), but it appears only here in Mark. The point was that dependent trust in God can accomplish humanly impossible things through prayer (cf. James 1:6).

God is the source of the power to change. "Moving a mountain" is a universal symbol of doing something that appears to be impossible (cf. Zech. 4:7). Jesus presupposed that overcoming the difficulty in view was God's will. A true disciple of Jesus would hardly pray for anything else (Matt. 6:10). The person praying can therefore believe that what he requests will happen because it is God's will. He will neither doubt God's ability to do what he requests, since God *can* do anything, nor will he doubt that God *will* grant his petition, since it is God's will. He will not have a divided heart about this matter.[503]

"What is here indicated by means of hyperbole is that one is to be absolutely confident in God's readiness to respond to faith."[504]

Why did Mark not explain what Jesus assumed, namely, that disciples would pray for God's will to happen? Evidently when he wrote, his original readers were committed Christians. The Roman Empire then weeded out professing-only Christians, much more than the world does today, at least in the West. The idea that a Christian would want anything but the will of God to happen was absurd, in a world where identifying oneself as a Christian meant severe persecution and possibly death.

11:24   Asking is a particular form of praying. As disciples, we can "believe" that we will have what we request in prayer, when we "ask" for God's will to take place (Matt. 6:10; 7:7), because God will accomplish His will.

11:25   Faith in God is not the only condition for answered prayer. One must also "forgive" his or her fellow human beings. The Jews commonly stood when they prayed (cf. 1 Sam. 1:26; Luke 18:11, 13). Forgiving our brothers and sisters is a precondition for obtaining family forgiveness from the Father (Matt. 6:14-15). This is the only place in Mark where Jesus referred to the disciples' ("your") "Father who is in heaven." This may have reminded them of His teaching in the Lord's Prayer (Matt. 6:9-15; Luke 11:2-4).

11:26   This verse does not appear in the most important ancient manuscripts of Mark's Gospel. Evidently scribes inserted it later, because they associated the preceding verse with Matthew 6:14.

---

[501]Gundry, p. 641.

[502]Wiersbe, 1:151.

[503]See David DeGraaf, "Some Doubts about Doubt: The New Testament Use of *Diakrino*," *Journal of the Evangelical Theological Society* 48:8 (December 2005):744-49.

[504]Cranfield, p. 361.

B. JESUS' TEACHING IN THE TEMPLE 11:27—12:44

This entire section contains Jesus' teaching in the temple courtyard on Wednesday. The religious leaders first questioned Jesus' authority (11:12—12:12), and then His teaching (12:13-37). Finally, Jesus condemned their hypocrisy, and commended a widow's action that demonstrated reality (12:38-44). Jesus functioned as a faithful servant of the Lord in the role of a prophet here.

1. The controversy over Jesus' authority 11:27—12:12

This controversy consisted of a discussion with the religious leaders over John the Baptist's authority (11:27-33), followed by a parable that illustrated the religious leaders' irresponsibility (12:1-12).

The authority of John the Baptist 11:27-33 (cf. Matt. 21:23-27; Luke 20:1-8)

11:27-28   The "chief priests," teachers or "scribes," and "elders" constituted the three components of the Sanhedrin. This was a very official inquiry prompted by Jesus' presence and made necessary by His cleansing of the temple. Israel's official leaders wanted to know about Jesus' credentials and who gave Him the right to say and do what He did. They questioned the nature and source of His authority. Their questions were legitimate, since the leaders were responsible for supervising Israel's religious life. Yet their question was a challenge to Jesus' honor.[505]

"The essence of the depiction of the opponents [of Jesus in Mark] lies in that they are self-serving; that is, they are preoccupied with preserving their power, their importance, their wealth, and their lives."[506]

11:29-30   Essentially, Jesus asked these leaders if they believed God was behind John's ministry (was "from heaven"). John had taught that God was behind Jesus' ministry. If the critics said they believed God was behind John's ministry, they would have had to agree that God was behind Jesus' ministry. Jesus challenged them to respond. "Answer Me" (v. 30) is unique in Mark, and reflects Jesus' superiority to these men.

"As on the earlier question of Sabbath observance (2:23—3:6), the counterquestion [sic] implies that Jesus stands not under the Sanhedrin but over it. His counterquestion demonstrates the authority about which he is questioned."[507]

11:31-33   The critics' concern for their own position—rather than for the *truth*—is obvious in their refusal to answer Jesus. Clearly, they rejected *both John and Jesus* as God's authorized prophets! Jesus had already answered their question in a veiled way, by claiming that His authority was the same as John's. He refused to give them a more obvious answer, knowing that they were trying to discredit Him. Their failure to reply to Him released Him from His conditional promise to reply to them (v. 29)—since they failed to meet the condition. Rejection of revelation shut the door on further revelation.

"In his assault on the demonic, forgiveness of sins, supremacy over Torah and temple, speech about God as Father, and grounding pronouncements about matters in which God is sovereign in his own authority, Jesus exercises an authority that is God's prerogative.... Coming from anyone else it would have signaled utter madness—as it did in the eyes of his enemies. What the devout Jew saw in Torah, or perhaps in the temple, the gospels see in Jesus, for Jesus replaces Torah and temple as the *locus Dei* [place of God]. When questioned about the source of his authority, Jesus points to his baptism by John, wherein the voice declaring Jesus Son of God and the Spirit empowering him as servant of God confer on him the *exousia* [authority] of God.

"Thus in the gospel of Mark, as in John, Jesus appears as God incarnate in his bearing, speech and activity. This astonishes, baffles, and even offends his contemporaries, from his closest circles outward. The religious leaders in particular regard his laying claim to a realm that belonged properly to God as the gravest possible trespass. Jesus gives the distinct impression, however, that he is not a trespasser but is entering into his rightful property."[508]

---

[505]See Joseph H. Hellerman, "Challenging the Authority of Jesus: Mark 11:27-33 and Mediterranean Notions of Honor and Shame," *Journal of the Evangelical Theological Society* 43:2 (June 2000):213-28.
[506]Rhoads and Michie, p. 121.
[507]Edwards, p. 226.
[508]Ibid., pp. 232-33.

The parable of the wicked tenant farmers 12:1-12 (cf. Matt. 21:33-46; Luke 20:9-19)

"The other major example of the concentric [chiastic] pattern in Mark's story [beside 2:1—3:6] is the series of Jesus' conflicts with the authorities in Jerusalem [ch. 12], comprised of seven episodes: Episodes A and A[1] involve Jesus' statement of judgment against the authorities (the riddle of the wicked tenants and the warning against the scribes). Episodes B and B[1] include a quotation from the psalms followed by a reaction to that citation (the quotations about the cornerstone and David's son); and episodes C and C[1] are both legal discussions about love for God and neighbor (Caesar and God, and love for God and neighbor). Episode D is the central episode; its topic is the resurrection, and its theme illuminates all the episodes: the failure of the authorities to understand either the writings or the power of God."[509]

Matthew's account of this parable is fuller than Mark's, because Matthew evidently wanted to show the Jews how wicked and irresponsible their leaders were. Mark probably included the story because it contrasts the behavior of Israel's official servants, the religious leaders, with God's Servant, Jesus.

"Recent study of the Zenon papyri and of the rabbinic parables has shown that situations very closely analogous to that of the parable actually existed in Palestine both around 280 years prior to Jesus' ministry and for some time afterward."[510]

12:1   Jesus addressed this parable to all the people present (Luke 20:9), but particularly to the religious leaders. The "man" in the parable represents God, the "vineyard" is Israel (Ps. 80:8-19; Jer. 2:21), and the tenants ("vine-growers") are Israel's leaders. The parable develops the scene presented in Isaiah 5:1-2, which is part of a prophecy of God's judgment on Israel (cf. Ps. 80:8-16). God spared no expense or effort to make Israel a choice nation. He had left Israel on its own, so to speak, after He had established the nation.

"Since the whole of the upper Jordan valley and a large part of the Galilean uplands were in the hands of foreign landlords at this time, such a practice was common."[511]

12:2-5   The "*harvest* time" stands for the time when God expected to obtain some reward for His investment in Israel. The servants ("slaves") represent the prophets, whom Israel's leaders typically rejected, persecuted, and even in some cases murdered. The main point of the parable is the wicked treatment Israel's leaders had given the servants whom God had sent to them.

12:6-8   The sending of the owner's son constituted the supreme test for the tenant farmers. The tenant farmers ("vine-growers") in the parable may have believed that the owner of the vineyard had died, and that he had only one son who was his heir. They rationalized that if they killed the son, there would be no one else to inherit the vineyard, and they could retain control of it. The tenants evidently "threw" the son "out of the vineyard," and *then* "killed him" (Matt. 21:39; Luke 20:15). Mark's order of events (v. 8) shows that his murder was also an act of rejection.[512]

The religious leaders certainly behaved as though God was dead. He really had only one uniquely beloved Son (cf. 1:11; 9:7).

12:9   The tenant farmers' rejection of the owner's "son" was equally a rejection of "the owner." His predictable reaction would be to remove them and give the care of his vineyard to other tenants. As in the parable, God would remove ("destroy" Jerusalem, the temple, and religious leaders in A.D. 70) Israel's leaders and replace them with other leaders, the leaders of the church.

"This prediction was fulfilled in the church where the spiritual leadership became entrusted mainly to those of Gentile origin. But the determining factor is their faithfulness, not their national origin."[513]

12:10-11 Jesus carried His revelation, concerning the fate of the Son, further by referring to Psalm 118. This is the same psalm the crowds chanted at the Triumphal Entry (11:9; cf. Ps. 118:22-23). The "stone" in view is probably the capstone for the building that God is constructing. In its original use, the stone represented Israel. Here, Jesus made Himself the Stone (cf. Acts 4:11; 1 Pet. 2:7). The Father's reversal of the Son's fate elicited wonder from the beholders, because it was an unexpected turn of events that demonstrated divine sovereignty.

It appears that Israel's leaders rejected the Stone that was to be the capstone to complete Israel, God's temple, through which He would work to bring blessing to all mankind (Gen. 12:3). The Stone rejected has become, not the capstone, but the most important Stone ("chief corner stone") in the foundation of a new temple that God is now building, namely, the church (Matt.

[509]Rhoads and Michie, p. 53.
[510]Lane, p. 416.
[511]Ibid., p. 417.
[512]Lenski, p. 512.
[513]Hiebert, p. 290.

16:18; Eph. 2:20; 1 Pet. 2:4-10). After God removes the church from the earth (1 Thess. 4:13-18), the Stone will return to the earth (cf. Dan. 2:34-35, 44-45; Rev. 19:11-16), and Israel will accept Him (Zech. 12:10). Then He will complete Israel (Isa. 59:20), and Israel will, during the Millennium, function as the temple that God intended her to be (Dan. 7:22). He will then bring blessing to the whole earth through Israel.

12:12	The meaning of Jesus' parable was clear to the religious leaders. Jesus had exposed their murderous plot to kill Him. The favor of the multitude shielded Jesus from their wrath temporarily.

Jesus' claims to being God's beloved Son were becoming increasingly clear to everyone. As they became clearer, opposition from Israel's leaders intensified.

2. The controversy over Jesus' teaching 12:13-37

Controversy over Jesus' authority led to controversy over His teaching. The Jewish religious leaders attacked Him three times, trying to destroy His credibility and popularity. They plied Him with questions about the poll tax (vv. 13-17), the resurrection (vv. 18-27), and the greatest commandment (vv. 28-34). Then Jesus took the initiative and questioned them about Messiah's sonship (vv. 35-37). This ended their attacks. The whole encounter happened on Wednesday following the events just recorded. It recalls the similar earlier sequence of conflicts with Jesus in Galilee (cf. 2:1—3:6)

Jesus' teaching about the poll tax 12:13-17 (cf. Matt. 22:15-22; Luke 20:20-26)

12:13	Sanhedrin members took the initiative in sending the "Pharisees" and "Herodians." They united against Jesus, whom they perceived as a common threat, even though they differed among themselves politically. They asked Jesus about a political issue that divided them.
12:14-15a	The critics' preamble was hypocritical flattery, but what they said about Jesus was true. They intended to impale Jesus on the horns of a dilemma.[514] Since Judea had become a Roman province in A.D. 6, the Romans had required the Jews to pay a yearly "poll (head) tax" into the emperor's treasury. The Zealots later refused to pay it, claiming that payment acknowledged Rome's right to rule over them. The Pharisees paid it but objected strongly to it. The Herodians paid it willingly since they supported Roman rule.

Jesus' critics asked Him what was the right or lawful thing to do. In their eyes Messiah would never sanction foreign rule, but if Jesus publicly opposed Rome He would be in a dangerous position. They thought that either answer would hurt Jesus.

12:15b-16	Jesus exposed their question for what it was, malicious entrapment rather than honest inquiry. The small silver "denarius" was the only coin the Romans accepted in payment for taxes.[515] The images on the coin showed that Rome had political authority over those who used it.

> "The denarius of Tiberius portrayed the emperor as the semi-divine son of the god Augustus and the goddess Livia and bore the (abbreviated) inscription 'Tiberius Caesar Augustus, Son of the Divine Augustus' on the obverse and 'Pontifex Maximus' on the reverse. Both the representations and the inscriptions were rooted in the imperial cult and constituted a claim to divine honors."[516]

12:17	Jesus avoided the "either or" problem with a "both and" response. God has authority over those who bear His image. Therefore, the Jews should "give ("render to") Him" His due, namely: complete personal submission. Caesar also had some authority over those who used "his image" by using his coins. Therefore the Jews should pay their tax.

> "Though the obligation to pay to Caesar some of his own coinage in return for the amenities his rule provided is affirmed, the idolatrous claims expressed on the coins are rejected. God's rights are to be honored. Here Jesus is not saying that there are two quite separate independent spheres, that of Caesar and that of God (for Caesar and all that is his belongs to God); but he is indicating that there are obligations to Caesar which do not infringe the rights of God but are indeed ordained by God."[517]

This answer "amazed" (Gr. *exethaumazon*) Jesus' critics. He had avoided the trap they had laid for Him, and had given a profound though simple answer to their question.

---

[514]Hunter, p. 116.

[515]Grassmick, p. 162.

[516]Lane, p. 424.

[517]Cranfield, p. 372.

This teaching would have been especially helpful to Mark's original Roman readers. It helped them and all subsequent disciples understand that Christianity does not advocate disloyalty to the state (cf. Rom. 13:1-7; 1 Tim. 2:1-6; 1 Pet. 2:13-17). Duty to God does not eliminate duty to government. Nevertheless, duty to government does not eliminate one's higher duty to God, either.

Jesus' teaching about the resurrection 12:18-27 (cf. Matt. 22:23-33; Luke 20:27-40)

12:18   The "Sadducees" were mainly urban, wealthy, and educated Jews. Their numbers were comparatively few, but they occupied important positions including many in the priesthood. Their influence was greater than their size as a party within Judaism. This is the only place Mark mentioned them. They claimed to believe only what the Old Testament taught, and they did not follow the traditions of the elders that the Pharisees observed. They did not believe in the "resurrection," because they said they could find no clear revelation about it in the Old Testament.

"It is probable that the Sadducees began as a political faction which supported the legitimacy of the Hasmonean throne over the protest of the purists who insisted on a separation of the priestly and royal prerogatives or who looked for a revival of the Davidic kingdom."[518]

The Hasmonean throne refers to rule by the Herods.

12:19-23   The Sadducees posed their hypothetical case to make any view of the resurrection but their own look absurd.[519]

12:24-25   The Sadducees did not understand the Scriptural revelation about resurrection. Furthermore, they did not realize that God's "power" was sufficient to raise people and to raise them to a different type of life. Marriage as we know it will not exist when we have immortal bodies, and deathless existence will not require propagation of the human race. The Sadducees denied the existence of the angelic race (Acts 23:8), which belief Jesus also corrected. They considered their views enlightened, but Jesus said they needed enlightening. Jesus did not say that when people die they become angels, which they do not, nor that we will be "like angels" *in every respect*, which we will not.

12:26-27   In concluding that the Old Testament did not teach the resurrection, the Sadducees had overlooked an important passage in the Torah (Pentateuch). They regarded the Torah as particularly authoritative. Exodus 3:6 taught continued human existence after death. Abraham, Isaac, and Jacob were still alive in Moses' day. The Sadducees not only rejected the resurrection, but also the afterlife in heaven or hell.[520] The Jews had a more holistic view of man than most modern westerners do (cf. Gen. 2:7). The Sadducees concluded that if the material part of man died, the whole person ceased to exist. Jesus, who held the same unified view of man, argued that if the immaterial part of man lived on, the whole person would live on.

The major error of the Sadducees was their "greatly mistaken" understanding of scriptural revelation. Jesus' final rebuke (v. 27), unique in the second Gospel, stressed that flaw.

"If the death of the patriarchs is the last word of their history, there has been a breach of the promises of God guaranteed by the [Abrahamic] covenant, and of which the formula 'the God of Abraham, of Isaac and of Jacob' is the symbol. It is in fidelity to his covenant that God will resurrect the dead."[521]

Jesus' teaching about the greatest commandment 12:28-34 (cf. Matt. 22:34-40)

The third attack by Jesus' enemies involved a question about the greatest commandment (cf. Luke 10:25-28).

12:28   The rabbis counted 613 commands in the Mosaic Law: 365 positive and 248 negative. They recognized that all were not equally important or equally foundational. They debated which were the "heavy" commands and which were the "light" ones. They also tried to formulate principles that comprehended the rest of the Law.[522] These were the concerns of the law teacher who asked Jesus what type (Gr. *poia*) of command He regarded as first in importance ("foremost").

"The scribe desired Jesus to indicate a principle of classification."[523]

---

[518]Lane, p. 426.

[519]Swete, p. 278.

[520]Josephus, *Antiquities of . . .*, 18:1:4; idem, *The Wars . . .*, 2:8:14. See the *Zondervan Pictorial Encyclopedia of the Bible*, s.v. "Sadducees," by D. A. Hagner, 5:214-15.

[521]Lane, p. 430.

[522]Wessel, p. 737.

[523]Hiebert, p. 303.

Matthew viewed his question as coming from the scribe who spoke as a spokesman for the Pharisees, whereas Mark presented it as the inquirer's personal concern. This difference reflects Mark's interest in individuals.

12:29-30   Mark's account included Deuteronomy 6:4, which Matthew omitted. This verse, the first in the *Shema* (Deut. 6:4-5; cf. Deut. 11:13-21; Num. 15:37-41) that the Jews repeated twice daily, provides a basis for Deuteronomy 6:5. *Shema* is the first Hebrew word in this passage, and it means "Hear." Matthew's Jewish readers would have understood this, but Mark's Gentile readers probably would not have. Verse 4 is an affirmation of belief in the unity of God (i.e., in monotheism). Many of Mark's original readers had formerly been polytheists.

> "God is to be loved completely and totally (v. 30) because he, and he alone, is God and because he has made a covenant of love with his people. In the covenant God gives himself totally in love to his people; therefore he expects his people to give themselves totally ('soul,' 'mind,' and 'strength') in love to him."[524]

"Heart" represents the control center of human personality, "soul" the self-conscious thought life, "mind" the thought capacity, and "strength" all of one's bodily powers.[525] These are to be the sources out of which love for God should flow. We should love God with all our will (decisions), emotions (desires), minds (thoughts), and bodies (actions).

> "A comparison of the order—heart, soul, mind (Matthew); heart, soul, mind, strength (Mark); heart, soul, strength, mind (Luke); heart, soul, strength (the Masoretic Text); and mind, soul, strength (the Septuagint)—among the various lists suggests that Mark and Luke added 'mind' to the Hebrew/Septuagintal formula whereas Matthew substituted 'mind' for 'strength.'"[526]

12:31   The scribe had requested one commandment, but Jesus gave him two. Love for man, in Leviticus 19:18, grows out of love for God, in Deuteronomy 6:4-5, and is inseparable from it philosophically. The Jews regarded only fellow Jews and full proselytes as their neighbors, but Jesus taught that a neighbor is anyone with whom we have any dealings whatsoever (cf. Luke 10:25-27). "Neighbor" (Gr. *plesion*, lit. one nearby) is a generic term for fellow man.

We are to love all others as we love ourselves. The Law assumed that every person has a fundamental love for himself or herself. We demonstrate this love by caring for ourselves in many different ways.[527] "Loving our neighbors as ourselves" does not mean spending the same amount of time or money to meet the needs of others, that we do to meet our own needs, since this would be impossible. It means treating others as we treat ourselves.

These are the greatest commandments, in that they summarize the two basic responsibilities regarding the Law: our duties toward God and our duties those toward other people. These are basic human responsibilities. The termination of the Mosaic Code does not invalidate them. They have been primary since creation, and will continue as such forever—because of man's relationship to God, and because of the unity of the human race.

12:32-33   Mark alone recorded the scribe's response and Jesus' comment (v. 34). These words underscore the importance of Jesus' teaching. The scribe believed Jesus' answer was correct. He, too, viewed love as more important than the observance of religious ritual (cf. 1 Sam. 15:22; Hos. 6:6). This was not typical of the Pharisees, who regarded ritual observance as more important than attitude, and ceremony as more important than morality.

> ". . . the 'friendly scribe' himself puts his finger on the fundamental difference separating Jesus and the religious authorities in terms of what it is to do the will of God: Whereas the essential matter for Jesus is loving God and neighbor, for the authorities it is strict adherence to law and tradition as they define this.

> ". . . Mark is in effect using the friendly scribe to identify the two contrasting positions of Jesus and the authorities on doing the will of God."[528]

12:34   Jesus meant that the scribe was "not far from" *entering* "the kingdom." His openness to Scriptural revelation and his positive orientation to Jesus, if continued, would bring him to faith in Jesus and ultimately entrance into His kingdom.

Jesus' skillful answers discouraged His critics from trying to trap Him. So they stopped asking Him questions.

---

[524]Wessel, p. 737.

[525]Grassmick, p. 164.

[526]Eugene H. Merrill, "Deuteronomy, New Testament Faith, and the Christian Life," in *Integrity of Heart, Skillfulness of Hands*, p. 26.

[527]For refutation of the view that this command implies that we must learn to love ourselves before we can love others, see Robert L. Thomas, *Evangelical Hermeneutics*, pp. 130-31.

[528]Kingsbury, pp. 17, 124.

It was clear that Jesus derived His authority from God's Word (cf. 11:28). All the answers He gave went back to the Old Testament. Since this is the authority all the Jewish leaders claimed to follow, though they did not, they failed to discredit Jesus.

Jesus' question about Messiah's sonship 12:35-37 (cf. Matt. 22:41-46; Luke 20:41-44)

Until now the religious leaders had questioned Jesus about His teaching. Now He asked them about theirs (Matt. 22:41). Matthew's account of this incident is the longest.

12:35	Jesus responded to the situation before Him. He wanted to know the sense in which the teachers of the law believed that Messiah was David's son. The Old Testament clearly taught that Messiah would be a descendant ("son") "of David" (2 Sam. 7:8-16; et al.). The leaders believed this, but their understanding of Messiah's relationship to David was only that of another victorious Jewish king from David's dynasty.

12:36-37   Mark focused the readers' attention on Jesus' authoritative teaching by omitting the Pharisees' answer, which Matthew included to discredit them (Matt. 22:42). Here only in the sayings of Jesus did He trace the authority of an Old Testament passage to its divine inspiration. How could Messiah be both *less* than David (his son) and *greater* than David (his lord) at the same time? A father does not refer to his own son as his "lord." It is more natural for a son to call his father "lord."[529]

> ". . . Jesus uses his superior knowledge of the legal and prophetic writings to justify his actions and to defend against criminal accusations."[530]

Psalm 110:1 showed that the Messiah was not only David's junior in age, but also his senior in rank.[531] He is the *Son of God:* God as well as Man.

> "Only through the Virgin Birth does Jesus possess the dual nature that allows Him to be both David's Son and David's Lord."[532]

Mark's record of the crowd's positive response to Jesus' teaching further stressed its authority. Israel's religious leaders challenged it, but the multitudes acknowledged it.

3. Jesus' condemnation of hypocrisy and commendation of reality 12:38-44

Jesus proceeded to condemn His accusers who had condemned Him. They had condemned Him because He did not fit their ideas of Messiah. He had shown that the Old Testament presented a different Messiah than the one they wanted. Now He condemned them for failing to measure up to what the Old Testament required of them. This section concludes Mark's account of Jesus' public ministry and resumes Jesus' teaching of His disciples.

Jesus' condemnation of hypocrisy 12:38-40 (cf. Matt. 23:1-39; Luke 20:45-47)

Mark condensed Jesus' comments, that Matthew recorded extensively, to give the essence of Jesus' criticism. These words signal Jesus' final break with Israel's official leaders.

12:38-39   Jesus condemned the religious leaders for having the attitude of lords rather than that of servants. He spoke of the religious teachers as a group, though there were exceptional individuals, of course (cf., e.g., v. 34). Most Israelites of this time venerated the scribes with unbounded respect.[533]

12:40   This verse "passes from their ostentatious manners to their corrupt morals."[534] Teachers of the law did not receive an income from the state; they depended on voluntary contributions.[535] This led some of them to prey on ("devour") the sympathy of others, even "widows," who needed all their income simply to survive. This reference sets the stage for the next incident (vv. 41-44).

---

[529]Cranfield, pp. 382-83.

[530]Rhoads and Michie, p. 85.

[531]Moule, p. 99.

[532]Bailey, p. 90.

[533]See Lane, pp. 339-40, for some examples.

[534]Hiebert, p. 310.

[535]Wessel, p. 740.

Their typically "long prayers" presented an impression of piety that masked greed. They pretended to love God greatly, but their aim was to get people to love them greatly. The result would be "greater condemnation" when they stood before God's judgment bar. Here is another indication that there are degrees of punishment (cf. Matt. 11:20-24; James 3:1; et al.).

Jesus' commendation of reality 12:41-44 (cf. Luke 21:1-4)

This incident contrasts the spiritual poverty and physical prosperity of the scribes, with the physical poverty and spiritual prosperity of the widow. It also contrasts the greed of the scribes with the generosity of the widow. It resumes Jesus' instruction of His disciples (12:41—13:37). This pericope brings the themes of true piety (the woman) and hardened unbelief (the scribes) to a climax.[536]

12:41-42   There were 13 trumpet-shaped receptacles (Heb. *shofar*) that the priests had placed against the north, east, and south walls of the women's courtyard to receive the Jews' offerings.[537] The court of the women (temple's "treasury") was within the court of the Gentiles, the outermost court of the temple. A low barrier separated the court of the Gentiles from the other courtyards and the temple building that lay within this enclosure. The court of the women was farther from the temple building than the court of Israel, which only Jewish men could enter, or the court of the priests, which only the priests could enter. Jesus had given His preceding teaching in the court of the Gentiles. Now He evidently moved into the court of the women.

While there, He observed "how" (Gr. *pos*) the Jewish men and women, who had come to celebrate Passover, were putting their voluntary contributions into the receptacles.

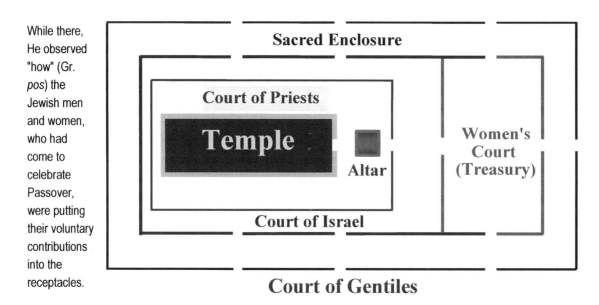

The woman whom Jesus observed was not only a widow, but "a poor widow." She contrasted with the many wealthy people there. The "two small" bronze ("copper") "coins" (Gr. *lepta*) that the widow contributed were together worth about one sixty-fourth of a denarius, the day's wage of a working man in Palestine. Mark told his Roman readers that they were worth "a fraction of" (NIV) one Roman cent (Gr. *kodrantes*, a transliteration of the Latin *quadrans*).

12:43-44   Mark stressed the importance of this lesson for disciples, by first noting that Jesus called "His disciples to Him," and then that He prefaced His statement with "Truly I say to you" (NASB). The poor widow's offering was worth more than the others, because it cost her more to give it, and most of all because she gave it willingly. Since she gave two coins, she could have kept one for herself. Her sacrifice expressed her love for God and her trust in God to sustain her (cf. 1 Kings 17:8-16).

> "The means of the giver and the motive are the measure of true generosity."[538]

> "The test of liberality is not what is given, but what is left."[539]

Here is another instructive example of a person with a servant's attitude who gave *all*, as little as that was, to God (cf. 10:45). Jesus and Mark taught disciples how God values wholehearted commitment to Himself with this incident.

---

[536]See Geoffrey Smith, "A Closer Look at the Widow's Offering: Mark 12:41-44," *Journal of the Evangelical Theological Society* 40:1 (March 1997)27-36.

[537]Mishnah *Shekalim* 6:5. See also Alfred Edersheim, *The Temple*, pp. 48-49.

[538]Plummer, p. 290.

[539]William Kelly, *An Exposition of the Gospel of Mark*, p. 179.

C. JESUS' TEACHING ON MT. OLIVET CH. 13

The Olivet Discourse is the longest section of Jesus' teaching that Mark recorded (cf. 4:1-34; 7:1-23). Mark used this discourse as a bridge between Jesus' controversies with Israel's leaders (11:27—12:44) and the account of His passion (chs. 14—15). It provides assurance that the leaders who had plotted against Jesus would suffer God's judgment.

> ". . . chap. 13 greatly enhances Mark's portrayal of Jesus as a predictor."[540]

Matthew and Mark both stressed Jesus' teaching that focused on His second coming. Matthew and Mark also recorded more about Jesus' answer to the disciples' second question, "What will be the sign when all these things are going to be fulfilled?" (13:4b). Luke concentrated more on His answer to their first question, "When will these things be?" (13:4a). Matthew wrote to answer the questions of Jewish unbelievers. Mark wrote primarily to respond to those of Gentile Christians living under Roman persecution and in a hostile world. Mark stressed Jesus' exhortations to watchfulness and His preparation of the disciples for future hardships.

1. The setting 13:1-4 (cf. Matt. 24:1-3; Luke 21:5-7)

13:1   This discourse evidently followed Jesus' departure from the temple on Wednesday with His disciples. The "wonderful (beautiful) stones" that caught the disciple's eye were probably those above the floor of the temple courtyard. Herod the Great had enlarged the temple esplanade and supported it with huge foundation stones. At the southeast corner, the temple complex rose about 200 feet above the Kidron Valley below. Some of those stones are still in place. In view of what Jesus predicted and what happened, the disciples apparently referred to the stones of the buildings and porches, not the foundation stones. The colonnades that surrounded the temple courtyard were also very beautiful. The whole temple complex was magnificent.[541] Mark probably called attention to the stones in view of what Jesus would say about them (v. 2).

13:2   Jesus predicted the complete destruction of the temple buildings (cf. Jer 7:11-14). This happened in A.D. 70 when Titus the Roman destroyed the city of Jerusalem. He razed the buildings and porches on the temple esplanade so thoroughly that no trace of them remains today. Not even their exact location on the temple mount is certain.

> "Up to this point during this day, Jesus had acted as God's Forthteller, applying the truth of God to the scene before Him; with this statement, He turned to predictive prophecy, declaring the near future."[542]

However, this prophecy has not yet attained complete fulfillment. There are still many stones standing on one another in the temple complex, specifically in its foundations. What Jesus proceeded to predict shows that complete fulfillment would not come until the future (i.e., the Tribulation).

13:3-4   Evidently the disciples pondered Jesus' prophecy as they crossed the Kidron Valley that separated the temple complex from Mt. Olivet to the east. When they sat down on the mountain and looked west into the temple courtyard, Jesus' first four disciples (1:16-20) asked two questions.

The first question dealt with the time of the temple's destruction. Matthew's account shows that their second question had two parts: They asked what the sign of Jesus' coming, and of the end of the present age, would be. Mark combined these two parts into one simple question about the sign of "all these things" being fulfilled. The disciples viewed the destruction of the temple and the end of the present age as occurring together. In His answer, Jesus taught them that these events would not happen at the same time. Again a question from the disciples led to a teaching session (cf. 4:10-32; 7:17-23; 9:11-13, 28-29; 10:10-12).

2. Warnings against deceptions 13:5-8 (Matt. 24:4-8; Luke 21:8-11)

Jesus first answered the disciples' second question about the sign of the end of the present age. He did so negatively, by warning them of false signs—"the beginning of birth pangs" (vv. 5-13). Then He gave them positive information about the event that will signal great "tribulation," followed by His Second Coming (vv. 14-27). Finally, Jesus answered their first question—about the destruction of Jerusalem—with a parable (vv. 28-32). The central part of this revelation is eschatological (vv. 14-27), flanked by moral exhortations. Verses 5-37 contain 19 imperative verbs in the Greek text. This discourse is a good example of the practical nature of biblical prophecy.

---

[540]Gundry, p. 734.

[541]See Josephus, *Antiquities of . . .*, 15:11:3-7; and Edersheim, *The Temple*, ch. 2.

[542]Hiebert, pp. 315-16.

"The conditions associated with the impending local crisis of Jerusalem's fall foreshadow those connected with the worldwide end-time crisis. Thus Jesus' words, relevant to His first disciples, remain so for all disciples who face similar conditions throughout this Age."[543]

13:5-6   The first word of the discourse proper means "take heed" (Gr. *blepete*). This word occurs four times in the following verses, indicating that *warning* is an important theme (vv. 9, 23, 33). Here, Jesus warned the disciples about people who would claim to be the Messiah ("I am He"). There would be "many" of them before He would return. Mark's "I am" is a divine name (cf. Exod. 3:14; John 8:58). Jesus said these false messiahs would claim to be "God" as well as "Messiah."

13:7-8   "Wars," "rumors of wars," "earthquakes," and "famines" would precede Jesus' return, but they are not signs of the end of the age. There will be many of these things before the end comes. The messianic kingdom will appear in history similar to an infant who emerges from a very painful birthing experience (cf. Isa. 66:8; Jer. 22:23; Hos. 13:13; Mic. 4:9-10). Jesus compared wars, rumors of war, earthquakes, and famines to the beginning of these pains. These phenomena show that the kingdom is coming, but they do not enable observers to date its arrival precisely. They are part of God's program for the present age that includes judgment as well as salvation. They do not necessarily indicate that the Tribulation has begun. However, these things will also mark the first part of the Tribulation (cf. Rev. 6). Verses 5-8 probably describe conditions before and during the first half of the Tribulation, and verses 9-23 describe conditions during the second half.[544]

3. Warnings about personal danger during persecution 13:9-13 (cf. Matt. 24:9-13; Luke 21:12-19)

These warnings also occur in other contexts of Jesus' ministry (cf. Matt. 10:17-22; Luke 12:11-12). Jesus evidently voiced them more than once.

Mark stressed the idea of persecution by recording the Greek word *paradidomi* three times in this pericope. The NASB translated this word "deliver up" in verses 9, 11, and 12. The NIV rendered it "handed over" in verse 9, "arrested" in verse 11, and "betray" in verse 12.

13:9   The disciples could anticipate persecution from the Jews and the Gentiles, from religious and secular courts. However, such treatment would provide opportunity to bear witness for Jesus. This warning is appropriate for all disciples in the inter-advent era, as are all the warnings in this discourse.

13:10   "Unto all the nations" is in the emphatic first position in the Greek text. "All" the nations must hear the gospel before the end of the age (cf. Matt. 24:14). This is the responsibility of every generation of disciples (Matt. 28:19). The generation of believers alive during the Tribulation, immediately preceding Jesus' return, will accomplish this task *in their generation* (Rev. 7). "Must" (Gr. *dei*) indicates divine necessity. God wants this to happen, and it will happen.

> "It is part of God's eschatological purpose that before the End [of this age] all nations shall have an opportunity to accept the gospel."[545]

This verse is not a promise, that if disciples will preach the gospel to all nations in a particular generation, God will then begin the kingdom—as postmillennialists teach. Man cannot bring in the kingdom by the universal preaching of the gospel. God will bring it in at His appointed time. This is not a promise that everyone will become a believer in Jesus, either.

13:11   Jesus promised that God will give special grace (help) to disciples, who want to bear a good testimony, when they are arrested and tried for their faith (v. 9). The "Holy Spirit" will give such disciples the appropriate words to "speak" then. Jesus did not forbid careful thought, but just anxious care (cf. Luke 21:15).[546] This promise should give disciples in these situations freedom from unnecessary anxiety. However, Jesus did not promise release from suffering.

> "History bears ample witness to the fact that Christians on trial for their faith have been amazed themselves at the aptness of the answers that flashed into their minds at the opportune moment."[547]

13:12-13   Betrayal even by family members will be another trial disciples may have to bear (cf. Mic. 7:2-6; Luke 12:51-53). Persecution would come through official channels but also from blood relatives. All kinds of people would hate them for their testimony.

> "As there is nothing that excites such love as the gospel, when intelligently received, so there is nothing that occasions such hate as this same gospel, when passionately rejected."[548]

---

[543]Grassmick, p. 167.

[544]Cf. Bailey, p. 91.

[545]Cranfield, p. 399.

[546]Taylor, p. 508.

[547]Hiebert, p. 321.

[548]Morison, p. 359.

The last part of verse 13 states a general principle. Faithful endurance of persecution to its end results in deliverance. Disciples who endure their persecution faithfully, to the end of that persecution, will experience deliverance from it while they are alive. Disciples who endure their persecution faithfully, to the end of their lives, will experience deliverance from it by death. Disciples living just before Jesus returns, who endure their persecution faithfully to the end of the present age, will experience deliverance at Jesus' Second Coming.

Faithful endurance of persecution also results in the privilege of reigning with Jesus in His kingdom (cf. 2 Tim. 2:12). Note that Jesus did not teach that all will endure to the end faithfully. Unfortunately some disciples do not (2 Tim. 2). Notwithstanding, our ultimate salvation does not depend on enduring persecution faithfully, but on God's faithfulness to His promises to keep us secure (2 Tim. 2:13; cf. John 10:27-28; Rom. 8:31-39; et al.).

This pericope should be a special encouragement for disciples undergoing persecution for their faith, including Mark's original readers. It is easier to endure suffering for our faith when we view it in the context of God's plan for the future. This perspective gives us hope.

4. The coming crisis 13:14-23 (cf. Matt. 24:14-28)

Having clarified what the sign of the coming destruction would not be, Jesus now explained what it would be. Matthew and Mark both described the destruction preceding Jesus' second coming. Luke recorded Jesus' teaching about the destruction of Jerusalem in A.D. 70 (Luke 21:20-24).

13:14   "But" identifies the contrast between the false and true signs. The true sign was the appearance of "the abomination of desolation" (cf. Dan. 9:27; 11:31; 12:11; Matt. 24:15).

The "abomination of desolation" would be something *abominable* that desecrates, associated with idolatry, that would defile the temple—resulting in its desertion by the godly.[549] The ultimate abomination would be the *Antichrist*, the "abomination" in view primarily in Matthew and Mark's accounts. The immediate abomination would be the polluting of the temple preceding its destruction in A.D. 70. A former abomination was the Syrian, Antiochus Epiphanes, who erected a pagan altar over the brazen altar, and sacrificed a pig on it to Zeus in 167 B.C. (1 Macc. 1:41-64; 6:7).[550]

The "abomination" would be "standing where it" did not belong ("should not be," i.e., in the temple). Mark described Jesus saying that the "abomination" (Gr. *bdelygma*, a neuter noun) would stand (*estekota*, a masculine participle) as a *person*—who set himself up *as God*—in the temple. The fact that Jesus used a masculine participle to modify a neuter noun suggests that the abomination is *a man*.

Mark avoided referring specifically to the temple sanctuary, though Matthew did refer to it (Matt. 24:15). Perhaps Mark did this to avoid planting the idea of polluting the temple in any Roman reader's mind. His parenthetical instruction to the reader would have encouraged Roman Christians to look up the identity of the place in Daniel's prophecy (Dan. 9:25-27).

When the Zealots occupied the temple in A.D. 67-68 and installed a usurper, Phanni, as high priest, Jewish Christians fled from Jerusalem to Pella, a Transjordanian mountain town.[551] This flight prefigured the one that will take place in the future (i.e., the Tribulation).

13:15-18   The point of these somber instructions is that the appearance of the abomination of desolation will require immediate flight from Jerusalem. The situation will be urgent.

13:19   This verse clarifies that the time of the appearance of the abomination will be in the Tribulation (Gr. *thlipsis*, Dan. 12:1; Jer. 30:7). Jesus looked beyond the destruction of Jerusalem to a much greater Tribulation.[552]

13:20   God will not shorten the Tribulation to a period less than the seven years He has already announced (Dan. 9:26-27). He has already chosen to shorten it to a period of seven years.[553] If He did not limit the Tribulation to this relatively brief duration, no one would survive. God's special love for believers led Him to shorten His judgment on the world then to only seven years.

13:21-23   Jesus repeated His warning about people who will claim to be the Messiah (cf. vv. 5-6), so that His disciples would not believe them. "If possible" (v. 22) is not intended to imply that the elect will inevitably continue to believe in Jesus and follow Him faithfully. If that were so, Jesus' repeated warnings would be meaningless. It means instead that the false messiahs will do

[549]Cf. C. E. B. Cranfield, "St. Mark 13," *Scottish Journal of Theology* 6 (July 1953):298-99.

[550]Cf. Josephus, *Antiquities of . . .*, 12:5:4.

[551]Idem, *The Wars . . .*, 4:3:7-10; 4:6:3; Eusebius, 3:5:3.

[552]Cf. Taylor, p. 514.

[553]See Renald E. Showers, *Maranatha: Our Lord, Come! A Definitive Study of the Rapture of the Church*, pp. 50-54.

miracles with the intent of leading the elect into error *if they*—the false messiahs—can (cf. 2 Tim 3:1-15). In view of this possibility, Jesus' disciples need to be discerning (Gr. *blepete*, v. 23).

"So for us the fulfillment of these verses [vv. 14-20] is past, present and future, and they are rightly included under the heading 'Signs of the End' or 'Characteristics of the Last Times'. The key to their understanding is the recognition that there is here a double reference. The impending judgement [*sic*] on Jerusalem and the events connected with it are for Jesus as it were a transparent object in the foreground through which he sees the last events before the End, which they indeed foreshadow."[554]

5. The Second Coming of the Son of Man 13:24-27 (cf. Matt. 24:29-31; Luke 21:25-28)

These verses do not describe the destruction of Jerusalem in A.D. 70, but rather the Tribulation at the end of the present age, and the Second Coming that will follow it. The Second Coming is the climax of the Olivet Discourse. It is also the climax of the Book of Revelation, especially chapters 6—19, that is an expanded revelation of the Olivet Discourse.

13:24-25   In contrast to the appearance of false messiahs, the true Messiah will appear after the predicted Tribulation.[555] This is, of course, a reference to the Second Coming, not the Rapture. The Rapture terminates the Church Age, a period of time within the inter-advent age. The Olivet Discourse deals with the larger period, the inter-advent age, and does not refer to the church, though the church has existed throughout most of the inter-advent age. The Book of Revelation gives further information about the celestial phenomena that will happen then (Rev. 6—18; cf. 2 Pet. 3:10). However, the Old Testament prophets also predicted these things (Isa. 13:10; 24:23; 34:4; Ezek. 32:7-8; Joel 2:10, 30-31; 3:15; Amos 8:9). If we take the wars, earthquakes, and famines of verses 7-8 literally, and I think we should, we should probably understand these phenomena literally too.

13:26   Jesus described His return by referring to Old Testament prophecies of it (Dan. 7:13; Deut. 30:4; Zech. 2:6). The unveiling and triumph of Jesus are the major emphases (cf. Rev. 19:11-16).[556] Jesus will no longer appear primarily as the Suffering Servant, but as the glorified "Son of Man"—"coming . . . with great power and glory"!

13:27   Evidently Jesus will bring all the elect together. This implies the resurrection of Old Testament saints (Dan. 12:2) and Tribulation saints who have died (Rev. 6:9-11). Probably Christians, saints of the Church Age who have gone to heaven at the Rapture or death, will return with Him (1 Thess. 4:17). Saints living on the earth when Jesus returns will also assemble to Him (cf. Matt. 25). Jesus pictured all believers converging to Him at His Second Coming—whether alive or dead, on earth or in heaven. He will become the universal center of attention, and then He will begin reigning. Unbelievers will not experience resurrection until the end of Jesus' millennial reign (Rev. 20:7-15).

6. The time of Jesus' return 13:28-32 (cf. Matt. 24:32-41; Luke 21:29-33)

Jesus began this discourse with exhortation (vv. 4-13), and He ended it the same way (vv. 28-37).

13:28-29   The parable of the fig tree appears in all the synoptic versions of the Olivet Discourse. Jesus had previously used a fig tree to illustrate the generation of Israelites that failed to believe in Him at His first advent (11:14). Here He used it to illustrate the fact that perceptive people can anticipate coming events by the signs that precede those events. Persecution (vv. 9-13), culminating in the Tribulation (vv. 14-25), pointed to the commencement of Jesus' kingdom (vv. 26-27; cf. Luke 21:31).

13:30   Jesus probably meant that the fulfillment of "all these things" (v. 4b) would begin in the generation of His present disciples, but complete fulfillment would not come until later.[557] A second view is that Jesus was referring to the specific generation in the future who would observe the signs He just spoke about. A third view is that Jesus meant His contemporaries were those who would see all these things coming to pass.[558] A fourth view is that by "generation," Jesus meant the entire Jewish race.[559] "All" those things began during *that* generation, if one interprets "all those things" to be the signs as a whole (vv. 9-25). The Greek word *genetai*, translated "take place" (NASB) or "have happened" (NIV), means "have come into existence"—and permits this interpretation. One could therefore translate this Greek verb: "have begun to come into existence."

---

[554]Cranfield, pp. 404-5.

[555]Bruce, "The Synoptic . . .," 1:431.

[556]Wessel, p. 750.

[557]E.g., C. E. Stowe, "The Eschatology of Christ, With Special Reference to the Discourse in Matt. XXIV. and XXV.," *Bibliotheca Sacra* 7 (July 1850):471.

[558]Gundry, p. 747.

[559]E.g., Wiersbe, 1:158.

13:31 | "Heaven and earth" is a figure of speech (merism) for all creation (cf. Gen. 1:1).[560] The universe *as we know it* will end one day (Rev. 21:1), but Jesus' "words" will remain. Jesus was referring specifically to His predictions in this chapter, but at the same time, His statement was general and includes *all* His "words." By saying this about His "words" (Word), Jesus was implying that He was God (cf. Ps. 102:25-27; Isa. 40:6-8; 51:6). The fulfillment of this prophecy is certain.

13:32 | "That day" is the day of Jesus' return, contrasted with "those days" preceding it (vv. 17, 19, 24). Jesus was distinguishing between knowing that an event was approaching or near at hand (vv. 28-29), from knowing the exact time of its arrival. God the "Father" *alone* "knows" the "day" and the "hour" of the Son's return (cf. Acts 1:7). Jesus' ignorance of this information was a result of His incarnation (Phil. 2:6-8).[561] Jesus may not have known this information when He made this statement, but He probably knows the time of His return now.

7. The concluding exhortation 13:33-37 (cf. Matt. 24:42; Luke 21:34-36)

Matthew recorded much more of what Jesus taught the disciples, following His statement in verse 32, than Mark or Luke did. They just included the essence of His exhortation to be vigilant.

13:33 | For the fourth time, Jesus urged His disciples to "take heed" (Gr. *blepete*, vv. 5, 9, 23). He underlined this warning by adding: "Be vigilant" (Gr. *agrypneite*) (or "Keep on the alert"). Watchfulness is necessary because we do not know the exact time of Jesus' return.

In view of God's revelations concerning the Rapture, the Tribulation, and the Second Coming, were Jesus' exhortations to remain watchful unnecessarily urgent? Christians who know their Bibles are aware that many events will precede the Second Coming. Is it realistic or necessary to live as though Jesus' return is imminent?

Jesus' return was not less than seven years away from His departure from the earth, because the Old Testament prophesied the Tribulation before the messianic kingdom (Dan. 9:24-27). Therefore, the 12 disciples to whom Jesus gave this discourse, could have been only a few years away from His return. They needed to be vigilant. That generation of disciples, and all succeeding generations of disciples, learned later that Jesus would return for His own at the Rapture before He comes at the Second Coming (1 Cor. 15:51-58; 1 Thess. 4:13-18). Thus, while His Second Coming is at least seven years away, His return at the Rapture will be sooner. Pretribulationists believe it could be at any moment. Therefore, all that Jesus said about the importance of being vigilant—anticipating His return—is applicable to and relevant for us.

13:34-36 | Jesus told another parable about a doorkeeper. Mark is the only evangelist who recorded it. It is similar to the parable of the talents (Matt. 25:14-30) and the parable of the minas (Luke 19:12-27), though much shorter.

In this parable, the "doorkeeper" is the focus of attention. A doorkeeper or porter was responsible to guard the entrance to his master's house. Entrusted with his master's goods, this doorkeeper did "not know when" his "master" would return. However, *whenever* the master returned, the doorkeeper would have to be ready to admit him to a well-managed house. Evening, midnight, rooster crowing, and dawn were the names that the Romans gave the four watches of the night.[562] The porter had to remain watchful (Gr. *gregore*) at night, when the Light of the World was absent from His estate. The opposite of watchfulness is insensibility, lethargy, and inactivity—pictured here as *sleep* (cf. Rom. 13:11; 1 Thess. 5:1-11). Likewise, it is necessary for Jesus' disciples to remain watchful ("on the alert," looking for, Gr. *gregoreite*, v. 35).

"The element of surprise is ineradicable from the parousia expectation."[563]

13:37 | Jesus concluded this discourse as He began it, with a final call to watchfulness (Gr. *gregoreite*, vv. 34, 35). "You" may refer to the four disciples who asked Jesus the initial question (vv. 3-4), or it may refer to all the Twelve who sat before Him. "All" could refer to all the disciples present, or to all disciples including those not present. In any case, the point is clear. What Jesus taught here is something every disciple of His needs to apply. We "all" need to "be on the alert," in view of the Lord's return—like the doorkeeper in Jesus' parable (vv. 34-36).

The previous parable of the fig tree (vv. 28-32) taught that disciples need to recognize the signs that the time of the Lord's return is drawing near. This parable of the doorkeeper (vv. 33-37) clarified that they would not be able to tell exactly when He would return at His Second Coming. Even

---

[560]See Appendix 7 "Some Figures of Speech" at the end of my notes on Matthew for a list of some of the more frequently used figures and their meanings.

[561]See Harold F. Carl, "Only the Father Knows: Historical and Evangelical Responses to Jesus' Eschatological Ignorance in Mark 13:32," a paper presented at the Annual Meeting of the Evangelical Theological Society, Nov. 16, 2000, Nashville, Tenn.

[562]Wessel, p. 753.

[563]G. R. Beasley-Murray, *A Commentary on Mark Thirteen*, p. 117.

though Daniel's prophecy specified the length of the Tribulation as seven years (Dan. 9:24-27), the exact day and hour of Christ's return remains unknown (cf. Matt. 24:50).

The outstanding emphasis in Mark's account of this discourse is clear. Disciples need to take heed (Gr. *blepo*, to be aware, to observe, to discern; vv. 5, 9, 23, 33), to be vigilant (Gr. *agrupneo*, to be awake, to watch; v. 33), and to be watchful (Gr. *gregoreo*, to be awake, attentive, vigilant, and circumspect; vv. 33, 35, 37).

VII. THE SERVANT'S PASSION MINISTRY CHS. 14—15

This section of Mark's Gospel records the climaxes of many themes that the writer had introduced. Mark chose to concentrate on the passion, or sufferings of Jesus, rather than simply give a record of all the events of the last week of Jesus' life. Out of Mark's 661 verses, 242 (37 percent) deal with the last week, from the Triumphal Entry through the Resurrection, and 128 concern Jesus' passion and resurrection.[564] Over half the events Mark recorded in the last week (53 percent) deal with Jesus' sufferings and triumph, the two major themes in the last three chapters.

A. THE SERVANT'S ANTICIPATION OF SUFFERING 14:1-52

Several themes peak in this section. Here we have the clearest evidence that Jesus was the Messiah and the Son of God (cf. 1:1; 8:29). Here, too, Jesus' conflict with the religious leaders, His foes, came to a head (cf. 3:1, 6; 11:18; 12:12). The ignorance and selfishness of Jesus' disciples, His friends, also peaked (cf. 3:19; 6:1-6; 8:31—10:52). Finally, the Servant's ministry climaxed in His giving His life as a ransom for many (cf. 10:45).[565]

1. Jesus' sufferings because of betrayal 14:1-11

This is another section of the Gospel that has a chiastic or "sandwich" structure (cf. 3:20-35; 5:21-43; 6:7-31; 11:12-26; 14:27-52). Mark's account of the conspiracy to kill Jesus (vv. 1-2, 10-11) surrounds Jesus' anointing in Bethany (vv. 3-9).

The plot to arrest Jesus 14:1-2 (cf. Matt. 26:1-5; Luke 22:1-2)

These verses introduce the whole passion narrative. Passover commemorated the Israelites' redemption from slavery in Egypt through the Exodus (Exod. 12:1—13:16). It anticipated a greater deliverance from the consequences of slavery to sin. The Jews began to celebrate Passover on the fourteenth of Nisan, and the Feast of Unleavened Bread followed on the fifteenth through the twenty-first of Nisan. Mark dated the events that follow immediately as occurring "two days" before Passover. This would have been Wednesday, April 1, A.D. 33.[566]

Passover, like the feasts of Tabernacles and Pentecost, was a pilgrim feast. Many Jewish families from all over the world traveled to Jerusalem to observe these feasts as the Mosaic Law required (Deut. 16:16). The Jews could observe the Passover only in Jerusalem (Deut. 16:5-6). Consequently mobs of people choked the city. One writer claimed that the population of Jerusalem swelled from 50,000 to 250,000.[567] Jesus enjoyed a large popular following, so the religious leaders wanted to avoid a riot by executing Jesus inconspicuously. Evidently they wanted to postpone further confrontation with Jesus until after the feasts when the pilgrims would have returned to their homes. However, Judas' offer to betray Jesus (vv. 10-11) was too good to refuse.

The anointing at Bethany 14:3-9 (cf. Matt. 26:6-13; John 12:1-8)

14:3   For thematic reasons, Matthew and Mark both placed this event within the story of the hostility of Jesus' enemies. It is apparently out of chronological order (cf. John 12:1). This rearrangement of the material highlighted the contrast between the hatred of unbelievers and the love of believers for Jesus. The incident probably occurred the previous Saturday evening.[568]

John added that the woman was Mary, the sister of Lazarus and Martha, and that she anointed Jesus' feet as well as His head. Anointing a guest's head was a common way to honor such a person at a festive occasion (cf. Ps. 23:5; Luke 7:46). Mary appears in three scenes in the Gospels, and each time she is at Jesus' feet (cf. Luke 10:38-42; John 11:31-32). She is a good model for all disciples to emulate. The high value of her perfume and its expensive container may suggest that this was an heirloom passed from one generation to another.[569]

[564]Wessel, p. 754.

[565]See J. P. Heil, "Mark 14, 1-52: Narrative Structure and Reader Response," *Biblica* 71:3 (1990):305-32.

[566]Hoehner, *Chronological Aspects . . .*, pp. 92, 143.

[567]Lane, p. 490.

[568]Hoehner, *Chronological Aspects . . .*, p. 91.

[569]Lane, p. 492.

14:4-5   Apparently Judas Iscariot voiced the disciples' violent objection (Gr. *embrimaomai*, cf. 10:14) to Mary's act of loving sacrifice (Matt. 26:8; John 12:4-5). Customarily, Jews gave gifts to the poor on the evening of Passover.[570] Mary's gift to Jesus was worth a year's wages. The disciples could see no reason for this "waste" because they did not understand that Jesus' death was imminent. Their concern for the poor contrasts with her concern for Jesus.

14:6-8   Jesus defended Mary's act and explained why it was appropriate. It was an act of devotion to Jesus, and it was an anointing for His burial. We cannot tell how much about Jesus' death Mary understood. She probably anointed Him only as an act of love. We should not interpret Jesus' statement as expressing disregard for the poor (cf. Matt. 5:3; 6:2-4; 19:21; Luke 6:20, 36-38; 21:1-4; John 13:29).

14:9   This statement is a further evaluation of the greatness of Mary's act. It implies the continuance of "the gospel" proclamation, after Jesus' death and resurrection, to "the whole world."

> "The Lord erected a memorial for all time to her who had done her best to honour Him."[571]
> "Wherever the gospel is truly preached, the story of the anointing is sure to be prized as the best possible illustration of the spirit which moved Jesus to lay down His life, as also of the spirit of Christianity as it manifests itself in the lives of sincere believers."[572]

Judas' betrayal of Jesus 14:10-11 (cf. Matt. 26:14-16; Luke 22:3-6)

If the preceding incident happened on Saturday evening, and Judas betrayed Jesus on Wednesday, then Mary's act of extravagance did not lead Judas to betray Jesus immediately. The Gospel writers did not explain Judas' reasons for betraying Jesus explicitly. It was evidently Judas' initiative, in offering "to betray" Jesus, that led the Sanhedrin ("chief priests") to move up their timetable for Jesus' execution. If Judas handed Jesus over to them, they could avoid the hostility of the crowds (cf. v. 2; Luke 22:6).

Even though Mary's act of devotion is the high point of this section, providing an excellent example for disciple readers, the dark undercurrent of betrayal is its dominant feature. The religious leaders, Judas, and even the disciples manifested opposition to glorifying Jesus. This attitude was a source of suffering for the Servant.

2. Jesus' sufferings because of desertion 14:12-52

The Servant's sufferings in anticipation of His death continue in this section of the text. They centered around two events: Jesus' observance of the Passover with His disciples, and His agony in the Garden of Gethsemane with His Father.

Jesus' farewell in the upper room 14:12-26

Mark's account of what happened in the upper room is divisible into three parts: the preparations for the meal, Jesus' announcement of His betrayal, and His institution of the Lord's Supper.

Preparations for the Passover meal 14:12-16 (cf. Matt. 26:17-19; Luke 22:7-13)

The main feature of this pericope is the unusual method by which Jesus' directed His disciples.

14:12   The Jews commonly referred to the first day of the combined Passover and Unleavened Bread feasts as the Feast of Unleavened Bread.[573] Mark clarified for his Gentile readers that this was the day the Jews slew the Passover lamb, namely, the fourteenth of Nisan. This would have been Thursday, April 2. Mark could say that from Wednesday, the Passover was "two days away" (v. 1), because the Jews ate the Passover lamb between sunset and midnight on the evening of the day they slew the lamb. For the Jews, this was two days later since they began each day with sunset. The disciples had to prepare to eat the Passover within Jerusalem (Deut. 16:5-6) that very evening.

[570]Wessel, p. 756.
[571]Swete, p. 326.
[572]Bruce, *The Training* . . ., pp. 299-300.
[573]Josephus, *Antiquities of* . . ., 2:15:1.

Wednesday	Thursday		Friday	
	Midnight	April 2	Midnight	April 3
	3:00 a.m.		3:00 a.m.	
	6:00 a.m.		6:00 a.m.	
April 1	9:00 a.m.		9:00 a.m.	Jesus was crucified
	Noon		Noon	
	3:00 p.m.	The Jews slew their Passover lambs	3:00 p.m.	Jesus died
14 Nisan	6:00 p.m.	15 Nisan	6:00 p.m.	16 Nisan
	9:00 p.m.	The Jews ate their Passover lambs	9:00 p.m.	

14:13-16   The two disciples were Peter and John (Luke 22:8). Normally, women carried the water, so a man carrying a water jar would not be hard to find. Perhaps the man carrying a water jar was a prearranged signal. Obviously Jesus had made arrangements to provide for His disciples' needs, but the Twelve had certain responsibilities in addition, namely, the preparation of the food.

"He Who was born in a 'hostelry'—*Katalyma*—was content to ask for His last Meal in a *Katalyma*."[574]

The whole record shows Jesus' sovereign control over the destinies of Himself and His disciples. Even as He approached the Cross, Jesus was aware of, and caring for, His disciples. Nevertheless they had responsibilities as well. All of this is instructive for the teachable disciple who reads this account.

The announcement of Jesus' betrayal 14:17-21 (cf. Matt. 26:20-25; Luke 22:14, 21-23; John 13:21-30)

Mark did not record all that happened in the upper room. He stressed the announcement of Jesus' betrayal and Jesus' explanation of the significance of the bread and wine.

14:17   This would have been Thursday evening. Because the Jews began their days at sundown, this incident would have happened at the beginning of the fifteenth of Nisan. Jesus came with the Twelve to the upper room. Luke 22:15-16, 24-30 and John 13:1-20 record what happened next.

14:18   Originally the Jews ate the Passover standing (cf. Exod. 12:11). However, in Jesus' day they customarily reclined to eat it.[575]

"To feel this pathos we should recall that in ancient near eastern culture, eating with someone connotes an almost sacred trust of friendship."[576]

"To betray a friend after eating a meal with him was, and still is, regarded as the worst kind of treachery in the Middle East [cf. Ps. 41:9]."[577]

The disciples heard for the first time that one of them would betray Jesus. Mark's account stresses Jesus' identification of His betrayer as "one of the Twelve" (v. 20).

"Perfidy on the part of an intimate, not criminality on the part of Jesus, put Jesus on a cross."[578]

14:19-20   The disciples' grief expressed sadness at this announcement. Their question was a protestation of innocence, but with a tinge of self-distrust. It expected a negative answer, but it was a question. Judas' motive in asking was obviously different from the

---

[574]Edersheim, *The Life . . .*, 2:483.

[575]Mishnah *Pesachim* 10:1.

[576]Gundry, p. 827.

[577]Wessel, p. 759.

[578]Gundry, p. 832.

others. Jesus' answer again implied the treachery of the betrayer. It also gave him an opportunity to repent since Jesus did not name him.

14:21   Jesus explained that His betrayal was part of divine purpose that the Old Testament had predicted (e.g., Ps. 22; Isa. 53). Nevertheless the betrayer would bear the responsibility for his deed and would pay a severe penalty.

"The fact that God turns the wrath of man to his praise does not excuse the wrath of man."[579]

The seriousness of Judas' act was in direct proportion to the innocence of the Person he betrayed (cf. v. 9). "By whom the Son of Man is betrayed" (NASB) views Judas as Satan's instrument.

The institution of the Lord's Supper 14:22-26 (cf. Matt. 26:26-30; Luke 22:17-20; 1 Cor. 11:23-26)

Matthew and Mark's accounts of this event are similar, but Paul's is more like Luke's.

14:22   The "bread" Jesus ate would have been the unleavened bread that the Jews used in the Passover meal. The "blessing" Jesus pronounced was a prayer of thanksgiving to God for the bread, not a consecration of the bread itself. People, not places or things, are always the objects of blessings in the Bible. Jesus' distribution of the bread to the disciples was more significant than His breaking of it. By passing it to them, He symbolically shared Himself with them. When Jesus said, "This is My body," He meant the bread represented His body (cf. Luke 12:1; John 6:32-35). The disciples could hardly have eaten the literal flesh of Jesus since He was physically reclining among them. Moreover, the Jews abhorred eating human flesh, and would never consume animal blood, much less human blood (cf. Lev. 3:17; 7:26-27; 17:10-14).[580]

"The bitter herbs served to recall the bitterness of slavery, the stewed fruit, which possessed the consistency and color of clay, evoked the making of bricks as slaves, while the paschal lamb provided a reminder of God's gracious 'passing over' of Israel in the plague of death that came to Egypt."[581]

14:23-24   The common "cup," likewise, symbolized Jesus' sharing of Himself with the disciples, and their unity as disciples. Judas had apparently left the upper room before the institution of the Lord's Supper. Jesus' viewed His "blood" as the ratifying agent of the New Covenant (cf. Jer. 31:31-34), as animal blood had made the Old (Mosaic) Covenant valid (Exod. 24:8). The Greek word translated "covenant" is *diatheke*, a word that describes an agreement made by one person for others. A different word, *syntheke*, describes an agreement that two parties made in which both had obligations to each other. The diluted wine in the cup was also a reminder of the covenant's existence.[582] Jesus' blood "poured out" is an obvious allusion to His death. "For" translates the Greek preposition *hyper* meaning "in behalf of" or "instead of," a clear reference to vicarious atonement (cf. Matt. 26:28). "Many" means all (cf. 10:45; Isa. 53:11-12).

"By the word *many* he means not a part of the world only, but the whole human race."[583]

14:25   The phrase "the fruit of the vine" may have been a liturgical formula describing wine used at a feast.[584] In any case, Jesus was saying He would not "drink" wine "again" until He did so "in the kingdom." Jesus was anticipating the messianic banquet at the beginning of His kingdom (cf. Isa. 25:6). This was a welcome promise in view of Jesus' announcement of His coming death.

"The cup from which Jesus abstained was the fourth, which ordinarily concluded the Passover fellowship. The significance of this can be appreciated from the fact that the four cups of wine were interpreted in terms of the four-fold promise of redemption set forth in Exod. 6:6-7: 'I will bring you out . . . I will rid you of their bondage . . . I will redeem you . . . I will take you for my people and I will be your God' (TJ *Pesachim* X. 37b)."[585]

"Jesus seldom spoke of His death without also speaking of His resurrection (8:31; 9:31; 10:34)."[586]

[579]Cranfield, *The Gospel* . . ., p. 424.
[580]Riddle, p. 194.
[581]Lane, p. 505.
[582]Taylor, p. 546.
[583]Calvin, 3:214.
[584]Wessel, p. 761.
[585]Lane, p. 508.
[586]Hiebert, p. 355.

"New" or "anew" means in a qualitatively different way (Gr. *kainon*). Now Jesus and the disciples anticipated suffering and death, but then they would anticipate joy and glory.

14:26   The "hymn" was probably the second part of the *Hallel* (lit. praise, Ps. 115—118) that the Jews sang antiphonally at the end of the Passover. The other evangelists recorded more that Jesus said and did in the upper room (e.g., John 13—16). By the time they left, it was probably quite late at night.

> "When Jesus arose to go to Gethsemane, Ps. 118 was upon his lips. It provided an appropriate description of how God would guide his Messiah through distress and suffering to glory."[587]

Jesus' agony in the garden 14:27-52

Jesus experienced suffering as He said farewell to His disciples in Jerusalem (vv. 12-26), but His suffering increased as He anticipated the Cross on the Mount of Olives (vv. 27-52).

The prediction of Peter's denial 14:27-31 (cf. Matt. 26:31-35; Luke 22:31-34; John 13:36-38)

Evidently Jesus made this prediction in the upper room before the institution of the Lord's Supper. Mark probably inserted it here in his narrative because of its logical connection with Jesus' arrest in Gethsemane.

14:27-28   We should understand the meaning of "fall away" (Gr. *skandalisthesesthe*, cf. 4:17; 6:3; 9:42-47) in the light of the prophecy that Jesus said predicted it (Zech. 13:7). Zechariah did not mean that the sheep would abandon the Shepherd permanently, much less that they would cease to be what they were—followers. He pictured the flock fleeing from the Shepherd because someone attacked Him. That is precisely what the disciples did when the authorities arrested and executed Jesus. Later those sheep rallied around the Shepherd. Jesus announced His leading them as a shepherd "to Galilee" later (v. 28). Again He spoke of His resurrection immediately after announcing His death (vv. 24-25).

Jesus attributed the Shepherd's striking to God. He changed the Zechariah passage slightly. Clearly Jesus viewed Himself as God's Suffering Servant (Isa. 53:4-6). This point would have helped the disciples accept Jesus' fate.

14:29-30   Peter refused to allow the possibility that he would forsake Jesus, even though the other disciples ("all") might (cf. John 21:15). Jesus informed Peter that his defection would actully be worse than that of the other disciples. He introduced His warning with the customary solemn affirmation, and explained that the denial was not only certain but imminent. Furthermore Peter would utter it "three times"—in spite of the rooster's double warning. Mark alone referred to the second crowing, probably because of Peter's recollection of the event. The word Jesus used for "deny" or "disown" (Gr. *aparnese*) is a strong one meaning "deny utterly."

14:31   Jesus' reply should have caused Peter to realize his weakness and seek help. Instead, he dug in his heels, and virtually told Jesus that he would "die with" Him and prove Him wrong. He kept affirming excessively (Gr. *ekperissos*, used only here in the New Testament) that he would definitely not deny Jesus. Peter did not know how weak he was, a problem most disciples of Jesus share with him. He would have to learn the hard way, through failure. Peter led the other disciples in denying that they would deny Jesus.[588] Later, he denied Jesus with the same vehemence with which he professed that he would *not deny Him!*

This pericope is a strong warning for all disciples. When facing persecution for one's allegiance to Jesus, one should not trust in the strength of his or her commitment. He or she should trust in God, who can supply the grace needed to remain faithful (cf. 9:14-29).

Jesus' sufferings in Gethsemane 14:32-42 (cf. Matt. 26:36-46; Luke 22:40-46)

This incident contrasts Jesus' humility and dependence on the Father with Peter's self-confidence (vv. 27-31). It is a remarkable revelation of the humanity of Jesus.

> "So far from sailing serenely through his trials like some superior being unconcerned with this world, he is almost dead with distress."[589]

This is Mark's third mention of Jesus praying (cf. 1:35; 6:46). In each instance, Jesus affirmed His commitment to the Father's will that Satan was constantly testing.

[587]Lane, p. 509.
[588]W. N. Clarke, "Commentary on the Gospel of Mark," in *An American Commentary*, p. 214.
[589]Moule, p. 117.

14:32-34   Jesus apparently took His inner circle of disciples (cf. 5:37; 9:2) with Him, in order to teach them about suffering, and to receive help from their intercession for Him (cf. Matt. 26:38). The other disciples were to pray as well (Luke 22:40). Perhaps they were also to keep watch so that He might be able to give Himself entirely to prayer.[590]

> "Since in that culture people prayed with their eyes open, the command to pray does not work against the command to keep awake, as it would if the three disciples were to close their eyes in prayer."[591]

This was apparently a favorite place that Jesus and the disciples had visited previously (cf. Luke 22:39; John 18:2).

The words "distressed" (Gr. *ekthambeisthai*) and "troubled" (Gr. *ademonein*) together "describe an extremely acute emotion, a compound of bewilderment, fear, uncertainty and anxiety, nowhere else portrayed in such vivid terms as here."[592] The prospect of bearing God's wrath for the world's sins and experiencing separation from His Father grieved Jesus deeply (Gr. *perilypos*, cf. 6:26). This was much more than any mere martyr has ever had to endure.

14:35-36   The Jews did not address God with "Abba" (lit. Daddy) because they considered such intimacy disrespectful. Jesus used the word because He—as the Son of God—was on intimate terms with the Father (cf. Rom. 8:15; Gal. 4:6). In the first prayer session, Jesus evidently prayed for the better part of an hour (v. 37), though Mark only recorded the essence of His request (cf. Heb. 5:7). In the ancient world, almost everyone prayed aloud, and this is how Jesus probably prayed.[593] His submission to His Father here recalls Genesis 22:7, where Isaac addressed his father Abraham in a very similar situation quite near this very place.[594]

Jesus expressed faith in God, with whom all things—consistent with His nature—are possible (cf. 9:23). The unclear issue to the God-man, who voluntarily limited His knowledge in the Incarnation, was not God's ability but God's will.

> "It is this complete dependence on God for his own salvation which is the source of Jesus' courage to renounce himself, be least, and lose his life."[595]

Jesus referred to the Cross as the "hour" and the "cup." The first expression includes everything involved in the Cross (cf. John 7:30; 8:20; et al.). The "cup" figuratively particularized God's judgment in the Cross (cf. 10:38-39; 14:29). Jesus' human will was distinct from the Father's will, but never opposed to it.

> "Though the Lord Jesus did praise God (Luke 10:21) and thank the Father (8:6, 7) in His praying, most of His recorded prayers were petitions and intercessions."[596]

14:37   Perhaps Jesus spoke specifically "to Peter," in verse 37, because Peter had boasted that he would never deny Jesus (vv. 29, 31). Jesus' use of the name "Simon," Peter's original name, may imply his natural weakness. Peter was not living up to the meaning of his new name; he was not behaving like a rock.

> "True friendship as we experience it—the sharing of inmost thoughts, the exchange of feelings, hopes, sorrows, joys—was a reality that Jesus seems not to have enjoyed, with any continuity, with the Twelve."[597]

14:38   Jesus then addressed all three disciples. He commanded them to be continually watchful (Gr. *gregoreite*, cf. 13:34, 35, 37) and to pray (Gr. *proseuchesthe*, the general word for prayer). These activities are necessary to overcome temptation. This use of "flesh" is probably literal (i.e., the body) rather than metaphorical (i.e., the sinful human nature), since it contrasts with the human spirit (i.e., man's volitional powers; cf. Ps. 51:12).

Mark wrote that Peter was asleep three times (vv. 37, 40, 41), and later he wrote that Peter denied Jesus three times (vv. 68, 70, 71). The disciples should have been praying for themselves, as well as for Jesus, in view of what Jesus had told them was coming.

---

[590]Gundry, p. 854.

[591]Ibid., p. 856.

[592]R. G. Bratcher and E. A. Nida, *Translator's Handbook on Mark*, p. 446.

[593]Lane, p. 515.

[594]See Joseph A. Grassi, "*Abba*, Father (Mark 14:36): Another Approach," *Journal of the American Academy of Religion* 50:3 (September 1982):449-58.

[595]Rhoads and Michie, p. 108.

[596]*The Nelson . . .*, p. 1674.

[597]Lane, p. 518.

"In the passion account, the disciples are ironic figures: Because of their incomprehension, they badly misconstrue the true nature of things. Thinking themselves to be astute, courageous, and loyal, they are in reality imperceptive, cowardly, and faithless. Entering upon the passion, the disciples yet follow Jesus in commitment to him. As events unfold, however, they will renounce their commitment through word or deed and apostatize."[598]

"Spiritual wakefulness and prayer in full dependence upon divine help provide the only adequate preparation for crisis (cf. Ch. 13:11)."[599]

14:39-40   Jesus returned from the disciples—who gave Him no support—to the Father, who sustained Him. The disciples did not have anything to say to ("did not know what to answer") Jesus, probably because they felt ashamed. They had boasted great spiritual strength, but they were demonstrating great spiritual weakness. There seems to be an inverse relationship between how self-confident we feel and how much we pray.

14:41-42   Mark alone recorded that Jesus made three separate forays into the depths of the garden to pray.

"The Temptation of the Garden divides itself, like that of the Wilderness, into three acts, following close one on another."[600]

Jesus' perseverance in prayer demonstrated the extent of His dependence on the Father. Jesus' question convicted the disciples again. He probably intended His words as an ironic (or cryptic) command—"Keep on sleeping and resting"—rather than as a question or simply to express surprise (cf. Matt. 26:45).

Less clear is the meaning of, "It is enough."[601] He could have meant that Judas had received the betrayal money from the chief priests, since the Greek word *apechei* can mean "he has received it." Another possibility is that He meant that He now understood that the Cross was inevitable. Perhaps Jesus meant the disciples had had enough sleep and it was time to wake up.[602] Fourth, He may have meant that He had finished His praying. I prefer the third and fourth views, because they are the simplest explanations and they make good sense.

"The hour" that had "come" was the time of Jesus' arrest and death (cf. v. 35). The "sinners" in view were Satan's agents who would slay Jesus. Jesus' short sentences reflect the tension and urgency of the moment.[603]

Mark described Jesus' movements in a somewhat chiastic form. Jesus came to the garden with His disciples, left most of them evidently at the entrance, took three of them farther, and proceeded even farther into its depths alone. Then He withdrew. At the center, Jesus communed with His Father. The center of the garden and the center of the pericope correspond to the center of His spiritual conflict. This description helps the reader identify Jesus' praying as at the very heart of His preparation for the Cross. It accounts for the remarkable poise with which Jesus handled Himself throughout the tumultuous events that followed.

"Perhaps the most commonly recognized pattern of narration in Mark is the threefold repetition of similar actions and events. . . . Some series are obvious because they occur in direct sequence: at Gethsemane, Jesus returns from prayer three times to find the disciples sleeping; Peter denies Jesus three times; Pilate asks the crowd three leading questions, each of which is rejected; and the narrator recounts events of the crucifixion at three, three-hour intervals (nine o'clock, noon, and three o'clock."[604]

Here, "This threefold pattern of narration underscores the definitive failure of the disciples."[605]

Jesus' betrayal, arrest, and abandonment 14:43-52 (cf. Matt. 26:47-56; Luke 22:47-53; John 18:2-12)

14:43   All the synoptic writers apparently repeated that "Judas" was "one of the Twelve," even though the reader already knows this, to stress the tragedy of Jesus' betrayal.[606] Judas guided the mob (Acts 1:16) that had come with authority from the Sanhedrin.

---

[598]Kingsbury, p. 111.

[599]Lane, p. 520.

[600]G. F. Maclear, "The Gospel According to St. Mark," in *Cambridge Bible for Schools and Colleges*, p. 163.

[601]Cranfield, *The Gospel . . .*, pp. 435-36, listed eight different interpretations.

[602]Ibid., p. 435.

[603]Hiebert, p. 362.

[604]Rhoads and Michie, p. 54.

[605]Ibid.

Part of the crowd consisted of Jewish temple police (Luke 22:52) and Roman soldiers (John 18:12). The police carried clubs and the soldiers had short swords.

14:44-46   The disciples of rabbis customarily greeted their teachers with a "kiss" on the hand.[607] This prearranged "signal" enabled Judas to identify Jesus to the soldiers without arousing the suspicion and opposition of the other disciples.

14:47   Perhaps shame led Mark to conceal the fact that it was Peter who cut off Malchus' ear, evidently in a misdirected attempt to cut off his head (cf. John 18:10). Peter's lack of prayer resulted in a lack of poise that contrasted sharply with Jesus' behavior. He had not only boasted too much (vv. 29, 31), and prayed too little (vv. 37, 40, 41), but he also acted too violently.

14:48-50   Jesus' reply pointed out that He was not a dangerous criminal. The Sanhedrin's action was totally unjustified and indefensible. Nevertheless it fulfilled prophecy. The Scriptures Jesus referred to included Isaiah 53:3, 7-9, 12 and Zechariah 13:7 (cf. v. 27). Verse 50 documents the failure of the disciples, including Peter, and their abandonment of Jesus to preserve their own safety. The writer's interest was the disciples' action more than that of the mob.

14:51-52   Only Mark recorded this strange event. He described the "young man" (Gr. *neaniskos*, between 24 and 40 years old) as one who was "following" Jesus. This description could mean he was one of the Twelve, or simply someone who was sympathetic with Jesus. He was wearing a rather costly linen outer garment (Gr. *sindon*) without an undergarment (Gr. *chiton*). It may have been his sleeping garment. Perhaps he had been in bed in Jerusalem, when he awoke to sounds of the mob leaving the city, and heard people talking about arresting Jesus—and decided to go along. When one of the soldiers "seized him," he was so intent on abandoning Jesus that he was willing to run through the crowd "naked" rather than staying with Jesus. This man's action further illustrates how eager Jesus' followers were to save their own skins at the cost of Jesus' safety and companionship. His naked condition highlights his fear and embarrassment (cf. Amos 2:16).

This incident makes little contribution to the story of Jesus' arrest, apart from illustrating that everyone fled. Therefore some of the church fathers and most of the modern commentators have concluded that the young man was Mark, the writer of this Gospel. However, there is no solid evidence for this.[608]

B. THE SERVANT'S ENDURANCE OF SUFFERING 14:53—15:47

Jesus' sufferings until now had been anticipatory and psychological. Now He began to experience physical pain resulting from His trials and crucifixion. As the faithful Servant of the Lord who came to do His Father's will, His sufferings continued to increase.

Jesus underwent two trials: a religious one before the Jewish leaders, and a civil one before the Roman authorities. This was necessary because under Roman sovereignty, the Sanhedrin did not have the authority to crucify.[609] The Sanhedrin wanted Jesus to suffer crucifixion (John 18:31). Each trial had three parts.

Jesus' Religious Trial	
Before Annas	John 18:12-14, 19-24
Before Caiaphas	Matt. 26:57-68; Mark 14:53-65; Luke 22:54, 63-65
Before the Sanhedrin	Matt. 27:1; Mark 15:1; Luke 22:66-71
Jesus' Civil Trial	
Before Pilate	Matt. 27:2, 11-14; Mark 15:1-5; Luke 23:1-5; John 18:28-38
Before Herod Antipas	Luke 23:6-12
Before Pilate	Matt. 27:15-26; Mark 15:6-15; Luke 23:13-25; John 18:39—19:16

[606]Gould, p. 273.

[607]Bishop, p. 246.

[608]See Abraham Kuruvilla, "The Naked Runaway and the Enrobed Reporter of Mark 14 and 16: What Is the Author Doing with What He Is Saying? *Journal of the Evangelical Theological Society* 54:3 (September 2011):527-45.

[609]See Josephus, *Antiquities of . . .*, 20:9:1: footnote b.

1. Jesus' Jewish trial 14:53—15:1

Mark omitted reference to Jesus' preliminary hearing before Annas (John 18:12-14, 19-24).

The hearing before Caiaphas 14:53-65 (cf. Matt. 26:57-68; Luke 22:54, 63-65; John 18:24)

14:53   The "high priest" in view here was Caiaphas. Interestingly Mark never mentioned him by name. He was the high priest that the Romans had appointed in A.D. 18, and he served in this capacity until A.D. 36. He seems to have been the person most responsible for the plot to do away with Jesus.

This was an unscheduled meeting of the Sanhedrin, since Jewish law required that official meetings take place during the daytime. It transpired before dawn on Friday, the fifteenth of Nisan, a feast day. Normally the Sanhedrin did not conduct hearings of this type on a feast day. The Jewish leaders probably met at this unorthodox hour because the Romans conducted their civil trials shortly after sunrise. The Sanhedrin wanted to deliver Jesus over to Pilate for a hasty trial before public sentiment built in favor of Jesus. Normally the Sanhedrin did not pass sentence on an accused capital offender until the day following his trial. They made an exception in Jesus' case. Usually the Sanhedrin met in a hall on the west side of the temple enclosure.[610] However, now they met in Caiaphas' house or palace (Luke 22:54). "All" the Sanhedrin may mean every one of its 71 members or, probably, all that were necessary for a quorum, at least 23.[611]

14:54   This notation helps the reader understand that Peter was in the high priest's residence throughout Jesus' trial there. It prepares us for the account of Peter's denial (vv. 66-72), which happened while the Sanhedrin was examining Jesus. It also helps us appreciate the fact that Peter's desertion of Jesus was only temporary. The synoptic evangelists did not mention that another disciple accompanied Peter into the courtyard (John 18:15). The officers ("servants") would have been the temple police, since the Roman soldiers would not have guarded the high priest's palace.

14:55-56   Even though this hearing, or grand jury investigation, took place at night, the Sanhedrin eventually found two witnesses against Jesus (Matt. 26:60). It seems that they had been planning their case for the prosecution carefully. However, the witnesses, who testified separately in Jewish trials, contradicted each other. Consequently their testimony was useless (cf. Num. 35:30; Deut. 17:6; 19:15).

"It is harder to agree on a consistent lie than to tell the simple truth."[612]

14:57-59   These verses provide a specific example of what Mark just described generally. Evidently the witnesses misunderstood Jesus' statements about the destruction of the temple (Gr. *naos*, temple building) of His body (John 2:19) and the future destruction of the Jerusalem temple (13:2). Anyone who destroyed a temple in the ancient world was subject to capital punishment (cf. Jer. 26:1-19).[613] This was evidently one of the most serious charges against Jesus (cf. v. 61; 15:29).

14:60-61   Apparently Caiaphas decided to question Jesus, hoping to get Him to incriminate Himself, since he could not get two witnesses to agree against Jesus. Jesus did not need to respond to the high priest's first question. No one had offered any real proof against Him.

"His [Jesus'] resolute silence loudly declared to the Sanhedrin His disdain for their lying efforts to establish a charge against Him."[614]

Then Caiaphas, trying a new strategy, asked if Jesus was the Messiah. "The Blessed One" is a synonym for God that the Jews used instead of the holy name of God.[615] The popular Jewish concept of Messiah was that he would be a human descendant of David. Caiaphas was not asking if Jesus claimed to be God, but only a human "Messiah": "the Son of the Blessed."

"In the formulation 'the Messiah, the son of the Blessed One,' the second clause stands in apposition to the first and has essentially the same meaning. In Jewish sources contemporary with the NT, 'son of God'

---

[610]Josephus, *Antiquities of* . . ., 5:4:2.

[611]Mishnah *Sanhedrin* 1:1.

[612]Cole, p. 226.

[613]Josephus, *Antiquities of* . . ., 10:6:2.

[614]Hiebert, p. 371.

[615]Mishnah *Berachoth* 7:3.

is understood solely in a messianic sense. Jewish hopes were situated in a messianic figure who was a man."[616]

"A Messiah imprisoned, abandoned by his followers, and delivered helpless into the hands of his foes represented an impossible conception. Anyone who, in such circumstances, proclaimed himself to be the Messiah could not fail to be a blasphemer who dared to make a mockery of the promises given by God to his people."[617]

14:62   Previously Jesus had veiled His messiahship because publicly claiming to be the Messiah would have precipitated a premature crisis (cf. 1:43-44; 8:29-30; 9:9; 11:28-33; 12:12). Now He openly admitted His messiahship because the time for crisis had arrived. Matthew may have given us Jesus' exact words (Matt. 26:64), and Mark their substance. Jesus added that He was not only a human Messiah, but the divine "Son of Man." The passages He claimed to fulfill predicted His enthronement in heaven following His resurrection (Ps. 110:1), and His return to earth with God's authority to establish a worldwide kingdom (Dan. 7:13-14; cf. 8:38; 13:24, 26; Rev. 1:7). As such, He was claiming to be the Judge of those who sat to judge Him. Jesus knew that this confession would seal His conviction. "Power" was a recognized circumlocution for "God."[618]

14:63-64   Rending one's garments expressed indignation or grief (cf. Gen. 37:29; Judg. 14:19; 2 Kings 18:37). It had become the high priests' traditional response to blasphemy (cf. Acts 14:14).[619] However, it was illegal for the high priest to rend his garments (Lev. 21:10). The hypocrisy of the religious leaders is clear throughout their trial of Jesus. The Jews regarded blasphemy as any serious affront to God, not just speech that reviled Him (cf. 2:7; 3:28-29; John 5:18; 10:33). At this time, "blasphemy" consisted of claiming for oneself a unique association with God, reflected in sitting at God's right hand, not just misusing God's name.[620] The Mosaic Law prescribed death by stoning for blasphemers (Lev. 24:14), but this was not harsh enough for Jesus. Jesus had foreseen this, and had predicted death at the hands of the Gentiles as well as the Jews (10:33).

14:65   Having judged Jesus guilty, some of the Sanhedrin members vented their anger by attacking Him bodily. The temple guards present joined them in beating Jesus. Spitting and hitting were traditional Jewish ways of expressing repudiation (cf. Num. 12:14; Deut. 25:9; Job 30:10; Isa. 50:6). Even today, spitting in someone's face is one of the grossest forms of personal insult. They blindfolded Jesus, and challenged Him to identify His assailants—evidently because of a traditional belief that Messiah did not need to see but could judge by smell (Isa. 11:2-4).[621] The Old Testament predicted this type of abuse for Messiah (Isa. 53:5, 7-8, 10).[622] Peter recorded that through all this suffering, Jesus did not protest or retaliate (1 Pet. 2:21-23; cf. Isa. 53:7).

Peter's denial of Jesus 14:66-72 (cf. Matt. 26:69-75; Luke 22:55-62; John 18:16-18, 25-27)

This event was happening in the courtyard *below*, while the hearing just described continued on the floor *above*. These verses resume what Mark introduced in verse 54. The events were contemporaneous with Jesus' examination by the Sanhedrin (vv. 55-65).

"The irony inherent in the situation is evident when the force of juxtaposing verse 65 and verses 66-72 is appreciated. At the precise time when the court attendants were heaping scorn and derision upon Jesus' claim to be the Messiah, the prophecy that Peter would deliberately deny him was being fulfilled."[623]

14:66-68   Peter's presence was a testimony to His love for Jesus. Unfortunately his love could not stand the test of fear.[624] The servant-girl's description of Jesus ("that Nazarene, Jesus") made it clear that Peter was among enemies. She had probably seen Peter with Jesus in the temple or the city during that week. Peter "denied" being one of Jesus' disciples: "using the form common in rabbinical law for a formal, legal denial."[625] Peter then left the warmth and light of the fire, in the center of the courtyard, and sought refuge in the shadows of the archway that led into the street.

---

[616]Lane, p. 535.

[617]Ibid., p. 536.

[618]Ibid., p. 537.

[619]Mishnah *Sanhedrin* 7:5.

[620]See Darrell L. Bock, *Blasphemy and Exaltation in Judaism and the Final Examination of Jesus*, pp. 30-183.

[621]Lane, p. 540.

[622]See Laurna L. Berg, "The Illegalities of Jesus' Religious and Civil Trials," *Bibliotheca Sacra* 161:643 (July-September 2004):330-42.

[623]Lane, p. 541.

[624]Wessel, p. 771.

[625]Lane, p. 542.

> "Being built on the slope of the hill, there was under the principal apartments [of the high priest's palace] a lower story, with a porch in front, so that we can understand how on that eventful night Peter was 'beneath in the palace.'"[626]

> Some later manuscripts add "and a rooster crowed" at the end of verse 68. Probably scribes added these words in view of Jesus' prediction in verse 30 and the fulfillment in verse 72.

14:69-70a   Evidently "the maid" was a different person than the servant-girl (v. 66; cf. Matt. 26:71). Instead of accusing Peter to his face, this girl whispered her charge to bystanders. Peter heard her. Again Peter denied being one of Jesus' disciples. This time he kept on denying it, as the Greek imperfect tense indicates.

14:70b-71   The third challenge came from the "bystanders," several people instead of just one, about an hour later (Luke 22:59). This time Peter went further. He denied that he even knew Jesus (cf. 8:29). He even called down God's judgment on himself if he was lying. "Cursing" means he put himself under a curse. "Swearing" means he affirmed the truthfulness of his words with oaths.

14:72   Mark alone noted that this was the "second time" that "a rooster" crowed (cf. v. 68). Peter had evidently received an earlier warning but had disregarded it. Now he remembered Jesus' prediction and broke down (Gr. epibalon, cf. Luke 22:61). He remembered too little and too late.

Peter now drops out of the picture until after Jesus' resurrection. He had finally learned and experienced his own weakness—and consequently seems to have felt unable to face the pressure of public identification with Jesus.

The parallels between Peter's behavior and Jesus' are all too evident. Both men faced a three-fold temptation. One defeated the tempter, and the other fell before him. While Jesus served God faithfully as His Servant on the upper floor, Peter failed to serve God faithfully on the lower floor. The reason for the difference goes back to Gethsemane. Disciples must learn from Peter's failure as well as from Jesus' success.

> "The importance and relevance of Peter's denial for the church to which Mark writes is obvious. To a church under severe pressure of persecution it provided a warning. If denial of Jesus Christ was possible for an apostle, and one of the leaders of the apostles at that, then they must be constantly on guard lest they too deny Jesus. The story also provided assurance that if anyone did fail Jesus under the duress of persecution, there was always a way open for repentance, forgiveness, and restoration (cf. 16:7)."[627]

The verdict of the Sanhedrin 15:1 (cf. Matt. 27:1-2; Luke 22:66-71)

Matthew and Mark described this meeting as though it was separate from the earlier one (14:53-65). They probably did so to bring the reader back from the courtyard to the upper room in Caiaphas' house. Yet the decision seems to have been a separate one from the conviction for blasphemy. The Roman authorities would not have prosecuted Jesus as a blasphemer. Consequently the Sanhedrin ("Council"), evidently now at full strength or close to it, decided to charge Jesus with treason against the Roman government. This verse does not explain that decision, but Pilate's examination of Jesus that follows, shows that this was the charge the Sanhedrin had made against Him.

> "Jesus, who is, indeed, king of the Jews in a deeply spiritual sense, has refused to lead a political uprising. Yet now, condemned for blasphemy by the Jews because of his spiritual claims, he is accused by them also before Pilate by [sic] being precisely what he had disappointed the crowds for failing to be—a political insurgent."[628]

Mark did not explain who Pilate was, as Matthew did, evidently because his Roman readers knew about Pilate.

> "Pilate belonged to a special group of imperial administrators, consisting of men beneath the rank of senator, the so-called equestrian class or Roman 'knights.' These magistrates, who owned a moderate minimum of property, were used to govern relatively small areas that required careful supervision. Their official title in the period prior to Claudius was not procurator but prefect (praefectus). . . . Pilate came to Judea in the year A.D. 26 as the fifth of the provincial prefects and remained in office ten years. He showed himself a harsh administrator who despised the Jewish people and their particular sensitivities."[629]

---

[626]Edersheim, The Temple, p. 34.
[627]Wessel, pp. 771-72.
[628]Moule, p. 124.
[629]Lane, pp. 548-49.

When Pilate visited Jerusalem from his provincial capital of Caesarea, he normally stayed either in Herod's palace, on the northwest corner of the city, or in the Fortress of Antonia, just northwest of the temple.[630] It was apparently to one of these places that the guards led Jesus in the early morning hours of Friday, the fifteenth of Nisan (April 3). Christian tradition favors the Fortress of Antonia, but modern commentators usually favor Herod's palace.[631]

> "As Friday morning arrives and the death of Jesus approaches, Mark will slow time from days to hours. Such slowing of time is yet another way of calling attention to the pivotal importance of Jesus' death."[632]

The Sanhedrin involved the Romans in Jesus' trial, because although the Jewish Council could *pass* a death sentence, they could not carry out any executions without Roman permission. The Jews probably bound Jesus to make Him look like a dangerous criminal. He would not have tried to escape.

2. Jesus' Roman trial 15:2-20

During the Jewish trial, Jesus had affirmed His messiahship—and the Sanhedrin had condemned Him for blasphemy. During His Roman trial, Jesus affirmed His kingship—and Pilate condemned Him for treason. The Roman trial, like the Jewish trial, had three stages: an interrogation before Pilate, an attempted interrogation before Herod, and an arraignment and sentencing before Pilate.[633]

Jesus' first appearance before Pilate 15:2-5 (cf. Matt. 27:11-14; Luke 23:1-5; John 18:28-38)

15:2   Pilate had absolute authority over Jesus' fate under Roman law. Customarily trials such as this one took place in public.[634] They also took place "as soon after dawn as possible because the working day of a Roman official began at the earliest hour of daylight."[635] First, the plaintiffs or accusers made their charges against the defendant. Then the prosecutor, in this case Pilate, examined the defendant—who could speak in his own defense—and he heard the testimony of any witnesses. Next, the prosecutor consulted with his legal advisers; and finally, he pronounced his verdict. The execution of the sentence followed immediately.[636]

Pilate's question shows that the Jews had charged Jesus with claiming to be a king. Claiming to be a king was tantamount to treason against Caesar and was a capital offense. Jesus admitted that He was "the King of the Jews," but He implied that He was a different kind of king than Pilate thought (cf. Matt. 27:11). John wrote that Pilate discussed the nature of Jesus' kingship with Him further, and even concluded that Jesus was not guilty of treason (John 18:34-38).

15:3-5   The "chief priests," speaking for the Sanhedrin, brought "many" other "charges" against Jesus, some of which Luke mentioned (cf. Luke 23:2). Jesus' refusal to defend Himself against so many accusations "amazed" Pilate (cf. Isa. 53:7).

Ironically, Pilate himself declared who Jesus was with his inscription over His cross: The King Of The Jews (v. 28). Jesus did not need to tell Pilate who He was. Pilate was going to give Him His proper title anyway. This is another indication of Jesus' authority in the political realm.[637]

Mark used a double negative in the Greek text (*ouketi ouden*) to describe Jesus' absolute silence. In English, two negatives make a positive, but in Greek, two negatives strengthen the force of the negative. Mark recorded Jesus replying only briefly to Caiaphas (14:62) and to Pilate. This is consistent with Mark's emphasis on Jesus as the Servant of the Lord.

Only Luke recorded that Pilate now sent Jesus to Herod Antipas, who was also in Jerusalem for the feast, since Jesus was a Galilean and Herod ruled over Galilee (Luke 23:6-12). Herod then sent Jesus back to Pilate.

---

[630]Hiebert, p. 379.

[631]Cranfield, p. 449, favored the Antonia Fortress.

[632]Kingsbury, p. 49.

[633]For helpful insights into Roman law as it affected Jesus' trial, see R. Larry Overstreet, "Roman Law and the Trial of Christ," *Bibliotheca Sacra* 135:540 (October-December 1978):323-32.

[634]Grassmick, p. 185.

[635]Lane, p. 549.

[636]Grassmick, p. 185.

[637]Edwards, p. 224.

Jesus' second appearance before Pilate 15:6-15 (cf. Matt. 27:15-26; Luke 23:13-25; John 18:39—19:16)

Mark's brief account of Jesus' arraignment and sentencing concentrates on Pilate's offer to release Jesus or Barabbas.

15:6   Evidently this custom served to improve relations between the Roman ruler and his subjects. Dictatorial governments such as Rome sometimes imprisoned popular rebel leaders. The Roman governor of Egypt practiced a similar custom.[638]

> "Amnesties at festival times are known in many parts of the world and in various periods."[639]

> "Two forms of amnesty existed in Roman law, the *abolitio* or acquittal of a prisoner not yet condemned, and the *indulgentia*, or pardoning of one already condemned. What Pilate intended in the case of Jesus, who at this stage of the proceedings had not yet been sentenced by the court, was clearly the first form."[640]

> "The historicity of the paschal amnesty has been disputed often, primarily because Josephus offers no evidence that such a custom ever existed. There is, however, a parallel in Roman law which indicates that an imperial magistrate could pardon and acquit individual prisoners in response to the shouts of the populace."[641]

15:7   This verse and the next provide more background information. "The man named Barabbas" was one of the popular Jewish freedom fighters whom the Romans had "imprisoned" for participating in an uprising against Rome. Later a large number of these revolutionaries organized and became known as the Zealots. Barabbas had also committed robbery, probably as part of his "insurrection" (John 18:40). Mark's use of the definite article before his name implies that his original readers had heard of Barabbas. However, "Barabbas" was a common name.[642]

> "Barabbas comes into play and accomplishes Mark's purpose of making a foil against which the injustice of Jesus' crucifixion may stand out."[643]

15:8   Evidently there was a large "crowd" of Jews that had come to request the customary amnesty from Pilate. There is no indication in the text that they had come because they knew of Jesus' arrest or because they wanted to observe the outcome of His trial. They appear to have been there for reasons unrelated to Jesus.[644]

15:9-10   Pilate responded to this crowd's request by asking if they wanted him "to release" Jesus, whom he contemptuously called "the King of the Jews" (cf. v. 2). He recognized the chief priests' motives in arresting Jesus as being self-seeking ("envy"), rather than loyalty to Rome. He hoped to frustrate the "chief priests" by getting the people to request the release of someone Pilate viewed as innocent (Jesus). He could thereby retain real criminals such as Barabbas. Matthew wrote that Pilate gave the people the choice of Jesus or Barabbas (Matt. 27:17). He evidently believed that Jesus had the greater popular following and would be the people's choice.

15:11   Many of the people in the crowd were residents of Jerusalem, and many were pilgrims from far away. The "chief priests" were able to persuade them ("stirred up the crowd") to ask for Barabbas' "release." The people may have accepted the advice of their leaders because Barabbas had already tried to lead a rebellion, but Jesus had only hinted at an overthrow. Moreover it would have been very unusual for the crowd to side with Pilate and oppose their leaders.

> "In Judea it was customary to confront the Roman authorities with as large and boisterous a delegation as could be mustered (cf. Acts 24:1; Josephus, *Antiquities* XVIII. viii. 4)."[645]

15:12-14   The people's choice left Pilate with a problem. What would he do with innocent Jesus? Pilate's wife had just warned him to have nothing to do with that righteous man (Matt. 27:19). He put the question to the crowd. The religious leaders probably started the chant calling for Jesus' *crucifixion*—not just any capital punishment—but it quickly spread through the crowd. The mob ignored Pilate's request for reasonable reconsideration and continued chanting and "shouting."

---

[638]Taylor, p. 580.

[639]S. E. Johnson, *A Commentary on the Gospel According to St. Mark*, p. 249.

[640]Lane, p. 552.

[641]Ibid., pp. 552-53.

[642]See Gundry, p. 926, for sources.

[643]Ibid., p. 927.

[644]Swete, p. 371.

[645]Lane, p. 555.

15:15   Pilate had had problems in his relations with the Jewish people that he governed (cf. Luke 13:1-2). He saw the present situation as an opportunity to gain popular support. This overrode his sense of justice and his wife's warning.

         Evidently Pilate flogged Jesus in the presence of the crowd, hoping that that punishment would satisfy them. John recorded that after the scourging, Pilate tried again to persuade the people against crucifixion (John 19:1-7). Scourging was not a necessary preparation for crucifixion, but it quickened an otherwise slow, lingering death.[646] Probably two soldiers stripped Jesus and tied His hands above Him to a post. Then they whipped Him with a leather scourge, containing pieces of bone and or metal embedded in the leather strips. Victims of Roman floggings seldom survived.[647]

> "The heavy whip is brought down with full force again and again across Jesus' shoulders, back and legs. At first the heavy thongs cut through the skin only. Then, as the blows continue, they cut deeper into the subcutaneous tissues, producing first an oozing of blood from the capillaries and veins of the skin, and finally spurting arterial bleeding from vessels in the underlying muscles. . . . Finally the skin of the back is hanging in long ribbons and the entire area is an unrecognizable mass of torn, bleeding tissue."[648]

         Mark's use of the phrase "delivered Him over" (NASB) or "handed Him over" (NIV) may be an allusion to Isaiah 53:6 and 12 where the same expression occurs in the Septuagint translation. This reminder of Jesus' position as the Suffering Servant is the emphasis in Mark's account of this aspect of His trial.

The Roman soldiers' mockery of Jesus 15:16-20 (cf. Matt. 27:27-31; John 19:16-17a)

15:16   "Praetorium" is a Latin loan word that describes a Roman governor's official residence (cf. Matt. 27:27; John 18:28, 33; 19:9; Acts 23:35). The Roman soldiers escorted Jesus to the *courtyard* (Gr. *aule*, cf. vv. 54, 66) of "the palace." This could have been either the Antonia Fortress or Herod's palace, but it was probably Herod's palace. There, a group of soldiers assembled around Jesus, probably those who were nearby and available. A "cohort" consisted of 600 men.

15:17-19   The reddish "purple" robe and the "crown of thorns" mocked Jesus' claim to be the Jews' king. The Greek word *porphyran* elsewhere describes colors from bright red to deep blue.[649] The crown of thorns was probably not a torture device but part of Jesus' mock royal attire.

> "It may well have been an improvised caricature of the radiate crown signifying divine kingship and frequently depicted on coins then in circulation."[650]

> "With this 'crown' the soldiers unwittingly pictured God's curse on sinful humanity being thrust on Jesus (cf. Gen. 3:17-18)."[651]

         Mark did not mention the staff that they placed in Jesus' hand as a mock scepter (Matt. 27:29). "Hail, King of the Jews" is a parody of "Hail, Caesar." Their repeated beatings, spitting, kneeling as if in worship, and bowing as before a great person, intensified Jesus' sufferings.

> "Irony is a dominant feature of Mark's story. *Verbal irony* occurs when a speaker self-consciously says one thing but means the opposite."[652]

15:20   Normally the Romans forced criminals condemned to crucifixion to walk naked to their place of execution, and flogged them along the way.[653] Evidently the soldiers concluded that Jesus would not live through such treatment in view of the abuse that He had already suffered. Therefore they "put His own garments" back "on Him."

Mark's original readers faced subjection to similar mockery and abuse from pagan authorities. This pericope would have been an encouragement to them to remain faithful to Jesus. As a Servant, Jesus allowed other people to treat Him as a condemned criminal, because this was a part of His obedience to God (cf. Phil. 2:5-8; 1 Pet. 5:6-7).

---

[646]Wessel, p. 775.

[647]Ibid.

[648]C. Truman Davis, "The Crucifixion of Jesus. The Passion of Christ from a Medical Point of View," *Arizona Medicine* 22:3 (March 1965):185.

[649]J. A. Alexander, *The Gospel According to Mark*, p. 418.

[650]Lane, pp. 559-60.

[651]Grassmick, p. 187.

[652]Rhoads and Michie, pp. 59-60.

[653]Josephus, *Antiquities of . . .*, 19:4:5.

3. Jesus' crucifixion, death, and burial 15:21-47

Jesus' sufferings continued to increase as He drew closer to the Cross.

The crucifixion of Jesus 15:21-32 (cf. Matt. 27:32-44; Luke 23:26-43; John 19:17b-27)

15:21   Probably only Mark mentioned Simon's sons ("Alexander and Rufus") because the Christians in Rome knew them or knew of them (cf. Rom. 16:13). Evidently Simon became a believer in Jesus. Mark mentioned very few people by name other than the Twelve. Simon was evidently a North African Jew who had come to Jerusalem for the Passover season. Since there was a large population of Jews in Cyrene, it is probable that Simon was racially a Semite rather than a black man.[654] Simon had to do literally what all followers of Jesus must do figuratively, namely, bear His cross (cf. 8:34; Luke 23:26). Normally the condemned had to carry the crosspiece of his cross to the place of execution.[655] The fact that Jesus did not, or could not, may reflect the unique character of His sufferings.[656] It also dignifies Jesus.[657]

15:22-23   "Golgotha" is a loose transliteration of the Aramaic word for "skull." Evidently the place resembled a skull or had some association with a skull or skulls or death. An ancient tradition that Jerome referred to identified the place as the one where Adam's skull lay. If you visit the Church of the Holy Sepulchre in Jerusalem, you can see this traditional site of Adam's grave under what the authorities claim is the site of the crucifixion.

> "According to an old tradition, respected women of Jerusalem provided a narcotic drink to those condemned to death in order to decrease their sensitivity to the excruciating pain (TB [Babylonian Talmud] *Sanhedrin* 43a)."[658]

"They" (v. 23) could refer to the soldiers, but it seems unlikely that *they* would have done anything to ease Jesus' pain.

15:24   Mark probably only mentioned Jesus' actual crucifixion, without description, because his Roman readers would have been only too familiar with its horrors. Yet for modern readers some explanation is helpful. Davis described it as follows.

> "Simon is ordered to place the patibulum [crosspiece] on the ground and Jesus is quickly thrown backwards with His shoulders against the wood. The legionnaire feels for the depression at the front of the wrist. He drives a heavy, square, wrought-iron nail through the wrist and deep into the wood. Quickly, he moves to the other side and repeats the action, being careful not to pull the arms too tightly, but to allow some flexion and movement. The patibulum is then lifted in place at the top of the stipes [the vertical beam]. . . .
>
> "The left foot is pressed backward against the right foot, and with both feet extended, toes down, a nail is driven through the arch of each, leaving the knees moderately flexed. The Victim is now crucified. As He slowly sags down with more weight on the nails in the wrists, excruciating, fiery pain shoots along the fingers and up the arms to explode in the brain—the nails in the wrists are putting pressure on the median nerves. As He pushes Himself upward to avoid this stretching torment, He places His full weight on the nail through His feet. Again there is the searing agony of the nail tearing through the nerves between the metatarsal bones of the feet.
>
> "At this point, another phenomenon occurs. As the arms fatigue, great waves of cramps sweep over the muscles, knotting them in deep, relentless, throbbing pain. With these cramps comes the inability to push Himself upward. . . . Air can be drawn into the lungs, but cannot be exhaled. Jesus fights to raise Himself in order to get even one small breath. Finally carbon dioxide builds up in the lungs and in the blood stream and the cramps partially subside. Spasmodically He is able to push himself upward to exhale and bring in the life-giving oxygen. . . .
>
> "Hours of this limitless pain, cycles of twisting, joint-rending cramps, intermittent partial asphyxiation, searing pain as tissue is torn from His lacerated back as He moves up and down against the rough timber. Then another agony begins. A deep crushing pain deep in the chest as the pericardium slowly fills with serum and begins to compress the heart. . . .

---

[654]Hiebert, p. 389; Wessel, p. 778.

[655]Cranfield, p. 454.

[656]Ibid.

[657]Gundry, p. 944.

[658]Lane, p. 564.

"It is now almost over—the loss of tissue fluids has reached a critical level—the compressed heart is struggling to pump heavy, thick, sluggish blood into the tissues—the tortured lungs are making a frantic effort to gasp in small gulps of air. . . .

"The body of Jesus is now in extremis, and He can feel the chill of death creeping through His tissues. . . .

"His mission of atonement has been completed. Finally He can allow His body to die."[659]

Mark's quotation of Psalm 22:18, the psalm that predicted more detail of Messiah's sufferings in death than any other passage, contrasted the soldiers' callous actions with Jesus' agony.

"While the use of nails to fasten a body to the cross is not widely attested, in June, 1968, a team of Israeli scholars discovered at Giv'at ha-Mivtar in northeastern Jerusalem a Jewish tomb which produced the first authenticated evidence of a crucifixion in antiquity. Among the remains in an ossuary [dating from the first century before A.D. 70] were those of an individual whose lower calf bones had been broken and whose heel bones had been transfixed with a single iron nail."[660]

15:25	This time reference is unique to Mark's Gospel. The third hour was 9:00 a.m. John located Jesus' trial before Pilate at "about" the sixth hour (John 19:14). This would have been noon (Jewish time), or 6:00 a.m. (Roman time).[661] Consequently we should probably understand Mark's reference as being to the approximate beginning of Jesus' crucifixion, rather than the precise time when the soldiers nailed Him to the cross.[662]
15:26	Typically, Mark recorded only the essence of "the charge" that Pilate wrote and had displayed over Jesus' head on the cross. It was probably written in red or black letters on a whitened background.[663]
15:27-28	Jesus' position between the two insurrectionists (John 18:40), perhaps cohorts of Barabbas, portrayed Him as the chief offender. The soldiers probably put Jesus in this position as a further insult to the Jews as well as to Jesus.

"Thus the temple-cleanser is crucified with bandits as though he were a temple-desecrator . . ."[664]

Most ancient manuscripts of Mark's Gospel omit verse 28. Many textual experts consider it an interpolation from Luke 22:37. Mark rarely pointed out the fulfillment of Old Testament prophecies.[665]

15:29-30	Evidently Jesus' predictions about destroying and raising "the temple" were well known (cf. 14:58-60). Unbelieving Jews seem to have focused on those statements as proof that Jesus could not be their Messiah. They viewed the temple with extreme veneration.

"The jest was the harder to endure since it appealed to a consciousness of power held back only by the self-restraint of a sacrificed will."[666]

This public abuse heaped further suffering on the Suffering Servant. The Greek word Mark used to describe their abuse was *eblasphemoun* meaning "they were blaspheming." Earlier the high priest had charged Jesus with blasphemy of which He was innocent (14:64). Now the people did blaspheme God. Their comments fulfilled Psalm 22:7 and Lamentations 2:15.

15:31-32	The "chief priests" and "scribes" also blasphemed by "mocking" Jesus and claiming: "He saved others; He cannot save Himself." Their abuse must have wounded Jesus grievously since they were Israel's leaders. Their sarcastically meant title for Jesus, "King of *Israel*," focused on the added apparent irony of Jesus being the leader, not only of the "Jews" (people), but of their *nation*. *They* were the leaders of the nation, not Jesus. The fact that Jesus was apparently helpless on the cross was the supreme joke from their viewpoint. Their Messiah of all people needed to be in control. This was the climax of the religious leaders' opposition to Jesus (cf. 3:6; 11:18; 12:12; 14:1, 64; 15:1, 11-13).

---

[659]Davis, pp. 186-87.

[660]Lane, pp. 564-65.

[661]See my comments on John 19:14 for an explanation.

[662]See *A Dictionary of the Bible*, 1906 ed., s.v. "Numbers, Hours, Years, and Dates," by W. M. Ramsay, extra volume: 478-79.

[663]Lane, p. 568.

[664]Gundry, p. 946.

[665]Plummer, p. 355.

[666]Swete, p. 383.

"*Situational irony* occurs when there is a discrepancy between what a character naively expects to happen and what actually happens, or between what a character blindly thinks to be the case and what the real situation is. . . .

"In situational irony the speaker is confident that what he or she says or expects is true, but is unaware that the real situation is, in fact, the opposite. The characters in the story are blind victims of the irony of the situation, while the reader sees the ironic contrast between what the speaker says and the way things really are."[667]

The rebels "who were crucified with" Jesus joined the others who were "insulting Him." Rejection, abuse, and derision assailed Jesus from the highest to the lowest in society.

The total humiliation of Jesus, which this pericope records, presents Him as the completely submissive Servant of the Lord, even to the point of dying on a cross. What an example He is for all whom God has called to be His servants!

The death of Jesus 15:33-41 (cf. Matt. 27:45-56; Luke 23:44-49; John 19:28-30)

Mark's account of Jesus' death included five climactic events: the darkness, two of Jesus' cries, the tearing of the temple veil, and the Roman centurion's confession. All of these events happened during the last three of the six hours of Jesus' sufferings on the cross.

"For the first three of Jesus' six hours on the cross he suffered in daylight at the hands of humans (15:21-32). In the darkness of the second three hours He suffered at the hands of God."[668]

15:33   All three synoptic evangelists recorded the supernatural "darkness" that covered all of Judah from 12:00 noon to 3:00 p.m. None of them explained it. They all evidently viewed it as a sign of God's judgment on Jesus (cf. Isa. 5:25-30; 59:9-10; Joel 2:31; 3:14-15; Amos 8:9-10; Mic. 3:5-7; Zeph. 1:14-15). The Father withdrew the light of His presence from His Son during the hours when Jesus bore the guilt of the world's sins (Isa. 53:5-6; 2 Cor. 5:21). Perhaps darkness covered "the whole land" of Israel because it *also* symbolized God's judgment on *Israel*—for rejecting His Son.[669] The ninth plague in Egypt was a plague of darkness, and it too was followed by the death of the firstborn (Exod. 10:22—11:9).

15:34   This cry came at the ninth hour, namely, 3:00 p.m. Jesus' cry expressed what the darkness depicted. "Jesus cried out" *loudly*, not weakly, with His last available energy. His great agony of soul was responsible for this cry. Mark recorded Jesus' words in Aramaic. Probably Jesus spoke in Aramaic in view of the crowd's reaction (cf. Matt. 27:46-47).

"The depths of the saying are too deep to be plumbed, but the least inadequate interpretations are those which find in it a sense of desolation in which Jesus felt the horror of sin so deeply that for a time the closeness of His communion with the Father was obscured."[670]

Jesus quoted Psalm 22:1: "My God, My God, why have You forsaken Me?" That is why He expressed His agony of separation as a question. Jesus was not asking God for an answer; the question was rhetorical. As Jesus used this verse, it expressed an affirmation of His relationship to God as His Father and an acknowledgment that the Father had abandoned Him. God abandoned Jesus in the judicial sense that He focused His wrath on the Son (cf. 14:36). Jesus bore God's curse and His judgment for sin (cf. Deut. 21:22-23; 2 Cor. 5:21; Gal. 3:13). God, who cannot look on sin (Hab. 1:13), turned His back, so to speak, on Jesus who bore that sin in His own body on the cross. Jesus experienced separation from God when He took the place of sinners (10:45; Rom. 5:8; 1 Pet. 2:24; 3:18).

"The burden of the world's sin, his complete self-identification with sinners, involved not merely a felt, but a real, abandonment by his Father. It is in the cry of dereliction that the full horror of man's sin stands revealed. But the cry also marks the lowest depth of the hiddenness of the Son of God—and so the triumphant *tetelestai* ["It is finished"] of Jn xix. 30 is, paradoxically, its true interpretation. When this depth had been reached, the victory had been won."[671]

[667]Rhoads and Michie, p. 60

[668]Bailey, p. 96.

[669]Grassmick, p. 189.

[670]Taylor, p. 549.

[671]Cranfield, pp. 458-59.

Even though the physical sufferings that Jesus experienced were incomparable, the spiritual agony that He underwent—as the Lamb of God taking away the sins of the world—was infinitely greater. We need to remember this when we meditate on Jesus' death, for example at the Lord's Supper.

15:35-36 "Elijah" had delivered several people in distress during his ministry. It is difficult to know if the "bystanders" did what they did, because they sincerely misunderstood Jesus, or if they were cruelly twisting His words to persecute Him further. In either case, they *did* wound Him more deeply. Perhaps one of the soldiers gave Jesus the sour wine (Gr. *oxos*) to prolong His life, so that the onlookers could see if Elijah would come and help Jesus.[672] In Mark's account, the soldier spoke (v. 36), and in Matthew's, the people did (Matt. 27:49). Both evangelists were undoubtedly accurate.

15:37 Jesus' strong "loud cry" indicates that this was not simply the last gasp of an exhausted, demoralized, or defeated man. Jesus' "cry" was a *shout of victory*. He triumphantly announced: "It is finished!" (John 19:30). Then He dismissed His spirit (Matt. 27:50; Luke 23:46; John 19:30)—"and breathed His last." Normally it took as long as two or three days for crucified people to die.[673] Jesus' relatively short period of suffering on the cross surprised Pilate (v. 44).

> "His comparatively early death was not due to His physical sufferings alone, and it is a mistake to center major attention on the physical agonies of our Lord."[674]

15:38 All the synoptic writers also recorded the symbolic act of the tearing of the "veil of the temple"—"from top to bottom." They did not explain it, but the writer of the Epistle to the Hebrews did (Heb. 6:19-20; 9:1-14; 10:19-22). It represented God opening a way into His presence by the death of His Son. The veil was probably the great outer one that separated the holy place from the courtyard.[675] If so, it would have been observed by many people. Priests would have been preparing the evening sacrifices in the temple when this event occurred near 3:00 p.m.

15:39 The "centurion" (Gr. *kentyrion*, a transliteration of the Latin *centurio*, that only Mark used) was the soldier in charge of Jesus' crucifixion (cf. v. 44). Elsewhere in the New Testament, the customary Greek word *hekatontarchos* ("centurion") appears. Mark's word choice here is another indication that he wrote for Romans. This centurion spoke more truly than he likely understood. He evidently meant that Jesus was a "righteous man" (Luke 23:47). Still, his words spoken as he stood directly in front of Jesus—as He died—were literally true! His statement constitutes the climax of Mark's demonstration that Jesus was God's divine Son (cf. 1:1; 8:29-30). This man was not a disciple of Jesus, but a Roman soldier, who had probably witnessed many crucifixions. The torn veil was a Jewish testimony to Jesus' identity, and the centurion's confession was a Gentile testimony to the same thing. Taken together they provide a double witness that Jesus was the Son of God.

> "Here Judaism and the Gentile world, each in its own way, acknowledges Jesus' sovereign dignity."[676]

15:40-41 Matthew referred to the same three women, and Luke mentioned them generally. "James the Less" may have been the son of Alphaeus mentioned in 3:18—who was one of the Twelve. "Salome" was the mother of Zebedee's sons, James and John—who were Jesus' cousins. These women, like the soldiers, also witnessed Jesus' death. Their loving example contrasts with the enemies of Jesus who ridiculed Him. However, verse 41 is unique to Mark. It should be a special encouragement to all female disciples. Many women followed Jesus and served Him throughout His ministry. John mentioned that he was present at the crucifixion (John 19:26-27), but none of the other male disciples appear to have been there. Women can serve Jesus—as disciples—as well as men. Their roles may be somewhat different from their male counterparts', today, as they were then, but their ministry is just as important. Mark's introduction of these three women prepares the reader for their roles as eyewitnesses of Jesus' burial (v. 47) and resurrection (16:1-8).

[672]Gould, p. 295.
[673]Grassmick, p. 190.
[674]Hiebert, p. 397. Cf. Clarke, p. 246.
[675]Lane, p. 574-75.
[676]Ibid., p. 488.

Some Women Who Observed the Crucifixion		
Matthew 27:56	**Mark 15:40**	**John 19:25**
Mary Magdalene	Mary Magdalene	Mary Magdalene
		Jesus' mother (Mary)
Mary the mother of James and Joseph =	Mary the mother of James the Less and Joses =	Mary the wife of Clopas
Mother of Zebedee's sons =	Salome =	Jesus' mother's sister

The burial of Jesus 15:42-47 (cf. Matt. 27:57-66; Luke 23:50-56; John 19:31-42)

The burial of Jesus was an important part of the preaching of the early church (cf. 1 Cor. 15:3-4). It forms a connection between Jesus' death and His resurrection. More important, it proved the reality of Jesus' death.

15:42   By "evening" Mark meant late afternoon. Friday was the day the Jews prepared ("preparation day") for their Sabbath observance, which began at sundown on Friday. Mark took special pains to explain this for his Gentile readers.

15:43   The shortness of time evidently spurred "Joseph of Arimathea" into action (cf. Deut. 21:23). The location of Arimathea is questionable, but it may have been the same as Ramah (Ramathaim), the birthplace of Samuel, about 5 miles north of Jerusalem.[677] Joseph was "a prominent member" of the Sanhedrin. Mark's description of him, as one who "was waiting for the kingdom of God," presents him as a devout Jew. He had also become a believer in Jesus (John 19:38). Mark's original readers were citizens of Caesar's kingdom, but they were also waiting for the kingdom of God. Mark stressed the courage that Joseph mustered to make his request. Joseph's bold action would have inspired Mark's readers to take a stand for Jesus too. Joseph had to gather up his "courage," since he faced much opposition on the Council. Similarly, Mark's Roman readers would have had to summon their courage—in order to side with Jesus against powerful officials who opposed Him.

> "To erase the shame of the Cross, Mark dignifies Jesus in burial as well as in death. . . . It speaks well of Jesus that despite the disgraceful manner of his death such a man as Joseph should dangerously seek to bury his body."[678]

15:44-45   It was unusual that a crucified person died so quickly. So Pilate verified Jesus' death. Mark noted that a Roman "centurion" confirmed Jesus' death, in order to prove to his Roman readers that Jesus really had died. Perhaps some Romans who had observed crucifixions would have had trouble believing that Jesus was dead, since they knew of crucified criminals who had lingered for days.

It was also unusual to give the corpse of a person condemned for treason to anyone but a near relative.[679] Consequently, Pilate's willingness to give (grant) Jesus' "body" to Joseph, suggests that he really did not believe that Jesus was guilty of treason (cf. vv. 14-15). This is the only place in the New Testament where someone referred to Jesus' dead body as a corpse (Gr. *ptoma*). Mark's use of the word further stressed the reality of Jesus' death.[680]

15:46   Nicodemus assisted Joseph with these tasks (cf. John 19:39), and perhaps other people, such as their servants, helped them. Mark's simple description stressed the wrapping of Jesus' body in "a linen cloth," or sheet (Gr. *sindon*). Perhaps this also indicated a genuine burial to his original readers.

> "The purchase of a linen cloth dignifies Jesus with a brand new shroud."[681]

15:47   The writer mentioned the presence of the two "Marys" at the tomb, during Jesus' burial, to set up his later statement that they were also present to witness the empty tomb (16:1, 5). They had seen Jesus die (v. 40), and now they saw Him buried. There

[677] *The New Bible Dictionary*, 1962 ed., s.v. "Arimathaea," by J. W. Meiklejohn.

[678] Gundry, p. 980.

[679] Wessel, p. 785.

[680] Cf. Nineham, p. 435.

[681] Gundry, p. 981.

was no question that they went to the right tomb on Sunday morning, since they had been there Friday afternoon. Once again, Mark guarded against any wrong conclusion that the disciples were mistaken about Jesus' resurrection.

The Servant of the Lord had paid the ultimate price for the sins of humankind, namely, His own life. Mark's narrative stressed Jesus' exemplary service and the reality of His death.

VIII. THE SERVANT'S RESURRECTION CH. 16

The resurrection of Jesus Christ is the climax of Mark's Gospel, as it is the high point of all the other Gospel accounts. Jesus vindicated His claims to being the divine Son of God, not simply a human messiah, by His resurrection from the dead.

A. THE ANNOUNCEMENT OF JESUS' RESURRECTION 16:1-8 (CF. MATT. 28:1-8; LUKE 24:1-8; JOHN 20:1)

16:1   The Sabbath ended with sundown Saturday evening. The women did not come to the tomb until Sunday morning (v. 2, cf. Matt. 28:1). Why did Mark refer to the Sabbath at all? Probably he did so to clarify that Jesus had been in the tomb for some time.

The women Mark mentioned coming to the tomb were the same ones he said observed Jesus on the cross (15:40-41). Two of them had already visited Jesus' tomb late Friday afternoon (15:47). However, there were several other women who accompanied them now (cf. Luke 24:10).

Women Who Visited the Tomb Easter Morning			
Matthew 28:1	**Mark 16:1**	**Luke 24:10**	**John 20:1**
Mary Magdalene	Mary Magdalene	Mary Magdalene	Mary Magdalene
The other Mary =	Mary the mother of James	Mary the mother of James	
	Salome		
		Joanna	
		others	

They went to "anoint" Jesus' corpse with "spices." The Jews did not practice embalming.[682] These women simply wanted to honor Jesus by making His corpse as pleasant smelling as possible. Perhaps Mary of Bethany's example had encouraged them to make this sacrifice for Him (cf. 14:3-9). Obviously they did not understand that Jesus would rise from the dead.

"In the final scenes, in Jerusalem, the little people [i.e., the minor characters in Mark's story] exemplify especially the teaching about being 'servant of all.' Earlier, Jesus served others. Now in his time of need others serve him: Simon the leper receives him in his house; a woman anoints him with ointment worth a worker's annual salary; Simon Cyrenean takes up his cross; Joseph takes his body from the cross and buries him; and a group of women go to the tomb to anoint him after his death. These actions are acts of service done for Jesus by people who courageously sacrifice or risk something—money or arrest or reputation—to carry them out. . . .

"Thus, the little ones serve throughout as 'foils' for the disciples. . . .

". . . the little people actually fulfill the functions expected of disciples. Because the disciples of John had buried John's corpse, the reader expects the same of Jesus' disciples. Instead, the little people do what might have been expected of the disciples . . ."[683]

[682]Hiebert, p. 408.
[683]Rhoads and Michie, pp. 132-33.

16:2-3   Mark dated their visit even more precisely.[684] Apparently the women left their homes before dawn and arrived at the tomb just after sunrise (Matt. 28:1; Luke 24:1; John 20:1). Their concern was the removal of the heavy "stone" that blocked their "entrance" into "the tomb." They evidently knew nothing about the sealing of the tomb and the posting of the guard there (Matt. 27:62-66).

16:4-5   Mark apparently included this story to impress the reader with the supernatural element represented by the angel. The women would have said to one another, "Who rolled the stone away? It must have been someone very strong." When they entered the antechamber of the tomb, they would have thought, "Who is this young man (Gr. *neaniskos*)? He must be very unusual." He appeared as a youth, but his strength and his unusual dress indicated that he was an angel (cf. 9:3). He terrified the women.

> "It may be suggested that the purpose of the angel's presence at the tomb was to be the link between the actual event of the Resurrection and the women. Human eyes were not permitted to see the event of the Resurrection itself. But the angels as the constant witnesses of God's action saw it. So the angel's word to the women, 'He is risen', is, as it were, the mirror in which men were allowed to see the reflection of this eschatological event."[685]

16:6   The angel first calmed the women's fears. They needed to stop being "amazed" (alarmed), since Jesus had predicted His resurrection—and now it had happened. Then the angel explained where Jesus was ("not here" in the tomb; however, He showed Himself to Mary Magdalene near the tomb shortly after this). He "has been resurrected" (Gr. passive tense, implying that God had raised Him)! The empty tomb and "place where they laid Him" testified to His resurrection. The same Person who was crucified was now alive!

> "It is significant that early Jewish polemicists never sought to dispute this fact."[686]

16:7   "Peter," especially, needed this good news, in view of his triple denial of Jesus and his consequent despair. Mark only recorded this special reference to Peter probably because it meant so much to Peter. Jesus still regarded Peter as one of His leading disciples, in spite of his failure.

Jesus had predicted the scattering of His sheep and their regathering in Galilee (14:27-28). Galilee was the appropriate place to launch a worldwide mission to Gentiles as well as Jews. As He had called His disciples to be fishers of men in Galilee (1:17), now He would commission them to be shepherds of sheep there (John 21:15-19).

> "Too many other predictions of Jesus have reached fulfillment in Mark to leave any doubt that this one will likewise reach fulfillment."[687]

> "The final scene points back to Galilee, back to the beginning of the story. The young man's message at the tomb with instructions for the disciples to go to Galilee suggests perhaps a fresh start for the disciples or for anyone in the future of the story world who chooses to follow Jesus. By implication, this fresh journey will result in the same complications and the same hostility met in Galilee by John and then by Jesus. Furthermore, Galilee points away from Jerusalem, the center of Judaism, toward gentile nations, where Jesus had said the good news was to be proclaimed before the end came."[688]

However, the disciples did not go immediately "to Galilee." They needed further proof of Jesus' resurrection, which Jesus provided, before they went.

16:8   The women were so upset by what had happened, that when they left the tomb, they told no one what they had seen—at first. However, it was not long before they were spreading the news that Jesus was alive again (Matt. 28:8; Luke 24:9).

> "The ending of Mark . . . punctures any self-confident superiority the reader might feel, for the ending turns irony back upon the reader. Throughout the story when Jesus commanded people to be quiet they talked anyway. But at the end when the young man commands the women to go tell the message—the crucial

---

[684]See Zane C. Hodges, "The Women and the Empty Tomb," *Bibliotheca Sacra* 123:492 (October-December 1966):301-9.

[685]Cranfield, *The Gospel . . .*, pp. 465-66.

[686]Lane, p. 588.

[687]Gundry, p. 1009.

[688]Rhoads and Michie, p. 71.

message—in an ironic reversal they are silent. The fear of the women dominates the ending of the story. At this point fear forces the reader to face once again the fear in his or her own situation. No matter how much the reader 'knows' or 'sees,' he or she still must make the hard choice in the end—whether to be silent like the women or to proclaim the good news in the face of persecution and possible death."[689]

"With his closing comment he [Mark] wished to say that 'the gospel of Jesus the Messiah' (ch. 1:1) is an event beyond human comprehension and therefore awesome and frightening. In this case, contrary to general opinion, 'for they were afraid' is the phrase most appropriate to the conclusion of the Gospel. The abruptness with which Mark concluded his account corresponds to the preface of the Gospel where the evangelist begins by confronting the reader with the fact of revelation in the person of John and Jesus (Ch. 1:1-13)."[690]

B. THE APPEARANCES AND ASCENSION OF JESUS 16:9-20

Many modern interpreters believe Mark ended his Gospel with verse 8.[691] This seems unlikely to some others, since if he did, he ended it with an example of disciples too fearful and amazed to bear witness to the resurrected Jesus. Throughout this Gospel, we have noted many unique features that appeal to disciples to serve God by bearing bold witness to Jesus, even in spite of persecution and suffering. The other interpreters believe the women's example would hardly be a good example for Mark to close his Gospel with.

The ending of Mark's Gospel is one of the major textual problems in the New Testament. The main reason some interpreters regard verses 9-20 as spurious is this. The two oldest Greek uncial manuscripts of the New Testament (fourth century), Codex Sinaiticus (*Aleph*) and Codex Vaticanus (B), plus many other old manuscripts, do not contain them. Moreover, the writings of some church fathers reflect no knowledge of these verses. On the other hand, verses 9-20 do appear in the majority of the old manuscripts, and other church fathers do refer to them—including Justin Martyr (A.D. 155), Tatian (A.D. 170), and Irenaeus (A.D. 180).[692] Some interpreters believe the vocabulary, style, and content of these verses argue against Mark's authorship of them.[693] This has led many modern scholars to conclude that verses 9-20 were not part of Mark's original Gospel.[694]

If they were not part of Mark's original Gospel, where did they come from, and are they part of the inspired Word of God or not inspired?

It may be that verses 9-20 were part of Mark's original Gospel and, for reasons unknown to us today, they were not included in some ancient copies of it. *Aleph* and "B" leave space for all or some of these verses.[695] If so, these verses are probably as fully authoritative as the rest of the Gospel.[696]

Another view is that someone added verses 9-20 to give this Gospel a more positive ending. He could have done so without divine inspiration, in which case these verses lack the divine authority that marks the rest of Scripture.

Alternatively, someone could have added verses 9-20 under the superintending influence of the Holy Spirit, in which case these verses have equal authority with the rest of the Gospel.[697] There are other passages of Scripture that seem to have been written somewhat later than the body of the book in which they appear, but which the Jews and later the Christians regarded as inspired. For example, the record of Moses' death appears at the end of Deuteronomy, which most conservatives believe Moses wrote (cf. Deut. 34:5-12). Another example is the references to the town of Dan in the Book of Genesis, which town did not go by that name until after Moses' time. Evidently someone after Moses' day updated the name of that town. Several other examples of this nature could be cited.

The view of many evangelicals, including myself, is that even though we may not be able to prove that verses 9-20 were originally part of Mark's Gospel, though they could have been, they appear to have been regarded as inspired and therefore authoritative early in the history of the church.

There are two other short endings to Mark's Gospel that follow verse 8 in some ancient copies, but almost all textual scholars reject these as being spurious.

---

[689]Ibid., pp. 61-62.

[690]Lane, p. 592.

[691]E.g., Carson and Moo, pp. 187-90; Cranfield, pp. 470-72; et al.

[692]For more details, see Bruce M. Metzger, *A Textual Commentary on the Greek New Testament*, pp. 122-26.

[693]E.g., Wessel, p. 792; Bratcher and Nida, pp. 517-22; et al.

[694]E.g., Swete, p. cxiii; A. F. Hort, *The Gospel According to St. Mark*, p. 199; B. B. Warfield, *An Introduction to the Textual Criticism of the New Testament*, p. 203; Joel F. Williams, "Literary Approaches to the End of Mark's Gospel," *Journal of the Evangelical Theological Society* 42:1 (March 1999):21-35; The NET Bible note on 16:9; Lane, pp. 591, 601-5; et al.

[695]*The Nelson . . .*, p. 1680.

[696]John W. Burgon, *The Last Twelve Verses of the Gospel According to S. Mark*; Morison, pp. 446-49, 463-70; Lenski, pp. 750-55; et al.

[697]Grassmick, p. 194.

1. Three post-resurrection appearances 16:9-18

These three accounts stress the importance of disciples believing what Jesus had taught, specifically that He would rise from the dead, with increasing urgency.

Jesus' appearance to Mary Magdalene 16:9-11 (cf. John 20:11-18)

16:9   The NIV has supplied "Jesus." The Greek text says, "Now after He had risen." The antecedent of "He" is obviously Jesus, but the lack of this antecedent in the immediately preceding context seems to some interpreters to indicate a major break between verses 8 and 9. Perhaps the writer did not feel he needed to name Jesus since He is the obvious antecedent.[698]

The writer may have described "Mary Magdalene" as he did here to explain why she was at the tomb. Jesus had done a great thing for her, and her love for Him was consequently very great. Perhaps the writer described her as he did, to identify her more precisely, since she becomes an important figure here for the first time in Mark's Gospel. Mary had returned to the tomb by herself after she and the other women had left it (vv. 1-8). Evidently people could not naturally perceive Jesus for who He was unless Jesus revealed Himself to them (cf. Luke 24:16, 31).[699]

16:10-11   Mary "reported to" the disciples that she had seen the risen Christ (cf. v. 7). While the rest of the Jews rejoiced, celebrating the Passover season, Jesus' disciples mourned His death. They would not believe Mary's eyewitness testimony. This should encourage other disciples who find that unbelievers will not believe their witness about the resurrection of Jesus.

Jesus' appearance to two men 16:12-13 (cf. Luke 24:13-32)

This is a condensed version of Jesus' appearance on the Emmaus road. The "different (immortal) form" in which Jesus "appeared" accounted in part for the failure of these men to recognize Him at first. The writer's point seems to be the unbelief of the disciples again. Neither the report of an eyewitness nor a personal appearance opened these men's eyes. God had to do that supernaturally, and He still does.

Jesus' appearance to the Eleven 16:14-18 (cf. Luke 24:36-43; John 20:19-23)

The writer said that Jesus "appeared to the Eleven" on this occasion. However, John qualified that statement by explaining that Thomas was absent (John 20:24). The writer was speaking of the Eleven as a group.

16:14   This event evidently happened on Easter Sunday evening. This is the most severe rebuke that Jesus ever gave His disciples that the Gospels record. They had not only disbelieved the reports of His resurrection, but they had also hardened their hearts against the *possibility* of His resurrection. The disciples' own unbelief would help them understand and appreciate the unbelief of many with whom they would share the gospel as eyewitnesses.

> "The Apostles may have been allowed to hear of the Resurrection before seeing the risen Christ in order that they might know from personal experience what it was to have to depend upon the testimony of others, as would be the case with their converts."[700]

16:15   The stating of the Great Commission, on this occasion, seems to have preceded the giving of it that Matthew recorded (Matt. 28:19-20). The account in the second Gospel stresses the universal scope of the disciples' responsibility (cf. 14:9). "All" in "all the world" is an especially strong form of the Greek word for "all," namely, *hapanta*. Every part of the world needs the gospel.

16:16   This is a verse that some people believe teaches the necessity of water baptism for salvation. However, *Christian baptism* elsewhere in the New Testament is always defined by an outward confession of belief in Jesus Christ. This verse also regards baptism as such. The second part of the verse clearly teaches that unbelief results in condemnation (cf. 9:43-48), not belief and failure to undergo baptism. In the first part of the verse, one article governs both participles: has believed and has been baptized (NASB) or believes and is baptized (NIV). This indicates the close relationship between believing and being baptized. However, they are not inseparable (cf. Rom. 3:21-28; 1 Cor. 1:17; Eph. 2:8-9). Baptism is not a condition for salvation, but it is an important step of obedience for a believing disciple.

---

[698]Morison, p. 450.
[699]S. J. Andrews, *The Life of Our Lord Upon the Earth*, p. 590.
[700]Plummer, p. 372.

16:17-18   These verses also support the primary importance of believing. Those who believe, not just the Eleven, would continue to perform supernatural acts. Throughout Scripture such "signs" always signified that something of supernatural origin was happening, and they authenticated the message that the witness bore (cf. v. 20).

> "The signs authenticated the faith the early believers proclaimed, not the personal faith that any one of them exercised."[701]

The Twelve had already cast out demons and healed people in Jesus' name (6:7, 12-13). They would continue to have these abilities (cf. Acts 5:16; 8:7; 16:18; 19:12; 28:8). This is the only reference to the disciples speaking in "tongues" (i.e., languages) in the Gospels (cf. Acts 2:4; 10:46; 19:6; 1 Cor. 12:10, 28, 30; 13:1; 14:2, 18-19). There is no textual basis for distinguishing the unlearned languages, spoken in Acts, from the gibberish that some claim the epistles refer to. Tongues in the New Testament were evidently always languages.[702] Immunity from the bite of poisonous snakes was another privilege the disciples would enjoy (cf. Acts 28:3-6). There are no examples of disciples drinking something deadly and surviving in the Book of Acts.

Jesus did not say how long the disciples would be able to do these things. Previous periods of miracle-working had all been fairly short (cf. Exod. 7—14; 1 Kings 17—2 Kings 10). Therefore that was what the disciples could expect (cf. 1 Cor. 13:8). Church history has confirmed that the period of miracle-working that existed in the first century passed away about the same time as the completion of the New Testament canon (cf. 2 Cor. 12:12; Heb. 2:3-4). Some Christians claim these promises are valid today, for example the snake-handling and poison-drinking sects of Appalachia. However, these were mainly promises of divine protection for occasions when the disciples' persecutors compelled them to do these things.

God still sometimes convinces people of the truth of the gospel, or confirms the truth of His Word to people, with supernatural experiences. Nevertheless these are not the same experiences as what Jesus promised here. Some of the early Christians could perform miracles whenever they wanted to do so in God's will (e.g., Acts 3:6; 16:18). That is not the case today, though God still performs miracles today.

2. Jesus' ascension 16:19-20 (cf. Luke 24:50-53; Acts 1:9-12)

16:19   This event happened 40 days after the appearances that the writer just recorded (cf. Acts 1:3). He narrated the ascension and session of Jesus without elaborating. The title "Lord Jesus" occurs only here and in Luke 24:3 in the Gospels. Jesus of Nazareth became "Lord" to His disciples, in the sense of sovereign master, following His resurrection. He was that always, but the Resurrection taught the disciples that that is what He was.

Jesus had predicted His ascension in veiled terms (14:7). The disciples witnessed this. They did not witness His seating in heaven. The Old Testament anticipated Messiah's seating in heaven before His return to reign (Ps. 110:1). The disciples learned that that session would occur between Jesus' two advents, not before His first advent (cf. Acts 2:33-35; 7:56). Jesus' present seated position, at the Father's right-hand side, pictures His finished work on earth—for the time being—and His authority as the Executor of God's will in this age. Jesus' present rule over the church, from His Father's right-hand side in heaven, is not the same as His future rule over the Davidic kingdom—from David's throne on earth.[703]

16:20   However, Jesus' work on earth was also continued through the first generation of His disciples. It was a continuation of Jesus' work on earth in a real sense, because He continued to work with them, and confirmed their preaching with signs (cf. Acts 1:1-2). Those first disciples provided a positive example for all succeeding generations of disciples to follow. Thus the Gospel ends on a positive note.

The task of evangelizing continued in Rome among the disciples who first received this Gospel. This account of the good news about Jesus Christ (1:1) would have been a particular encouragement to the new Roman disciples. They faced the choice of whether to take a public stand as Christians—and suffer the loss of real estate, personal property, employment, and even their lives—or to lay low. They were required by law to offer a pinch of incense in worship of "divine" Caesar, as Roman citizens. Doing so compromised their exclusive commitment to Jesus as Lord. To fail to worship Caesar cost them dearly. This Gospel is particularly helpful for disciples who face similar challenges in their own time and place in history.

Wiersbe pointed out that the Gospel of Mark parallels Paul's great servant passage in Philippians 2. Jesus came as a servant (Mark 1—13; Phil. 2:1-7), He died on a cross (Mark 14—15; Phil. 2:8), and God exalted Him to glory (Mark 16; Phil. 2:9). Both Mark and Paul stressed the need for

---

[701]Grassmick, p. 196.

[702]See S. Lewis Johnson Jr., "The Gift of Tongues and the Book of Acts," *Bibliotheca Sacra* 120:480 (October-December 1963):309-11.

[703]See Cleon L. Rogers Jr., "The Davidic Covenant in Acts-Revelation," *Bibliotheca Sacra* 151:601 (January-March 1994):81-82.

Jesus' disciples to carry the gospel to all nations (Mark 16:15-16; Phil 2:10-11). And both of them gave assurance that God is at work in and through us (Mark 16:19-20; Phil. 2:12-13).[704]

---

[704]Wiersbe, 1:168.

End Map

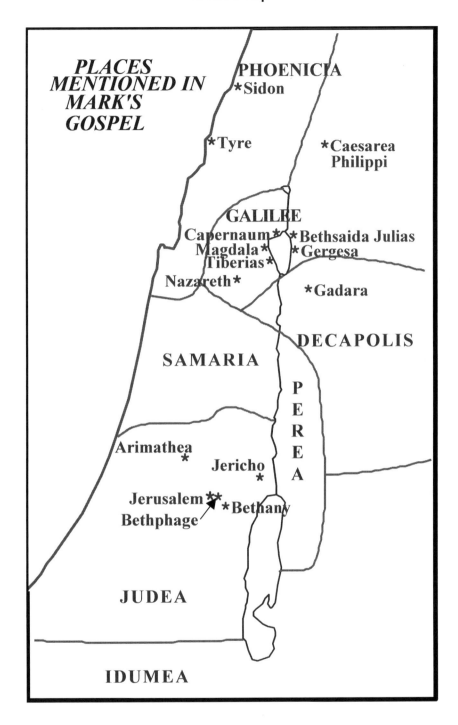

PLACES MENTIONED IN MARK'S GOSPEL

PHOENICIA
*Sidon

*Tyre

*Caesarea Philippi

GALILEE

Capernaum* *Bethsaida Julias
Magdala* *Gergesa
Tiberias*
Nazareth*

*Gadara

DECAPOLIS

SAMARIA

P
E
R
E
A

Arimathea
*

Jericho
*

Jerusalem**
*Bethany
Bethphage

JUDEA

IDUMEA

Bibliography

Adams, J. McKee. *Biblical Backgrounds*. Nashville: Broadman Press, 1965.

Alexander, Joseph Addison. *The Gospel According to Mark*. 1881. Reprint ed. London: Banner of Truth, 1960.

Alexander, William M. *Demonic Possession in the New Testament: Its Relations Historical, Medical, and Theological*. Edinburgh: T. & T. Clark, 1902.

Anderson, Hugh. *The Gospel of Mark*. New Century Bible series. Greenwood, S.C.: Attic Press, 1976.

Andrews, Samuel J. *The Life of Our Lord Upon the Earth*. 1862. Reprint ed. Grand Rapids: Zondervan Publishing House, 1954.

Bailey, Mark L., and Thomas L Constable. *The New Testament Explorer*. Nashville: Word Publishing, 1999. Reissued as *Nelson's New Testament Survey*. Nashville: Thomas Nelson Publishers, 1999.

Bateman, Herbert W., IV. "Defining the Titles 'Christ' and 'Son of God' in Mark's Narrative Presentation of Jesus." *Journal of the Evangelical Theological Society* 50:3 (September 2007):537-59.

Beasley-Murray, G. R. *A Commentary on Mark Thirteen*. London: Macmillan, 1957.

Berg, Laurna L. "The Illegalities of Jesus' Religious and Civil Trials." *Bibliotheca Sacra* 161:643 (July-September 2004):330-42.

Best, E. *The Temptation and the Passion*. Cambridge: Cambridge University Press, 1965.

Bishop, Eric F. F. *Jesus of Palestine: The Local Background to the Gospel Documents*. London: Lutterworth, 1955.

Blunt, A. W. F. *The Gospel According to Saint Mark*. The Clarendon Bible series. Oxford: Clarendon Press, 1929.

Bock, Darrell L. *Blasphemy and Exaltation in Judaism and the Final Examination of Jesus: A Philological-Historical Study of the Key Jewish Themes Impacting Mark 14:61-64*. Wissenschaftliche Untersuchungen zum Neuen Testament, number 106. Tübingen, Germ.: Mohr Siebeck, 1998.

Boobyer, G. H. "Mark II, 10a and the Interpretation of the Healing of the Paralytic." *Harvard Theological Review* 47 (1954):115-20.

Bratcher, R. G., and E. A Nida. *Translator's Handbook on Mark*. Leiden, Netherlands: E. J. Brill, 1961.

Brown, William E. "The New Testament Concept of the Believer's Inheritance." Th.D. dissertation, Dallas Theological Seminary, 1984.

Bruce, Alexander Balmain. "The Synoptic Gospels." In *The Expositor's Greek Testament*. Edited by W. Robertson Nicoll. Grand Rapids: Wm. B. Eerdmans Publishing Co., 1910.

_____. *The Training of the Twelve*. 8th ed. N. c.: A. C. Armstrong and Son, 1894; reprint ed. Grand Rapids: Kregel Publications, 1971.

Burgon, John W. *The Last Twelve Verses of the Gospel According to S. Mark*. 1871. Reprint ed. N. c.: Sovereign Grace Book Club, 1959.

Calvin, John. *Commentary on a Harmony of the Evangelists*. 3 vols. Grand Rapids: Baker Book House, 1979.

Carl, Harold F. "Only the Father Knows: Historical and Evangelical Responses to Jesus' Eschatological Ignorance in Mark 13:32." A paper presented at the Annual Meeting of the Evangelical Theological Society, Nov. 16, 2000, Nashville, Tenn.

Carrington, P. *According to Mark*. Cambridge: Cambridge University Press, 1960.

Carson, Donald A., and Douglas J. Moo. *An Introduction to the New Testament*. 2nd ed. Grand Rapids: Zondervan, 2005.

Chantry, Walter J. "Does the New Testament Teach the Fourth Commandment?" *The Banner of Truth* 325 (October 1990):18-23.

Clarke, W. N. "Commentary on the Gospel of Mark." In *An American Commentary*. 1881. Reprint ed. Phildelphia: American Baptist Publication Society, n. d.

Cole, R. A *The Gospel According to Mark*. Tyndale New Testament Commentaries series. 2nd ed. Leicester, England: Inter-Varsity Press, and Grand Rapids: Wm. B. Eerdmans Publishing Co., 1989.

Cranfield, C. E. B. *The Gospel According to Saint Mark*. Cambridge Greek Testament Commentary series. Cambridge: Cambridge University Press, 1959.

_____. "St. Mark 13." *Scottish Journal of Theology* 6 (April 1953):165-96; (July 1953):287-303; 7 (April 1954):284-303.

Davis, C. Truman. "The Crucifixion of Jesus. The Passion of Christ from a Medical Point of View," *Arizona Medicine* 22:3 (March 1965):185-87.

Decker, Rodney J. "The Use of *euthys* ('immediately') in Mark." *Journal of Ministry and Theology* 1:1 (Spring 1997):90-121.

DeGraaf, David. "Some Doubts about Doubt: The New Testament Use of *Diakrino*." *Journal of the Evangelical Theological Society* 48:8 (December 2005):733-55.

A Dictionary of the Bible. Edited by James Hastings. 1906 ed. S.v. "Numbers, Hours, Years, and Dates," by W. M. Ramsay, extra volume: 473-84.

Dillow, Joseph C. *The Reign of the Servant Kings*. Miami Springs, Fla.: Schoettle Publishing Co., 1992.

Donahue, J. R. "Tax Collectors and Sinners: An Attempt at Identification." *Catholic Biblical Quarterly* 33 (1971):39-61.

Doriani, Daniel. "The Deity of Christ in the Synoptic Gospels." *Journal of the Evangelical Theological Society* 37:3 (September 1994):333-50.

Earle, Ralph. *The Gospel According to Mark*. The Evangelical Commentary on the Bible series. Grand Rapids: Zondervan Publishing House, 1957.

The Ecclesiastical History of Eusebius Pamphilus. Twin Brooks series. Popular ed. Grand Rapids: Baker Book House, 1974.

Edersheim, Alfred. *The Life and Times of Jesus the Messiah*. 2 vols. Grand Rapids: Wm. B. Eerdmans Publishing Co., 1971.

_____. *The Temple: Its Ministry and Services As They Were at the Time of Jesus Christ*. Reprint ed. Grand Rapids: Wm. B. Eerdmans Publishing Co., 1972.

Edwards, James R. "The Authority of Jesus in the Gospel of Mark." *Journal of the Evangelical Theological Society* 37:2 (June 1994):217-33.

Ellenburg, B. Dale. "A Review of Selected Narrative-Critical Conventions in Mark's Use of Miracle Material." *Journal of the Evangelical Theological Society* 38:2 (June 1995):171-80.

English, E. Schuyler. "A Neglected Miracle." *Bibliotheca Sacra* 126:504 (October-December 1969):300-5.

Eppstein, V. "The Historicity of the Gospel Account of the Cleansing of the Temple." *Zeitschrift für die Neutestamentliche Wissenschaft* 55 (1964):42-58.

Farmer, William Reuben. *The Synoptic Problem*. New York: Macmillan, 1964.

Garlington, Don B. "Jesus, the Unique Son of God: Tested and Faithful." *Bibliotheca Sacra* 151:603 (July-September 1994):284-308.

Gianoulis, George C. "Did Jesus' Disciples Fast?" *Bibliotheca Sacra* 168:672 (October-December 2011):413-25.

Gould, Ezra P. *A Critical and Exegetical Commentary on the Gospel According to St. Mark*. Internationa Critical Commentary series. Edinburgh: T. & T. Clark, 1896.

Grassi, Joseph A. "*Abba*, Father (Mark 14:36): Another Approach." *Journal of the American Academy of Religion* 50:3 (September 1982):449-58.

Grassmick, John D. "Mark." In *The Bible Knowledge Commentary: New Testament*, pp. 95-197. Edited by John F. Walvoord and Roy B. Zuck. Wheaton: Scripture Press Publications, Victor Books, 1983.

Green, Michael P. "The Meaning of Cross-Bearing." *Bibliotheca Sacra* 140:558 (April-June 1983):117-33.

Guelich, Robert A. *Mark 1—8:26*. Word Biblical Commentary series. Dallas: Word Books, 1989.

Gundry, Robert H. *Mark: A Commentary on His Apology for the Cross*. Grand Rapids: Wm. B. Eerdmans Publishing Co., 1993.

Heil, John Paul. "Mark 14, 1-52: Narrative Structure and Reader Response." *Biblica* 71:3 (1990):305-32.

Hellerman, Joseph H. "Challenging the Authority of Jesus: Mark 11:27-33 and Mediterranean Notions of Honor and Shame." *Journal of the Evangelical Theological Society* 43:2 (June 2000):213-28.

Hengel, Martin. *Studies in the Gospel of Mark*. Philadelphia: Fortress Press, 1985.

Hiebert, D. Edmond *Mark: A Portrait of the Servant*. Chicago: Moody Press, 1974.

Hodges, Zane C. "The Blind Men at Jericho." *Biblitheca Sacra* 122:488 (October-December 1965):319-30.

_____. "The Women and the Empty Tomb." *Bibliotheca Sacra* 123:492 (October-December 1966):301-9.

Hoehner, Harold W. *Chronological Aspects of the Life of Christ*. Contemporary Evangelical Perspectives series. Grand Rapids: Zondervan Publishing House, 1977.

_____. *Herod Antipas*. Society for New Testament Studies Monograph Series 17. Cambridge: Cambridge University Press, 1972.

Hort, A. F. *The Gospel According to St. Mark*. 1902. Reprint ed. Cambridge: Cambridge University Press, 1928.

Hunter, A. M. *The Gospel According to Saint Mark*. Torch Bible Commentary series. London: SCM, 1967.

Hutchison, John C. "Servanthood: Jesus' Countercultural Call to Christian Leaders." *Bibliotheca Sacra* 166:661 (January-March 2009):53-69.

Jamieson, Robert; A. R. Fausset; and David Brown. *A Commentary Critical and Explanatory on the Old and New Testaments*. 2 vols. Hartford, Conn.: S. S. Scranton, n. d.

Jeremias, Joachim *The Eucharistic Words of Jesus*. 2nd ed. New York: Scribners, 1966.

_____. *New Testament Theology*. New York: Scribners, 1971.

_____. *The Parables of Jesus*. Translated by S. H. Hooke. London: SCM, 1963.

Johnson, S. Lewis, Jr. "The Gift of Tongues and the Book of Acts." *Bibliotheca Sacra* 120:480 (October-December 1963):309-11.

Johnson, Sherman E. *A Commentary on the Gospel According to St. Mark*. Black's New Testament Commentaries series. London: Adam & Charles Black, 1960.

Josephus, Flavius. *The Works of Flavius Josephus*. Translated by William Whiston. London: T. Nelson and Sons, 1866; reprint ed. Peabody, Mass.: Hendrickson Publishers, 1988.

Kelly, William. *An Exposition of the Gospel of Mark*. Reprint ed. London: C. A. Hammond, 1934.

Kingsbury, J. D. *Conflict in Mark: Jesus, Authorities, Disciples*. Minneapolis: Fortress Press, 1989.

Kuruvilla, Abraham. "The Naked Runaway and the Enrobed Reporter of Mark 14 and 16: What Is the Author Doing with What He Is Saying? *Journal of the Evangelical Theological Society* 54:3 (September 2011):527-45.

Lane, William L. *The Gospel According to Mark*. New International Commentary on the New Testament series. Grand Rapids: Wm. B. Eerdmans Publishing Co., 1974.

Lenski, Richard C. H. *The Interpretation of St. Mark's Gospel*. Minneapolis: Wartburg Press, 1946.

Lowery, David K. "A Theology of Mark." In *A Biblical Theology of the New Testament*, pp. 65-86. Edited by Roy B. Zuck. Chicago: Moody Press, 1994.

MacArthur, John A., Jr. *The Gospel According to Jesus*. Grand Rapids: Zondervan Publishing House, Academie Books, 1988.

Maclaren, Alexander. "St. Mark." In *Expositions of Holy Scripture*. Vol. 8. Reprint ed. Grand Rapids: Wm. B. Eerdmans Publishing Co., 1944.

Maclear, G. F. "The Gospel According to St. Mark." In *Cambridge Bible for Schools and Colleges*. Cambridge: Cambridge University Press, 1890.

Martin, R. P. *Mark: Evangelist and Theologian*. Grand Rapids: Zondervan Publishing House, 1972.

Matera, Frank J. "The Prologue as the Interpretive Key to Mark's Gospel." *Journal for the Study of the New Testament* 34 (October 1988):3-20.

McComiskey, Douglas S. "Exile and the Purpose of Jesus' Parables (Mark 4:10-12; Matt 13:10-17; Luke 8:9-10)." *Journal of the Evangelical Theological Society* 51:1 (March 2008):59-85.

Merrill, Eugene H. "Deuteronomy, New Testament Faith, and the Christian Life." In *Integrity of Heart, Skillfulness of Hands*, pp. 19-33. Edited by Charles H. Dyer and Roy B. Zuck. Grand Rapids: Baker Book House, 1994.

Metzger, Bruce M. *A Textual Commentary on the Greek New Testament*. London: United Bible Societies, 1971.

Meyer, Heinrich August Wilhelm. "Critical and Exegetical Hand-Book to the Gospels of Mark and Luke." In *Meyer's Critical and Exegetical Commentary on the New Testament*. Translated, revised, and edited by William P. Dickson. New York: Funk & Wagnalls, 1884.

The Mishnah. Translated by Herbert Danby. London: Oxford University Press, 1933.

Morgan, G. Campbell. *Living Messages of the Books of the Bible*. 2 vols. New York: Fleming H. Revell Co., 1912.

Morison, James. *A Practical Commentary on the Gospel According to St. Mark*. 8th ed. London: Hodder & Stoughton, 1896.

Moule, C. F. D. *The Gospel According to Mark*. The Cambridge Bible Commentary series. Cambridge: Cambridge University Press, 1965.

Moulton, James Hope, and George Milligan. *The Vocabulary of the Greek Testament*. Grand Rapids: Wm. B. Eerdmans Publishing Co., 1930.

Murray, John. *Divorce*. Philadelphia: Presbyterian and Reformed Publishing Co., 1974.

The Nelson Study Bible. Edited by Earl D. Radmacher. Nashville: Thomas Nelson Publishers, 1997.

The New Bible Dictionary. 1962 ed. S.v. "Arimathaea," by J. W. Meiklejohn.

_____. S.v. "Judas Iscariot," by R. P. Martin.

The New Scofield Reference Bible. Edited by Frank E. Gaebelein, William Culbertson, et al. New York: Oxford University Press, 1967.

Nineham, D. E. *Saint Mark*. Pelical Gospel Commentary series. Baltimore: Penguin Books, 1963.

Overstreet, R. Larry. "Roman Law and the Trial of Christ." *Bibliotheca Sacra* 135:540 (October-December 1978):323-32.

Page, Sydney H. T. "Satan: God's Servant." *Journal of the Evangelical Theological Society* 50:3 (September 2007):449-65.

Pentecost, J. Dwight. *The Parables of Jesus*. Grand Rapids: Zondervan Publishing House, 1982.

_____. *The Words and Works of Jesus Christ: A Study of the Life of Christ*. Grand Rapids: Academie Books, Zondervan Publishing House, 1981.

Peterson, Robert A. "Does the Bible Teach Annihilationism?" *Bibliotheca Sacra* 156:621 (January-March 1999):13-27.

Plummer, Alfred. "The Gospel According to St. Mark" In *The Cambridge Greek Testament*. 1914. Reprint ed. Cambridge: Cambridge University Press, 1938.

Rawlinson, A. E. J. *The Gospel According to St. Mark*. Westminster Commentaries series. London: Methuen, 1949.

Rhoads, David M., and Donald M Michie. *Mark as Story: An Introduction to the Narrative of a Gospel*. Philadelphia: Fortress Press, 1982.

Riddle, Matthew B. "The Gospel According to Mark." In *International Revision Commentary on the New Testament*. New York: Scribner, 1881.

Rogers, Cleon L., Jr. "The Davidic Covenant in Acts-Revelation." *Bibliotheca Sacra* 151:601 (January-March 1994):71-84.

Ryrie, Charles C. *The Miracles of our Lord*. Dubuque, Iowa: ECS Ministries, 2005.

Santos, Narry F. "Jesus' Paradoxical Teaching in Mark 8:35; 9:35; and 10:43-44." *Bibliotheca Sacra* 157:625 (January-March 2000):15-25.

_____. "The Paradox of Authority and Servanthood in the Gospel of Mark." *Bibliotheca Sacra* 154:616 (October-December 1997):452-60.

Schweizer, Eduard. *The Good News According to Mark*. London: SPCK, 1971.

Shanks, Monte A. "An Alternative Solution to an Alleged Contradiction in the Gospels." *Bibliotheca Sacra* 169:675 (July-September 2012):317-27.

Showers, Renald E. *Maranatha Our Lord, Come: A Definitive Study of the Rapture of the Church*. Bellmawr, Pa.: Friends of Israel Gospel Ministry, 1995.

Skinner, Christopher W. "'Whom He Also Named Apostles': A Textual Problem in Mark 3:14." *Bibliotheca Sacra* 161:643 (July-September 2004):322-29.

Smith, Geoffrey. "A Closer Look at the Widow's Offering: Mark 12:41-44." *Journal of the Evangelical Theological Society* 40:1 (March 1997)27-36.

Smith, George Adam. *The Historical Geography of the Holy Land*. New York: Armstrong and Son, 1909.

Stauffer, Ethelbert. *Jesus and His Story*. Translated by Richard and Clara Winston. New York: Alfred A. Knopf, 1960.

Strack, H. L., and P. Billerbeck. *Kommentar zum Neuen Testament aus Talmud und Midrasch*. 4 vols. Munich: Beck'sche, 1922-28.

Sugirtharajah, R. S. "The Syrophoenician Woman." *The Expository Times* 98:1 (October 1986):13-15.

Swete, Henry Barclay. *The Gospel According to St. Mark*. 1898. Reprint ed. London: Macmillan, 1905.

Taylor, Vincent. *The Gospel According to St. Mark*. 2nd ed. New York: St. Martins Press, 1966.

Theological Dictionary of the New Testament. Edited by Gerhard Kittel. S.v. "basilia," by K. L. Schmidt.

_____. S.v. "pais," by Albrecht Oepke.

Thomas, Robert L. *Evangelical Hermeneutics: The New Versus the Old*. Grand Rapids: Kregel Publications, 2002.

Unger, Merrill F. *Biblical Demonology: A Study of the Spiritual Forces Behind the Present World Unrest*. Wheaton: Van Kampen Press, 1952.

_____. *Demons in the World Today*. Wheaton: Tyndale, 1971.

_____. "Divine Healing." *Bibliotheca Sacra* 128:511 (July-September 1971):234-44.

Van der Loos, H. *The Miracles of Jesus*. Supplements to Novum Testamentum series. Vol. VIIII. Leiden, Netherlands: E. J. Brill, 1965.

Warfield, Benjamin B. *An Introduction to the Textual Criticism of the New Testament*. London: Hodder & Stoughton, 1899.

Wessel, Walter W. "Mark." In *Matthew-Luke*. Vol. 8 of *The Expositor's Bible Commentary*. 12 vols. Edited by Frank E. Gaebelein and J. D. Douglas. Grand Rapids: Zondervan Publishing House, 1984.

Wiarda, Timothy. "Story-Sensitive Exegesis and Old testament Allusions in Mark." *Journal of the Evangelical Theological Society* 49:3 (September 2006):489-504.

Wiersbe, Warren W. *The Bible Expositon Commentary*. 2 vols. Wheaton: Scripture Press, Victory Books, 1989.

Williams, George. *The Student's Commentary on the Holy Scriptures*. 5th ed. London: Oliphants, 1949.

Williams, Joel F. "Discipleship and Minor Characters in Mark's Gospel." *Bibliotheca Sacra* 153:611 (July-September 1996):332-43.

_____. "Does Mark's Gospel Have an Outline?" *Journal of the Evangelical Theological Society* 49:3 (September 2006):505-26.

_____. "Literary Approaches to the End of Mark's Gospel." *Journal of the Evangelical Theological Society* 42:1 (March 1999):21-35.

Wrede, William. *The Messianic Secret*. 1901. Reprint ed. Cambridge: James Clarke, 1971.

Zondervan Pictorial Encyclopedia of the Bible. Edited by Merrill C. Tenney. S.v. "Sadducees," by D. A. Hagner.

72672027R20235

Made in the USA
Lexington, KY
03 December 2017